C000124501

1 MONTH OF
FREE
READING

at

www.ForgottenBooks.com

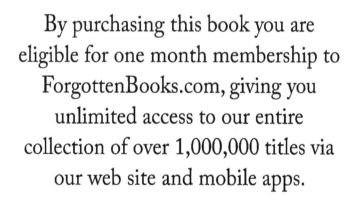

By purchasing this book you are eligible for one month membership to ForgottenBooks.com, giving you unlimited access to our entire collection of over 1,000,000 titles via our web site and mobile apps.

To claim your free month visit:

www.forgottenbooks.com/free910571

ISBN 978-0-266-92437-1
PIBN 10910571

FORT WAYNE CITY

AND

ALLEN COUNTY

DIRECTORY

1890-91.

CONTAINING

AN ALPHABETICALLY ARRANGED LIST OF BUSINESS FIRMS AND PRIVATE
CITIZENS IN FORT WAYNE—A MISCELLANEOUS DIRECTORY OF CITY AND
COUNTY OFFICERS, PUBLIC AND PRIVATE SCHOOLS, CHURCHES,
BANKS, INCORPORATED INSTITUTIONS, SECRET AND BENEV-
OLENT SOCIETIES, ETC., ETC.—A CLASSIFIED LIST
OF ALL TRADES, PROFESSIONS AND PUR-
SUITS—A FARMERS' DIRECTORY
OF ALLEN COUNTY.

SOLD ONLY BY SUBSCRIPTION.

VOLUME XIII.

R. L. POLK & CO., PUBLISHERS,

40 TO 44 LARNED STREET WEST, DETROIT, MICH.

For List of Publications, see back fly leaf.

INTRODUCTORY.

The thirteenth volume of the FT. WAYNE AND ALLEN COUNTY DIREC-TORY is presented to the public with the belief that the result attained must reflect credit upon the thorough system and faithful efforts of the publishers; no class of work requires more diligence and carefulness than the compilation of such information as the directory contains, a letter or figure misplaced often rendering it unserviceable ; with these facts in view the work has been prosecuted with a determination to make it a complete and reliable representative of the city with all its various institutions and organizations, its incorporated companies, societies, churches, schools, banks, etc., its business firms and private citizens. It is the purpose of the publishers that the directory shall keep pace with the rapid development of the population and resources of the city and county, and with each succeeding issue improvements and additions will be made.

The first 56 pages are devoted to useful miscellaneous information relating to the city and county in general, comprising a street and avenue guide, lists of city and county officers, fire department, churches, schools, banks, railroads, incorporated institutions, miscellaneous insti-tutions and societies, newspapers, secret and benevolent societies, etc. Succeeding these, are 516 pages containing an alphabetically arranged directory of all the inhabitants of the city, followed by 74 pages con-taining a list of all persons engaged in business or the professions, clas-sified under their respective callings. The remaining pages contain name, number of section, number of acres, assessed valuation of same, name of township, and postoffice address of all farmers, etc., in Allen county.

This edition of the Ft. Wayne City Directory shows 17,129 names, which, with the multiplier of three persons to one directory name—the lowest used in any city in the United States—gives a total population of 51,387. Sincere thanks are tendered to those who, by their patronage and support, materially aided and encouraged the publishers in their work, and also to those who kindly assisted in collecting the informa-tion required in the preparation of this volume; and, in conclusion, the publishers would say, that in due time the fourteenth volume of the Ft. Wayne City and Allen County Directory will be issued, and that noth-ing shall be wanting on their part to maintain the high standard already attained, and they confidently hope to meet with the recognition the work deserves.

GENERAL INDEX.

	Page.
Abbreviations	57–649
Alphabetical List of Names—	
County	649–817
Alphabetical List of Names—	
Fort Wayne	57–573
Bands of Music	31
Banks	31
Board of Health	25
Board of School Trustees	49
Board of Police Commissioners	25
Building, Loan and Savings	
Associations	31
Cemeteries	32
Churches	33–36
City Government	25
City Officers	25
Classified Business Directory	
	575–647
Colleges	53
Council	25
County Directory	649–817
County Officers	29
Courts	30
Farmer's Directory — Allen	
County	649–817
Federal Officers	29

	Page.
Fire Department	26
Incorporated Institutions	36–39
Libraries	39
Military	39
Miscellaneous Institutions	39–43
Miscellaneous Schools	52
Names received too late for	
regular insertion	9–11
Newspapers	43–44
Parks	44
Police Department	27
Postoffice	45–46
Public Buildings, Halls, etc.	46–48
Public Schools	49–52
Railroads	48–49
Rates of Fare	28
Secret and Benevolent Socie-	
ties	53–56
Street Railroads	29
Streets and Avenues	13–24
Teachers in Public Schools	49–52
Telegraph and Telephone Cos	56
Township Trustees	30
Ward Boundaries	24
Water Works Trustees	25

43759

INDEX TO ADVERTISEMENTS.

	Page.
Albrecht M L	63
Barkley I L	left top lines
Binkley F C	right side lines
Boerger C R & Bro	65
Boltz F C	2
Borcherding & Toensing	601
Bowman Charles	left top lines
Brames L & Co	3
Carter & Son	bottom end and 61
Chicago, Milwaukee & St Paul	
Ry Co	back fly leaf

	Page.
Chicago & Grand Trunk Ry	
	back fly leaf
Clark M & Co	right top lines
Cline J F	left bottom lines
Crow J A	65
Curtice J F	front cover and 63
Dennison Mnfg Co, Boston,	
Mass	backbone and 574
Derheimer Joseph	592
Detroit, Grand Haven & Mil-	
waukee Ry	back fly leaf

Page.

Detroit & Cleveland Steam
 Navigation Co.........opp 820
Diether L & Bro...right side lines
Flagler Mrs E A...right top lines
Fleming Mnfg Co.......... 6
Fletcher J F............... 65
Ft Wayne, Cincinnati & Louis-
 ville R R..opp inside back cover
Foster A....... ....left top lines
Grand Rapids & Indiana R R
 inside back cover
Harr & Zimmerly..right side lines
Hattersley A & Son line front cover
Hilgemann E H & Son....... 67
Hilgemann J W............ 67
Horstman Louis............ 65
Hull L O..........right top lines
Illinois Central R R.......... 820
Iron Mountain Route......... 819
Jaap George...............
 left bottom lines and 593
Jones F L & Co..left bottom lines
Junk L..........left bottom lines
Kaag M F......left bottom lines
Keller & Braun 7
Kendrick F B........back cover
Kline C W.................. 579
Liebman & Henry........... 67
McDermut W E, back cover
 and 8
Madden James....right side lines
Matson H W........front cover
Meyer Bros & Co............ 59

Page.

Missouri Pacific Ry........ 818
Moellering Wm..front edge and 5
Muhler C F & Son.top edge and 59
Muldoon John W.line back cover
Northern Pacific R R, back fly leaf
Ogden Robert, back cover and 631
Perrin A C................. 63
Peters Box and Lumber Co... 6
Pfeiffer & Schlatter.right top lines
Polk R L & Co.back fly leaf
 12 and 648
Pressler John........left top lines
Renner, Cratsley & Co.front cover
Riedel J M E.......front cover
Ruchel Wm................. 69
Scherzinger G............... 61
Schroeder A H............. 69
Siemon Wall Paper Co .....
 left bottom lines
Siemon & Brother.....back cover
Sites E F.. ....right top lines
Spice Robert..,.....left top lines
Stahn & Heinrich..right top lines
Umstead H D.............. 583
Wah, Kee & Co............. 67
Walda H B & Bro.......... 69
Wells W D.....left bottom lines
Wisconsin Central Lines
 back fly leaf
Wise Wm 609
Young & Carter.... 4
Zuber Philip............... 7

Names Received too Late for Regular Insertion.

Ackerman John, sawyer, res 79 Summit.

Adams Frank H, sec Western Gas Construction Co, rms 26 Pixley & Long bldg.

Ames Milo E, engineer G R & I R R, res 282 S Webster.

Bacher Elizabeth (wid Conrad), res s w cor Allen and Calhoun.

Barcus Anzella (wid Isaac), bds n w cor LaSalle and Monroe.

Barnett Wm, cooper, res 22 Burgess.

Benjamin Aaron, editor German Freie Presse, res 88 W Lewis.

Berndt Charles A, cigar mnfr, 176 Calhoun, res same.

Berning Conrad, laborer, res 40 Summit.

Biddle Christophor, clerk, res 234 Francis.

Biddle Dora (wid George), res 234 Francis.

Bilgerig Andrew, cooper C Rosenberger, res 66 Murray.

Bley John E G, clerk Mendel Frank, bds 208 Hanna.

Boaeus Julian, carpenter, res s w cor Erie and Hanover.

Brabandt Robert, laborer Bass F & M Works, bds 98 Gay.

Braden David, farmer, res 270 W Jefferson.

Braden Jesse S, student, bds 270 W Jefferson.

Braden Mary D, bds 270 W Jefferson.

Braun Charles G, cigar mkr C A Berndt, res 162 Mont.

Brown Nathaniel T, carpenter, res 90 Maumee road.

Brunson Priscilla (wid Abraham), nurse, bds 8 Brandriff.

Bryant George W, dryer Olds' Wagon Works, res Wayne township.

Bryant Wm H, contractor, res 228 W Creighton ave.

Budde Magdalena (wid Herman), res 43 St Martin's.

Bullerman Henry F, county commissioner, Court house, res St Joseph township.

Burnett Alfred, cook Rich's Hotel.

Callahan Wilda, domestic Rich's Hotel.

Cohagen Wm E, stripper C A Berndt, bds s w cor E Lewis and Clinton.

Cunz Charles, res 90 Maumee road.

Doehla John, laborer, res 77 Hayden.

Eiter August, laborer, res 21 John.

Felitz Charles J, laborer, Olds' Wagon Works, res Wayne
township.
Forrest John L, car inspector Penn Co, res Adams township.
French R Morgan (French & Jefferds), res 148 E Washington.
French & Jefferds (R Morgan French, Oliver W Jefferds),
proprs Summit City Woolen Mills, 96 E Superior.
Frimute Charles, boilermaker, res rear 80 Broadway.
Garrison Albert, res 18 Colerick.
Gerry Miss Annie E, res n s E Washington bet Harmer
and Monroe.
Goeckle John, letter carrier, res 7 Monroe.
Good Stories (newspaper), Foster block.
Gutermuth John, lab, res s e cor Archer ave and Hensch.
Haag Louisa (wid John), res rear 329 W Washington.
Hael Martha A (wid John D), res n s Savilla place 3 e of
Broadway.
Hamilton-Williams Mrs Mary, bds Hamilton homestead, s e
cor Clinton and Lewis.
Hatfield Miss Della, stenographer McDermut's Business Col-
lege, res 91 W Superior.
Henkel Catherine (wid Henry), res 9 Elm.
Henzler Eva (wid Adam), bds 113 E Creighton ave.
Jackson John (Flinn & Jackson), res 79 E Columbia.
James Elizabeth (wid Daniel), bds 157 Fox.
Jefferds Oliver W (French & Jefferds), res 131 E Wayne.
Johnson Mary E (wid Andrew J), rms 94 Wells.
King George, res 125 Montgomery.
Kinney Oscar P, engineer Penn Co, res 123 W DeWald.
Kirbach Frederick, stone mason, res 159 Gay.
Kirkhoff Caroline (wid Frederick), bds 157 Broadway.
Klock Wm, fireman, res 168 Taylor.
Kramer Gottlieb, lab, res 19 Huron.
Krauhs J Charles, lab, res 61 Fox.
Kress Elizabeth (wid Isaac), res 133 W DeWald.
Kretzinger Christian, res 35 Putnam.
Krieg Michael, lab Bass F and M Wks, res 143 Buchanan.
Lahr George W, teacher McDermut's Business College, res
62 Calhoun.
Lininger John, switchman Penn Co, res Walton ave 5 s of
P, Ft W & C R R.
Loucks Ernest, carpenter, res 141 Fox.
McCollum Lydia (wid John), res 163 Webster.
McKay David, manager Brookside farm, res same.
McKee Archibald, res 131 W 3d.
Maerz George, blacksmith, res 102 Putnam.
Maley Bridget (wid Patrick), bds 69 Grand.

Markey Miss Mary D, teacher, bds 286 Broadway.
Meyers Wm F, veterinary surgeon, 112 Webster.
Miller Alvina (wid Charles T), res 64 Wall.
Miller John H, foreman Hoffman Bros, res Wayne tp.
Miner School, s w cor Miner and DeWald.
Mintz David, lab Olds' Wagon Works, res 67 John.
Nelson Henry, actionmaker, res 43 Miner.
Nohe Wm, shoemaker J F Noll, res 21 Nirdlinger ave.
Oalis Otto, mason, bds 111 Hanna.
Oberlin Lydia (wid Wm), bds n s Howell nr Runnion ave.
O'Connell Dennis, lab, res s s Wheeler 2 w of Runnion ave.
Pauley Edward, bartender, res 76 Williams.
Raeff Mary (wid George), res 56 Williams.
Raidy David, engineer Penn Co, res 20 Bass.
Ramm Louis G, spoke polisher Olds' Wagon Works, res 38 Gay
Reidmiller Catherine (wid John M), res cor Taylor and Eagle.
Roach Kate (wid Richard), res 7 Walnut.
Robinson Henry, res 70 Melita.
Rose Frederick J, machine hand Olds' Wagon Works, res
　　120 Buchanan.
Rose Louisa (wid Anthony), res 28 Pritchard.
St Patrick's School, in charge of the Sisters of Providence,
　　Rev Joseph Delaney director, cor Fairfield av and Duryea.
St Vincent's Orphan Asylum, e s Wells 1 n of Putnam.
Sanders Elizabeth (wid Edward), res 148 Fairfield ave.
Schifferly Conrad, trav agt, res 9 Buchanan.
Siebold Herman, bds 173 W DeWald.
Sine Amos, engineer Penn Co, res 77 Dawson.
Slagle Julia A (wid Samuel), res e s Metz 1 n of Wabash R R.
Spiegel August T, tailor, res 40 Wall.
Squires Grant, helper Ft Wayne Iron Works, res 29 Elm.
Stemen Henry B, brakeman, res 65 Boone.
Stevens Catherine (wid Jacob), res 21 Miner.
Welker Andrew, carpenter, res 59 Wall.
Wilhelm Peter, lab, res 5 Pine.

. L. POLK, President.   A. C. DANSER, Vice-President.   ALBERT DUFFILL, Sec'y and Treasur

INCORPORATED 1885.

ESTABLISHED 1870.

R. L. POLK & CO.

AZETTEER AND DIRECTOR

PUBLISHERS.

ublishers of Gazetteers and Business Directorie

FOR THE STATES OF

ILLINOIS,	WEST VIRGINIA,	CALIFORNIA,
MICHIGAN,	KENTUCKY,	WASHINGTON,
PENNSYLVANIA,	INDIANA,	COLORADO,
NEW JERSEY,	IOWA,	WYOMING,
MINNESOTA,	WISCONSIN,	NEW MEXICO,
MONTANA and	TEXAS,	UTAH,
DAKOTA,	MARYLAND,	NEVADA,
KANSAS,	OREGON,	ARIZONA,
MISSOURI,	TENNESSEE,	ARKANSAS
ALABAMA, and the DOMINION OF CANADA.		IDAHO,

MEDICAL AND SURGICAL REGISTER OF THE UNITED STATES,
ARCHITECTS AND BUILDERS' DIRECTORY OF THE UNITED STATES

AND CITY DIRECTORIES

—FOR—

Baltimore, Maryland; Detroit, Grand Rapids, Saginaw, Bay City, Jackson, Lansing, Muskego Port Huron, Sault Ste. Marie, Ann Arbor, Ypsilanti, Kalamazoo, Flint, Alpena, Cheboygar and Big Rapids, Mich.; Toledo, Columbus, Findlay, Newark and Lima, Ohio; Atlanta, Columbus and Augusta, Ga.; Birmingham and Montgomery, Ala.; Memphis, Tenn.; Indianapolis and Fort Wayne, Ind.; St. Paul, Minneapolis and Duluth, Minn.; Ashland, Oshkosh and Eau Claire, Wis.; Sioux City, Iowa; Portland, Ore.; Stockton, Cal.; Bismarck and Mandan, Dak.; Helena and Butte, Mont.; Seattle, Tacoma, Spokane Falls and Walla Walla, Wash.; London and Toronto, Ont.; Puget Sound; and Marine Directory of the Great Lakes.

40 TO 44 LARNED STREET WEST, DETROIT, MICH.

OFFICES:

CHICAGO, ILL., 150 Dearborn Street.
PHILADELPHIA, PA., Ledger Building, corner Chestnut and Sixth Streets.
TOLEDO, OHIO, 403 Jefferson Street.
COLUMBUS, OHIO, 80 North High Street.
INDIANAPOLIS, IND., Corner Circle and Meridian Streets.
BALTIMORE, MD., 112 N. Charles Street.
ST. PAUL, MINN., New Chamber of Commerce Building.
MINNEAPOLIS, MINN., 257 First Ave. South.
TORONTO, ONT., Victoria Chambers.
PORTLAND, ORE., First National Bank Building.
ATLANTA, GA., Chamber of Commerce.
SAN FRANCISCO, CAL., 606 Montgomery St.

R. L. POLK & CO.'S

FORT WAYNE DIRECTORY

1890-91.

MISCELLANEOUS DIRECTORY.

STREETS AND AVENUES.

Abbott, from Pontiac south, second east of Walton ave.

Aboit, from Sherman west to Franklin ave, first south of Barthold ave.

Alexander, from Pontiac south, first east of Walton ave.

Allen, from Lafayette west to Webster, first north of Pontiac.

Alliger, from Maumee road south to Wayne Trace, second east of Walton ave.

Andrew, from Archer ave south, third east of St Mary's ave.

Antoinette, from Walton ave east, fourth south of P, Ft W & C Ry.

Archer ave, changed to Pfeiffer ave.

Baker, from Calhoun west to Fairfield ave, first south of Brackenridge.

Barr, from Water south to Pontiac, second east of Calhoun.

Barthold, from St Mary's river north to canal feeder, fourth west of Wells.

Bass, from Fairfield ave east to Hoagland, first south of Wabash R R.

Beck, *see Koch.*

Begue, from E Wayne north to N Y, C & St L Ry, first east of Harmer.

Bell ave, from Fox west to Miner, first south of W Creighton ave.

Berry, from Francis east, first north of E Wayne.

3

Berry (East), from Calhoun east to W & E Canal, first south of Main.

Berry (West), from Calhoun west to St Mary's river, first south of Main.

Bond, from New Haven road south to Wabash R R, second east of tollgate.

Boone, from Cherry west to L S & M S R R, first north of Main.

Bowser, from Wells west, first north of High.

Brackenridge, from Calhoun west to Broadway, second north of Penn R R.

Brandriff, from Hoagland ave east to Webster, first south of Melita.

Breck, from St Mary's river at Van Buren Street bridge, west to canal basin.

Broadway, from N Y, C & St L Ry south to city limits, seventh west of Calhoun.

Brooklyn ave, west of St Mary's river, running parallel with Lavina ave.

Buchanan, from Lafayette east to Hanna, fifth south of Wabash R R.

Burd ave, second east of tollgate near Haven road, south to New Haven road.

Burgess, from St Mary's ave west, first south of Ft W, C & L Ry.

Butler (East), from Calhoun east to Lafayette, first south of Williams.

Butler (West), from Calhoun west to Fairfield ave, first south of Williams.

Calhoun, from St Mary's river south to city limits, first west of Clinton.

Canal, from N Y, C & St L Ry south to E Wayne.

Caroline, from Suttenfield south to Pontiac, first east of Lafayette.

Cass, from Wells north to canal feeder.

Cedar, from E Lewis north to Maumee road, first east of Ohio.

Centlivre ave, from Spy Run ave west to canal feeder, first north of Randolph.

Centre, from St Mary's river north to canal basin, second west of Main Street bridge.

Charles, from Lafayette east to Hanna, first south of Wallace.

Cherry, from St Mary's river north to old canal basin, first west of the river.

Chestnut, from Calhoun east to Clinton, first south of Holman.

Chestnut, from Strawberry ave west to Piqua road.

Chicago, from Calhoun west, first north of P, Ft W & C Ry.

Chute, from Maumee road south to Wabash R R, second east of Harmer.

Clark, from High north to Third, third west of Wells.

Clay, from Main south to Laselle, first east of Lafayette.

Clinton, from Superior south to Pontiac, first east of Calhoun.

Cochran, from Coombs east to Hanover, first north of N Y, C & St L Ry.

Colerick, from Fairfield ave east to Hoagland ave, second south of Wabash R R.

College, from W Berry south across Jones, first west of Rockhill.

Coln, from Maumee river, south to Dwenger ave.

Columbia, from Harrison east to Lafayette, first north of Main.

Comparet, from Wayne south to Maumee road, second east of Harmer.

Coombs, from Wayne north to N Y, C & St L Ry, second east of Harmer.

Cour, from Webster east to Piqua ave, south of limits.

Court, from Main south to Berry, first east of Calhoun.

Creighton ave (East), from Calhoun east to limits, first south of DeWald.

Creighton ave (West), from Calhoun west to city limits, first south of DeWald.

Dawson, from Calhoun west to Hoagland ave, first north of Williams.

DeGroff, from Ft W, C & L Ry south to Burgess, first west of St Mary's ave.

DeWald (East), from Calhoun east to Hanna, first north of Creighton ave.

DeWald (West), from Calhoun west to Broadway, first north of Creighton ave.

Diamond, from Walton ave east, second south of P, Ft W & C Ry.

Division, from Maumee road south to Wabash R R, third east of Hanna.

Dougal, from Maumee river south, second south of Glasgow ave.

Douglas ave, from Calhoun west to McClellan, second south of Jefferson.

DuBois, from Maumee road south to Wabash R R, fourth east of Walton ave.

Duck, from Calhoun east to Barr, first north of Superior.

Duryea, from Fairfield ave to Hoagland ave, first south of Butler, continuation of Poplar.

Dwenger ave, from Glasgow ave east, first north of Nickel Plate track.

Eagle, from Taylor south, second west of Broadway.

Eckart, from Hanna east to Smith, fourth south of Pontiac.

Edgerton, from Winter east to Walton ave, first south of P, Ft W & C Ry.

Edna, from Spy Run ave to canal feeder, first north of Centlivre ave.

Edsall, *see Union*.

Eliza, from Francis east across Ohio, second south of Lewis, and from Walton ave east to Euclid.

Elizabeth, from Spy Run ave west to Spy Run, at north city limits.

Elm, from St Mary's river west to same, first south of Main.

Emily, from Spy Run ave west to Spy Run, first south of Elizabeth.

Emily, from Thomas west to Gay, second south of E Creighton ave.

Erie, from junction of Francis and N Y, C & St L Ry east, first north of Wayne.

Euclid, from Maumee road south to Mercer, second east of Walton ave.

Eva, from Huestis ave south to Maple ave, first west of Broadway.

Evans, from Hartman west to Queen, third south of Pontiac.

Ewing, from W Superior south to Brackenridge, third west of Calhoun.

Fair, from St Mary's river to same, third south of Main.

Fairfield ave, from Brackenridge to south city limits, continuation of Griffith.

Ferguson ave, from Miner west to Broadway, first south of W Creighton ave.

Fifth, from Wells east to N Calhoun, fifth north of St Mary's river.

Fisher, from Holton ave west, second south of E Creighton ave.

Fletcher ave, from Maumee road south to Wayne Trace, first east of Range road.

Force, from Herndon south to Pontiac, fourth east of Lafayette.

Fourth, crosses Wells, fourth north of St Mary's river.

Fox, crosses Creighton ave, second east of Broadway.

Francis, from N Y, C & St L Ry south to Wabash R R, fourth east of Lafayette.

Franklin, from Holton ave west to Smith, fourth south of Pontiac.

Franklin ave, from canal feeder north to Archer ave, first west of St Mary's ave.

Frederick, from Holton ave west to Smith, second south of Pontiac.

Fry, from W Main north to Boone, first west of Osage.

Fulton, from W Superior south to Jefferson, first east of Broadway.

Garden, south from M E College grounds across Jefferson, first west of Nelson.

Gay, from Hayden south to Pontiac, third east of Hanna.

George, east from Broadway to Fairfield ave, fourth north of P, Ft W & C R R.

Gerke, from Holton ave west to Smith, first south of Pontiac.

Glasgow, from Maumee river south to Maumee road, fourth east of Walton ave.

Grand, from Calhoun west, along south side of Wabash R R.

Grant ave, from Hanna east to P, F W & C Ry, first south of Wallace.

Grant ave, from Wayne south to Maumee road, second east of Walton ave.

Greely, from Fulton west to Jackson, first north of N Y, C & St L Ry.

Greene, from John east to Holton ave, first south of Samuel.

Griffith, from W Superior south to Brackenridge, second east of Broadway.

Hamilton, from Calhoun east to Lafayette, first south of Murray.

Hanna, from N Y, C & St L Ry south to city limits, third east of Lafayette.

Hanover, from Wayne north to W & E canal, first east of College.

Harmer, from N Y, C & St L Ry south to Hayden, second east of Hanna.

Harmony Court, from W Berry north to W Main, first west of Calhoun.

Harrison, from St Mary's river south to city limits, first west of Calhoun.

Hartman, from Pontiac south, fourth east of Walton ave.

Hayden, from Francis east, third south of Lewis.

Hendricks, from Fairfield ave west to Broadway, first north of P, Ft W & C Ry.

Henry ave, from Holton west to Smith, fifth south of Pontiac.

Hensch, from Pfeiffer ave south, third west of Wells.

Herndon, from Hanna east to Gay, first south of Wabash R R.

High, from Wells west to St Mary's, second north of the river.

Highland, from Calhoun west to Webster, second south of Wabash R R.

Hoagland ave, from Wabash R R shops south, third west of Calhoun.

Hoffman, from Wells at canal feeder, west to Tyler ave.

Holman, from Calhoun east to Hanna, second south of Lewis.

Holton ave, from P, Ft W & C Ry to south city limits, seventh east of Hanna.

Home ave, from Fairfield ave west to Broadway, fourth south of W Creighton ave.

Hood, *see Union.*

Horace, from John east to Holton ave, first south of Grant.

Hough, from Clay east to Hanna, first south of Holman.

Howell, from G R & I R R east, second north of Burgess at canal feeder.

Huestis ave, from Broadway west, second south of Creighton ave.

Hugh, from Hanna east to Alliger, first south of Lewis.

Hugh, from Walton ave east of Euclid, first south of Maumee road.

Humphrey, from Grant east to Glasgow, first south of Washington.

Hurd, from Holton ave east, first south of E Creighton ave.

Huron, from St Mary's river west to same, second south of Main.

Indiana ave, from Seneca south across Home ave, second west of Fairfield ave.

Jackson, from N Y, C & St L Ry south to P, Ft W & C Ry, second west of Broadway.

Jane, from Leith south, first east of Calhoun.

Jefferson (East), from Calhoun east to Division, first south of Washington.

Jefferson (West), from Calhoun west to Fair Ground, first south of Washington.

Jenison, from Holton ave east, second south of E Creighton ave.

Jesse, from G R & I R R east, third north of Burgess at canal feeder.

John, from P, Ft W & C Ry south to Pontiac, second east of Hanna.

Jones, from West west to Nelson, second south of Jefferson.

Julia, from Holton ave west, first south of E Creighton ave.

Kansas, from Wabash R R south to Melita, first east of Hoagland ave.

Killea, from Calhoun west to Hoagland ave, first south of Pontiac.

King, from E Wayne south to Maumee road, first east of Harmer.

Koch, from Archer ave south, first west of Wells.

Koenig, from Meegan north, first west of Hanna.

Lafayette, from Superior south to city limits, third east of Calhoun.

Lake, from St Mary's ave at canal feeder, west to Franklin ave.

Laselle, from Lafayette east to Hanna, first south of Charles.

Leith, from Calhoun east to Lafayette, first south of Pontiac.

Lewis (East), from Calhoun east to Walton ave, first south of Jefferson.

Lewis (West), from Calhoun west to Ewing, first south of Jefferson.

Liberty, from Begue east two blocks, second north of Wayne.

Lillie, from Grant south to Pontiac, third east of Holton ave.

Lillie, from Maumee road south to Wabash R R, first west of Walton ave.

Lincoln ave, from Broadway east, third south of W Creighton ave.

Line, from Lumbard east to Burd ave, first south of New Haven road.

Locust, from Fairfield ave west, first south of Wabash R R.

Lumbard, from New Haven road south, first east of tollgate.

McClellan, from W Lewis south to Chicago, first west of Webster.

McCulloch, from Maumee road south to Wabash R R.

McLaughlin, from Leith south, second east of Calhoun.

Madison, from Barr east to Division, first south of Jefferson.

Maiden Lane, from N Y, C & St L Ry south to Berry, first west of Harrison.

Main (East), from Calhoun east to N Y, C & St L Ry, first north of Berry.

Main (West), from Calhoun west to city limits, first north of Berry.

Maple ave, from Broadway west, second south of Creighton ave.

Marchell, from Piqua ave west to Webster, first south of Killea.

Maria, from G R & I R R east, second south of Spring.

Marion, from High north to Third, first west of Wells.

Mary, from Runnion ave west, first north of canal feeder.

Masterson, from Calhoun east to Lafayette, first south of Hamilton.

Maud, from Holton ave west, first north of Pontiac.

Maumee road, from near corner of Washington and Harmer, southeast to city limits.

Mechanic, from Fair north to canal basin, third west of Main Street bridge.

Meegan, from Hanna west, first south of Pontiac.

Melita, from Harrison west to Hoagland ave, first south of Grand.

Mercer, from Walton ave east, third south of P, Ft W & C Ry.

Meridian, from Archer ave south, fourth west of Wells.

Metz, from Taylor south to Wabash R R, first west of Broadway.

Meyer, from Holton ave west to Smith, third south of Pontiac.

Milan, from Edgerton east to Walton ave, first south of Creighton ave.

Miner, from W De Wald south, first east of Broadway.

Montgomery, from Calhoun east to Hanna, first south of Lewis.

Monroe, from Berry south to Laselle, second east of Lafayette.

Muncie, from Pape east, first east of Ft W, C & L Ry.

Murray, from Calhoun east to Lafayette, first south of Wabash
R R.

Nelson, from W Wayne south to P, Ft W & C Ry, fourth
west of Jackson.

Nirdlinger ave, from Broadway west, second south of P, Ft
W & C Ry.

N Calhoun, from Superior north to canal feeder, third east of
Wells.

N Cass, from Wells north to canal feeder.

N Fisher, from Maumee river south to N Y, C & St L Ry,
third east of Glasgow ave.

N Harrison, from Superior north to canal feeder, second east
of Wells.

New Haven ave, from Pioneer ave east to city limits.

Oak, from Division east to Ohio, first south of Maumee road.

Oakland, from canal feeder north to Archer ave, first east of
St Mary's.

Oakley, from Taylor south to W De Wald, first west of
Fairfield ave.

Ohio, from Maumee road south to Wabash R R, third east of
Harmer.

Oliver, from P, Ft W & C Ry south to city limits, first east
of Smith.

Orchard, from High north to Third, second west of Wells.

Osage, from Main north to canal basin, four west of Main
Street bridge.

Pape, from Ft W, C & L Ry south to Breck, first east of St
Mary's ave.

Park, from Maumee river south to Nickel Plate R R, fourth
east of Glasgow ave.

Park ave, from Broadway west, fourth south of Creighton
ave.

Pearl, from Harrison west to Broadway, first north of Main.

Perin, from Alliger east to limits, first south of Maumee road.

Pfeiffer ave (formerly Archer ave), from Wells west to Tyler
ave at north city limits.

Pine, from Taylor north, first west of Fairfield ave.

Pioneer ave, from Walton ave east to Summer.

Piqua ave, from a point on Calhoun 1½ miles from Court
House south.

Pittsburg, from Walton ave east to Burd ave, third south of
New Haven road.

Plum, *see Wells*.

Polk, from canal feeder east, parallel with Ft W, C & L Ry.

Pontiac, from Hoagland ave east to Walton ave, fourth south
of Creighton ave.

Poplar, from Fairfield ave west to Oakley, second south of Taylor.

Prince, from Bass south to Colerick, first east of Fairfield ave.

Pritchard, from Fairfield ave west to Rockhill, second north of P, Ft W & C Ry.

Prospect ave, from Spy Run ave east to St Joe river, first north of Wagner.

Purman, from Warsaw east, first north of Pontiac.

Putnam, from Wells west to Tyler ave, first south of Pfeiffer ave.

Queen, from Pontiac south, third east of Walton ave.

Railroad, from Calhoun east to Pittsburg shops, first north of P, Ft W & C Ry.

Randall from Grant east to Glasgow, second south of Washington.

Randolph, from Spy Run ave to canal feeder, first north of Burgess ave.

Rebecca, from G R & I R R east, third south of Spring.

Reed, from E Creighton ave south to Pontiac, first east of Holton ave.

Reynolds, from Glasgow ave east to Summer.

Richardson, from canal feeder west to G R & I R R, first north of Wheeler.

Riedmiller, from Metz west to Eagle, first south of Taylor.

Rockhill, from W Main south of Pritchard, second west of Jackson.

Ross, from St Mary's river south to W Superior, first west of Fulton.

Rudisill ave, from Calhoun west to Broadway, first south of Home ave.

Rumsey ave, from canal feeder north to Spring, third east of G R & I R R.

Runnion ave, from Main north to Spring, second east of G R & I R R.

Ruth, from Spy Run ave west, second north of St Mary's bridge.

St Martin, from Lafayette east to Hanna, first south of Buchanan.

St Mary's ave, from old canal basin north to city limits, sixth west of Wells.

St Michael ave, from Ross west to Van Buren.

Savilla Place, from Broadway east to Indiana ave.

Samuel, from Hanna east to Holton ave, fifth south of Wabash R R.

Sand, from Maumee river south to N Y, C & St L Ry, first west of Glasgow.

Schick, from N Y, C & St L Ry south to Maumee road, fifth east of Harmer.

Seneca, from Fox west to Broadway, second south of W
Creighton ave.

Sherman, from canal feeder north to Pfeiffer ave, second east
of St Mary's ave.

Short, from Archer ave south, second west of Wells.

Siemon, from Pontiac south to Leith, east of Calhoun.

Simon, from P, Ft W & C Ry east to Walton ave, first south
of Wabash R R.

Sixth, from Wells east to N Calhoun, sixth north of St Mary's
river.

Smith, from P, Ft W & C Ry south to city limits, fourth
east of Hanna.

South Wayne ave, from W Creighton ave south across Home
ave, first west of Fairfield ave.

Spring, from Sherman west to city limits, second north of
canal feeder.

Spring, from canal feeder north to Mary, first west of Runnion ave.

Spy Run ave, from St Mary's river at junction of Superior
and Lafayette, north to city limits.

Stophlet, from Broadway west, first south of Nirdlinger ave.

Sturgis, from Fulton west half block, first south of West
Jefferson.

Summer, from Wabash R R to P, Ft W & C Ry, sixth east
of Walton ave.

Summit, from Division east across McCulloch, first north of
Lewis.

Superior (East), from Calhoun east to Clay, first north of
N Y, C & St L Ry.

Superior (West), from Calhoun west, first north of N Y, C &
St L Ry.

Suttenfield, from Webster east to Hanna, second south of
Creighton ave.

Swinney ave, from Nirdlinger ave west to city limits, first
north of Stophlet.

Taber, from Webster east to Hanna, first south of Creighton
ave.

Taylor, from Fairfield ave west to Lavina ave, fourth south
of P, Ft W & C Ry.

Third, from N Calhoun west to St Mary's ave, third north
of the river.

Thomas, from P, Ft W & C Ry south to Meyer, first west of
Holton ave.

Thomasetta, from Thomas west to Gay, first south of East
Creighton ave.

Thompson ave, from Wabash R R south, first west of Broadway.

Toledo, from Hanna to Lafayette, first south of Wabash R R.

Tons, from Maumee river south, first east of Glasgow ave.

Tyler ave, from Spring south to Howell, first west of Runnion ave.

Union, from Main south to P, Ft W & C Ry, first west of Jackson.

University, from West Wayne south to Maumee road, third east of Harmer.

Van Buren, from St Mary's river south to Pritchard, first west of Broadway.

Victoria ave, from Piqua ave south, first east of Calhoun.

Vine, from Walton ave east, first south of P, Ft W & C Ry.

Virginia, from Lafayette east to Monroe, second south of Wabash R R.

Wabash (Vordermark's addition), from city limits east, first south of Wabash R R.

Wabash ave, from East Wayne south to Maumee road, third east of Walton ave.

Wall, from Broadway west, first south of P, Ft W & C Ry.

Wallace, from Lafayette east to Smith, first south of Virginia.

Walnut, from Fairfield ave west, first south of Taylor.

Walter, from Wayne south to Maumee road, fourth east of Harmer.

Walton ave, from Maumee road south to city limits, tenth east of Hanna.

Warren, from Wabash R R south to P, Ft W & C Ry, first east of Glasgow ave.

Warsaw, from Laselle south to limits, first east of Lafayette.

Washington (East), from Calhoun east to city limits, third south of Main.

Washington (West), from Calhoun west to Fair Grounds, third south of Main.

Watkins, from W Main north to Boone.

Wayne (East), from Calhoun east to city limits, second south of Main.

Wayne (West), from Calhoun west to Schick, second south of Main.

Wayne Trace, from Walton ave south of Wabash Ry, southeast to city limits.

Webster, from St Mary's river south to city limits, second west of Calhoun.

Wefel, from High north to Third, first west of Barthold.

Wells, from W Superior north to city limits.

West, see Rockhill.

Wheeler, from canal feeder west to G R & I R R, first north of Mary.

Wiebke, from Lafayette east to Hanna, 1¾ miles south of Court House.

Williams (East), from Calhoun east to Lafayette, fourth south of Wabash R R.

Williams (West), from Lafayette west to Fairfield ave, fourth south of Wabash R R.

Wilt, from Broadway west to Nelson, first south of Jefferson.

Winch, from Maumee road south to Wayne Trace, third east of Walton ave.

Winter, from Edgerton south to limits, second east of Holton ave.

Wright, from G R & I R R east, first south of Spring.

Zollinger, from Glasgow ave east to Coles.

WARD BOUNDARIES.

No. 1. Bounded on the north by the St Mary's river between Lafayette and Hanna streets, on the east by Hanna, on the south by the P, Ft W & C Ry, and on the west by Lafayette.

No. 2. Bounded on the north by the St Mary's river between Calhoun and Lafayette streets, on the east by Lafayette, on the south by the P, Ft W & C Ry, and on the west by Calhoun.

No. 3. Bounded on the north by the St Mary's river between Calhoun and Cass streets, on the east by Calhoun, on the south by the P, Ft W & C Ry, and on the west by Cass and Webster streets.

No. 4. Bounded on the north by the St Mary's river between Cass and the continuation of Broadway, on the east by Cass and Webster, on the south by the P, Ft W & C Ry, and on the west by Broadway.

No. 5. Bounded on the north by the St Mary's river and canal basin, on the east by Broadway, on the south by the W, St L & P Ry, on the west by Eagle, Taylor, Cherry and Allen County Fair Grounds.

No. 6. Bounded on the north by the W, St L & P Ry, on the east by Calhoun, on the south by Pontiac, Webster and Creighton ave, and on the west by the W, St L & P Ry.

No. 7. Bounded on the north by the P, Ft W & C Ry, on the east by the city limits, on the south by Pontiac and Leith, and on the west by Calhoun.

No. 8. Bounded on the north by the Maumee river, on the east by Glasgow ave, DuBois, Wayne Trace and Grange road, on the south by the P, Ft W & C Ry, and on the west by Hanna.

No. 9. Bounded on the north by Barthold, Archer ave and Spy Run creek, on the east and south by the St. Mary's river, on the west by canal basin and Rumsey ave.

No. 10. Bounded on the north by the P, Ft W & C Ry, on the east by the city limits, on the south by the city limits, and on the west by Hanna street.

CITY GOVERNMENT.

Municipal Election, first Tuesday in May.

Council meets on the second and fourth Tuesday evenings of each month, and at the call of five members.

Council Chamber, City Hall building, Barr street, between Berry and Wayne.

CITY OFFICERS.

Mayor—Daniel L Harding.
Clerk—Rudolph C Reinewald.
Treasurer—Charles J Sosenheimer.
Attorney—Henry Colerick.
Marshal—Henry C Franke.
Assessor—Charles Reese.
Street Commissioner—Dennis O'Brien.
Chief of Police—Frank Wilkinson.
Chief of Fire Department—Henry Hilbrecht jr.
City Engineer—Ochmig B Wiley.
Weighmaster—Patrick Ryan.
Marketmaster—Wm Ropa.
Poundmaster—Wm F Rippe.
Secretary Board of Health—Louis T Sturgis, M D.

COUNCILMEN.

First Ward—John Scheffer, Wm D Meyer.
Second Ward—Maurice Cody, H P Michael.
Third Ward—Joseph L Gruber, Wm F Meyer.
Fourth Ward—Geo W Ely, Henry F Hilgeman.
Fifth Ward—Henry Hilbrecht, Louis P Huser.
Sixth Ward—Frederick Dalman, Robert Cran.
Seventh Ward—Peter J Scheid, G B Gordon.
Eighth Ward—John Smith, Henry P Vordermark.
Ninth Ward—Fred C Boltz, Louis Hazzard.
Tenth Ward—Valentine Ofenloch, J E de La Grange.

BOARD OF HEALTH.

The Mayor, *ex officio* Chairman.
Executive Committee—M Cody, George P Gordon, H F Hilgeman.
Louis F Sturgis, M D, Secretary.

BOARD OF POLICE COMMISSIONERS.

The Mayor, *ex officio* Chairman.
Commissioners—Herman P Michael, Henry Hilbrecht, George P Gordon, John Smith.

WATER WORKS TRUSTEES.

Christian Boseker, Pres ; Wm Bittler, Charles McCulloch.

FIRE DEPARTMENT.

Chief Engineer—Henry Hilbrecht, jr; office cor Court and E Berry.

Assistants—John McGowan, Fred Becker.

Commissioners—Robert Cran, George W Ely, Lewis P Huser, Peter J Scheid.

Hook and Ladder Company No 1—Northwest cor Clinton and Berry. John Baker, foreman ; Robert T Waggner, driver ; Ferdinand Schroeder, tillerman; James T McElfatrick, Peter Freiburger, Edwin L Kirkendall, laddermen.

Hook and Ladder Company No 2—Wallace, bet Lafayette and Clay. August Tremmel, driver.

Steamer No 1—Northeast cor Court and Berry. John Schroeder, engineer ; Christian Rohyans, driver.

Steamer No 2—Wallace bet Lafayette and Clay. Michael Connors, engineer ; John Stahlhout, driver.

Hose Company No 1—Northwest cor Clinton and Berry. Charles Becker, foreman ; George Wesson, driver ; Frederick Reinking, hoseman.

Hose Company No 2—Wallace bet Lafayette and Clay. George Klingman, driver ; Emanuel Hoch, hoseman.

Hose Company No 3—Northeast cor Court and Berry. Charles Sheldon, foreman ; Edward Moody, driver ; John D. Carl, hoseman.

Chemical Engine Co—N E cor Court and Berry. Louis Steup, driver.

FIRE ALARM TELEGRAPH STATIONS.

6—S E Corner Calhoun and Columbia streets.
7—Corner St Mary's ave and Spring street.
8—   "   Wells and Hoffman streets.
12—   "   Wells and Third streets.
13—   "   High and Clark streets.
14—   "   Superior and Ewing streets.
15—   "   Calhoun and Jefferson streets.
16—   "   Calhoun and Chicago streets.
17—   "   Calhoun and Williams streets.
18—   "   Calhoun and Leith streets.
23—   "   Washington and Clay streets.
24—   "   Washington and Harmer streets.
25—   "   Lewis and Hanna streets.
26—   "   Summit and Division streets.
27—   "   Maumee ave and Schick street.
28—White's Factory.
31—Corner Douglas ave and Webster street.
32—   "   Jefferson and Griffith streets.

34—Corner Broadway and Wilt streets.
35— " Washington and VanBuren streets.
36— " Union and Pritchard streets.
37— " Broadway and Wall streets.
38— ⏹ " Washington and College streets.
41—Olds & Sons' Works.
42—Engine House No 2.
43—Corner Hanna and Wallace streets.
45— " Grant and Smith streets.
46— " Hanna street and Creighton ave.
47— " Lafayette and DeWald streets.
48— " Creighton ave and Thomas street.
51— " Wayne and Webster streets.
52— " Main and Griffith streets.
53— " Main and Van Buren streets.
54— " Main and Cherry streets.
56— " Boone and Osage streets.
61—Engine House No 1.
62—Corner Harrison and Columbia streets.
63— " Columbia and Barr streets.
64— " Barr and Madison streets.
65— " Lafayette and Holman streets.
67—Pittsburgh Round House.
71—Corner Fairfield ave and Bass street.
72— " Butler street and Hoagland ave.
73— " Broadway and Taylor street.
74— " Fox and DeWald streets.
81— " Wayne and Walter streets.
82— " Lewis and Lillie streets.
83— " Washington and Grant avenue.

POLICE DEPARTMENT.

Headquarters, City Hall Building, Barr street, between Berry
and Wayne.
Chief—Frank Wilkinson.
Clerks—Wilmer Wilkinson, Andrew Schearer.
Patrolmen—Henry Lapp, Lieutenant; John O'Connell, John
Siebold, Joseph Gushing, Stephen Fletcher, Henry
Shroeder, George Humbrecht, John Kenelly, Edward
Quinn, George McCrorey, Michael Singleton, George D
Lee, John Tremmel, John Trautman, Patrick O'Ryan,
Wm Kramer, Frank Rohle, Frederick Stahlhut, Charles
M· Romey, Enoch Richter, Frederick Bandau, Henry
Harkenrider, Jesse Patton, Frederick Daseler, Henry
Stohl, Frederick Limecooly.
Marshal—Henry C Franke.
Drivers Patrol Wagon—Henry Sanders, George Swain.

RATES OF FARE.

AS ESTABLISHED BY CITY ORDINANCES, RELATIVE TO PUBLIC CARRIAGES.

Sec. 7. The prices to be charged by the owner or driver of any vehicle, except an omnibus, for the conveyance of passengers for hire, within said city, shall be as follows, to be regulated and estimated by the distance on the most direct routes, namely:

For conveying a passenger not exceeding one mile..... 50c
For conveying a passenger any distance over a mile and less than two miles..........................$1.00

For conveying children between five and fourteen years of age, half the above prices may be charged for like distances, but for children under five years of age no charge shall be made, unless such child is the only passenger, in which case full charge may be made.

The distance from any railroad depot or hotel to any other railroad or hotel shall, in all cases, be estimated as not exceeding one mile.

For the use of coaches drawn by two horses, with one or more passengers, by the day............. $8.00

For the use of any vehicle by the hour, with one or more passengers, with the privilege of going from place to place, and stopping when required, as follows:

For the first hour..................................... $1.50
For each succeeding hour........................... 1.00

Every passenger shall be allowed to have conveyed upon such vehicle, without charge, his ordinary traveling baggage, not exceeding in any case one trunk.

Sec. 13. Any person who shall violate any or either of the provisions of this chapter, or any section, clause or provision of any section of this chapter, or who shall fail or neglect to comply with any or either of the requirements thereof, shall, upon conviction, pay a fine of not more than one hundred dollars.

FORT WAYNE STREET RAILROAD CO.

President—John H Bass.
Vice-President—S B Bond.
Secretary—J M Barrett.
Treasurer—A S Bond.
Superintendent—L D McNutt.

Office, corner Main and Calhoun streets. Operate the following lines:

Route No 1—Belt line. Commencing at Main and Calhoun streets on Calhoun, then south on Calhoun street passing the

Pittsburgh, Grand Rapids and Wabash depots and on to Creighton ave, then west on Creighton ave to Broadway, north on Broadway to Main street, then east on Main street to Calhoun, forming a belt line.

Route No 2—Bloomingdale, Hanna and Walton ave line. Commencing at the corner of Wells and Third streets, to Cass street, west on Cass, passing the Lake Shore and Muncie depot to Wells street, south on Wells to Superior street, east on Superior to Calhoun street, south on Calhoun, passing the Pittsburg, Grand Rapids and Wabash depots to Hamilton street, east on Hamilton to Lafayette, north on Lafayette to Wallace street, east on Wallace to John street, south on John to Creighton ave, east on Creighton ave to Walton ave or the new yards.

Route No. 3—Main street line. Commencing at Glasgow ave on east Washington street, then west on Washington to Harmer, south on Harmer to Jefferson street, west on Jefferson to Lafayette street, north on Lafayette on Main street, then west on Main to Linwood Cemetery.

Route 4—Commencing at Garden street, running east on Jefferson to Broadway, connecting with the Belt Line.

FEDERAL OFFICERS.

GOVERNMENT BUILDING.

Postmaster—C R Higgins.
Collector of Internal Revenue—John S Cravens.
Division Deputy Collector Internal Revenue—Wm O Butler.
Deputy Collector Internal Revenue—Claude C Miller.
U S Gauger—James Liggett.
U S Commissioner—Elmer Leonard.
U S District Attorney—Smiley Chambers, Indianapolis.
U S Deputy Marshal—Robert B Hanna.
Deputy Clerk U S District Court—John Morris, jr.

COUNTY OFFICERS.

Court House, bet Calhoun and Court, south of Main and north of Berry.
Judge of the Circuit Court—Hon Edward O'Rourke.
Judge of the Superior Court—Hon Augustus A Chapin.
Clerk—Jacob J Kern.
Prosecuting Attorney—James M Robinson.
Sheriff—George H Viberg.
Recorder—Milton Thompson.
Treasurer—Isaac Mowrer.
Auditor—John B Niezer.
Surveyor—Henry E Fischer.

5

Supt of Bridges—W H Goshorn.
Coroner—Abraham J Kesler.
Commissioners—Jasper W Jones, John H Brannan and
    Henry F Bullermann.
Attorney for County Commissioners—Robert C Bell.
School Superintendent—George F Felts.

COURTS.

TIME OF HOLDING COURTS IN ALLEN COUNTY.

Circuit Court—First Monday in February, third Monday in
    April, first Monday in September, and third Monday in
    November. Hon Edward O'Rourke, Judge ; James M
    Robinson, Prosecuting Attorney.
Superior Court—Second Monday in January, first Monday in
    April, second Monday in September and second Monday
    in November. Hon Augustus A Chapin, Judge.

U. S. COURTS.

COURT ROOMS IN GOVERNMENT BUILDING.

District Court of United States—Second Tuesdays in June
    and December. Hon W A Woods, Judge ; Noble C
    Butler, Clerk ; John Morris, jr, Resident Deputy Clerk;
    Wm L Dunlap, Marshal ; Robert B Hanna, Resident
    Deputy Marshal.
Circuit Court of United States—Second Tuesdays in June
    and December. Hon W Q Gresham, Judge ; Noble C
    Butler, Clerk ; John Morris, jr, Resident Deputy Clerk ;
    Wm L Dunlap, Marshal ; Robert B Hanna, Resident
    Deputy Marshal.

COUNTY BOARD OF TRUSTEES, WITH POST-OFFICE ADDRESS.

Aboite—Thomas Covington, Fort Wayne.
Adams—Martin P Habecker, Fort Wayne.
Cedar Creek—Wm C Howey, Leo P O.
Eel River—John Holmes, Wallen P O.
Jefferson—Edward Harper, Gar Creek P O.
Jackson—John McConnel, Monroeville P O.
Lafayette—Jacob Kuyser, Zanesville P O.
Lake—John G Clapesattle, Arcola P O.
Madison—Wm Franke, Hoagland P O.
Marion—David Gibson, Root P O.
Maumee—Robert B Shirley, Woodburn P O.
Milan—Gottleib Schafer, Goeglein P O.
Monroe—Sylvanus F Baker, Dixon, O, P O.

Perry—Florentine Roy, Fort Wayne.
Pleasant—Wm Dalman, Sheldon P O.
St Joseph—C H Rose, Fort Wayne.
Scipio—Benjamin F Rose, Hicksville, O, P O.
Springfield—Clarence F Swift, Harlan P O.
Washington—Matthew A Ferguson, Fort Wayne.
Wayne—George W Brackenridge, Fort Wayne.

BANDS OF MUSIC.

First Regiment Band and Orchestra, Harry Achenbach
leader and manager ; office 212 Calhoun.
Fort Wayne City Band, brass and string, Prof Philip Keinz
leader ; office 12 W Main.
Reineke's Orchestra, Frederick J Reineke leader; office 12
W Main.

BANKS AND BANKERS.

First National Bank, s e cor Court and Main. Capital and
surplus, $415,000. Organized May, 1863 ; re-organized
May, 1882. John W Bass, Pres ; M. W. Simons, Vice-
Pres ; L R Hartman, Cash ; W L Pettit, Asst Cash.
Hamilton National Bank, 44 Calhoun. Capital, $200,000 ;
surplus, $200,000. Organized 1874. Charles McCulloch,
Pres ; John Mohr, jr, Cash ; C W Orr, Asst Cash.
Nuttman & Co (private), 32 E Main. Organized 1883.
Old National Bank The, s w cor Calhoun and Berry. Cap-
ital, $350,000 ; surplus, $70,000. Organized 1885. S B
Bond, Pres ; O P Morgan, Vice-Pres ; J D Bond, Cash ;
J C Woodworth, Asst Cash.

BUILDING, LOAN AND SAVINGS ASSOCIA-
TIONS.

Allen County Loan and Savings Association.—Organized
April 7th, 1890. Capital stock, $1,000,000. Meets first
and third week each month at White's Block. Edward
White, Pres ; Gottlieb Haller, Vice-Pres ; L Gruber,
Sec ; Thomas C Rogers, Acting Sec ; Charles W Orr,
Treas.
Fidelity Building and Savings Bank Union. H Hohnholz,
Pres ; H L Studer, Vice-Pres ; W A Speice, Sec ; Daniel
Krapf, Treas. Meets Wednesday before the 20th of
each month at Union Hall, 7 E Main.
Fort Wayne Building, Loan-Fund and Savings Association.
Organized April 11, 1884. Capital stock, $500,000.
Meets first Tuesday after the 18th of each month at Odd
Fellows' Hall (new). Stockholders' meeting to elect

officers, etc, second Wednesday in May. F D Lasanave,
Pres ; O E Bradway, Vice-Pres ; C W Howey, Sec;
Christopher Hettler, Treas.
German Building, Loan-Fund and Savings Asssciation, No 1.
Organized June, 1886. Meets last Monday of each
month at Custer House. Otto P Herbst, Pres and
Sec ; George Motz, Treas.
German Building, Loan-Fund and Savings Association, No 3.
Organized September, 1884. Meets fourth Friday in
each month at Custer House. Stockholders' meeting
to elect officers, etc, first Monday in October. Wm.
Meyers, Pres ; John H Pranger, Sec ; Charles Stellhorn,
Treas.
German Building, Loan and Savings Association, No
4.—Organized November 20, 1887. Meets first Wed-
nesday of each month at Custer House. Otto Nich-
ter, Pres ; Henry Zur Muehlen, Sec ; A Fuelber, Treas.
German Building, Loan-Fund and Savings Association, No 5,
Organized January 10, 1885. Meets fourth Tuesday
of each month at the Custer House. Peter G Holmhaus,
Pres ; Otto P Herbst, Sec ; George Motz, Treas.
Summit City Building, Loan-Fund and Savings Association.
Organized October 14, 1886. Meets first Monday of
each month at Custer House. J B Monning, Pres; Otto
P Herbst, Sec; George Motz, Treas.
Tri-State Building and Loan Association—Organized July,
1889. Capital stock $2,000,000 ; 13 and 14 Pixley &
Long Building. George W Pixley, Pres; A D Cressler,
Vice-Pres; C A Wilding, Sec; Joseph W Bell, Treas.
Washington German Building, Loan-Fund and Savings
Association—Organized December, 1887. Meets first
Tuesday of each month at Custer House. Stockholders'
meeting to elect officers, etc, second Tuesday in Decem-
ber. Otto Nichter, Pres; John H Pranger, Sec; Charles
Liebenguth, Treas.
Wayne Building, Loan and Savings Association—Organized
October 24, 1887. Meets third Friday of each month at
Custer House. Jacob Hartman, Pres; Otto P Herbst,
Sec; George Motz, Treas.

CEMETERIES.

Achduth Veshalom Congregation (Jewish), e s Broadway,
bet Wabash and P, Ft W & C R R's.
German-Lutheran (St John's), Bluffton road, 3 miles s w from
city.
Concordia, n s Maumee ave, e of Concordia College. Wm.
Meinzen, Supt.

Lindenwood, on Huntington road, half mile west of city
limits. John H Doswell, Supt.
New Catholic, Hicksville State road, 1½ miles e of city limits.

CHURCHES.

BAPTIST.

First Baptist Tabernacle of the People, W Jefferson, bet
Harrison and Webster. Rev S A Northrop, Pastor.
Sunday Services 10:30 a m and 7:30 p m; Sunday School
2 p m; prayer meeting Wednesday evening at 7:30.
Young People's Society meets Monday evening at 7:30.

CATHOLIC.

Cathedral of the Immaculate Conception, Cathedral Square,
Calhoun, bet Lewis and Jefferson. Rt Rev Joseph
Dwenger, D D, Bishop of the Diocese and Rector of the
Cathedral; Very Rev Joseph H Brammer, V G; Rev
John F Lang, Chancellor and Bishop's Secretary; Rev
Michael J Burns, Rev J F Delaney. Sunday services 6,
7:30, 8:30 (children's services) and 10:30 a m; Sunday
school 1:30 p m; Vespers 3 p m.
St Joseph's Chapel (in connection with St Joseph's Hospital).
Thomas Eisenring, C, P P, S, Chaplain. Sunday services
8:00 a m and 4 p m. Week day services 8 a m.
St Mary's (German) Church southeast cor Jefferson and
Lafayette. Rev John H Oechtering, Rector. Sunday
services 10 a m and 3 p m ; Sunday school 2 p m.
St Paul's (German) Church, southeast cor Griffith and W
Washington. Rev Edward Koenig, Rector. Sunday
services 10 a m and 2.30 p m ; Sunday school 2 p m.
St Peter's (German) Church, south side St Martin's, bet
Warsaw and Hanna. Rev A Messman, Rector. Sunday
services 8 and 10 a m and 2 p m ; Sunday school 9 a m.

CHRISTIAN.

Christian Chapel, southeast cor W Jefferson and Griffith.
Elder G H Sims, Pastor. Sunday services 10:30 a m and
7:30 p m ; Sunday school 9:15 a m.

CHURCH OF GOD.

Cor Hoagland ave and DeWald. Sunday services 10:30 a m
and 7:30 p m ; Sunday school 9 a m.

CONGREGATIONAL.

Plymouth Congregational Church, northwest cor W Washington and Fulton. Rev James S Ainslie, Pastor. Sunday services 10:30 a m and 7:30 p m ; Sunday school 12
noon. Prayer meeting Wednesday 7:30 p m.

EPISCOPAL.

Trinity Church, southwest cor Fulton and W Berry. Rev A W Seabrease, Rector. Sunday services 10:45 a m and 3 and 7:30 p m, from October to June, and 9:30 a m from June to October; Sunday school 2:30 p m.

EVANGELICAL ASSOCIATION.

Church northeast cor, Holman and Clinton. Rev Charles Hansing, Pastor. Sunday services 10:30 a m and 7 p m; Sunday school 9:30 a m.

GERMAN REFORM.

St John's Church, southeast cor W Washington and Webster. Rev Carl Schaaf, Pastor. Sunday services 10:30 a m and 7:30 p m; winter 7 p m. Sunday school 9 a m.

Salem Church, east side Clinton, bet Wayne and Berry. Rev C F Kriete, Pastor. Sunday services 10:30 a m and 7:30 p m; Sunday school 2 p m in winter, and 9 a m in summer.

ENGLISH.

Grace Reformed Church, south side E Washington, bet Barr and Lafayette. Rev A K Zartman, Pastor. Sunday services 10:30 a m and 7:30 p m; Sunday school 9:30 a m. Week-day services Wednesday 7:30 p m.

HEBREW.

Achduth Veshalom Temple, s w cor Harrison and Wayne. Services Friday 7 p m, and Saturday 10 a m. Children's instruction, Sunday 10 to 12 a m and 1 to 2 p m.

LUTHERAN.

Emanuel Church, south side W Jefferson, bet Union and Jackson. Rev Charles Gross, Pastor. Sunday services 10 a m and 2 p m.

Evangelical Lutheran Zion's Congregational Church, southwest cor E Creighton ave and Force. Rev Henry Juengel, Pastor. Services Sunday 10 a m and 2 p m, and Friday 7:30 p m.

St John's German Lutheran Church, southeast cor Washington and Van Buren. Rev Henry P Donncekir, Pastor. Sunday services 10 a m and 2:30 p m, Wednesday 7:30 p m.

St Paul's German Lutheran Church, west side Barr bet Jefferson and Lewis. Rev Henry G Sauer, Pastor. Services Sunday 10 a m and 2:30 p m, Wednesday 7:30 p m.

Trinity Church (English Lutheran), southeast cor Wayne and Clinton. Rev Samuel Wagenhals, Pastor. Sunday services 10:30 a m and 7:30 p m; Sunday school 2 p m.

METHODIST EPISCOPAL.

Berry Street Church, northeast cor W Berry and Harrison. Rev Wm M Van Slyke, Pastor. Sunday services 10:30 a m and 7:30 p m; Sunday school 2:15 p m. Prayer meeting Wednesday 7:30 p m.

St Paul's Church, west side Walton ave south of Wabash R R. Rev M C Cooper, Pastor. Sunday services 10:30 a m and 7:30 p m. Sunday school 2:30 p m.

Simpson M E Church, southeast cor Dawson and Harrison. Rev John M Drives, Pastor. Sunday services 10:45 a m and 7:30 p m; Sabbath school 9:30 a m. Prayer meeting Thursday 7:30 p m.

Trinity Church, northeast cor Cass and Fourth. Rev Nathan D Shackelford, Pastor. Sunday services 10:30 a m and 7:30 p m. Sunday school 2 p m.

Wayne Street Church, southwest cor Broadway and W Wayne. Rev R Monroe Barnes, Pastor. Sunday services 10:30 a m and 7:30 p m; Sunday school 2 p m. Prayer meeting Wednesday 7:30 p m. Epworth League service 6:30 p m.

Free Methodist Church, south side Creighton ave east of Thomas. Sunday services 10:30 a m and 8 p m. Sunday school 2.30 p m. Prayer meeting Thursday, 8 p m.

African Methodist Church, northeast cor E Wayne and Francis. Rev Cyrus F Hill, pastor. Sunday services 10:30 a m and 7:30 p m; Sunday school 2 p m.

PRESBYTERIAN.

First Presbyterian Church, northeast cor Clinton and E Washington. Rev D W Moffat, D D, Pastor. Sunday services at 10:45 and 7:30 p m; Sunday school 9:30 a m. Prayer meeting Wednesday 7:30 p m.

Second Presbyterian Church, south side Berry bet Webster and Ewing. Rev James L Leeper, Pastor. Sunday services 10:45 a m and 7:30 p m; Sunday school 12 noon. Prayer meeting Wednesday evening 7:30.

Third Presbyterian Church, northeast cor Calhoun and Holman. Rev J M Boggs, Pastor. Sunday services 10:30 a m and 7:30 p m; Sunday school 2 p m. Prayer meeting Wednesday evening 7:30.

Glenwood Chapel Mission of the Second Presbyterian Church, S Broadway s of city limits. Has no pastor. Sunday school 3:30 p m.

UNITED BRETHREN.

First U B Church, southeast cor E Lewis and Harmer. Rev John W Lower, Pastor. Sunday services 10:30 a m and 7:30 p m. Prayer meeting Wednesday and Friday evenings at 8.

Second U B Church, southwest cor Boone and Fry. Sunday services 10:30 a m and 7:30 p m.

INCORPORATED INSTITUTIONS.

Anthony Wayne Manufacturing Co, cor Lafayette and W, St L & P Ry, incorporated January 27, 1886, capital $18,000. John Rhinesmith, Pres; James H Simonson, Sec and Treas; Albert C F Wichman, Supt.

Bash S & Co, incorporated June 4, 1890, capital $100,000. S Bash, Pres; C S Bash, Vice-Pres; W B Bash, Sec; P D Smyser, Treas.

Bass Foundry and Machine Works, Hanna s of.Wabash R R established 1853, incorporated 1873, capital $500,000, John H Bass, Pres; J I White, Sec; R J Fisher, Treas.

Berghoff Herman Brewing Co The, incorporated April, 1887,. capital $100,000. Herman Berghoff, Pres; Hubert Berghoff, Sec and Treas; e s Grant ave, near E Washington.

Brookside Farm Co, 1½ miles west of city, incorporated March, 1884. John H Bass, Pres; David McKay, Sec; Frank S Lightfoot, Treas.

Dreibelbiss Abstract Co, rooms 3 and 4 Pixley & Long bldg, incorporated January, 1887, capital $10,000. John Dreibelbiss, Pres; R B Dreibelbiss, Sec-Treas.

First Regiment Light Artillery Band, 212 Calhoun, organized August 8, 1888, capital $2,500. Charles Deirstein, Pres; Herman Wichman, Sec; Samuel Talbot, Treas.

Fort Wayne Business Men's Exchange, 98 Calhoun, incorporated January 11, 1887. John B Monning, Pres; W D Page, Vice-Pres; A S Lauferty, Treas; A J Moynihan, Fin and Rec Sec.

Fort Wayne City Band, 12 W Main, organized 1874, capital $2,000. John Dennison, Pres; Fred Goebel, Sec; F J Reineke, Treas; Philip Keinz, Leader.

Fort Wayne City Bill Posting Co, incorporated December, 1884. C B Woodworth, Pres; H J Seibold, Sec-Treas; George C Richard, Supt. Office 1 Aveline House Block.

Fort Wayne City Hospital, incorporated November 2, 1878. M L Albrecht, Pres; W D Page, Sec; E F Yarnelle, Treas; Mrs C L Smith, Supt; s w cor Barr and Washington.

Fort Wayne Conservatory of Music, incorporated 1871. L M Ninde, Pres; Fred J Hayden, Sec; C F W Meyer, Prin; 22, 24 and 26 E Main.

Fort Wayne Electric Co,. incorporated August 12, 1889, capital $3,000,000. H G Olds, Pres; P A Randall, Vice-Pres; R T McDonald, Treas and Genl Mgr; Brainard Rorison, Sec; Broadway and Wabash R R.

Fort Wayne Furniture Co The, incorporated November, 1887, capital $75,000. D N Foster, Pres; P A Randall, Vice-Pres; E C Hedekin, Sec; D B Kehler, Treas; Office and factory e end of Columbia.

Fort Wayne Gas Light Co, s e cor Superior and Barr; organized 1855, capital $225,000. James Cheney, Pres, Treas and Supt; Wm J Probasco, Sec.

Fort Wayne Land Improvement Co, incorporated February, 1890, capital $250,000. D N Foster, Pres; P A Randall, Vice-Pres; C A Wilding, Sec; George W Pixley, Treas; 12 Pixley & Long bldg.

Fort Wayne Newspaper Union (eastern branch Chicago Newspaper Union), J F Cramer, Pres; C E Strong, Treas; Charles D Tillo, Manager. Office 55 and 57 E Columbia.

Fort Wayne Organ Co, incorporated 1871, office and factory e s Fairfield ave, s of Creighton ave. S B Bond, Pres; C E Bond, Sec; A S Bond, Treas and Supt.

Fort Wayne Relief Union, office 144 Pritchard, incorporated 1882. Mrs H F Guild, Pres; Mrs A R Henderson, Vice-Pres; Mrs G E Bursley, Sec; Miss C Hamilton, Treas.

Fort Wayne Street Railroad Co, incorporated 1887. J H Bass, Pres; S B Bond, Vice-Pres; J M Barrett, Sec; A S Bond, Treas; L D McNutt, Supt. Office s w cor Main and Calhoun.

Fort Wayne Transfer & Storage Co, 47 East Columbia, incorporated 1888, capital $5,000. James Wilding, Pres; D S McCarthy, Sec and Treas.

Fort Wayne Water Power Co, J H Bass, Pres; H J Miller, Sec; Lew R Hartman, Treas.

Foster D N Furniture Co, incorporated August 9, 1884, capital $80,000. D N Foster, Pres; S M Foster, Sec; W J Kettler, Treas. Office 11 Court.

Hoffman Lumber Co, office 200 W Main, incorporated 1887, A E Hoffman, Pres; Wm H Hoffman, Vice-Pres; John W Sale, Treas; M P Longacre, Sec.

Hoosier Manufacturing Co, office and factory 28 and 30 East Berry, incorporated April, 1882, capital $30,000. Amos S Evans, Pres; John P Evans, Treas; George P Evans, Sec; J F Budd, Supt.

Horton Manufacturing Co, cor Main and Osage, incorporated 1883, capital $30,000. H C Paul, Pres; W A Bohn, Sec-Treas; J C Peters, Genl Mngr.

Indiana Machine Works, Osage near W Main. J C Peters, Pres; P A Randall, Vice-Pres; E H McDonald, Sec; J M Landenberger, Treas and Mngr.

Inter-State Fair Association, incorporated 1886, capital $25,000, office 32 East Berry. Wm D Page, Pres; J W Pearse, Vice-Pres and Supt; D C Fisher, Sec and Treas.

"Jenney" Electric Light and Power Co, Spy Run ave, office rooms 38 and 39 Pixley & Long Bldg, incorporated 1883, capital $50,000. H C Graffe, Pres; G W Pixley, Treas; Emmet H McDonald, Sec; Charles G Guild, Supt.

Journal Co The, 30 E Main, incorporated May 12, 1884, capital $10,000. W W Rockhill, Pres and Mngr; A J Moynihan, Sec and Treas.

Kerr-Murray Manufacturing Co, n e cor Calhoun and Murray, incorporated 1881, capital $100,000. A D Cressler, Pres and Genl Mngr; G A Schust, Sec; G L Hackius, Treas.

Masonic Temple Association, capital $50,000, incorporated February, 1878. Edward O'Rourke, Pres; W W Rockhill, Sec; A H Dougall, Treas; n e cor Clinton and Wayne.

Master Builders' Association, incorporated March 14, 1890, capital $2,000. Wm Geake, Pres; Levi Griffith, Vice-Pres; J W Wilding, Sec and Treas. Office 195 Calhoun.

Mayflower Mills The, incorporated October 1889, capital $20,000. Charles S Bash, Pres; Joseph Hughes, Mngr; 20 W Columbia.

Old Fort Manufacturing Co, office 3 and 4 Pixley & Long Bldg, incorporated September 17, 1888, capital $20,000. Francis A Lamont, Pres; John Dreibelbiss, Sec and Treas.

Olds' Wagon Works, incorporated 1882, capital $200,000. Henry G Olds, Pres; A H Hamilton, Vice-Pres; Wm Johnston, jr, Sec; W H Olds, Treas; s s Murray bet Calhoun and Lafayette.

Peters Box and Lumber Co, 79 to 101 High, established 1870, incorporated Nov 26, 1873, capital $55,000. Charles Pape, Pres and Genl Mngr; W H Murtaugh, Vice-Pres; Wilson McQuiston, Sec.

Salamonie Mining & Gas Co, 50 Clinton, incorporated 1887, capital $750,000. Henry C Paul, Pres; Charles S Bash, Vice-Pres; Charles McCulloch, Sec; F E W Scheimann, Treas; G Max Hofmann, Supt.

Standard Medical & Surgical Institute, incorporated 1890, capital $100,000. J W Younge, A M, M D, Pres; W J Carter, A M, M D, Genl Mngr; N B Smith, M D, Treas; W W Smith, Ph D, Sec. Office 210 Calhoun.

Star Iron Tower Co, incorporated February, 1884, capital $25,000. J H Bass, Pres; H G Olds, Vice-Pres; R T McDonald, Sec; P A Randall, Treas; cor Plum and Nickel Plate R R.

Taylor Bros Piano Co The, incorporated January, 1885, capital $4,000. S R Taylor, Pres; I N Taylor, Sec. Office 138 Calhoun.

Taylor University of Fort Wayne, foot of Wayne, C B Stemen, Pres; H C Schrader, Sec; Charles McCulloch, Treas.

Western Gas Construction Co, incorporated May 20, 1890, capital $50,000. Olof N Guldlin, Pres; Gordon W Lloyd, Vice-Pres and Treas, Detroit, Mich; Frank H Adams, Sec; John Sunger, Engineer. Offices 24 to 27 Pixley & Long Bldg.

LIBRARIES.

Allen County Teachers' Library, 7 Trentman Blk. George F Felts, Librarian.

Catholic Young Men's Reading Halls and Club Rooms; open every evening in Library Hall.

Fort Wayne Catholic Circulating Library and Association, 8,000 volumes, established July 1st, 1871, incorporated August 4th, 1874; Library Hall, n e cor Calhoun and E Lewis. Kilian Baker, President (*ex officio*) ; George A Fry, Pres; M J Houlihan, Sec; George A Litot, Treas; Rev M J Byrne, Librarian. Association meets first Thursday in each month. Library open Sundays from 3 to 5, and 7 to 9 p m.

Woman's Free Reading Room, 23½ W Wayne, 1,300 volumes. Laura Goshorn, Librarian.

MILITARY.

Fort Wayne Rifles, meet every Tuesday evening at 166 Calhoun. W H Peltier, Capt; Charles J Bulger, 1st Lieut; W W Kerr, 2d Lieut; Charles J Bulger, Sec; C E Reese, Company Clerk and Treas.

German Military Co. Henry Heine, Sec; 26 W Main; meets last Sunday in each month.

Zollinger Battery The. W W Munger, Capt; Wm F Ranke, 1st Lieut; F J Rooney, Sec.

MISCELLANEOUS INSTITUTIONS AND SOCIETIES.

Academy of Medicine. Dr G W McCaskey, Pres; Dr A P Buchman, Sec; meets every alternative Monday evening.

Allen County Asylum, n s Bluffton rd, opp toll gate. John Wilkinson, Supt.

Allen County Bible Society, Dr Wm T Ferguson, Pres; W E Griffith, Vice-Pres; H C Schrader, Sec; F D Paulus, Treas. 46 Harrison.

Allen County Licensed Liquor Dealers' Protective Association, meets first Tuesday in each month at 2 p m, in hall

64 E Main. Jacob Hartman, Pres; George J Ortlieb, Cor Sec; B Weber, Fin Sec; Christ Entemann, Treas.

Allen County Medical Society, Dr A P Buchanan, Pres; Dr Howard McCullough, Sec. Meets first Tuesday evening in each month.

Barbers' Union No 14, meets in hall in Bank Block every second and fourth Tuesday of each month. I J Swinehart, Pres; Wm G Miller, Fin Sec; Charles Yeakley, Treas.

Bricklayers' Union, meets every Monday evening at 30 E Main.

Brickmakers' Association. Office 55 Clinton; James S Field, Agent.

Brotherhood of Locomotive Engineers, Division No 12, meets every Sunday afternoon at 2, at hall, 140 Calhoun.

Brotherhood of Locomotive Firemen, meets every Wednesday evening at n w cor Berry and Calhoun.

Brotherhood of Railroad Brakemen, meets every alternate Sunday afternoon and every alternate Monday evening of each month, at 27 Calhoun.

Bruederlicher Unterstuetzungs Verein, meets third Sunday of each month at Carpenters' Union Hall. Frederick Schmetzer, Pres ; Charles H Buck, Sec ; Wm Schmidt, Treas.

Butchers' Association, meets first Tuesday in each month, in Nimrod Hall, 54 E Main. Gottlieb Haller, Pres ; David Shaw, Sec.

Caledonian Society, meets first and third Mondays of each month at 76 Calhoun. J B White, Pres ; A H Dougal, Vice-Pres ; Wm Lawson, Sec and Treas.

Carpenters' Union, meets every Saturday at 7:30 p m, at room 7, 30 E Main.

Catholic Knights of America, St Bernard Branch No 103, meets first and third Sundays of each month at Library Hall, n e cor Calhoun and E Lewis. Very Rev J H Brammer, Spiritual Director ; Frank H Fink, Pres ; Patrick Ryan, Rec Sec.

Catholic Young Mens' Amusement Society, Library Hall, rooms open from 8 a m to 10 p m. Rev M J Byrne, director.

Commandry No. 73, Knights of St. John, under the control of Branch 103, C K of A. Fred Graffe, jr, Capt ; Louis H Gocke, Rec Sec.

Crow Club meets in hall 195 Calhoun second and fourth Sundays of each month. Louis Schmoe, Pres ; Fred Krebs, Fin Sec ; John Winbaugh, Treas.

Eureka Social Club, organized Sept, 1885. O W Tresselt, Pres ; J A Thieme, Vice-Pres ; F Wise, Sec ; F Tresselt, Treas ; s w cor Calhoun and Main.

Fort Wayne Amateur Athletic Club, 14 W Berry; James B White, jr, Pres; Edward N Detzer, Vice-Pres; Samuel W Albratt, Sec. ; Frederick W Beach, Treas.

Fort Wayne Bicycle Club, 142 Calhoun, organized 1884. Membership, 60. C W Edgerton, Pres; John L Hannah, Sec ; F M Smith, Treas.

Fort Wayne Cigar Maker's Union No 37, meets every Saturday evening and first and third Friday evenings of each month, in rooms 30 E Main. Charles Sauer, Pres; Thomas Major, Vice-Pres; W T Jeffries, Sec; Fred Krebs, Treas.

Fort Wayne City Hospital, cor Barr and Washington. M L Albrecht, $_{Pres}$; W D Page, Sec; E F Yarnelle, Treas.

Fort Wayne College of Medicine. C B Stemen, M D, Dean of the Faculty; W P Wherry, M D, Sec.

Fort Wayne Electric Club, meets first Tuesday in each month, in Schmitz Blk. Charles C Miller, Pres; Harry C McKinley, Vice-Pres; Eugene McLachlin, Sec; Lewis Freyer, Treas.

Fort Wayne Saenger Bund, organized Feb 10, 1869, meets every Tuesday for rehearsal. Regular meeting first Sunday after first Tuesday in each month at Nimrod Hall, 54 E Main. Adam Schlegel, Pres; August Laghorst, Sec; Nicholas Moster, Director.

Fort Wayne Trades Assembly, meets in Carpenters' Union Hall, Bank Block, 30 E Main. L T Marsh, Pres; Philip Rapp, Vice-Pres; George R Hench, Fin Sec; Henry Koch, Cor Sec.

Fort Wayne Typographical Union, meets first Sunday afternoon of every month at 30 E Main. Wm P Duffy, Pres; J T Ferguson, Vice-Pres; Lew H Green, Sec.

Fort Wayne Vocal Society, meets every Monday evening at the Conservatory of Music, 22, 24 and 26 E Main. C F W Meyer, Director.

Hod Carriers' Union, meets at Union Hall, 7 E Main, every Monday evening.

Humane Society, organized Jan 23, 1888. Annual meetings fourth Monday in January of each year. Charles McCulloch, Pres; Dr Edward J McOscar, Sec and Treas. (This incorporation still exists, but is inactive.)

Journeymen Plasterers' Union, meets every Wednesday evening at 30 E Main.

Kekionga Council National Union, meets second and fourth Thursday of each month, in Hall, Bank Blk. O E Bradway, Pres; C O Essig, Sec; J H Tibbles, Treas.

Morton Club, meets n e cor Wayne and Calhoun, on first Monday of each month. Charles W Orr, Pres; Owen N Heaton, Rec Sec; C D Tillo, Fin Sec; W J Kettler, Treas.

Northern Indiana Poultry Association, meets second Monday in each month. D Christian, Pres; J B Niezer, Vice-Pres; John H Welch, Sec; G Knisely, Treas.

Order of Railway Conductors, meets every second Monday evening and fourth Sunday afternoon of each month at 106 Calhoun. B F Stonecifer, Sec.

Plumbers, Steam and Gas Fitters' Union, meets every Tuesday at Carpenters' Union Hall, 30 E Main.

Q & O Club, organized December, 1886. Frank H Rohrer, Pres; Albert W Hazzard, Sec; Daniel F Hauss, Treas; meets first Tuesday of each month at n e cor Calhoun and Main.

Relief Union The, 144 Pritchard. Mrs. A D Guilds, Pres; Miss Emma E Eckels, Supt.

St Agnes Young Ladies' Society, meets first Sunday in each month at 3 p m at St Peter's Church. Regina Wiegand, Pres.

St Aloysius Society of St Mary's Catholic Church, meets the last Sunday in each month. C Schuler, Pres; George App, Sec; John G Kramer, Treas.

St Boniface Society, meets every fourth Sunday at n e cor W Washington and Griffith.

St Charles Boromeo Benevolent Society, meets second Sunday in each month at St Mary's Hall, s w cor Lafayette and Jefferson. Michael Baltes, Pres; Henry Brink, Sec.

St Charles Uniform Rank, meets first Sunday in each month at St Mary's Catholic School. Jacob Hartman, Pres; George Masbaum, Sec.

St Joseph's Hospital, s w cor W Main and Broadway. Sister Secunda, Superior; Rev Thomas Eisenring, C P P S, Chaplain.

St Joseph's Catholic Benevolent Society, meets second Sunday in each month at Library Hall, n e cor Calhoun and Jefferson. Kilian Baker, Pres; Patrick Ryan, Sec.

St Joseph's School Society, meets first Sunday in each month at St Mary's Hall, s w cor Lafayette and Jefferson. Fred Woehnker, Pres; Edward Van der Leeuw, Sec.

St Martinus Benevolent Society, meets second Sunday in each month at St Peter's school, s w cor Hanna and St Martin's. Valentine Ofenloch, Pres.

St Mary's, No 14 (col'd), meets first Monday in each month in hall, n e cor Francis and Wayne. Furney Turman, W M; James Smith, Sec.

St Patrick's Catholic Benevolent Association, meets the fourth Sunday in each month at Library Hall, n e cor Calhoun and E Lewis. Daniel McKendry, Pres; Patrick Ryan, Sec.

St Rosa Society, meets first Sunday of each month at St Mary's church. Miss Lizzie Snilker, Pres; Miss Mary Zurburch, Sec.

St Stanislaus' Society, meets last Sunday of each month at
St Mary's school. Albert Uhl, Pres; Clement Shuck-
man, Sec and Treas.

St Stephen's Young Men's Society, meets third Sunday of
each month at St Peter's church. John Koehl, Pres.

St Vincent de Paul Society, instituted for relief of the poor,
rooms Library Hall, n e cor Calhoun and E Lewis. Very
Rev J Brammer, Spiritual Director; Kilian Baker, Pres;
George J Litot, Sec; Albert Dittoe, Treas.

St Vincent Orphan Asylum, e s Wells n of Putnam. Rev
B T Borg, Chaplain; Sister Eudoria, Sister Superior.

Standard Club, cor Berry and Harrison; Max J Fisher, Pres;
Julius Nathan, Vice-Pres; Joseph Tribus, Sec; Benjamin Lehman, Treas; I Mautner, Louis Wolf, A S Lauferty, Board of Managers.

Stone Cutters' Union meets first and second Tuesday of each
month at 28 W Main.

Stone Masons' Union meets every Tuesday evening at 26 W
Main. August Pulls, Pres; Louis Arion, Sec.

Switchmans' Mutual Aid Association meets every second
and last Thursday of each month at 27 Calhoun.

Tinners' Union meets every Tuesday evening at Union Hall,
7 E Main.

Trades and Labor Council meets last Friday evening of each
month at 30 E Main.

Tri-State Veterans' Association, headquarters 210 Calhoun.
Alvin P Hovey, Pres; Colonel J W Younge, Adjt-Gen-
eral.

Young Men's Christian Association, organized March 18,
1886. 105 Calhoun.

Young Men's Christian Association (Railroad Department),
C H Newton, Chairman; Z T Esmond, Gen Sec.

NEWSPAPERS.

American Farmer (monthly), E A K Hackett, propr, 107
Calhoun; issued first of each month; $1.00 per annum.

Business Guide, The, established September, 1887. The
Business Guide Co, publishers, 55 and 57 E Columbia.
Issued monthly at 50 cents per annum.

Fort Wayne Dispatch (weekly, Ind), James Mitchel, propr
and pub, 26 Clinton; issued every Thursday.

Fort Wayne Freie Presse (daily), Otto F Cummerow, propr,
n e cor Calhoun and Main.

Fort Wayne Gazette (daily, weekly and Sunday, Rep), R
N Leonard, propr, 41 E Berry. Daily issued every morning at 10 cents per week; weekly issued every Thursday,
$1.00 per annum.

Fort Wayne Journal (daily and weekly, Dem), The Journal Co, pubs, 30 E Main. Daily issued every morning at 10 cents per week; weekly issued every Thursday, $1.00 per annum.

Fort Wayne Journal of the Medical Sciences (quarterly), subscription $1.00 per annum. C B Stemen, editor; George C Stemen, assistant editor; Charles E Archer & Bro, publishers, Clinton.

Fort Wayne News (daily and weekly, Ind), Wm D Page, propr, 19 E Main. D$_{aily}$ issued every evening, $3.00 per annum; weekly every Friday, $1.00 per annum.

Fort Wayne Sentinel (daily and weekly, Dem), E A K Hackett, propr, 107 Calhoun. Daily every evening, 10 cents per week; weekly every Wednesday, $1.00 per year.

Gospel Tidings, A R Wheeler, propr, 9 Foster block; issued first day of each month.

Indiana Deutsche Press (weekly), Otto F Cummerow propr, n e cor Calhoun and Main.

Indiana Staats Zeitung (daily and weekly), John D. Sarnighausen, editor; A Louis Greibel, business manager, n e cor Columbia and Clinton. Daily $4.00 per year; weekly $2.00 per year.

Journal of the National Association of Railway Surgeons (monthly, Medical), $3.00 per annum. B Stemen, editor.

Poultry and Pets. Devoted to Poultry, Pigeons and Pet Stock. Published monthly by Wm D Page, 19 E Main. Terms, $1.00 per year.

Press The, (daily and weekly), Fred J Wendell, Pres. 17 Court. Daily issued every morning.

Watchman The (monthly), Mrs H A Berry, propr, e s Fairfield ave, 1 s of organ factory.

PARKS.

Allen County Fair Grounds, west end Washington, bet St Mary's river and P, F W & C Ry.

Anthony Wayne Park, on north side of Maumee river, e of Main st bridge. A summer resort for parties, picnics, etc.

Centlivre's Park, west side Spy Run ave, n of canal feeder. A summer resort for parties, picnics, etc.

City Park, cor Broadway and Taylor.

McCulloch Park, Broadway opp Nirdlinger ave.

Swinney's Park, see Fair Grounds.

Tivoli Garden, w s Spy Run ave, ½ mile north of Court House. A summer resort for parties, picnics, etc.

Vordermark's Grove, s s Maumee road 1 e of Glasgow ave.

Williams Park, s s Creighton ave, bet Webster and Hoagland ave.

POSTOFFICE.

Southeast cor Berry and Clinton.

Postmaster—C R Higgins.

Assistant Postmaster—Charles W Howey.

Office hours—Week days, 7:30 a m to 7 p m; Sundays, 9 to 10 a m.

Money Order Department—Clerk, George D Adams; office hours 8 a m to 5 p m.

Orders are issued in sums of not more than $100. Larger amounts may be transmitted to the same person by additional orders.

Rates for Orders to any part of the United States.—Not exceeding $10, eight cents; over $10 and not exceeding $15, ten cents; over $15 and not exceeding $30, fifteen cents; over $30 and not exceeding $40, twenty cents; over $40 and not exceeding $50, twenty-five cents; over $50 and not exceeding $60, thirty cents; over $60 and not exceeding $70, thirty-five cents; over $70 and not exceeding $80, forty cents; over $80 and exceeding $100, forty-five cents. Postal notes to any amount not exceeding $4.99, three cents.

Rates on all International Money Orders—On orders not exceeding $10, ten cents; over $10 and not exceeding $20, twenty cents; over $20 and not exceeding $30, thirty cents; over $30 and not exceeding $40, forty cents; over $40 and not exceeding $50, fifty cents.

Mailing Department—Chief Clerk, S L Lewis; Assistants, T W Blair, C S Swann.

General Delivery Department—Chief Clerk, F J Drake.

Registered Letter Department—Clerks, George D Adams and James Harper. Office hours, 8 a m to 5 p m.

Stamp Department—Clerk, P F Poirson. Office hours, 7:30 a m to 7 p m.

Distributing Clerk—George Humphrey.

Free Delivery Department—Superintendent of Letter Carriers—C F Kettler.

Carriers:

No 1—C F Kettler.
No 2—Wm Slate.
No 3—John Gloeckle.
No 4—F W Gallmeier.
No 5—George L Ashley.
No 6—Charles Rau.
No 7—P M Lindsley.
No 8—F M Morgan.
No 9—C D Bourie.
No 10—Wm Griswold.
No 11—C M Rouzer.

No 12—John Soliday.
No 13—H C Niedhammer.
No 14—Wm Stahl.
No 15—F R Reilma.
No 16—J K Carson.
No 17—Frank Horstman.
Substitute—N W Wright.
Special Delivery Messenger—Fred Etzold.
Four deliveries daily in the business portion of the city, viz:
   at 7:15 a m, 1, 2:30 and 4:30 p m.
Two deliveries daily outside the business portion of the city,
   viz: 7:30 a m and 3 p m.
Factory Delivery—Three deliveries, viz: 7:15 a m, 1 and 3
   p m.
Sundays, office open from 9 to 10 a m. Two city collections
   by the carriers are made at 4 and 6 p m. One delivery
   outside business portion at 6 p m.
Postage—The postage on letters to be forwarded in the mails
   to any part of the United States is two cents per ounce,
   prepaid by stamp. The postage for letters dropped in
   this office for delivery in the city, two cents per ounce,
   prepaid by stamp.
Canada and the British Provinces—Two cents per ounce;
   prepayment compulsory.
Postage to all countries included in Universal Postal Union—
   For prepaid letters, five cents per half ounce; for unpaid
   letters received, ten cents per half ounce; for postal cards,
   two cents each; for newspapers, if not over two ounces
   in weight, one cent each; for books, other printed matter,
   legal and commercial documents, pamphlets, music, visit-
   ing cards, photographs, prospectuses, announcements and
   notices of various kinds, whether printed, engraved or
   lithographed, one cent per each weight of two ounces or
   fraction of two ounces; merchandise, ten cents for each
   eight ounces or fraction thereof, and parcel not to exceed
   that weight.
Registration—Valuable letters to any part of the United
   States and Canada and the Universal Postal Union, will
   be registered on application, for which a charge of ten
   cents (in addition to postage) will be made.

PUBLIC BUILDINGS, HALLS, ETC.

Allen County Jail, w s Calhoun nr Superior.
Anderson's Block and Hall, n w cor Broadway and Jefferson.
Arion Hall, cor Main and Harrison.
Aveline House Block, s e cor Berry and Calhoun.
Barr Street Market House, s e cor Barr and Berry.
Bank Block, s e cor Main and Court.

Bursley Block, e s Calhoun bet Washington and Jefferson.
Centennial Block, 197 and 199 Broadway.
Certia Block, w s Calhoun bet Wayne and Berry.
City Hall, w s Barr bet Berry and Wayne.
Colerick's Hall, over 49 and 53 Columbia.
Court House, e s Calhoun bet Main and Berry.
Driscoll's Hall, s e cor Calhoun and Wabash Ry.
Esmond Block, 298 Calhoun.
Eureka Hall, 43 W Superior.
Evans Block, s s Berry bet Calhoun and Clinton.
Ewing Block, s w cor W Main and Harrison.
Fleming Block, e s Calhoun bet Washington and Jefferson.
Foellinger's Block, 34 and 36 Calhoun.
Fort Wayne City Hospital, 166 Barr.
Foster's Block, e s Court bet Main and Berry.
G A R Hall, n w cor Calhoun and Main.
Government Building, s e cor Berry and Clinton.
Hackett Block, e s Calhoun bet Wayne and Washington.
Hamilton Homestead, s e cor Clinton and Lewis.
Herrington Block, e s Fairfield ave bet Williams and Bass.
Hibernia Hall, 176 Calhoun.
Kane's Block, s s Main bet Calhoun and Harrison.
Keystone Block, s w cor Calhoun and Columbia.
Library Hall, n w cor Calhoun and E Lewis.
McDougal's Block, n w cor Calhoun and Berry.
Masonic Hall, n w cor Calhoun and Berry.
Masonic Temple, cor Wayne and Clinton.
Miller Block, w s Clinton between Berry and Main.
Miner Block, n e cor Clinton and Wayne.
Myer's Block, 108 Fairfield ave.
Nestle's Block, s w cor Broadway and W Jefferson.
Nierman's Block, 5 and 7 N Harrison.
Nill's Hall, 80 Calhoun.
Nimrod Hall, 54 E Main.
Ninde Building, 40 to 44 W Berry.
Odd Fellows' Hall, Bank Block.
Odd Fellows' Hall (new), n s Berry bet Calhoun and Harrison.
Phœnix Block, w s Calhoun n of Main.
Pixley & Long Block, e s E Berry bet Calhoun and Clinton.
Postoffice s e cor Berry and Clinton.
Princess Roller Rink, s e cor Main and Fulton.
Remmel's Block, s w cor Broadway and Washington.
Rich Block e s Calhoun bet Washington and Jefferson.
Schott's Block, n w cor Barr and Washington.
Schroeder's Block (old), 242 Calhoun.
Schroeder's Block (new), s e cor Broadway and W Washington.
Seidel Block, 52 Calhoun.

Shuman Block, n s Main bet Barr and Clinton.
St. Joseph's Hospital (Catholic), s w cor Broadway and E Maine.
St. Mary's Hall, s w cor Lafayette and Jefferson.
Standard Hall, 40–44 W Berry.
Studer Block, 228 W Main.
Swinney Block, 11, 13 and 15 E Main.
Temperance Hall, 94 Harrison.
Trentman Block, e s Calhoun bet Berry and Wayne.
Union Block, n w cor Main and Clinton.
Verth's Hall, 267 E Wayne.
Wolke Block, s w cor Calhoun and Wayne.
Young Men's Christian Association Building, 105 Calhoun.

RAILROADS.

Cincinnati, Richmond and Ft Wayne, leased and operated by the Grand Rapids & Indiana.

Ft Wayne, Cincinnati & Louisville. Passenger depot and office First nr Wells; George L Bradbury, Genl Mngr.

Grand Rapids and Indiana, offices, freight and passenger depots with Pittsburgh, Ft Wayne & Chicago Ry. W Odne Hughart, Pres and Genl Manager; J H P Hughart, Assistant to President; W R Shelby, Vice-Pres and Treas; F A Gorham, Auditor; E C Leavenworth, Acting Genl Freight Agent; C L Lockwood, Genl Passenger Agent; W B Stimson, Supt Northern Division—General Offices Grand Rapids, Mich. P S O'Rourke, Supt Southern Division—Office, Ft Wayne, Ind. R B Rossington, Freight Agent; John E Ross, Ticket Agent.

Lake Shore & Michigan Southern, office, freight and passenger depots, cor First and Railroad. John Newell, Pres and Manager, Cleveland, O; T F Whittelsey, Division Supt, Hillsdale, Mich; E S Philley, Freight and Ticket Agent, Ft Wayne, Ind.

New York, Chicago & St Louis ("Nickel Plate"), general offices Cleveland, O; passenger depot on old W & E canal, bet Calhoun and Clinton; freight depot w s Harrison nr Superior. D W Caldwell, Pres, New York; Lewis Williams, Genl Manager, Cleveland, O; C D Gorham, Supt; H C Moderwell, Freight Agent; F W Gardener, Ticket Agent, Ft Wayne, Ind.

Pennsylvania Company, operating the P, Ft W & C Ry, office e s Clinton, bet Holman and Railroad; freight depot n e cor Clinton and Railroad. Joseph Wood, Genl Manager, Pittsburgh, Pa; E B Taylor, Genl Supt Transportation, Pittsburgh, Pa; Charles Watts, Genl Supt, Pittsburgh, Pa; C D Law, Supt Western Division;

F D Casanave, Supt Motive Power; R B Rossington, Freight Agent, Ft Wayne, Ind; John E Ross, Ticket Agent.

Pittsburgh, Fort Wayne & Chicago, leased and operated by Pennsylvania Co, office e s Clinton, bet Holman and Railroad; freight depot n e cor Clinton and Railroad. Charles Watts, Genl Supt, Pittsburgh, Pa; C D Law, Supt Western Division; R B Rossington, Freight Agent, Ft Wayne, Ind; John E Ross, Ticket Agent.

Wabash, general offices St Louis, Mo; Master Mechanic's office cor Fairfield ave and Wabash R R; passenger depot s e cor Calhoun and Wabash R R; freight depot s w cor Calhoun and Wabash R R. Charles M Hayes, Genl Manager; H L Magee, Genl Supt; F Chandler, Genl Passenger Agent; M Knight, Freight Traffic Mngr, St Louis, Mo; E A Gould, Supt, Peru, Ind; J M Osborn, Divisional Freight Agent, Toledo, O; C H Newton, Local Freight Agent, office, Freight Depot; R G Thompson, Passenger Agent, Fort Wayne, Ind.

SCHOOLS.

BOARD OF SCHOOL TRUSTEES.

President—John M Moritz.
Secretary—A Ely Hoffman.
Treasurer—Oliver S Morgan.
Superintendent—John S Irwin, M D, LL D.
Office Clerk and Librarian—Miss Mary Irwin.
Janitor-in-Chief—James A Gavin.

SPECIAL TEACHERS.

Drawing—Miss Charlotte J Emmins.
Reading—Miss Lucia M Vail.
Music—Wilbur F Heath.
Writing—John L Tyler.
Stenography—Wilson E McDermut.
Book-keeping—J Frank Whiteleather.

BLOOMINGDALE SCHOOL.

N W CORNER MARION AND BOWSER STREETS.

Principal—Miss Margaret M McPhail.
Teachers—Miss Alice L Hamil, Miss Emilie S Weber, Miss Elizabeth J Bowman, Miss Victoria Carter, Miss Mary E Freeman, Miss Mary A Hill, Miss Emma Stanley, Mrs. Sarah J Stahl, Miss Margaret L Goshorn, Miss Emma H Ersig, Miss Jessie Robison.
Janitor—Miss Catherine Sheridan.

CENTRAL GRAMMAR SCHOOL.

EAST WAYNE STREET.

Principal—Chester T Lane, B A.
Teachers—Melvin A Brannon, A B; Miss Hannah E Evry, Miss Mary L Jay, Miss Ellen McKeag, Miss E Louisa Hamilton, Miss Sarah A Updegraff.
Janitor—Conrad Leidolf.

CLAY SCHOOL.

N W CORNER CLAY AND WASHINGTON STREETS.

Principal—Miss Mary McClure.
Teachers—Miss Anna Habecker, Miss M Georgina Wadge, Miss Rose E Kohn, Miss Georgiana Boyd, Miss Elizabeth Collins, Miss Louvie E Strong, Miss Annette Gaskins, Miss Sarah E McKean, Miss M Belle Clark, Miss Emma L Armstrong, Mrs Jennie S Woodward.
Janitor—Michael L Brannan.

EAST GERMAN SCHOOL.

IN HARMER SCHOOL BUILDING.

Principal—Miss Emma C Weber.
Assistant—Miss Bertha Ritter.

HANNA SCHOOL.

S W CORNER HANNA AND WALLACE STREETS.

Principal—Belle R Lloyd.
Teachers—Mrs Marion H Brenton, Miss Jennie M Abel, Miss Margaret A Wade, Miss Martha E Wohlfort, Miss Mary E Hedekin, Miss Clara F Humphrey, Miss Sadie L Sturgis, Miss Cecelia Foley, Miss Katherine Freeman, Miss Addie H Williams, Miss Elizabeth O Collins.
Janitor—Mrs Maria Parrett.

HARMER SCHOOL.

CORNER HARMER AND JEFFERSON STREETS.

Principal—Mrs Mary S Waldo.
Teachers—Miss Matilda E Knight, Miss Edith M Boseker, Miss Mary E Christie, Miss Lelia H Seybold, Miss Henrietta M Wirbaugh, Miss Edith M Cothrell.
Janitor—Mrs Anna J Clark.

HOAGLAND SCHOOL.

N E CORNER HOAGLAND AVENUE AND BUTLER STREET.

Principal—Miss Frances Hamilton.
Teachers—Miss M A Abel, Miss K A Ross, Miss M E Dick, Miss E F Gaskins, Miss M F Homsher, Miss Emma F

Kinnaird, Miss Addie F Davis, Miss M Ella Orff, Miss Mary B Lincoln, Miss E B Mitchell, Miss L B Beaber, Miss Miriam Cohen, Miss Grace M Waldo.

Janitor—Mrs Ann O'Callahan.

HOLTON AVENUE SCHOOL.

S W CORNER HOLTON AND CREIGHTON AVENUES.

Principal—Miss E M Brewster.

German—Miss Martha Stumpf.

Janitor—Mrs J Richards.

JEFFERSON SCHOOL.

S W CORNER JEFFERSON AND GRIFFITH STREETS.

Principal—Miss Harriet E Leonard.

Teachers—Miss Clara Phelps, Miss Janet A McPhail, Miss Mary Smyser, Miss R Etta Cothrell, Miss Elizabeth E Chapin, Miss Elizabeth M Biegler, Mrs Mabel E Clayton, Miss Katherine H Bryan, Miss Prudence L Bowman, Miss Helen Brenton.

Janitor—John Immel.

McCULLOCH SCHOOL.

N W CORNER MCCULLOCH AND ELIZA STREETS.

Principal—Miss Edith E Ersig.

Assistant—Miss Clara Green.

Janitor—Mrs Mary E Dolan.

MINER SCHOOL.

CORNER MINER AND DE WALD STREETS.

Principal—Miss Alice M Habecker.

Teachers—Mrs Delia Wilson, Miss Mary J Smith, Miss Anna M Trenman.

Janitor—Mrs Orpha Clippinger.

NEBRASKA SCHOOL.

S E CORNER BOONE AND FRY STREETS.

Principal—Miss Susan S Sinclair.

Teacher—Miss Lillie V Bowen.

Janitor—Mrs A Rouzer.

WASHINGTON SCHOOL.

S W CORNER WASHINGTON AND UNION STREETS.

Principal—Miss Margaret S Cochrane.

Teachers—Miss Jessie L Humphrey, Miss Luella C Boles, Miss Lizzie F Irwin, Miss Marianne J Geake, Miss Lettie A Van Alstyne, Miss Effie B Richey, Miss Mary E

McClure, Miss Carrie A Snively, Miss Josephine Updegraff, Effie Lumbard.
Janitor—Mrs Annie Luhrmann.

WEST GERMAN SCHOOL.

WEBSTER STREET, SOUTH OF WASHINGTON STREET.

Principal—Carl Schwarz.
Assistant—Miss Sarah Schaaf.
Janitor—Mrs Elizabeth Rohlman.

MISCELLANEOUS SCHOOLS.

CATHOLIC.

Academy of Our Lady of the Sacred Heart. Conducted by the Sisters of the Holy Cross, Mother Arsere, Superior. P O address, Academy, Allen Co, Ind.
Cathedral Schools, in charge of the Brothers of the Holy Cross. Rev M J Byrne, Director; Brother Engelbert, Superior. Cathedral Square, s w cor Clinton and Jefferson.
St Patrick's School, under the direction of the Sisters of Providence, South Side.
St Augustine's Academy (for girls), under the direction of the Sisters of Providence. Cathedral Square, s e corner Calhoun and E Jefferson. Mother Mary Ephrem, Superior.
St Mary's (for boys), under direction of Sisters of Notre Dame, s w cor Jefferson and Lafayette. Rev J H Oechtering, Director.
St Mary's (for girls), under the direction of the Sisters of Notre Dame. Rev J H Oechtering, Director.
St Patrick's School, conducted by the Sisters of Providence. Rev Joseph Delaney, director, cor Fairfield ave and Duryea.
St Paul's (for boys), s e cor W Washington and Griffith. J Hauk, Director.
St Paul's (for girls), under the direction of Sisters of the Poor Handmaids.
St Peter's s s St Martin's, bet Warsaw and Hanna, conducted by the Sisters of Notre Dame. Rev A Messman, Director.

GERMAN LUTHERAN.

Emanuel's, northeast cor Union and Wilt. Rev Charles Gross, Principal.
St John's, s e cor W Washington and Van Buren. Rev Henry P Dannuken, Principal.

St Paul's, n e cor Barr and Madison. Rev Henry G Sauer, Director.

Zion German Lutheran, s w cor Creighton ave and Force. Rev Frederick A Klein, Principal.

COLLEGES.

Concordia College (German Lutheran), e s Schick, bet Washington and Maumee road. Organized in Missouri in 1839. Established in Fort Wayne in 1861. Rev Andrew Baepler, Director.

Fort Wayne College of Medicine, Medical Department of Taylor University. Christian B Stemen, M D, Dean; W P Whery, Sec.

Indiana School for Feeble Minded Youth, located 1¾ n e of Court House, opened July 10, 1890. John G Blake, Supt; Mrs Mary E Orr, Matron.

McDermut & Whiteleather's Business College, n w corner Calhoun and Berry. W E McDermut, Professor Shorthand and Typewriting; J F Whiteleather, Professor Bookkeeping, Penmanship, Arithmetic, Commercial Law, etc. Average number of pupils, 125. Day and evening sessions. Evening sessions, from September 1st to June 1st.

Taylor University of Fort Wayne, west end of W Wayne. C B Stemen, Pres.

Westminster Seminary (for young ladies), 251 W Main. Mrs D B Wells, Principal.

SECRET AND BENEVOLENT SOCIETIES.

MASONIC.

Hall northeast cor Clinton and Wayne.

Wayne Lodge, No 25, F & A M. Meets first Tuesday on or before full moon; Edward O'Rourke, W M; D L Harding, Sec.

Summit City Lodge, No 170, F & A M. Meets first Friday in each month; W Geake, W M; Daniel W Souder, Sec.

Home Lodge, No 342, F & A M. Meets first Tuesday in each month; Louis C Kasten, W M; De Mott C Gardner, Sec.

Sol D Bayless Lodge, No 359, F & A M. Meets second Monday in each month; C B Stemen, W M; Wm E Hood, Sec.

Fort Wayne Chapter, No 19, R A M. Meets first Wednesday in each month; James M Henry, H P; Levi Griffith, King; Ernest F Liebman, Scribe; G W Spencer, Capt of the Host.

Fort Wayne Council, No 4, R & S M. Meets second Wednesday in each month; Levi Griffith, Ill M; J M Henry, Dep'y Ill M.

Fort Wayne Commandery, No 4, K T. Meets third Thursday in each month; C D Law, E C; H B Granger, Rec.

Fort Wayne Grand Lodge of Perfection, A & A S Rite, N M J. Meets first and third Tuesdays of each month; Wm Geake, T P G M; C A Wilding, Sec.

Darius Council, Princes of Jerusalem, A & A S Rite, N M J. Meets second and fourth Tuesday of each month; C M Dawson, S P G M; C A Wilding, Sec.

ODD FELLOWS.

Hall in Bank Block.

Fort Wayne Lodge, No. 14. Meets every Monday evening; Valentine Gutesmuth, N G; Herman Michaels, Sec.

Canton Lodge, No 17, Patriarch Militant; H L Williamson, Capt; Brookfield Gard, Clerk.

Concordia Lodge, No 228. Meets every Wednesday evening in hall in Bank Block; A Lemmerman, N G; Edward Younghas, Sec.

Concordia Rebecca Lodge, No 41 (German). Meets first and third Thursdays in each month at hall in Postoffice Building; Mrs Adolph Schulz, N G; Mrs Charles Haag, Sec.

Deborah Rebecca Degree Lodge, No 110. Meets first and third Tuesdays in each month at Harmony Hall; Mrs Alice Sharp, N G; Mrs Craig, Rec Sec and Fin Sec.

Queen Esther Rebecca Degree Lodge, No 324. Meets second and fourth Saturdays of each month in hall in Bank Block; Mrs Dinah Carl, N G; Mrs Sarah Hamilton, V G; Mrs T J Hammond, Rec Sec.

Fort Wayne Encampment, No 152. Meets second and fourth Friday evenings in each month; John Shuster, C P; Christian Burns, H P; John Dorman, S H; F T Weitzman, J H; Frank Benoy, R S; D L Harding, P S; T J Rodabaugh, T; George S Carl, O S G.

Harmony Lodge, No 19. Meets every Thursday evening at Harmony Hall; Charles Stapleford, N G; George Doswell, V G; Lawrence Bittinger, R S; Thomas Greer jr, Asst R C; H H Barcus, F C; Wm Myers, T.

Summit City Encampment, No 16. Meets first and third Friday evenings in each month at Harmony Hall; R P Sharp, C P; Albert Barbier, Rec Sec.

GRAND ARMY REPUBLIC.

Anthony Wayne Post, No 271. Meets in Will's Hall, 80 Calhoun first and third Fridays of each month; P Dickinson, P C; A H Dougall, Q M; S W Stirk, Adjt.

George Humphrey Post, No 530. Meets at Foster Hall, Foster Blk, first and third Thursdays of each month; George D Adams, P C; Patrick Ryan, Adjt; R G Renfrew, Q M.

Sion S Bass Post, No 40. Meets at Mill's Hall, 80 Calhoun, second and fourth Fridays of each month; W H McClellan, P C; Enos White, Adjt, Sol Soliday, Q M.

Union Veteran Legion, Encampment No 51. Meets second and fourth Thursdays of each month, in Hall, Mill Blk. James E Graham, Col Com; M M Thompson, Q M; S W Stirk, Adjt.

A. O. U. W.

Fort Wayne Lodge, No 19. Meets every Wednesday evening at their hall, 80 Calhoun. John M Kelly, P M W; J W Younge, M W, S G Throckmorton, Recorder; G N Soliday, Foreman; W A Diether, Financier; W F Reitz, Receiver.

Summit City Lodge, No 36. Meets every Thursday evening at their hall, 106 Calhoun. G R Hench, P M W; J M Amiss, M W; N W Lambert, Recorder; C W Holverstott, Foreman; J B Saunders, Financier; J P Merrilot, Receiver.

IMPROVED ORDER OF RED MEN.

Me-che-can-noch-qua Tribe, No 106. Meets every Tuesday night in Trentman Bldg. R B Rossington, Sachem, A L Bond, Senior Sagamore; C O Essig, Chief of Record.

INDEPENDENT ORDER OF B'NAI B'RITH.

B'nai B'rith Lodge, organized April 15, 1865. Meets every first and third Sunday in each month in hall in Bank block; Charles Young, Pres; A Guttmacher, Vice-Pres; E Strass, Sec; J Lohman, Treas.

KNIGHTS OF HONOR.

Fort Wayne Lodge, No 1547. Meets second and fourth Wednesdays in each month, at 30 Calhoun; Abraham G Barnett, Dictator; Wm L Pettit, Reporter.

KNIGHTS OF LABOR.

No 2315, Liberty Assembly. Meets every Thursday evening at K of L Hall, Postoffice Bldg.

KNIGHTS OF PYTHIAS.

Goethe Lodge, No 99. Meets every Thursday evening in Seidel Blk. Frederick Schmueckle, C C; John Koenig, V C; B Hartmann, Prelate.

Phœnix Lodge, No 101. Meets every Monday evening in Seidel Blk. Daniel Hulse, C C; Frank Tower, V C; Frederick Grosline, Prelate.

Fort Wayne Lodge, No 116. Meets every Tuesday evening
in Seidel Blk. F J Bechtold, C C; Walter Lyman,
V C; Theo Thorward, K of R & S.

Loyal Lodge, No 182. Meets in Trentman Building every
Wednesday evening; Frank Challenger, C C; A T Lipes,
V C; C J Lose, K of R & S.

Summit City Uniform Rank. Camp meets second and fourth
Fridays of each month at Seidel Block; E L Siver, S K C;
Judson Ross, S K T; F N Kollock, S K R.

KNIGHTS OF THE GOLDEN EAGLE.

Wayne Castle, No 2. Meets every Friday evening at Seidel
Hall; Charles P Pens, N C; John Kellen, H P; Alfred O
Buchman, Sec; George H Seabold, Treas.

ORDER OF CHOSEN FRIENDS.

John H Bass Council, No 3. Meets second and fourth Tuesday evenings in each month at 34 Calhoun; C C Gum-
per, C C; Harry Hamill, V C; H P Vordermark, Rec Sec
and Financier; Peter Morganthaler, Treas.

PATRIOTIC CIRCLE.

Fort Wayne Circle, 101. Meets every Wednesday evening
at Phœnix Lodge Room, Phœnix Block; George Jaap, O;
Charles M Compart, V O; Wm J Barr, Sec.

ELKS.

P B O E. Meets every Friday evening in hall, Trentman
Building; G W Wilson, E R; George Renner, E L K; J
Seibold, E L K; J J Williams, E L K.

ROYAL ARCANUM.

Howard Council, No 246. Meets first and third Fridays of
each month at Odd Fellows' Hall; William Tiger,
Regent; George Reiter, Past Regent; H C Moderwell,
Sec and Treas.

SONS OF ST. GEORGE.

Robin Hood Lodge. Meets second and fourth Tuesdays of
each month in hall, Bank Block; John Slater, Pres; Harry
Smith, Sec.

TELEGRAPH AND TELEPHONE COMPANIES.

Edison Mutual Telegraph Co, C G Harrison, Mngr; office,
Wayne Hotel.

Western Union Telegraph Co, Oscar L Perry, Mngr; office,
Aveline House Block.

Central Union Telephone Co, W P Chapman, Mngr; office, 34
Calhoun.

FORT WAYNE DIRECTORY

1890-91.

ABBREVIATIONS.

adv......................advertisement	n e cor....................... .....northeast cor
agt..............................agent	nr...................................near
assn......................association	n s............................north side
asst..............................assistant	n w cor....................northwest cor
ave .... avenue	opp ....opposite
bds................................boards	pres........ ....president
bet ....between	propr ....proprietor
bldg......................building	publr.... ....publisher
blksmith........ ....blacksmith	res........................resides
carp.... ....carpenter	Rev............................Reverend
cash..............................cashier	rd..................................road
col'd..............................colored	s....... ....south or south of
cor..............................corner	s e cor...................southeast cor
e ....east or east of	sec............................secretary
e s................................east side	s s....... ....south side
lab..............................laborer	supt..................... superintendent
mach........................machinist	treas ....treasurer
mkr........... ....maker	whol............................wholesale
mnfg ....manufacturing	w........................west or west of
mnfr.... ....manufacturer	w s............................west side
mngr.....................manager	wks ....works
n......................north or north of	

ALPHABETICAL LIST OF NAMES.

A

Abbott Wm T, real estate, 1 and 2 Foster blk, res 172 E Berry.

Abdon George, plumber James Madden, bds Diamond hotel.

Abel, *see also Ebel and Habel.*

Abel Miss Jennie M, teacher Hanna school, bds 405 Calhoun.

Abel John C, lawyer, 19 Court, res 405 Calhoun.

Abel Miss Mary A, teacher Hoagland school, bds 405 Calhoun.

Abel M Kate, teacher, bds 405 Calhoun.

Aborn Thomas E, printer Archer, Housh & Co, res 107 · W Main.

Academy of Our Lady of the Sacred Heart, conducted by the Sisters of the Holy Cross, Mother Arsene Superior, 6 miles n of Court house.

Acbie J R, laborer Penn Co, res cor Dubois and Maumee ave.

Achduth Veshalom Congregation (Jewish) cemetery, e s
Broadway bet P, Ft W & C and Wabash R R's.

Achduth Veshalom Temple (Jewish), s w cor Harrison and
W Wayne.

Achenbach Harry, mngr Fort Wayne Music Co, and leader
First Regiment band, office 212 Calhoun, res same.

Achenback Edward, works Indiana School for feeble-minded
youth.

Acker, *see also Eicher*.

Acker Wm J, painter J W Muldoon, res 163 E Jefferson.

Ackerman Charles L, lab White's Wheel Works, res 64
Summit.

Ackerman John, lab White's Wheel Works, bds 64 Summit.

Ackerman Martin, lab, res rear 88 Madison.

Adams Andrew J, millwright Bass Foundry and Machine
Works, res 107 John.

Adams Charles C, engineer, res 226 E Lewis.

Adams Express Company, M G Stimmel Agent,
95 Calhoun.

Adams Frank H, sec Western Gas Construction Co.

Adams George D, chief clerk register letter dept P O, res 165
Griffith.

Adams Israel, finisher E B Kunkle & Co, res Huntington
road nr Lindenwood cemetery.

Adams Israel B, engineer, res 48 Brackenridge.

Adams James C, artist Wm Salzmann, res 64 Force.

Adams James H (Adams & Armstrong), res Adrian, Mich.

Adams John H, dentist, 106 Calhoun, res same.

Adams Kate, domestic 389 E Wayne.

Adams Mrs Louisa (col'd), bds 33 W Lewis.

Adams Minnie, bds 165 Griffith.

Adams Oscar, driver Ft Wayne City Railroad Co, bds 101
Glasgow ave.

Adams Oscar S, moulder E B Kunkle & Co, res 101 Clay.

Adams Thomas, brakeman, res s s Hayden bet Ohio and
Chute.

Adams Wm, carpenter, res 319 Hanna.

Adams Wm, painter Penn Co, bds 14 Union.

Adams Wm M, laborer Fort Wayne Electric Co, bds 183
Calhoun.

Adams Wm R, sawyer Winch & Son, res 39 Winch.

Adams & Armstrong (James H Adams, James A Armstrong),
wholesale millinery, 109 Calhoun.

Adamson George, laborer Penn Co, res 54 Walnut.

Adamson Lewis R, dynamo winder Ft Wayne Electric Co,
res 16 Walnut.

Aderman Christina (wid Carl), bds 19 Wall.
Adkins Albert C, finisher American Wheel Co, res 45 Laselle.
Adkins Mary (wid Armus W), bds 353 Lafayette.
Adler Anna (wid Andrew), res 61 Wall.
Adler Fredericka, bds 61 Wall.
Aehnelt Adelbert, steward Concordia College, res same.
Aehnelt Ottilie, bds Adelbert Aehnelt.
Affder Louis, laborer Bass Foundry and Machine Works, res 10 Buchanan.
African M E Church, n e cor E Wayne and Francis.
Agenbroad John, teamster, res 123 Harrison.
Ager Amelia, bds 176 E Lewis.
Ager Louisa (wid Romer), res 176 E Lewis.
Ager Mary, bds 176 E Lewis.
Agster Annie M (wid Gottlieb), res 42 W Jefferson.
Agster Charles A, machinest Wabash R R, res 206 Hoagland avenue.
Ahern Dennis, switchman Wabash R R, bds 199 Barr.
Ahern Johanna (wid Eugene), res 199 Barr.
Ahern Mary, bds 199 Barr.
Ahern Patrick T, operator, bds 199 Barr.
Ahern Thomas, plasterer, res 93 W Williams.
Ahern Thomas W, saloon, 226 Calhoun, res same.
Ahlers John, laborer, res 117 Montgomery.
Ahlers Otto, bricklayer, bds 323 Hanna.
Ahlersmeyer Wm, stonemason, res 20 Winch.
Ahner Charles, carpenter, res 61 Winter.
Ahner Jacob, car builder Penn Co, res 141 Walton ave.
Aichele George F, polisher Brunner & Hoag, res 79 St Mary's ave.
Aiken, see also Eakin.
Aiken Charles, yardmaster L S & M S Ry, res 36 E 2d.
Aiken John, res 281 W Main.
Aiken Margaret (wid Wm), bds 281 W Main.
Aiken Wm A, clerk G E Bursley & Co, res 301 E Lewis.
Aiker Wm, laborer Ft Wayne Artificial Ice Co.
Aikins Henry W J, insurance, 80 Calhoun, res 65 Pfeiffer ave.
Ainslie Rev James S, pastor Congregational Church, res 330 W Washingtan.
Ainsworth Amos, teamster, bds 124 Union.
Ainsworth Wm N, laborer S Bash & Co, res 76 Wells.
Airhart David, fireman, rms 47 Elm.
Ake Elias (Ake & McQuown), res n s Savilla pl 1 w of Indiana ave.
Ake Zedekiah, res 17 Lincoln.

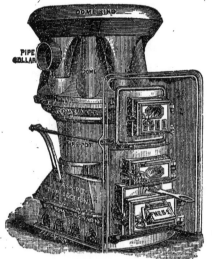

Ake & McQuown (Elias Ake, John S McQuown), poultry, w s Calhoun 1 n of county jail.

Aker Mrs Amanda J, dressmaker, 178 W Washington, res same.

Aker Ambrose B, carpenter Indiana Machine Works, res 178 W Washington.

Aker Frank, carpenter, res 11 Duck.

Albers Herman, laborer Penn Co, res 69 Force.

Albers Herman jr, molder Bass Foundry and Machine Works, bds 69 Force.

Albers Mary, dressmaker L A Worch, bds 69 Force.

Albers Philip E, clerk, res 299 E Lewis.

Albersmeier Charles, molder Bass Foundry and Machine Works, bds 192 Madison.

Albersmeier Christian H, clerk F J Miller, bds 192 Madison.

Albersmeier Frederick, clerk R Steger & Co, bds 192 Madison.

Albersmeier Louisa (wid Frederick), res 192 Madison.

Albert Miss Josephine A, teacher Westminster Seminary, bds 15 E Washington.

Albert Mary L (wid Nicholas J), res 164 E Lewis.

Alberty Adolph, foreman J Lohman & Co, res 209 W Jefferson.

Albrecht Anthony, cigarmaker A N Ehle, res 516 E Lewis.

Albrecht Charles F, cigarmaker John Zern, bds 516 E Lewis.

Albrecht Frank, coachman 252 W Wayne.

Albrecht Frank L, supt M L Albrecht, bds 112 E Main.

Albrecht Martin L, Mnfr of and Dealer in Fine Carriages, cor Main and Barr, res 112 E Main. (*See adv, opp.*)

Albrecht Miss Mary, bds 516 E Lewis.

Albrecht Otto, finisher Fort Wayne Furniture Co, bds 23 Julia.

Albrecht Paulina (wid John), res 12 Wilt.

Albrecht Peter, shoemaker, 117 Broadway, res 14 Elm.

Albrecht Samuel W, bookkeeper M L Albrecht, bds 112 E Main.

Albrecht Wm F, cigarmaker Louis Bender, res 334 Hanna.

Albreight Wm, hostler W W Shryock, bds 157 E Berry.

Albro Francis, driver U S Ex Co, res S Webster 1 s of Court.

Alden Samuel R, lawyer, 18 Bank blk, res 135 E Washington.

Alderman Dayton (Shordon & Alderman), res 324 W Jefferson.

Alderman Miss Edna, bds 324 W Jefferson.

Alderman Frank (Louis Schmidt & Co), res 303 W Washington.

Aldine Hotel, James Humphrey Propr, n s E Berry bet Clinton and Barr.

Aldrich Bessie, bds 29 Lillie.

Aldrich Elisha M, res e s Fairfield av 1 n of Pontiac.

Aldrich George, butcher, res 29 Lillie.

Alexander Elsie O (wid Perry), bds 80 N Harrison.

Alexander Frank E, car builder Penn Co, res 65 Buchanan.

Alexander Robert B, printer Fort Wayne Journal, bds Windsor Hotel.

Alexander Samuel M, laborer, bds 80 N Harrison.

Alexander Stephen F, hostler, res s s 5th 1 w of N Cass.

Alfelt Emil, coremaker Bass Foundry and Machine Works, bds 22 W Main.

Allen Benjamin, painter, bds 85 Wells.

Allen Charles B, brakeman, res 204 Hanna.

Allen County Asylum, John Wilkinson supt, n s Bluffton road, opp toll gate.

Allen County Fair Grounds, w end of W Wayne.

Allen County Jail, w s Calhoun nr Superior.

Allen County Loan and Savings Association, Edward White Pres, Gottlieb Haller Vice-Pres, Joseph L Gruber Sec, T C Rogers Acting Sec, Charles W Orr Treas, White's Blk.

Allen County Teachers' Library, George F Felts librarian, 7 and 8 Trentman blk, Calhoun.

Allen Cyrus W, carpenter, 324 W Washington, res same.

Allen David E, sec American Wheel Co, res Chicago, Ill.

Allen Ethan, carpenter, bds 324 W Washington.

Allen Frank, supt public works, res 189 W DeWald.

Allen Frank F, foreman, bds 324 W Washington.

Allen Jennie M, bds 324 W Washington.

Allen Louis P, cigarmaker, res 11 McClellan.

Allen Lyman, overseer Fair grounds, res 360 W Washington.

Allen Mrs Maggie, dressmaker, 204 Hanna, res same.

Allen Mary (wid George), res 80 Fairfield ave.

Allen Nellie (wid James), bds 124 E Lewis.

Allen Richard, engineer White's Wheel Works, res 39 Wabash ave.

Allen Robert, painter, bds 206 E Lewis.

Allen Rose (wid Daniel M), res s e cor Simon and Winter.

Allen Wm, barber Oscar Wobrock, bds 49 W Washington.

Allen Wm, conductor, bds Rose Allen.

Allen Wm, laborer, bds 80 Fairfield ave.

Allgeier Anton, teamster, res 162 Taber.

Allgeier Charles, tinsmith S F Bowser & Co, res 264 E Washington.

Allgeier Frank J, tinsmith Ft W, C & L R R, res 36 E 4th.
Allgeier Henry, tinsmith, res 262 E Washington.
Allgeier Mary, market stall No 84.
Alliger Frank, driver Ft Wayne Artificial Ice Co, bds 103
    Erie.
Alpaugh Eliza, domestic Aveline house.
Alt Anton, laborer Bass Foundry and Machine Works, res
    149 Suttenfield.
Altekruse Henry R, carbuilder Penn Co, res s w cor Warren
    and Reynolds.
Altekruse Wm'E, carpenter, res 29 N Calhoun.
Alternau Charles E, plasterer, res 82 Hanna.
Altenburger Basilius, res 183 Montgomery.
Alter Albert C, clerk A C Kalt, bds 133 E Main.
Alter Annie, bds 20 Wilt.
Alter Bros (Jacob A jr and Henry A), painters, 20 Wilt.
Alter George J, bartender Philip Graf, res 18 Buchanan.
Alter Henry A (Alter Bros), bds 20 Wilt.
Alter Jacob A, res 20 Wilt.
Alter Jacob A jr (Alter Bros), bds 20 Wilt.
Alter John, painter Alter Bros, bds 20 Wilt.
Alter John P, molder Bass Foundry and Machine Works, bds
    27 John.
Alter Lizzie, bds 20 Wilt.
Alter Nicholas, clerk Redlich Bros, res 133 E Main.
Alter Peter, asst foreman Penn Co, res 27 John.
Altevogt Henry F, clerk R Steger & Co, bds 38 Allen.
Altevogt Herman F, res 38 Allen.
Altevogt Lewis W, laborer, bds 38 Allen.
Altevogt Wm R, machinist Bass Foundry and Machine
    Works, res 42 Allen.
Alvord Frances D (wid Alwyn A), bds 154 W Berry.
Alway Edward, laborer Nickel Plate, res 27 Richardson.
Amann Cecilia, bds 215 E Washington.
Amann John H, helper Bass Foundry and Machine Works,
    bds 215 E Washington.
Amann Joseph, clerk Root & Co, bds 215 E Washington.
Amann Louis, plasterer, res 215 E Washington.
Ambler Alice, domestic 124 Wells.
Ambler Emmet E, gas inspector, res 12 W 5th.
Ambuster Laurence, blacksmith Bass Foundry and Machine
    Works, res 136 Horace.
American Electrical Directory, Star Iron Tower Co publrs,
    cor Plum and Nickel Plate R R.
American Express Company, George S Howard
    Agent, Court opp Court House.

American Farmer, E A K Harkett Propr, 107 Calhoun.

American Wheel Co, H G Olds Pres, J F Pratt, Vice-Pres and Treas, Addison Bybee Genl Mngr, D E Allen Sec, John D Olds Mngr Ft Wayne Branch, s e cor Lafayette and Wabash R R.

Ames George W, res 15 Hamilton.

Ames Milo E, engineer, res 75 W Williams.

Amon Charles, conductor, res 168 E Jefferson.

Amon Frank, molder Kerr-Murray Mnfg Co, bds 168 E Jefferson.

Amon Maud N, boxmaker Davis & Bro, bds 202 Francis.

Amoss Jasper M, collector New York Installment Co, res 110 W Main.

Andersen August, laborer Bass Foundry and Machine Works, bds 41 Miner.

Andersen A Thorwald, machine hand Olds' Wagon Works, bds 28 E Williams.

Andersen Peter, foremen Olds' Wagon Works, res 28 E Williams.

Anderson Andrew, brakeman, res 69 Wells.

Anderson Annie (wid Wm H), res 85 W Superior.

Anderson's Block and Hall, n w cor Broadway and Jefferson.

Anderson Calvin, res 123 W Wayne.

Anderson Charles A, laborer Joseph Fremion, bds cor Lafayette and Piqua ave.

Anderson C August, filer The Peters Box and Lumber Co, res 154 High.

Anderson Eli G, clerk Penn Co, res 123 W Wayne.

Anderson Essie (col'd), waiter Randall Hotel.

Anderson Frederick, machine hand American Wheel Co.

Anderson George A, engineer, res 17 Pritchard.

Anderson George D, porter G E Bursley & Co, res 5 Riverside av.

Anderson Goldie I, clerk, bds 69 Wells.

Anderson Harry A, shipping clerk Standard Oil Co, res 161 W Main.

Anderson James, blacksmith Olds' Wagon Works, res 458 Calhoun.

Anderson James R, engineer, res 411 Calhoun.

Anderson John N (col'd), laborer, res 31 Pearl.

Anderson Louis N, student, rms 27 Pritchard.

Anderson Miss Minnie M (Anderson & Large), res 36 W Wayne.

Anderson Neddie, conductor, bds 14 Lafayette.

Anderson Peter, blacksmith Bass Foundry and Machine
Works, res 300 E Washington.

Anderson Robert E, machinist E B Kunkle & Co, bds 123 W
Wayne.

Anderson Sarah, cashier Renner, Cratsley & Co, bds 123 W
Wayne.

Anderson Thomas P, res e s Spy Run ave 8 n of Wagner.

Anderson Wilson D, watchman, bds 189 Ewing.

Anderson Zora G, binder Archer, Housh & Co, bds 165 High.

Anderson & Large (Minnie M Anderson, Josephine Large), School of Music, 36 W Wayne, cor Harrison.

Andreasen Andreas J, machine hand Olds' Wagon Works, bds 28 E Williams.

Andreasen Hans, wheelmaker Olds' Wagon Works, bds 28 E Williams.

Andreasen Villads P, gearmaker Olds' Wagon Works, res 28 E Williams.

Andrew David, boilermaker Penn Co, res 201 Barr.

Andrew Jennette, bds 201 Barr.

Andrew Lizzie, clerk V E Wolf, bds 201 Barr.

Andrews Charles, painter, bds 57 Barr.

Andrews James N, laborer Shordon & Alderman, res 68 E Columbia.

Andrews Josephine, bds 339 W Main.

Andrews Minnie E, bds 26 Poplar.

Andrick Lizzie, domestic Miss Theresa Swinney.

Andruss Cora A, bds 78 Douglass ave.

Andruss George H, engineer, res 78 Douglass ave.

Angebine George E, blacksmith Fleming Mnfg Co, res 82 Force.

Angelbeck Louisa, domestic 103 E Washington.

Angell Byron D (Strack & Angell), res 242 W Berry.

Angell John J, brakeman, res 9 Pape ave.

Angell Mary C (wid Orange), res 166 W Berry.

Angst Joseph, packer Root & Co, bds 56 Madison.

Angst Kittie, boxmaker Davis & Bro, bds 56 Madison.

Angst Theresa (wid Leonard), res 56 Madison.

Ankenbruck Catherine (wid Bernard), res 172 E Washington.

Ankenbruck Frank M, driver L Brames & Co, bds 172 E Washington.

Ankenbruck John, carpenter J W Hilgeman, bds 314 E Wayne.

Ankenbruck Joseph, driver Monning & Baker, res 30 Erie.

Ankenbruck Louis, driver, bds 172 E Washington.

Ankenbruck Martin H, molder Bass Foundry and Machine Works, res 314 E Wayne.

Ankney Mary, bds 15 Caroline.

Annex Sample Room, H B Hammill Propr, 60 Calhoun.

Anstead Miss Emma C, bds 12 E Columbia.

Anstett George B, driver J P Tinkham, res 80 Huron.

Anthony Senes S, driver Fort Wayne Street Railroad Co, bds Monroe House.

Anthony Wayne Mnfg Co, John Rhinesmith pres, James H Simonson sec and treas, Albert C F Wichman supt, washing machine mnfrs, cor Lafayette and Wabash R R.

Anweiler George W, carpenter Penn Co, bds 22 Charles.

Anweiler Minnie (wid Louis), res 35 Fairfield ave.

App Block, 106 Calhoun.

App Clement P, clerk Mathias App, bds 104 W Washington.

App George J, clerk Mathias App, bds 104 W Washington.

App Henry J, clerk Mathias App, res 362 E Washington.

App Martin, pressman The Journal Co, res 360 E Washington.

App Mathias, shoes, 106 Calhoun, res 104 W Washington.

App Nicholas, stone mason, res 89 Summit.

Appele Pequinot, laborer, res e s Chestnut s of city limits.

Apple Emery, brakeman Penn Co, rms 268 Calhoun.

Applegate Charles W, mngr Central Mutual Fire Insurance Co, bds cor Lafayette and Berry.

Arantz Emma, bds 58 E Washington.

Arantz Mollie, bds 58 E Washington.

Arantz Philip, res 58 E Washington.

Arantz Simon P, carp Olds' Wagon Works, res 447 Lafayette

Arantz Wm F, filer American Wheel Co, res 166 Hanna.

Archer Charles E (Archer, Housh & Co), res 152 Wells.

Archer David L, laborer S Bash & Co, res 45 E 2d.

Archer Frank, fireman, res 53 Madison.

Archer Frederick R, student, bds 45 E 2d.

Archer, Housh & Co (Charles E Archer, John Housh, R S Taylor, W Sherman Archer), Printers and Publishers, 82 Clinton.

Archer John H, real estate, 82 Clinton, res 39 E 2d.

Archer Mary L, binder Archer, Housh & Co, bds 39 E 2d.

Archer Miss Olive E, clk Archer, Housh & Co, bds 39 E 2d.

Archer Perry J (Coverdale & Archer), res 117 E Wayne.

Archer Wm L, shipping clk B W Skelton, res 35 E 4th.

Archer W Sherman (Archer, Housh & Co), res 74 S Wayne.

Archibald Abraham F, clk Wabash R R, res 468 S Harrison.

Arens Anton, lab, res 52 Laselle.

Arens Bernard, machine hand American Wheel Co, res n w cor Buchanan and John.

Arens Edward J, finisher, bds 52 Laselle.

Arens Herman, laborer, bds Bernard Arens.

Arens Herman J, lab American Wheel Co, bds 52 Laselle.

Arens John, grocer, 124 Madison, res 122 same.

Arens Mary, operator Hoosier Mnfg Co, bds John Bentham.

Arens Tillie (wid Anton), res 122 Laselle.

Arentz Wm, laborer Penn Co, res 167 Hanna.

Argerbright James, cabinetmkr, res 196 E Jefferson.

Argo Martin E, insurance n w cor Calhoun and Berry, bds Wayne Hotel.
Arieon James L, foreman, res 204 Madison.
Arieon Lewis, stone mason, res 232 E Jefferson.
Arion Hall, cor Main and Harrison.
Armack Benjamin, asst foreman Penn Co, res 142 Holman.
Armack Dora (wid Albert), bds 73 W Jefferson.
Armack Frederick, fireman Chemical Engine Co, rms Engine house No 1.
Armel Charles, laborer, res 143 Wallace.
Armel Wm, bds 47 Laselle.
Armel Wm jr, switchman, res 47 Laselle.
Armstrong Charles E, finisher American Wheel Co, res 101 Maumee ave.
Armstrong Charles G, brakeman Penn Co, bds 320 Calhoun.
Armstrong Miss Emma L, teacher Clay school, bds 113 W Wayne.
Armstrong James A (Adams & Armstrong), res 148 W Berry.
Armstrong Matilda (wid Moses), res s e cor Dubois and Maumee road.
Armstrong Wm B, agt Prudential Life Ins Co, bds Union House.
Arney Scott M, spoke driver White's Wheel Works, res e s Glasgow ave bet E Washington and Maumee.
Arney Wm H, teamster, bds 544 E Wayne.
Arnold Amos W, driver Troy Laundry, res 60 Home ave.
Arnold Anson, cabinetmaker Fort Wayne Organ Co, res 480 Harrison.
Arnold Anthony A, machinist Indiana Machine Works, bds 480 Harrison.
Arnold Anthony N, cabinetmaker Fort Wayne Organ Co, res 480 Harrison.
Arnold Budd, hostler, bds 309 W Washington.
Arnold Charles W, clerk, bds 27 1st.
Arnold David A, cabinetmaker Fort Wayne Organ Co, res 415 Lafayette.
Arnold Miss Dolly, milliner Mrs E A Flagler, bds 480 Harrison.
Arnold Emma A, milliner, bds 480 Harrison.
Arnold Harry A, clerk Root & Co, bds 480 Harrison.
Arnold John J, mason, res 112 W Creighton ave.
Arnold John J, truckman, res 101 Barr.
Arnold Margaret A (wid Jacob), bds 101 Barr.
Arter Ephraim, teamster David Tagtmeyer, res 79 W Superior.
Arter Joseph, teamster, res 87 St Mary's ave.

Artis James (col'd), laborer, res 7 Dwenger av.
Ash Cora H, bds 104 E Main.
Ash Henry J, Mnfr of Pieced Tinware and Jobber of Tinners' Stock and Trimmings, Stoves, Hollowware and House Furnishing Goods; also Natural Gas and Steam Fitting, 9 and 11 E Columbia, res 104 E Main.
Ash Luella F, bds 104 E Main.
Ashley Amandus E, instrument maker Fort Wayne Electric Co, bds 28 Nirdlinger ave.
Ashley George L, letter carrier P O, res 106 Hanna.
Ashley Philo P, lumber, res 160 W Washington.
Ashley Sarah (wid Wm H), bds 155 Hayden.
Astry Jonas, carpenter, res 44 Pritchard.
Atkins Mrs Rosella, bds 20 Francis.
Atkinson John A, agent, bds Hedekin House.
Aubrey Alfred J, clerk J H Hartman, res 165 Hayden.
Aubrey Frank J, rimmer White's Wheel Works, res 34 Smith.
Aubry John J, laborer White's Wheel Works, res 132 Horace.
Aubry Joseph, machine hand, res 15 Hough.
Aubry Joseph J, laborer, res rear Leikauf's packing house.
Auer Charles, laborer American Wheel Co, bds 17 Nirdlinger ave.
Auer Conrad, table turner Penn Co, res 17 Nirdlinger ave.
Auer Daniel, laborer, res 108 Wells.
Auer Daniel jr, tailor John Rabus, bds 108 Wells.
Auer Emma, bds 17 Nirdlinger ave.
Auer Frank, lab Fort Wayne Artificial Ice Co, bds 108 Wells.
Auer George C, conductor, bds 17 Nirdlinger ave.
Auer Henry, hostler Concordia College, bds A Aehnelt.
Auer Jacob, mach Olds' Wagon Works, res 49 E Williams.
Auer John, laborer, res w s Walton ave 3 s of Pontiac.
Auer John H, carpenter, bds 108 Wells.
Auer Sophia, capper, bds 108 Wells.
Auer Wm, machine hand American Wheel Co, bds 17 Nirdlinger ave.
Aufrecht Charles F, saloon 36 W Main, res same.
Aufrecht Mary J (wid Jacob), res 36 W Main.
Auger Block, n s E Main 3 w of Barr.
Auger B Louis, Propr City Greenhouse, 16 E Washington, and South Wayne Greenhouse, cor Creighton ave and Webster, res 16 E Washington.
Auger Charles, res 453 E Wayne.
Auman Ricka, clerk, bds 251 E Jefferson.
Aumann Charles, section hand L S & M S Ry, res 28 Orchard.
Aumann Conrad, helper Penn Co, res 118 Gay.

Aumann Henry, clerk Siemon & Bro, bds 7 N Cass.
Aumann Henry F (Gerding & Aumann Bros), bds 118 Gay.
Aumann Louis F, cigarmaker F J Gruber, bds 118 Gay.
Aumann Louisa, bds 118 Gay.
Aumann Minnie, bds 118 Gay.
Aumann Wilhelmina, domestic 76 W Berry.
Aumann Wm, watchman, res 7 N Cass.
Aumann Wm jr, clerk, bds 7 N Cass.
Aumann Wm H (Gerding & Aumann Bros), bds 118 Gay.
Aurentz Anna, bds 79 W Main.
Aurentz Augustus B C, clerk Louis Fox & Bro, bds 79 W Main.
Aurentz Emma, bds 79 W Main.
Aurentz Frank, clerk, bds 79 W Main.
Aurentz Robert J, clerk S A Aurentz, bds 79 W Main.
Aurentz Skelley P, clerk S A Aurentz, bds 79 W Main.
Aurentz Solomon A, grocer, 31 W Main, res 79 same.
Austin Clarence R, brakeman, bds 288 Calhoun.
Austin Daniel S, photographer, 156 Horace, res same.
Austin Jaline (wid Wm M), bds 156 Horace.
Austin Louise (wid John C), res 288 Calhoun.
Austin Richard A, res 199 W Wayne.
Austrub Frederick, res 216 E Wayne.
Auth John H, bartender John Christen, res 135 W Wayne.
Autz Mrs Catharine, res 23 W 4th.
Aveline House, Miller & Moritz Proprs, s e cor Calhoun and E Berry.
Aveline House Block, s e cor Calhoun and Berry.
Avels Mary, works Indiana School for Feeble-Minded Youth.
Avis John, laborer, res 134 Francis.
Axt Andrew, painter, res 173 W Superior.
Axt August W, clerk Henry Dicke, bds 129 Francis.
Axt Charles W, molder Bass Foundry and Machine Works, bds 88 Summit.
Axt Mrs Melissa, bds 100 E Lewis.
Axt Moritz, res 129 Francis.
Axt Wm T, car builder Penn Co, bds 186 Francis.
Ayers Gertrude, bds 49 Grand.
Ayers Philip G, res 82 W DeWald.
Ayres James D, carpenter, bds Clifton House.

B

Baade, *see also Bade and Bahde.*
Baade Conrad H, grocer, 2 Fairfield ave, res 4 same.
Baade Ernest, carpenter, res n w cor Hugh and Gay.

Baade Fred C, clk Salimonic Mining and Gas Co, res 261 E Jefferson.

Baade Frederick, driver, rms 13 E Williams.

Baade Henry, car repairer, res 17 Barthold.

Baade Henry C (Kayser & Baade), res 19 Pritchard.

Baade Henry F, clerk Root & Co, bds 17 Barthold.

Baade Miss Lizzie, bds 263 E Jefferson.

Baade Wm, teamster, res 263 E Jefferson.

Baade Wm C, clerk Penn Co, res 251 E Jefferson.

Baals August (August Baals & Co), res 94 W Main.

Baals Barbara (wid George), res 150 Montgomery.

Baals John G, laborer Penn Co, res 302 W Jefferson.

Baals Mina, clerk Alexander Goodman, bds 302 Jefferson.

Baals Sadie, trimmer A C Keel, bds 302 W Jefferson.

Baals & Co (August Baals), furniture, 59 E Main.

Baatz Ernest, laborer, res rear 65 Hendricks.

Babcock Mrs Anna M, res 114 Clinton.

Babcock Mary (wid John), res 27 Butler.

Babcock Thomas Z, engineer Fort Wayne Electric Co, res 43 Locust.

Bach Savannah (wid Peter R), bds 594 Lafayette.

Bachon W H, car builder Penn Co, res 292 Hanna.

Backes, see also Beckes.

Backes Annie, bds 129 Wilt.

Backes Charles, laborer Bass Foundry and Machine Works, 124 Wilt.

Backes Jacob, boilermaker Penn Co, bds 30 E 3d.

Backes John, drill pressman Penn Co, res 30 E 3d.

Backes John J, boilermaker Penn Co, res 129 Wilt.

Backes Mathew, boilermaker Penn Co, res 58 Melita.

Backes Philip, boilermaker Penn Co, bds 58 Melita.

Backes Wm, rivet heater Penn Co, bds 129 Wilt.

Backofen Julian, laborer Horton Mnfg Co, res 2 s Jesse 2 e of Miller.

Bacome Frank, printer The Press, rms 128 Lafayette.

Bacon Miss Adeline E, bds 241 W Washington.

Bade, see also Baade and Bahde.

Bade Frederick, deliverer Markey & Mungovan, bds 13 E Williams.

Bade Wm C F, machine hand Hoffman Bros, res 162 W 3d.

Baepler Andrew, Director Concordia College, res College Grounds.

Baer, see also Baier, Bair and Bayer.

Baer Alvin E, engineer, res 329 W Washington.

Baer August, tailor, res 40 Oak.

Baer Essie, operator Hoosier Mnfg Co, bds 80 W Creighton.

Baer Frances, operator Hoosier Mnfg Co, bds 80 W Creighton.
Baer Joseph G, wagonmaker Olds' Wagon Works, bds 80 W Creighton ave.
Baer Wm M, lab Fort Wayne Organ Co, bds 80 W Creighton.
Bagby Albert L, constable, rms 85 W Superior.
Bagby Mrs Mary M, nurse, bds 302 W Jefferson.
Babde, *see also Baade and Bade.*
Bahde Mrs Dora, domestic 54 W Berry.
Bahret, *see also Barrett.*
Bahret Christian, sheet iron worker Kerr-Murray Mnfg Co, res 22 Pritchard.
Baier, *see also Baer, Bair and Bayer.*
Baier Catherine, tailoress, rms 21 Foster blk.
Baier John, molder, res 178 W Washington.
Baier Lena, domestic 178 Barr.
Bail Anthony, laborer, bds Joseph Bail.
Bail Joseph, carpenter, res n w cor Reed and Pontiac.
Bail Joseph F, wood turner, bds Joseph Bail.
Bailer Jacob, pedler, res 138 Maumee rd.
Bailey, *see also Baillie and Baily.*
Bailey Alexander, barber, 21 Grand, res 6 Melita.
Bailey August, foreman White's Wheel Works, res 130 Maumee rd.
Bailey Charles A, laborer White's Wheel Works, bds 24 Winch.
Bailey Ettie, domestic Clifton House.
Bailey Frank, brakeman, res 146 W Main.
Bailey Frank, laborer, bds George Sult.
Bailey Ladiz, laborer, bds 91 E Washington.
Bailey Louis A, barber, bds 6 Melita.
Baillie, *see also Baily and Baily.*
Baillie Andrew, boilermaker Bass Foundry and Machine Works, bds 166 Jackson.
Baillie John W, blacksmith Wabash R R, res 65 Stophlet.
Baillie Thomas S, foreman, bds 166 Jackson.
Baily, *see also Bailey and Baillie.*
Baily Alpheus H, harnessmaker F Hilt, res n s Grogly-1 e of Fulton.
Baily Charles F, printer, bds Alpheus H Baily.
Baily Frank C, stereotyper The Press, bds Alpheus H Baily.
Baily Harry B, painter F W Robinson, bds Alpheus H Baily.
Baily James A, printer Ft Wayne Newspaper Union, bds Alpheus H Baily.
Baily Mary R, clerk, bds Alpheus H Baily.
Bain John, rms 144 E Berry.
Bain John E, gas fitter Robert Spice, rms 157 Harrison.

E. F. Sites, ⬯ Dentist, 86 Calhoun St., Four Doors North of Wayne.

FORT WAYNE DIRECTORY.   77

Bainbridge Charles W, laborer, bds 154 Broadway.
Bainbridge Daniel W, laborer, res 57 E Superior.
Bair, see Baer, Baier and Bayer.
Bair Ada, milliner, bds 340 W Main.
Bair Allen, harnessmaker A L Johns & Co, res s e cor Clinton and Superior.
Bair Charles, teamster, res 340 W Main.
Bair Elva, dressmaker, bds 340 W Main.
Bair Frank, foreman Wayne Paint & Painting Co, rms 191 Calhoun.
Bair John E, driver J A M Storm, bds 340 W Main.
Bair Wm M, teamster, bds 340 W Main.
Baird Clarence H, laborer Penn Co, bds 39 Melita.
Baird Julius W, laborer Penn Co, res 39 Melita.
Baker, see also Becker and Boecker.
Baker Albert, rms. 124 Harrison.
Baker Albert G E, teamster, bds 40 Miner.
Baker Alexander J, blacksmith Charles Ehrmann, res 193 W Berry.
Baker Alice, bds 196 E Jefferson.
Baker Ambrose C, Mnfr of Fine Havana Cigars; Brands: B & B, 10 cents; Bluff and Jim & Fatty, 5 cents. The best in the Market, 31 E Main, res St Joe Road 1 Mile n e of City Limits.
Baker Amelia E, bds 139 Clinton.
Baker Andrew J, driver U S Express Co, res 33 Barr.
Baker Barnard H, carriages, 16 Lafayette, res 139 Clinton.
Baker Bridget (wid Conrad), res 193 W Berry.
Baker Conrad, butcher, res 82 Buchanan.
Baker Edward J, painter S E Smith, bds 139 Clinton.
Baker Emma (wid Cornelius), res 196 E Jefferson.
Baker Eva, domestic Wayne Hotel.
Baker Mrs Frances (John Baker & Co) res 18 Laselle.
Baker Frank J, sawmill, res 361 E Wayne.
Baker Henry J, clerk, res 75 N DeWald.
Baker Isaac W, car builder Penn Co, res 102 Butler.
Baker Jacob, res n s St Joe Road e of city limits.
Baker John (John Baker & Co), res 18 Laselle.
Baker John, res 139 Clinton.
Baker John, helper Olds' Wagon Works, bds 249 Gay.
Baker John A, foreman Hook and Ladder Co No 1, res 33 Barr.
Baker John G (Monning & Baker), res 347 E Wayne.
Baker John S, teamster, res 174 Taylor.
Baker John & Co (John and Mrs Frances Baker), galvanized iron cornice, slate and tin roofing, rear 377 Lafayette.

8

Baker Jonas E, carpenter, bds 79 W De Wald.

Baker Joseph J jr, clerk U S and Pacific Express Cos, bds ½ mile n e of city limits.

Baker Joseph L, saloon, 34 E Columbia, res same.

Baker Josiah C M, ticket agt Penn Co, res 16 W Creighton.

Baker Kilian, mnfr hardwood lumber, cor Superior and Lafayette, res 92 E Main.

Baker Lawrence A, cigarmaker A C Baker, bds same.

Baker Mary J (wid Henry), res St Joe road 1 mile e of city limits.

Baker Minnie C, boxmaker City Book Bindery, bds 196 E Jefferson.

Baker Noah A, carpenter, res 79 W De Wald.

Baker Vincent, plumber A Hattersley & Sons, bds 193 W Berry.

Baker Wm H, machinist Penn Co, res 97 Montgomery.

Balbach Maggie, domestic 25 E Main.

Balcer Kate, domestic 272 W Wayne.

Balcer Valentine, watchman, res 14 Force.

Balcome Sarah (wid Rodney), rms 70 W Wayne.

Baldock Lydia, bds 144 Wallace.

Baldock Wm R, printer Fort Wayne News, res 27 Hanna.

Baldwin D H & Co, Pianos, Organs, Music and Musical Instruments, 98 Calhoun.

Baldwin Elbert, clerk Penn Co, bds 239 W Berry.

Baldwin Frances (wid Elbert), res 239 W Berry.

Baldwin George H, brakeman, res 5 Aboit.

Baldwin Lindley J, salesman Singer Mnfg Co, res 104 St Mary's ave.

Baldwin Merchant H, operator N Y, C & St L Ry, bds 239 W Berry.

Ball, see also Boll.

Ball Emma, bds 172 W Main.

Ball Jason L, general agent Fidelity Mutual Life Insurance Co, 7 Schmitz block, rms same.

Ball Jennie, clerk E Shuman & Sons, bds 91 E Washington.

Ball Lillian, bds 172 W Main.

Ball Magdalena (wid Rudolph), grocer, 172 W Main, res same.

Ballard Levi, driver, res 38 Baker.

Ballmann, see also Bollman and Bolman.

Ballmann Joseph P, res 28 Nirdlinger ave.

Ballmann Kate M, converter worker Fort Wayne Electric Co, bds 28 Nirdlinger ave.

Ballmann Rosa A, converter worker Fort Wayne Electric Co, bds 28 Nirdlinger ave.

Ballmann Theresa, candy wrapper B W Skelton, bds 28 Nird-linger ave.

Balls John L, carpenter, res 302 W Jefferson.

Balsey Everett, tel operator, bds 40 E 5th.

Baltes Miss Clara, bds 63 Harrison.

Baltes Edward M, clerk Michael Baltes, bds 63 Harrison.

Baltes Jacob, res n e cor Spy Run ave and Wagner.

Baltes John, bricklayer, bds Jacob Baltes.

Baltes Michael, Mnfr White Lime and Dealer in Stone, Cement, Sewer Pipe, etc, cor Harrison and Nickel Plate Track, res 63 Harrison.

Baltes Peter, bricklayer, bds 157 E Washington.

Baltzer Ferdinand, laborer, res s s Wiebke 4 e of Lafayette.

Balzèle Dayton, teamster, bds 418 E Washington.

Balzer Valentine, barber, res 14 Force.

Bandau Frederick, policeman, res 27 Pritchard.

Bandel Minnie, domestic 443 Lafayette.

Bandelier L August, laborer Penn Co, res 17 Gay.

Bandenburger Gustav, laborer, bds 7 Walnut.

Bandenburger Rosina (wid Samuel), res 7 Walnut.

Bandt Frederick, carpenter, res 87 W DeWald.

Bandtel George F, clk Pfeiffer & Schlatter, res 358 E Wayne.

Banet Louis E, saloon, 72 E Columbia, res Riverside.

Bangert Bonifacius, grocer, 34 Fairfield ave, res same.

Bank Block, s e cor Main and Court.

Banker Edward B, barber S G Hubbard, bds 63 W Main.

Banks Creed T, res 219 W Washington.

Banks Elmer, res 351 E Wayne.

Banks Joseph V, bookkeeper White's Wheel Works, bds s w cor E Berry and Lafayette.

Banta, see Bente.

Banthum Charles, mason, bds 91 E Washington.

Baptist John, laborer, bds 26 Harrison.

Baral Gottlieb, clk Kimball & Webb, bds 183 Calhoun.

Barber, see also Barbour.

Barber Asphalt Paving Co, J C Jennings supt, rms 22 and 23 Pixley & Long building.

Barber Frederick J, clerk H W Carles, rms 18 Colerick.

Barber George K, machinist Penn Co, res 131 E Washington.

Barber Harlow E, fireman, res 11 Colerick.

Barbier Leon, florist Markey Bros, bds New Haven road near city limits.

Barbier Alfred, painter Penn Co, res 33 Madison.

Barcus George, candymaker H H Barcus, bds 96 Calhoun.

Barcus Henry H, confectioner, 96 Calhoun, res same.

Bard Samuel, res 39½ W Berry.

Barden Wm N, engineer Penn Co, res 28 W Creighton ave.
Bardin Louis, carpenter, bds Lake Shore Hotel.
Barge James, brakeman, bds Brokaw House.
Bargemann Mary (wid Diederich), bds 100 Smith.
Barjarow Augustus J, carpenter, bds James L Smith.
Barker Dwight W, yardmaster, bds 62 Buchanan.
Barker Summer P, telegraph operator L S & M S Ry, res 108 E Wayne.
Barkley Ira L, Real Estate, Loans, and General Agent Ætna Life Ins Co of Hartford, Conn, 18 Schmitz Block, res 297 E Lewis.   (*See left top lines.*)
Barlow Dora (wid Joseph H), res 82 W 3d.
Barlow Mrs Jennie, dressmaker, bds 194 W De Wald.
Barnard, *see also Bernard.*
Barnard Horace, clerk T E Covington, bds 77 Lafayette.
Barnard John, painter Olds' Wagon Works, res 137 Holman.
Barnard Wm M, clerk Pfeiffer & Schlatter, res 77 Lafayette.
Barner Addie H, seamstress P E Wolf, bds 155 Montgomery
Barner Charles F, patternmaker Fort Wayne Furniture Co, res 155 Montgomery.
Barner Emma, bds 155 Montgomery.
Barner Henry C, machinist Fort Wayne Electric Co, res 153 Montgomery.
Barner Lillie, bds 155 Montgomery.
Barnes Arthur, laborer Winch & Son, bds Winch.
Barnes Charles, transfer agent Fort Wayne Street Railroad Co, bds 427 Calhoun.
Barnes Charles E, boltmaker Penn Co, res 50 McClellan.
Barnes Horace M, bds 197 W Wayne.
Barnes James W, clerk Peter Morganthaler, res Clinton s e cor Tabor.
Barnes Jessie, bds 165 E Lewis.
Barnes Joseph, lather, res 165 E Lewis.
Barnes Joseph jr, lather, bds 165 E Lewis.
Barnes Rev R Monroe, pastor W Wayne St M E Church, res 195 W Wayne.
Barnes Wm, lather, bds 165 E Lewis.
Barnett Abraham G (Powers & Barnett), res 18 E Wayne.
Barnett Byron H, clerk Ft Wayne Transfer and Baggage Line, bds 18 E Wayne.
Barnett James W, clerk Ft Wayne Transfer and Baggage Line, bds 18 E Wayne.
Barnett Simon, tailor, 152 Calhoun, bds W Jefferson nr Hood.
Barnett W Wynn, physician, 434 Calhoun, rms same.
Barnette Samuel, expressman, res 148 Fairfield ave.
Barney Frank M, conductor, res 33 E 1st.

Barney Harvey L, brakeman, bds S Current.
Barnhardt Louisa, domestic 306 Maumee rd.
Barnhart James, bds 199 Broadway.
Barnum George P, Veterinary Surgeon, Livery and Hack Barn, 91 E Columbia, res same.
Barr, *see also Berr.*
Barr Albert, harnessmaker, bds s e cor Clinton and Superior.
Barr Miss Anna, teacher Indiana School for Feeble-Minded Youth.
Barr Bros (Wm J and James), grocers, 32 W Main.
Barr James (Barr Bros), res 130 W Jefferson.
Barr James S, farmer, bds Custer House.
Barr Mary A (wid Thomas), res 330 W Jefferson.
Barr St Market House, s e cor Barr and Berry.
Barr Wm J (Barr Bros), res 63 W DeWald.
Barrand August, plasterer, res 99 Laselle.
Barrand Frank, lather, res rear 99 Laselle.
Barrand John, lather, res 500 E Washington.
Barrand John B, supt Louis Diether & Bro, res 30 Oak.
Barrand Julius, lather, bds rear 99 Laselle.
Barrand Peter, lather, bds rear 99 Laselle.
Barrett, *see also Bahret.*
Barrett Erva E, stenographer, bds 135 Wells.
Barrett Miss Florence, teacher, bds 135 Wells.
Barrett Frederick, bartender, bds 26 W Jefferson.
Barrett Frederick C, carpenter, res 135 Wells.
Barrett Mrs Harriet, laundress, res 66 Murray.
Barrett James M (Morris & Barrett), res 255 Fairfield ave.
Barrett Oliver, laborer, bds 66 Murray.
Barrow George H, stonecutter Wm & J J Geake, bds 312 W Main.
Barrow Henry, lab Penn Co, res Spy Run ave 1 s n of Ruth.
Barrow John, teamster, res w s Spy Run ave 1 n of Ruth.
Barrows Charles V, photographer, 16 W Berry, res 106 W Wayne.
Barrows Frank R (Diether & Barrows), photographer, 62 Calhoun, res 242 W Wayne.
Barrus Timothy, carpenter, res 22 Winch.
Barry, *see also Berry.*
Barry Daniel, laborer, res 74 Melita.
Barry John M, teamster, res 16 Barthold.
Barry Owen, forgeman Penn Co, res 154 Holman.
Barsoe Charles, section hand, bds 27 E 1st.
Barsoll Joseph, lab Ft Wayne Furniture Co, res W Lewis.
Bartel Robert, bds 42 W Washington.
Bartele Adele, bds 167 Harmer.

Bartele Emma (Bartele Sisters), bds 167 Harmer.
Bartele Kate (Bartele Sisters), bds 167 Harmer.
Bartele Maggie (Bartele Sisters), bds 167 Harmer.
Bartele Michael, physician, 167 Harmer, res same.
Bartele Sisters (Maggie, Kate and Emma), hair dressers, 167
    Harmer.
Bartels, *see also Bertels.*
Bartels Annie (wid Wm), res 58 Hayden.
Bartels Henry, polisher White's Wheel Works, res 179 Gay.
Bartels Maggie, dressmaker, bds 58 Hayden.
Bartels Mary, bds 58 Hayden.
Bartels Wm, hodcarrier, res 58 Hayden.
Barter George W, boilermaker, res 326 Hanna.
Barthold Frederick L, res 80 Baker.
Bartlett Laura E, janitor 1st U B church, res 205 Madison.
Bartley Miss Anna, res 159 Harrison.
Bartley Charles S, lab F D Paulus, res 137 Holman.
Bartley Frank, teamster, bds 137 Holman.
Bartley John S, boarding house, 137 Holman, res same.
Barton Daniel, flagman Penn Co, res 415 Lafayette.
Baschelier Christina (wid George), bds 366 W Main.
Base Christina (wid Amand), res 150 E Jefferson.
Bash Charles S, pres The Mayflower Mills, res 280 W Wayne.
Bash Daniel F, with S Bash & Co, bds 240 W Berry.
Bash George J, carpenter, res 160 Fairfield ave.
Bash Harry E, clerk, bds 240 W Berry.
Bash Solomon, pres S Bash & Co, res 240 W Berry.
Bash S & Co, Solomon Bash Pres, C S Bash Vice-Pres,
    W B Bash Sec, Produce Commission and Seeds, 22 and
    24 W Columbia.
Bash Wm, res 286 W Wayne.
Bash Willis B, sec S Bash & Co, bds 260 W Berry.
Bash Winfield S, with S Bash & Co, res 286 W Wayne.
Bashelier Philip, painter, res s w cor Webster and Pearl.
Basil Miss Ida, bds 133 Holman.
Basil Margaret (wid Martin), res 133 Holman.
Bass Alfred (col'd), barber 32 E Columbia, res n s E
    Wayne 1 e of Hanover.
Bass Foundry and Machine Works (Capital,
    $500,000), John H Bass Pres, John I White Sec, Robert-
    son J Fisher Treas, Hanna s of Railroad Crossing.
Bass Henry (col'd), works Indiana School for Feeble-Minded
    Youth, res 100 E Columbia.
Bass John H, pres Bass Foundry and Machine Works, Hanna
    s of railroad crossing and pres First National Bank, res
    113 W Berry.

Stahn & Heinrich, Leading Dealers in ARTISTS' MATE- RIALS AND DRAUGHTING INSTRU- MENTS. 116 Calhoun Street.

FORT WAYNE DIRECTORY. 83

Bass Matison (col'd), wks Indiana School for Feeble-Minded Youth.

Bassett Frank (Wm H Bassett & Son), bds Wm H Bassett.

Bassett John M, foreman American Wheel Co, res 118 Jackson.

Bassett Wm H (Wm H Bassett & Son), res n e cor Runnion ave and Rebecca.

Bassett Wm H & Son (Wm H and Frank), dairy, n e cor Runnion ave and Rebecca.

Bassett Wm O, machinist Penn Co, res 187 E Lewis.

Bastien Jacob, clk M R Yohey, res 205 Madison.

Bastues John M, molder Bass Foundry and Machine Works, res 399 E Lewis.

Batchelder Jesse S, foreman B W Skelton, res 20 W Lewis.

Bates A, car builder Penn Co, res cor Wayne and Clay.

Bates Ida E, bds 390 E Wayne.

Bates Miss Jennie, stenographer Carnahan & Co, bds 262 E Washington.

Bates John, laborer, res 48 E Columbia.

Bates Lycurgus, bridge builder Penn Co, res 28 Buchanan.

Bates Wm G, bkkpr Fort Wayne Gazette, bds 390 E Wayne.

Bates Wm H, res 390 E Wayne.

Batius Julius, stonecutter, bds Washington House.

Battenberg Jacob, bds 125 St Mary's ave.

Battenberg Otto J, laborer Kerr Murray Mnfg Co, res 125 St Mary's ave.

Battenberg George, carpenter, bds Monroe House.

Battershall Jennie, works Indiana School for Feeble-Minded Youth.

Battershall John M, conductor, res 170 Greeley.

Battles Wm, laborer American Wheel Co, res e s Hanna s of city limits.

Baty Wm E, machine hand Horton Mnfg Co, res 160 Greeley.

Bauch Rosa (wid Charles E), res 203 Taylor.

Bauchle John, clerk Fred Eckart, bds 91 E Wayne.

Bauer, see also Bougher, Bour and Bower.

Bauer Henry, Dealer in Ladies', Gents', Misses' and Childrens' Fine Shoes; Repairing Neatly Done, 321 Lafayette, res same.

Bauer Jacob, molder, res 117 Force.

Bauer Joseph A, bds 242 E Lewis.

Bauer Joseph K, real estate, res 244 E Lewis.

Bauer Kajetan J (Glutting & Bauer), res 242 E Lewis.

Bauer Richard, confectioner, bds Washington House.

Baughman, see also Bowman.

Baughman Jeremiah, carpenter Frederick Kraft, res 63 W 4th.

Baughman Julia R, music teacher, 63 W 4th, bds same.
Baughman Newton J, engineer, res 334 W Jefferson.
Baulmer Alfred, laborer, bds 46 E Columbia.
Baum Joseph, saloon, 14 E Columbia, res same.
Bauman Maggie, domestic 362 Fairfield ave.
Baumann David, laborer, res 169 N Harrison.
Baumann John, shoemaker, 374 Calhoun, res 41 W Lewis.
Baumann Paul, Steam Dye House, 51 E Main, res same.
Baumeister Frederick, molder Bass Foundry and Machine Works, res 12 Force.
Baumgard Max, baker J H Schwieters, res St Joe gravel road 1 mile east of city limits.
Baumgratz Charles, car repairer Penn Co, res e s Calhoun 4 s of Marchell.
Baur Jacob J, molder Bass Foundry and Machine Works, bds 117 Force.
Baus Adam, laborer, res 65 Hoffman.
Baus Adam jr, laborer, bds 65 Hoffman.
Baus Frederick, upholsterer, res 89 Hanna.
Bauss Conrad, saloon, 36 Fairfield ave, res 106 Chicago.
Baxter Belle, bds 9 Emily.
Baxter James, works J O Keller, bds 9 Emily.
Baxter Joseph, painter B H Baker, bds 9 Emily.
Baxter Phœbe (wid Joseph), res 9 Emily.
Baxter Thomas, chief engineer City Water Works, res s e cor Barr and 7th.
Bayer, *see also Baer, Baier, Bair and Boyer.*
Bayer Annie, bds Conrad Bayer.
Bayer Conrad, cigarmaker H W Ortmann, bds 34 Sherman.
Bayer Frederick, laborer, bds 34 Sherman.
Bayer Jacob, gate keeper Maysville and St Joe roads, res junction same.
Bayer John M, carpet weaver, 34 Sherman, res same.
Bayer Wm, cigarmaker, J Lohman & Co, bds 34 Sherman.
Bayless Absalom, laborer, res 117 John.
Bayless August E, trav agent, res 171 Van Buren.
Bayless Cora, clerk, bds s e cor Clinton and Taber.
Bayless Emma, milliner A Mergentheim, bds s e cor Clinton and Taber.
Bayless Frank O, clerk, bds s e cor Clinton and Taber.
Bayless Gustavus S, died July 3, 1890.
Bayless Jennie N, dressmaker, bds 102 Franklin ave.
Bayless Leah E (wid Gustavus), res 102 Franklin ave.
Beaber, *see also Bieber.*
Beaber Abraham G, bds 514 Broadway.

Beaber Daniel, carpenter Liebman & Henry, res 15 W De Wald.

Beaber Jacob, carpenter, res 342 Broadway.

Beaber Miss Lillie B, teacher Hoagland school, bds 342 Broadway.

Beaber Michael, painter F H Treep, bds 21 Francis.

Beach August, finisher Fort Wayne Furniture Co, bds 444 Broadway.

Beach Edward A, clerk Coombs & Co, bds 133 E Berry.

Beach Fred J, awnings and tents, 171 Broadway, res same.

Beach Frederick (Morgan & Beach), res 133 E Berry.

Beach Frederick E, checker L S & M S Ry, res 124 W 3d.

Beach Frederick W, stenographer Morgan & Beach, bds 133 E Berry.

Beach George, harnessmaker A L John & Co, bds 375 Lafayette.

Beach Henry, machine hand American Wheel Co, res 375 Lafayette.

Beach John, laborer Penn Co, res 444 Broadway.

Beach John H, driver F P Mensch, res 60 Hoffman.

Beadell Henry (Dozois, Beadell & Co), res 343 E Wayne.

Beahler John E, trav agt Central Mutual Fire Insurance Co, bds cor Lafayette and Berry.

Beahrs Emma, bds s e cor Glasgow ave and Maumee road.

Beahrs John, watchman, res s e cor Glasgow ave and Maumee road.

Beals Miss Augusta D, teacher McDermut & Whiteleather, bds 157 Ewing.

Beals Melvin M, watchman, res 157 Wells.

Beals Thomas C, machinist, res 19 Baker.

Beam Calvin, fitter Fort Wayne Furniture Co, res 242 E Wayne.

Beam Rebecca (wid David), bds 242 E Wayne.

Beaman Richard H, laborer American Wheel Works, bds 435 Lafayette.

Beaman Wm G, driver, res 435 Lafayette.

Bear Francis J, bds 80 W Creighton ave.

Bear Frank, rms 458 Calhoun.

Bear George J, brakeman, res 80 W Creighton ave.

Bear John H, helper Penn Co, bds 290 Calhoun.

Bear Joseph G, laborer, bds 80 W Creighton ave.

Bear Wm M, bds 80 W Creighton ave.

Bear Zeta C, bds 80 W Creighton ave.

Beard Albert, driver Ryan Bros, bds same.

Beard C Wm, driver Fort Wayne Newspaper Union, bds 153 E Berry.

Beard Frank, fireman, rms 38 Brackenridge.

Beardsley Andrew F, fireman, res 26 Poplar.

Bearinger George W, caller Penn Co, res 55 W De Wald.

Bearinger Harry, messenger Penn Co, bds 55 W De Wald.

Bearley Frank, laborer, rms 303 Calhoun.

Beaston Harry S, clk Markey & Mungovan, res 13 E Williams.

Beaton Peter, laborer, res 26 Harrison.

Beatch George, harnessmaker, bds 375 Lafayette.

Beatch Henry, mortiser, bds 375 Lafayette.

Beattie Joseph, laborer A Hattersley & Sons, res 21 W 4th.

Beattie Walter, laborer, bds 595 Calhoun.

Beattie Wm, boiler maker Fort Wayne Iron Works, res 595 Calhoun.

Beattie Wm jr, rivet boy Fort Wayne Iron Works, bds 595 Calhoun.

Beaubien Albert L, office boy T J Dills, bds 5 Monroe.

Beaubien Cleophas J, assistant J C Peltier, res 5 Monroe.

Beaubien Eva, bds 5 Monroe.

Beaubien Marie, bds 5 Monroe.

Beaucha Frank, switchman Nickel Plate, bds Clifton House.

Beavens Wm, laborer, bds 101 Glasgow ave.

Beaver Augustus C (Beaver, Miller & Co), res e s Broadway opp Glenwood Chapel.

Beaver Charles B, Agent U S and Pacific Express Cos, 79 Calhoun, res 176 Ewing.

Beaver Edward L, traveling agent Coombs & Co, res 116 Jackson.

Beaver, Miller & Co (Augustus C Beaver, John M Miller, John B Krudop, Julius Knothe, Henry M Williams), lumber, n e cor Francis and Hayden.

Beaver Miss Minnie A, bds 305 W Washington.

Beaver Minnie M, bds 176 Ewing.

Beaver Montgomery G, bookkeeper Fort Wayne Lumber Co, bds E Jefferson.

Beaver Wm, teamster, bds 815 Broadway.

Beazley John, brakeman Penn Co, res w s Holton ave 4 s of Creighton ave.

Beberstine George W, carpenter, res s s Rudisill ave 3 w of Piqua ave.

Bechman, see Beckman.

Bechener Frederick, laborer Hoffman Bros, res Pape.

Bechmann John, bds 268 E Jefferson.

Bechtel John A, machine hand Louis Rastetter, res 96 Wall.

Bechtel Lena, works Model Steam Laundry, bds 416 E Washington.

Bechtol John G, engineer, res 354 W Washington.

MILLINERY GOODS ——LATEST STYLES—— MRS. E. A. FLAGLER, 14 W. BERRY STREET.

FORT WAYNE DIRECTORY. 87

Bechtold Frederick J, bookkeeper McDonald, Watt & Wilt, bds 120 Harrison.
Bechtold Louis, grocer, 152 Maumee road, res same.
Bechtoldt J H, laborer Penn Co.
Beck Abraham R, res 48 Centre.
Beck Charles, res 124 Wilt.
Beck Henry, patternmaker Penn Co, res 13 West.
Beck Leopold, carpet weaver, 136 Barr, res same.
Beck Miss Minnie, seamstress P E Wolf, bds 424 E Wayne.
Beck Pauline, dressmaker, bds 13 Rockhill.
Beck Peter, stone mason, res 1 Walnut.
Beck Susannah C (wid Wm L), bds 48 Centre.
Beck Wm, bookkeepr G De Wald & Co, bds 39 Pritchard.
Beck Wm, engineer, bds 13 Rockhill.
Becker Abbott Z, engineer, res 169 High.
Becker Anna (wid Peter), bds 212 E Wayne.
Becker August E C, grocer, 160 Fairfield ave, res 107 Williams.
Becker Charles (Fred Becker & Bro), bds 11 E Washington.
Becker Charles G, carp Penn Co, res 170 W Washington.
Becker Charles M, bds 220 W Berry.
Becker Conrad, sausagemaker F Eckart, res 80 Buchanan.
Becker Emma L, clerk Frank & Co, bds 220 W Berry.
Becker Fred (Fred Becker & Bro), res 11 E Washington.
Becker Fred & Bro (Fred and Charles), horseshoers, 13 E Washington.
Becker George, driver Adams Express Co.
Becker Helen, domestic Paul E Wolf.
Becker Henry W (Griebel, Wyckoff & Becker), res 51 E Jefferson.
Becker Herman, laborer American Wheel Co, res 56 Thomas.
Becker Jacob, res 119 W Washington.
Becker John, laborer, bds 249 Gay.
Becker John J, machinist S F Bowser & Co, res 83 Monroe.
Becker Joseph, porter G De Wald & Co, bds 249 Gay.
Becker Leon, cook Hotel Randall.
Becker Lorenz, grocer, 91 John, res same.
Becker Louis, res 249 Gay.
Becker Margaret (wid Frederick), bds 11 E Washington.
Becker Mary, domestic 252 W Wayne.
Becker Minnie A, milliner A Mergentheim, bds 11 E Washington.
Becker Sophie, housekeeper 220 W Berry.
Becker Susan (wid Henry), domestic 218 W Jefferson.
Becker Theresa, domestic August L Fox.
Becker Wilhelmina (wid Christian), res 220 W Berry.

Becker Wm F, tinsmith Penn Co, res Pontiac.
Beckes, *see also Backes.*
Beckes Jacob, saloon, 221 Lafayette, res same.
Beckes John, hostler, res 183 Fairfield ave.
Beckett Wm M, hostler J G Hooper, res St Joseph tp.
Beckman, *see also Bechman.*
Beckman Ellen (wid John C), res 6 Bass.
Beckman Franklin, sewer contractor, res 63 E Superior.
Beckman Frederick, laborer, res 173 Gay.
Beckman Frederick G, clerk, res 160 W Wayne.
Beckman George, grocer, 56 Thomas, res 55 same.
Beckman Martin, polisher, bds 103 Force.
Beckus John, servant John M Coombs.
Becks Rev Julius, res St Joseph Hospital.
Becquette Elizabeth (wid John B), res 498 W Main.
Becquette Elizabeth C, bds Elizabeth Becquette.
Becquette Henry, brass finisher, bds 104 Barr.
Becquette John A, truckman, res 498 W Main.
Becquette Mary E, bds Elizabeth Becquett.
Beebe Charles H, res 62 Brackenridge.
Beebe Dewitt C, brakeman, res 46 McClellan.
Beeckman Martin, machine hand American Wheel Co, bds
    103 Force.
Beekner Lotta, works Troy Steam Laundry, bds 19 Catherine.
Beemer Jamison, laborer, bds 104 Barr.
Beemer M D Jameson, laborer The Remington-Lawton Co,
    bds 106 Barr.
Beerman, *see also Biermann.*
Beerman Frederick, laborer, res 39 Boone.
Beers Harry C, converter worker Fort Wayne Electric Co,
    bds 103 Wilt.
Beezley Edwin J, brakeman, res 28 Holton ave.
Begue Miss Alice, clerk, bds 164 E Wayne.
Begue Mary (wid John C), res 164 E Wayne.
Behl Mary (wid Charles), res 56 E 3d.
Behn Charles, car builder Penn Co, res 69 Holman.
Behrens Christian, coremaker Bass Foundry & Machine
    Works, res 3 Metz.
Behrens Herman, laborer, res 84 Gay.
Behret Christian, boilermaker, res 22 Pritchard.
Beidler Wm S, conductor, res 27 E 3d.
Beierlein George, carpenter, bds 49 W Main.
Beierlein John G, laborer, res 107 N Cass.
Beilgerig Andrew, cooper Frederick Sauertieg, res 66 Mur-
    ray.
Beinhardt Johan C, helper Penn Co, res 29 John.

Beirau, *see Baerau.*

Bejont John, laborer, bds 88 Hayden.

Belchner Frederick, helper John Orff, res 101 Putnam.

Belger Michael F (Belger & Lennon), res 140 Calhoun.

Belger & Lennon (Michael F Belger, Edwin J Lennon), Proprs The Exchange, 140 Calhoun.

Bell Charles W, conductor, bds 80 W 3d.

Bell Edgar L, traveling agent J W Bell, rms 56 E Wayne.

Bell George A, clerk J W Bell, rms 56 E Wayne.

Bell George E, conductor, bds 80 W 3d.

Bell Horace L, stock buyer, res 35 Boone.

Bell Hulda E (wid Wm H), res 22 Fairfield ave.

Bell Jacob, clerk, bds 141 Madison.

Bell Jane (wid Alexander G), bds 91 W Superior.

Bell Joseph W, saddlery hardware, 13 E Columbia, res 285 W Wayne.

Bell Julia A (wid Wm M), res 80 W 3d.

Bell J Alva, clerk J W Bell, rms 56 E Wayne.

Bell Robert C (Bell & Morris), bds Wayne Hotel.

Bell Thomas H, conductor, bds 80 W 3d.

Bell Wm E, laborer, res 132 Wells.

Bell Wm F, brakeman Penn Co, res 231 Barr.

Bell & Morris (Robert C Bell, Samuel L Morris), Lawyers, 32 E Berry.

Bellamy Ada A, clerk Root & Co, bds 135 Cass.

Bellamy Albert F, res 135 N Cass.

Bellamy Miss Carrie A, music teacher, bds 135 N Cass.

Bellamy Frank A, circulator, bds 135 N Cass.

Bellamy John, teamster, res 31 Prince.

Bellamy Mary E, bds 135 N Cass.

Belling Nicholas A, cutter Hoosier Mnfg Co, bds 21 W Jefferson.

Belmont Stables, A C Perrin Propr, 88 E Main. (*See adv p 63.*)

Belnap Catherine (wid James), bds 41½ W Berry.

Belot John C, res 211 W Jefferson.

Belshner Frederick, laborer, res 101 Putnam.

Belvick Ernst J, bds 303 Calhoun.

Belvick Fanny M, bds 303 Calhoun.

Belvick James A, carpenter, res 303 Calhoun.

Belvick Mrs Minnie R, dressmaker, 303 Calhoun, res same.

Beman Richard H, laborer Olds' Wagon Works, res 435 Lafayette.

Beman Wm G, coil winder Fort Wayne Electric Co, res 435 Lafayette.

Bence Wm C, carpenter, res 486 Hanna.

Bender Albert, servant 391 Fairfield ave.
Bender Caroline (wid John), res 204 Francis.
Bender Charles, cigarmaker Reuben Bender, bds 27 Grand.
Bender Christoph P, wagonmaker H A Rose, res n e cor Lillie
    and Creighton ave.
Bender Dennis, bds 275 E Washington.
Bender Elizabeth, stripper Reuben Bender, bds 27 Grand.
Bender Elmer, carpenter, bds 49 W Main.
Bender Emma, cigarmaker, bds 27 Grand.
Bender Ephraim, laborer, res 27 Brandriff.
Bender George, laborer, res 206 Francis.
Bender George T, coil winder Fort Wayne Electric Co, bds
    20 Poplar.
Bender John F P, machine hand American Wheel Co, bds 75
    W Jefferson.
Bender Levi, cigarmaker Reuben Bender, bds 27 Grand.
Bender Levi, plumber, res rear 152 E Wayne.
Bender Louis, cigars, 166 E Washington, res 168 same.
Bender Louis, painter, bds 154 Clay.
Bender Margaret, bds 160 Ewing.
Bender Minnie, bds 168 E Washington.
Bender Peter, laborer, res 14 Fulton.
Bender Reuben, cigar mnfr, 19 Grand, res 27 same.
Bender Samuel F, brakeman, res 12 Melita.
Bender Ursula (wid Adam), res 20 Poplar.
Bender Willard L, teamster, bds 124 Union.
Bender Wm, fireman, res 83 Broadway.
Bendorf Herman, cigarmaker G F Yergens, bds 69 Charles.
Bendure Wm H, carpenter, res 241 E Washington.
Benedict Ambrose, machinist Penn Co, bds 197 E Lewis.
Benedict Mrs Charlotte L, res 304 E Creighton ave.
Benedict Edward R, conductor Penn Co, res 147 John.
Benedict Jacob, driver C L Centlivre, res 24 Randolph.
Benedict Jacob, pedler, res 87 Wells.
Benedict Wm, carpenter, res 197 E Lewis.
Benedict Wm L, conductor Penn Co, bds 304 E Creighton
    ave.
Beneke Frederick W, car builder Penn Co, res 225 W
    Creighton ave.
Beneke Henry, machine hand Fort Wayne Organ Co, bds 225
    W Creighton ave.
Beneke Miss Louisa A, bds 225 W Creighton ave.
Beneke Wm F (Beneke & Co), res 443 Broadway.
Beneke & Co (Wm F Beneke), druggists, 210 Calhoun.
Bengs Gustav, boilermaker Bass Foundry and Machine
    Works, bds 240 Smith.

Stahn & Heinrich, Booksellers and Stationers, Schmitz Block News Stand, 116 Calhoun Street.

FORT WAYNE DIRECTORY. 91

Bengs Herman, stone cutter, res s e cor John and E Creighton ave.

Bengs Otto F, carpenter, res e s John 4 s of E Creighton ave.

Benhower Simon, carpenter, bds 22 W Main.

Beninghoff Daniel R (Beninghoff & Futter), res 37 Hugh.

Beninghoff & Futter (Daniel R Beninghoff, Charles Futter), barbers, Hotel Pearse.

Benjamin Adolph, editor Freie Presse, res 59 W Main.

Benner Conrad, painter, res 94 Montgomery.

Bennet Winton, res 36½ Lillie.

Bennett Asa, car builder Penn Co, res 157 Tabor.

Bennett Fannie M, dressmaker, bds 336 W Main.

Bennett George R, cook C Entemann, rms 68 W Main.

Bennett John C, machine hand American Wheel Co, bds 69 Charles.

Bennett Joseph F, laborer, res 500 Hanna.

Bennett J George, lab Bass Foundry and Machine Works, res 104 E Wayne.

Bennett Mary E (wid Adam J), res s e cor Wallace and Monroe.

Bennett Wm, bds n e cor Oliver and Buchanan.

Bennett Wm B, carriage trimmer, bds 320 Calhoun.

Bennett Wm M, packer Olds' Wagon Works, res 320 Calhoun.

Bennigan Joseph A, finisher, res 34 Summit.

Bennigen Laura, bds 83 Baker.

Bennigen Mary, bds 83 Baker.

Bennigen Mollie, domestic 216 W Berry.

Bennigin Charles F, machine hand American Wheel Co, bds 92 Force.

Bennigin Edward, machine hand Olds' Wagon Works, bds 92 Force.

Bennigin Henry E, machinist American Wheel Co, res 92 Force.

Bennigin Hugh, molder, res 207 E Lewis.

Bennigin Julius J, machinist Penn Co, res 207 E Lewis.

Bennigin Lena, bds 207 E Lewis.

Bennigin Mary, bds 207 E Lewis.

Benoy Charles W, machinist Bass Foundry and Machine Works, res 155 Force.

Benoy Frank T, res 179 Hanna.

Benroth Ferdinand, machinist Fort Wayne Electric Co, bds 46 Wall.

Bensberger, *see Bonsberger.*

Bensman Elizabeth (wid Rudolph), bds 76 Madison.

Bensman Mary C, clerk J F Gerke & Co, bds 76 Madison.

Bensman Rudolph, boilermaker, res 92 Madison.

Bensman Wm H, clerk Bass Foundry and Machine Works,
    bds 92 Madison.
Bensman Wm J, boilermaker Wabash R R, res 76 Madison.
Bente Charles W, painter Wabash R R, res 249 W Wash-
    ington.
Bente Frank, machinist Wabash R R, bds 125 Griffith.
Bente George F, painter Wabash R R, bds 155 Griffith.
Bente Harry, wks Rippe & Son, bds 155 Griffith.
Bente Harmon F, foreman Wabash R R, res 165 Griffith.
Benz Charles F, cigarmaker John Eckert, res 88 Dawson.
Benz Henry, checker Penn Co, res 318 Hanna.
Benz Otto M, machine hand American Wheel Co, res 169
    Holman.
Berbiller George, cigarmaker J Sohman & Co, bds 11 Melita.
Bercot Ella F, dressmaker, 37 Barr, bds same.
Bercot Joseph, res 41 W Lewis.
Berdelman Ernest, teamster John Orff, res 66 Barthold.
Berdelman John H, laborer, bds 66 Barthold.
Berg, *see Burg.*
Berg Lena, domestic H A Philley.
Berg Maggie, domestic 289 Fairfield ave.
Berg Nicholas, laborer Penn Co, res 594 Lafayette.
Bergel Melinda (wid Valentine), res 23 Boone.
Berger, *see also Boerger and Burger.*
Berger Emil, baker C C Gumpper, bds 238 Calhoun.
Berger Paul, blacksmith White's Wheel Works, res 252 Erie.
Berghoff Gustave, trav agent The Herman Berghoff Brewing
    Co, bds 100 E Jefferson.
Berghoff Henry C (Berghoff & Rothschild), res 100 E
    Jefferson.
Berghoff Herman Brewing Co The, Herman J
    Berghoff Pres, Hubert Berghoff Sec and Treas, e s Grand
    ave nr E Washington.
Berghoff Herman J, pres The Herman Berghoff Brewing Co,
    res 181 E Jefferson.
Berghoff Hubert, sec and treas The Herman Berghoff Brew-
    ing Co, res 91 Madison.
Berghoff & Rothschild (Henry C Berghoff, Aaron Roths-
    child), proprs Fort Wayne Artificial Ice Co, cor Wells
    and Cass nr Lake Shore depot.
Berghorn Frederick, car builder Penn Co, res 34 Hugh.
Berghorn Frederick, laborer, bds 169 Holman.
Berghorn Henry, carpenter, res 56 Maumee road.
Berghorn Louis H F, tailor F Hardung, bds 169 Holman.
Bergk Charles, physician, 52 W 4th, res same.
Bergmann, *see also Borgmann.*

E. F. Sites, 🦷 **Dentist,** 86 Calhoun St., Four Doors North of Wayne.

FORT WAYNE DIRECTORY.   93

Bergmann Henry, laborer, res w s Calhoun s of Rudisill ave.

Berkhold Matthew, cook, res 41 Williams.

Berleman Christina (wid Frederick), res 24 Van Buren.

Berlin Henry J, flour packer John Orff, res 45 Boone.

Berlin Wm, laborer Penn Co, res 69 Charles.

Berlonge Jennie, operator Hoosier Manufacturing Co, bds 210 E Washington.

Berlonge Susan, operator Hoosier Manufacturing Co, bds 210 E Washington.

Bernard, *see also Barnard.*

Bernard Mrs Nancy J, nurse, bds 48 W Williams.

Bernard Simeon, machinist, res 88 W Superior.

Bernhard Benjamin, musician, bds 309 Hanna.

Bernhard Newman, trav agt S M Foster, res 136 W Wayne.

Bernhardt Christian, coppersmith, res 29 John.

Bernhardt Frank, laborer, res 205 Gay.

Bernhardt Frederick J, saloon, 27 E Main, res same.

Berning Charlotte (wid Conrad), res 420 E Washington.

Berning Miss Dora, clerk Emma Wichman, bds 41 Summit.

Berning Henry, laborer, res 50 Smith.

Berning John, boilermaker, bds 420 E Washington.

Berning Lizzie M, domestic 203 W Wayne.

Berning Wm, machinist, res 16 McClellan.

Berr, *see also Barr.*

Berr Edward M, finisher, res 19 E Washington.

Berry, *see also Barry.*

Berry Charles, laborer, bds 182 E Jefferson.

Berry Charles W, laborer American Wheel Co, bds s e cor Putnam and Beck.

Berry Mrs Hattie A, editor The Watchman, res 575 Fairfield.

Berry Henry D, machine hand, bds 409 Lafayette.

Berry James H, asst foreman Fort Wayne Organ Co, res 575 Fairfield ave.

Berry Street M E Church, n w cor W Berry and Hanson.

Bertelmen John, boxmkr Davis & Bro, bds 66 Barthold.

Bertels, *see also Bartels.*

Bertels John, contractor, 160 Harmer, res same.

Berth Quirnus, domestic J D Nuttman.

Barthold Emil, grocer, s w cor Hanna and E Creighton ave, res same.

Berthold Gottfried J, wheelwright, res 156 Gay.

Berthold Louis E, baker, 37 W Berry, res same.

Bertsch Louise, domestic 15 W Jefferson.

Bertt Elizabeth, domestic 25 Berry.

Besancon Alexander F, brakeman, res 197 Hayden.

9

Besancon Josephine (wid Frank), res n s Parnell ave 1 n of St Joe road.
Bescheles Christina (wid George), bds 366 W Main.
Besson Ellen, bds 136 Monroe.
Besson John B, res 136 Monroe.
Besson Joseph J, clerk H J Ash, res 22 Summit.
Besson May, bds 136 Monroe.
Bestues Christina, bds 228 Hugh.
Bestues Michael, res 228 Hugh.
Betts Ellen (wid John), res 29 Charles.
Betts Maggie, dressmkr Mary L Sherin, bds 29 Charles.
Betts Thomas J, machine hand American Wheel Co, res 29 Charles.
Betz Ella, waiter McKinnie House.
Betz Frederick A, baker Wm F Geller, res 52 Nirdlinger av.
Betz John, laborer Hoffman Bros, res 50 Nirdlinger ave.
Betz Samuel J, carpet layer Foster Furniture Co, bds 50 Nirdlinger ave.
Betzler Crescynthia (wid George), bds 296 Broadway.
Betzler George A, filer, res 296 Broadway.
Betzold Rosa, domestic 18 Butler.
Beuch August, varnisher, bds 444 S Broadway.
Beuch John, bookkeeper, res 444 S Broadway.
Beuchel Otto, carpenter, res 514 E Lewis.
Beuchel Robert, carpenter, bds 512 E Lewis.
Beugnot Miss Alice, clk County Recorder, bds 164 E Wayne.
Beugnot Clara, bds 67 Harrison.
Beugnot John C, laborer, rms 18 Madison.
Beugnot Joseph E, saloon, 65 E Main, res same.
Beuke Christian F, truckman, res 155 Harrison.
Beuret Charles A, clerk Coombs & Co, bds 174 E Berry.
Beuret Charles A, mach hand American Wheel Co, res 34 E 2d.
Beuret Frank L, laborer, bds 34 E 2d.
Beuret Henry J, with Coombs & Co, bds 174 E Berry.
Beuret John B, mach Fort Wayne Electric Co, res 34 E 2d.
Beuret John P, wheel facer American Wheel Co, bds 34 E 2d.
Beuret Mary E (wid Xavier), res 390 Duck.
Beuret Mary P, seamstress, bds 34 E 2d.
Beuret Philomine, operator S M Foster, bds 34 E 2d.
Beuret Sylvester, laborer American Wheel Co, bds 34 E 3d.
Bevan Wm, wheelmaker American Wheel Co, res w s Glasgow ave nr Washington.
Bevelhaimer Daniel, carpenter, res 167 W De Wald.
Bevelhaimer Dayton, bridge carpenter, res 71 Butler.
Bevelhaimer Edward, actionmaker Fort Wayne Organ Co, bds 167 W De Wald.

Beverforden August, bds 175 Griffith.
Beverforden August, brewer, res 30 Schick.
Beverforden Henry F, Druggist, 286 Calhoun, res 284 Harrison. Telephone No 286.
Beverforden Rudolph, saloon, 294 Calhoun, res 11 Brandriff.
Bewlah Harry J, brakeman, res 215 W Washington.
Bewley John M, porter Hotel Randall.
Beyer Charles A, laborer, res 80 Barthold.
Beyer Paul, draughtsman J M E Riedel, bds same.
Beyerlein, *see also Beierlein.*
Beyerlein Charles F, clerk F M Smaltz, bds 107 Mechanic.
Beyerlein Frederick, supt city parks, res 45 N Calhoun.
Beyerlein George F, apprentice Penn Co, bds 30 Jones.
Beyerlein John L, laborer American Wheel Co, res 30 Jones.
Beyerlein Julius H, clerk F M Smaltz, res 59 Boone.
Beyers Dean L, lamp repairer, res 16 Hoffman.
Beyrau August, machine hand American Wheel Co, res 226 John.
Beyrau Wm, machine hand American Wheel Co, bds 54 Thomas.
Biard Clarence, laborer Penn Co, bds 39 Melita.
Biard Julius, laborer Penn Co, res 39 Melita.
Bibler Wm, laborer Penn Co, res 29 Hough.
Bickel Charles, cabinetmaker Fort Wayne Furniture Co, bds 71 Buchanan.
Bickenbeul Henry, wiper, res 34 Charles.
Bickford John D, saloon, 11 N Harrison, res same.
Bicknese Frederick C, saloon, 86 Barr, res 171 E Lewis.
Bicknese Frederick F, bartender, res 171 E Lewis.
Bicknese Frederick W E, clerk J B White, res 73 W Williams.
Bickness Henry, helper Penn Co, res 18 Madison.
Biddle C I, perfumer, 169 Ewing, res same.
Biddle Edward F, news agt, bds 169 Ewing.
Biddle Miss Mary, bds 169 Ewing.
Biddle Parker S, instrument maker, res 163 Clinton.
Biddle Thomas M, trav agt, res 169 Ewing.
Biddlecome John A, driver Fort Wayne Street Railroad Co, res 25 Grand.
Bidwell Emma A (wid George), res 9 N Calhoun.
Bidwell Wm P, painter, bds 77 N Cass.
Bidwell Wm S, carpenter, res 77 N Cass.
Bieber, *see also Beaber.*
Bieber Harvey F, carpenter, res 20 W Superior.
Bieber Wm L, teamster, res 21 Boone.
Bieberick Mary, domestic 224 W Berry.

Biedenweg Gottfried, laborer Bass Foundry and Machine Works, res 27 Smith.

Biegel Julius T, painter, res 52 Hugh.

Biegler Daniel, clerk Anthony Kalbacher, res 78 S Wayne av.

Biegler Miss Elizabeth M, teacher Jefferson school, bds 78 S Wayne ave.

Biemer George, wagonmaker Olds' Wagon Works, res 9 Clay.

Biemer Martin, blacksmith American Wheel Co, res 9 Clay.

Bierbaum Frederick G, laborer, bds 51 Taylor.

Bierbaum F Wm, car repairer Nichel Plate, res 184 Greely.

Bierbaum Frederika (wid Herman), res 51 Taylor.

Bierbaum Henry, laborer, bds 229 W Superior.

Bierbaum Wm, car repairer, res 184 Greely.

Bierley Wm W, clerk, res John nr Creighton ave.

Bierman, see also Beermann.

Bierman Ernest, janitor Taylor University, bds same.

Biermann Frederick, laborer, res 39 Boone.

Biewend Mrs Celestine, bds 333 E Washington.

Biewend Sophie, bds August Crull.

Bigbee Heber, painter L H Johnson, bds 72 Chicago.

Biggs Rebecca, domestic 9 E Wayne.

Bikel, see Bickel.

Bikels Charles, carpenter, bds 71 Buchanan.

Bilcer Jacob, truckman, res Rockhill Heirs' add.

Bilcer John, finisher, res Rockhill Heirs' add.

Bill Anna, operator Hoosier Mnfg Co, bds 141 Madison.

Bill Jacob, laborer, res 141 Madison.

Bill Jacob jr, clk H G Sommers, bds 141 Madison.

Bill Louisa, operator Hoosier Mnfg Co, bds 141 Madison.

Billman Henry, barber, bds 33 Monroe.

Billman Tillie (wid Ray), res 33 Monroe.

Bilser John, finisher The Peters Box and Lumber Co, res s s Spring w of Runion ave.

Bimer Charles, teamster, res 58 Barthold.

Bindel George, laborer Olds' Wagon Works, res 204 Smith.

Binder Jacob, gluer Fort Wayne Organ Co, bds 518 Fairfield.

Binkley Frank C, Electrician and Professor of Telegraphy, Rooms 17 to 20 Foster Block, res 293 W Jefferson. (See right side lines.)

Biper E, laborer Penn Co, res 88 W Jefferson.

Birbeck Edward, machinist Wabash R R, bds 97 W De Wald.

Birbeck Elizabeth (wid John), bds 97 W De Wald.

Birbeck Wm, machinist Wabash R R, res 97 W De Wald.

Bireley Luther, foreman, bds 116 E Columbia.

Bireley Wm W, asst foreman, res 288 E Wayne.

Birg N, laborer Penn Co, res 594 Lafayette.

Birk, *see also Burk and Burke.*
Birk Anna, bds 58 Elm.
Birk John G, carpet weaver, 58 Elm, res same.
Birkenbeul Henry, laborer Penn Co, res 34 Charles.
Birning Henry, laborer, res 50 Smith.
Bischoff Charles W, lawyer, res 63 Elm.
Bischoff Wm, well digger, bds 63 Elm.
Bischoff Wm, res 73 St Mary's ave.
Bischoff Rudolph, tchr Concordia College, res College grounds.
Bishop Charles, carp, res n s Riverside ave nr St Joseph river.
Bishop Charles, huckster, bds 13 Erie.
Bishop Harry, lab, bds n s Riverside ave nr St Joseph river.
Bishop Katie, dressmaker, bds n s Riverside ave near St
    Joseph river.
Bishop Martha (wid Martin), res 13 Erie.
Bishop Nellie D, folder Fort Wayne Sentinel, bds 13 Erie.
Bissell Frank P, clerk Penn Co, bds Rich Hotel.
Bissinger Henry, bds Clifton House.
Bitler Samuel D, Truss Hoop Mnfr, cor E Wayne and
    Schick, res 319 E Wayne.
Bitler Wm, clerk Star Grocery, bds 248 Calhoun.
Bitner A James, molder Penn Co, res Butler.
Bitner Clark A, molder Penn Co, res 67 E DeWald.
Bitner David W, clk Markey & Mungovan, rms 13 E Williams.
Bitner Eliza M (wid Andrew J), res 60 E Williams.
Bitner John R, machinist Penn Co, res 175 E Lewis.
Bitner Mattie A, seamstress, bds 60 E Williams.
Bitner Willard D, clerk, rms 13 E Williams.
Bitsberger Emanuel F, conductor, res 102 Wallace.
Bitsberger Mrs E F, dressmaker, 102 Wallace, res same.
Bitsberger Hallie E, machine hand Olds' Wagon Works, bds
    102 Wallace.
Bitsberger Wm H, machine hand American Wheel Co, bds
    102 Wallace.
Bittenger Jacob R, lawyer, 26 Court, res 262 W Washington.
Bittenger Lawrence E, clerk Penn Co, res 2 Erie.
Bittenger Miss Adah, teacher, bds 262 W Washington.
Bittinger Adam H (Bittinger & Edgerton), res 44 Pfeiffer av.
Bittinger Miss Marcia, teacher, bds 262 W Washington.
Bittinger & Edgerton (Adam H Bittinger, Dixon
    Edgerton), Lawyers, 27 and 28 Bank Block.
Bittler Wm M, res 301 N Jefferson.
Bittmann Carl, laborer Bass Foundry and Machine Works,
    res 150 Smith.
Bitzinger Henry, molder, res 436 E Wayne.
Bitzinger John, laborer White's Wheel Wks, res 26 Dubois.

Bitzinger John jr, laborer White's Wheel Wks, bds 26 Dubois.
Bitzler George A, finisher Fort Wayne Organ Co, res 296 Broadway.
Bixler Wm, teamster, res n s Richardson nr canal feeder.
Bixler Wm A, laborer Hoffman Bros, bds 20 Richardson.
Black Albert, deputy sheriff, res 178 E Washington.
Black Edward (col'd), porter J W Bell, res Bloomingdale.
Black Frank E, brakeman Penn Co, res 219 Lafayette.
Black Herman, helper Bass Foundry and Machine Works, bds 42 John.
Black John, janitor N Y, C & St L Ry, bds 153 High.
Black Marion, clerk Pfeiffer & Schlatter, bds 19 E Washington.
Black Oliver E, machine hand Winch & Son, bds Winch.
Blackburn James A, conductor Penn Co, res 25 Gay.
Blackburn James H, brakeman Penn Co, res 77½ Hoagland.
Blair Henry B, fireman, bds Camilla Schilling.
Blair Solon K, train marker N Y C & St L R R, res 221 W Wayne.
Blair Thomas W, asst chief clerk mailing dept Postoffice, res 220 E Wayne.
Blaising John, machinist, res 269 E Washington.
Blaising J Philip, laborer J A Koehler, res w s Lafayette 9 s of Pontiac.
Blake Mrs Ermina A F, res 22 W Berry.
Blake John B, foreman A L Johns & Co, res 255 E Wayne.
Blake John G, Supt Indiana School for Feeble-Minded Youth, 1 mile east of limits.
Blake Miss Lillian, bds 22 W Berry.
Blakeley Homer, clerk, bds 326 Harrison.
Blakeley Mary (wid Wm), res 326 Harrison.
Blakesley Charlotte, bds 105 Wallace.
Blakesley Harry A, flagman, bds 105 Wallace.
Blakesley James E, conductor, res 130 Horace.
Blakesley John H, res 105 Wallace.
Blakesley Lottie, milliner Mrs Adolph Schulte, bds 105 Wallace.
Blakesley Lyman M, conductor Penn Co, bds 105 Wallace.
Blakesley Wm, bds 20 Huron.
Blakley Wm F, gunsmith, 88 Broadway, res same.
Blank John, laborer Penn Co, res 15 St Martin.
Blase Wilhelmina (wid Louis), res 82 E Washington.
Bledsoe Miss Bessie, bookkeeper, bds 125 E Main.
Bledsoe Nathaniel H, Manager The Singer Mnfg Co, 4 Aveline House Block, res 125 E Main.
Bledsoe Miss Valeria, bds 125 E Main.

* Blee Edward, laborer White's Wheel Works, bds 95 Clay.

Blee John A, laborer American Wheel Co, res s e cor Washington and Clay.

Bleeke Miss Emma, bds 263 E Jefferson.

Bleeke Frederick W, clerk Wm Moellering & Sons, bds 200 E Jefferson.

Bleich John, laborer, res 45 Smith.

Bleki Diedrich, sweeper Penn Co, res 131 Madison.

Bleki Frederick L D, upholsterer The Pape Furniture Co, bds 131 Madison.

Bley George W, carpenter, 152 Hanna, res 173 Montgomery.

Bley Henry, switchman, bds Theodore Bley.

Bley Joseph, switchman, bds Theodore Bley.

Bley Theodore, yardmaster P, Ft W & C R R, res s s Old Piqua rd nr car shops.

Bligh Carolina (wid Stephan), bds 42 John.

Bligh Emil, laborer, res 42 John.

Blimm John N, tuner Ft Wayne Organ Co, res 23 W Butler.

Blitz Max J, city ticket agent Nickel Plate R R 5 Aveline House block, bds 30 E Wayne.

Bloch George, setter American Wheel Co, res 296 Hanna.

Bloch George A, laborer, bds 296 Hanna.

Block Frederick, laborer Wm Bruns, res 135 Gay.

Block Henry, bds 148 Ewing.

Block Mary (wid Frederick), res 87 Maumee road.

Block Sophie, domestic 267 W Wayne.

Block Wm F, helper C W Bruns & Co, bds 87 Maumee road.

Bloemker Frederick H, car inspector, res 55 Baker.

Bloemker Henry, carpenter, res 110 W Superior.

Bloemker Herman F, car inspector, res 55 Baker.

Bloemker John H, finisher, bds 110 W Superior.

Bloemker Wm, teamster, bds 110 W Superior.

Blombach Hugo, plasterer, bds 181 Gay.

Blombach Otto, plasterer, res 131 Gay.

Blomenberg Christ, carpenter, res 123 Union.

Blondell August E, machine hand Fort Wayne Organ Co, res n s Cornelia 1 w of Calhoun.

Blondiot Felix, res 8 Short.

Blondiot Wm H, tailor, res 47 E Lewis.

Blood John L, lab Wm Moellering & Co, res 38 E Pontiac.

Bloom Miss Caroline, bds 112 E Main.

Bloom John A, bookkeeper E F Clausmeier & Co, res 199 Montgomery.

Bloomfield Clemence C (wid Frederick A), res 30 E DeWald.

Bloomfield Frederick A jr, clk Penn Co, bds 30 E DeWald.

Bloomhuff Samuel H, res 281 E Washington.

Bloomingdale Mills, Pilliod & Brown proprs, cor Wells and 6th.
Bloomingdale School, n w cor Bowser and Marion.
Blopp Peter, lab White's Wheel Works, bds 85 Lillie.
Blotkamp Frank J, machinist Penn Co, res 26 Bass.
Blount Ambrose C, clerk, bds 9 N Calhoun.
Blount James A, laborer, res 9 N Calhoun.
Blue John O, conductor, res 320 Hanna.
Blum Catherine (wid Henry), res 19 Walnut.
Blum Charles, polisher White's Wheel Works, bds 11 Erie.
Blum Henry, boilermkr, bds 420 E Washington.
Blum Henry jr, machine hand, bds 19 Walnut.
Blum John, student, bds 11 Erie.
Blum Kate, operator Hoosier Mnfg Co, bds 11 Erie.
Blum Margaret, bds 11 Erie.
Blum Nicholas, mason, res 11 Erie.
Blum Nicholas jr, molder Bass Foundry and Machine Wks, bds 11 Erie.
Blum Peter, laborer, bds 11 Erie.
Blumenthaler Louis M, laborer L S & M S Ry, res 56 3d.
Blynn Harriet (wid Wm), dressmaker, 23 W Wayne, res same.
Blynn Miss Katherine H, teacher Jefferson school, bds 23 W Wayne.
Blystone Cyrus, sawyer, res 435 Lafayette.
Blystone Isaac, res 16 Holman.
Blystone Oliver A, carpenter, res 197 High.
Boag Mary L, bds 69 W Lewis.
Boag Wm G, machinist Penn Co, res 69 W Lewis.
Board of Health Office, L T Sturgis, M D, med sup, 275 Hanna.
Boatman David J, carpenter Penn Co, res 131 Suttenfield.
Bobay Peter, market stall No 72, res St Joe township.
Bobee Laura, chambermaid Aldine Hotel.
Bobilya Louis J, trav agt, bds 159 Griffith.
Bobs Christopher, finisher Horton Mnfg Co, res 81 St Mary's ave.
Bock, see also Buck and Buuck.
Bock Wm C, carpenter, res 35 Nirdlinger ave.
Bock Wm F, laborer American Wheel Company, res 39 Nirdlinger ave.
Bockeloh Mrs Emma, bds 78 Dawson.
Bockeloh Miss Lizzie, bds 83 W Washington.
Bocksberger Francis T, laborer, bds 36 Koch.
Bocksberger Louis, barber Louis Uplegger, res 48 Pfeiffer av.
Bocksberger Veroneka (wid Valentine), janitor Hamilton Nat Bank, res 36 Koch.

Printers. M. CLARK & CO.,
16 WEST COLUMBIA STREET.

FORT WAYNE DIRECTORY. 101

Bode Frank, laborer Bass Foundry and Machine Works, res 56 Smith.

Bode Frederick, driver, bds 248 Calhoun.

Boecker Frederick W, druggist, 108 Fairfield ave, res same.

Boecker Henry, laborer Wabash R R, res 58 Pritchard.

Boedeker August W, teamster Wm Moellering, bds 128 Montgomery.

Boedeker Diedrich, car builder Penn Co, res 29 Stophlet.

Boedeker Wm C, packer Pottlitzer Bros, res 195 High.

Boedike Deidrich, car builder Penn Co, res 67 Stophlet.

Boegel Ernest, laborer Hoffman Bros, res 212 Broadway.

Boegel Frederick E, lab Hoffman Bros, res 212 Broadway.

Boehm Christian, res 120 Rockhill.

Boehrer Alexis, wheel molder Bass Foundry and Machine Works, res 147 Force.

Boensot Jacob, cellarman, res cor n e Grant ave and Humphrey.

Boerger, *see also Berger and Burger.*

Boerger Charles R (C R Boerger & Bro), res 194 E Washington.

Boerger C R & Bro (Charles R and Wm H), House Movers, House and Roof Raisers, 194 E Washington. (*See adv, p 65.*)

Boerger Emma, bds 194 E Washington.

Boerger Florenz, asst flanger Penn Co, bds 42 Monroe.

Boerger Gustav W, leather, 39 E Main, res 24 McClellan.

Boerger Rudolph, clk G W Boerger, bds 183 E Washington.

Boerger Sarah S, bds 183 E Washington.

Boerger Simon J, clk G W Boerger, bds 183 E Washington.

Boerger Wm H (C R Boerger & Bro), res 312 Hanna.

Boerschinger Henry J, laborer Penn Co, res St Joe road.

Boerschinger Henry L, gardener, res n s St Joe road east city limits.

Boes Louis, molder Bass Foundry and Machine Works, res 510 E Lewis.

Boese Christina (wid Amond), res 150 E Jefferson.

Boese Clara, bds 135 Montgomery.

Boese Frederick, barnman, res s e cor Penn and Dubois.

Boese Fredrick, clerk Fredrick Dick, res 137 Force.

Boese Frederick W, laborer Penn Co, res 98 Stophlet.

Boese Mary, domestic 201 W Wayne.

Boese Wm C, car builder Penn Co, res 18 Hough.

Boese Wm C jr, carpenter, bds 18 Hough.

Boester Frederick, contractor, res 164 Griffith.

Boester John, clerk C F Reinkensmeier, bds 164 Griffith.

Boettcher Charles, forgeman, bds 53 Hugh.

Boeversen Louisa, domestic 59 Maumee road.

Bogash Frank, hostler C L Centlivre, res w s Leo pike 2 n of canal feeder.

Bogenhuelz Charles, bartender J T Wagner, res 208 Lafayette.

Bogenhuelz Joseph, bartender C Entemann.

Boggs Rev John M, pastor Third Presbyterian Church, res 13 Butler.

Bohanan Rose, tailoress Frederick Kayser, bds 333 Lafayette.

Bohde Augusta (wid Wm), res 225 Madison.

Bohde Charles H, polisher Fort Wayne Electric Co, res 53 Wall.

Bohde John, machine hand American Wheel Co, bds 225 Madison.

Bohde Louisa, bds 225 Madison.

Bohen, *see also Bowen.*

Bohen Michael, laborer, res, 245 E Jefferson.

Bohen Michael jr, slater, bds 245 E Jefferson.

Bohen Thomas, tinner John Baker Co, res 55 E Williams.

Bohen Wm, slater, bds 245 E Jefferson.

Bohler George, helper Wabash R R, res 79 Nirdlinger ave.

Bohler Jacob, painter, res 28 Murray.

Bohling F Wm, clerk, bds Wm Bohling.

Bohling Henry F C, bookbinder City Book Bindery, bds Wm Bohling.

Bohling Wm, laborer, res e s Force 2 s of E Creighton ave.

Bohn Adolph T, printer Archer, Housh & Co, bds 20 Allen.

Bohn Charles J P, canvasser, bds 20 Allen.

Bohn Christian P, printer Ft Wayne Newspaper Union, res 20 Allen.

Bohn Wm A, sec and treas The Horton Mnfg Co, res 285 W Berry.

Bohne Carl, foreman Kerr-Murray Mnfg Co, res 42 W Williams.

Bohne Frederick H, clerk Wm Meyer & Bro, bds 25 Boone.

Bohne Louis, bookkeeper F M Smith & Co, res 68 W Washington.

Boisnet Mary, domestic 110 Grant ave.

Boisno Philomena, domestic 22 E Columbia.

Bokaw Joseph, laborer, res 37 Duck.

Boland Asa H, plasterer, res 187 Suttenfield.

Boland Annie E, milliner A Mergentheim, bds 24 Oliver.

Boland John, engineer, res 24 Oliver.

Bolar Josie, domestic Wayne Hotel.

Boldt Bernard J, res 209 E Jefferson.

Bolender Levi, bds 222 W Wayne.

Boles, *see also Bolz.*

Ladies and Gentlemen's Garments, Plush and Velvet Wraps Cleaned and Dyed by the Celebrated Old Staten Island Dyeing Establishment. Mrs. E. A. Flagler, Agt., 14 W. Berry St.

FORT WAYNE DIRECTORY. 103

Boles Miss Luella C, teacher Washington School, bds 280 W Berry.

Boles Mrs Rachael C, teacher, bds 280 W Berry.

Boley George, helper, bds 79 Nirdlinger ave.

Boley John N, laborer Penn Co, bds James L Smith.

Boling Francis, bds 132 Wells.

Boling Lemuel R, painter, res 132 Wells.

Bolinger Jacob, carpenter, res 90 E Main.

Boll, *see also Ball.*

Boll Victor, tuner D H Baldwin & Co, bds 26 E Wayne.

Bollman August, laborer Indiana Machine Works, res 283 W Main.

Bolman Albert F, cigar mnfr 138½ Broadway, res 284 same.

Bolman Christ, foreman Olds' Wagon Works, res 47 W Lewis.

Bolman Frederick, carpenter, bds 47 W Lewis.

Bolman Frederick A, conductor, res 188 Jackson.

Bolman Minnie, domestic 104 E Main.

Bolman Otto F, brakeman Penn Co, bds 25 Hood.

Bolton Nehemiah, machinist Fort Wayne Electric Co, res 407 S Broadway.

Bolton Richard, actionmaker Fort Wayne Organ Co, rms 51 Hendricks.

Boltz Ferdinand F, res 250 W Jefferson.

Boltz Fred C, Wholesale Dealer in Fine Whiskies, Wines, Liquors, Tobaccos and Cigars, 27 Calhoun, Branch Store, 92 Calhoun, res 87 N Cass. (*See adv, p 2.*)

Boltz George C, gardener, bds 87 N Cass.

Bolyard Charles W, teamster, res 64 W Wayne.

Bolz, *see also Boles.*

Bolz Frank A, machine hand, res 505 Hanna.

Bolz Hugh, mach hand American Wheel Co, bds Frank Bolz.

Bonche Sophie, domestic, 259 W Wayne.

Bond Albert L, photographer, res 43 Butler.

Bond Albert S, supt Fort Wayne Organ Co, res 362 Fairfield.

Bond Charles E, sec Fort Wayne Organ Co, res 289 Fairfield.

Bond Charles Z, machinist, bds 164 Brackenridge.

Bond Frank E, messenger Old National Bank, bds 322 Fairfield ave.

Bond Henry W, flour, 65 E Columbia, bds 132 E Berry.

Bond Herbert W, actionmaker Fort Wayne Organ Co, bds 322 Fairfield ave.

Bond Hugh McC, traveling agent S F J Bowser & Co, res w s Fairfield ave 2 s of Creighton ave.

Bond Jared B, Cashier Old National Bank, res s w cor Calhoun and De Wald.

Bond Jennie M (wid Alonzo S), res 164 Brackenridge.
Bond John, hostler Christian Martz, rms 15 W Jefferson.
Bond Levina A (wid Charles D), bds Wayne Hotel.
Bond Stephen B, pres Old National Bank and pres Fort Wayne Organ Co, res 322 Fairfield ave.
Bond Stephen D, res 155 W Wayne.
Bond Wm J, dry goods, 376 Calhoun, res same.
Bonfield Mary (wid Kennedy), res 180 E Wayne.
Bonker Frederick, carpenter, bds 397 W Main.
Bonnet George J, helper, res 104 E Wayne.
Bonter George W P, conductor Penn Co, res 73 W DeWald.
Bonter Wm F C, conductor, rms 17 W Lewis.
Bookwalter, see also Buckwalter.
Bookwalter Mrs Alice, res s e cor Jefferson and Clinton.
Bookwalter Charles C, car painter Penn Co, res 40 E Jefferson.
Bookwalter Elias H, pressman Fort Wayne Gazette, res 15 W Williams.
Bookwalter John A, agent, res 134 E Lewis.
Booth Wm, well driller Robert Spice, bds Monroe House.
Bopp Andrew, laborer Winch & Son, res 30 Buchanan.
Bopp Charles, bellboy, bds 69 Melita.
Bopp George, painter, bds 97 Taylor.
Bopp Henry C, wagonmaker Olds' Wagon Works, res 69 Melita.
Bopp John, billiard clerk J M Klingenberger, bds 95 Clay.
Bopp Maggie, domestic Wayne Hotel.
Borcherding Ferdinand (Borcherding & Toensing), res 58 Liberty.
Borcherding & Toensing (Ferdinand Borcherding, Henry Toensing), Foundry, n e cor Superior and Barr. (See adv in classified Founders and Machinists.)
Borchert Frederick A, painter, res 59 Indiana ave.
Borg Rev Theodore, chaplain St Vincent Orphan Asylum, res same.
Borg Wm, machinist Penna Co, res 69 W Lewis.
Borgman, see also Bergmann.
Borgman August, teamster, res 202 Ewing.
Borgman Christian, clk Peter Pierre, res 35 Pritchard.
Borgman Christian, teamster, bds 200 Ewing.
Borgman Fredericka (wid Christian), res 35 Pritchard.
Borgman Fredericka E K, milliner A Mergentheim, bds 35 Pritchard.
Borgman Lizzie, bds 35 Pritchard.
Borgman Mary, bds 35 Pritchard.
Borgman Wm, teamster, res 200 Ewing.
Borgman Wm F, fireman, res e s Koch 1 n of Putnam.

Bork, *see Birk and Burke.*

Borkenstein Bernhard, carpenter, res 44 Baker.

Borneman Charles, tailor, res 98 W Harrison.

Bornemann Frederick C, clk Isaac Lauferty, res 98 Harrison.

Bornkamp Ferdinand, bricklayer, res 25 Smith.

Borts Albert, car builder Penn Co, rms 152 E Wayne.

Boscheg John, laborer Ranke & Gergens, res 127 W Superior.

Boschet Gottlieb, well borer, res 68 Butler.

Boschet Henry, carpenter J A Crow & Co, bds 68 Butler.

Boseker Catherine (wid John), bds John Barrow.

Boseker Charles F, contractor, res 62 McClellan.

Boseker Christian, contractor, res 37 Brackenridge.

Boseker Miss Edith, teacher Harmer School, bds 66 W De Wald.

Boseker Frank H, carpenter, res 131 Shawnee ave.

Boseker Harry, clerk, bds 37 Brackenridge.

Boseker Henry, traveling agent American Wheel Co, res 66 W De Wald.

Boseker Lincoln, conductor, res 37 Elm.

Boseker Wm, machine hand Horton Mnfg Co, res 40 Wall.

Boseker Wm G, blacksmith Penn Co, res 138 Shawnee ave.

Boshler Charles W, clerk J A M Storm, res 70 Butler.

Bosler Edward, fireman, bds 335 W Main.

Bosler Wm, hostler Lee & Fulton, rms 22 W Main.

Boss Annie, bds 138 E Main.

Boss Mary (wid Henry), res 138 E Main.

Bosselman Dietrich, boilermaker Ft Wayne Iron Works, res Madison.

Bossler Henry H, real estate, 34 Clinton, res w s Spy Run ave 1 n of St Mary's bridge.

Bossler Joseph, fireman Penn Co, res 22 Gay.

Bossler Joseph jr, molder, bds 22 Gay.

Boster Lena, works Troy Steam Laundry, bds 17 Baker.

Bostick Emanuel, manager, res 170 E Wayne.

Bostick John W, res 130 E Wayne.

Bostick Reuben J, clerk, bds 170 E Wayne.

Bostick Wm D (E B Kunkle & Co), res 170 E Wayne.

Boston Willis, washer Fort Wayne Bottling Works, bds 166 Holman.

Boswell Andrew J, physician, 96 Barr, res 199 E Lewis.

Boswell Asa C, physician, 96 Barr, res 199 E Lewis.

Boswell John, hoopmaker, res e s Grant ave 1 s of Maumee road.

Both Ottilie (wid Theodore), bds 23 E Jefferson.

Bothner Anna, bds 141 Lafayette.

Bothner John G, saloon, 136 Calhoun, res same.

Bott Anna, bds 32 W 5th.
Bott Edward, machine hand Kerr-Murray Mnfg Co, bds 26
    Walnut.
Bott Frank J, clerk Louis Fox & Bro, bds 26 Walnut.
Bott Herman, helper, res 46 Taylor.
Bott Innocent, blacksmith Penn Co, res 26 Walnut.
- Bott Joseph, laborer, bds 24 Murray.
Bott Maurice, laborer, bds 26 Walnut.
Bott Nellie, dressmaker, bds 46 Taylor.
Bott Urban, machinist Wabash R R, res 46 Taylor.
Bottenberg Andrew J (Bottenberg & Miller), res 13 Liberty.
Bottenberg Benjamin F, foreman G K Hubbard, bds 13
    Liberty.
Bottenberg Daniel (Heller & Bottenberg), res Monroe twp.
Bottenberg & Miller (Andrew J Bottenberg, Wm Miller),
    junk, 305 Canal.
Bottger John E, engineer, res 54 Jackson.
Bougher, see also Bauer, Bour and Bower.
Bougher Frank (Riegel & Bougher), res 130 Lafayette.
Bouillon Jennie, domestic 32 Maple ave.
Boumeister Frederick, molder, res 12 Force.
Bourie Miss Adelle F, bds 115 W Washington.
Bourie A Ophelia, stenographer American Wheel Co, bds
    115 W Washington.
Bourie Brutus A, bookkeeper Olds' Wagon Works, res 18 W
    De Wald.
Bourie Clinton D, letter carrier, res 32 E DeWald.
Bourie George W, clerk Pixley & Co, res 115 W Washington.
Bourie Louis J, bds 115 W Washington.
Bourie Louis T, res 115 W Washington.
Bouse Jane M (wid Lorenz), res 35 E 1st.
Bovine David F, laborer, res 62 Home ave.
Bowen Miss Alberta, bds 229 E Washington.
Bowen Daniel, lawyer, res 229 E Washington.
Bowen George R, bookkeeper John Pressler, res 108 Barr.
Bowen George W, physician, 12 W Main, res 232 E Wash-
    ington.
Bowen James, laborer McKinnie House.
Bowen Miss Lillie V, teacher Nebraska School, bds 229 E
    Washington.
Bowen Michael, slate roofer J H Welch, bds 245 E Jefferson.
Bowen Wm, slate roofer J H Welch, bds 245 E Jefferson.
Bower, see also Bauer, Bougher and Bowers.
Bower Annie R, student, bds 210 Fairfield ave.
Bower Daniel F, Gen'l Sec Young Men's Christian
    Association, 103 Calhoun, rms 72 Harrison.

Stahn & Heinrich, **Booksellers and Stationers,**
Schmitz Block News Stand, 116 Calhoun Street.

FORT WAYNE DIRECTORY. 107

Bower Frank D, bds 67 Harrison.
Bower George B M, physician, 72 Harrison, res 116 W Main.
Bower Harry H, flagman Penn Co, res 41 Walton ave.
Bower Jacob M, carpenter, res 19 N Cass.
Bower Mary A, domestic 406 S Clinton.
Bowers Agnes M, domestic 104 Barr.
Bowers Benjamin, carpenter, res 184 Hayden.
Bowers Charles A, asst engineer Olds' Wagon Works, res 47 Bass.
Bowers Clara, domestic 77 W Williams.
Bowers David, carp, bds n s Prospect ave 1 w of St Joseph river.
Bowers Emma, domestic 67 W DeWald.
Bowers Jacob J, laborer Fort Wayne Iron Works, bds 57 Williams.
Bowers John W, painter Wayne Paint and Painting Co, bds 251 Calhoun.
Bowers Maria (wid James), res 268 W Washington.
Bowers Mary, domestic 75 W Williams.
Bowers Racy, pedler, bds Brokaw House.
Bowersock Andrew, hotel, 31 W Columbia, res same.
Bowker Mrs Adelpha, bds 37 Elizabeth.
Bowman, *see also Baughman and Bauman.*
Bowman Arthur F, driver Fort Wayne Street Railroad Co, res 163 Clinton.
Bowman Charles, Saw Repairer, also Tinners' Shears, Lawn Mowers, Butchers' Tools, Scissors, Plow Points and All Kinds of Edged Tools Ground and put in First-Class Order, 18 Harrison, res 146 High. (*See left top lines.*)
Bowman Clark, machine hand Olds' Wagon Works, bds 30 W Williams.
Bowman Miss Elizabeth J, teacher Bloomingdale School, bds 160 W Superior.
Bowman Mrs Emeline D, res 160 W Superior.
Bowman Harriet, domestic 77 E Berry.
Bowman Jennie, teacher, bds 160 W Superior.
Bowman Lee, clk Isaac Lauferty, bds Central House.
Bowman Miss Prudence L, teacher Jefferson School, bds 160 W Superior.
Bowman Wm, clk C Tresselt & Sons, bds 43½ E Columbia.
Bowser Alexander, mach S F Bowser & Co, res 264 E Creighton ave
Bowser Allen A (S F Bowser & Co), bds 264 E Creighton ave.
Bowser Augustus (S F Bowser & Co), res 5 Julia.
Bowser Clark, carpenter, bds 51 E Superior.
Bowser Deliah (wid Jacob C), res 86 E Washington.

Bowser Delmore, driver S F Bowser & Co, bds 5 Julia.
Bowser Ernest M, laborer, bds G. W Bowser.
Bowser George W, fireman, res n s Julia 1 e of Thomas.
Bowser Isaiah, laborer, bds 264 E Creighton ave.
Bowser Mrs Margaret, res 95 Summit.
Bowser Mary F, domestic 29 E 2d.
Bowser Nelson J, teamster, bds G W Bowser.
Bowser Orra J, painter, res 266 E Creighton ave.
Bowser Sarah M, bds 86 E Washington.
Bowser Sylvanus F (F S Bowser & Co), res 152 Force.
Bowser S F & Co (Sylvanus F, Augustus, Allen A Bowser),
    oil tanks and pumps, 260 E Creighton ave.
Bowsher Amos, transfer clerk Wabash R R depot, res 42 Mc-
    Clellan.
Bowsher Nellie V, bds 42 McClellan.
Boxberger Frances, works Model Steam Laundry, bds 36
    Koch.
Boyce Myrtle, bds 26 E Williams.
Boyd Miss Georgina, teacher Clay School, bds 223 Lafayette.
Boyd Minnie, bds 87 Ewing.
Boyd Sarah (wid Benjamin F), res 223 Lafayette.
Boyd Seymour D, clerk Bass Foundry and Machine Works,
    bds 223 Lafayette.
Boyd Thomas L, brakeman, res 171 High.
Boyer, *see also Bayer.*
Boyer Frederick, waiter Aveline House.
Boyer Ida F, nurse Fort Wayne City Hospital.
Boyer Lulu J, nurse Fort Wayne City Hospital.
Boylan Etta L, bds 225 Calhoun.
Boylan John, Propr Jewel House, 225 Calhoun, res
    same.
Boylan Rufus A, bds 225 Calhoun.
Boyle Mrs Anna, cook W H Pease, res 47 Superior.
Boyle John, iceman, res 62 Summit.
Boyle John, car repairer Penn Co, res New Haven road.
Boyle Maggie, chambermaid Randall Hotel.
Boyle Mary J, domestic 38 E Williams.
Boyle Sadie, clerk L Dessauer & Co, bds 118 E Wallace.
Boyle Wm M, carpenter, res 47 E Superior.
Boyles Miss Aggie, bds 47 E Superior.
Boyles Richard, rms 51 Hendricks.
Boyles Robert C, finisher Ft Wayne Organ Co, res 35 Miner.
Boyles Robert D, cabinetmaker Fort Wayne Organ Co, res
    35 Miner.
Brabandt Henry B, molder Bass Foundry and Machine
    Works, res 228 Gay.

Bracht Joseph C, engineer, res 33 Butler.
Brackenridge Charles S, res 144 W Wayne.
Brackenridge George W, Trustee Wayne Township, Office 13 Foster Block, res 31 Douglas ave.
Brackenridge Joseph, lawyer, 20 W Berry, res 77 W Wayne.
Brackenridge Robert E, bds 77 W Wayne.
Brackenridge Wm T, clerk Joseph Brackenridge, bds 77 W Wayne.
Brackett Mary, cook, bds 201 Calhoun.
Brackett W A, bds 378 Calhoun.
Bradbury Agnes E (wid Thomas), bds 21 Lincoln ave.
Bradbury James, machine hand American Wheel Co, bds 183 Montgomery.
Braden Daniel D, barber H Guenther, bds 225 Calhoun.
Braden David, farmer, res 131 Griffith.
Brademeyer Henry, canvasser, res 38 E 4th.
Bradfield Lafayette, depot agt Adams Express Co.
Bradley Archie, architect, bds 68 Charles.
Bradley Edgar O, engineer, bds 233 E Lewis.
Bradley George, painter, res 37 Laselle.
Bradley George O, carpenter, res 68 Charles.
Bradley Harry J, draughtsman F B Kendrick, bds 101 Calhoun.
Bradley Howard, painter, bds 37 Laselle.
Bradley James K, machinist Penn Co, res 233 E Lewis.
Bradley Nelson L, machine hand Fort Wayne Furniture Co, res 233 E Lewis.
Bradley Robert A, apprentice Wing & Mahurin, bds 68 Charles.
Bradley Mrs Sarah A, propr Grand Central Hotel, 101 Calhoun.
Bradley Wm N, engineer, bds Grand Central Hotel.
Bradshaw Charles, painter E E Schuman & Sons, bds 91 E Main.
Bradshaw Jeremiah, teamster, res 61 Garden.
Bradshaw Samuel (col'd), porter S G Hubbard, bds 145 E Erie.
Bradshaw Wm (col'd), porter S G Hubbard, bds 61 Gardner.
Bradtmueller Charles H, horseshoer Fort Wayne St Railroad Co, res 172 Madison.
Bradtmueller Gottlieb, cab builder Penn Co, bds 59 Douglas.
Bradtmueller Henrietta, bds 59 Douglas ave.
Bradtmuller Mrs Elizabeth, res 99 Summit.
Bradway Orlando E, foreman Penn Co, res 216 E Lewis.
Brady Jane (wid Samuel A), bds 142 E Berry.
Brady Richard E, machinist, res 67 Rockhill.

10

Brady Wm H (Root & Co), res 260 W Berry.
Braeuer, *see also Breuer.*
Braeuer Conrad, shoes 358 S Broadway, res same.
Braeuer John C, shoemaker Conrad Braeuer, res 184 Griffith.
Brahs John, clerk McKinnie House, res 297 Harrison.
Brainard Annie, rms 135 Lafayette.
Braithwait Charles F, engineer, res 178 Greeley.
Braithwait Elijah, driver Hoffman Bros, bds 178 Greeley.
Braithwait George, laborer Hoffman Bros, bds 178 Greeley.
Braithwait George W, caller, bds 178 Greeley.
Braithwait Wm H, machinist, bds 178 Greeley.
Braitinger George, collector Metropolitan Mnfg Co, res 338 Broadway.
Brake Edward, laborer White's Wheel Works, res 170 Maumee road.
Brake Henry, polisher Winch & Son, res 172 Maumee road.
Brake Henry, laborer, bds 521 E Lewis.
Brake Olin, laborer, bds 25 Lillie.
Brake Theodore, machine hand American Wheel Co, bds 34 Gay.
Brake Ulrich G, wheelmaker American Wheel Co, res 176 Maumee road.
Brake Ulrich G jr, rimmer, res 172 Maumee road.
Brames Charles, laborer, bds 88 Hayden.
Brames Louis (L Brames & Co), res 162 E Jefferson.
Brames L & Co (Louis Brames), Propr Summit City Bottling Works, 123, 125 and 127 Clay. (*See adv, p 3.*)
Brammer Very Rev Joseph H, vicar general Diocese Fort Wayne, res 172 Clinton.
Brandenberger G, laborer Penn Co, res 7 Walnut.
Brandt August, cigarmaker, bds 158 Harrison.
Brandt Caroline, domestic 171 Harmer.
Brandt Charles, buyer, res 34 McClellan.
Brandt Christian, machinist Indiana Machine Works, res 15 Boone.
Brandt Miss Clara, bds 158 Harrison.
Brandt Diedrich, foreman Bass Foundry and Machine Works, res n w cor John and Creighton ave.
Brandt Dora, bds 76 Hayden.
Brandt Miss Emma, bds 158 Harrison.
Brandt Frederick, res 158 Harrison.
Brandt Gottlieb F, sawyer, res 9 Marion.
Brandt Henry, laborer Weil Bros & Co, res 76 Hayden ave.
Brandt Herman, laborer, res 187 Taber.
Brandt Lizzie, bds 34 McClellan.
Brandt Miss Minnie, clerk J M Kane, bds 34 McClellan.

Brandt Mollie, clerk Stewart & Hahn, bds 34 McClellan.

Brandt Theodore W, clerk G De Wald & Co, bds 45 W Jefferson.

Brandt Wm, cigarmaker, res 69 Wilt.

Brandtmeyer Carrie, bds 168 Ewing.

Brandtmeyer Frederick, molder, res 168 Ewing.

Branican Beverly, laborer Bass Foundry and Machine Works, res 165 Clinton.

Brannan, *see also Brennan.*

Brannan John H, county comur, res 195 E Lewis.

Brannan Julia (wid Thomas), res 185 Monroe.

Brannan Miss Mary, bds 195 E Lewis.

Brannan Michael L, tchr Clay school, res 171 E Washington.

Brannan Richard, plumber, bds 195 E Lewis.

Brannan Thomas L, fireman, res 160 W Main.

Brannen Michael J, driver Fred Eckert, bds 91 E Wayne.

Branner Charles B, lawyer, 4 Schmitz blk, rms 46 Douglas av.

Branning Conrad, laborer, res 89 Wall.

Branning Ernst, farmer, res w s Fairfield ave s of organ factory.

Branning Henry C, clerk, bds 537 Broadway.

Branning Minnie, domestic 284 W Wayne.

Brannon Melvin A, asst Central Grammar school, res 102 E Berry.

Branstator Frank, laborer, bds 87 W Superior.

Branstator Leander, laborer, bds 87 W Superior.

Branstraitor Jason, laborer, bds 71 Maumee road.

Brasch Charles, porter, rms 55 W Main.

Brase August C, grocer, 73 W Jefferson, res same.

Brase Frederick C, teamster, res 75 W Jefferson.

Brase Theodore F, teamster, res 176 W Jefferson.

Brase Wm C, teamster The Herman Berghoff Brewing Co, res 415 E Washington.

Braum John, laborer Bass Foundry and Machine Works, bds 88 Hayden.

Braum L, helper Penn Co, res Holton ave.

Braun, *see also Brown.*

Braun Carrie, works Troy Steam Laundry, bds 78 Wall.

Braun Charles G (Keller & Braun), res 46 Pritchard.

Braun Charles G, cigarmaker G F Yergens, res 80 N Harrison.

Braun Elizabeth (wid Philip), bds 168 E Washington.

Braun Frederick, stone mason, res 233 John.

Braun Frederick J, blacksmith L C Zollinger, bds 78 Wall.

Braun George, baker, 135 Fairfield ave, res same.

Braun George, machine hand Fort Wayne Furniture Co, bds 135 Fairfield ave.

Braun Henry, pressman Fort Wayne Newspaper Union, bds 342 E Washington.

Braun John, carpenter, res 342 E Washington.

Braun John G, bds 54 Pritchard.

Braun Stephen M, engineer Fort Wayne Artificial Ice Co, res 15 Oak.

Brauneisen Joseph, grocer, 137 Fairfield ave, res same.

Braunsberger Alonzo, laborer, bds 322 Broadway.

Brauntmeyer Carrie, clerk Eleanor Kratzch, bds 168 Ewing.

Brauntmeyer Charles H, machinist A Hattersley & Sons, res 202 Ewing.

Brauntmeyer Frederick W, molder Kerr-Murray Mnfg Co, res 168 Ewing.

Brawley George, paver, bds 29 E Main.

Brawley George H, foreman The Remington-Lawton Co, bds 106 Barr.

Breaden Ida (wid James E), res 143 Holman.

Breaugh John E, brakeman, res 69 W 4th.

Bredemeyer Annie D (wid Wm), res 8 Marion.

Bredemeyer Henry E, carpenter, res 38 E 4th.

Bredemeyer H Wm, painter Fleming Mnfg Co, res 8 Marion

Bredemeyer Wm, laborer, bds 41 Gay.

Breed Alvin, laborer Hoffman Bros, bds 49 St Mary's ave.

Breen Ella H, dressmaker, bds 15 Bass.

Breen Henry E, switchman, bds 15 Bass.

Breen James E, conductor, bds 15 Bass.

Breen Kate, stenographer J O Keller, bds 91 W Washington

Breen Maria (wid Michael), res 15 Bass.

Breen Maria E, dressmaker, bds 15 Bass.

Breen Michael J, seal clerk, bds 15 Bass.

Breen Wm P, Lawyer, over 44 Calhoun, res 121 Main.

Breer Ferdinand, wood carver Fort Wayne Furniture Co, bd 137 E Washington.

Breese George H, driver J M Moderwell, res 60 Wall.

Breese Samuel E, painter, res 217 Broadway.

Breidenstein Mathias, carp J Wagner, bds 25 W Wayne.

Breidenstein Simpson, real estate, 25 W Wayne, res same.

Breimeier Ernst (Breimeier & Son), res 221 W Creighton av

Breimeier Ernst F H (Breimeier & Son), res 207 W DeWal

Breimeier Gustav, mach Indiana Machine Works, bds 221 Creighton ave.

Breimeier Herman, bricklayer, bds 221 W W Creighton av

Breimeier Louis C, clerk, res 128 W Williams.

Breimeier & Son (Ernst and Ernst F H), builders, 221 W Creighton ave.

Breimeyer Miss Clara, bds 219 W Jefferson.

Breimeyer Henry, res 219 W Jefferson.

Breimeyer John, laborer, bds Washington House.

Breimeyer Miss Minnie, bds 219 W Jefferson.

Breimeyer Wm F, clk G DeWald & Co, bds 219 W Jefferson.

Bremer Henry H, blacksmith, bds 47 Archer ave.

Bremer Henry J, clerk J B White, res 47 Archer ave.

Bremer Wm F, clerk, bds 47 Archer ave.

Brendel Anna T, bds 12 St Mary's ave.

Brendel George C, brakeman Nickel Plate, bds 12 St Mary's.

Brendel Jacobine (wid John), res 12 St Mary's ave.

Brendel John, brakeman, bds 12 St Mary's ave.

Brendel Joseph, caller Nickel Plate, bds 12 St Mary's ave.

Brendel Josephine, bds 12 St Mary's ave.

Brendt Charles, cigarmaker, res 162 Montgomery.

Brennan, see also Brannan.

Brennan Bernard T, cigarmaker G F Yergens, res n e cor High and St Mary's ave.

Brennan Wm T, machinist, res 198 E Lewis.

Brenner Charles F, machinist Kerr-Murray Mnfg Co, bds 78 Wilt.

Brenner Frank, lumber, res 218 W Jefferson.

Brenner George, printer Freie Presse, bds 108 Madison.

Brenner Jacob, bartender Fritz Hotel, bds 10 E Berry.

Brenner Mary (wid John), res 78 Wilt.

Brenner Mollie, dressmaker Mary L Sherin, bds 78 Wilt.

Brenton Eliza (wid Samuel), res 220 W Wayne.

Brenton Miss Helen, teacher Jefferson School, bds 220 W Wayne.

Brenton Mrs Marion H, teacher Hanna School, res 19 Madison.

Bresler Albert, brakeman, res 64 Elm.

Bresnihan Johanna, bds 145 Holman.

Bresnihan John J, fireman, bds 145 Holman.

Bresnihan Mary, tailoress G Scheffler, bds 145 Holman.

Bresnihan Patrick, machinist Indiana Machine Works, bds 145 Holman.

Bresnihan Thomas A, bds 145 Holman.

Bretmiller George, horseshoer Ft Wayne City Railroad Co, res 172 Madison.

Breuer, see also Braeuer.

Breuer Wm, foreman The Herman Berghoff Brewing Co, res 570 E Washington.

Brewer Wm L, traveling agent S Bash & Co, bds 73 Holman.

John Pressler, Hot Air and Hot Water Furnaces. Columbia, Barr and Dock Streets.

114   R. L. POLK & CO.'S

Brewster Miss Edith M, principal Holton Avenue School, bds 139 E De Wald.

Brewster Lucy, operator Hoosier Manufacturing Co, bds 141 E De Wald.

Briant Miss Julia M, bookkeeper, bds 228 W Creighton ave.

Briant Wm H, res 228 W Creighton ave.

Brice James F, clerk Hotel Randall, res 98 W Superior.

Brice James F, conductor, res 159 W Superior.

Brick Christina (wid Adam), bds 122 W Jefferson.

Bricker Charles F, laborer, res 34 Chicago.

Bricker Charles P, laborer, bds 34 Chicago.

Bricker Conrad, engineer Penn Co, res n w cor Thomas and Green.

Bricker David, engineer, res 25 Oliver.

Bricker D Edwin, shipping clerk S M Foster, bds n w cor Thomas and Green.

Bricker Homer A, clerk Foster Furniture Co, bds 53 Thomas.

Bricker Ida, bds 22 Oliver.

Bricker John M, feed stable, res 37 Barr.

Bricker Lincoln, driver B W Skelton, res 40 Laselle.

Bricker Servard D, fireman, res s s E Williams 1 w of Lafayette.

Brickmakers' Association, James S Fields agent, 55 Clinton.

Brickner Clements, helper Bass Foundry and Machine Works, bds 141 Erie.

Brickner Herman, stone mason, res 141 Erie.

Brickner Oswald, laborer Bass Foundry and Machine Works, bds 141 Erie.

Briddon Sarah C (wid John V), bds 237 W Wayne.

Brieggaman Fredericka W, domestic 54 E Wayne.

Briggeman Wm, car builder Penn Co, res 21 Euclid ave.

Briggs Charles E, driver Ft Wayne Street Railroad Co, bds 248 Calhoun.

Briggs Frank, bds 199 Broadway.

Briggs Hattie (wid Alfred), res 120 Ewing.

Briggs Lillie, clerk Root & Co, bds 120 Ewing.

Briggs Martin E, porter Pearse Hotel.

Bright Benjamin W, molder Bass Foundry and Machine Works, bds 229 E Wayne.

Bright Wm J, car builder Penn Co, res 229 E Wayne.

Brigmannn Wm, carpenter, res 21 Euclid ave.

Brill Henry F, conductor, res 265 E Creighton ave.

Brillhart Andrew, res 275 E Jefferson.

Brimmer Joseph H, sign painter, 33 W Main, res 265 W Jefferson.

Brink Aileen I, dressmaker Wm Malloy, res 39 E Berry.

Stahn & Heinrich, Leading Dealers in ARTISTS' MATE-RIALS AND DRAUGHTING INSTRUMENTS. 116 Calhoun Street.

FORT WAYNE DIRECTORY. 115

Brink Miss Elizabeth M, dressmaker 320 E Washington, res same.

Brink Henry H, machinist, res 298 E Washington.

Brink Mrs Ida A, trimmer A C Keel, bds 24 W Berry.

Brink John J, Druggist, 44 Wells, res same.

Brink Mary E, bds 320 E Washington.

Brinker Theodore, baggage master Nickel Plate depot, res 312 W Jefferson.

Brinkman Frederick, harnessmaker A L Johns & Co, bds 140 Eliza.

Brinkman John, cigarmaker, bds 63 Baker.

Brinkman Wm E, painter S W Hull, res 28 Park ave.

Brinkmann Henry, mason, res 177 Gay.

Brinkroeger Frederick, clk H P W Brinkroeger, bds 50 W 4th.

Brinkroeger Herman P W, grocer, 48 Harrison, bds 50 W 4th.

Brinsley George C (G C Brinsley & Son), res 264 W Washington.

Brinsley George C jr (G C Brinsley & Son), res 85 W Main.

Brinsley G C & Son (George C and George C jr), oils and gasoline, office cor Pearl and Maiden lane. Tel 225.

Brinsley Herbert G, draughtsman Wing & Mahurin, bds 90 E Wayne.

Brinsley John C, Propr Red Lyon Boarding, Feed and Sale Stable and Feed Yard; Horses Bought and Sold, also on Commission. Office and Stables cor Pearl and Maiden Lane, res 90 E Wayne. Tel No 225.

Brinsley Mary A, bds 264 W Washington.

Brintzenhofe Ammon S, machinist Wabash R R, res Wayne township.

Britcher Charles, switchman, bds 83 Broadway.

Britcher Edward, carpenter, res 83 Broadway.

Britt Mary, works Indiana School for Feeble-Minded Youth.

Brittingham John S, turner American Wheel Company, res 467 S Harrison.

Britz Jacob, watchman, bds 78 Grant ave.

Brockerman Jacob R, plasterer, res 106 Riverside ave.

Brockerman Leonard S, plasterer, res 40 Riverside ave.

Brockerman Rudy, printer, bds 75 Riverside ave.

Brockerman Thomas W, flagman, res 75 Riverside ave.

Brockerman Wm C, lather, bds 40 Riverside ave.

Brockman Henry, laborer, res n w cor Horace and Oliver.

Brockman Wm, polisher, bds n w cor Horace and Oliver.

Brockmeyer Edward, wheel molder Bass Foundry and Machine Works, bds 87 Wall.

Brockmeyer Minnie, domestic 240 W Berry.

Brockriede Annie M, domestic 83 Clinton.

Brockway Jennie (wid Clarence), res 11 Melita.
Broderick Margaret (wid David), bds 93 W Williams.
Broeking Augusta, bds C Broeking.
Broeking Charles, grocer, n e cor Gay and E Creighton ave, res same.
Broeking Deidrich, whitewasher, res 26 Wall.
Broeking Emma, clerk Charles Broeking, bds n e cor Gay and E Creighton ave.
Broeking Mary, clerk Alexander Goodman, bds 30 Wall.
Broeking Wm, clerk Charles Broeking, bds same.
Brokaw Agnes F, bds 251 Calhoun.
Brokaw Bud F, caller Penn Co, bds s s W Columbia 4 w of Wayne Hotel.
Brokaw House, L T Brokaw propr, 31 W Columbia.
Brokaw James H, conductor, res 20 W Creighton ave.
Brokaw Leander, messenger, bds 251 Calhoun.
Brokaw Leonard, laborer, bds 69 Lillie.
Brokaw Lewis, machine hand American Wheel Company, bds 69 Lillie.
Brokaw Louis T, propr Brokaw House, 31 W Columbia, res same.
Brokaw Robert, carpenter, res 69 Lillie.
Brokaw Samuel L, baggagemaster, res 105 Gay.
Brokaw S Frank, machine hand American Wheel Co, bds 69 Lillie.
Brokmeyer Minnie, domestic 286 W Wayne.
Brokriede, *see Brockriede.*
Bronenkant Dionysius, shoemkr, 14 Nirdlinger ave, res same.
Bronson Almon, driver Fort Wayne Street Railroad Co, res 67 Smith.
Broockmen Minnie, domestic 16 Smith.
Brooks Abraham B C, cabinetmaker The Peters Box and Lumber Co, res 102 Webster.
Brooks Bryant (col'd), barber, 48 E Columbia, res same.
Brooks Mrs Edith, rms 213 E Wayne.
Brooks Ernst, barber, bds 3 E Superior.
Brooks Frank L, shipping clerk Fort Wayne Electric Co, bds 22 Baker.
Brooks George H, carpenter, res 3 E Superior.
Brooks Henry, printer Indiana Staats Zeitung, res 49 W Jefferson.
Brooks Henry C, builder, res 187 W DeWald.
Brooks John, cabinetmaker, res 102 Webster.
Brooks Kate (wid Walter F), bds 148 E Lewis.
Brooks Milo H, contractor, res 22 Baker.

Brooks Oscar H, supt Olds' Wagon Works, bds McKinnie House.
Brooks Richard, bds McKinnie House.
Brooks Robert, saloon, 52 W Main, res same.
Brooks Wm, carpenter, res 336 E Washington.
Brooks Wm H, bds 107 W Berry.
Brooks Wm H, printer, bds 336 E Washington.
Brookshire Isaac, brakeman Penn Co, bds 19 Grand.
Broom Harry, finisher, bds 31 Gay.
Broom John N, shipping clk S F Bowser & Co, res 31 Gay.
Broom Willard, laborer, bds 31 Gay.
Brosius Aaron, teamster, res 206 W Superior.
Brosnahan Thomas, laborer, bds Monroe House.
Brosnahan Timothy, tel operator, bds Monroe House.
Brosowske Edward, finisher Winch & Son, res n e cor Pittsburg and Lumbard.
Brosowske Martin, lab, e s Lumbard 1 s of New Haven road.
Brosowske Maud, bds Martin Brosowske.
Brossard Clara, operator S M Foster, bds 82 Wells.
Brossard George, blacksmith Wm Thiel, res 18 W 5th.
Brossard George, clerk, bds 82 Wells.
Brossard John, grocer, 84 Wells, res 82 same.
Brossard Josephine, dressmaker, bds 33 Wefel.
Brossard Tracy, dressmaker, 33 Wefel, bds same.
Brossard Wm, blacksmith Penna Co, res 33 Wefel.
Brothers of the Holy Cross, s w cor Clinton and Jefferson.
Browand Mary, res 355 E Lewis.
Browand Norman C, barber, 192 Calhoun, bds 355 E Lewis.
Browand Reuben M, barber N C Browand, bds 355 E Lewis.
Brower Cain, sawyer Fort Wayne Furniture Co, res e s Broadway s of Glenwood Chapel.
Brown, see also Braun.
Brown Adelbert C, brakeman, res n w cor Thomas and Holton ave.
Brown Albert L, hostler, bds 251 Calhoun.
Brown Alfred H, laborer, bds 70 Dawson.
Brown Asa O, laborer, res 70 Dawson.
Brown August C, foreman L S & M S Ry, res 40 E 3d.
Brown Barbara (wid John), res 78 Wall.
Brown Charles E, laborer, bds 70 Dawson.
Brown Charles H B, tailor Andrew Foster, res 152 Griffith.
Brown Charles S, barber J W Brown, bds John S Brown.
Brown Charles W (Pilliod & Brown), bds 141 N Cass.
Brown David J, lab Hoffman Bros, res 174 Greeley.
Brown Edward H, well digger Frederick Weidel, res 165 Wells.

Brown Elfa L, student, bds 69 Pfeiffer ave.
Brown Elizabeth (wid Wm H), bds 139 Montgomery.
Brown Ella (wid Charles), res 10 Oliver.
Brown Flora (wid John), res 29 Prince.
Brown Frank, apprentice L O Hull, bds 10 Oliver.
Brown Frank G, cabinetmaker Fort Wayne Organ Co, res e s Shawnee ave 3 n of Home ave.
Brown Frank I, timber inspector N Y C & St L Ry, res cor W Wayne and Ewing.
Brown Frank L (Kime & Brown), res 90 Wilt.
Brown Frederick S, printer, res 244 W Creighton ave.
Brown George F, res e s Shawnee ave 2 n of Home ave.
Brown George H (Heilbroner & Brown), res 142 W Wayne.
Brown Gertrude, res 67 McCulloch.
Brown Harvey H, foreman Bass Foundry and Machine Works, res 269 E Jefferson.
Brown Howard H, brakeman, res 11 High.
Brown James, laborer, res 22 Hough.
Brown James D, dentist, bds Clifton House
Brown James E, conductor, res 270 E Lewis.
Brown Jessie C, bookkeeper Pilliod & Brown, bds 141 N Cass.
Brown John, blacksmith, res 71 Holman.
Brown John, carpenter, res 342 E Washington.
Brown John, coachman, 232 W Wayne.
Brown John, helper Penn Co, bds 192 Lafayette.
Brown John, laborer, bds 29 Prince.
Brown John, shoemaker August Henry, res 212 Lafayette.
Brown John A, hack driver Fort Wayne Transfer and Baggage Line, bds 71 Harrison.
Brown John B, iron inspector Penn Co, res cor Taylor and Pine.
Brown John E, chief clerk Penn Co, res 166 W Berry.
Brown John H, stonecutter W & J J Geake, bds 342 E Washington.
Brown John O, carpenter, res 60 Boone.
Brown John S, section foreman Penn Co, res 164 Walton ave.
Brown John W, barber, 42 E Columbia, res s s Riverside ave 5 e of Spy Run ave.
Brown John W (col'd), cook Aveline House, res 31 Grand.
Brown Mrs Kate, bds 283 W Berry.
Brown Kate, domestic 302 W Washington.
Brown Kate, operator Hoosier Mnfg Co, bds 25 Randolph.
Brown Leonard, brakeman, res 31 Boone.
Brown Louis, laborer, res 2 Holton av.
Brown Louis B, conductor, res 4 Jackson.

Brown Margaret (wid Joseph), res 4 Kansas.

Brown Martin, boilermaker, bds 342 E Washington.

Brown Miss Mary, res n s Cochrane 3 e of Coombs.

Brown Mary E (wid John), res 247 W Washington.

Brown Mrs Mattie L, propr Clifton House, 12 Harrison.

Brown Nettie, wks Indiana School for Feeble-Minded Youth.

Brown Ora J, bds 70 Dawson.

Brown Peter M, patternmaker Bass Foundry and Machine Works, res 142 Madison.

Brown Sarah, dressmaker, bds 22 Hough.

Brown Sarah, bds 174 Greely.

Brown Seneca B, Dentist, 15 Bank Block, res 100 W Berry.

Brown Thomas, fireman, res 139 Montgomery.

Brown Wm, laborer Fort Wayne Electric Co, res 37 W De Wald.

Brown Wm C, helper Fort Wayne Electric Co, bds 213 Broadway.

Brown Rev Wm H (col'd), res n w cor Ohio and Eliza.

Brown Wm H, teamster S Bash & Co, res 73 Holman.

Browne Augustus C, foreman, res 40 E 3d.

Browne Edith J, bds 40 E 3d.

Browne Robinson, flagman Penn Co, bds 213 Broadway.

Browne Samuel H, harnessmaker, bds 40 E 3d.

Browning Wm F, collector James Madden, bds Rich Hotel.

Browning Willis M, machine hand American Wheel Co, bds 318 S Harrison.

Brownsberger Charles, cigarmaker J Lohman, bds 57 E Main.

Brownsberger Charles E, brakeman Penn Co, res 38 W Williams.

Brownsberger Samuel W, laborer Fort Wayne Electric Co, bds 209 Harrison.

Brownsberger Wm, watchman Fort Wayne Transfer and Baggage Line, res 57 E Main.

Bruce Robert, painter Penn Co, bds 43½ E Columbia.

Brucker Frank X, cooper n s Butler 2 w of Calhoun, res 251 W Wayne.

Brucker Michael, cooper, res 62 Nelson.

Bruder August, Watchmaker, Jeweler and Dealer in Watches, Clocks, Diamonds and Silverware, etc, 93 Calhoun, bds 94 same.

Brudi Henry, baker C W Jacobs, bds 62 E Main.

Brudi J George, miller H W Bond, res 203 High.

Brudi Wm H, agent Pilliod & Brown, res 29 Miner.

Bruebach Amelia E (wid George T), res 171 Clinton.

Brueck Theodore, driver Pickard Bros, bds 53 Hugh.

Brueggemann John, laborer, bds 119 Force.
Brueggemann Wm, car builder Penn Co, res 21 Euclid ave.
Bruening Francis, domestic John McCoombs.
Bruggemann Henry, clerk Henry Busching, bds 148 Wallace.
Brumbaugh Harry L, brakeman, res 370 W Main.
Brumfiel Wm, fireman, bds 33 St Mary's ave.
Brundige David jr, laborer, res 68 Franklin ave.
Brune Wm, teamster, res 35 Ewing.
Bruner Alexander, cigarmaker Christian Wenninghoff, res 275 W Washington.
Bruner Angeline (wid Owen), bds 275 W Washington.
Bruner Martin, cleaner, res 13 Union.
Brunett Andrew, carpenter, bds 51 W 4th.
Brunett Charles, engineer J Klett & Son, res 51 W 4th.
Brunett Mary (wid Joseph), res 51 W 4th.
Brunka Wm, helper, res 558 Lafayette.
Brunkhart Henry A, laborer, res 146 High.
Brunne Wm, driver Ranke & Yergens, res 35 Ewing.
Brunner Amelia, bds 47 Pritchard.
Brunner Annie, bds 184 W Main.
Brunner Cornelius (Brunner & Haag), res 184 W Main.
Brunner John, shoemaker Isidor Lehman, res 47 Lavina.
Brunner Joseph A, jeweler H C Graffe, bds 185 Calhoun.
Brunner J Louis, painter, 79 Nirdlinger ave, res same.
Brunner Martin, laborer Penn Co, res 13 Hood.
Brunner Minnie M, packer Louis Fox & Bro, bds 184 W Main.
Brunner Rose, tailoress F H Koenig, bds 184 W Main.
Brunner & Haag (Cornelius Brunner, Charles J Haag), marble works, 124 W Main.
Bruns Annie E (wid Christian F), res 224 E Jefferson.
Bruns Christ, blacksmith Penn Co, res 152 Wallace.
Bruns Christian E H, cab builder Penn Co, bds 332 Wallace.
Bruns Christian W (C W Bruns and Co), res 160 Griffith.
Bruns C W & Co (Christian W and Wm Bruns), plumbers, 166 Calhoun.
Bruns George W, meats, 350 Calhoun, bds 332 Harrison.
Bruns Harmon, laborer Wm Bruns, bds 130 Gay.
Bruns John W, clerk, bds 224 E Jefferson.
Bruns Philip C, molder, bds 224 E Jefferson.
Bruns Wm (C W Bruns & Co), res 130 Gay.
Bruns Wm, laborer Wm Miller, res 36 Johns.
Bruns Wm J, boilermaker, bds 224 E Jefferson.
Brunshen John, wiper Penn Co, res 145 Holman.
Brunskill James, boilermaker, res 46 Pontiac.
Brunskill John, barber, 318 Lafayette, res 46 Pontiac.
Brunskill Rebecca L, bds 46 Pontiac.

Brunson Allan, driver, res 67 Smith.
Brunson Lizzie, dressmaker, bds 67 Smith.
Bruntmeyer Charles, carpenter, bds 319 Hanna.
Brush Mary L (wid Edward), rms s w cor Calhoun and Highland.
Bryan A, laborer, bds 22 W Main.
Bryan Elijah, barnman Stapleford & Co, rms 1 Lafayette.
Bryan Eliza (wid Henry), res 119 Fairfield ave.
Bryant Addie W (wid John F), res 213 E Wayne.
Bryant Joseph H, wheelwright American Wheel Co, res 204 Lafayette.
Bryant Miss Julia, clerk Kuhne & Co, bds 228 W Creighton
Bryant Otto R, finisher American Wheel Co, res 156 Metz.
Bryant Ralph O, finisher, res 178 Metz.
Bryant Wm, pedler, res 122 Hanna.
Brye Theodore, blacksmith John Rupp, res 62 E Superior.
Bube Frank, porter Aveline house.
Buchanan James B, hostler Pearse & Loag, bds Hotel Pearse.
Buche Anna, seamstress D S Redelsheimer & Co, bds 54 Charles.
Buche Catherine (wid Henry), res 54 Charles.
Buche Frederick J, painter Olds' Wagon Works, bds 54 Charles.
Buche Louisa, forelady D S Redelsheimer & Co, bds 54 Charles.
Buchele Frank, clerk A C Trentman, bds Windsor Hotel.
Bucher Adam F, car builder Penn Co, res 15 Ross.
Bucher Benjamin, driver, bds 73 Holman.
Bucher Matthew, painter, res 88 Home ave.
Bucher Mollie, domestic 64 Barr.
Buchheit Adam, carpenter, res 20 Union.
Buchheit Alois J, clerk Glutting & Bauer, bds 20 Hood.
Buchheit Louis, bds 20 Union.
Buchheit Salome, bds 20 Union.
Buckman Alfred O, General Agent Connecticut Indemnity Assn and The Manufacturers' Accident Indemnity Co, Geneva, N Y; Office 20 Schmitz Blk, res 83 Force.
Buck, *see also Buuck.*
Buck Ada, bds 188 Hanna.
Buck Carrie (wid Frederick), res 10 McClellan.
Buck Charles H, foreman Indiana Staats Zeitung, res 29 Nirdlinger ave.
Buck Charles W, foreman Wabash R R, res 188 Hanna.
Buck Charles W jr, telegraph operator, bds 188 Hanna.
Buck Eliza (wid John), res 211 St Mary's ave.
Buck Henry W, clerk Siemon & Bro, bds 290 W Jefferson.
Buck Sophie (wid Diedrich), res 290 W Jefferson.

Buck Wm, car builder Penn Co, res 10 Hough.
Buckley Charles, printer American Farmer, bds 29 Baker.
Buckley Frederick, laborer, bds 199 Broadway.
Buckley Henry S, blacksmith, res 29 Baker.
Buckley Joseph, heater, bds 29 Baker.
Buckley Walter, laborer, bds 104 Barr.
Buckwalter, *see also Bookwalter.*
Buckwalter Corwin, painter Penn Co, bds 219 W Wayne.
Buckwalter Louis R, machinist Penn Co, res 54 W Jefferson.
Budd Frank F, supt Hoosier Mnfg Co, res 219 W Wayne.
Budde John F C, machine hand American Wheel Co, bds 43
St Martin.
Budde Magdalena (wid Herman), res 43 St Martin.
Buddemeyer Emma, bds 14 Fairfield ave.
Buddemeyer Ernest, car repairer, res 14 Fairfield ave.
Buddemeyer Kate, works Troy Steam Laundry, bds 14 Fair-
field ave.
Bueche Frederick E, clerk C Tresselt & Sons, bds 15 Clark.
Bueche George, laborer, res 15 Clark.
Buechner Casper, bds n s Cochrane 3 w of Coombs.
Buechner Conrad, carpenter, res n s Cochrane 3 w of Coombs.
Buechner Frederick G, laborer, res 3 Pape.
Buehfink John G, machine hand, bds 67 High.
Buehfink Mary A, bds 67 High.
Buehfink Sibylla (wid George), res 67 High.
Buehler Diedrich, helper Penn Co, res 22 Oak.
Buehler Samuel E, blacksmith J A Spereisen, bds 56 Taylor.
Buehler Wm C, helper Penn Co, bds 22 Oak.
Bueker Ernest, plasterer, res 46 Walter.
Bueker Henry E (Dudenhoefer, Bueker & Scherer), res 409 E
Washington.
Buell Miss Lena A, stenographer Fort Wayne Electric Co,
bds 28 W Creighton ave.
Buellow Frederick, laborer Bass Foundry and Machine Wks,
res 234 Smith.
Buelow Kate, domestic 106 E Washington.
Buesching Henry, saloon, 207 Lafayette, res same.
Bucsking Conrad, boots and shoes, 302 Hanna, res same.
Buettel A Christian, clk G H Wilson & Son, bds 234 Francis.
Buettel Dora (wid George), res 234 Francis.
Buettel Henry W, fireman American Wheel Co, res 1 Eliza.
Buff Julian, carpenter, res 158 Erie.
Buffalo German Insurance Co, Buffalo, N Y,
Edward Seidel Agent, 52½ Calhoun.
Buffenberger Jacob, laborer L D Collins, bds n e cor Francis
and Hugh.

Stahn & Heinrich, Dealers in BOOKS and FINE STATIONERY, Blank Books, Etc. 116 Calhoun Street.

FORT WAYNE DIRECTORY. 123

Buffington Jesse C, laborer J A Koehler, res e s Piqua ave 3 n of Richardville ave.

Buffink Charles C, laborer, bds 104 Barr.

Buffink George, laborer, bds 104 Barr.

Buffink John M, laborer, bds 104 Barr.

Bufford Edward, pumps, 88 E Columbia, res 8 St Mary's av.

Bufford Norman, machine hand Louis Rastetter, bds 8 St Mary's ave.

Bufink Emma, domestic, 60 Nirdlinger ave.

Bufink George F, teamster, res 24 E Williams.

Buford John C, laborer, bds 8 St Mary's ave.

Bugbee John, section hand Penn Co, res Maumee road nr toll gate.

Bugert George, car builder Penn Co, res 155 E Creighton av.

Bugert Matthew (Rear & Bugert), res 88 Home ave.

Buhr Catherine (wid Nicholas), bds 244 E Lewis.

Buhr Charles H, clerk Pfeiffer & Schlatter, bds 18 Oak.

Buhr Frederick, clerk Doehrmann & Hitzeman, bds 18 Oak.

Buhr James W, saloon, 202 Broadway, res 23 Pritchard.

Buhrkuhl Henry, res 87 Monroe.

Bulger Charles, shipping clk A C Trentman, bds 176 Griffith.

Bulger John H, teamster, bds 176 Griffith.

Bulger Mrs Martin L, res 146 W Berry.

Bulger Patrick J, truckman A C Trentman, res 176 Griffith.

Bull John, driver Ft Wayne Street Railroad Co, bds 290 Calhoun.

Bulla Mrs Sarah A, bds 415 Calhoun.

Bullerman Charles, laborer Ranke & Yergens, bds 286 W Jefferson.

Bullerman Charlotte S, bds 286 W Jefferson.

Bullerman Henry F, teamster, res 286 W Jefferson.

Bullerman Lizzie, tailoress Charles Kruse, bds 286 W Jefferson ave.

Bullerman Louisa C, tailoress, bds 286 W Jefferson.

Bulmahon Fritz G, clerk Siemon & Bro, bds 90 Baker.

Bulmahn Henry C, paperhanger Keil & Keil, res 90 Baker.

Bulo Emma, clerk Alexander Goodman, bds 112 Griffith.

Bulow, see also Buelow.

Bulow John C, milk pedler, res 149 Wells.

Bulow Mary, bds 149 Wells.

Bultemeyer Ernst H, carpenter, res 90 Wall.

Bultemeier Frederick, carp Wabash R R, res 25 Rockhill.

Bunce Almon A, machine hand American Wheel Co, res 94 Oliver.

Bunce Anna L (wid Theodore L), clerk, res 134 Lafayette.

Bunce Hetty (wid Anson A), res s s E Creighton ave 2 w of Winter.

Bunce Minnie, seamstress, bds Hetty Bunce.

Bunce Wm S, laborer, bds Hetty Bunce.

Bundy Joseph, carpenter, res e s Calhoun 3 s of Marshall.

Bund Joseph (col'd), waiter, rms 67 W Superior.

Burchard Charles A, car builder Penn Co, res 64 Madison.

Burchard George C, helper Kerr–Murray Mnfg Co, bds 64 Madison.

Burdell Charles H, gas fitter Salimonie Mining and Gas Co, bds 43½ E Columbia.

Burdett Samuel H, tuner Fort Wayne Organ Co, res 93 W Jefferson.

Burdick Louis B, carpenter, res 133 Oliver.

Buret Charles A, laborer, res 34 E 2d.

Burg Frederick, laborer, bds 159 Hayden.

Burg Henry A, laborer, bds 159 Hayden.

Burg Jacob, laborer, bds 159 Hayden.

Burg John, whitewasher Penn Co, res 159 Hayden.

Burg Nicholas, res 159 Hayden.

Burger Emma C, clerk J C Figel, rms 224 W Jefferson.

Burger Edward W, machinst Fort Wayne Electric Co, bds 146 W Berry.

Burger Frederika, domestic J H Jacobs.

Burger George C, engineer, res 331 S Harrison.

Burger Gottlieb, clerk Frank & Co, bds 224 W Jefferson.

Burger Joseph A, barber Hotel Randall, bds 63 W Main.

Burger Miss Kate, bds 224 W Jefferson.

Burger Louis A, feeder Archer, Housh & Co, bds 224 W Jefferson.

Burger Mary (wid Louis), res 224 W Jefferson.

Eurger Michael, helper A Vogely, bds 52 Oak.

Burgert Milton H (Renner, Cratsley & Co), bds 110 E Berry.

Burgess Miss Elizabeth T, teacher, bds 178 W Jefferson.

Burgess Francis, machinist Wabash R R, res 178 W Jefferson,

Burgett Harley, molder Bass Foundry and Machine Works. res 196 Smith.

Burgett Wm H, painter Olds' Wagon Works, res 216 Francis.

Burhenn Clara, clerk, bds 122 W Creighton ave.

Burhenn Kate, works Fort Wayne Electric Co, bds 122 W Creighton ave.

Burbenn Mary (wid Edward A), res 122 W Creighton ave.

Burhenn Olive, bds 122 W Creighton ave.

Burk, *see also Birk and Burke.*

Burk Emma, operator Hoosier Manufacturing Co, bds 55 Thomas.
Burk Julius, laborer, res 55 Thomas.
Burkas Albert C, laborer Penn Co, res 22 McClellan.
Burkas John A, res 22 McClellan.
Burkas Louis C, molder Bass Foundry and Machine Works, bds 22 McClellan.
Burkas Nettie E, milliner A Mergentheim, bds 22 McClellan.
Burke, *see also Birk*.
Burke Annie (wid Edward), res 83 Buchanan.
Burke Edward T, laborer, bds 83 Buchanan.
Burke Maggie, domestic Diamond Hotel.
Burke Nellie, domestic Aveline House.
Burke Wm, clerk O B Fitch, res 27 Elizabeth.
Burkhart Thomas, laborer, bds 39 W 4th.
Burkholder John, hostler C L Centlivre, bds Albert Eckerle.
Burlag Frederick, bds 122 Maumee road.
Burlag John, laborer, bds 122 Maumee road.
Burlag Mary, domestic 521 E Lewis.
Burlag Joseph L, bds 122 Maumee road.
Burlage John, tinsmith, res 75 Madison.
Burlage John W, tinsmith Penn Co, res 75 Madison.
Burlager Christina, bds 210 E Washington.
Burlager George, res 137 E Washington.
Burlager Henry H, spoke polisher, res 161 E Washington.
Burlager Herman, laborer, bds 210 E Washington.
Burlager John, machine hand American Wheel Company, res 43 Summit.
Burlager Oliver C, cigarmaker John Gronendyke, bds 110 Maumee road.
Burlager Sherman, machine hand American Wheel Co, bds 220 E Washington.
Burlager Wm, laborer, res 210 E Washington.
Burnett Frank B, laborer, res 64 Home ave.
Burnett George W, boilermaker, bds 148 Fairfield ave.
Burnett Miss Lizzie S, dressmaker, 148 Fairfield ave, bds same.
Burnett Samuel, truckman, res 148 Fairfield ave.
Burnett Wm, boilermaker Fort Wayne Iron Works, res 148 Fairfield ave.
Burnie David A, brakeman Penn Co, bds Henton Restaurant.
Burnie Wm R, flagman Penn Co, res 222 E Madison.
Burns Arthur, laborer, bds 44 W Williams.
Burns Arthur, tender, res 152 Holman.
Burns Christian, blacksmith, res 152 Wallace.
Burns Frank J, machinist Penn Co, res 43 W Williams.
Burns James, tooldresser Penn Co, res 335 Lafayette.

11

Burns James J, fireman, res 62 W Williams.
Burns Kate, domestic Aveline house.
Burns Michael, agt Journal, bds 43 W Williams.
Burns N, carpenter Penn Co, res 44 W Williams.
Burns Patrick, machinist Wabash R R, res 41 W Williams.
Burns Thomas E, instrument maker Ft Wayne Electric Co, res 20 Fairfield ave.
Burns Virgil R, carpenter Penn Co, res 44 W Williams.
Burns Wm P, fresco painter S O Hull, rms 181 Calhoun.
Burrell Duff G, machine hand, res 312 Lafayette.
Burrell Naomi, bds 312 Lafayette.
Burrowes Stephen A, bookkeeper Morgan & Beach, res 377 Fairfield ave.
Bursley Block, e s Calhoun bet Washington and Jefferson.
Bursley Gilbert E (G E Bursley & Co), res 301 Fairfield ave.
Bursley G E & Co (Gilbert E Bursley, James M McKay, Frank L Smock, Frank K Safford), Wholesale Grocers, 129, 131, 133 Calhoun.
Burt Alice, cushion maker Louis Horstman, bds 48 Barr.
Burt Harry, books, bds 110 E Berry.
Burton Wm, brakeman, bds 33 St Mary's ave.
Burwell Peter, teamster, res 235 Lafayette.
Busch Charles, coffee essence mnfr, 126 Franklin ave, res same.
Busch John, carpenter, res 72 Wilt.
Busch Louisa, bds 72 Wilt.
Busch Miss Sophia C, clerk Wm F Geller, bds 72 Wilt.
Buscher Henry, laborer Robert Spice, bds Butler.
Busching Henry, grocer, 272 Hanna, res 148 Wallace.
Busching Henry, laborer American Wheel Co, res 50 Smith.
Busching Henry, cupola tender Borcharding & Tonsing, res s e cor Canal and Erie.
Busching Wm, clerk Henry Busching, res 122 Wallace.
Buser Joseph, student, bds 342 Hanna.
Bush, *see also Busch.*
Bush Emanuel K, clerk J B White, res 74 Douglas ave.
Bush James L, saloon, 36 E Columbia, res same.
Busher John, laborer, res 127 W Superior.
Bushing Minnie, housekeeper 37 Miner.
Bushley Theodore, laborer, bds 100 Montgomery.
Bushor Eva, bds 139 Holman.
Bushor Narcissus, painter Fleming Mnfg Co, res 50 Chicago.
Bushor Wm, cook, bds 139 Holman.
Bushor Wm N, painter, bds 50 Chicago.
Business Guide Co The, Clarence G Smith mngr, publrs The Business Guide, 55 and 57 E Columbia.

Business Guide The (monthly), The Business Guide Co publrs, 55 and 57 E Columbia.

Busking Henry, Boots and Shoes, 90 Harmer, res same.

Busse Amelia, dressmaker, bds 156 Ewing.

Busse Charles H, fireman, bds 156 Ewing.

Busse Charlotte (wid Wm), res 156 Ewing.

Busse Clara, bds 156 Ewing.

Busse Ferdinand, painter, res 200 Ewing.

Busse Frederick, blacksmith Olds' Wagon Works, res 218 E Jefferson.

Busse Frederick C, blacksmith, bds 156 Ewing.

Busse George W, printer Archer, Housh & Co, res 156 Ewing.

Busse Lizzie, dressmaker, bds 156 Ewing.

Busser Wm H, engineer Indiana School for Feeble-Minded Youth.

Butcher George, machine hand Winch & Son, res 81 Winch.

Buter Herman, bds 56 Thomas.

Butke Henry, Grocer, 141 Broadway, bds 143 same.

Butler Alexander, laborer, res 6 Oliver.

Butler Burton, porter Aldine Hotel.

Butler Mrs Dora, bds 237 W Berry.

Butler Ira, market stall No 98, res New Haven road.

Butler Jacob A, market stall No 98, res New Haven.

Butler James P (Lichtenwalter & Butler), res 233 Broadway.

Butler Lewis F, grocer and saloon, 7 N Calhoun, res 46 Wells.

Butler Wm O, deputy revenue collector, bds Aldine Hotel.

Butte Frank, bds 56 Smith.

Buttenbender Miss Addie, bds 287 W Berry.

Buttenbender Caroline (wid Henry), bds 287 W Berry.

Butz Frederick, tailor, res s e cor Calhoun and Marchell.

Butz Jacob, tailor, res 145 Wells.

Buuck, *see also Bock and Buck.*

Buuck Frederick, car builder Penn Co, res 134 Force.

Buuck Wm, car builder Penn Co, res 10 Hough.

Buuk Conrad, shoemaker, bds 25 Rockhill.

Byall Carrie L, druggist, 52 Oliver, res 54 same.

Byall Isaac A, postal clerk, res 54 Oliver.

Byanskie Joseph D, machinist Penn Co, res 57 Force.

Bybee Addison, gen'l mngr American Wheel Co, res Indianapolis, Ind.

Byer Sophia M, laundress Riverside Hotel.

Byers Charity E (wid Hiram A), boarding house, 57 Barr.

Byers Emma, bds 48 Charles.

Byers George, switchman, res 48 Charles.

Byers George L, agt D C Fisher, res 323 W Washington.

Bymer Christian, stone mason, bds 231 Barr.

Byrd Ellis, driver Ryan Bros, bds Aldine Hotel.
Byrne Rev Michael J, asst The Cathedral, res 172 Clinton.

C

Cadwallader Lizzie, bds 339 Lafayette.
Cadwallader Thomas, lab Penn Co, res 339 Lafayette.
Cahill Della, dressmaker, bds 16 Huffman.
Cain Augustus, bds 1 Pape ave.
Cain Wm, laborer, res 10 St Mary's ave.
Cairl J Frank, driver, res 38 Baker.
Cairns, *see also Karns, Kearns and Kern.*
Cairns Frank M, machinist Penn Co, res 410 Broadway.
Cairns James, machinist Penn Co, res 430 S Broadway.
Cairns Michael, conductor, bds 415 Lafayette.
Cairns Rufus J, rimmer, bds 20 Murray.
Caldewlay Carrie, domestic 322 W Washington.
Caldwe l David H, chief despatcher N Y, C & St L R R, bds 154 Harrison.
Caldwell James, physician 20 Schmitz block, res 154 Harrison.
Caldwell Miss Laura B, bds 154 Harrison.
Caldwell Miss Sadie, bds 154 Harrison.
Calhoun David, bds Windsor Hotel.
Calhoun Jacob A, clerk August Bruder, bds 94 Calhoun.
Caledonian Hall, 76 Calhoun.
Calkins Wm H, painter, res 372 E Lewis.
Callaghan Daniel, laborer Penn Co, res 30 Bass.
Callaghan John, section hand, res 18 Bass.
Callaghan John P, laborer, bds 30 Bass.
Callaghan Patrick D, flagman, res 30 Bass.
Callahan, *see also O' Callahan.*
Callahan James T, despatcher N Y, C & St L R R, res 114 W Washington.
Callahan Mary A, waitress Pearse Hotel.
Callahan Wm, bellowsmaker Fort Wayne Organ Co, res 237 Indiana ave.
Callahan Wm jr, laborer, res 83 W Williams.
Calloway Allen, laborer, bds 39 Duck.
Calmelat Louis, bartender Joseph Baum, res 153 Madison.
Calvert Burton T, lawyer, n w cor Calhoun and Berry, bds 108 E Berry.
Cameille Jennie, operator Hoosier Mnfg Co, bds 51 E Superior.
Camp, *see also Kamp, Kemp and Komp.*
Campbell Benjamin F, engineer, res 259 W Jefferson.
Campbell Mrs Bessie, dressmaker 259 W Jefferson, res same.

Campbell Charles, farmer, bds 51 Force.

Campbell Charles, sign painter Ernest Kramer, bds 193 E Washington.

Campbell Daniel, foreman Wabash R R, res 53 Brackenridge.

Campbell Delbert, painter, bds 51 Force.

Campbell Ellison T, shoemkr, 156½ Fairfield av, res 51 Force.

Campbell Elton, brakeman, bds 193 E Washington.

Campbell Miss Elva, bds 193 E Washington.

Campbell Emma, operator S M Foster, bds 51 Force.

Campbell George E, clerk, bds 361 E Washington.

Campbell George W, car builder Penn Co, res 193 E Washington.

Campbell Lydia (wid George B), res 361 E Washington.

Campbell Mary M (wid Charles B), bds 9 Elm.

Campbell Mary S (wid Joseph C), rms 47 W Washington.

Campbell Rachael, res 3 Rockhill.

Campbell Vincent, lineman, bds 29 E Main.

Campion John J, clerk, res 293 S Harrison.

Cannady Ransom, driver, res 68 Riverside.

Canning, see Kanning.

Cantwell Ozias R, conductor, bds 314 Harrison.

Cap, see Kapp and Kopp.

Cappeller George, stone cutter, res 35 W 5th.

Carball Oliver, laborer, bds 77 Huestis ave.

Carbaugh Alonzo W, machine hand American Wheel Co, bds 17 Baker.

Carbery Henry P, laborer, res 15 Burgess.

Carey, see also Carray, Carry and Cary.

Carey Charles W, flagman Penn Co, res 133 Walton ave.

Carey George, with Coombs & Co, res 61 Broadway.

Carey John S, flagman Penn Co, res 208 Walton ave.

Carey Mary (wid Thomas), res 123 Fairfield ave.

Carey Michael, helper Penn Co, bds 104 E Wayne.

Carey Thomas, laborer, bds 112 Mechanic.

Carey Thomas J, clerk Rich's Hotel, bds same.

Carey Wallace F, student, bds 71 Oakley.

Carey Wm R, truckman Wabash R R, res 71 Oakley.

Carier Clemence (wid August), res 178 E Berry.

Carier Miss Clemence, bds 178 E Berry.

Carier Miss Helena, bds 178 E Berry.

Carl, see also Carll and Carroll.

Carl George, lab, res n s New Haven ave 3 w of Lumbard.

Carl John, Dealer in Cigars, Tobacco and Smokers' Articles, 259 Calhoun, res 9 Chestnut.

Carl John D, fireman Hose Co No 3, bds 82 Calhoun.

Carl Margaret (wid Patrick), res 14 Walnut.
Carles Horace W, grocer, 40 W Berry, res 287 W Berry.
Carll George S, cabinet maker J M Miller, res 433 Lafayette.
Carll Harriet R (wid Hiram D), res 397 Lafayette.
Carll Miss Sarah, stengphr T E Ellison, bds 433 Lafayette.
Carman Caleb, machinist Penn Co, res 77 Douglas ave.
Carman James G, engineer, res 168 Hanna.
Carmedy Catharine, bds 54 Hendricks.
Carmedy Cornelius, engineer, res 54 Hendricks.
Carmody F G, res 43 John.
Carnahan Wm L (Carnahan & Co), res 119 E Wayne.
Carnahan & Co (Wm L Carnahan), wholesale boots and
    shoes, 76 Clinton.
Carnrike George W, laborer Wabash R R, bds 70 Indiana av.
Carpenter Aaron, brakeman, bds Monroe House.
Carpenter Albert L, livery, n e cor Duck and Clinton, res
    same.
Carpenter Amanda, bds 237 E Wayne.
Carpenter Charles, cook, rms 36 N Main.
Carpenter Dimon L, carpenter, res 82 Putnam.
Carpenter Homer, messenger, bds 82 Putnam.
Carpenter John D, telegraph operator, bds 82 Putnam.
Carpenter Warren, fireman Fort Wayne Electrice Co, res 41
    N Calhoun.
Carpenter Wesley, laborer, bds 156 Taylor.
Carpenters' Union Hall, 7 Bank Block.
Carr John W, car builder Penn Co, res 106 Barr.
Carr Joseph, barber Mathias Momper, res 578 S Lafayette.
Carr Wm W, carpenter, bds 104 Barr.
Carray, *see also Carey, Carry and Cary.*
Carray Edward J, delivery clerk Penn Co, bds 294 E
    Creighton ave.
Carray Frank J, helper Penn Co, res 294 E Creighton ave.
Carray John E, helper Penn Co.
Carret G, laborer Penn Co, res New Haven ave.
Carrigan Wm, cigarmaker, bds 86 Montgomery.
Carrigan Wm H, cigarmaker L Dessauer & Co, bds 137
    Holman.
Carroll, *see Carl and Carll.*
Carroll Denandy A, carpenter, res 24 Colerick.
Carroll Harry, mach Star Iron Tower Co, bds 94 W Superior.
Carroll John, bricklayer, res 228 E Washington.
Carroll John M, whol wood, 58 W 5th, res same.
Carroll Miss Julia L, milliner, 222 Calhoun, bds 95 Thomas.
Carroll Kate, bds 95 Thomas.
Carroll Margaret (wid Patrick), res 94 W Superior.

Carroll Margaret A, milliner J L Carroll, bds 95 Thomas.

Carroll Mary (wid Thomas), res 24 Colerick.

Carroll .Mary A, works Troy Steam Laundry, bds 94 W Superior.

Carroll Maurice, molder, bds 95 Thomas.

Carroll Nellie, bds 95 Thomas.

Carroll Patrick, watchman, res 95 Thomas.

Carroll Patrick J, molder, bds 95 Thomas.

Carroll Susan F, bds 24 Colerick.

Carroll Thomas, conductor Penn Co, res 38 Buchanan.

Carroll Wm J, pressman Archer, Housh & Co, bds 94 W Superior.

Carry Adolphus, contractor, res 74 Fletcher ave.

Carry Joseph A, blacksmith Penn Co, res 153 E Lewis.

Carson John E, clerk J K Carson, bds same.

Carson John K, grocer, s e cor Spy Run and Riverside aves, res same.

Carson Wm W, lawyer, res 95 E Berry.

Carter B Frank, brakeman, bds 248 Calhoun.

Carter Charles E, salesman Singer Mnfg Co, bds 71 Harrison.

Carter Charles L (Carter & Son), res 29 Clinton.

Carter Frank, tailor A F Schoch, bds 224 Calhoun.

Carter Isaac, bds 127 E Main.

Carter James, boilermaker Penn Co, res 57 Prince.

Carter James, salesman, bds 71 Harrison.

Carter James M, carpenter, res 187 Jackson.

Carter Jerome B, laborer The Remington-Lawton Co, bds Star Restaurant.

Carter Josephine, student, bds 34 Miner.

Carter J B, laborer, bds 22 W Main.

Carter Martha A, bds 83 Butler.

Carter Oliver, blacksmith Penn Co, bds Monroe House.

Carter Rebecca A (wid James W), res 34 Miner.

Carter Rosa, clerk, bds 299 E Lewis.

Carter Samuel, driver B Gutermuth, bds 29 Columbia.

Carter Miss Victoria, teacher Bloomingdale school, bds 34 Miner.

Carter Wm (Carter & Son), res 127 E Main.

Carter Wm J, A M, M D, General Mngr Standard Medical and Surgical Institute; Office 135 Calhoun, res 537 Broadway.

Carter & Son (Wm and Charles L), Hot Air Furnaces, Ranges, Mantels and Grates, 29 Clinton. (*See bottom edge and p 61.*)

Cartwright Ada, bds 23 Lillie.

Cartwright Alice, bds 73 Baker.

Cartwright Anna L, cook Monroe House.

Cartwright Charles, lumber inspector, res 50 E Washington.

Cartwright Charles A, broom mnfr, s e cor E Lewis and Lillie, res 27 Lillie.

Cartwright Edward E, wheelmaker American Wheel Co, res 202 Lafayette.

Cartwright Ella (wid John), res 73 Baker.

Cartwright George, barber, bds 63 W Main.

Cartwright George W, laborer, res 39 Wall.

Cartwright James, harnessmaker, bds 20 N Harrison.

Cartwright James, teamster, res 23 Lillie.

Cartwright John F, laborer, res 69 Baker.

Cartwright Porter D, baggageman, res 22 W DeWald.

Carver John F, real estate, res 320 W Washington.

Carver Mary, teacher District School No 3, Adams twp.

Cary, *see also* Carey, *Carray 'and Carry.*

Cary Alice V, bds 200 E Washington.

Cary Benjamin, carpenter, bds 61 Winter.

Cary David B, physician, 200 E Washington, res same.

Cary Ira L, laborer, bds 200 E Washington.

Casanave Francis D, supt motive power Penn Co, res 57 W Berry.

Casanave John H, bds 57 W Berry.

Casanave Miss Julia, bds 57 W Berry.

Casanave Miss Zetta, bds 57 W Berry.

Case Charles A, fireman, bds 36 Colerick.

Case David, foreman N Y, C & St L R R, res n w cor Howell and Rumsey ave.

Case Edward, laborer, bds 160 Greeley.

Case Flora, seamstress, bds 36 Colerick.

Case Isaac H, clerk D H Baldwin & Co, res 65 Brackenridge.

Case John W, laborer, bds 36 Colerick.

Case Wm H, tinsmith, bds 36 Colerick.

Case Wm L, fireman, res 36 Colerick.

Casey Christopher, conductor, res 28 John.

Casey Mrs Emma, res 38 E Williams.

Casey John, machinist Penn Co, bds 38 E Williams.

Casey Margaret (wid James L), bds 13 Hamilton.

Casey Timothy, conductor Penn Co, bds Hinton's Restaurant.

Cashman John, section foreman L S & M S Ry, res 41 E 4th.

Caskey Archibald, brakeman, rms 16 Chicago.

Cassady Jacob, blksmith S W Bowser & Co, res 152 Griffith.

Cassady Miss Maggie, bds 152 Griffith.

Cassidy Patrick, table turner Penn Co, bds 82 Montgomery.

Casso Frank A, fruits, 156 Calhoun, res 42 Laselle.

Casson Jacob, rimmer, res 521 E Lewis.

Casteel Mrs Mary, boarding house, 28 Chicago.

Casteel Samuel W, baker, bds 28 Chicago.

Casteel Wm M, polisher American Wheel Co, bds 38 Hamilton.

Casterline Cassius C, printer, res 186 W Washington.

Castle, *see also Kassel and Kestel.*

Castle Calvin, wheel molder Bass Foundry and Machine Works, res 94 Thomas.

Castle Cora B, bds 34 Oliver.

Castle Della E, domestic Joseph Arter.

Castle Edwin, washer, bds 34 Oliver.

Castle Henry, lab White's Wheel Works, bds n e cor Tons and Dwenger ave.

Castle James F, washer, bds 34 Oliver.

Castle Minnie, domestic 69 Lillie.

Castle Robert, laborer White's Wheel Works, res n e cor Tons and Dwenger ave.

Castle Samuel, laborer Fort Wayne Organ Co, res 34 Oliver.

Caston Phœbe J (wid Hiram), cook Hyer House.

Caswell Frank A, trav agt, res 341 E Wayne.

Caswell John W, clk Bass Foundry and Machine Works, bds 341 E Wayne.

Cathedral of the Immaculate Conception, Calhoun bet Lewis and Jefferson.

Cathedral School (Catholic), s w cor Clinton and Jefferson.

Catholic Orphan Asylum, cor Wells and city limits.

Catholic Young Men's Reading Hall and Club Rooms, n e cor Calhoun and Lewis.

Catlin Albert P, clerk, res 48 McClellan.

Cattez Frank, lab Penn Co, bds Julia Cattez.

Cattez John, laborer, bds Julia Cattez.

Cattez Joseph, fireman, bds Julia Cattez.

Cattez Julia (wid Joseph), res n s Buchanan 5 e of Thomas.

Cattez Julian J, driver Francis Sallier, bds Julia Cattez.

Cattez Mary, bds Julia Cattez.

Cattez Peter, tel operator, bds Julia Cattez.

Caurdway Leonard, painter, bds 252 E Lewis.

Cavanaugh, *see also Kavanaugh.*

Cavanaugh George, bds 57 Barr.

Cavanaugh Julia, works Troy Steam Laundry, bds 22 Gay.

Cavanaugh Thomas, blacksmith Wabash R R, res 34 Bass.

Cellers Andrew, harnessmaker A L Johns & Co, bds 98 Archer ave.

Celt Theodore, carpenter, res 75 Maumee road.

Centennial Block, 197 and 199 Broadway.

Center Spencer H, boilermaker Penn Co, res 2 Warsaw.

Centlivre Charles F, supt C L Centlivre, res n end Spy Run av.

Centlivre Charles L, Propr French Brewery and Bottling Works, n end Spy Run ave, res same.

Centlivre Louis A, Propr Home Billiard Hall and Mngr C L Centlivre Brewery, Harmony court bet Berry and Main, bds C L Centlivre.

Centlivre's Park, w s Spy Run ave n of canal feeder.

Central Grammar School, E Wayne bet Calhoun and Clinton.

Central Mutual Fire Insurance Co The, D N Foster Pres, P A Randall Sec, Charles McCulloch Treas, Aldine Hotel Bldg.

Central Press Association The, proprs The Press, 17 Court.

Central Union Telephone Co, W P Chapman Mngr, 34 Calhoun.

Certia Block, w s Calhoun bet Wayne and Berry.

Certia Jacob, grocer, 116 Wells, res 114 same.

Certia Peter, saloon, 70 Calhoun, res 126 W Washington.

Chalat Lettie R, dressmaking school, s w cor Calhoun and Highland, res same.

Challenger Charles, clerk Penn Co, bds 232 Harmer.

Challenger D Edward, clerk, res 232 Harmer.

Chamberlain Miss Eliza J, res 163 Clinton.

Chamberlain James, helper Penn Co, bds 41 Baker.

Chamberlain Porter, engineer Olds' Wagon Works, res 71 Butler.

Chamberlain Richard C, paperhanger, res 20 Chicago.

Chamberlain Sarah C R (wid Wm), bds 24 Brandriff.

Chambers Mrs Jennie C, music teacher 16 Brackenridge, res same.

Chambers John D, physician, 16 Brackenridge, res same.

Chandler Charles, horse radish mnfr, bds 29 E Main.

Chandler Nancy E, works Indiana School for Feeble-Minded Youth.

Chandler Wm H, carpenter Ft W, C & L R R, res 95 W 4th.

Chapin Miss Angeline F, stenographer Fort Wayne Electric Co, bds 16 Douglas ave.

Chapin Miss Artina M, bds 16 Douglas ave.

Chapin Augustus A, judge of Superior court, office Court house, res 16 Douglas ave.

Chapin Bertha, works Troy Steam Laundry, bds 18 Harrison.

Chapin Miss Catherine B, bds 16 Douglas ave.

Chapin Miss Elizabeth E, teacher Jefferson School, bds 16 Douglas ave.

Chapin Henry W, laborer Nickel Plate, res 22 Boone.

Chapman Catherine (wid John V), res 83 E Berry.

Chapman Clark, carpenter, res 56 Madison.

Chapman Frank M, township assessor, res 150 Fairfield ave.
Chapman George, carpenter, res 69 Garden.
Chapman Ira, teamster, bds 44 South Wayne ave.
Chapman Jason S, driver Ft Wayne Street R R Co, res 430 E Washington.
Chapman Maggie B, milliner 150 Fairfield ave, res same.
Chapman Nathaniel L, machinist Fort Wayne Electric Co, res 322 W Main.
Chapman W Platt, mngr Central Union Telephone Co, res 228 Fairfield ave.
Charles Isaac, laborer, res 297 Fairfield ave.
Charleswood Sheridan G, helper Penn Co, res 55 Walter.
Chase Miss Abbie S, bds 40 Garden.
Chase Emily B (wid Ira F), bds 40 Garden.
Chase Harry S, tailor A F Schoch, bds 224 Calhoun.
Chase Reuben C, fireman Penn Co, res 77 Hoagland ave.
Chase Stephen W, res 176 Huffman.
Chaska Samuel, trav agt Charles Falk & Co, res 110 E Wayne.
Chasky Harry, fruits, res 388 E Wayne.
Chauvanne Joseph, bottler L Brames & Co, res 276 E Jefferson.
Chauvey Bros (Charles and Francis), wagon mnfrs, 35 E Superior.
Chauvey Charles (Chauvey Bros), res 51 E Superior.
Chauvey Charles E, blacksmith Chauvey Bros, bds 150 N Clinton.
Chauvey Francis (Chauvey Bros), res 150 N Clinton.
Chauvey John, res 223 E Wayne.
Chauvey Joseph, blacksmith Chauvey Bros, bds 150 N Clinton.
Chauvey Mary, bds 223 E Wayne.
Cheney Frank, waiter Randall Hotel.
Cheney James, Pres and Treas Fort Wayne Gas Light Co, bds e s Spy Run ave 2 s of Riverside ave.
Chenney Julia (wid Jonas), bds 142 W Jefferson.
Cherry Charles P, clerk, bds 109 W DeWald.
Cherry Frank C, painter, bds 160 E Washington.
Cherry Frank M, manager Penn Co, bds 160 E Washington.
Cherry Henry Y, boilermaker apprentice Penn Co, bds 104 E Lewis.
Cherry Howard, engineer, res 108 College.
Cherry Rowland T, brakeman, res 38 St Mary's ave.
Cherry Wm C, rivet heater Penn Co, bds 104 E Lewis.
Cherry Wm H, boilermaker Penn Co, res 104 E Lewis.
Cheviron Amelia, bds 190 E Wayne.
Cheviron Louise, bds 190 E Wayne.

Cheviron Xavier, res 190 E Wayne.

Chinworth Ida, bds Jane Chinworth.

Chinworth Jane (wid Robert), res e s Spy Run ave 6 n of Wagner.

Chisten Anthony, laborer, res w s Walton ave 2 s of Pontiac.

Chnitzler Mary, domestic 50 E Washington.

Chorpening Ida, clerk J O Keller, bds 35 1st.

Chorpening Thomas R, works J O Keller, bds 35 1st.

Chriss Edward (col'd), bds 227 W Washington.

Christ Frederick, boilermaker, res 333 E Lewis.

Christ Frederick jr, molder, 333 E Lewis.

Christ Frederick, sawyer American Wheel Co, bds 44 Grant av.

Christ Gottlieb A, teamster The Herman Berghoff Brewing Co, res 44 Grant ave.

Christ Henry, molder, bds 333 E Lewis.

Christ Minnie, bds 333 E Lewis.

Christen Edward, driver, bds w s Walton ave 2 s of Pontiac.

Christen George, shipping clerk, bds w s Walton ave, 2 s of Pontiac.

Christen John, Propr Fort Wayne Ale House, Bottler and Dealer in Foreign and Domestic Ale, Porter, Beer, Wines and Liquors, 100 Calhoun, res same.

Christen John C, laborer, bds w s Walton ave 2 s of Pontiac.

Christen Joseph, driver, bds w s Walton ave 2 s of Pontiac.

Christen Wm, clerk John Christen, bds same.

Christensen Christopher E, painter Olds' Wagon Works, res 317 S Harrison.

Christian Anthony, farmer, res w s Walton ave 2 s of Pontiac.

Christian Chapel, s e cor W Jefferson and Griffith.

Christie James B, molder Fort Wayne Iron Works, res 48 Walnut.

Christie Joseph, laborer American Wheel Company, res 123 E DeWald.

Christie Miss Mary E, teacher Harmer School, bds n w cor Creighton and Hoagland aves.

Christie Wm P, machinist Fort Wayne Electric Co, res 356 S Calhoun.

Christleib John, teamster, res rear 382 W Main.

Chronister Anna, domestic John Mohr jr.

Church of the Evangelical Assn, n e cor Clinton and Holman.

Church of God, n e cor Hoagland ave and De Wald.

Church of the Holy Trinity (English Lutheran), s e cor E Wayne and Clinton.

Church Perry, laborer, res 10 Huron.

Churchill Charlotte (wid Samuel), bds 120 Clinton.

Cincinnati, Richmond & Fort Wayne R R, operated by Grand Rapids & Indiana R R. (*See G R & I R R.*)

City Attorney's Office, Henry Colerick attorney, City Hall, e s Barr.

City Bookbindery, George W Winbaugh propr, 13 E Main.

City Carriage Works, Dudenhoefer, Bueker & Scherer Proprs, 11 and 13 Clay.

City Clerk's Office, R C Reinewald clerk, City Hall e s Barr.

Coal City Co, M M Smick mngr, 80 E Columbia.

City Engineer's Office, O Bird Wiley city engineer, office 68 Barr.

City Fire Department, Henry Hilbrecht chief, office cor Court and E Berry.

City Greenhouse, B L Auger Propr, 16 E Washington.

City Hall, w s Barr bet Berry and Wayne.

City Hospital, M L Albrecht pres, s w cor Barr and Washington.

City Market, Barr bet Wayne and Berry.

City Mills, C Tresselt & Sons proprs, cor Clinton and Nickel-Plate R R.

City Park, e s Broadway bet Taylor and P, Ft W & C R R.

City Pound, Wm Rippe poundmaster, w s Calhoun n of County Jail.

City Treasurer's Office, C J Sosenheimer treas, City Hall.

City Water Works, P J McDonald sec, 68 Barr.

City Weigh Scales, P Ryan weighmaster, s end City Hall.

Clanke August, machine hand White's Wheel Works, bds 411 E Lewis.

Clanke Henry, carpenter, res 411 E Lewis.

Clapham Edward, fireman Hoffman Bros, res 213 W Superior.

Clapesattle George A, teacher, bds 11 Wagner.

Clark Alanson W, machine hand J Klett & Son, res 38 Wells.

Clark Mrs Anna J, janitor Harmer School, res 280 E Washington.

Clark Miss M Belle, teacher, bds 113 W Wayne.

Clark Charles, bartender Thomas Clark, bds Oliver House.

Clark Edward, finisher Winch & Son, bds I G Clark.

Clark Elizabeth (wid Daniel), bds 125 Monroe.

Clark Mrs Ella, bds 65 W Superior.

Clark Eva, bds 237 E Wayne.

Clark Horace R, teamster, res 24 Dubois.

Clark Isaac G, painter, res 208 Thomas.

Clark Jacob W, trainmaster Penn Co, res 11 Holman.

Clark Miss Jessie O, bds 111 W Wayne.

Clark John, hostler, bds 309 W Washington.

Clark John A, saloon, 213 Lafayette, res same.

Clark John E, operator, res rear 344 E Wayne.

Clark Joseph, painter Indiana Machine Works, bds 280 E Washington.

Clark Joseph M (Joseph M Clark & Co), res Kent, Ohio.

Clark Joseph M & Co (Joseph M Clark, Perry N DeHaven), Merchant Tailors and Dealers in Fine Cloths, Cassimeres and Vestings, 34 E Berry.

Clark Kenton A, laborer Penn Co, res 117 E Wayne.

Clark Lewis N, carpenter, res 125 Monroe.

Clark Lydia M (wid John H), res 111 W Wayne.

Clark Miss Martha M, teacher, bds 280 E Washington.

Clark Marvin J, conductor, res 92 Thomas.

Clark Mary R, clerk Louis Fortriede, bds 280 E Washington.

Clark Mrs Mattie T, res 5 DeGroff.

Clark Mortimer (M Clark & Co), bds 111 W Wayne.

Clark Miss M Belle, teacher Clay School, bds 113 W Wayne.

Clark M & Co (Mortimer Clark), Printers, 16 W Columbia. (*See right top lines.*)

Clark Oliver, draughtsman F B Kendrick, bds 111 W Wayne.

Clark Miss Rose M, teacher, bds 280 E Washington.

Clark Thomas, saloon, 102 E Columbia, bds Oliver House.

Clark Victoria (wid James), res 5 Brandriff.

Clark Wm, machinst Wabash R R, res 5 Brandriff.

Clarke Franklin D, Notions, 5 E Main, res Chicago, Ill.

Claus J August, carpet weaver, 16 University, res same.

Claus Max G, wheel molder Bass Foundry and Machine Works, res 79 Hayden.

Clausmeier Edward F (E F Clausmeier & Co), res 157 Montgomery.

Clausmeier E F & Co (Edward F Clausmeier, Wm Kaough), farm implements, 50 E Columbia.

Clay, *see also Klee and Kley.*

Clay Jacob (col'd), teamster, res 3 Dwenger ave.

Clay Miss Minnie, bds 105 W Jefferson.

Clay Sarah (wid Henry), bds 180 Griffith.

Clay School, n w cor Clay and Washington.

Claymiller Rudolph, engineer City Carriage Works, bds 197 Barr.

Clayton Miss Ella, milliner Mrs E A Flagler, bds 14 W Berry.

Clayton George L, res 22 E DeWald.

Clayton Mrs Mabel E, teacher Jefferson School, bds C L Hill.

Claytor J Edward, boilermaker, res 153 E Lewis.

Clear John, tinner H J Ash, res 26 Orchard.

Clear Wm H, laborer, bds 28 Marion.

Stahn & Heinrich, Leading Dealers in ARTISTS' MATE-RIALS AND DRAUGHTING INSTRU-MENTS. 116 Calhoun Street.

FORT WAYNE DIRECTORY. 139

Cleary Dennis, plumber P E Cox, bds 51 Oakley.
Cleary Edward, res 141 Shawnee ave.
Cleary John, helper Penn Co, bds 3 Eliza.
Cleary Martin, printer, bds 39 W Washington.
Clem Isaiah, engineer, res 30 Butler.
Clemans Louis L, printer Fort Wayne News, bds 94 W Main.
Clements Agnes M, bds 57 W Williams.
Clements Daisy P, bds 57 W Williams.
Clements Etta, operator S M Foster, bds 57 W Williams.
Clements John, market stall 61, res Sand Point rd nr County
    Poor House.
Clements Wm, clerk Penn Co, res 57 W Williams.
Clements Wm H, laborer, bds 57 W Williams.
Clemmer Benjamin R, patternmaker Fort Wayne Electric Co,
    res 124 Chicago.
Clido May, waitress 248 Calhoun.
Clifford Thomas, attendant Allen County Asylum, bds same.
Clifford Timothy, gasfitter Salimonie Mining and Gas Co,
    bds Diamond Hotel.
Clifton House, Mrs Mattie L Brown propr, 12 Harrison.
Cline John F, Restaurant, 99 Calhoun, res 39 Bracken-
    ridge. (*See left bottom lines.*)
Clinton Abraham, plumber, bds 19 W Jefferson.
Clinton Albert B, plumber Robert Ogden, res 19 W Jefferson.
Clippinger Orpha (wid Alexander), res 20 Miner.
Clirbe Lemuel L, cashier Penn Co, res 221 W Wayne.
Close Charles F, molder Bass Foundry and Machine Works,
    res 271 E Lewis.
Close Edward C, engraver, n w cor Main and Clinton, bds
    271 E Lewis.
Close Wm, coremaker Bass Foundry and Machine Works,
    res 196 Hanna.
Closs Lemuel, laborer, res 88 Fairfield ave.
Cloud Richard M, car builder Penn Co, res 31 Brandriff.
Clough Mollie (wid Charles), domestic 151 Broadway.
Clow Charles L, teamster, bds 57 W Superior.
Clusserath M, laborer Penn Co, res 54 Smith.
Clutter Adelbert F (Clutter & Purcell), bds 8 Cass.
Clutter Lulu M, student, bds 8 Cass.
Clutter Phœbe A (wid Caspar), bds 290 Harrison.
Clutter Sarah J (wid Ryan), res 8 Cass.
Clutter & Purcell (Adelbert F Clutter, Frank E Purcell),
    commission, 37 E Main.
Coates Arthur, cook, rms 65 Baker.
Coates Wm, cook, rms 65 Baker.
Coblentz Jacob W, physician, 41 W Berry, res 103 W Main.

Cochrane, *see also Corcoran.*
Cochrane Miss Agnes J, bds 258 W Berry.
Cochrane Edward, laborer Penn Co, res 265 Hanna.
Cochrane John, res 258 W Berry.
Cochrane Miss Margaret S, bds 258 W Berry.
Cody John H, foreman, res 288 W Main.
Cody Miss Mary R, bds Morris Cody.
Cody Morris, res n w cor Barr and E Superior.
Cody Thomas, machinist Indiana Machine Works, bds Monroe House.
Coe Amos, agent Griebel, Wyckoff & Becker, bds 35 Douglas.
Coffman, *see Kaufmann.*
Cohagan Laura, cook Clifton House.
Cohen, *see also Koehn and Kohn.*
Cohen Benjamin, clerk Redlich Bros, bds 73 Webster.
Cohen Mrs Fannie, res 73 Webster.
Cohen Henry, cigarmaker, bds 73 Webster.
Cohen Miss Marian, teacher Hoagland School, bds 73 Webster.
Cohen Simon, bds 73 Webster.
Colbach John, butcher F Eckart, res Rockhill heirs' add.
Colclesser F P, car builder Penn Co, res 29 Lillie.
Cole, *see also Koehl.*
Cole Rose, cook, rms 191 Calhoun.
Cole Sherman, bds 248 Calhoun.
Coleman, *see also Kohlmann.*
Coleman Stella L, domestic Monroe House.
Coleman Sylvanus S, market stall 59, res s s County road 8 miles w of city limits.
Colerick Miss Antoinette M, res 85 E Jefferson.
Colerick Charles E, clerk Penn Co, bds 266 W Wayne.
Colerick Henry (Colerick & Oppenheim), City Attorney, res 117 E Main.
Colerick Mrs Margaret, bds 266 W Wayne.
Colerick Philamon B (Colerick & France), res 108 E Berry.
Colerick Walpole G, Lawyer, 22 Court, res 88 E Berry.
Colerick & France (Philamon B Colerick, James E K France), Lawyers, 17 and 18 Pixley & Long Bldg.
Colerick & Oppenheim (Henry Colerick, Wm S Oppenheim), lawyers, 5 and 6 Pixley & Long bldg.
Colerick's Hall, over 49 and 53 E Columbia.
Coling Charles, butcher G W Bruns, bds 338 Harrison.
Coling George, brakeman, bds 338 Harrison.
Coling John C, clerk, bds 338 Harrison.
Coling Peter, res 338 Harrison.
Collar George W, laborer Kilian Baker, res 121 Lafayette.

Collier Ammon B, die sinker Fort Wayne Electric Co, bds 72 Dawson.

Collier Clara, bds 243 E Wayne.

Collier John W, bricklayer, res 243 E Wayne.

Collier Thomas, baker B W Skelton, bds 243 E Wayne.

Collins Charles, turner, bds 171 Madison.

Collins Dennis, laborer Penn Co, res 31 Baker.

Collins Edward, barber, n e cor Buchanan and Thomas, bds Sullivan House.

Collins Miss Elizabeth, teacher Clay School, bds 201 Barr.

Collins Miss Elizabeth O, teacher Hanna School, bds e s Monroe 2 s of Wallace.

Collins Elmer, brakeman, bds 248 Calhoun.

Collins Lindsay D, feed mill, 21 N Harrison, res 5 N Calhoun.

Collins Lizzie, cigarmaker F J Gruber, bds 31 Baker.

Collins Mary L, domestic 278 Calhoun.

Collins Mollie, operator S M Foster, bds 177 Hanna.

Collis Adam, machinist Penn Co, res 51 St Martin.

Collis Frank M, driver Dozois, Beadell & Co, bds 51 St Martin.

Colmey Christopher R, engineer, res 39 Douglas ave.

Colmey Mrs Christopher R (Mrs C R Colmey & Ripley), res 39 Douglas ave.

Colmey Mrs C R & Ripley (Mrs Christopher R Colmey, Mrs Elizabeth L Ripley), notions, 201 Calhoun.

Colson Charles E, fireman Nickel Plate R R, bds 329 W Main.

Colson Gustav, laborer, bds 15 Pearl.

Colson Nicholas, res 12 Short.

Columbia House, J P Ross & Sons proprs, 25 and 27 W Columbia.

Colvin Elbert, mason, res 137 Franklin ave.

Colvin Miss Evangeline, bds 120 Harrison.

Colvin Joseph, carpenter, res 11 Wagner.

Comady J, oiler Penn Co, res 43 John.

Combs Eugene V, flagman, bds 51 W Superior.

Combs Herbert A, brakeman, bds 51 W Superior.

Combs Wm V, res 51 W Superior.

Comer Lineas A, traveling agent, bds 209 E Wayne.

Comincavish Felix, machinist Ft Wayne Electric Co, res s s Bluffton road w of St Mary's river.

Comincavish Marshall, res 85 Baker.

Comparet Charles M (C M Comparet & Co), res 47 Harmer.

Comparet C M & Co (C M Comparet), shirt mnfrs, 36 E Berry.

Comparet David F, commission, 76 E Columbia, res 59 Erie.

12

Comparet Thomas L, clerk, bds 59 Erie.

Compton Edgar, conductor, res 208 Madison.

Compton Howard P, flagman Penn Co, bds cor Clay and Holman.

Compton Jasper, rms 133 Holman.

Conahan John J, clk Massachusetts Shoe Co, res 65 Hoffman.

Conard Wm H, carriage painter M L Albrecht, bds Hedekin House.

Concanon Wm, fireman, rms 23 Baker.

Concordia Cemetery (St Paul's), n s Maumee road e of Concordia College.

Concordia College (German Lutheran), e s Schick bet e Washington and Maumee road.

Congdon Hattie E, bds 104 Ewing.

Congdon Horton E, laborer, bds 104 Ewing.

Congdon Joanna L (wid Joshua E), res 104 Ewing.

Conklin Charles S, engineer, res 11 N Calhoun.

Conklin Elizabeth A (wid Theodore), res 207 W De Wald.

Conklin Ella, bds 278 W Creighton ave.

Conklin George W, laborer, bds 278 W Creighton ave.

Conklin Guy, piano tuner, bds 66 W Main.

Conklin John J, engineer, res 278 W Creighton ave.

Conklin Miss Josie, teacher, bds 207 W De Wald.

Conklin Wm E, fireman Ft W, C & L R R, bds 9 N Calhoun.

Conley James, wheel inspector, res 131 Wallace.

Conley Thomas J, machinist Fort Wayne Electric Co, res 110 W Main.

Conn Benjamin F, conductor, res 19 W 3d.

Connelly, *see also Connelly.*

Connelly James, laborer, res 14 Melita.

Connelly Maggie, dressmaker Mary L Sherin, bds 14 Melita.

Conners, *see also Conners and O'Connor.*

Conners Anna, bds 43 Charles.

Conners Emma, domestic 73 W Main.

Conners Frank, helper, bds 43 Charles.

Conners Michael, engineer Engine Co No 2, res 43 Charles.

Connett Allen, market stall 23 and 25, res s s Miller nr Muncie R R.

Connett David, teamster Fort Wayne Lumber Co, res n w cor Broadway and Bluffton road.

Connett Leota M, bds 60 Wilt.

Connett Martin V, foreman Fort Wayne Electric Co, res 171 Holman.

Connett Mary E, bds 60 Wilt.

Connett Milon T, carpenter, res 60 Wilt.

Connolly, *see also Connolly.*

Connolly Wilson J, machinist Wabash R R, bds 24 Baker.
Connors, *see also* Connors, O' Conners and O' Connor.
Connors John, helper Penn Co, bds 255 Webster.
Connors Mary, clk Dozois, Beadell & Co, bds 251 Webster.
Connors Michael, engineer Fire Co No 2, res 43 Charles.
Connors Wm H, machinist Penn Co, bds 43 Charles.
Conover Alice (wid Addison V D), res 130 W Jefferson.
Conover Edward, trav agt, bds 152 Griffith.
Conover Fannie, bds 381 E Wayne.
Conover Norton, foreman job rooms Fort Wayne Sentinel,
    res 381 E Wayne.
Conover Wm A, clerk McDonald, Watt & Wilt, bds 130
    W Jefferson.
Conrad John, laborer White's Wheel Works, bds e s Lillie
    near Creighton ave.
Conrad Mrs Mary, res 103 Lafayette.
Conrad Mary, domestic 117 E Main.
Conrad Susan, domestic 213 W Berry.
Conrad Wm, car builder Penn Co, res 47 John.
Conrad Wm F, carpenter, res 38 South Wayne ave.
Conrod Mathias, engineer, res 53 Lillie.
Conrod Wm H, wheelmaker American Wheel Co, bds 53
    Lillie.
Conrady Frederick G, car builder Penn Co, res 43 John.
Conrady John G, car repairer Penn Co, res 43 John.
Conrady Kate, bds 43 John.
Conrady Rosa, tailoress A F Schoch, bds 43 John.
Conrady Sophie, tailor, bds 43 John.
Conroy James, blacksmith Wabash R R, res 42 Melita.
Contant August, machinist Penn Co, res 72 Laselle.
Converse Geneva I, domestic 290 Calhoun.
Converse Maggie, operator, bds 18 Gay.
Conway Bryan, machine hand American Wheel Co, res 84
    Fairfield ave.
Conway Catherine (wid Edward), res 84 Fairfield ave.
Conway Edward, conductor, res 51 Baker.
Conway Frank, Wine and Beer Saloon ; Best Brands
    of Wines, Liquors and Cigars, 55 E Main, res same.
Cook, *see also* Cooke and Koch.
Cook Albert H, res 47 E Lewis.
Cook Annie, bds 34 John.
Cook Catherine (wid Adam), res 34 John.
Cook Charles F, helper Fort Wayne Electric Co, bds 231 S
    Webster.
Cook Charles O, machinist Electric Light Works, res 231 S
    Webster.

Cook Christian F, machinist, res 157 College.
Cook Clarence F, city edr Ft Wayne Sentinel, bds 49 E
Lewis.
Cook Ernest W, cashier Wabash R R, res 70 Indiana ave.
Cook Edward C, instrument maker Fort Wayne Electric Co,
bds 157 College.
Cook Frederick C, shoemaker J A Walter, rms 40 Harrison.
Cook John F, fireman, res 38 Elm.
Cook John M, wagonmaker Olds' Wagon Works, res 85
Butler.
Cook Mary, bds 34 John.
Cook Miss Rose L, bookkeeper L O Hull, bds 47 E Lewis.
Cook Theodore D, printer The Journal Co, bds 46 E Jefferson.
Cooke John H, engineer, res 359 W Main.
Coolican Ellen B (wid Patrick), res 21 Poplar.
Coolican John, coil winder Fort Wayne Electric Co, bds 21
Poplar.
Coolican Mary T, dressmaker, bds 21 Poplar.
Coolman George W, carpenter, res 13 Wagner.
Coomb Wm, carpenter, bds 91 E Washington.
Coombs Miss Alice, bds 336 W Washington.
Coombs Edmund H, traveling agent Coombs & Co, bds s w
cor Fairfield and Creighton aves.
Coombs John M (Coombs & Co), res s w cor Fairfield and
Creighton aves.
Coombs Wm H, res 336 W Washington.
Coombs & Co (John M Coombs, F A Newton), Iron and
Heavy Hardware, 38, 40 and 42 E Main.
Coon Alonzo, laborer, res n s Wagner 3 w of St Joseph River.
Coon Nathan, laborer, res 163 E Jefferson.
Cooney Patrick, bds 38 Buchanan.
Coonrad John C, laborer White's Wheel Works, res New
Haven road 2 miles east of limits.
Cooper Cornelius G, machinist Penn Co, res 191 Jackson.
Cooper Fanny L E, Cooper Kennels, res and kennels 787 S
Broadway.
Cooper George J, engineer, res 284 W Jefferson.
Cooper Rev Malachi C, pastor St Paul M E Church, res 136
Walton ave.
Cooper Mary (wid Cornelius), bds 191 Jackson.
Cooper Wm F, brakeman Penn Co, bds 270½ Calhoun.
Cooper Wm P, clerk S C Lumbard, res 182 W Washington.
Cooper Winfield S, machinist Penn Co, res 787 Broadway.
Cope Abraham, bds 51 Barr.
Cope Daniel C, res 204 E Wayne.
Cope David F, laborer, bds 51 Barr.

Cope Miss Eva, bds 204 E Wayne.
Copenhaver Alfred, laborer, res 42 Force.
Copp, *see Kopp.*
Copper Grant, laborer, bds 533 E Wayne.
Copinus Albert, traveling agent Pottlitzer Bros, bds 47 W
    Wayne.
Corbett Wm H, carpenter, bds 229 E Wayne.
Corbin Rosa (wid Amos C), bds 96 Wells.
Corcoran, *see also Cochran and Cochrane.*
Corcoran Anthony, molder, bds 159 Harrison.
Corcoran Bridget (wid Patrick), bds 23 Grand.
Corcoran James E, printer The Press, bds 159 Harrison.
Corcoran John, printer, bds 159 Harrison.
Corcoran John, molder, res 41 E De Wald.
Corcoran Julia, bds 159 Harrison.
Corcoran Mary, bds 159 Harrison.
Corcoran Mary (wid John), res 159 Harrison.
Corcoran Owen H, clerk Dreier Bros, res rear 23 Grand.
Corcoran Thomas, truckman, res e s Spy Run ave 4 n of
    Wagner.
Cordeway Henry J, laborer, res e s Spy Run ave 4 n of St
    Mary's bridge.
Cordrey Elmer E, molder Kerr-Murray Mnfg Co, bds 196
    Hanna.
Cork Martin, watchman, bds 59 Boone.
Corl Ida J, works Troy Steam Laundry, bds 18 Harrison.
Corneille August L, White's Wheel Works, res 41 E Superior.
Corneille Casimir F, clerk Francis Sallier, res 51 E Superior.
Corneille Jennie E, domestic 96 E Wayne.
Corneille John B, notary public, res 45 E Superior.
Corneille Louis J, harnessmaker G R Wells, res 21 Erie.
Corneille Paul E, florist, bds 41 E Superior.
Cornelley Jeremiah, switchman, bds 56 Baker.
Cornelley John, policeman, res 56 Baker.
Cornelley Margaret (wid Michael), res 56 Baker.
Cortwright Stanley S, printer The Press, bds 35 E Wayne.
Corwin Lydia A (wid Theodore), bds 226 Fairfield ave.
Cose A R, laborer Penn Co, res 225 Calhoun.
Cosgrove Frank K, res 103 W Superior.
Cosper Miss Laura, milliner Mrs E A Flagler, bds 259 E
    Washington.
Costigan James V, clerk, bds 121 E Washington.
Costillo Ida, domestic 226 W Creighton ave.
Cothrell Allen B, brakeman, res 35 Buchanan.
Cothrell Andrew J, bds 71 Douglas ave.
Cothrell Belle (wid Wm), res 84 Brackenridge.

John Pressler, Plumbing, Gas and Steam Fitting
Columbia, Barr and Dock Streets.

146   R. L. POLK & CO.'S

Cothrell Clinton J, engineer, bds 71 Douglas ave.
Cothrell Miss Edith M, tchr Harmer School, bds 71 Douglas.
Cothrell Miss R Etta, tchr Jefferson School, bds 71 Douglas.
Cothrell Ready (wid Charles), res 132 Lafayette.
Cothrell Ruthetta (wid Jared), res 71 Douglas ave.
Cotner Edmund G, car painter Penn Co, res 23 Walnut.
Cotter Bartlett E, engineer, res 23 Van Buren.
Couderet Jacob, laborer Penn Co, bds 305 Hanna.
Couderet Jean, laborer Penn Co, bds 305 Hanna.
Councell Charles E, bookkeeper Leikauf Bros, bds 19 E Jefferson.
Council Chambers, City Hall, Barr.
County Clerk's Office, Jacob J Kern clerk, Court House.
County Jail, George H Viberg sheriff, n end Calhoun.
County Surveyor's Office, Court House.
Couples Myra, domestic n e cor Penn and Dubois.
Cour Alexander W, shipping clerk Fort Wayne Newspaper Union, res 24 Schick.
Cour Cecila, domestic John Mohr jr.
Cour Eugene, laborer, res 19 Buchanan.
Cour Claude J A, res 261 E Washington.
Cour Ella, bds 47 Douglas ave.
Cour Frank, horseshoer Fort Wayne Street Railroad Co, res 330 E Jefferson.
Cour Frank V, bartender James Summers, bds 47 Douglas avenue.
Cour George E, machinist Kerr-Murray Mnfg Co, bds 261 E Washington.
Cour John H, helper Kerr-Murray Mnfg Co, bds 261 E Washington.
Cour Joseph P, machine hand, bds 261 E Washington.
Cour Wm, boilermaker Penn Co, res 139 E Lewis.
Courdevay John L, coil winder Fort Wayne Electric Co, res 11 Wall.
Courdevey Edward, teamster, bds 73 N Cass.
Courdevey Henry, engineer Borcherding & Tonsing, res 340 E Wayne.
Courdevey Jerome, laborer Jenny Electric Light and Power Co, bds 73 Cass.
Courdevey Joseph, fireman Jenney Electric Light and Power Co, res 73 N Cass.
Courdevey Serphine, res 73 N Cass.
Courdveay Francis S, fireman, bds n s Howell e of Rumsey avenue.
Courdveay Louis, teamster, res s s Rebecca w of Runnion ave.
Court House, e s Calhoun bet Main and Berry.

Courter Charles A, bricklayer, res 139 Walton ave.

Courter George, caller, bds 139 Walton ave.

Cousar Charles, clerk Bass Foundry and Machine Works, res 205 E Wayne.

Covault Wm M, driver Fort Wayne Transfer and Baggage Line, res 70 Madison.

Coverdale Asahel S (Coverdale & Archer), res 29 2d.

Coverdale & Archer (Asahel S Coverdale, Perry J Archer), grocers, 24 Harrison.

Covey Wm H, printer Fort Wayne Newspaper Union, res 55 E Wayne.

Covington Miss Prudence K, artist, 11 Schmitz blk, bds 19 Madison.

Covington Thomas E, Market Gardener, Charlotte n of Indiana Asylum, res 188 Ewing.

Cowan Robert, engineer, res 314 Clay.

Cowder Bernard, laborer, res 131 Taber.

Cowell Nettie J, waiter Riverside Hotel.

Cowl Wm H, brakeman, bds 27 E 1st.

Cowles Edwin N, bds 57 Butler.

Cox, *see also Kocks.*

Cox Arthur P, laborer Penn Co, bds 225 Calhoun.

Cox Bessie S, stenographer Wabash R R, bds 15 Park pl.

Cox Ellis, driver Pottlitzer Bros, res 40 W Main.

Cox Eliza, operator S M Foster, bds 183 Hanna.

Cox Eliza W (wid Delos A), bds 103 W Superior.

Cox Enoch, storekeeper Penn Co, res n s Suttenfield 2 e of Calhoun.

Cox James B, plumber P E Cox, bds 183 Hanna.

Cox John, laborer Penn Co, res 183 Hanna.

Cox Kate, pastry cook KcKinnie House.

Cox Patrick E, plumber, 29 W Main, res 35 same.

Cox Wm R, rms 94 Calhoun.

Coy Commodore P, mngr Summit City Soap Works, bds 248 Calhoun.

Coy James O, teamster Summit City Soap Works, bds 6 Glasgow ave.

Coy John A, bookkeeper Summit City Soap Works, res 6 Glasgow ave.

Coyle Bernard J, machinist Penn Co, res 78 Montgomery.

Coyle J David, dentist, 84 Calhoun, res 157 E Washington.

Coyle Mary (wid Daniel), res 78 Montgomery.

Crabill Levi, fireman, res 95 John.

Craft, *see Kraft.*

Cragg Charles, laborer, res n s Tabor 1 e of Lafayette.

Cragg Charles, laborer American Wheel Cobds 94 Laselle.

Cragg Thomas, foreman, res 130 Wallace.

Cragg Wm J, wheelmaker American Wheel Company, bds 130 Wallace.

Crago James E, machine hand American Wheel Company, bds 158 W Main.

Craig Andrew, carpenter, res 27 Boone.

Craig Atchison D, brakeman Penn Co, res 141 Horace.

Craig Calvin, caller N Y, C & St L R R, bds 345 W Main.

Craig Charles, machinist, res 356 Calhoun.

Craig Christian, engineer, res 149 E Jefferson.

Craig Della M, milliner J L Carroll, bds 124 Horace.

Craig James C, conductor Penn Co, res 208 E Lewis.

Craig John, carpenter, res 345 W Main.

Craig Rawson, fireman, rms 149 E Jefferson.

Craig Sidney, engineer, rms 94 Calhoun.

Craig Wm W, salesman Singer Mnfg Co, bds Clifton House.

Crall Charles E, reporter Fort Wayne Sentinel, res 147 W Washington.

Crall Fred L, bookkeeper Hoosier Mnfg Co, bds 310 W Washington.

Cram Robert, foreman Bass Foundry and Machine Works, res 398 Calhoun.

Cramer, *see also Kramer.*

Cramer Andrew S, laborer, res 78 St Mary's ave.

Cramer Charles B, machinist Penn Co, res 35 Force.

Cramer David C, engineer, res 29 E Williams.

Cramer Eli, engineer, res 395 Lafayette.

Cramer Frank, laborer American Wheel Co, res 91 Laselle.

Cramer Frederick, driver Ryan Bros, bds 245 W Wayne.

Cramer George, yardman J M Moderwell, bds 78 St Mary's.

Cramer Henry C, driver J Klett & Son, res 21 Melita.

Cramer Jennie, nurse, bds 21 Melita.

Cramer Marcus, laborer, bds 91 Laselle.

Cramer Martin, foreman Penn Co, res 167 W De Wald.

Cramer Mathias, foreman American Wheel Co, res 465 S Lafayette.

Cramer Theresa (wid Solomon), res 91 Laselle.

Cramer Wm M, laborer American Wheel Co, res 64 Hayden.

Cramp Wm S, hair goods, 128 Calhoun, res 96 E Wayne.

Cran Charles, molder Kerr-Murray Mnfg Co, res 158 Wallace.

Cran Charles W, patternmaker Fort Wayne Iron Works, bds 158 Wallace.

Cran Robert, comur Fire dept, res 398 Calhoun.

Crance, *see also Kranz.*

Crance Crawley, laborer, bds 319 Hanna.

Crance D Frank, laborer, res 498 Hanna.

Crance Frank, laborer, bds 80 Thomas.
Crance George W, grocer, s w cor Smith and Creighton ave, res same.
Crance James, laborer, res n w cor Hanna and Pontiac.
Crance John, laborer, bds 80 Thomas.
Crance Louis J, wheelmaker American Wheel Company, bds 104 Gay.
Crance Rachel, domestic 162 E Wayne.
Crance Richard, laborer, res 80 Thomas.
Crance Wm, finisher White's Wheel Works, bds 80 Thomas.
Crane Mrs Bridget M, res 5 Bass.
Crane Charles, pipe liner Salimonic Mining and Gas Co, bds Peter Killinger.
Crane Eugene T, finisher Fort Wayne Organ Co, bds 5 Bass.
Crane George D, Lawyer, s w cor Clinton and Berry, res 305 W Jefferson.
Crane John J, finisher, bds 5 Bass.
Crane Wm M, lawyer, res 235 W Washington.
Cranston Alice (wid John), res 28 Marion.
Cranston James J, engineer Ft W, C & L R R, res 28 Marion.
Cranston Lizzie A, milliner A Mergentheim, bds 28 Marion.
Cranston Margaret E, dressmaker, bds 28 Marion.
Cratsley Frank C (Renner, Cratsley & Co), res 65 Douglas ave.
Craw, see also Krah.
Craw Edward L, real estate, res 71 W Wayne.
Crawford Chloe, domestic Jewel House.
Crawford Clara (wid Elbert J), res 37 E 1st.
Crawford Frank B, plasterer, bds 14 Chicago.
Crawford Frederick E, machine hand American Wheel Co bds 54 John.
Crawford George L, carpenter, res 102 Putnam.
Crawford John, rivet heater Penn Co, bds 66 Melita.
Crawford John T, carpenter, res 439 S Broadway.
Crawford Martin J, helper Penn Co, bds 66 Melita.
Crawford Nelson, converter worker Fort Wayne Electric Co, res 1 Rockhill.
Crawford Richard, painter, res 19 Nirdlinger ave.
Crawford Samantha S, bds 386 E Washington.
Crawford Samuel, laborer, bds 182 E Jefferson.
Crawford Samuel M, laborer, res 68 Melita.
Creag Charles A, machinist Bass Foundry and Machine Works, bds Windsor Hotel.
Creagh Annie, domestic, 278 Calhoun.
Creane John J, finisher, Fort Wayne Organ Co, bds 5 Bass.
Cregan Alfred, printer The Press, bds 95 Lafayette.

Creig James, machine hand, bds 38 Hamilton.
Creigh Andrew, helper Penn Co, res 25 Baker.
Creigh Michael, engineer Penn Co, res 110 Force.
Creigh Peter, helper Penn Co, res 25 Baker.
Creighton Miss Margaret T, bds 96 W Wayne.
Cresler Anna, housekeeper Aveline House.
Cressler Alfred D, pres and gen'l mngr Kerr-Murray Mnfg
    Co, res 141 W Berry.
Cressler Lizzie, domestic 126 E Main.
Cretzer Leona, domestic 25 E Main.
Crick Reuben W, carpenter, res 161 W DeWald.
Crighton Jennie, bds 49 Brackenridge.
Crighton Wm jr, draughtsman Penn Co, bds 49 Brackenridge.
Crighton Wm, master mechanic Kerr-Murray Mnfg Co, res
    49 Brackenridge.
Crimmans Dennis J, fireman, res 47 Butler.
Crimmans Margaret, domestic McKinnie House.
Crist Ira B, clerk F J Beach, bds 171 Broadway.
Crist John, switchman, res 105 John.
Cristlieb John E, driver J C Peters, res n w cor Osage and
    Main.
Critchfield Orrin, fireman, bds 16 Brackenridge.
Croft John, bds 400 E Washington.
Cromwell Clarence W, Wholesale Hardwood Logs
    and Lumber, 224 W Berry, res same.
Cromwell Joseph C, lumber, res 261 W Wayne.
Cromwell Joseph W, Wholesale Hardwood Logs and
    Lumber, 224 W Berry, res same.
Cromwell Wm O, stenographer Bass Foundry and Machine
    Works, bds 224 W Berry.
Cronan Nora, bds 274 Calhoun.
Croninger Edward, laborer, res 82 W Creighton ave.
Cronk Cleora, trimmer City Carriage Works, bds St Joe
    township.
Crook Charles, bench hand Louis Rastetter, bds 72 E North.
Crosby Anna J (wid Thomas H), res 128 N Cass.
Crosby Edwin G, machinist Wabash R R, res 63 Charles.
Crosby Elbert W, engineer, res 100 St Mary's ave.
Crosby George T, machinist Wabash R R, res 111 W DeWald.
Crosby Henry H, trainmaster Ft W, M & C Ry, bds 128 N Cass
Crosby Hiram O, clerk Penn Co, res 612 S Calhoun.
Crosby Mary (wid Nathan), bds 11 W DeWald.
Cross Charles W, asst master mechanic Penn Co, res 63 W
    Jefferson.
Crossen George W, watchman Penn Co, res 113 Williams.
Crouse, *see also Krauhs, Kraus and Krouse.*

Mrs. E. A. Flagler, Cheapest, Best and Most Fashionable MILLINERY STORE in Town. 14 West Berry Street.

FORT WAYNE DIRECTORY. 151

Crouse Miss Augusta, housekeeper Westminster Seminary.

Crouse Charles R, machine hand Louis Diether & Bro, res w s Begue cor Liberty.

Crout Henry, laborer, bds 57 John.

Crow Anna F, bds 74 Gay.

Crow Charles D, laborer, bds 11 Force.

Crow Club Rooms, 195 Calhoun.

Crow James A, Carpenter, Contractor and Practical Builder, 82 Fairfield ave, res 74 Gay. (*See adv, p 65.*)

Crow Jennie, clerk E Shuman & Sons, bds 74 Gay.

Crow John C, apprentice, bds 74 Gay.

Crow John L, carpenter, res 11 Force.

Crow John W, finisher Horton Mnfg Co, res 296 W Main.

Crow Wm, carpenter Edward Suter, bds n s Grace ave 1 e of Broadway.

Crowe Hattie, works Indiana School for Feeble-Minded Youth.

Crowe Louis, teamster, res 253 E Jefferson.

Crowley Mrs Margaret, housekeeper 85 Butler.

Croxton M E, car oiler Penn Co, res 13 McClellan.

Croxton Worthington A, res 215 W Wayne.

Croy Wesley B, car builder Penn Co, res 96 Oliver.

Crull August, teacher of German, Concordia College, res same.

Crumby John, fireman, rms 38 Brackenridge.

Cruse Charles A, tuck pointer, bds 56 Pontiac.

Cruse Demetrius A, tuck pointer, res 56 Pontiac.

Crutchfield Ernest, hostler B Rorison.

Crutchfield John, laborer Hoffman Bros, res 5 Breck.

Crutchfield Wm H, section hand, res 15 Pape.

Crystal Billiard Hall and Sample Room, C W Kline Propr, 242 Calhoun. (*See adv in classified Billiard Halls.*)

Culbertson Frank B, mngr R G Dun & Co, res 425 Calhoun.

Culbertson Harry R, clerk R G Dun & Co, bds 425 Calhoun.

Cull, *see Kull.*

Cullen Michael, laborer, bds Elizabeth Becquette.

Cullison Charles E, engineer, res 416 S Clinton.

Culver Augustus C, engineer Wm & J J Geake, bds Philip Bashelier.

Culver Burt, painter, bds 274 E Lewis.

Culver Wm, laborer Penn Co, bds 103 Broadway.

Cummerow George, collector Freie Presse, bds 121 W Superior.

Cummerow Otto F, propr Fort Wayne Daily Freie Presse and Weekly Indiana Deutsche Presse, n e cor Calhoun and Main, res 121 W Superior.

Cummerow Rudolph M, saloon, 276 Calhoun, res 122 Butler.

Cummings Jerry, flagman, res n w cor Charles and Clay.

Cummings Judith L (wid Theodore), bds 29 Grand.

Cummings Miss Nellie, clerk Fowler Mnfg Co, bds 29 Grand.

Cummings Rachel, domestic Grand Central Hotel.

Cummings Thomas J T, mngr Fowler Mnfg Co, 152 Calhoun, res 29 Grand.

Cummins Abner, section hand, res 54 Walnut.

Cunningham James F, brakeman, bds Racine Hotel.

Cunningham Robert R, foreman, res 31 E 2d.

Curdes Louis F, tuner Fort Wayne Organ Co, res s e cor Creighton ave and Webster.

Curran, *see also Kern.*

Curran Isabella, bds 71 Charles.

Curran Lorenzo, laborer the Remington-Lawton Co, bds 43½ E Columbia.

Curran Michael, conductor Penn Co, res 415 Lafayette.

Curran Timothy, laborer Penn Co, res 71 Charles.

Curran Wm, flagman Penn Co, rms 224 Calhoun.

Currel George, laborer Penn Co, res New Haven ave.

Current Samuel W, laborer Penn Co, res Wayne Trace.

Current Sylvanus S, car builder Penn Co, res n s Wayne Trace nr car shops.

Currier Charles A, operator W U Tel Co, bds 332 E Wayne.

Currier Charles H, Dealer in Staple and Fancy Groceries, 72 E Main, res 332 E Wayne.

Currier Miss Clara M, bds 332 E Wayne.

Currier John L, operator W U Tel Co, bds 315 E Wayne.

Currier Miss Leah G, bds 332 E Wayne.

Curry James, switchman Wabash R R.

Curtice John F, Real Estate and Loans, Rooms 1 and 2 Trentman Block, res 142 Montgomery. (*See front cover and p 63.*)

Curtis Joseph F, painter, bds 35 E De Wald.

Curtis Samuel H, laborer Penn Co, res 35 E De Wald.

Curwin Henry G, brakeman L S & M S Ry, res 46 E 5th.

Cushing John J, machinist, bds 9 Ohio.

Cushing Miss Nellie, milliner Mrs E A Flagler, bds 9 Ohio.

Cushing Timothy J, engineer, res 76 Butler.

Custer House, Gerson Scherzinger Propr, 16 and 18 W Main. (*See adv, p 61.*)

Cutler Alice, bds Wm M Cutler.

Cutler Elmer L, coil winder Ft Wayne Electric Co, bds Wm M Cutler.

Cutler Mary E, operator Hoosier Mnfg Co, bds 72 W 4th.

Cutler Wm, laborer Winch & Son, bds Wm M Cutler.

Cutler Wm M, foreman Winch & Son, res n s New Haven ave 3 e of Lumbard.

Cutshall Joseph H, night watchman Troy Steam Laundry, res 103 Wilt.

Cutshall Sherman, molder Bass Foundry and Machine Works, bds e s Monroe 2 s of Wallace.

Cutshall Theodore, bds e s Monroe 2 s of Wallace.

Cutshall Wm H, meat market, 61 Wells, res e s Monroe 2 s of Wallace.

Cutter Michael, bricklayer, res 7 Oak.

Cutter Milo O, clerk Penn Co, res 222 Madison.

Cypher Rufus, fireman David Tagtmeyer, res 30 Clinton.

D

Dager Maggie, domestic, 306 Calhoun.

Daib Adelinda, dressmaker, bds 58 Division.

Daib Rev John L, res 58 Division.

Dailey, *see also Daily.*

Dailey Ephraim, bookkeeper Root & Co, bds 37 Bass.

Dailey John H, helper Penn Co, res 37 Bass.

Dailey Michael, flagman Penn Co, res 38 Baker.

Dale James M, clerk N Y, C & St L Ry, res 244 W Main.

Daler Louis P, painter Olds' Wagon Works, res Adams township.

Daley John, bds 219 Lafayette.

Daley John, machinist Penn Co, res 73 Charles.

Dallman Ernst, blacksmith Ft Wayne Iron Works, res 88 Wall.

Dalman Miss America E, teacher, bds 368 Fairfield ave.

Dalman Edwin F, clerk F M Smith & Co, bds 368 S Fairfield.

Dalman Frederick, res 116 W Williams.

Dalman John, farmer, res 368 Fairfield ave.

Dalman Robert, fish pedler, res 533 E Wayne.

Dalman Sophie, bds 533 E Wayne.

Dalman Theodore F, blacksmith, bds 116 W Williams.

Dalte Christian, mach hand Horton Mnfg Co, res 7 Rockhill.

Dalton Catherine, bds 32 Wilt.

Dalton Edmund, carpenter Louis Diether & Bros, res 32 Wilt

Dalton James, laborer, res 58 W Williams.

Dalton James, section hand, res w s St Mary's ave 1 s of Huffman.

Dalton John E, trav agent Clutter & Purcell, bds 32 Wilt.

Dalton Mollie, bds 32 Wilt.

Dalton Nicholas, paver, bds 41 Wallace.

Dalton Wm F, turner Fort Wayne Organ Co, bds 60 W Williams.

Daly, *see also Dailey and Daily.*

Daly Alice L, bds 93 E Lewis.
Daly Margaret R, janitor Trentman block, rms 51 Melita.
Daly Mary C (wid Wm G), res 93 E Lewis.
Dammeier Wm, res 63 Douglas ave.
Dammeyer Emma, dressmaker, bds 201 Ewing.
Dammeyer Henry, cutter Hoosier Mnfg Co, bds 201 Ewing.
Dammeyer Henry C, blacksmith Penn Co, res 201 Ewing.
Dammeyer Louisa, dressmaker, bds 201 Ewing.
Damon Wm, laborer, res 21 Buchanan.
Dandaro Philip, fruits, res 28 Columbia.
Danehy, *see also Denehy.*
Danehy James, engineer, res 4 Bass.
Daniels Rena A C (wid Samuel S), res 46 W Berry.
Dannecker Rev Henry P, pastor St John's Evangelical Luth-
eran Church, res 212 W Washington.
Danner Hattie, bds 127 Montgomery.
Danner Robert, conductor, res 96 Montgomery.
Danzer John, carpenter, res 151 E Jefferson.
Darker George U, clerk Bass Foundry and Machine Works,
bds 77 Butler.
Darker Martha E (wid Wm), res 77 Butler.
Darling John W, boilermaker Penn Co, res 14 Murray.
Darling Joseph L, piano tuner, res 28 E Wayne.
Darrow House, F M Johnson Propr; Rates $1 per
Day ; 2 Squares only from Pittsburgh Depot, 248
Calhoun.
Dartnell E W, laborer Penn Co, res 22 Charles.
Dartnell Wm, clerk, bds 22 Charles.
Daseler Charles H, sweeper Penn Co, bds 163 Montgomery.
Daseler Christian, res 16 Liberty.
Daseler Christian L, clerk Penn Co, bds 163 Montgomery.
Daseler Conrad E, machinist Penn Co, res 211 Madison.
Daseler Dora, bds 163 Montgomery.
Daseler Frederick G, policeman, res 199 Lafayette.
Daseler George, driver, bds 163 Montgomery.
Daseler Henry, clerk Hartman & Bro, bds 163 Montgomery.
Daseler Henry C, laborer Penn Co, res 163 Montgomery.
Daseler Henry J, boilermaker Wabash R R, res 201 John.
Daseler Lizzie, bds 163 Montgomery.
Daseler Sophia, bds 163 Montgomery.
Dau August, carpenter, bds 478 Hanna.
Dau Frederick, carpenter, res 478 Hanna.
Daub Joseph, printer The Press, bds 95 Lafayette.
Daugharty Alfred, transfer clerk Wabash R R, res 227 Wells.
Daugharty Ulysses E, bookkeeper A L Johns & Co, bds 227
Wells.

Daugherty, *see also Doherty and Dougherty.*

Daugherty Anna, bds 151 Holman.

Daugherty Charles J S, stove mounter, res 14 N Cass.

Daugherty Ellen, works Troy Steam Laundry, bds 151 Holman.

Daugherty George B, engineer, res 116 High.

Daugherty James, shoemaker O B Fitch, res 151 Holman.

Daugherty Maggie, domestic Rich's Hotel.

Daugherty Mary, bds 151 Holman.

Daukins Henry G, vegetables, market stall 97, res s s New Haven rd e of city limits.

Davenport Charles, engineer Jenny Electric Light and Power Co, res

Davenport Edward N, carpenter, res n e cor Oliver and Buchanan.

Davenport Frederick, night clerk Pearse Hotel.

David F, laborer Penn Co, res 226 Gay.

David Wm, brickmaker, bds 106 Gay.

Davis Miss Addie F, teacher Hoagland school, bds 308 E Wayne.

Davis Alfred A, carbuilder Penn Co, res 96 E Lewis.

Davis Amos, sewing machines, 138 Calhoun, res 148 E Lewis.

Davis Benjamin, bds 103 W Main.

Davis Miss Blanche, bds 176 Jackson.

Davis Charles E, Bookbinder and Blank Book Mnfr, 84 Calhoun, res 262 E Main.

Davis Clarence E, painter Wayne Paint and Painting Co, bds 23 Holman.

Davis Miss Chrissie, clerk Amos Davis, bds 148 E Lewis.

Davis Delbert C, clerk Fort Wayne Electric Co, bds 176 Jackson.

Davis Edward, fireman N G Olds & Co, res 326 E Wayne.

Davis Edward T, foreman Penn Co, res 249 E Jefferson.

Davis Edwin G, fireman American Wheel Co, res 10 Erie.

Davis Eliza (wid Amos), res 148 E Lewis.

Davis Eugene, teamster Standard Oil Co, res St Mary's ave nr G R & I R R.

Davis Frank L, fireman, bds 176 Jackson.

Davis Gail N, laborer, bds 1 McLaughlin.

Davis George, painter, res 112 Griffith.

Davis G Bert, conductor, bds 120 Harrison.

Davis Harry S, wheel inspector American Wheel Co, bds 308 E Wayne.

Davis Harry W, res 126 E Wayne.

Davis Hezekiah M, driver Stapleford & Co, rms 1 Lafayette.

Davis John, car repairer Penn Co, res 191 E Lewis.

Davis John J, car repairer Penn Co, bds 191 E Lewis.
Davis Mary J (wid Calvin), res 18 Chicago.
Davis Nettie, domestic Clifton House.
Davis Oscar, caller Penn Co, res 1 McLaughlin.
Davis Miss Rosa, res 268 Calhoun.
Davis Theodore G, hostler Pearse & Loag, bds Hotel Pearse.
Davis Thomas A, machinist Bass Foundry and Machine Works, bds 308 E Wayne.
Davis Villroy, conductor N Y, C & St L R R, res 176 Jackson.
Davis Washington W, painter, bds 251 Calhoun.
Davis Wesley T, engineer American Wheel Company, res 308 E Wayne.
Davis Wilbur E, train dispatcher Penn Co, rms 55 Brackenridge.
Davis Wm H, Propr Empire Box Factory and Mnfr Empire Letter Files, 3d floor Bank Block, res 253 W Creighton ave.
Davis Wm T, laborer, res 84 Barr.
Dawkins Miss Ellen E, bds 96 W Wayne.
Dawson Amanda M (wid John W), res 140 E Berry.
Dawson Andrew, conductor Penn Co, res 46 Chicago.
Dawson Charles M, Lawyer, 5 and 6 Bank Block, res 287 W Wayne.
Dawson G Wallace, musical merchandise, 27 W Main, res 187 E Jefferson.
Dawson John W, conductor Ft W, M & C Ry, res 102 Broadway.
Dawson Michael, laborer, res 46 Chicago.
Day Adolph C, painter, bds 137 W Superior.
Day Amelia, bds 137 W Superior.
Day Charles, finisher Horton Mngf Co, bds 137 W Superior.
Day Henry D, painter Horton Mnfg Co, bds 137 W Superior.
Day John, brakeman, res 39 Grand.
Dayton Charles F, laborer, bds 74 Walton ave.
Dayton Louisa (wid Charles F), bds 552 E Washington.
Deady Edwin R, molder Kerr-Murray Mnfg Co, bds 312 S Harrison.
Deady Emmett A, molder, bds 312 S Harrison.
Deady Jeremiah P, painter, 312 S Harrison.
Deagan Edward, laborer, res 52 Leith.
Deagan Elizabeth J, milliner, bds 52 Leith.
Deagan John, blacksmith Penn Co, res 177 Hanna.
Deagan Wm H, clerk Sam, Pete & Max, bds 90 Summit.
Deahl, see also Deihl.
Deahl Edward W, carpenter The Peters Box and Lumber Co, res 17 St Mary's ave.

Deahl Frederick T, helper H J Ash, bds 17 St Mary's ave.
Deahm Elizabeth (wid George), res 132 Wells.
Deal Nora N, domestic 104 Barr.
Dealer Herman, laborer, bds 27 Force.
Dean Anna, operator Central Union Telephone Co, bds 138 Broadway.
Dean Charles, laborers The Peters Box & Lumber Co, res 10 Barthold.
Dearstine Charles, painter, rms 73 E Berry.
Deaveny John, laborer, bds 76 Baker.
Deaveny Kate, bds 76 Baker.
Deaveny Martin, laborer, res 76 Baker.
Debrey Henry, gasfitter A Hattersley & Sons, bds 73 Laselle.
Deck David, bench hand Fort Wayne Electric Co, res 232 Thomas.
Deck Frank, laborer Bass Foundry and Machine Works, bds 70 Pontiac.
Deck John, res 70 Pontiac.
Deck Sophia, bds 70 Pontiac.
Decker Mary, wks Indiana School for Feeble-Minded Youth.
Decker Sophia, domestic 52 E Jefferson.
Dedolph Wm, saloon, 61 Wells, res same.
Deel George P, laborer, bds 156 Taylor.
Deem Henry, laborer J A Koehler, res same.
Deems Barney, plasterer, bds 22 Winch.
Deens John, watchman, res s s Pontiac nr Penn new yards.
DeFraine Francis, car builder Penn Co, res West place, Maysville road.
Degalues Henry J, carpenter, res 70 St Mary's ave.
Degitz Charles, laborer, res 15 Colerick.
Degitz Charles, wheel molder Bass Foundry and Machine Works, res 160 Force.
Degitz Charles A, lab Bass Foundry and Machine Works, bds 160 Force.
Degitz Frank, laborer, res 72 Leith.
Degitz Frank, lab American Wheel Co, res 544 S Calhoun.
Degitz Frank, wheelmkr American Wheel Co, bds 160 Force.
Degitz Joseph, mach hand American Wheel Co, bds 160 Force.
Degitz Louis, watchman, res 15 Colerick.
Degitz Margaret, domestic 570 Broadway.
DeGrattery Elizabeth (wid James E), res n w cor Division and Hayden.
DeHart Wm, lab Kerr-Murray Mnfg Co, bds 202 W Superior.
DeHaven Harrison D, laborer Penn Co, res 107 Holman.
DeHaven Perry N (Joseph N Clark & Co), res 153 W Washington.

13

DeHaven Samuel H, switchman Wabash R R, res 58 Oakley.
Deheny Cornelius, laborer Penn Co, res 70 Force.
Dehm Elizabeth (wid George), res 132 Wells
Dehms John, watchman, res s s Pontiac 1 e of Walton ave.
Dehne Ernst, patternmaker Penn Co, res 114 Gay.
Deibel Ella, tailoress Thieme Bros, bds 133 Holman.
Deibel Maggie, bds 133 Holman.
Deihl, *see also Deahl.*
Deihl Alice, bds 49 Harmer.
Deihl Hugh M, machinist Penn Co, res 49 Harmer.
Deihl Lillie, bds 49 Harmer.
Deitrich Wm O, driver Fort Wayne Street Railroad Co, res
    s e cor Harrison and Grand.
De La Grange Frank, laborer, res 68 Laselle.
De La Grange Frank J E, Dry Goods, Notions and
    Saloon, 273 Hanna, res same.
De La Grange Jescon, clerk F J E De La Grange, bds same.
Delaney John, laborer P E Cox, rms 29 W Main.
Delaney Rev Joseph F, asst pastor Cathedral, res 172 Clinton.
De Laney Richard W, bartndr J A Clark, bds 213 Lafayette.
Delano Elizabeth D (wid Thomas), res 76 E Wayne.
Delano Timothy, gas fitter, bds 91 E Washington.
Delker Caroline (wid Jacob), res 74 E Columbia.
Delker Minnie, bds 74 E Columbia.
Delker Wm, driver, bds 74 E Columbia.
Dell Mrs Annie, works Indiana School for Feeble-Minded
    Youth.
Delle George, machinist, bds 199 Broadway.
Delph Alice, operator Hoosier Mnfg Co, bds 107 Lafayette.
Delph Milton F, carpenter, res 107 Lafayette.
De Mass Charles C, bds 39 Duck.
De Mass Mrs Ollie J, res 39 Duck.
De Maulpied Martin, brakeman, bds 237 Barr.
Demma Olive, waitress Hedekin House.
Demeyer August, sawyer American Wheel Co, res s s Eckert
    nr Hanna.
Demeyer Christian D, laborer Olds' Wagon Works, bds 9
    Eckert.
Demeyer Frederick, laborer, bds s s Eckart 3 e of Hanna.
Dence Andrew, laborer, res 416 E Washington.
Dender Levi, plumber James Madden, res 152 E Wayne.
Denehy, *see also Danehy.*
Denehy Michael, painter L C Zollinger, res 12 Bass.
Denges Frederick, res 413 E Washington.
Denner Mrs Margaret, res rear 409 W Main.
Dennio Cordelia (wid Wm), bds 146 Wallace.

Builders' Hardware, PFEIFFER & SCHLATTER, 38 and 40 EAST COLUMBIA ST.

FORT WAYNE DIRECTORY. 159

Dennis Albert, laborer, res 235 Barr.

Dennis J Frederick, works Rippe & Son, bds 199 Broadway.

Dennis Michael, driver J B White, res 10 St Mary's ave.

Dennis Wm, teamster The Herman Berghoff Brewing Co, res Grant ave near brewery.

Dennison Miss Georgie L, teacher, bds 293 W Jefferson.

Dennison John, machinist Fort Wayne Electric Co, res 293 W Jefferson.

Dennler Frederick, laborer, res 281 E Washington.

Denno Mrs Ellen, bds 101 Harmer.

Denny Watts P, lawyer, 34 E Berry, res 70 Jackson.

Denz Joseph, watchmaker H Marriotte, res 103 Lafayette.

Denzel John, works Keil Bros, bds 151 E Jefferson.

Depler Hugh H, car builder Penn Co, res 165 Hoagland ave.

Depler John A, brakeman Penn Co, bds 103 Fairfield ave.

Depner George J, painter Olds' Wagon Works, bds 51 Hugh.

De Poy Mollie, domestic 271 W Wayne.

Deppelter Rudolph, physician, 18 E Columbia, res same.

Deppen Bennedena (wid August), res 37 E 3d.

Dereck Rosa, domestic 56 Smith.

Derheimer Joseph, General Contractor; Dredging a Specialty, Office 55 Clinton, res 177 E Jefferson. (*See adv in classified Contractors.*)

Derheimer Kate, bds 177 E Jefferson.

Derig Joseph, laborer, res 68 Smith.

Dern Cyrus, bartender W H Pease, rms 11 W Columbia.

De Rome Charles, laborer Penn Co, bds 75 W Washington.

De Rome Solomon, res 75 W Washington.

Derr George W, printer The Press, bds 61 Winter.

Desprez August, plumber, bds 73 Laselle.

Desprez Rosa, works Troy Steam Laundry, bds 73 Laselle.

Desprez Victor, night watchman, res 73 Laselle.

Desprez Victoria, bookbinder City Book Bindery, bds 73 Laselle.

Dessauer Carrie, bds 90 W Main.

Dessauer Henrietta (wid Louis), res 90 W Main.

Dessauer Jacob, clerk Sam, Pete & Max, bds 90 W Main.

Dessauer Louis, cash boy L Wolf & Co, bds 90 W Main.

Dessauer L & Co (Isaac Trauerman), cigar mnfrs, 23 Calhoun.

Desser Joseph P, harnessmaker A L Johns & Co, res 247 E Washington.

De St Aubin Albert, trav agt, bds 157 E Berry.

Dettmann Charles F, wheelmaker Bass Foundry and Machine Works, bds 75 John.

DeTurk Lebanon, machine hand, res 57 W 3d.

Detzer August J (Klinkenberg & Detzer), bds 9 E Wayne.

Detzer Edward N, clerk First National Bank, bds 260 Calhoun.
Detzer Gustave G, bookkeeper Old National Bank, rms 30 Douglas ave.
Detzer Martin, Druggist, 260 Calhoun, res same.
Devald Catharine (wid Nicholas), bds 175 E Wayne.
Devany Edward M, polisher American Wheel Co, res 152 Holman.
Devany Martin, deputy street commissioner, res 76 Baker.
Devaux David, section hand, rms 60 E Columbia.
Devaux Frank, laborer, bds Lake Shore Hotel.
Devendorf Alberta (wid Harry C), bds 197 Montgomery.
Devenport Nelson, engineer Louis Fox & Bro, res 48 W Lewis.
De Vere Daniel W, driver Ft Wayne Transfer & Baggage Line, res 125 Harrison.
Deveveaux Edward F, bartender J H Nolan, res 23 Laselle.
Deveveaux Felicia (wid Xavier), dressmaker, res 23 Laselle.
Deveveaux Mary, forewoman Hoosier Mnfg Co, bds 23 Laselle.
De Vilbiss Thomas D, carpenter, res 265 E Creighton ave.
De Vilbiss Wm F, res 58 Thomas.
Deville Frank, switchman, bds 60 E Williams.
Devlin Robert J, laborer American Wheel Company, bds 110 W DeWald.
Devlin Wm, coil winder Fort Wayne Electric Co, res 106 W DeWald.
DeWald Anna, clerk Root & Co, bds 404 S Calhoun.
DeWald Anthony, clerk George DeWald & Co, res 26 Clay.
DeWald Miss Caroline L, bds DeWald square.
DeWald Miss Elizabeth M, bds DeWald square.
DeWald George, bds 26 Clay.
DeWald George (George DeWald & Co), res DeWald square.
DeWald George L, bill clerk G DeWald & Co, bds DeWald square.
DeWald George & Co (George DeWald, Effingham T Williams, Amelius J Lang, Robert W T DeWald), Wholesale and Retail Dry Goods and Notions, n e cor Columbia and Clinton.
DeWald Henry, Tin, Copper and Sheet Iron Ware, Roofing and Spouting, 80 Barr, res 141 same.
DeWald Lizzie, clerk Foellinger Bros, bds 41 Locust.
DeWald Miss Mamie E, bds DeWald square.
DeWald Mary, dressmaker L A Worch, bds 404 Calhoun.
DeWald Mary A (wid Frank), res 41 Locust.

DeWald Michael, carpenter, res 116 Fulton.

DeWald Nicholas, laborer Bass Foundry and Machine Works, res 404 Calhoun.

DeWald Robert W T (George DeWald & Co), res 162 E Wayne.

DeWald Miss Sophia, clerk Siemon & Bro, bds 404 Calhoun.

DeWald Square, n s E Creighton ave, bet Hanna and Lafayette.

DeWitt Lorenzo B, laborer, res 281 E Washington.

DeWitt Mrs Wealthy, trimmer Adams & Armstrong, bds 103 W Berry.

Dexter Wm, fireman Penn Co, res 48 W Williams.

Diamond Adolph, clerk Pottlitzer Bros, res 99 E Wayne.

Diamond Henry, traveling agent Pottlitzer Bros, bds 99 E Wayne.

Diamond Hotel, James Wilkinson Propr, 233 and 235 Calhoun.

Diamond John, farmer, res s s Huntington rd w of Lindenwood cemetery.

Dibber Charles W, laborer, bds 78 Melita.

Dibbern Ferdinand, painter Wayne Paint and Painting Co, res 78 Melita.

Dick Arthur L, feeder The Press, bds 89 W Butler.

Dick Charles, engineer Model Steam Laundry, res 7 Dwenger ave.

Dick Daniel, engineer, res 89 W Butler.

Dick John H, laborer Wm & J J Geake, res 25 Wall.

Dick Katie, domestic 248 Calhoun.

Dick Miss Mary E, teacher Hoagland School, bds 87 W Butler.

Dick Wm E, fireman G R & I R R, bds 87 W Butler.

Dicke Frederick, grocer, 29 Smith, res same.

Dicke Henry, grocer, 119 E Lewis, res 192 same.

Dickey Anna, domestic 232 W Wayne.

Dickerson, *see also Dickinson.*

Dickerson Andrew F (col'd), porter Fort Wayne Newspaper Union, bds 33 W Lewis.

Dickerson Jefferson, res 19 Lafayette.

Dickerson Sarah (col'd, wid Andrew), res 33 W Lewis.

Dickie Robert, res 586 Calhoun.

Dickinson, *see also Dickerson.*

Dickinson Miss Mamie, bds 18 W Washington.

Dickinson Philemon, mngr D H Baldwin & Co, res 18 Washington.

Dickman Harry W, machine agent, rms 51 E Main.

Dickman Wm, helper, res 75 John.

Dickmeier Charles, helper Bass Foundry and Machine Works, res 99 Gay.

Dickmeier Henry, laborer, res 93 Gay.

Dickmeyer Wm, foreman Beaver, Miller & Co, res 168 Greely.

Dickson James M, engineer Penn Co, res 26 W DeWald.

Dickson Joseph, laborer, bds 16 Clay.

Didier Ellen, operator Central Union Telephone Co, bds 410 E Wayne.

Didier Emeline (wid Francis,) res 410 E Wayne.

Didier Frank X, clk Francis Sallier, res 92 Montgomery.

Didier James, car builder Penn Co, res 347 E Creighton ave.

Didier Joseph C, clerk C H Currier, res 66 E Columbia.

Didier Julian J, laborer, bds 410 E Wayne.

Didier Julian T, harnessmaker A L Johns & Co, bds Philomine Nommay.

Didier Kate, works Troy Steam Laundry, bds 91 Laselle.

Didier Rosa M, bds 66 E Columbia.

Didier Wm H, harnessmaker A L Johns & Co, bds Philomine Nommay.

Didier Louis, plumber, bds 104 Maumee road.

Didierjohn Joseph (Didierjohn & Co), res 104 Maumee road.

Didierjohn Louis, plumber Robert Ogden, bds 104 Maumee road.

Didierjohn Rosa, seamstress, bds 104 Maumee road.

Didierjohn & Co (Joseph Didierjohn, John Hunter), broom mnfrs, 102 Maumee road.

Didion Amelia, paster Ruesewald & Dedion, bds 208 Madison.

Didion Martin A (Ruesewald & Didion), bds 208 Madison.

Didion Olivia, bds 508 Madison.

Diebold Catherine (wid Joseph), res 275 E Washington.

Diebold Clara, dressmaker, bds 275 E Washington.

Diebold Henry, laborer, res 68 Boone.

Diebold Henry A, clk H G Sommer, bds 275 E Washington. ·

Diebold Joseph, bds 68 Boone.

Diebold Mary, bds 275 E Washington.

Dieckman, *see Dickman.*

Dieckmeyer Ferdinand, blacksmith, res n e cor Nirdlinger ave and Metz.

Diederick Prof Henry W, U S Minister to Germany, res Concordia College grounds, E Washington.

Diedrick Wm, brakeman Penn Co, rms Windsor Hotel.

Diehl, *see Deahl and Deihl.*

Diehm George, molder Penn Co, res w s Lafayette 7 s of Pontiac.

Diehm Henry, brick molder, bds w s Lafayette 10 s of Pontiac.

Diek Frank, tinsmith, bds 56 Smith.

Diek John B, finisher Fort Wayne Organ Có, bds 25 Wall.

Diek John H, laborer, res 25 Wall.

Diekmeyer Ferdinand, boltmkr Penn Co, res 157 Broadway.

Diem Charles, musical instruments, 75 Harrison, res same.

Diener Henry G, teamster Olds' Wagon Works, bds 17 Colerick.

Dierkes Anthony J, finisher American Wheel Co, res 94 Laselle.

Dierkes Catherine (wid Frederick W), res 72 Barthold.

Dierstein Charles A, carriage painter M L Albrecht, bds 91 E Washington.

Dierstein Frederick C, tailor John Wasserbach, bds 36 Fairfield ave.

Dierstein Frederika (wid Christian), res 12 Fairfield ave.

Dierstein George C, upholsterer Foster Furniture Co, bds 12 Fairfield ave.

Dierstein Henry G, saloon, 24 E Berry, res same.

Dierstein Miss Mary, bds 12 Fairfield ave.

Dierstein Philip, upholsterer The Pape Furniture Co, bds 36 Fairfield ave.

Dierstein Samuel W J, mach hand, bds 36 Fairfield ave.

Dierstein Wilhelmina (wid Samuel), res 36 Fairfield ave.

Diether Carl F, res 267 W Wayne.

Diether Edward, machine hand, res 128 Griffith.

Diether John H (Louis Diether & Bro), res 165 W Superior.

Diether Louis (Louis Diether & Bro), res 267 W Wayne.

Diether Louis & Bro (Louis and John H), Dealers in Rough and Dressed Lumber and Shingles; Mnfrs and Dealers in Sash, Doors, Blinds and Mouldings; All Kinds of Factory Work; Office and Yards bet City Mills and Gas Works on E Superior, Factory 100 Pearl. (*See right side lines.*)

Diether Wm A, clk Louis Diether & Bro, res 29 W Columbia.

Diether & Barrows(Louis Diether, Frank R Barrows), Mnfrs Weisell Washer, 100 Pearl. (*See right side lines.*)

Dietrich Wm, driver Ft Wayne Street Ry Co, res 25 Grand.

Diffenderfer Isabella A (wid Benjamin O), res 33 W DeWald.

Diffenderfer John H, dispatcher Penn Co, bds Pearse House.

Diffenderfer Miss Mary, clerk; bds 33 W DeWald.

Diffenderfer Thomas H, despatcher Penn Co, bds Pearse House.

Diffenderfer Wm A, bookkeeper Mossman, Yarnelle & Co, res 33 W DeWald.

Digan John, laborer, bds 34 Chicago.

Diggins Charlotte (wid Wm G), bds 159 Griffith.
Dignan Lawrence, foreman, res 215 E Wayne.
Dignan Lawrence jr, bds 215 E Wayne.
Dildine Frank, managing editor Ft Wayne Sentinel, res 66 W Jefferson.
Dill Charles, works Indiana School for Feeble-Minded Youth.
Dille Martin, servant 243 W Creighton ave.
Dilling Wm, gas fitter, bds 22 E Columbia.
Dillon James E N, blue printer Penn Co, bds 139 Broadway.
Dillon Nettie, laandress, bds 59 Grand.
Dills Thomas J, Physician and Surgeon, Office 42 W Berry, res 40 Douglas ave.
Dimon John, live stock, s s Huntington road nr. Lindenwood cemetery.
Dincher John, bartender T J Schuler, rms 130 W Main.
Dingman Daniel, rms 281 E Washington.
Dingman Hiram, gardener, res 199 W Washington.
Dinkel Charles, carpenter, res 65 Wabash.
Dinklage Herman L, machine hand Olds' Wagon Works, bds 11 Gay.
Dinklage Margaret (wid Henry), bds 271 E Washington.
Dinklage Mary (wid Herman), res 30 Gay.
Dinklage Patrick O, conductor Penn Co, bds 30 Gay.
Dinklager Anthony, harnessmaker A L Johns & Co, res 249 E Washington.
Dinkmeyer Charles, laborer, res 97 Gay.
Dinkmeyer Henry, laborer, res 97 Gay.
Dinnen James M, physician, 67 W Wayne, res 69 same.
Dirig Alios, lab Bass Foundry and Mach Works, bds 68 Smith.
Dirig Henry, laborer, bds 68 Smith.
Dirig Joseph, laborer Bass Foundry and Machine Works, res 68 Smith.
Dirig Jeseph jr, section hand, bds 68 Smith.
Disbrow Frank W, carpenter, res 89 N Cass.
Disler Mahala, domestic 57 Barr.
Disser Joseph P, harnessmaker A L Johns & Co, res 247 E Washington.
Distel Edward, clerk Coombs & Co, bds 38 Hendricks.
District School No 3, Adams Township, s s Wayne Trace 5 e of Walton ave.
Diter Henry, molder, res 37 Force.
Ditmann Charles F, laborer, res 150 Smith.
Dittman Henry, machine hand White's Wheel Works, bds 75 John.
Dittman Wm, laborer Bass Foundry and Machine Works, res 75 John.

Dittmer Jacob, tailor J G Thieme & Son, bds 122 Smith.
Dittoe Albert J (A J Dittoe & Co), res 195 E Wayne.
Dittoe A J & Co (Albert J Dittoe), grocers, 20 W Berry.
Dittoe Charles W, clerk A J Dittoe & Co, bds 195 E Wayne.
Dittoe James A, res 195 E Wayne.
Dittoe Mary, bds 195 E Wayne.
Dix Frank G, inspector Jenny Electric Light and Power Co, bds n w cor Lafayette and 7th.
Dix Hugh J, pressman, bds n w cor Lafayette and 7th.
Dix Seth, teamster, res n w cor Lafayette and 7th.
Dixson, *see Dickson.*
Dobberkan Frederick, car builder Penn Co, res 59 Hugh.
Dobler Louis, laborer, bds 154 John.
Dobler Theodore, tool inspector Penn Co, res 154 John.
Dobson Richard, painter, res 21 Taylor.
Doctor Henry T, laborer C L Centlivre, bds 25 Randolph.
Doctor Matthias, driver G E Bursley & Co, bds 324 E Washington.
Doctor Wm A, driver C L Centlivre, res 25 Randolph.
Doctorman Mrs Carrie, works Indiana School for Feeble-Minded Youth.
Dodane Amede L, grocer, 92 Wells, res same.
Dodane Minnie, bds 18 W Creighton ave.
Dodez Edward W, student J E Waugh, bds 113 W Wayne.
Dodez Gustavus C, trav agt, res 113 W Wayne.
Dodge Arthur, Veterinary Surgeon, Office with Red Lion Stables, with Infirmary Attached, res 143 W Berry. Tel 225.
Dodge Charlotte (wid John W), bds 181 E Wayne.
Dodge Isabella (wid Norman), res s e cor Wabash R R and Broadway.
Doebler Charles H, asst foreman Penn Co, bds 233 W Berry.
Doehring John, finisher White's Wheel Works, bds 546 E Wayne.
Doehring John H, laborer White's Wheel Works, res w s Grant ave 2 s of E Washington.
Doehrman Charles, car builder Penn Co, res 165 Holman.
Doehrman Lizzie, domestic 255 Fairfield ave.
Doehrman Lottie, domestic 255 Fairfield ave.
Doehrmann Ernest, blacksmith, res 88 Wall.
Doehrmann Frederick S S, laborer, res 16 Rockhill.
Doehrmann Frederick W, carpenter, res 39 Nirdlinger ave.
Doehrmann Henry A, tailor J G Thieme & Son, bds 18 Rockhill.
Doehrmann Wm (Doehrmann & Hitzeman), res 329 E Washington.

Doehrmann & Hitzeman (Wm Doehrmann, George Hitzeman), grocers, 56 Barr.
Doelker Caroline (wid Jacob), res 74 E Columbia.
Doell Wm, blacksmith Ft W, C & L R R, res 88 Hanna.
Doenges Christian, contractor and builder, 126 Maumee road, res same.
Doenges Ferdinand, tilemaker, bds s e cor Oliver and Greene.
Doenges G Frederick, carriagemaker City Carriage Works, res 413 E Washington.
Doenges Herman, carpenter, res s w cor Oliver and Grant.
Doenges John, res s e cor Oliver and Greene.
Doenges Louis, carpenter Christian Doenges, res 59 Winter.
Doenges Peter, carpenter, res rear 80 Hayden.
Doenges Philip, carpenter Christian Doenges, res Winch.
Doenges Wm, carpenter, n w cor Grant and Oliver, res same.
Doermann Frederick, machinist Wabash R R, res 16 Rockhill.
Doermer Miss Anna, teacher, bds 55 Wilt.
Doermer Lyda, converter worker Fort Wayne Electric Co, bds 55 Wilt.
Doermer Peter, farmer, res n s New Haven ave above junction of Piqua road.
Doherty, *see Daugherty and Dougherty.*
Dolan Bessie, bds 353 W Main.
Dolan Charles, engineer Horton Mnfg Co, res 8 Runnion ave.
Dolan Edward A, res 46 Centre.
Dolan John P, machinist Penn Co, res 109 Fairfield ave.
Dolan Miss Lizzie, clerk F M Smaltz, res 46 Centre.
Dolan Margaret, bds Mary Dolan.
Dolan Mary A, bds 46 Centre.
Dolan Mrs Mary E, janitor McCulloch School, res n e cor Lewis and Walton ave.
Dolan Theresa, bds 316 W Main.
Dominico Louis, fruit dealer, res 70 Riverside ave.
Donahoe Bridget, dressmaker Mary L Sherin, bds 75 Baker.
Donahoe Peter, brakeman Penn Co, res 16 Smith.
Donahue Daniel J, molder, bds 44 Brandriff.
Donahue Florance, foreman, res 44 Brandriff.
Donahue Mary S (wid John), bds 16 Smith.
Donahue Patrick W, engineer, res 12 Jackson.
Donahue Thomas, laborer Penn Co, res 39 Walnut.
Donahue Timothy, machinist Penn Co, bds 44 Brandriff.
Donald George, plumber James Madden, bds Custer House.
Donaldson Alexander W, cabinetmaker Fort Wayne Organ Co, bds 23 Poplar.
Donaldson Anna F, bookkeeper, bds 23 Poplar.
Donaldson Ebenezer R, bailiff, res 23 Poplar.

Donaldson John, res 307 Calhoun.
Donaldson Matthew K, clerk, res 21½ Poplar.
Donaldson Wm A, student H C Sites, bds 23 Poplar.
Dondero George, res 12 E Columbia.
Dondero Philip, fruit stand, res 28 E Columbia.
Donges Frederick, machine hand American Wheel Co, res 63 Buchanan.
Donnell Edward R, helper Fort Wayne Electric Co, bds 181 Fairfield ave.
Donnell Wm, machinist Fort Wayne Electric Co, res 181 Fairfield ave.
Donnell Wm B, laborer Fort Wayne Electric Co, bds 181 Fairfield ave.
Donnelly Ambrose, shoemaker, res 348 Calhoun.
Donnelly Amelia (wid Harry), bds 108 W Jefferson.
Donnelly Miss Claudia L, bds 108 W Jefferson.
Donnelly Jennie, bds 348 Calhoun.
Donnelly John, brakeman, bds 348 Calhoun.
Donner, see Dorner.
Donovan John W, conductor, bds 177 Griffith.
Donovan Peter, laborer, bds 34 Chicago.
Donovan Wm, undertaker, bds 208 Madison.
Donze Charles, bds 281 E Washington.
Dooley John, painter, bds 199 Broadway.
Dooley Philip, shoemaker, bds 5 S Hoagland ave.
Doran Wm, flagman Penn Co, bds Pearse Hotel.
Doriot Cora, bds 58 Charles.
Doriot Frank, clerk Wm Scheiman, bds 58 Charles.
Doriot Harry W, brakeman Penn Co, bds 196 Hanna.
Doriot Harry W, machine hand American Wheel Co, res 58 Charles.
Doriot Julius, molder Bass Foundry and Machine Works, res 58 Charles.
Dornberg Wm, saloon, 91 Harmer, res same.
Dornbush Henry, artist, room 14 Schmitz blk, res Fritz Hotel.
Dornte August, helper Penn Co, res 221 E Washington.
Dornte Carrie, bds 77 Maumee road.
Dornte Edward, laborer, bds 77 Maumee road.
Dornte George F, car repairer Penn Co, res rear 24 Van Buren.
Dornte Henry, laborer Penn Co, res 31 Maumee road.
Dornte Wm, laborer, res 77 Maumee road.
Dornte Wm H, car repairer Penn Co, res 37 Chestnut.
Dorr Everett K, traveling agent, res 115 Barr.
Dossler Henry, laborer, res 201 John.
Doswell Alfred E, gardener, bds 110 W Main.

Doswell Arthur C, gardener G W Doswell, bds J H Doswell.
Doswell George W, florist, n s W Main nr Lindenwood Cemetery, res same.
Doswell Henry J, asst supt Lindenwood Cemetery, res J H Doswell.
Doswell John H, Superintendent Lindenwood Cemetery, res same.
Dothage Dinah (wid Ernest), res 71 Webster.
Dothage Sophia (wid Ernest), res 23 Wilt.
Dothage Wm, machine hand J Klett & Son, res 71 Webster,
Doty Amelia (wid Willis P), res 170 E Jefferson.
Doty Richard E, engineer, res 342 Hanna.
Doty Wm W, engineer, res 26 Leith.
Doubler Louis, fireman Penn Co, res 154 John.
Doudrick Charles A, saloon, 250 Calhoun, res same.
Doudrick James S, brakeman, res 40 W Williams.
Dougall Allan H (Miller & Dougall), res 323 E Wayne.
Dougall Miss Inez, bds 323 E Wayne.
Dougall John T, city editor Fort Wayne News, bds 323 E Wayne.
Dougherty, *see also Daugherty and Doherty.*
Dougherty Catherine (wid Christopher), res 320 Lafayette.
Dougherty John, teamster Jenson & Sargent, bds Racine Hotel.
Doughman Newton D (Swayne & Doughman), res 189 Ewing.
Doughty Cora, bds 21 John.
Doughty Grace, milliner V E Wolf, bds 21 John.
Doughty Wm L, time keeper Penn Co, res 21 John.
Douglas Joseph H, saloon, 284 Calhoun, res 399 same.
Douglas Robert F, asst passenger and ticket agent Wabash R R depot, res 399 Calhoun.
Douglas Wm B, res 262 W Jefferson.
Douglass Wm V, real estate, and agent Merchants' Despatch Transportation Co, 3 Schmitz blk, res 116 College.
Douings Lavinia, seamstress, bds 52 E 3d.
Douings Sarah A (wid Henry), res 52 E 3d.
Dowell John P, gas fitter Salimonie Mining and Gas Co, bds 22 W Main.
Dowie Wm A, machinist Bass Foundry and Machine Works, res 120 Fairfield ave.
Downer George W, brakeman Nickle Plate Ry, res 140 High.
Downing Myron S, traveling agent Louis Fox & Bro, res 45 W DeWald.
Downing Wm E, base ball player, rms 25 Grand.
Doyle Annie, operator Hoosier Mnfg Co, bds 237 Clay.
Doyle Bernard, bds 248 Calhoun.

Doyle Catherine (wid Patrick), res 237 Clay.

Doyle Daniel M, traveling agent G E Bursley & Co, res 47 Home ave.

Doyle James, wheelmaker Olds' Wagon Works, res 198 Hanna.

Doyle James C, butcher, bds 70 Wilt.

Doyle John P, brakeman, res 8 Melita.

Doyle John W, driver Fort Wayne Transfer and Storage Co, res 83 Holman.

Doyle Joseph, machinist Indiana Machine Works, bds 237 Madison.

Doyle Joseph D, flagman Penn Co, res 308 E Creighton ave.

Doyle Mary (wid Patrick), res 159 Harrison.

Doyle Minnie, operator Hoosier Mnfg Co, bds 237 Clay.

Doyle Thomas, patternmaker Indiana Machine Works, res 237 Madison.

Doyle Tillie, operator Hoosier Mnfg Co, bds 237 Clay.

Dozois, Beadell & Co (P Omer Dozois, Henry Beadell), Dealers in Staple and Fancy Dry Goods, Gents' Furnishing Goods, Hosiery, Notions, Etc, 22 E Berry.

Dozois Charles, clerk Dozois, Beadell & Co, bds 96 E Wayne.

Dozois P Omer (Dozois, Beadell & Co), res 146 E Wayne.

Draeger Amelia C, tailoress, bds 31 E 2d.

Draeger Charles E, fireman, res 133 High.

Draeger Emma N (wid Charles F), res 31 E 2d.

Draeger Frank B, machinist, bds 31 E 2d.

Draeger Matilda M, tailoress, bds 31 E 2d.

Drake Frankie (wid George W), res 3 Harrison.

Drake Frederick J, chief clerk P O, bds Aldine Hotel.

Drake Jackson C, coil winder Fort Wayne Electric Co, res 145 Fairfield ave.

Drake Theodore, cook, rms 65 Baker.

Drake Thomas F, engineer, res 151 Wallace.

Draker Frank A, teamster, res 134 W 3d.

Draker John J, feed barn, 42 Pearl, res same.

Dratt John A, saloon, 36 Barr, res same.

Drebert Frank, carpenter, 91 W DeWald, res same.

Drecker, *see Drucker.*

Dreibelbiss Abstract of Title Co The, John Dreibelbiss Pres, Robert B Dreibelbiss Sec and Treas, Abstracts of Title, 3 and 4 Pixley & Long Building.

Dreibelbiss Anna (wid John P), res 169 W DeWald.

Dreibelbiss Conrad W, real estate, res 113 Wallace.

Dreibelbiss Edward D, tel opr Penn Co, res 134 W Creighton

Dreibelbiss John, pres The Dreibelbiss Abstract of Title Co, and sec and treas Old Fort Mnfg Co, res 17 Holman.

Dreibelbiss Robert B, sec and treas The Dreibelbiss Abstract of Title Co, res 169 W DeWald.

Dreier, *see also Dreyer and Dryer.*

Dreier Lissette, domestic 240 S Hoagland ave.

Dreier Wm H (Dreier & Bro), res 178 W Berry.

Dreier & Bro (Wm H Dreier), druggists, 10 Calhoun.

Drerup John, laborer 135 E Berry.

Dressel Henry F, carpenter, res 63 Melita.

Dressel Maria T (wid George), res 158 Montgomery.

Dressel Sarah M, clerk Root & Co, bds 158 Montgomery.

Dressel Valentine, brakeman, bds 158 Montgomery.

Drew Stephen A, saloon, 317 W Main, res 316 same.

Drew Wm E, carpenter, res 391 W Main.

Drewett George J, foreman Horton Mnfg Co, res w s Osage 2 n of Main.

Dreyer, *see also Dreier and Dryer.*

Dreyer Conrad, shoemaker Charles Stillhorn, res 9 Union.

Dreyer Henry F W, helper Penn Co, bds 36 Charles.

Dreyer Wm F H, helper Penn Co, res 116 Hanna.

Driftmeyer August F, watchman, res 190 W Main.

Driftmeyer Emma L, domestic 115 N Cass.

Driftmeyer Ernest, car builder Penn Co, res 154 Madison.

Driftmeyer Henry W, trav agt, bds 16 Walnut.

Driftmeyer Louisa M, bds 216 W Washington.

Driscoll Ellen C, bds 281 Calhoun.

Driscoll's Hall, s e cor Calhoun and Wabash R R.

Driscoll Margaret E, dressmaker, bds 281 Calhoun.

Driscoll Wm, bds 281 Calhoun.

Driver Alanson, conductor Nickel Plate, res 63 W Main.

Driver George R, machinist, res 130 Franklin ave.

Driver Rev John M, pastor Simpson M E Church, res 319 S Harrison.

Driver Margaret (wid Henry), bds 186 W Main.

Driver Samuel C, fireman Hoffman Bros, res 125 Franklin av.

Droegemeyer Charles F, paper hanger The Siemon Wall Paper Co, rms 191 Calhoun.

Droegemeyer Clara, bds 25 Nirdlinger ave.

Droegemeyer John A, clerk Pixley & Co, res 25 Nirdlinger.

Droegemeyer John F W, painter, rms 10 W Main.

Droegemeyer Theodore F, apprentice Robert Spice, bds 25 Nirdlinger ave.

Droegemeyer Walter F H, cigarmaker H W Ortmann, bds 98 W Superior.

Droegemeyer Wm J, laborer, bds 25 Nirdlinger ave.

Droste Diedrich, plasterer, res 100 W Jefferson.

Drucker Elizabeth (wid Henry), res 66 W Washington.

Druhot Addie (Druhot Sisters), bds 324 E Jefferson.
Druhot Dade (Druhot Sisters), bds 324 E Jefferson.
Druhot Elizabeth (wid Claude), res 324 E Jefferson.
Druhot Frank C, molder Bass Foundry and Machine Works, res 28 Force.
Druhot John F, molder Bass Foundry and Machine Works, res 140 Wallace.
Druhot Joseph N, molder Bass Foundry and Machine Works, res e s Monroe 3 s of Wallace.
Druhot Joseph T, molder Bass Foundry and Machine Works, res 28 Force.
Druhot Miss May (Druhot Sisters), bds 324 E Jefferson.
Druhot Sisters (May, Addie and Dade), dressmakers, 324 E Jefferson.
Druids James, laborer, res rear 382 W Main.
Drukenbrod Rufus, tinsmith S F Bowser & Co, res w s Thomas 2 s of E Creighton ave.
Druley Charles, teamster, res 592 Calhoun.
Druly Annie (wid Joseph), res rear 98 Baker.
Drummond Arthur, apprentice Robert Spice, bds 71 Garden.
Drummond Charles L, editor, res 47 Baker.
Drummond Harry E, printer Ft Wayne Sentinel, res 391 E Wayne.
Drummond Sylvester D, plasterer, res 71 Garden.
Drury Michael M, calker A Hattersley & Son, res 163 E Jefferson.
Dryer, *see also Dreier and Dreyer.*
Dryer Charles R, chemist Fort Wayne Electric Co, res 32 Maple ave.
Dubberkenn Frederick, laborer, res 59 Hugh.
Duber Albert, laborer, res 74 E Columbia.
Dubois Kate, cook Wm C Seidel & Bro, rms 52½ Calhoun.
Dubois Philip, res 54 E 3d.
Dudenhaefer Anna M (wid Philip), res 123 Maumee road.
Dudenhoefer Miss Amelia, clerk Louis P Scherer, res 336 E Wayne.
Dudenhoefer, Bueker & Scherer (George P Dudenhoefer, Henry E Bueker, Henry P Scherer), Proprs City Carriage Works, 11 and 13 Clay.
Dudenhoefer George P (Dudenhoefer, Bueker & Scherer), res 336 E Wayne.
Dudenhoefer Philip G, laborer City Carriage Works, res 336 E Wayne.
Duell Lizzie, domestic 261 W Berry.
Duemling Dr Herman, teacher Concordia College, res 441 E Washington.

Duemling Herman jr, student, bds 441 E Washington.
Duerr Jacob, clerk The Pape Furniture Co, res 22 Ewing.
Duffy James E, laborer Winch & Son, bds 410 E Wayne.
Duffy Mary, operator Hoosier Mnfg Co, bds 95 W Superior.
Duffy Sarah (wid James), bds 95 W Superior.
Duffy Thomas E, photographer, res 100 W 3d.
Duffy Wm P, printer Fort Wayne News, res 100 W 3d.
Dugan Daniel W, switchman, res 62 Chicago.
Dugan Mrs Savannah, res 62 Chicago.
Dukeman Samuel, watchman Root & Co, res 224 E Jefferson.
Dun R G & Co, The Mercantile Agency, F V Culbertson Mngr, 21 Pixley and Long Bldg.
Dunanu Emma E (wid John J), res 216 W Jefferson.
Dunann George L, engineer Nickel Plate, res 216 W Jefferson.
Dunfee Alice M, bds 58 W Berry.
Dunfee Charles H, trav agent S F Bowser & Co, res 58 W Berry.
Dunfee Ernst W, foreman Olds' Wagon Works, res 89 W De Wald.
Dunfee Harry E, cutter S M Foster, bds 58 W Berry.
Dunham Charles W, machine hand American Wheel Co, bds 100 Montgomery.
Dunham Eugene, conductor, res 26 Van Buren.
Dunham Frank W, supt American Wheel Co, res 202 E De Wald.
Dunlap Harvey, laborer H W Bond, bds 289 E Wayne.
Dunlap Jason C, fireman, res 109 Van Buren.
Dunlap Margaret (wid Collar), res 298 E Wayne.
Dunlap Wm, driver Kilian Baker, res 1 Lafayette.
Dunlop Andrew W, lumber inspector, res 313 Hanna.
Dupont Emma, domestic 172 Clinton.
Dupont Louisa, bds 347 E Creighton ave.
Durbin Charles W, brakeman, bds 47 W Superior.
Durbin Dennis, brakeman, res 204 Francis.
Durbin John W, laborer, bds 92 Franklin ave.
Durbrow Charles, teamster C F Muhler & Son, res cor N Calhoun and Superior.
Durbrow Lydia (wid James), res 22 N Calhoun.
Durfee George A, trav agt B W Skelton, res 77 Douglas av.
Durfee Lulu, bds 258 Calhoun.
Durfee Mary L, bds 258 Calhoun.
Durfee Sarah A, gents' furnishing goods, 258 Calhoun, res same.
Durfee Wm R, clk S A Durfee, res 258 Calhoun.
Durkee Edward, machine hand American Wheel Co.
Durnall Jane (wid George), res 17 Burgess.

Durnell Miss Addie, teacher, bds 27 Duryea.
Durnell Alfred S, tinsmith Penn Co, res 111 Madison.
Durnell Chester, engineer, res 49 W DeWald.
Durnell Herman, engineer, res 177 Calhoun.
Durnell Luke, market gardener, e s Spy Run ave 1 n of brewery, res same.
Durnell Marshall H, fireman, res 27 Duryea.
Durr Jacob, clerk, res 22 Ewing.
Durst Matthias, mason, bds 22 W Main.
Duryee George W, baggageman, res n w cor Fisher and Holton ave.
Duryee Sadie, paper boxmaker City Book Bindery, bds cor Fisher and Holton ave.
Dushow Rhinebolt, laborer Luke Durnell, bds same.
Dustman George G, sawyer, bds 533 E Wayne.
Dustman Sarah A, bds 533 E Wayne.
Duval Catherine (wid Nicholas), bds 175 E Wayne.
Dwelly Charles, machinist Wabash R R, res 20 McClellan.
Dwelly Lotta, bds 20 McClellan.
Dwenger Rt Rev Joseph, D D, Bishop of the Roman Catholic Diocese of Fort Wayne, res 172 Clinton.
Dwenger Joseph H, laborer Penn Co, res 22 Charles.
Dwyer John, agent, bds Hedekin House.
Dyche Mrs Leota A, bds 90 E Wayne.
Dyer Charles F, coppersmith, bds Brokaw House.
Dyer Thomas jr, apprentice Fort Wayne Newspaper Union, bds 273 W Jefferson.
Dyer Thomas, engineer, res 273 W Jefferson.
Dyke Anton, laborer Penn Co, res 53 John.
Dykes Agnes, bds 321 E Wayne.
Dynes James, painter, bds 302 E Creighton ave.

E

Eagle Warren, carpenter, res n s Howell w of Runnion ave.
Eakin, *see also Aiken.*
Eakin A Avery, clerk, res 28 Clinton.
Eakin Ella, dressmaker, 28 Clinton, bds same.
Eakin James W, laborer, res 71 Monroe.
Earl Ella, domestic Aveline House.
Earle Wm B, servant J H Jacobs.
Early Michael, wheelmaker American Wheel Co, res 9 Ohio.
Easley Charles, carpenter, res 206 W Jefferson.
East End Bottling Works, Herman Berghoff Brewing Co proprs, cor E Washington and Wabash ave.

14

East End Street Car Barn, n w cor E Washington and Glasgow ave.

East German School, n w cor Harmer and Jefferson.

Eastwood Harry C, traveling agent S F Bowser & Co, res 173 Ewing.

Eastwood Raphael W, butcher Frank Parrot, res 283 Webster.

Eaton, *see also Heaton.*

Eaton Wm T, engineer, res 39 W Washington.

Ebby Mollie (wid Oliver P), bds 225 W Main.

Ebel, *see also Abel.*

Ebel Louis F, painter Olds' Wagon Works, res 151 Gay.

Eberhardt John, clerk Anton Kalbacher, res 82 Barr.

Eberhardt Wm E, molder Bass Foundry and Machine Works, res 125 N Cass.

Eberline Mrs Sophia, dressmaker, res 86 E Jefferson.

Eberly Anna M (wid Daniel), res 40 E 5th.

Ebert, *see also Hebert.*

Ebert Adam, laborer Horton Mnfg Co, res 127 Franklin ave.

Ebert Douglas F, brakeman, bds 219 Lafayette.

Ebert Edward, brakeman, bds 219 Lafayette.

Eberwine Christian, res 96 Walton ave.

Ebner Caroline, bds 145 E Lewis.

Ebner Froney, bds 145 E Lewis.

Ebner George, car builder Penn Co, res 39 Force.

Ebner George, car builder Penn Co, res 205 Hanna.

Ebner Jacob, machinist Penn Co, res 145 E Lewis.

Ebner John, clerk R Steger & Co, bds 145 E Lewis.

Ebner Kate, bds 39 Force.

Ebner Lorenz, car oiler Penn Co, res 145 E Lewis.

Ebner Verona, tailoress Charles Vestermeier, bds 145 E Lewis.

Echelberry George, laborer J C Peters, res 10 Short.

Echelberry Wm G, brakeman, res 117 Wells.

Eobrick Peter, helper Penn Co, bds 7 Smith.

Eck Wm M, stone cutter, bds Hedekin House.

Eckard Ernest, laborer J A Koehler, res w s Lafayette south of city limits.

Eckardt Gustave, laborer, res s e cor Thomas and Fisher.

Eckart Block, s e cor Main and Harrison.

Eckart David, cigarmaker, bds 19 W Williams.

Eckart Frederick, Meat Market and Pork Packer, 35 W Main, res 91 E Wayne.

Eckart Frederick jr, mngr Eckart's Packing House, res 470 W Main.

Eckart Henry, supt Frederick Eckart, bds 91 E Wayne.

Eckart John C (Eckart & O'Connor), res 19 W Williams.

Eckart John C jr, butcher Gottlieb Haller, bds 19 W Williams.

Eckart Wm E, cigarmaker, bds 19 W Williams.

Eckart & O'Connor (John C Eckart, Bernard O'Connor), proprs Princess Roller Skating Rink, s e cor W Main and Fulton.

Eckart's Packing House, Frederick Eckart jr mngr, 474 W Main.

Eckelburger Samuel, laborer, res 143 Taber.

Eckels Miss Emma E, clerk Woman's Reading Room, bds 57 Riverside ave.

Eckels Harry C, telephone inspector, res 5 Riverside ave.

Eckels James M, carpenter, res 57 Riverside ave.

Eckels Willis J, bookkeeper Hoffman Bros, res 115 N Cass.

Eckenrod David N, foreman news room Fort Wayne Gazette, res 243 W Washington.

Ecker, see *Acker, Aiker and Eicher.*

Eckerle Albert, laborer C L Centlivre, res n s Spy Run ave 1 n of Edna.

Eckermann John, turner White's Wheel Works, res 64 Summit.

Eckhart Anton, section hand, res rear 19 Walnut.

Eckhart Gustav, laborer, res s e cor Fisher and Thomas.

Eckles Henry C, inspector Central Union Telephone Co, res 27 Riverside ave.

Eckley Eliza A (wid Peter), bds 24 W Jefferson.

Edelman John, helper Penn Co, res 70 Charles.

Edgerton Alfred P, res 154 W Berry.

Edgerton Miss Clara, bds 87 W Wayne.

Edgerton Clement W, bicycles, 57 W Main, bds 87 W Wayne.

Edgerton Dixon (Bittinger & Edgerton), res 44 Pfeiffer ave.

Edgerton Edward C, bds 87 W Wayne.

Edgerton Joseph K, Real Estate and Agricultural Implements, 57 W Main, res 87 W Wayne.

Edgerton Miss Josephine, bds 87 W Wayne.

Edison Mutual Telegraph Co The, C G Harris Mngr, Wayne Hotel.

Edler, see *Adler.*

Edmunds Harry M, tel opr Nickel Plate, bds 131 Jackson.

Edmunds Mary (wid James E), dressmaker, 131 Jackson, res same.

Edmunds Minnie, clerk Alexander Goodman, bds 21 Cass.

Edmunds Wm, buyer L Bash & Co, res 21 Cass.

Edsall Clarence W, Lawyer, 5 and 6 Bank Block, res s s Maumee road, 1 e of Lillie.

Edsall Frank N, machine hand Fort Wayne Furniture Co,
    bds 61 Oliver.
Edsall Jasper, laborer, res 61 Oliver.
Edsall Tecumseh, switchman Wabash R R, bds 61 Oliver.
Edwards Charles W, res 247 W Berry.
Edwards Daniel, foreman Penn Co, res 229 W Creighton ave.
Edwards Ella, domestic 90 Thompson ave.
Edwards Emery, gluer Ft Wayne Organ Co, bds 28 Chicago.
Edwards Miss Jennie, bds 229 W Creighton ave.
Effert Mary, domestic 116 College.
Effert Rose, domestic 284 W Berry.
Eggemann Peter, shoemaker, 17 E Main, res 20 W Jefferson.
Eggemann Tillie, bds 20 W Jefferson.
Eggiman Peter J, clerk, res 63 High.
Eggimann Charles, clerk, bds 52 John.
Eggimann Conrad, checker Penn Co, res 52 John.
Eggimann David, laborer Nickel Plate Ry, bds 29 E Main.
Ehinger Adolph, plasterer, res n s Riverside ave 7 w of St
    Joseph river.
Ehinger Charles, laborer Hoffman Bros, res 148 High.
Ehinger Emma M, bds 112 Clay.
Ehinger Felix, laborer, res 72 E Columbia.
Ehinger Frank O, clerk Kerr-Murray Mnfg Co, bds 112 Clay.
Ehinger Joseph, helper Wabash R R, res 143 W 3d.
Ehinger Louisa (wid Roman), res 176 E Lewis.
Ehinger Mary (wid Michael), bds 148 W 3d.
Ehinger Othman, car builder Penn Co, res 112 Clay.
Ehle Albert N, cigars and tobacco, 178 Broadway, res 180
    same.
Ehle Edward T, bricklayer, res 306 W Washington.
Ehle Ernest, cigarmaker A N Ehle, bds 180 Broadway.
Ehle Ernest H, contractor (brick), 529 Broadway, res same.
Ehle Frank, cigarmaker A N Ehle, bds 180 Broadway.
Ehle Frederick E, laborer Penn Co, res 27 Rockhill.
Ehle Henry C, bricklayer, res 18 Nirdlinger ave.
Ehle Michael, res 224 W Creighton ave.
Ehle Sophie M, bds 27 Rockhill.
Ehrhardt Leonard, butcher F Eckart, res 51 Pfeiffer ave.
Ehrman Amelia, operator S M Foster, bds 132 Greely.
Ehrman Caroline (wid Mattice), res 132 Greely.
Ehrman Charles F (Ehrman & Geller), res 175 Van Buren.
Ehrman Coleman, saloon, 64 E Main, res same.
Ehrman Edward J, bds 64 E Main.
Ehrman Emelie, seamstress Foster's Waist Factory, bds 132
    Greely.
Ehrman George J, carriage painter M L Albrecht, bds 42 Elm.

Ehrman John G, laborer, res 42 Elm.
Ehrman John W M, car builder Penn Co, res New Haven ave.
Ehrman Michael, machinist Penn Co, res 17 Taylor.
Ehrman Miss Rickie, res 175 Van Buren.
Ehrman Wm H, stereotyper, bds 64 E Main.
Ehrman & Geller (Charles F Ehrman, Charles C Geller), barbers, 12 W Main.
Ehrmann Charles Blacksmith and Wagonmaker, 149 W Main, res 339 W Jefferson.
Ehrmann Charles W, blacksmith Charles Ehrmann, bds 339 W Jefferson.
Ehrmann Charles W, machine hand, bds 123 Taylor.
Ehrmann C Frederick, collarmaker Aime Racine, res 36 E 4th.
Ehrmann Henry, teamster, res 153 Taylor.
Ehrmann Louisa, bds 339 W Jefferson.
Ehrmann Michael, laborer, res 24 Hoffman.
Ehrmann Minnie, bds 339 W Jefferson.
Eichel Andrew, brewer C L Centlivre, res 50 Randolph.
Eichel Charles, cook Edwin Rich, res 497 E Wayne.
Eichel John, cook, res 497 E Wayne.
Eichelberger Samuel, laborer Penn Co, res 143 Taber.
Eicher George, brakeman, rms 151 Holman.
Eicher Gottlieb, res 108 Hoffman.
Eickhoff Bernard H, machinist Fort Wayne Electric Co, res 72 W 4th.
Eickhoff Charles A, foreman Fort Wayne Electric Co, res 270 Webster.
Eickmeyer Charles L, car builder Penn Co, res 33 Duryea.
Eickstead Gustav, fireman, rms 366 W Main.
Eider August, coremaker Indiana Machine Works, res 22 John.
Eihl Christian, boilermkr, bds 21 Force.
Eihl Virgil, baker, res 21 Force.
Eikart Gustav, laborer American Wheel Co, res s e cor Thomas and Fisher.
Eiker Louis, laborer, bds rear 3 Oak.
Eikes Henry, helper Bass Foundry and Machine Works, res 58 Hayden.
Einsiedel Andrew, blacksmith Olds' Wagon Works, res 69 Stophlet.
Einsiedel Frederick, laborer Kerr-Murray Mnfg Co, res 69 Stophlet.
Einsiedel Michael, pipe liner Salimonic Mining and Gas Co, res 69 Stophlet.
Eisenhauer Andrew, watchmaker August Koenig, bds same.

John Pressler, Mantels, Grates and Tile Floor.
Columbia Barr and Dock Streets.

178   R. L. POLK & CO.'S

Eisenhut Wm, cigarmaker John Zern, bds 374 Calhoun.
Eisennacher Frederick, carpenter, res 197 Taylor.
Eising Henry, molder Bass Foundry and Machine Works, bds 73 Force.
Eising John, car builder Penn Co, res 73 Force.
Eising John, toolkeeper Kerr-Murray Mnfg Co, bds 73 Force.
Eising Maggie, operator, bds 73 Force.
Eising Mary, res 73 Force.
Eissensig Rev Thomas, chaplain St Joseph Hospital, res same.
Eiter Frank, molder Kerr-Murray Mnfg Co, bds 22 John.
Eiter Henry, molder Kerr-Murray Mnfg Co, res 37 Force.
Eiter Joseph, molder Bass Foundry and Machine Works, res 22 John.
Eiter Peter, laborer, res 22 John.
Eitzinger George, molder Bass Foundry and Machine Works, res w s Winter 2 s of Pontiac.
Eitzinger Rose (wid George), res w s Winter 2 s of Pontiac.
Eix August, helper Penn Co, res 81 Hayden.
Eix August F, blacksmith Frederick Roesener, res 191 Hanna.
Eix Ernest, hammerer, bds 197 Hanna.
Eix Frederick, laborer, res 60 W Washington.
Eix John, blacksmith helper Penn Co, bds 197 Hanna.
Eix Lottie, domestic 254 W Main.
Eix Sophia (wid August), bds 60 W Washington.
Eix Wm, laborer, res n e cor Spruce and Elm.
Elberson George, driver Ryan Bros, bds same.
Elbert Anthony, boilermaker, bds 40 Pritchard.
Elder Cynthia, seamstress, bds 138 Jackson.
Eldred Danford P, engineer, res 24 Baker.
Eldridge Carl W, bench hand Fort Wayne Electric Co, bds 219 W Main.
Eldridge Lotta, works Troy Steam Laundry, bds 15 Ross.
Eldridge Nettie, works Troy Steam Laundry, bds 15 Ross.
Elett John, carp Christian Doenges, bds 126 Maumee road.
Elion Charles J, molder Bass Foundry and Machine Works, res 55 Oliver.
Ell Adam J, polisher American Wheel Co, bds 22 Hough.
Ell Charles, laborer, res 22 Hough.
Ell Frederick G, laborer, rms 22 Hough.
Ellenwood Bertie A, bds 230 Francis.
Ellenwood Charles A, conductor Penn Co, res 134 E Lewis.
Ellenwood Cloyd C, helper Penn Co, bds 96 Laselle.
Ellenwood George W, laborer Penn Co, res 124 Harrison.
Ellenwood Horace D, engineer, res 230 Francis.
Ellenwood O Rodney, engineer, bds 185 Hanna.
Ellenwood Warren S, brakeman, bds 230 Francis.

Ellenwood Webster D, brakeman, bds 230 Francis.

Ellert Benoit (Walter & Ellert), res 135 Lafayette.

Elligsen Henry, tailor, res 19 Clark.

Elling Mary, domestic B J Trentman.

Elliott Enoch W (col'd), engineer The Peters Box and Lumber Co, res 153 High.

Elliott Fennimore F, mach hand, res 47 Buchanan.

Elliott Frank, laborer, bds 87 E Lewis.

Elliott Frederick H, clerk, res 127 N Cass.

Elliott Miss Leota M, clk Standard Medical and Surgical Institute, bds 57 Butler.

Elliott Loyal D, conductor, res 66 Boone.

Elliott Margaret J (wid George W), bds 66 Boone.

Elliott Nelson, caller, bds 57 Butler.

Elliott Samuel B, carpenter, res 57 Butler.

Ellis John F, cigarmkr, bds 148 Wells.

Ellis Robert H, carpenter, res 148 Wells.

Ellison George R, driver C J La Vanway, bds 320 E Jefferson.

Ellison Jacob L, carpenter, Park ave Lumbard's Park add.

Ellison John, bds Jacob L Ellison.

Ellison John S, laborer, bds 320 E Jefferson.

Ellison Richard, laborer, res 320 E Jefferson.

Ellison Thomas E, lawyer, 23 and 24 Bank block, res 167 W Wayne.

Elsner Albert, vegetables, market stand 68, res n s St Joseph road e of city limits.

Ely George W, commissioner fire dept, res 105 W Berry.

Emanuel German Lutheran School, n e cor Wilt and Union.

Emanuel Lutheran Church, s s W Jefferson bet Union and Jackson.

Embrey Anna G (wid Louis), res 336 Broadway.

Embrey Joseph, bds Charles H Titus.

Embry Edward, paperhanger The Siemon Wall Paper Co, rms 191 Calhoun.

Eme Claude F (Eme & Son), res 175 E Wayne.

Eme Constant J, fireman, res 40 St Mary's ave.

Eme Julius J (Eme & Son), res 93 Montgomery.

Eme Louis J, carp Nickel Plate, res s s Jesse e of Runnion.

Eme & Son (Claude F and Julius J), Real Estate, Insurance, Loans and House Renting, Rooms 1 and 2 Foster Blk.

Emerick, *see also Emrich.*

Emerick August, watchman, res 46 Walton ave.

Emerick Dora, fireman, rms 34 W Main.

Emerick Emma, bds 46 Walton ave.

Emerick Frederick, section hand, bds 46 Walton ave.
Emerick Jacob, laborer American Wheel Co, res 38 Smith.
Emerick Kate, machine hand, bds 46 Walton ave.
Emerick Preston L, plasterer, res n s Prospect ave 8 e of Spy
Run ave.
Emly Frank, carpenter, bds 18 McClellan.
Emerson Almeron, driver, res 10 Highland.
Emerson Charlotte M, bds 10 Highland.
Emery Edward, paperhanger, rms 191 Calhoun.
Emery J Wesley (S B Thing & Co), res Troy, N Y.
Emme Wm, car builder Penn Co, res 141 Montgomery.
Emmer Frederick, bridge builder, res 136 Maumee road.
Emmons Charles, brakeman Nickel Plate, res 253 W Wayne.
Empire Box Factory, Wm H Davis Propr, Mnfr of
All Kinds of Pasteboard, Shelf and Cigar Boxes, 3d floor
Bank Block.
Empire Flour Mills, John Orff Propr, near W Main
Street Bridge.
Empire Line (Fast Freight), Angus McPherson
Agent, 26 Court.
Emrich, *see also Emerick.*
Emrich Henry, laborer, res 183 Madison.
Emy Julius, carpenter, bds 91 E Washington.
Ench John, laborer, res 9 Caroline.
Ench John, laborer, bds 150 Suttenfield.
Ench Mathias, res 150 Suttenfield.
Euch Mathias jr, laborer, bds 150 Suttenfield.
Engel Mrs Virginia, works Indiana School for Feeble-Minded
Youth.
Engelbeck Augusta, domestic 24 E Washington.
Engelbrecht Henry, carpenter, res 32 Union.
Engelking Charles, clerk Gross & Pellens, bds 172 Ewing.
Engelking Eliza A (wid Henry D), res 172 Ewing.
Engelking Frederick, helper Penn Co, bds rear 100 W Jef-
ferson.
Engelking F Deidrich, coil winder Fort Wayne Electric Co,
res 100 W Jefferson.
Engelking Henry C, machine hand, res 1 St Mary's ave.
Engelking Louisa (wid Henry), res 125 High.
Engelking Sophia, domestic Montgomery Hamilton.
Engelking Wm H, clerk T D Gerow, bds 172 Ewing.
Enghausen August, laborer American Wheel Co, bds 58
Hayden.
Engine House No 1, n e cor Court and Berry.
Engine House No 2, s s Wallace 4 e of Lafayette.
Engle Alexander, res 287 W Main.

Engle Edward, apprentice J O Keller, bds 35 Taylor.

Engle Emma M, machine hand, bds 35 Taylor.

Engle Gertrude, operator S M Foster, bds 35 Taylor.

Engle John F, laborer Wm Moellering & Co, res w s Piqua ave near Rudisill ave.

Engle J Edward, machinist, bds 35 Taylor.

Engle Lena E, domestic J A Koebler.

Engle Seldon E, photographer M L Jones, res 231 E Wayne.

Engle Wm, cabinetmaker Fort Wayne Furniture Co, res 229 W De Wald.

Engle Wm, engineer, res 35 Taylor.

Englert Carrie, operator, bds 49 Taylor.

Englert George, cooper F X Brucker, bds e s Harrison 2 n of Jefferson.

Englert Lena, operator, bds 49 Taylor.

Englert Louisa (wid George), res 49 Taylor.

Englert Wm F, laborer Penn Co, bds 49 Taylor.

English Maggie, domestic County Jail.

English Wm H, brakeman Penn Co.

Enright Mary, clerk J B White, bds 102 Webster.

Enslen Frank M, fireman, bds 493 Calhoun.

Enslen Wm M, physician, 286 Calhoun, rms same.

Ensley Ella (wid Albert), bds 26 E Columbia.

Entemann Christian, saloon, 13 E Main, res 149 W Berry.

Entradacher Sebastian, car builder Penn Co, res 72 Hayden.

Enz Albert, cooper, bds Washington House.

Enz Frederick J, laborer, res e s Winter 1 s of Pontiac.

Enz Wm H, laborer American Wheel Co, bds Frederick J Enz.

Epple Christian, laborer, res 40 Taylor.

Epple Gottlieb, res 188 Fairfield ave.

Epple Gottlieb jr, laborer, bds 188 Fairfield ave.

Epple Rosa (wid John), res 40 Allen.

Eppstein Babette (wid Maier), bds 54 W Berry.

Erb Henry, bds 56 Smith.

Erdel Emma, domestic John Orff.

Erdwin Paul, shoemaker Foellinger Bros, bds Riverside Hotel.

Erhardt Leonard, sausagemaker F Eckart, res 49 Pfeiffer ave.

Erickson Charles J E, cabinetmaker Fort Wayne Furniture Co, bds 43 Miner.

Erickson Edward, conductor Penn Co, res 335 S Harrison.

Erickson John E, foreman Fort Wayne Furniture Co, res 43 Miner.

Erion Jacob, coremaker Bass Foundry and Machine Works, res 228 John.

Erkell Wm, laborer Salimonie Mining and Gas Co, bds 98 Harrison.

Erlenbaugh Maude, domestic, 116 College.

Erlwein George, collarmaker, bds 27 N Cass.

Ernest Andrew, section hand, res 67 Grand.

Ernst Peter, coremaker Bass Foundry and Machine Works, res n s St Joseph road nr city limits.

Ernst Vina, cook Aldine Hotel.

Ernsting Charles H, res 16 Clark.

Ernsting Charles H, jr, grocer, 121 Wells, res same.

Ernsting Christian, helper Kerr-Murray Mnfg Co, bds 264 Webster.

Ersig Doretta (wid Wm), res 129 Monroe.

Ersig Miss Edith E, principal McCulloch School, bds 129 Monroe.

Ersig Miss Emma H, teacher Bloomingdale School, bds 129 Monroe.

Ersig Miss Kate A, bds 129 Monroe.

Ersig Wm A, horseshoer Gearey & Peney, res 123 Wilt.

Ersing J, car builder Penn Co, res 73 Force.

Ertel Bernard, res 39 Laselle.

Ertel Elizabeth (wid George), bds 36 John.

Ertel George, molder, res 53 John.

Ertel Louis, finisher White's Wheel Works, res 165 Erie.

Ertel Walter, laborer, res 85 Putnam.

Ertll Lizzie, bds 325 E Wayne.

Erwin, *see also Erwin and Irwin.*

Ervin Edward W, harnessmaker A L Johns & Co, bds 233 Wells.

Ervin John O, res 233 Wells.

Ervin Joseph F, mngr Fort Wayne Sentinel, res 202 W Wayne.

Ervin Wm H, student S B Hartman, bds 536 S Broadway.

Erwin, *see also Ervin and Irwin.*

Erwin Richard, carpenter, res s s Rebecca w of Runnion ave.

Esmond Block, 298 Calhoun.

Esmond Z Titus, gen sec Y M C A (R R dept), res 67 Brackenridge.

Esselstein Minerva (wid Levi), works Troy Steam Laundry, res 10 George.

Essick George, clerk, bds 91 E Washington.

Essier Melissa (wid Ives), bds 157 Wells.

Essig Adam P, res 39 E Superior.

Essig Charles O, res 163 E Washington.

Essig George, clk Indiana Installment Co, bds 152 Harrison.

Estry Albert G, conductor Penn Co, res 436 Broadway.

MILLINERY GOODS ——LATEST STYLES—— MRS. E. A. FLAGLER, 14 W. BERRY STREET.

FORT WAYNE DIRECTORY.   183

Estry Elwood T, conductor Penn Co, res s s Green 3 e of Thomas.

Etchel Clara M, domestic 60 E Main.

Etchey Frank, carpenter, res 37 Wefel.

Etchey Michael, clk F M Smith & Co, res 39 Wefel.

Etgen Daniel, bds 245 Clay.

Etgen Nicholas, res 245 Clay.

Etsoll Mary, dressmaker L A Worch, bds 173 W Jefferson.

Etzold Anna M, tailoress H C Meyer, bds 110 Webster.

Etzold Clara, tailoress John Rabus, bds 110 Webster.

Etzold Emma, bds 110 Webster.

Etzold Gustav, clerk, bds 46 Douglas ave.

Etzold Henry, shoemaker, 110 Webster, res same.

Etzold Minnie, bds 46 Douglas ave.

Etzold Paul W, bookkeeper, bds 46 Douglas ave.

Etzold Wm, grinder, res 46 Douglas ave.

Etzold Wm C, clerk Horton Mnfg Co, bds 110 Webster.

Eureka Hall, 43 W Superior.

Evangelical Association Church, n e cor Holman and Clinton.

Evangelical Lutheran German Church, s e cor Hanna and E Creighton ave.

Evangelical Lutheran Zion's Church and School, s w cor E Creghton ave and Force.

Evans Amos S, pres Hoosier Mnfg Co, res San Jose, Cal.

Evans Anna C (wid Josiah), res 241 S Webster.

Evans Bennett B, roof painter, res 66 W Main.

Evans Bertrand W, clerk, bds 241 S Webster.

Evans Block, s s Berry bet Calhoun and Clinton.

Evans Charles, machinist Kerr-Murray Mnfg Co, bds 43½ E Columbia.

Evans Edwin M, printer Archer, Housh & Co, bds 135 E Jefferson.

Evans Edwin, res 174 W Wayne.

Evans Edwin G, trav agt, bds 322 Fairfield ave.

Evans Frank D, clk Meyer & Niemenn, bds 162 E Jefferson.

Evans George P, sec Hoosier Mnfg Co, bds 126 E Main.

Evans Gertrude, clk Dozois, Beadell & Co, bds 174 W Wayne.

Evans Gordon M, clerk Ft W, C & L R R, bds 241 Webster.

Evans Ira P, clerk Rhinesmith & Simonson, res 109 W Washington.

Evans Irving D, draughtsman Kerr-Murray Mnfg Co, bds 241 Webster.

Evans Jenkins S, train dispatcher Nickel Plate Ry, res 157 E Berry.

Evans John M, clk Rhinesmith & Simonson, res 241 Webster.

Evans John P, treas Hoosier Mnfg Co, res 126 E Main.

Evans Miss Mary T, bds 174 W Wayne.
Evans Oliver F, bds 141 E Berry.
Evans Riley B, conductor, res 40 E Williams.
Evans Wm A, clk Carnahan & Co, bds 174 W Wayne.
Evarts Charles E, printer F R Barrows, bds 104 Wells.
Evarts Emma R, bds 104 Wells.
Evarts George C, candymaker B W Skelton, bds 104 Wells.
Evarts Nancy (wid Gilbert C), bds 104 Wells.
Evarts Sarah M (wid Gilbert C), bds 1 N Calhoun.
Evens Frank A, clk John Scheffer & Co, bds 135 E Jefferson.
Everets Edward, tel operator, bds Clifton House.
Everett Wm E, fireman, res 37 Marion.
Evers Avilla, domestic 279 Fairfield ave.
Evers Elizabeth (wid Henry), bds 73 Force.
Evers Henry, brick mason, res 199 John.
Evers John, bricklayer, bds 323 Hanna.
Evers Lizzie, bds 323 Hanna.
Everts Sarah M (wid Gilbert), bds 140 High.
Evry Miss Hannah E, asst Central Grammar School, bds 106 E Main.
Ewald Albert P, cratemkr Olds' Wagon Wks, bds 40 S Clay.
Ewell James A, printer Fort Wayne Journal, bds Custer House.
Ewing Aaron, laborer, res 19 Charles.
Ewing Block, s w cor Main and Harrison.
Ewing Mary C (wid George W), res 115 W Main.
Exner Robert, laborer, res 36 Chestnut.
Exchange The, Belger & Lennon Proprs, Sample and Lunch Room, 140 Calhoun.
Eyanson Miss Margaret F, bds 154 Griffith.

F

Fabian Adolph, carpenter, bds 112 Hanna.
Fabian Julius W, laborer, res 133 E Lewis.
Fahling, *see also Fehling.*
Fahling Christian, laborer, bds 45 Maumee rd.
Fabling Frederick, laborer, res 45 Maumee rd.
Fahling Frederick, teamster The Peters Box and Lumber Co, bds 8 Clark.
Fahling Henry C, carpenter, bds 45 Maumee rd.
Fahling Mary S, wrapper Summit City Soap Works, bds 45 Maumee rd.
Fahlsing Anna, milliner, bds W C F Fahlsing.
Fahlsing August K, boilermaker Fort Wayne Iron Works, res 87 Barthold.

Fahlsing Charles W, clk L Wolf & Co, bds 254 E Washington.
Fahlsing Charles W, clk D C Fisher, bds Wm C F Fahlsing.
Fahlsing Christina (wid Frederick), bds 87 Barthold.
Fahlsing Frederick, helper Olds' Wagon Works, res 9 Sturgis.
Fahlsing John W, apprentice M L Frankenstein, bds 9 Sturgis.
Fahlsing Minnie, wks Telephone Exchange, bds W C F Fahlsing.
Fahlsing Wm, clerk Riverside Hotel, res 108 Clinton.
Fahlsing Wm C F, bailiff circuit court, res e s Spy Run ave 3 n of Riverside ave.
Fahnestock James W, bookkeeper The Wayne, res 169 W Jefferson.
Failour Jacob, laborer, bds 109 E Creighton ave.
Fair Joseph, laborer, bds George Warner.
Fair The, E Shuman & Sons Proprs, 41 and 43 E Main.
Fairbank Clark, genl agent Penn Mutual Life Ins Co, 19 Court, res 115 E Berry.
Fairchild Fannie (wid George), shirtmaker P G Kuttner.
Fairfield Cyrus K, real estate, 7–9 Bell ave, res same.
Fairfield George, machinist Indiana Machine Works, bds 309 W Jefferson.
Fakar Mary, domestic 289 W Wayne.
Falconer John, blacksmith Kerr-Murray Mnfg Co, res 71 W Williams.
Falconer Richard, machinist Wabash R R, bds 71 W Williams.
Falk Charles (Charles Falk & Co), bds 80 W Washington.
Falk Charles & Co (Charles Falk), whol notions, 23 W Main.
Falk Leopold (Falk & Lamley), res 80 W Washington.
Falk & Lamley (Leopold Falk, Moses Lamley), liquors, 17 E Columbia.
Fallon Mary (wid John), res 237 Clay.
Fallon Peter J, clerk N Y, C & St L R R, bds 23 W Lewis.
Falls David M, tallow renderer, e end Dwenger ave 1 mile e of limits, res 163 W Wayne.
Falls Miss Olive M, bds 163 W Wayne.
Fally Wm W, engineer, res 66 Elm.
Falvy Daniel, res 285 W Main.
Fang J Frank, laborer Bass Foundry and Machine Works, res 68 Smith.
Fankhouser Andrew, lab, res s s Wayne Trace 3 e of Walton.
Farber N, laborer Penn Co, res 186 Taylor.
Fark Edward, car builder Penn Co, res 74 John.
Farland Albert C, conductor, bds 40 E 5th.
Farnan Miss Anna E, teacher Hoagland School, bds 305 Lafayette.

Farnan Owen, watchman Nickel Plate, res 305 Lafayette.
Farnan Owen, heater Bass Foundry and Machine Works, res 15 Caroline.
Farra Joseph C, lab Louis Diether & Bro, bds 21 Wagener.
Farrell John Z, mason, res 15 McLaughlin.
Farrell Richard, rms 38 Brackenridge.
Farrell Thomas, engineer, bds Lake Shore Hotel.
Farrell Wm T, stone cutter Wm & J J Geake, res 126 W Main.
Farrington David A, clerk The Wayne, bds same.
Farris, see also Ferris.
Farris Warren, engineer, res 120 Union.
Faulkner, see Falconer.
Faust Adam, res 5 Union.
Faust Henry, bartender J G Strodel, rms 54 E Main.
Faust Max, printer Freie Presse, bds 5 Hood.
Favery Kate, dressmaker Mrs G J Stier, bds 92 Madison.
Fay, see also Fey.
Fay John, switchman, bds 18 McClellan.
Fay Montford W, broker, bds Aveline House.
Fay Stephen, laborer, bds 10 Ewing.
Fears Henry B (col'd), laborer, res 29 Pearl.
Feasor Amos, hostler J F Fletcher, res 60 Riverside ave.
Fee Frank F, lumber, 181 W Wayne, res same.
Fee Thomas W, finisher The Peters Box and Lumber Co, res 57 N Cass.
Feeny John H, tinsmith C F Graffe & Co, res 127 Harrison.
Fehling, see also Fahling.
Fehling August, brick mason, res 13 Wall.
Fehling Frederick H (Freese & Fehling), res 33 Duryea.
Feighner George W, photographer B A Strawn, bds 150 Broadway.
Feipel Frank, laborer, res 164 Harmer.
Feist Kate, domestic 30 Madison.
Feist Louis J, tailor, 226 Lafayette, res same.
Feistkorn Charles, clerk Foster Furniture Co, res 8 Erie.
Felger Delia, operator S M Foster, bds 490 E Washington.
Felker Edward, driver Baals & Co, bds 94 W Main.
Felker Elizabeth (wid Peter), res 173 W Jefferson.
Felker Forest J, stone mason, res rear 73 High.
Felker Lizzie, bds 315 W Jefferson.
Felon Peter J, bookkeeper, rms 23 W Lewis.
Felt Frank A, teamster, res n e cor Lafayette and 7th.
Felt John, painter E P Nestel, bds 206 Francis.
Felt Warren B, teamster, res 68 Putnam.
Felts Charles E, painter, res 23 Erie.

Stahn & Heinrich, Leading Dealers in ARTISTS' MATE-RIALS AND DRAUGHTING INSTRU-MENTS. 116 Calhoun Street.

FORT WAYNE DIRECTORY.   187

Felts George F, county supt of schools, office rooms 7 and 8 Trentman building, res s e cor Loree and Lake ave.

Felts Herman W, foreman, res 60 Pontiac.

Felts Lena, seamstress, res 146 E Jefferson.

Fenker Herman, car builder Penn Co, res 340 E Wayne.

Fenker R G, car builder Penn Co, res New Haven ave.

Fenson Walter, machinist, bds 164 Brackenridge.

Fenton Miss Kate, tel opr Penn depot, bds 35 Douglas ave.

Ferber Henry, carpenter Frederick Kraft, res 269 E Lewis.

Ferch Christina, bds 205 Broadway.

Ferch Henry, res 205 Broadway.

Ferckel Adam, wheel molder Bass Foundry and Machine Works, res 224 John.

Ferckel Bertha, teacher, bds 31 Clinton.

Ferckel Emma, trimmer Eleanor Kratzch, bds 31 Clinton.

Ferckel John, bds 224 John.

Ferckel Martin, saloon, 31 Clinton, res same.

Ferckel Martin J, harnessmkr A L Johns & Co, bds 31 Clinton.

Ferckel Mary, domestic 246 S Hoagland ave.

Ferckel Tillie L, bookkeeper G K Hubbard, bds 31 Clinton.

Ferguson Mrs Anna J, dressmaker, 289 W Washington, res same.

Ferguson Charles D, driver Bass Foundry and Machine Works, res 15 Smith.

Ferguson Miss Cora M, bds 203 W Berry.

Ferguson George, machine hand Fort Wayne Organ Co, bds 105 Fairfield ave.

Ferguson John, plasterer, bds 57 Barr.

Ferguson John, res 203 W Berry.

Ferguson John K, bds 203 W Berry.

Ferguson John T, printer Ft Wayne Gazette, res 213 Madison

Ferguson Joseph E, painter, res 62 E Main.

Ferguson Miss Lida K, bds 203 W Berry.

Ferguson Miss Minnie E, bds 203 W Berry.

Ferguson Samuel T, brakeman, res 350 W Washington.

Ferguson Wm G, student, bds 82 W Berry.

Ferguson Wm H, music teacher, 851 Broadway, bds same.

Ferguson Wm T, Physician; Diseases of Women and Diseases of the Kidneys; Office Hours 9 to 10 a m and 1 to 2 p m, 82 W Berry, res same.

Ferks Albert, laborer Hoffman Bros, res 152 Greeley.

Ferris, *see also Farris.*

Ferris Ezekiel M, res 28 Wilt.

Ferris Frank C, brakeman, res 111 John.

Ferris Jennie, laundress Aldine Hotel.

Ferry Caroline P (wid Lucian P), res 119 W Washington.

Fessenden Charles E, clerk McDonald, Watt & Wilt, res 150,
    W Jefferson.
Fessenden Frederick, printer Fort Wayne Sentinel, bds 128
    Calhoun.
Fessenden Sylvanus C, carpenter, res 128 Calhoun.
Fessenden Mrs S C, dressmaker, 128 Calhoun, res same.
Fetters Martin, saw filer American Wheel Co, res 37 Maumee
Fetters Mary (wid John), bds 37 Maumee rd.
Fetters Wm, laborer White's Wheel Works, res 12 Oak.
Fetters Wm H, machinist White's Wheel Wks, res 12 Oak.
Feulner Anthony, hub inspector American Wheel Co, bds 33
    Laselle.
Feulner Eva, bds 33 Laselle.
Feulner Margaret (wid Frank), res 33 Laselle.
Feustel August F, gardener, res s s Elizabeth 1 w of Spy
    Run ave.
Feustel Edward L, clerk C H Currier, bds 21 Elizabeth.
Feustel Henry, gardener A F Feustel, bds same.
Feutz Peter, laborer, bds 46 E Columbia.
Fey, see also Fay.
Fey Conrad, bds 55 W Wayne.
Fey J, laborer Penn Co, res 317 Hanna.
Fichter Jacob, carpenter, bds 101 Taylor.
Fickel George W, clerk Penn Co, res 153 Harrison.
Fickes Mary E, res 97 Pearl.
Fidelity Mutual Life Association, J L Ball general agent, 7
    Schmitz block.
Fiedler Charles, laborer Olds' Wagon Works, res n w cor
    Winter and Creighton ave.
Fiedler Ella, domestic 204 Berry.
Fiedler Emil, janitor Concordia College, bds A Aehnelt.
Fiedler Emil, Olds' Wagon Works, bds Charles Fiedler.
Fiedler Joseph, candymaker Wm C Seidel & Bro, rms 52½
    Calhoun.
Fiedler Wm, laborer, Bass Foundry and Machine Works, res
    6 Force.
Fiegel Charles, laborer C L Centlivre, res Centlivre's Park.
Fields James S, agent Brickmakers' Association, bds 19 W
    Jefferson.
Fields Joseph W, cigarmaker H W Ortmann, bds 19 W Jef-
    ferson.
Figel Charles C, res n e cor Oakland and Aboit.
Figel Edward, wiper Ft W, C & L R R shop, res 20 W 4th.
Figel Frederick C, clerk Robert Figel, bds 121 Wells.
Figel Henry W, teamster The Herman Berghoff Brewing Co,
    res 53 Wabash ave.

Figel John C, grocer, 54 Wells, res same.
Figel Robert, grocer, 53 Wells, res same.
Figel Wm, tailor, res 89 Maumee road.
Fike Cyrus, collector Fort Wayne Transfer and Baggage
   Line, bds Windsor Hotel.
Filley Julia (wid Robert), rms 196 E Jefferson.
Filley Miss Nettie, rms 196 E Jefferson.
Findorff Henry, locksmith, bds Catherine Strodel.
Fink August, laborer, bds 13 Baker.
Fink Conrad, farmer, near n e cor Pontiac and Walton ave.
Fink Delia, seamstress, bds 29 Buchanan.
Fink Edward, res 109 Madison.
Fink Elenora T, boxmaker Davis & Bro, bds 176 E Jefferson.
Fink Frank H, foreman Bass Foundry and Machine Works,
   res 176 E Jefferson.
Fink Frederick, laborer Penn Co, bds 138 Fairfield ave.
Fink Frederick H, laborer Penn Co, bds 138 Fairfield ave.
Fink George B, flagman Penn Co, res 212 Walton ave.
Fink John B, barber, 56 E Main, rms same.
Fink John H, laborer Ranke & Yergers, res 138 Fairfield ave.
Fink May E, boxmaker Davis & Bro, bds 176 E Jefferson.
Fink Wilfred C, teamster, bds 37 Buchanan.
Fink Wm F, mason, res 21 Winch.
Finker Rudolph, car builder Penn Co, res New Haven ave.
Finkhouse Frederick, brakeman, bds Jewel House.
Finleyson John L, bartender Joseph Baum, bds 153 Madison.
Finn Miss Mary, bds 39 W Washington.
Finnell Miss Priscilla, stenographer The Remington-Lawton
   Co, bds 108 E Berry.
Finney Austin M, printer Fort Wayne Journal, bds 18 Melita.
Finney James A, conductor Penn Co, bds 135 Holman.
Finney Michael A, blacksmith Wabash R R, res 18 Melita.
Finze Christian, bartender F W A Hollenbeck, res 273 Web-
   ster.
Fireman's Insurance Co, Dayton, Ohio, Edward
   Seidel Agent, 52½ Calhoun.
Firgusson Elmer E, laborer, bds 224 Hugh.
Firgusson James, blacksmith, res 224 Hugh.
Firgusson Walter O, laborer, bds 224 Hugh.
Firks Albert, laborer Hoffman Bros, res 152 Greely.
Firks Frederick, laborer Hoffman Bros, res 100 Mechanic.
First Baptist Church, n s W Jefferson near Harrison.
First Light Artillery Band, H Achenbach leader, 64 E Main.
First National Bank, John H Bass Pres, M W Sim-
   ons Vice-Pres, Lem R Hartman Cashier, Wm L Pettit
   Asst Cashier, s e cor Main and Court.

Robert Spice, Waterworks and General Plumbing.
48 West Main and 11 Pearl Streets.

190 R. L. POLK & CO.'S

First Presbyterian Church, n e cor Clinton and E Washington.
First Regiment Band, Harry Achenbach leader, 212 Calhoun.
First United Brethren Church, s e cor Harmer and Lewis.
Firth Frederick, agent R L Polk & Co, res 248 Erie.
Fischer Anna C, bds 85 E Berry.
Fischer Anthony, blacksmith Penn Co, res 483 Fairfield ave.
Fischer Anthony jr, blacksmith Penn Co, bds 483 Fairfield.
Fischer C F, Adolph, bds C F W Meyer.
Fischer Frank, brass molder Fort Wayne Electric Co, bds 51 Home ave.
Fischer Frederick, laborer, bds 483 Fairfield ave.
Fischer Henry E, county surveyor, rms 96 Barr.
Fischer Herman E, clerk J B White, res 182 W Creighton av.
Fischer Miss Hermione, stenographer, bds 182 W Creighton ave.
Fischer John, laborer, bds 65 Charles.
Fischer Lizzie D, converter worker Fort Wayne Electric Co, bds 85 E Berry.
Fischer Michael, res 85 E Berry.
Fischer Otto, fireman, res w s Winter 2 n of Pontiac.
Fisher Abel, foreman Penn Co, res s s New Haven Road 2 e of toll gate.
Fisher Annie (wid Frederick), res 65 Charles.
Fisher Benjamin F, trav agent, res 289 W Washington.
Fisher Benjamin J, painter, bds 131 W Washington.
Fisher Bettie I (wid Isaac), res 133 W Washington.
Fisher Bros (Samuel S and Max B), paper, 23 E Columbia.
Fisher Christian, helper Penn Co, bds 49 Hugh.
Fisher David C, Real Estate, Loans, Insurance, Notary Public, 32 E Berry, res 24 W Wayne.
Fisher Edwin, trav salesman, bds 133 W Washington.
Fisher Miss Ellen C, bds 131 W Washington.
Fisher Frederick, machinist, res 126 Hoagland ave.
Fisher George H, carpenter Louis Diether & Bro, res 131 W Washington.
Fisher Miss Henrietta, bds 131 W Washington.
Fisher Jacob, tinsmith, res 125 Fairfield ave.
Fisher Jacob jr, baker Louis Fox & Bro, bds 125 Fairfield ave.
Fisher John, section hand, res rear 419 W Main.
Fisher Jonathan H, machinist Penn Co, res 127 Monroe.
Fisher Max B (Fisher Bros), res 79 Griffith.
Fisher Moses P, bookkeeper Fisher Bros, bds 133 W Washington.
Fisher Miss N, draughtsman Kerr-Murray Mnfg Co, bds 182 W Creighton ave.

Sewing Machines, Shears ⎱ Pfeiffer & Schlatter
— and Pocket Knives, — ⎰ 38 & 40 E. Columbia.

FORT WAYNE DIRECTORY. 191

Fisher Robertson J, treas Bass Foundry and Machine.Works, res 151 W Berry.

Fisher Samuel S (Fisher Bros), res 24 W Washington.

Fisher Walter, laborer Penn Co, bds Abel Fisher.

Fisk Wm W, clerk J M Miller, res 217 W DeWald.

Fissel George J, clerk, bds 61 Pfeiffer ave.

Fissel Philip, driver J M Miller, res 61 Pfeiffer ave.

Fitch Charles B, purchasing agt Fort Wayne Electric Co, res 52 Brackenridge.

Fitch Clarence M, laborer Penn Co, bds 83 Buchanan.

Fitch Herbert O, conductor, res 178 Wells.

Fitch Mary E (wid Nathaniel H), res 83 Buchanan.

Fitch Nathaniel H, watchman Penn Co, res 75 Douglas ave.

Fitch Otis B, shoes 52 Calhoun, res 407 same.

Fitch Steward E, machine hand, bds 178 Wells.

Fitzgerald Bridget, dressmaker, 27 W Columbia, bds same.

Fitzgerald Mrs Ellen, employment office and boarding house, 39 W Washington, res same.

Fitzgerald Francis, salesman, res 408 W Main.

Fitzgerald Laura E, wks Ft Wayne Electric Co, bds 42 Melita.

Fitzgerald Wm T, office boy The Press, bds 408 W Main.

Fitzgibbons Margaret (wid Michael), res rear 94 Baker.

Fitzhugh G, lab Penn Co, res cor Dubois and Maumee rd.

Fitzpatrick Bernard, machinist, res 241 E Lewis.

Fitzpatrick John, watchman, res 42 Bass.

Fitzpatrick Maggie, clerk Dozois, Beadell & Co, bds 46 Bass.

Fitzpatrick Michael, boarding house, 12 Chicago.

Fitzpatrick Thomas, machine hand American Wheel Co, bds 12 Chicago.

Fitzsimons Arthur, bkkpr Fleming Mnfg Co, bds 138 Wells.

Flachman Mrs Anna, bds 152 Ewing.

Flack, *see also Flock*.

Flack Cyrus I, carriagemkr M L Albrecht, res 315 Harrison.

Flagle Milton G, engineer, res 41 E 3d.

Flagler Mrs E A, Milliner; Agent for The Old Staten Island Dyeing Establishment, 14 W Berry, res same. (*See right top lines.*)

Flaig Engelbert, laborer Penn Co, res 172 Smith.

Flaig George J, laborer Penn Co), res 36 Miner.

Fleckenstein Elizabeth (wid Henry), res 74 Barr.

Fleckenstein Henry E, brass molder Fort Wayne Electric Co, bds 21 Pine.

Fleddermann Mary E (wid John G), res 185 E Jefferson.

Fleiger, *see Flieger and Pfleger*.

Fleischmann C Frederick, wheel molder Bass Foundry and Machine Works, res 2 Holton ave.

Fleischmann Eva D (wid Henry), res 30 Hoffman.

Fleischmann John B, helper Fort Wayne Iron Works, res 58 Wells.

Fleischmann John M, blacksmith Fleming Mnfg Co, res rear 10 Short.

Fleischmann & Co, Louis Fox & Bro agents, compressed yeast, n e cor Calhoun and Jefferson.

Fleming Block, e s Calhoun bet Washington and Jefferson.

Fleming Miss Celeste, bds 261 W Berry.

Fleming Harry D, printer The Press, rms 128 Lafayette.

Fleming Helen (wid Wm), res 261 W Berry.

Fleming James W, res 61 N Cass.

Fleming James W jr, clerk T J Fleming, bds 61 Cass.

Fleming Miss Josephine, bds 261 W Berry.

Fleming Mnfg Co (Charles Pape), Mnfrs Road Levelers and Graders, 78 High. (*See adv, p 6.*)

Fleming Miss Minnie, bds Aveline House.

Fleming Ollabell, clerk, bds 61 N Cass.

Fleming Robert, barber Alfred Bass, bds 32 E Columbia.

Fleming Stephen, bds 261 W Berry.

Fleming Thomas, stonecutter George Jaap, res Goshen road.

Fleming Thornton J, Dry Goods, Notions, Boots, Shoes, Hats, Caps, Gents' Furnishing Goods, Glass and Queensware, 25 Calhoun, bds 61 Cass.

Fleming Wm, fireman, bds 238 W Wayne.

Fleming Wm H (Rockhill Bros & Fleming), res 106 W Berry.

Fleminheischer Thomas, brakeman, res s e cor Winter and Edgerton.

Flemming Miss Erin, teacher Indiana School for Feeble-Minded Youth.

Fletcher Charles P & Jennie, proprs Geary's Museum, n s E Berry bet Clinton and Barr.

Fletcher Charles P, res 124 E Berry.

Fletcher Josiah F, Livery, 32 Barr, res 48 same. (*See adv, p 65.*)

Fletcher J Thomas (col'd), brakeman Penn Co, rms 72 Murray.

Fletcher Margaret A, dressmaker, 48 Barr, res same.

Fletcher Stephen, policeman, res 89 Erie.

Fletter Charles H, brakeman, res 58 Oliver.

Fletter Henry A, carpenter, res 101 Taylor.

Fletter Nancy M, bds 168 Hanna.

Fletter Wm S, boarding, 182 E Jefferson.

Flick Clara B, florist, bds 132 Thompson ave.

Flick George W, Florist, Propr Chestnut Slope Greenhouses, South Wayne, 132 Thompson ave, res same.

Flickinger John W, painter, res 400 W Main.
Flinn Charles M (Flinn & Jackson), res 11 N Cass.
Flinn Theodore, blacksmith Flinn & Jackson, bds 116 W Williams.
Flinn & Jackson (Charles M Flinn, John Jackson), blacksmiths, 81 E Columbia.
Flochmann Miss Anna, bds 152 Ewing.
Flock, *see also Flack.*
Flock Daniel J, coppersmith, res 182 E Lewis.
Flock Harry, clerk, bds 182 E Lewis.
Flood Luke J, pipe liner Salimonie Mining & Gas Co, bds 55 Barr.
Florence Thomas, gardener Frederick Nursery, res same.
Flowers Frank, brakeman, bds 53 Taylor.
Floxant Charles, laborer, res 206 Broadway.
Flynn Anthony, trav agent, res 164 Hayden.
Flynn Peter, conductor Nickel Plate, res 94 W Superior.
Foellinger Adolph G, bds 441 Fairfield ave.
Foellinger Augusta, clerk Foellinger Bros, bds 126 Harrison.
Foellinger Bros (Jacob Jr, Martin C and Louis F), Boot and Shoe Mnfrs, 36 Calhoun, 3d and 4th Floors.
Foellinger Jacob, farmer, res 441 Fairfield ave.
Foellinger Jacob jr (Foellinger Bros), res 36 Calhoun.
Foellinger Louis F (Foellinger Bros), res 126 Harrison.
Foellinger Martin C (Foellinger Bros), res 126 Harrison.
Foellinger's Block, 34 and 36 Calhoun.
Foernier Louis, machine hand American Wheel Co, bds 13 Furman.
Foerster Conrad, foreman White's Wheel Works, res 581 E Washington.
Foerster Henry, foreman White's Wheel Works, res 579 E Washington.
Folers Henry C, matcher Ranke & Yergens, res 63 E Superior.
Foley Miss Bridget, bds 236 W Jefferson.
Foley Miss Cecelia, tchr Hanna School, bds 236 W Jefferson.
Foley Hanorah (wid Patrick), bds 70 Chicago.
Foley Miss Jane, dressmaker, bds 236 W Jefferson.
Foley Jeremiah, laborer, res 48 Chicago.
Foley Jeremiah J, finisher Fort Wayne Organ Co, bds 48 Chicago.
Foley Jerry, driver Wm H Bassett & Son, bds same.
Foley John, watchman, res 236 W Jefferson.
Foley John W, carpenter, res 252 E Lewis.
Foley Miss Julia, bds 236 W Jefferson.
Foley Laura, bds 252 E Lewis.
Foley Mary, laundress Rich's Hotel, bds same.

John Pressler, Galvanized Iron Cornices and Slate Roofing
Columbia, Barr and Dock Streets.

194   R. L. POLK & CO.'S

Foley Thomas J, dispatcher Penn Co, res 236 W Jefferson.
Foley Timothy, laborer, bds 48 Chicago.
Foley Timothy, machinist Bass Foundry and Machine Works,
    bds Darrow House.
Foley Timothy, wiper Penn Co, res 11 Walnut.
Foley Wm, laborer, bds 48 Chicago.
Foltz James H, laborer, bds 73 Melita.
Foltz Samuel, carpenter, res 73 Melita.
Foncannon Oliver, yard foreman White's Wheel Works, res
    104 Glasgow ave.
Foncannon Oliver P, paperhanger Renner, Cratsley & Co,
    rms 37 W Berry.
Fonner Hiram J, stenographer, bds 238 W Wayne.
Fonner J Bernard, stenogr Bell & Morris, rms 159 Harrison.
Fontaine Louis D, clerk Dozois, Beadell & Co, rms 146 E
    Wayne.
Foote Mrs Helen, res 229 W Jefferson.
Forbing Gertrude (wid Michael), bds 366 Hanna.
Forbing John, real estate, 28 Bank block, res 385 Hanna.
Forche Joseph, carpenter Ft W, C & L R R, bds 121 Calhoun.
Ford Andrew J, engineer, res 109 Wallace.
Ford Blanche, bds 109 Wallace.
Ford John, laborer Penn Co, res 109 Wallace.
Ford John M, laborer Penn Co, res 109 Wallace.
Ford Wm O, foreman S M Foster, res 201 E Jefferson.
Fordham Martin E, barber, bds 248 Calhoun.
Fordmier Frederick, teamster Wm Moellering & Co, bds
    Henry Fritcha.
Fordney Alberta, tailoress John Rabus, bds 197 Montgomery.
Fordney Bessie, bds 197 Montgomery.
Fordney George M, wheel molder Bass Foundry and
    Machine Works, res 197 Montgomery.
Fordney Georgia, works Fort Wayne Electric Co, bds 197
    Montgomery.
Fordney Michael, molder, res 197 Montgomery.
Foreman Charles E, clerk, rms 35 W Main.
Forest Samuel, bds 64 W Wayne.
Forkes Caroline, domestic 287 Hanna.
Forks August, machine hand American Wheel Co, res 74
    John.
Forks Edward, machine hand, bds 74 John.
Forrest Joseph E, brakeman, res 65 Boone.
Fortriede Louis, Boots and Shoes, 19 Calhoun, res
    212 E Wayne.
Fort Wayne Advertising Co, Clarence G Smith mngr, 55 and
    57 E Columbia.

Fort Wayne Ale House, John Christian propr, 100 Calhoun.

Fort Wayne Artificial Ice Co, Berghoff & Rothschild Proprs, cor Wells and Cass, near Lake Shore Depot.

Fort Wayne Beef Co, 4 and 6 Calhoun.

Fort Wayne Bicycle Club, Frank Lightfoot capt, John Hanna sec, 142 Calhoun.

Fort Wayne Bottling Works, Fremion & Vollmer proprs, 9 N Harrison.

Fort Wayne Brass Works, A Hattersley & Sons Proprs, 48 E Main. (*See embossed line front cover.*)

Fort Wayne Business Men's Exchange, John B Monning pres, W D Page vice-pres, A J Moynihan sec, A S Lauferty treas, 98 Calhoun.

Fort Wayne Carpet Beating Works, Paul E Wolf Propr, 33 and 35 Clinton.

Fort Wayne Catholic Circulating Library and Association, n e cor Calhoun and E Lewis.

Fort Wayne, Cincinnati and Louisville Railway, Office and Depot, 1st near Wells. (*See p opp inside back cover.*)

Fort Wayne City Band, Philip Keinz leader, 12 W Main.

Fort Wayne City Bill Posting Co, C B Woodworth pres, H J Seibold sec-treas, G C Richard supt, 1 Aveline House block.

Fort Wayne City Directory, R L Polk & Co Publrs, 50 Calhoun.

Fort Wayne City Hospital, Mrs C L Smith supt, s w cor Washington and Barr.

Fort Wayne City Truck Co (Ryan Bros), 17 W Washington.

Fort Wayne College of Medicine, medical department of Taylor University, C B Stemen, M D, dean, W P Whery, M D, sec, foot of Wayne.

Fort Wayne Conservatory of Music, C F W Meyer Director, Bank Block, 22–24–26 E Main.

Fort Wayne Dispatch (weekly), James Mitchel propr, 24 Clinton.

Fort Wayne Electric Co, H G Olds Pres, R T McDonald Treas and Genl Mngr, Brainard Rorison Sec, Mnfrs Dynamo Electric Machines, Lamps and Motors, Broadway and P, Ft W & C Ry.

Fort Wayne Freie Presse (daily), Otto F Cummerow propr, n e cor Calhoun and Main.

Fort Wayne Furniture Co The, D N Foster pres and mngr, P A Randall vice-pres, W E Mossman sec, D B Kehler treas, mnfrs of folding beds, e end of E Columbia.

Fort Wayne Gas Light Co, James Cheney pres and treas, Wm J Probasco sec, s e cor Superior and Barr.

Fort Wayne Gazette (Daily and Weekly), N. R Leonard Propr, 41 E Berry.

Fort Wayne Iron Works, Mnfrs Engines, Boilers and Band Saw Mills, Office and Works s e cor Superior and Harrison.

Fort Wayne Journal (daily and weekly), Journal Co proprs, 30 E Main.

Fort Wayne Journal of Medical Science, Christian B Stemen editor and publr, 74 Calhoun.

Fort Wayne Land Improvement Co, D N Foster pres, P A Randall vice-pres, C A Wilding sec, George W Pixley treas, 12 Pixley & Long bldg.

Fort Wayne Lumber Co, Augustus C Beaver genl mngr, office and yard 106 W Main and 796 S Broadway.

Fort Wayne Music Co, Harry Achenbach Mngr, Band and Orchestra Instruments, Sheet Music and Musical Merchandise of all Kinds, 212 Calhoun.

Fort Wayne News (Daily and Weekly), Wm D Page Propr, 19 E Main.

Fort Wayne Newspaper Union (Eastern Branch Chicago Newspaper Union), John F Cramer Pres, Charles E Strong Treas, Charles D Tillo Resident Mngr, Ready Print Publishers and Paper Dealers, Printers' Supplies, Etc, 55 and 57 E Columbia.

Fort Wayne Organ Co, S B Bond Pres, Charles E Bond Sec, A S Bond Treas and Supt, Office and Factory e s Fairfield ave ½ Mile s of City Limits.

Fort Wayne Saengerbund Hall, 54 E Main.

Fort Wayne Safety Valve Works, E B Kunkle & Co Proprs, 87 Barr.

Fort Wayne Sentinel (Daily and Weekly), E A K Hackett Propr, 107 Calhoun.

Fort Wayne Soap Works, Jacob M Keyser propr, 91, 93 and 95 Glasgow ave.

Fort Wayne Spice Mills, H B Monning & Co proprs, 75 E Columbia.

Fort Wayne Steam Stone Works, Keller & Braun Proprs, 86 to 98 Pearl. (*See adv, p 7.*)

Fort Wayne Street Railroad Co, J H Bass Pres, S B Bond Vice-Pres, J M Barrett Sec, A S Bond Treas, L D McNutt Supt, Office s w cor Main and Calhoun.

Fort Wayne Street Railroad Stables, cor Glasgow ave and E Washington.

Fort Wayne Transfer and Baggage Line, Powers & Barnett Proprs, 16 to 24 E Wayne.

Fort Wayne Transfer and Storage Co, James Wilding Pres, F M McCarthy Sec, Treas and Genl Mngr, 47 E Columbia.

Fort Wayne Water Works, P J McDonald sec, office 68 Barr.

Fort Wayne Weekly Dispatch, James Mitchell editor and propr, 24 Clinton.

Foster Andrew, Merchant Tailor, 15 W Wayne, res 150 Griffith. (*See left top lines.*)

Foster Asa, car builder Penn Co, res 33 W Williams.

Foster's Block, e s Court nr Main.

Foster Burton, printer, bds 46 E Jefferson.

Foster Catherine P, clerk, bds 247 Lewis.

Foster Charlotte (wid James), res 443 Lafayette.

Foster David N, pres D N Foster Furniture Co and Fort Wayne Furniture Co, res 98 E Berry.

Foster D N Furniture Co, David N Foster Pres, S M Foster Sec, Wm J Kettler Treas, Furniture and Carpets, 11 and 13 Court.

Foster Frederick W, blacksmith, bds 292 E Lewis.

Foster George, packer Fort Wayne Organ Co, res 131 E De-Wald.

Foster Harry A, despatcher Penn Co, res 433 Lafayette.

Foster James A, machinist Penn Co, bds 443 Lafayette.

Foster John B, printer Fort Wayne Sentinel, bds 46 E Jefferson.

Foster Miss Kate P, clerk S W Hull, res 4 McClellan.

Foster Lydia (wid Wm T), res 292 E Lewis.

Foster Nathaniel H, clerk Penn Co, bds 292 E Lewis.

Foster N F Charles, painter Olds' Wagon Works, res 54 Hamilton.

Foster Sadie M, bds 292 E Lewis.

Foster Samuel M, mnfr shirts and shirt waists, n end Lafayette, and sec of D N Foster Furniture Co, res 96 E Berry.

Foster Wm M, tel opr, bds 443 Lafayette.

Fought Anna, bds 23 W Lewis.

Foulks Norve P, foreman B W Skelton, res 45 W Main.

Fournier Frank E, molder Bass Foundry and Machine Works, bds 13 Purman.

Fournier Frank J, laborer, bds 13 Purman.

Fournier Frank W, res 13 Purman.

Fowler Clarence C, brakeman Penn Co, bds 16 Colerick.

Fowler Josephine, converter worker Fort Wayne Electric Co, bds 17 Bass.

Fowler Manufacturing Co, T J T Cumings mngr, 152 Calhoun.

Fowles John W, Merchant Tailor, Fashionable Tailoring, Moderate Prices, 64 Barr near Berry, res same.

Fox Albert, teamster J M Moderwell, bds 20 Huron.
Fox Albert L, car builder Penn Co, res 27 Baker.
Fox Amelia, domestic 25 E Main.
Fox August L (Louis Fox & Bro), res s w cor Walnut and Fox.
Fox Catherine, clerk, bds 58 McClellan.
Fox Charles, propr Racine Hotel, n e cor Cass and 1st.
Fox Charles, plumber, steam and gasfitter, 123 Broadway, res 80 Taylor.
Fox Miss Charlotte, bds 110 Van Buren.
Fox Christian, barber, res 74 Barr.
Fox Edward, plumber C W Bruns & Co, res 58 McClellan.
Fox Ellsworth, machinist, bds 110 Van Buren.
Fox Frank E, machinist Indiana Machine Works, res 44 Elm.
Fox George, res 25 E Main.
Fox Henry, wagonmkr Olds' Wagon Works, bds 69 Stophlet.
Fox Henry A, meat market, 319 W Main, res 315 same.
Fox James, contractor, res 58 McClellan.
Fox James R, machinist Penn Co, res 110 Van Buren.
Fox Jeheïl, conductor Penn Co, res 514 Broadway.
Fox Joseph V, confectioner, 25 E Main, res 46 W Superior.
Fox Kate, clerk Frank & Co, bds 58 McClellan.
Fox Lawrence, expressman, res 28 Huron.
Fox Louis (Louis Fox & Bro), mngr The Fox Branch United States Baking Co, res s e cor Walnut and Fox.
Fox Louis & Bro (Louis and August), Mnfrs Crackers and Confectionery, Wholesale Dealers in Foreign Fruits, Fireworks, Etc, also Agents Fleischmann & Co, n e cor Calhoun and Jefferson.
Fox Mary, cashier, bds 58 McClellan.
Fox Mary A (wid Francis), bds 189 Madison.
Fox Miss Minnie, bds 110 Van Buren.
Fox Phœbe A (wid Henry C), res 9 E Wayne.
Fox Valentine, market stall 32, res s s Miller w of city limits.
Fox Wm W, grocer, 325 W Main, res 327 same.
Foxhuber John L, res 100 W Williams.
Fraelich Philip, laborer, res 67 W 5th.
Fraetag August, laborer, res 142 South Wayne ave.
Fraikin John J, machinist Bass Foundry and Machine Works, res 132 Madison.
Fraikin Oscar G, machinist Bass Foundry and Machine Works, res 132 Madison.
Fraine Alexander, helper, res 200 Hanna.
Fraine John, bds 141 Lafayette.
Fraine Mary, bds 141 Lafayette.
Fraine Prosper, plasterer, res 141 Lafayette.
France, *see also Franz.*

France Abraham, teamster, res Maumee road 1 e of Glasgow ave.

France Edward, brakeman, res 82 Gay.

France Frank, hostler, res 40 Harrison.

France Harry F, justice of the peace, 13 E Main, res 600 Calhoun.

France James E K (Colerick & France), res 496 S Harrison.

France Jesse W, laborer A McKernan, bds s e cor Maumee rd and Glasgow ave.

France Joseph S, carpenter, res 484 Hanna.

France Louisa, domestic 133 E Berry.

France Maude, domestic 43½ E Columbia.

France Philip L, machinist Fort Wayne Electric Co, res 83 Home ave.

France Rachel (wid Joseph), res 133 Fairfield ave.

France Wm O, teamster, res rear 537 E Wayne.

Franchie Marsh, harnessmaker, bds s e cor Clinton and Superior.

Frane Joseph, hub mortiser Winch & Son, res 66 Maumee rd.

Frane Margaret (wid Xavier), res 371 Lafayette.

Frane Miss Pauline, bds 371 Lafayette.

Frank Bessie, bds 206 Hanna.

Frank Charles F, carpenter Louis Diether & Bro, res s s Cochrane 3 w of Coombs.

Frank Ellen (wid Francis J), res 192 E Wayne.

Frank George A, tel operator Penn Co, res 60 W DeWald.

Frank George W, carpenter Louis Diether & Bro, res 124 E Lewis.

Frank Henry W, hostler, bds 107 W Berry.

Frank Jennie, bds 206 Hanna.

Frank Josephine T, tailoress Gottlieb Stauffer, bds 60 W DeWald.

Frank Manuel, plumber, bds 192 E Wayne.

Frank Marx (M Frank & Co), res 82 W Washington.

Frank Mendel, grocer, 208 Hanna, res 206 same.

Frank M & Co (Marx and Theodore Frank), Dry Goods and Notions, 60 Calhoun.

Frank Theodore (M Frank & Co), bds 82 W Washington.

Frank Wm T, painter, bds 142 E Wayne.

Franke August H, assistant engineer City Water Works, res 154 N Clinton.

Franke Charles (Wiegmann & Franke), res 129 Taylor.

Franke Charles, shoemkr Foellinger Bros, res 237 Broadway.

Franke Christian, carpenter, res 364 E Lewis.

Franke Edward G, bookkeeper C L Centlivre, bds same.

Franke Frederick, huckster, res n s Wiebke 2 e of Lafayette.

Franke Henry, carpenter, 362 E Lewis, res same.

Franke Henry, laborer J C Peters, res 21 Barthold ave.

Franke Henry jr, cabinetmaker The Peters Box and Lumber Co, bds 21 Barthold ave.

Franke Henry C, city marshal police station, res 408 E Washington.

Franke John H, machinist Penn Co, res 336 Hanna.

Franke Julia, clerk Kayser & Baade, bds 237 Broadway.

Franke Julian F, clerk The Dreibelbiss Abstract of Title Co, bds 366 Hanna.

Franke Martin G, conductor, bds 237 Broadway.

Franke Mary L, tailoress F H Luhmann, bds 19 Barthold.

Franke Ritchie, domestic 260 W Wayne.

Franke Wm, carpenter, bds 362 E Lewis.

Frankel Louis (Heller & Frankel).

Frankenstein Max L, Druggist, n w cor Barr and Washington, res same.   Telephone 100.

Frankling Anthony, laborer, bds 134 Madison.

Frankling Margaret (wid Bernard), res 134 Madison.

Franks Gustav, clk Belger & Lennon, res 67 Maumee rd.

Franks Henry, coachman Henry G Olds.

Franks Joseph F, asst J C Peltier, res 17 W Wayne.

Frans Frederick, cigarmkr John Gronendyke, bds Windsor Hotel.

Franz, *see also France.*

Franz Charles W, bds Windsor Hotel.

Franz George, cigarmkr F J Gruber, res 112 W DeWald.

Franz Mary A, propr Windsor Hotel, 302 Calhoun, res same.

Franz Wm P, cigarmaker, bds Windsor Hotel.

Frary Addie M, clerk, bds 14 Summit.

Frary Frank, machine hand American Wheel Co, bds 14 Summit.

Frary Frank, mach Wabash R R, res 19 Brooklyn ave.

Frary Henry A, clk American Wheel Co, res 14 Summit.

Frase Franklin B, laborer, bds 181 Oakland.

Frase Hannibal W, fireman, bds 181 Oakland.

Frase Jessie B, photographer, bds 181 Oakland.

Frase Mary E (wid Charles), res 181 Oakland.

Frase Mary S, seamstress, bds 181 Oakland.

Frase Sarah E, seamstress, bds 181 Oakland.

Frase Washington A, fireman Nickel Plate, res 181 Oakland.

Fratenburgh Abraham A, laborer, res 104 E Wayne.

Frauenfelder Jacob, sawyer American Wheel Co, res n e cor Hanna and Eckert.

Frawley John F, cigarmkr A C Baker, bds Racine House.

Frazier Edward, painter Wayne Paint and Painting Co, bds 180 W Jefferson.

Frech Sophia (wid Henry), res 289 W Jefferson.

Freck Henry, laborer, res n s Romey 3 e of Parnell ave.

Freck Wm, bench hand Louis Rastetter, bds 205 Broadway.

Frecke Augusta (wid Henry), res 175 Lafayette.

Frecke Wm, carp Louis Diether & Bro, res 91 Justus ave.

Fredenburg George, brakeman, res 190 W Superior.

Frederick Christina (wid Jacob), res 415 Lafayette.

Frederick George H, lab Robert Hood, res 17 W Lewis.

Frederick John W, machinist Fort Wayne Iron Works, res 43 Laselle.

Frederick Miss Maud, milliner Mrs E A Flagler, bds 17 W Lewis.

Frederick Wm R, bookkeeper J P Gray, bds 415 S Lafayette.

Fredericks Adolph, laborer, res 67 Oliver.

Frederickson Alexander, laborer C L Centlivre, bds w s Spy Run ave 2 s of Randolph.

Frederickson John, laborer F C Bicknese, rms 24 E Berry.

Frederickson Wm, lab, res w s Spy Run ave 2 s of Randolph.

Frederking Annie, domestic Hamilton homestead.

Fredrickson Annie, domestic Rich's Hotel.

Fredrickson Charles C, laborer, bds 104 E Wayne.

Free Katie, domestic 15 Butler.

Free Methodist Church, s s E Creighton ave e of Thomas.

Freeby George H, truckman Wabash R R, res 318 S Harrison.

Freece John, driver Ryan Bros, bds same.

Freeland Charles, laborer Wm & J J Geake.

Freeman Miss Bertha, bds w s Spy Run ave 1 n of Elizabeth.

Freeman Henry R, teller First National Bank, res w s Spy Run ave 1 n of Elizabeth.

Freeman Joseph E F, hostler Pearse & Loag, bds Hotel Pearse.

Freeman Miss Katherine, teacher Hanna School, bds w s Spy Run ave 1 n of Elizabeth.

Freeman Miss Mary E, teacher Bloomingdale School, bds w s Spy Run ave 1 n of Elizabeth.

Freeeman Mary N, janitor, bds 62 Wilt.

Freeman Newton B, trav agent, rms w s Spy Run ave 1 n of Elizabeth.

Freer Jennie (wid John W), res 19 N Cass.

Freer Laura A, dressmaker, 19 N Cass, bds same.

Freese August (Freese & Fehling), res 178 W Creighton av.

Freese Charles, blacksmith J C Winte, bds 213 Fairfield ave.

Freese Charles F, clerk Meyer Bros & Co, bds 177 W Washington.

Freese Charles W, blksmith Fleming Mnfg Co, res 32 Wefel.
Freese Fred, Grocer, 379 E Washington, res 381 same.
Freese Sophie (wid Wm), res 177 W Washington.
Freese Wm, teamster Kerr-Murray Mnfg Co, res 200 Fairfield.
Freese Wm A, solicitor, bds 177 W Washington.
Freese & Fehling (August Freese, Frederick H Fehling), grocers, 184 Fairfield ave.
Freiburger Anthony C, machinist E B Kunkle & Co, bds 92 Smith.
Freiburger Bernard, clerk J B White, res 28 Charles.
Freiburger George W, tinner, 55 Thomas, res same.
Freiburger Herman, bookkeeper S Freiburger & Bro, bds 91 W Berry.
Freiburger Ignatz, res 92 Smith.
Freiburger Ignatz jr, foreman J B White, res 152 W Jefferson.
Freiburger Joseph, bookkeeper S Freiburger & Bro, bds 91 W Berry.
Freiburger Joseph J, Tin, Copper and Sheet Iron Worker, 139 Broadway; res 92 Smith.
Freiburger Julius, clerk, bds 91 W Berry.
Freiburger Leopold (S Freiburger & Bro), res 91 W Berry.
Freiburger Mary, bds 92 Smith.
Freiburger Peter, fireman Hook and Ladder Co No 1, rms Engine House No 1.
Freiburger Samuel, merchant, res 95 W Berry.
Freiburger Simon (S Freiburger & Bro), res 95 W Berry.
Freiburger S & Bro (Simon and Leopold), leather, 24 E Main.
Freimuth August, laborer J C Peters, res 38 Watkins.
Freimuth Charles, boilermaker, res 199 W Washington.
Freinstein George, clerk J B White, bds 227 E Washington.
Freistroffer's Block, 41 W Main.
Freistroffer Henry, horseshoer, 41 W Main, res 43 W Berry.
Freistroffer Simon (Freistroffer & Jasper), res 261 E Wayne.
Freistroffer & Jasper (Simon Freistroffer, George W Jasper), livery, n e cor Clinton and Nickel Plate Ry.
Freitag Wm, laborer, bds 27 South Wayne ave.
Fremion Frank (Fremion & Vollmer), res n w cor High and Wells.
Fremion Gustav, laborer Joseph Fremion, bds same.
Fremion John, laborer Joseph Fremion, bds same.
Fremion Joseph, brick mnfr, w s Hanna 10 s of Pontiac, res same.
Fremion & Vollmer (Frank Fremion, Frederick C Vollmer), proprs Fort Wayne Bottling Works, 9 N Harrison.
French Albert R, baker H H Barcus, bds Grand Central House.

French Charles G, bds 87 Maumee road.

French Coval B, tel operator Wabash R R, res 90 Dawson.

French Edgar A, stopmaker Fort Wayne Organ Co, res 92 W Creighton ave.

French Edward, printer Fort Wayne Journal, bds 568 Calhoun.

French Miss Ella M, fancy goods, 87 Maumee road, res same.

French Mrs Emma, res 57 E Main.

French, Hanna & Co (R Morgan French, Oliver W Jefferds, estate of Charles Hanna), woolen mills, 96 E Superior.

French Jeremiah, laborer, res 57 Barr.

French Mary A, cashier Dozois, Beadell & Co, bds 558 Calhoun.

French Mary J (wid Samuel C), res 558 Calhoun.

French Mattie, bds 148 E Washington.

French Miss Nellie B, assistant S B Brown, bds 558 Calhoun.

French R Morgan (French, Hanna & Co), res 148 E Washington.

Frentzel John A N, picture frames, 90 E Main, res 14 Chicago.

Frentzel Rudolph W N, bds 14 Chicago.

Freund Wm H, janitor, res 33 E 3d.

Frey George C, clerk C Entemann, res 96 Clay.

Frey James, clerk, rms 32 E Berry.

Fricke Christian, helper Staub Bros, bds 91 Huestis ave.

Fricke Frederick W, carpenter, res 91 Huestis ave.

Fricke Joseph, market gardener, n s St Joe road 4 e of St Joe's bridge, res same.

Fricke Mary, domestic, 91 Huestis ave.

Friday Henry A, machinist Bass Foundry and Machine Works, res 1 Brandriff.

Friday Louis, laborer, bds 1 Brandriff.

Friday Mary, domestic Diamond Hotel.

Fridley Louis F, fireman, res 37 Buchanan.

Friedlich Isaac (Sam, Pete and Max), res Delaware, Ia.

Friedmann Frank, wheel molder Bass Foundry and Machine Works, res s e cor Thomas and Maud.

Friedmann Matthias, laborer, res s e cor Maud and Thomas.

Friedmann Wendlin, laborer Bass Foundry and Machine Works, res cor Holton ave and Fisher.

Friedrich Emma, operator Hoosier Mnfg Co, bds 65 Oliver.

Friek Lucy B, nurse Fort Wayne City Hospital.

Friemel Albert, laborer J M Riedmiller, bds same.

Friend Alfred I (A I & H Friend), res 190 W Berry.

Friend A I & H (Alfred I and Henry), clothing, 62 and 64 Calhoun.

Friend Henry (A I & H Friend), res 172 W Wayne.
Friend Jacob, res 190 W Berry.
Friend John T, trav agent, res 230 W Washington.
Friend Miss Stella, bds 190 W Berry.
Friend Wm, bds 190 W Berry.
Frisbie Frederick, laborer, res s s Spring 1 w of St Mary's av
Frisby Frank C, brakeman, res 26 Chicago.
Frisby Frank H, carpenter, res 40 E Wayne.
Frisinger Simon P, laborer, res 109 Huron.
Fritcha Henry, laborer Wm Moellering & Co, res w s Calhoun s of Rudisill ave.
Fritz Henry N, shoemaker H D Umstead, bds 183 Calhoun.
Fritz Hotel, Frederick Schmueckle Propr, European Plan; Special Inducements to the Traveling Public and Theatrical People, 10 E Berry, res same.
Froelich Charles, res 66 Nelson.
Froger Victor, labor, bds Lake Shore Hotel.
Frohmuth Gustave H, machinist Bass Foundry and Machine Works, res 93 Buchanan.
Frohmuth John jr, blacksmith Ft W, C & L R R, res 33 N Calhoun.
Frohmuth John M F, res 95 Buchanan.
Frohmuth Theodore, laborer, bds 95 Laselle.
Fronefield Reuben, machine hand, res 28 W Superior.
Frost Benjamin, res 313 Calhoun.
Frost Charles, bds 313 Calhoun.
Frost Edward, carpenter, res 41 Hough.
Frost James S, painter, res s s New Haven av 1 e of Lumbard.
Fruth Henry, laborer The Peters Box and Lumber Co, res 32 Sherman.
Fry Charles F, teamster Winch & Son, res 32 Lillie.
Fry Francis J, miller, res 90 E Main.
Fry Francis J jr, teamster, bds 90 E Main.
Fry Frederick, job Printer Fort Wayne Sentinel, bds 219 E Wayne.
Fry Grant, dyer Paul Baumann, bds 51 E Main.
Fry Harry, laborer, bds 9 Jones.
Fry Henry, laborer, bds 27 Force.
Fry Henry W, clerk Fred Eckert, res 219 E Wayne.
Fry Jacob, laborer, res 52 John.
Fry James H, clk Penn Co, bds McKinney House.
Fry John, truckman Wabash R R, res 52 John.
Fry Mary M (wid Jacob), bds 321 S Harrison.
Fry Tannery, O G Hutchinson propr, n e cor Boone and Cherry.
Fry Wm M, butcher, bds 219 E Wayne.
Frye George H, steam fitter, res 79 N Cass.

Frye Jerome B, conductor G, R & I R R, res 32 Brackenridge

Fryer David L, armature winder Fort Wayne Electric Co, res 312 Broadway.

Fryer Lewis E, foreman Fort Wayne Electric Co, res 52 Hendricks.

Fuchs Christian, barber, 76 Barr, res same.

Fuchs Francis J, machine hand, res 13 Force.

Fuchs George, res 167 E Jefferson.

Fuchs Rosina (wid Adam), bds 76 Barr.

Fuchshuber August, cook J T Wagner, bds 100 Williams.

Fuchshuber John L, res 100 Williams.

Fuelber Anselm, city editor Indiana Staats Zeitung, res cor Clinton and Creighton ave.

Fueling Mary, domestic 46 Erie.

Fuelling Frederick H, helper Bass Foundry and Machine Works, res 140 Eliza.

Fuhrman John, carpenter, bds 79 W DeWald.

Fulker Elizabeth (wid Peter), res 173 W Jefferson.

Fulker Mary E, dressmaker, bds 173 W Jefferson.

Fullan Mary (wid John), res 237 Clay.

Fuller Charles F, laborer, bds 21 W 4th.

Fuller Frank C, painter City Carriage Works, bds 106 Barr.

Fuller James G, bds Hotel Randall.

Fuller Louisa L (wid Job R), res 21 W 4th.

Fullmer Charles L, wheel molder Bass Foundry and Machine Works, res 106 Gay.

Fulton Ansel M, lab Kerr-Murray Mnfg Co, res nr Helling's ice house W Main.

Fulton Charles W (Lee & Fulton), res 182 Griffith.

Fulton Florence, bds 138 E Lewis.

Fulton John N, agt D C Fisher, res 153 Wells.

Fulton Walter B, mach hand American Wheel Co, bds 153 Wells.

Fultz Charles, lab A McKernan, res 184 Suttenfield.

Fultz John, laborer A Hattersley & Sons.

Funk Gustav, laborer, bds 46 E Columbia.

Funk Michael, cellarman C L Centlivre, res n s Centlivre ave 1 w of Spy Run ave.

Funk Miles, watchman, bds 310 Hanna.

Furche, *see Foerche.*

Furian Wm, laborer Penn Co, bds 5 Summit.

Furlong John, hostler J C Brinsley, bds 90 E Wayne.

Furste Miss Alice McA, newsdealer, 56 Calhoun, bds 209 E Wayne.

Furste Bridget (wid Francis L), res 209 E Wayne.

Furste Elizabeth B (wid Francis L), res 209 E Wayne.

16

Robert Spice, Pumps, Pipe, Hose, Fittings and Brass Goods
48 **WEST MAIN** and 11 **PEARL** STS.

206   R. L. POLK & CO.'S

Furste George A, clk A J Dittoe & Co, bds 209 E Wayne.
Furthmiller Albert, helper Penn Co, res 174 Hanna.
Furthmiller Freeman, laborer Penn Co, res 190 Taber.
Fussner Lizzie, domestic 19 W Williams.
Futter Charles (Beninghoff & Futter), res 72 Brackenridge.
Futter Helena, bds 93 W Superior.
Futter Joseph O, barber George Thain, bds 93 W Superior.
Futter Martin, laborer The Peters Box and Lumber Co, res
    93 W Superior.

G

Gabel Charles F, bartender Charles Such, bds 338 Harrison.
Gable, *see also Geble and Goebel.*
Gable Clara, bds 74 Lillie.
Gable George F, apprentice Bass Foundry and Machine
    Works, bds 74 Lillie.
Gable Mary (wid Christian), res 40 Madison.
Gable Peter F, stonecutter Fort Wayne Steam Stone Works,
    bds n s Lakeside 6 e of Toll Gate.
Gable Philip, machinist Bass Foundry and Machine Works,
    res 74 Lillie.
Gaddis Margaret (wid James), res 231 Calhoun.
Gaehringer John, laborer Penn Co, res w s Walton ave 1 n of
    Edgerton.
Gaetje John, saloon, 179 Calhoun, res same.
Gaff Perry O, laborer, res 143 Wallace.
Gaffney Catherine A, clerk, bds 402 Calhoun.
Gaffney Edward F, clerk, bds 33 Bass.
Gaffney Margaret, clerk Root & Co, bds 33 Bass.
Gaffney Mary (wid Edward), res 33 Bass.
Gaffney Tillie, clerk L Wolf & Co, bds 402 Calhoun.
Gaffney Wm, grocer, 378 Calhoun, res 402 same.
Gage Edward F, physician, res 41½ W Berry.
Gage Miss Fannie, res 268 Calhoun.
Gage Robert, Broom Mnfr, 318 W Main, res 320 same.
Gaide Carl J W, clerk Trenkley & Scherzinger, bds 118 W
    Wayne.
Galbraith John, laborer Bass Foundry and Machine Works,
    res 143 Holman.
Gales Simon (col'd), whitewasher, res 48 E Columbia.
Galland Edmund, laborer American Wheel Co, bds 18
    Brandriff.
Galland Henry, laborer, res 18 Brandriff.
Gallapoo Peter, laborer American Wheel Co, res 381 Lafay-
    ette.

Gallmeier Conrad, laborer, res 72 Organ ave.
Gallmeier Ernest, carpenter, res 69 Maumee road.
Gallmeier Frederick W, letter carrier, res 61 Maumee road.
Gallmeier Lizzie, domestic 242 W Wayne.
Gallmeier Louisa, bds 136 Francis.
Gallmeier Wm, carpenter, 136 Francis, res same.
Gallmeyer Minnie, domestic 310 W Washington.
Gallmeyer Sophie, domestic 310 W Washington.
Galvin Dennis, laborer, bds Monroe House.
Gamble Clara, operator Hoosier Mnfg Co, bds 119 Taylor.
Gamel Charles, laborer, bds 46 E Columbia.
Gamrath Annie, dressmaker, bds 374 W Main.
Gamrath Charles, machinist Indiana Machine Works, bds 374 W Main.
Gamrath Wm, packer F Eckart, res 374 W Main.
Gannon George H, carpenter, bds Custer House.
Gans Carrie, operator S M Foster, bds 3 Marion.
Gans Joseph, laborer Penn Co, res 3 Marion.
Gans Lizzie, seamstress, bds 3 Marion.
Gans Louis, helper, res 3 Marion.
Gans Michael, clerk, bds 3 Marion.
Gans Paul, laborer Penn Co, bds 3 Marion.
Gansepohl Henry, helper Penn Co, bds 296 E Washington.
Ganser Jacob, baker, res 66 W 5th.
Ganser Joseph, machinist Ft W, C & L R R, res 66 W 5th.
Ganser Louis, driver L Wolf & Co, bds 66 W 5th.
Ganzer Stephen, clerk J B White, res 222 E Wayne.
Garard Manasseh G, carpenter, res 31 Wagner.
Gard Albert W, helper Penn Co, bds 60 Williams.
Gard Brookfield, Physician and Mngr Guardian Medical and Surgical Institute, 13 W Wayne, res same.
Gard Margaret (wid Brookfield), res 27 Lillie.
Gardes Henry, bricklayer, bds 323 Hanna.
Gardiner Frederick W, cashier Nickel Plate Ry, res 15 W Washington.
Gardner De Motte C, printer Fort Wayne News, res 309 S Harrison.
Gardner Frederick W, car painter Penn Co, res 353 Lafayette.
Gardner George W, watchman Penn Co, res 120 Chicago.
Gardner Harry W, clerk East Shops Penn Co, res 120 Chicago.
Gardner Harvey J, messenger Nickel Plate, bds 111 W Superior.
Gardner Henry J, molder Penn Co, bds 60 Williams.
Gardner Henry J, switchman Penn Co, bds 155 Clay.

Gardner James (col'd), barber, res 32 E Columbia.
Gardner Maud, bds 155 Clay.
Gardner Melvin R, clerk, res 96 W Superior.
Gardner Ross, conductor, bds 155 Clay.
Gardt Henry, barber, 271 Hanna, res same.
Gardt Henry jr, machine hand American Wheel Co, bds 271 Hanna.
Gardt Kate, bds 271 Hanna.
Gardt Stephen J, molder Bass Foundry and Machine Works, bds 271 Hanna.
Garman Adam W, painter, res 63 Pontiac.
Garman Catherine (wid Wm), res 74 Melita.
Garman Howard L, painter, bds 63 Pontiac.
Garman John W, Dealer in Watches, Clocks and Jewelry; Repairing a Specialty, 207 Calhoun, res same.
Garrison Anna, operator Hoosier Mnfg Co, bds 41 Force.
Garrison John H, car painter Penn Co, res 41 Force.
Garrison Major, fireman, rms 17 W Lewis.
Garrison Mary (wid Albert), res 18 Colerick.
Garry Ellen, tailoress, bds 96 E Jefferson.
Garta Emma (wid James), bds 104 Maumee road.
Garta John, cigarmaker F J Gruber, bds 104 Maumee road.
Garver Franklin, farmer, res 231 Barr.
Garver Melvin, coachman W Bash, bds 334 W Jefferson.
Garver Richard H, teamster, res 154 Broadway.
Garvey John A, bds 26 Douglas ave.
Garvey May, bds 26 Douglas ave.
Garvey Patrick H, engineer Penn Co, res 26 Douglas ave.
Gary Peter, vegetables, market stall 95, res w of County Poor House.
Gaskell Frank, mach A Hattersley & Sons, bds St Mary's av.
Gaskill Charles M, plumber, bds 67 Franklin ave.
Gaskill Edward H, laborer The Remington-Lawton Co, bds 57 Barr.
Gaskill Emma L, domestic 111 N Cass.
Gaskill Harrison W, machine hand Louis Diether & Bro, res 10 Short.
Gaskill Ira, laborer, bds 30 Laselle.
Gaskill Kyle, veterinary surgeon, 159 Hoffman, res same.
Gaskill Leonard M, sawyer American Wheel Co, res 66 Hayden.
Gaskill Malcomb, lab Louis Fox & Bro, bds Wm Gaskill.
Gaskill Minard A, teamster F Muhler & Son, bds 67 Franklin.
Gaskill Wm, watchman, res 67 Franklin ave.
Gaskins Miss Annette, teacher Clay School, bds 188 W Creighton ave.

Gaskins Catherine (wid Joseph), res 188 W Creighton ave.

Gaskins Miss Emma F, teacher Hoagland School, bds 188 W Creighton ave.

Gaskins Harry M, finisher Fort Wayne Organ Co, bds 188 W Creighton ave.

Gaskins Joseph E, machinist Wabash R R, bds 188 W Creighton ave.

Gaskins Wm B, mach Wabash R R, bds 188 W Creighton av.

Gassert Anna, bds e s Lafayette 1 n of Pontiac.

Gassert Frederick, flagman, rms 74 E Williams.

Gassert Nicholas, lab Olds' Wagon Works, res E Lafayette 1 n of Pontiac.

Gaszner John P, clerk Renner, Cratsley & Co, res 83 W DeWald.

Gates Abraham, conductor, res 326 Harrison.

Gates Albert, carpenter, res 21 Duryea.

Gates George, cigarmaker F J Gruber, res 84 Barr.

Gates Horatio S, clk Penn Co, res 57 W DeWald.

Gates Wm H, engineer, res 412 S Clinton.

Gauff Eveline M (wid Henry D), bds 100 E Washington.

Gavin Frank W, student, res 311 E Wayne.

Gavin James A, janitor-in-chief school board, res 311 E Wayne.

Gavin Robert, miller C Tresselt & Sons, res 8 Harmer.

Gawhen Frederick A, tailor J G Thieme & Son, res 191 E Washington.

Gay Millard F, laborer Penn Co, res cor Home and Raymond.

Gay Munroe W, carpenter Winch & Son, bds 79 Winch.

Gaylord Meda A, bds 231 Lafayette.

Gaylord Orville, wood sawyer, res 231 Lafayette.

Gaylord Sylvester, wood sawyer, bds 23 Holman.

Geake Clara, bds J J Geake.

Geake Edward, stonecutter Wm & J J Geake, bds J J Geake.

Geake John J (Wm & J J Geake), res s e cor Ewing and Pearl.

Geake Miss Mariana J, teacher Washington School, bds J J Geake.

Geake Miss Maud, bds J J Geake.

Geake Walter G, stonecutter Wm & J J Geake, bds J J Geake.

Geake Wm (Wm & J J Geake), res 18 Union.

Geake Wm jr, bds 18 Union.

Geake Wm & J J (Wm and John J), stone yard, 76 Pearl.

Geard Sarah (wid John), res 130 Madison.

Gearhart Charles R, filer Hoffman Bros, bds 95 Putnam.

Gearhart Edward, laborer Hoffman Bros, bds 95 Putnam.

Gearhart Wm S, section hand L S & M S Ry, res 95 Putnam.

Geary Annie, bds 287 E Washington.
Geary Charles, sewer contractor, 287 E Washington, res same.
Geary Charles T, driver Fort Wayne City Railroad Co, res
    s e cor Grant ave and Humphrey.
Geary Edward, butcher, bds 287 E Washington.
Geary James P, propr World's Museum, res 55 E Wayne.
Geary Leona, bds Charles T Geary.
Geary Mabel, bds Charles T Geary.
Geary's Museum, Charles P and Jennie Fletcher, proprs, n s
    E Berry bet Clinton and Barr.
Geary Oliver, mason, bds 287 E Washington.
Geary Wm (Geary & Peney), res 241 Clay.
Geary & Perrey (Wm Geary, Frank J Perrey), horseshoers,
    5 Harrison.
Gebele Miss Adeline, bds 63 Harrison.
Gebele Miss Hannah, dressmaker, res 65 Harrison.
Gebele Miss Mary, dressmaker, bds 65 Harrison.
Gebert Frank (Ryan & Gebert), rms 60 E Columbia.
Gebert John L, driver C Tresselt & Sons, bds 105 Barr.
Gebfert Louis, clerk, res 24 Van Buren.
Gebhard Casper, laborer, res 66 Charles.
Gebhard George, harnessmaker G H Kurtz, res 27 Liberty.
Gebhard Henry, polisher White's Wheel Works, bds 156
    Maumee road.
Gebhard Theodore, laborer White's Wheel Works, bds 156
    Maumee road.
Gebhard Wm, bricklayer, res 156 Maumee road.
Gebhard Wm jr, machinist Penn Co, bds 156 Maumee road.
Gebhart Edward, clerk F J E De LaGrange, bds 273 Hanna.
Geble, *see Gable and Goebel.*
Geerken Charles, driver Monning & Baker, res 135 E Lewis.
Geerken Ernest W, janitor Penn Co, res 72 Pontiac.
Geerken Frederick, machinist Penn Co, res 200 Francis.
Geerken George, boilermaker Penn Co, res 37 Eliza.
Geerken George, clerk, res 80 Montgomery.
Geerken Henry, boilermaker Penn Co, res 169 Montgomery.
Gehle Ferdinand, laborer, bds 174 Gay.
Gehring Andrew J, foreman, res 206 W Creighton ave.
Gehring Louisa S, seamstress, bds 206 W Creighton ave.
Gehring Mary K, seamstress, bds 206 W Creighton ave.
Gehring Paul, machinist Fort Wayne Electric Co, res 18
    Walnut.
Gehring Samuel, laborer, bds 206 W Creighton ave.
Gehring Wm F, cigarmaker Christian Wenninghoff, bds 206
    W Creighton ave.
Gehrke, *see also Gerke.*

Gehrke Louis G, clerk Pottlitzer Bros, res 51 W Williams.
Geiger, *see also* *Gieger.*
Geiger Catherine (wid Herman), res 235 Barr.
Geiger Charles, bookbinder, res 125 E Jefferson.
Geiger Charles, bookkeeper The Herman Berghoff Brewing
    Co, bds 86 E Lewis.
Geiger Frank J, saloon, 288 Calhoun, res 292 same.
Geiger Joseph, laborer, bds 100 Putnam.
Geiger Louis, bookkeeper, bds 125 E Jefferson.
Geiger Wm, clerk Adams Express Co, res 57 Maumee rd.
Geiger Wm, laborer, bds 100 Putnam ave.
Geise Henry, car repairer Penn Co, res 186 Francis.
Geisman Charles, laborer, bds 40 Locust.
Geisman Elizabeth (wid Jacob), res 40 Locust.
Geisman George, mach hand Am Wheel Co, bds 40 Locust.
Geisman John, laborer, bds 40 Locust.
Geismar Adolph, trav agent, res 101 E Berry.
Geiss Emma, domestic Wayne Hotel.
Geiss Julia (wid Jacob), res 140 Lafayette.
Geiss Louis J, laborer, res 91 Ewing.
Geisteffer Ferdinand, market stall 48, res nr French Brewery.
Gelard Theodore, laborer, res 93 Hoffman.
Geller Charles C (Ehrman & Geller), res 186 Griffith.
Geller George, baker W F Geller, res 58 Maumee road.
Geller George, laborer Penn Co, res 2 Union.
Geller Gottlieb, saloon, 96 Broadway, res 53 Stophlet.
Geller Lizzie, domestic 305 W Jefferson.
Geller Mary, bds 2 Union.
Geller Theodore, market stall 39, res 93 Hoffman.
Geller Theodore jr, baker Wm F Geller, bds 98 Broadway
Geller Wm F, baker, 98 Broadway, res same.
Gellert Max, tinner J P Gray, res 34 Allen.
Genge Palmer, machine hand American Wheel Co, bds 114
    E Berry.
Genth Michael, wheel molder Bass Foundry and Machine
    Works, bds 50 Force.
George Ellwood H, traveling agent, res 155 Ewing.
George Eugene, bartender Russel George, bds 28 W Main.
George Russel, saloon, 28 W Main, res same.
Georget Charles, cigarmaker F J Gruber, bds 25 W Wash-
    ington.
Gephart Charles jr, market stall 55, res w s Bluffton rd w
    city limits.
Gephart David, laborer Wm Moellering & Co, res e s Piqua
    ave 2 s of Rudisill ave.
Gephart Margaret E, domestic Jewel House.

Gephart Ralph, market stall 41, res e s St Joseph rd e of city
    limits.
Gerard, *see also Girard.*
Gerard Anthony, helper Penn Co, bds 92 Lillie.
Gerard Anthony jr, clerk Penn Co, res 94 Lillie.
Gerard Benoit, flagman Penn Co, res 93 Lillie.
Gerard Kate, bds 92 Lillie.
Gerard Mary, bds 92 Lillie.
Gerard Nicholas, res 518 E Lewis.
Gerard Sarah (wid John W), res 130 Madison.
Gerardin Hippolyte, saloon, 70 Barr, res same.
Gerardin Mary, bds 70 Barr.
Gerber Conrad, driver G DeWald & Co, res 114 Erie.
Gerberding August, ice, res 103 Erie.
Gerberding Edward, teacher St Paul's German Lutheran
    School, res 201 E Lewis.
Gerberding Henry A, driver Fort Wayne Artificial Ice Co,
    bds 103 Erie.
Gerberding John H, laborer, bds 37 Barr.
Gerberding Joseph L, laborer, bds 37 Barr.
Gerberding Rudolph E, clerk M L Frankenstein, bds 201 E
    Lewis.
Gerberding Walter R, clerk Penn Co, bds 201 E Lewis.
Gerberding Wm A, laborer, res 37 Barr.
Gerdes Herman, bricklayer, res 86 Lillie.
Gerding Bros (Herman C and John P), livery, 66 Harrison.
Gerding Herman C (Gerding Bros), res 22 Union.
Gerding John P (Gerding Bros), res 122 John.
Gerding Wm E (Gerding & Aumann Bros), res 373 Hanna.
Gerding & Aumann Bros (Wm E Gerding, Wm H
    and Henry F Aumann), Hardware, Stoves and Tinware,
    and Tin, Copper and Sheet Iron Workers, 115 Wallace.
Gerdom Ernst H, foreman Bass Foundry and Machine Wks,
    res 160 Smith.
Gerdom Herman W, molder Bass Foundry and Machine Wks,
    bds 52 John.
Gerhard Wm, machinist Bass Foundry and Machine Works,
    res 353 Lewis.
Gerke, *see also Gehrke.*
Gerke Charles W, bookkeeper Fort Wayne Street Railroad
    Co, bds 161 Gay.
Gerke Christina (wid Henry), res 161 Gay.
Gerke Frederick H, clerk, res 209 Lafayette.
Gerke Henry C, bookkeeper Wm Moellering & Sons, bds 209
    Lafayette.
Gerke Henry F, clerk D Meyers, res 209 Lafayette.

Gerke Henry W, with J F Gerke & Co, bds 5 McClellan.

Gerke John F (J F Gerke & Co), res Goeglein, Ind.

Gerke John F, farmer, bds 25 Summit.

Gerke Julia, domestic 40 E Washington.

Gerke J F & Co (John F Gerke), Dry Goods, 191 Lafayette.

Gerke J Henry, res 25 Summit.

Gerke Kate, domestic 40 E Washington.

Gerke Louis, teamster Penn Co, res 161 Gay.

Gerke Louis H, mail service, res 5 McClellan.

Gerke Louise, domestic John F W Meyer.

Gerlach Emil, laborer, res s s Pontiac 1 e of Oliver.

Gerlach George, carpenter, bds 232 E Jefferson.

Gerlach Gustav, painter Olds' Wagon Works, res s s Pontiac 1 e of Holton.

Germain Roswell M, engineer, res 22 Richardson.

German Lutheran Cemetery, n s Maumee rd e of Concordia College.

German Lutheran Cemetery (St John's), Bluffton road 3 miles s w of city limits.

German Lutheran School, Rev Charles Gross principal, n e cor Union and Wilt.

Gerow Teles D, grocer, 120 Fairfield ave, res 23 Grand.

Gerry Edward, butcher Charles Jacobs, bds 116 Madison.

Gerwig Mary (wid Louis), res 12 Liberty.

Gessler Albert F, meats, 60 E Main, res same.

Gessler Victoria (wid Frederick), res 60 E Main.

Getty Christopher, res 73 Buchanan.

Getty Frank X, teamster, res 75 Buchanan.

Getty George, trunk maker Fisher Bros, res 27 Buchanan.

Getty Miss Lida I, music teacher 97 E Jefferson, bds same.

Getz George, blacksmith, bds 18 W 5th.

Getz Hubert, machinist Fort Wayne Iron Works, res Maumee road.

Getz John C, shoemaker, 174 Fairfield ave, res 86 Dawson.

Getz Joseph, driver, res 12 Sturgis.

Geye Henry, shoemaker 424 E Wayne, res same.

Geye Herman F W, shoemaker O B Fitch, res 428 E Wayne.

Gibford Mrs A W, works Indiana School for Feeble-Minded Youth.

Gibford Catherine (wid David), bds 58 Nelson.

Gibford Harry W, clerk O B Fitch, rms 50 W Superior.

Gibian Henry H, bds 104 Barr.

Gibson Eliza, dressmaker, bds 38 Oak.

Gibson Frank, traveling agent, res 13 Hamilton.

Gibson Frank P, brakeman Penn Co, bds 13 Hamilton.
Gibson Lena (wid Charles), res 57 W Williams.
Gibson Mary, dressmaker, 194 W De Wald, res same.
Gibson Mary J (wid Frank), res 38 Oak.
Gibson Matilda F (wid James), res 37 E 1st.
Gibson Rose, dressmaker, bds 38 Oak.
Gibson Theresa, domestic 22 Park ave.
Gick Amelia, bds 292 E Washington.
Gick George, clerk Pickard Bros, res 292 E Washington.
Gick Louis, clerk H J Ash, res 253 E Washington.
Gidley John A, machinist Fort Wayne Electric Co, bds 20 Pine.
Gidley Rebecca (wid Wm), res 20 Pine.
Gidley Richard, boilermaker, res 24 Pine.
Gidley Rosa M, clerk, bds 20 Pine.
Gieger Ernest, watchman, bds 3 Edgerton.
Gieger Frederick, section hand, bds 3 Edgerton.
Gieger George, laborer, res 3 Edgerton.
Gieger Jacob, section hand, bds George Gieger.
Gieger Wm, tailor, res 3 Edgerton.
Giesman Charles, rimmer, res 73 Buchanan.
Giffin Robert, fireman, res 53 Taylor.
Gifford Harry, clerk, bds 50 W Superior.
Gilb Nicholas, cigarmaker George Reiter, res 374 S Calhoun.
Gilbert Edward, pressman Fort Wayne Newspaper Union, bds 251 W DeWald.
Gilbert Glenn M, laborer Bass Foundry and Machine Works, bds 228 Calhoun.
Gilbert Miss Grace G, bds John V Gilbert.
Gilbert Harry W, traveling agent S F Bowser & Co, res 101 W Williams.
Gilbert James B, blacksmith Bass Foundry and Machine Works, res 173 W DeWald.
Gilbert John, mngr Standard Oil Co, res 246 W Washington.
Gilbert John V, fruit grower, res Vordermark's homestead.
Gilbert Leonard, bartender T W Ahern, bds same.
Gilbert Walter S, bds John V Gilbert.
Gilby John, machinist, res 16 W Williams.
Gilchrist Mrs Christopher, res 60 W Berry.
Gilchrist Elizabeth H (wid Wm L), bds 134 E Main.
Gilchrist Ernst P, clerk Stewart & Hahn, bds 60 W Berry.
Gill Lawrence, bds 393 E Wayne.
Gillen Bernard, wheelmaker American Wheel Co, res 76 Laselle.

Gillen Frank, candymaker, bds Grand Central Hotel.

Gillespie Asa E, painter City Carriage Works, bds 130 Broadway.

Gillespie Charles, bricklayer, bds 85 Wells.

Gillespie Charles, waiter, rms 65 Baker.

Gillespie Grace M, clerk J B White, bds 190 W Superior.

Gillespie Rufus R, bds 47 N Calhoun.

Gillespie Mrs Susanna, res 130 Broadway.

Gillespie Wm R, stonecutter, res 131 Griffith.

Gillett Hollis, bds 57 Barr.

Gillette Edwin A, insptr of engines Wabash R R, res 243½ W Washington.

Gillham Lewis O, mngr New York Installment Co, rms 43 E Columbia.

Gilliom Emma (wid Henry), res 192 E Wayne.

Gilliom Miss Lenore, clerk, bds 192 E Wayne.

Gilliom Miss Zella, assistant Dr Sites, bds 192 E Wayne.

Gillock Edward G, carpenter George W Bley, bds 232 E Jefferson.

Gilman Charles A, machine hand American Wheel Co, bds 33 Buchanan.

Gilman Cora H, bds 33 Buchanan.

Gilman Huldah (wid Jerome B), res 33 Buchanan.

Gilmartin Edward, telegraph poles, 31 W Williams, res same.

Gilmartin Michael J, clerk Fort Wayne Electric Co, bds 31 W Williams.

Gilmartin Wm, laborer, bds 31 W Williams.

Gilpin James W, carpenter, bds 36 Oak.

Gimpel Clara, seamstress, bds 119 Taylor.

Gimpel Henry, coremaker Bass Foundry and Machine Works, res 119 Taylor.

Ginder John A, brakeman, res 92 Chicago.

Gindlesparger Ida B, dressmaker, s w cor Pearl and Maiden Lane, bds same.

Gindlesparger Jacob, hostler, res s w cor Pearl and Maiden Lane.

Gindlesparger Mead, laborer, bds 8 Clark.

Ginther Charles H, helper, bds 203 E Wayne.

Ginty Charles, brakeman Penn Co, bds 196 Hanna.

Ginty Frederick, brakeman Penn Co.

Girard, *see also Gerard.*

Girard Frank, helper Penn Co, bds 413 E Lewis.

Girard Nicholas, car repairer Penn Co, res 518 E Lewis.

Gladbach Gottfried, cabinetmaker Fort Wayne Organ Co, res n s Killea 3 w of Calhoun.

Gladbach Joseph, carp, res e s Force 4 s of E Creighton ave.

Glah Henry, laborer Leikauf Bros, res Leikauf's packing house.

Glanowitch John, car builder Penn Co, res 3 Lumbard.

Glaser Edward F, grocer, 195 Hanna, res same.

Glaser Edward G, clerk, bds 195 Hanna.

Glaser Edward K, laborer Penn Co, bds 195 Hanna.

Glaser Frank E, driver, bds 195 Hanna.

Glaser John E, baker, bds 195 Hanna.

Glass Chester C, asst bookkeeper Root & Co, bds 193 W Washington.

Glass Eliza J (wid Randall S), res 193 E Washington.

Glass James, carpenter, bds 311 W Jefferson.

Glaze Wm, brakeman, res 23 Richardson.

Glenn Robert, clerk Martin Detzer, bds 266 Hoagland ave.

Glenn Thomas, conductor Penn Co, res 266 Hoagland ave.

Glenn Thomas M, Real Estate and Loan Agent, South Side Investments a Specialty; also Passenger Conductor Penn Co, Office 352½ Calhoun, res 266 Hoagland ave.

Glenn Wm M, engineer, res 67 W DeWald.

Glennwood Chapel, cor S Broadway and Bluffton road.

Glessner Charles, saloon, 192 Griffith, res same.

Glessner Cora, bds 192 Griffith.

Glissman Minnie, domestic 287 W Washington.

Glissmann Christian, laborer Ranke & Yergens, bds 23 Jones.

Globe Flour Mills, Monning & Baker proprs, 73 and 75 E Columbia.

Gloecke John, letter carrier, res 7 Monroe.

Gloyd Louis L, clerk Penn Co, res 410 S Clinton.

Gloyd Mary A, student, bds 410 S Clinton.

Glusenkamp Frederick, blacksmith Ft W, C & L R R, res 51 W 5th.

Glusenkamp Frederick, clerk, bds 397 W Main.

Glusenkamp Wm, wiper, res 397 W Main.

Glutting Andrew F (Glutting & Bauer), res 114 W Main.

Glutting Miss Elizabeth, res 15 W Washington.

Glutting Miss Frances M, bds 15 W Washington.

Glutting & Bauer (A F Glutting, K J Bauer), Real Estate and Insurance, 55 Clinton.

Glynn Miss Kate, dressmaker, res 53 E Main.

Gmeiner Bertha M, domestic 50 W 4th.

Gmeiner Charles, engineer Ft W, C & L R R, res 55 W 5th.

Gmeiner Michael F, laborer, bds 50 W 4th.

Gnau John, laborer Penn Co, res 15 Wabash ave.

Gnau Martin, laborer Penn Co, res 15 Wabash ave.

Gnau Peter, machine hand, res 13 Force.

Goble M Effie, bds 298 E Creighton ave.
Gocke Anthony, bds 162 Griffith.
Gocke August A, porter G E Bursley & Co, res 99 Grant av.
Gocke August C, clk B R Noll, bds 162 Griffith.
Gocke Frank A, trav agt A C Trentman, res 225 E Wayne.
Gocke Henry J, clerk L Wolf & Co, res 46 W Lewis.
Gocke Louis, helper Penn Co, bds 158 Holman.
Gocke Louis H, bkkpr A C Trentman, res 80 Brackenridge.
Godard Ruth P, bds 71 Douglas ave.
Godfrey Casper, conductor, res 179 W Jefferson.
Godfrey James P, engineer, res 236 W DeWald.
Goebel, *see also Gable.*
Goebel Christina (wid Peter), res 219 Lafayette.
Goebel Frank A, clerk J B White, res 219 Lafayette.
Goebel Frederick, musician, res 32 W Main.
Goebel Siebert, fireman, res rear 103 Force.
Goeglein Abraham, teamster, res 83 Smith.
Goeglein Andrew, helper Kerr-Murray Mnfg Co, res 21 Pritchard.
Goeglein Frederick, coremaker Bass Foundry and Machine Works, res 21 Pritchard.
Goeglein Jacob, teamster, res 6 Jones.
Goehren Joseph, tailor, res 320 E Washington.
Goeric Anna (wid Adolphus), res 10 W Wayne.
Goering Dora (wid Frederick), bds 107 Force.
Goers Wm, laborer Penn Co, res 89 Shauner ave.
Goertz Theodore, harnessmaker F Hilt, res 103 Wallace.
Goette Frederick, res 113 Gay.
Goetz George, helper Wm Thiel, bds 18 W 5th.
Goetz Hubert, helper, res 55 Maumee road.
Goings Wm H, checker Penn Co, res 166 Madison.
Golay Miss Linnie, teacher Indiana School for Feeble-Minded Youth.
Goldammer Charles, cigarmaker Louis Bender, res 336 Hanna.
Golden Anna, bds 32 Smith.
Golden Anthony W, clerk Golden & Monahan, res 200 Lafayette.
Golden Bridget (wid Patrick), res 32 Smith.
Golden Miss Bridget, res 29 Melita.
Golden Edward (Golden & Monahan), res 177 W Wayne.
Golden Frank, hostler Jenson & Sargent, bds Racine Hotel.
Golden John, brakeman, res 345 E Washington.
Golden John, flagman Penn Co, res 30 John.
Golden Joseph J, helper Wabash R R, res 38 Melita.
Golden Kate, works Fort Wayne Electric Co, bds 38 Melita.
Golden Margaret (wid Thomas), res 38 Melita.

Golden Mary (wid Patrick), bds 197 W De Wald.
Golden Mary, clerk V E Wolf, bds 177 W Wayne.
Golden Miss Mary M, bds 38 Melita.
Golden Patrick, brakeman Penn Co, bds 32 Smith.
Golden Samuel W, laborer, res 57 W Superior.
Golden Thomas F, car builder Penn Co, res 38 Melita.
Golden & Monahan (Edward J Golden, Dennis Monahan),
    hats, caps and gents' furnishing goods, 68 Calhoun.
Goldstine Harry, canvasser, bds 401 E Wayne.
Goldstine Himan, grocer, 401 E Wayne, res same.
Goldstine Samuel, pedler, bds 401 E Wayne.
Goldthait Howard H, canvasser, res 35 John.
Goleeke Josephine (wid Wm), res 74 Walton.
Gomoll Julius, machine hand American Wheel Co, res 23
    Julia.
Good George L, carpenter, bds Windsor Hotel.
Good Peter, laborer, bds 27 Force.
Goodell Doctor F, packer Olds' Wagon Works, res 75 Smith.
Goodenough George J, laborer Indiana Machine Works, bds
    215 Jefferson.
Goodes Eliza, dressmaker, bds 77 Brackenridge.
Goodfellow Bros (James F and Wm), saloon, 274 Calhoun,
    res same.
Goodfellow James F (Goodfellow Bros), res 274 Calhoun.
Goodfellow Wm (Goodfellow Bros), res 274 Calhoun.
Goodman Alexander, gents' furnishings, 38 Calhoun, res 49
    W Berry.
Goodman Carrie, clerk Peter Pierre, bds 254 W Washington.
Goodman Francis X, cigars, 139 E Jefferson, res same.
Goodman Kate, bds 139 E Jefferson.
Goodman Mary, bds 139 E Jefferson.
Goodrich Miss Cecile, bds 49 Pixley and Long bldg.
Goodrich Janette (wid Jules), stenographer, 49 Pixley &
    Long bldg, res same.
Goodsell George, carpenter, bds 40 Wells.
Goodsell George M, gasfitter A Hattersley & Sons, res 40
    Wells.
Goodwin Monroe A, wheel molder Bass Foundry and Machine
    Works, res 200 S Thomas.
Gophert Bernhard, market stall No 74, res n s Plank road.
Gordon Daniel D, stereotyper Ft Wayne Newspaper Union,
    res 16 Locust.
Gordon Eugene B, printer, res 204 E Wayne.
Gordon George P, baggage agent Penn Co, res 16 Leith.
Gordon Hugh K, baggage agent Penn Co, res 375 E Wash-
    ington.

Stahn & Heinrich, Booksellers and Stationers, Schmitz Block News Stand, 116 Calhoun Street.

FORT WAYNE DIRECTORY. 219

Gordon James S, clerk F W Robinson, bds 16 Leith.
Gordon John F, stock clerk Coombs & Co, bds 16 Leith.
Gordon Wm D, shipping clerk Coombs & Co, bds 16 Leith.
Gordon Wm H, watchman, res 375 E Washington.
Gorel Burt, domestic 133 E Berry.
Gorham Charles D, supt W Div N Y, C & St L R R, bds Aveline House.
Gorham Marquis D L F, saw repairer, 19 W Berry, res same.
Gorham Wm, laborer Fort Wayne Steam Stone Works, bds 160 Greely.
Gorman Dennis, clerk county auditor, bds Diamond Hotel.
Gorman Patrick J, sectionman Wabash R R, bdse 102 Webster.
Gormley John H, brakeman, res 35 Burgess.
Gorrell Albert, driver Morgan & Beach, bds 133 E Berry.
Gorsline Frederick, brakeman, res 312 Clay.
Gorsline Homer A, clerk, bds 473 Lafayette.
Gorsline Sylvester L, baggageman, res 473 Lafayette.
Gosda August, laborer, res 44 Smith.
Goshorn Benjamin F, carpenter, res 164 Hoffman.
Goshorn Jacob S, Civil Engineer and Surveyor, 26 Court, res 386 E Washington.
Goshorn Miss Laura, librarian Women's Free Reading Room, bds 102 E Washington.
Goshorn Miss Margaret L, teacher Bloomingdale School, bds 386 E Washington.
Goshorn Wm H, res 102 E Washington.
Goshway Joseph, helper Penn Co, bds 68 Laselle.
Gospel Tidings Publishing Co, A R Wheeler Propr, 9 Foster Blk.
Gospel Tidings The, Gospel Tidings Publishing Co Publrs, 9 Foster Blk. (*See left bottom lines.*)
Gossow August, market stall No 58, res e s Lima rd.
Gotsch Christ C, clk F M Smith & Co, bds Columbia Hotel.
Gotsch Theodore, clk Morgan & Beach, res 50 W Superior.
Gotta Mitchel, stonecutter, res 7 Oak.
Gotte Conrad, tailor, res s s Pontiac 1 w of Pittsburgh Ry.
Gottmacher Rev Adolph, bds 110 E Wayne.
Gould Carroll C, stenographer Penn Co, bds 86 W DeWald.
Gould Mrs Jennie M, dressmaker, 47 W Main, res same.
Gould Oscar P, barber G J Nichter, bds 164 Broadway.
Gould Theodore H, engineer, res 86 W DeWald.
Gould Wm A, machinist Bass Foundry and Machine Works, bds 86 W DeWald.
Gouty Benjamin F, foreman Hoffman Bros, res s e cor Howell and Rumsey ave.
Gouty Emma S, music teacher, 252 Calhoun, bds same.

Gouty James M, res 179 W Superior.
Gouty Laura B, clerk A Mergentheim, bds 179 W Superior.
Gouty Louis E, laborer Hoffman Bros, bds 179 W Superior.
Gouty Mary, dressmaker, 179 W Superior, bds same.
Gouty Thomas A, cigars, 252 Calhoun, res same.
Gouty Walter O, laborer Hoffman Bros, bds 101 Franklin ave.
Gouty Wm F, collector, bds 252 Calhoun.
Gouty Wm H, driver J Klett & Son, res 101 Franklin ave.
Government Building The, s e cor Berry and Clinton.
Gowen Henry, carpenter, res 349 W Main.
Grable John, res 111 Fairfield ave.
Grable John jr, engineer, bds 111 Fairfield ave.
Grable Samuel A, res 152 W Wayne.
Grace Reformed Church, s s Washington bet Barr and Lafayette.
Grady Emma, dressmaker, bds 30 Lillie.
Grady Mary (wid Henry), bds 30 Lillie.
Grady Oney, bds 30 Lillie.
Grady Richard E, machinist Indiana Machine Works, res 67 Rockhill.
Grady Thomas, brakeman Penn Co, res 30 Lillie.
Graf John, laborer Penn Co, res 18 Buchanan.
Graf Philip, grocer, 337 Lafayette, res 401 same.
Graffe Miss Carrie, res 134 Calhoun.
Graffe Charles F (C F Graffe & Co), res 24 W Jefferson.
Graffe Charles F & Co (Charles F Graffe), hardware, and sheetiron workers, 132 Calhoun.
Graffe Miss Clara J, bds 26 W Jefferson.
Graffe Edward J, clk Charles F Graffe & Co, bds 24 W Jefferson.
Graffe Frederick jr, jeweler H C Graffe, res 25 W Berry.
Graffe George W, engraver, bds 24 W Jefferson.
Graffe Henry C, Watches, Diamonds and Jewelry and President Jenny Electric Light and Power Co, cor Calhoun and Columbia, res 156 W Jefferson.
Graffe Joseph E, printer, bds 24 W Jefferson.
Graffe Mary E (wid George W), res 26 W Jefferson.
Graffe Miss Regina, bds 134 Calhoun.
Graffe Miss Rosa M, bds 26 W Jefferson.
Graffe Wm H, watchmaker, bds 24 W Jefferson.
Grage Emma L, opr Hoosier Mnfg Co, bds 52 Buchanan.
Grage Frederick, drayman, res 185 W Jefferson.
Grage Henry, trav agent, bds 99 E Berry.
Grage Sophia C, operator, bds 52 Buchanan.
Grage Wm A, clerk G W Seavey, res 185 W Jefferson.

Grage Wm H, laborer, res 52 Buchanan.

Graham Belle, clerk Root & Co, bds 103 Madison.

Graham Charles A, barber Louis Uplegger, bds 160 Greely.

Graham Elizabeth C (wid Wm), res 126 E Berry.

Graham Elizabeth J, dressmaker, bds 593 Calhoun.

Graham Frederick V (James E Graham & Son), res n e cor Williams-and Calhoun.

Graham George B, harnessmaker G H Kuntz, bds Clifton House.

Graham George E, painter Penn Co, bds 178 E Lewis.

Graham George W, laborer, res 313 E Washington.

Graham Howard M, printer Fort Wayne Journal, bds 313 E Washington.

Graham Jacob, market stall 10, res w s Bluffton s of city lmts.

Graham James A, foreman Penn Co, res 230 E Lewis.

Graham James E (James E Graham & Son), law and pension claim atty, 26 Bank block, res 405 Hanna.

Graham James E & Son (James E and Frederick V), Abstracts of Title, Real Estate, Loans, Insurance and Steamship Agents, 26 Bank Block.

Graham John W, shoemaker, 174 Calhoun, bds 17 Baker.

Graham Miss L Maud, bds 405 Hanna.

Graham Robert L, horse trainer, bds Clifton House.

Graham Samuel D, carpenter, res w s Webster 1 s of Pontiac.

Graham Wm F, clerk Penn Co, res 74 E Williams.

Grahl Otto, clerk A W Miller, bds 6 Summit.

Grahl W Clemens, teacher St Paul's German Lutheran School, res 6 Summit.

Gralah Emil, laborer Bass Foundry and Machine Works, res n e cor Pontiac and Holton ave.

Gramlich John, laborer C W Bruns & Co, bds John Stier.

G A R Hall, n w cor Calhoun and Main.

Grand Central Hotel, Mrs Sarah A Bradley propr, 101 Calhoun.

Grand Rapids & Indiana Railroad, operating Cincinnati, Richmond & Fort Wayne R R; P S O'Rourke supt, R B Rossington freight agent, John E Ross ticket agent; offices and depots with Pennsylvania Co, cor Clinton and Railroad.

Graney Conrad J, boilermaker Bass Foundry and Machine Works, res 139 E DeWald.

Graney Dennis S A, finisher, bds 107 Fairfield ave.

Graney Michael G, molder Bass Foundry and Machine Works, bds 107 Fairfield ave.

Graney Patrick J, laborer, bds 107 Fairfield ave.

Graney Wm, laborer, res 107 Fairfield ave.

17

Graney Wm J, helper American Wheel Co, bds 107 Fairfield.
Granger Claude E, brakeman, bds 271 Webster.
Granger Frank T, brakeman, bds 271 Webster.
Granger Horace G, storekeeper Wabash R R, bds 202 W Washington.
Granger Priscilla (wid Charles), res 271 Webster.
Grannemann Anna, bds 235 S Webster.
Grannemann Charles, carp Wabash R R, res 235 S Webster.
Grannemann Emma, bds 235 S Webster.
Grannemann Henry C, clerk C B Woodworth & Co, bds 235 S Webster.
Gransenbau Anna, domestic Wm B Smith.
Grant Daniel D, blksmith B H Baker, res 20 Lafayette.
Grant John H trav freight agt N Y, C & St L Ry, res 105 W Berry.
Grantz Valinda, lab Bass Foundry and Machine Works, res 258 John.
Graper Rekia, domestic 102 E Washington.
Gratt Frederick, clk G D Niswonger, bds 36 Barr.
Graue Frederick, bricklayer, res 86 Home ave.
Grauter Gottlieb, coremkr, res 224 Gay.
Graves Charles E, res 129 W Main.
Gray Albert, lab Hoffman Bros, bds 230 E Wayne.
Gray Anderson, laborer 263 Hanna.
Gray David S, sewing mach repairer, res 51 Barr.
Gray James P, Hardware, Etc, 364 Calhoun, res 90 W Williams.
Gray Jastie, bds 230 E Wayne.
Gray Jennie, bds 230 E Wayne.
Gray John W, contractor, res 230 E Wayne.
Greek Charles W, lab Kerr-Murray Mnfg Co, res nr Helling's ice house W Main.
Green Miss Clara, tchr McCulloch School, bds 30 Erie.
Green Emma L (Green Sisters), bds 179 Jackson.
Green Flora B (col'd), bds 232 Lafayette.
Green Frank R, clerk John Figel, bds 140 High.
Green George, brakeman Penn Co, res 62 Madison.
Green George M, coil winder Fort Wayne Electric Co, res 69 Thompson ave.
Green Hugh W, carpenter, res 179 Jackson.
Green John, whitewasher, res 31 Grand.
Green Joseph, molder Bass Foundry and Machine Works, bds 145 E Lewis.
Green Lawrence, cooper C H Stockman, bds Lake Shore House.
Green Letta M (Green Sisters), bds 179 Jackson.

Green Lewis H, compositor Fort Wayne Gazette, bds 179 Jackson.

Green Margaret (wid Johnson), res 62 Madison.

Green Mary A (wid Wm), bds 114 W Berry.

Green M Frances (wid Seth R), physician, 139 W Main, res same.

Green Miss M Gertrude, bds 139 W Main.

Green Noah (col'd), res 232 Lafayette.

Green Richard B, wood carver, res 32 Home ave.

Green Richard E, stopmaker Fort Wayne Organ Co, bds 32 Home ave.

Green Sisters (Emma L and Letta M), dressmakers, 179 Jackson.

Green S Frank, shipping clerk G E Bursley & Co, bds 139 W Main.

Green Thomas C, engineer Hoffman Bros, res 3 St Mary's ave.

Green Walter A, laborer Ranke & Yergens, bds 140 High.

Green Wm H, agent, res 109 Lafayette.

Greenawalt George L, Physician, 151 E Wayne, res same.

Greene Mrs Ella S, res 22 W 3d.

Greener John, laborer Bass Foundry and Machine Works, res 119 Eliza.

Greenick Abraham A, fireman, res 141 E DeWald.

Greening Edwin T, harnessmaker C B Neireiter, bds cor Pearl and Webster.

Greenisen Joseph, laborer, res 669 Broadway.

Greenlun Harry, flagman Penn Co, res 61 Maud.

Greenlun Helsel J, brakeman, bds 61 Maud.

Greenlun Herbert C, hostler, bds 61 Maud.

Greenlun Marion F, laborer J M Keyser, res 61 Maud.

Greensfelder Aaron, clerk J B White, bds 95 Ewing.

Greensfelder Gustav, res 95 Ewing.

Greensfelder Josias, cashier J B White, bds 95 Ewing.

Greenwood Henry, pipe liner Salimonie Mining and Gas Co, bds Wm Kelker.

Greer Charles E, laborer American Wheel Co, bds 20 Erie.

Greer Clara, bds 20 Erie.

Greer Frank J, clerk Penn Co, res 53 Shawnee ave.

Greer James L, bds 20 Erie.

Greer John, carpenter, res 36 Walnut.

Greer John W, carpenter, res 20 Erie.

Greer Laurence J, harnessmaker A L Johns & Co, bds 20 Erie.

Greer Thomas jr, clerk, res 53 High.

Gregg Anna (wid James S), res 176 E Wayne.

Gregg Stella M, bds 176 E Wayne.
Greibel, *see Griebel*.
Greiner Charles, laborer, res e s Hoagland ave 1 s of Organ Factory.
Greiner Henry, laborer, res s s Rudisill ave 1 w of Piqua ave.
Greist Albert B, grocer, res 34 W Main.
Grennell Melinda W (wid Hiram W), bds 392 Fairfield ave.
Grenouillet Margaret (wid Jacob), res 305 Hanna.
Grenzenbach Elizabeth (wid Frederick), bds Frederick Butz.
Grenzenbach Henry F, laborer, res 22 Jane.
Grenzenbach John, painter, bds Frederick Butz.
Grenzenbach Justus, laborer, bds Frederick Butz.
Gresham Frederick H (col'd), janitor Pixley & Long bldg, bds 67 W Superior.
Gresham Isaac, waiter, rms 67 W Superior,
Gretzinger Christian, res 35 Putnam.
Gretzinger Jacob, mach Ft Wayne Electric Co, res 12 Walnut.
Greve Frederick, cigarmaker Christian Wenninghoff, res 147 Broadway.
Greve George, street car driver, bds 290 Calhoun.
Greve John, collarmaker, res 11 Summit
Greve Joseph, foreman, res n s Cochrane 2 w of Coombs.
Greve Wm, carpenter, res 28 Erie.
Grey, *see Gray*.
Gribben Charles O, helper Penn Co, res 24 Douglas ave.
Gribben Elizabeth, bds 24 Douglas ave.
Gribben Hester, bds 24 Douglas ave.
Gribben John F, bds 24 Douglas ave.
Gribben Louis J, fireman, bds 24 Douglas ave.
Gribben Mary J (wid James M), res 24 Douglas ave.
Grieb John, tailor, res 182 E Lewis.
Grieb John N, conductor Penn Co, res 257 Hanna.
Griebe Henrietta (wid John), bds 106 W Washington.
Griebel A Louis (Indiana Staats Zeitung), res 211 W Berry.
Griebel Carrie E, works Troy Steam Laundry, bds 147 W 3d.
Griebel Charles (Griebel, Wyckoff & Becker), res 346 E Washington.
Griebel Christian, teamster, res w s Lavinia 2 s of Taylor.
Griebel Kate, works Troy Steam Laundry, bds 147 W 3d.
Griebel Louis (Griebel & Son), res 58 E Jefferson.
Griebel Louis, teamster, res 147 W 3d.
Griebel Wm, teamster, res 181 Taylor.
Griebel Wm J (Griebel & Son), res 168 Madison.
Griebel, Wyckoff & Becker (Charles Griebel, O C Wyckoff, H W Becker), Marble and Granite, 74 and 76 W Main.

Griebel & Son (Louis and Wm J), Dealers in Fine Furniture, Parlor Sets, Bedroom Suites and all Kinds of Chairs, 44 E Main.

Griener Catherine, domestic L A Fox.

Griener Christian C, laborer Wm Moellering & Co, res 19 Buchanan.

Griep John N, switchman, res 257 Hanna.

Grier Edna E, bds s w cor Pontiac and Oliver.

Grier Joseph H (Hayden & Grier), res s w cor Pontiac and Oliver.

Grier Viola L, bds s w cor Pontiac and Oliver.

Griffin John, brakeman, bds Monroe House.

Griffin Mary, cook Racine Hotel.

Griffin Nora, works Indiana School for Feeble-Minded Youth.

Griffith Chauncy L, carpenter, bds 77 W Williams.

Griffith David S, clk Stewart & Hahn, res 135 Holman.

Griffith James M (Griffith & Son), res n s Suttenfield bet Clinton and Calhoun.

Griffith Mrs Jennie E, dressmaker, rms 16 W Main.

Griffith Levi (Griffith & Son), res 77 W Williams.

Griffith Lewis, carpenter, res 509 E Lewis.

Griffith Miss Nellie M, bds 77 W Williams.

Griffith Miss Rosa V, bds 509 E Lewis.

Griffith Wm S, carpenter, bds 509 E Lewis.

Griffith & Son (Levi and James M), carpenters, 77 W Williams.

Griffiths Wm E, Hardware, 120 and 122 Broadway, res 348 W Washington.

Griftmeyer Frederick, laborer Hoffman Bros, bds 190 W Main.

Griftmeyer Wm, trav agt, res 16 Walnnt.

Grigsby George, switchman Penn Co, bds 414 S Hanna.

Grill Peter, constable Washington tp, res w s Spy Run ave 7 n of St Mary's bridge.

Grime Ferdinand, car builder Penn Co, res 229 Madison.

Grime John P, plumber Robert Ogden, bds 229 Madison.

Grimes Charles A, floor walker Root & Co, res 244 E Washington.

Grimm Clara, dressmaker Mary L Sherin, bds 222 Broadway.

Grimm Flora (wid John), res 222 Broadway.

Grimm Frank, clerk, bds 229 Madison.

Grimm Rose M, bds 229 Madison.

Grimm Theresa, dressmkr Mary L Sherin, bds 222 Broadway.

Grimme Gerhardt B (J H Grimme & Sons), res 162 Griffith.

Grimme John C (J H Grimme & Sons), res 2 McClellan.

Grimme John H (J H Grimme & Sons), res 83 Brackenridge.

Grimme J H & Sons (John H, Gerhardt B and John C), Merchant Tailors, 108 Calhoun.

Grindel Alfred, draughtsman Wing & Mahurin, res 208 W Creighton ave.

Gripton Wm C, laborer, res 44 Wall.

Griswold Crawford, foreman bridge builder, res 165 W De-Wald.

Griswold Maude, cook cor Clinton and Superior.

Griswold Wm H, letter carrier, bds 165 W DeWald.

Griver Isaiah, laborer Hoffman Bros, bds 130 Franklin ave.

Groat Josephine, bds 36 Lillie.

Groat Wm, laborer, res 151 Holman.

Grodzik Henry, wks Indiana School for Feeble-Minded Youth.

Groman Joseph E, painter, bds Jewel House.

Gronau Miss Augusta, bds Ludwig Gronau.

Gronau Frederick W, painter Olds' Wagon Works, res e s Lumbard nr Maumee road.

Gronau Ludwig, machinist Penn Co, res Lumbard 3 s of New Haven rd.

Gronau Wm, laborer, res 112 Hanna.

Gronau Wm, painter, bds Ludwig Gronau.

Gronendyke Mrs Belle, res 86 Montgomery.

Gronendyke John, cigar mnfr, 214 Calhoun, res same.

Groner Chauncey, laborer, res 32 Butler.

Groner Mrs Elsie, nurse, bds 32 Butler.

Groom Harry E, laborer American Wheel Co, bds 31 Gay.

Grosh Gustav, machinist Wabash R R, bds 501 Hanna.

Grosh Henry, car builder Penn Co, res 501 Hanna.

Grosh Joseph H, carpenter J A Crow & Co, bds 501 Hanna.

Grosh Martha K, bds 501 Hanna.

Grosh Minnie (wid John), res 501 Hanna.

Groshoff Frank, servant Hanna homestead.

Groshoff Lizzie, domestic Hanna homestead.

Grosjean Francis J, agent, res 7 Riverside ave.

Grosline Homer A, clk Heller & Frankel, bds 473 Lafayette.

Gross Rev Charles, pastor Emanuel Lutheran Church, res 241 W Jefferson.

Gross Charles, laborer, bds 163 Van Buren.

Gross Charles T, blacksmith Fleming Mnfg Co, res 75 W 3d.

Gross Frank, helper Olds' Wagon Works, res 178 Gay.

Gross Frederick, laborer, bds 163 Van Buren.

Gross Gottlieb, laborer, bds 163 Van Buren.

Gross Louis, machine hand Fort Wayne Furniture Co, res 34 South Wayne ave.

Gross Martin C, bookkeeper Fort Wayne Electric Co, res 128 Rockhill.

Gross Paulina (wid Frederick), res 163 Van Buren.

Gross Wm O (Gross & Pellens), res 159 W Washington.

Gross & Pellens (Wm O Gross, Joseph B Pellens), Druggists and Dealers in Barbers' Supplies, 94 Calhoun.

Grossenbacher Frederick, helper Wabash R R, res 7 Bass.

Grosskopf Carrie, domestic Aveline House.

Grosvenor Harry M, laborer, bds 17 Burgess.

Grote, *see also Grout.*

Grote Frederick, turner American Wheel Co, bds Windsor Hotel.

Grote Frederick H, carpenter, bds 3 Pape.

Grote Louisa, domestic 147 E Berry.

Grote Minnie, bds 120 Harrison.

Grothaus Elizabeth, tailoress Charles Kruse, bds 194 E Wayne.

Grothaus Frances, bds 194 E Wayne.

Grothaus George, laborer, bds 194 E Wayne.

Grothaus Henry, res 194 E Wayne.

Grothaus Joseph H, blacksmith Penn Co, res 194 E Wayne.

Grotholtman Henry A (H A Grotholtman & Co), res 28 E 4th.

Grotholtman H A & Co (Henry A Grotholtman, J Henry Meyers), contractors and builders, 48 W Jefferson.

Grotrian Mary, domestic 211 W Berry.

Grout, *see also Grote.*

Grout Wm H, conductor, res 333 S Harrison.

Grove Maxwell, boilermkr Penn Co, res 25 Butler.

Grove Wm B, rms 51 E Main.

Groves Oscar, conductor, res 11 Force.

Grovner Harry, laborer Hoffman Bros, bds Burgess.

Grubbs Daniel, fireman, rms 47 Elm.

Gruber Anthony, messenger, bds 108 Jackson.

Gruber August C, coppersmith Penn Co, res 62 Walnut.

Gruber Miss Bertha, bds 108 Jackson.

Gruber Caroline, bds 18 Wilt.

Gruber Charles, machine hand Fort Wayne Electric Co, bds 108 Jackson.

Gruber Clementine, drsmkr E A Waltemath, bds 108 Jackson.

Gruber Edward J, machine hand The Peters Box and Lumber Co, res 37 Wall.

Gruber Edward J jr, cigarmaker F J Gruber, bds 18 Wilt.

Gruber Frank J, boilermaker Bass Foundry and Machine Works, res 85 Force.

Gruber Frank J, Cigar Mnfr, 110 Calhoun, res 60 Brackenridge.

Gruber John V, boilermkr Kerr–Murray Mnfg Co, res 1 Pine.

Gruber Joseph A, machinist Fort Wayne Electric Co, res 108 Jackson.

Gruber Joseph L, sec Allen County Loan and Savings Assn,
res 21 Brackenridge.
Gruber Josephine (wid Valentine), bds 37 Wall.
Gruber J Michael, res 18 Wilt.
Gruber J Michael jr, cigarmaker, F J Gruber, bds 18 Wilt.
Gruber Veronica, operator S M Foster, bds 18 Wilt.
Grueneisen Joseph, laborer, res e s Broadway 2 s of Home.
Gruhler Mary (wid Andrew), res 201 Calhoun.
Grummett Wm, agt Prudential Life Ins Co, bds Union House.
Grund Clara, operator S M Foster, bds 59 Melita.
Grund Frederick, mason, res 59 Melita.
Grund John H, truss hoopmaker S D Bitler, res 24 Schick.
Grund Philip R, res 176 W De Wald.
Gruner John, res 119 Eliza.
Grusankamp Frederick, blacksmith, res 51 W 5th.
Guardian Medical and Surgical Institute, Brookfield Gard
physician and manager, 13 W Wayne.
Guebard John F, stone mason, bds 301 Calhoun.
Guenther, *see also Gunther*.
Guenther Anna, works Indiana School for Feeble-Minded
Youth.
Guenther Clara, bds 11 Maumee road.
Guenther Emma, bds 11 Maumee road.
Guenther Henry, barber, 318 E Washington, res 11 Maumee
road.
Guenther Jacob, tailor Leonhardt Jaxtheimer, bds Wells.
Guerne August, collarmaker, bds 27 N Cass.
Guetner Herman, car builder Penn Co, res 154 Smith.
Guffin Elmer, barber, 200 Broadway, res 108 same.
Guhte Joseph, cabinetmaker The Peters Box and Lumber Co,
res 88 4th.
Guida Carl J W, bds 113 W Wayne.
Guiff Fannie, domestic 287 W Berry.
Guiff James, bartender J L Bush, res 30 Duck.
Guiff Paul, market stall No 76, res w s Coldwater rd, 7 miles.
Guiff Sallasty, engineer Fort Wayne Gas Light Co, res 77 E
Superior.
Guiff Victor, mkt stall No 76, res e s Coldwater rd, 7 miles.
Guild Albert D, sec Bass Furnace Co, res 372 Fairfield ave.
Guild Charles G, Supt Jenney Electric Light and Power
Co, bds 372 Fairfield ave.
Guillaume August, driver C L Centlivre, bds John Kintz.
Guillaume James, carpenter, res 57 Wells.
Guldlin Olaf N, pres Western Gas Construction Co, res 148
Clinton.
Gulke Wm, laborer, res New Haven road, 1 w of toll gate.

Gumbert Henry, watchman, res 192 Jackson.

Gumpper Charles H, supply agent N Y, C & St L R R, bds 238 Calhoun.

Gumpper Christian C, baker, 238 Calhoun, res same.

Gumpper Jacob D, Fruit and Produce Commission Merchant, Wholesale Dealer in and Shipper of Oysters, Celery, Fruits and Vegetables, 240 Calhoun, res 16 E DeWald.

Gumpper John F, bricklayer, res 46 Home ave.

Gunder Emanuel, collarmaker Aime Racine, res 223 Wells.

Gunder Henry, laborer Hoffman Bros, res 215 Wells.

Gunkel Otto, laborer Michael Baltes, res 40 Nirdlinger ave.

Gunkel Otto jr, tinner, bds 40 Nirdlinger ave.

Gunkler John, cabinetmaker Fort Wayne Organ Co, res 140 Force.

Gunn Lucian, engineer, res 187 Hayden.

Gunther, *see also Guenther.*

Gunther Charles H, res 203 E Wayne.

Gunther Edward, driver Ryan Bros, bds same.

Gurjohn August, res 86 Smith.

Gurnett Thomas, molder, res 108 Gay.

Gurry Alice, bds Michael Ryan.

Gusching Balthazar, res rear 148 Holman.

Gusching Jacob, tallyman L S & M S Ry, res 137 Wells.

Gusching Joseph, policeman, res 148 Holman.

Gust August, laborer, res 44 Smith.

Gust John, blacksmith, res 65 Oliver.

Gust Matilda, bds 65 Oliver.

Gutermuth Benjamin, baker, 29 W Columbia, res 155 Broadway.

Gutermuth Carrie, operator S M Foster, bds 39 W Jefferson.

Gutermuth Caspar J, laborer, res 39 W Jefferson.

Gutermuth George, bartender Wm Simonton, bds 150 Archer.

Gutermuth George, bds 36 Wilt.

Gutermuth John G, bds 321 W Jefferson.

Gutermuth Valentine, mngr cloak dept Root & Co, res 321 W Jefferson.

Guth Henry, molder Bass Foundry and Machine Works, res 47 Buchanan.

Guthe Joseph, cabinetmaker Fort Wayne Furniture Co, res 88 4th.

Guttner H, car builder Penn Co, res 154 Smith.

Guy John, brakeman, bds 17 Burgess.

Guye Francisca (wid Henry), bds 332 E Washington.

Guyer Rudolph, vegetables, market stall No 18, res n s St Joseph River road e of city limits.

HH

Haag Charles (Brunner & Haag), res 155 Van Buren.

Haag Gottlieb L, stone cutter, Fort Wayne Steam Stone Wks, res 23 Rockhill.

Haag John G, asst supt Prudential Life Insurance Co, res s e cor Lafayette and DeWald.

Haak Theodore, market stall No 64, res e s Lima road, 3 miles out.

Haas, *see also Hass and Hess.*

Haas Rev Charles H, res 111 Wells.

Haas Charlotte (wid Jacob), res s w cor Lafayette and Leith.

Haas Flora (wid John), bds Rose Allen.

Haas Louis H, clerk Penn Co, res 51 Hugh.

Haas Simon, laborer, res 64 Baker.

Haas Wm J, clerk Penn Co, res 292 W Jefferson.

Haase Frank L, helper, res s s Liberty 2 w of Coombs.

Habbert J Henry, porter, res 5 Jones.

Habecker Miss Alice, teacher, bds 64 McClellan.

Habecker Miss Anna, teacher Clay School, bds 64 McClellan.

Habecker Charles W, brakeman, bds 80 Hayden.

Habecker Charles W, printer Fort Wayne Newspaper Union, bds 64 McClellan.

Habecker Elias, carpenter, res 64 McClellan.

Habecker Frank, printer, bds 64 McClellan.

Habecker Wm H, carpenter, res 80 Hayden.

Habel, *see also Abel.*

Habel Charles C, machinist Wabash R R, res 164 Taylor.

Habel John G, mach Kerr-Murray Mnfg Co, res 172 Taylor.

Habel Pauline, seamstress, bds 172 Taylor.

Haberkorn Amelia, bds 130 Harrison.

Haberkorn Emil F, machinist Penn Co, res 130 Harrison.

Haberkorn Henry, machinist Fort Wayne Electric Co, res 236 Hoagland ave.

Haberkorn Theodore, res 69 Douglas ave.

Hache Cecilia, res 222 Madison.

Hachman Frederick, laborer Winch & Son, res 61 Summer.

Hachmann Minnie, domestic 13 Butler.

Hachmeier Henry, brickmason, bds 46 Stophlet.

Hachmeier Minnie, domestic 441 Fairfield ave.

Hachmeier Wm, car builder Penn Co, res 46 Stophlet.

Hackett Block, e s Calhoun bet Wayne and Washington.

Hackett Edward A K, Propr Fort Wayne Sentinel, res 207 W Berry.

Hackius Amelia C, clerk G De Wald & Co, bds 71 Brackenridge.

Hackius F Wm, clerk Root & Co, bds 71 Brackenridge.
Hackius Gustav L, treas Kerr-Murray Mnfg Co, bds 71 Brackenridge.
Hackius Miss Lena M, bds 71 Brackenridge.
Hackius Marie (wid Andrew), res 71 Brackenridge.
Hackius Miss Paulina A, bds 71 Brackenridge.
Haddon Alfred H, machinist Fort Wayne Electric Co, res 25 W Creighton ave.
Hadley Arthur L, clerk Fort Wayne Electric Co, bds 50 W Washington.
Hadley Wm P, laundry, 63 Barr, res 73 E Berry.
Hadsell James, driver, bds 22 W Main.
Haegerman, *see Hagermann.*
Haetsch Simon, res 375 W Main.
Haffner Christian, baker, 105 E Lewis, res 30 Madison.
Haffner Emma, clerk Christian Haffner, bds same.
Haffner Frederick C, driver Christian Haffner, bds 105 E Lewis.
Haffner George M, pedler Christian Haffner, bds same.
Haffner Laurence, machinist, res 39 E De Wald.
Hagan, *see also Hagen.*
Hagan Edward, barber Ehrman & Geller, bds 46 Harrison.
Hagan Mary C (wid Frank), dressmaker, res 46 Harrison.
Hagan Milton, printer, bds 122 Wilt.
Hagan Minnie, bds 122 Wilt.
Hagan Robert W, laborer, res 122 Wilt.
Hagan Thomas W, agricultural impl'ts, res 174 N Harrison.
Hagedorn Ernest, laborer, bds 51 Locust.
Hagan Mrs Wm, bds 247 Webster.
Hagedorn Herman, checker Penn Co, res 51 Locust.
Hagemann Anna, bds 165 Jackson.
Hagemann Elizabeth, bds 188 Broadway.
Hagemann Frederick W, cigarmaker L Dessauer & Co, res 43 Wilt.
Hagemann Henry, clerk, bds 188 Broadway.
Hagemann Louis E, clerk Root & Co, res 165 Jackson.
Hagemann Wm, supervisor, res 188 Broadway.
Hagemann Wm F, cigarmaker, res 43 Wilt.
Hagen, *see also Hagan.*
Hagen Wm, blacksmith Fort Wayne Iron Works, res 105 Butler.
Hagerman, *see also Haegermann.*
Hagerman August, helper Penn Co, bds 363 E Lewis.
Hagerman Henry, laborer, bds 41 Gay.
Hagerman Henry, molder Bass Foundry and Machine Works, bds 92 Oliver.

Hagerty Ella, domestic Wayne Hotel.

Haggarty Jonathan, hostler Fort Wayne Street Railroad Co, res 24 Chicago.

Haggarty Thomas P, hostler Fort Wayne Street Railroad Co, res 26 Chicago.

Hagist Adolph, upholsterer Paul E Wolf, res 421 E Washington.

Hagist Henry, cigarmaker Lewis Bender, bds 433 E Washington.

Hagist John G, laborer, res 433 E Washington.

Hahn Henry, laborer, res 215 John.

Hahn John, car repairer Penn Co, res w s Abbott 2 s of Pontiac.

Hahn Wm, Saloon, Agent for Toledo and Cincinnati Beer, 148 W Main, res 157 same.

Hahn Wm (Stewart & Hahn), res 208 W Berry.

Haiber Charles F, grocer, 122 Wells, res 124 same.

Haiber Frederick, Notary Public and Collection Agent, 64 Wells, res same.

Haiber George W, grocer, s w cor Hanna and E DeWald, res same.

Haiber John J, butcher, res 17 Hoffman.

Haiber Lorenz, meat market, 15 High, bds 64 Wells.

Haiber Wm B, driver, bds 64 Wells.

Haight Garrison, carpenter, res 348 Calhoun.

Hail George S, paperhanger Keil & Keil, res 165 E Washington.

Haines, *see also Haynes.*

Haines Ada, bds 256 E Washington.

Haines Henry H, medicine mnfr, 120 E Lewis, res 256 E Washington.

Haines Morris M, cabinetmaker Fort Wayne Organ Co, bds 471 S Lafayette.

Hake Frank, saloon 26 Wells, res same.

Hake Robert, laborer Bottenberg & Miller, bds Wm Miller.

Hake Rosa (wid Herman), res 152 E Washington.

Hale Joseph, painter N Y, C & St L R R.

Hale Thomas N, conductor Penn Co, res 167 Holman.

Hale Wm S, miller, res 9 Hoffman.

Haley Andrew, laborer, res 74 Murray.

Haley Daniel P, trav agt L Brames & Co, res 197 E Jefferson.

Haley John, brakeman, bds 2 Thomas.

Haley Joseph A, engineer, res 339 W Washington.

Haley Michael, res 224 W Creighton ave.

Hall Albert H, rivetter American Wheel Co, res e s Fletcher ave 1 e of Walton ave.

Hall Edgar M, pedler, res 36 Chestnut.
Hall Edward, laborer Winch & Son, bds Winch.
Hall Mrs Ella, dressmaker, res 18 Hamilton.
Hall Elmira, res 18 Harrison.
Hall Eugene, machinist, bds Wm Hall.
Hall Frank C, flagman Penn Co, res 142 Fairfield ave.
Hall James E, carpenter, res 254 W Creighton ave.
Hall John S, machine hand Winch & Son, bds Wm Hall.
Hall John W, lawyer, bds 254 W Creighton ave.
Hall Mark E, brakeman, res 191 E Washington.
Hall Mrs Mary, res cor Spy Run ave and Elizabeth.
Hall Nelson, laborer, res 147 E Jefferson.
Hall Rinaldo, laborer Penn Co, res 147 E Jefferson.
Hall Samantha B, milliner, 34 W Main, res same
Hall Silas S, blacksmith, bds 34 W Main.
Hall Theodore, teamster, bds 100 Wilt.
Hall Wm, res w s Winch 2 n of Wabash R R.
Hall Wm A jr, foreman The Press, res 128 Lafayette.
Halleck Wm H, flagman Penn Co, res 182 Smith.
Haller Adolph, clerk Gottlieb Haller, res 34 Elm.
Haller Miss Frida, bookkeeper Gottlieb Haller, bds 366 Calhoun.
Haller Gottlieb, Dealer in Fresh and Salt Meats, Hams, etc, also Steam Sausage Manufacturer, 366 Calhoun and 277 Hanna, res 366 Calhoun.
Haller Wm, meat market, 109 E Lewis, bds 100 Montgomery.
Halstead Charles, barber, 70 Barr, bds same.
Halstein Henry D, clk M G Lade, res 188 E Washington.
Halter, *see Alter.*
Hambrock Frederick H, machine hand Olds' Wagon Works, bds 20 Jane.
Hambrock Frederick J, laborer, res 20 Jane.
Hambrock Henry C, machine hand Olds' Wagon Works, bds 20 Jane.
Hambrock Wm J, bricklayer, res 598 Lafayette.
Hamel Henry L, canvasser, rms s e cor Harrison and Washington.
Hamil Miss Alice L, teacher Bloomingdale School, bds 306 W Washington.
Hamil Anna J (wid John W), res 306 W Washington.
Hamilton Albert, hostler Frederick Myers, rms 62 E Wayne.
Hamilton Miss Alice, bds Montgomery Hamilton.
Hamilton Allen, machinist Penn Co, res 19 Holman.
Hamilton Andrew H, vice-pres Olds' Wagon Works, res s e cor Clinton and E Lewis.
Hamilton Bridget (wid John), res 151 W Wayne.

Hamilton Catherine S, bds n s Hanna 5 s of Pontiac.

Hamilton Charles E, harnessmkr G H Kuntz, bds 26 Harrison.

Hamilton Miss Edith, bds Montgomery Hamilton.

Hamilton Eliza (wid Benjamin), res 13 Belle ave.

Hamilton Miss E Louisa, assistant Central Grammar School, bds R J Hamilton.

Hamilton Miss Frances, principal Hoagland School, bds 151 W Wayne.

Hamilton Frederick R, mngr R J Hamilton, bds same.

Hamilton George, laborer, bds 29 Hough.

Hamilton Homestead, s e cor Clinton and Lewis.

Hamilton House, Wm H Jones propr, 103 W Berry.

Hamilton I Louise (wid James), bds 18 Chicago.

Hamilton Miss Jane A, res 235 E Wayne.

Hamilton Joseph F, driver J B White, res 158 W Main.

Hamilton Miss Margaret V, res s e cor Clinton and E Lewis.

Hamilton Montgomery, res n w cor Clinton and Montgomery.

Hamilton Moses, driver Wilding & Son, res 158 W Main.

Hamilton National Bank, Charles McCulloch Pres, John Mohr Jr Cash, Charles W Orr Asst Cash, 44 Calhoun.

Hamilton Peter, boilermaker Wabash R R, res w s Hanna 5 s of Pontiac.

Hamilton Robert J, dairy, n s Bluffton road 1 w of St Mary's river, res same.

Hamilton Robert J jr, bds R J Hamilton.

Hamilton Wm G, mach Wabash R R, bds Peter Hamilton.

Hamilton Wm J, brakeman Penn Co, bds 111 Hanna.

Hamilton Wm J, sawyer, res 407 S Clinton.

Hamlet Jesse, engineer, rms 94 Calhoun.

Hamlin Mattie, domestic 51 Butler.

Hamm Alexander, laborer, bds Andrew Hamm.

Hamm Andrew, laborer Penn Co, res 31 Maumee rd.

Hamm Andrew, market stall 9, res s s New Haven rd s e cor Burd ave.

Hamm Annie, bds Andrew Hamm.

Hamm John, laborer Penn Co, res 250 E Lewis.

Hamm Louisa, bds Andrew Hamm.

Hammer Charles H, cutter S M Foster, bds 22 Brackenridge.

Hammerle Otto, lab Indiana Machine Wks, bds 301 W Main.

Hammerle Xavier, grocer, 297 and 299 W Main, res 301 same.

Hammill Harry B, Propr The Annex Sample Room, 60 Calhoun, res 44 W Wayne.

Hammond James, pastry cook Randall Hotel.

Hammond Martin E, pipe liner Salimonie Mining and Gas Co, res 30 Butler.

Hammond Robert, bartender A Centlivre, res 8 Erie.
Hammond Thomas G, caller Penn Co, res 21 Miner.
Hanagan, *see also Hennigan.*
Hanagan John, fireman, res 344 W Main.
Hancil Wm, bds 2 Thomas.
Hancler A, laborer Penn Co, res 58 Lillie.
Handshiegel Anthony, laborer, res 217 Broadway.
Hanefeld Cord, carpenter, res 190 E Lewis.
Haneseld Carrie, domestic w s Burd ave 1 n of Wabash R R.
Haney Anna M (wid Anton), res 22 W 4th.
Haney Frank, machine hand, bds 22 W 4th.
Haney Isaac, laborer, bds 22 W 4th.
Haney Mrs Maggie S, res 117 Butler.
Hankel Tina, domestic 197 W Wayne.
Hankens Barney, mason, res 141 Suttenfield.
Hanker Hulda, operator S M Foster, bds 40 Charles.
Hanks Mary, seamstress, rms 114 Clinton.
Hanley Albert H, laborer, res 73 N Cass.
Hanley Ellen (wid James H), res rear 43 Baker.
Hanley James J, clk Penn Co, bds e s Monroe 4 s of Wallace.
Hanley John, brakeman, rms 36 Baker.
Hanley Maggie, bds e s Monroe 4 s of Wallace.
Hanley Mary E, bds e s Monroe 4 s of Wallace.
Hanley Paul J, foreman Penn Co, res e s Monroe 4 s of Wallace.
Hanline John M, painter L O Hull, res 25 W Columbia.
Hanna Miss Anna L, bds 135 E Berry.
Hanna Elizabeth C (wid Henry), res 135 E Berry.
Hanna Henry C, lawyer, 8 and 9 Bank blk, res 135 E Berry.
Hanna Homestead, s s Lewis opp Division.
Hanna Hugh T, res Hanna Homestead.
Hanna James T, res 266 W Wayne. —
Hanna John L H, clk Olds' Wagon Wks, bds 288 W Berry.
Hanna Miss Marguerite, artist J A Shoaff, bds 288 W Berry.
Hanna Martha E (wid Samuel T), res 288 W Berry.
Hanna Oliver S, with Nuttman & Co, res 245 W Berry.
Hanna Robert B, U S deputy marshal, res 135 E Berry.
Hanna School, s w cor Hanna and Wallace.
Hannamann Ernest, stone cutter Brunner & Haag, bds 65 Stophlet.
Hannink George, laborer 96 W Wayne.
Hanrahan Timothy, res rear 20 Bass.
Hans Adam, blacksmith Olds' Wagon Works, res 18 Charles.
Hans Bruno, tinsmith, bds 53 Hugh.
Hans Charles A, blacksmith Bass Foundry and Machine Works, res 253 Broadway.

ELECTION SLIPS, Headquarters for Perfect Slips
At JOHN F. EBY & CO.'S, Detroit.

236   R. L. POLK & CO.'S

Hans Laura M, domestic 16 E De Wald.

Hans Theresa (wid Carl), res 53 Hugh.

Hansen Henry F, machine hand American Wheel Co, bds 208 Monroe.

Hansen Joseph, saw filer Fort Wayne Iron Works, res 395 Broadway.

Hansen Peter C, machinist Penn Co, res 208 Monroe.

Hansen Richard C, steam fitter A Hattersley & Sons, res 58 N Harrison.

Hansen Wm E, machinist Fort Wayne Iron Works, bds 58 N Harrison.

Hansing Rev Charles, pastor Evangelical Association Church, res e s Clinton 2 n of Holman.

Hanson Albert P C, blksmith Olds' Wagon Works, res 40 Clay.

Happ, see App.

Harbauer Peter, driver, res rear 301 W Jefferson.

Harber, see also Harper and Herber.

Harber Henry J, flagman, bds 390 Hanna.

Harber Joseph W, helper Penn Co, bds 390 Hanna.

Harber Peter, machinist Penn Co, res 390 Hanna.

Harber Peter jr, painter Olds' Wagon Works, bds 390 Hanna.

Harber Valentine, laborer, res 97 John.

Hardendorf Charles, fireman American Wheel Works, res 169 Gay.

Hardendorf Eugene, bds 113 W Wayne.

Hardendorf Rosell, laborer Penn Co, bds 153 Hanna.

Hardendorf Theodore, turner Louis Diether & Bro, res 13 Barthold.

Harder Daniel B, hostler Lee & Fulton, rms same.

Hardesty Mary, cook Fort Wayne City Hospital.

Hardesty Mrs Mary A, bds 48 W Superior.

Hardesty Wm H, laborer, res 43 W Superior.

Harding Daniel L, Mayor, Insurance, Real Estate and Loans, City Hall, res 174 W DeWald.

Harding Joseph F, brakeman, rms 268 Calhoun.

Harding Perry, laborer, res 179 St Mary's ave.

Harding Robert F, clerk Fort Wayne Electric Co, bds 174 W DeWald.

Hardman Benjamin B, engineer, res 242 E Wayne.

Hardung Frederick, Merchant Tailor, 35 E Main, res 207 Madison.

Hardy Charles H, machinist Fleming Mnfg Co, bds 8 Clark.

Harges August, blacksmith, bds 329 E Washington.

Harges Edward, trimmer City Carriage Works, bds 329 E Washington.

Harges Theodore C, carriagemaker City Carriage Works, bds 329 E Washington.

Harges Wm F, blacksmith Olds' Wagon Works, res 329 E Washington.

Hargon Frederick, laborer, bds 364 E Lewis.

Harkemper Wm, bookkeeper H C Graffe, rms s e cor Calhoun and Columbia.

Harkenrider, *see also Hergenrather.*

Harkenrider Henry J, policeman, res 294 Hanna.

Harkenrider John, brakeman Penn Co, res 86 Force.

Harkenrider John M, car builder Penn Co, res s s Rebecca 3 w of G R & I R R.

Harkenrider Joseph, car builder Penn Co, bds 294 Hanna.

Harkenrider Wm, butcher, res 37 Charles.

Harkins Charles, carpenter, res 104 Guy.

Harlan Perry, tel opr, bds 40 E 5th.

Harlow Elizabeth, domestic 241 W Main.

Harman, *see Herman.*

Harmer School, cor Harmer and E Jefferson.

Harmeyer Frederick, foreman Louis Diether & Bro, res 39 Maiden Lane.

Harmeyer Henry J, helper Penn Co, bds 96 Oliver.

Harmeyer Wm, machine hand Louis Diether & Bro, res 17 Gay.

Harmon Blanche, bds 70 Douglas ave.

Harmon Daniel, res 46 Brackenridge.

Harmon Elma, bds 70 Douglas ave.

Harmon Jonathan C, bds 46 Brackenridge.

Harmon Mary, bds 46 Brackenridge.

Harmon Michael, bds 99 Laselle.

Harmon Samuel W., restaurant, 278 Calhoun, res 70 Douglas.

Harmsdorfer George, grocer, 279 W Jefferson, res 281 same.

Harnischfeger Elizabeth (wid Martin), bds 78 Buchanan.

Harnischfeger Joseph, machine hand Olds' Wagon Works, bds 78 Buchanan.

Harnischfeger Peter, laborer Penn Co, res 78 Buchanan.

Harp Wm, lab, bds 16 Holman.

Harper, *see also Harber.*

Harper Alfred, whitewasher Penn Co, bds 521 Lewis.

Harper Annie L (wid James), res 211 E Wayne.

Harper Benjamin F, lawyer, 10 Pixley & Long bldg, rms 365 W Main.

Harper George, conductor, bds 200 Greely.

Harper James jr, clerk Postoffice, res 211 E Wayne.

Harper James B, Attorney-at-Law, 12 and 13 Bank Block, res 76 E Washington.

Harper John, res 365 W Main.

18

Harper Oliver, machinist, bds 521 E Lewis.
Harper Thomas, conductor, res n e cor Fulton and Greely.
Harper Wm, rimmer, bds 521 E Lewis.
Harr Elmer E (Harr & Zimmerly), res 20 N Cass.
Harr & Zimmerly (Elmer E Harr, Wm A Zimmerly),
    Proprs Model Steam Laundry, cor Superior and Wells.
    (*See right side lines.*)
Harrall James, clerk Wayne Hotel, bds same.
Harries Miss Lydia, bds 63 W Jefferson.
Harries Mary (wid John), res 63 W Jefferson.
Harries Wm F G, clerk Baals & Co, res 79 Hanna.
Harris Albert O, machine hand The Peters Box and Lumber
    Co, res 56 Wells.
Harris Charles F, marker Fort Wayne Organ Co, bds 68 W
    Creighton ave.
Harris Charles G, mngr The Edison Mutual Telegraph Co,
    res 50 N Superior.
Harris Ella F, physician, 148 Calhoun, res same.
Harris Elwood E, plumber Robert Ogden, res 193 Calhoun.
Harris Emmett V, lawyer with Judge Ninde, res 150 Taylor.
Harris George, painter, bds Monroe House.
Harris Henry E, molder Penn Co, res 157 Taylor.
Harris Jesse, laborer, bds 17 N Cass.
Harris Lyman P, physician, 148 Calhoun, res same.
Harrison Miss Agnés, bds 172 Calhoun.
Harrison Grace, bds 22 Charles.
Harrison Edward M, clerk L S & M S Ry, res 82 W 3d.
Harrison Elwood A, switchman, bds 596 Calhoun.
Harrison Harry, bartender, rms 32 E Berry.
Harrison John (col'd), works Indiana School for Feeble-
    Minded Youth.
Harrison Miss Josephine, bookkeeper S M Foster, bds 88 E
    Lewis.
Harrison Michael, laborer, bds 172 Calhoun.
Harrison Robert H, foreman Penn Co, res 22 Charles.
Harrison Thomas, bds 145 Erie.
Harrison Viola, bds 22 Charles.
Harrison Walter S, sign painter, 32 E Columbia, res 39 Madi-
    son.
Harrison Wm, machinist Penn Co, res 88 E Lewis.
Harrison Wm H, res 145 Fairfield ave.
Harrod Eli, res 113 Madison.
Harrod Eulice, bds 113 Madison.
Harrod George W, bds 113 Madison.
Harrod H Seymour, carpenter, bds 113 Madison.
Harrod Melinda, bds 113 Madison.

Sewing Machines, Shears and Pocket Knives, {Pfeiffer & Schlatter 38 & 40 E. Columbia.

FORT WAYNE DIRECTORY. 239

Harsch, *see also Hersh and Hirsch.*
Harsch John, teamster, res 154 Maumee road.
Harsh George G, conductor, bds 164 Harrison.
Harshbarger Hulda L, bookkeeper H W Bond, rms 70 Pixley & Long bldg.
Harshman John N, molder Bass Foundry and Machine Works, res 200 Thomas.
Hart Alice M, domestic Pearse Hotel.
Hart Mrs Catherine, cook Riverside Hotel.
Hart Chauncey S, laborer Penn Co, res cor Maumee road and Dubois.
Hart Daniel, mason, bds 91 E Washington.
Hart George C, laborer Penn Co, res 35 Charles.
Hart Harry H, laborer, bds 27 Taylor.
Hart James, laborer, res 61 Wells.
Hart John C, car builder Penn Co, res 91 E Washington.
Hart John T, helper Penn Co, bds 196 Hanna.
Hart Wm P, baggageman Penn Co, res 60 Buchanan.
Hartel Wm, wheelmaker American Wheel Co, bds 521 E Lewis.
Hartendof Charles, laborer, res 169 Gay.
Harter Charles, laborer, bds 141 N Cass.
Harter George M, laborer Hoffman Bros, res 84 Van Buren.
Harter Joseph, blacksmith, 170 W Main, res same.
Harter Joseph M, brakeman, res 25 Richardson.
Harter Philip, clerk, res 202 W Washington.
Hartigan James, engineer, rms 337 W Main.
Hartley Egbert, laborer, bds rear 65 Hendricks.
Hartley Nelson L, laborer, res 63 Grand.
Hartman Apollonia (wid Valentine B), res St Joseph's Hospital.
Hartman Bessie, domestic 49 W Main.
Hartman Charles A, tel operator Fort Wayne Electric Co, bds 611 S Broadway.
Hartman Eliza (wid George R), bds 167 W Washington.
Hartman Frederick, baker J P Ross & Sons, bds Columbia House.
Hartman George B, postal clerk, res 611 Broadway.
Hartman Gottfried, baker, res 54 Force.
Hartman Henry (Hartman & Bro), bds 344 E Wayne.
Hartman Herman, res 130 E Washington.
Hartman Homer C, lawyer 32 W Berry, res 65 Maple ave.
Hartman Jacob, Saloon, 267 E Wayne, res same.
Hartman John, laborer, res n s Howell e of Rumsey ave.
Hartman John G, cigarmaker Schele Bros, bds 344 E Wayne.

Hartman John H, Groceries, Provisions, Wines and Liquors, also Flour and Feed, 126 E Washington, res same.

Hartman Joseph H (Hartman & Bro), res 63 E Wayne.

Hartman Joseph R, laborer Nickel Plate, bds 44 Burgess.

Hartman Miss Josephine, music teacher, 65 Maple ave, bds same.

Hartman Lem R, cashier First National Bank, res 241 W Wayne.

Hartman Lena, waiter Rich's Hotel, bds same.

Hartman Nancy A (wid George), bds 141 E De Wald.

Hartman Philip, wheel molder Bass Foundry and Machine Works, res w s Lillie 3 s of Creighton ave.

Hartman Stephen, painter, bds John Hartman.

Hartman S Brenton, dentist 1 Schmitz blk, res 536 S Broadway.

Hartman Theresa (wid Adolph), res 344 E Wayne.

Hartman Valentine, coremaker, res 135 Force.

Hartman Wilton W, trav salesman, res 167 W Washington.

Hartman & Bro (Joseph H and Henry), grocers, 63 E Wayne.

Hartmann Anna, seamstress D S Redelsheimer & Co, bds 53 W Jefferson.

Hartmann Charlotte (wid Christian), res 53 W Jefferson.

Hartmann Henry F, helper Penn Co, bds 162 John.

Hartnett Ellen, domestic 416 Fairfield ave.

Hartnett Frank, boilermaker M A Miller, res 68 Baker.

Hartnett James, yard foreman Wabash R R, res 14 Melita.

Hartnett John, porter Grand Central Hotel.

Hartnett Margaret (wid James), res 25 Baker.

Hartnett Murray, bookkeeper S C Lumbard, res 140 E Main.

Hartnett Nellie, bds 68 Baker.

Hartnett Peter R, laborer Penn Co, res 68 Baker.

Hartnett Richard, machinist Penn Co, res 68 Baker.

Hartnett Richard E, printer, bds 25 Baker.

Hartnett Wm, painter, bds 25 Baker.

Hartrup Alonzo C, brick mason, res 156 Taylor.

Hartshorn Alzina M (wid Luther), res room 7 s e cor of Harrison and W Main.

Hartshorn Salem J, res 114 Butler.

Hartstein Andrew, action maker Ft Wayne Organ Co, res 6 Cottage ave.

Hartstein George H, bds 6 Cottage ave.

Hartstein Lewis, laborer Ft Wayne Steam Stone Works, bds 6 Cottage ave.

Hartsuff Wm D, clerk Penn Co, res 235 W Jefferson.

Hartwig, see also Hertwig.

Hartwig Herman H (C Schiefer & Son), res 99 E Main.
Hartzell James D, bartender J H Douglas, res 34 W Butler.
Hartzell Susan, domestic 230 W Washington.
Hartzler Leroy, dispatcher N Y, C & St L R R, bds Rich's Hotel.
Harz Christina, domestic 26 E Washington.
Hascall Miss Hannah B, teacher Westminster Seminary, bds 251 W Main.
Hasel Julius J, laborer, res 121 Fairfield ave.
Hasenfuss John, Propr Riverside Hotel, 2 N Cass.
Hasenfuss Otto A, clerk, bds Riverside Hotel.
Hasenfuss Walter D, clerk Riverside Hotel.
Haskell Edward, laborer, bds 57 Barr.
Haskell George W, painter L O Hull, res 36 Leith.
Haskell James, bds 126 W Williams.
Haskell James M, clerk Penn Co, res 126 W Williams.
Haslanger Phœbe (wid Michael), bds 233 Broadway.
Haslup James, helper Penn Co, res 163 Hanna.
Hass, *see also Haas and Hess.*
Hass Jacob, wheel molder Bass Foundry and Machine Works, res 88 Madison.
Hass Jacob N, machinist Fort Wayne Iron Works, res 2 Thomas.
Hassel George A, cabinetmaker Fort Wayne Furniture Co, res 102 W Superior.
Hassert, *see also Hazzard and Hessert.*
Hassert Thomas, laborer American Wheel Co, bds 27 Maumee ave.
Hassinger Wm H, conductor, res 63 St Martin's.
Hassler Miss Bessie H, stenographer Fort Wayne Organ Co, bds 249 E Jefferson.
Hassler Charles G, fireman, bds 72 Brackenridge.
Hassler Miss Hattie E, bds 72 Brackenridge.
Hassler Kositt D, driver Troy Steam Laundry, res 72 Pearl.
Hassler Sarah J (wid Joseph B), res 72 Brackenridge.
Hasty John, expressman, bds 134 Francis.
Hasty Webster S, plasterer, res 99 N Cass.
Haswell Burton S, newsvender, bds 50 Oliver.
Haswell Emma, operator S M Foster, bds 50 Oliver.
Haswell Frankie, operator S M Foster, bds 50 Oliver.
Haswell George I, finisher Fort Wayne Organ Co, res 50 Oliver.
Hatch Jennie, domestic 29 E Main.
Hatch John E, carpenter, res 38 Walnut.
Hatch Nettie, canvasser, bds 124 Union.
Hatch Wm, carpenter, bds 29 E Main.

Hatfield Jacob, laborer J Klett & Son, res 105 Taylor.
Hathaway James M, carpenter, bds 248 Calhoun.
Hathaway Sarah A (wid John), res 419 W Main.
Hattendorf Caroline (wid Wm), res 30 St Mary's ave.
Hattendorf Henry, cabinetmaker, bds 110 High.
Hattendorf Henry G, laborer, res 9 Herman.
Hattendorf Minnie L, clerk, bds 30 St Mary's ave.
Hattendorf Wm H, laborer, bds 30 St Mary's ave.
Hattersley Alfred (A Hattersley & Sons), res 173 W Wayne.
Hattersley Alfred I, bookkeeper A Hattersley & Sons, bds
    173 W Wayne.
Hattersley A & Sons (Alfred, Willis and Byron E)'
    Plumbers, Steam and Gas Fitters, 48 E Main. (*See em
    bossed line front cover.*)
Hattersley Byron E (A Hattersley & Sons), res 131 E Main.
Hattersley Willis (A Hattersley & Sons), res 60 E Washington.
Hauck, *see also Hawk.*
Hauck John J, teacher, res 111 Griffith.
Haudenschild Jacob, laborer, bds 80 St Mary's ave.
Haudenschild John, section hand, res 80 St Mary's ave.
Haudenschild John jr, plumber, bds 80 St Mary's ave.
Hauenstein Julius, harnessmaker A L Johns & Co, bds 224
    W Main.
Hauk Benjamin, engineer, bds 64 E Berry.
Hauke Frederick, helper, res 108 Maumee road.
Hausbach Jacob, blksmith Bass Foundry and Machine Wks,
    res 76 Leith.
Hausbach Joseph, machinist, bds 34 Leith.
Hausbach Michael, mach Wabash R R, res 181 W De Wald.
Hausback Nicholas, bds 1 Fair.
Hause Christopher C, blacksmith, bds 365 Force.
Hauser, *see also Houser.*
Hauser Elizabeth, bds rear 278 E Jefferson.
Hauser Henry, laborer, res w s Hanna 8 s of Pontiac.
Hausmann Charles, market stall 31, res w of County poor-
    house.
Hauss Daniel F, steamfitter A Hattersley & Sons, bds 8
    McClellan.
Hauss Frederick, bds 8 McClellan.
Hauss Louisa, bds 8 McClellan.
Hauss Susan (wid David), res 8 McClellan.
Hautch George A, stenographer, bds 375 W Main.
Hautch Peter, finisher Horton Mnfg Co, bds 375 W Main.
Hautch Simon, stone cutter, res 375 W Main.
Havens Cora L, operator Central Union Telephone Co, bds
    53 Maumee road.

Havens Frank E, coil winder Fort Wayne Electric Co, bds 53 Maumee road.

Havens Gertrude, bds 53 Maumee road.

Havens Isaac B, bookkeeper McDonald, Watt & Wilt, res 49 Maumee road.

Havens Nathaniel, shoemaker, cor Calhoun and Railroad, res 53 Maumee road.

Havens Tella E, operator Central Union Telephone Co, bds 53 Maumee road.

Haverley Anthony, forgeman Penn Co, bds 138 Lafayette.

Haverley George N, helper Penn Co, bds 138 Lafayette.

Haverley Jennie, tailoress Simon Barnett, bds 138 Lafayette.

Haverley Margaret F, clerk Dozois, Beadell & Co, bds 86 E Main.

Havert Alphonse, res 146 Holman.

Havert Louis J, brakeman, bds 119 Holman.

Havert Mary M (wid Theodore), res 119 Holman.

Hawk, *see also Hock.*

Hawk Bina, seamstress D S Redelsheimer & Co, bds Melita.

Hawk Ionia, seamstress D S Redelsheimer & Co, bds Melita.

Hawk Wm, laborer, bds 163 Francis.

Hawkins Edward, cigarmaker, bds 96 Wells.

Hawley Kate, operator Hoosier Mnfg Co, bds 47 Barr.

Hawthonton Miss Ida, dressmaker, 110 Calhoun, res same.

Hay Hannah M (wid Augustus A), res 236 W Main.

Hay Lizzie, dressmaker, bds 30 Laselle.

Haycock James, butcher, res 43 Grand.

Hayden Mrs Elizabeth (wid Isaac), res 144 Pritchard.

Hayden Frank M, mngr S E Hayden, res 166 Calhoun.

Hayden Frederick J, real estate, res Hanna homestead.

Hayden Miss Grace G, teacher, bds 68 Thompson ave.

Hayden John W (Hayden & Grier), Lawyer, 22 Bank Block, res 68 Thompson ave.

Hayden Park, e s Harmer bet Maumee road and E Jefferson.

Hayden Susan E, furniture, 184 Calhoun, res 166 same.

Hayden & Grier (John W Hayden, Joseph H Grier), Real Estate and Loans, 22 Bank Block.

Hayes, *see also Hays.*

Hayes Bridget (wid Dennis), res 92 Calhoun.

Hayes Daniel M, conductor, rms 17 W Lewis.

Hayes Dennis T, yardmaster Wabash R R, res 31 Colerick.

Hayes Harry, machinist, bds Windsor Hotel.

Hayes James J, conductor, res 46 Oliver.

Hayes James J, fireman, rms 23 Douglas ave.

Hayes Miss Jennie M, bds 346 W Washington.

Hayes John, helper Penn Co, bds 172 Montgomery.

Hayes John H, carpenter, res 19 Elm.
Hayes Neil, section hand L S & M S Ry, res 16 Clark.
Hayes Richard M (evangelist), res 346 W Washington.
Hayes Tena, domestic 136 E Berry.
Hayes Thomas D, res 25 Colerick.
Haynes, *see also Haines.*
Haynes Frank, engineer Penn Co, res 36 W Williams.
Hays, *see also Hayes.*
Hays Charles A, justice of peace, 13 E Main, res Rockhill
     hill heirs' addition.
Hays John B, brakeman, bds 282 S Harrison.
Hays Wm H, conductor, res 10 Jackson.
Hazzard, *see also Hassert.*
Hazzard Albert W, cigarmaker L Dessauer & Co, res 39
     Marion.
Hazzard Henry, grinder American Wheel Co, bds 37 Maumee
     road.
Hazzard John, machinist, bds 37 Maumee rd.
Hazzard Louis N, res 39 Marion.
Hazzard Wm, dairyman, e s Lumbard 1 s of Wabash R R,
     res same.
Head Irving, carpenter, res 42 Harmer.
Heany, *see also Heine.*
Heany Anna M (wid Antoine), res 22 W 4th.
Heany Isaac, sawyer Hoffman Bros, bds 22 W 4th.
Hearlihie Ellen (wid Thomas), res 48 Baker.
Heath Benjamin F, painter, res 86 Barr.
Heath Edward, res 64 E Columbia.
Heath Herbert W, clk Pixley & Co, rms Pixley & Long bldg.
Heath Wilbur F, supt music public schools, res 68 Pixley &
     Long bldg.
Heathman Charles, laborer Ranke & Yergens, bds n w cor
     Franklin and Pfeiffer ave.
Heathman David, laborer, res 129 Franklin ave.
Heathman Lee E, machine hand Louis Rastetter, bds David
     Heathman.
Heaton, *see also Eaton.*
Heaton Charles E, druggist, 36 E Berry, res 88 N Harrison.
Heaton Ellis J, stenographer O N Heaton, bds Owen N
     Heaton.
Heaton Owen N, Lawyer, over 44 Calhoun, res 260 S
     Hoagland ave.
Heaton Samantha C (wid Jesse), bds 260 S Hoagland ave.
Hebbison George M, watchman, res 28 W Williams.
Heber John, laborer, bds 325 E Lewis.
Hebert, *see also Ebert.*

Hebert Herman, brakeman Penn Co, bds 219 Lafayette.
Hebert Josephine, bds 73 Thomas.
Hebert Oliver, engineer, res 73 Thomas.
Hebrew Cemetery, west of Lindenwood Cemetery.
Heck Christina, domestic Fritz Hotel.
Heck Louis C, cigar mnfr, 79 E Washington, res 49 W
 Washington.
Heck Mary, operator Hoosier Mnfg Co, bds 152 E Washington.
Heck Regina, domestic 16 E Washington.
Heck Sophie, domestic Aveline House.
Hecke Rose (wid Herman), res 152 E Washington.
Heckey Daniel, conductor, bds Lake Shore Hotel.
Heckey Morris, engineer, bds Lake Shore Hotel.
Heckler Charles W, hostler J S Hooper, bds 15 Pearl.
Heckler Elmer, apprentice Robert Spice, bds 15 Pearl.
Heckler George, boarding house, 15 Pearl.
Heckman Wm C, traveling agent, res 157 W Berry.
Hedekin Miss Bessie, bds 94 W Wayne.
Hedekin Edwin C, bds 94 W Wayne.
Hedekin House, J W Swaidner propr, 25 Barr.
Hedekin Miss May C, tchr Hanna School, bds 94 W Wayne.
Hedekin Thomas B, res 94 W Wayne.
Hedges Bailey S, fireman, res 19 Colerick.
Hedges Edward, laborer, res 40 Chicago.
Hedges John P, agent L Bash & Co, res 20 W 3d.
Hedges Thomas J, laborer Penn Co, res 323 W Main.
Heffelfinger Arthur I, blacksmith M L Albrecht, bds 200
 Greely.
Heffelfinger Jay, setter The Peters Box and Lumber Co, bds
 200 Greely.
Heffelfinger John M, clerk Pixley & Co, res 200 Greely.
Heffelfinger John W, brakeman, bds 200 Greely.
Heffert John, laborer, res 100 Montgomery.
Heffert Matilda, bds 100 Montgomery.
Hefter Annie (wid George), res 218 Broadway.
Hefter Henry, machine hand Louis Rastetter, bds 218 Broad-
 way.
Heger Edith E M, dressmaker, bds 391 E Washington.
Heger Emma H, bds 391 E Washington.
Heger George M, clerk J B White, res 391 E Washington.
Heger George W F, clerk H J Ash, bds 391 E Washington.
Hegerfeld Charles, teamster Wm Moellering, bds 120 Mont-
 gomery.
Heibler Emma L (wid Frank), res 14 E Columbia.
Heibler Jane P (wid George W), bds 116 Butler.
Heid, *see Heit and Hite.*

Heidenreich Amand J, laborer Bass Foundry and Machine Works, res 110 W De Wald.

Heidenreich Jacob, rivetter, bds 110 W De Wald.

Heidenreich Joseph, helper Bass Foundry and Machine Works, bds 116 W De Wald.

Heider Albert, bricklayer, res 87 Wall.

Heiger Wm, bricklayer, res s s Maysville road near toll gate.

Heikowski Florentina (wid Ferdinand), res 211 John.

Heilbroner Abraham, res 62 W Main.

Heilbroner Carrie, clerk Redlich Bros, bds 56 W Wayne.

Heilbroner Clara, bds 62 W Main.

Heilbroner Louis (Heilbroner & Brown), res 56 W Wayne.

Heilbroner Louis, clerk Isidor Lehman, bds 62 W Main.

Heilbroner Samuel, res 56 W Wayne.

Heilbroner Samuel A, shoemaker, 27 Pearl, res 62 W Main.

Heilbroner & Brown (Louis Heilbroner, George H Brown), Saloon, 18 W Berry.

Heimroth Andrew, laborer Penn Co, res 60 E Washington.

Heine Anna C, domestic 410 Lafayette.

Heine Christina (wid Frederick), res 96 Madison.

Heine Ernest, clerk, bds 52 Douglas ave.

Heine Frederick C, painter, res 130 Wallace.

Heine Frederick W, laborer Penn Co, bds 53 Douglas ave.

Heine Gottlieb W, boilermaker Bass Foundry and Machine Works, res 191 Hanna.

Heine Henry, blacksmith helper Penn Co, bds 52 Buchanan.

Heine Henry, engineer The Herman Berghoff Brewing Co, bds 17 Wabash ave.

Heine John C, machinist Bass Foundry and Machine Works, res 98 Madison.

Heine Minnie, domestic 25 W De Wald.

Heine Nicholas, salesman A C Trentman, res 122 E Wayne.

Heine Wm, watchman Penn Co, res 167 Hanna.

Heine Wm jr, laborer Penn Co, res 167 Hanna.

Heine Wm C D, truss hoopmaker S D Bitler, bds 167 Hanna.

Heineman Matilda, dressmkr Mary Edwards, bds 131 Jackson.

Heiney Lizzie, bds 122 E Wayne.

Heiney Maggie, bds 122 E Wayne.

Heiney Nicholas, salesman, res 122 E Wayne.

Heingartner Emma, tailoress, bds 155 W Main.

Heingartner Eugene, bds 155 W Main.

Heingartner Frederick, teamster, bds 155 W Main.

Heingartner Sivella (wid Martin), res 155 W Main.

Heinig Max F, painter Olds' Wagon Works, bds 266 E Creighton ave.

Heinlen Arthur, machinist Wabash R R, bds 128 Butler.

Heinlen Eugenie M, milliner Wm Malloy, bds 128 Butler.
Heinlen Wm J, machinist Wabash R R, res 128 Butler.
Heinrich Elizabeth, bds 85 Monroe.
Heinrich Louis (Stahn & Heinrich), res 85 Monroe.
Heinrich Rudolph, clerk H F Beverforden, bds 85 Monroe.
Heiskel Amandus, laborer, res 46 S Wayne ave.
Heisner Charles, teamster, res 170 Gay.
Heisner Charles jr, clerk, bds 170 Gay.
Heist Frederick, machinist Penn Co, res 305 Calhoun.
Heisterman John, fireman, rms 27 Baker.
Heit, *see also Hite.*
Heit Alexander, butcher, res 74 Wells.
Heit Amos, foreman C F Muehler & Co, res 129 W De Wald.
Heit Anthony W, trav agt Louis Fox & Bro, res 60 Douglas.
Heit Catherine, packer, bds 74 Wells.
Heit Charles F J, clerk Zoeller & Merz, bds 129 W De Wald.
Heit Christopher, trav agt Louis Fox & Bro, res 188 Griffith.
Heit Elizabeth, bds 74 Wells.
Heit Frank, cutter Hoosier Mnfg Co, bds 21 Nirdlinger av.
Heit George H, tinner J P Gray, bds 129 W De Wald.
Heit Joseph J, trav agt Louis Fox & Bro, res 190 Griffith.
Heit Josephine (wid Anthony), res 190 Griffith.
Heit Kate, works J O Keller, bds 74 Wells.
Heit Lena, opr Hoosier Mnfg Co, bds 74 Wells.
Heit Matilda, tailoress A F Schoch, bds 74 Wells.
Heit Wm, carpenter, bds 21 Nirdlinger ave.
Heitkam Charles P, machinist Fort Wayne Electric Co, res
        37 Walnut.
Heitkam Eliza (wid Charles A), bds 37 Walnut.
Heitkam Martin, whitewasher Penn Co, res 27 Taylor.
Heitwinkel Henry, bds 43 Charles.
Heitzler Elizabeth M, bds 48 Walter.
Heitzler Joseph, brakeman, bds 48 Walter.
Heitzler Mrs Margaret M, res 48 Walter.
Heitzman, *see Hitzemann.*
Helbig Charles E, tinner Pickard Bros, bds 53 Hugh.
Heldt Barbara (wid John M), bds 182 E Wayne.
Heldt Miss Elizabeth M, bds 182 E Wayne.
Heldt John, barber C A Shidel, bds 182 E Wayne.
Helker, *see also Hilker.*
Helker J Frederick, laborer, res 175 W Washington.
Helker Wm, driver Fort Wayne Transfer & Baggage Line,
        res 175 W Washington.
Hellbert Mary, domestic, 139 Force.
Helle Andrew, helper Bass Foundry and Machine Works, res
        74 Murray.

Heller Miss Ada M, stenographer Fort Wayne Newspaper
. Union, bds 32 W Washington.
Heller Flora A, bds 32 W Washington.
Heller George W (Heller & Frankel), bds 22 W Washington.
Heller John C, deputy recorder Allen county, res 32 W
    Washington.
Heller John W, traveling agent, res 71 College.
Heller Lulu C, bds 32 W Washington.
Heller Mahlon, deputy sheriff, res 72 Cass.
Heller Martin, helper, res 71 Buchanan.
Heller Paul, lab Ft Wayne Steam Stone Works, res 55 Wall.
Heller Thomas S (Heller & Bottenberg), res 32 W. Wash-
    ington.
Heller Wm E, clerk, bds 32 W Washington.
Heller Wm L, foreman The Peters Box and Lumber Co, res
    89 Barthold.
Heller & Bottenberg (Thomas S Heller, Daniel Bottenberg),
    implements, 58 E Columbia.
Heller & Frankel (George W Heller, Louis Frankel), cloth-
    ing, 40 Calhoun.
Helley Charles, laborer, bds 185 Jackson.
Helling Frederick W, ice dealer, res 189 Griffith.
Helling John F W, teamster, bds 83 W Washington.
Helling Miss Minnie, bds 83 W Washington.
Helling Miss Mollie, bds 83 W Washington.
Hellinger J, laborer Penn Co, res 15 Erie.
Helmer Fannie (wid Harry), housekeeper R M Cloud.
Helmes August, patternmaker, res 54 Smith.
Helmes John, laborer, bds 54 Smith.
Helmick Ida, dressmaker Druhot Sisters, bds 99 E Lewis.
Helmkamp Henry, carpenter, res 344 Broadway.
Helmke Edward, cabinetmaker, bds 13 Douglas ave.
Helmke F W Edward, shoes, 212½ Calhoun, res 13 Douglas av.
Helmke Herman, shoes, 45 W Main, res same.
Helwig Bertha, seamstress D S Redelsheimer & Co, bds 227
    Gay.
Helwig Julia (wid Emil), carpet weaver, 227 Gay, res same.
Hemmann Benjamin M, teacher St Paul's German-Lutheran
    School, res 166 Barr.
Henaman Miles, laborer Salimonie Mining and Gas Co, bds
    43½ Columbia.
Hench, *see also Hensch*.
Hench George R, foreman news room Fort Wayne Sentinel,
    res 383 E Wayne.
Hench Robert H, printer Fort Wayne Sentinel, res 383 E
    Wayne.

Hench Samuel M, Attorney-at-Law, 31 E Main, bds 9 E Wayne.

Henderson Alexander, engineer Wabash R R, res 407 S Broadway.

Henderson Andrew R, supt, res 115 E Wayne.

Henderson Angeline M (wid Wm D), res 86 E Main.

Henderson Anna, bds 106 W Superior.

Henderson Arthur, cutter Hoosier Mnfg Co, bds 100 E Superior.

Henderson Charles F, lawyer, 204 E Wayne, res same.

Henderson Charles W, trav agt S F Bowser & Co, res 115 E Wayne.

Henderson David, laborer Hoffman Bros, res 106 W Superior.

Henderson David, watchman French, Hanna & Co, res 100 E Superior.

Henderson Henry C, brass finisher E B Kunkle & Co, res 149 Barr.

Henderson Milton J, driver Model Steam Laundry, bds 100 E Superior.

Henderson Samuel C, foreman Penn Co, res 29 W Wayne.

Henderson Thomas J, truckman Wabash R R, bds 31 Colerick.

Henderson Wm (col'd), laborer, bds 31 Pearl.

Henderson Wm D, feed, 69 E Columbia, res 86 E Main.

Hendler Gilbert, mach hand American Wheel Co, bds 24 Murray.

Hendler John, brakeman, bds 248 Calhoun.

Hendler Joseph, laborer, bds 24 Murray.

Hendrix George A, conductor Penn Co, res 136 Buchanan.

Hendrix Miss Georgie, bds 26 Van Buren.

Heneline Wm D, carpenter, res 36 Pritchard.

Hener Christopher, watchman, res 107 Force.

Hengsteler Charles, shoemkr L P Huser, bds 199 Broadway.

Hengsteter Martin, blacksmith Bass Foundry and Machine Works, res 222 Gay.

Henker Charles F, barber Walter & Ellert, bds 40 Charles.

Henker Clara, bds 40 Charles.

Henker Ferdinand, wagonmaker, res 83 Shawnee ave.

Henker Hulda, bds 40 Charles.

Henker Laura, bds 40 Charles.

Henker Minnie (wid Charles), res 40 Charles.

Henker Wm C, machine hand Olds' Wagon Works, bds 40 Charles.

Henline John H, carpenter, bds 65 Barthold.

Henline Samuel, carpenter, res 65 Barthold.

Hennessey Alexander, section hand, res 11 Pape.

Hennessey Michael, plasterer, bds 22 Winch.

Henning George, laborer Louis Rastetter, bds Wm Hampton.

Henninger Gottfried, laborer, res 99 Riverside ave.

Hennings Frederick J jr, laborer Rockhill Bros & Fleming, bds same.

Henry Miss Alma A, bds 34 Chicago.

Henry August, shoemaker, 24 Barr, rms same.

Henry Carrol B, brakeman, bds 325 W Jefferson.

Henry Jacob, Pictures and Frames, 379 Lafayette, res same.

Henry James M (Liebman & Henry), res s s Grace 3 e of Broadway.

Henry John, laborer Penn Co, res 14 Oak.

Henry John A, boarding house, 34 Chicago.

Henry John G, laborer, bds 34 Chicago.

Henry John M, carpenter, res 325 W Jefferson.

Henry John W, shoemaker, s e cor Creighton and Oliver, res same.

Henry Julius A, carpenter, res 14 Oak.

Henry Mary A, bds 93 Shawnee ave.

Henry Wm H, hostler, res 93 Shawnee ave.

Hensch, *see also Hench.*

Hensch August, laborer Penn Co, res s s Eckart 2 e of Hanna.

Henschen Mrs Belle, res 418 E Washington.

Henschen Edward, brakeman, bds 164 Ewing.

Henschen Ernst H, coremaker Bass Foundry and Machine Works, res 242 E Jefferson.

Henschen George H, car repairer Penn Co, res n s Chestnut 1 w of Glasgow ave.

Henschen Henry F, driver C H Waltemath & Sons, res 52 Charles.

Henschen Henry G, car repairer Penn Co, res 40 Chestnut.

Henschen Henry J, clerk Coombs & Co, res 164 Ewing.

Henschen John H, res 164 Ewing.

Henschen Mary, packer Pottlitzer Bros, bds 222 Francis.

Henschen Wm R, laborer Penn Co, res 222 Francis.

Henschleger Anton, potash maker C Strasburg & Sons, res Broadway.

Hensel Anna, bds 37 Gay.

Hensel Frederick W, machinist Fort Wayne Iron Works, res 37 Gay.

Hensel Peter, contractor, 37 Miner, res same.

Hensel Wm, molder Bass Foundry and Machine Works, bds 37 Gay.

Hensel Wm F, machinist Fort Wayne Iron Works, res 37 Gay.

Henshaw Lillie, works Indiana School for Feeble-Minded Youth.
Hensler Irvin, machine hand American Wheel Co, res 103 Force.
Henson Thomas, waiter, rms 65 Baker.
Hentzell Wm, carpenter, res 339 Hanna.
Henz Charles, laborer Bass Foundry and Machine Works, res 344 Force.
Henze Wm, shoemaker, 102 Wells, res same.
Henze Wm jr, molder Ft Wayne Iron Works, bds 102 Wells.
Henzel John G, gasfitter Salimonie Mining and Gas Co, bds 29 E Main.
Hepnor Wm, bell boy Aveline House.
Herber, see also Harber.
Herber Fred E, car builder Penn Co, res 210 Lafayette.
Herber Frederick I, car builder Penn Co, res 144 Force.
Herber Gerhard, carpenter, bds 86 Walton ave.
Herber Jacob, carpenter, bds 86 Walton ave.
Herber John F, carpenter, res 86 Walton ave.
Herbert Valentine, blacksmith Olds' Wagon Works, res 96 John.
Herbst Dora (wid Frederick), res 507 E Lewis.
Herbst Otto P, bookkeeper Hamilton National Bank, res 319 Lafayette.
Herderhorst Ernest, carpenter, bds 136 Francis.
Hergenrader Michael, laborer, res 43 Wall.
Hergenrather, see also Harkenrider.
Hergenrather Joseph, bricklayer, res 389 E Washington.
Hergenrather Joseph jr, laborer, bds 43 Nirdlinger ave.
Hergenrather Maggie (wid Joseph), bds 43 Nirdlinger ave.
Hergenrother Henry, cooper, 76 Murray, res same.
Hergenrother Wm, machine hand Olds' Wagon Works, bds 76 Murray.
Herman, see also Hermon and Herrmann.
Herman David, brakeman Penn Co, res 310 S Hanna.
Herman John, engineer John Orff, res 40 Boone.
Herman John A, carpenter, res 339 Hanna.
Herman Nicholas, laborer Penn Co, res 55 Thomas.
Hermann D Alexander, res 353 E Washington.
Hermann Theodore, instrument maker Fort Wayne Electric Co, res 144 Taylor.
Hermas August, pattern maker Bass Foundry and Machine Works, res 54 Smith
Hermas John, laborer Penn Co, bds 54 Smith.
Hermeler Delia, bds 28 Huron.
Hermeler Henry, laborer Hoffman Bros, bds 28 Huron.

Hermeler Henry jr, bds 28 Huron.

Hermeler Sophia, bds 28 Huron.

Hermsdorfer Frederick C, res 222 W Washington.

Hermsdorfer George A, grocer, 281 W Jefferson, res same.

Hermsdorfer John, machine hand, bds 222 W Washington.

Herold Daniel J, laborer, bds e s Spy Run ave 2 n of St Mary's bridge.

Herr Charles, laborer, res 590 Lafayette.

Herr James, bricklayer, bds 91 E Washington.

Herr Mary, domestic 327 Lafayette.

Herres Mathias, section hand Penn Co, res cor Euclid ave and Milan.

Herrick Ruth (wid Wm R), res n s Ruth 1 west of Spy Run.

Herring, *see also Hering.*

Herring George, teamster, res 15 Rockhill.

Herring Howard L, canvasser Indiana Installment Co, rms 127 Calhoun.

Herring Isaac, laborer, bds 3 Glasgow ave.

Herring Jemima, bds 3 Glasgow ave.

Herring John P, conductor, res 204 Walton ave.

Herring Oliver, bds 3 Glasgow ave.

Herring P C, conductor Penn Co, res w s Walton ave 5 s of P, F W & C Ry.

Herring Zachariah, laborer, res 3 Glasgow ave.

Herrington Block, e s Fairfield ave bet Williams and Bass.

Herrmann, *see also Herman.*

Herrmann George, laborer, res 82 Walton ave.

Herrmann George jr, clerk, bds 82 Walton ave.

Herron Isaac, farmer, bds 23 Thompson ave.

Herron Isaac, laborer, bds J W H Hummel.

Herrs Mary, domestic 327 Lafayette.

Hersche John, laborer Bass Foundry and Machine Works, res 78 John.

Herschfelder, *see Hirschfelder.*

Hersh, *see also Harsch and Hirsch.*

Hersh Joseph W, clk G H Wilson & Sons, res 328 Lafayette.

Hershey Charles C, fireman, bds 329 W Main.

Hershey Christian, tanner, res 329 W Main.

Hershey J Milton, carriage painter M L Albrecht, bds 12 Harrison.

Hershey Philip, laborer, res 261 Hanna.

Hershman John N, molder Bass Foundry and Machine Works, res 200 Thomas.

Hertwig, *see also Hartwig.*

Hertwig Paul, carpet weaver, 287 E Lewis, res same.

Hesemeier Henry, bricklayer, res 15 Pritchard.

Hess, *see also Haas and Hass.*

Hess Charles F, machine hand Fort Wayne Electric Co, bds 28 Nirdlinger ave.

Hess Charlotte (wid Jacob), res s w cor Lafayette and Leith.

Hess Frank J, painter Olds' Wagon Works, bds Nicholas Hess.

Hess George F, machinist Penn Co, bds 132 E Creighton av.

Hess John, truckman, res 40 Wefel.

Hess John R, cornicemaker, bds 40 Wefel.

Hess Laura F, bds N W Hess.

Hess Lee, clerk F D Clarke, bds 46 W Wayne.

Hess Nicholas W, carriagemaker B H Baker, res s s Elizabeth 7 w of Spy Run ave.

Hess Philip, painter E P Nestel, res n s Pontiac nr Hanna.

Hess Philip J, mach Penn Co, res 133 E Creighton ave.

Hess Wm E, machine hand Fort Wayne Electric Co, bds 40 Wefel.

Hess Wm E J, clk Penn Co, bds 132 E Creighton ave.

Hess Wm H, painter Old Fort Mnfg Co, bds s s Elizabeth 8 w of Spy Run ave.

Hessert, *see also Hassert and Hazzard.*

Hessert Bernard, teamster, res 103 N Cass.

Hessert George, teamster, res 225 W Superior.

Hessert John B, clk Fort Wayne Transfer and Storage Co, bds 103 N Cass.

Heth Annie, bds 206 Lafayette.

Heth Miss Emma, milliner Mrs E A Flagler, bds 206 Lafayette.

Heth Jacob, res 206 Lafayette.

Heth Tillie, clerk Wm Moellering & Sons, bds 206 Lafayette.

Hetrick Jacob (J Hetrick & Co), res 160 E Wayne.

Hetrick Miss Julia E, bds 160 E Wayne.

Hetrick J & Co (Jacob Hetrick, John M Neufer), druggists, 303 E Washington.

Hetrick Miss Minnie M, bds 160 E Wayne.

Hettendorf Henry, cabinetmkr The Peters Box and Lumber Co, bds 110 High.

Hettler Albert, laborer, bds 61 Laselle.

Hettler Christopher F, agent, res 99 E Lewis.

Hettler Clara, bds 61 Laselle.

Hettler Ehinger, polisher, bds 61 Laselle.

Hettler Gottlieb, sewer builder, 84 Charles, res same.

Hettler Mrs Harriet, res 61 Laselle.

Hetzel Mathias, laborer Penn Co, res 208 Lafayette.

Heuber Isidore, driver Fort Wayne Artificial Ice Co.

Heuer Ernst, boilermaker Ft W, C & L R R, res 59 Maumee.

Heuer Fredericka (wid Herman), res 55 W Wayne.

19

Heuer Martin, bds 55 W Wayne.
Heuer Wm F, carpenter Wm Bruns, res 326 Hanna.
Heugnard, see Huguenard.
Heur Christian, watchman, res 107 Force.
Heur Wm, sawyer, bds 107 Force.
Hewes, see also Hughes.
Hewes James C, foreman, res 142 E Lewis.
Hewitt Allie, bds 17 Euclid ave.
Hewitt Etta, operator S M Foster, bds 17 Euclid ave.
Hewitt George, flagman, res 17 Euclid ave.
Hey Wm B, laborer The Remington-Lawton Co, bds 57 Barr.
Heymann J, car builder Penn Co, res 225 Calhoun.
Hibbert Henry, laborer, res 5 Jones.
Hibbins Thomas H, roofer, res 74 Baker.
Hibernia Hall, 176 Calhoun.
Hibler Anthony, laborer J A Koehler, res e s Lafayette 5 s of Pontiac.
Hibler Bernard, teamster, res e s Lafayette 4 s of Pontiac.
Hibler Bernard A, blacksmith Wabash R R, res 46 Miner.
Hibler Henry, helper Wabash R R, res e s Lafayette 4 s of Lee.
Hibler Lewis, sawyer, res 41 Wallace.
Hickman Alfred M, laborer, res 127 Franklin ave.
Hickman Arthur E, machine hand Hoffman Bros, bds 195 Sherman.
Hickman Miss Cora B, bds 216 W Washington.
Hickman Daniel, teamster, res 195 Sherman.
Hickman Edward A, machine hand, bds 195 Sherman.
Hickman Eugene, sawyer, res 33 Elm.
Hickman George, laborer, bds 118 Franklin ave.
Hickman James, fruit, res 216 W Washington.
Hickman John C, machinist Penn Co, bds 49 Indiana ave.
Hickman John W, carpet weaver, 157 Wells, res same.
Hickman Laura E, clerk J O Keller, bds 216 W Washington.
Hickman Rosa D, seamstress, bds 195 Sherman.
Hickman Wm, res 118 Franklin ave.
Hicks Wm, laborer Paul Koehler, bds same.
Hieche, see Heche.
Hieber Isidore, laborer bds 103 Erie.
Hiefner Jacob, cabinetmaker Fort Wayne Organ Co, res 71 Oakley.
Hiel Frederick, barn man Fort Wayne Transfer and Baggage Line, bds 43 W Superior.
Hielkier Richard, machine hand Olds' Wagon Works, res 63 Buchanan.
Hierholzer Mary M (wid Kolmanus), bds 50 W Main.

Hiesner Charles, teamster Rhinesmith & Simonson, res 186 Gay.

Higgins C R, Postmaster, Government Bldg, res 160 E Berry.

Higgins Frank P, engineer, res 143 E Jefferson.

Higgins Miss Maggie, bds 143 E Jefferson.

Highland Henry, laborer, bds 221 John.

Higley Joseph E, laborer, bds 365 Force.

Higley Martha J (wid Edward D), res 365 Force.

Hilbrecht Henry, bds 256 W Jefferson.

Hilbrecht Henry jr, chief fire dept, cor Court and E Berry, res 61 Clinton.

Hilbrecht Miss Louisa S, bds 256 W Jefferson.

Hild Albert D, machinist Kerr-Murray Mnfg Co, bds 159 Van Buren.

Hild Henry, Sign and Carriage Painter, 149 W Main, res 159 Van Buren.

Hild Otto G, tel insptr, bds 159 Van Buren.

Hild Valentine, cigarmaker, res 282 Broadway.

Hildebrand Frederick, carpenter, res 215 Madison.

Hildebrand Frederick W, fireman, bds 234 W Washington.

Hildebrand Louisa (wid Joseph), bds 92 Wilt.

Hildebrand Wm H, res 234 W Washington.

Hildebrand Frank, traveling agent, rms 303 Calhoun.

Hildeman Ernest, laborer, res 24 Fulton.

Hildinger Caroline, bds 15 Erie.

Hildinger John J, laborer Penn Co, res 15 Erie.

Hiler Frank E, bookkeper, bds J V Hiler.

Hiler John V, carpenter, 470 Fairfield ave, res n s Killea 2 e of Hoagland ave.

Hilgemann August, brakeman, res 37 W Main.

Hilgemann August H, hostler Fort Wayne Transfer and Baggage Line, res 163 E Jefferson.

Hilgemann Emma, packer Pottlitzer Bros, bds cor Baker and Fairfield ave.

Hilgemann Ernst, laborer Wm & J J Geake, res 24 Fulton.

Hilgemann Ernst H (Ernst H Hilgemann & Son), res s s Baker 3 e of Fairfield ave.

Hilgemann Ernst H & Son (Ernst H and Louis), Carpenters, Contractors and Practical Builders, s e cor Baker and Fairfield ave. (See adv, p 67.)

Hilgemann Ernst R, car repairer, res 559 Broadway.

Hilgemann Florance W, machinist Fort Wayne Electric Co, bds 24 Walnut.

Hilgemann Frederick, laborer, res 66 Smith.

Hilgemann Frederick jr, laborer, bds 66 Smith.

Hilgemann Frederick, machine hand White's Wheel Works, bds 66 Smith.

Hilgemann Frederick G, coil winder Fort Wayne Electric Co, res 24 Walnut.

Hilgemann Frederick H, laborer Bass Foundry and Machine Works, res 66 Smith.

Hilgemann Frederick W, carpenter, res 399 E Washington.

Hilgemann Gustave F, carpenter J W Hilgemann, bds 216 E Washington.

Hilgemann Henry, laborer, bds 66 Smith.

Hilgemann Henry, laborer White's Wheel Works, bds 216 E Washington.

Hilgemann Henry, watchman, res 91 W Jefferson.

Hilgemann Henry F, Grocer and Saloon, 121 and 123 W Jefferson, res same.

Hilgemann Henry W, carpenter Bass Foundry and Machine Works, res 184 Ewing.

Hilgemann Jacob W, Carpenter, Contractor and Practical Builder, 216 E Washington, res same. (*See adv, p 67*.)

Hilgemann Louis (Ernst H Hilgemann & Son), res s s Baker 2 e of Fairfield ave.

Hilgemann Louise, domestic 234 W Berry.

Hilgemann Louise, packer Pottlitzer Bros, bds 216 W Washington.

Hilgemann Matilda, bds 66 Smith.

Hilgemann Minnie, operator S M Foster, bds 180 Ewing.

Hilgemann Rudolph, car repairer Wabash R R, res 559 Broadway.

Hilgemann Wm, carpenter, res 180 Ewing.

Hilker, *see also Helker*.

Hilker Anthony, laborer, bds 58 John.

Hilker Carl D W, laborer Penn Co, res 137 Francis.

Hilker Charles, machine hand J Klett & Son, res 166 Harmer.

Hilker Charles C, machine hand American Wheel Co, bds 231 John.

Hilker Diedrich F W, machine hand, res 63 Buchanan.

Hilker Frank, laborer, bds 58 John.

Hilker Henry, boilermaker Penn Co, res 44 Hendricks.

Hilker Herman, machine hand, res 231 John.

Hilker Herman H, clerk J B White, res 36 Koch.

Hilker Mrs Margaret, res 58 John.

Hilker Wm, molder Bass Foundry and Machine Works, bds 223 John.

Hill Miss Alice M, teacher, bds C L Hill.

Hill Andrew, engineer Louis Rastetter, res 65 Hendricks.

Hill Arthur L, clerk C L Hill, res same.

Hill Barbara (wid Valentine), bds 22 Pritchard.

Hill Charles A, clerk S A Karn, res 47 Hendricks.

Hill Charles E, tel opr, res 29 Boone.

Hill Charles L, Pianos and Organs, 38 Clinton, res Prospect ave 4 e of Spy Run ave.

Hill Rev Cyrus F, pastor African M E Church, res 273 E Wayne.

Hill David, laborer, res 64 W 3d.

Hill David, restaurant, 29 E Main, res same.

Hill Edward C, mach Penn Co, res-93-Fairfield-ave. *NO 8*

Hill Edward E, lab Hoffman Bros, bds 100 W 3d.

Hill Etta, operator Hoosier Mnfg Co, bds 65 Hendricks.

Hill Frank H, clerk, bds 90 W 4th.

Hill Frank W, fireman, bds 295 W Jefferson.

Hill Fremont, asst city engineer, bds Aveline House.

Hill George, carpenter, bds 206 Lafayette.

Hill George, driver Wm & J J Geake, res 22 Pritchard.

Hill George, laborer, bds n s Spy Run ave nr Randolph.

Hill George, machinist Penn Co, res 2 Erie.

Hill Henry, lab Louis Rastetter, bds 65 Hendricks.

Hill John C, bds 152 E Berry.

Hill John D, laborer Louis Diether & Bro, bds 64 W 3d.

Hill John M, laborer, bds 137 Walton ave.

Hill John W, plumber, bds 123 St Mary's ave.

Hill Kate, milliner A Mergentheim, bds 22 Pritchard.

Hill Louis H, mach hand Louis Diether & Bro, bds 81 Rockhill.

Hill Louisa K, wks Troy Steam Laundry, bds 64 W 3d.

Hill Lydia, bds 65 Hendricks.

Hill Mandeville E, stopmaker Fort Wayne Organ Co, bds 45 Butler.

Hill Maria A (wid Edward), res 45 Butler.

Hill Martha (wid John), res s s Hayden 2 w of McCulloch.

Hill Miss Mary A, tchr Bloomingdale School, bds Prospect pl.

Hill Minnie M, works J O Keller, bds 90 W 4th.

Hill Onslow G, res 316 W Jefferson.

Hill Paulina T, clk J O Keller, bds 90 W 4th.

Hill Rachel A, dressmaker Mrs G J Stier, bds 31 Bass.

Hill Thomas, foreman Fort Wayne Organ Co, res 130 E Berry.

Hill Thomas W, insurance, bds Racine Hotel.

Hill Wm, works Indiana School for Feeble-Minded Youth.

Hill Wm W, weighmaster Nickel Plate, res 295 W Jefferson.

Hillabrand Frederick, trav agt A C Trentman, res Perrysburg, Ohio.

Hille Henry, machinist Wabash R R, res 256 W Jefferson.

Hille Henry, car builder Penn Co, res 310 S Harrison.
Hille Henry W, machinist Bass Foundry and Machine Works,
   bds 310 S Harrison.
Hille Wm, carpenter, res 72 Baker.
Hilleka Anthony J, boilermaker Wabash R R, res 78 W
   Williams.
Hilleke August, porter A C Trentman, bds 114 Fairfield ave.
Hilleke Henry, porter A C Trentman, res 114 Fairfield ave.
Hilliard Miss Etta, teacher Indiana School for Feeble-Minded
   Youth.
Hilliker Wm H, engineer, res 78 Brackenridge.
Hills Anna R (wid Frank M), notions, 15 E Main, res 17 same.
Hills Leslie W, clerk A R Hills, res 17 E Main.
Hills Sarah E (wid Ambrose A), res 125 Fairfield ave.
Hills Waldo, bds 39 W Washington.
Hilt Frederick, Saddles, Harness, Blankets, Robes and
   Trunks, 18½ E Columbia, res 26 Baker.
Hilt John, laborer, bds 26 Baker.
Hilt Louis J, harnessmaker F Hilt, bds 26 Baker.
Hilt Miss Ricka, bds 26 Baker.
Hilton Charles S, supt Fort Wayne Electric Co, res 227 W
   DeWald.
Hilton Hattie, stenographer, bds 227 W DeWald.
Himbert John, teamster, bds 14 Pritchard.
Himbert John M, fireman The Herman Berghoff Brewing
   Co, res 620 E Wayne.
Himbert Michael, truckman, res 14 Pritchard.
Himbert Wm, painter, bds 55 E Main.
Himes Lucian M, painter, res 97 Taylor.
Hinch August, laborer Penn Co, res Eckart.
Hine, *see Heine.*
Hines Clement, stone mason, bds 29 E Main.
Hines John, plumber Robert Ogden, res 37 Maiden Lane.
Hines Philip, carpenter, res 6 Short.
Hinkle Kate (wid Henry), res 9 Elm.
Hinkson Samuel, laborer, res n s Wagner 9 e of Spy Run ave.
Hinton Alice, clk J C Hinton, bds 270½ Calhoun.
Hinton Hattie, housekeeper 270½ Calhoun.
Hinton John C, restaurant, 270½ Calhoun, res 39 Bracken-
   ridge.
Hinton Samuel, bds 270½ Calhoun.
Hinz Charles, laborer, res 344 Force.
Hipp Christ, car builder Penn Co, bds Windsor Hotel.
Hipp Edward, car builder Penn Co, res 57 John.
Hippard George R, city editor The Press, rms 90 E Wayne.
Hippenhammer John W, clk county audtr, res 159 Harrison.

Stahn & Heinrich, Dealers in BOOKS and FINE STATIONERY, Blank Books, Etc. 116 Calhoun Street.

FORT WAYNE DIRECTORY. 259

Hire Elias, laborer, res n s Prospect ave 6 e of Spy Run ave.
Hire Elma D, artist, bds Elias Hire.
Hirsch, *see also Harsch and Hersh.*
Hirsch Bertha, cashier L Wolf & Co, bds 75 Webster. ·
Hirsch Caroline (wid George), res 65 Stophlet.
Hirsch David, bookkeeper Alexander Goodman, bds 49 W Berry.
Hirsch Frederick, molder Bass Foundry and Machine Works, res 208 John.
Hirsch Hannah (wid Leopold), res 75 Webster.
Hirsch Henrietta (wid Moses), res 87 W Jefferson.
Hirsch Herman, salesman, bds 75 Webster.
Hirsch Jane (wid Joseph), res 71 Melita.
Hirsch Louis, clerk L Wolf & Co, bds 75 Webster.
Hirsch Samuel C, laborer Electric Light Works, res 35 Walnut.
Hirsch Seymour, clerk Fisher Bros, bds 75 Webster.
Hirschfelder Caroline (wid Michael), res 240 E Wayne.
Hirschfelder Henry, stone mason, bds 360 E Wayne.
Hirschfelder Lucas, stone mason, res 360 E Wayne.
Hirschman John, cabinetmaker Fort Wayne Organ Co, res 14 Union.
Hirt Jacob, bartender J D Bickford, bds 11 N Harrison.
Hirt Wm F, screwmaker Fort Wayne Electric Co, bds 26 Nirdlinger ave.
Hiser Ella, cook 29 E Main.
Hiser Samuel A, engineer, res 23 W Lewis.
Hislop Catherine (wid Robert), res 31 Grace ave.
Hislop Hugh W, brass molder Fort Wayne Electric Co, res 31 Grace ave.
Hislop John S, brass molder Fort Wayne Electric Co, res 31 Grace ave.
Hisner Lizzie, bds 68 Wilt.
Hisner Wm F, carpenter, res 68 Wilt.
Hisner Wm F jr, carpenter, bds 68 Wilt.
Histon Thomas, brakeman, bds 196 Hanna.
Hitberg Wm, driver Ryan Bros, bds same.
Hite, *see also Heit.*
Hite Samuel E, laborer, bds 614 Calhoun.
Hite Samuel H, elevator man Fort Wayne Organ Co, res 614 Calhoun.
Hiteke Henry, porter A C Trentman, res 114 Fairfield ave.
Hitzeman Charles, bds 24 Summit.
Hitzeman Charles, laborer, bds 36 Pritchard.
Hitzeman Christian, clerk G De Wald & Co, res 290 W Washington.

Hitzeman Ernest F, finisher Fort Wayne Organ Co, bds 36 Pritchard.
Hitzeman Frederick, stone mason, res 36 Pritchard.
Hitzeman Frederick H D, clerk A E C Becker, bds 36 Pritchard.
Hitzeman George (Doehrmann & Hitzeman), res 24 Summit.
Hitzeman Louisa (wid Henry), res 244 E Washington.
Hitzeman Sophia, dressmaker M A Fletcher, bds 24 Summit.
Hitzeman Sophia E (wid Wm), bds 219 W Jefferson.
Hitzemann Frederick J, cutter G H Hitzemann, bds 49 Wilt.
Hitzemann Gottlieb, clerk Henry Butke, bds 49 Wilt.
Hitzemann Gottlieb H, tailor, 133 Broadway, res 49 Wilt.
Hitzemann Henry C, clerk Pfeiffer & Schlatter, bds 49 Wilt.
Hitzemann Lizzie C, domestic 133 W Wayne.
Hitzemann Sophia, dressmaker Mary L Sherin, bds 49 Wilt.
Hively Adam H, helper Bass Foundry and Machine Works, bds 29 Hough.
Hively Anna, laundress Wm P Hadley, bds 73 E Berry.
Hoadley Miss Annie (Rich & Hoadley), bds 46 W Berry.
Hoadley Jennie B, bds 46 W Berry.
Hoadley Mary, dressmaker, bds 46 W Berry.
Hoag George, printer, bds 104 Barr.
Hoagland Frank H, printer Fort Wayne Gazette, res 37 Bass.
Hoagland Miss Merica, bds 106 W Berry.
Hoagland School, n e cor Hoagland ave and Butler.
Hoagland Susan C (wid Americus), bds 235 W Washington.
Hoalle Andrew, laborer Bass Foundry and Machine Works, res 74 Murray.
Hobbs John, brickmaker A McKernan, bds Wm A Smith.
Hobbs Julia (wid Reuben), res 237 E Wayne.
Hobbs Oscar L, res 298 S Hoagland ave.
Hobrock Albert, machine hand American Wheel Co, bds 50 Buchanan.
Hobrock August C, machinist Penn Co, bds 94 Fairfield ave.
Hobrock Cora, operator Hoosier Mnfg Co, bds 50 Buchanan.
Hobrock Edward L, messenger Penn Co, bds 94 Fairfield av.
Hobrock Eva (wid Wm), res 50 Buchanan.
Hobrock Henry A, machine hand American Wheel Company, bds 50 Buchanan.
Hobrock J Henry, machine hand, bds 50 Buchanan.
Hobrock J Herman, carpenter Penn Co, res 94 Fairfield ave.
Hobrock J Herman jr, clerk Penn Co, bds 94 Fairfield ave.
Hobrock Martin H, laborer Penn Co, res 168 Ewing.
Hobrock Minnie, bds 94 Fairfield ave.
Hobrock Wm H, furnace tender Penn Co, res 134 E De Wald.
Hoch Emanuel, fireman Hose Co No 2, bds 31 Charles.

Hoch Henry J, laborer Penn Co, res e s Monroe 5 s of Wallace.

Hoch Wm, saloon, 313 Lafayette, and meat market, 121 Wallace, res 313 Lafayette.

Hoch Wm F, clerk, bds 313 Lafayette.

Hochstetter Phillip A, driver Ft Wayne St Railroad Co, rms 38 Hough.

Hochstetter Wilhelm, painter Penn Co, res Romy road.

Hochstrasser John jr, laborer C L Centlivre.

Hock, *see Hawk*.

Hockaday Deborah (wid Samuel L), res 60 Chicago.

Hockaday James M, cooper F X Brucker, bds 60 Chicago.

Hockemeyer Charles F, printer Ft Wayne Newspaper Union, bds 317 W Washington.

Hockemeyer Henry, bricklayer, res 115 Madison.

Hockemeyer Lizzie, wks J O Keller, bds 317 W Washington.

Hockemeyer Mary (wid Charles), res 317 W Washington.

Hockemeyer Sophia (wid Christian), bds 51 Holton ave.

Hockemier Louisa, bds 319 E Wayne.

Hockley Mrs Kate, bds 305 S Harrison.

Hoctor Henry, helper Wabash R R, res 5 Hoagland ave.

Hodges Frank, fireman res n e cor Highland and Webster.

Hodges Isaac, hostler John Stirling, rms 29 N Clinton.

Hoelle Martin, laborer Bass Foundry and Machine Works, res 69 Buchanan.

Hoeltje Henry C, cigarmaker A C Baker, bds 13 Elm.

Hoeltje Lizzie (wid August), res 13 Elm.

Hoemeyer, *see also Homeyer*.

Hoemeyer Henry, driver, bds 66 Douglas ave.

Hoeniesen Jacob, laborer, res 11 W Jefferson.

Hoeppner Mrs Catherine, res s s Pontiac opp Smith.

Hoeppner Charles, laborer Penn Co, res 160 Gay.

Hoeppner Herman, boilermaker Penn Co, res 160 Gay.

Hoeppner Wm, laborer, bds 160 Gay.

Hoerner Peter, laborer, res 69 Buchanan.

Hoewischer Frederick, carpenter, res 79 W Jefferson.

Hofacker August, laborer Hoffman Bros, bds 120 Rockhill.

Hofacker George, laborer J C Peters, bds 391 W Main.

Hofer John, laborer, res w s Van Buren 1 n of W Superior.

Hofer Theobold, janitor, res 140 N Cass.

Hoff Anna M (wid Anthony), res 17 Wefel.

Hoffer Andrew, butcher, res n s Maysville road nr toll gate.

Hoffer Carrie B, metre tester Ft Wayne Electric Co, bds 37 N Cass.

Hoffer Celia L, clk Stewart & Hahn, bds 37 N Cass.

Hoffer Edward, butcher A F Gessler, bds Andrew Hoffer.

Hoffer Frederick, molder Fort Wayne Iron Works, bds 224
    W Main.
Hoffer John, laborer, bds n w cor W Main and Runnion ave.
Hoffer John, machinist Star Iron Tower Co, res 37 N Cass.
Hoffer John G, carpenter, res 37 N Cass.
Hoffer Robert, blacksmith City Carriage Works, bds Lake
    Side Park add.
Hoffer Sophie J, clerk L Wolf & Co, bds 37 N Cass.
Hoffman, *see also Hoffmann, Hofmann and Huffmann.*
Hoffman Adam J, molder Bass Foundry and Machine
    Works, res 142 Wallace.
Hoffman A Ely (Hoffman Bros and J R Hoffman & Co), pres
    Hoffman Lumber Co, res 188 W Wayne.
Hoffman Barbara, operator Hoosier Mnfg Co, bds 31 Force.
Hoffman Bros (A Ely and Wm H), Lumber Mnfrs,
    200 W Main,
Hoffman Charles, car builder Penn Co, res 515 E Washington.
Hoffman Cynthia, clerk Root & Co, bds 2 Riverside ave.
Hoffman Daniel, painter, res s w cor Reed and Jennison.
Hoffman George, wagonmaker L C Zollinger, res 2 River-
    side.
Hoffman Henry, packer F Eckart, res e s Runnion ave bet W
    Main and Canal Feeder.
Hoffman Henry A, carpenter, 52 W Creighton ave, res same.
Hoffman Jacob R (J R Hoffman & Co), res Charleston, W
    Virginia.
Hoffman J R & Co (Jacob R, A Ely and Wm H Hoff-
    man), Patent Band Saw Mills, 200 W Main.
Hoffman Lena, domestic 261 W Wayne.
Hoffman Louisa, domestic 340 W Jefferson.
Hoffman Lumber Co, A E Hoffman Pres, Wm H
    Hoffman Vice-Pres, John W Sale Treas, M P Longacre
    Sec, Hardwood Lumber and Logs, 200 W Main.
Hoffman Margaret (wid Adam), bds 31 Force.
Hoffman Martin, carpenter, bds 34 Allen.
Hoffman Miss Mary E, bookkeeper S M Foster, bds 2 River-
    side ave.
Hoffman Nicholas, clerk J B White, res 31 Force.
Hoffman Peter, laborer Penn Co, res 167 Clinton.
Hoffman Susan C (wid Frank), bds 279 Fairfield ave.
Hoffman Urban S, clerk Root & Co, res 8 Riverside ave.
Hoffman Wm H (Hoffman Bros and J R Hoffman & Co),
    vice-pres Hoffman Lumber Co, res 200 W Berry.
Hoffmann, *see also Hoffman, Hofmann and Huffmann.*
Hoffmann Adolph, laborer Bass Foundry and Machine Works,
    res 163 Hayden.

Hoffmann Charles A, Wholesale and Retail Dealer in Cider, Apple Wine and Cider Vinegar, 183, 185 and 187 Calhoun, res same.

Hoffmann George, stone mason, res 72 Gay.

Hoffmann George, teamster, res 464 E Wayne.

Hoffmann Henry, market stall No 66, res nr Adams station.

Hoffmann Mary B, waitress Custer House.

Hoffmeister Henry, cooper, 12 W 3d, res same.

Hofmann, *see also Hoffman, Hoffmann and Huffmann.*

Hofmann Alois, stone mason, res 52 Force.

Hofmann G Max, supt Salimonie Mining and Gas Co, res 23 Madison.

Hogan Alexander, plumber, bds 11 Grand.

Hogan Catherine (wid Michael), res 58 Prince.

Hogan Dennis, bds 12 Chicago.

Hogan Eliza, bds 176 Fairfield ave.

Hogan Hugh, foreman Penn Co, res 92 Baker.

Hogan Jane (wid Samuel B), res 93 Ewing.

Hogan John P, plumber A Hattersley & Sons, bds 176 Fairfield ave.

Hogan Mary (wid Timothy), res 11 Grand.

Hogan Michael, laborer Penn Co, res 58 Prince.

Hogan Michael jr, upholsterer, bds 58 Prince.

Hogan Patrick, laborer, res 176 Fairfield ave.

Hogan Stephen A, bartender J A Dratt, bds 93 Ewing.

Hogle Isabella (wid George), bds 29 Grand.

Hogston James M, cabinetmaker Fort Wayne Furniture Co, res 21 Wagner.

Hoham Frederick D, druggist, 298 Calhoun, res same.

Hoham Wm H, trav agent M F Kaag, res 106 W Superior.

Hohmann Emily, dressmaker M A Fletcher, bds 175 High.

Hohmann Frank, tailor, res 175 High.

Hohmann Henry, barber Oscar Wobrock, bds 175 High.

Hohnhaus Miss Emma, seamstress P E Wolf, bds 63 Wall.

Hohnhaus George, awningmaker, res 125 High.

Hohnhaus George, patternmaker Bass Foundry and Machine Works, res s e cor Hanna and Eckart.

Hohnhaus Peter G, patternmaker Indiana Machine Works, res 63 Wall.

Hohnhaus Wm J, machinist Fort Wayne Iron Works, bds 63 Wall.

Hohnhausen G Peter, mason Bass Foundry and Machine Works, res 33 Taylor.

Hohnhausen Magdalena (wid Nicholas), bds 33 Taylor.

Hohnholz Herman, implements, 46 W Main, res same.

Hoke Anna, seamstress, bds 52 Pontiac.

Hoke George S, wheel insptr American Wheel Co, bds 52 Pontiac.
Hoke Mary, operator, bds 52 Pontiac.
Hoke Nicholas, laborer, res e s Hanna 3 s of Pontiac.
Hoke Rosanna (wid Jacob), res 52 Pontiac.
Hokemeyer Henry, carpenter, bds 239 Madison.
Holchaucr Anna, domestic 215 W Berry.
Holiday Francis M (col'd), kalsominer, res 14 Lafayette.
Holipeter Charles E, machine hand Louis Diether & Bro, bds 15 Pearl.
Holland Henry, laborer, bds 82 Fairfield ave.
Holland Margaret (wid Patrick), bds 457 Lafayette.
Holland Richard, car builder Penn Co, res 15 Euclid ave.
Hollenbacher Louis, shipping clerk, res 141 Francis.
Hollenbeck Amelia E G, milliner Margaret Koch, bds 137 E Jefferson.
Hollenbeck Annie M, bds 137 E Jefferson.
Hollenbeck Frederick W A, Saloon, 144 Calhoun, res 137 E Jefferson.
Hollenbeck Garret F, laborer, res 273 Webster.
Holley John, conductor, res 41 Boone.
Hollinger Elizabeth (wid Daniel), res 76 E Columbia.
Hollinger Harry M, laborer Clutter & Purcell, bds 76 E Columbia.
Hollinger Wm, bartndr Edward Lennan, bds 76 E Columbia.
Hollister A Judson, cigar mnfr, 104 W Williams, res same.
Hollister Clara, bds 104 W Williams.
Hollister Edwin J, cigar mnfr, res 82 W Williams.
Hollmann August, carpenter, res 394 E Washington.
Hollmann Frederick, carpenter, res 46 Wall.
Holloway C Peter, flagman, bds 51 W Superior.
Holm Nils, action maker, res 18 Park ave.
Holman Henry, carpenter J W Hilgemann, bds 216 E Washington.
Holmes Abiram T, engineer Penn Co, res 189 Barr.
Holmes Byron, engineer, res 189 Barr.
Holmes Charles, brakeman, bds 12 St Mary's ave.
Holmes Fountain, machinist Penn Co, bds 323 S Calhoun.
Holmes George W, gardener, res 18 Gay.
Holmes Joanna (wid Wm J), res 323 Calhoun.
Holmes Joshua, bds 18 Gay.
Holmes Lillian K, clerk A Mergentheim, bds 323 Calhoun.
Holmes Mabel, operator S M Foster, bds 18 Gay.
Holmes Otis, hostler, bds 544 E Wayne.
Holmes Simon, sawyer Kerr-Murray Mnfg Co, res 616 Calhoun.

Holmes Wm A, clerk Zoeller & Merz, bds 616 Calhoun.

Holmes Wm E, laborer Penn Co, res cor Hayden and Ohio.

Holmes Wm L, laborer Fort Wayne Artificial Ice Co, bds Riverside Hotel.

Holsworth, *see also Holzwarth and Holzworth.*

Holsworth Addie, clerk Root & Co, bds 158 W Wayne.

Holsworth Lizzie, domestic Wayne Hotel.

Holt John, res 266 W DeWald.

Holtermann Frederick, laborer, res 169 Gay.

Holton Avenue School, s w cor Holton and Creighton aves.

Holton Sabina B (wid Thomas J), bds 151 W Berry.

Holtzman Samuel, engineer Standard Oil Co, res s s Wheeler nr Runnion ave.

Holverstott Miss Belle, bds 33 W Williams.

Holverstott Charles H, res 13 Duryea.

Holverstott Clinton W, clerk McDonald, Watt & Wilt, res 319 W Washington.

Holverstott Wm Z, machinist Fort Wayne Electric Co, res 33 W Williams.

Holz Mathias, laborer Penn Co, bds Hoffman House.

Holzborn Adolph, keeper station D, res 848 S Broadway.

Holzhauer Henry, helper Kerr-Murray Mnfg Co, res 143 Oliver.

Holzwarth, *see also Holzworth.*

Holzwarth Christian E, brakeman, res 11 Bass.

Holzworth, *see also Holzwarth.*

Holzworth Addison, clk County Auditor, res 158 W Wayne.

Holzworth Floyd, laborer, bds John A Holzworth.

Holzworth Frank P, clk Klinkenberg & Detzer, bds 158 W Wayne.

Holzworth George A, stopmaker Fort Wayne Organ Co, res 6 Cottage ave.

Holzworth John A, carpenter, res s s Canal 1 e of N Y, C & L R R.

Home Billiard Hall, L A Centlivre propr, Harmony Court bet Berry and Main.

Homeyer Ernst, teamster, res 200 Fairfield ave.

Homeyer Frederick C, teamster Fort Wayne Organ Co, res 188 DeWald.

Homeyer Frederick Wm, watchman, res 57 High.

Homeyer Henry C D, machinist Bass Foundry and Machine Works, res 184 W DeWald.

Homeyer John, carriage trimmer E C Smith, bds 57 High.

Homeyer Lizzie, seamstress D S Redelsheimer & Co, bds 57 High.

Homeyer Louisa C, clk A E C Becker, bds 188 W DeWald.

Homeyer Minnie, seamstress D S Redelsheimer & Co, bds 57 High.

Homke, *see Humbke, Humeke and Humk.*

Homsher Benjamin F, lab Penn Co, res 255 S Webster.

Homsher Miss Bertie A, teacher, bds 255 S Webster.

Homsher Miss Minnie F, teacher Hoagland School, bds 255 Webster.

Honeck, *see also Ohneck.*

Honeck Fredericka, tailoress F Kayser, bds 58 Elm.

Honeck George, laborer, res 39 N Calhoun.

Honeck Henry, laborer, res 58 Elm.

Honeck Henry, carpenter, res 151 Montgomery.

Honeck Louisa (wid Henry), bds 115 Madison.

Honeick Herman, carpenter, bds 155 Madison.

Honeick Wm, machinist Bass Foundry and Machine Works, res 380 E Washington.

Hontheim, *see also Huntheim.*

Hontheim John J, mach Wabash R R, res 12 McClellan.

Hontheim Peter T, wheelmaker American Wheel Co, bds 12 McClellan.

Hood Miss Emilie, bds 34 Garden.

Hood Florence, bds 21 W Jefferson.

Hood Frank, cutter Hoosier Mnfg Co, bds 21 W Jefferson.

Hood John O, laborer Penn Co, res 130 W 3d.

Hood Julia (wid James), res 21 W Jefferson.

Hood Martha (wid George B), res 130 W 3d.

Hood Miss Minnie, bds 34 Garden.

Hood Robert, meats, 98 Barr, res 25 W Lewis.

Hood Wm E, bookkeeper Carnahan & Co, res 34 Garden.

Hood Wm E jr, bds 34 Garden.

Hook and Ladder Co No 2, s s Wallace 4 e of Lafayette.

Hooper John G, Propr Wayne Stables, 13 and 15 Pearl, res 143 W Berry.

Hooper Samuel T, engineer, res 101 Wilt.

Hoopingarner George C, laborer Penn Co, res 210 Fairfield.

Hoopingarner Wm H, painter, res 49 Walnut.

Hoormann Diedrich C, coremaker Bass Foundry and Machine Works, res 115 Eliza.

Hoormann Henry F C, coremaker Bass Foundry and Machine Works, res 115 Eliza.

Hoosier Mnfg Co, Amos S Evans Pres, John P Evans Treas, George P Evans Sec, F F Budd Supt, Mnfrs of Diamond Staid Overalls, Sack Coats, Jumpers, Jeans Pants and Lined Duck Clothing, 28 and 30 E Berry.

Hoover Abraham, car builder Penn Co, res 91 E Lewis.

Hop Lee Henry, laundry, 154½ and 180 Calhoun, res 180 same.

Hope David F, laborer, bds Hedekin House.
Hopp Nicholas, res 91 Summit.
Hopkins Zelous, well digger, res 30 Huron.
Hoppe Dora (wid Henry W), res 20 Wall.
Hoppe Edwin, clerk, bds 20 Wall.
Hoppe Henry, car builder Penn Co, res 393 S Hanna.
Hoppe Herman, carpenter Ft W, C & L R R, res 393 Hanna.
Hoppe Paul O, clerk C B Woodworth & Co, bds 20 Wall.
Hoppe Selina, seamstress, bds 20 Wall.
Hopple Martin V B, driver G E Bursley & Co, bds 137 W 3d.
Hoppner Frederick, laborer American Wheel Co, res 161 Broadway.
Horen Mrs Electa, tailoress, res 63 W Superior.
Horland Henry, coremaker Bass Foundry and Machine Works, res 225 John.
Hormann Henry W, helper Bass Foundry and Machine Works, res e s Force nr E Creighton ave.
Hormel George, teacher Emanuel School, res 3 McClellan.
Horn Ferdinand, res 102 Smith.
Horn John L (John L Horn & Co), res 202 High.
Horn John L & Co (John L Horn), second-hand goods, 13 W Berry, res 202 High.
Horn Mrs Nettie, res 202 High.
Horn Rebecca E, res 54 Hamilton.
Horn Wm, laborer Bass Foundry and Machine Works, res 35 Smith.
Horn Wm jr, cigarmaker Christian Wenninghoff, bds 35 Smith.
Horn Wm, laborer Winch & Sons, bds 102 Smith.
Horner Peter, helper Bass Foundry and Machine Works, res 69 Buchanan.
Horning Emma (wid Wm), res 166 Holman.
Hornung Max, engineer, res 312 S Harrison.
Horstman Carrie, bds 272 E Washington.
Horstman Cecilia, bds 203 Hanna.
Horstman Frank, letter carrier, res 14 Clay.
Horstman Henry C, car builder Penn Co, res 203 Hanna.
Horstman Henry G, stripper L C Heck, bds 203 Hanna.
Horstman Louis, Mnfr of Buggy Tops and Cushions, 9 E Superior, rms 48 Barr. (See adv, p 65.)
Horstmann Charles, laborer Amerian Wheel Co, res 227 John.
Horstmann Frederick H, tailor, 351 Calhoun, res 266 S Wayne.
Horstmann John B, laborer Wm Moellering, res 90 Force.
Horstmeyer Charles, clerk, bds 197 Ewing.
Horstmeyer Frederick, carpenter, bds 79 Oakley.
Horstmeyer Frederick, carpenter, bds 244 Beaver ave.

Horstmeyer Henry, res 30 Savilla place.

Horstmeyer Louis, carpenter, res 244 Beaver ave.

Horstmeyer Louis J, laborer, bds 244 Beaver ave.

Horstmeyer Marie, clerk Alexander Goodman, bds 197 Ewing.

Horstmeyer Wilhelmina (wid Frederick), res 80 Nirdlinger.

Horstmeyer Wm, carpenter, res 197 Ewing.

Horstmeyer Wm, carpenter, bds 213 Fairfield ave.

Horstmeyer Wm F, boilermaker Ft Wayne Iron Works, bds 197 Ewing.

Horton Edward W, brakeman, bds 33 St Mary's ave.

Horton Manufacturing Co The, Henry C Paul Pres, Wm A Bohn Sec and Treas, John C Peters Mngr, Mnfrs of Wooden Novelties and the Western Washer, w s Osage n of Main.

Hose Co No 2, s s Wallace 4 e of Lafayette.

Hosenfeld Amelia, domestic 262 W Jefferson.

Hosenfeld Bertha, domestic 264 W Wayne.

Hosey Wm, machinist Penn Co, res 131 E Washington.

Hosier Charles, paperhanger L O Hull, res 365½ E Lewis.

Hoskins Wm A, flagman Penn Co, res 42 Walnut.

Hosler Abraham, carpenter, bds 71 Melita.

Hosler Calvin, teamster, res 71 Melita.

Hosler John W, night watch, bds 43 Pritchard.

Hosler Reginald H, driver Fort Wayne City Railroad Co, bds 544 E Wayne.

Hossfield Frederick, laborer American Wheel Works, rear 65 Hendricks.

Hostedler Mano, bds 104 Barr.

Hoster Perry E, clerk Clutter & Purcell, rms Aldine Hotel.

Hostetter Daniel, helper Penn Co, bds 290 Calhoun.

Hostman Charles W H, clerk D J Spencer, bds 86 W Jefferson.

Hostman Christian F, res 86 W Jefferson.

Hostman Frederick J, bds 86 W Jefferson.

Hostman Mary (wid Christian), res 88 W Jefferson.

Hotel Pearse, F D Pearse Propr; Strictly First-Class, n w cor Calhoun and Chicago opp Pittsburgh Depot.

Hotel Randall, R B Hughes Propr, cor Harrison and Columbia.

Houck Cory, clerk, bds 353 W Main.

Houck Robert C, bookkeeper, bds 353 W Main.

Hough, *see also Huff.*

Hough Frank L, clerk Fort Wayne Electric Co, bds 32 Brackenridge.

Houk Frank E, upholsterer, 36 Clinton, res same.

Houlihan Bridget A, milliner Wm Malloy, bds s w cor Hoagland ave and Williams.

Houlihan James J, clerk Morgan & Beach, bds 93 W Williams.

Houlihan Johanna, bds 28 Locust.

Houlihan John J, machinist Bass Foundry and Machine Works, res 93 Williams..

Houlihan Michael J, deputy county clerk, bds 93 Williams.

Houlihan Thomas W, bookkeeper, bds 93 Williams.

Hourigan John, laborer, res 53 Home ave.

House Christian C, helper Penn Co, bds 355 Force.

House John S, clerk, res 32 Oak.

House Joseph M, canvasser New York Installment Co.

Houser, *see also Hauser.*

Houser Carrie, domestic 106 E Main.

Houser Charles H A, clerk McDonald, Watt & Wilt, bds 24 E Washington.

Houser David E, machinist Fort Wayne Electric Co, res 24 Poplar.

Houser John A, foreman, res 88 Wells.

Houser Lizzie, works Troy Steam Laundry, bds 278 E Jefferson.

Housh Ella, domestic Mason Long.

Housh John E (Archer, Housh & Co), res 40 Home ave.

Howard Charles, laborer, bds 8 Clark.

Howard George S, Agent American Express Co, Court St opp Court House, rms 44 Brackenridge.

Howard Herman, brewer, bds 101 Glasgow ave.

Howard Jane (wid Charles), bds s s Eckart 4 E of Hanna.

Howell Charles A, machinist Penn Co, res 39 Miner.

Howell Ella, domestic 43½ E Columbia.

Howell Eva, domestic 29 E Main.

Howenstine John, trav agent, bds 171 E Wayne.

Howey Aaron B, bookkeeper, res 67 Wilt.

Howey Charles W, asst postmaster, res 87 E Berry.

Howey I Frank, clerk Penn Co, bds 232 W DeWald.

Howey Mary (wid Isaac), bds 232 W DeWald.

Howey Wm T, Saloon, 354 Calhoun, res same.

Howland Mary, domestic 341 W Washington.

Howley Bernard C, helper Penn Co, bds 47 Barr.

Howley Catherine (wid Thomas), res 47 Barr.

Howley Kate A, operator, bds 47 Barr.

Howley Martin A, helper, bds 47 Barr.

Howley Martin J, helper, bds 47 Barr.

Hoy Frank L, cashier L S & M S Ry, res 266 E Lewis.

Hoyner D J, fireman, bds 248 Calhoun.

Hoynes Wm J, trav agent Mossman, Yarnell & Co, rms W Superior.

Hoyt Clara (wid Clark), bds 43 Shawnee ave.

Hubbard Alvin L, clerk L F Butler, res 9 Harrison.

Hubbard Clifford S, draughtsman Fort Wayne Electric Co, bds 9 Harrison.

Hubbard George K, bee hives, 277 Harrison, res 124 Hoagland ave.

Hubbard John H, machine hand White's Wheel Works, res 48 Penn.

Hubbard Sidney G, barber, 21 W Columbia, res 48 Wells.

Hnbbs Wm H, porter C Entemann, rms 51 E Main.

Huber Anton J, machinist Penn Co, bds 126 E Lewis.

Huber Bertha, operator Hoosier Manufacturing Co, bds 403 E Washington.

Huber Caroline (wid George), res 126 E Lewis.

Huber Frederick, lab J Klett & Son, res 403 E Washington.

Huber George, fireman, res 38 Chicago.

Huber Johanna, bds 403 E Washington.

Huber John, finisher, bds 126 E Lewis.

Huber Kate, bds 126 E Lewis.

Huber Louisa, bds 403 E Washington.

Huber Martha, operator Hoosier Mnfg Co, bds 403 E Washington.

Huber Matilda, bds 403 E Washington.

Huber Theresa, dressmaker Mrs G J Stier, bds 403 E Washington.

Huber Ulrich, teamster, res n s Cochrane 5 e of Coombs.

Hubner John, machinist Kerr-Murray Mnfg Co, res 66 Baker.

Hudgel Daniel R, traveling agent A C Trentman, res 271 W Jefferson.

Hudrey Louis W, machinist Bass Foundry and Machine Wks, bds 186 Montgomery.

Hudrey Nicholas, car builder Penn Co, res 186 Montgomery.

Hudson, see also Hutson.

Hudson Charles R, bartender George Jacobs, bds 138 Wells.

Hudson Hamilton, fireman, res 22 Ewing.

Hudson Oliver, switchman, bds 22 Ewing.

Hue Constant, machinist Fort Wayne Electric Co, res 68 Laselle.

Hueber Barbara (wid Tobias), bds n s 4th 7 w of Wells.

Huebner Reinholdt, laborer, res 49 Smith.

Huelf Johanna S (wid Nicholas), res 52 W 4th.

Huer, see also Heuer.

Huer Baade, carpenter, bds 59 Maumee road.

Huer Ernest, boilermaker, res 59 Maumee road.

Huesner Wm, carpenter Frederick Bandt, res 68 Wilt.

Huestis Alexander C, res 205 W Berry.

Huestis Charles D C, res 205 W Berry.

Huestis Wm H, traveling agent McDonald, Watt & Wilt, res 16 Monroe.

Huff, *see also Hough.*

Huff Anna J, bds 28 E Columbia.

Huff Hiram, fireman Nickel Plate R R, res 5 Brandriff.

Huff Jessie L, laundress Fort Wayne City Hospital.

Huff Udney, brakeman, res e s Winter 2 s of Creighton ave.

Huffert, *see Heffert.*

Huffman, *see also Hoffman, Hoffmann and Hofmann.*

Huffman Bert W, printer, bds 248 Calhoun.

Huffman George C, carpenter Old Fort Mnfg Co, res 393 E Wayne.

Huffman Henry, brakeman, bds 219 Lafayette.

Huffman Jacob O, finisher Fort Wayne Furniture Co, res 362 W Main.

Huffner Anthony, laborer, bds 15 Poplar.

Hughes, *see also Hewes.*

Hughes Alice, clerk Dozois, Beadell & Co, bds 25 Walnut.

Hughes Anna A, tailoress Gottlieb Stauffer, bds 25 Walnut.

Hughes Edward H, clerk Hotel Randall.

Hughes James, cabinetmaker Fort Wayne Organ Co, bds 518 Fairfield ave.

Hughes James, laborer, bds 290 Calhoun.

Hughes James E, fireman, bds 25 Walnut.

Hughes Joseph, mngr The Mayflower Mills, res 284 W Wayne.

Hughes Miss Lulu E, student, bds 145 Fairfield ave.

Hughes Maggie, bds 196 Hanna.

Hughes Mary (wid Edwin), res 196 Hanna.

Hughes Mrs Mary (wid James), res 25 Walnut.

Hughes Ollie, operator Hoosier Mnfg Co, bds 293 W Main.

Hughes Robert B, Propr Hotel Randall, cor Harrison and Columbia.

Hughes Rose, bds 196 Hanna.

Hughes Thomas E, boilermaker Wabash R R, bds 25 Walnut.

Hughston John, laborer Penn Co, res 65 W Williams.

Huguenard August C, res 152 High.

Huguenard Frank, laborer Penn Co, bds 29 Hough.

Huguenard Frank, section hand, bds 152 High.

Huguenard Julia (wid Charles), res 29 Hough.

Huguenard Julius C, grocer, 107 Maumee road, res same.

Huguenard Mollie, domestic Diamond Hotel.

Huguenard Victor A, feed stable, 62 E Superior, res 61 same.

Huhn Amand, cabinetmaker Fort Wayne Organ Co, res 70 Nirdlinger ave.

Huhn August, coremaker Bass Foundry and Machine Works, res 72 Nirdlinger ave.

Huhn Edward, laborer, bds 236 Smith.

Huhn E Frederick, wiper, res 236 Smith.

Huhn Frank, laborer American Wheel Co, res w s Lillie 1 s of E Creighton ave.

Huhn Frederick, stonecutter Fort Wayne Steam Stone Works, res 51 Nirdlinger ave.

Huhn Henry, coremaker Bass Foundry and Machine Works, res 215 John.

Huhn Henry, stonecutter Fort Wayne Steam Stone Works, res n e cor Fox and Walnut.

Huhn John, wiper Penn Co, res 236 Smith.

Huhn Pius, laborer Bass Foundry and Machine Works, res 70 Nirdlinger ave.

Huhnhaus Henry, cigarmaker, bds 11 Melita.

Hull Frederick A, stockman Fort Wayne Newspaper Union, res e s Spy Run ave 2 n of Riverside ave.

Hull Isaac P, paperhanger, res 288 W Jefferson.

Hull Joseph P, laborer Fort Wayne City Railroad Co, res 544 E Wayne.

Hull Lewis O, Wall Paper, Paints, Painting and Artists' Materials, 90 Calhoun, res 201 W Wayne. (*See right top lines.*)

Hull Martin, laborer, bds Wm Hull.

Hull Sylvester W, wall paper, 134 Broadway, res 247 E Lewis.

Hull W H, carpenter, res n s Killea 1 e of Hoagland ave.

Hullinger Neal, laborer South Wayne Brick Co, bds 26 Thompson ave.

Hullinger Wm J, laborer South Wayne Brick Co, bds 26 Thompson ave.

Hulse Lula, bds 44 Brackenridge.

Hulse Wm L, machinist Penn Co, res 44 Brackenridge.

Hulse Wm S, draughtsman Fort Wayne Electric Co, bds 44 Brackenbridge.

Humbel John, laborer Hoffman Bros, res 50 Butler.

Humbel Rudolph, machine hand Fort Wayne Organ Co, res 50 Butler.

Humbert James, laborer J F Fletcher, rms 32 Barr.

Humbrecht George H, policeman, res 44 W 3d.

Humcke Diedrich, blacksmith helper Penn Co, bds 225 John.

Hume Wm Thompson, conductor, res 35 Williams.

Humke Frederick, laborer Ranke & Yergens, bds 354 E Washington.

Humke Richard, helper, res 221 John.

Hummel John W H, laborer, res 23 Thompson ave.

Hummel J George, teamster, res 192 E DeWald.

Humphrey Miss Clara E, teacher Hanna School, bds 175 W Berry.

Humphrey George B, clerk P O, bds 175 W Berry.

Humphrey Hannah (wid John), res 38 Brackenridge.

Humphrey James, Propr The Aldine Hotel, n s E Berry bet Clinton and Barr.

Humphrey James A, car tracer Penn Co, res 270 W Jefferson.

Humphrey Miss Jane, bds 171 W Berry.

Humphrey Jane (wid James), res 171 W Berry.

Humphrey Miss Jessie L, teacher Washington School, bds 175 W Berry.

Humphrey Louisa (wid George), res 175 W Berry.

Humphrey Lucena W (wid Noah), res 19 Madison.

Humphrey Matthew, bds 171 W Berry.

Humphreys Miss Fannie L, teacher, bds 166 Barr.

Hungry Charles, molder Kerr-Murray Mnfg Co, res 362 E Wayne.

Hunsche Carrie, works Troy Steam Laundry, bds 41 Wells.

Hunsche Frederick, carpenter, res 65 Elizabeth.

Hunsche Frederick, clerk, bds 19 Koch.

Hunsche Frederick, clerk, bds Wm F Borgmann.

Hunsche Henry J, machine hand Louis Diether & Bro, res 41 Wells.

Hunsche Wm, clerk J C Figel, bds same.

Hunt Albert F, laborer C L Centlivre, bds 16 Randolph.

Hunt Charles E, brakeman, res 76 Chicago.

Hunt Edward, bds 6 Smith.

Hunt Edward T, dispatcher Penn Co, rms 188 Calhoun.

Hunt Hoyt B, general agent Northwestern Mutual Life Insurance Co, 1 Trentman block, res 331 W Jefferson.

Hunt John T, sales stables, 14 Randolph, res same.

Hunt Leonard R, dispatcher Penn Co, rms 188 Calhoun.

Hunt Patrick, teamster, res 6 Smith.

Hunt Robert, porter, rms 55 W Main.

Hunt Thomas R, lab American Wheel Company, bds 6 Smith.

Hunter Charles, laborer, American Wheel Co, res 320 Hanna.

Hunter James L, res 153 Hayden.

Hunter James W, master of transportation G R & I R R, rms 26 McClellan.

Hunter John L (Didierjohn & Co), res 153 Hayden.

Hunter Lewis C, olerk County Treasurer, res 67 N Cass.

Hunter Mnfg Co, merchant tailors, Wm M Smith manager, 15 W Columbia.

John Pressler, Mantels, Grates and Tile Floor. Columbia, Barr and Dock Streets.

274   R. L. POLK & CO.'S

Hunter Miss Tillie, bds 153 Hayden.
Hunter Wm E, clerk G R & I R R, bds 196 Calhoun.
Hunthein, *see also Hondheim.*
Hunthein Jacob, carpenter, res 31 Pine.
Hunthein Jacob jr, finisher, bds 31 Pine.
Hunthein Michael, boilermaker Kerr-Murray Mnfg Co, res 13
    Brandriff.
Hunthein Michael, plumber, res 51 Hendricks.
Hunting Frederick S, engineer Ft Wayne Electric Co, res 144
    W Main.
Hunting Harlen, machine hand American Wheel Company,
    bds 163 Harmer.
Hunting Wm H, fireman American Wheel Company, res 163
    Harmer.
Huntley Wm H, barber J B Fink, res 60 Force.
Huntoon Loudean P, civil engineer, res 110 W Washington.
Huntsman Elizabeth (wid Israel), res 142 E Wayne.
Huntsman Vina, bds 142 E Wayne.
Hunziker Jacob, saloon, 25 Force, res 27 same.
Hupner Jacob, carpenter, res 69 Oakley.
Hurd Oscar D, assistant custodian Government building, bds
    Wayne Hotel.
Hurd Wm T, laborer, bds 22 W Main.
Hurlburt Isabella, bds 104 Barr.
Hurlburt Sidney C, machine hand Old Fort Mnfg Co, res 365
    E Lewis.
Hurlbut Edward S, shipping clerk Olds'. Wagon Works, res
    188 W DeWald.
Hurlbut Oscar B, painter, res 177 Barr.
Hurlbut Wm R, lab American Wheel Co, bds 188 W DeWald.
Hurlbut Wm R, machine hand American Wheel Co, bds 181
    W DeWald.
Hurless James O, brakeman Penn Co, res cor Madison and
    Monroe.
Hurley Daniel, asst fireman boiler shop Penn Co, res 45 W
    Williams.
Hurley Maggie (wid Michael), bds 309 Lafayette.
Hurley Timothy J clerk Kerr-Murray Mnfg Co, bds 73
    Madison.
Hursche Herman, laborer, res 78 John.
Hursh Annie (wid Luther E), bds 118 Eliza.
Hursh Samuel C, machine hand Fort Wayne Electric Co, res
    35 Walnut.
Hurshour Louis B, laborer, res 52 Chicago.
Hurst Emma, bds 91 Montgomery.
Hurst James M, lab Wm Moellering, res 9 Bass.

Huser Louis P, shoemkr, 178 Broadway, res 167 Jackson.
Hushour Clara, bds 92 Chicago.
Hushour Nora, bds 92 Chicago.
Huston Archibald H, clk Union Line, bds 322 W Washington.
Huston John, laborer, res 65 W Williams.
Hutchins Wm, inspector, bds 29 E Main.
Hutchinson Mrs Blanche, dressmkr, 130 W 3d, res same.
Hutchinson Chief, produce buyer, bds Hyer House.
Hutchinson Frank M, painter Wayne Paint and Painting Co,
    bds 198 Lafayette.
Hutchinson John, agt, res 185 E Jefferson.
Hutchinson Mahlon R, cabinetmaker Fort Wayne Organ Co,
    res 7 Caroline.
Hutchinson Mrs Mate M, res 135 Calhoun.
Hutchinson Mrs Mate, res 37½ W Berry.
Hutchinson Oliver G, tanner, s e cor Cherry and Boone, res
    296 W Main.
Hutchinson Wm, wood turner Fort Wayne Organ Co, res s w
    cor Clinton and Murray.
Hutchison Alonzo, plasterer, res 31 John.
Huth Louis, cigarmaker Reuben Bender, bds Windsor Hotel.
Hutker Louise, domestic 296 W Jefferson.
Hutson, see also Hudson.
Hutson Charles, laborer, res 104 Gay.
Hutton Clara B, bds 517 Broadway.
Hutton D Edwin, traveling agent A L Johns & Co, res 517
    Broadway.
Hutton Rebecca (wid Samuel), bds 517 Broadway.
Hutzell Daniel, Saloon, 378 W Main, res 376 same.
Hutzell John, res 200 W Washington.
Hutzell Valentine, molder Indiana Machine Works, bds 376
    W Main.
Huxley Frank S, engineer, res 361 W Main.
Huxoll August, Dealer in Staple and Fancy Groceries,
    Provisions, Flour, Feed, etc, 92 Barr and 65 E Wayne,
    res 173 Harmer.
Huxoll Frederick, clk August Huxoll, bds 171 Harmer.
Hyde Alexander W, teamster, res 12 Marion.
Hyde Charles, transfer agent Fort Wayne Street Railroad
    Co, bds 55 Melita.
Hyer Edward A, propr Hyer House, 3 Railroad.
Hyer House, Edward A Hyer propr, 3 Railroad.
Hyland Patrick J, inspector, bds 55 Barr.
Hyle Louise, domestic 126 E Berry.
Hyman Philip H, lumber, res 338 Calhoun.
Hynes, see Hines.

I

Iba Elizabeth (wid Wm), res 129 Fairfield ave.

Iba Etta, bds 129 Fairfield ave.

Iba George S, fireman City Water Works, res 39 W Jefferson.

Iebold Henry, baker B W Skelton, res 68 Boone.

Ifel John, helper Penn Co, res 7 Smith.

Iliff David H, works Winch & Son, res 30 Winch.

Iliff John, teamster Winch & Son, res n e cor Penn and Dubois.

Imbody Adam, wood turner Ft Wayne Organ Co, res 83 W DeWald.

Imbody Daniel, molder Bass Foundry and Machine Works, res 189 Ewing.

Imbody Dorothy (wid Harrison), res 83 W DeWald.

Imbody Eliza, clerk, bds 83 W DeWald.

Imbody Henry A, finisher Ft Wayne Organ Co, bds 103 W Williams.

Immel Amelia, bds 568 E Washington.

Immel Edward A H, fireman City fire dept, bds 568 E Washington.

Immel John, janitor Jefferson School, res 63 McClellan.

Immel John, bds 568 E Washington.

Immel Louisa (wid Henry), res 568 E Washington.

Immel Mary, bds 568 E Washington.

Immel Walter H, shipping clerk The Herman Berghoff Brewing Co, bds 568 E Washington.

Imperial Hotel, Martin S Stantz propr, s e cor Clinton and E Superior.

Imswiler Wm H, laborer, res w s Indiana ave 5 s of Home ave.

Inch John, laborer Winch & Son, res 9 Caroline.

Indiana Deutsche Presse (weekly), Otto F Cummerow propr, n e cor Calhoun and Main.

Indiana Installment Co, John V Reul mngr, 127 Calhoun.

Indiana Machine Works, J C Peters pres, P A Randall vice-pres, E H McDonald sec, J M Landenberger treas and mngr, office and works Osage near Main.

Indiana School for Feeble-Minded Youth, 1¾ miles n e of Court house.

Indiana Staats Zeitung (daily and weekly), Indiana Staats Zeitung Co publrs, n e cor Columbia and Clinton.

Indiana Staats Zeitung Co (John D Sarnighausen, A Louis Griebel), publrs Indiana Staats Zeitung, n e cor Columbia and Clinton.

Indiana State Asylum for Feeble-Minded, St Joe road 1 mile n e of Court house.

Indiana State Gazetteer, R L Polk & Co Publrs, 50 Calhoun.

Industrial Life Association, A O Buchman agt, 20 Schmitz block.

Inman Charles W, painter, res 68 Riverside ave.

Inter-State Fair Association, W D Page pres, J W Pearse vice-pres, D C Fisher sec and treas, grounds located 1 mile w of city, office 32 E Berry.

Irey Alfred K, foreman, res 86 Wells.

Irey Frank J, clerk J M Clark & Co, bds 86 Wells.

Irey Sarah (wid Wm), bds 86 Wells.

Irmscher Max, bricklayer, res 504 E Lewis.

Irvin Anna R (wid Robert), bds 18 Hamilton.

Irvin Lee, laborer, res 43 E Superior.

Irvin Michael, laborer, bds 43½ E Columbia·

Irwin George B, dry goods, 125 Broadway, res 30 Wilt.

Irwin George H, foreman Olds' Wagon Works, res 49 Gay.

Irwin George U, bds 241 W Main.

Irwin John S, M D, L L D, Superintendent Public Schools, Central Grammar School Bldg, res 241 W Main.

Irwin Miss Lizzie F, teacher Washington School, bds 30 Wilt.

Irwin Miss Mary, clerk School board, bds 241 W Main.

Irwin Miss Rose, bds 241 W Main.

Irwin Thomas L jr, clerk H W Mordhurst, bds same.

Irwin Wm J, boilermaker, res 98 Baker.

Isaby Ellen, domestic, 101 Glasgow ave.

Isaby George, farmer, bds Louis Isaby.

Isaby Joseph, farmer, bds Louis Isaby.

Isaby Louis, farmer, res n s New Haven rd 1 e of toll gate.

Isaby Maggie, bds Louis Isaby.

Isaby Rosa, bds Louis Isaby.

Isett John, painter Penn Co, bds 369 Lafayette.

Israel Bros (Henry and Frederick), blacksmiths, 5 Pearl.

Israel Charles, painter, res 16 Sturgis.

Israel Emil, laborer George Newcomer, bds same.

Israel Frederick (Israel Bros), bds 215 W Main.

Israel Henry (Israel Bros), res 119 Broadway.

Israel Wm, bottler The Herman Berghoff Brewing Co, res s w cor Wabash ave and Humphrey.

Iten Catherine (wid John), bds 112 E Creighton ave.

Iten Frank, inspector, res 51 Buchanan.

Iten John C, carpenter, res 13 Begue.

Iten Frank, inspector City Water Works, res 51 Buchanan.

J

Jaap George, Cut and Ornamental Stone Contractor, 79 and 81 E Columbia, res 180 Wells. (*See left bottom lines and card in classified Cut Stone Contractors.*)

Jabas Emil, bricklayer, res 361 E Lewis.

Jabas Emil jr, apprentice E Jabas, bds 361 E Lewis.

Jackson Alexander, brickmaker, bds 182 E Jefferson.

Jackson Allen T, carp S F Bowser & Co, res 82 S Wayne.

Jackson Augustus B, bartender Hotel Randall, bds same.

Jackson Brownell, clerk Keil & Keil, bds 197 E Jefferson.

Jackson Daniel J, baggageman, rms 34 W Main.

Jackson Edward M, janitor Young Men's Christian Assn, res 68 Dawson.

Jackson Edwin, reporter, bds 50 E Washington.

Jackson Miss Effie A, asst T H McCormick, bds 82 S Wayne.

Jackson Emma (wid Jacob), dressmaker, 197 E Jefferson, res 601 Calhoun.

Jackson Frank B, machinist Ft Wayne Electric Co, res 46 W Williams.

Jackson Ira C, carpenter, bds 82 S Wayne ave.

Jackson John (Flinn & Jackson), res 35 Douglas ave.

Jackson John A, brickmaker A McKernan, bds 35 Douglas.

Jackson John P, conductor Penn Co, res 16 W De Wald.

Jackson Kirby C, engineer, res 55 Brackenridge.

Jackson Lillian, bds 155 W Washington.

Jackson Marlin F, coil winder Fort Wayne Electric Co, bds 82 S Wayne ave.

Jackson Samson, res 35 Douglas ave.

Jackson Thomas, Engineer Maintenance of Way Penn Co, res e s Fairfield ave 4 s of W Creighton ave.

Jackson Wm, watchman, res 103 W Williams.

Jackson Wm A, traveling agent, res n w cor Hoagland and W Creighton aves.

Jackson Wm A, tinsmith, bds 103 W Williams.

Jackson Wm H, carpenter, res 13 Bell ave.

Jackson Wm T, engineer, res 155 W Washington.

Jacob Anna B, candymaker, bds 73 Wall.

Jacob Carrie A, bds 73 Wall.

Jacob Gustav, watchman Nickel Plate, res 38 Watkins.

Jacob Henry, laborer Penn Co, res 115 Hayden.

Jacob Johanna (wid George), res 73 Wall.

Jacobs Andrew, grocer, 354 Broadway, res 42 Stophlet.

Jacobs Caroline (wid Peter), bds 116 Madison.

Jacobs Charles, meats, 197 E Washington, res 116 Madison.

Jacobs Charles W, baker, 62 E Main, res 297 W Washington.

Jacobs Christian C, driver C W Jacobs, bds 297 W Washington.

Jacobs George, saloon, 30 W Main, res same.

Jacobs George H, baker C W Jacobs, bds 297 W Washington.

Jacobs Harry N, compounder J Nathan & Co, bds Aveline House.

Jacobs Henry, laborer Hoffman Bros, res 19 Richardson.

Jacobs Henry G, blacksmith, bds 297 W Washington.

Jacobs James, foreman Ryan Bros, bds same.

Jacobs John H, res w s Spy Run ave 1 n of Brewery.

Jacobs John W, baker C W Jacobs, res rear Leikauf's packing house.

Jacobs Lizzie, bds 297 W Washington.

Jacobs Miss Mary E, res 171 E Wayne.

Jacobs Philanda (wid John), bds 22 Fulton.

Jacobs Sophie, bds 297 W Washington.

Jacobs Thomas, driver Hoffman Bros, res 22 Fulton.

Jacobs Wm F, baker C W Jacobs, bds 297 W Washington.

Jacobson Miss Laura, bds 136 W Wayne.

Jacobson Rosalie (wid Victor), res 136 W Wayne.

Jacobson Miss Sarah, bds 136 W Wayne.

Jacoby Frederick, carpenter, res 40 Buchanan.

Jacoby George, carpenter, res 78 Murray.

Jacoby Mary, operator S M Foster, bds 40 Hanna.

Jacoby Tillie, clerk Dr T J Dills, bds 40 Buchanan.

Jacot August, laborer, bds 70 E Columbia.

Jaebker August, blacksmith, res 15 Summit.

Jaeger, *see also Yager and Yeager.*

Jaeger Charles, laborer Penn Co, res 59 Force.

Jaeger Christian, clerk Freese & Fehling, bds 178 W Creighton ave.

Jahn, *see also John.*

Jahn Charles C, car builder Penn Co, res Wayne Trace.

Jahn Elizabeth (wid Herman), bds 123 Union.

Jahn Herman F, painter, res 84 Buchanan.

Jahn Nicholas, carpenter, res 1 Rockhill.

James Eliza (wid Elisha), res 83 St Mary's ave.

James Frank B, machine hand American Wheel Co, res 223 Madison.

James George A, laborer, bds 83 St Mary's ave.

James George H, painter Penn Co, bds 197 Barr.

James H Lednum, painter Fleming Mnfg Co, res 31 W 4th.

James Mrs Jane, res 197 Barr.

James Jesse N, carpenter, res 157 Shawnee ave.

James Jonathan, bds 143 Wells.

James Steven, driver C L Centlivre, bds Centlivre's Park.

James Wm, engineer H W Bond, bds 43½ E Columbia.

James Wm H, teamster, res 161 Shawnee ave.

James Wm S, laborer, res 197 Barr.

Jamey Emiel, engineer, res 85 Greene.

Jamey Frederick, laborer, res 42 Boone.

Janorschke Frank, cabinetmaker Fort Wayne Furniture Co, res 47 Wagner.

Jansen Thomas J, tailor John Wasserbach, bds 202 John.

Jarrard Harry R, photographer, 86 Calhoun, res same.

Jarrett Cyrenius F, clerk, res 24 Brandriff.

Jarrett James V, laborer, bds 24 Brandriff.

Jasper Elizabeth (wid Rudolph), bds 49 W Washington.

Jasper Frederick, car builder Penn Co, res 49 W Washington.

Jasper Frederick, laborer, bds 197 W Superior.

Jasper George W (Freistroffer & Jasper), res 51 W Washington.

Jasper Wm F, carpenter Frederick Kraft, res 197 W Superior.

Jautz, see also Yautz.

Jautz Charles L, car repairer Wabash R R, res 113 High.

Jautz Christian, gardener, res 3 Polk.

Jautz Louis, teamster, bds 113 High.

Jaxtheimer Alexander W, cutter Leonhard Jaxtheimer, bds 31 Wefel.

Jaxtheimer Leonhard, merchant tailor, 83 Calhoun, res 31 Wefel.

Jay Burt, carpenter, bds 91 Montgomery.

Jay Miss Mary L, asst Central Grammar School, bds 19 E Jefferson.

Jefferds Oliver W (French, Hanna & Co), res 131 E Wayne.

Jefferies Wm T, cigarmkr George Reiter, res 7 McClellan.

Jefferson Lewin T, car repairer Penn Co, res 9 Hayden.

Jefferson School, s w cor W Jefferson and Griffith.

Jeffery Ephraim R, chief clerk Wabash R R shops, res 94 Wilt.

Jehl Virgil, baker Christian Heffner, bds same.

Jenkins Mary (wid Barnett), bds 105 W Berry.

Jenkinson Miss Emma, bds 89 W Berry.

Jenkinson Mrs Harriet E, res 32 Brackenridge.

Jenkinson Joseph J, Lawyer, 15 and 16 Pixley & Long Bldg, res 89 W Berry.

Jenkinson Wm E, clerk Fort Wayne Electric Co, res 32 Brackenridge.

Jenne Chauncey R, agt Hercules Powder Co, 18 W Columbia, res same.

Jenney Electric Light and Power Co, H C Graffe Pres, E H McDonald Sec, G W Pixley Treas, Charles G Guild Supt, Office 38 and 39 Pixley & Long Bldg, Plant, Spy Run ave n of Burgess ave.

Jenson Abigail J (wid John), bds 36 Marion.

Jenson James O (Jenson & Sargent), res 36 Marion.

Jenson Wm A, bartender H B Hammill, res 47 W Superior.

Jenson & Sargent (James O Jenson, Thomas P Sargent), livery, 16 and 18 Wells.

Jeretzky Anton, laborer, res n w cor Liberty and Coombs.

Jewel House, John Boylan Propr, 225 Calhoun.

Jewell Mrs Elizabeth, res 58 W Berry.

Jewell Frank, clerk Robert Spice, rms 74 W Main.

Jobst, *see also Yobst.*

Jobst Anna, machine hand, bds 11 Oak.

Jobst Balbina (wid Alexander), res 11 Oak.

Jobst Charles, laborer City Water Works, bds 11 Oak.

Jobst Elizabeth, machine hand, bds 11 Oak.

Jobst Frank H, laborer City Water Works, res 303 Hanna.

Jobst John, operator Hoosier Mnfg Co, bds 14 Oak.

Jobst Theresa, bds 11 Oak.

Jockel Leonard, stonecutter, res 45 Force.

Jocquel John J, bds 168 Calhoun.

Jocquel Louis, books, 168 Calhoun, res same.

Joerns Frank, cigarmkr Schele Bros, bds 197 Barr.

Johann Andrew, laborer Penn Co, res 248 E Jefferson.

Johann Andrew H, baker Louis Fox & Bro, bds 248 E Jefferson.

Johann George N, machine hand Fort Wayne Furniture Co, res 374 W Washington.

Johanny George B, cigarmkr John Zern, bds 342 Hanna.

John, *see also Jahn.*

John Robert, engineer, res 398 W Main.

Johnell Frank, bds 155 High.

Johnell Henry J, wiper, res 137 High.

Johnell Lawrence, section hand, res 155 High.

Johns Alfred L (A L Johns & Co), res 287 W Washington.

Johns Alfred S, res 308 W Washington.

Johns A L & Co (Alfred L Johns), saddlery hardware, 51 E Columbia.

Johns Edward B, editor The Symposium Taylor University, res same.

Johnson Alfred S, clk N Y, C & St L R R, res 255 W Wayne.

Johnson Andrew J, lumber, res 96 Wells.

Johnson August, coremaker Bass Foundry and Machine Works, res 301 Calhoun.

Election Slips. Headquarters for PERFECT SLIPS
at JOHN F. EBY & CO.'S, DETROIT.

282   R. L. POLK & CO.'S

Johnson Augustine, engineer, res 203 Barr.

Johnson A Lincoln, machinist Fort Wayne Electric Co, res 154 W DeWald.

Johnson Miss Belle, bds 203 Barr.

Johnson Benjamin, laborer, bds 108 High.

Johnson Bernard, helper Bass Foundry and Machine Works, res 87 Holman.

Johnson Byron J, laborer Penn Co, res 150 Force.

Johnson B Frank, hostler A Hattersley & Sons, res 103 Barr.

Johnson Charles, oiler Penn Co, res 42 Wells.

Johnson Charles, painter J W Muldoon, res 137 Holman.

Johnson Charles E, res 41 Harmer.

Johnson Cynthia (wid Edward), bds 41 Harmer.

Johnson Cyrus, driver, bds 101 Glasgow ave.

Johnson Della, laundress 248 Calhoun.

Johnson Miss Edith M, bds 276 W Washington.

Johnson Elizabeth (wid George W), res 32 Butler.

Johnson Miss Ella A, operator W U Tel Co, bds 276 W Washington.

Johnson Emmet, helper Penn Co, bds 42 St Mary's ave.

Johnson Frank (col'd), barber Gerney Winslow, bds 68 Chicago.

Johnson Frank, fireman, res 26 Melita.

Johnson Frank M, Propr Darrow House, 248 Calhoun, res same.

Johnson Frederick W, mngr National Portrait Co, res 67 E Main.

Johnson George, laborer, res 202 John.

Johnson George E, laborer Salimonie Mining and Gas Co, bds 32 Butler.

Johnson Hans P, blksmith Olds' Wagon Works, res 28 Gay.

Johnson Henry, coachman 255 Fairfield ave.

Johnson Henry C, bds 266 W Jefferson.

Johnson Henry E, laborer Penn Co, res 217 John.

Johnson Henry J F W, laborer, bds 136 W DeWald.

Johnson Jacob, carpenter Penn Co, res 214 John.

Johnson Jane, domestic 308 S Harrison.

Johnson John W, res 136 W DeWald.

Johnson Josiah, car oiler Penn Co, res 33 Walnut.

Johnson Laura J, vestmaker Charles Kruse, res 161 Griffith.

Johnson Loren H, grocer, rear 262 Calhoun, res same.

Johnson Lydia, opr Hoosier Mnfg Co, bds 61 W Pontiac.

Johnson Marcus R, machinist Fort Wayne Electric Co, res 231 W Jefferson.

Johnson Mary, seamstress D S Redelsheimer & Co, bds 202 John.

Stahn & Heinrich, Booksellers and Stationers, Schmitz Block News Stand, 116 Calhoun Street.

FORT WAYNE DIRECTORY. 283

Johnson Melvin A, painter Olds' Wagon Works, bds 42 St Mary's ave.

Johnson Milton R, lab American Wheel Co, bds 41 Wallace.

Johnson Minnie C, bds 421 Calhoun.

Johnson Ollie (wid Albert), tailoress P D Swick, bds 509 E Washington.

Johnson Oscar B, clerk, res 276 W Washington.

Johnson Oscar B jr, bds 276 W Washington.

Johnson Peter H, blacksmith Fort Wayne Electric Co, res 73 Shawnee ave.

Johnson Miss Sadie, bds 32 Butler.

Johnson Sarah E (wid Elias), res 35 Pixley & Long bldg.

Johnson Thomas, tailor, bds 202 John.

Johnson Thomas F, carpenter, res 39 Wilt.

Johnson Wesley H, laborer L S & M S Ry, res 5 Marion.

Johnston Lee, bartender, rms 51 E Main.

Johnston Lucy, bds 136 Barr.

Johnston Monroe, laborer Penn Co, res 71 W 3d.

Johnston Wm jr, sec Olds' Wagon Works, res 109 W Berry.

Jolly, *see also Jully.*

Jolly Frank, clerk John Langard, res Randolph nr Centlivre's Brewery.

Joly Emma F, bds 61 E Columbia.

Jones Alice, wks Indiana School for Feeble-Minded Youth.

Jones Ambrose F, clerk J B White, res 301 Harrison.

Jones Arthur L, clerk, bds 112 Wells.

Jones Belle M (wid Maurice L), res 35 E Wayne.

Jones Benjamin F, machine hand Kerr-Murray Mnfg Co, bds 63 Butler.

Jones Catherine (wid Paul), res 51 Oliver.

Jones Charles (col'd), laborer Bass Foundry and Machine Works, bds 31 Pearl.

Jones Charles, fireman, res n s High 1 w of St Mary's ave.

Jones Charles A, physician, 87 Maumee rd, res same.

Jones Charles M, clerk Penn Co, res 116 Force.

Jones Cornelius B, teamster, res rear 349 W Washington.

Jones David W, job printer, 13 E Main, res 21 Leith.

Jones Edward, clk Pottlitzer Bros, bds 47 W Wayne.

Jones Edward S, engineer, res 83 Butler.

Jones Eva, domestic 25 Brandriff.

Jones Frederick W, res 309 W Washington.

Jones Fremont L (F L Jones & Co), res w s Hoagland ave 2 s of Creighton ave.

Jones F L & Co (Fremont L Jones, Ogden Pierce), Proprs Troy Steam Laundry, 48 and 50 Pearl. (*See left bottom lines.*)

Jones George A, clerk G W Seavey, res 274 E Wayne.

Jones George W, mach hand American Wheel Company, res 81 Buchanan.

Jones George W, real estate, 33 Calhoun, res 146 Jackson.

Jones Harry A, bookkeeper M L Jones, bds cor Clinton and Wayne.

Jones Harvey P, clk Troy Steam Laundry, res 21 Leith.

Jones Miss Hattie, teacher, bds 146 Jackson.

Jones Henry, brakeman, bds 51 Oliver.

Jones Henry, checkman, res 166 Madison.

Jones Henry, engineer, res 47 E DeWald.

Jones Isaac, conductor Penn Co, res 228 Francis.

Jones Ivins E (col'd), porter Hotel Randall, bds 205 Calhoun.

Jones Jane (wid Henry), res 91 E Main.

Jones John, farmer, res e s Lafayette 2 s of Piqua ave.

Jones John, laborer, bds Monroe House.

Jones John, mach Wabash R R, res 63 Butler.

Jones John G, laborer, res 27 Taylor.

Jones John L, molder, bds 63 Butler.

Jones Joseph H, physician, 320 W Jefferson, res same.

Jones Kate (wid John), bds 22 John.

Jones Levi N, real estate, res 152 E Berry.

Jones Lloyd, clerk, res 112 Wells.

Jones Lucelle F, res 246 S Hoagland ave.

Jones Mary (wid David W), bds 53 W Superior.

Jones Maurice L, Photographers' Supplies, 44 Calhoun, res 2 E Columbia.

Jones Oliver S, painter, bds 63 Butler.

Jones Paris D, teamster, bds rear 349 W Washington.

Jones Robert M, engineer, res 146 Wallace.

Jones Silas E, expressman, bds 266 E Creighton ave.

Jones Thomas, clk Coombs & Co, res 30 Pine.

Jones Thomas, conductor, rms 38 Brackenridge.

Jones Wilbur, brakeman, bds Monroe House.

Jones Wilbur (col'd), coremaker Bass Foundry and Machine Works, bds 31 Pearl.

Jones Wm, laborer Robert Spice, bds 68 Butler.

Jones Wm, laborer, bds 182 E Jefferson.

Jones Wm H, laborer Kilian Baker, bds 3 Railroad.

Jones Wm H, Propr Hamilton House, 103 W Berry.

Jones Wm S (col'd), barber J H Roberts, rms 31 Pearl.

Joost, *see also Yoast.*

Joost Albert, music teacher, res 132 W Jefferson.

Jordain Charles, photographer J O Shoaff, bds same.

Jordan, *see also Jourdain.*

Jordan George S, engineer, res 60 Barthold.

Jordan Joseph, machinist, res 142 Madison.
Jordan Joseph A, helper Penn Co, bds 328 Harrison.
Jornod Ernest, driver Fort Wayne Street Railroad Co, bds 42 Division.
Joseph Louis, bartender Charles Noirot, rooms 64 E Columbia.
Joshlin Enoch, deputy sheriff, bds Hedekin House.
Joslin Hiram, laborer, bds 57 Huffman.
Josse Charles P, painter, res n s 4th 1 w of Cass.
Josse Frederica (wid Edward), res 61 Meridian.
Josse Louisa C (wid John M), res 138 Wells.
Jourdain, *see also Jordan.*
Jourdain Celestian J, grocer, 98 Maumee road, res 94 same.
Jourdain Mary, bds 94 Maumee road.
Jourdain Minnie, bds 94 Maumee road.
Jourdain Sophie, bds 94 Maumee road.
Journal Co The, W W Rockhill Manager, A J Moynihan Editor, Publrs Fort Wayne Daily and Weekly Journal, 30 E Main.
Journal of the National Association of Railway Surgeons, Christian B Stemen editor and publr, 74 Calhoun.
Judt George, turner White's Wheel Works, res 28 Lillie.
Judy David L, machinist Penn Co, bds 157 Holman.
Judy George H, foreman, res 157 Holman.
Judy Lloyd W, laborer Penn Co, bds 157 Holman.
Judy Oscar B, blacksmith Penn Co, res 32 Brackenridge.
Juengel Rev Henry, pastor Evangelical Lutheran Zion's Congregational Church, res s e cor Creighton ave and Force.
Juergens August H, brickmkr, res w s Lafayette road 2 n of Piqua.
Juergens Wm, carpenter, bds Fritz Hotel.
Julliard Francis, dressmaker, 103 Broadway, res same.
Jully, *see also Jolly.*
Jully Louis, barber, 112 St Mary's ave, res same.
Jump Edward D, finisher P E Wolf, bds 22 Ewing.
Junge Clements J, painter, res 174 Suttenfield.
Jungles Wm F, fireman, res 467 Lafayette.
Junk Beecher W, Mngr L Junk, res 66 Monroe.
Junk Gertude (wid Nicholas), res 74 Leith.
Junk Jacob, labor Penn Co, bds 74 Leith.
Junk Joseph, laborer Penn Co, bds 74 Leith.
Junk L, Dealer in Mouldings, Pictures, Frames, Mirrors, Chromos, Easels etc, 181 Calhoun, res 66 Monroe. (*See left bottom lines.*)
Junk Peter, helper Penn Co, bds 74 Leith.

21

Robert Spice, Waterworks and General Plumbing. 48 West Main and 11 Pearl Streets.

286 R. L. POLK & CO.'S

Jurgensen Peter K, clerk Morgan & Beach, res s s St Joe road 1 e of St Joe bridge.

Just, *see Yost.*

K

Kaade August, boilermaker, res 71 Nirdlinger ave.

Kaade Ferdinand, laborer Bass Foundry and Machine Works, res 166 W Creighton ave.

Kaade Herman, laborer South Wayne Brick Co, bds 71 Nirdlinger ave.

Kaade Wm, coremaker Bass Foundry and Machine Works, bds 166 W Creighton ave.

Kaag Miss Bertha A, bds 45 N Cass.

Kaag Carrie E, clerk A C Keel, bds 283 W Jefferson.

Kaag Lillie E, bds 283 W Jefferson.

Kaag Margaret (wid Jacob C), res 283 W Jefferson.

Kaag Mathias F, Crockery, Glassware, Bar Goods, Lamps and Chandeliers, 5 E Columbia, res 45 Cass. (*See left bottom lines.*)

Kaag Pauline R, clerk M F Kaag, bds 283 W Jefferson.

Kaag Wm, laborer Hoffman Bros, bds s e cor Spring and Oakland.

Kabisch Frederick C (Kabisch & Son), res 180 W DeWald.

Kabisch John H, barber, 137 Fairfield ave, res 108 Williams

Kabisch Rudolph (Kabisch & Son), res 182 Fairfield ave.

Kabisch & Son (Rudolph and Frederick C), meat market, 156 Fairfield ave.

Kaeck Eliza, bds s e cor Oakland and Spring.

Kaeck Peter, carpenter Wm Ruchel, res s e cor Spring and Oakland.

Kaeck Wm, laborer, bds s e cor Oakland and Spring.

Kafnel Jacob, carpenter Bass Foundry and Machine Works, res 525 Hanna.

Kah George, saloon, 41 Harrison, res same.

Kahl Wendling, laborer, res 336 Force.

Kahlbacher, *see Kalbacher and Kohlbacher.*

Kahler, *see also Kaler, Kayler, Keeler, Kehler, Keller and Kohler.*

Kahler Henry, bds 30 Huffman.

Kahnlein, *see Koehnlein.*

Kahoe Wm, fireman, res 57½ Laselle.

Kain, *see Kane.*

Kaiser, *see also Kayser, Keiser, Keyser and Kiser.*

Kaiser Annie, domestic 164 Calhoun.

Sewing Machines, Shears | Pfeiffer & Schlatter
—and Pocket Knives,—— 38 & 40 E. Columbia.

FORT WAYNE DIRECTORY. 287

Kaiser Anthony W, clerk Penn Co, res 127 Madison.
Kaiser Charles, blacksmith Wabash R R, res 6 Union.
Kaiser Conrad, foreman Ranke & Yergens, res 43 N Cass.
Kaiser Ernest, machinist Penn Co, res 186 E Lewis.
Kaiser Frederick, boilermaker Penn Co, bds 148 Force.
Kaiser Frederick F, helper Bass Foundry and Machine Works, bds 148 Force.
Kaiser George, machinist Indiana Machine Works, bds 252 W Jefferson.
Kaiser Henry D, clerk Ranke & Yergens, bds 43 N Cass.
Kaiser John, laborer Penn Co, res rear 43 Wells.
Kaiser Louise, domestic 301 Fairfield ave.
Kaiser Minnie (wid Henry), bds 127 Madison.
Kaiser Wm G, patternmaker Fort Wayne Iron Works, bds 43 N Cass.
Kalbacher, see also Kahlbacher and Kohlbacher.
Kalbacher Anton, grocer, 13–15 Grand, res 234 E Wayne.
Kalbacher A & Co (Anton Kalbacher, Wm Potthoff), flour and feed, 296 Calhoun.
Kalbacher Edward H, clerk, bds 234 E Wayne.
Kalbacher Kate, bookkeeper, bds 234 E Wayne.
Kalbacher Theresa, bds 234 E Wayne.
Kalbus John, laborer, res 153 Pfeiffer ave.
Kaler, see also Kahler, Kayler, Keeler, Kehler, Keller and Kohler.
Kaler Charles P, conductor, res 202 W Jefferson.
Kales Henry, laborer, bds 72 Gay.
Kallen Peter, inventor, res n e cor Richardson and Rumsey.
Kallenbach George, laborer Neil Bros & Co, bds 32 Charles.
Kallenbach Hattie (wid George), res 32 Charles.
Kallenbach Lottie, milliner Mrs Adolph Schulte, bds 32 Charles.
Kallenbach Louis, laborer, bds 14 Force.
Kamm Julius, helper, bds 512 E Lewis.
Kamm Wm, engineer, res 512 E Lewis.
Kammeier, see also Kohlmeyer.
Kammeier Henry, laborer Nickel Plate, res 87 St Mary's ave.
Kammer Henry, laborer, res 133 Madison.
Kammer Louis, wagonmaker, res 181 Madison.
Kammeyer Diedrich, laborer, bds 80 Nirdlinger ave.
Kammeyer Ernest, driver Kayser & Baade, bds 57 Baker.
Kammeyer Richard, machine hand Fort Wayne Electric Co, bds 81 Wall.
Kamp, see also Kemp and Komp.
Kamp George, machinist, res 26 Nirdlinger ave.

Kamp Kate J, bds 390 Hanna.
Kamp Wm F, laborer, bds 26 Nirdlinger ave.
Kampe Charles A, res 50 W Lewis.
Kampe Christian J, clerk Penn Co, bds 50 W Lewis.
Kampe Ernest, clerk Root & Co, bds 50 W Lewis.
Kampe Gustave, tchr Emanuel School, res 306 W Jefferson.
Kampe Otto F, upholsterer P E Wolf, bds 50 W Lewis.
Kamphues Henry, butcher Leikauf Bros, res Leikauf's packing house.
Kamphues John, laborer, bds 38 Wall.
Kamphues Mary (wid Joseph), res 38 Wall.
Kanaga Francis J, conductor, res 86 W Williams.
Kanaga Lee A, conductor Penn Co, res 88 Williams.
Kanamann Catherine (wid Frederick), res 11 McLaughlin.
Kane, *see also Kain.*
Kane's Block, s s Main bet Calhoun and Harrison.
Kane Charles E, clerk James M Kane, bds 88 W Berry.
Kane Daniel W, clerk James M Kane, bds 88 W Berry.
Kane Frederick, laborer, bds 72 Gay.
Kane Hannah (wid James), bds 50 W Berry.
Kane James M, notions, 24 Calhoun, res 88 W Berry.
Kane John P, conductor Penn Co, res 504 Hanna.
Kane Miss Mary, bds 50 W Berry.
Kane Patrick H, cigars, res 50 W Berry.
Kanne August F, foreman L O Hull, res 68 E Pontiac.
Kanne Caroline (wid Frederick), bds 315 E Washington.
Kanne Frederick H, clerk Fisher Bros, res 95 Montgomery.
Kanney John, bricklayer, res 94 Barr.
Kanney Rose, clerk E Shuman & Sons, bds 94 Barr.
Kanning Henry, bricklayer, bds 15 Pritchard.
Kanning Henry, shipping clk Fred Eckert, bds 59 E Wayne.
Kanning Henry F, springmaker E B Kunkle & Co, bds 135 E Lewis.
Kanning Louis, molder E B Kunkle & Co, bds 59 E Wayne.
Kanning Miss Louise A, bds 59 E Wayne.
Kanning Sophia (wid Lewis), res 135 E Lewis.
Kanning Sophia (wid Wm), res 59 E Wayne.
Kanning Wm, helper Penn Co, bds 59 E Wayne.
Kanst Siemon, laborer C L Centlivre, bds Albert Eckerle.
Kaomer Gottlieb, laborer J C Peters, res 19 Huron.
Kaough Elizabeth, bds 166 Montgomery.
Kaough Richard, helper, bds 166 Montgomery.
Kaough Wm (E F Clausmeier & Co), res 166 Montgomery.
Kapp, *see Kapp and Cap.*
Kappel Henry (J H Kappel & Bro), bds 180 E Washington.
Kappel Henry, helper Penn Co, bds 349 E Lewis.

Kappel Herman G, clerk G De Wald & Co, bds 180 E Washington.

Kappel John, paperhanger Keil & Keil, res 180 E Washington.

Kappel John H (J H Kappel & Bro), bds 180 E Washington.

Kappel John H, apprentice M L Frankenstein, bds 349 E Lewis.

Kappel John H & Bro (John H and Henry), painters, 180 E Washington.

Karber Erastus, bds 26 Grant ave.

Karber Frederick, jeweler, res 156 Wells.

Karber George D, carpenter White's Wheel Works, res s e cor Grant ave and Humphrey.

Karber James H, laborer White's Wheel Works, bds 104 Glasgow ave.

Kariger Catherine (wid Peter), bds 141 Cass.

Kariger Samuel, farmer, res 187 Harmer.

Karkhoff Frank J, carpenter, res 15 Leith.

Karman, see Carman.

Karn, see also Kern and Kirn.

Karn Kaim (Rich & Karn), res 168 Griffith.

Karn Samuel A, pianos, 118 Calhoun, res 58 W Berry.

Karns Calvin H, wagonmaker, bds 301 Calhoun.

Karns Rufus J, wheelmaker Olds' Wagon Works, bds 20 Murray.

Karns Wilson, photographer, res 55 Smith.

Karp Helena, bds 223 Walton ave.

Karrer John, laborer, bds George Gieger.

Karrer Lucy A, domestic 56 E Wayne.

Karte John, laborer, res w s Hanna 6 s of Pontiac.

Kartholl Caroline (wid Joseph), bds 112 Clay.

Kasbaum Charles, wheelmaker American Wheel Co, res n s Spy Run ave nr Wagner.

Kasch Adam, boilermaker, bds 78 Wilt.

Kassans Christian, carpenter, res 56 Thomas.

Kassel, see also Kestel and Castle.

Kassel Robert, laborer White's Wheel Works, res 1 Glasgow.

Kasser John, laborer, bds 27 Force.

Kassman Benjamin, turner, bds 24 Murray.

Kasten Louis C (Kasten & Kohlmeyer), res 116 W Jefferson.

Kasten & Kohlmeyer (Louis C Kasten, Edward Kohlmeyer), cigars, 173 Broadway.

Katt August C, Books and Stationery and News Stand 82 Calhoun, res 69 W Berry.

Katt Claud, stone mason, res 41 Maumee road.

Katt Gustav E, printer Indiana Staats Zeitung, bds 41 Maumee ave.

Kauffman Harry S, telegraph operator, bds 262 W Berry.

Kauffman Julia, operator Hoosier Manufacturing Co, bds 348 Hanna.

Kaufman Catherine (wid Christian), res 348 Hanna.

Kaufman John, waiter, bds 38 Clinton.

Kaufmann Valentine, laborer Kerr-Murray Mnfg Co, res 40 Charles.

Kauter Christian, baker C W Jacobs, bds 62 E Main.

Kavanaugh, *see also Cavanaugh.*

Kavanaugh May, clerk, bds 167 N Harrison.

Kavanaugh Rose, works J O Keller, bds 167 N Harrison.

Kavanaugh Thomas, collector, res 167 N Harrison.

Kavanaugh Thomas J, laborer, bds 167 N Harrison.

Kay, *see also Key.*

Kay Mrs Amanda E, res 37 Bass.

Kay Benjamin, machinist, res 44 Hoagland ave.

Kay Herbert, machine hand, bds 44 Hoagland ave.

Kay John, machine hand, bds 44 Hoagland ave.

Kaylor, *see also Kahler, Kaler, Keeler, Keller and Kohler.*

Kaylor John, baker L P Scherer, bds 145 John.

Kaylor Lester, bds 21 Force.

Kaylor Lyman, laborer David Tagtmeyer, res cor Lewis and Lillie.

Kaylor Mary (wid Peter), bds 21 Force.

Kaylor Peter, brickmaker A McKernan, res 525 E Lewis.

Kaylor Reuben, laborer, res 21 Force.

Kaylor Rosa, bds 21 Force.

Kaylor Wm, lumber, res 145 John.

Kayser, *see also Kaiser, Keiser, Keyser and Kiser.*

Kayser Anton, tailor, res 252 W Jefferson.

Kayser Charles E, stripper F J Gruber, bds 346 E Wayne.

Kayser Diederich, laborer, res 148 Broadway.

Kayser Ernest, driver Pottlitzer Bros, res 179 W Washington.

Kayser Frederick, tailor, 42 Harrison, res same.

Kayser Frederick C, bed-spring maker, bds 346 E Wayne.

Kayser Frederick D, shoemaker Peter Eggemann, res 346 E Wayne.

Kayser Helen L, bds 346 E Wayne.

Kayser Mary, dressmaker E A Waltemath, bds 252 W Jefferson.

Kayser Minnie, dressmaker E A Waltemath, bds 252 W Jefferson.

Kayser Oscar, laborer, res 332 Force.

Kayser Peter, works D M Foster Furniture Co, res 374 E Washington.

Kayser Theodore, clk, bds 252 W Jefferson.

Kayser Wm (Kayser & Baade), res 27 Pritchard.
Kayser Wm, tailor, bds 42 Harrison.
Kayser Wm D, printer Indiana Staats Zeitung, bds 346 E
Wayne.
Kayser & Baade (Wm Kayser, Henry C Baade), grocers, 129
Broadway.
Kearns, see also Karn, Karns, Kern and Kerns.
Kearns Bridget (wid Thomas), res 2 Brandriff.
Kearns Dennis, flagman Penn Co, bds 2 Brandriff.
Kebach Emil, lab, res n s Eckart 2 e of Hanna.
Keberger Henry, driver I C Youngker, bds same.
Kee Wah, laundry, 203 Calhoun, res same.
Keech Arthur S, laborer, bds 471 Lafayette.
Keech J Edward, machinist Kerr-Murray Mnfg Co, res 471
Lafayette.
Keefe John, brakeman Nickel Plate, res 1 N Calhoun.
Keefe Mary (wid Cornelius), res 74 Montgomery.
Keefer, see also Keever, Keffer and Kiefer.
Keefer Christian, stone cutter Fort Wayne Steam Stone
Works, res 275 W Jefferson.
Keefer Emma, bds 275 W Jefferson.
Keefer Frederick, lab Horton Mnfg Co, res 143 Fairfield ave.
Keefer John, laborer Paul Koehler, res w s Lafayette 5 s of
Pontiac.
Keefer Susan, seamstress, bds 143 Fairfield ave.
Keegan Abbie C, bds 147 W Washington.
Keegan Edward A, messenger Penn Co, bds 147 W Wash-
ington.
Keegan Hugh G, clk Coombs & Co, bds 147 W Washington.
Keegan Patrick H, engineer, res 147 W Washington.
Keehner Katie, cook, 270½ Calhoun.
Keel, see also Keil, Kiel and Kyle.
Keel Mrs Aurora C, milliner, 22 and 24 W Berry, res same.
Keel George C, student W W Shryock, bds 24 W Berry.
Keel Miss Minnie, bds 24 W Berry.
Keeler, see also Kahler, Kaler, Kayler, Kehler, Keller, Koeh-
ler and Kohler.
Keeler Joseph W, conductor Penn Co, bds Hinton's Rest.
Keeley, see also Keiley and Kieley.
Keeley Wm, boilermaker Penn Co, res 75 Baker.
Keenhert August, market stall 21, res e s Plank rd n of city
limits.
Keep Louis, machine hand American Wheel Co, res 176
Maumee rd.
Kees, see also Keys and Kies.
Kees Christian, clerk, bds 35 Wilt.

Kees Frank, wiper Ft W, C & L R R, res 35 Wilt.
Kees John, helper, bds 35 Wilt.
Keever, *see also Keefer, Keffer and Kiefer.*
Keever Samuel, laborer, res n s Wagner 1 w of St Joseph
    river.
Keffer, *see also Keefer, Keever and Kiefer.*
Keffer Isaac P, machine hand American Wheel Co, bds 69
    McCulloch.
Keffer Nicholas, pedler, res 39 Duck.
Keffer Nicholas F, laborer, res 27 Euclid ave.
Kegelman Julius, mattressmaker Paul E Wolf, res n s E
    Wayne 3 w of Walton ave.
Kegelman Kate, bds 539 E Wayne.
Kegg Emanuel, carpenter, res 116 Butler.
Kegg Judson D, machine hand American Wheel Co, bds 116
    Butler.
Kegg Wm A, carpenter, res 108 Butler.
Kehler, *see also Kahler, Kaler, Kayler, Keeler, Keller, Koeh-
    ler and Kohler.*
Kehler Daniel B, treas Fort Wayne Furniture Co, bds cor
    Spy Run and Prospect aves.
Kehler Frank C, machine hand Fort Wayne Furniture Co,
    res cor Spy Run and Prospect aves.
Kehler George A, laborer Fort Wayne Furniture Co, res
    385 E Wayne.
Kehler Joseph W, machine hand Fort Wayne Furniture
    Co, res n s Prospect ave 7 e of Spy Run ave.
Keifer H, car builder Penn Co, res Piqua.
Keiffer Joseph, laborer, bds 160 Greely.
Keihl Adam jr, coremaker, res 111 E Creighton ave.
Keihl Anna (wid Adam), bds 111 E Creighton ave.
Keil, *see also Keel, Kiel and Kyle.*
Keil Miss Emma J, bds 145 W Superior.
Keil Frederick W (Keil & Keil), res 145 W Superior.
Keil George, hostler, bds 251 Calhoun.
Keil Henry, coachman, 82 W Berry.
Keil Jacob H (Keil & Keil), res 143 W Superior.
Keil Louis D (Keil & Keil), res 145 W Superior.
Keil Luther H, clerk Hoffman Bros, bds 143 W Superior.
Keil Miss Mary A, bds 145 W Superior.
Keil Miss Sophia S, bds 145 W Superior.
Keil & Keil (Jacob H, Louis D and Frederick W Keil),
    Wall Paper, 116 Calhoun.
Keintz Celia, clerk F J E De La Grange, bds 293 Hanna.
Keintz John, engineer, res 293 Hanna.
Keinz Leona, bds 307 Lafayette.

Keinz Philip, saloon, 307 Lafayette, res same.
Keiser, *see also Kaiser, Kayser, Keyser, Kiser and Kyser.*
Keiser Charles, plasterer, bds 492 W Main.
Keiser Isaac G, plasterer, res 492 W Main.
Kelker Anthony, engineer, res 174 Griffith.
Kelker Harry O, engineer, res 100 Chicago.
Kelker John, laborer, res 71 Holman.
Kelker Orlo L, barkeeper L A Centlivre, res 16 Randolph.
Kelker Mattie, bds 16 W Lewis.
Kelker Samuel S, engineer, res 16 W Lewis.
Kelker Wm, res 120 Clinton.
Kelker Wm C, engineer, res 89 Baker.
Kelleher Joseph F, machinist Kerr-Murray Mnfg Co, bds 6
   Kansas.
Keller, *see also Kahler, Kaler, Kaylor, Keeler, Kehler and
   Kohler.*
Keller Abraham, carpenter, res 124 Union.
Keller Albert, upholsterer Foster Furniture Co, res 224 W
   Main.
Keller Andrew J, Druggist, 97 Broadway, rms same.
Keller Caspar, laborer Bass Foundry and Machine Works,
   res 68 Force.
Keller Charles, res rear 224 W Main.
Keller Charles, baker C W Jacobs, bds 62 E Main.
Keller Charles E, laborer, bds 92 Wilt.
Keller Cornelius, teamster, bds 92 Wilt.
Keller Edwin W, bds 26 E Williams.
Keller Elmer E, printer Fort Wayne Newspaper Union, bds
   Clifton House.
Keller Frederick J, farmer, res 26 E Williams.
Keller Harry, printer, bds Clifton House.
Keller Henry (Keller & Braun), res 141 W Superior.
Keller Isaac E, teamster, res 342 W Jefferson.
Keller James, brakeman Penn Co, bds Henton's Restaurant.
Keller Josiah O, medicine mnfr, e s Barr 1 n of Wayne, res
   154 E Berry.
Keller Louisa A, seamstress D S Redelsheimer & Co, bds 57
   Grand.
Keller Mary, domestic McKinnie House.
Keller Mattie, seamstress D S Redelsheimer & Co, bds 57
   Grand.
Keller Maurice, res 29 Melita.
Keller Medicine Co, J O Keller pres and treas, e s Barr 1 n
   of Wayne.
Keller Paul, laborer, res 75 Wall.
Keller Samuel Y, mngr Mary McAfee, res 90 Wilt.

Keller Wm A, laborer, res 100 Wilt.

Keller Wm E, teamster, bds 124 Union.

Keller & Braun (Henry Keller, Charles G Braun), Proprs Fort Wayne Steam Stone Works, 86 to 98 Pearl. *(See adv, p 7).*

Kellermann Frederick, laborer Bass Foundry and Machine Works, res 57 Winter.

Kellermeyer Christian H, car inspector, res 16 Sturgis.

Kelley, *see also Kelly.*

Kelley Anna (wid Michael), res 28 Douglas ave.

Kelley Daniel, laborer, res 204 E Wayne.

Kelley Emma (wid Michael), res 8 Mechanic.

Kelley George W, clerk Salimonie Mining and Gas Co, bds 28 Douglas ave.

Kelley Harry, laborer, res 74 Nelson.

Kelley John M, switchman, res s e cor Horace and Holton av.

Kelley Mrs Sarah A, bds 116 W Main.

Kelley Wm, fresco painter, rms 158 Holman.

Kells Joseph M, Medical Examiner for the Relief Dept Penn Co, Office Penn Depot, res 397 Calhoun.

Kelly, *see also Kelley.*

Kelly Abbie, bds 20 Brandriff.

Kelly Andrew, laborer, bds 20 Brandriff.

Kelly Anna, dressmaker, bds 313 S Harrison.

Kelly Christopher, res 82 Madison.

Kelly Dennis, laborer, res 60 Leith.

Kelly Frank, finisher, res 69 McCulloch.

Kelly Frank, fireman, bds 17 Burgess.

Kelly James, driver Fort Wayne Street Railroad Co, res 115 John.

Kelly John, heater Penn Co, bds 313 S Harrison.

Kelly John jr, elevator man Fort Wayne Electric Co, bds 81 Hoagland ave.

Kelly John H, laborer, bds 9 Walnut.

Kelly John J, bookkeeper Fort Wayne Electric Co, bds 82 Madison.

Kelly John T, laborer, res 81 Hoagland ave.

Kelly Lewis, wheelmaker, bds 41 Wallace.

Kelly Lillie, operator Hoosier Mnfg Co, bds 41 Wallace.

Kelly Maggie, operator Hoosier Mnfg Co, bds 313 S Harrison.

Kelly Mary, tailoress Simon Barnett, bds 313 S Harrison.

Kelly Mary A, converter worker Fort Wayne Electric Co, bds 81 Hoagland ave.

Kelly Patrick, clerk Penn Co, bds 9 Walnut.

Kelly Patrick jr, laborer Penn Co, res 9 Walnut.

Kelly Patrick J, helper Penn Co, bds 81 Hoagland ave.
Kelly Richard, brakeman, bds 20 Brandriff.
Kelly Robert E, engineer, bds 108 W 3d.
Kelly Thomas F, res 108 W 3d.
Kelly Timothy, laborer, res 20 Brandriff.
Kelly Timothy jr, laborer Penn Co, bds 20 Brandriff.
Kelly Wm F, brakeman, res 98 Ewing.
Kelsey Alfred N, trav agt, res n w cor Putnam and Sherman.
Kelsey Bertha, clk Alexander Goodman, bds 141 Cass.
Kelsey Bros (Elias M and Elva C), meat market, 17 Grand.
Kelsey Charles, carpenter, bds 122 S Wayne ave.
Kelsey Charles, laborer J Kelsey, bds 40 Pearl.
Kelsey Elias M (Kelsey Bros), res 122 S Wayne ave.
Kelsey Elva C (Kelsey Bros), res 122 S Wayne ave.
Kelsey Henry, butcher, res rear 409 W Main.
Kelsey Jesse M, laborer Rousseau & Pfeiffer, rms 37½ W Berry.
Kelsey Joseph, feed yard, 40 Pearl, res same.
Kelsey Phœbe (wid James T), res 22 Harrison.
Kelsey Sarah (wid James), bds 122 S Wayne ave.
Kelsey Walter D, driver Clutter & Purcell, bds 22 Harrison.
Kelsey Wm A, barber L B Pegg, res 40 Pearl.
Kelsey Wm H, butcher, res rear 417 W Main.
Keltch Adam, boilermkr Kerr-Murray Mnfg Co, res 78 Wilt.
Keltsch Nicholas, cabinetmaker The Peters Box and Lumber Co, res 120 High.
Kemmel, see Kimmel.
Kemmer Louis, laborer Bass Foundry and Machine Works, res 181 Madison.
Kemp, see also Kamp and Komp.
Kemp Charles M, clk G DeWald & Co, bds 169 E Wayne.
Kemp Edgar, trav agt, res 169 E Wayne.
Kemp Herbert L, clerk Mossman, Yarnell & Co, bds 169 E Wayne.
Kemp John W, machine hand American Wheel Co, res 223 Madison.
Kemp Jonathan, laborer, bds 162 Hoffman.
Kemp Martin, laborer Penn Co, res 214 Madison.
Kemp Whitley, carpenter, res 162 Hoffman.
Kemp Wm F, finisher, res 223 Madison.
Kempf Anna, operator Hoosier Mnfg Co, bds 17 High.
Kempf Charles, laborer American Wheel Co, bds 17 High.
Kempf Etta, operator Hoosier Mnfg Co, bds 17 High.
Kempf Wm, laborer, res 17 High.
Kenaugh Wm, machine hand, bds 13 Force.
Kenawell Ella S, dressmaker, bds 108 W DeWald.

Kendall Wallace E, armature winder Fort Wayne Electric Co, res 114 Jackson.

Kendrick Frank B, Architect, Rooms 23, 24, 25, 26 Schmitz Block, res 42 W Washington. (*See back cover.*)

Kendrick Harriet, stenographer J F Rodabaugh, bds 147 Griffith.

Kendrick Louisa, bds 147 Griffith.

Kendrick Wm G, heating, res 147 Griffith.

Kendrick Wm H, supt F B Kendrick, res 68 W Creighton.

Kenlin Henry, barber, res 14 Wilt.

Kennedy John, engineer, res 80 Boone.

Kennedy Kate, domestic Hanna Homestead.

Kennedy Wm (col'd), waiter, rms 227 W Washington.

Kennelly Jeremiah, laborer, bds 56 Baker.

Kennelly John, policeman, res 56 Baker.

Kennelly Michael E, conductor, res 145 Walton ave.

Kennerk Celia, operator S M Foster, bds 26 Murray.

Kennerk John, produce buyer, res 26 Murray.

Kensill Catherine, bds 173 Holman.

Kensill Emma, works Fort Wayne Electric Co, bds 173 Holman.

Kensill George, fireman, res 147 Fairfield ave.

Kensill George W, engineer Penn Co, res 148 Montgomery.

Kensill John C, boilermaker Penn Co, res 173 Holman.

Kensill John C, engineer, res 213 Hanna.

Kensill Kate D, dressmaker L A Worch, bds 148 Montgomery.

Kepler, *see also Kapler.*

Kepler John H, machine hand Olds' Wagon Works, bds 26 Gay.

Kepler Louisa (wid John G), res 26 Gay.

Keplinger Frank E D, bookkeeper First National Bank, bds 15 Douglas ave.

Keplinger Harry A, teller Hamilton National Bank, res 21 W Creighton ave.

Keplinger Maud, milliner V E Wolf, bds 118 Force.

Kepner Peter, cigarmaker J Lohman Co, bds cor Calhoun and Murray.

Kerbach Frederick C, laborer, res 159 Gay.

Kerbach Wm, carpenter, bds 159 Gay.

Kern, *see also Karn and Kirn.*

Kern Jacob J, County Clerk, res 107 W Washington.

Kern Samuel E, fireman Nickel Plate, bds 12 St Mary's ave.

Kern William, brakeman, bds Monroe House.

Kerns Franklin, laborer, bds 88 Fairfield ave.

Kerp Joseph W, painter Olds' Wagon Works, res 102 Gay.

Kerr David, bds 40 E Williams.

Kerr Florence, dressmaker, bds 362 W Main.

Kerr Lacey, hostler, bds 309 W Washington.

Kerr-Murray Manufacturing Co, Alfred D Cressler Pres and Gen Mngr, G A Schust Sec, Gustav L Hackius Treas, Mnfrs of Gas Works Machinery, Gas Holders and Apparatus of All Descriptions, cor Calhoun and Murray.

Kerr Wm J, Pension, Bounty and War Claim Attorney, 13 E Main, res 186 Jackson.

Kerr Wm W, Notary Public and Conveyancer, 13 E Main, bds 186 Jackson.

Kerr W Clarence, tel operator N Y, C & St L R R, bds 353 E Wayne.

Kershaw Thomas M, pianist World's Museum, bds 55 E Wayne.

Kesler Dr Abraham J, coroner, 286 Calhoun, res s e cor Wallace and Monroe.

Kesman Bernard, turner Fort Wayne Organ Co, bds 24 Murray.

Kess John, helper Wabash R R, bds 35 Wilt.

Kessens Christian, laborer, bds 363 E Washington.

Kessens Jacob, rimmer N G Olds & Son, res 521 E Lewis.

Kessens John N, laborer Penn Co, bds 363 E Washington.

Kessens Lena, bds 363 E Washington.

Kessens Mary, domestic C Entemann, bds 363 E Washington.

Kessens Wm, laborer, res 363 E Washington.

Kessler Annie (wid Andrew), bds 10 Force.

Kessler Henry S, molder, res 359 E Lewis.

Kestel Louis, helper Penn Co, res 163 Montgomery.

Kester, *see also Koester.*

Kester Morris R, clerk J P Gray, res 84 W DeWald.

Ketcher Barbara, seamstress D S Redelsheimer & Co, bds 23 Charles.

Ketcher John, laborer, res 23 Charles.

Ketcher Paul, machinist Kerr-Murray Mnfg Co, bds 104 W Washington.

Ketchum Clement V, caller Penn Co, res 37 Grand.

Kethner Getto, painter Wayne Paint and Painting Co, res 198 Lafayette.

Ketker Elizabeth (wid Frederick), res 18 Pritchard.

Ketker Frederick W, brass molder Fort Wayne Electric Co, res 168 Taylor.

Ketker Frederica, bds 18 Pritchard.

Ketker Sophie, bds 18 Pritchard.

Kettern Peter, section hand Penn Co, res s e cor Winter and Edgerton.

Kettler Conrad F, supt letter carriers Postoffice, res 205 E Jefferson.

Kettler Eliza (wid Conrad), bds 205 E Jefferson.

Kettler Miss Mary E, bds 205 E Washington.

Kettler Wm J, treas D N Foster Furniture Co, res 46 Erie.

Key, *see also Kay.*

Key Clayton H, wheelmaker American Wheel Co, res 37 Holman.

Key John (col'd), porter Hotel Randall.

Keyes Dora, works J O Keller, bds 143 Griffith.

Keys, *see also Kees and Kies.*

Keys Morris, lab South Wayne Brick Co, bds 26 Thompson.

Keyser, *see also Kaiser, Kayser, Keiser, Kiser and Kyser.*

Keyser August, machinist, bds 179 W Washington.

Keyser Charles H, polisher Winch & Son, res 95 Glasgow.

Keyser Jacob M, propr Fort Wayne Soap Works, res 95 Glasgow ave.

Keyser Wm A, painter, bds 95 Glasgow.

Keystone Block, s w cor Calhoun and Columbia.

Kibiger Edward, laborer, bds 105 Barr.

Kibiger George, driver H J Ash, res e s Barr bet Wayne and Washington.

Kibiger Henry, coil winder Fort Wayne Electric Co, bds 105 Barr.

Kibiger John, laborer, bds 105 Barr.

Kibiger Louisa (wid George), res 105 Barr.

Kibiger Wm, clerk E Shuman & Sons, bds 105 Barr.

Kickley, *see also Kikly.*

Kickley Charles M, machinist, res 133 Fairfield ave.

Kickley Ida, bds 90 Chicago.

Kickley Isadore, conductor Penn Co, res 53 De Wald.

Kickley Joseph, molder Wabash R R, res 90 Chicago.

Kickory Emil, section hand, res n s New Haven ave 4 e of Lumbard.

Kickory Paul, laborer Winch & Son, bds n s New Haven av 4 e of Lumbard.

Kidd John, stonecutter Wm & J J Geake, res 3 Liberty.

Kidd Julia (wid Robert G), bds 205 W Jefferson.

Kidd Kate, dressmaker, bds 205 W Jefferson.

Kief, *see Keefe.*

Kiefer, *see also Keefer and Keffer.*

Kiefer Adolph, driver, res 69 Elizabeth.

Kiefer Christian, carpenter, bds 16 Wilt.

Kiefer Christian F, carpenter, bds 490 Fairfield ave.

Kiefer Edward, driver, bds 63 Elizabeth.

Kiefer George A, driver, res cor Spy Run and Riverside ave.

Stahn & Heinrich, Booksellers and Stationers,
Schmitz Block News Stand, 116 Calhoun Street.

FORT WAYNE DIRECTORY. 299

Kiefer Henry, clerk Mossman, Yarnell & Co, res s s Elizabeth 9 w of Spy Run ave.

Kiefer Julius G, laborer C L Centlivre, res s s Elizabeth 9 w of Spy Run ave.

Kiefer Oscar P, laborer C L Centlivre, bds Rufus Cypher.

Kiefer Philip F, saloon, 16 Wilt, res same.

Kiefhaber Frederick J, coil winder Fort Wayne Electric Co, res 22 Pritchard.

Kiel, *see also Keel, Keil and Kyle.*

Kiel Henry F, policeman, res 264 Webster.

Kiel Wm, helper Kerr-Murray Mnfg Co, res 397 Hanna.

Kiel Wm C, clerk, bds 264 Webster.

Kiely, *see Keeley and Kiley.*

Kienzle, *see also Kuentzel.*

Kienzle Christian, teamster, res 105 Hoffman.

Kiep John, helper Henry DeWald, bds 137 E Washington.

Kiep Theodore, machine hand American Wheel Co, bds 254 E Jefferson.

Kiep Wm, soapmaker Summit City Soap Works, res 137 E Washington.

Kiernan Joseph, clk Dozois, Beadell & Co, bds 96 E Wayne.

Kiersey John C, carpenter, bds 24 Winch.

Kierspe Charles W, mach Wabash R R, res 39 Locust.

Kierspe Frederick, carver Fort Wayne Organ Co, res 346 Broadway.

Kierspe George J, bookkeeper Root & Co, bds 39 Locust.

Kies, *see Kees and Keys.*

Kiesling Ferdinand W, baker, 142 Broadway, res 255 same.

Kiess John F, storekeeper Fort Wayne Electric Co, res 17 Pritchard.

Kiess Joseph A, clerk Fort Wayne Electric Co, bds 165 Holman.

Kiest Laura, domestic 24 Brandriff.

Kietzman Albert, teamster, res s s Illinois road opp Lindenwood cemetery.

Kiger Perry A, relief agent N Y, C & St L R R, res 114 W Washington.

Kikley, *see also Kickley.*

Kikley J C Francis, helper Penn Co, res 237 Lafayette.

Kiley Dennis T, laborer, bds 33 Colerick.

Kiley John J, fireman, bds 33 Colerick.

Kiley Mary (wid Thomas), electrician Fort Wayne Electric Co, bds 33 Colerick.

Kilgore Gershom D, conductor, res 142 Buchanan.

Kilgore Wm R, fireman, res 11 Butler.

Killen George G, helper Penn Co, bds 365 E Creighton ave.

Killen Wm, blacksmith Penn Co, res 331 E Creighton ave.
Killer Frank, cabinetmkr Fort Wayne Organ Co, res 50 Leith.
Killer Gottlieb, cabinetmaker, res 50 Leith.
Killer Henry E, electrician Penn Co, res 164 Harrison.
Kilpatrick Grace, dressmkr I J Trisch, bds Oscar B Kilpatrick.
Kilpatrick Harry E, fireman, res 142 N Cass.
Kilpatrick James S, clerk Wabash R R, res 60 Prince.
Kilpatrick Oscar D, engineer, res 136 N Cass.
Kimball Fred N (Kimball & Webb), res 61 Douglas ave.
Kimball Laura E, cashier Pixley & Co, res 29 West.
Kimball Mary E, res 29 Rockhill.
Kimball & Webb (Fred N Kimball, Reuben Webb), cigars, 81 Calhoun.
Kime Frank C, brakeman G R & I R R, res 102 South Wayne.
Kime Rachel A (wid Isaac M), bds 20 Bell ave.
Kime Wesley, waiter C Entemann, bds W Main.
Kime Wm T (Kime & Brown), res 20 Bell ave.
Kime & Brown (Wm T Kime, Frank L Brown), barbers, 352 Broadway.
Kimmel, *see also Kemmel.*
Kimmel Alice, waiter Rich's Hotel.
Kimmel Christian, car builder Penn Co, res 69 Oliver.
Kimmel Edward, car builder Penn Co, res 69 Oliver.
Kimmel Frank, brakeman, res 160 Smith.
Kimmel Jacob C, laborer Fort Wayne Organ Co, res 63 Home ave.
Kimmel John, farmer, res 266 Beaver ave.
Kimmel Kinzie, conductor Penn Co, res 128 Chicago.
Kimmel Milton G, engineer Fort Wayne Organ Co, res 172 Indiana ave.
Kimmel Nancy, dressmaker L A Worch, bds John Kimmel.
Kinder Michael, car builder Penn Co, res 169 Warsaw.
Kinder Paul P, carpenter, res 39 E 4th.
Kindt Wm P, laborer, res 172 W Jefferson.
Kinerk Frisbie S, carpenter, bds 93 Shawnee ave.
King Arthur, bds 65 Harrison.
King Carrie M, bds 62 Clinton.
King Eliza M (wid George E), res 125 Montgomery.
King Frances (wid Diamond), bds 203 W Berry.
King Frank D, rod man Penn Co, bds 67 S Harrison.
King Frank W, cutter S M Foster, res 17 N Cass.
King Miss Grace I, stenographer Central Mutual Fire Insurance Co, bds 334 E Washington.
King Henry J, clk Scheffer & Geiger, bds 271 E Washington.
King Ida C, bds 125 Montgomery.

King John E, molder Bass Foundry and Machine Works, bds 271 E Washington.

King John T, harnessmaker A L Johns & Co, res 22 Brackenridge.

King Kate, bds 11 Monroe.

King Sarah J, bds 62 Clinton.

King Victor, car inspector Ft W, C & L R R, res 271 E Washington.

King Wm F, cutter, res 17 N Cass.

Kingel Philip, blacksmith, bds 56 Smith.

Kinkelberg Arthur, blacksmith Olds' Wagon Works, res 68 Force.

Kinkiad Joseph, flue worker Penn Co, bds 248 Calhoun.

Kinley Christian, laborer, bds Hyer House.

Kinley Frederick J, machine hand American Wheel Company, bds 193 Barr.

Kinley Paul, laborer, bds 185 Lafayette.

Kinnaird Alexander, machinist Penn Co, res 25 W Williams.

Kinnaird Miss Emma F, teacher Hoagland School, bds 25 W Williams.

Kinnaird Louis S, draughtsman Penn Co, bds 25 W Williams.

Kinnaird Robert, mach Wabash R R, res 25 W Williams.

Kinnan Harry, stage mngr World's Museum, bds 57 Barr.

Kinnan John W, molder, bds 392 Calhoun.

Kinnan Martha (wid John), res 392 Calhoun.

Kinnard Sarah (wid James), bds 232 E Jefferson.

Kinnie James J, laborer, bds 123 W DeWald.

Kinnie Michael, laborer Penn Co, res 123 W DeWald.

Kinsman James A, bartender F C Boltz, bds 114 Calhoun.

Kintz, *see also Koontz and Kuntz.*

Kintz Alexander, bds 52 E 3d.

Kintz Alice, operator S M Foster, bds 52 E 3d.

Kintz Ambrose W, mason, res 149 Pfeiffer ave.

Kintz Charles, driver C L Centlivre, res w s Leo rd 4 n of Canal Feeder.

Kintz Henry, engineer C L Centlivre, res e s Canal Feeder 1 n of Edna.

Kintz Jacob J, conductor, res 111 N Cass.

Kintz John, car builder Penn Co, res 11 Lillie.

Kintz John, driver C L Centlivre, res w s Spy Run ave 3 n of Edna.

Kintz Miss Laura, bds 11 Lillie.

Kintz Phœbe (wid Alexander), bds 45 E 4th.

Kirbach Emil R, wheelmaker American Wheel Co, res n s Eckart 2 e of Hanna.

Kirbach Ernst, laborer American Wheel Co, res e s John 2 s of E Creighton ave.

Kirbach Frank, helper S F Bowser & Co, bds Ernst Kirbach.

Kirbach Robert, painter, res 333 Hanna.

Kirby Michael, engineer, res 7 Colerick.

Kirchheimer Joseph, bookkeeper Charles Falk & Co, bds 144 W Berry.

Kirchifer Harmon, painter Penn Co, res 114 Force.

Kirchner Carl, farmer, res 44 Oak.

Kirchner Elenora, mach hand, bds Ernest Kirchner.

Kirchner Ernst, laborer, res n s Eliza bet McCulloch and Ohio.

Kirchner Ferdinand, watchman Winch & Son, res 40 Winch.

Kirchner Gottlieb W, laborer Hoffman Bros, res 16 Nirdlinger ave.

Kirchner Mary, mach hand, bds Ernest Kirchner.

Kirkbride James, painter, rms 191 Calhoun.

Kirkbride John E, painter, rms 191 Calhoun.

Kirkendall Edwin, fireman Hook and Ladder Co No 1, rms engine house No 1.

Kirkendall Jacob G, Wine and Beer Saloon; also Billiard and Pool Room, 26 E Columbia, res same.

Kirkendall John, porter, 87 W Wayne.

Kirkham Mary (wid John), bds 253 W Creighton ave.

Kirkland Emily (wid John), bds 62 Greene.

Kirkley James B, roof painter, bds 40 Pearl.

Kirkpatrick Charles A L, Ry P O clerk, bds 106 N Cass.

Kirn, *see also Karn and Kern.*

Kirn John M, cabinetmaker Fort Wayne Electric Co, res 158 Fairfield ave.

Kirn John M, engineer Bass Foundry and Machine Works, res 56 W Williams.

Kiser, *see also Kaiser, Kayser, Keiser, Keyser and Kyser.*

Kiser Angie L (wid Daniel), res 96 Ewing.

Kiser Byron A, bds 70 W Wayne.

Kiser Charles S, patternmaker Fort Wayne Electric Co, bds 70 W Wayne.

Kiser Christ, painter Penn Co, bds 148 Broadway.

Kiser Peter, res 70 W Wayne.

Kispe Frederick, carpenter, res 346 Broadway.

Kist Frank, laborer American Wheel Co, res 147 E DeWald.

Kitselman John, res 9 Smith.

Kitselman Leander, engineer, bds 9 Smith.

Kitselman Wm B, conductor, res 2 Center.

Klaas John A, carpet weaver, res 16 University.

Klachn W Robert (Schueman & Klachn), res 225 W Jefferson.

Builders' Hardware, PFEIFFER & SCHLATTER, 38 and 40 EAST COLUMBIA ST.

FORT WAYNE DIRECTORY. 303

Klaffei Charles, bartender G J Ortlieb, res 148 Ewing.
Klages Albert, bds 16 Clay.
Klanar George, saloon, res 109 Wells.
Klanke, *see also Klenke.*
Klanke Conrad, laborer C Tresselt & Sons, res 58 W Lewis.
Klar Adam W, carpenter, bds 230 Harmer.
Klebe Bertha E, seamstress, bds 146 Franklin ave.
Klebe Elizabeth M, seamstress, bds 146 Franklin ave.
Klebe Henry jr, clk A L Johns & Co, bds 146 Franklin ave.
Klebe Maggie A, wks Troy Steam Laundry, bds 146 Franklin ave.
Kleber Sebastian, engineer, res 64 Boone.
Klee, *see also Kley and Clay.*
Klee Miss Frenie, seamstress, bds 378 E Washington.
Klee John, carp Ft W, C & L R R, res 378 E Washington.
Klee John J, harnessmaker A L Johns & Co, bds 378 E Washington.
Kleeberg Paul, brickmaker, res 300 E Wayne.
Kleemeier Dietrich, tailor George Motz, res 346 Broadway.
Klein, *see also Kline and Cline.*
Klein Christian, res 562 Lafayette.
Klein Conrad, sawyer Wm Bruns, bds 131 Taber.
Klein Frederick A, principal Zion German Lutheran School, res 412 Hanna.
Klein Jacob, woodworker City Carriage Works, bds 336 E Wayne.
Klein Mary, domestic 307 Lafayette.
Klein Peter, shoemaker J F Noll, bds 273 W Jefferson.
Kleindinst Edwin S, fireman, bds 286 Calhoun.
Kleindinst Lydia (wid Christian C), res 286 Calhoun.
Kleindinst Minnie I, dressmaker, bds 286 Calhoun.
Kleinegees Ada, clk Frank & Co, bds 155 Harrison.
Kleinegees Henrietta (wid Adolphus), res 155 Harrison.
Kleinmiller Henry, res 55 Madison.
Klenrichert Lizzie, bds 9 Summit.
Kleinschmidt Wm, laborer The Peters Box and Lumber Co, res 8 Clark.
Kleinsorge Herman, res 164 High.
Kleinsorge John, painter, res 16 Barthold.
Kleinsorge Louise, seamstress D S Redelsheimer & Co, bds 164 High.
Kleinsorge Minnie, tailoress Charles Kruse, bds 164 High.
Kleinsorge Wm, clk C J Pierre, bds 164 High.
Klenke, *see also Klanke.*
Klenke August H, machine hand American Wheel Co, bds 241 Barr.

Klenke Frederick, car builder Penn Co, res 241 Barr.
Klenke Henry, car builder Penn Co, res 241 Barr.
Klepper Charles, cab builder Penn Co, res 92 Oliver.
Klepper Henry, carpenter, bds 92 Oliver.
Klepper Wm, laborer Bass Foundry and Machine Works. bds 93 John.
Klepson August, brickmaker, bds 14 Force.
Klerner George, saloon, 156 E Washington, res 109 Wells.
Klett Edward (Jacob Klett & Son), bds 328 S Broadway.
Klett Jacob & Son (Jacob and Edward), lumber, 54 Pearl.
Klett John A, bookkeeper, bds 328 Broadway.
Klett Wm B, bkkpr J Klett & Son, bds 328 Broadway.
Kley, *see also Klee and Clay.*
Kley Carrie, clk L Wolf & Co, bds 336 W Main.
Kley Frederick, cooper, res 336 W Main.
Kley Frederick jr, cooper C H Stockman, res 97 Cass.
Kley Lizzie, clk L Wolf & Co, bds 336 W Main.
Klienline Wm, blacksmith Fleming Mnfg Co, res 14 Cass.
Kline, *see also Klein and Cline.*
Kline Anna M, bds 118 E Berry.
Kline Bernard, market stall 28 and 30, res n s Miller nr city limits.
Kline Charles W, blacksmith Olds' Wagon Works, res 91 E Washington.
Kline C W, Propr Crystal Billiard Hall and Sample Room, 242 Calhoun, res same. (*See adv in classified Billiard Halls.*)
Kline Christina, cook Wm C Seidel & Bro, rms 52½ Calhoun.
Kline Edward, plumber, bds 11 Pritchard.
Kline Frederick, clerk, res 11 Pritchard.
Kline Henry, clerk Jacob Kline, bds 118 E Berry.
Kline Henry E, helper Ft Wayne Electric Co, bds 11 Lavina.
Kline Jacob, grocer, 30 E Columbia, res 118 E Berry.
Kline Jacob, painter City Carriage Works, bds 336 E Wayne.
Kline John J, brakeman, bds 194 E Lewis.
Kline Maria M (wid John), res 91 E Washington.
Kline Matilda, bds 118 E Berry.
Kline Milton F, car builder Penn Co, res 2 Fairfield ave.
Kline Orin, blacksmith, bds 91 E Washington.
Kline Peter, clerk Jacob Certia, res 32 E 5th.
Kline Wm, clerk Jacob Kline, bds 118 E Berry.
Kline Wm C, laborer Penn Co, res 136 Maumee road.
Klinedinst Wm, laborer Bass Foundry and Machine Works, bds 37 Buchanan.
Kling Peter, laborer Bass Foundry and Machine Works, res 213 John.

Klingel Eva B (wid John M), res 76 Laselle.
Klingel John M, coremaker Fort Wayne Iron Works, res 76 Laselle.
Klingenberger Chester, carpenter, bds 285 Hanna.
Klingenberger John, car builder Penn Co, res 285 Hanna.
Klingenberger John H, car builder Penn Co, bds 285 Hanna.
Klingenberger Joseph M, Saloon and Billiard Hall, First-class Beer of Grasser & Brand Brewing Co of Toledo, O, always on tap, 9 E Main, res 95 Clay.
Klingenberger Mandes J, driver, res 95 Clay.
Klingenberger Xavier, painter Olds' Wagon Works, bds 285 Hanna.
Klinger James E, second-hand gds, 67 E Columbia, res same.
Klinger John, laborer, res 329 E Lewis.
Klinger Joseph, laborer, res 217 Broadway.
Klinger Wm E, apprentice George Jaap, bds 67 E Columbia.
Klingerbaugh Caroline M, domestic Pearse Hotel.
Klingerman Annie, bds 30 Euclid ave.
Klingerman David, laborer, bds 30 Euclid ave.
Klingerman Delbert, brickmaker, bds 30 Euclid ave.
Klingerman Dora, bds 30 Euclid ave.
Klingerman Joseph, laborer, res 30 Euclid ave.
Klingerman Stella, bds 30 Euclid ave.
Klingman George W, driver Hose Co No 2, rms Engine House No 2.
Klingmann Albert M, helper American Wheel Co, bds 373 Lafayette.
Klingmann John, cattle buyer, res 373 Lafayette.
Klingmann John E, machine hand, bds 373 Lafayette.
Klingmann Minette K, clerk C H Waltemath & Sons, bds 373 Lafayette.
Klingmann Wm, molder Bass Foundry and Machine Works, bds 373 Lafayette.
Klinkel Michael, conductor, res 36 Lillie.
Klinkel Wm, clk E Vordermark & Sons, bds 25 W Washington.
Klinkenberg Otto (Klinkenberg & Detzer), res 62 Clinton.
Klinkenberg & Detzer (Otto Klinkenberg, August J Detzer), Druggists and Photographic Supplies, 80 Calhoun.
Klippert George, grocer, 393 Lafayette, res same.
Klochberg Paul, laborer Wm Miller, res 300 E Wayne.
Kloepper Henry, machine hand Horton Mnfg Co, res 19 Wilt.
Kloepper Henry C, boilermkr Ft Wayne Iron Works, bds 19 Wilt.
Kloger Joseph, machinist Ft Wayne Electric Co, res 73 Oakley.
Klomp Wm, mach hd Ft Wayne Organ Co, res 606 S Calhoun.

Klotz Daniel, dry goods 372 Calhoun, res 546 same.
Klotz Daniel, painter L O Hull, bds Herman Klotz.
Klotz Elizabeth, converter worker Fort Wayne Electric Co,
　　bds Herman Klotz.
Klotz Frank G, clk Daniel Klotz, bds 546 Calhoun.
Klotz Herman, laborer Penn Co, res w s Calhoun 1 s of Cour.
Klotz Joseph, painter, bds Herman Klotz.
Klug Charles, carpenter, res 112 Erie.
Klug Gregor, shoemaker, 194 Hanna, res 190 same.
Klug G Nicholas, trav agt, bds 190 Hanna.
Klug Henry J, shoemaker, bds 190 Hanna.
Klug Joseph, machine hand American Wheel Co, bds 293 E
　　Wayne.
Klug Martin, carpenter Nickel Plate R R, res 293 E Wayne.
Kluppel Gerhard, carpenter, bds 77 Smith.
Kluppel John, stone mason, res 77 Smith.
Kluppel Sophia, bds 77 Smith.
Klusmann Frederick, laborer, res 229 John.
Knaack Charles, finisher, bds 39 Elm.
Knaack Frederick, laborer, res 39 Elm.
Knaasa August, carpenter, res s s Packard ave 1 w of Fairfield.
Knase Charles, painter, res 31 Union.
Knause Miss Alice, teacher Taylor University, bds same.
Knave Isaac, carpenter, bds 231 Barr.
Knecht Frank J, florist, 301 E Wayne, bds 27 Erie.
Knecht John, saw filer American Wheel Co, bds 104 Barr.
Knedeler Frederick, market gardener, 815 Broadway, res same.
Kneese, *see also Ness, Neise and Nies.*
Kneese August, cabinetmaker Fort Wayne Organ Co, res w
　　s Fairfield ave.
Knepper J Daniel, laborer White's Wheel Works, res 74
　　Maumee road.
Knepper Margaret, market stall 73, res Illinois road, Aboit
　　township.
Knepper Wm J, laborer N Y,C & St L R R, res 71 St Mary's.
Knight Charles S, general agent Fort Wayne Electric Co, res
　　777 Spy Run ave.
Knight John H, fireman, rms 39 Baker.
Knight Joseph S, driver Fort Wayne City Railroad Co, res
　　s e cor Grant ave and Humphrey.
Knight Miss Maggie, res 12 E Columbia.
Knight Miss Matilda E, teacher Harmer School, bds 35 Eckart.
Knight Sarah J, res 199 W Washington.
Knight Sarah J (wid Noel), res 31 Randolph.
Knight Thomas H, foreman Ft W, C & L R R, res 45 E 4th.
Knight Willard C, clerk, bds Charles S Knight.

Stahn & Heinrich, Dealers in BOOKS and FINE STATIONERY,
Blank Books, Etc. 116 Calhoun Street.

FORT WAYNE DIRECTORY. 307

Knight Wm, foreman Penn Co, res 5 Eckart.
Kniseov Wm H, teamster, bds 12 Clark.
Knispel Emil, driver, bds 106 Chicago.
Knobel Gottlieb, shoemaker, 110 Wells, res 30 same.
Knoche August D, painter Olds' Wagon Works, bds 112 Thomas.
Knoche Frederick, carpenter, bds 112 Thomas.
Knoche Henry, laborer, bds 112 Thomas.
Knoche Johanna, bds 112 Thomas.
Knoche John, laborer Bass Foundry and Machine Works, res 112 Thomas.
Knoche Peter, laborer Bass Foundry and Machine Works, res 112 Thomas.
Knock Wm F, fireman, res 168 Taylor.
Knode Ernest H, fireman, bds 74 Douglas ave.
Knoder George W, painter Penn Co, res 29 Hugh.
Knoll Anna, boxmaker Davis & Bro, bds 15 Miner.
Knoll Minnie, domestic Aveline House.
Knoll Wm H, machinist, res 15 Miner.
Knothe Charles F, asst master mechanic Fort Wayne Electric Co, res 72 Dawson.
Knothe Julius A (Beaver, Miller & Co), bds Paul E Wolf.
Knox Thomas E, laborer Jenney Electric Light and Power Co, res s s Elizabeth 5 w of Spy Run ave.
Knox Wm R, traveling agent, res 19 W De Wald.
Knuth Henry, driver Fort Wayne Gas Light Co, res 69 Hoffman.
Koby Joseph, painter, res 66 Walton ave.
Koby Viola, bds 66 Walton ave.
Koch, see also Cook.
Koch Andrew, laborer Olds' Wagon Works, res 57 W Lewis.
Koch Augusta, tailoress F Kayser, bds 57 W Lewis.
Koch Benedict, laborer Kerr-Murray Mnfg Co, res 265 Hanna.
Koch Catherine (wid Adam), res 34 John.
Koch Charles, carpenter Bass Foundry and Machine Works, res 146 E Creighton ave.
Koch Charles K, cabinetmaker Fort Wayne Furniture Co, res 25 W Washington.
Koch Christian, machinist Fort Wayne Electric Co, res 157 College.
Koch Christopher, wheelmaker Olds' Wagon Works, res 72 Brackenridge.
Koch Elizabeth (wid Christian), res 45 W Jefferson.
Koch Elizabeth (wid John W), res 119 Lafayette.
Koch Frank, carpenter, bds 21 Euclid ave.
Koch Henry, cigarmaker, res 9 Duryea.

Koch Henry, laborer Penn Co, res 16 Hamilton.
Koch Henry, painter, bds rear 72 Brackenridge.
Koch John, helper Kerr-Murray Mnfg Co, res 97 Laselle.
Koch John B, res 124 E Washington.
Koch John D C, cigarmaker G F Yergens, bds 72 Brackenridge.
Koch Julius, machinist, res 16 Hamilton.
Koch Margaret (wid John), notions, 74 Barr, res same.
Koch Minnie, bds 57 W Lewis.
Koch Sophia (wid Anthony), res 58 W Lewis.
Koch Sophia, dressmaker J M Gould, bds 57 W Lewis.
Koch Wm, carpenter, bds 148 Taylor.
Koch Wm, clerk Louis Schirmeyer, bds 124 E Washington.
Koch Wm, saloon, 117 E Lewis, bds 58 W Lewis.
Kochel Frederick, instrument maker Fort Wayne Electric Co, bds 28 Nirdlinger ave.
Kochen Richard, engineer, res 76 Wells.
Kocher George, laborer, bds 21 Force.
Kocher John, carpenter, res 128 Greely.
Kocks, *see also Cox.*
Kocks Frank, carpenter Penn Co, res 28 3d.
Kocks Frank C, painter Penn Co, res n s St Joe road é of city limits.
Kocks Frank J, machine hand The Peters Box and Lumber Co, res 27 High.
Kocks Henry B, shoemaker Louis Fortriede, res 28 W 3d.
Kocks John B, sawyer Hoffman Bros, res 35 Marion.
Kocks Mary E, tailoress, bds 27 High.
Koeble Charles, helper J H Welch, bds 224 E Jefferson.
Koeble Emma, bds 224 E Jefferson.
Koeble Eva (wid John G), res 224 E Jefferson.
Koegel Emma, bds 54 Pritchard.
Koegel Mary, bds 54 Pritchard.
Koegel Mary (wid Christian), res 54 Pritchard.
Koehl, *see also Kuhl and Cole.*
Koehl Adam, coremkr Penn Co, res 111 E Creighton ave.
Koehl Jacob, stonecutter Wm & J J Geake, res 125 E De Wald.
Koehl John, machine hand American Wheel Co, bds 111 E Creighton ave.
Koehl Michael, stonecutter Fort Wayne Steam Stone Works, res 30 Buchanan.
Koehl Wendlin, molder Bass Foundry and Machine Works, res 336 Force.
Koehlein August, helper Penn Co, res 24 Hoffman.

Koehler Alfred J, laborer Paul Koehler, bds same.
Koehler Frederick, laborer Paul Koehler, bds same.
Koehler Henry, baker, res 50 John.
Koehler John A, brick mnfr, e s Lafayette n of Wiebke, res w s Lafayette 10 s of Pontiac.
Koehler John M, foreman J A Koehler, bds same.
Koehler Lewis, lab, res e s Piqua ave opp Rudisill ave.
Koehler Paul, brick mnfr, cor Rudisill ave and Webster, res same.
Koehlinger E, car builder Penn Co, res 322 Broadway.
Koehlinger Gustav A, clk Root & Co, res 65 Wall.
Koehlinger Peter, boarding house, 64 E Berry.
Koehn, *see also Kohn, Kuhn and Cohen.*
Koehn Regina, domestic 321 W Jefferson.
Koehn Wm, lab Olds' Wagon Works, res 11 Wiebke.
Koehn Wm, lab White's Wheel Wks, bds 101 Glasgow ave.
Koehn Wm C F, shoemkr C Schiefer & Son, res 217 E Jefferson.
Koehnlein Emma, seamstress, bds 12 Wilt.
Koehnlein Henry J, barber, res 12 Wilt.
Koehnlein Julia, bds 12 Wilt.
Koehnlein Mary, operator S M Foster, bds 12 Wilt.
Koehnlein Ricka, bds 12 Wilt.
Koehnlein Wm F, blksmith, res 14 Cass.
Koekly John, fireman, bds 33 St Mary's ave.
Koelmann Henry, lab American Wheel Co, bds 229 John.
Koenemann Edward F, boilermkr Kerr-Murray Mnfg Co, res 284 Webster.
Koenemann John, excavator, 32 Colerick, res same.
Koenemann Wm, carpenter, bds Washington House.
Koenemann Wm F, painter Olds' Wagon Works, bds 11 McLaughlin.
Koenig August, jeweler, 176 Calhoun, res same.
Koenig Charles, carpenter, bds 21 Summit.
Koenig Charles F, clerk F Koenig, res 335 E Washington.
Koenig Christian F, grocer, 89 Harmer, res 187 Madison.
Koenig Rev Edward, Pastor St Paul's Church, res 95 Griffith.
Koenig Frederick A, clk Isaac Lauferty, res 332 E Washington.
Koenig Frederick G, tailor, 98 W Main, res same.
Koenig Frederick H, tailor, 176 Greely, res same.
Koenig Henry, carpenter, res 48 Oak.
Koenig John N, cabinetmaker Fort Wayne Furniture Co, res 393 E Washington.
Koenig Theresa, housekeeper, res 95 Griffith.
Koenig Wm, carpenter, bds 21 Summit.

Koenig Wm, bds 335 E Washington.
Koenig Wm jr, boilermaker Fort Wayne Iron Works, res 332 E Jefferson.
Koenlein Andrew, laborer, bds 24 Hoffman.
Koepf Amelia, domestic 303 E Washington.
Koepf Jacob, boilermaker Fort Wayne Iron Works, bds 309 W Washington.
Koerber Frederick, watchmaker H C Graffe, res 156 Wells.
Koerss Christian, teamster Herman Berghoff Brewing. Co, res Erie nr Hanover.
Koester, *see also Kester.*
Koester J Bernard, clerk S Freiburger & Bro, res 160 Calhoun.
Koester Martin, draughtsman, res 160 Calhoun.
Koester Minnie, domestic Montgomery Hamilton.
Kofmehl Jacob, laborer, res 525 Hanna.
Kohl Jacob, stonecutter, res 125 E De Wald.
Kohlbach John, pork packer, res 30 Richardson.
Kohlbach Wm, painter Wayne Paint and Painting Co, bds 30 Richardson.
Kohlbacher, *see also Kahlbacher and Kalbacher.*
Kohlbacher Adam, laborer Penn Co, res 65 1st.
Kohlbacher John H, clerk Philip Graf, bds 65 Force.
Kohler, *see also Kahler, Kaler, Kaylor, Keeler, Kehler, Keller and Koehler.*
Kohler Andrew J, fireman, bds 461 Calhoun.
Kohler Miss Catherine A, bookkeeper, bds 461 Calhoun.
Kohler Catherine A (wid Daniel), res 461 Calhoun.
Kohler Emma E, chambermaid Pearse Hotel.
Kohler Miss Jennie A, clerk, bds 461 Calhoun.
Kohler Uriah H, fireman, bds 461 Calhoun.
Kohlhebb Moritz, section hand Penn Co.
Kohlman Henry, laborer, bds 92 Montgomery.
Kohlman John, res 92 Montgomery.
Kohlmann Annie, seamstress, bds 11 Marion.
Kohlmann Edward, driver Michael Baltes, bds 11 Marion.
Kohlmann Elizabeth (wid Conrad), res 11 Marion.
Kohlmann John F, sawyer, bds 11 Marion.
Kohlmann Mary (wid Jacob W), res 147 E Jefferson.
Kohlmeier Henry, helper Wabash R R, res 21 Jones.
Kohlmeier Henry, laborer Ranke & Yergens, bds 21 Jones.
Kohlmeyer Christian, stripper, bds 275 Webster.
Kohlmeyer Edward (Kasten & Kohlmeyer), res 275 Webster.
Kohlmeyer George E, cigarmkr Kasten & Kohlmeyer, bds 275 Webster.
Kohlmeyer Henry C E, clerk F D Hoham, bds 275 Webster.

Kohlmeyer John H, cigarmkr Kasten & Kohlmeyer, bds 275 Webster.

Kohn, *see also Koehn, Kuhn and Cohen.*

Kohn Charles, meat market, 42 Maumee road, res same.

Kohn Miss Rose E, teacher Clay School, bds 42 Maumee rd.

Kohrmann Andrew, tailor, res 312 E Wayne.

Kohrmann Henry M, laborer Hoffman Bros, bds 215 W Superior.

Kohrmann Henry W, clk White's Wheel Works, res 312 E Wayne.

Kohrmann John J, clk Louis Fox & Bro, bds 215 W Superior.

Kohrmann Mary (wid John B), res 215 W Superior.

Kohte Ernst, molder Bass Foundry and Machine Works, res 192 Montgomery.

Kolb Adam, car builder Penn Co, res 83 Montgomery.

Kolb Caroline (wid George A), res 16 Bell ave.

Kolb Miss Carrie, cashier Kayser & Baade, bds 16 Bell ave.

Kolb John A, car builder Penn Co, res 83 Montgomery.

Kolkmann Dora (wid Henry), res 229 John.

Kolkmann Frederick, laborer, res 179 Gay.

Kollman M, laborer Penn Co, res 207 Broadway.

Kollock Fred N, Agt Union Line 79 Calhoun, res 215 W Berry.

Kollock John K, bds 215 W Berry.

Kolthoff Frederick, wiper, res 23 Wall.

Kolthoff Louisa, dressmaker J M Gould, bds 23 Wall.

Kolthoff Wm F C, turner Fort Wayne Organ Co, bds 23 Wall.

Komp, *see also Kamp and Kemp.*

Komp Daniel (Komp & Scarlet), res s s Pontiac 2 e of Hoagland ave.

Komp Miss Sarah D, bds Daniel Komp.

Komp & Scarlet (Daniel Komp, Chester A Scarlet), Real Estate, Loans and Insurance, 27 and 28 Bank Blk.

Koons Andrew, engineer, res 212 Francis.

Koons Christian, teamster, res 116 Erie.

Koons Edgar, teamster, bds Henry Koons.

Koons Henry, teamster, res n s Prospect ave 1 e of Spy Run.

Koons John, res 90 Maumee road.

Koontz, *see also Kintz and Kuntz.*

Koontz Edna, bds 260 S Harrison.

Koontz Wm K, brakeman, res 204 Thomas.

Koop Frederick H W, molder Bass Foundry and Machine Works, res 53 Buchanan.

Koop Henry, teamster American Wheel Co, res 91 Smith.

Koopman Henry, boilermaker Wabash R R, res 23 Jones.

Koorsen Adelina, bds 80 Smith
Koorsen George H, turner American Wheel Co, res 76 Gay.
Koorsen Henry, laborer, bds 80 Smith.
Koorsen John, foreman, res 291 Hanna.
Koorsen John M, laborer American Wheel Co, res 80 Smith.
Kopp, *see also Kapp and Cap.*
Kopp John H, machinist Bass Foundry and Machine Works, pbds Michael Kopp.
Kopp Joseph, clk J B White, bds 177 Jackson.
Kopp Louis C, machinist Bass Foundry and Machine Works, bds Michael Kopp.
Kopp Michael, laborer, res s e cor Lillie and Creighton ave.
Koppenhoefer Frederick, butcher Leikauf Bros, res 40 Schick.
Korn August, saloon, 194 Broadway, res 60 Nirdlinger ave.
Korn Frederick, butcher, res 20 Ohio.
Korn John, meat market, 136 Fairfield ave, res same.
Korn Katie, domestic 212 W Washington.
Korte Frederick, carpenter, res 65 Maumee road.
Korte Frederick, laborer, res 174 Gay.
Korte John, laborer American Wheel Co, res w s Hanna s of city limits.
Korte Miss Louisa, bds 65 Maumee road.
Korte Wm, carpenter, bds 65 Maumee road.
Korte Wm, molder Bass Foundry and Machine Works, bds 50 Smith.
Kortrey Kunigunda (wid John), bds 104 E Wayne.
Kortum Henry, coremkr Bass Foundry and Machine Works, res 39 Hoffman.
Koselitz Gustav H, lab American Wheel Co, res 144 Erie.
Kossenjans Helena, bds 497 E Wayne.
Kover Edward W, painter, res s w cor Howell and Rumsey.
Kover Obadiah J, painter, res s w cor Howell and Rumsey.
Kowiansky Abraham, bds 290 E Washington.
Kowiansky Kate, bds 290 E Washington.
Kowiansky Max, real estate, 28 Bank block, res 290 E Washington.
Kraft Charles, molder Indiana Machine Works, bds 317 S Lafayette.
Kraft Conrad, laborer, res 271 W Washington.
Kraft Frederick, carpenter, n s Montgomery 4 e of Lafayette, res 317 Lafayette.
Kraft Frederick, flue setter Penn Co, bds 333 E Lewis.
Kraft Frederick C, molder Bass Foundry and Machine Works, bds 333 E Lewis.
Kraft Henry, molder Bass Foundry and Machine Works, bds 333 E Lewis.

Kraft Lula, apprentice, bds 271 W Washington.
Kraft Lizzie, bds 317 Lafayette.
Kraft Minnie, bds 271 W Washington.
Kraft Minnie C, dressmaker Mrs G J Stier, bds 333 E Lewis.
Krah, *see also Craw.*
Krah Christian F, stone mason, res 159 Griffith.
Krah Christian H, printer, bds 159 Griffith.
Krah Henry, brick mason, res 82 Wilt.
Krah Henry W, printer Indiana Staats Zeitung, bds 115 Madison.
Krah John, bricklayer, bds 159 Griffith.
Krainor George J, wheel molder Bass Foundry and Machine Works, res 208 E Lewis.
Krakenberger Pauline, cook Custer House.
Kramer, *see also Cramer.*
Kramer Adam, section hand Penn Co, res cor Thomas and Greene.
Kramer Anna, operator Hoosier Mnfg Co, bds 465 Lafayette.
Kramer Arthur A, painter, res 145 John.
Kramer Bernard, bookkeeper The Herman Berghoff Brewing Co, res 49 Madison.
Kramer Bernard J, clerk A C Trentman, bds 49 Madison.
Kramer Caroline, domestic S B Bond.
Kramer Christian, teamster, res 123 Ewing.
Kramer Christian C, clerk Root & Co, res 380 E Wayne.
Kramer Conrad, painter Penn Co, res 3 Summit.
Kramer Edward M, molder Bass Foundry and Machine Works, res 28 John.
Kramer Ernest, Sign Painter; all Kinds of Gilding, Decorating, Frescoing and Fancy Painting done to order at Lowest Prices, 247 Calhoun, res 216 Shawnee ave, S Wayne.
Kramer Frederick, painter Penn Co, res 126 John.
Kramer Frederick, teamster, res 134 Harrison.
Kramer George, tinsmith Penn Co, res 135½ Force.
Kramer Henry, laborer Wm H Bassett & Son, bds same.
Kramer Henry C, bookkeeper A C Trentman, bds 49 Madison.
Kramer Herman, coil winder Fort Wayne Electric Co, bds 199 Broadway.
Kramer Jacob, painter L O Hull, bds 74 Murray.
Kramer John A, cutter Hoosier Mnfg Co, res Spy Run ave.
Kramer John G, clerk J B White, bds 49 Madison.
Kramer Joseph, feeder The Journal Co, bds 49 Madison.
Kramer J William, policeman, res 350 E Wayne.
Kramer Lena, domestic 322 Fairfield ave.

Kramer Lizzie, candy wrapper B W Skelton, bds 350 E Wayne.

Kramer Louis A, clerk G H Loesch, bds 49 Madison.

Kramer Mary, bds 126 John.

Kramer Mathias, foreman, res 465 Lafayette.

Kramer Minnie, operator S M Foster, bds 350 E Wayne.

Kramer Peter, road supervisor, res cor Spy Run av and Ruth.

Kramer Ricka, works Troy Steam Laundry, bds 164 Harrison.

Kramer Wm A, helper, res 92 Hanna.

Kramer Wm C, car builder Penn Co, res 21 Summit.

Kramer Wm P, carpenter, bds 61 Pontiac.

Krane, *see Crane.*

Kranichfeld Magdalena (wid John), bds 184 Wells.

Kranichfeld Theodore F, sawyer Hoffman Bros, res 175 Wells.

Kranz, *see also Crance.*

Kranz Frank, painter, res 88 Summit.

Kranzman Wm H, bellowsmaker Ft Wayne Organ Co, bds 268 Calhoun.

Krapf Daniel, shipping clerk Morgan & Beach, res 238 E Jefferson.

Kratzmann, carpenter, res w s Abbott 3 s of Pontiac.

Kratzmann Simon, shoemaker, res 267 Hanna.

Kratzsch Charles, clerk A I & H Friend, res 93 Baker.

Kratzsch Eleanor (wid Herman), milliner 114 Calhoun, res 15 W Wayne.

Kratzsch Emil, clerk Eleanor Kratzsch, bds 114 Calhoun.

Kratzsch Frederick C, clerk Root & Co, bds 168 Greely.

Kratzsch Herman, agent, res 15 W Wayne.

Krauhs, *see also Kraus, Krouse and Crouse.*

Krauhs Charles, shoemaker, 169 Jackson, res same.

Krauhs Dora, bds 169 Jackson.

Krauhs Frederick J, machinist Kerr-Murray Mnfg Co, bds 169 Jackson.

Krauhs Henry J, shoemaker G Spiegel, bds 169 Jackson.

Krauhs John C, barber J H Kabisch, bds 169 Jackson.

Krauhs John T, laborer Ranke & Yergens, res 61 Shawnee av.

Krauhs Wm C, piler, bds 169 Jackson.

Kraus, *see also Krauhs, Krouse and Crouse.*

Kraus Amelia (wid Ferdinand), res w s Hanover 3 n of Erie.

Kraus Edward, driver Fort Wayne Transfer and Storage Co, bds s s Madison bet Clay and Hanna.

Kraus Frank, driver Neil Bros & Co, res 87 E Lewis.

Kraus George, res 139 Madison.

Kraus Jacob, laborer, res 33 Charles.

Kraus Martin, fireman, res rear 178 Hanna.

Stahn & Heinrich, Leading Dealers in ARTISTS' MATE-RIALS AND DRAUGHTING INSTRU-MENTS. 116 Calhoun Street.

FORT WAYNE DIRECTORY. 315

Krause Annie, bds 409 E Washington.

Krause Frederick, cigarmaker John Gronendyke, bds 86 Montgomery.

Krause Joseph, res 15 Elm.

Krauskopf Carl G W, student, bds 88 W Washington.

Krauskopf Henry, laborer, res 42 Oak.

Krauskoph Mary A (wid Henry), bds 114. W Main.

Krauss Wm, driver, res 37 Taylor.

Krauter Gottlieb, laborer, res 224 Gay.

Krauter John, blacksmith Bass Foundry and Machine Works, res 68 Force.

Krautzman Wm, rms 268 Calhoun.

Krebs Edward jr, foreman Olds' Wagon Wks, res 46 Butler.

Krebs Frederick G, cigarmaker C A Berndt, bds 162 Montgomery.

Kreckmann Amelia, domestic A H Hamilton.

Kreckmann Jacob, boilermaker Fort Wayne Iron Works, bds 377 E Washington.

Kreckmann Mary, bds 377 E Washington.

Kreibaum Frederick, wall paper, 90 Barr, res same.

Kreis Eustacius, laborer, res 213 W DeWald.

Kress Catherine, domestic Custer House.

Kress George, laborer, Salimonie Mining and Gas Co, res cor Taylor and Eagle.

Kress Jacob M, helper Wabash R R, res 191 W DeWald.

Kress Jacob W, wagonmkr Olds' Wagon Works, bds George Kress.

Kress John, woodworker Olds' Wagon Works, res 112 Butler.

Kress John N, laborer, res 191 W DeWald.

Kress Michael, res 29 Pine.

Kress Philip, laborer, bds 29 Pine.

Kress Theodore, tinsmith Penn Co, res e s Harrison 1 n of 2d.

Kress Walter B, laborer, res 119 Fairfield ave.

Kress Wm N, laborer, bds 191 W DeWald.

Kretsinger Constantine, laborer Penn Co, bds 1 Piqua ave.

Kretsinger Henry R, Real Estate and Loan Agent, 1 Piqua ave, res same.

Kretsinger John R, foreman Penn Co, res 267 E Jefferson.

Kreutzer Charles, cigarmaker F J Gruber, res 170 Madison.

Krickeberg Frederick, teamster White's Wheel Works, bds 65 Lillie.

Krickeberg Frederick H C, finisher White's Wheel Works, bds 65 Lillie.

Krieg Albert, wagonmaker Fleming Mnfg Co, bds 43½ Columbia.

Krieg George, polisher Underhill's Monumental Works, res 132 Wells.

Kriete Rev Charles F, pastor Salem Reformed Church (German), res 83 Clinton.

Krimmel Carrie, bds 55 Douglas ave.

Krimmel Charles A T (Root & Co), bds 55 Douglas ave.

Krimmel Christian, cabbuilder Penn Co, res 55 Douglas ave.

Krimmel Wm, cigarmaker, res 86 N Harrison.

Kring Frank M, laborer Penn Co, bds Jewel House.

Krock Anselm, res 325 E Lewis.

Krock Benedict, laborer Kilian Baker, bds 325 E Lewis.

Krock George J, laborer, res 364 E Wayne.

Krock Jessie A, dressmaker Mrs Anna White, bds 416 E Wayne.

Krock John, carpenter, 416 E Wayne, res same.

Krock Mary, bds 364 E Wayne.

Krock Wm, carpenter, bds 416 E Wayne.

Krockenberger Jacob, helper Olds' Wagon Works, bds 174 Della.

Kroeger Wilhelmina (wid Carl), bds 3 Summit.

Kroesch Frederick, boilermaker Bass Foundry and Machine Works, res 136 John.

Kroft John, bds 400 E Washington.

Krohn August, laborer, res 200 Smith.

Krohn Charles C, bartender J G Voors, res w s Grant ave 3 s of E Washington.

Krohn Frederick, plumber, bds 49 W 4th.

Krohn Louisa (wid Henry), res 49 W 4th.

Krohn Wm, bartender F C Boltz, res 49 W 4th.

Krohne Herman, guns, 13 W Berry, res 96 E Jefferson.

Krokaiberger Jacob, teamster, res 174 Taylor.

Krokaiberger John, helper, bds 174 Taylor.

Kromm Curtis, mortiser White's Wheel Works, res 542 E Wayne.

Krone Carrie L, waitress Riverside Hotel.

Kronk George, laborer Bass Foundry and Machine Works, res 364 E Wayne.

Kronmiller Charles, machine hand American Wheel Co, bds w s Hanna 3 s of Pontiac.

Kronmiller Charles W, harnessmaker G H Kuntz, bds Columbia House.

Kronmiller Edward, machinist A Hattersley & Sons, bds 43 Taylor.

Kronmiller George, carpenter, res 105 High.

Kronmiller George, laborer American Wheel Co, res w s Hanna 3 s of Pontiac.

E. F. Sites, 🦷 Dentist, 86 Calhoun St., Four Doors North of Wayne.

FORT WAYNE DIRECTORY. 317

Kronmiller George A, brakeman, bds 43 Taylor.
Kronmiller George N, laborer Penn Co, res 43 Taylor.
Kronmiller Harry, molder Kerr-Murray Mnfg Co, bds George
   W Kronmiller.
Kronmiller Kate, bds w s Hanna 3 s of Pontiac.
Kropp Frank J, truckman L S & M S Ry, res 96 3d.
Krouse, *see also Krauhs, Kraus and Crouse.*
Krouse Wm F, machine hand, res 127 Fairfield ave.
Krudop Anna F, milliner, 33 E Main, bds 29 W Jefferson.
Krudop Charles F, wood and coal, n e cor Harmer and Hay-
   den, res 33 Lillie.
Krudop George H, bookkeeper C F Krudop, bds 29 W Jef-
   ferson.
Krudop Gottlieb D, clerk, bds 29 W Jefferson.
Krudop John B (Beaver, Miller & Co), res 29 W Jefferson.
Krudop John E, boilermaker Wabash R R, res 2 S Monroe.
Krudop Wm, teamster Beaver, Miller & Co, bds 2 S Monroe.
Krueger August C, bookkeeper Siemon & Bro, res 183 Calhoun.
Krueger Charles, car builder Penn Co, res 170 Suttenfield.
Krueper August E, traveling agent, res 53 N Cass.
Krull, *see also Crull.*
Krull Bernard J, harnessmaker A L Johns & Co, bds 266 E
   Washington.
Krull Lena A (Krull Sisters), bds 266 E Washington.
Krull Margaret A (Krull Sisters), bds 266 E Washington.
Krull Rudolph, car inspector Penn Co, res 266 E Washington.
Krull Rudolph L, jeweler, 128 E Washington, res 266 same.
Krull Sisters (Lena A and Margaret A), Milliners, 268
   E Washington.
Krummelbein Adam, bds Jacob Zuber.
Kruse August, clerk G Riethmiller & Son, bds George Rieth-
   miller.
Kruse August, laborer Bass Foundry and Machine Works, res
   364 E Lewis.
Kruse Charles, bds 161 Montgomery.
Kruse Charles, Merchant Tailor, 13 Harrison, res same.
Kruse Ferdinand, machinist Bass Foundry and Machine
   Works, res 169 Gay.
Kruse Frederick, laborer S D Bitler, bds 415 E Wayne.
Kruse Henry C, laborer Penn Co, res 161 Montgomery.
Kruse Henry F W, carpenter, res 415 E Wayne.
Kruse Henry W, fireman, res 159 Montgomery.
Kruse Lena, domestic 142 Montgomery.
Kruse Louis F, oil, res 159 Montgomery.
Kruse Minnie, domestic 229 W Berry.
Kruse Wm, laborer Wm Moellering, res 67 E Jefferson.

Kruse Wm C, clerk O B Fitch, bds 415 E Wayne.
Krusmann Frederick, laborer Wm Miller, res 229 John.
Krusse Wm F, res 67 E Jefferson.
Krutz Lena, waitress Hedekin House.
Kucher Herman N, clk Penn Co, bds 39 Savilla pl.
Kucher Rev John J, res 39 Savilla pl.
Kucher Paul C, laborer Penn Co, res 39 Savilla pl.
Kucher Theodore N, lab Penn Co, res 39 Savilla pl.
Kucher Theophilus J, clk Penn Co, bds 39 Savilla pl.
Kuckuck Charles A, laborer Bass Foundry and Machine
     Works, res 150 John.
Kuehn Wm, lab, res s s Wiebke 2 e of Lafayette.
Kuentzel, see also Kienzle.
Kuentzel Frank J, machinist, res 136 Wallace.
Kuhfuss Julius, machinist, bds 18 Colerick.
Kuhl, see also Koehl and Cole.
Kuhl Edward, clerk, bds 9 Line.
Kuhl Martin, laborer, res 9 Line.
Kuhlbach Elizabeth (wid Wm), res 119 Lafayette.
Kuhlbach Wm, checker Penn Co, res 231 Harmer.
Kuhn Wm H, car builder Penn Co, res New Haven ave.
Kuhne, see also Koehn and Kohn.
Kuhne Charles W, Lawyer, 19 Court, rms 144 E Berry.
Kuhne Frederick W (Kuhne & Co), res 124 W Jefferson.
Kuhne H Richard (Kuhne & Co), rms 144 E Berry.
Kuhne Paul F (Kuhne & Co), res 124 W Jefferson.
Kuhne & Co (Frederick W Kuhne), The Abstract Office;
     Insurance, Loan, Real Estate and Steamship Agents;
     Agent Remington Standard Typewriter, 19 Court.
Kuhns John M, Bookkeeper Fort Wayne Iron Works,
     res 364 Field ave.
Kukkuck Dorothea (wid Louis), res 181 Jackson.
Kukuk Joseph, shoemkr, res 162 Madison.
Kull, see also Cull.
Kull Christina (wid Gottlieb), bds 105 Hoffman.
Kull Dora (wid George F), res s w cor St Mary's ave and Lake.
Kull John, laborer, res 147 W 3d.
Kumfer Owen, carpenter, res 96 Smith.
Kummer Albert, mach Penn Co, res 114 E Creighton ave.
Kummer Elizabeth, cook Fritz Hotel.
Kunan Anna (wid Bernard), res e s Hanna 4 s of Eckart.
Kunkle Miss Ella, bds 138 E Wayne.
Kunkle Miss Eva, bds 138 E Wayne.
Kunkle Erastus B (E B Kunkle & Co), res 138 E Wayne.
Kunkle E B & Co (Erastus B Kunkle, Wm D Bostick),
     Proprs Fort Wayne Safety Valve Works, 87 Barr.

Kuns Peter, laborer Bass Foundry and Machine Works, bds Jacob Hunziker.
Kunse August, laborer, bds 364 E Lewis.
Kuntz, *see also Kintz and Koontz.*
Kuntz Adam, butcher, res 362 W Main.
Kuntz Elizabeth (wid Peter), res 550 Calhoun.
Kuntz Eva (wid Adam), res w s Hanna 7 s of Pontiac.
Kuntz Frank B, harness, 14 Pearl, res 204 W Superior.
Kuntz George, upholsterer Penn Co, res 156 E Jefferson.
Kuntz George H, harness, 11 Harrison, res same.
Kuntz Mary (wid Jacob), res 32 Brandriff.
Kuntz Mattie, bds 550 Calhoun.
Kuntz Philip, works Jenney Electric Light and Power Co, bds s w cor Allen and Calhoun.
Kuntz Philip H (Kuntz & Bro), res 550 Calhoun.
Kuntz Samuel (Kuntz & Bro), bds 550 Calhoun.
Kuntz & Bro (Philip H and Samuel), saloon, 548 Calhoun.
Kurns Christian, laborer, res 116 Erie.
Kurth Robert, cigarmkr G F Yergens, bds 63 Baker.
Kurtom Henry, laborer, res 39 Hough.
Kuttner Joseph G, car inspector Penn Co, res 237 E Jefferson.
Kuttner Peter G, shirt mnfr, 144 Calhoun, res 237 E Jefferson.
Kutz Wm, foreman James Madden, bds Grand Central Hotel.
Kyle, *see also Keel, Keil and Kiel.*
Kyle Abraham P, flagman Penn Co, res 72 Chicago.
Kyle Allen C, brakeman Penn Co, bds 72 Chicago.
Kyle Dale W, brakeman Penn Co, res 72 Chicago.
Kyle Ethel B, bds 72 Chicago.
Kyle Julia W, domestic 58 Maple ave.
Kyle Wm D, music dealer, 82 Calhoun, res 58 W Wayne.
Kyser, *see Kaiser, Kayser, Keiser, Keyser and Kiser.*
Kyser Oscar, laborer Penn Co, res 332 Force.

L

Laaser, *see Leeser.*
Laback Elizabeth (wid John), res 50 Wall.
Laback Frank, laborer, bds 50 Wall.
Labbe, *see Lobbe.*
Labe, *see Loeb.*
La Boub Julian, painter L O Hull, res 201 S Hanna.
Lacey Harry P, brakeman, bds 17 Burgess.
Lackey Alfred, carpenter, res 414 Hanna.
Lackey Madison, carpenter, bds 414 Hanna.
Lackey Melvin, car builder Penn Co, res 39 John.
Lacklin Charles L (col'd), cook, bds 169 Harrison.

Ladd Nettie, domestic Fort Wayne City Hospital.
Lade Max G, guns, 58 E Main, res 176 W Washington.
Ladenberger, see *Landenberger.*
Laemmle, see also *Lemmle.*
Laemmle David, potter, res 284 W Main.
Laemmle Mary, domestic 23 E Main.
Laepple Christian, carpenter, res 51 Grand.
Lafferty, see *Lauferty.*
La France Henry, res 294 W Jefferson.
La France Sophie, domestic 208 W Berry.
Lagemann Frederick, helper Penn Co, bds 45 St Martin.
Lagemann Henry, boilermaker Penn Co, res 45 St Martin.
Lagemann Henry E, machine hand American Wheel Co, bds 45 St Martin.
Lagemann Lizzie, domestic 46 W Superior.
Lagemann Rudolph, laborer, res 45 St Martin.
La Graw, see *Le Graw.*
Lahmann Charles, molder Brass Foundry and Machine Wks, res 166 E Creighton ave.
Lahmayer, see also *Lahmeyer and Lohmeier.*
Lahmayer Frederick, laborer, bds Henry Lahmayer.
Lahmayer Henry, res e s Lillie 1 s of Milan.
Lahmayer Henry jr, molder Bass Foundry and Machine Works, bds Henry Lahmayer.
Lahmayer John, molder Bass Foundry and Machine Works, res e s Winter s of Creighton ave.
Lahmayer Louis W, helper Bass Foundry and Machine Works, bds Henry Lahmayer.
Lahmayer Wm, molder Bass Foundry and Machine Works, res Henry Lahmayer.
Lahmeyer, see also *Lahmayer and Lohmeier.*
Lahmeyer Caroline (wid Daniel), bds 67 Union.
Lahmeyer Charles F, res 67 Union.
Lahmeyer Christian, carpenter, res 41 Taylor.
Lahmeyer Frederick, farmer, res 64 W Williams.
Lahmeyer Frederick C, bds 64 W Williams.
Lahmeyer Henry B, clerk, bds 61 W Lewis.
Lahmeyer John, car builder Penn Co, res 61 W Lewis.
Lahmeyer John G D, clerk Salimonie Mining and Gas Co, bds 61 W Lewis.
Lahmeyer Miss Mary, bds 64 W Williams.
Lahr, see *Laier and Lehr.*
Lahr George W, teacher Taylor University, rms 322 W Washington.
Laib Frank, machine hand American Wheel Co, res 19 Fletcher.

Laib Maria, bds 19 Fletcher ave.
Laible Christian F, laborer Penn Co, res 96 W De Wald.
Laible Paul L (Laible & Muehlfeith), res 10 W Main.
Laible & Muehlfeith (Paul L Laible, Charles A Muehlfeith), Saloon, 10 W Main.
Laier, *see also Lauer, Lehr and Loyer.*
Laier Adam, laborer, res 499 Lafayette.
Laisure Daniel C, fireman, res 45 Locust.
Laisure John C, laborer, bds 45 Locust.
Lake Robert H (Ryan & Lake), bds 599 Calhoun.
Lake Shore Hotel, J B Lassus propr, 6 N Cass.
Lake Shore and Michigan Southern Ry, office, passenger and freight depot cor 1st and Railroad.
Lakeside Park, n s of Maumee river e of Main St bridge.
Lallow Charles F, carpenter, bds 61 Pontiac.
Lallow Jennie, opr Hoosier Mnfg Co, bds 61 Pontiac.
Lallow Louis J, carpenter, 61 Pontiac, res same.
La Mar John, engineer, res 144 Wallace.
La Master George W, clk Dreier Bros, bds 25 W Washington.
Lamay Elijah, laborer, res 13 Hoffman.
Lamb David, machinist, res 139 Fairfield ave.
Lamb George A, fireman, res 215 W Jefferson.
Lamb J L, bds 248 Calhoun.
Lambert Jennie (wid Walter L), res 24 Murray.
Lambert Norris W, regulator Fort Wayne Organ Co, bds 68 W Jefferson.
Lamboley Eugenia I, milliner A F Krudop, bds 42 E 3d.
Lamboley Joseph, student, bds 42 E 3d.
Lamley, *see also Lemley.*
Lamley Moses (Falk & Lamley), res 128 W Wayne.
Lamont, *see also Lomont.*
Lamont Tilla, waitress Aldine Hotel.
La Mott Israel, laborer, res 10 W Wayne.
La Mott Maggie A, bds 10 W Wayne.
Lampke Conrad, porter Coombs & Co, res 128 Madison.
Lancaster Charles J, molder Kerr-Murray Mnfg Co, res 67 Butler.
Lancaster John, res e s Piqua ave 4 n of Rudisill ave.
Lancaster Nelson W, yardmaster Nickel Plate, res 213 W Main.
Landenberger Frederick G, clerk Horton Mnfg Co, bds 165 W Washington.
Landenberger John M, treas and mngr Indiana Machine Works, res 296 S Fairfield ave.
Landgraff Elizabeth (wid John), res 101 Smith.
Landgraff Mary, opr Hoosier Mnfg Co, bds 101 Smith.

John Pressler, Mantels, Grates and Tile Floor.
Columbia, Barr and Dock Streets.

322   R. L. POLK & CO.'S

Landman Louis W, manager C P Webber, bds 108 E Berry.

Landon Hal D, telegraph editor The Press, rms 90 E Wayne.

Landon Henry, laborer Wm & J J Geake, bds 38 Ewing.

Landsdown, *see Lansdown.*

Landstofer George, driver Bass Foundry and Machine Works, res 17 Laselle.

Lane Chester B, principal Central Grammar School, res 61 Maple ave.

Lane John W, piano tuner, res 57 Garden.

Lane Theodore M, painter J W Muldoon, bds 92 Dawson.

Lane Wm, laborer, res 56 Chicago.

Lang, *see Long.*

Lang Aemilius J (George DeWald & Co), res 304 W Washington.

Lang Albert F, clerk, bds 4 Marion.

Lang Annie (wid George), bds 30 Wells.

Lang Christian W, engineer Fort Wayne Steam Stone Works, res 6 Hensch.

Lang Gustav, laborer, bds 6 Hensch.

Lang Rev John F, Chancellor and Secretary Diocese of Fort Wayne, res 172 Clinton.

Lang John, clk M F Kaag, res 4 Marion.

Lang Leonard, engineer, res 75 Butler.

Lang Maggie, clk Dozois, Beadell & Co, bds 165 Ewing.

Lang Wm, laborer Fort Wayne Steam Stone Works, bds 2 Hensch.

Langard Clara, bds 70 E Columbia.

Langard John, grocer, 70 E Columbia, res w s Spy Run ave 3 n of St Mary's bridge.

Langard Joseph, res 70 E Columbia.

Langard Minnie, bds 70 E Columbia.

Lange Christian (J H Lange & Sons), bds 327 Calhoun.

Lange Ernest, bds 124 Harrison.

Lange Herman (J H Lange & Sons), bds 327 Calhoun.

Lange John (J H Lange & Sons), bds 327 Calhoun.

Lange John H (J H Lange & Sons), res 327 Calhoun.

Lange J H & Sons (John H, Herman, Christian and John), grocers, 327 Calhoun.

Lange Miss Lizzie, bds 30 Pritchard.

Lange Minnie, bds 327 Calhoun.

Lange Wm, clk Root & Co, res 30 Pritchard.

Langenbacher Mathias, res 21 Wall.

Langenfeld John, finisher American Wheel Co, res 67 Charles.

Langer Charles H, cabinetmkr The Peters Box and Lumber Co, res 133 W 3d.

Stahn & Heinrich, Dealers in BOOKS and FINE STATIONERY, Blank Books, Etc. 116 Calhoun Street.

FORT WAYNE DIRECTORY. 323

Langhals John, tailor J H Grimme & Sons, res 146 E Washington.
Langheinrich Rachel F (wid Ernst), res 13 St Martin.
Langhenry Wm, fireman, rms 37 Baker.
Langhorst August W, cigarmaker George Reiter, res 372 E Wayne.
Langle John T, trav agt D H Baldwin & Co, bds 37 E 3d.
Langohr Amelia (wid John), res 129 Wells.
Langohr Andrew J, saloon, 144 Broadway, res same.
Langohr John, driver C L Centlivre, res w s Leo rd 2 n of Canal feeder.
Langohr Louis E, laborer, res 85 Wells.
Langson Miriam (wid Richard), res 72 Madison.
Langstaff Walter H, laborer, res 44 S Wayne ave.
Langtry Walter, veterinary surgeon, 7 N Harrison, bds 40 W Superior.
Lanigan James, engineer, res 290 S Harrison.
Lanigan Patrick, flagman Penn Co, res 67 Melita.
Lanigan Thomas J, bookkeeper F C Boltz, bds 67 Melita.
Lankenau Addie, domestic 229 W Jefferson.
Lankenau Catherine (wid Francis), res 80 W Jefferson.
Lankenau Christian, clerk Frank & Co, bds 80 W Jefferson.
Lankenau Miss Clara, bds 83 Wilt.
Lankenau Frederick W, bookkeeper Indiana Machine Works, res 83 Wilt.
Lankenau Wm J, clerk Root & Co, res 40 Wilt.
Lankenau Wm J jr, draughtsman Penn Co, bds 83 Wilt.
Lannan Annie (wid Wm), res 103 W Washington.
Lannan Augustus J, fireman, bds 103 W Washington.
Lannan Edward, saloon, 7 Harrison, bds 103 W Washington.
Lannen James, Sample Room; Choice Wines, Liquors and Cigars, 268 Calhoun, rms 226 Calhoun.
Lansdown Job A, car builder Penn Co, res w s Rumsey nr Richardson.
Lansing Harry, engineer, res 218 E Washington.
Lanterman Frank E, printer Fort Wayne News, rms 68 E Main.
Lanternier August, market stalls 36 and 38, res s e cor Walton ave and Wayne Trace.
Lanternier Clara, bds August Lanternier.
Lanternier Joseph, gardener, bds s e cor Walton ave and Wayne Trace.
Lanternier Lena, bds August Lanternier.
Lanternier Louis, gardener, bds August Lanternier.
Lantz Louisa (wid Wm), res 310 Hanna.
Lapier Leonard, laborer, bds 67 Baker.

Lapoint George C, brakeman, res s s Jesse e of Runnion ave.
Lapp Albert, stone mason, res 57 Hoffman.
Lapp Charles J, molder, bds 52 W Williams.
Lapp Henry, lieut of police, res 52 W Williams.
Lapp Henry G V, machinist A Hattersley & Sons, bds 52 W
Williams.
Lapp Henry J, carpenter, res 34 Stophlet.
Lapple, see also Laepple.
Lapple Gottlieb, car inspector, res 17 Duryea.
Laprell Amos, tailor L J Feist, bds Johanna Ahern.
Lapshire, see Lopshire.
Large Miss Josephine (Anderson & Large), res 36 W Wayne.
Larimore Bernard L, packer Olds' Wagon Works, res 127
Grant.
Larimore George W, decorator L O Hull, res 296 W Jefferson.
Larimore James, fireman, res n s E Williams 1 w of Lafayette.
Larimore Levi B, engineer, res s s Howell 1 e of Runnion av.
La River Joseph, cabinetmaker The Peters Box and Lumber
Co, res 198 Lafayette.
Larrabee Thomas, laborer Penn Co, res 74 E Lewis.
Larson Magnus, wagonmaker Olds' Wagon Works, res 143
Holman.
Larwill John S, res 93 E Berry.
Lasen Andrew, laborer, res 235 E Wayne.
Lasher Edgar H, cigarmaker, res 57 Wells.
Lassus John B, propr Lake Shore Hotel, 6 N Cass.
Latenberger Peter, laborer, res 81 Shawnee ave.
Latham Edward (col'd), cook McKinnie House.
Latham Harry, bds 66 Wilt.
Latham John, brakeman, res 101 Harmer.
Latham Maria (wid Joseph), res 28 E Columbia.
Latham Nimmons C, laborer, bds 28 E Columbia.
Latham Zachariah, brakeman, res 208 W Superior.
Lathamer A, laborer Penn Co, res 143 Holman.
Lathrop Elias L, traveling agent, res 143 Wells.
Latta Charles S, wtchmn White's Wheel Works, res 24 Winch.
Lau, see also Law and Low.
Lau Miss Agatha, bds 122 Calhoun.
Lau Julian, bds 122 Calhoun.
Lau Miss Maggie M, milliner, 31 E Main, res 122 Calhoun.
Lau Miss Mary, milliner, bds 122 Calhoun.
Lau Thomas, res 122 Calhoun.
Lau Thomas jr, bookkeeper, bds 122 Calhoun.
Laubach A J, Physician and Surgeon; Office Hours 7 to
8 a m, 1 to 2.30 and 7 to 8 p m, n w cor Barr and Washington, res 127 E Washington.

Laubach Miss Blanche W, bds 127 E Washington.
Laubach Miss Gertrude L, bds 127 E Washington.
Laubcher John, machine hand, res 25 Laselle.
Lauer, *see also Laier and Loyer.*
Lauer Annie, operator Hoosier Mnfg Co, bds 289 E Washington.
Lauer August, laborer, bds 113 Hanna.
Lauer Barbara (wid Paul), res 70 E Jefferson.
Lauer Conrad, res 116 Maumee road.
Lauer Edward, laborer Penn Co, bds 206 Gay.
Lauer Ferdinand, butcher Wilkens Bros, res 126 Chicago.
Lauer Frank, laborer, bds 116 Maumee road.
Lauer Frank X, car inspector Penn Co, res 159 Taber.
Lauer Frederick, laborer, bds 166 Smith.
Lauer Frederick, molder Bass Foundry and Machine Works, res 370 E Lewis.
Lauer George, apprentice, bds 84 Maumee road.
Lauer Gertrude, bds 347 Lafayette.
Lauer Gregory, carpenter, res 84 Maumee road.
Lauer Gustav, carpenter, res 159 Taber.
Lauer Henry, car builder Penn Co, res 129 Lafayette.
Lauer Henry, cigarmkr Louis Bender, bds 289 E Washington.
Lauer Henry, laborer, res 118 Maumee road.
Lauer Henry, mason, res 206 Gay.
Lauer Henry P, barber, 562 E Washington, bds 113 Barr.
Lauer John, confectioner, 152 Barr, res 70 E Jefferson.
Lauer John G, res 113 Hanna.
Lauer John H, molder Bass Foundry and Machine Works, bds 206 Gay.
Lauer Joseph, carpenter, 1 University, res same.
Lauer Joseph, laborer, rms 113 Barr.
Lauer Justin, carpenter, 151 Hanna, res same.
Lauer Lizzie, milliner Margaret Koch, bds 159 Taber.
Lauer Lizzie, operator Hoosier Manufacturing. Co, bds 289 E Washington.
Lauer Louis M, carpenter Nickel Plate, res 77 Erie.
Lauer Martha, operator Hoosier Mnfg Co, bds 159 Taber.
Lauer Miss Mary, res 13 E Wayne.
Lauer Mathias W, laborer, res 156 E Creighton ave.
Lauer Michael, carpenter, res 200 Gay.
Lauer Nicholas, stonemason, res 202 Gay.
Lauer Peter, finisher Fort Wayne Organ Co, bds 126 Chicago.
Lauer Peter, laborer Bass Foundry and Machine Works, res 289 E Washington.
Lauer Peter, molder Bass Foundry and Machine Works, res 83 Summit.

Lauer Sarah (wid John), res 62 E Main.

Lauer Wm C, machine hand American Wheel Co, bds 166 Smith.

Lauer Wm P, molder Bass Foundry and Machine Works, res 166 Smith.

Lauferty, *see also Lafferty*.

Lauferty Alexander S, mngr I Lauferty, bds 75 W Berry.

Lauferty Isaac, Clothing, Furnishing Goods, Hats, etc, 73 to 77 Calhoun, res 75 W Berry.

Laughlin Catherine M, stenographer Mossman, Yarnell & Co, bds 49 E Lewis.

Laughlin John, furnace tender Penn Co, bds 60 E Williams.

Laughlin Miss Minnie, clerk Standard Medical and Surgical Institute, bds 49 E Lewis.

Laughlin Michael, engineer, res 332 Lafayette.

Laumann, *see also Lohman and Lohrmann*.

Laumann Herman J, carpenter, res 127 W 3d.

Laumann Minnie A, dressmaker, bds 127 W 3d.

Laumann Rudolph H, carpenter, bds 127 W 3d.

Laun Mary, domestic 51 E Main.

Laurent Charles, machinist, res 206 Broadway.

Laurents Alexander, butcher, res 1 Glasgow ave.

Laurentz, *see also Lorenz*.

Laurentz Frank, clerk Lake Shore Hotel.

Lauschner Herman, laborer, res 266 E Creighton ave.

Lauterberg Charles J, machinist Indiana Machine Works, res 11 St Mary's ave.

Lavack, *see Levack*.

La Vanway Alexander, carpet layer Root & Co, res 123 Madison.

La Vanway Charles J, feed, 20 Harrison, res same.

La Vanway Frank, painter, res 74 E Columbia.

La Vanway Louisa, bds 68 E Columbia.

La Vanway Luke, res n s Cochrane 1 e of Coombs.

La Vanway Sherman, driver U S Express Co, bds 68 E Columbia.

La Vanway Silas E (La Vanway & Le Graw), res 68 E Columbia.

La Vanway Theresa, bds 153 Madison.

La Vanway & Le Graw (Silas E La Vanway, Augustus Le Graw), meats, 68 E Columbia.

Lavenburger John H, car repairer Penn Co, res 43 Force.

Law, *see also Lau and Lew*.

Law Charles D, supt Western Division Penn Co, res 151 E Berry.

Law David, bds 302 W Washington.

Law Herbert J, electrician Ft Wayne Electric Co, res 302 W Washington.
Lawler Stephen, laborer American Wheel Co, res 88 Laselle.
Lawrence, *see Lorenz.*
Lawson Wm, clerk G E Bursley & Co, res 45 Home ave.
Lawton Daniel H, The Remington-Lawton Co, bds 151 W Wayne.
Lawyer, *see also Lauer and Layer.*
Lawyer Esther, bds Mark Lawyer.
Lawyer Mark, lab, res 1 w of s w cor Buchanan and Smith.
Layer John, painter Olds' Wagon Works, bds 156 E Creighton ave.
Layer Joseph, painter Olds' Wagon Works, bds 156 E Creighton ave.
Layhe Nellie, domestic 265 W Jefferson.
Layman, *see also Lehman, Lehmann and Luhman.*
Layman George, conductor, res n e cor Howell and Runnion.
Layton James, works Indiana School for Feeble-Minded Youth.
Lazzerini Amadeo, saloon, 37 Barr, res same.
Lazzerini Carrie, bds 37 Barr.
Lea, *see Lee.*
Leach Edward, carpenter Penn Co, res 64 Eckart.
Leach Etta, bds 64 Eckart.
Leach James, bds 83 Laselle.
Leach John T, boilermaker Penn Co, res 83 Laselle.
Leach Rebecca (wid John), res 190 W De Wald.
Leach Richard, fireman, rms 366 W Main.
Leach Thomas, laborer Penn Co, res 64 Eckart.
Leach Walter, packer Olds' Wagon Works, res 64 Eckart.
Leach Wm, helper Penn Co, bds 83 Laselle.
Leader Wm, tuck pointer, res 414 E Washington.
Leafstone John, cigarmaker A C Baker, bds Hedekin House.
League Park (base ball), e s Calhoun n of E Superior.
Learch, *see also Lerch and Lersch.*
Learch Frank, watchman, res 79 Force.
Learmonth Robert, chief clerk Penn Co, rms 15 Douglas.
Leary Daniel, clerk, rms 32 E Berry.
Leary James T, clerk Penn Co, rms 32 E Berry.
Leathers W Creighton, student, bds 326 Hanna.
Lebracht Frederick, laborer, res 346 Force.
Lechler Henry M, res 335 W Jefferson.
Lechler James A, convertor worker Fort Wayne Electric Co, bds 335 W Jefferson.
Lechr Mary, domestic A Aehnelt.
Le Claire Wilfred W, printer, bds 46 E Jefferson.
Lee Arnold A, carpenter, res 173 St Mary's ave.

Lee Charles W, car builder Penn Co, bds 381 Hanna.
Lee George D, policeman, res 138 W Berry.
Lee Jeffery J, car builder Penn Co, res 22 Madison.
Lee John, brakeman, res 15 Euclid ave.
Lee John, laborer, bds 38 Bass.
Lee John M, laborer, res 178 Oakland.
Lee John O (Lee & Fulton), res 105 W Jefferson.
Lee John S, clerk Lee & Fulton, bds 105 W Jefferson.
Lee Louis H, laborer Joseph Fremion, res cor Lafayette and Piqua ave.
Lee Mac, carpenter Louis Diether & Bro, res 178 Oakland.
Lee Maggie (wid Samuel), bds 178 Hanna.
Lee Maurice J, machinist Penn Co, res 381 Hanna.
Lee Samuel, bds 170 Hoffman.
Lee Samuel S, carpenter, res 170 Hoffman.
Lee Sophie C (wid Israel), res 120 Harrison.
Lee Wm (col'd), waiter, rms 67 W Superior.
Lee & Fulton (John O Lee, Charles W Fulton), livery, 18 W Wayne.
Leech Wm, laborer, bds 34 Chicago.
Leedy Wm M, circulator Fort Wayne Gazette, bds 120 Harrison.
Leek George W, machinist, res n e cor Fletcher ave and Wayne Trace.
Leeper, see also Leper.
Leeper Rev James L, pastor Second Presbyterian Church, rms 105 W Berry.
Leeper Joseph J, engineer Penn Co, res 85 E Washington.
Leese John, engineer, bds 25 W Washington.
Leeser Amelia, dressmaker, bds 14 Wall.
Leeser Miss Emma, bds 6 Summit.
Leeser Mary (wid Charles), res 14 Wall.
Leeser Pauline, milliner A Mergentheim, bds 14 Wall.
Leeuw Edward, shoemkr Mathias App, res 368 E Washington.
Leffers John, molder Bass Foundry and Machine Works, res 23 Oak.
Leffler Wm, steam fitter, res 189 E Wayne.
Lefler Otto, plumber, bds 104 Barr.
Le Graw Augustus (La Vanway & Le Graw), res 4 Spy Run.
Le Graw Emil F, clk A J Dittoe & Co, bds August Le Graw.
Le Graw Mrs Julia, housekeeper 172 Clinton.
Le Graw Margaret (wid Louis), res e s Spy Run ave 2 n of Wagner.
Lehman, see also Lahman, Lehmann and Luhmann.
Lehman Ada M (wid Samuel H), res 67 Harrison.
Lehman Benjamin, clothing, 72 Calhoun, rms 20 W Berry.

Lehman Charles, molder, bds 166 E Creighton ave.
Lehman Charles L, coil winder Fort Wayne Electric Co, bds 290 Hoagland ave.
Lehman Conrad, carpenter, res 608 Calhoun.
Lehman Miss Ellen, bds 290 S Hoagland ave.
Lehman Eugenia H, clk G De Wald & Co, bds 67 Harrison.
Lehman Frank, brickmaker A McKernan, res 85 Lillie.
Lehman Frederick, laborer, res 166 E Creighton ave.
Lehman Henry, laborer White's Wheel Wks, res 520 E Lewis.
Lehman Isaac, clerk B Lehman, rms 20 W Berry.
Lehman Isidor, Boots and Shoes, 17 Calhoun, res 138 W Main.
Lehman Jacob J, farmer, res 290 S Hoagland ave.
Lehman John, laborer C L Centlivre, res Centlivre Park.
Lehman Julius, wheel molder Bass Foundry and Machine Works, res 185 Hayden.
Lehman Louis, laborer White's Wheel Wks, bds 520 E Lewis.
Lehman Louis E, carpenter, bds 608 Calhoun.
Lehman Magdalena (wid Jacob), res 54 W Williams.
Lehman Oliver W, gearmaker Olds' Wagon Works, bds 290 Hoagland ave.
Lehman Samuel, paperhanger Keil & Keil, res 35 Walnut.
Lehman Sophie, domestic 148 E Washington.
Lehmann Emma, domestic 183 Calhoun.
Lehmann Frederick, laborer Bass Foundry and Machine Wks, res 102 Gay.
Lehmann John C, res 222 E Washington.
Lehmann John D, drayman, res 71 Huron.
Lehmann Kate, bds 222 E Washington.
Lehmann Louise, bds 222 E Washington.
Lehmkuhler Casper, helper Penn Co, res 324 Hanna.
Lehnart, see Lennart and Leonard.
Lehnemann John, laborer Hoffman Bros, bds 1 Fair.
Lehnemann Kate, bds 1 Fair.
Lehnemann Rosina (wid John), res 1 Fair.
Lehneke Edward, switchman, rms 19 Baker.
Lehnert, see also Lennart and Leonard.
Lehnert Henry C, finisher Fort Wayne Organ Co, bds 344 Broadway.
Lehnert Martin, bench hand Louis Rastetter, bds 344 Broadway.
Lehr, see also Laier.
Lehr Addie, waiter Rich's Hotel, bds same.
Lehr Charles A, engineer, res 152 E Lewis.
Lehr Eliza A, clerk Charles Falk & Co, bds 66 N Cass.
Lehr Frankie, dressmaker Mary L Sherin, bds 66 N Cass.

Election Slips. Headquarters for PERFECT SLIPS at JOHN F. EBY & CO.'S, DETROIT.

330   R. L. POLK & CO.'S

Lehr George P, wiper Penn Co, res 216 Francis.
Lehr Hannah (wid Justus J), res 66 N Cass.
Lehr Miss Hattie M, milliner, bds 91 W Washington.
Lehr John J, res 91 W Washington.
Lehr Susan, domestic 328 W Washington.
Lehrmann, see Lohrmann and Luhrmann.
Leib Charlotte (wid Ferdinand), res 81 Madison.
Leiben James B, salesman Singer Mnfg Co, res 113 Holman.
Leichner Conrad, molder Bass Foundry and Machine Works,
    res 53 W 4th.
Leichner Gustav, blacksmith, bds 27 Force.
Leidolf Conrad, janitor Central Grammar School, res 15 E
    Wayne.
Leifels Margaretha (wid Joseph J), res 239 Barr.
Leighler Wm, laborer, bds 29 Hough.
Leighton James W, bds 12 Chicago.
Leikauf, see also Leykauf.
Leikauf Bros (John J and Frank), meats, 94 Barr.
Leikauf Frank (Leikauf Bros), bds 86 E Wayne.
Leikauf Henry W, foreman Leikauf Bros, res 110 Erie.
Leikauf John J (Leikauf Bros), res 86 E Wayne.
Leinbarger Mary (wid Joseph), domestic 48 Barr.
Leinker Charles F, teamster, bds 19 Marion.
Leinker Christopher H, carpenter, res 19 Marion.
Leinker Ernst, laborer, bds 19 Marion.
Leinker Henry F, carpetlayer Root & Co, bds 19 Marion
Leising Mrs Dorothea, res 119 Lafayette.
Leitz Herman, clerk Meyer Bros & Co, res 56 Miner.
Leitz Joseph P, laborer J Klett & Son, res 11 Jones.
Leitze, see Leutze.
Lembach Charles, teamster The Herman Berghoff Brewing
    Co, res Grant ave nr brewery.
Lemke Charles, laborer, res 96 Franklin ave.
Lemley, see also Lamley.
Lemley Mrs Annie, res 25 Poplar.
Lemmelet Celestin, fireman C L Centlivre, res s s Edna 1 w
    of Spy Run ave.
Lemmerm Adolph, brewer, res 15 Wabash ave.
Lemmle, see also Laemmle.
Lemmle Caroline, bds 295 W Main.
Lemmle Johanna (wid John), res 295 W Main.
Lemon Anna M, physician, 80 Calhoun, res same.
Lempke, see Lampke.
Lenfestor Edward S, laborer Penn Co, res 4 Thomas.
Lenfestor Solon, conductor Penn Co, res 4 Thomas.
Lenk, see also Link.

Stahn & Heinrich, Leading Dealers in ARTISTS' MATE-RIALS AND DRAUGHTING INSTRU-MENTS. 116 Calhoun Street.

FORT WAYNE DIRECTORY. 331

Lenk Bernard, boxmrker Olds' Wagon Works, res 114 Chicago.

Lenk George, meat market, 198 Broadway, bds 199 same.

Lenligan Miss Ellen, bds 23 W Lewis.

Lenligan John, res 23 W Lewis.

Lenligan Miss Mary, bds 23 W Lewis.

Lennart John, clerk Kerr-Murray Mnfg Co, bds 364 E Washington.

Lennart John E, car builder Penn Co, res 364 E Washington.

Lennart Mary, bds 364 E Washington.

Lennart Wm J, stenogphr Penn Co, res 358 E Washington.

Lennington Jacob, driver, bds 38 Baker.

Lennon Edwin J (Belger & Lennon), bds 140 Calhoun.

Lenocker John, yardmaster, res 194 E Lewis.

Lenox Ida, domestic 231 Calhoun.

Lentz Henry, clk Wm Moellering & Sons, bds 212 Lafayette.

Lenz, *see also Lintz.*

Lenz Brainard, brewer The Herman Berghoff Brewing Co, res same.

Lenz Charles F, molder Bass Foundry and Machine Works, bds 41 Smith.

Lenz Ernst, machinist Penn Co, res 212 Lafayette.

Lenz Frederick, meat market, 170 Hanna, res 172 same.

Lenz Henry, lab Bass Foundry and Machine Works, res 41 Smith.

Lenz Joseph, helper Penn Co, res 21 Gay.

Lenz Leonard, brewer, res 46 Grant ave.

Lenz Wm, harnessmaker A L Johns & Co, bds n s St Mary's ave 4 w of Runnion ave.

Lenz Wm F, car builder Penn Co, res Rockhill's add.

Leonard, *see also Lenhart and Lennart.*

Leonard Barbara (wid Henry), res 346 Broadway.

Leonard Elmer (W & E Leonard), bds e s Spy Run ave n of Brewery.

Leonard Miss Harriet E, principal Jefferson School, bds 142 W Jefferson.

Leonard Miss Hattie M, teacher, bds 61 Brackenridge.

Leonard Ivers W, clk Penn Co, res 61 Brackenridge.

Leonard J H, bkkpr Indiana School for Feeble-Minded Youth.

Leonard Martin G, laborer, bds 346 Broadway.

Leonard Miss Mary J, typewriter, bds 61 Brackenridge.

Leonard Minnie E, bds 112 E Wayne.

Leonard Nathan R, Propr Fort Wayne Gazette, 41 E Berry, res 112 E Wayne.

Leonard Park M, physician, 61 Brackenridge, res same.

Leonard Wm, gunsmith, 71 W Superior, res same.

Leonard Wilmer (W & E Leonard), bds e s Spy Run avé n of Brewery.
Leonard W & E (Wilmer and Elmer), lawyers, 25 Bank blk.
Lepker Wm, traveling agent, res 73 Grand.
Lepper, *see also Leeper.*
Lepper Anna C, bds 95 Summit.
Lepper Charles O, druggist, 66 W Jefferson, res 176 Calhoun.
Lepper Daniel, carpenter, bds 117 Force.
Lepper Edmund B, machinist Fort Wayne Electric Co, res 164 Broadway.
Lepper Elizabeth (wid Christian), res 324 E Washington.
Lepper Frederick, cabinetmaker Penn Co, res 443 E Wayne.
Lepper Frederick G, clerk C H Waltemath & Sons, bds 95 Summit.
Lepper Henry C, blacksmith Penn Co, res 44 Harmer.
Lepper Henry W, clerk G DeWald & Co, bds 242 E Jefferson.
Lepper Jennie S, domestic 90 E Wayne.
Lepper John, carpenter, bds 117 Force.
Lepper Louis H, teamster White's Wheel Wks, res 65 Lillie.
Lepper Miss Louisa, housekeeper, bds Otto Siemon.
Lepper Louisa (wid Henry), res 242 E Jefferson.
Lepper Minnie, domestic 260 Calhoun.
Lepper Peter, machinist Penn Co, res 186 Francis.
Lepper Susan, domestic 338 Calhoun.
Lepper Wm, laborer Penn Co, res 37 Hough.
Lepper Wm D, carriage trimmer M L Albrecht, bds 112 E Main.
Lepper Wm H, carpenter, res 490 Fairfield ave.
Lepple G, car oiler Penn Co, res 17 Duryea.
Leppler Joseph, laborer American Wheel Co, bds 16 Locust.
Lerch, *see also Learch and Lersch.*
Lerch Archibald, machinist Bass Foundry and Machine Wks, bds 401 S Clinton.
Lerch Barbara, bds 55 Thomas.
Lerch Casper, switch tender, res 121 Force.
Lerch Frank, watchman, res 79 Force.
Lerch Henry, helper Penn Co, res 350 Force.
Lerch Joseph, shoemaker, 127 Fairfield ave, res 401 Clinton.
Lerch Mary, clerk, bds 79 Force.
Lerch Wm M, machinist Bass Foundry and Machine Works, res 165 Harmer.
Lersch, *see Learch and Lerch.*
Lesh Cora, domestic 334 W Jefferson.
Leslie Clement M, tel operator Penn Co, res 317 Hanna.
Leslie J Carson, carpenter, bds 12 E Columbia.

Lester George H, turner The Peters Box and Lumber Co, bds Daniel Cope.

Leu, *see also Lau, Law and Lew.*

Leu Frederick, teamster, res 8 Cottage ave.

Leu George jr, tinner, bds 8 Cottage ave.

Leu John, pedler, bds Washington House.

Leuschner Herman, cabinetmaker Fort Wayne Organ Co, 266 W Creighton.

Leuthner Barbara, res rear 278 E Jefferson.

Leutweiler Wm, meat market, 544 Calhoun, res same.

Leütze Gottlieb, laborer, res e s Hoagland ave 1 s of organ factory.

Levack Elizabeth (wid John), res 50 Wall.

Levack Frank, laborer Penn Co, bds 50 Wall.

Leveck John M, laborer Kerr-Murray Mnfg Co, res w s S Broadway s of city limits.

Level John, hostler, bds Brokaw House.

Levenburgh John H, car inspector, res 43 Force.

Levenburgh Lizzie, bds 43 Force.

Levensparger John B, carpenter, bds 22 W Main.

Levi August, pedler, res 78 W Main.

Levi Belle, clerk Frank & Co, bds 78 W Main.

Levi Carl, clerk Sam, Pete & Max, res 78 W Main.

Levi Leon, stonecutter Fort Wayne Steam Stone Works, bds 78 W Main.

Levy Abraham, pedler, res 278 E Washington.

Lew, *see also Lau and Law.*

Lew Charles W, painter, bds 182 E Jefferson.

Lew Peter, bds C F Sweny.

Lewis B Asa, dyer, res 16 Madison.

Lewis Catherine, bds 142 Montgomery.

Lewis Miss Cora G, bds Sylvester Lewis.

Lewis David M, hostler A C Perrin, bds 57 Barr.

Lewis Dominick, fruit stand, res s s Riverside ave 5 n of St Joseph river.

Lewis Edwin W, mngr Massachusetts Shoe Co, res 334 W Washington.

Lewis Frank, engineer Indiana Machine Works, res 227 Madison.

Lewis Frank, painter Archer, Housh & Co, res s e cor Pearl and Griffith.

Lewis Frederick W, clerk Massachusetts Shoe Co, rms 334 W Washington.

Lewis Henry H, huckster, res 8 Buchanan.

Lewis James D, Druggist and Pharmacist, 434 Calhoun cor DeWald, res 18 W Creighton ave.

Lewis Jonathan, Washing Machines, 142 Pearl, res 142 W. Main.
Lewis John A, laborer, res n s Pontiac 1 e of Lafayette.
Lewis John J, plumber Robert Ogden, bds 16 Madison.
Lewis Laura A (wid Levi), bds 600 Calhoun.
Lewis Lulu, bds 101 Glasgow ave.
Lewis Mrs Mary, res 38 Clinton.
Lewis Mary A (wid John), bds J A Lewis.
Lewis Matilda (wid David), res 101 Glasgow ave.
Lewis Nora, bds 101 Glasgow ave.
Lewis Oris B, teamster The Herman Berghoff Brewing Co, bds cor E Washington and Glasgow ave.
Lewis R Curtis, laborer, bds Sylvester Lewis.
Lewis Sylvester L, clerk Postoffice, res s w cor E Washington and Glasgow ave.
Lewis Mrs S J, teacher Indiana School for Feeble-Minded Youth.
Leykauf, *see also Leikauf.*
Leykauf Henry N, plumber A Hattersley & Sons, res 25 Union.
Leykauf John N, brakeman Penn Co, bds 198 Broadway.
Leykauf Lizzie, clerk Nicholas Leykauf, bds 23 Union.
Leykauf Nicholas, grocer, 209 Broadway, res 23 Union.
Libes, *see Lipes.*
Libkeman Frederick, tailor Andrew Foster, bds 227 E Madison.
Library Hall, n w cor Calhoun and E Lewis.
Lichtenwalter Albert L, barber Lichtenwalter & Butler, bds 260 E Lewis.
Lichtenwalter George, laborer Penn Co, bds 260 E Lewis.
Lichtenwalter Orrin J, flagman, res 185 Jackson.
Lichtenwalter Solomon M, res 260 E Lewis.
Lichtenwalter Wallace A (Lichtenwalter & Butler), res 181 Montgomery.
Lichtenwalter Wm M, clerk C F Reinkensmeier, bds 170 Brackenridge.
Lichtenwalter & Butler (Wallace A Lichtenwalter, James P Butler), barbers, 272 Calhoun.
Lichtle Paul, laborer Bass Foundry and Machine Works, bds Peter P Lichtle.
Lichtle Peter P, laborer Bass Foundry and Machine Works, res n s Ruth 3 w of Spy Run ave.
Lichtsinn Henry, clk A W Miller & Co, bds 382 E Washington.
Lichtsinn Henry, laborer Penn Co, res w s Cochrane 4 e of Coombs.

Lichtsinn Henry H, teamster, res 382 E. Washington.
Lichtsinn Johanna (wid Wm), res 15 Summit.
Lichy Aaron, sawyer White's Wheel Works, bds 551 E
Washington.
Lickly George B, fireman, bds 92 Dawson.
Lieb Henry, res 81 Madison.
Lieb Herman, bds 81 Madison.
Liebe Louis, carpenter, bds 172 Suttenfield.
Liebenguth Albert, molder, res 89 Laselle.
Liebenguth Charles, saloon, cor Calhoun and Railroad, res
same.
Liebenguth Charles C, machinist Bass Foundry and Machine
Works, bds 46 W Wayne.
Liebenguth Frank, clerk, bds 46 W Wayne.
Liebenguth Jennie, bds 46 W Wayne.
Liebenguth Mrs Rosa, res 46 W Wayne.
Lieberenz Frederick C, plasterer, res 283 Hanna.
Liebig Charles, mason, res 1 Tam.
Liebig Emil, machinist Penn Co, bds 1 Tam.
Liebig Herman C, bricklayer, res s s Simon 3 e of Winter.
Liebig Richard, clerk, bds 1 Tam.
Liebman Ernst F (Liebman & Henry), res 106 W Wayne.
Liebman & Henry (Ernst F Liebman, James M
Henry), Carpenters, Contractors and Practical Build-
ers, s e cor W Jefferson and Fulton. (*See adv p 67.*)
Liebmann Reinhold, shoemaker, res 113 Barr.
Liedtke John J, porter Meyer Bros & Co, res 110 High.
Liedtke Louisa H, tailoress, bds 110 High.
Liggett Bros (James and Robert A), livery, 5 N Harrison.
Liggett James (Liggett Bros), U S Gauger, res 89 W
Superior.
Liggett James, driver, res 291 S Harrison.
Liggett Robert A (Liggett Bros), res 73 Wells.
Light John, truckman, res 81 W Washington.
Light Lewis C, laborer, bds 81 W Washington.
Lightfoot Frank S, bookkeeper Bass Foundry and Machine
Works, res 185 W Wayne.
Lightfoot Miss Laura, bds 158 W Berry.
Lightfoot Melinda (wid George), res 158 W Berry.
Liiken Barney, machine hand American Wheel Co, res 5 Oak.
Lile, *see also Lyles.*
Lile Alfred, laborer, res 70 Gay.
Lill Martin, saloon, 150 Calhoun, res 149 E DeWald.
Lill Peter, watchman, res 147 E DeWald.
Lilly John S, fireman, bds 125 Walton ave.
Lilly Merritt B, brakeman Penn Co, res 125 Walton ave.

Limbach Charles, teamster, res s s Grant ave 1 s of brewery.
Limbach Herman, blacksmith Wabash R R, res 79 Wall.
Limecooly Casper, laborer, res 324 Hanna.
Limecooly Charles G, clerk Penn Co, res 453 Lafayette.
Limecooly Frederick R, policeman, res 453 Lafayette.
Limecooly Frederick W, traveling agent, res 562 Calhoun.
Limecooly Henry, stripper, bds 324 Hanna.
Limecooly Louis F, grocer, 546 Calhoun, res 453 Lafayette.
Limecooly Wm H, blacksmith, res 49 W Williams.
Linck, *see Lenk and Link.*
Lincoln Caroline B (wid Edmund), res 22 Butler.
Lincoln Charles, laborer Penn Co, res 117 Holman.
Lincoln Miss Elizabeth C, bds 22 Butler.
Lincoln Etta, operator S M Foster, bds 47 Lillie.
Lincoln George W, pedler, res n e cor Lillie and Milan.
Lincoln Miss Mary B, teacher Hoagland School, bds 22 W
    Butler.
Lindeman Dora, domestic 84 W Creighton ave.
Lindeman Frederick H, clerk F W Boecker, bds 106 Wilt.
Lindeman George, apprentice Penn Co, bds 106 Wilt.
Lindeman George, laborer C L Centlivre, bds 85 Cass.
Lindeman Gottlieb, car builder Penn Co, bds 106 Wilt.
Lindeman Henry, bookkeeper G E Bursley & Co, res 106 Wilt.
Lindeman Henry J, carpenter P, F W & C Ry, res 106 Wilt.
Lindeman John H, car builder Penn Co, res 106 Wilt.
Lindeman Mary E, bds 106 Wilt.
Lindeman Wm, machinist, bds 106 Wilt.
Lindemann Bernard, cabinetmaker Thé Peters Box and Lum-
    ber Co, res 183 Oakland.
Lindemann Clara, dressmaker Mary L Sherin, bds 81 Wilt.
Lindemann Daniel, teacher Emanuel School, bds 81 Wilt.
Lindemann Elizabeth (wid Eberhardt), bds 18 Pritchard.
Lindemann Rev Frederick, Pastor St Paul's Ger-
    man Evangelical Lutheran Church, res 178 Barr.
Lindemann Frederick, wiper Penn Co, res 166 Broadway.
Lindemann Gustav, clerk, bds 404 E Washington.
Lindemann John, laborer Penn Co, res 21 Charles.
Lindemann Miss Matilda, music teacher, 81 Wilt, bds same.
Lindemann Oscar A H, engineer Bass Foundry and Machine
    Works, res 363 E Lewis.
Lindemann Theodore, molder Indiana Machine Works, bds
    81 Wilt.
Lindemann Wm E, saloon, res 83 N Cass.
Lindemann Wm R, carpenter J W Hilgemann, res 404 E
    Washington.
Lindenberg Christian, clerk H F C Rust, bds 24 Union.

Lindenberg Christian, machinist Fort Wayne Iron Works, res 24 Union.

Lindenberg Frederick, brick mason, res 55 Stophlet.

Lindenberg Frederick W, clerk Kimball & Webb, bds 55 Stophlet.

Lindenberg Wm F, bookkeeper J Wilding & Son, bds 24 Union.

Lindenmeyer Adam, laborer Kerr-Murray Mnfg Co, res 21 Pritchard.

Lindenmeyer Minnie, domestic 233 W Berry.

Lindenwood Cemetery, John H Doswell supt, Huntingdon road w of city limits.

Lindermeyer, *see also Linnemeier.*

Lindermeyer Richard, bds 244 E Washington.

Lindermeyer Sophie, domestic 316 W Jefferson.

Lindlag Philip, collector, bds 123 Ewing.

Lindman Edward J, clerk Penn Co, bds 171 Clinton.

Lindman Harry J, brakeman, bds 171 Clinton.

Lindner Andrew, shoemaker Louis Fortriede, res 89 Putnam.

Lindsey Charles W, turnkey County Jail, res 3 E Superior.

Lindsey James E, engineer, bds 234 W Main.

Lindsley Percy M, letter carrier, res 210 E Jefferson.

Line, *see Lyne.*

Ling Maggie, works Troy Steam Laundry, bds 11 Mary.

Lingle Theodore, laborer, res 85 St Mary's ave.

Linhardt Ernest, clerk A Koon, bds 60 Nirdlinger ave.

Lininger Frank E, conductor Penn Co, res 210 Walton ave.

Lininger Miss Ollie M, bds 73 Grand.

Link, *see also Lenk.*

Link Ad, trav agt, res 102 E Main.

Link Ament, bds 116 Chicago.

Link Andrew J, carpenter, bds 236 E Jefferson.

Link Annie M (wid George N), res 236 E Jefferson.

Link Carrie R, clerk, bds 236 E Jefferson.

Link Frederick, stone mason, res 116 Chicago.

Link Henry J, cashier Root & Co, bds 236 E Jefferson.

Link John, laborer, bds 11 Mary.

Link Kate, operator Hoosier Mnfg Co, bds 116 Chicago.

Link Mary (wid Thomas), res 11 Mary.

Link Wm B, tallyman Nickel Plate, res 12 N Cass.

Linker Christina (wid Henry E), res 46 W Berry.

Linker John V, clerk The Herman Berghoff Brewing Co, bds 70 Grant ave.

Linker Miss Kate, res 46 W Berry.

Linker Valentine, watchman The Herman Berghoff Brewing Co, res 70 Grant ave.

John Pressler, Galvanized Iron Cornices and Slate Roofing
Columbia, Barr and Dock Streets.

338   R. L. POLK & CO.'S

Linn Henry F, carpenter J A Crow & Co, bds 223 Calhoun.
Linn Ida J, domestic 399 Calhoun.
Linn Vincent, teacher, bds 581 Broadway.
Linnemann, see *Lindemann.*
Linnemeier, see also *Lindermeyer.*
Linnemeier Charles, carpenter, bds 131 Monroe.
Linnemeier Mrs Minnie, midwife, 131 Monroe, res same.
Linnemeier Wm, coachman 76 W Berry.
Linnemeier Wm, helper Penn Co, res 131 Monroe.
Linnemeyer Charles, sawyer, bds 58 Hayden.
Linsky Timothy, spoke selector Winch & Son, res n e cor
    Thomas and Fisher.
Lintlag Jacob, feed yard 10 Pearl, res 6 Pritchard.
Lintner, see *Lindner.*
Linton Jacob, bds 360 W Washington.
Linton John, car repairer Fort Wayne City Railroad Co, res
    185 N Lafayette.
Lintz, see also *Lenz.*
Lintz Anthony W, foreman Fort Wayne Street Railroad Co,
    res 34 Baker.
Lintz Delia (wid Anthony), res 14 E Columbia.
Lintz Miss Josephine, bds 14 E Columbia.
Lintz Theodore L, crockery, 12 E Columbia, res 14 same.
Lipes Alexander T, printer Fort Wayne Newspaper Union.
Lipes Andrew, bds 69 Archer ave.
Lipes Charles J, driver Adams Express Co, res 22 W DeWald.
Lipes David D, res 303 E Lewis.
Lipes John M, works J O Keller, bds 37 Elizabeth.
Lipsett Edgar W, conductor, bds 223 Lafayette.
Lischy, see *Lichy.*
Liscum John R, conductor, res e s St Mary's ave 1 n of High.
Lisenberger George, machinist Fort Wayne Electric Co, res
    167 Metz.
Lisenop Meta, domestic 58 Maple ave.
Lish Carl, brakeman, bds 17 Burgess.
List Emma, bds 395 E Washington.
List Herman, teamster L P Scherer, bds 99 Maumee road.
List John J, carpenter, res 395 E Washington.
Litot Edward L, boilermaker Fort Wayne Iron Works, bds
    cor Randolph and Spy Run ave.
Litot George A, glazier, res s w cor Spy Run ave and Ran-
    dolph.
Litot Joseph V, employee Fort Wayne Electric Co, res 165
    Clinton.
Litot Miss Mary, bds George A Litot.
Litt George O, clerk, bds 220 W Jefferson.

Litt George W, grocer 132½ Broadway, res 220 W Jefferson.
Little, *see also Lyttle.*
Little Alfred, painter Penn Co, res 164 Madison.
Little John, wheel inspector Olds' Wagon Works, res 317 S
 Harrison.
Little Rebecca (wid George), res 34½ John.
Little Wm A, mach hand American Wheel Co, bds 34½ John.
Littlejohn David M, machinist Wabash R R, bds 19 Poplar.
Littlejohn Jennie, domestic 250 W Creighton ave.
Littlejohn Wm, blacksmith Wabash R R, res 19 Poplar.
Livelsberger Albert M, traveling agent, res 47 N Calhoun.
Lloyd, *see also Loyd.*
Lloyd Miss Belle R, prin Hanna School, bds 121 E Main.
Lloyd Rev John P, res 121 E Main.
Lloyd Thomas M, clerk G DeWald & Co, bds 121 E Main.
Loag Anna R (wid George W), bds Hamilton House.
Loag & Mungen (Est of George W Loag, W Wallace
 Mungen), Dentists, 2 E Columbia.
Lobbe Joseph, fireman Penn Co, res 198 Madison.
Lobdell Effie, nurse, bds 94 W Main.
Lobdell John D, brakeman, res 253 W Wayne.
Lobsige r Frederick, laborer Fort Wayne Steam Stone Wks,
 bds 46 Calhoun.
Lochert Emil H, finisher American Wheel Co, res 218 John.
Lochner Henry, bds 19 Francis.
Loebert Frederick, wiper Penn Co, res 216 John.
Loeffler Otto, steamfitter A Hattersley & Sons, bds 106 Barr.
Loeffler Wm M, steamfitter A Hattersley & Sons, res 189 E
 Wayne.
Loesch George H, drugs, 96 Barr, res 52 W Washington.
Loftus John B, laborer, bds 199 Broadway.
Logan Hugh, engineer, bds 12 St Mary's ave.
Logan Elizabeth, electrician Fort Wayne Electric Co, bds 42
 Baker.
Logan Lot A, carpenter, res 314 S Harrison.
Logan Margaret, bds 42 Baker.
Logan Thomas J, stenographer, 16 W Main, res 99 Madison.
Logan Wm H, engnr Star Iron Tower Co, res 314 Harrison.
Logan Wm L, blacksmith, res 42 Baker.
Lohman, *see also Laumann and Luhmann.*
Lohman Joseph (Joseph Lohman & Co), res 98 W Berry.
Lohman Joseph & Co (Joseph Lohman), cigar mnfrs, 137
 Calhoun.
Lohmeier, *see Lahmeyer.*
Lohmeyer Henry, molder Bass Foundry and Machine Works,
 bds Diedrich Brandt.

Lohrman, *see Laumann and Luhrmann.*

Lohrman Wm, engineer, bds 154 John.

Lombard Joseph, insurance, res 128 Fairfield ave.

Lombard Louis, machine hand Fort Wayne Organ Co, bds 128 Fairfield ave.

Lomeyer, *see also Lahmeyer and Lohmeier.*

Lomeyer Frederick machine hand Winch & Son, res n e cor Lillie and Milan.

Lommatzsch Gustave, stone cutter Fort Wayne Steam Stone Works, res 19 Pritchard.

Lommatzsch Herman, bricklayer, bds 300 E Wayne.

Lomont, *see also Lamont.*

Lomont Epolyet A, laborer, bds 83 Putnam.

Lomont Francis A, pres Old Fort Mnfg Co, res n s E Wayne 2 e of Hanover.

Lomont Louisa (wid V Peter), res 83 Putnam.

Lomont Margaret (wid Adolphus), res 551 E Washington.

Lomont Mary E, seamstress, bds 83 Putnam.

Lomont Mary P (wid Francis T), res 87 Putnam.

Lonergan Cecil A, clerk A Mergentheim, bds 168 Harmer.

Lonergan James E, binder Fort Wayne Sentinel, res 400 E Wayne.

Lonergan John V, machinist, res 168 Harmer.

Lonergan J Charles, conductor, res 100 E Lewis..

Lonergan Margaret J (wid Thomas D), bds 100 E Lewis.

Lonergan Wm J, machinist Kerr-Murray Mnfg Co, bds 168 Harmer.

Loney Alexander J, baggageman, res 119 W Williams.

Loney George, carpenter, res 140 W De Wald.

Loney Peter J, draughtsman, res 274 W Jefferson.

Long, *see also Lang.*

Long Anna (wid George), res 30 Wells.

Long Claud H, bds 77 E Berry.

Long Cora E, bds 19 Pine.

Long Edward M, carpenter, bds 248 Calhoun.

Long Emma (wid Charles A), res 262 E Lewis.

Long Harry M, wall paper, 11 W Berry, res 77 E Berry.

Long James B, clerk Stewart & Hahn, res 77 E Berry.

Long John E, engineer, res 19 Pine.

Long Mary, domestic 11 N Calhoun.

Long Mason, lecturer, res 33 Pixley & Long bldg.

Long Nancy V (wid John C W), res 20 Williams.

Longacre Milton P, sec Hoffman Lumber Co, res 29 Garden.

Longan George M D, harnessmaker A L Johns & Co, bds Edsall House.

Longfield Edward J, clerk D C Fisher, bds 67 Charles.
Longfield John, finisher, res 67 Charles.
Longhenry, *see Langheinrich.*
Longstaff W H, laborer Penn Co, res 30 S Wayne ave.
Lonsbury Frank, wheelmaker, bds 104 Barr.
Loomis Emerson N, brakeman, res 47 High.
Loomis Ray M, salesman Singer Mnfg Co, rms 59 E Wayne.
Loos, *see also Lase.*
Loos Anna, bookkeeper Henry Loos, bds 419 Lafayette.
Loos Charles H, machinist Penn Co, bds 419 Lafayette.
Loos Henry, grocer, 421 Lafayette, res 419 same.
Loos Henry jr, boilermaker, bds 419 Lafayette.
Loos John, bds 419 Lafayette.
Loos Joseph, clerk, res 57 Charles.
Loos Joseph, saloon, 162 Holman, res same.
Loos Matilda P, bds 419 Lafayette.
Lopshire, *see also Lapshire.*
Lopshire A Lincoln, fireman, bds 13 St Martin.
Lopshire Frederick H, clerk, bds 31 Duck.
Lopshire John, turner, bds 23 Laselle.
Lopshire Lemuel, bartender Russel George, res 31 Duck.
Lord Edmond P, asst engineer motive power Penn Co, rms
    122 E Main.
Lordier August F, res 537 E Wayne.
Lordier Clara, bds 37 Baker.
Lordier Felix, section hand, bds 22 E Columbia.
Lordier Francis J, bds 537 E Wayne.
Lordier Phillip, shoemaker, 37 Baker, res same.
Lorenz Charles, wireworker, res n s Spring 2 w of Franklin.
Lorenz Joseph, laborer Penn Co, res 14 Buchanan.
Lorey Jesse, carpenter, bds 248 Calhoun.
Lose, *see also Loos.*
Lose Cyrus J, printer The Journal Co, bds 43 Douglas ave.
Lose Levi H, car builder Penn Co, res 43 Douglas ave.
Loss Joseph, clerk, res 57 Charles.
Lott John B, inventor, bds 26 W Jefferson.
Lotti Wm, clerk Clifton House.
Lotz, *see also Lutz.*
Lotz Charles O, painter F W Robinson, bds G W Riley.
Lotz George C, packer F Eckart, res 37 Breck.
Lotz John H, tailor A F Schoch, res 279 W Jefferson.
Lotz Philip G, cook, rms 129 Wells.
Lotz Wm, laborer Hoffman Bros, bds 47 St Mary's ave.
Loucks Amos, carpenter, res 139 Shawnee ave.
Loudenbach Truman B, painter, bds 251 Calhoun.
Loughlin, *see also Laughlin.*

Loughlin Alonzo, machine hand Fort Wayne Organ Co, bds 101 Williams.

Louis, *see Lewis.*

Lour Lee, stone cutter, rms 14 Clay.

Lounsberry Frank W, laborer White's Wheel Works, res 199 E Washington.

Lounsberry Frederick J, bds 53 Madison.

Lounsberry George H, bds 53 Madison.

Lounsberry John H, finisher White's Wheel Works, res 53 Madison.

Lourain Catherine (wid Nicholas), bds 92 Madison.

Lourent, *see also Laurent.*

Lourent August, bartender J H Schele, res 163 W Superior.

Louth Maggie, wks J O Keller, bds 115 Hayden.

Louttet Kate (wid James), domestic 260 W Berry.

Love Wm, expressman, res e s Force 5 s of E Creighton ave.

Lovell John, hostler Fort Wayne St Railroad Co, bds Brokaw House.

Lowder Maggie, domestic Monroe House.

Lowe Clara (wid Josephus), res 130 Broadway.

Lowe George W, farmer, res 280 W Washington.

Lowe Samuel D, fireman, res 31 Boone.

Lower Edward, laborer, bds 288 Calhoun.

Lower Rev John, pastor First U B Church, res 54 Division.

Lowman, *see Laumann.*

Lown Allen W, cabinetmaker Fort Wayne Furniture Co, res 115 W DeWald.

Lowrey Martin, laborer, bds 20 W Superior.

Lowry Anna A, clerk Penn Co, bds 92 W Berry.

Lowry Fannie, bds 65 Douglas ave.

Lowry James W, saloon, 6 E Columbia, res same.

Lowry Miss Lida C, bds 92 W Berry.

Lowry Miss Lotta C, bds 92 W Berry.

Lowry Mary E, wks Indiana School for Feeble-Minded Youth.

Lowry Morton, flue cleaner Penn Co, res 82 Montgomery.

Lowry Robert, lawyer, 5 Court, res 92 W Berry.

Loyd, *see also Lloyd.*

Loyd George, mach, White's Wheel Works, res 3 Hanover.

Loyd Thomas W, finisher White's Wheel Works, res 435 E Washington.

Loyer, *see also Lauer and Lawyer.*

Loyer Esther, works Troy Steam Laundry, bds 1 Buchanan.

Loyer Mark, laborer, res s s Buchanan 1 e of Gay.

Loyer Stephen, laborer, res 88 Laselle.

Lubbenjans Anna (wid Henry) res 82 Smith.

Lubbenjans Annie, bds 82 Smith.

Mrs. E. A. Flagler, Cheapest, Best and Most Fashionable MILLINERY STORE in Town. 14 West Berry Street.

FORT WAYNE DIRECTORY. 343

Lubbenjans Bernard, laborer American Wheel Co, bds 82 Smith.

Lubbenjans Minnie, bds 82 Smith.

Luce, *see also Loos and Lose.*

Luce Adelbert G, butcher, bds Hedekin House.

Luce Lura O (wid George L), bds 89 E Lewis.

Luce Samuel, blacksmith City Carriage Works, bds 89 E Lewis.

Lucey Daniel, clerk, bds 40 Hood.

Lucey Michael, laborer, bds 40 Hood.

Lucey Timothy, laborer, res 40 Hood.

Luckey Elizabeth (wid John), bds 106 Wallace.

Luckey Henry, laborer La Vanway & Le Graw, rms 68 E Columbia.

Lucky Jacob, teamster Louis Diether & Bro, res 12 Franklin.

Ludford Thomas, painter, bds 22 E Columbia.

Ludington James A, machinist Penn Co, res 84 Baker.

Ludington Kissie, clerk Root & Co, bds 84 Baker.

Luegel Herman J, student, bds 342 Hanna.

Luegring Anthony, tinner, res 16 Cedar.

Luehrmann, *see Lohrmann and Luhrmann.*

Luessinhop Louis, truckman Wabash R R, bds 310 S Harrison.

Luhmann, *see also Layman, Lehman and Lehmann.*

Luhmann August H, carriage painter M L Albrecht, bds Wm C Luhmann.

Luhmann Ernest, carpenter, bds 144 Erie.

Luhmann Frederick E D, laborer, res 144 Erie.

Luhmann Frederick H, tailor, 125 Calhoun, bds e s Canal 1 s of Erie.

Luhmann Henry C, clerk J G Thieme & Son, res 51 Maumee road.

Luhmann Minnie, bds 144 Erie.

Luhmann Wm, carpenter, bds Wm C Luhmann.

Luhmann Wm C, tailor, res e s Canal 1 s of Erie.

Luhn C, laborer Penn Co, res Walton ave.

Luhrmann, *see also Lohrmann and Luehrmann.*

Luhrmann Mrs Annie M, janitor Washington School, res 213 W Washington.

Luhrmann Christian, plumber, bds 213 W Washington.

Luhrmann Christian jr, hostler Winkelmeyer Bros, bds 213 W Washington.

Luhrmann Henry C, machinist Fort Wayne Electric Co, bds 213 W Washington.

Luhrmann Wm C, carpenter George W Bley, bds 407 E Wayne.

Luhrs Charles, laborer Penn Co, res Walton ave.
Luken Bernard, finisher, res 5 Oak.
Lukens Alfred T, solicitor Ft Wayne News, res 236 W Berry.
Lukens Miss Clara M, bds 236 W Berry.
Luley Annie, bds 279 Hanna.
Luley Anton, machinist Indiana Machine Works, bds 279 Hanna.
Luley Anthony B, bookkeeper Pickard Bros, bds 171 E Jefferson.
Luley Frank J, foreman Bass Foundry and Machine Works, res 171 E Jefferson.
Luley Frank P, patternmaker Fort Wayne Iron Works, res 256 E Jefferson.
Luley Henry W, patternmaker Bass Foundry and Machine Works, bds 171 E Jefferson.
Luley Jacob J, machinist, bds 171 E Jefferson.
Luley John, machinist Ft Wayne Electric Co, res 279 Hanna.
Luley Joseph J, molder Fort Wayne Iron Works, bds 171 E Jefferson.
Luley Philip, molder Indiana Machine Works, res 279 Hanna.
Luley Wm J, machinist Indiana Machine Works, bds 279 Hanna.
Lumbard, *see also Lombard.*
Lumbard Miss Effie, teacher Harmer School, bds 164 W Wayne.
Lumbard Miss Georgie, bds 137 W Wayne.
Lumbard Mary A (wid Sanford), res 164 W Wayne.
Lumbard Sidney C, Insurance, Real Estate and Loans, 3 Aveline House Block, res 137 W Wayne.
Lund Hans M, cabinetmaker, 172 W Creighton ave, res same.
Lunger Frank, laborer, rms 49 E Main.
Lunn James, laborer, res 230 Lafayette.
Luntenberger Peter, laborer Olds' Wagon Works, res 81 Shawnee ave S Wayne.
Lunz John G, market stall 33, res Maysville road.
Lupton Lawson T, machinist Fort Wayne Electric Co, bds 82 Montgomery.
Lupton Patrick, fireman, rms 17 W Lewis.
Luther Maggie, works Indiana School for Feeble-Minded Youth.
Luttrell Rev John L, Presiding Elder United Brethren Church, res s s E Creighton ave 3 w of Winter.
Lutz, *see Lotz.*
Lutz Peter, stonecutter Wm & J J Geake, bds 312 W Main.
Lutz Philip, cook J T Wagner.
Lutze Julia F (wid John H), res 35 E 1st.
Lydolph Eliza (wid Frederick), bds 99 E Main.

Lying-in Institution and Sanitarium, Frederick Thayer M D propr, 57 Walton ave.

Lyles John Q, blacksmith Bass Foundry and Machine Works, res 328 E Jefferson.

Lyles Stella, bds 328 E Jefferson.

Lyman Burke W, stereotyper The Press, bds 74 E Lewis.

Lyman Charles H, res 98 W Superior.

Lyman Mrs Jennie R, nurse Fort Wayne City Hospital.

Lyman Walter F, blacksmith M L Albrecht, bds 98 W Superior.

Lynch Barton, laborer, bds 251 Calhoun.

Lynch Frank, agt Metropolitan Mnfg Co, res 192 E Wayne.

Lynch Jackson, works Indiana School for Feeble-Minded Youth.

Lynch Jeremiah C, engineer, bds 335 W Main.

Lynch Johanna (wid Patrick), bds 195 Barr.

Lynch John, helper Penn Co, bds 322 Lafayette.

Lynch John, janitor Catholic Reading, Bath and Club Rooms, res 195 Barr.

Lynch John, laborer, bds w s Spy Run ave 2 s of Randolph.

Lynch John J, coppersmith Penn Co, res 12 Kansas.

Lynch Matthew, laborer Penn Co, res 12 Kansas.

Lyne Wm, florist, res 111 W Jefferson.

Lynn Martha (wid Lewis), res 203 W Washington.

Lyonberg Miss Adelaide, student, bds 179 W Jefferson.

Lyons Frederick, brakeman, bds 17 Burgess.

Lyons Robert J, engineer, res 161 Hanna.

Lyons Winfield G, engineer, res 16 Chicago.

Lyttle, *see also Little.*

Lyttle Benjamin, teamster, res 84 Taylor.

Mc

McAfee Mrs Mary, livery, 36 E 1st, res Bluffton, Ind.

McAfee Rose, ice cream parlors, 331 Hanna, res same.

McAfee Samuel, blacksmith Penn Co, res 354 Hanna.

McAfee Wm A, helper Penn Co, bds 25 Grand.

McAfee Winfield P, brakeman Penn Co, bds 331 Hanna.

McAllister Jessie W, emp Massachusetts Shoe Co, bds 334 W Washington.

McArdle Thomas P, conductor, res 38 Buchanan.

McAssey Frank J, clerk Penn Co, res 74 Pontiac.

McBennett Frank, carpenter, 410 Lafayette, res same.

McBennett Frank J, clerk Root & Co, bds 410 Lafayette.

McBride George, laborer Penn Co, res 309 Lafayette.

McCaffery George, brakeman, bds 22 E Columbia.

McCaffrey Arminda M (wid Wm), res s e cor Jenison and Holton.

McCaffrey Daniel, machine hand American Wheel Co, bds 72 Melita.

McCaffrey John C, works Penn Co, bds 263 E Webster.

McCaffrey John F, fireman Wabash R R, bds 72 Melita.

McCaffrey Mary (wid Cormick), res 72 Melita.

McCaffrey Thomas, helper Penn Co, bds 263 Webster.

McCaffrey Thomas J, laborer, bds 72 Melita.

McCain Mrs Emma J, res 378 Calhoun.

McCain John H, res 378 Calhoun.

McCain Margaret (wid Wm), bds 84 E Berry.

McCall Charles, conductor, rms 34 W Main.

McCamley Edward F, molder Bass Foundry and Machine Works, bds 341 W Washington.

McCann John, contractor, res 65 Grand.

McCann Maggie, cigarmkr F J Gruber, bds 65 Grand.

McCann Patrick, laborer, bds 65 Grand.

McCann Wm, teamster, res 179 E Washington.

McCarthy Ann J (wid Andrew), n s W Main 3 w of Runnion.

McCarthy Dennis, brakeman Penn Co, bds Hinton's Rest.

McCarthy Dennis, engineer, res 160 W Superior.

McCarthy Dennis F, mngr Fort Wayne Transfer and Storage Co, bds 3 Colerick.

McCarthy Dennis S, laborer Penn Co, res 27 Bass.

McCarthy F M, sec and treas Fort Wayne Transfer and Storage Co, 47 E Columbia.

McCarthy James, blksmith Kerr-Murray Mnfg Co, res 290 Calhoun.

McCarthy James, laborer Penn Co, bds 27 Bass.

McCarthy John C, fireman, bds 160 W Superior.

McCarthy Maggie, waiter McKinnie House.

McCarthy Michael, engineer, bds 25 Baker.

McCarthy Patrick, engineer, res 51 Melita.

McCarthy Patrick, watchman, res 3 Colerick.

McCarthy Patrick F, brakeman, bds 51 Baker.

McCarthy Timothy, brakeman Penn Co, bds 310 Hanna.

McCarthy Timothy, fireman, bds 27 Bass.

McCarty Daniel D, helper Penn Co, res 48 Lillie.

McCaskey George W, Physician, 38 W Wayne, res same.

McCausland John W, physician,113 Lewis, res 133 Barr.

McClain, see McLain and McLean.

McCleery Isaac, laborer, res 9 Duck.

McCleish Duncan, helper, res 7 Liberty.

McClellan Hattie, bds 136 E Lewis.

McClellan John A, helper Penn Co, bds 144 Horace.
McClellan John Q, engineer, res 136 E Lewis.
McClellan Wm, brakeman, bds 136 E Lewis.
McClelland Samuel W, barber S G Hubbard, bds 15 N Cass.
McClelland Wm H, clerk Morgan & Beach, res 15 N Cass.
McClintock Elizabeth (wid John), res 98 Montgomery.
McClisch Leander, coachman 301 Fairfield ave.
McClish Adam, gardener, res e s S Wayne ave 1 s of Home.
McClish Anna, domestic 43½ E Columbia.
McClure Andrew (McClure & Paulus), res 20 Douglas ave.
McClure Annie, bds 59 Butler.
McClure David B, millwright, res 225 W Main.
McClure David C, machinist Wabash R R, bds 59 Butler.
McClure James H, brakeman, res 2 Thomas.
McClure Jennie, trimmer A C Keel, bds 59 Butler.
McClure John H, clerk Fort Wayne Beef Co, bds 22 W Main.
McClure J Rosser, adv solicitor Fort Wayne Gazette, res 340 W Washington.
McClure Martha A (wid Joseph), bds 20 Douglas ave.
McClure Miss Mary, principal Clay School, bds 23 Douglas.
McClure Miss Mary E, teacher Washington School, bds 20 Douglas ave.
McClure Wm C, helper Penn Co, bds 24 Force.
McClure & Paulus (Andrew McClure, Frank D Paulus), Proprs Rich's Hotel, n w cor Calhoun and Douglas ave.
McCollen Harry A, machinist Fort Wayne Electric Co, bds 177 W Superior.
McCollen John, engineer, res 177 W Superior.
McColloch, see also McCulloch.
McColloch Kate A (wid Samuel), res 230 Harmer.
McColloch Robert H, bookkeeper James M Kane, bds 230 Harmer.
McConahy Bertie, works Indiana School for Feeble-Minded Youth.
McConnell Joseph, conductor, res 13 St Michael's ave.
McConnell Thomas G, hostler Fort Wayne Street Railroad Co, bds 38 Baker.
McCormick George B, conductor, res 14 Jackson.
McCormick P John, laborer, bds 182 E Jefferson.
McCormick Thomas H, Physician and Surgeon, 7, 8 and 9 Pixley & Long Bldg, rms same.
McCoy John W, machinist Penn Co, res 80 Chicago.
McCoy Peter, laborer, bds 43½ E Columbia.
McCoy Thomas, caller, bds 6 Kansas.
McCracken Henry W, bds 58 Maple ave.

Election Slips. Headquarters for PERFECT SLIPS at JOHN F. EBY & CO.'S, DETROIT.

348 R. L. POLK & CO.'S

McCracken James K, res 271 W Wayne.

McCracken Walter H, asst chemist Fort Wayne Electric Co, bds 58 Maple ave.

McCray Jesse, brakeman, res 104 John.

McCreary A, canvasser Indiana Installment Co, res 274 Calhoun.

McCrimmon Annie G (wid Samuel), res 46 E Jefferson.

McCrory George, policeman, res 140 Barr.

McCubbin Wm, teamster Bass Foundry and Machine Works, bds 29 Hough.

McCulloch, *see also Mc Colloch.*

McCulloch Charles, pres Hamilton National Bank, sec Salimonie Mining and Gas Co, and treas Taylor University, res 122 W Wayne.

McCulloch John R, clerk Hamilton National Bank, bds 122 W Wayne.

McCulloch School, n w cor McCulloch and Eliza.

McCullough Gustine, dentist, 27 Calhoun, res 61 Madison.

McCullough Howard, Physician and Surgeon, Office 42 W Berry, res 180 Harrison.

McCullough Mrs Millie, res 73 Grand.

McCullough Thomas P, Physician, 180 Harrison, res 34 Douglas ave.

McCullough Wm J, messenger, res 401 E Washington.

McCumsey Ancel M, engineer, res 47 E DeWald.

McCurdy Andrew R, clerk G DeWald & Co, bds 45 E 3d.

McCurdy Delbert K, cabinetmaker Fort Wayne Furniture Co, bds 45 E 3d.

McCurdy George A, clerk Ohnhaus & Co, bds 45 E 3d.

McCurdy John S, dentist, 25 Bank block, res 45 E 3d.

McCurdy Melvin J, conductor, res 69 High.

McCurdy Mildred F, bds 45 E 3d.

McDaniel Alexander, justice, w s Spy Run ave 6 n of St Mary's bridge.

McDaniel Anna, nurse, bds Alexander McDaniel.

McDaniel Jennie, nurse, bds Alexander McDaniel.

McDaniels Frank O, flagman Penn Co, res 24 Euclid ave.

McDarby Matthew C, cigarmaker F J Gruber, res 278 E Jefferson.

McDermott James, res 317 Calhoun.

McDermut Nancy V (wid Josiah S), res 119 W Washington.

McDermut Wilson E (Successor to McDermut & Whiteleather), Business College, Stenographer and Dealer in Typewriters, 62 and 64 Calhoun, res 29 W Lewis. (*See back cover and p 8.*)

McDole H G, helper Penn Co, res 274 E Lewis.

E. F. Sites, Dentist, 86 Calhoun St., Four Doors North of Wayne.

FORT WAYNE DIRECTORY. 349

McDonald Duncan D, bartender F J Geiger, res 13 Caroline.
McDonald Emmet H (McDonald, Watt & Wilt), sec Jenney
  Electric Light and Power Co and Indiana Machine Wks,
  res 272 W Wayne.
McDonald John, blacksmith Fleming Mnfg Co, res 231 Wells.
McDonald John, laborer, bds George Rudert.
McDonald John G, gasfitter, res 17 N Calhoun.
McDonald John W, porter, bds 17 N Calhoun.
McDonald Margaret H (wid Archibald J), res 321 E Wayne.
McDonald Mary C, bds 321 E Wayne.
McDonald Mary J (wid David), res n s Spring 1 w of Frank-
  lin ave.
McDonald Milo, laborer, bds 11 Force.
McDonald Patrick J, sec City Water Works, 68 Barr, res 108
  W Jefferson.
McDonald Ronald T, treas and gen mngr Fort Wayne Elec-
  tric Co and sec Star Iron Tower Co, res 252 W Wayne.
McDonald Sarah M, bds 321 E Wayne.
McDonald Stephen A, brakeman Penn Co, rms 23 Baker.
McDonald Thomas, carriagemaker City Carriage Works, bds
  25 W Washington.
McDonald, Watt & Wilt (Emmet H McDonald, Wm H
  Watt, Franklin P Wilt), grocers, 141 and 143 Calhoun.
McDonough John, road supervisor N Y, C & St L R R, bds
  Clifton House.
McDonough Wm, section hand Wabash R R, res 6 Kansas.
McDorman John E, helper Penn Co, bds 167 Van Buren.
McDorman Mary J (wid John E), res 167 Van Buren,
McDougal's Block, n w cor Calhoun and Berry.
McDowell Edward C, bds 248 Calhoun.
McDowell Henry, helper, res 3 Duryea.
McElfatrick Charles L, machinist Penn Co, res 156 Wallace.
McElfatrick James T, ladderman Hook and Ladder Co No 1,
  rms Engine House No 1.
McElfatrick Mary (wid John), res 103 W Main.
McFee Daniel T, engineer, bds 328 W Jefferson.
McFee Margaret (wid Wm), res 328 W Jefferson.
McFeely Dennis, saloon, res 8 W Wayne.
McFeely John, bds 8 W Wayne.
McFerran George H, bookkeeper, bds 345 W Jefferson.
McFerran Jane (wid Milton), res 345 W Jefferson.
McGath Ida, domestic B B Wickliffe.
McGaw Amelia (wid Thomas), res 169 W Jefferson.
McGaw Miss Anna, bds 169 W Jefferson.
McGaw Cassius H, coil winder Fort Wayne Electric Co, bds
  169 W Jefferson.

McGee, *see also McKee and Mackie.*

McGee Kittie, dressmaker, bds 175 Clinton.

McGee Lizzie, dressmaker, bds 175 Clinton.

McGee Miss Maria, dressmaker, 175 Clinton, res same.

McGee Martha, clerk A Mergentheim, bds 175 Clinton.

McGeehon John, baggageman, res 72 Thomas.

McGinnis B, laborer Penn Co, res Wayne Trace.

McGinnis Daniel, roofer, res 24 Miner.

McGinnis Michael, pipe liner Salimonie Mining and Gas Co, bds Wm Keller.

McGlennon Edward F, cigarmaker George Reiter, res 13 Marion.

McGlennon Peter, cigarmaker, bds 13 Marion.

McGovern Thomas, agt Metropolitan Mnfg Co, res 132 Wells.

McGowan John, asst chief engineer fire dept, res 107 Wallace.

McGowan Mary (wid Hugh), bds 107 Wallace.

McGrady Charles E, laborer, res 74 E Columbia.

McGrady Mrs Eliza, 59 W Superior.

McGrady John D jr, hostler, bds 85 N Cass.

McGrady John G, livery, bds 59 W Superior.

McGreevy Richard, brakeman Penn Co, bds 310 Hanna.

McGuire, *see also Maguire.*

McGuire Ann (wid Edward), res 338 W Main.

McGuire Anna M, bds 338 W Main.

McGuire Bessie, bds 16 Baker.

McGuire Frank, packer Fort Wayne Organ Co, res 34 Leith.

McGuire John B, postal clerk, res 185 Ewing.

McGuire Owen, switchman Penn Co, res 16 Baker.

McGuire Patrick, laborer, bds 57 Barr.

McGuire Peter, messenger Penn Co, bds 16 Baker.

McGuire Samuel C, carpenter, bds 187 Jackson.

McGuire Theodore, gasfitter S F Bowser & Co, bds 225 S Calhoun.

McGuire Theodore, laborer, bds 43½ E Columbia.

McIlvaine Wm, plumber James Madden, res 163 Francis.

McIntee John, foreman, bds 55 Barr.

McIntosh Miss Alice, stenographer Fleming Mnfg Co, bds 65 W 4th.

McIntosh Miss Helen I, stenographer Indiana Machine Wks, bds 65 W 4th.

McIntosh Wm, farmer, res 65 W 4th.

McIntyre Lillie L, domestic 416 Calhoun.

McKay, *see also McKee and Mackie.*

McKay Miss Christina B, bds 134 W Main.

McKay Florentine, machinist Fort Wayne Electric Co, res 49 Grand.

Builders' Hardware, PFEIFFER & SCHLATTER, 38 and 40 EAST COLUMBIA ST.

FORT WAYNE DIRECTORY. 351

McKay James M (G E Bursley & Co), res 134 W Main.

McKay Miss Nellie M, bds 134 W Main.

McKeag Agnes (wid Wm), res 149 Fairfield ave.

McKeag Agnes T, dressmaker, 149 Fairfield ave, bds same.

McKeag Miss Ellen, teacher Central Grammar School, bds 149 Fairfield ave.

McKean, see also McKeon.

McKean Miss Anna M, bds Eliza W McKean.

McKean Eliza W (wid Wm T), res w s Spy Run ave opp Riverside ave.

McKean Hugh S, machinist Fort Wayne Iron Works, bds n s Spy Run ave opp Riverside ave.

McKean John L, enginr C L Centlivre, bds Eliza W McKean.

McKean Milton H, bookkeeper J C Peltier, bds w s Spy Run ave opp Riverside ave.

McKean Miss Sarah E, tchr Clay School, bds Spy Run ave.

McKee, see also McGee, McKay and Mackie.

McKee Alonzo W, candymaker Louis Fox & Bro, bds 35 Ewing.

McKee Charles W, jewelry, 120 Calhoun, res 54 E Washington.

McKee Edwin P, clerk C W McKee, bds 54 E Washington.

McKee Jefferson F, laborer Hoffman Bros, res 224 W Main.

McKee John L, laborer Hoffman Bros, bds 35 Ewing.

McKeeman Alexander, laborer, rms 124 S Wayne ave.

McKeeman Wm, carpenter, res 124 S Wayne ave.

McKendry Charles A, timekeeper, bds 282 Harrison.

McKendry Daniel, asst city engineer, res 282 Harrison.

McKendry Daniel jr, deputy city clerk, res 362 E Wayne.

McKenzie George, machinist Wabash R R, res 121 Butler.

McKenzie James S, Mngr The Wonderland, 5 E Main, res 142 W Jefferson.

McKenzie Jane (wid Robert), bds 193 W Superior.

McKeon, see also McKean.

McKeon Charles, clerk, bds 152 W Wayne.

McKeon James, res 152 W Wayne.

McKering Dennis L, section foreman, bds 59 Boone.

McKering Jerry D, laborer, bds 59 Boone.

McKernan Alexander, brickmkr, w s Burd ave 1 n of Wabash R R, bds same.

McKillit Minnie P, student, bds 106 N Cass.

McKinley Harry, teamster, res 141 N Cass.

McKinley Harry C, foreman Fort Wayne Electric Co, res 72 Dawson.

McKinley Perry, teamster, res 141 N Cass.

McKinley Reginald, teamster, bds 141 N Cass.

McKinley Thomas S, collector Indiana Installment Co, rms 127 Calhoun.

McKinney Nathaniel C, line repairer, res 39 Butler.

McKinnie Daniel, teacher, res 35 Duck.

McKinnie George B, propr McKinnie House, Penn depot, res same.

McKinnie House, George B McKinnie propr, Penn depot.

McKinnie Wm M (Wm M McKinnie & Co), res 170 W Wayne.

McKinnie Wm M & Co (Wm M McKinnie), Proprs The Wayne, s s W Columbia bet N Calhoun and Harrison.

McKinzie Caleb I, painter, res 11 St Martin.

McKinzie John L, student, bds 11 St Martin.

McKletchey John, foreman, res 29 Hanna.

McLachlan Annie J, bds 209 Barr.

McLachlan Miss Coralyn, bds 51 W Berry.

McLachlan Jane (wid Neal), res 66 W Creighton ave.

McLachlan John B, machinist Fort Wayne Electric Co, res 123 Williams.

McLachlan Mary E (wid James C), bds 209 Barr.

McLachlan Miss Nannie, bds 66 W Creighton.

McLachlan Neil, supt, res 66 W Creighton ave.

McLachlan Wm, trav agt, res 51 W Berry.

McLachlin Edward, laborer, bds 130 Maumee road.

McLain Benoni P, res n s Prospect ave 3 e of Spy Run ave.

McLain Charles C, dep Co auditor, res 132 W Creighton ave.

McLain Miss Clara, bds n s Prospect ave 5 e of Spy Run av.

McLain Miss Zeruiah E, teacher Bloomingdale School, bds Prospect pl.

McLane Hannah L, bds 40 Marion.

McLane Mary A (wid Robert), res 40 Marion.

McLaren Jesse, hostler Fort Wayne City Railroad Co, res 544 E Wayne.

McLauchlin Eugene F, coil winder Fort Wayne Electric Co, res 95 Wall.

McLaughlin, *see also Laughlin.*

McLaughlin George W, armature winder Fort Wayne Electric Co, res 50 Taylor.

McLaughlin Mary A (wid James), bds 107 Wallace.

McLaughlin Wm, coremaker Bass Foundry and Machine Works, bds 16 Gay.

McLaughlin Wm, salesman Fort Wayne Iron Works, res 51 W Berry.

McLaughlin Wm S, laborer Hoffman Bros, bds 5 Pape.

McLean Henry C, printer Ft Wayne Journal, bds 291 W Main.

McLean Mary A (wid Robert), res 40 Marion.
McLeish Duncan, delivery clerk Penn Co, res 7 Liberty.
McLeish Francis M, clerk J B White, res 16 McClellan.
McLeod George, stone cutter George Jaap, bds 47 Barr.
McLetchie Hugh, clerk J B White, bds 103 W Main.
McLetchie John D W, bookkeeper White's Wheel Works, res 29 Hanna.
McMacken Frank, plumber Robert Spice, res 48 W Main.
McMahon Catherine A (wid Wm), res 167 Gay.
McMahon Mrs John, res 273 W Main.
McMahon John W, driver J B White, res 66 Butler.
McMahon Mrs Sophia, res 273 W Main.
McMahon Sylvester, conductor Penn Co, res 324 Broadway.
McMaken Anna, bds 351 E Wayne.
McMaken Delia, bds 351 E Wayne.
McMaken Dorothy (wid Joseph G), res 351 E Wayne.
McMaken Lizzie, bds 351 E Wayne.
McManigal George M, caller, bds 161 Webster.
McManigal Harry, brakeman, bds 161 Webster.
McManigal James L, laborer, bds 161 Webster.
McManigal Mrs Mahala, res 161 Webster.
McMillan James B, well driver, n s Richardson 1 w of Runnion ave, res same.
McMillan John V, foreman, res 34 E 5th.
McMullan Henry, reporter The Press, rms 38 Brackenridge.
McMullen James, engineer, res s s Monroe 1 n of Charles.
McMullen John, contractor, 70 Charles, res same.
McMullen John H, clerk Olds' Wagon Works, bds Rich's Hotel.
McMullen Louis, barber Ehrman & Geller, bds 75 W 3d.
McMullen Mary (wid Michael), bds 410 Lafayette.
McNair Charles, car builder Penn Co, res 138 W De Wald.
McNalley Miss Blanch, bds 63 Baker.
McNalley Mary (wid John), res 63 Baker.
McNally Oliver, bartender C A Doudrick, bds 250 Calhoun.
McNamara John, laborer, res 33 Walton ave.
McNamara Monroe, finisher American Wheel Co, res 46 E Butler.
McNamara Peter, section foreman, res 10 Runnion ave.
McNamara Thomas, laborer, res 194 Broadway.
McNamara Washington, foreman American Wheel Company, res E Williams.
McNaught Duncan, stone cutter George Jaap, res 62 W 5th.
McNearney John, laborer, res 81½ Smith.
McNearney Mary, attendant Penn Co depot, bds 84 Baker.
McNearney Mary J, bds 84 Baker.

McNearney Thomas, res 84 Baker.
McNearney Thomas A, laborer Penn Co, bds 84 Baker.
McNulty Delia, boxmaker Wm H Davis, bds 245 S Webster.
McNulty Frank J, foreman John Pressler, res 108 Wallace.
McNulty John, molder Bass Foundry and Machine Works, bds 178 Hanna.
McNulty John, plumber A Hattersley & Sons, res 247 S Webster.
McNulty Mary (wid Anthony), res 245 S Webster.
McNulty Neil, helper Penn Co, res 245 S Webster.
McNulty Wm H (McNulty & Weber), res 178 Hanna.
McNulty & Weber (Wm H McNulty and Adam Weber), shoemakers, 211 Lafayette.
McNutt Henry T, clerk Ft Wayne St Railroad Co, bds 427 Calhoun.
McNutt Lorenzo D, supt Ft Wayne St Railroad Co, res 427 Calhoun.
McNutt Wm C, painter Ft Wayne St Railroad Co, res 427 Calhoun.
McOscar Amos J, teacher, bds 16 W Jefferson.
McOscar Edward J, physician, 16 W Jefferson, res same.
McOscar Mary S (wid John), res 16 W Jefferson.
McPhail Mrs Janet A, tchr Jefferson school, bds 192 Ewing.
McPhail Miss Margaret M, principal Bloomingdale School, bds 192 Ewing.
McPhail Miss Mary, bds 192 Ewing.
McPhail Wm, machinist, res 192 Ewing.
McPhail Wm B, master mechanic Ft W, C & L R R, res 38 E 5th.
McPherson Angus, Agent Empire Line, 26 Court, rms same.
McPherson John, brakeman, bds 33 St Mary's ave.
McQuarrie Allan, cabinetmaker Fort Wayne Organ Co, res 28 Home ave.
McQuarrie Samantha (wid Duncan), nurse, bds 115 Barr.
McQuiston Allen P, bds 70 Wells.
McQuiston Jane, bds 70 Wells.
McQuiston John, res 70 Wells.
McQuiston Wilson, sec The Peters Box and Lumber Co, res 43 E 2d.
McQuown John S (Ake & McQuown), res e s Franklin ave 2 s of High.
McTavish Angus, tailor John Rabus, bds 25 W Washington.
McTigue Mary (wid Patrick), bds 30 Melita.
McTigue Rose, res 18 Burgess.
McVey John H L, clerk, bds 3 De Groff.

McVey Mary A, seamstress, bds 3 De Groff.
McVey Michael, fireman Nickel Plate, res 3 De Groff.
McWhorter Lawrence, printer Fort Wayne Gazette, bds 15 W Williams.

M

MacDougal Miss Catherine, bds 143 W Wayne.
MacDougal John, res 143 W Wayne.
MacDougal Michael C (Root & Co), res 143 W Wayne.
Mack Gottfried, paperhanger, bds 75 W 3d.
Mack John, brakeman, bds 248 Calhoun.
Mack John jr, laborer The Herman Berghoff Brewing Co, bds John Mack.
Mack John, shoemaker E Vordermark & Sons, res 106 Boone.
Mackie, see McGee, McKay and McKee.
MacKinzie, see McKenzie.
Madden Frederick, laborer Nickel Plate, bds 88 E Columbia.
Madden Jacob, laborer, res 94 Franklin ave.
Madden James, Plumber, Steam and Gas Fitter, and Dealer in the Perfect Hot Water Heater, Gas Fixtures, Brass Goods, Plumbers' Supplies, etc; Sanitary Plumbing a Specialty, 101 Calhoun, res 39 Baker. (*See right side lines.*)
Madden Jennie, bds 10 Oliver.
Madden John, laborer, res 37 W Williams.
Madden John, watchman, res 88 E Columbia.
Madden Martin G, baker Louis Fox & Bro, bds 88 E Columbia.
Madden Matilda (wid Allen), res 10 Oliver.
Madden Patrick M, bartender R M Cummerow, rms 226 Calhoun.
Maddes Jacob, watchman, res 31 Julia.
Maddox Joseph, driver J C Peters, res 1st cor Harrison.
Maddux Wm A, foreman, res 28 Sherman.
Madison Wm J, machinist Penn Co, res 155 Wallace.
Madison Wm J jr, machinist Penn Co, res 297 E Lewis.
Maerz, see Martz and Mertz.
Maest Gottlieb, laborer, res 57 W 5th.
Magers D Merrin, janitor Taylor University, bds same.
Magers Frank, carpenter, res 37 Wilt.
Magers Frank X, gardener, res 91 Thompson ave.
Magers John F, bds 91 Thompson ave.
Magner Clara, domestic 133 E Berry.
Magner Oliver J, lab Kerr-Murray Mnfg Co, bds 67 Butler.
Magner Wright, driver, bds 64 W Wayne.

Magnus Charles W B, physician, 124 Buchanan, bds same.
Magnus Ella, bds 124 Buchanan.
Magnus Wm, engineer, res 124 Buchanan.
Maguer Frank, helper Penn Co, bds 80 Gay.
Maguire, see McGuire.
Mahan Bridget M (wid Dominick), res 176 W Jefferson.
Mahan James, blacksmith, bds 176 W Jefferson.
Mahanke, see Marhenke.
Maher James V, stenographer S C Lumbard, res 23 Douglas.
Mahin Rev Augustus E, presiding elder Fort Wayne M E
    Church, res 269 W Jefferson.
Mahin John W, bds 269 W Jefferson.
Mahin Miss May, bds 269 W Jefferson.
Mahin Miss Sadie, bds 269 W Jefferson.
Mahl, see also Mehl.
Mahl Frank, machine hand White's Wheel Works, res 5
    Dwenger ave.
Mahl John, laborer, res 5 Dwenger ave.
Mahoney Viola, bds 86 Montgomery.
Mahony James, cigarmaker Reuben Binder, rms 21 Hamilton.
Mahony Mary, domestic 31 W Williams.
Mahrt Conrad, harnessmaker F Hilt, res 42 Pritchard.
Mahrt Louisa (wid Wm), bds 42 Pritchard.
Mahurin Marshall S (Wing & Mahurin), res 161 Griffith.
Maibucher Joseph, salesman Singer Mnfg Co, rms 92 Calhoun.
Maier, see also Mayer, Meier, Meyer and Myer.
Maier Dora (wid Frederick), res 99 Wilt.
Maier Henry, laborer M Orr, bds 112 Mechanic.
Maier Louis, tailor, res 99 Wilt.
Maier Louisa, domestic 171 Clinton.
Maier Mary, domestic 100 E Washington.
Maier Wm, farmer, bds 99 Wilt.
Mailand Christian, laborer Penn Co, res 310 Harrison.
Mailey Annie, dressmaker, bds 61 Melita.
Mailey John, laborer, bds 69 Grand.
Mailey Kate, dressmaker, bds 61 Melita.
Mailey Patrick, flagman Nickel Plate R R, res 61 Melita.
Maines Charles C, conductor, res 218 Walton ave.
Maisch August C, clerk, bds 172 Gay.
Maisch Jacob, stone cutter, res 172 Gay.
Maisch Jacob jr, cigarmkr A C Baker, bds 172 Gay.
Major Belle Z, milliner A F Krudop, bds 29 W Jefferson.
Major David H, fireman, res 57 Smith.
Major James E, conductor Penn Co, res 143 Horace.
Major John F, lab Fort Wayne Electric Co, bds 90 Maple ave.
Major Roxena, converter Ft Wayne Electric Co, bds 57 Smith.

Major R Roy, feeder Fort Wayne Newspaper Union, bds 132 Broadway.

Major Wm S, res 132 Broadway.

Majors Lucy, works Troy Steam Laundry, bds 77 W 3d.

Majors Phoebe (wid John), res 77 W 3d.

Majors Thomas J, letter carrier, res 117 W DeWald.

Makepeace Augustus K, conductor, res 71 W 4th.

Malcolm Sherman E, canvasser, res w s Lillie 1 n of Milan.

Malin James, trimmer Jenney Electric Light and Power Co, bds 22 E Columbia.

Malle Lizzie, bds 187 E Jefferson.

Malle Mary (wid Henry), res 187 E Jefferson.

Malle Wm, clerk, bds 187 E Jefferson.

Malloy Wm, milliner, 16 Calhoun, res 107 E Main.

Malnowski Gustav, res 65 John.

Malone, *see also Molone.*

Malone Christina (wid John), bds 290 W Main.

Malone John, brakeman, bds 196 Hanna.

Malone Joseph W, insurance, 16 W Main, bds 22 W Jefferson.

Malone Peter, grocer, 167 Broadway, res same.

Maloney John, helper Penn Co, bds 1 Thomas.

Maloney Michael, watchman Penn Co, res 1 Thomas.

Maloney Walter, laborer, res 110 John.

Maltman John, stone cutter George Jaap, bds 63 E Columbia.

Manaray Arthur J, helper A Hattersley & Sons, bds 4 Riverside ave.

Manaray John C, car builder Penn Co, res 4 Riverside ave.

Manaray Robert H, printer, bds 4 Riverside ave.

Manchester Alfred E, supt machine department Bass Foundry and Machine Works, bds Aldine Hotel.

Manchester Frank A, machinist Indiana Machine Works, bds 110 W Main.

Manet Adeline, cook, 22 E Columbia.

Manet Ida, domestic, 130 Maumee road.

Manett Alonzo, fireman, bds 102 E Lewis.

Mangan Bridget (wid Patrick), res 3 Walnut.

Mangan Thomas J, caller, res 64 W Main.

Mangels Anna, bds 63 Maumee road.

Mangels Mary (wid Claude), res 63 Maumee road.

Mangelsdorf John D, teacher Zion German Lutheran School, res 124 John.

Manier Frank, carpenter Penn Co, res 144 Holman.

Manier Joseph, clerk, bds 144 Holman.

Manier Minnie J, stripper John Gronendyke, bds 144 Holman.

Manley Asa (col'd), laborer, res 5 Glasgow ave.

Mann Elizabeth (wid Wm), bds 62 Buchanan.

Charles Bowman Keeps in Stock E. C. Atkins' Celebrated SAWS, 18 Harrison Street.

358   R. L. POLK & CO.'S

Mann Miss Ida M, bds Jesse E Mann.
Mann Isaac, laborer, res 225 E Wayne.
Mann James K, clerk Root & Co, bds Grand Central Hotel.
Mann Jesse E, physician, 37 Pixley & Long bldg, res 456 S
    Calhoun.
Manner Louis, blacksmith, bds 22 Ewing.
Manning, *see also Monning.*
Manning Bridget M, bds 15 Brandriff.
Manning Thomas, laborer, res 15 Brandriff.
Manning Tillie (wid Andrew), res 173 Wells.
Mannix Charles, cigarmaker, res 195 Jackson.
Mannix Frank J, machinist, bds 10 Holman.
Mannix Thomas, deputy sheriff, res 10 Holman.
Mannix Wm T (Mannix & Wiebke), res 376 Calhoun.
Mannix & Wiebke (Wm T Mannix, Henry A Wiebke),
    saloon, 33 Calhoun.
Mannweiler Anthony C, instrument maker Fort Wayne Elec-
    tric Co, bds 23 Duryea.
Mannweiler Christian, blacksmith Fort Wayne Electric Co,
    res 23 Duryea.
Mannweiler Herman, flue setter Penn Co, res 21 Duryea.
Mannweiler Mary (wid Martin E F), bds 1 Walnut.
Manok Charles, cigarmaker L Dessauer, res 95 Jackson.
Manok Crescentia (wid Simon), res 21 E Williams.
Manok Edward J, clerk O B Fitch, bds 21 E Williams.
Manok Julia, packer Louis Fox & Bro, bds 21 E Williams.
Manon Wm A, clk Mossman, Yarnell & Co, res 182 E Wash-
    ington.
Manoncil John, whitewasher Penn Co, bds 88 Chicago.
Manor Alexander P, carp Frederick Weidel, res 9 Hoffman.
Mansdorfer George J, lab Horton Mnfg Co, bds 375 W Main.
Mansing Charles, laborer, res s w cor Mary and Runnion ave.
Manth Albert F W, clerk, bds 56 Buchanan.
Manth Julius G, sewing machines, 27 W Main, res 56 Bu-
    chanan.
Manuel Frank A, plumber A Hattersley & Sons, bds 192 E
    Wayne.
Manuel Jules P, clerk Isaac Lauferty, res 223 W Jefferson.
Mapel Lewis, brakeman, bds 213 W Main.
Mapes Benjamin F, laborer, res 12 E Columbia.
Maple Benjamin F, plasterer, res 14 Cedar.
Maple Charles E, machine hand Olds' Wagon Works, bds 139
    Griffith.
Maple Wm, laborer, res 139 Griffith.
Maples Birdie, bds 17 Baker.
Maples Mary (wid Lemuel), res 17 Baker.

Marahrens Charles F, lab American Wheel Co, res 36 Smith.

Marc Rosa, domestic 225 W Washington.

Marceau Delphis, harnessmaker A L Johns & Co, res s e cor Clinton and Superior.

Marchal, *see Marshall.*

Marhenke Augusta (wid Frederick), res 145 High.

Marhenke Christian, engineer, res 110 Madison.

Marhenke Christian H, clk G DeWald & Co, bds 110 Madison.

Marhenke John, carpenter, res 75 Force.

Marhenke Wm F, laborer Penn Co, res 110 Madison.

Mariotte Benjamin, clerk H Mariotte, rms 20 E Columbia.

Mariotte George, clerk H Mariotte, res 41 W Main.

Mariotte Horace, pawnbroker, 20 E Columbia, res 166 N Harrison.

Mariotte Josephine M, dressmaker Wm Malloy, bds 166 N Harrison.

Market Charles L, molder Kerr-Murray Mnfg Co, res n w cor Wallace and Gay.

Market Master's Office, Wm Ropa market master, City Hall e s Barr.

Markey Andrew J, insurance, bds 286 Broadway.

Markey Bros (Edward J and Willis J), florists, 117 W Jefferson.

Markey Edward J (Markey Bros), res 109 W Jefferson.

Markey Frederick F, fireman, bds 286 Broadway.

Markey Lawrence, res 344 Calhoun.

Markey Richard F (Markey & Mungovan), bookkeeper A C Trentman, res 414 Calhoun.

Markey Willis J (Markey Bros), bds 109 W Jefferson.

Markey & Mungovan (Richard F Markey, Franklin Mungovan), Grocers and Bakers, 256 Calhoun. Tel 81.

Markley Daniel (Markley Medicine Co), bds 176 Ewing.

Markley Medicine Co (Daniel Markley), 50 Harrison.

Marks Charles Q, brakeman, res 26 Fisher.

Marks Louis B, clk E Shuman & Sons, res 91 E Main.

Marks Maggie, domestic 29 W Lewis.

Marks Simon L, barber, 47 Maumee road, res 264 E Washington.

Marks Simon P, engine inspector Penn Co, res 264 E Washington.

Marquardt Catherine (wid John), bds 59 W Washington.

Marquardt Frederick, lab J Wilson & Sons, res 186 Hayden.

Marquardt Henry, driver Fort Wayne City Railroad Co, bds 101 Glasgow ave.

Marsh Thomas J, carpenter Frederick Kraft, res w s Metz 1 n of Wabash R R.

Marshall George, car repairer Penn Co, res Piqua road.
Marshall Peter, gardener, res n e cor Lumbard and New Haven ave.
Marshall Wesley, engineer, res 227 E Jefferson.
Martens, *see also Mertens.*
Martens Frederick W, upholsterer P E Wolf, res n e cor Liberty and Canal.
Martin Alexander A, saloon, 74 E Columbia, res same.
Martin Alice (wid Bernard), res 52 Baker.
Martin Alonzo, painter Frank Treep, bds 117 Butler.
Martin Anna M (wid Lambert), bds 206 W Washington.
Martin Anthony D, clk Penn Co, res 206 W Washington.
Martin August, laborer, res 169 N Harrison.
Martin Bernard H, wheelmkr American Wheel Co, bds 355 Lafayette.
Martin Charles, molder, bds 16 Gay.
Martin Christian, bds 225 Broadway.
Martin Daniel, res 355 Lafayette.
Martin Daniel, asst bkkpr C L Centlivre, bds 355 Lafayette.
Martin Diedrich, janitor, res 57 Wilt.
Martin D, laborer Penn Co, res cor Chestnut and Reynolds.
Martin Edward, helper Penn Co, res 307 Washington.
Martin Emma, bds 115 W Superior.
Martin Emmet, plumber, bds 359 Hanna.
Martin Eugene, messenger Penn Co, bds 359 Hanna.
Martin Frank J A, laborer, bds 169 N Harrison.
Martin Frederick, laborer, res 73 John.
Martin Henry W, car builder Penn Co, res 126 Smith.
Martin Jacob, laborer, bds 91 Montgomery.
Martin Jane (wid Francis H), res 115 W Superior.
Martin John, cook C Entemann, rms 57 E Main.
Martin John, laborer, bds 52 Baker.
Martin John C, gasfitter A Hattersley & Sons, res 103 E Main.
Martin John L, laborer, bds 169 N Harrison.
Martin Joseph L, carpenter, res 246 Erie.
Martin Joseph P, plumber P E Cox, bds 359 Hanna.
Martin J F, carpenter, bds 43½ E Columbia.
Martin Miss Lizzie M, bds 206 W Washington.
Martin Lotta, bds 11 W Jefferson.
Martin Louis E, clerk Stewart & Hahn, res 110 Chicago.
Martin Mamie, works Troy Steam Laundry, bds 36 Oak.
Martin Terrence, blacksmith Penn Co, res 359 Hanna.
Martin Victor, lab Penn Co, res s w cor Chestnut and Summer.
Martin Wilhelmina, bds 57 Wilt.
Martin Wm, helper, res 110 Chicago.

Martin Wm, house mover, res 225 Broadway.

Martin Wm, laborer American Wheel Co, bds 73 John.

Martin Wm, engineer, bds 57 Barr.

Martin Wm W, engineer, res 53 Charles.

Martline Frederick, laborer, bds 69 Stophlet.

Martz, *see also Maerz and Mertz.*

Martz Christian, Physician and Surgeon, 15 W Jefferson, res same.

Martz Susan, dressmaker, 176 W Washington, res same.

Masbaum Anton H, carpenter Penn Co, res 177 Madison.

Masbaum George G, bookkeeper Michael Baltes, res 253 E Jefferson.

Masel Martin, fireman, res 162 Hoffman.

Mason David L, fireman, res 298 Calhoun.

Mason George W, hostler, bds 298 Calhoun.

Mason Henry M, clerk Penn Co, res 203 W Jefferson.

Mason Melville A, bds 203 W Washington.

Mason Nancy (wid John F), res s e cor Williams and Clinton.

Mason Nellie, domestic 90 W Williams.

Mason Sidney A, laborer Penn Co, bds 298 Calhoun.

Masonic Hall, n w cor Calhoun and Berry.

Masonic Temple, cor Wayne and Clinton.

Massachusetts Shoe Co, S B Thing & Co Proprs, 36 Calhoun.

Mast Agnes, rms 383 E Washington.

Mast Augusta, operator S M Foster, bds 383 E Washington.

Mast Josephine, operator S M Foster, bds 383 E Washington.

Mastbaum Anthony, car builder Penn Co, res 177 Madison.

Master Builders' Association, J W Wilding Sec and Treas, 195 Calhoun.

Masterson Ellis H, watchman, res 426 E Washington.

Match, *see also Matsch.*

Match John, tank inspector Nickel Plate, res 240 W Washington.

Mathews George, laborer, bds 49 E Main.

Mathews John, shoemaker, res 49 E Main.

Mathis Eugene T, machinist Ft Wayne Electric Co, bds 391 S Hanna.

Matott Charles, conductor, res 19 Buchanan.

Matsch Catherine (wid Wm), res 82 Montgomery.

Matsch Dora, clerk G W Haiber, bds same.

Matsch J Christopher, clerk Bass Foundry and Machine Works, res 165 E Creighton ave.

Matsch Martha, tailoress Gottlieb Stauffer, bds 82 Montgomery.

Matsch Wm, helper Penn Co, res 35 Hough.

Matson Harry W, Architect, Ninde Bldg, 40 to 44 W Berry, res 318 E Wayne. (*See front cover.*)

Mattern Christian, yardmaster Hoffman Bros, res 202 Greely.

Mattes Joseph, blksmith City Carriage Works, res 59 Greene.

Matthews David, conductor, res 160 Ewing.

Matthews Henry, plumber James Madden, bds Swift House.

Matthews John (col'd), laborer, res 33 W Lewis.

Matthews Wm C, driver Fort Wayne Street Railroad Co, res 48 Oliver.

Matthews Wm S, painter City Carriage Works, bds 106 W Berry.

Matthias G, car builder Penn Co, res Walton ave.

Matthiew Joseph, section hand, res n s New Haven ave 4 w of Lumbard.

Mattiz John, watchman Penn Co, res 31 Julia.

Matzdorf Frederick, trav agt Summit City Soap Works, bds 248 Calhoun.

Maugey Ernest, laborer Penn Co, res 298 Hanna.

Maurer Gottlieb, helper Wabash R R, res 179 Oakland.

Maurer Jacob, laborer Hoffman Bros, res 621 E Washington.

Maurer Margaret (wid Ferdinand), res n s E Washington opp Wabash ave.

Maurice, *see Morris.*

Mauser Frederick, laborer, bds 46 E Columbia.

Mauthe John, teamster, res n s E Washington, bet Walton and Grant aves.

Mauthe John jr, laborer, bds n s E Washington bet Walton and Grant aves.

Mauthe Martin, fireman Jenney Electric Light and Power Co, res 5 St Mary's ave.

Mauthe Mary, bds n s E Washington bet Walton and Grant aves.

Mautner Isidor (Sam, Pete & Max), res 171 W Wayne.

Mawer Wm J, machine hand American Wheel Co, res 10 Oak.

Max Teleka (wid Francis), res 173 Wells.

Maxfield Charles W, machine hand American Wheel Co, res 206 E Lewis.

Maxfield Mrs Charlotte, bds 11 W Harrison.

Maxfield Esther, bds 206 E Lewis.

Maxfield Frederick, bds 11 N Harrison.

Maxwell Edward, machine hand, res 271 W De Wald.

Maxwell M, bds 63 Winter.

May Mary, domestic Wayne Hotel.

May Villa J, car builder Penn Co, res 71 Melita.

Maybee George, janitor Ft Wayne City Hospital.

Mayer, *see also Maier, Meier, Meyer and Myer.*

Stahn & Heinrich, **Booksellers and Stationers,**
Schmitz Block News Stand, 116 Calhoun Street.

FORT WAYNE DIRECTORY. 363

Mayer Charles H L, machinist, bds 148 Taylor.
Mayer Christian, plasterer, bds 61 Stophlet.
Mayer Clara (wid Louis), bds 203 E Washington.
Mayer Eugene, clerk J T Mayer, bds 6 Force.
Mayer George, laborer, bds 61 Stophlet.
Mayer Henry, wheel molder Bass Foundry and Machine
    Works, res 41 Gay.
Mayer Jacob T, saloon, 6 Force, res same.
Mayer Julia (wid Andrew), res 29 W Wayne.
Mayer Lawrence, res 47 E Jefferson.
Mayer Mrs Lizzie C, teacher Fort Wayne Conservatory of
    Music, rms 40 Harrison.
Mayer Sophie, bds 47 E Jefferson.
Mayer Theodore W H, plasterer, res 61 Stophlet.
Mayers Eleanor M (wid Louis), res 33 Madison.
Mayflower Mills The, Charles S Bash president, Joseph
    Hughes manager, flour and feed, 20 W Columbia.
Mayhew Allen, carpenter, bds 57 Barr.
Mayhew Mary, domestic 221 W Wayne.
Mayhew Mary E, clerk Penn Co, bds 271 W Wayne.
Mayhew Nannie, domestic 221 W Wayne.
Mayhue Lizzie, emp Indiana School for Feeble-Minded Youth.
Mayland August F, machine hand Fort Wayne Electric Co,
    bds 236 W Washington.
Mayland Henry F, laborer Louis Rastetter, bds 236 W Wash-
    ington.
Mayland Louisa, bds 236 W Washington.
Mayland Mary (wid Frederick), res 236 W Washington.
Mayland Paulina, dressmaker, bds 236 W Washington.
Mayland Sophie, housekeeper 236 W Washington.
Mayor's Office, Daniel L Harding mayor, City Hall e s Barr
    bet Berry and Wayne.
Mazrine John, bds 254 E Lewis.
Meads Zachariah (col'd), brakeman Penn Co, res 292 E Wayne.
Medawl Watson, plasterer, bds B B Wickliffe.
Medsker Isaac N, traveling agent, bds 473 Lafayette.
Medsker James R, machinist Penn Co, res 70 Baker.
Medsker John H, traveling agent, bds 75 W Lewis.
Meegan Thomas, clerk Penn Co, res 15 Douglas ave.
Meehan Charles, laborer, bds 36 Brandriff.
Meehan Fannie, tailoress L J Feist, bds 260 E Jefferson.
Meehan James, laborer, bds 36 Brandriff.
Meehan James, laborer White's Wheel Works, bds 260 E
    Jefferson.
Meehan John M, molder Bass Foundry and Machine Works,
    res 395 E Lewis.

Meehan Joseph N, molder Bass Foundry and Machine Wks, bds 260 E Jefferson.
Meehan Margaret (wid James), res 36 Brandriff.
Meehan Mary, bds 260 E Jefferson.
Meehan Mary A (wid Laurence), bds 87 E Jefferson.
Meehan Michael, res 260 E Jefferson.
Meehan Wm, laborer, bds 36 Brandriff.
Meek Wm H, laborer Clutter & Purcell, res 18 W Columbia.
Meeks U S Grant, coil winder Fort Wayne Electric Co, bds 29 Union.
Mehl, *see also Mahl.*
Mehl Amos K, teacher, res e s Spy Run ave 3 n of Riverside.
Mehl Frank W J, clerk Frank & Co, bds 95 W Superior.
Mehl George J, machinist, bds 95 W Superior.
Mehl Mary (wid John), res 95 W Superior.
Meier, *see also Maier, Mayer, Meyer and Myer.*
Meier Adolph, cabinetmaker Foster Furniture Co, res 55 Wabash ave.
Meier Diedrich, carpenter, bds 190 E Lewis.
Meier Edward H, car builder Penn Co, res 310 Harrison.
Meier Ferdinand, blacksmith, 123 Wallace, res 46 Smith.
Meier Frederick, molder Bass Foundry and Machine Works, bds 89 Maumee road.
Meier Karl, car builder Penn Co, res 149 Ewing.
Meier Leonard J, laborer, res 39 Franklin ave.
Meier Pius, stone mason, bds 230 Thomas.
Meier Wm, teamster, bds 382 E Washington.
Meierding Catherine (wid Christian), res 420 E Wayne.
Meierding Lizzie, seamstress P E Wolf, bds 420 E Wayne.
Meiers Gottlieb, laborer, res 356 Calhoun.
Meinzen August (Meinzen & Toensing), res 25 Maumee road.
Meinzen Henry, bricklayer, bds 50 Smith.
Meinzen Henry, tailor, bds 25 Maumee road.
Meinzen Henry W, clerk, bds 327 Lafayette.
Meinzen & Toensing (August Meinzen, Henry Toensing), Merchant Tailors, 227 Calhoun.
Meiser Benjamin, laborer, res 21 Wagner.
Meiser Bessie, artist M L Jones, bds 21 Wagner.
Meiser Miss Elsie, teacher, bds 21 Wagner.
Meisner Jacob, laborer Hoffman Bros, res 172 Greely.
Meister Henry, laborer, res s w cor Liberty and Canal.
Meiz Nicholas, carpenter, res 125 W De Wald.
Melching Charlotte (wid Wm), res 41 High.
Melching Wm A, Feed Yard, 20 N Harrison, res same.
Mellinger Christian, shoemaker, res 86 Lillie.
Mellinger John, helper White's Wheel Works, bds 86 Lillie.

Mellinger Joseph F, helper, bds 86 Lillie.

Mellon Jennie, domestic 320 Calhoun.

Melsheimer Henry G, tinner J H Welch, bds Washington House.

Melsheimer Louis, printer, res 206 E Washington..

Melshcimer Martha, bds 207 W Berry.

Melsheimer Matilda (wid John M), bds 240 W Washington.

Melsheimer Phaphat D, mngr American Farmer, res 328 E Wayne.

Melzer Henry, barber, bds 24 Erie.

Melzer Herman, lab Salimonie Mining & Gas Co, res 24 Erie.

Mendenhall Isaac, machine hand Fort Wayne Furniture Co, res 107 Lafayette.

Mendenhall Lotta, bds 107 Lafayette.

Mender Gottfried, harnessmaker A L Johns & Co, res 249 E Washington.

Menebracker Matilda (wid Henry), res 195 W Superior.

Menefee Charles M, molder Bass Foundry and Machine Works, res 202 Thomas.

Mengels Mary (wid Claus), res 63 Maumee road.

Mennewisch Edward, helper Penn Co, res 160 Holman.

Mennewisch Frederick, car builder Penn Co, res 168 Francis.

Mennewisch Frederick W, machinist Penn Co, res 37 Hough.

Mennewisch Henry, blacksmith Bass Foundry and Machine Works, res 289 Hanna.

Mennewisch Henry, driver Charles Schwier & Son, bds 59 Gay.

Mennewisch Henry A, laborer Penn Co, res 65 Oliver.

Menning, *see Manning*.

Mensch Frank P, Grocer, 23 W Columbia, res 164 Wells.

Mensch Henry S, res 43 W DeWald.

Mensing Charles, laborer J C Peters, res n w cor Runnion ave and Mary.

Mensing Sophie C, domestic, 205 W Berry.

Menze Charles H, cigarmaker, bds 338 E Washington.

Menze Frederick, coremaker Bass Foundry and Machine Works, res 108 Eliza.

Menze Minnie, tailoress John Rabus, bds 338 E Washington.

Menze Wm C, tailor John Rabus, res 338 E Washington.

Merchants' Despatch Transportation Co, Wm V Douglass agt, 3 Schmidt block.

Mergel Martin, bds 324 Calhoun.

Mergel Reinhard, cigars, 17½ W Main, res 324 S Calhoun.

Mergel Reinhard T, clerk, res 244 W Washington.

Mergentheim Alexander, milliner, 38 Calhoun, res 84 W Washington.

Mergott Adolph, bds 38 Hough.
Mergott Mrs Minnie, res 38 Hough.
Merillat Joseph P, clerk Coverdale & Archer, res 62 N Harrison.
Merillet Emily, bds 63 Boone.
Merillet John, laborer, res 63 Boone.
Meriwether James R, clerk Penn Co, res 76 Lafayette.
Merlet Matthew, laborer White's Wheel Works, res 239 E Washington.
Merneiser Christian, clerk John Suelzer, bds 287 Hanna.
Merrell Mrs Ellen D, music teacher, 26 Chute, res same.
Merrell Frank R, printer, res 26 Chute.
Merriam Ann J (wid Cyrenus), res 174 E Creighton ave.
Merriett Charles F, engineer, res 234 W Main.
Merrifield Kate, domestic 60 W DeWald.
Merritt Della, bds 55 E Main.
Merry Elizabeth, dressmaker, bds 65 W Superior.
Merry Ida, dressmaker, bds 65 W Superior.
Merry Wm, painter, res 65 W Superior.
Mertens Frederick, tailor J G Thieme & Son, res cor Canal and Liberty.
Mertz, see *Maerz, Martz and Merz.*
Merz Albert, tinner J H Welch, res 41 Pine.
Merz D, car builder Penn Co, res 196 E Lewis.
Merz George, laborer, res 3 Short.
Merz Joseph, res 25 Pine.
Merz Lizzie, bds 196 E Lewis.
Merz Louis (Zoeller & Merz), res 25 W DeWald.
Merz Matilda, bds 196 E Lewis.
Merz Nicholas, car builder Penn Co, res 125 W DeWald.
Merz Peter, car builder Penn Co, res 196 E Lewis.
Merz Theodore, bartender Zoeller & Merz, res 37 Pine.
Messerschmidt John, res 149 Hayden.
Messerschmidt J Martin, wheel molder Bass Foundry and Machine Works, res 106 Francis.
Messerschmidt Wm, baker L P Scherer, bds 157 Hayden.
Messmann Rev Anthony, pastor St Peter's German Catholic Church, res s e cor Warsaw and DeWald.
Messmann Miss Catherine, bds Rev Anthony Messmann.
Metcalf Samuel C, physician, 10 Calhoun, res 109 W Superior.
Metcalf Samuel S, brakeman Penn Co, bds 128 E Lewis.
Metcalfe John, engineer, res 55 Force.
Metker Barnard, stone mason, res 70 Leith.
Metker Emma, operator Hoosier Mnfg Co, bds 357 E Washington.
Metker John, carriage painter M L Albrecht, bds 72 Lee.

Metker Joseph, bds Wm Hazard.

Metker Joseph, plasterer, res 357 E Washington.

Metley Elizabeth, works Troy Steam Laundry, bds 37 Barr.

Metley George F, molder Bass Foundry and Machine Works, bds 37 Barr.

Metropolitan Mnfg Co, Harry B Ridgley mngr, 19 W Wayne.

Metsker Allen W, truckman Wabash R R, res 243 S Webster.

Metting Wm C, driver Ft Wayne Street Ry Co, res 55 Melita.

Mettler Bernhard, cigarmaker Christian Wenninghoff, bds w s Spy Run ave 7 n of St Mary's bridge.

Mettler John, clerk, bds Peter Mettler.

Mettler Joseph, machine hand, bds 16 Locust.

Mettler Katie, operator S M Foster, bds 261 E Wayne.

Mettler Mathias, cabinetmaker Fort Wayne Furniture Co, res 127 Francis.

Mettler Peter, carpenter res w s Spy Run ave 2 s of Ruth.

Mettler Peter J, bartender M N Webber, res 146 E Jefferson.

Metty Mrs Elizabeth, wks Troy Steam Laundry, res 37 Barr.

Metzger Elizabeth (wid Andrew), bds 40 Brackenridge.

Metzger Harry M, clerk, bds 40 Brackenridge.

Metzler Charles J, baker L E Berthold, bds 37 W Berry.

Metzler Leo, tailor L J Feist, res 81 Holman.

Metzner Jasper, conductor, res 358 Hanna.

Metzzer Emma, bds John Metzzer.

Metzzer John, laborer, res w s Walton ave 1 s of Wabash R R.

Meyer, *see also Maier, Mayer, Meier and Myer.*

Meyer Adolph, tailor, 54 W Wayne, res same.

Meyer Anna M (wid John M), bds 443 E Wayne.

Meyer Anthony G, laborer American Wheel Co, bds 94 Buchanan.

Meyer Bertha, bds 54 W Wayne.

Meyer Bros & Co (Christian F G and John F W Meyer), Druggists and Proprietors Prickly Ash Bitters, 2 and 9 Keystone Block, s w cor Calhoun and Columbia. (*See adv, p 59.*)

Meyer Bruno, molder Bass Foundry and Machine Works, res 127 Gay.

Meyer Caroline R, domestic 61 Maumee rd.

Meyer Charles, bartender, bds 45 W Washington.

Meyer Charles, laborer, res 71 Wilt.

Meyer Charles, painter, bds 127 Gay.

Meyer Charles F, machinist Penn Co, res 338 Force.

Meyer Charles F W, Director Fort Wayne Conservatory of Music, res s s Pontiac 3 e of Hoagland ave.

Meyer Charles W, grocer, n w cor W Creighton ave and Miner, bds 76 W Washington.

Meyer Christian F G (Meyer Bros & Co), res St Louis, Mo.
Meyer Conrad, laborer Fort Wayne Electric Co, res 84 Wall.
Meyer Diedrich J, res 22 W Wayne.
Meyer Emma, bds 127 Gay.
Meyer Ernst, clerk, res 36 Hood.
Meyer Ernst C, res 91 Force.
Meyer Ernst H, carpenter, res 310 S Harrison.
Meyer Frank H, res 76 W Washington.
Meyer Frank J C, gunsmith M G Lade, res 142 Erie.
Meyer Frederick, blacksmith, bds 50 Smith.
Meyer Frederick, boilermkr Penn Co, res 5 Summit.
Meyer Frederick, helper Penn Co, res 62 Hugh.
Meyer Frederick, helper Penn Co, bds 213 Fairfield ave.
Meyer Frederick, laborer, res 88 Gay.
Meyer Frederick H, saloon, 104 Calhoun, res same.
Meyer F Wm, instrument maker Fort Wayne Electric Co,
    bds 338 Force.
Meyer George, laborer, res 39 Wells.
Meyer George M, molder Bass Foundry and Machine Works,
    res 254 E Washington.
Meyer Gustav, porter Hamilton homestead.
Meyer Miss Hannah, stenographer Pottlitzer Bros, bds 54
    W Wayne.
Meyer Henry, bds 76 W Washington.
Meyer Henry, cigars and tobacco, 88½ Barr, res same.
Meyer Henry, res 183 E Lewis.
Meyer Henry helper, res 41 Gay.
Meyer Henry, tailor John Rabus, bds 49 Hugh.
Meyer Henry, whitewasher, res 200 E Lewis.
Meyer Henry C, tailor, 44 Harrison, res 281 W Washington.
Meyer Henry J (Wm Meyer & Bro), res 37 Madison.
Meyer Henry jr, bookkeeper Wm Meyer & Bro, res Madison
    2 w of Lafayette.
Meyer Henry W, draughtsman Penn Co, bds 18 Oak.
Meyer Henry W, foreman Bass Foundry and Machine
    Works, res 18 Oak.
Meyer Jacob, clerk Pottlitzer Bros, bds 54 W Wayne.
Meyer John, bds 76 W Washington.
Meyer John, driver C L Centlivre, res w s Leo rd 3 n of
    canal feeder.
Meyer John, laborer Weil Bros & Co, bds 64 E Berry.
Meyer John F W (Meyer Bros & Co), res 8 S Fairfield ave.
Meyer John H, stone mason, res 519 E Lewis.
Meyer John H, contractor, res 138 Harrison.
Meyer J Henry, packer Meyer Bros & Co, res 100 Harrison.
Meyer Lena, domestic 42 Stophlet.

Meyer Lizzie, bds 129 E Lewis.
Meyer Louis G, sawyer David Tagtmeyer, res 76 N Harrison.
Meyer Martin, laborer Ranke & Yergens, res 119 E Washington.
Meyer Mary (wid Ernest), bds 51 Maumee rd.
Meyer Matilda, domestic 241 W Jefferson.
Meyer Miss Minnie, bds 76 W Washington.
Meyer Minnie (wid Arndt), bds 36 Hood.
Meyer Otto C, clk A W Miller & Co, bds 254 E Washington.
Meyer Ray, clerk Frank & Co, bds 54 W Wayne.
Meyer Robert, clerk J G Thieme & Son, bds 53 E Wayne.
Meyer Wessel, bds 323 Hanna.
Meyer Wm (Wm Meyer & Bros), res 100 Harrison.
Meyer Wm, bds 395 Hanna.
Meyer Wm, boilermaker, bds 183 E Lewis.
Meyer Wm, mach Indiana Machine Works, bds 396 E Wayne.
Meyer Wm, laborer, res 28 Union.
Meyer Wm C, blksmith Olds' Wagon Works, bds 56 Charles.
Meyer Wm D, Groceries, Provisions, Wines and Liquors, 227 Lafayette, res 129 E Lewis.
Meyer Wm F (Meyer & Niemann), res 91 Wilt.
Meyer Wm H, clerk L S & M S Ry, bds 127 Gay.
Meyer Wm H C, tailor, res 396 E Wayne.
Meyer William & Bro (Wm and Henry J), gents' furnishing goods and hats, 34 Calhoun.
Meyer & Niemann (Wm F Meyer, Gottlieb Niemann jr), gents' furnishing goods, 142 Calhoun.
Meyerhoefer Henry, tinner, bds 164 Broadway.
Meyerhoffer John, filer, res 180 Greely.
Meyers, see also Myers.
Meyers Anna, domestic 21 W Creighton ave.
Meyers Bernard, laborer A McKernan, res New Haven road 1½ miles e of city limits.
Meyers Catherine (wid Frederick C), res 24 McClellan.
Meyers Charles F F, clk Root & Co, res 45 W Washington.
Meyers Christina, domestic 142 E Wayne.
Meyers Edward, laborer A McKernan, bds Wm A Smith.
Meyers Ernest, clerk Wm Moellering & Sons, res 36 Hood.
Meyers Ethel, bds 45 W Washington.
Meyers E L, laborer Penn Co, res 29 Hough.
Meyers Frederick, laborer, bds 52 John.
Meyers Frederick G, clk Henry Dicke, res 241 Madison.
Meyers George, cigarmaker, res 354 Broadway.
Meyers George L, wood turner Horton Mnfg Co, bds 165 Ewing.
Meyers Henry F, laborer Penn Co, res 132 Force.

John Pressler, Mantels, Grates and Tile Floor.
Columbia, Barr and Dock Streets.

370   R. L. POLK & CO.'S

Meyers Henry F, carriage trimmer M L Albrecht, bds 76 W
     Washington.
Meyers J Henry (H A Grotholtman & Co), res 138 Harrison.
Meyers Kate, domestic George DeWald.
Meyers Leander H, res s s Riverside ave 6 e of Spy Run av.
Meyers Lulu, bds 45 W Washington.
Meyers Maggie, seamstress, bds 8 Clark.
Meyers Margaret (wid Ferdinand), res 165 Ewing.
Meyers Wilhelmina (wid Christian), res 47 W Washington.
Meyne John H, hostler Ft Wayne Street Railroad Co, bds
     290 Calhoun.
Michael Daniel W, laborer, res 132 Wells.
Michael Frederick, saloon, 20 Clinton, res same.
Michael George, wagonmaker, res 517 E Lewis.
Michael George jr, machine hand, bds 517 E Lewis.
Michael Herman, clerk Meyer Bros & Co, bds Herman P
     Michael.
Michael Herman P, real est, 19 Court, res over Gazette office.
Michael John C, carpenter, bds H A Philley.
Michaelis Charles D, cigarmkr J Lohman & Co, bds 297 W
     Jefferson.
Michaelis Charles J, clerk E Shuman & Sons, res 297 W Jef-
     ferson.
Michaelis Herman, feeder Fort Wayne Sentinel, bds 297 W
     Jefferson.
Michel, *see also Mitchell.*
Michel Adam, laborer, res 48 Taylor.
Michel Andrew, printer, res 404 E Wayne.
Michel Andrew J, printer Indiana Staats Zeitung, bds 404 E
     Wayne.
Michel Charles J, bookkeeper J B White, bds 130 N Cass.
Michel Frank J, cooper, res 130 N Cass.
Michel Frederick, machinist Indiana Machine Works, bds 130
     N Cass.
Michel George, laborer, res 23 Walnut.
Michel George, wagonmaker A Vogely, res 517 E Lewis.
Michel George H, mach hand Winch & Son, res 517 E Lewis.
Michel John, laborer, bds 130 N Cass.
Michel Joseph, mach Indiana Machine Wks, bds 130 N Cass.
Michel Maggie, trimmer Eleanor Kratzch, bds 517 E Lewis.
Michel Wm, section hand, res 13 Pape.
Mick Abraham C, conductor, res 62 Greene.
Mick Tillie, bds 69 Smith.
Mick Wm, switchman, res 69 Smith.
Middendorf Bernard, contractor, res 276 E Wayne.
Middendorf Herman, mason, bds 276 E Wayne.

Middleton George W, carpenter, res 36 Buchanan.
Middleton Matilda, domestic 138 Shawnee ave.
Miedhammer George, machinist Fort Wayne Electric Co, res 35 Melita.
Mienzen Sophie, bds Wm Mienzen.
Mienzen Wm, supt Concordia Cemetery, res same.
Mienzen Wm jr, bds Wm Mienzen.
Mier Charles, carpenter, res 149 Ewing.
Mier Christina (wid Bernard), bds 20 W Jefferson.
Mier John, candymaker, bds 49 Hugh.
Miers Lotta, boxmaker W H Davis, bds s s Superior e of Wells.
Miles Arthur, laborer, res n s Huron 2 w of Cherry.
Miles Miss Carolina, bds 221 W Washington.
Miles Charles, engineer, res 221 W Washington.
Miles David, laborer, res 105 Wells.
Miles John, fireman, bds 221 W Washington.
Miles Miss Lydia C, teacher, bds 221 W Washington.
Miles Mary H, bds 221 W Washington.
Miles Wm B, laborer, bds 105 Wells.
Milledge Corrilda, domestic 278 W Berry.
Millenbruck Henry, res 148 Greely.
Miller, *see also Moeller, Mueller and Muller.*
Miller Abraham C, conductor Penn Co, res 165 Van Buren.
Miller Albert F, carpenter, res 337 Hanna.
Miller Albert T, machinist, bds 169 E Washington.
Miller Albert W, conductor, res 165 Van Buren.
Miller Alfred, res 14 Huron.
Miller Alois, foreman Weil Bros & Co, res 557 Hanna.
Miller Alvin L, machine hand American Wheel Co, bds Hyer House.
Miller Amelia, bds 38 Hendricks.
Miller Amos A, laborer Winch & Son, bds Wm Hale.
Miller Andrew E, fireman, res 39 Pine.
Miller Andrew W (A W Miller & Co), res 170 Montgomery.
Miller Anna M, bds 222 W Creighton ave.
Miller Annie, bds 65 Boone.
Miller Anthony A P, student, bds 342 Hanna.
Miller Asenath (wid Wm F), bds e s Miner 6 n of De Wald.
Miller August, carpenter, bds 64 E Berry.
Miller August, gunsmith C H Miller, res s s Riverside 1 e of Spy Run ave.
Miller A W & Co (Andrew W and James E Miller), druggists, 210 Calhoun.
Miller Benjamin F, bds 50 W Main.
Miller Miss Bertha, bds 161 Harmer.

Miller Block, w s Clinton bet Berry and Main.
Miller Calvin, laborer Fort Wayne Artificial Ice Co, bds
    Racine House.
Miller Carl L, student, bds 125 N Cass.
Miller Caspar, trav agent G E Bursley & Co, res 161 Harmer.
Miller Cassius A, clerk J M Miller, res 103 E Washington.
Miller Catherine (wid John J), res 81 E Washington.
Miller Charles, fireman, res 86 Laselle.
Miller Charles, helper Bass Foundry and Machine Works, bds
    28 Brandriff.
Miller Charles, painter, res 15 Hamilton.
Miller Charles, patternmaker Bass Foundry and Machine
    Works, res 59 Charles.
Miller Charles, pedler, res 122 Maumee road.
Miller Charles A, clerk James Madden, bds Aldine Hotel.
Miller Charles C, clerk, bds 169 E Washington.
Miller Charles H, guns, 20 W Main, res 50 same.
Miller Charles L, bookkeeper Adams & Armstrong, res 51
    Douglas ave.
Miller Charles L, engineer, res 126 N Cass.
Miller Charles O, machine hand Louis Diether & Bro, bds 513
    Broadway.
Miller Charlotte H, grocer, s w cor E Lewis and Walton ave,
    res same.
Miller Chauncy O, finisher Fort Wayne Organ Co, res 23
    Miner.
Miller Christian, horseshoer Geary & Perrey, bds 28 Brandriff.
Miller Christian, laborer, res 66 Chicago.
Miller Christian, saloon, res 63 Wells.
Miller Christian H, foreman Bass Foundry and Machine
    Works, res 9 Force.
Miller Christina, bds 122 Maumee road.
Miller Christopher H, car repairer Penn Co, res 55 Williams.
Miller Clara (wid Jacob), artist, res 100 W Main.
Miller Clark, butcher, bds 100 W Main.
Miller Claude C, asst revenue collector, res 101 Lafayette.
Miller Clement E, clerk J B White, bds 38 Hendricks.
Miller Conrad, laborer, res 38 Watkins.
Miller Conrad, packer F Eckart, bds George Jacobs.
Miller Cyrus E, laborer, res 25 Lincoln ave.
Miller Cyrus S, laborer Wabash R R, bds 222 W Creighton.
Miller Cyrus W, res s s Killea 1 w of Calhoun.
Miller Mrs C C, dressmaker, res 101 Lafayette.
Miller Daniel B, carpenter, bds 49 W Main.
Miller Daniel M (Miller & Moritz), res Aveline House.
Miller David E, laborer, res 408 W Main.

Miller D Nathan C, fireman, res 108 Fairfield ave.
Miller Edward, prntr Ft Wayne Gazette, bds Windsor Hotel.
Miller Edward D, bookkeeper Robert Ogden, bds 251 E
Washington.
Miller Edwin W, grocer, 2 Lincoln ave, res 16 same.
Miller Effie, bds 124 E Berry.
Miller Eliza, bds 28 Brandriff.
Miller Eliza (wid Henry D), bds Charles Josse.
Miller Emil, bds 169 E Washington.
Miller Miss Emma, bds 83 Monroe.
Miller Emma, bds 54 Elm.
Miller Ernest, boilermaker, res 51 W Williams.
Miller Ernst F, clerk, bds 21 N Calhoun.
Miller Erwin, shipping clerk McDonald, Watt & Wilt, res 81
E Washington.
Miller Esther (wid James B), bds 22 Scott ave.
Miller Ethan A, teamster, bds C W Miller.
Miller Miss Flora E, stenographer Strack & Angell, bds 68
W Jefferson.
Miller Frank, blacksmith, res 383 Lafayette.
Miller Frank, carpenter, res 69 E DeWald.
Miller Frank, driver Joseph Fremion, bds same.
Miller Frank, laborer, bds 290 Calhoun.
Miller Frank, plumber James Madden, bds St Joseph Hos-
pital.
Miller Frank H, helper M L Albrecht, bds 54 Elm.
Miller Franklin M, res 796 Broadway.
Miller Franz, laborer, bds 103 Erie.
Miller Frederick, carpenter, 8 Summit, res same.
Miller Frederick, carpenter Fort Wayne Electric Co, res 107
Jackson.
Miller Frederick, laborer, bds 66 Chicago.
Miller Frederick, laborer Bass Foundry and Machine Works,
res 5 Force.
Miller Frederick C, bricklayer, bds 8 Summit.
Miller Frederick C, engineer The Herman Berghoff Brewing
Co, res 424 E Washington.
Miller Frederick E, candy maker Louis Fox & Bro, bds 21 N
Calhoun.
Miller Frederick J, druggist, 327 Lafayette, res same.
Miller Frederick M, asst cashier Penn Co, res 111 Taylor.
Miller Frederick N, clerk J B White, bds 9 Force.
Miller Frederick R, helper Penn Co, bds 383 Lafayette.
Miller George, brakeman Penn Co, res 15 Hood.
Miller George, clerk Markey & Mungovan, res s w cor E
Lewis and Walton ave.

Miller George, coil winder Fort Wayne Electric Co, res 15 Rockhill.

Miller George, roofer, bds 28 Brandriff.

Miller George A, engineer, res 185 Montgomery.

Miller George E, bds 182 E Washington.

Miller George F, flue welder Penn Co, res 18 Marion.

Miller George F, patternmaker Bass Foundry and Machine Works, res 67 Force.

Miller George S, clerk Massachusetts Shoe Co, res 48 Harmer.

Miller Gilbert C, grocer, 230 W Main, res same.

Miller Gilbert S, laborer Penn Co, res 103 Broadway.

Miller G Theodore, machinist Wabash R R, bds Wm F Miller.

Miller Harvey D, laborer, res 122 Fairfield ave.

Miller Hattie (wid Daniel E), res 87 Ewing.

Miller Henry, cabinetmaker Fort Wayne Organ Co, res s e cor Fairfield ave and Organ.

Miller Henry, machinist Penn Co, res 20 Marion.

Miller Henry C, res 621 Fairfield ave.

Miller Henry C, grainer, rms 82 Baker.

Miller Henry D, carriagemkr, bds 273 E Jefferson.

Miller Henry D, pressman Fort Wayne News, res 145 Broadway.

Miller Henry J, asst treas Fort Wayne Electric Co, res 57 Douglas ave.

Miller Henry J, trav agt Coombs & Co, res 36 E DeWald.

Miller Henry M, painter, res e s Calhoun 2 s of Marchell.

Miller Herman, laborer, res 21 N Calhoun.

Miller Herman F W, brick mason, res 416 Hanna.

Miller Herman J, clerk J B White, bds 296 E Washington.

Miller Isaac, grocer, 406 Calhoun, res same.

Miller Jacob J, truss hoopmkr S D Bitler, res 403 E Wayne.

Miller James, clerk J B White, res Howell, Rockhill's add.

Miller James, laborer, res s s Howell nr Runnion ave.

Miller James, rivet driver American Wheel Co, bds 315 Hanna.

Miller James E (A W Miller & Co), physician, 210 Calhoun, res same.

Miller James N F, clerk, bds 9 Force.

Miller John, blacksmith helper Penn Co, bds 51 W Williams.

Miller John jr, brakeman, res 31 Bass.

Miller John, cigarmkr John Gronendyke, bds 28 Brandriff.

Miller John, clerk, bds 63 Wells.

Miller John, laborer, res s s Howell nr Runnion ave.

Miller John, laborer S D Bitler, bds 408 E Wayne.

Miller John, teamster, res 22 W 3d.

MILLINERY GOODS — LATEST STYLES — **MRS. E. A. FLAGLER,** 14 W. BERRY STREET.

FORT WAYNE DIRECTORY. 375

Miller John, teamster, res 29 Bass.
Miller John A, res 222 W Creighton ave.
Miller John A, laborer, res 5 Sturgis.
Miller John A, laborer, res 12 Lafayette.
Miller John E, carpenter, res 65 Winter.
Miller John E, trav agt, res 22 Scott ave.
Miller John H, carpenter, res n s New Haven ave 2 e of Lumbard.
Miller John H, contractor, res 106 Fairfield ave.
Miller John H, machinist, res 20 Marion.
Miller John H, teamster, res 54 Elm.
Miller John M (Beaver, Miller & Co), Fine Furniture, 50 and 52 E Main, res 52 E Jefferson.
Miller John S, foreman Louis Diether & Bro, res 418 Broadway.
Miller Joseph, laborer, res 43 Nirdlinger ave.
Miller Joseph A, boarding house, 49 W Main.
Miller Joseph F, fireman Wabash R R, res 20 W Creighton.
Miller Joseph F, trav agt Louis Fox & Bro, res 38 Hendricks.
Miller Joseph L, engineer, res 105 Wilt.
Miller Julia (wid Wm H), res 68 W Jefferson.
Miller Julius L, meat market, 109 Maumee road, res 122 same.
Miller J Wm, painter, res 160 Greely.
Miller Laura J, clk Isaac Miller, bds 406 Calhoun.
Miller Lee, bridge builder, bds 35 Douglas ave.
Miller Lena, bds 122 Maumee road.
Miller Levi H, plasterer, res 10 Marion.
Miller Levi H jr, laborer, bds 10 Marion.
Miller Lizzie, bds 182 E Washington.
Miller Lorenzo D, clerk, bds 10 Marion.
Miller Lorin, laborer, bds 199 Broadway.
Miller Louis, laborer White's Wheel Works, bds 65 Winter.
Miller Louis, boilermaker, bds 51 W Williams.
Miller Louis C, brakeman Penn Co, bds 66 Chicago.
Miller Louis J, molder Kerr-Murray Mnfg Co, res 70 W Williams.
Miller Louis L, lab White's Wheel Works, res 63 Hayden.
Miller Louis L, machinist Penn Co, res 20 Marion.
Miller Louise M (wid Samuel), res s w cor Erie and Begue.
Miller Miss Louise J, music teacher, 145 Broadway, res same.
Miller Mary, bds 111 Wilt.
Miller Mary, bds 169 E Washington.
Miller Mary, domestic 340 W Washington.
Miller Mary L, bds 20 Marion.
Miller Mathias A, boilermkr e s Barr 1 n of E Superior, res 274 E Lewis.

Miller Matilda (wid Samuel), res 251 E Washington.
Miller Michael, laborer, res 224 W Washington.
Miller M, car repairer Penn Co, res 53 Hugh.
Miller Nathaniel C (Miller & Dougall), res 273 E Jefferson.
Miller Nicholas, car repairer Penn Co, res 296 E Washington.
Miller Nicholas, teamster J E Remus, bds 442 S Broadway.
Miller Ollis, foreman, res 507 Hanna.
Miller Oscar, supt B L Auger, bds 16 E Washington.
Miller Otto, machine hand American Wheel Co, bds 507
     Hanna.
Miller Paul, teamster, res e s Winter 1 s of Pontiac.
Miller Peter, res 28 Brandriff.
Miller Philip, helper Penn Co, res 3 Duryea.
Miller Rachel, seamstress E C Smith, bds 96 Ewing.
Miller Robert E, bds 49 W Main.
Miller Robert F, conductor, rms 323 W Main.
Miller Rosa, domestic Wayne Hotel.
Miller Rowland M, waiter Edwin Rich, bds 16 W Main.
Miller Samuel, brakeman, res 40 Hough.
Miller Samuel D, solicitor F X Schuhler, res 102 N Harrison.
Miller Seraphine C, carpenter Penn Co, res 139 John.
Miller Silas E, carpenter, res 43 Shawnee ave.
Miller Simon, painter, bds 160 Greely.
Miller Sophia, convertor worker Fort Wayne Electric Co, bds
     21 N Calhoun.
Miller Sophia M (wid Wm), res 305 Calhoun.
Miller Theodore, bds 315 Hanna.
Miller Theodore N, tinner, res 64 Wall.
Miller Urban U, tinner, bds 101 Lafayette.
Miller Walter D, foreman Nickel Plate round house, res 70
     W Main.
Miller Wm (Bottenberg & Miller), res Washington turnpike.
Miller Wm, bartender Hartman & Bro, bds 63 E Wayne.
Miller Wm, boilermaker, bds 274 E Lewis.
Miller Wm, Brick Mnfr, e s Hanna s of city limits, res
     same.
Miller Wm, carpenter, res 89 W Jefferson.
Miller Wm, gardener School for Feeble-Minded, res n s St
     Joe road 1 n of St Joe bridge.
Miller Wm, laborer, bds 43½ E Columbia.
Miller Wm, laborer Penn Co, res 81 Force.
Miller William, Real Estate and Loans, District Land
     and Emigration Agent, 5 W Main, res 169 E Washington.
Miller Wm F, res s s Columbia bet Lafayette and Clay.
Miller Wm F, finisher Ft Wayne Organ Co, res 85 Shawnee.
Miller Wm G, bartender Ulrich Stotz, bds 23 E Main.

Miller Wm G, carp Fort Wayne Electric Co, res 29 Wall.
Miller Wm L, meat market, 228 W Main, res same.
Miller Wm M, boilermaker M A Miller, bds 274 E Lewis.
Miller & Dougall (Nathaniel C Miller, Allan H Dougall),
    lawyers, real estate and insurance, 4 Foster block.
Miller & Moritz (Daniel M Miller, John M Moritz),
    Proprs Aveline House, s e cor Calhoun and E Berry.
Millet Wm C, varnish mnfr, 149 Barr, bds same.
Millholen Henry, cigarmaker C A Berndt, res 176 E Lewis.
Millhouse Charles, porter G E Bursley & Co, res 54 John.
Millhouse Samuel, bridge carpenter, res 54 John.
Millikin Thomas R, agent, rms 58 W Berry.
Mills Arthur A, finisher American Wheel Co, res 73 Home ave.
Mills Bella M, organist, bds 63 Brackenridge.
Mills Bluford A, wheelmaker American Wheel Co, res n s
    Prospect ave near Spy Run ave.
Mills Charles J, bds 678 Broadway.
Mills Elizabeth, dressmaker, bds 678 Broadway.
Mills George, machinist Fort Wayne Iron Works, bds 95 W
    Superior.
Mills Horatio T, machinist Penn Co, res 63 Brackenridge.
Mills Joseph L, machinist Wabash R R, bds 35 Fox.
Mills Katie, domestic, 330 W Washington.
Mills Maggie, domestic, 9 E Wayne.
Mills Mary A, dressmaker, bds 678 Broadway.
Mills Mary B, bds 35 Shawnee ave.
Mills Percival E, car builder Penn Co, res 343 E Jefferson.
Mills Samuel, porter Aveline House.
Mills Theodore H, painter L O Hull, res 95 Riverside ave.
Mills Thomas, machinist Wabash R R, res 35 Shawnee ave.
Mills Wm, machinist Fort Wayne Electric Co, res 678 S
    Broadway.
Mills Wm G, wheel inspector American Wheel Co, res w s S
    Walton near city limits.
Millspaugh Miss Helen G, teacher Westminster Seminary,
    bds 251 W Main.
Mimpy David, machine hand Olds' Wagon Wks, res 67 John.
Minark Louis J, bookkeeper The Press, bds 107 E Main.
Mincer A A, car painter Penn Co, res 110 Superior.
Minder Gottfried, harnessmaker, res 39 E Superior.
Mine Henry, bds 290 Calhoun.
Miner Block, n e cor Clinton and Wayne.
Miner Eli, teamster, res 228 Lafayette.
Miner Miss Etta, bds 62 Douglas ave.
Miner George E (Wm E and George E Miner), bds 62 Doug-
    las ave.

Miner John J, engineer Troy Steam Laundry, res 123 Harrison.
Miner Miss Leonora, bds 62 Douglas ave.
Miner Michael, car repairer Ft W, C & L Ry, bds 50 W 4th.
Miner Sarah (wid Byron B), res 62 Douglas ave.
Miner Samuel R, barber, 311½ W Main, res 313 same.
Miner Wm E (Wm E & George E Miner), Dealer in Flour, Feed, Hay, Straw, Oats, etc, 45 E Columbia, res High nr City Limits. Telephone 253.
Miner Wm E & George E, real estate and insurance, 45 E Columbia.
Mingot Adrien, hostler, bds 22 E Columbia.
Minick Frank E, helper Penn Co, res 389 E Lewis.
Minneker Henry J, blacksmith Olds' Wagon Works, res 80 Montgomery.
Minnerley Joseph M, laborer, res 100 E Columbia.
Minnich Harry F, painter F W Robinson, bds Philip Minnich.
Minnich James W, ticket agent L S & M S Ry, res 72 Douglas ave.
Minnich Philip, car builder Penn Co, res 208 Hanna.
Minnich Philip J, laborer, res 115 Barthold.
Minnick Frank E, laborer, res 389 E Lewis.
Minnix Frank J, machinist Penn Co, res 10 Holman.
Minot Jane (wid Samuel), bds 341 E Wayne.
Minser Edward, machine hand Hoffman Bros, bds 175 W Superior.
Minser George W, teamster Hoffman Bros, res 175 W Superior.
Minser Lawrence, painter, res n w cor Superior and Van Buren.
Minser Mitchel, painter A Vogely, bds 175 W Superior.
Minskey Samuel, traveling agent, res 290 E Wayne.
Mintch Martin, confectioner, 172 Calhoun, res same.
Mischo Catherine (wid Nicholas), res 33 Pritchard.
Mischo Catherine (wid Michael), res 158 Broadway.
Mischo Elizabeth, dressmaker, bds 158 Broadway.
Mischo John A, machine hand Fort Wayne Electric Co, bds 33 Pritchard.
Mischo Kate, dressmaker, 33 Pritchard, bds same.
Mischo Mary, dressmaker, bds 158 Broadway.
Mischo Minnie, bds 33 Pritchard.
Miser Miss Rilla, res 114 Calhoun.
Misner Annie (wid Seymour D), res n w cor Julia and Holton ave.
Misner Clarence E, fireman, bds 311 Lafayette.
Misner George W, painter, res 39 E Williams.
Misner James A, engineer, res 311 Lafayette.

Stahn & Heinrich, Leading Dealers in ARTISTS' MATE-RIALS AND DRAUGHTING INSTRU-MENTS. 116 Calhoun Street.

FORT WAYNE DIRECTORY. 379

Misting Charles, hostler, 198 W Wayne.

Mitchel, *see also Michel.*

Mitchel James, propr Fort Wayne Dispatch, 24 Clinton, res same.

Mitchell Miss Elizabeth B, teacher Hoagland School, bds 313 Calhoun.

Mitchell Harry J, city mngr Singer Mnfg Co, bds 59 E Wayne.

Mitchell James W, laborer, res 209 W Superior.

Mitchell John C, file cutter, res 140 Lafayette.

Mitchell Lydia F, domestic 235 W Jefferson.

Mitchell Walter J, hostler Hoffman Bros, res 209 Greely.

Mitchell Wm, engineer, res 186 Montgomery.

Mitchell Wm G, machinist E B Kunkle & Co, bds 46 W Wayne.

Mittendorf, *see also Middendorf.*

Mittendorf Herman, lab C L Centlivre, bds Albert Eckerle.

Mix Moritz, stonecutter Fort Wayne Steam Stone Works, res 2 Elm.

Mock John, brakeman Penn Co, bds 51 Hendricks.

Model Steam Laundry, Harr & Zimmerly Proprs, cor Superior and Wells. (*See right side lines.*)

Moderwell Hiram C, freight agent Nickel Plate R R, res 93 W Wayne.

Moderwell Jay M, coal, Plum nr Wells street bridge, res 53 W Superior.

Moeller, *see also Miller, Mueller and Muller.*

Moeller Christian, carpenter, res 239 Madison.

Moeller Frederick, teamster, bds 239 Madison.

Moellering Anna, bds 120 Montgomery.

Moellering August H F, tailor Thieme Bros, bds 33 Madison.

Moellering Charles B, clerk W L Moellering, bds 33 Madison.

Moellering Charles E, clerk, bds 120 Montgomery.

Moellering Henry A, machinist Penn Co, res 33 Madison.

Moellering Henry F (Wm Moellering & Sons), bds 120 Montgomery.

Moellering Minnie, domestic 106 Broadway.

Moellering Sophie, clerk, bds 120 Montgomery.

Moellering Wm (Wm Moellering & Sons), Contractor, Builder, Brick Mnfr, Stone Quarrier and Dealer in Lime, Plaster, Cement, Sewer Pipe, etc ; Office 53 to 59 Murray; Brick Yard, Fairfield ave; Stone Quarries at Wabash, Ind; res 120 Montgomery. (*See front edge and p 5.*)

Moellering Wm F (Wm Moellering & Sons), res 118 Montgomery.

Moellering Wm H F (Wm Moellering & Co), bds Henry Fritcha.

Moellering Wm L, Druggist; Agent for King's German Heave Cure and Clipper Corn Cure, n w cor Lewis and Lafayette, res 100 E Washington.

Moellering Wm & Co (Wm and Wm H F Moellering), Brick Mnfrs, w s Calhoun s of Rudisill ave.

Moellering Wm & Sons (Wm, Wm F and Henry F), wholesale and retail grocers, 215 and 217 Lafayette and 116 Montgomery.

Moering Henry J, laborer, res 181 Monroe.

Moering Johanna, bds 181 Monroe.

Moering Lillie, bds 181 Monroe.

Moering Margaret, bds 181 Monroe.

Moering Minnie, bds 181 Monroe.

Moffat Rev David W, pastor First Presbyterian Church, res 126 E Berry.

Mohl George, mattressmaker P E Wolf, res 150 Walton ave.

Mohl Philip, driver P E Wolf, res 429 E Washington.

Mohler Albert D, bds 120 Harrison.

Mohler Orion E, editor Ft Wayne Gazette, bds 120 Harrison.

Mohn Mrs Rachel, bds 23 Holman.

Mohr, *see also Moore.*

Mohr John, bds s w cor Clinton and Washington.

Mohr John jr, cash Hamilton National Bank, res s w cor Clinton and Washington.

Moiser Stephen, laborer, res 310 E Wayne.

Molan James, machine hand American Wheel Co, res 54 Chicago.

Molitor Adam, lab Penn Co, res w s Hanna 4 s of Pontiac.

Molitor Annie M, dressmaker, bds w s Hanna 4 s of Pontiac.

Molitor Charles, painter Olds' Wagon Works, bds 69 Charles.

Molitor Charles E, laborer Olds' Wagon Works, bds Adam Molitor.

Molitor John, lab Olds' Wagon Works, bds Adam Molitor.

Molitor Leonard, laborer, res 69 Charles.

Molitor Miss Lizzie, bds w s Hanna 4 s of Pontiac.

Mollet Henry, carpenter, bds 60 Walnut.

Mollet Peter, market stall 69, res w s Bluffton road 5 miles s of limits.

Molone, *see also Malone.*

Molone Bridget (wid Patrick), res 57 Laselle.

Molone Patrick E, fireman, bds 57 Laselle.

Molone Rosa, seamstress, bds 57 Laselle.

Mommer Benjamin H, dentist, 76 Calhoun, res same.

Mommer Carrie, bds 174 E Lewis.

Mommer Edward J (Mommer & Stevenson), bds 180 E Lewis·

Mommer John, mach Ft Wayne Iron Works, res 174 E Lewis.

Mommer John W, foreman Kerr-Murray Mnfg Co, res 4 Mc-Clellan.

Mommer Joseph jr, boots and shoes, 76 Calhoun, res 133 W Main.

Mommer Joseph C, molder, bds 180 E Lewis.

Mommer J Franklin, clerk J Mommer jr, res 99 W Washington.

Mommer Louis, molder Bass Foundry and Machine Works, res 180 E Lewis.

Mommer Wm J, molder Bass Foundry and Machine Works, bds 174 E Lewis.

Mommer & Stevenson (Edward J Mommer, Wm L Stevenson), barbers Aveline House.

Momper Mathias, barber, 24 W Main, res 7 Fulton.

Monahan, *see also Moynihan.*

Monahan Dennis (Golden & Monahan), res 65 E Jefferson.

Monahan Helen (wid Daniel), carpet sewer Root & Co, res 6 Kansas.

Monahan John, boilermaker Wabash R R, res 102 Webster.

Monahan John J, clerk Golden & Monahan, bds 65 E Jefferson.

Mong George E, painter, res s s Riverside ave 4 w of St Joseph river.

Mongey Ernest, helper, res 298 Hanna.

Monger Sebastian, bench hand Fort Wayne Electric Co, bds 28 Nirdlinger ave.

Monnesmith Nancy, domestic 202 W Main.

Monnier Joseph, laborer Bass Foundry and Machine Works, res 42 Force.

Monnier Seraphim, laborer, res 29 Duck.

Monning, *see also Manning.*

Monning Agnes (wid Henry), res 143 E Wayne.

Monning Henry B (J B Monning & Co), res 143 E Wayne.

Monnning John B (J B Monning & Co), res 163 E Wayne.

Monning J B & Co (John B and Henry B Monning, August C Trentman Special), Proprs Fort Wayne Spice Mills and Globe Flour Mills, 73 and 75 E Columbia.

Monning Miss Louise, bds 143 E Wayne.

Monnot Louis C, blacksmith H A Rose, res 33 Harrison.

Monroe Angeline (wid Wm), res 92 Franklin ave.

Monroe Mrs Elizabeth, propr Monroe House, 224 Calhoun, res same.

Monroe House, Mrs Elizabeth Monroe propr, 224 Calhoun.

Monteith Millard, tel operator G R & I R R, rms 209 Harrison.

Robert Spice, Waterworks and General Plumbing, 48 West Main and 11 Pearl Streets.

382   R. L. POLK & CO.'S

Montgomery David, switchman Wabash R R, res 71 Baker.
Montgomery Edward (col'd), driver Renner, Cratsley & Co, res w s Hoffman 1 n of St Mary's ave.
Montgomery Emma (wid Wm), res 81 Holman.
Montgomery George, brass finisher E B Kunkle & Co, bds 126 Madison.
Montgomery George M, bds 81 Holman.
Montgomery Noah, finisher American Wheel Co, res 71 Baker.
Mood Moses, carpenter, bds 102 Putnam.
Moodey Cornelia C, laundress Wm P Hadley, bds 73 E Berry.
Moody Edward, driver Hose Co No 3, rms Engine House No 1.
Moon Christopher C, carpenter Indiana Machine Works, res 18 Burgess.
Mooney Flora (wid Wm), rms 192 Lafayette.
Mooney Isabella (wid Enos T), res 213 Fairfield ave.
Mooney John, engineer, res 275 E Lewis.
Mooney John, janitor Gov't bldg, res rear 47 W Main.
Mooney Lizzie, rms 192 Lafayette.
Moore, *see also Mohr.*
Moore Abbie E, works Troy Steam Laundry, bds 24 Harrison.
Moore Alvin O, brakeman, res 51 N Calhoun.
Moore Asa L, laborer, bds Hyer House.
Moore Chauncey, helper Olds' Wagon Wks, bds 27 St Martin.
Moore David H, engineer, res 27 St Martin.
Moore Elias B, laborer Penn Co, res 24 Harrison.
Moore Eugene, painter, bds 21 Taylor.
Moore George, brakeman, rms 20 Chicago.
Moore George W, market stall No 90, res New Haven, Ind.
Moore George W, engineer, res 328 W Main.
Moore Harry, bds 27 St Martin.
Moore James, laborer, bds 84 Fairfield ave
Moore James C, clerk, res 281 W Jefferson.
Moore Jesse, driver, bds 57 Barr.
Moore Jonathan A, brakeman Penn Co, bds 208 Lafayette.
Moore John, brakeman, rms 20 Chicago.
Moore John, laborer, bds 312 W Main.
Moore John, wiper, bds 320 Calhoun.
Moore John W, trav agent Fred Eckart, res n w cor Superior and Barr.
Moore Mabel, works Troy Steam Laundry, bds 24 Harrison.
Moore Margaret (wid John), res 84 Fairfield ave.
Moore Mary H (wid Thomas C), bds 13 Walnut.
Moore Nathan, flagman Penn Co, bds 168 Brackenridge.
Moore Samuel A, brakeman Penn Co, bds 208 Lafayette.
Moore Samuel C, conductor, res n s Suttenfield 3 e of Calhoun.
Moore Wm H, fireman, res 13 Walnut.

Sewing Machines, Shears ∫ Pfeiffer & Schlatter
—and Pocket Knives,—— ∫ 38 & 40 E. Columbia.

FORT WAYNE DIRECTORY. 383

Moore Wm H, machinist Fort Wayne Electric Co, res 154 W De Wald.

Moore Wm S, laborer Kilian Baker, res 12 Lafayette.

Moore Wm W, teamster, res 108 High.

Moorehead Glenn W, fireman, bds 407 W Main.

Moormann Benjamin, laborer Bass Foundry and Machine Works, bds 164 Harmer.

Moos Emil, butcher F Eckart, res Rockhill's heirs add.

Moran Clifford, laborer Fort Wayne Organ Co, bds cor Oakland ave and Killea.

Moran Dominick C, carver Fort Wayne Organ Co, res cor Oakland ave and Killea.

Moran Dominick C j r, draughtsman, bds D C Moran.

Moran Julia T, bds 201 E Wayne.

Moran Nora (wid John), domestic J D Nuttman.

Moran Peter A, ice dealer, res 201 E Wayne.

Moran Rachel A (wid Peter), bds 201 E Wayne.

Moran Wm J, collector, res 435 Hanna.

Mordhurst Henry W, druggist, 72 Calhoun, res same.

More, see Mohr and Moore.

Morell Eleanor, market stall 43, res s w of County Poor Farm.

Morell Henry, clerk C Schiefer & Son, res 255 Broadway.

Moresi Emile P, machinist, bds Riverside Hotel.

Morey Louisa A (wid Edwin), res 438 Fairfield ave.

Morey Miss Marian, bds 438 Fairfield ave.

Morey Seldon S, tel opr Nickel Plate, bds 438 Fairfield ave.

Morgan Charles E, dining car conductor, res 60 Hamilton.

Morgan Frank M, letter carrier, bds 184 E Jefferson.

Morgan George W, oil dealer, res 184 E Jefferson.

Morgan Miss Lena, rms 39½ W Berry.

Morgan Louise, dressmaker Wm Malloy, res 39½ W Berry.

Morgan Nancy (wid John), bds 28 Chicago.

Morgan Oliver P (Morgan & Beach), vice-pres Old National Bank, res 40 E Washington.

Morgan & Beach (Oliver P Morgan, Frederick Beach), Wholesale and Retail Hardware, 19 and 21 E Columbia.

Morganthaler Clifford, clerk, bds 141 W Wayne.

Morganthaler Peter, clothing and gents' furnishing goods, 52½ Calhoun, res 141 W Wayne.

Moring August J, teamster American Wheel Co, res 135 Wallace.

Moring John, laborer, res 192 John.

Moring Lottie (wid John), bds 26 Wallace.

Moring Louis W, wheelmaker Olds' Wagon Works, res 26 Wallace.

Moritz August, laborer, bds 1 Sturgis.

Moritz Miss Charlotta, bds 79 W Berry.
Moritz Elizabeth (wid Peter), res 79 W Berry.
Moritz John M (Miller & Moritz), res 79 W Berry.
Moritz Vincent, fruits, res 1 Sturgis.
Morrell Frank L, wheel molder Bass Foundry and Machine Works, bds 196 Hanna.
Morrey, *see also Murray*.
Morrey A Richard, confectioner, 322 Calhoun, bds 382 Lafayette.
Morris, *see also Maurice*.
Morris Charles M, laborer, bds 315 Hanna.
Morris Edward J, switchman Wabash R R, res 62 Oakley.
Morris James J, switchman, res 10 Bass.
Morris John (Morris & Barrett), res 77 Maple ave.
Morris John jr (Worden & Morris), dep clerk U S District Court, res 77 Maple ave.
Morris Louis W, stone mason, res 335 Hanna.
Morris Miss Lulu, teacher Indiana School for Feeble-Minded Youth.
Morris Margaret (wid James), res 315 Hanna.
Morris Miss Mary, bds 77 Maple ave.
Morris Samuel L (Bell & Morris), res 282 W Washington.
Morris Sarah G, bds 315 Hanna.
Morris Stephen, bookkeeper Old National Bank, res 340 W Jefferson.
Morris Wm P, engineer, res 337 W Main.
Morris & Barrett (John Morris, James M Barrett), Lawyers, 52½ Calhoun.
Morrison Charles E, mach hand American Wheel Co, bds 315 Hanna.
Morrison M Henry, heater Penn Co, res 155 Wallace.
Morrison Robert, painter Ft W, C & L R R, res 60 N Harrison.
Morrow Louisa, domestic 28 Wilt.
Morrow Nora, domestic McKinnie House.
Morsch John, watchman, res 69 Wall.
Morse Anna E (wid John B), bds Aldine Hotel.
Morse Frank W, master mechanic Wabash R R, bds Aldine Hotel.
Morse Harold, bds 303 E Lewis.
Morton Club, Charles W Orr pres, Owen N Heaton sec, n e cor Wayne and Calhoun.
Morton Thomas, grocer, 302 E Wayne, res same.
Morton Wm H, laborer Penn Co, res w s Grant ave 1 s of Maumee road.
Morvilius Frank W, cigarmkr Schele Bros, res 75 E Wayne.

Moscrop Richard, porter Wayne Hotel.
Moscrop Wm, laborer, bds 43½ E Columbia.
Moser Ambrose, stonecutter Fort Wayne Steam Stone Wks, bds 157 W Main.
Moser Andrew, cooper, res 7 Clark.
Moser Elizabeth, domestic 25 E Main.
Moser John G, laborer, res 68 Oakley.
Moser Stephen, lab American Wheel Co, res 310 E Wayne.
Moses John S, carpenter, res 178 W DeWald.
Mosher Mary, milliner F Tait & Sister, bds 26 E Wayne.
Moshier George K, engineer, res 33 E Williams.
Moslander Asa J, baker D J Shaw, bds 26 Smith.
Moslander Wm A, baker D J Shaw, bds 26 Smith.
Moss Frederick, watchman Wabash R R, res 38 Bass.
Moss Martin, wheel molder Bass Foundry and Machine Wks, res 59 Gay.
Moss Mary, bds 205 E Washington.
Mosser Andrew, cooper Frederick Sauertieg, res 11 Clark.
Mosshammer Bertha, midwife, died May 20, 1890.
Mosshammer Gustav M, bartender J G Strodel, res 109 Barr.
Mosshammer Jacob, coremaker Bass Foundry and Machine Works, res 359 E Washington.
Mosshammer John M, laborer, res 113 Barr.
Mossman Paul B, bds 328 W Washington.
Mossman Wm E (Mossman, Yarnelle & Co), sec Fort Wayne Furniture Co, res 330 W Washington.
Mossman, Yarnelle & Co (Wm E Mossman, Edward F Yarnelle, W S Sponhauer), whol hardware, 10 and 12 W Columbia.
Moster Nicholas J, laborer, res 18 Runnion ave.
Moten Moses (col'd), engineer Kerr-Murray Mnfg Co, res 70 Murray.
Motherwill Henry J, tinner G H Wilson & Sons, bds 57 Barr.
Motherwill Wm, driver, bds 106 Riverside ave.
Motsch Frederick J, boarding house, 518 Fairfield ave.
Motz George, Dealer in Cigars and Tobacco, 47 W Main, res 30 E 2d.
Motz George jr, clerk George Motz, bds 30 E 2d.
Mounsir Ada, clerk Frank & Co, bds 50 Brackenridge.
Mourning John E, teamster, bds 61 Garden.
Moutner Isadore, clothing, res 171 W Wayne.
Mouzin Ernest, laborer Olds' Wagon Works, res 298 Hanna.
Mowrer Emma, bds Margaretta Mowrer.
Mowrer Henry, polisher White's Wheel Works, bds Margaretta Mowrer.
Mowrer Isaac, County Treasurer; Office Court House, res 221 W Main.

John Pressler, Galvanized Iron Cornices and Slate Roofing
Columbia, Barr and Dock Streets.

386   R. L. POLK & CO.'S

Mowrer Jacob, bartender The Herman Berghoff Brewing Co,
 res E Washington opp East End brewery.
Mowrer Jacob jr, bds Jacob Mowrer.
Mowrer Margaretta (wid Lorenz), res n-s E Washington nr
 street car barn.
Mowrer Miss May V, clerk county treas, bds 221 W Main.
Moynihan, *see also Monahan*.
Moynihan Andrew J, editor Fort Wayne Journal, res 159 E
 Wayne.
Moynihan Johanna (wid Martin), bds 159 E Wayne.
Mudge Jeremiah C, carpenter, res 108 W DeWald.
Mudge John A, carpenter, bds 108 W DeWald.
Muehlfeith Charles A (Laible & Muehlfeith), res 42 3d.
Muehlfeith John, tailor George Motz, res 42 3d.
Mueller, *see also Miller, Moeller and Muller*.
Mueller August, carpenter, bds 10 Pritchard.
Mueller Charles F W, engineer Wabash R R, res 10 Prit-
 chard.
Mueller Charles M, tailor J G Thieme & Son, bds 120 High.
Mueller Ernst J, draughtsman, rms 123 W Jefferson.
Mueller F Wm, bartender R Beverforden, res 23 Brandriff.
Mueller F Wm jr, painter Olds' Wagon Works, bds 23 Brand-
 riff.
Mueller Henry, baker L P Scherer, bds 120 High.
Mueller Henry, blacksmith Louis Schwartz, rms 84 Barr.
Mueller John G, finisher, bds 120 High.
Mueller Julius, car builder Penn Co, res 53 Hugh.
Mueller Wm G, barber Mathias Momper, bds 10 Pritchard.
Muenster Fina, domestic 254 W Washington.
Muhlenbrock Richard, driver Fort Wayne Street Railroad
 Co, bds 81 Wall.
Muhlenbruch Charles, clerk Carnahan & Co, res 213 E Jef-
 ferson.
Muhlenbruch Charles F, machine hand, bds 20 Burgess.
Muhlenbruch Diedrich, cabinetmaker Penn Co, res 213 E
 Jefferson.
Muhlenbruch D F Wm, wagonmaker Fleming Mnfg Co, res
 19 Burgess.
Muhlenbruch Frederick, helper Penn Co, bds 213 E Jefferson.
Muhlenbruch F Gottreich, mngr The Pape Furniture Co, res
 238 E Washington.
Muhlenbruch Gustav, clk J B White, bds 238 E Washington.
Muhlenbruch Louisa, bds 213 E Jefferson.
Muhlenbruch Louisa, bds 238 E Washington.
Muhlenbruch Wm, carpenter, bds 238 E Washington.
Muhlenbruch Wm D, carpenter, res 20 Burgess.

Muhler August T, messenger Hamilton National Bank, bds 166 W Wayne.

Muhler Bernard C (Charles F Muhler & Son), bds 166 W Wayne.

Muhler Charles B, clerk A C Trentman, bds 166 W Wayne.

Muhler Charles F (Charles F Muhler & Son), res 166 W Wayne.

Muhler Charles F & Son (Charles F and Bernard C), Lime, Plaster and Cement, Fire Brick and Clay, Builders' Supplies, Sewer Pipe and Stone Yard, 1 N Calhoun. (*See adv top edge and p 59.*)

Muhler Mrs George M, bds 79 W Main.

Muhler Miss Kate, bds 166 W Wayne.

Muhlfeith, *see Muehlfeith.*

Muirhead Alexander, machinist Wabash R R, res 505 S Calhoun.

Mulcahy Richard, watchman Olds' Wheel Works, res w s Spy Run ave 5 n of St Mary's bridge.

Mulcahy Wm J, blacksmith M L Albrecht, bds Richard Mulcahy.

Muldary Andrew J, conductor Penn Co, res 53 Baker.

Muldoon Angeline, bds 280 E Lewis.

Muldoon Charles, rms 37 W Main.

Muldoon John W, Practical Painter, Kalsomining, Graining, Hard Oil Finishing and Papering, 12 E Berry, res 280 E Lewis. (*See embossed line back cover.*)

Muldoon Margaret (wid Patrick), bds 280 E Lewis.

Mulhearn Thomas, grocer, 117 Fairfield ave, res 115 same.

Muller, *see also Miller, Moeller and Mueller.*

Muller August, shoemaker, n s New Haven ave 5 w of Lumbard, res same.

Muller Conrad, laborer, res rear 31 Smith.

Muller Ernst J, draughtsman Fort Wayne Iron Works, rms 123 W Jefferson.

Muller Francis, teamster, bds 324 E Washington.

Muller Gustav, driver Frank & Co, bds 215 W Main.

Muller Henry, res 215 W Main.

Muller Herman, coremaker Bass Foundry and Machine Wks, res 110 Eliza.

Muller John, car builder Penn Co, res 53 Hugh.

Muller Josephine, domestic 216 W Wayne.

Muller Paul, bds rear 31 Smith.

Muller Wm S, tinnner, bds 3 E Superior.

Mulligan Miss Alice, bds n e cor Calhoun and Williams.

Mulligan Alice (wid Henry), res n e cor Calhoun and Williams.

Mulligan John W, cigars, 272 Calhoun, res n e cor Calhoun
 and Williams.
Mulligan Rose, seamstress, bds n e cor Calhoun and Williams.
Mullins Lizzie, bds 115 Fairfield ave.
Mulnofski Gustave, laborer, res 65 John.
Mulqueen John W, brakeman, res 220 W Washington.
Munch, *see also Muench and Muensch.*
Munch August, tinner Staub Bros, bds 52 N Harrison.
Munch Henry, laborer, bds 52 N Harrison.
Munch Philip, laborer, res 52 N Harrison.
Munch Philip J, blacksmith Indiana Machine Works, res 115
 Barthold.
Mundt Christian, student E F Sites, bds 82 St Mary's ave.
Mundt Edward, laborer Penn Co, res 122 Chicago.
Mundt Ernest, laborer, res 122 Chicago.
Mundt Wm H, section hand, res s w cor St Mary's ave and
 Aboit.
Mungen John J, trav agent, res 50 W Superior.
Mungen Miss Linnie, stenographer Star Iron Tower Co, bds
 50 W Superior.
Mungen W Wallace (Loag & Mungen), bds 50 W Superior.
Mungovan Franklin J (Markey & Mungovan), res 321 Harri-
 son.
Mungovan Thomas C, steel worker Wabash R R, res 607 S
 Calhoun.
Mungovan Wm E, fireman, res 59 W Williams.
Munich John, barber, 352 Calhoun, res 41 Williams.
Munroe, *see Monroe.*
Munson Charles A, res 22 W Wayne.
Murbaugh Caroline, domestic 37 Maumee rd.
Murphy Amos W, foreman Rivers & Son, res 277 E Wayne.
Murphy Bernard, laborer A Hattersley & Sons, res 163 E
 Jefferson.
Murphy Charles W, cigarmaker J Lohman, bds 11 Melita.
Murphy Daniel, laborer, bds 104 E Wayne.
Murphy Dennis C, switchman Nickel Plate, res 51 Prince.
Murphy Edward, fireman, bds 219 Lafayette.
Murphy Frank A, engineer, bds 12 St Mary's ave.
Murphy George, gardener, res 11 Colerick.
Murphy Johanna (wid Dennis), res 7 Colerick.
Murphy John, machinist Fort Wayne Electric Co, res 138
 Holman.
Murphy John C, engineer, rms 34 W Main.
Murphy John H, painter, bds 53 Force.
Murphy John J, boilermaker Wabash R R, res 72 South
 Wayne ave.

Murphy Kate, dressmaker L A Worch, bds 171 Madison.
Murphy Michael, engineer, res 151 Fairfield ave.
Murphy Minnie, bds 138 Holman.
Murphy Nicholas E, machinist, bds 151 Fairfield ave.
Murphy Patrick, brakeman, bds 138 Holman.
Murphy Patrick, laborer, res 54 Melita.
Murphy Samuel C, painter Penn Co, res 53 Force.
Murphy Sarah E, bds 53 Force.
Murphy Thomas J, machinist Penn Co, res 138 Holman.
Murphy Timothy, laborer American Wheel Co, bds 171 Madison.
Murphy Wm, brakeman Penn Co, res 138 Holman.
Murphy Wm H, bds 53 Force.
Murphy Wm J, coil winder Fort Wayne Electric Co, res 14 Bass.
Murray, *see also Morrey.*
Murray Charles M, teamster, res s e cor Putnam and Koch.
Murray David, helper Wabash R R, res 29 Pritchard.
Murray Harry, brakeman, rms 23 Baker.
Murray James, plumber, 63 E Main, res same.
Murray Jane (wid Kerr), res 141 W Berry.
Murray John, cabinetmaker Louis Diether & Bro, res 282 E Washington.
Murray Maggie, domestic 62 Summit.
Murray Mary M, tailoress Charles Kruse, bds 55 W Jefferson.
Murray Nellie, bds 15 Baker.
Murray Newton, lineman Telephone Exchange, res 76 E Columbia.
Murray Ophelia M (wid Americus W), res 15 Baker.
Murray Patrick, bricklayer, bds s e cor Clinton and Superior.
Murtagh Wm H, vice-pres The Peters Box and Lumber Co, res Peoria, Illinois.
Musilek Joseph, cabinetmaker Fort Wayne Organ Co, res e s Piqua ave 2 n of Rudisill ave.
Mussebaum Nettie, domestic Hotel Randall.
Myer, *see also Maier, Mayer, Meier and Meyer.*
Myer Christian, finisher Horton Mnfg Co, bds 391 W Main.
Myer George, gardener Miss Theresa Swinney.
Myers, *see also Meyers.*
Myers Miss Alice, bds 109 Holman.
Myers August, carpenter, res n s Wagner 6 w of St Joseph river.
Myers Block, 108 Fairfield ave.
Myers Charles, cigarmaker, bds 11 Melita.
Myers Charles, engineer, rms 34 W Main.
Myers Charles F, horse dealer, res 66 Douglas ave.

Myers Charles J, helper A Hattersley & Sons, bds 10 Jackson.
Myers Christopher, carpenter, bds 124 Union.
Myers Cornelius C, helper Penn Co, bds 139 Francis.
Myers Darwin S, stenographer Fort Wayne Electric Co, bds 157 W Wayne.
Myers Edward, laborer, bds 29 Hough.
Myers Frederick, Propr East Wayne Street Livery and Sale Stables, 62 E Wayne, res 49 Douglas ave.
Myers Frederick C, molder Bass Foundry and Machine Wks, res 31 Hugh.
Myers Frederick W, finisher Horton Mnfg Co, res 391 W Main.
Myers George, cigarmkr John Gronendyke, res 9 Sturgis.
Myers George S, laborer American Wheel Co, bds 109 Holman.
Myers George W, lab Penn Co, bds 98 W Williams.
Myers Hallie, converter worker Fort Wayne Electric Co, bds 157 Holman.
Myers Henrietta, domestic 50 W Superior.
Myers Henry, carpenter, bds 18 McClellan.
Myers Henry, lab J C Peters, res s s Main opp Osage.
Myers Henry, teamster, res 385 W Main.
Myers Henry C, bds 66 Douglas ave.
Myers Herschel S, physician, 12 Schmitz block, bds 157 W Wayne.
Myers John, barber S R Miner, bds 76 W Washington.
Myers John A, patent rights, res 29 Buchanan.
Myers Lewis C, brakeman Penn Co, res 200 E Creighton ave.
Myers Lizzie, cook J F Cline, bds 7 Duryea.
Myers Louis, bds 290 Calhoun.
Myers Martin V, carpenter, res 409 Lafayette.
Myers Mary (wid Christian W), grocer, 1 St Mary's ave, res same.
Myers Mrs Mary A, res 109 Holman.
Myers Minnie, domestic 77 Maple ave.
Myers P J Harry, clerk Nickel Plate, res 170 W Jefferson.
Myers Sherman, brakeman, bds Hyer House.
Myers Sophie, domestic, 232 W Wayne.
Myers Wm, blacksmith Penn Co, res 98 W Williams.
Myers Wm, nurse, bds 72 Calhoun.
Myers Wm F, Veterinary Surgeon, 112 Webster, bds 66 Douglas ave.
Myers Wm H, physician, 157 W Wayne, res same.
Myers Wm M, helper Penn Co, bds 109 Holman.
Myron Frank C, conductor Penn Co, bds 313 S Calhoun.
Myron John, brakeman, rms 209 Harrison.

N

Nablo Ephraim, clerk Stewart & Hahn, rms 24 E Washington.

Nagel Catherine, vestmaker, bds 41 N Cass.

Nagel Frederick, storekeeper Wabash R R, res 99 W Jefferson.

Nagel Joseph M, horseshoer F Becker & Bro, bds 41 N Cass.

Nagel Lawrence E, cigarmaker F J Gruber, bds 41 N Cass.

Nagel Minnie, seamstress, bds 41 N Cass.

Nagel Xavier, wagonmaker Chauvey Bros, res 41 N Cass.

Nahrwold, *see also Norwald.*

Nahrwold Charles, carpenter, res 126 Eliza.

Nahrwold Charles, carpenter, bds 267 E Lewis.

Nahrwold Charles, plasterer, 265 E Lewis, res same.

Nahrwold Christian, boilermaker, res 147 E Lewis.

Nahrwold Conrad, carpenter, res 150 E Creighton ave.

Nahrwold Conrad, machinist Penn Co, res 267 E Lewis.

Nahrwold Diedrich, carpenter, res 164 Smith.

Nahrwold Emma, domestic 232 W Wayne.

Nahrwold Frederick, carpenter, bds 137 Force.

Nahrwold Frederick C, blacksmith helper Penn Co, bds 25 Wilt.

Nahrwold Frederick C jr, rivet heater Penn Co, bds 25 Wilt.

Nahrwold Lizzie, bds 29 Wilt.

Nahrwold Minnie, dressmaker, bds 29 Wilt.

Nahrwold Richard, carpenter Bass Foundry and Machine Works, res 164 Smith.

Nahrwold Richard, driver Fort Wayne Street Railroad Co, bds 166 Gay.

Nahrwold Sophie, bds 29 Wilt.

Nahrwold Wm F, foreman Horton Mnfg Co, res 29 Wilt.

Narr Kate, domestic 280 W Wayne.

Nasch Henry C, blacksmith, res 72 Hamilton.

Nash Frederick E, traveling agent, res 266 W Jefferson.

Nathan Charles, bookkeeper Frank & Co, bds 142 W Berry.

Nathan Julius (Julius Nathan & Co), res 142 W Berry.

Nathan Julius & Co (Julius Nathan, Max Rubin), wholesale liquors, 137 and 139 Calhoun.

Nathan Miss Rose, bds 142 W Berry.

National Portrait Co, Frederick W Johnson mngr, 67 E Main.

Nave Mrs Catherine A, teacher Indiana School for Feeble-Minded Youth.

Nave House, *see New Yards House.*

Neabor Henry, laborer, res 86 Summit.

Nead Frank, laborer, res 71 McCulloch.

Neal, *see also Neil.*
Neal Caleb J, driver W F Geller, res 112 Broadway.
Nease Ulysses S, lab Hoffman Bros, bds 178 W Washington.
Nebraska School, s e cor Boone and Fry.
Nebur John, laborer Penn Co, res 25 Lillie.
Neeb August, candymaker Louis Fox & Bro, bds 54 Oakley.
Neeb Catherine (wid John G), res 54 Oakley.
Neeb John G, baker Louis Fox & Bro, bds 60 Walnut.
Neeb Wm G, clerk Louis Fox & Bro, bds 54 Oakley.
Needham Fred F, propr Rich's Hotel, n w cor Calhoun and
    Douglas ave.
Nees, *see also Kneese, Neise, Ness and Nies.*
Nees Albert, bds 28 Schick.
Nees Miss Eliza, bds 28 Schick.
Nees Henry B, tinsmith Penn Co, res 36 Wilt.
Nees Henry C C, cabinetmaker Penn Co, res 28 Schick.
Neff August, laborer Penn Co, res 66 Boone.
Neff John, farmer, res 461 W Main.
Neff John, harnessmaker A L Johns & Co, bds 20 Huron.
Neff Mrs Martha T, physician, 461 W Main, res same.
Neff Rebecca (wid Enoch), bds 461 W Main.
Neff Wm, laborer, res 20 Huron.
Neher Frank, machine hand American Wheel Co, bds 12
    Francis.
Neher Joseph, shoemaker, res 12 Francis.
Neher Lizzie M, dressmaker Mrs G J Stier, bds 12 Francis.
Neibel John, laborer Penn Co, res 79 Putnam.
Neice Mary (wid Adam), res 58 Maumee road.
Neidhart Joseph, carpenter, res 60 Madison.
Neidhofer Anna, clerk Philip Graf, bds 273 Hanna.
Neier O Clay, physician, 113 E Lewis, rms 3 Summit.
Neiman, *see also Nieman.*
Neiman John, conductor, res 276 W Jefferson.
Neireiter Casper B, harness, 28 Clinton, res 226 W Washing-
    ton.
Neireiter Charles W, clerk L F Limecooly, bds 34 Allen.
Neireiter Christian A, vegetables, market stall 62, res w s
    Bluffton road s of city limits.
Neireiter Clara B, milliner Mrs F C Spiegel, bds 226 W Wash-
    ington.
Neireiter Conrad, insurance, 269 W Washington, res same.
Neireiter Miss Emma, bds 269 W Washington.
Neireiter Jessie, bds 226 W Washington.
Neireiter Rebecca (wid John), res 294 W Jefferson.
Neise, *see also Kneese, Nees, Ness and Neise.*
Neise Frederick K, clerk A J Dittoe & Co, res 151 Barr.

Neiswonger, *see also Niswonger.*
Neiswonger David H, brakeman, res 296 E Lewis.
Neiswonger Henry W, physician, 284 E Jefferson, res same.
Neiswonger Rolland, laborer, bds 284 E Jefferson.
Neiter Herman, laborer, bds 100 Montgomery.
Nelligan John, res 23 W Lewis.
Nelligan Michael, machinist Penn Co, res 58 Douglas ave.
Nels Philip, laborer Olds' Wagon Works, res 54 Smith.
Nelson Elizabeth (wid Elmore N), res 60 W Wayne.
Nelson Miss Eva T, bds 262 W Berry.
Nelson Helen E (wid DeGroff), res 262 W Berry.
Nelson Isaac D G, res 132 E Berry.
Nelson John, cabinetmaker Fort Wayne Organ Co, res 41 Miner.
Nelson Miss Julia D, bds 262 W Berry.
Nelson Mark A, foreman pressroom Fort Wayne Newspaper Union, res 59 Wilt.
Nelson Nels K, blksmith Olds' Wagon Works, res 33 Charles.
Nelson Peter, laborer Olds' Wagon Works, bds 33 Charles.
Nelson Thomas, tinsmith, bds 104 Barr.
Nepp Louisa, bds 111 Wilt.
Nergott Adolph J, machine hand American Whee lCo, bds 38 Hough.
Nerhood James J, carpenter, bds 438 S Broadway.
Nerhood Lillian F, bds 438 S Broadway.
Nerhood Mathias, plasterer, res 438 S Broadway.
Nerkler Anton, laborer, res 34 Buchanan.
Nern Conrad, laborer, res s w cor Cochrane and Coombs.
Nern Conrad jr, teamster, bds s w cor Cochrane and Coombs.
Nern John, laborer, bds s w cor Cochrane and Coombs.
Nesbit David N, driver W D Henderson, bds 91 Montgomery.
Nesbit Mollie (wid Isaac), res 251 Calhoun.
Ness, *see Neise and Nies.*
Nessel Carrie, packer Louis Fox & Bro, bds 463 Lafayette.
Nessel Christina (wid Michael), res 463 Lafayette.
Nessel John A, laborer, bds 463 Lafayette.
Nessel Minnie, packer Louis Fox & Bro, bds 463 Lafayette.
Nessler John, car cleaner, res 1 Lumbard.
Nestel Adolph G, boots and shoes, 189 Lafayette, res 187½ same.
Nestel's Block, s w cor Broadway and W Jefferson.
Nestel Charles W, bds 243 W Creighton ave.
Nestel Daniel, nursery, w s Broadway opp Creighton ave, res 243 W Creighton ave.
Nestel Daniel jr, painter, res 165 Wells.
Nestel Edward P, painter, 115 E Lewis, bds 187 Lafayette.

Nestel Miss Eliza, bds 243 W Creighton ave.
Nestel Miss Henrietta C, bds 243 W Creighton ave.
Nestel Oscar W, traveling agent, res 273 W DeWald.
Nestel Philip, res 187 Lafayette.
Neu Joseph, sawyer Olds' Wagon Works, res 501 Lafayette.
Neuenschwander Isaac M, saloon, 46 E Columbia, res same.
Neuenschwander Matilda, bds 46 E Columbia.
Neufer John M (J Hetrick & Co), rms 303 E Washington.
Neuhaus Frank, gardener, res 61 Hoffman.
Neuhaus Frank A, bds 61 Hoffman.
Neuhaus Henry, trav agent, bds Barney T Brennan.
Neuhaus Lucy, bds 61 Hoffman.
Neuhaus Reinhard H, shoemaker Foellinger Bros, res cor St
    Mary's and Pfeiffer aves.
Neumann, *see also Newman.*
Neumann Anna, bds 62 Lillie.
Neumann August, miller, res 208 Broadway.
Neumann Clara, opr Hoosier Mnfg Co, bds 208 Broadway.
Neumann John, oiler Penn Co, res 480 Hanna.
Neumann Lena, hair dresser, bds 62 Lillie.
Neumann Mathias, laborer, res 167 E Creighton ave.
Neumann Wm, mach Kerr-Murray Mnfg Co, res 62 Lillie.
Neumeier Adam, grocer, 38 Maumee road, res same.
Neuroth Louis, foreman Wabash R R shops, res 160 Taylor.
Neuroth Mary, bds 37 Stophlet.
New Catholic Cemetry, Hicksville State road 1½ miles e of
    city limits.
New Government Building and Postoffice, s e cor Berry and
    Clinton.
Newcomer Christian, solicitor J E Graham & Son, res 145
    Griffith.
Newcomer George, dairy, w s Smith 2 s of Pontiac, res same.
Newcomer John, laborer George Newcomer, bds same.
Newell Charles D, engineer, res 79 Douglas ave.
Newell Hans, res 46 Park ave.
Newhart Charles E, machinist Fort Wayne Electric Co, bds
    42 Brandriff.
Newhart Louisa (wid Edward), res 42 Brandriff.
Newhart Wm L, fireman Fort Wayne Electric Co, bds 42
    Brandriff.
Newhouse Henry, farm impts, 56 E Columbia, res same.
Newman, *see also Neuman.*
Newman Bernhard, bds 136 W Wayne.
Newman George, laborer, bds 16 Clay.
Newman Horace J, solicitor Fort Wayne Sentinel, res 114 W
    Wayne.

Stahn & Heinrich, Leading Dealers in ARTISTS' MATE-
RIALS AND DRAUGHTING INSTRU-
MENTS. 116 Calhoun Street.

FORT WAYNE DIRECTORY. 395

Newman Lewis D, car builder Penn Co, res 119 Force.

Newman May, domestic Hyer House.

New Oddfellow Block, n e cor Calhoun and Wayne.

Newport Catherine (wid Henry), bds Wm Wilkin.

Newton Charles H, Local Freight Agent Wabash R
R, res 130 W Creighton ave.

Newton Frederick A (Coombs & Co), res 213 W Berry.

Newton Reuben W, clerk Coombs & Co, bds 213 W Berry.

New York, Chicago & St Louis R R (Nickel Plate), passenger depot, s s Superior bet Calhoun and Clinton; freight
depot w s Harrison nr Superior.

New York Installment Co, L O Gillham Manager,
Dealers in Household Specialties, 43 E Columbia.

Nicholls Otis S, cigarmaker H W Ortmann, res cor Barr and
Wayne.

Nichols George M, res 42 Wells.

Nichols Nancy, works Troy Steam Laundry, bds 42 Wells.

Nichols Wm, bartender, res 119 Lafayette.

Nicholson Sarah (wid John M), res 30 E Columbia.

Nichter Francis, bds 34 Hendricks.

Nichter George J, barber, 153 Broadway, res 34 Hendricks.

Nichter John J, carpenter, res 35 St Martin.

Nichter Joseph, machinist Wabash R R, res 34 Hendricks.

Nichter Lizzie, bds 34 Hendricks.

Nichter Otto, molder Bass Foundry and Machine Works, res
48 Hendricks.

Nichter Peter P, machinist Wabash R R, res 22 Nirdlinger.

Nick Herman C, mngr Meyer Bros & Co, res 7 W Columbia.

Nick Otto L, clk Meyer Bros & Co, bds 7 W Columbia.

Nickel Plate Hotel, Andrew Bowersock propr, 31 W Columbia.

Nickel Plate Railway Depot, *see N Y, C & St L R R Depot.*

Nickel Plate Restaurant, Wm C Seidel & Bro proprs, Nickel
Plate depot.

Nickell Andrew J, engineer, bds Rose Allen.

Nickell John F, engineer, res 130 W Washington.

Nickels Alexander, bds 71 Smith.

Nickels Grace, bds 71 Smith.

Nickels James, laborer Fort Wayne Electric Co, bds 71 Smith.

Nickels Wm, boots and shoes, 71 Smith, res same.

Nickels Wm C, boxmaker W H Davis, bds 71 Smith.

Nickerson Christopher, checker Wabash R R, res 308 S
Harrison.

Nickerson Ezra, laborer, res 81 Home ave.

Nickerson Lorenzo H, laborer, res 79 W 3d.

Nickerson Margaret (wid Joshua), works Troy Steam Laundry, bds 79 W 3d.

Nickey Addison B, lumber, res s w cor Webster and Park place.

Nickey Alfred J (Soest, Nickey & Co), rms 493 Calhoun.

Nickle Frederick, laborer, bds n s New Haven ave 3 w of Lumbard.

Nickols Anna O, bds 100 Riverside ave.

Nickols Jay T, engineer County Jail, res 100 Riverside ave.

Nicodemus Charles, carp, res n s Grace ave 1 e of Broadway.

Nicoll Frederick, truck repairer Penn Co, res New Haven av.

Niebel John, helper, res 88 Putnam.

Niebergall Henry, grocer, 201 E Washington, res same.

Niedermeyer Frederick, wheel molder Bass Foundry and Machine Works, bds 24 Laselle.

Niedermeyer Joseph, wheel molder Bass Foundry and Machine Works, bds 24 Laselle.

Niedermeyer Mary, domestic J C Hinton, bds 24 Laselle.

Niedermeyer Paul, laborer, res 24 Laselle.

Niedhammer Charles H, clerk, bds 35 Melita.

Niedhammer George, machinist, res 35 Melita.

Niedhammer Hervey C, letter carrier, bds 35 Melita.

Nieman, see also Neiman.

Nieman August H, harnessmaker A L Johns & Co, bds 140 Eliza.

Nieman Bernhard, clerk, bds 272 E Washington.

Nieman Louis J, pedler, res 6 Oak.

Nieman Theodore, grocer, 272 E Washington, res same.

Niemann Edward, bds 326 E Washington.

Niemann Gottlieb, Grocer, 148 Calhoun, res 68 Brackenridge.

Niemann Gottlieb H (Meyer & Niemann), bds 68 Brackenridge.

Niemann Henry D, clerk Gottlieb Niemann, bds 68 Brackenridge.

Niemann John, meter repairer Ft Wayne Gas Light Co, res 326 E Washington.

Niemann John jr, clk J H Hartman, bds 326 E Washington.

Niemann Louise, bds 68 Brackenridge.

Niemeier Christian, res n s New Haven ave 6 w of Lumbard.

Niemeyer Emily, tailoress G Scheffler, bds 155 Madison.

Niemeyer Henry, res 155 Madison.

Niemeyer Henry C jr, clk Isidore Lehman, bds 155 Madison.

Niemeyer Miss Mary, bds 155 Madison.

Niemeyer Wm, teamster, bds 155 Madison.

Nierman's Block, 507 N Harrison.

Niermann August C, finisher Horton Mnfg Co, bds 72 Nelson.

Niermann Herman, res 142 Erie.

Niermann Martin, cigarmkr J Lohman & Co, res 26 Poplar.

E. F. Sites, 🦷 Dentist, 86 Calhoun St., Four Doors North of Wayne.

FORT WAYNE DIRECTORY. 397

Niermann Mary (wid Martin), res 72 Nelson.
Nies, *see also Kneese, Nees, Neise and Ness.*
Nies Mary, domestic 126 E Main.
Nieschang Charles C F, physician, 298 Calhoun, res same.
Niesz Miss Barbara E, bds 39½ W Berry.
Nieter Frederick, helper, res 118 Madison.
Nieter Henry, carpenter, res 51 Holton ave.
Nieter Lizzie, bds 118 Madison.
Nietert Edward, clk Henry Buesking, bds same.
Nietert Herman, table turner Penn Co, bds 100 Montgomery.
Niezer John B, County Auditor, Office Court House, bds 20 W Jefferson.
Niezer Wm J, tinsmith Penn Co, res 20 W Jefferson.
Nikolai Dora, bds 155 Holman.
Nikolai Edward F, helper Penn Co, bds 155 Holman.
Nill Conrad, truckman, res 13 Clark.
Nill George E, shoemaker, 191 Broadway, res 11 Wall.
Nill's Hall, 80 Calhoun.
Nill Regina B (wid Conrad), res 34 W Washington.
Nille Miss Emma, bds 29 W Wayne.
Nimick Frank, boilermkr Penn Co, bds 389 E Lewis.
Nimrod Hall, John G Strodel propr, 54 E Main.
Nimtz David, laborer, res 67 John.
Ninde Benjamin F, student L M & H W Ninde, bds 18 Monroe.
Ninde Building, 40 to 44 W Berry.
Ninde Henry W (L M & H W Ninde), res 93 W Main.
Ninde James W, student, bds 278 W Berry.
Ninde Miss Jane R, bds 416 Fairfield ave.
Ninde Lindley M (L M & H W Ninde), res 416 Fairfield ave.
Nine L M & H W (Lindley M and Henry W), lawyers 42 W Berry.
Ninde Wm M, student Bell & Morris, bds 18 Monroe.
Nirter Frederick, blksmith helper Penn Co, bds 118 Madison.
Niswonger, *see also Neiswonger.*
Niswonger George D, Fish, Oysters and Fruits, 17½ W Berry, res 77 E Berry.
Nitche Emil, wheel molder Bass Foundry and Machine Works, res 43 Smith.
Nix Abbie M, domestic 62 Clinton.
Nix Charles, molder Bass Foundry and Machine Works, bds 80 E Jefferson.
Nix Henry, shoemkr Peter Eggemann, res 531 E Wayne.
Nix John, carpenter, bds 172 E Washington.
Nix John A, laborer, bds 80 E Jefferson.
Nix Joseph J, shoemkr Peter Eggemann, res 142 Barr.
Nix Lizzie, dressmkr, bds 80 E Jefferson.

Nix Selina, milliner A Mergentheim, bds 80 E Jefferson.
Nix Valentine, shoemkr, 80 E Jefferson, res same.
Nixon Sherman, clk Fort Wayne Beef Co, bds 248 Calhoun.
Noack Augusta, domestic 287 W Wayne.
Noag Edward G, tailor Andrew Foster, bds 21 Nirdlinger av.
Noag John, machinist, res 19 Nirdlinger ave.
Noag Wm, shoemkr, res 21 Nirdlinger ave.
Noble Charles, turner White's Wheel Works, n e cor Pitts-
    burg and Bond.
Noble Edward, mach hand Winch & Son, res 80 Walton av.
Noble Hemy E, clk J M Moderwell, bds 348 W Main.
Noble Hubert E, bookkeeper J M Moderwell, bds 348 W
    Main.
Noble James E, agt, res 33 Brackenridge.
Noble Jane (wid Wm), bds 49 Shawnee ave.
Noble Miss Jennie L, bds 33 Brackenridge.
Noble John E, electrician, n e cor Winter and E Creighton
    ave, res same.
Noble Miss Nettie E, stenographer, bds 138 Jackson.
Noble Sarah (wid Lester), res 138 Jackson.
Noble Wm H, machinist Ft W, C & L R R, res 348 W Main.
Noble Wm K, bds 33 Brackenridge.
Noecker James L, brakeman Penn Co, bds 49 Baker.
Noecker Mary (wid Ferdinand), res 49 Baker.
Noecker Millie, bds 49 Baker.
Noesler John, laborer Penn Co, res 1 Lumbard.
Noftzger Arthur R, feeder Fort Wayne Newspaper Union,
    bds 144 W DeWald.
Noftzger Charles E, trav agt Mossman, Yarnelle & Co, res
    382 Fairfield ave.
Nogal Leslie H, Dealer in New and Second-Hand Fur-
    niture; Tinware and Furniture Promptly Repaired;
    Stoves and Household Goods Stored at Moderate Prices,
    246 Calhoun, res 103 Madison.
Nohe John, machinist Fort Wayne Iron Works, bds 19 Nird-
    linger ave.
Nohe Rosina (wid Joseph), bds 48 Hendricks.
Nohe Miss Veronica, bds 48 Hendricks.
Nohrwald, *see Nahrwold and Norwald.*
Noirot Charles, saloon, 64 E Columbia, res same.
Noirot George, saloon, 49 E Main, rms same.
Noish Henry, blacksmith Olds' Wagon Works, res 72 Ham-
    ilton.
Nolan Garrett, laborer, rms 21 W 4th.
Nolan James, laborer, res 54 Chicago.
Nolan John, machinist Penn Co, res 328 Lafayette.

Nolan John A jr, machinist Penn Co, bds 24 Charles.
Nolan John H, saloon, 330 Lafayette, res 328 same.
Nolan Kate, bds 24 Charles.
Nolan Michael, engineer, res 24 Charles.
Nolan Nora, bds 24 Charles.
Nolan Rosa, milliner, bds 328 Lafayette.
Noll Albert, mach hd Olds' Wagon Works, bds 11 Simon.
Noll Albert J, clerk B R Noll, bds 97 W Wayne.
Noll Alfred F, clerk Adams & Armstrong, bds 239 E Jefferson.
Noll Alphonse A, broommaker, res 63 E Jefferson.
Noll Anton, stonecutter, res 231 W Washington.
Noll Barbara (wid Martin), bds 129 E Jefferson.
Noll Benedict R, druggist, 10 E Columbia, res 97 W Wayne.
Noll Benedict R & Co (Benedict R Noll), Druggists, 128 Broadway.
Noll Charles, butcher, res 109 Barthold.
Noll Charles jr, clerk, bds 109 Barthold.
Noll Charles A, clk Adams & Armstrong, bds 97 E Jefferson.
Noll Clement, bds 231 W Washington.
Noll Edward M, organist, res 68 Clay.
Noll Emma, clerk, bds 11 Simon.
Noll Ferdinand, helper, res 49 Nirdlinger ave.
Noll Frank J, traveling agent Adams & Armstrong, res 239 E Jefferson.
Noll George, clerk, bds 7 Harmer.
Noll John, stonecutter Fort Wayne Steam Stone Works, bds 240 E Wayne.
Noll John F, boots and shoes, 22 Clinton, res same.
Noll John G, bookkeeper J Nathan & Co, res 7 Harmer.
Noll Mrs Julia, res 63 E Jefferson.
Noll Kate, bds 7 Harmer.
Noll Martin A, traveling agent Adams & Armstrong, res 97 E Jefferson.
Noll Martin F, plumber Robert Ogden, bds 129 E Jefferson.
Noll Peter, painter Penn Co, bds 129 E Jefferson.
Noll Mrs Theresa, meat market, 109 Barthold, res same.
Noll Upton W, grocer, s w cor E Creighton ave and Lillie, res 11 Simon.
Noll Wm, farmer, res s s Main w of G R & I R R.
Noll Wm E, machinist, bds 11 Simon.
Noll Wm H, clerk, bds 97 W Wayne.
Noll Wm H, flagman, bds 11 Simon.
Noll Wm H, stonecutter George Jaap, bds 7 Harmer.
Nolz C, helper Penn Co, res 184 Suttenfield.
Nomdran C, laborer Penn Co, res 178 Gay.

Nommay Philomine (wid Frank), res w s Spy Run ave 4 n of St Mary's bridge.

Nones Mary L (wid Jefferson), res 333 E Washington.

Nonnamaker Andrew, bookkeeper, res 205 W Jefferson.

Nonnamaker Miss Lizzie, music teacher, 205 W Jefferson, bds same.

Nonnamaker Robert G, bookkeeper Charles F Muhler & Son, bds 205 W Jefferson.

Noonan David, laborer, res 39 E Superior.

Noonan Joseph, laborer, res 2 Madison.

Noonan Josephine (wid David), res 39 Duck.

Nordlinger Walter, trav agt J Lohman & Co.

Norris Calvin, laborer, bds 28 E Columbia.

Norris Mary (wid Calvin), res 28 E Columbia.

North David B, fireman, res 16 Murray.

North Sanford E, brakeman, bds 26 Harrison.

Northrop James L, engineer Nickel Plate, res 177 St Mary's.

Northrop Maud C L, seamstress, bds 187 St Mary's ave.

Northrop Rev Stephen A, D D, Pastor First Baptist Church, res 36 Montgomery.

North Western Mutual Life Ins Co, H B Hunt general agent, 1 Trentman block.

Norton Susan (wid John T), res 155 Holman.

Norwald, *see also Nahrwold*.

Norwald Frederick, molder Bass Foundry and Machine Wks, res 395 Hanna.

Norwald John E, machine hand Olds' Wagon Works, bds 327 Hanna.

Norwald Joseph W, machine hand Olds' Wagon Works, bds 327 Hanna.

Norwald Wm, machine hand Olds' Wagon Works, res 327 Hanna.

Notestine John H, clerk John Langard, res 48 W 3d.

Noviski Veronica (wid Joseph), res 267 Hanna.

Noweck Edward, carpenter, res 234 John.

Noze Christian, coremaker Bass Foundry and Machine Wks, res 12 Pine.

Nuffer Leonard, hostler, res 419 Calhoun.

Nulf Amanda, dressmaker, bds 110 Thomas.

Nulf Clarence, brakeman, bds 110 Thomas.

Nulf Edward L, conductor Penn Co, res 137 E De Wald.

Nulf Philip, fireman, res 110 Thomas.

Null John, laborer A McKernan, bds Wm A Smith.

Null Wm T, carpenter, res 334 E Washington.

Nunamaker Miss Dora, bds 264 W Washington.

Nunemaker Cyrilius, res 66 John.

Nussbaum Peter, foreman C L Centlivre, res cor Spy Run ave and Emily.

Nussmann Anthony, harnessmaker A L Johns & Co, bds 231 E Wayne.

Nussmann Catherine (wid John), res 231 E Wayne.

Nussmann Josephine B, clk Henry Treseler, bds 231 E Wayne.

Nusstorfer John P, teamster, res 4 Colerick.

Nuttle Wm, carpenter, res 12 E Columbia.

Nuttman Joseph D (Nuttman & Co), res 130 W Berry.

Nuttman & Co (Joseph D Nuttman), Bankers, 32 E Main.

Nyboer John H, car builder Penn Co, res 94 Force.

Nye Louis S, conductor, res 189 W Superior.

Nyland Frances, seamstress, bds 95 Smith.

Nyland Henry, helper, res 95 Smith.

O

Oacks Etta, domestic 110 E Berry.

Oakes Sumner, conductor Penn Co, res 76 Buchanan.

Oakley Chauncey B, bookkeeper J C Peters, res 240 W Main.

Oats Holland, stone carver Fort Wayne Steam Stone Works, bds Clifton House.

Oats James W, stone carver Fort Wayne Steam Stone Wks, bds Clifton House.

Oats Julian, stone carver Fort Wayne Steam Stone Works, bds Clifton House.

Oats Robert, stone carver Wm & J J Geake, bds Clifton House.

Oberlin Otto, clerk Hotel Pearse, bds same.

O'Brady Richard, flagman Penn Co, bds Hinton's Restaurant.

O'Brien, see also Bryan.

O'Brien Dennis, street commissioner, office 68 Barr, res 225 W Washington.

O'Brien Frank, fireman, bds 164 Broadway.

O'Brien James, driver Fort Wayne Artificial Ice Co, bds 11 W Columbia.

O'Brien James J, bartender C J Riedmiller, rms 51 Oakley.

O'Brien Jane (wid Thomas), res 157 Van Buren.

O'Brien John, plumber James Madden, bds 157 Van Buren.

O'Brien Kate, clk Alexander Goodman, bds 157 Van Buren.

O'Brien Martin, fireman, bds 157 Van Buren.

O'Brien Miss Mary, bds 83 Hoagland ave.

O'Brien Mary (wid Michael), res 22 Charles.

O'Brien Mary E, clerk G De Wald & Co, bds 157 Van Buren.

O'Brien Michael, fireman, bds 415 Lafayette.

John Pressler, Hot Air and Hot Water Furnaces.
Columbia, Barr and Dock Streets.

402   R. L. POLK & CO.'S

O'Brien Michael, fish-pedler, res 319 Hanna.
O'Brien Nanny, operator S M Foster, bds 86 Oakland.
O'Brien Patrick, blacksmith Penn Co, res 83 Hoagland ave.
O'Brien Patrick G, helper Penn Co, bds 83 Hoagland ave.
O'Brien Thomas, paper carrier, bds 157 Van Buren.
O'Brien Wm, bds 110 W Main.
O'Callahan, *see also Callahan.*
O'Callahan Mrs Anna, janitress Hoagland School bldg, res
    83 W Williams.
O'Connell Agnes, bds 99 W Main.
O'Connell Catherine (wid Daniel), res 25 9 Webster.
O'Connell Dennis, laborer, res s s Wheeler 2 w of Runnion.
O'Connell Edward J, clerk Penn Co, bds 259 Webster.
O'Connell Francis A, bds 259 Webster.
O'Connell George C, machine hand Horton Mnfg Co, bds 259
    S Webster.
O'Connell Hugh, plumber A Hattersley & Sons, bds 99 W
    Main.
O'Connell James, finisher Fort Wayne Furniture Co, res 395
    E Wayne.
O'Connell John, policeman, res 99 W Main.
O'Connell Thomas, machinist Indiana Machine Works, bds
    259 S Harrison.
O'Connell Thomas, messenger, bds 41 Hugh.
O'Connor, *see also Conners.*
O'Connor Bernard, res 156 W Wayne.
O'Connor Bernard (Eckart & O'Connor), s e cor W Main and
    Fulton.
O'Connor Bernard S (Summit City Soap Works), bds 9 E
    Wayne.
O'Connor Bridget (wid Jeremiah), res 184 Madison.
O'Connor Charles, car painter Penn Co, res 163 Hanna.
O'Connor Dennis, laborer Penn Co, res 12 Poplar.
O'Connor Frederick B, train despatcher Penn Co, bds 188
    Calhoun.
O'Connor Isabella M, bds 19 E Jefferson.
O'Connor Jeremiah, blacksmith Penn Co, res 46 Baker.
O'Connor John, helper, res 251 S Webster.
O'Connor John G, printer Fort Wayne Sentinel, bds 251 S
    Webster.
O'Connor Joseph M, res 19 E Jefferson.
O'Connor Julia, bds 184 Madison.
O'Connor Mary, clerk, bds 251 S Webster.
O'Connor Louisa (wid Stephen), res 19 W Jefferson.
O'Connor Wm F, blacksmith American Wheel Co, bds 251
    Webster.

Odd Fellows' Block, n e cor Wayne and Calhoun.

Odd Fellows' Hall, Postoffice bldg.

Odd Fellows' Hall (new), 20 W Berry.

Oddou Frank E, clerk J F Oddou, bds 207 E Jefferson.

Oddou Joseph F, grocer, 44 E Columbia, res 207 E Jefferson.

Oddou Louis, clerk J F Oddou, bds 207 E Jefferson.

Oddou Peter, carpenter, res 36 W 5th.

Oechtering Miss Antoinette, bds 142 E Jefferson.

Oechtering Rev John H, pastor St Mary's German Catholic Church, res 142 E Jefferson.

Oelschlaeger Caroline, bds 66 Baker.

Oelschlaeger Frederick, tailor, res 66 Baker.

Oertel Herman, laborer, res 71 Gay.

Oesterheld Frederick, hub turner Winch & Son, res 199 E Washington.

Oesterheld Frederick, tailor, res 126 Gay.

Oesterheld Lena, bds 126 Gay.

Oestermann, see also Osterman.

Oestermann George L, cornicemaker J H Welch, res 239 E Washington.

Oestermeier Charles, tailor, s e cor Calhoun and Montgomery, res 48 Leith.

Oestermeier Frederick, laborer, res 99 Smith.

Oetting Frederick, teamster, bds 126 Eliza.

Oetting Frederick D, saloon, 186 Fairfield ave, res 277 Webster.

Oetting Henry, bricklayer, res 374 E Lewis.

Oetting Wm, laborer, res 39 Hough.

Oetting Wm, baker B Gutermuth, bds 29 W Columbia.

Ofenloch Frank, meats, 100 Barr, res 213 E Wayne.

Ofenloch Mary A, converter worker Fort Wayne Electric Co, bds 130 Francis.

Ofenloch Michael, machinist Fort Wayne Electric Co, res 130 Francis.

Offenloch Kate, milliner Mrs Adolph Schulte, bds 32 Force.

Ofenloch Peter A, clerk V Ofenloch, bds 32 Force.

Ofenloch Valentine, grocer and saloon, 30 Force, res 32 same.

Offerle Joseph, laborer, bds 68 Smith.

Offerle Louis, laborer C L Centlivre, res n s Edna 1 w of Spy Run ave.

Offner John, machinist Wabash R R, res 46 Miner.

Ogden Robert, Plumber, Steam and Gas Fitter, and Natural Gas; Dealer in Iron and Lead Pipe, Sheet Lead, Hydrants, Bath Tubs, Pumps, Brass Goods, etc, 26 E Berry, res 64 Barr. (See adv back cover and in classified Plumbers.)

Ogier Thomas F, engineer, res 326 W Main.
Ogle John J, Physician and Surgeon, 13 W Wayne, res cor Creighton and Holton aves.
O'Harra Kate, domestic Rich's Hotel.
O'Hearn Edward, helper Penn Co, bds 128 Lillie.
O'Hearn James, blacksmith Penn Co, res 51 Prince.
O'Hearn James, blacksmith, res 430 E Wayne.
O'Hearn James B, helper Penn Co, bds 128 Lillie.
O'Hearn John, res 128 Lillie.
Ohneck, *see also Honeck.*
Ohneck Edward, student, bds 87 E Jefferson.
Ohneck George A, laborer The Peters Box and Lumber Co, res 39 N Calhoun.
Ohneck George D, trav agent C L Centlivre, res n w cor Clinton and Chestnut.
Ohneck John P, painter, res 58 W Williams.
Ohnhaus Frank J, trav agent, bds 25 Clay.
Ohnhaus John E, insurance, 10 Pixley & Long bldg, bds 25 Clay.
Ohnhaus Louis (Ohnhaus & Co), res 25 Clay.
Ohnhaus Scholastika (wid John E), res 25 Clay.
Ohnhaus & Co (Louis Ohnhaus, Charles G Guild), hats and gents' furnishing goods, 86 Calhoun.
Ohse John, laborer, res w s Abbott 3 s of Pontiac.
Ohse John jr, molder Bass Foundry and Machine Works, bds John Ohse.
O'Keefe, *see Keefe and Kief.*
Old Fort Manufacturing Co, Francis A Lomont pres, John Dreibelbiss sec-treas, pulley mnfrs, 3 and 4 Pixley & Long bldg.
Old Ladies' Home The, 144 Pritchard.
Old National Bank, S B Bond Pres, O P Morgan Vice-President, J D Bond Cashier, J C Woodworth Asst Cashier, s w cor Calhoun and Berry.
Olds Charles H, machinist Ft Wayne Electric Co, res 131 E De Wald.
Olds Charles L, res 213 Barr.
Olds Charles M, bds 198 W Wayne.
Olds Egbert G, foreman American Wheel Co, bds 198 W Wayne.
Olds Frederick G, machinist Penn Co, res 130 E De Wald.
Olds Henry G, pres Olds' Wagon Works, American Wheel Works and Fort Wayne Electric Co, res 107 W Berry.
Olds John D, mngr Ft Wayne Branch American Wheel Co, res 198 W Wayne.
Olds Noble G, clerk Olds' Wagon Works, bds 107 W Berry.

Olds' Wagon Works, Henry G Olds Pres, Andrew H Hamilton Vice-Pres, Wm Johnston Jr, Sec, Wm H Olds Treas, Mnfrs of Farm and Wayne Road Wagons, s s Murray bet Calhoun and Lafayette.

Olds Wm H, treas Olds' Wagon Works, bds 107 W Berry.

O'Leary Bartholomew, res 202 Francis.

O'Leary Bartholomew jr, laborer, bds 202 Francis.

O'Leary Elizabeth (wid Timothy), bds 171 W Berry.

O'Leary James, foreman, res 32 Hugh.

O'Leary Rev Thomas M, died October 24, 1889.

Olinger Albert, carpenter George W Bley, bds 232 E Jefferson.

Olinger John B, car builder Penn Co, res New Haven ave 1 w of Lumbard.

Olive James, helper Wabash R R, res 35 Bass.

Olive James jr, bellowsmaker Fort Wayne Organ Co, bds 35 Bass.

Oliver House, Mrs J B Wickliffe propr, 107 E Columbia.

Olmstead Leslie, lab, bds w s Spy Run ave 2 s of Randolph.

Olmstead Mary A, tailoress P D Swick, bds 509 E Washington.

Olson Nelson, actionmaker Ft Wayne Organ Co, res 18 Park.

Olson Olof, steamfitter, bds 104 Barr.

Olson Simon, fireman N Y, C & St L R R, bds 323 W Main.

O'Neil Daniel J, engineer, res 341 W Washington.

O'Neil Sarah, waiter Rich's Hotel, bds same.

O'Neil Timothy, molder Borcherding & Tonsing, res 36 Hamilton.

O'Neill John, laborer, bds 29 Colerick.

O'Neill Mrs Margaret, res 29 Colerick.

O'Neill Mary, clerk McKinnie House.

O'Neill Patrick, caller, bds 29 Colerick.

O'Neill Patrick, night clerk, bds 29 Colerick.

O'Neill Patrick W, brakeman, res 17 Bass.

Opatz Frank A, blacksmith Penn Co, res 150 Holman.

Openheimer Jacob, lab Weil Bros & Co, bds 47 E Columbia.

Oppelt George, barber George Thein, bds 26 W Superior.

Oppelt Joseph, polisher Griebel, Wyckoff & Becker, res 26 W Superior.

Oppenheim Wm S (Colerick & Oppenheim), res 9 E Wayne.

Oppenheimer Abraham, res 54 W Berry.

Oppenheimer Frederick, notions, bds 54 W Berry.

Oppenheimer Laura, bds 54 W Berry.

Oppenheimer Mrs Maggie, bds 105 Lafayette.

Oppliger, see also *Uplegger*.

Oppliger Annie M (wid Daniel), res 72 Pontiac.

Oren Solomon, laborer, bds 28 W Main.
Orff Charles E, cashier John Orff, bds same.
Orff Miss Flora B, bds John Orff.
Orff George E, clerk, bds 233 S Webster.
Orff Henry, music teacher, res 80½ W Creighton ave.
Orff John, Propr Empire Flour Mills, nr W Main Street Bridge, res The Cedars, Junction Columbia City and Huntington Roads.
Orff John R, miller John Orff, res 313 W Washington.
Orff Mary (wid Gottlieb), res 148 Clinton.
Orff Miss Mary E, tchr Hoagland School, bds 233 Webster.
Orff Montgomery C, bookkeeper John Orff, bds same.
Orlinskey Christian, milk pedler, res 49 Smith.
Ormiston Alexander, brick mnfr, res w s Piqua 4 s of Rudisill ave, res same.
Ormiston Christina (wid James), res w s Lafayette 8 s of Pontiac.
Ormiston Francis L, laborer, bds Lewis Ormiston.
Ormiston James, laborer Paul Koehler, res w s Lafayette s of city limits.
Ormiston Lewis, labor Wm Miller, res w s Piqua avs 3 s of Rudisill ave.
Ormiston Mark, laborer, bds Alexander Ormiston.
Ormiston Rufus, laborer, bds Lewis Ormston.
Orns Herman, laborer, bds 56 Thomas.
O'Rourke Edward, judge Circuit Court, res 134 E Washington.
O'Rourke Jeremiah, conductor Penn Co, bds 33 Lafayette.
O'Rourke John, brakeman, bds 2 Thomas.
O'Rourke John, conductor, res 235 E Lewis.
O'Rourke John B, plumber Robert Ogden, bds 235 E Lewis.
O'Rourke John C, res 268 E Lewis.
O'Rourke Josephine, domestic McKinnie House.
O'Rourke Miss Kate, teacher, bds 235 E Lewis.
O'Rourke Mary (wid Michael), res 236 Harmer.
O'Rourke Patrick S, supt Southern Division G R & I R R, res 30 McClellan.
Orr Charles W, asst cashier Hamilton National Bank, pres Morton Club, res 312 W Washington.
Orr Clinton H, bds Clifton House.
Orr H Clark, instrument maker Fort Wayne Electric Co, bds 377 Lafayette.
Orr James, electrician, bds 377 Lafayette.
Orr James A, stenogr Bash & Co, bds 28 Butler.
Orr James H, works Indiana School for Feeble-Minded Youth.
Orr John W, res 28 Butler.

Orr Joseph, teamster, res 109 Mechanic.

Orr Joseph H, bkkpr First National Bank, res 21 Butler.

Orr Mrs Mary E, matron Indiana School for Feeble-Minded Youth.

Orr Michael, teamster, res 112 Mechanic.

Orr Rezin, car driver, res 129 Broadway.

Orr Wm, res 377 Lafayette.

Orr Zachariah, driver Ft Wayne City Railroad Co, res 26 Grant ave.

Orrock Wm, rms 144 E Berry.

Ort Wm, farmer, bds 231 Barr.

Orth Christian, painter S F Bowser & Co, res 124 E DeWald.

Ortlieb George J, saloon, 88 Calhoun, res 125 W Jefferson.

Ortman Henry R, foreman L Dessauer & Co, res 55 E Lewis.

Ortmann Henry W, cigar mnfr, 26 Clinton, res 22 W Superior.

Ortmann Henry W jr, cigarmkr H W Ortmann, bds 22 W Superior.

O'Ryan, *see also Ryan.*

O'Ryan James, machinist, bds 50 Baker.

O'Ryan John, fireman, bds 50 Baker.

O'Ryan Patrick, policeman, res 50 Baker.

Osborne Miss Ida R, bds 91 E Main.

Osborn Murlin C, agt lightning rods, res 386 Calhoun.

Osborne John C, harnessmkr, bds 319 S Harrison.

Osborne Wm, switchman, rms 27 Baker.

Osenbaugh George I, brakeman, res s s Wayne Trace 3 e of Walton ave.

Osenbaugh Isaac, upholsterer Penn Co, res s s Wayne Trace 3 e of Walton ave.

Osenbaugh John, brakeman, res 113 Gay.

Oser Miss Josephine, domestic 142 E Jefferson.

O'Shaughnessy, *see also Shaughnessy.*

O'Shaughnessy Nora, bds 143 W Wayne.

Ossaforth Bernhardt, laborer Penn Co, res 80 Oliver.

Ossaforth Maggie, operator Hoosier Mnfg Co, bds 80 Oliver.

Ossaforth Rosa, domestic 126 E Wayne.

Osterhouse Herman, cigarmkr, bds Diamond Hotel.

Osterman, *see also Oestermann.*

Osterman John, fireman, res 4 St Mary's ave.

Ostermann Henry, cooper Louis Fox & Bro, res 320 E Wayne.

Ostermann John H, laborer, res 320 E Wayne.

Ostermann Lambert, res 235 E Washington.

Osthouse Herman, cigarmkr G F Yergens, bds Diamond Hotel.

Ostmann Charles, fireman, res 36 Burgess.

Oswald George, laborer, res 130 Erie.
Oswald Joseph, teamster Ft Wayne Iron Works, res 52 Smith.
Oswald Peter, laborer, bds s e cor Clinton and Superior.
Otis Eugene L, brakeman Penn Co, bds 190 Taber.
Otis Thomas, laborer, res 209 E Jefferson.
Ott Frank, painter, 90 E Main, res e s St Joe Gravel rd nr
    Institution for Feeble-Minded Youth.
Ott James, painter F Ott, bds Frank Ott.
Otten Christiana, tailoress L J Feist, bds 34 Gay.
Otten Henry, bds 56 Thomas.
Otten John, turner White's Wheel Works, res 70 Summit.
Otten Louis, wheelmkr American Wheel Co, res 122 Madison.
Otten Lucas, mach hand American Wheel Co, res 34 Gay.
Otten Lucas jr, molder American Wheel Co, bds 34 Gay.
Otten Nicholas, laborer Bass Foundry and Machine Works,
    res 44 Force.
Otten Otto H, plasterer, res 141 E Washington.
Otten Theodore, tinsmith Henry DeWald, bds 34 Gay.
Otten Tracy, bds 34 Gay.
Otto Anthony, laborer Penn Co, res 52 Baker.
Overholzer Irving, carpenter, res 121 W Washington.
Overly Didymus, plasterer, res 76 Smith.
Owen Luella M, bds 260 S Hoagland ave.
Owens Alice (wid Peter), res 51 Oakley.
Owens James, clerk Hunter Mnfg Co, bds 51 Oakley.
Owens John, machine hand American Wheel Co, res 89 Force.
Owens Michael J (Sherman & Owens), bds 54 W Main.
Owens Owen, conductor, res 143 Walton ave.
Owens Wm M, painter, res 18 Monroe.

P

Pacific Express Co, C B Beaver Agent, 79 Calhoun.
Pacius Julius P, stonecutter George Jaap, bds Peter Lutz.
Page John L, flagman, res 84 Chicago.
Page Wm D, Propr Fort Wayne News, 19 E Main, res
    316 E Jefferson.
Page Wm G, laborer Penn Co, res 4 Kansas.
Pageler Frederick H, clerk American Wheel Co, bds 177
    Montgomery.
Pageler Frederick J, spoke driver, res 177 Montgomery.
Pageler Henry H, laborer, bds 177 Montgomery.
Pageler John A, laborer, bds 177 Montgomery.
Pahl, see also Paul and Pohl.
Pahl Wm, machinist Bass Foundry and Machine Works, res
    106 Force.

Pailliotet Josephine, domestic Lake Shore Hotel.

Pailliotet Laura, bds 537 E Wayne.

Pallaton L, laborer Penn Co, res New Haven ave.

Palmer Albert, helper Frank Veith, res 20 Francis.

Palmer Albert D, plasterer, res s s Pontiac 2 w of Webster.

Palmer D S, clerk, rms 94 Calhoun.

Palmer Earl, res 31 N Cass.

Palmer George W, bds 114 E Berry.

Palmer Hiram, bricklayer, res 114 E Berry.

Palmer Jennie, dressmaker, 57 E Main, res same.

Palmer John W, engineer Nickel Plate, res 8 Pritchard.

Palmer Milford S, machine hand American Wheel Co, bds 110 E Berry.

Palmer Oscar, brakeman, res 63 High.

Palmer R Dilworth, clerk American Electric Co, rms 10 Thiemen & Gross Block.

Palmer Wm W, hammersmith, res 105 Force.

Panister, *see Bannister.*

Pantlind Henry D, laborer, res 33 E Main.

Pantlind Mrs Martha, res n s Cochrane 3 e of Coombs.

Panyard John, bds 599 E Wayne.

Panyard Joseph, painter L O Hull, res 599 E Wayne.

Panyard Mary C, seamstress, bds 599 E Wayne.

Pape, *see also Pepe and Pope.*

Pape Alfred, clerk A J Dittoe & Co, rms 20 W Berry.

Pape Miss Amelia, bds 56 St Mary's ave.

Pape Charles (Fleming Mnfg Co), Pres The Peters Box and Lumber Co, and Propr The Pape Furniture Co, res 56 St Mary's ave.

Pape Charles G, clerk The Peters Box and Lumber Co, bds 56 St Mary's ave.

Pape Furniture Co The, Charles Pape Propr, 28 and 30 E Berry.

Pape Miss Lizzie, bds 56 St Mary's ave.

Pape Miss Sophia, bds 56 St Mary's ave.

Pape Wm, res 151 High.

Pape Wm C, foreman, res 185 Taber.

Pappert Amand, res 252 E Wayne.

Pappert Amand jr, cigarmaker, bds 252 E Wayne.

Pappert Henry, res 279 W Main.

Pappert Maria, bds 252 E Wayne.

Pappert Wm F, molder Bass Foundry and Machine Works, res 250 E Wayne.

Pardee Wm McKay, civil engineer Nickel Plate, res 171 W Wayne.

Parham Frederick C (F C & J M Parham), res 153 W De Wald.

Parham F C & J M (Frederick C and John M), farm impts, 29 Barr.

Parham John M (F C & J M Parham), res 1 Riverside ave.

Parisian Millinery and Cloak House, Victor E Wolf Propr, 26 Calhoun.

Parisoe Emma, rms 74 Montgomery.

Parisoe Mary, rms 74 Montgomery.

Parisot Alexander J, clk Wabash R R, res 74 Buchanan.

Parisot Edward F, photographer, bds 322 Hanna.

Parisot Frank S, rimmer, bds 322 Hannna.

Parisot Joseph, foreman Wabash R R, res 322 Hanna.

Parker Charles (col'd), night watchman Ryan Bros, bds Jacob Clay.

Parker James, laborer Lindenwood Cemetery, res s s Wheeler nr Runnion ave.

Parker Joshua, res 130 Franklin ave.

Parker Samuel, machinist Fort Wayne Electric Co, res 55 W, Main.

Parker Wm, machine hand Hoffman Bros, bds 22 W Main.

Parkes Emanuel, brakeman, rms 23 Baker.

Parkinson Wm F, packer Olds' Wagon Works, bds 43½ E Columbia.

Parks John, printer, bds 46 E Jefferson.

Parks Volney, bds 49 W Main.

Parmalee Robert H (Pixley & Co), res Bloomington, Ill.

Parnin Louis F, hostler V A Huguenard, bds 61 E Superior.

Parr Andrew J, tailor A F Schoch, bds 90 W 4th.

Parr Charles J, car repairer, res 90 W 4th.

Parr Frederick, apprentice John Pressler, bds 90 W 4th.

Parr John B, clerk L S & M S Ry, bds 90 W 4th.

Parrant Annie, bds F E Parrant.

Parrant Frank A, wheelmaker American Wheel Co, bds F E Parrant.

Parrant Frank E, market stall 35, res e s Walton ave 1 n of P, F W & C Ry.

Parrant Joseph, bartender C J Jourdain, bds e s Walton ave 1 n of P, F W & C Ry.

Parrant Julian, section hand, res 9 Simon.

Parrant Lena, bds F E Parrant.

Parrant Peter J, painter L O Hull, bds F E Parrant.

Parrett, *see also Parrott and Perett.*

Parrett Mrs Maria, janitor Hanna School, res 290½ Hanna.

Parrin Josie, bds 223 E Wayne.

Parrish Leo J, engineer, res 87 W Williams.

Parrish Theodore G, fireman, bds 87 W Williams.
Parrish Wm A, bds 87 W Williams.
Parrisot Miss Louise, teacher, bds 29 Duck.
Parrot Frank, Dealer in Fresh, Salt and Smoked Meats, Poultry, Butter, Eggs, etc, 28 E Columbia, res 385 E Washington.
Parrott, *see also Parrett and Perett.*
Parrott George J, clerk J A Shoaff, bds 27 Oak.
Parrott Julia, clerk H H Barcus, bds 27 Oak.
Parrott Louis A, laborer American Wheel Co, res 283 E Washington.
Parrott Mary, dressmaker, bds 27 Oak.
Parrott Peter, res 27 Oak.
Parry, *see also Perrey and Perry.*
Parry Gaylord T, clerk, bds 264 W Wayne.
Parry George W, boilermaker, res 330 Harrison.
Parry John W, conductor, rms 29 W Lewis.
Parry Wm S, trav salesman, res 264 W Wayne.
Passage Elmer, laborer, bds 91 Franklin ave.
Passage Levi H, res 91 Franklin ave.
Passino Alpha, clerk J P Gray, bds 19 Jane.
Passino Frank, coil winder Fort Wayne Electric Co, bds 19 Jane.
Passino George, conductor G R & I R R, res 47 Thomas.
Passino Joseph P, machinist Bass Foundry and Machine Works, res 405 Lafayette.
Passino Peter, flagman, res 19 Jane.
Patee Wm H, painter Fleming Mnfg Co, res 22 Barthold.
Pattee Torrance D, brakeman Penn Co, res 206 Walton ave.
Patterson Mrs Calista, res 50 Brackenridge.
Patterson Elizabeth (wid John), bds 82 Barr.
Patterson George A, machinist E B Kunkle & Co, res 32 Baker.
Patterson George M, engineer, res 304 S Harrison.
Patterson James, harnessmaker F Hilt, bds 87 Ewing.
Patterson Jesse F, train despatcher Penn Co, rms 30 Douglas.
Patterson Minnie M, clk A Mergentheim, bds 304 S Harrison.
Patterson Robert, bds 32 Baker.
Patterson Thomas R, clerk Wm E Miner, bds 10 Oliver.
Patterson Virgil, machine hand American Wheel Co, bds 105 John.
Patton Miss Alice, dressmaker, 10 W Superior, bds same.
Patton George D, trav agent, res 526 E Wayne.
Patton Jesse T, policeman, res 193 Ewing.
Patton Joshua, laborer, bds Hedekin House.
Patton Wm S, carpenter, res 58 Brackenridge.

Paul, *see also Pahl and Pohl.*

Paul Augusta, clerk L Wolf & Co, bds 38 W Jefferson.

Paul Charles, laborer, res 45 High.

Paul Charles A, bookkeeper Tri-State Building and Loan Association, bds 38 W Jefferson.

Paul Christian, machinist Old Fort Mnfg Co, bds 296 S Harrison.

Paul Emil F C, apprentice Fort Wayne Newspaper Union, bds 45 High.

Paul Ernst, engineer, res 298 S Harrison.

Paul Frederick, machinist Penn Co, res 296 S Harrison.

Paul Frederick jr, clerk C Schiefer & Son, res 178 Ewing.

Paul Henry C, pres The Horton Mnfg Co and Salimonie Mining and Gas Co, res 119 W Wayne.

Paul Miss Justa, bds 38 W Jefferson.

Paul Miss Lena, bds 296 S Harrison.

Paul Miss Lizzie, bds 38 W Jefferson.

Paul Wm, res 38 W Jefferson.

Paul Wm jr, fitter Salimonie Mining and Gas Co, bds 38 W Jefferson.

Pauley Eugene J, machine hand Fort Wayne Electric Co, bds 76 W Williams.

Pauley James, laborer, bds 76 W Williams.

Pauley John J, chief clerk The Randall, res 60 W Williams.

Pauley Thomas, blksmith Penn Co, res 76 W Williams.

Pauley Thomas jr, laborer Penn Co, bds 76 W Williams.

Paulus Frank D (McClure & Paulus), farm implements, 16 Columbia, res 222 W Wayne.

Paus Albert, helper C W Bruns & Co, bds 107 High.

Paxton George L, stenographer Indiana School for Feeble-Minded Youth.

Paxton James, brakeman, bds 33 St Mary's ave.

Payne Aurelius T, machine hand Louis Diether & Bro, res 148 St Mary's ave.

Payne Charles, laborer, bds 64 E Berry.

Payne Edward I, clerk, bds 407 E Wayne.

Payne Elmer E, livery, bds 407 E Wayne.

Payne Eva, domestic Windsor Hotel.

Payne Frank D, driver F W Robinson, bds 148 St Mary's av.

Payne George C, bds 290 Calhoun.

Payne Harry A, hostler, bds 290 Calhoun.

Payne Ira S, laborer, res 148 St Mary's ave.

Payne James W, laborer The Remington-Lawton Co, bds 57 Barr.

Payne John H, clerk G W Seavey, res 337 E Wayne.

Payne John H, hostler Winkelmeyer Bros, bds Clifton House.

Payne Mary E (wid Charles L), res 70 Dawson.
Payne Matilda (wid Rutherford S), bds 30 Calhoun.
Payne Seymour, laborer American Wheel Co, res 78 Melita.
Payne Wm C, boarding house, 290 Calhoun.
Payne Wm C jr, fireman, bds 290 Calhoun.
Payne Wm R, laborer, res 407 E Wayne.
Payne Wm S, laborer, res 78 Melita.
Payton Alfred B, laborer, bds 332 W Main.
Payton Jefferson W, laborer, bds Wm B Payton.
Payton Wm B, laborer, res e s St Mary's ave 1 n of canal
  feeder.
Pearl Minnie, domestic 68 W Berry.
Pearse Edward, engineer, res 332 W Washington.
Pearse Frank D, Propr Hotel Pearse, n w cor Calhoun
  and Chicago, res same.
Pearse James W (Pearse & Loag), res 22 Chicago.
Pearse & Loag (J W Pearse, est of G W Loag), livery, 18
  Holman.
Pearson, *see also Pierson.*
Pearson John C, fireman, res 54 Hugh.
Pease Wm H, saloon, 11 W Columbia, res 7 same.
Peck John M, machine hand American Wheel Co, res e s
  Monroe 5 s of Wallace.
Peck Solon L, res 148 W Wayne.
Peckham Charles T, teamster John Wilson & Son, res 8
  Thomas.
Peckham Harlan R, teamster John Wilson & Son, res 18
  Colerick.
Peckham Wm T, agent, res 244 Creighton ave.
Peckstein, *see Beckstein.*
Peek Henry A, machinist Bass Foundry and Machine Works,
  bds 20 Jones.
Pegeler Frederick, wheelmaker American Wheel Co, res 177
  Montgomery.
Pegensic Ralph, billiard room, rms 55 W Main.
Pegg Henry, carpenter, res 20 Jones.
Pegg Loren B, barber, 136 Broadway, res 208 W Jefferson.
Peigh Simon, bds Clifton House.
Peion Louis, carpenter C L Centlivre, res 18 Randolph.
Peirot James, boilermaker, res 57 Prince.
Pelkin Louis, lab, bds n s New Haven ave 3 w of Lumbard.
Pellens Joseph B (Gross & Pellens), res 228 W Washington.
Peltier James C, Undertaker and Embalmer, 17 W
  Wayne, res 137 E Berry.
Peltier Louis, assistant J C Peltier, res 49 E Lewis.
Peltier Wm H, clerk J C Peltier, bds 137 E Berry.

Pelton Theodore, toolmaker Fort Wayne Electric Co, res 233 W Jefferson.

Pelz Albert, wiper Penn Co, bds 40 Laselle.

Pelz August, laborer, res 40 Laselle.

Pelzer Frederick, section foreman, res 41 Nirdlinger ave.

Pembroke Mary M, converter worker Fort Wayne Electric Co, bds 51 Oakley.

Pence Frank, porter Aveline House.

Pence Sarah E (wid Robert H), res 16 Marion.

Penkin Rudolph, car inspr, res n w cor Warren and Chestnut.

Penn Mutual Life Insurance Co, Clark Fairbank general agent, 19 Court.

Penningrot August, laborer, bds 81 Wall.

Pennsylvania Company, Operating the Pittsburgh, Ft Wayne & Chicago Railway, C D Law Supt Western Division, R B Rossington Freight Agent, John E Ross Ticket Agent, Offices e s Clinton bet Holman and Railroad, Passenger Depot cor Calhoun and Clinton, Freight Depot cor Clinton and Railroad.

Penoyer Frank, fireman, bds 202 Hanna.

Pens Albert, helper C W Bruns & Co, bds 107 High.

Pens Charles W, laborer Louis Rastetter, res 1 Indiana ave.

Pens Henry D, engineer Ft Wayne Iron Works, res 107 High.

Pens Wm F, plumber C W Bruns & Co, res 107 High.

Peppe Albert C, clerk, bds 67 Harrison.

Peppe Edward L, car repairer Ft W, C & L R R, bds 73 N Cass.

Peppers John L, janitor Y M C A (R R dept), res 94 Wells.

Perett, see also Purrett and Parrott.

Perett Emily, bds rear 290 Hanna.

Perett Margaret, bds rear 290 Hanna.

Perett Richard W, res rear 290 Hanna.

Perkins L B, laborer Penn Co.

Perrey, see also Parry and Perry.

Perrey Adele (wid Joseph), res 2 Oak.

Perrey Edward, photographer J A Shoaff, bds 2 Oak.

Perrey Emma, dressmaker, 2 Oak, bds same.

Perrey Flora, bds 2 Oak.

Perrey Frank J (Geary & Perrey), bds 174 Jackson.

Perrey Joseph, laborer, bds 2 Oak.

Perrin Ashley C, Propr Belmont Stables, 88 E Main, res 181 E Wayne. (See adv, p 63.)

Perrin Elias H, pressman The Press, bds 15 W Williams.

Perrin Hiram F, pressman, bds 15 W Williams.

Perrin John W, pressman Fort Wayne Sentinel, res 32 E 4th.

Perrin Mattie, dressmaker, bds 15 W Williams.

Perrin May, bds 181 E Wayne.
Perrine Anna (wid Wm H), res 58 Chicago.
Perrine Charles A, laborer, bds 320 Calhoun.
Perrine Harvey J, conductor, res 320 Calhoun.
Perriquay Felix, brickmaker, res 187 W Superior.
Perriquay Frank, section hand, bds 22 E Columbia.
Perriquay Julian, fireman, res 12 Sturgis.
Perriquay Peter, gardener, res n w cor Lumbard and New Haven ave.
Perrman Robert P, lumber, rms 144 E Berry.
Perry, *see also Parry and Perrey.*
Perry Anna, bds 100 Walton ave.
Perry A C, car builder Penn Co, res 46 Madison.
Perry Edward, caller, bds 159 Erie.
Perry Ella I, bds 100 Walton ave.
Perry Frank, engineer, res 127 Montgomery.
Perry Franklin L, laborer, bds 159 Erie.
Perry George H, fur dealer, 22 W Columbia, bds Aveline House.
Perry Henry, street paver, bds 22 E Columbia.
Perry John T, bricklayer, res 39 Shawnee ave.
Perry Madison, finisher Olds' Wagon Works, res 100 Walton,
Perry Oscar L, Manager Western Union Telegraph Co. res 164 Lafayette.
Perry Philip, lab White's Wheel Works, res 100 Walton.
Perry Wm W, carpenter, res 159 Erie.
Perry Zelma G, opr S M Foster, bds 159 Erie.
Peterman Wm H, laborer, res 161 High.
Peters Box and Lumber Co The, Charles Pape Pres, Treas and Gen'l Mngr, W H Murtagh Vice-Pres, Wilson McQuiston Sec, Mnfrs Hardwood Lumber and Furniture; Office and Factory 79 to 105 High; Furniture Salesroom 28 and 30 E Berry. (*See adv, p 6.*)
Peters Frederick, butcher, bds 1 Glasgow ave.
Peters Frederick H, sawyer J C Peters, res 20 Pritchard.
Peters Frederick R, machinist Ft Wayne Iron Works, res 219 W Superior.
Peters Jacob, lab, res s s Riverside ave on St Joseph river.
Peters Jacob A, plasterer, bds 106 Riverside.
Peters Jerome (col'd), barber, cor Columbia and Barr.
Peters John C, pres Indiana Machine Works, mnfr hardwood lumber, and mngr Horton Mnfg Co, w s Osage n of Main, res 232 W Wayne.
Peters John F, laborer, bds Jacob Peters.
Peters Matilda S, tailoress G Scheffler, bds 20 Pritchard.
Peters Simon J, paperhanger, res 67 W Superior.

Peters Wm H, clk Dreier Bros, bds 178 W Berry.
Peterson Charles, foreman, res s s Pontiac 1 e of Hoagland.
Peterson Charles E. teamster, res 132 Wells.
Petgen Daniel, coppersmith Penn Co, res 245 Clay.
Petgen Frank, boilermaker Kerr-Murray Mnfg Co, bds 64 Melita.
Petgen Frank A, brakeman Penn Co, res 95 Baker.
Petgen John H, laborer, bds 64 Melita.
Petgen Mrs Mary E, res s e cor Winter and Edgerton.
Petgen Nicholas, checker, res 64 Melita.
Petgen Nicholas, helper Penn Co, res 245 Clay.
Pettit August, section hand, bds 22 E Columbia.
Pettit Benjamin F, printer, bds 221 W DeWald.
Pettit Charles A, teamster, res 113 Barthold.
Pettit Edward, laborer Penn Co, bds 91 E Washington.
Pettit Joseph E, laborer, bds Wm Pettit.
Pettit Joseph S, publisher, 19 Schmitz blk, res 268 W Washington.
Pettit Sadie, bds Wm Pettit.
Pettit Sherman E, brakeman, res 73 E Berry.
Pettit Wm, res w s Francis 2 n of Wayne.
Pettit Wm L, asst cashier First National Bank, res 221 W DeWald.
Pettit Wm V, teamster, bds Wm Pettit.
Petzinger Charles, apprentice Penn Co, bds 76 Pontiac.
Petzinger Frederick L, boilermaker, res s s Pontiac 2 e of Lafayette.
Petzinger George W, boilermaker Penn Co, bds s s Pontiac 1 e of Lafayette.
Peulvermueller Henrietta, res 57 John.
Pevert Frank, laborer, res 32 Elm.
Peyton Clara, domestic 55 E Wayne.
Pfeiffer Benjamin F, carpenter, res 25 Schick.
Pfeiffer Charles F, mngr Fleming Mnfg Co, res e s Spy Run ave 2 n of Brewery.
Pfeiffer Christian J, farmer, res e s Spy Run ave 2 n of Brewery.
Pfeiffer Edward, laborer Nickel Plate, res s e cor Richardson and Rumsey ave.
Pfeiffer Eva (wid Joseph), res 61 Elm.
Pfeiffer Henry (Pfeiffer & Schlatter), res 386 E Wayne.
Pfeiffer Henry G, clerk Pfeiffer & Schlatter, bds 386 E Wayne.
Pfeiffer John N (Rousseau & Pfeiffer), bds 37 W Berry.
Pfeiffer Louis M, fireman, res 29 Gay.
Pfeiffer Robert D, butcher, res 37½ W Berry.

Pfeiffer Thomas, laborer Ranke & Yergens, res 5 Wall.

Pfeiffer & Schlatter (Henry Pfeiffer, Christian C Schlatter), Hardware, Farm Implements and Sewing Machines, 38 and 40 E Columbia. (*See right bottom lines.*)

Pfister Alexander, stone mason, res 218 Broadway.

Pfister John, laborer Louis Rastetter, bds 218 Broadway.

Pfleager Mrs Carrie L, bds 74 Barr.

Pfleiderer Henrietta, bds 536 E Wayne.

Pfleiderer Jacob, grocer, 529 E Wayne, res 536 same.

Pfleiderer Wm, clk Jacob Pfleiderer, bds 536 E Wayne.

Pflieger Joseph, express, res n w cor Mary and Runnion ave.

Phelps Charles, carpenter, res 1 Diamond.

Phelps Miss Clara, teacher Jefferson School, bds 258 W Wayne.

Phelps George A, fireman, bds 9 N Calhoun.

Phelps George W, truckman, res 168 Putnam.

Phelps John W, conductor, res 5 West.

Phelps Nellie, packer Summit City Soap Works, bds 367 E Lewis.

Phelps Whitcomb, physician, 367 E Lewis, res same.

Philabaum Alice, opr S M Foster, bds 42 Wells.

Philabaum Frank, messenger Empire Line, bds 42 Wells.

Philabaum Sarah (wid David), res 42 Wells.

Philbin Wm H, laborer Wabash R R, bds 4 Kansas.

Phillabaum Mrs Ann J, laundry, 168 Francis, res same.

Philley Miss Anna M, teacher elocution Westminster Seminary, bds 251 W Main.

Philley Eli S, freight agt L S & M S Ry, res 40 Brackenridge.

Philley Miss Emily L, res 20 W Superior.

Philley Hiram A, clk Penn Co, res w s Victoria ave 6 s of Calhoun.

Phillips Caroline W (wid Bernhardt), res 121 W Main.

Phillips Frank B, bookkpr Bass Foundry and Machine Works, bds 121 W Main.

Phillips Patrick, blacksmith helper Penn Co, bds 71 Dawson.

Phillips Siley P, physician, 123 E Main, res same.

Phillips Thomas, section hand Wabash R R, bds 71 Dawson.

Phipps John A, conductor Penn Co, res 36 Thomas.

Phipps Robert, conductor, res 8 Jackson.

Phœnix Block, w s Calhoun n of Main.

Piatt Cyrus H, laborer Penn Co, res 505 Lafayette.

Pichon Alexander, bds 329 E Wayne.

Pichon George, carpenter, bds 192 E Wayne.

Pichon Hattie, shirtmaker P G Kuttner, bds Euclid ave.

Pichon Joseph, carpenter, bds 192 E Wayne.

John Pressler, Mantels, Grates and Tile Floor.
Columbia, Barr and Dock Streets.

418   R. L. POLK & CO.'S

Pichon Margaret, bds 329 E Wayne.

Pichon Sadie, domestic, rms 16 W Main.

Pickard Artemus W, clk Bass Foundry and Machine Works, bds 106 E Washington.

Pickard Bros (Peter E, Thomas D and Harry R), Stoves, Tinware and House Furnishing Goods, 29 E Columbia.

Pickard Harry R (Pickard Bros), bds 106 E Washington.

Pickard Peter E (Pickard Bros), res 149 E Berry.

Pickard Thomas D (Pickard Bros), res Chicago, Ill.

Pickard Thomas R, supt foundry dept Bass Foundry and Machine Works, res 106 E Washington.

Pickering Charles, bds 290 Calhoun.

Pidgeon Charles T, traveling agent Adams & Armstrong, bds 148 W Berry.

Pieber Ernest, laborer, res 88 W Jefferson.

Piepenbrink Albert J, machinist Jenney Electric Light and Power Co, res 19 Clark.

Piepenbrink Charles, vegetables, market stall 34, res s s New Haven rd e of city limits.

Piepenbrink Christian, clerk county treasurer, res n s Prospect ave 2 e of Spy Run ave.

Piepenbrink Clara C, bds 48 W Washington.

Piepenbrink Conrad D, assessor, res 48 W Washington.

Piepenbrink Emma, domestic 64 McClellan.

Piepenbrink George D, clerk E S Thomas, bds 48 W Washington.

Piepenbrink Henry (Gombert & Piepenbrink), res 84 Lillie.

Piepenbrink Henry P, bartender Heilbroner & Brown, bds 48 W Washington.

Piepenbrink Wm, section hand, res 82 Lillie.

Pieper, *see also Piper*.

Pieper Frederick C, carpenter, res 214 W Jefferson.

Pieper John F, machinist Wabash R R, res 71 W Jefferson.

Pieper Sophia, bds 71 W Jefferson.

Pierce, *see also Pearce and Peirce*.

Pierce Andrew W, painter, res 156 Greely.

Pierce Austa (wid Franklin J), bds 171 Wells.

Pierce Charles E, machinist Penn Co, bds 245 E Lewis.

Pierce Daniel, sawyer Kilian Baker, bds 109 E Columbia.

Pierce Edward, engineer, res 332 W Washington.

Pierce Everett, machinist Penn Co, res 245 E Lewis.

Pierce Harry W, student, bds 245 E Lewis.

Pierce James S, bds 29 E 2d.

Pierce Mrs L L, teacher Indiana School for Feeble-Minded Youth.

Pierce Ogden (F L Jones & Co), res 240 Hoagland ave.

Pierce Ogden jr, clerk Troy Steam Laundry, bds 240 Hoagland ave.

Pierre Charles J, Dry Goods, Notions, Gents' Furnishings, Groceries, Glass and Tinware, s w cor Wells and 2d, res same.

Pierre Joseph M, clerk Peter Pierre, res 173 Van Buren.

Pierre Kate, clerk Peter Pierre, res 254 W Washington.

Pierre Peter, dry goods, 166 and 168 Broadway, res 254 W Washington.

Pierson, *see also Pearson.*

Pierson Calvin J, engineer, res 155 Hanna.

Pierson Elizabeth, (wid Nicholas), bds 144 Maumee road.

Pierson Jacob B, sewer contractor, res 144 Maumee road.

Pierson Jennie A, milliner Mrs G J Stier, bds 144 Maumee road.

Pierson Lottie M, bds 144 Maumee road.

Pierson Ulietta D (wid John), dressmkr, 153 Hanna, res same.

Pietz J Ferdinand, jeweler, 138 Calhoun, res 222 Lafayette.

Piggott Wm, driver Ryan Bros, res 180 W Jefferson.

Pike Iva, bds 34 Walton ave.

Pike James E, machine hand Louis Diether & Bro, res 34 Walton.

Piles Theodore, stone cutter, res 27 Brandriff.

Pilliod Charles J (Pilliod & Brown), bds 141 N Cass.

Pilliod Frank, engineer Pillod & Brown, bds 141 N Cass.

Pilliod & Brown (Charles J Pilliod, Charles W Brown), proprs Bloomingdale Mills, cor Wells and 6th.

Pimbroke Mary, bds 51 Oakley.

Pinnegar George, stone cutter Wm & J J Geake, bds 312 W Main.

Piper, *see also Pieper.*

Piper Julius A, cigarmaker G F Yergens, bds 162 Montgomery.

Pitcher Ledger, laborer, bds 301 Calhoun.

Pittijohn Louise, domestic Diamond Hotel.

Pittsburgh, Fort Wayne & Chicago and Grand Rapids & Indiana Ry Passenger Depot cor Calhoun and Railroad.

Pittsburgh, Fort Wayne & Chicago Railway Freight Depot, cor Clinton and Railroad.

Pittsburgh, Fort Wayne & Chicago Railway, operated by the Pennsylvania Co, offices e s Clinton bet Holman and Railroad. (*See Pennsylvania Co.*)

Pixley Frank J, machine hand American Wheel Co, res 53 Madison.

Pixley George K, clerk Pixley & Co, bds 133 W Wayne.

Pixley George W (Pixley & Co), treas Jenney Electric Light
    and Power Co, and Fort Wayne Land Improvement Co,
    res 133 W Wayne.

Pixley George W jr (Pixley & Co), res Utica. N Y.

Pixley Henry D (Pixley & Co), res Utica, N Y.

Pixley & Co (Henry D, George W and George W Pixley
    jr, Charles E Read, Robert H Parmalee), Clothing, Gents'
    Furnishing Goods, Hats and Caps, 16 and 18 E Berry.

Pixley & Long Block, e s Berry bet Calhoun and Clinton.

Plasterer Purl C, clk Dozois, Beadell & Co, bds 110 W Main.

Platter Ananias, conductor, bds 49 Grand.

Plattor Edwin, polisher White's Wheel Works, bds 34 Hay-
    den.

Plattor George J, fireman G R & I R R, res 34 Hayden.

Pleasant Hill Dairy, n s Maysville road 2 miles n e of city
    limits.

Plengey George, teamster, res Centlivre Park.

Pliett Christina (wid Carl), res 206 John.

Pliett Conrad, laborer Bass Foundry and Machine Works, res
    206 John.

Pliett Edward J, helper Bass Foundry and Machine Works,
    bds 206 John.

Plock, *see also Block.*

Plock Bernard, fireman, res 204 W Jefferson.

Plock Edward J, painter City Carriage Works, bds 63 Co-
    lumbia.

Plock Herman H, finisher Ft Wayne Furniture Co, bds 20
    N Harrison.

Plock John, finisher Foster Furniture Co, bds 61 Columbia.

Ploor Margaretta (wid Christian F), res 96 E Jefferson.

Plogstart John A, gardener, junction Old Piqua rd and New
    Haven ave.

Plogstart Wm, trav agent, bds John A Plogstart.

Plumadore Horton, clerk Root & Co, bds 40 Madison.

Plumadore Marshall N, teacher Ft Wayne Conservatory of
    Music, res 9 E Wayne.

Plummer Caroline, domestic A B Nickey.

Plunkett George A, gasfitter Salimonie Mining and Gas Co, bds
    Monroe House.

Plymouth Congregational Church, n w cor W Washington
    and Fulton.

Poch August F, driver Root & Co, bds 165 Broadway.

Poch Emil F, weaver M E Poch, bds 165 Broadway.

Poch Emma, domestic 198 W Wayne.

Poch Moritz E, carpet weaver, 165 Broadway, res same.

Pocock Miss Jennie, clerk C W McKee, bds 56 Douglas ave.

Pocock Major, fireman, rms 303 Calhoun.

Poeple Henry, rms 59 E Wayne.

Poenitz Robert, clerk F J E De LaGrange, res 71 Ohio.

Poetsch Agnes (wid Frederick), res 32 Pritchard.

Poetsch Lena, seamstress, bds 32 Pritchard.

Pohl, *see also Pahl and Paul.*

Pohl Bernardina, bds George Pohl.

Pohl George, car builder Penn Co, res n s Chestnut 2 e of .Lumbard.

Pohlman Christian, carpenter, res 144 Greely.

Pohlmeier Minnie, domestic 241 W Wayne.

Pohlmeyer Frederick C, bricklayer, res 57 Baker.

Poinsatte Joseph, laborer The Herman Berghoff Brewing Co.

Poirson Frank J, setter David Tagtmeyer, res 215 Wells.

Poirson Peter F, clerk P O, bds 70 E Columbia.

Polhamus Albert H, foreman Penn Co, res 73 Dawson.

Polhamus Allen Z, machinist Penn Co, res 302 Harrison.

Polhamus John G, stereotyper Fort Wayne Newspaper Union, bds 73 Dawson.

Polhamus Wm H, fireman, res 25 Julia.

Police Headquarters, Frank Wilkinson chief, City Hall.

Polison Elizabeth, laundress Hotel Pearse.

Polk R L & Co, Ralph L Polk Pres, Jacob W Weeks Sec and Treas, Publishers Fort Wayne City Directory, 50 Calhoun.

Polley James, coachman 289 Fairfield ave.

Pollison Samuel, brakeman, res 79 W DeWald.

Pollitz Frederick, laborer, res 236 Gay.

Pollock Cleveland, hostler Lee & Fulton, rms same.

Pollock Frank, carpenter, res w s Shawnee ave 1 n of Home.

Pollock James H, carpenter, res 581 Broadway.

Pollock Wm H, carpenter, res 43 Indiana ave.

Polson Henry, gardener, 261 W Berry.

Polson John, sewer builder, res 148 Wells.

Polzen Michael, engine inspector Penn Co, res 36 Force.

Pombaugh Thomas C, laborer Fort Wayne Organ Co, res 108 W Creighton ave.

Pomper Herman, carpet weaver, 229 Lafayette, res same.

Pomper Otto, stripper C A Berndt, bds 229 Lafayette.

Pomper Richard, cigarmaker C A Berndt, bds 229 Lafayette.

Pomroy Wm J W, paperhanger, res 193 High.

Ponfot Emile, meats, bds 105 Summit.

Pool Asa D, laborer Penn Co, bds 16 Colerick.

Pool Charles, laborer Penn Co, res 16 Colerick.

Poole Emery O, keeper tool room Wabash R R, res 17 W Creighton ave.

Poole Frank H, asst cashier Hamilton National Bank, res 17 W Creighton ave.

Poor Handmaids of Jesus Christ in charge of St Joseph's Hospital, s w cor Broadway and W Main.

Pope, *see also Pape.*

Pope James F, train despatcher Nickel Plate, res 75 Lafayette.

Popp, *see also Bopp.*

Popp Adam, laborer, res 208 High.

Popp Charles, bartender Henry Ranke, bds 42 Harmer.

Popp George L, machine hand American Wheel Co, bds 158 Wallace.

Poppel Henry D F, Groceries and Dry Goods, 302 E Washington, rms 59 E Wayne.

Porseh Amelia, works Troy Steam Laundry, bds 140 W 3d.

Porsch George B, machinist Indiana Machine Works, res 18 W Burgess.

Porsch Johanna (wid Wm), res 140 W 3d.

Porsch John, candymaker Louis Fox & Bro, bds 140 W 3d.

Porsch Laura, works Troy Steam Laundry, bds 142 W 3d.

Porter Cora, operator Hoosier Mnfg Co, bds 71 Purman.

Porter Elizabeth (wid Humphrey), res 39 Pritchard.

Porter George, painter J W Muldoon, rms 181 Calhoun.

Porter John L (Romy & Porter), res 59 W Wayne.

Porter Miles F, Physician, 80 Calhoun, res 100 Fairfield ave.

Porter R Lee, bds 17 Purman.

Porter Wm B, bookkeeper, bds 39 Pritchard.

Porter Wm P, carpenter, res 17 Purman.

Postoffice, s e cor Berry and Clinton.

Post Bernhard L, saloon, 308 W Main, res same.

Poston John, laborer, res 139 Griffith.

Potter Frank J, driver, res n s Wagner 4 w of St Joseph river.

Potter George E, asst civil engineer N Y, C & St L R R, bds 220 W Washington.

Potter George L, master mechanic Penn Co, bds 148 E Washington.

Potter John, bridge builder, res 30 Sherman.

Potter Millie E (wid Orange E), res 154 Broadway.

Potter Philip L, Real Estate, Loans, Notary Public and Conveyancer, 28 Bank Block, res 142 Jackson.

Potter Thomas, carpenter, res 45 Baker.

Potthoff Wm (A Kalbacher & Co), res 170 E Washington.

Pottlitzer Bros (Leo, Herman and Julius), commission merchants, 25 E Columbia.

Pottlitzer Herman (Pottlitzer Bros), res Lafayette, Ind.

Pottlitzer Isidor, bookkeeper Pottlitzer Bros, bds 47 W Wayne.

Pottlitzer Julius (Pottlitzer Bros), res 50 W Wayne.

Pottlitzer Leo (Pottlitzer Bros), res Lafayette, Ind.

Pottlitzer Max, trav agt Pottlitzer Bros, bds 47 W Wayne.

Pottlitzer Selig, with Pottlitzer Bros, res 47 W Wayne.

Poulson Britton, patternmkr, res e s Spy Run ave 3 n of Wagner.

Poulson Edward, painter Old Fort Mnfg Co, res 5 Spy Run ave.

Poulson Elmer, bds Britton Poulson.

Poulson George N, bds Britton Poulson.

Poultry and Pets (Monthly), Wm D Page Propr, D Charles A Robinson Associate Editor, 19 E Main.

Powell Isaac B, laborer, bds 12 Barthold.

Powell John M, laborer The Peters Box and Lumber Co, res 12 Barthold.

Powers Ellen (wid James), res 62 Hamilton.

Powers Emmet M (Powers & Barnett), res 31 Barr.

Powers James F, laborer, bds 62 Hamilton.

Powers John A, res 156 E Wayne.

Powers J, laborer, bds 43½ E Columbia.

Powers Thomas E, molder Kerr-Murray Mnfg Co, bds 62 Hamilton.

Powers & Barnett (Emmet M Powers, Abraham G Barnett), Proprs Fort Wayne Transfer and Baggage Line, 16 to 24 E Wayne.

Poyncer George W, physician, 114 Calhoun, res same.

Poyser George E, machinist Wabash R R, res 77 Wall.

Poyser Henry J, machinist Wabash R R, res 47 Miner.

Poyser Hiram, foreman Wabash R R, res 566 S Broadway.

Poyser Wm F, patternmkr Wabash R R, bds 566 S Broadway.

Prabandt Ernst R, molder Bass Foundry and Machine Works, bds 98 Gay.

Prabandt Henry, molder, res 228 Gay.

Prange Charles W, teamster, res 422 Hanna.

Prange Frederick, teamster, bds 422 Hanna.

Prange Henry, blacksmith Fleming Mnfg Co, res 588 S Calhoun.

Prange Lizzie C, seamstress Paul Baumann, bds 51 E Main.

Pranger Annie, bds 310 E Wayne.

Pranger Christian, carpenter, bds 18 Jones.

Pranger Edward, car builder Penn Co, res 66 Summit.

Pranger Herman, section hand, bds 67 Lillie.

Pranger John H, carpenter, 226 E Washington, res same.

Pranger John H jr, car builder Penn Co, res 297 E Washington.

Pranger Susie, bds 310 E Wayne.
Pranger Theke (wid Conrad), res 206 E Washington.
Pranger Wm, roofer J H Welch, res 206 E Washington.
Pranger Wm, stone mason, bds 67 Lillie.
Pranger Wm, tinner, bds 206 E Washington.
Pratt Benjamin D, bricklayer, res 14 Hoffman.
Pratt Hannah (wid George H), bds 14 Hoffman.
Pratt John W, street car driver, res 429 E Washington.
Pratt Julius F, vice-pres and treas American Wheel Co, res
    Indianapolis, Ind.
Pratt Nellie, bds 14 Hoffman.
Pratt Wm T, inspector, bds 75 Baker.
Prentiss Patrick, laborer, res 97 Baker.
Press The, Ferd J Wendell Pres, John F Rodabaugh
    Manager, 17 Court.
Pressler Charles F, gasfitter John Pressler, bds 99 E Jefferson.
Pressler Edward C, carpenter, bds 52 W DeWald.
Pressler Miss Emma, bds 52 W DeWald.
Pressler George, carpenter, 52 W DeWald, res same.
Pressler John, Propr Summit City Galvanized Iron
    Works; Mnfr of Galvanized Iron Work of Every Des-
    cription; Plumbing, Gas and Steam Fitting; Dealer in
    Mantels and Grates of All Kinds; Hot Air and Hot
    Water Furnaces, Columbia, Barr and Dock Streets;
    Telephone 249; Residence 99 E Jefferson. (*See left top
    lines.*)
Prill August, molder Bass Foundry and Machine Works, res
    88, Hayden.
Prince Charles A, fireman, res 261 S Webster.
Prince Isaac, car inspector L S & M S Ry, res 44 W 5th.
Princess Roller Skating Rink, Eckart & O'Connor proprs, s e
    cor W Main and Fulton.
Prior Wm A (S B Thing & Co), res Troy, N Y.
Pritchard Edward P, hostler J G Hooper, bds 16 Harrison.
Pritchard Harry, bds 57 Barr.
Pritchard Lizzie, dressmkr Mrs G J Stier, bds 3 Holton ave.
Pritchard Samuel, agent Griebel, Wyckoff & Becker, res S
    Whitley, Ind.
Pritchard Thomas, molder Bass Foundry and Machine Wks,
    res e s Holton ave nr Mott.
Pritchard Thomas jr, apprentice Bass Foundry and Machine
    Works, bds Thomas Pritchard.
Probasco Luciana (wid Aaron C), res 30 Douglas ave.
Probasco Wm J, secretary Fort Wayne Gas Light Co, bds
    101 Lafayette.
Proegler Carl, physician, 137 Broadway, res same.

Proegler Mrs Carl, milliner 137 Broadway, res same.
Prudential Life Insurance Co The, Charles Sauer Supt, Room 30 Pixley & Long Building.
Prullage Henry, laborer, bds 22 E Columbia.
Pryor Joseph F, clerk Model Steam Laundry, bds 34 W Superior.
Puff Adolph C (Puff Bros), bds 338 Hanna.
Puff Bros (Edwin C and Adolph C), saloon, 340 Hanna.
Puff Bros (Robert C and Edwin C), boots and shoes, 338 Hanna.
Puff Charles B, shoes, 134 Maumee road, res same.
Puff Edwin C (Puff Bros), bds 338 Hanna.
Puff Mary T, bds 338 Hanna.
Puff Robert C (Puff Bros), bds 338 Hanna.
Puff Theresa M (wid Charles), res 338 Hanna.
Puls August, stone mason, res 92 Wilt.
Pultz G Conrad, market stall No 56, res 87 N Cass.
Pulver Dexter, wheelmaker American Wheel Co, bds 248 Calhoun.
Purcell Frank E (Clutter & Purcell), res cor 4th and Harrison.
Purman Algernon A, lawyer, 1 and 2 Foster block, res 259 W Wayne.
Purman Bertha M, operator, bds 63 W 5th.
Purman Nathaniel N, blacksmith, res 63 W 5th.
Puterbaugh Jennie, works Model Steam Laundry, bds e s Wagner.
Putnam Charles, teamster M M Smick, res 8 Short.
Putnam Charles H, cabinetmaker Rhinesmith & Simonson, res 90 E Lewis.
Pyke Charles W, real estate, res 144 E Berry.
Pyke Frank H, clerk, bds 144 E Berry.
Pyke Miss Lillie M, music teacher, 144 E Berry, bds same.
Pyle Frank, painter, res n s New Haven ave 5 w of Lumbard.
Pyle Minerva (wid Isaac M), res 125 Fairfield ave.
Pyles Dorie, driver Henry Scheele, res 27 Brandriff.
Pyles Erastus, laborer, bds 68 Dawson.
Pyles Wm, carpenter, res 68 Dawson.

Q

Quealy Wm A, blacksmith Olds' Wagon Works, bds 91 Washington.
Quick Andrew, laborer, bds 91 E Washington.
Quick O L, tel operator, bds Windsor Hotel.
Quicksell Harry M, clerk Penn Co, bds 16 Jones.
Quicksell Peter, coal and wood, 196 Jackson, res 16 Jones.

Quidor George B, engineer, bds 150 W Wayne.
Quidor Nathan K, engineer, res 150 W Wayne.
Quidor Sidney C, bds 150 W Wayne.
Quigley Emmett, section hand, res n s New Haven ave nr Cutler.
Quillinan James J, clerk Penn Co, bds 23 Colerick.
Quince James A, bookkeeper Louis Diether & Bro, res 513 Broadway.
Quinlan Mary, domestic Aveline House.
Quinn Bridget (wid Thomas), bds 21 Hamilton.
Quinn Daniel, fireman Bass Foundry and Machine Works, res 44 Chicago.
Quinn Edward, policeman, res 42 Chicago.
Quinn James, heater Penn Co, res 194 Lafayette.
Quinn Kate, dressmaker M E Quinn, bds 181 W DeWald.
Quinn Louisa (wid Patrick), bds 90 Thomas.
Quinn Maggie, dressmaker M E Quinn, bds 181 W DeWald.
Quinn Mary E, milliner, 119 Fairfield ave, bds 181 W De Wald.
Quinn Michael, laborer, res 157 W DeWald.
Quinn Michael, laborer Wabash R R, res 181 W DeWald.
Quinn Patrick, helper Wabash R R, res 122 Chicago.
Q & O Club, Albert W Hazzard sec, n e cor Calhoun and Main.

R

Raab Mrs Christina, milliner, 175 E Washington, res same.
Raab Miss Emma, bds 112 W Jefferson.
Raab Edward H, clk S C Lumbard, bds 112 W Jefferson.
Raab Frederick, laborer, res 175 E Washington.
Raab John, res 112 W Jefferson.
Raab John G, bds 112 W Jefferson.
Raab Miss Josie, milliner Mrs C Raab, bds 175 E Washington.
Raab Miss Kate, milliner Mrs C Raab, bds 175 E Washington.
Raab Miss Mary E, bds 112 W Jefferson.
Raab Miss Monna, milliner Mrs C Raab, bds 175 E Washington.
Rabel Christian, switchman, res 105 Beaver ave.
Rabel Wm, flagman Penn Co, res 90 Fairfield ave.
Raber Charles, laborer, bds 199 Broadway.
Raber Jacob, stonecutter, bds 199 Broadway.
Rabisch Rudolph jr, tinner Staub Bros, bds 92 Fairfield ave.
Rabus Charles, cutter John Rabus, bds 156 W Washington.
Rabus George J, cutter John Rabus, bds 156 W Washington.
Rabus Gustave A, mngr John Rabus, res 284 W Berry.

Rabus John, merchant.tailor, 16 W Berry, res 156 W Washington.
Rabus John F, foreman W H Davis, res 50 W 3d.
Rabus Miss Louise, bds 156 W Washington.
Rabus Magdalena (wid Mathias), res 56 W 3d.
Rabus Samuel, tailor John Rabus, bds 156 W Washington.
Race Elizabeth G, printer, bds 34 E 3d.
Race Gertrude E, clerk, bds 34 E 3d.
Race John L, harnessmkr A L Johns & Co, res 34 E 3d.
Race Olive L, bds 34 E 3d.
Race Walter H, clk Fort Wayne Furniture Co, bds 34 E 3d.
Racht Albert, laborer, bds Joseph Racht.
Racht Joseph, res n s Killea 2 w of Calhoun.
Racine Aime, horse collar mnfr, res 27 N Cass.
Racine Frederick L, horse collar mkr, 36 N Cass, res 34 same.
Racine Herman, fireman, rms 37 Baker.
Racine Hotel, Charles Fox propr, n e cor Cass and 1st.
Racine Jacob F, collarmaker Aime Racine, res 124 N Cass.
Racine John F, woodworker Fort Wayne Iron Works, res 22 E Columbia.
Racine John W, carpenter, res 18½ E Columbia.
Racine Virgil, brakeman, res 154 Walton ave.
Rader Gustav, baker, res 55 Madison.
Radtke Herman R, teamster Louis Rastetter, res 5 Wall.
Radtke Louis, laborer Penn Co, res 5 Wall.
Rady David, engineer, res 20 Bass.
Raeber George J, laborer, res 31 Wagner.
Rafter James, brakeman Penn Co, rms 14 Chicago.
Ragan Barney A, clerk Mossman, Yarnelle & Co, bds 10 W Superior.
Ragan Charles K, bds 368 W Main.
Ragan Daniel, brakeman, bds 50 Melita.
Ragers Adelbert, music teacher, 102 E Jefferson, res same.
Ragsdale Thomas H, miller, res 230 W De Wald.
Rahe August, molder Bass Foundry and Machine Works, res 45 Gay.
Rahe Mrs Catherine, dressmaker, 241 Broadway, res same.
Rahe Edward, bricklayer, bds 176 E Washington.
Rahe Frank H, cigar mnfr, 241 Broadway, res same.
Rahe Frederick H, machinist, res e s Spy Run ave 7 n of Wagner.
Rahe Henry, stone mason, res 176 E Washington.
Rahe J Henry, Dealer in all Kinds of Furniture, 34 Clinton, res 161 Broadway.
Rahe Lizzie, bds 176 E Washington.
Rahe Wm, clerk, bds n e cor Gay and Horace.

Rahe Wm F, city salesman Louis Fox & Bro, res 243 Broadway.

Raidy, *see Ready.*

Raifsnyder Alfred, yardmaster, res 26 W Williams.

Railing, *see also Reehling, Rehling, Reiling, Roehling and Ruehling.*

Railing Jacob, laborer, bds Brokaw House.

Rains Charles (col'd), waiter Aldine Hotel, rms 65 Baker.

Rains Rhoda, bds 65 Baker.

Rains Solomon (col'd), cook Aldine Hotel, res 65 Baker.

Raiserman Lizzie, domestic 254 W Jefferson.

Rambo Benjamin W, res 124 W Washington.

Rambo Ilian K, jeweler, bds 124 W Washington.

Ramer August, farmer, res St Joe road 1 miles e of city limits.

Ramm Anthony, machine hand American Wheel Co, res 229 Gay.

Ramm Emil, machine hand American Wheel Co, res 229 Gay.

Ramm Ida, domestic 50 W Wayne.

Rampes Jacob F, sawyer Olds' Wagon Works, res 126 Eliza.

Ramsay Bertha V, bds 205 W Main.

Ramsay Martha M (wid Charles), res 205 W Main.

Ramsbottom Jasper F, plasterer, res 58 Riverside ave.

Ramsey Alonzo, fireman, res 107 Gay.

Ramsey Peter, machinist, res 245 Indiana ave.

Randall Alfred L, bookkeeper G W Seavey, bds 115 E Berry.

Randall David, laborer Paul Koehler, bds same.

Randall David J, broker, bds 115 E Berry.

Randall Frank M, civil engineer, res 326 Broadway.

Randall Franklin P (F P Randall & Son), res 115 E Berry.

Randall F P & Son (Franklin P and Irwin), Real Estate and Insurance, 24 Clinton.

Randall Irwin (F P Randall & Son), bds 115 E Berry.

Randall Miss May, bds 115 E Berry.

Randall Perry A (Randall & Vesey), treas Star Iron Tower Co and vice-pres Indiana Machine Works, res 58 Maple.

Randall & Vesey (Perry A Randall, Wm J Vesey), Lawyers, 19 Bank Block.

Rank Jessie, bds 161 Erie.

Rank Lena, operator S M Foster, bds 161 Erie.

Rank Margaret (wid John), res 161 Erie.

Ranke Henrietta (wid Frederick), bds 127 W Washington.

Ranke Henry, Propr The Bank Sample Room, 37 Calhoun, bds 55 W Wayne.

Ranke Henry J, clerk A J Keller, bds 127 W Washington.

Ranke Miss Louisa, bds 127 W Washington.

Ranke Wm F (Ranke & Yergens), res 127 W Washington.

E. F. Sites, 🦷 Dentist, 86 Calhoun St., Four Doors North of Wayne.

FORT WAYNE DIRECTORY. 429

Ranke Wm F jr, clerk Meyer Bros & Co, bds 127 W Washington.

Ranke & Yergens (Wm F Ranke, Wm Yergens), stave and buggy bow mnfrs, s e cor Superior and Griffith.

Rankin Christian, teamster Wm Bruns, res 168 Smith.

Ransom Lyman H, res 56 Douglas ave.

Ransom Newell H, clerk Mossman, Yarnelle & Co, res 191 Griffith.

Rapman Michael, butcher F Eckart, res 17 Elm.

Rapole, *see Raypole.*

Rapp, *see also Rupp.*

Rapp Frederick G, packer Louis Fox & Bro, bds 82 Taylor.

Rapp Henry, laborer, bds 82 Taylor.

Rapp Henry, teamster, res 19 Boone.

Rapp Louis, market stall 17, res w s Fairfield ave s of city limits.

Rapp Philip, helper Wabash R R, res 37 Stophlet.

Rapp Wilhelmina (wid Wm), res 82 Taylor.

Rappold Martin L, fireman, res 47 Elm.

Raquet Annie, works Troy Steam Laundry, bds n e cor Meridian and Pfeiffer ave.

Raquet Carrie, cigarmaker F J Gruber, bds 35 W 5th.

Raquet Charles C, machinist Ft W, C & L R R, bds 113 Barthold.

Raquet Charles H, clerk, bds Peter Raquet.

Raquet Lena, works Troy Steam Laundry, bds n w cor Meridian and Pfeiffer ave.

Raquet Lizzie, works Model Steam Laundry, bds n e cor Pfeiffer ave and Meridian.

Raquet Peter, gunsmith, res s w cor Pfeiffer ave and Meridian.

Raquet Rose, operator, bds 113 Barthold.

Raquet Wm A, washer Fort Wayne Bottling Works, bds Peter Raquet.

Rarick John, engineer Old Fort Mnfg Co, res 157 Erie.

Rarig Elijah A, res 74 Cherry.

Rasmus Jacob, oil pedler, rms 37 Baker.

Rastenburg Charles, painter, bds 65 John.

Rastenburg Frank, bds 65 John.

Rastenburg Frederick, watchman, res 65 John.

Rastenburg Rudolph, finisher, bds 65 John.

Rastetter Louis, Mnfr Buggy Bows, s w cor Broadway and P, Ft W & C Ry, res 246 Broadway.

Rathert Mrs Amelia, midwife, 51 Wilt, res same.

Rathert August H A, baker, res 55 Madison.

Rathert Christian, blacksmith Fort Wayne Electric Co, res 194 Smith.

Rathert Frederick, bricklayer, res 51 Wilt.
Rathert Frederick C, student, bds 212 E Washington.
Rathert Frederick W, machinist Indiana Machine Works, res 180 Metz.
Rathert Gustav, baker H Wiegman & Sons, res 55 Madison.
Rathert Henry, blacksmith helper Penn Co, bds 13 Summit.
Rathert Henry C, helper Penn Co, res 212 E Washington.
Rathert Henry W, clerk Gross & Pellens, bds 212 E Washington.
Rathert Lizzie, domestic 68 W Berry.
Rathert Robert, hostler, bds 212 E Washington.
Rathert Sophia, apprentice Mary Edmonds, bds 51 Wilt.
Rattenbury John W, cigarmaker Kasten & Kohlmeyer, bds 199 Broadway.
Rau Casper, res 299 E Washington.
Rau Charles, letter carrier, bds 46 Erie.
Rau Wm, driver H D F Poppel, bds 299 E Washington.
Raub Jacob H, car builder Penn Co, res 232 E Jefferson.
Rauch Abraham J, dentist, 48 Harrison, res 171 Wells.
Rauch Clara I, binder Archer, Housh & Co, bds 171 Wells.
Rauch Horatio S, dentist, bds 171 Wells.
Rauen Matthews, tank inspector, res 207 Broadway.
Rauen M, carpenter Penn Co, res 594 Lafayette.
Rauh Emma, clk Stewart & Hahn, bds 49 N Cass.
Rauh Gustav A, plasterer, res 49 N Cass.
Rauh Gustave, tailor J Rabus, bds 49 N Cass.
Rauh Matthias, clk Root & Co, bds 49 N Cass.
Rauh Pauline, tailoress, bds 49 N Cass.
Rauh Philip, barber, bds 49 N Cass.
Rauner Aloysius, blacksmith Penn Co, res s s Eliza 1 e of Hillside ave.
Rauner George, carpenter, res 118 Fulton.
Rauner Joseph, painter, res 126 Wilt.
Rauner Joseph F, candymaker Louis Fox & Bro, bds 126 Wilt.
Rauner Joseph H, laborer, res 13 Poplar. •
Rauth Martin, res 35 Gay.
Raven Miss Lina, bds 49 Walter.
Rawley Bridget, cook McKinnie House.
Rawwer Henry, painter L O Hull, res 41 Webster.
Ray John W, molder, res 64 E Columbia.
Ray S Wm, helper Kerr-Murray Mnfg Co, bds 237 E Wayne.
Rayal Jerry, switchman, bds 196 Hanna.
Rayhouser Miss Addie T, stenographer Coombs & Co, bds 188 Ewing.
Rayhouser Charles, driver Ryan Bros, bds 245 W Wayne.

Rayhouser Gideon I Z, printer The Press, bds 245 W Washington.

Rayhouser Josephine (wid Gredaliah), bds 245 W Wayne.

Rayhouser Rufus C F, Printer, 34 E Berry, res St Joe road near City Limits.

Rayhouser Wm E, brakeman, res 245 W Washington.

Rayman John, switchman, rms 27 Baker.

Raypole John, butcher Edwin Rich, res 168 Griffith.

Read, *see also Reed and Reid.*

Read Asahel J, res 16 W Wayne.

Read Charles E (Pixley & Co), res 214 E Wayne.

Read Henry A, veterinary surgeon, 66 Harrison, res 64 same.

Read James M, news stand, bds 278 E Lewis.

Read Moses, clk Penn Co, res 278 E Lewis.

Ready, *see also Raidy.*

Ready Ella, bds 80 Hoagland ave.

Ready John, machine hand Fort Wayne Electric Co, bds 80 Hoagland ave.

Ready Mary, bds 80 Hoagland ave.

Ready Wm, laborer, res 80 Hoagland ave.

Ready Wm M, machine hand Fort Wayne Electric Co, bds 80 Hoagland ave.

Ream Daniel, carpenter, bds 18 McClellan.

Reamsnider Nellie, domestic 200 W Berry.

Rear Eben (Rear & Bugert), res 55 Ferguson ave.

Rear Jesse M, painter Rear & Bugert, bds 116 Fairfield ave.

Rear Nicholas, wagonmaker Olds' Wagon Works, res 116 Fairfield ave.

Rear & Bugert (Eben Rear, Matthew Bugert), painters, 185 Broadway.

Reardon Mrs Elizabeth, res 14 Brandriff.

Reardon James, brakeman, res 25 Brandriff.

Reardon Timothy J, packer Olds' Wagon Works, bds 14 Brandriff.

Reaser John J, finisher Horton Mnfg Co, res 110 Boone.

Rebar Joseph P, driver, bds 439 E Washington.

Reber George, market stall 50, res nr County Poor House.

Reber John, laborer Fort Wayne Electric Co, res 107 Taylor.

Rebman Anna, works Fort Wayne Electric Co, bds 17 Elm.

Rebman John, laborer, bds cor Elm and Cherry.

Rebman Lizzie, domestic 17 Elm.

Rebman Michael, res 17 Elm.

Reddin Lexemerald, carpenter Edward Sutter, bds n s Grace ave 1 e of Broadway.

Reddingius Peter, machine hand Fort Wayne Organ Co, bds 50 Oakley.

Redelsheimer David S (D S Redelsheimer & Co), res Monroeville, Ind.
Redelsheimer D S & Co (D S Redelsheimer), overall mnfrs, 30 Clinton.
Redelsheimer Sigmund, res 144 W Berry.
Redlich Bros (Joseph and Solomon B), shoes, 20 Calhoun.
Redlich Joseph (Redlich Bros), rms 20 W Berry.
Redlich Solomon B (Redlich Bros), rms 20 W Berry.
Redmann Louis, molder Borcherding & Tonsing, bds 17 Elm.
Redrup Charles E, laborer, res 25 Duck.
Redwood Frederick R, bookkpr Louis Diether & Bro, res 24 W Berry,
Redwood Miss Maud, teacher, bds 24 W Berry.
Reed, *see also Read.*
Reed Abbie (wid James), res 5 Rockhill.
Reed Miss Beatrice A, bds 312 E Jefferson.
Reed Elvy, laborer, bds 49 St Mary's ave.
Reed Frank, plasterer, bds 248 Calhoun.
Reed George, carpenter, bds 29 Buchanan.
Reed George F, switchman, bds 323 Calhoun.
Reed Henry, laborer, bds 199 Broadway.
Reed James W, blacksmith City Carriage Works, res 59 Wells.
Reed John, bds 139 Montgomery.
Reed John, laborer Hoffman Bros, bds 49 St Mary's ave.
Reed John J, clerk Francis Sallier, res 37 Barr.
Reed Louis, insurance, 12 E Berry, res 312 E Jefferson.
Reed Lucinda, bds 10 Jackson.
Reed Margaret (wid Isaac N), res 302 Hoagland ave.
Reed Mary, domestic 200 W Berry.
Reed Mrs Mary A, res 275 E Washington.
Reed Sylvanus, laborer, res 19 St Mary's ave.
Reed Wm, stone cutter, bds Hedekin House.
Reed Wm D, brakeman Penn Co, bds 302 Hoagland ave.
Reehling, *see also Railing, Rehling, Reiling and Rueling.*
Reehling Caroline, dressmkr Druhot Sisters, bds 97 Madison.
Reehling Catherine (wid Conrad), res 97 Madison.
Reehling Conrad, engineer, res 127 Wallace.
Reehling Emma, bds 97 Madison.
Reehling Henry, grocer, 220 Madison, res 222 same.
Reehling Lizzie S, domestic 179 Clinton.
Reehling Philip J, res 221 Madison.
Reehling Wm, fireman, bds 127 Wallace.
Reehling Wm V, machinist Fort Wayne Electric Co, bds 97 Madison.
Reeley George, teamster, bds Charles M Murray.
Reeley Jacob, teamster, bds Charles M Murray.

Reeps Charles F W, cabinetmaker Penn Co, res 158 W De Wald.

Reese Benjamin, agent, bds Hedekin House.

Reese Charles, city assessor City Hall, res 131 Montgomery.

Reese Charles E, bookkeeper The Journal Co, bds 131 Montgomery.

Reese Frederick C, clerk Foster Furniture Co, res s s Leith 2 W of Calhoun.

Reffelt Charles H, upholsterer P E Wolf, bds 235 Madison.

Reffelt Miss Flora, bds 170 W Wayne.

Reffelt Wm, painter L O Hull, res 225 Madison.

Reffelt Wm R, cabinetmaker Louis Diether & Bro, res 235 Madison.

Regedanz Charles, clerk Meyer Bros & Co, res 58 Jefferson.

Regel Henry E, machinist Penn Co, res 36 Summit.

Regel Herman, machinist Brass Foundry and Machine Wks, bds 36 Summit.

Regel Mary (wid Edward), res 36 Summit.

Regenauer Wm, pulley builder Old Fort Mnfg Co, res rear 3 Oak.

Rehling, *see also Railing, Reehling, Reiling and Ruehling.*

Rehling Conrad, storekeeper Kerr-Murray Mnfg Co, bds 93 Smith.

Rehling C Ernest, machinist Wabash R R, bds 161 E Lewis.

Rehling Ernest, foreman Wabash R R shops, res 161 E Lewis.

Rehling Frederick, bds 127 John.

Rehling Frederick H, boilermkr Wabash R R, res 193 John.

Rehling Henry K, boilermkr Wabash R R, res 139 E Lewis.

Rehling John, watchman, res 93 Smith.

Rehling Josephina, bds 93 Smith.

Rehling Lizzie, dressmaker Druhot Sisters, bds 139 E Lewis.

Rehling Louis E, blacksmith Penn Co, res 127 John.

Rehling Wm, bds 104 Glasgow ave.

Rehling Wm, fireman, bds 127 Wallace.

Rehm Christian J, res 247 W Washington.

Rehm Daniel, gardener, res s s St Joe road 1 mile e of city limits.

Rehm Elizabeth (wid Peter), res 41 Barthold.

Rehm Herman F, coil winder Fort Wayne Electric Co, res 24 Scott ave.

Rehm Philip, painter, res n e cor Warsaw and Pontiac.

Rehrer Collins S, foreman Fort Wayne Electric Co, res 310 Broadway.

Rehrer Robert W, brakeman, res 196 Broadway.

Rehrer Wm S, armature winder Fort Wayne Electric Co, res 34 Wall.

Reiber G, laborer Penn Co, res 53 Baker.

Reichard Henry L, printer Fort Wayne Newspaper Union, res 153 W Main.

Reichardt Henry, driver, bds 129 Clay.

Reichardt John, boilermaker Wabash R R, res 154 Clay.

Reichert Herman, traveling agent, res 570 Broadway.

Reichter Emil, laborer, bds 85 Holman.

Reid, *see also Read and Reed.*

Reid Clement C, machinist, bds 195 E Lewis.

Reidel John, helper Penn Co, res 338 Force.

Reidel Margaret, domestic 266 W Jefferson.

Reider Frederick, buyer, res 96 W Jefferson.

Reidt, *see also Wright.*

Reidt Bernard, engineer, res 9 Summit.

Reidt Herman, res 407 E Lewis.

Reidt Herman jr, machinist, bds 407 E Lewis.

Reidt Wm J, machinist A Hattersley & Sons, bds 407 E Lewis.

Reifeine Jonathan, plumber Robert Ogden, res 140 E Washington.

Reiling, *see also Railing, Reehling, Rehling, Roehling and Ruehling.*

Reiling August, locksmith, 66 Pearl, res 70 Pearl.

Reiling Frederick R, letter carrier, res 3 West.

Reiling George, laborer Ranke & Yergens, bds 111 Wilt.

Reiling Gustav A, brakeman, bds 70 Pearl.

Reiling Margaret (wid Frederick), res 111 Wilt.

Reiling Meinhardt, locksmith, bds 70 Pearl.

Reiling Richard, laborer, bds 46 E Columbia.

Reilly, *see also Riley.*

Reilly Miss Annie, dressmaker, 58 Walton ave, bds same.

Reilly Daniel J, foreman Louis Fox & Bro, res 51 W Lewis.

Reilly James A, dairyman, 58 Walton ave, res same.

Reilly John, fireman Penn Co, bds 82 Montgomery.

Reilly Matilda, bds 58 Walton ave.

Reilly Oscar, cook Edwin Rich, bds 11 Gay.

Reilly Peter, engineer, res 169 Harmer.

Reilly Robert, clerk Nickel Plate, rms 15 Douglas ave.

Reiman, *see Riemann.*

Reincamp Henry, brakeman, bds 33 St Mary's ave.

Reineke Frederick, molder Bass Foundry and Machine Wks, bds 81 Smith.

Reineke Frederick J, upholsterer Foster Furniture Co, res 119 E Main.

Reineke John, coremaker Bass Foundry and Machine Works, res 81 Smith.

Reineke's Orchestra, Frederick J Reineke leader, 30 W Main.

Reinemeyer John D, blksmith Penn Co, res 123 Walton ave.

Reinewald Charlotte, dressmaker, bds 328 Harrison.

Reinewald Henry, Ry P O clerk, bds 328 Harrison.

Reinewald Henry F, butcher C Kohn, bds 124 Williams.

Reinewald Henry W, res 338 E Wayne.

Reinewald John, painter Chauvey Bros, res 106 John.

Reinewald Lizzie, operator S M Foster, bds 338 E Wayne.

Reinewald Miss Mary H, cashier Wm C Seidel & Bro, bds 328 S Harrison.

Reinewald Rudolph C, City Clerk, City Hall, res 353 Calhoun.

Reinewald Mrs Rudolph C, milliner, 353 Calhoun, res same.

Reinewald Wm, cigarmkr F J Gruber, bds 338 E Wayne.

Reinewald Wm F, laborer, res 328 Harrison.

Reinewald Wm H, molder Indiana Machine Works, res 34 Burgess.

Reinhardt, *see Reinhart, Rhinehart and Rinehart.*

Reinhardt John, finisher White's Wheel Works, res 101 Maumee road.

Reinhart, *see also Rhinehart and Rinehart.*

Reinhart Aloysius S, clerk Renner, Cratsley & Co, bds 258 E Washington.

Reinhart Henry, laborer J A Koehler, bds same.

Reinhart John A, fireman, bds 48 Pontiac.

Reinhart John R, clk J B White, bds 258 E Washington.

Reinhart Louisa (wid John), res 48 Pontiac.

Reinhart Mary R, tailoress, bds 258 E Washington.

Reinhart Mathias, lab Penn Co, res 258 E Washington.

Reinheimer Carl, porter Adams Express Co.

Reinheimer Valentine, carpenter, res 41 E Creighton ave.

Reinholt Louis, laborer, res rear 537 E Wayne.

Reiniche Frank, wheelmaker American Wheel Co, bds 68 Laselle.

Reiniche Joseph, laborer, bds 68 Laselle.

Reiniche Mary, wks Troy Steam Laundry, bds 68 Laselle.

Reinkensmeier Christian F, Grocer, 124 Broadway, res 175 Griffith.

Reinkensmeier Henry, grocer, res 175 Griffith.

Reinking Albert, helper Wabash R R, bds 7 Jones.

Reinking Amelia, tailoress Charles Kruse, bds 7 Jones.

Reinking Christian F, car builder Penn Co, res 37 John.

Reinking Ernést, carpenter, res 59 Brackenridge.

Reinking Ferdinand C, molder Bass Foundry and Machine Works, bds 10 McClellan.

Reinking Frederick W, machinist Fort Wayne Electric Co, rms No 1 Engine House.
Reinking Matilda, bds 67 Baker.
Reinking Wm, helper Olds' Wagon Works, res 7 Jones.
Reinking Wm F, carpenter, res 157 E Creighton.
Reinking Wm G, laborer, bds 7 Jones.
Reinmeyer Mollie, operator S M Foster, bds 123 Walton ave.
Reiter, *see also Rider.*
Reiter Charles H, driver Root & Co, bds 148 Taylor.
Reiter Christina (wid Wm), res 148 Taylor.
Reiter Frederick, buyer, res s s Columbia bet Clay and Lafayette.
Reiter Frederick C, clerk, bds 49 Wall.
Reiter George, Cigar Mnfr, 30 Calhoun, res same.
Reiter John F, wheel molder Bass Foundry aud Machine Works, bds 96 W Jefferson.
Reiter John H, teamster McDonald, Watt & Wilt, res 54 Wall.
Reiter Louis, molder Kerr-Murray Mnfg Co, bds Ferdinand Prang.
Reiter Louise, domestic 372 Fairfield ave.
Reiter Minnie, domestic 297 Fairfield ave.
Reiter Pauline, dressmaker, bds 49 Wall.
Reiter Wm, blacksmith Bass Foundry and Machine Works, bds 19 Union.
Reiter Wm, carpenter Wabash R R, res 49 Wall.
Reitnouer Jacob F, clerk U S Express, res 140 Beaver.
Reitnouer Jeremiah B, laborer Fort Wayne Organ Co, res 140 Beaver ave.
Reitnouer Margaret (wid Peter S), bds 140 Beaver ave.
Reitze John B, patternmaker, res 258 W Jefferson.
Reitze Mrs Minnie, milliner, 118 Calhoun, res 258 W Jefferson.
Reitze Wm F, teller Old National Bank, res 283 W Berry.
Rekers, *see also Riker.*
Rekers Bernhard J, carpenter, res 121 W Washington.
Rekers Charles E, clerk Peter Morganthaler, bds 110 W Washington.
Rekers Clemens A, clerk Peter Morganthaler, res 123 W Washington.
Rekers Clemens A jr, clerk, res 123 W Washington.
Rekers Edward A, clerk Gerhard Rekers, bds 116 W Washington.
Rekers Frank H, tailor, res 82 W Main.
Rekers Gerhard, grocer, 116 W Washington, res same.
Rekers Henry G V, finisher Fort Wayne Organ Co, bds 121 W Washington.

Rekers H Bernhard, clerk Gerhard Rekers, bds 116 W Washington.

Rekers Miss Josephine, bds 116 W Washington.

Rekers Miss Lizzie, bds 116 W Washington.

Relue Newton, res 22 Grant ave.

Remington-Lawton Co The, Remington & Lawton Proprs, Contractors, Artificial Stone, Asphalt Roofers, Sidewalks, 19 and 20 Pixley & Long Building.

Remington Paul G (The Remington-Lawton Co), res 164 W Berry.

Remington & Lawton (Paul G Remington, Dan H Lawton), proprs The Remington-Lawton Co, 19 and 20 Pixley & Long bldg.

Remmel's Block, s w cor Broadway and Washington.

Remmert Herman, laborer, res 30 W 3d.

Remmert Herman jr, tool keeper Kerr-Murray Mnfg Co, bds 30 W 3d.

Remmert Herman J, supt Kerr-Murray Mnfg Co, res 157 W Washington.

Remmert John H, machinist, res 38 E 3d.

Remmert Joseph, laborer Bass Foundry and Machine Works, res 410 E Washington.

Remmert Miss Mamie, stenographer Wing & Mahurin, bds 157 W Washington.

Remus Julius E, contractor, res 442 S Broadway.

Renaud Emil, paver, bds Fred Rosselot.

Rencker Joseph, laborer Bass Foundry and Machine Works, res 56 Smith.

Renfrew Benton B, machinist E B Kunkle & Co, res 32 Pritchard.

Renfrew Rea K, laborer Penn Co, res 169 Madison.

Renfrew Robert G, foreman American Wheel Co, res 189 Madison.

Renner, Cratsley & Co (George A Renner, Frank C Cratsley, Milton H Burgert), Jobbers and Dealers in Books, Stationery, Wall Paper, Toys, Notions and Artists' Materials, 56 Calhoun. (*See front cover.*)

Renner George A (Renner, Cratsley & Co), res 110 E Berry.

Rensberger Alpheus, carpenter, res 64 Walton ave.

Rensberger Cephas, laborer, bds 64 Walton ave.

Rensman Bernard, salesman A C Trentman, res 47 Wall.

Rensman Bernard C, patternmaker Kerr-Murray Mnfg Co, bds 47 Walnut.

Rensman Clara, packer Louis Fox & Bro, bds 47 Walnut.

Rentschler Anna M, domestic 150 Clinton.

Rentschler Carrie, bds 48 Wall.

CHARLES BOWMAN, Saw Gumming, FILING and SETTING.
No. 18 Harrison Street.

438   R. L. POLK & CO.'S

Rentschler Charles, laborer Penn Co, res 138 Broadway.
Rentschler David, laborer Penn Co, res 48 Wall.
Rentschler Lottie, domestic 36 Montgomery.
Rentschler Mrs Mary, confectioner, 138 Broadway, res same.
Rentschler Philip J, machine hand Olds' Wagon Works, res 168 W De Wald.
Renz Adam, book agent, res 257 E Washington.
Renz Alexander J, clerk G De Wald & Co, bds 257 E Washington.
Renz Edward A, hostler Lee & Fulton, rms same.
Repine John, yardmaster, res 20 Hough.
Repp, see Rapp and Rupp.
Resselt Charles, upholsterer, bds 235 Madison.
Resselt Wm C, painter, bds 235 Madison.
Resselt Wm R, carpenter, res 235 Madison.
Reuesewald Joseph, printer, bds 71 Harrison.
Reul John V, mngr Indiana Installment Co, rooms 127 Calhoun.
Reuss John B, collector C L Centlivre, res e end Spy Run av.
Revels Rev John (col'd), bds 145 Erie.
Revert Henry, teamster, bds August Meyers.
Reyelt Peter H, clerk C H Baade, bds 4 Fairfield ave.
Reynold Mrs Anna, res n w cor Maumee road and Glasgow.
Reynolds Mrs Florence (Frank Tait & Sister), res 26 E. Wayne.
Reynolds Joseph, plumber James Madden, bds 252 E Lewis.
Reynolds Rev Marcus L, pastor Free Methodist Church, res 268 E Creighton ave.
Reynolds Wm J, bds 75 Douglas.
Rhea, see Ray.
Rheels Peter, carpenter, bds 58 Hayden.
Rhein Charles, brickmaker, res 599 Calhoun.
Rhine Christian, helper Penn Co, bds 17 Union.
Rhine Gustav, laborer Lindenwood Cemetery, res s s Mary near Wheeler.
Rhine Jacob, laborer, bds 11 Mary.
Rhine Philip, laborer Lindenwood Cemetery, bds Gustav Rhine.
Rhine Sarah (wid Calvin), res 301 Hanna.
Rhinehart, see also Reinhard, Reinhart and Rinehart.
Rhinehart Calvin S, wheel facing American Wheel Co, res 34 E 2d.
Rhinehart Isaac W, laborer American Wheel Co, res 13 McLaughlin.
Rhinesmith Elizabeth (wid George), bds 231 W Wayne.
Rhinesmith George, bds 231 W Wayne.

Rhinesmith John (Rhinesmith & Simonson), pres Anthony Wayne Mnfg Co, res 231 W Wayne.

Rhinesmith Susan, bds 231 W Wayne.

Rhinesmith & Simonson (John Rhinesmith, James H Simonson), Sash, Door and Blind Mnfrs and Stair Builders; Planing Mill s w cor Lafayette and Wabash R R.

Rhoades Daniel W, fireman, res n e cor Milan and Walton av.

Rhoades George N, brakeman Penn Co, res s w cor Reed and E Creighton ave.

Rhoades Harry, mach hand Olds' Wagon Works, bds Daniel W Rhoades.

Rhoades Mary (wid Samuel), bds 27 Oliver.

Rhode John, section hand, bds 41 Nirdlinger ave.

Rhode Mary, works Troy Steam Laundry, bds 41 Nirdlinger ave.

Rhodes Alexander, teamster, res 30 Baker.

Rhodes Chapman (col'd), brakeman Penn Co, bds 292 E Wayne.

Rhodes Charles, bds 292 E Wayne.

Rhodes Frank M, printer Fort Wayne News, bds 30 Baker.

Rhodes Milton A, woodworker, res 36 Hamilton.

Rhodes Sadie (wid Wm), res 113 Holman.

Rhodes Oscar, brakeman, bds 153 Madison.

Rhodes Robert B (col'd), brakeman Penn Co, rms 70 Murray.

Rhodes Sarah (wid Wm), res 113 Holman.

Rhodes Wm, bds 292 E Wayne.

Rhodes Ulysses G, clk J C Hinton, res 30 Baker.

Riblet Frank E, trav agt, res 483 Harrison.

Riblet Hiram F, bds 483 Harrison.

Rice Charles, helper Penn Co, res Lafayette s of Pontiac.

Rice John, teamster Hoffman Bros, res 17 St Mary's ave.

Rice Joseph A, driver Hoffman Bros, bds 17 St Mary's ave.

Rice Mary (wid Benjamin F), res 851 Broadway.

Rich Block, e s Calhoun bet Washington and Jefferson.

Rich Della, bds 25 W Jefferson.

Rich Edward (Rich & Karn), res 196 Calhoun.

Rich Edwin, res 25 W Jefferson.

Rich Edwin (Rich & Karn), res 25 W Jefferson.

Rich Elgie J, butcher, res 596 Calhoun.

Rich Ellsworth, butcher Gottlieb Haller, res 596 Calhoun.

Rich Frank J, clk, bds 25 W Jefferson.

Rich's Hotel, Andrew McClure and Frank D Paulus Proprs, n w cor Calhoun and Douglas ave.

Rich Miss Linnie D (Rich & Hoadley), bds 25 W Jefferson.

Rich Miss Lotta, clerk Rich & Karn, bds 196 Calhoun.

Rich Sanford, mngr Fort Wayne Beef Co, res 196 Calhoun.

Rich & Hoadley (Miss Linnie D Rich, Miss Annie Hoadley), fancy goods, 170 Calhoun.

Rich & Karn (Edward Rich, Kaim Karn), meat market, 254 Calhoun.

Richard Charles, laborer, bds 412 E Wayne.

Richard Christian, res 240 E Wayne.

Richard David, res 148 Smith.

Richard George C, supt Fort Wayne City Bill Posting Co, res rear 19 W Wayne.

Richard James, fireman, rms 36 Baker.

Richard James C, machine hand American Wheel Co, res 59 Laselle.

Richard John B, blacksmith Fort Wayne Electric Co, res 101 Wallace.

Richard Joseph, machine hand, bds 148 Smith.

Richard Louis, brakeman, res 86 Chicago.

Richard Philip, spoke selector, res 412 E Wayne.

Richards Andrew, carbonmaker, res 35 Elm.

Richards Catherine (wid Wm C), res 596 Calhoun.

Richards Della, bds 23 Euclid ave.

Richards Eliza (wid Henry), res 23 Euclid ave.

Richards George W, carpenter J A Crow & Co, res 91 4th.

Richards Mrs Julia, janitor Holton Ave School, res 148 Smith.

Richards Louis, flagman Penn Co, bds 86 Chicago.

Richards May, bds 23 Euclid ave.

Richards Orion F, mantel setter Carter & Son.

Richards Philip T, laborer, res 412 E Wayne.

Richards Reuben, deliverer J D Gumpper, bds 16 E DeWald.

Richards Sylvester W, watchman, res 372 Calhoun.

Richardson Hannah (wid Thomas), res 167 Hayden.

Richardson Ida, bookkeeper D N Foster Furniture Co, bds 101 E Berry.

Richardson James A, carpenter, bds 167 Hayden.

Richardson Viola, works Model Steam Laundry, bds n w cor Main and Harrison.

Richey Amos, clerk Morgan & Beach, res 87 W Main.

Richey Amos jr, clerk Old National Bank, bds 87 W Main.

Richey Miss Effie B, teacher Washington School, bds 87 W Main.

Richey Otho R, checker Penn Co, res 170 Francis.

Richie Wm, cabinetmaker Fort Wayne Organ Co, res 492 Fairfield ave.

Richter Bernard D, tinner, res 29 E 3d.

Richter Emil P, wood turner Horton Mnfg Co, bds 85 Holman.

Richter Erich J B, policeman, res 39 Buchanan.

Richter Ernest, finisher Horton Mnfg Co, res 20 Jesse.

Richter Max A, instrument maker Ft Wayne Electric Co, res 60 Miner.

Richter Paul, instrument-maker Ft Wayne Electric Co, res 28 Jones.

Riddell John J, conductor Nickel Plate, res Bellevue, Ohio.

Rider, *see also Reiter.*

Rider F A, bds Aldine House.

Rider Jacob, teamster L S & M S Ry, res 73 Holman.

Ridgley Harry B, mngr Metropolitan Mnfg Co, rms 19 W Main.

Ridley Daniel, whitewasher, res 145 Erie.

Ridley John (col'd), barber Gerney Winslow, bds 68 Chicago.

Ridley Wm, paperhanger, bds 68 Chicago.

Ridt John H, fireman, res 228 Francis.

Riedel George J, carpet weaver 338½ Force, res same.

Riedel John, laborer, bds 338½ Force.

Riedel John jr, machinist, bds 338½ Force.

Riedel John, teacher St Paul's German Lutheran School, res s s St Joseph road nr Centlivre Brewery.

Riedel John M E, Architect, 79 and 81 Calhoun, res Washington Township. (*See front cover.*)

Rieder Wm, helper, bds 18 McClellan.

Riedmiller Charles J, saloon, 16 Harrison, res same.

Riedmiller John M, Bottling Works s e cor Taylor and Eagle, res same.

Riedmiller John W, pedler John M Riedmiller, res 207 Taylor.

Rieg Alois, laborer, Wm & J J Geake, res 257 Hoffman.

Rieg Anton, laborer, res 100 Putnam.

Riegel Alois L (Riegel & Bougher) res 39 W Washington.

Riegel Tracey, domestic 173 Van Buren.

Riegel & Bougher (Alois Riegel, Frank Bougher), saloon, 12 Calhoun.

Rieger Emilie, domestic 212 W Washington.

Riehl Edward, painter, res 33 John.

Riehl Frank, coil winder Ft Wayne Electric Co, res 666 W 3d.

Riehl Wm, coil winder Ft Wayne Electric Co, res 140 Lafayette.

Rieke Edmund J, carver Fort Wayne Organ Co, bds 100 Indiana ave.

Rieke Henry jr, cabinetmaker Fort Wayne Organ Co, bds 100 Indiana ave.

Rieke Henry S, carpenter Penn Co, res 100 Indiana ave.

Riemann Mary, bds 185 E Jefferson.

Riemann Regina (wid August), res 231 Harmer.

Riemen Joseph H, packer Ft Wayne Electric Co, bds 162 Brackenridge.

Ries Clara, bds 365 E Washington.

Ries Philip A, tailor, res 365 E Washington.

Rietdorf Ernst C G, finisher Fort Wayne Organ Co, bds 338 Broadway.

Rietdorf Ernest J, carpenter, res e s Shawnee ave 2 s of Grace.

Riethmiller August (G Riethmiller & Son), res 318 Broadway.

Riethmiller George (G Riethmiller & Son), res w s Lavina, 3 s of Taylor.

Riethmiller George jr, caller Penn Co, res 139 Taylor.

Riethmiller G & Son (George and August), grocers, 139 Taylor.

Riggle Grant, car driver, bds 71 Melita.

Riker, see also Rekers.

Riker Edward, bds 61 Brackenridge.

Riley, see also Reilly.

Riley Edward, brakeman Penn Co, res 46 Force.

Riley George N, watchman Nickel Plate, bds 216 W Jefferson.

Riley George W, painter J W Muldoon, res n s Breck 5 w of St Mary's ave.

Riley Jennie M, bds 116 Walnut.

Riley Loban J, laborer Hoffman Bros, res 27 Clinton.

Riley Mary J, bds 11 Gay.

Riley Nettie, bds 11 Gay.

Riley Wm H, engineer Fort Wayne Artificial Ice Co, res 11 Gay.

Rimes Myron, hostler Jenson & Sargent, bds Racine Hotel.

Rindemann Ernst W, bartndr Christian Schafer, res 83 N Cass.

Rinehart, see also Reinhard and Rhinehart.

Rinehardt Martin, clerk L Wolf & Co, bds 46 E Pontiac.

Rinehart Wm A, blacksmith J Zurbuch, bds 387 W Main.

Rinewald Henry, hub turner White's Wheel Works, res 338 E Wayne.

Ring John, fireman, rms 82 Baker.

Ringer Joseph, laborer, res 56 Smith.

Ringer Wm J, laborer, res 355 Calhoun.

Ripley Mrs Elizabeth L (Mrs C R Colmey & Ripley), bds 39 Douglas ave.

Rippe Charles (Rippe & Sons), res 113 Broadway.

Rippe Charles H, boilermaker Kerr-Murray Mnfg Co, res 115 Taylor.

Rippe Christian (Rippe & Sons), res 91 Wilt.

Rippe Christian H, stair builder Louis Diether & Bro, res 89 Wilt.

Stahn & Heinrich, Leading Dealers in ARTISTS' MATE-RIALS AND DRAUGHTING INSTRU-MENTS. 116 Calhoun Street.

FORT WAYNE DIRECTORY. 443

Rippe Frederick, brick contractor, 176 Madison, res same.

Rippe Frederick, carpenter, res 79 Oakley.

Rippe Frederick C (Rippe & Sons), res 184 W Jefferson.

Rippe Henry C, clerk J A M Storm, bds 176 Madison.

Rippe Henry F, helper Bass Foundry and Machine Works, bds 9 Jones.

Rippe Sophie, apprentice, bds 89 Wilt.

Rippe Wm, city pound master, res 9 Jones.

Rippe Wm F jr, carpenter, res 56 Wall.

Rippe & Son (Christian and Frederick C), livery, 86 Broadway.

Rippe & Sons (Christian, Charles and Frederick C), livery, 111 Broadway.

Rissing John F, tinsmith, bds 123 High.

Rissing John H, cabinetmaker Foster Furniture Co, res 123 High.

Rissing Magdalene (wid John), bds 123 High.

Ritchie Jennie (wid Silas), res 116 High.

Ritchie Albert, cabinetmaker, bds 492 Fairfield ave.

Ritchie John H, cabinetmaker, bds 492 Fairfield ave.

Ritchie Wm H, cabinetmaker, res 492 Fairfield ave.

Ritter Miss Bertha A, teacher Harmer School, bds 116 E Creighton ave.

Ritter Cyrus, wagonmaker L C Zollinger, res 18 Cass.

Ritter Jacob, machinist Penn Co, res 116 E Creighton ave.

Ritter Miss Kate, asst W W Shryock, bds 259 E Washington.

Ritter Max, bookkeeper Frederick Eckart, res 35 W Main.

Ritter Miss Nellie A, bds 116 E Creighton ave.

Ritto Joseph, res 165 Clinton.

Ritzius Albert, cabinetmaker Fort Wayne Organ Co, bds 492 Fairfield ave.

Ritzius John H, cabinetmaker Fort Wayne Organ Co, bds 492 Fairfield ave.

Rival Peter, brakeman, rms 16 Chicago.

Rivers Charles (Rivers & Son), res 217 E Wayne.

Rivers Wm (Rivers & Son), bds 217 E Wayne.

Rivers & Son (Charles and Wm), painters, 70 Calhoun.

Riverside Hotel, John Hasenfuss propr, 2 N Cass.

Roach, see Roche.

Robb Wm, bricklayer, res 24 W 4th.

Robbe Alphonse F, foreman Ft Wayne Bottling Works, res 151 Wells.

Robbins John L, rivetter, res 20 Murray.

Robbins John V, porter Sam, Pete & Max, bds 186 Francis.

Robel John, shoemaker, 15½ Grand, res Whitmore ave 3 s of Illinois rd.

Roberts Albert G, painter Olds' Wagon Wks, res 320 Calhoun.

Roberts Charles, carpenter, res 105 Walton ave.
Roberts Emma H, domestic 87 N Cass.
Roberts Frank, laborer, bds 235 Lafayette.
Roberts George I, brakeman Penn Co, res 392 S Calhoun.
Roberts Joseph, clerk, bds 18 McClellan.
Roberts Joseph H (col'd), barber, 205 Calhoun, res same.
Roberts Mary (col'd, wid Wm), bds 205 Calhoun.
Robertson Henry H, helper Penn Co, bds 70 Melita.
Robertson Leonora, carpet sewer Root & Co, res 70 Melita.
Robertson Louisa (wid Wm G), res 86 Brackenridge.
Robertson Nicholas A, bds 179 W Berry.
Robertson Robert S, lawyer, 20 W Berry, res 179 same.
Robertson Robert S jr, clk Hoffman Bros, bds 179 W Berry.
Robertson Walter, bds 86 Brackenridge.
Robinette Ida (wid George), res 63 W Main.
Robinette James B, machine hand Olds' Wagon Works, res 96 Oliver.
Robinette Newton, carpenter, bds 30 W Williams.
Robinson Charles A, associate editor Poultry and Pets, res Morrstown, Ind.
Robinson David A, watchman, res 21 High.
Robinson Elijah, book agent, res 168 Hoffman.
Robinson Elmer B, barber S G Hubbard, bds 108 E Wayne.
Robinson Frank, driver Ryan Bros, bds same.
Robinson Frank A, clerk, bds 150 W Jefferson.
Robinson Frank W, Dealer in Wall Paper, Paints, Ground Glass, etc, House and Sign Painter, 68 Wells, res n w cor St Mary's ave and Hoffman.
Robinson Frederick, teamster, res 225 W Superior.
Robinson Henry H, Lawyer, 55 and 56 Pixley & Long Bldg, bds Hotel Randall.
Robinson James H, accountant, bds Hotel Randall.
Robinson James M, Lawyer, s w cor Main and Calhoun, res 95 E Main.
Robinson Jane, domestic 126 E Wayne.
Robinson Jesse S, teamster, res 162 Brackenridge.
Robinson Miss Jessie, teacher Bloomingdale School, bds 21 High.
Robinson Joseph M, wiper, res 73 High.
Robinson Lydia S (wid Irving T), bds 50 W Superior.
Robinson Miss Maud, bds 70 Harrison.
Robinson Nellie, domestic 11 Holman.
Robinson Oscar, rms 108 E Wayne.
Robinson Otis B, telegraph operator, bds 285 Webster.
Robinson Sarah, domestic Hotel Randall.
Robinson Samuel, waiter, res 23 Melita.

Robinson Samuel B, brakeman, bds 325 W Jefferson.
Robinson Wm, res 11 Mechanic.
Robinson Wm L, molder, res 31 Euclid ave.
Robinson Winston, clerk, bds 186 Francis.
Robison Caroline B (wid John), boarding house, 301 Calhoun.
Robke Frederick, carpenter, res 81 Wall.
Roche David, helper Wabash R R, bds 60 Baker.
Roche James, helper Wabash R R, res 60 Baker.
Roche James P, blacksmith American Wheel Co, bds 60 Baker.
Roche Margaret, works Model Steam Laundry, bds 60 Baker.
Roche Mary, tailoress, bds 60 Baker.
Roche Wm F, blacksmith American Wheel Co, bds 60 Baker.
Rocholl Bertha C, clk J B White, bds 49 E Butler.
Rocholl Matilda O (wid Morris A), res 49 E Butler.
Rocholl Valentine, blacksmith B H Baker, res 49 Butler.
Rocholl Valentine C, helper Penn Co, bds 49 E Butler.
Rockhill Bros & Fleming (W Wright, Howell C, Hugh M and Jesse B Rockhill, Wm H Fleming), stock farm, ½ mile w of city limits, office 30 E Main.
Rockhill Emily (wid Wm), res 295 W Wayne.
Rockhill Howell C (Rockhill Bros & Fleming), bds 71 W Wayne.
Rockhill Hugh M (Rockhill Bros & Fleming), res ½ mile w of city limits.
Rockhill Jesse B (Rockhill Bros & Fleming), res ½ mile w of city limits.
Rockhill W Wright (Rockhill Bros & Fleming), bds 71 W Wayne.
Rockmann Christian H, engineer, bds 397 Lafayette.
Rodabaugh Charity D (wid Adam), bds 309 S Harrison.
Rodabaugh John F, lawyer and mngr The Press, 5 Foster blk, res The Aldine.
Rodabaugh Miss Rosa, music teacher, 286 W Washington, res same.
Rodabaugh Thomas J, foreman painter Penn Co, res 286 W Washington.
Rodebaugh Franklin, fruit tree agent, res 525 E Lewis.
Rodeheaver Mrs Delilah, bds 533 E Wayne.
Rodeheaver Miss Flora, stenogr G W Seavey, bds 515 E Lewis.
Rodeheaver Henry, finisher, bds 533 E Wayne.
Rodeheaver Horace, fireman, res 8 Hendricks.
Rodeheaver Miss Maggie, bds 515 E Lewis.
Rodeheaver Wm H, res 515 E Lewis.
Rodemeier Frederick, res 325 E Washington.

Rodemeier Frederick G, presser American Wheel Co, bds 325 E Washington.
Rodemeier Hannah, bds 325 E Washington.
Rodemeier Wm, bds 325 E Washington.
Rodenbeck Amelia, domestic 127 E Washington.
Rodenbeck August, carpenter, bds 171 Harmer.
Rodenbeck Carrie, domestic 127 E Washington.
Rodenbeck Catherine, bds 168 E Lewis.
Rodenbeck Charles, bds 168 E Lewis.
Rodenbeck Charles, carpenter, bds 140 Eliza.
Rodenbeck Charles, helper Penn Co, bds 201 Madison.
Rodenbeck Charles H, boilermaker, bds 67 Madison.
Rodenbeck Christian, car builder Penn Co, res 513 E Lewis.
Rodenbeck Christina, domestic 119 E Wayne.
Rodenbeck Conrad, helper Penn Co, bds 168 E Lewis.
Rodenbeck Diedrich, laborer, res 23 Hough.
Rodenbeck Emma C, dressmkr Druhot Sisters, bds 210 E Jefferson.
Rodenbeck Frederick, boilermkr, res 210 E Jefferson.
Rodenbeck Frederick H, clk Root & Co, bds 67 Madison.
Rodenbeck F Wm, helper Wabash R R, res 18 Jones.
Rodenbeck Hannah, bds 67 Madison.
Rodenbeck Henry, blacksmith Bass Foundry and Machine Works, bds 345 E Lewis.
Rodenbeck Louis, bds 168 E Lewis.
Rodenbeck Louisa, bds 168 E Lewis.
Rodenbeck Mena, domestic 119 E Wayne.
Rodenbeck Sophia M, tailoress G Scheffler, bds 110 Madison.
Rodenbeck Wm, boilermkr Wabash R R, res 67 Madison.
Rodenbeck Wm, machine hand American Wheel Co, bds 513 E Lewis.
Rodenbeck Wm F, helper Penn Co, bds 168 E Lewis.
Rodenbeck Wm G, helper Bass Foundry and Machine Wks, bds 345 E Lewis.
Rodermond John, laborer, res 54 Smith.
Rodewald Carrie (wid Frederick), bds 570 E Washington.
Rodewald Frank F, bartender F D Oetting, res 260 Webster.
Rodewald Miss Sophia, bds 91 W DeWald.
Rodgers, *see Rogers.*
Roe, *see also Rowe.*
Roe Dora B, domestic Joseph Fricke.
Roebuck Asa, lab Penn Co, res s e cor Purman and Warsaw.
Roebuck Homer, laborer, bds Asa Roebuck.
Roeger Charles, saloon, 26 W Main, res same.
Roeger Christian, saloon, n w cor Spy Run ave and Randolph, res same.

Builders' Hardware, PFEIFFER & SCHLATTER, 38 and 40 EAST COLUMBIA ST.

FORT WAYNE DIRECTORY. 447

Roehling, *see Railing, Reehling, Rehling, Reiling and Ruehling.*

Roehrs Henry, expressman, res 261 W Jefferson.

Roehrs Margaret (wid Henry), bds 261 W Jefferson.

Roelle G Frank, policeman, res 13 W Jefferson.

Roelle Jacob, machinist Wabash R R, res 86 E Lewis.

Roembke, *see also Rombke.*

Roembke August, laborer Penn Co, res 75 Wilt.

Roembke August H, clerk Root & Co, bds 118 Union.

Roembke Frederick, clerk Gottlieb Niemann, bds 57 Wall.

Roembke Frederick H, molder Kerr-Murray Mnfg Co, bds 57 Wall.

Roembke Henry, blacksmith Bass Foundry and Machine Works, res 25 Wilt.

Roembke Henry J E, janitor Court House, res 118 Union.

Roembke Wm H, clerk B Lehman, bds 57 Wall.

Roemermann Henry, res 141 Broadway.

Roemermann Henry jr, engineer, bds 143 Broadway.

Roempke Ernest, fireman, res 100 Smith.

Roenke Minnie S, domestic 203 W Wayne.

Roepke Charles W, junk dealer, res e s Indiana ave 1 s of Home ave.

Roepke Frederick, laborer, res New Haven road 1 w of tollgate.

Roesener Christian, laborer Penn Co, res 35 Stophlet.

Roesener C H Frederick, clerk J A M Storm, re s 35 Stophlet.

Roesener Frederick, blacksmith, 356 Broadway, res same.

Roesener Frederick, section hand, bds 35 Stophlet.

Roesener Henry F, driver Olds' Wagon Works, res 35 Stophlet.

Roesler Agatha (wid Henry C), bds 116 W Jefferson.

Roeuelle Carrie, cook Lake Shore Hotel.

Roeuelle Mary, waitress Lake Shore Hotel.

Roff Charles, bds 56 W Williams.

Roff Mary (wid George), bds 56 W Williams.

Rogers Alexander, driver J Klett & Son, bds 98 Baker.

Rogers Amelia, domestic 202 W Washington.

Rogers Andrew, foreman American Wheel Co, res 180 Montgomery.

Rogers A Lincoln, draughtsman Thomson Electric Welding Co, Lynn Mass, res 64 E Jefferson.

Rogers Charles, teamster, bds 2 Thomas.

Rogers Elmer H, engineer, res 137 Buchanan.

Rogers Frank, conductor Penn Co, bds 227 E Lewis.

Rogers Frederick H, switchman, res 32 Marion.

Rogers Henry, brakeman, bds 186 Francis.

Rogers Herbert, printer, res 81 Wells.

Rogers James, bridge supervisor Nickel Plate, res cor Jefferson and Garden.
Rogers Mary, domestic 2 Thomas.
Rogers Thomas C, sec Allen County Loan and Savings Association, White's block, res 64 E Jefferson.
Rogers Warren, propr Sullivan House, res 2 Thomas.
Rogers Wm H, asst foreman boiler shop Penn Co, res 162 E Lewis.
Rogge August, janitor Penn Co depot, res 32 Brandriff.
Rogge Frederick, car repairer, res 16 Jackson.
Rogge Louise, opr S M Foster, bds 52 McClellan.
Rogge Sophie, opr S M Foster, bds 52 McClellan.
Rogge Wm, laborer, res 195 W Superior.
Rogge Wm, laborer Hoffman Bros, res 114 Orange.
Rogge Wm R, laborer, res 52 McClellan.
Rohan, *see also Rowan.*
Rohan Frank C, finisher Fort Wayne Organ Co, bds 386 Fairfield ave.
Rohan John H, foreman Fort Wayne Organ Co, res 386 Fairfield ave.
Rohan Lottie T, bds 386 Fairfield ave.
Rohan Wm H, asst cashier G DeWald & Co, bds n w cor Fairfield and Home aves.
Rohlfing Edward, laborer, res 180 Gay.
Rohlman Elizabeth (wid Wm), janitress West German School, res 190 Brackenridge.
Rohlman Frederick W, cigarmkr George Reiter, bds 109 Brackenridge.
Rohlman Henry F, painter, res 59 E DeWald.
Rohlmann John H W, laborer Louis Diether & Bro, bds 190 Brackenridge.
Rohrbach John, laborer Coombs & Co, res 148 Maumee rd.
Rohrbach Louis, bds 241 Madison.
Rohrer Frank H, cigarmkr H W Ortmann, bds 36 Wells.
Rohrer Jacob, collarmkr Aime Racine, res 40 Wells.
Rohrer John, chairmkr, res 36 Wells.
Rohrer Wm, blacksmith Ft W, C & L Ry, res 49 N Calhoun.
Rohs Charles, clk, bds 519 E Washington.
Rohs Henry, res 519 E Washington.
Rohyans Christian, driver Fire Engine No 1, res 60 Clinton.
Rohyans Gesina (wid Christian), res 363 E Washington.
Rohyans John N, clk Penn Co, res 401 E Lewis.
Rohyans Rosa, bds 363 E Washington.
Rohyans Wm, laborer Penn Co, res 363 E Washington.
Rolape Angeline (wid John), res 157 E Washington.

Rolf August W, bds 53 Wall.
Rolf Frederick A, mason, res 53 Wall.
Rolf Frederick H, mach hand Fort Wayne Electric Co, bds 53 Wall.
Rolf Henry, teacher Emanuel School, res 36 Hendricks.
Rolling ouisa, domestic 199 Broadway.
Rolling Mina, domestic 199 Broadway.
Rollins Wm, laborer, bds 182 E Jefferson.
Rolshausen Henry, cigarmkr J Lohman & Co, bds 11 Melita.
Romary Armand, laborer Louis Diether & Bro, res n w cor Coombs and Cochrane.
Romary August, painter, bds n s Cochrane 1 w of Coombs.
Romary Charles, helper City Carriage Works, bds 128 Erie.
Romary Clara, bds 128 Erie.
Romary Joseph A, clerk Morgan & Beach, bds 128 Erie.
Romary Joseph J, clerk Morgan & Beach, res 128 Erie.
Romary Mary, bds n s Cochrane 1 w of Coombs.
Rombke, *see also Roembke.*
Rombke Eugene, fireman Penn Co, res 100 Smith.
Rombke Heinrich, blacksmith Penn Co, res 243 Madison.
Rombke Henry, broommaker, 68 Madison, res same.
Rombke Herman E, painter Olds' Wagon Works, res 97 Buchanan.
Rombolt Helen (wid Gottlieb), res 55 Wilt.
Romer Rev Charles, asst pastor St Mary's German Catholic Church, bds 142 E Jefferson.
Romick John, painter, res 1 Bass.
Romy Alfred B, carpenter, res 104 E Wayne.
Romy Charles M, policeman, res 140 Maumee rd.
Romy Edward, laborer, res n e cor Lafayette and Wiebke.
Romy Miss Eleanor, bds 157 Ewing.
Romy James L, clerk Romy & Porter, bds 157 Ewing.
Romy James L, laborer Olds' Wagon Works, bds 157 Ewing.
Romy Lewis H, brakeman, res 31 Lillie.
Romy Louis, grocer, 142 Maumee rd, bds 140 same.
Romy Robert L (Romy & Porter), res 157 Ewing.
Romy & Porter (Robert L Romy, John N Porter), Real Estate and Loan Brokers, 4 Bank Block.
Rondot Charles, bds 22 E Columbia.
Rondot Charles, engineer Fort Wayne Gas Light Co, res 8 Mary.
Rondot Joseph, fireman, res 44 Summit.
Roney Julia, wks Indiana School for Feeble-Minded Youth.
Ronk Wm, conductor Penn Co, rms 224 Calhoun.
Rooney Robert H, upholsterer F E Houk, bds 36 Clinton.
Roos, *see also Ross.*

Roos George, barber, 377 E Washington, res same.

Roos George jr, barber, bds 377 E Washington.

Roos Henry, baker, bds 377 E Washington.

Roos Jacob F, laborer The Remington-Lawton Co, bds Washington House.

Roos Philip, baker, bds 377 E Washington.

Root Darwin F, bookkeeper S Bash & Co, bds 270 W Washington.

Root Herbert V, lumber, res 43 Harmer.

Root John H, cook Aveline House, res 165 E Jefferson.

Root Lewis B (Root & Co), res 113 W Main.

Root Vandoren (Vandoren Root & Co), res 270 W Washing-

Root Vandoren & Co (Vandoren Root, Charles S Bash), wholesale hardwood lumber, 22 W Columbia.

Root Velorus, res 45 Harmer.

Root & Company (Lewis B Root, Ernest C Rurode, Wm H Brady, Michael C MacDougal, Charles A T Krimmel), Wholesale and Retail Dry Goods and Notions, 46 and 48 Calhoun.

Ropa Frederick W, machinist Penn Co, res 116 John.

Ropa George C, machine hand, bds 27 Wall.

Ropa Henry W, clerk Ohnhaus & Co, bds 27 Wall.

Ropa Hermann, boilermkr Ft Wayne Iron Works, res 27 Wall.

Ropa Wm, laborer American Wheel Co, bds 116 John.

Ropa Wm, market master City Hall, res 27 Wall.

Ropa Wm F, clerk A I & H Friend, bds 27 Wall.

Rorbergh George, Singer Sewing Machine agent, bds 43½ E Columbia.

Rorison Miss Arda B, bds 186 W Berry.

Rorison Brainard, sec Fort Wayne Electric Co, res 186 W Berry.

Rorison Miss Marabel V, bds 186 W Berry.

Roscher Diedrich W, teacher Emanuel School, res 310 W Jefferson.

Roscoe Wm, brakeman, bds 33 St Mary's ave.

Rose Anthony, clerk Charles Rose, res 286 E Jefferson.

Rose Charles, grocer, 75 E Wayne, res 196 Ewing.

Rose Christian B, clerk Sam, Pete & Max, res 28 Pritchard.

Rose Henry A, Practical Blacksmith and Horseshoer, 10 N Calhoun, res 84 Madison cor Clay.

Rose John, res 92 Laselle.

Rose Wm, clerk Charles Rose, res 17 Summit.

Rosenberger Anthony, cigarmkr John Zern, bds 134 Wallace.

Rosenberger Charles, grocer, 342 Force, res 340 same.

Rosenberger Charles, painter Penn Co, res 134 Wallace.

Rosenberger Frank C, car painter Penn Co, res 290 Hanna.

Rosenberger John C, wheelmaker American Wheel Co, bds 134 Wallace.

Rosener Christian, teamster David Tagtmeyer, bds same.

Rosener Frederick, laborer, bds 77 W Superior.

Rosenstiel Morris, stengphr Weil Bros & Co, bds 53 W Wayne.

Rosenthal Charles, clerk E Shuman & Sons, bds 60 W Main.

Rosenthal Emanuel, clerk G De Wald & Co, bds 60 W Main.

Rosenthal Emil, clerk A I & H Friend, bds 96 W Berry.

Rosenthal Emma, clk Alexander Goodman, bds 60 W Main.

Rosenthal Ephraim, horse dealer, res 60 W Main.

Rosenthal Miss Hattie, bds 96 W Berry.

Rosenthal Isaac M, physician, 96 W Berry, res same.

Rosenthal Max, res 105 W Wayne.

Rosenthal Minnie, clerk G DeWald & Co, bds 60 W Main.

Ross, *see also Roos*.

Ross Ella M, bds 12 Chicago.

Ross George A, physician, 84 Calhoun, res same.

Ross James P (J P Ross & Sons), res 25 W Columbia.

Ross John, laborer, bds Washington House.

Ross John E, passenger and ticket agent Penn Co, res 403 Calhoun.

Ross Judson K (J P Ross & Sons), res 70 W 3d.

Ross J P & Sons (James P, Judson K and Wilbert A), Grocers and Proprs Columbia House, 25 and 27 W Columbia.

Ross Miss Kate A, teacher Hoagland School, bds 18 Brackenridge.

Ross Martha (wid Donald), res 18 Brackenridge.

Ross Orion Q, clerk Penn Co, bds McKinnie House.

Ross Oscar, bartender, rms 102 E Columbia.

Ross Richard C, yardmaster, res 48 E 4th.

Ross Wilbert A (J P Ross & Sons), res 60 W Berry.

Ross Wm M, telegraph operator, bds 13 Brackenridge.

Ross W Albert, traveling agent S F Bowser & Co, res Maiden lane bet Main and Berry.

Rosseau Melinda, seamstress, bds 165 Clinton.

Rossell Joseph A, traveling agent, res 138 W Wayne.

Rossell Louis, bds 138 W Wayne.

Rosselot Charles, plumber A Hattersley & Sons, bds 101 Riverside.

Rosselot Frederick, saloon, 22 E Columbia, res same.

Rosselot Henry, painter Old Fort Mnfg Co, bds 101 Riverside ave.

Rosselot Julia A (wid Louis), res 101 Riverside ave.

Rosselot Oliver J, fireman Jenney Electric Light and Power Co, bds 22 E Columbia.

Rosselot Peter F, laborer, res 85 Putnam.
Rossington Annie, bds 117 Hanna.
Rossington Charles H, clerk, bds 96 E Wayne.
Rossington Mrs Linnie, boarding house, 96 E Wayne.
Rossington Richard, res 96 E Wayne.
Rossington Rudolphus B, Local Freight Agent Penn Co and G R & I R R, Office cor Clinton and Railroad, res 179 Clinton.
Rossington Wm W, clerk Penn Co, res 228 E Lewis.
Ross-Lewin Edward A, carpenter, 181 E Lewis, res same.
Ross-Lewin Miss Ida L, bookkeeper Fort Wayne Furniture Co, bds 181 E Lewis.
Rossman Jane (wid August), res 24 Erie.
Rost August, laborer Penn Co, bds 38 Charles.
Rost Emil, mach hand Olds' Wagon Works, bds 38 Charles.
Rost Herman, machinist, res 67 Gay.
Rost Hugo, helper Penn Co, bds 110 Gay.
Rost John D, heater Penn Co, bds 110 Gay.
Rostenburg Charles, painter Olds' Wagon Works, bds 263 Hanna.
Rostenburg Eugene, finisher Fort Wayne Furniture Co, bds 65 John.
Roth Bernhardt, laborer Bass Foundry and Machine Works, res 20 Force.
Roth Clara, bds 20 Force.
Roth Ernst, stone cutter Fort Wayne Steam Stone Works, bds 131 W Main.
Roth Mary, bds 20 Force.
Roth Peter, laborer Penn Co, res 20 Force.
Roth Susan (wid Frederick), res 131 W Main.
Rothenbeck Minnie, domestic 101 E Berry.
Rothenberger Frederick, tinsmith Penn Co, res 181 Griffith.
Rothenberger George, res 190 Ewing.
Rothman Joseph, laborer, bds 46 E Columbia.
Rothschild Aaron (Fort Wayne Artificial Ice Co), res 68 W Berry.
Rothschild Belle, bds 68 W Berry.
Rothschild Benjamin, res 144 W Berry.
Rothschild Henry, res 152 W Washington.
Rothschild Ida (wid Bernard), bds 138 W Main.
Rothschild Joseph, cashier Isaac Lauferty, bds 68 W Berry.
Rothschild Solomon, res 68 W Berry.
Rousey Amanda, opr Hoosier Mnfg Co, bds 165 Clinton.
Roush Frederick, carpenter, bds n s Prospect ave 1 w of St Joseph river.
Roush Sadie, wks Model Steam Laundry, bds Prospect ave.

Rousseau Benjamin F, bookkeeper Fort Wayne Beef Co, bds 110 W Main.
Rousseau Francis M, market stall 47, res S Huntington road.
Rousseau Robert D (Rousseau & Pfeiffer), res 37 W Berry.
Rousseau & Pfeiffer (Robert D Rousseau, John N Pfeiffer), meats, 44 W Berry.
Roussel Annie, domestic 229 W Berry.
Roussel Francis, clk J P Ross & Sons, bds Columbia House.
Roussel Mary, domestic County Jail.
Roussey Ellen, bds 92 Montgomery.
Roussey Joseph, laborer, bds 55 Lillie.
Routh Wm, laborer, Fort Wayne Iron Works.
Roux Charles, butcher, bds 105 Summit.
Roux Emilie, bds 105 Summit.
Roux George, butcher, res 105 Summit.
Rouzer Mrs Anna,-janitor Nebraska School, res 55 Boone.
Rouzer Cassius M, letter carrier, res 55 Boone.
Rowan, *see also Rohan.*
Rowan Barbara A (wid Benjamin C), bds 76 E Washington.
Rowan Belle, operator S M Foster, bds 13 Euclid.
Rowan James, conductor Penn Co, res 457 S Lafayette.
Rowan James E,feeder Archer, Housh & Co, bds M H Rowan.
Rowan Kate, bds 13 Euclid ave.
Rowan Mark H, brakeman Penn Co, res East Yards.
Rowe, *see also Roe.*
Rowe Mrs Mary (Rowe & Williams), res 294 W Washington.
Rowe Nicholas B, meat market, 189 Broadway, res 294 W Washington.
Rowe & Williams (Mrs Mary Rowe, Mrs Lizzie Williams), milliners, 84 Calhoun.
Roy Amelia, domestic 61 E Columbia.
Roy John B, laborer, res n s New Haven ave 5 e of Lumbard.
Roy Joseph C, machine hand American Wheel Co, bds 315 Hanna.
Rubin Eliza (wid Edward), bds 140 W Main.
Rubin Max (Julius Nathan & Co), res 140 W Main.
Ruch Catherine (wid Louis), res 2 St Mary's ave.
Ruch Clara, milliner, 389 W Main, res same.
Ruch Elizabeth L, operator S M Foster, bds 2 St Mary's ave.
Ruch Frank, gasfitter, bds 2 St Mary's ave.
Ruch Henry L, laborer, res 59 W 5th.
Ruch Joshua, fireman, res 274 E Lewis.
Ruch Samuel, laborer Penn Co, res 339 W Main.
Ruchel Wm, Carpenter, Contractor and Practical Builder, 209 E Lewis, res same. (*See adv, p 69*).

Ruck John, car builder Penn Co, res 117 Taylor.
Rudert Edward, packer F Eckart, bds George Rudert.
Rudert George, packer F Eckart, res n e cor W Main and Runnion ave.
Rudisill Miss Eliza, bds w s Spy Run ave 1 n of Elizabeth.
Rudisill Elizabeth (wid Henry), res w s Spy Run ave 1 n of Elizabeth.
Rudolph Alvin, carpenter, bds 104 Hoffman.
Rudolph Charles, upholsterer, bds 104 Hoffman.
Rudolph Christina (wid Charles), res 104 Hoffman.
Rudolph Franklin, harnessmkr Wm Schaper, res 58 Hoffman.
Rudolph Henry G, pressman Fort Wayne Newspaper Union, bds 7 Short.
Rudolph Louisa, works Troy Steam Laundry, bds 58 Hoffman.
Rudolph Minnie, opr Hoosier Mnfg Co, bds 104 Hoffman.
Rudolph Philip, pressman Ft Wayne Sentinel, bds 7 Short.
Rudolph Wm, res 7 Short.
Rudolph Wm L, pressman Journal, res 51 Hillside ave.
Rue Henry, laborer, res 59 W 5th.
Ruehling, *see also Railing, Reeling, Rehling and Reiling.*
Ruehling Philip J, res 221 Madison.
Ruesewald Joseph (Ruesewald & Didion), res 208 Madison.
Ruesewald & Didion (Joseph Ruesewald, Martin A Didion), Union Cigar Box Factory and Printers, 49 E Main.
Rufner Samuel, conductor Penn Co, res 44 Buchanan.
Rugar Miss Jennie A, teacher Westminster Seminary, bds 261 W Wayne.
Ruggaber Joseph, cabinetmaker, res 99 W Williams.
Ruhl Charles, laborer C L Centlivre, res e s Edna 1 n of Spy Run ave.
Rumler James E, cashboy, bds 315 S Harrison.
Rumm Amelia, bds 38 Gay.
Rumm Lena, bds 38 Gay.
Rumm Louis, machine hand American Wheel Co, res 38 Gay.
Rump Clara, bds 29 Pritchard.
Rump Ernest F, carpenter, res 29 Pritchard.
Rump Ernest H, carpenter, res 202 Fairfield ave.
Rump Frederick, carpenter, bds 202 Fairfield ave.
Rump Frederick, laborer, bds 29 Pritchard.
Rump Rickie, bds 29 Pritchard.
Rumpf Daniel, stone cutter Ft Wayne Steam Stone Works, bds 199 Broadway.
Rumrill Mollie, laundress Rich's Hotel.
Rumsey Helen E (wid Henry B), bds 87 W Wayne.

Rumsill Amelia, domestic Wayne Hotel.
Rundel Charles B, clerk S W Harmon, bds 181 Lafayette.
Rundel Martin, machinist, res 181 Lafayette.
Runion Frank, laborer, bds 544 E Wayne.
Runner Minnie, domestic Aveline House.
Runtz Mary (wid Jacob), bds 32 Brandriff.
Runyan James W, clerk Aldine Hotel.
Rupert Harry, bds 356 Calhoun.
Rupert Ira, real estate, res 234 W De Wald.
Rupert John E, helper Fort Wayne Electric Co, bds 356 Calhoun.
Rupert Lydia M, converter worker Fort Wayne Electric Co, bde 356 Calhoun.
Rupp, *see also Rapp.*
Rupp Miss Ida, bds n w cor Penn and Dubois.
Rupp John, blacksmith, res n w cor Penn and Dubois.
Rupp John, blacksmith Penn Co, res 113 E Creighton ave.
Rupp John, Propr Summit City Steel Works, n end Barr, res cor Maumee road and Glasgow ave.
Rupp Philip, fireman Penn Co, res 149 E DeWald.
Rupp Wm H, clerk Dreier Bros, bds John Rupp.
Ruppel Anna, operator Hoosier Mnfg Co, bds 20 Locust.
Ruppel Carrie, operator Hoosier Mnfg Co, bds 20 Locust.
Ruppel Clemens J, machine hand Olds' Wagon Works, bds 20 Locust.
Ruppel Fabian, brick mason, res 20 Locust.
Ruppel John, grocer, 268 E Wayne, res 264 same.
Ruppel Josephine, bds 258 E Wayne.
Ruppel Lena, bds 389 E Washington.
Ruppel Paul, res 258 E Wayne.
Ruppel Wm, driver J E Klinger, res 46 E Columbia.
Rupple Wm, driver J E Klinger, bds 48 E Columbia.
Rurode Ernest C (Root & Co), res 76 W Berry.
Rush George D, res 55 W Main.
Rusher Miss Laura, stenographer D N Foster Furniture Co, bds 110 W Main.
Rushton Olive, domestic 7 Bell ave.
Rushton Samuel, bds Windsor Hotel.
Russell Charles M, insurance agent, res 415 Calhoun.
Russell Dominick, machine hand Fort Wayne Organ Co, res 110 W Creighton ave.
Russell Frank E, switchman Nickel Plate, res 136 Jackson.
Russell Henry O, conductor, bds 170 Greely.
Russell John, pipe liner Salimonie Mining and Gas Co, bds Wm Keller.
Russell Louis, laborer, res 28 Rockhill.

Russell Thomas G, cigarmaker F J Gruber, res 93 Fairfield.
Rust Henry F C, gents' furnishing goods, 126 Broadway, res 150 Ewing.
Ryan, *see also* O'Ryan.
Ryan Agnes B, bds 118 Barr.
Ryan Andrew, helper Penn Co, bds 69 Grand.
Ryan Bros (Oliver F Ryan), teaming, 21 W Wayne.
Ryan Catherine (wid John), res 164 Indiana ave.
Ryan Catherine (wid Michael), res 79 Hoagland ave.
Ryan Charles, laborer, res 599 Calhoun.
Ryan Christian, rms 15 W Washington.
Ryan Cornelius M (Ryan & Gebert), res 60 E Columbia.
Ryan Daniel, Justice of the Peace and Lawyer, 24 E Berry, res 121 E Washington.
Ryan Edith, bds 121 E Washington.
Ryan Frank J, painter Olds' Wagon Works, bds 36 Hayden.
Ryan George W, laborer, res s e cor Tons and Dwenger ave.
Ryan Hannah H, bds 118 Barr.
Ryan James, cabinetmaker Ft Wayne Organ Co, res 164 Indiana ave.
Ryan Jane M, bds 9 Clay.
Ryan John (Ryan & Lake), res s s Pontiac ½ mile e of limits.
Ryan John, laborer, bds 492 W Main.
Ryan John, teamster, res n e cor Alexander and Franklin.
Ryan John B, molder, bds 118 Barr.
Ryan John B, fireman, bds Windsor Hotel.
Ryan John J, apprentice Penn Co, bds 79 Hoagland ave.
Ryan Joseph D, helper A Hattersley & Sons, bds 118 Barr.
Ryan Lawrence, carpet layer L Wolf & Co, res 21 Hamilton.
Ryan Margaret (wid James W), bds 22 W Washington.
Ryan Michael, lab American Wheel Co, res 320 Lafayette.
Ryan Michael S, car builder Penn Co, res cor Runnion and Wheeler.
Ryan Oliver F (Ryan Bros), res 22 W Washington.
Ryan Oscar D, plumber Robert Ogden, bds 121 E Washington.
Ryan Patrick, city weighmaster, res 118 Barr.
Ryan Patrick H, fireman, res 71 Charles.
Ryan Paul, car builder Penn Co, res s s Jesse e of Rumsey.
Ryan Thomas, comn merchant, 406 S Calhoun, res same.
Ryan Wm H, section hand, res 35 Hoagland ave.
Ryan & Gebert (Cornelius M Ryan, Frank Gebert), saloon, 60 E Columbia.
Ryan & Lake (John Ryan, Robert H Lake), wood dealers, n e cor Grant and Oliver.
Ryus Wm H, machinist Penn Co, res 143 E DeWald.

S

Saahmon Charles, laborer, res 395 W Main.
Saahmon Charles jr, painter, bds 395 W Main.
Sack Regina (wid Jacob) res 119 Lafayette.
Saer Wm M, painter Wayne Paint and Painting Co, bds 225 Calhoun.
Saffen Birdie A, bds 390 E Washington.
Saffen Francis S, mach Bass Foundry and Machine Works, res 100 Madison.
Saffen George B, molder Ft Wayne Iron Works, res 387 E Washington.
Saffen Samuel, bds 390 E Washington.
Saffen Thomas D, machinist, res 390 E Washington.
Saffen Thomas W, foreman Ft Wayne Iron Works, res 390 E Washington.
Saffen Wm, bds 390 E Washington.
Safford Frank K (G E Bursley & Co), res 210 W Wayne.
Safford J W, laborer, bds 43½ E Columbia.
Safford Miss Kate P, teacher Kindergarten, bds 210 W Wayne.
Safford Lucy C (wid Dr Jonas P), bds 210 W Wayne.
Sage Arthur E, teamster, res 38 Marion.
Sage W J, rms 196 Calhoun.
Sahner, *see also Sayner and Zauner.*
Sahner Marcus, res 431 E Washington.
Sailor, *see Saylor.*
St Augustine's Academy for Girls, cor Calhoun and Jefferson.
St John's German Lutheran Church and School, s e cor W Washington and Van Buren.
St John's Reformed Church, s e cor W Washington and Webster.
St Joseph's Hospital, s w cor W Main and Broadway, Sister Secunda superior, Rev Thomas Eisenring, C S S S, chaplain.
St Mary's German Catholic Church, s e cor Lafayette and Jefferson.
St Mary's Hall, s w cor Lafayette and Jefferson.
St Mary's School for Boys, s w cor Lafayette and Jefferson.
St Mary's School for Girls, e s Lafayette s of St Mary's Church.
St Paul's Catholic Church (German), n e cor Griffith and Washington.
St Paul's German Lutheran Church, w s Barr head of Madison.
St Paul's German Lutheran School, n e cor Madison and Barr.
St Paul's M E Church, w s Walton ave 2 s of Wabash R R.
St Paul's School, s e cor Washington and Griffith.

St Peter's German Catholic Church and School, s s St Martin west of Hanna.

Sale John W, treas Hoffman Lumber Co, res 203 W Wayne.

Salem Reformed (German) Church, e s Clinton near Wayne.

Salge Christian, machine hand, res 7 West.

Salge Christian, painter Horton Mnfg Co, bds 7 West.

Salge Frederick, boilermaker Bass Foundry and Machine Works, bds 7 West.

Salge Henry, carpenter, res 23 West.

Salge Louisa, bds 7 West.

Salimonie Mining and Gas Co, Henry C Paul Pres, Charles S Bash Vice-Pres, Charles McCulloch Sec, F E W Scheimann Treas, G Max Hofmann Supt, 50 Clinton.

Salley George E, printer Fort Wayne Newspaper Union, bds Clifton House.

Sallier Francis, Groceries, Provisions, Wines and Liquors, 66 E Columbia, res 30 Hough.

Sallier Joseph, clerk Francis Sallier, res 28 Hough.

Sallot Jacob F, carpenter, res rear 164 E Lewis.

Sallot Victor A, supt Indiana Machine Works, res 4 Summit.

Salmon Daniel F, reporter, bds n e cor Butler and Barr.

Salmon John, clerk, bds n e cor Butler and Barr.

Salmon Margaret (wid Daniel T), res n e cor Butler and Barr.

Salter Mary A (wid John), bds 74 Baker.

Salter Wm, brakeman, res 46 Burgess.

Saltzgaber Henry, lab Hoffman Bros, rms 22 Foster block.

Salzmann Wm, photographer, 164 Calhoun, res same.

Sam, Pete & Max (Stern, Mautner & Friedlich), clothing, 58 Calhoun.

Sams John W, section hand, res 59 Grand.

Sams Uriah, watchman Wabash R R, bds 59 Grand.

Samse Caroline (wid Wm), res 40 W Superior.

Samse Miss Rose, stenographer Randall & Vesey, bds 40 W Superior.

Sanburn Amos H, res 34 W Superior.

Sanburn John W, bds 34 W Superior.

Sanburn Lillie M, bds 34 W Superior.

Sander Charles W, clerk Siemon & Bro, res 187 Griffith.

Sander Miss Lena, bds 86 W Washington.

Sander Miss Sophie, bds 86 W Washington.

Sander Wm, res 86 W Washington.

Sanders, *see also Saunders.*

Sanders Catherine (wid Ernest), res rear 103 W Jefferson.

Sanders Henry, driver patrol wagon, res 72 Barr.

Sanders John, laborer Penn Co, res 38 Baker.

Stahn & Heinrich, Leading Dealers in ARTISTS' MATE-
RIALS AND DRAUGHTING INSTRU-
MENTS. 116 Calhoun Street.

FORT WAYNE DIRECTORY. 459

Sanders John, painter, bds 166 Holman.
Sanders Wm F, clerk Stewart & Hahn, res 103 W Jefferson.
Sandkuhler Henry, coremaker Bass Foundry and Machine Works, bds 226 Gay.
Sanford Philip, laborer Joseph Fremion, res s s Wiebke 1 e of Lafayette.
Sanger Jacob, lab C L Centlivre, res Centlivre Park.
Sarasien Sophia L, seamstress D S Redelsheimer & Co, bds 62 E Superior.
Sarazen, *see also Sarraizen and Sarrazin.*
Sarazen George E, laborer, res 34 Smith.
Sarber Thomas J, brakeman Penn Co, res 16 Euclid.
Sargent, *see also Sergeant.*
Sargent Archie, cigarmaker Schele Bros, bds 322 E Wayne.
Sargent John (col'd), porter, res 33 Grand.
Sargent Thomas P (Jenson & Sargent), res 12 Marion.
Sargent Wm, res 14 Marion.
Sargent Wm jr, blacksmith, res 322 E Wayne.
Sarnighausen John D (Sarnighausen & Griebel), res n e cor Columbia and Clinton.
Sarnighausen & Griebel (John D Sarnighausen, A Louis Griebel), publrs Indiana Staats Zeitung, n e cor Columbia and Clinton.
Sarraizen, *see also Sarazen and Sarrazin.*
Sarraizen Emil, laborer Penn Co, res 98 Maumee road.
Sarraizen Julian E, lab Penn Co, res 200 E Washington.
Sarrazin, *see also Sarazen and Sarraizen.*
Sarrazin Carrie, works Troy Steam Laundry, bds 37 Barr.
Sarrazin Mary (wid Joseph), res 37 Barr.
Satoris, *see Sutoreus.*
Sauer Charles, cigarmaker F J Gruber, bds 284 Broadway.
Sauer Charles, Supt The Prudential Life Insurance Co, 30 Pixley & Long Bldg, res 106 Barr.
Sauer Christian, conductor, res 356 W Main.
Sauer C Herman, clerk, bds 170 Barr.
Sauer Gottlieb M, conductor Penn Co, res 138 Horace.
Sauer Rev Henry G, Pastor St Paul's German Lutheran Church, res 170 Barr.
Sauerbier W A, cigarmaker Louis Bender, res 62 E Williams.
Sauertieg Frederick, cooper, 17 E Superior, bds same.
Sauerwein Ernst A, barber, bds 58 Barthold.
Sauerwein Ernst H S, machinist Ft W, C & L R R, res 56 Barthold.
Sauerwein Frank, springmaker Penn Co, res 86 W Lewis.
Saunders, *see also Sanders.*
Saunders Benjamin, clerk, bds 164 Broadway.

Saunders Joseph (col'd), waiter, rms 67 W Superior.
Saunders Joseph B, machinist, res 55 W Lewis.
Saunders Maud M, bds 55 W Lewis.
Saurbaugh Marion A, bartender L E Banet, res 13 Barthold.
Saurs James T, engineer, res 226 Fairfield ave.
Saurs Mary A (wid George J), bds 226 Fairfield ave.
Saurs Samuel P, res 226 Fairfield ave.
Sauser Louis, jeweler, 188 Calhoun, res same.
Sautter Frederick W, conductor, res 130 Buchanan.
Savio Frank, brakeman Penn Co, bds Hinton's Restaurant.
Sawtell Henry P, res 3 Oak.
Sawyer Charles, laborer, bds 27 E 1st.
Sawyer Frank M, laborer, bds 27 E 1st.
Sawyer James T, boarding house, 27 E 1st.
Saylor George B, trav agent Adams & Armstrong, res 173
    Griffith.
Saylor Jacob K, switchman, res 67 Grand.
Sayner, *see also Sahner and Zauner.*
Sayner Henry, fireman, res 106 W Williams.
Scalf Lizzie, clerk C J Pierre, bds same.
Scanlin Hannah, domestic Fort Wayne City Hospital.
Scarlet Chester (Komp & Scarlet), res 56 N Harrison.
Scarlet Rosa E, clerk J O Keller, bds 56 N Harrison.
Scarlett Bertha, bds 41 Jesse.
Scarlett Henry O, carpenter, res 41 Jesse.
Scarlett Reuben W, machine hand Fort Wayne Furniture
    Co, res 40 Miner.
Scarlett Washington C, plasterer, bds 41 Jesse.
Schaaf Rev Carl, pastor St John's Reformed Church, res 59
    W Washington.
Schaaf Miss Rosalia, bds 59 W Washington.
Schaaf Miss Sarah, teacher West German School, bds 59 W
    Washington.
Schaaf Wm G, laborer, bds 815 Broadway.
Schacher Charles, molder Bass Foundry and Machine Works,
    res 80 Wall.
Schacher Christian F, helper, bds 41 Stophlet.
Schacher Leonard, laborer Wm & J J Geake, res 41 Stophlet.
Schacher Wm H, laborer, bds 41 Stophlet.
Schack Augusta (wid Wm), res 55 Charles.
Schack George H, store keeper Bass Foundry and Machine
    Works, res 231 Madison.
Schack Wm, fireman Hook and Ladder Co No 2, rms same.
Schad Frederick, gas fitter, res 85 Wells.
Schaden Peter W, lawyer, n w cor Calhoun and Berry, res
    349 W Jefferson.

E. F. Sites, 🦷 Dentist, 86 Calhoun St., Four Doors North of Wayne.

FORT WAYNE DIRECTORY. 461

Schadle Henry, bds 309 Hanna.
Schadle Louisa, bds 309 Hanna.
Schadle Paulina (wid August), res 309 Hanna.
Schaedel Jacob, laborer C L Centlivre, res w s Spy Run ave
  3 n of Edna.
Schaefenacker Fritz, truck builder Penn Co, res n s New
  Haven ave 2 w of Lumbard.
Schaefenacker Jacob F, car builder Penn Co, res 60 Smith.
Schaefer, *see also Schafer, Schaffer, Scheffer, Shafer and
  Shaffer.*
Schaefer Miss Amelia, bds 26 Wilt.
Schaefer Augusta, milliner A Mergentheim, bds 26 Wilt.
Schaefer Charles, clerk, bds 26 Wilt.
Schaefer Christian F, carpenter, res 171 W Superior.
Schaefer John H W, bds John H W Schaefer jr.
Schaefer John H W jr, grocer, rear 147 W 3d, res same.
Schaefer Reinhardt, clerk Siemon & Bro, bds 26 Wilt.
Schaefer Wm, brass molder Fort Wayne Electric Co, bds 26
  Wilt.
Schaefer Wm E, machinist Penn Co, res 26 Wilt.
Schaenle Theodore, cabinetmaker Fort Wayne Furniture Co,
  bds 46 E Columbia.
Schafer, *see also Schaefer, Schaffer, Scheffer, Shafer and
  Shaffer.*
Schafer Christian, broommkr C A Cartwright, bds 67 Grand.
Schafer Christian, car builder Penn Co, res 296 W Main.
Schafer Christian, saloon, 201 Lafayette, and 99 Calhoun,
  res 171 E Main.
Schafer Christian F W, bartender Christian Schafer, bds 171
  E Main.
Schafer Christian M, bartndr Henry Dierstein, rms 24 E Berry.
Schafer Edward A, Druggist, 277 E Washington,
  res same.
Schafer Ernst, clerk, bds 314 Lafayette.
Schafer Frank, plumber P E Cox, bds 186 Francis.
Schafer Frederick, clerk, bds 90 St Mary's ave.
Schafer Frederick C, driver Fort Wayne Artificial Ice Co,
  bds foot E Main.
Schafer George G, chief clerk East Car Shops Penn Co, res
  147 Madison.
Schafer Henry, laborer, bds 193 Montgomery.
Schafer Henry, teamster, res 90 St Mary's ave.
Schafer Henry C, clk G DeWald & Co, bds 90 St Mary's av.
Schafer John, res 314 Lafayette.
Schafer John G, barber Walker & Ellert, bds 314 Lafayette.
Schafer Joseph, upholsterer, bds 314 Lafayette.

Schafer J Christian, car repairer, res s e cor Wall and Metz.

Schafer Lizzie, operator Hoosier Mnfg Co, bds 193 Montgomery.

Schafer Minnie E, tailoress, bds 90 St Mary's ave.

Schafer Olive, waitress Aldine Hotel.

Schafer Sophia, tailoress G Scheffler, bds 186 Francis.

Schafer Wm, helper Penn Co, bds 186 Francis.

Schafer Wm F, setter Penn Co, bds 193 Montgomery.

Schaffer, *see also Schaefer, Schafer, Scheffer, Shafer and Shaffer.*

Schaffer Ferdinand, car builder Penn Co, res 289 E Jefferson.

Schaffer Henry, driver Wm Moellering & Sons, bds 120 Montgomery.

Schafman Louis, umbrella repairer, res 281 E Washington.

Schaich Anna M, dressmaker M J Schaich, bds 190 Taber.

Schaich Maggie J, dressmaker, 190 Taber, res same.

Schallenberger Stephen, car repairer Penn Co, res 316 Lafayette.

Schandly Theresa, domestic 393 Lafayette.

Schank, *see also Shank.*

Schank Emil, clerk Sam, Pete and Max, res 173 Madison.

Schank John, laborer, bds n s Cochrane 5 e of Coombs.

Schank Mary (wid Louis), bds 374 E Washington.

Schanz Felix, artist and photographer, 112 Calhoun, res same.

Schaper Christian, carpenter, bds 69 Maumee rd.

Schaper John, carpenter, bds 345 E Lewis.

Schaper Wm, harnessmaker, 20 N Harrison, bds same.

Schaphorst Engal (wid Herman), res 22 Orchard.

Schaphorst Frederick F, laborer, bds 12 Orchard.

Schaphorst Henry, car builder Penn Co, res 12 Orchard.

Schaphorst John, clerk Siemon & Bro, bds 26 Orchard.

Schaphorst John F, car builder Penn Co, res 128 W 3d.

Schaphorst Lizzie, domestic 76 W Berry.

Schaphorst Wm, carpenter Ft W, C & L R R, res 26 Orchard.

Schaphorst Wm, laborer, bds 12 Orchard.

Scharf, *see also Sharp.*

Scharf Charles A, tinner, 195 Lafayette, res 202 Madison.

Scharf Lena, bds 202 Madison.

Scharf Louisa (wid Adam), res 150 E Jefferson.

Scharmann Philip, teacher St John's German Lutheran School, res 212 W Washington.

Schearer, *see also Scherer.*

Schearer Andrew, clerk police station, res 6 Erie.

Scheek John, laborer Salimonie Mining and Gas Co, bds Frederick Bizeler.

Scheele, *see also Schele.*

Scheele August W, driver Henry Scheele, bds 284 Webster.

Scheele Emma, dressmaker, bds 284 Webster.

Scheele Henry, coal, 68 Murray, res 284 Webster.

Scheele Henry W, driver, bds 284 Webster.

Scheele Wm F, machinist, bds 284 Webster.

Scheer Wm, laborer Penn Co, res 96 Wilt.

Scheer Wm jr, clerk Penn Co, res 96 Wilt.

Scheere John C, laborer, bds 50 Oakley.

Scheere Louis T, machine hand, Fort Wayne Organ Co, bds 50 Oakley.

Scheere Margaret (wid Patrick), res 50 Oakley.

Scheetz, *see also Sheetz.*

Scheetz James B, helper Penn Co, bds Monroe House.

Scheffer, *see also Schaefer, Schafer, Schaffer, Shafer and Shaffer.*

Scheffer John (Scheffer & Geiger), res 135 E Jefferson.

Scheffer & Geiger (John Scheffer, Frank J Geiger), grocers, 292 Calhoun.

Scheffler, *see also Shefler.*

Scheffler Gustav, tailor 43 W Main, res 15 Sturgis.

Scheib Edward J, clerk J B White, bds 91 Summit.

Scheib John, car builder Penn Co, res 91 Summit.

Scheid Frank, machinist Penn Co, res 55 E De Wald.

Scheid Peter J, commissioner fire dept, res 129 E De Wald.

Scheid Wm H, tinsmith, bds 129 E De Wald.

Scheiferstein, *see Schieferstein.*

Scheiman, *see also Scheumann Schumann and Shuman.*

Scheiman Caroline (wid Ernst), res 338 Broadway.

Scheiman Charles, printer Fort Wayne Journal, bds 338 Broadway.

Scheiman Ernst D, foreman Fort Wayne Journal, res 37 E Williams.

Scheiman Wm, grocer, 362 Calhoun, res same.

Scheimann Charles J, bookkeeper Fort Wayne Organ Co, bds 86 E Jefferson.

Scheimann Dora, bds 86 E Jefferson.

Scheimann Frederick E W, treas Salimonie Mining and Gas Co, res 321 E Washington.

Scheimann Sophia (wid Frederick), res 86 E Jefferson.

Scheimann Wm H, bookkeeper G E Bursley & Co, res 86 E Jefferson.

Scheirer John C, machine hand Fort Wayne Organ Co, bds 50 Oakley.

Scheirman Frederick, pulley finisher Old Fort Mnfg Co, bds 3 Oak.

Schele, *see also Scheele.*

Schele Albert F, waiter, bds 33 St Mary's ave.
Schele Arnold J, cigarmaker, bds August Schele.
Schele August, bricklayer, res n e s Pitsburgh New Yards on Wayne Trace.
Schele Bernard H, trav agent Mossman, Yarnelle & Co, bds August Schele.
Schele Bros (Martin and Clemens), cigar mnfrs, 52 Barr.
Schele Carrie (wid Conrad), res w s Lumbard 3 s of Wabash R R.
Schele Catherine (wid John B), bds 286 E Wayne.
Schele Catherine M, bds August Schele.
Schele Cecilia, bds Henry Schele.
Schele Charles H, clerk, bds 33 St Mary's ave.
Schele Clemens (Schele Bros), bds 286 E Wayne.
Schele Edward, barber, 121 E Lewis, bds August Schele.
Schele Frank, saloon, 14 Harrison, res same.
Schele Henry, laborer, res s s Wayne Trace 2 e of Walton.
Schele Henry F, brick mason, bds 20 Locust.
Schele John H, saloon, 26 Harrison, res same.
Schele Joseph J, works H H Barcus, bds Julius Schele.
Schele Julius, mason, res 33 St Mary's ave.
Schele Louisa, bds August Schele.
Schele Margaret, bds August Schele.
Schele Martin (Schele Bros), res 32 W 4th.
Schele Theresa, bds 33 St Mary's ave.
Schele Wm J, fireman, bds 33 St Mary's ave.
Schelker Louis, laborer, res 12 Buchanan.
Schell, *see also Shell.*
Schell Frank K, clerk County Auditor, rms 132 Lafayette.
Schell George O, clerk J D Gumpper, bds 235 Calhoun.
Schell Myron J, clerk J D Gumpper, res 15 Holman.
Scheller, *see Sheeler.*
Schellhammer Charles, molder Bass Foundry and Machine Works, bds s w cor Pontiac and Walton.
Schellhammer Robert, lab, res w s Walton ave 1 s of Pontiac.
Schellhammer Robert C, lab, bds w s Walton ave 1 s of Pontiac.
Schelveur Thomas J, clerk County Auditor, bds 72 Nelson.
Schemer Emma, domestic 269 W Main.
Schemmele George, teamster, res 258 Hoffman.
Schenk Carl, laborer Louis Rastetter, bds 11 Caroline.
Schenk Mary, domestic Peter Nusbaum.
Schenk Peter, machine hand Louis Rastetter, res 11 Caroline.
Schenk Wm, helper Kerr-Murray Mnfg Co, bds Hoffman House.
Schenkel Peter, stone mason, res 128 Franklin ave.
Schenkle Fannie, domestic Diamond Hotel.

Schepper Wm G, mach A Hattersley & Sons, bds 64 Wall.
Schept Anna R, domestic 199 Broadway.
Scherer, *see also Schearer.*
Scherer Charles W, grocer, 56 Walton ave, res same.
Scherer Frederick, cabinetmaker Penn Co, res 95 E Washington.
Scherer Henry P (Dudenhoefer, Bueker & Scherer), res 355 E Washington.
Scherer Henry T, teamster L P Scherer, bds 99 Maumee road.
Scherer John, res 12 Erie.
Scherer John, clerk Hartman & Bro, bds 95 E Washington.
Scherer Lizzie, dressmaker, 28 Lillie, bds same.
Scherer Louis, res 28 Lillie.
Scherer Louis P, baker, market stall 46, res 99 Maumee road.
Scherer Thomas J, mach American Wheel Co, bds 236 E Lewis.
Scherer Wm F, tinner H J Ash, bds 95 E Washington.
Scherschel Valentine, laborer, res 180 Force.
Scherzinger Gerson, Propr Custer House, 16 and 18 W Main, res same. (*See adv, p 61.*)
Scherzinger Primus (Trenkley & Scherzinger), rms 78 Calhoun.
Scheumann, *see also Scheiman, Schumann and Shuman.*
Scheumann August, hostler A Melching, bds same.
Scheumann Christian, cabinetmkr Penn Co, res 315 E Washington.
Scheumann Christian D, clk W D Meyers, bds 129 E Lewis.
Scheumann Edw F, clk First National Bank, bds 1 W Butler.
Scheumann Frederick H (Scheumann & Klaehn), res 321 S Calhoun.
Scheumann F W, car builder Penn Co, res 168 Ewing.
Scheumann Jacob, yardman Aveline House.
Scheumann Wm, molder Bass Foundry and Machine Works, res 16 Butler.
Scheumann & Klaehn (Frederick H Scheumann, W Robert Klaehn), undertakers, 39 W Main.
Schick George, teacher Concordia College, res College grounds.
Schick Miss Gertrude, bds George Schick.
Schiefer Charles W, blacksmith, res s w cor Wabash R R and Warren.
Schiefer Christian (C Schiefer & Son), res 8 E Columbia.
Schiefer C & Son (Christian Schiefer, Herman H Hartwig), Boots and Shoes, Slippers and Rubbers, 8 E Columbia.
Schiefer Diedrich, tinner Wabash R R, res 135 Montgomery.
Schiefer Elizabeth, bds Wm D Schiefer.
Schiefer George H, bookkpr C W Bruns & Co, bds 135 Montgomery.

John Pressler, Mantels, Grates and Tile Floor. Columbia, Barr and Dock Streets.

466   R. L. POLK & CO.'S

Schiefer George W, mngr The Siemon Wall Paper Co, rms 191 Calhoun

Schiefer Lillie, bds 135 Montgomery.

Schiefer Wm C, machinist Wabash R R, bds 135 Montgomery.

Schiefer Wm D, clk C Schiefer & Son, res e s Spy Run ave s of Riverside ave.

Schiefer Wm F, bds 442 E Wayne.

Schieferdecker Jacob, truckmkr, res 60 Smith.

Schieferstein Albert, laborer, bds n w cor W Main and Runnion ave.

Schieferstein Frederick, carpenter, bds 53 Walton ave.

Schieferstein Henry, driver, bds 53 Walton ave.

Schieferstein Henry, laborer, bds n w cor W Main and Runnion ave.

Schieferstein Louis, fireman, bds 53 Walton ave.

Schieferstein Philip, butcher F Eckart, res cor W Main and Runnion ave.

Schieferstein Philip jr, butcher F Eckart, bds Philip Schieferstein.

Schieferstein Wm, blacksmith, bds n w cor W Main and Runnion ave.

Schieman, *see Scheiman.*

Schiemer Annie, bds 43 N Calhoun.

Schiemer Frank, Dealer in Pure Wines and Liquors, Lager Beer and Cigars, 264 Calhoun, res 43 N Calhoun.

Schiemer Pauline, dressmkr, bds 43 N Calhoun.

Schienlein Charles B, tailor Thieme Bros, res 350 W Main.

Schifferdecker Wm, brewer The Herman Berghoff Brewing Co, res 548 E Wayne.

Schild Jesse S, wks J O Keller, res 15 Emily.

Schildmeyer Louisa (wid Christian), res 180 W Jefferson.

Schilling Camilla (wid Jacob), res s s Howell e of Rumsey.

Schilling Carl, phys, 15 E Washington, res 69 E Jefferson.

Schilling Charles F, dairy, n s Howell e of Rumsey, res same.

Schilling Frank J, clerk, bds 255 W Jefferson.

Schilling Frank X, stonecutter Wm & J J Geake, res 255 W Jefferson.

Schilling John, market stall 53, res w s Lima road n of city limits.

Schilling John, clk A J Dittoe & Co, bds 255 W Jefferson.

Schilling Kate, bds 255 W Jefferson.

Schilling Mary, milliner M M Lau, bds 255 W Jefferson.

Schilling Miss Mary B, res 88 W Washington.

Schilling Sophia, market stall 51, res w s Bluffton road w of city limits.

Schimmele George, laborer, res 253 Hoffman.

Stahn & Heinrich, Dealers in FANCY GOODS, ALBUMS, Etc. 116 CALHOUN STREET.

FORT WAYNE DIRECTORY. 467

Schimmelpfennig Gustave, wheel molder Bass Foundry and Machine Works, res 348 Force.

Schimming Mrs Sophia, bds 195 W Superior.

Schirmeyer Albert J, clerk Louis Schirmeyer, bds 127 E Jefferson.

Schirmeyer Anthony, wiper Penn Co, res 22 W Jefferson.

Schirmeyer Charles W, messenger Penn Co, bds 22 W Jefferson.

Schirmeyer Louis, clk Sam, Pete & Max, res 127 E Jefferson.

Schirmeyer Louis, grocer, 122 E Washington, res 127 E Jefferson.

Schirmeyer Otto A, cashier Root & Co, bds 127 E Jefferson.

Schermeyer Werner T, dentist, 27 Calhoun, res 22 W Jefferson.

Schisler, see also Shisler.

Schisler Albert, brakeman, res 272 W Jefferson.

Schisler Milton S, brakeman, res 272 W Jefferson.

Schlabacker George, res 129 Clay.

Schlack W Frederick, cigarmkr George Reiter, res 89 E Lewis.

Schlage Christian, tailor, res 104 E Wayne.

Schlatter, see also Schlotter.

Schlatter Christian C (Pfeiffer & Schlatter), res 111 E Wayne.

Schlatter David D, clk Pfeiffer & Schlatter, bds 337 E Wayne.

Schlatter Kate, bds 337 E Wayne.

Schlatter Noah W, clerk G W Seavey, bds 337 E Wayne.

Schlaudraff George, lab, res w s Lafayette 8 s of Pontiac.

Schlaudraff Louis P, laborer Paul Koehler, bds same.

Schlebacher Elizabeth (wid George), bds 415 E Washington.

Schlegel Adam J, carriagemkr M L Albrecht, res 31 Barr.

Schlegel John, carp Christian Doenges, bds 126 Maumee rd.

Schlenker Andrew, laborer, bds 115 Taylor.

Schlenker George, machinist Fort Wayne Electric Co, res 64 Wall.

Schlie Christian, car repairer, res 73 Oakley.

Schliebitz Frederick W, jeweler, bds Custer House.

Schlink Frank H, barber John Brunskill, bds 340 E Wayne.

Schlotter, see also Schlatter.

Schlotter Alois, coil winder Fort Wayne Electric Co, bds 316 Broadway.

Schlotter Frank, coil winder Fort Wayne Electric Co, res 36 Wall.

Schlotter Joseph, armature winder Fort Wayne Electric Co, bds 316 Broadway.

Schlotter Joseph jr, machinist, bds 316 Broadway.

Schmall, see Schmoll and Small.

Schmalz, see also Smaltz.

Schmalz Carrie, tailoress, bds 32 W Williams.

Schmalz Charles, tailor, res 32 W Williams.

Schmalz Lizzie, tailoress, bds 32 W Williams.

Schmalz Mary, tailoress, bds 32 W Williams.

Schmalzriedt Sophie (wid George), res 287 E Lewis.

Schmeling Agnes, tailoress G Scheffler, bds 168 Maumee rd.

Schmeling George C, laborer, res 168 Maumee road.

Schmeling Herman, laborer, bds 168 Maumee road.

Schmenck Gerrat, machinist Fort Wayne Electric Co, res 10 Nirdlinger ave.

Schmetzer Adolph, machinist, bds 240 W Washington.

Schmetzer Gustav W, machinist Fort Wayne Electric Co, bds 240 W Washington.

Schmetzer John G, clerk Stahn & Heinrich, bds 240 W Washington.

Schmetzer Michael F, clerk Pixley & Co, res 240 W Washington.

Schmid August C, laborer Bass Foundry and Machine Works, res 54 Melita.

Schmidt, *see also Schmit and Smith.*

Schmidt Adolph, laborer Paul Koehler, bds same.

Schmidt Anna, bds 33 Wilt.

Schmidt August M, yardmaster Wabash R R, res 216 E Jefferson.

Schmidt Charles (Schmidt & Bro), res 318 E Jefferson.

Schmidt Charles, laborer The Herman Berghoff Brewing Co, bds 119 Eliza.

Schmidt Charles, machinist, res 173 Fairfield ave.

Schmidt Conrad, laborer, bds 41 Gay.

Schmidt Elizabeth S (wid Peter), bds 43 St Martin.

Schmidt Emma, bds 33 Wilt.

Schmidt Frank, machinist Indiana Machine Works, res 84 Summit.

Schmidt Frederick, car builder Penn Co, res Euclid ave.

Schmidt Frederick W, tool mnfr, 181 W Jefferson, res same.

Schmidt Gottfried (Schmidt & Bro), res 75 Monroe.

Schmidt Helena (wid John W), bds 231 Madison.

Schmidt Henry R, laborer, bds 7 Colerick.

Schmidt Herman, truss hoopmaker S D Bitler, bds 84 Lillie.

Schmidt Jacob, bricklayer, res 33 Wilt.

Schmidt Jacob jr, bds 33 Wilt.

Schmidt John, stone mason, bds 41 Gay.

Schmidt Joseph, baker Concordia College, res college grounds.

Schmidt Lorenz, car builder Penn Co, res 135 Force.

Schmidt Louis, brewer The Herman Berghoff Brewing Co, res 24 Grant ave.

Schmidt Louis W (Louis Schmidt & Co), res 274 W Washington.

Schmidt Louis & Co (Louis W Schmidt, Frank Alderman), Druggists, 120 Calhoun.

Schmidt Lucy, tailor, bds 318 E Jefferson.

Schmidt Ludwig S, carpenter, bds 43 St Martin.

Schmidt Margaret (wid John), bds 233 John.

Schmidt Martin, clerk Baals & Co, res 93 Summit.

Schmidt Peter C, res 135 Van Buren.

Schmidt Peter S, foreman, res 29 St Martin.

Schmidt Philip H, saloon, 168 W Main, res same.

Schmidt Rachel (wid Andrew), bds s e cor Barr and 7th.

Schmidt Wm, blacksmith Ferdinand Meier, bds 126 Smith.

Schmidt Wm, clerk Morgan & Beach, res 127 Erie.

Schmidt Wm J, cigarmaker A N Ehle, res 50 Nirdlinger av.

Schmidt & Bro (Gottfried and Charles), merchant tailors, 70 E Main.

Schmieders Frederick, cigarmaker L Dessauer & Co, res 282 W Jefferson.

Schmieman Gustav, trav agent A C Trentman, res 181 Ewing.

Schmit, *see also Schmidt and Smith.*

Schmit John, laborer Penn Co, res 44 John.

Schmit John jr, lab American Wheel Co, bds John Schmit.

Schmit Joseph, machine hand American Wheel Co, bds John Schmit.

Schmitt Adam P, molder Bass Foundry and Machine Works, bds 16 Gay.

Schmitt Eva M (wid Pankratz), res 22 Clark.

Schmitt Jacob, wheel molder Bass Foundry and Machine Works, res 129 Taber.

Schmitt Joseph P, laborer, bds 16 Gay.

Schmitz Block, 116 to 120 Calhoun.

Schmitz Frederick W, laborer, res w s Lafayette 11 s of Pontiac.

Schmitz Henrica (wid Charles), res 116 College.

Schmitz Philip, machine hand American Wheel Co, bds 212 John.

Schmitz Theodore, res 212 John.

Schmitz Theodore jr, machine hand American Wheel Co, res 495 S Lafayette.

Schmoe Catherine, bds 161 Ewing.

Schmoe Louis, shoemaker, 161 Ewing, res same.

Schmoe Louis jr, clerk Isaac Lauferty, bds 161 Ewing.

Schmoll, *see also Small.*

Schmoll George A, asst foreman Penn Co, res 78 Force.

Schmoll Rheta, milliner E Wolf, bds 78 Force.

Schmuck, *see also Smock.*

Schmuck Asa, laborer J C Peters, bds 105 Mechanic.

Schmuck Mrs Mary, res 105 Mechanic.

Schmucker Alfred P, machinist Penn Co, res s e cor DeWald and Calhoun.

Schmueckle Frederick, Propr Fritz Hotel, 10 E Berry, res same.

Schnabel Miss Mary E, bds 170 W Washington.

Schnarr, *see Schnurr.*

Schnee Joseph J, wheel molder Bass Foundry and Machine Works, res 19 E Williams.

Schneider, *see also Snider and Snyder.*

Schneider Adam, cigarmaker F J Gruber, res 173 High.

Schneider Charles, bds 16 Clay.

Schneider Christian, farmer, res 111 Putnam.

Schneider Conrad, laborer Bass Foundry and Machine Works, res 68 Force.

Schneider Frederick, cigarmaker Wm Schneider, bds 104 Webster.

Schneider George, saloon, e s Piqua ave 1 n of Rudisill ave res same.

Schneider Gottlieb F, tailor, res 52 Wells.

Schneider Henry, laborer Ranke & Yergens, res 52 Wells.

Schneider Henry, cigarmkr Wm Schneider, bds 104 Webster.

Schneider Henry J, foreman Fleming Mnfg Co, res 77 St Mary's.

Schneider John M, janitor, res 33 W Jefferson.

Schneider Julia, tailoress H C Meyer, bds 104 Webster.

Schneider Louis C, driver Fort Wayne Transfer and Baggage Line, bds 33 W Jefferson.

Schneider Martin, laborer American Wheel Co, res 5 Pine.

Schneider Mary (wid Olof), bds 6 Hoffman.

Schneider Mary, domestic 14 Harrison.

Schneider Mathias, teamster, res 324 E Wayne.

Schneider Maurice, heater Kerr-Murray Mnfg Co, res 61 Elm.

Schneider Otto A, helper Kerr-Murray Mnfg Co, bds 33 W Jefferson.

Schneider Wm, cigar mnfr, 104 Webster, res same.

Schneider Wm, laborer, bds 119 Eliza.

Schneider Wm H, cigarmaker Wm Schneider, res 97 Wall.

Schnelker Mrs Adeline, res 64 Maumee road.

Schnelker Agnes, bds 64 Maumee road.

Schnelker Elizabeth, bds 257 E Wayne.

Schnelker Harmon, bds 64 Maumee road.

Schnelker Henry, mason, res 257 E Wayne.

Schnelker Henry F, driver, bds 64 Maumee road.

Schnelker John B, laborer, bds 64 Maumee road.

Schnieders Annie E, bds 193 Barr.

Schnieders Bernhard H, shoemaker, 197 Calhoun, res 193 Barr.

Schnieders Clement A, bookkeeper, bds 107 Wallace.

Schnieders Mary E, clerk Root & Co, bds 193 Barr.

Schnitker Christian F, bartender Frank Schele, res 202 W Superior.

Schnorberger Charles, clerk Frank & Co, bds 216 Lafayette.

Schnorr John, laborer, res 33 Lillie.

Schnorr Tobias, carpenter, res n e cor Grant ave and Maumee road.

Schnurr Anna, domestic 55 E Superior.

Schnurr Kate, market stall 45, res w s Broadway road.

Schnurr Lena (wid Stephen), res 55 E Superior.

Schoch August F, Merchant Tailor, 41½ W Main, res 46 E 2d.

Schoch Wm F, tailor A F Schoch, bds 46 E 2d.

Schoell Adam, car repairer Penn Co, res Pontiac opp Smith.

Schoen, *see also Schone.*

Schoen Gustav, carpenter, bds 76 Maumee road.

Schoen Wm, carpet weaver, 76 Maumee road, res same.

Schoenbein Alice (wid Wm), bds 164 E Wayne.

Schoene Theodore, bds 46 E Columbia.

Schoenfeld Wm, machine hand Horton Mnfg Co, res 59 Stophlet.

Schoenherr Albert J, car repairer Penn Co, res 109 Smith.

Schoenherr August, laborer, res n w cor Erie and Canal.

Schoenle Joseph, molder Bass Foundry and Machine Works, bds 1 Lumbard.

Schoenlein Charles B, tailor, res 350 W Main.

Schoenlein John A, tailor Leonhardt Jaxtheimer, res 7 Union.

Schoenlein Max A, tailor Leonhardt Jaxtheimer, bds n w cor Osage and Main.

Schoepf Mathias, helper Penn Co, bds 46 Taylor.

Schoepke Anna, bds 89 Shawnee ave.

Schoepke Wm H, laborer, res 89 Shawnee ave.

Schof Joseph J, tinner, bds 180 Fairfield ave.

Schof Valentine, painter, res 180 Fairfield ave.

Schofield Charles B, brakeman, res 7 Pape.

Schondel George, engineer Kilian Baker, res 243 Clay.

Schone, *see also Schoen.*

Schone Annie M (wid Henry), res 227 E Washington.

Schone Henry H (Schone & Wellman), res 225 E Washington.

Schone & Wellman (Henry H Schone, Henry Wellman), Funeral Directors and Embalmers, 39 W Berry.

Schook Edward E, works Indiana School for Feeble-Minded Youth.

Schooley John, laborer Penn Co, res 76 Melita.

Schoonover Owen, laborer Penn Co, res 135 Wallace.
Schoonover Samuel E, carpenter J Klett & Son, res 57 Barr.
Schoonover Zachariah L, laborer American Wheel Co, bds 292 Hanna.
Schophorst, *see Schaphorst.*
Schoppman Charles, laborer Bass Foundry and Machine Works, bds 215 Hanna.
Schoppman Emma, bds 215 Hanna.
Schoppman Henry jr, blacksmith helper Penn Co, bds 141 E Lewis.
Schoppman Henry, laborer, res 141 E Lewis.
Schoppman Henry, market stall No 56, res e s St Joseph road.
Schoppman Johanna, bds 12 Hough.
Schoppman Kate (wid Wm), res 12 Hough.
Schoppman Louise, bds 215 Hanna.
Schoppman Minnie, bds 12 Hough.
Schoppman Wm, saloon, 209 Hanna, res 215 same.
Schotemeyer Harmon J, car repairer, res 82 Oakley.
Schotemeyer Sophia L, seamstress, bds 82 Oakley.
Schotemeyer Wm H, car repairer, bds 82 Oakley.
Schottmen Philip, boilermaker, res 41 Eliza.
Schott's Block, n w cor Barr and Washington.
Schowe Frederick R, stone mason, res 86 Oakley.
Schrack, *see also Schreck.*
Schrack Joseph, laborer American Wheel Co, res 185 Hanna.
Schrader, *see also Schroeder.*
Schrader A Lillian, bds 149 Griffith.
Schrader Miss Carrie B, music teacher, w s Rockhill bet Berry and W Main, bds same.
Schrader Frederick, laborer Bass Foundry and Machine Works, bds 183 Gay.
Schrader Henry, laborer Olds' Wagon Works, res 183 Gay.
Schrader Henry C (Schrader & Wilson), notary public, 46 Harrison, res w s Rockhill bet Berry and Main.
Schrader Wm, finisher Ft Wayne Furniture Co, bds 183 Gay.
Schrader Wm H, clerk Root & Co, bds 149 Griffith.
Schrader & Wilson (Henry C Schrader, Edward M Wilson), Insurance, Real Estate and Loans, 46 Harrison bet Berry and Main.
Schrage Mary A (wid August), res 55 Lillie.
Schram Frank, machinist Penn Co, res 28 Wallace.
Schramm George M, student, bds 86 Madison.
Schramm John, clerk L P Sharp, bds 86 Madison.
Schramm Martin, clerk J B White, res 86 Madison.
Schramm Martin F, helper Bass Foundry and Machine Wks, bds 86 Madison.

Schramm Max, laborer American Wheel Co, bds 41 Summit.
Schramm Minnie, bds 223 E Jefferson.
Schramm Nora (wid John), res 223 E Jefferson.
Schramm Peter, tailor L J Feist, bds 86 Madison.
Schramm Philip, machinist, res 205 Taylor.
Schramm Wm, helper Wabash R R, res 82 Fairfield ave.
Schrantz Adelaide (wid Edward), res 49 Melita.
Schrantz Bernard, laborer Olds' Wagon Works, res 3 Mc-Laughlin.
Schrantz Delia, dressmaker, bds 49 Melita.
Schrantz Frank, engineer Fort Wayne Furniture Co, bds 49 Melita.
Schrantz Maggie, bds 49 Melita.
Schrantz Sophronia, bds 49 Melita.
Schreck, *see also Schrack.*
Schreck Agnes (wid Adam), res 69 Melita.
Schreck Charles, contractor, res 75 W Washington.
Schreck Frank, laborer, bds 69 Melita.
Schremser John, laborer, res 38 John.
Schroeder, *see also Schrader.*
Schroeder Amelia, bds Henry J Schroeder.
Schroeder Andrew L, agt Prudential Life Insurance Co, res 102 Summit.
Schroeder Anna, bds 21 Charles.
Schroeder August H, Taxidermist, also Mnfr of Fancy Feathers, 38 Clinton, res 125 Calhoun. (*See adv, p 69.*)
Schroeder's Block (new), s e cor Broadway and W Washington.
Schroeder's Block (old), 242 Calhoun.
Schroeder Charles J H (Schroeder Bros), res 181 W Washington.
Schroeder C Louis (Schroeder & Sons), res 119 Superior.
Schroeder Edmond, carpenter, bds 286 E Jefferson.
Schroeder Mrs Eliza M, res 19 Miner.
Schroeder Ferdinand, fireman Hook and Ladder Co No 1, rms engine house No 1.
Schroeder Gottfried, res 170 E Jefferson.
Schroeder Henry F, helper Penn Co, bds 112 St Mary's ave.
Schroeder Henry H, feed yard, n e cor Duck and Calhoun, bds H J Schroeder.
Schroeder Henry J, policeman, res e s N Calhoun 1 n of Duck.
Schroeder Herman, contractor, n w cor Walnut and Fox, res same.
Schroeder John, laborer Penn Co, res 21 Charles.
Schroeder John H, laborer, bds 597 Calhoun.

Election Slips. Headquarters for PERFECT SLIPS at JOHN F. EBY & CO'S., DETROIT

474   R. L. POLK & CO.'s

Schroeder John S, engineer Hose Co No 1, res 80 Clinton.
Schroeder Louis, teamster, res 106 St Mary's ave.
Schroeder Louis S C (Schroeder & Sons), res 109 Broadway.
Schroeder Margaret E (wid J Frederick), res 597 Calhoun.
Schroeder Mary, domestic 183 Calhoun.
Schroeder Wilhelmine (wid Wm), res 33 Hough.
Schroeder Wm, bricklayer, res 33 Hough.
Schroeder & Sons (C Louis, Louis S C and Charles J H), real
    estate, 99 Broadway.
Schrumm Frank, plasterer, res 41 Summit.
Schu John, painter, res 594 Lafayette.
Schubert C August, molder Bass Foundry and Machine
    Works, res 230 Gay.
Schuck Albert A, clerk Isaac Lauferty, bd 842 Pontiac.
Schuck Mary A (wid Louis), res 42 Pontiac.
Schuckman Anna, clerk Root & Co, bds 105 E Washington.
Schuckman Elizabeth C (wid John J), res 105 E Washington.
Schuckman George jr, packer, bds 105 E Washington.
Schuckman Henrietta, bds 211 E Washington.
Schuckman Henry, tinner, res 211 E Washington.
Schuckman Henry J, clk Root & Co, res 105 E Washington.
Schuckman Miss Katie, bds 105 E Washington.
Schuckman Lizzie, bds 211 E Washington.
Schuckman Tillie, works J O Keller, bds 19 Buchanan.
Schuelke August, teacher Concordia College, res College
    grounds.
Schuewerk August, foreman D M Falls, res 531 E Wayne.
Schuhler Frank H, ins, 4 Pixley & Long bldg, res 107 Wells.
Schuler Clara, bds 268 E Jefferson.
Schuler Constantine, bookkeeper P E Wolf, bds 268 E
    Jefferson.
Schuler John, car builder Penn Co, bds 111 Hanna.
Schuler Mrs Mary, operator S M Foster, bds 268 E Jefferson.
Schuler Mathias, night watchman, res 268 E Jefferson.
Schuler Theodore J, saloon, 36 W Columbia, rms same.
Schulke Louis, laborer Bass Foundry and Machine Works,
    res 12 Buchanan.
Schulte Adolph, foreman Olds' Wagon Works, res 334 S
    Calhoun.
Schulte Mrs Adolph, milliner, 332 Calhoun, res 334 same.
Schulte Ernest, carp J W Hilgeman, res 42 Summit.
Schulte John H, laborer, res 131 Oliver.
Schulte Wm, laborer S Bash & Co, res 24 Clark.
Schultheis August, clk John Christen, bds 211 E Jefferson.
Schultheis Louis, clerk, bds 211 E Jefferson.
Schultheis Pius, porter Coombs & Co, res 211 E Jefferson.

Stahn & Heinrich, Booksellers and Stationers, Schmitz Block News Stand, 116 Calhoun 'Street.

FORT WAYNE DIRECTORY. 475

Schultz, *see also Shultz and Shulze.*
Schultz Annie, bds 140 Francis.
Schultz Carrie, bds 298 E Lewis.
Schultz Elizabeth (wid Wm), res 71 John.
Schultz Ferdinand, cooper, bds 299 Hanna.
Schultz Frederick, sewer contractor, 140 Francis, res same.
Schultz Frederick H, molder Bass Foundry and Machine Wks, bds 71 John.
Schultz Gustav, laborer, bds 71 John.
Schultz Henry, plasterer, res 298 E Lewis.
Schultz Miss Lizzie, bds 298 E Lewis.
Schultz Martha, bds 140 Francis.
Schultz Rosalia, bds 37 W Berry.
Schultz Sophia, operator Hoosier Mnfg Co, bds 71 John.
Schultz Wm H, clk Wm L Moellering, bds 298 E Lewis.
Schultz Wm H, machinist Fort Wayne Electric Co, res 76 Taylor.
Schulz, *see also Schulze and Shultz.*
Schulz Adolph F, foreman Kerr-Murray Mnfg Co, res 5 Sturgis.
Schulz Christopher F, helper Bass Foundry and Machine Works, bds 152 Horace.
Schulz Ernst, bds 43 Wagner.
Schulz Frederick C, helper Bass Foundry and Machine Wks, bds 162 Gay.
Schulz Henry, foreman, res 162 Gay.
Schulz Herman, bricklayer, res 38 Hugh.
Schulz John, printer, bds 70 Barr.
Schulz Peter, bds 70 Barr.
Schulz Wm, clerk C W Scherer, bds 56 Walton ave.
Schulz Wm, pedler, res 152 Horace.
Schulz Wm F, helper Fort Wayne Electric Co, bds 162 Gay.
Schumacher, *see also Shoemaker.*
Schumacher Mollie C, bds 134 Lafayette.
Schumacker Christina (wid Adam), res 23 Baker.
Schumann, *see also Scheiman, Scheuman and Shuman.*
Schumann Herman A, blksmith Olds' Wagon Works, res w s Lima road, Washington township.
Schunk, *see Shunk.*
Schuricht Herman, laborer Bass Foundry and Machine Works, res 230 John.
Schuricht Max, laborer, bds 230 John.
Schust Andrew, carpenter, res 182 Wells.
Schust Ferdinand H, machinist Kerr-Murray Mnfg Co, bds 230 W Jefferson.
Schust George A, fireman City Water Works, res 184 Wells.

Schust G Adolph, sec Kerr-Murray Mnfg Co, res 32 W Creighton ave.

Schnst Harry S, machinist, bds 230 W Jefferson.

Schust Louis H, machinist Kerr-Murray Mnfg Co, bds 230 W Jefferson.

Schust Michael J, patternmaker Kerr-Murray Mnfg Co, res 230 W Jefferson.

Schust Minnie, bds 230 W Jefferson.

Schuster, *see also Shuster.*

Schuster Della, domestic Aveline House.

Schuster Henry G, carpenter, res 201 Taylor.

Schuster Wm G, laborer, res 18 Allen.

Schwab Annie, bds 392 E Wayne.

Schwab Edward, truckman Penn Co, bds Monroe House.

Schwab John, meat market, n e cor Buchanan and Thomas, res same.

Schwab Kate (wid John), res 392 E Wayne.

Schwab Martin G, painter, res 143 Erie.

Schwabe Julius, patternmaker Bass Foundry and Machine Works, res 59 Summit.

Schwalm Elizabeth (wid George), bds 148 Maumee road.

Schwaninger Peter, laborer, res 90 Franklin,

Schwanz Frank J, laborer, bds 207 Taylor.

Schwanz Matthew, carpenter, res 130 University.

Schwartz Charles A, harnessmaker A L Johns & Co, res 442 E Wayne.

Schwartz Christian, plasterer, res 113 Boone.

Schwartz Frederick, collarmkr F L Racine, res 42 W Butler.

Schwartz George, fireman, bds 42 Butler.

Schwartz George, laborer, res 350 Broadway.

Schwartz George M, car inspector Penn Co, res 36 Taylor.

Schwartz Henry, fireman, bds 42 Butler.

Schwartz Henry W, plasterer, res 542 Calhoun.

Schwartz John, lab, res n s St Joe road 1 e of St Joe bridge.

Schwartz John A, bds 104 Butler.

Schwartz Louis, blacksmith, 84 Barr, res 102 Madison.

Schwartz Rosa, bds 42 Butler.

Schwarz Carl, prin West German School, res n e cor Howard and Dubois.

Schwarz Miss Carrie, bds Carl Schwarz.

Schwarz Frank C, cashier J B White, bds Carl Schwarz.

Schwarz John G, bds Carl Schwarz.

Schwarze Henry, carpenter, res 13 St Mary's ave.

Schwarze Sophie (wid Wm), tailoress, bds 197 Lafayette.

Schwarzmann Frederick, laborer Olds' Wagon Works, bds 248 Calhoun.

Schwarzmann Henry, laborer Olds' Wagon Works, bds 248 Calhoun.

Schwegmann Gustav A, bookkeeper Old National Bank, res 35 E Jefferson.

Schwegmann John F, plumber, bds 35 E Jefferson.

Schwegmann Lydia, bds 23 E Jefferson.

Schwegmann Matilda (wid Rudolph H), res 35 E Jefferson.

Schwegmann Paul R, trav agt, bds 35 E Jefferson.

Schwehn Conrad jr, boilermkr, res 135 W 3d.

Schwehn Conrad, machinist Wabash R R, res 18 Orchard.

Schwehn Henry W, upholsterer P E Wolf, bds 18 Orchard.

Schwehn John, blacksmith Wabash R R, res 168 Gay.

Schweigel Frederick, carpenter, res 171 Gay.

Schweigel Ida, domestic 280 W Wayne.

Schweiniger Peter, mach hand Louis Rastetter, res 90 Franklin ave.

Schweitzer Rosa (wid Frederick), res 312 W Main.

Schwertz Wm, laborer Hoffman Bros, res 112 Hanna.

Schwertzgen Joseph, bds 157 E Wayne.

Schwertzgen Joseph jr, press opr, res 157 E Wayne.

Schwier Charles (Charles Schwier & Son), res 174 Montgomery.

Schwier Charles & Son (Charles and Wm C), grocers, 176 Montgomery.

Schwier F Wm, boilermkr Penn Co, bds 159 Holman.

Schwier Henry C, boilermkr Bass Foundry and Machine Works, res s w cor Thomas and Pontiac.

Schwier Wm C (Charles Schwier & Son), bds 174 Montgomery.

Schwier Wm F, res 186 E Jefferson.

Schwieters Charles, clk A B White Cycle Co, bds 151 Ewing.

Schwieters Frank W, driver J H Schwieters, bds 41 E Columbia.

Schwieters Hermann, baker, res 151 Ewing.

Schwieters John H, baker, 41 E Columbia, res same.

Schwieters Kate, cashier J B White, bds 151 Ewing.

Schwieters Rosa, bds 151 Ewing.

Schwind Albert A, engineer, res 106 Butler.

Scott Alice, works Indiana School for Feeble-Minded Youth.

Scott Arza W, watchman, res 466 E Wayne.

Scott Charles A, flagman Penn Co, rms 224 Calhoun.

Scott Duane, carpenter, bds 49 Walnut.

Scott George, machinist Penn Co, res 241 E Lewis.

Scott George T, clk Penn Co, bds 241 E Lewis.

Scott James, molder, bds 241 E Lewis.

Scott James W, car builder Penn Co, res 101 Maumee road.

Scott Jefferson W, shaft trimmer Olds' Wagon Works, bds 122 Ewing.

Scott Jennie, bds 241 E Lewis.

Scott Jessie, bds 241 E Lewis.

Scott John, car builder Penn Co, res 122 Ewing.

Scott Mrs Julia A, dressmaker, bds 83 E Berry.

Scott Mattie, bds 241 E Lewis.

Scott Nellie, res cor Main and Clinton.

Scott Orville M, clk John Gronendyke, bds Diamond Hotel.

Scott Stephen D, meat market, 352 Broadway, res 364 same.

Scott Miss Susan A, bds 101 Maumee road.

Scott Wm L, engineer, res 118 Wallace.

Scotton Chester, supt South Wayne Brick Co, res 26 Thompson ave.

Scoville Seth S, engineer Wabash R R, res 95 W DeWald.

Scranton Israel, turner Louis Diether & Bro, bds 110 W Main.

Screen George, laborer, res s s Wheeler nr Runnion ave.

Screen John, laborer, res n s Wheeler nr Runnion ave.

Screen Thomas, laborer Luke Durnell, bds same.

Scully John, laborer Penn Co, res 76 Melita.

Seabold, *see also Seibold, Seybold and Siebold,*

Seabold Adam, res 27 Elm.

Seabold Christian, teamster, res 211 W Main.

Seabold George C, machine hand Louis Diether & Bro, bds 211 W Main.

Seabold George H, restaurant, 22 W Main, res same.

Seabold John, res 165 Wells.

Seabold John G, sawyer Winch & Son, res 92 Hayden.

Seabold Louis K, clerk Siemon & Bro, bds 211 W Main.

Seabold Theodore, laborer, bds 211 W Main.

Seabrease Rev Alexander W, Rector Trinity Episcopal Church, res Trinity Rectory 167 W Berry.

Seabrease Alexander W jr, clerk Carnahan & Co, bds 167 W Berry.

Seabrease McLean, clk Ft Wayne Electric Co, bds 167 W Berry.

Seacrist Harvey, saloon, 223 Calhoun, res same.

Seaman Rev Joseph W, steward Taylor University, res same.

Searney Carl E, millinery, 164 Calhoun, bds 53 Walter.

Search S Cleophas, conductor, res 10 W Superior.

Search Wm N, clerk Ft W, C & L R R, bds 10 W Superior.

Seaton John, oculist, 10 Calhoun, res 91 W Superior.

Seaton Robert L, driver Ft Wayne St Railroad Co, res 225 Lafayette.

Seavey Gideon W, Wholesale and Retail Hardware, Stoves and Tinware, 19 and 21 W Main, res 235 same.

Sewing **Machines,Shears** Pfeiffer & Schlatter
and Pocket Knives, 38 & 40 E. Columbia.

FORT WAYNE DIRECTORY. 479

Sebold Henry, engineer, res 22 Pritchard.

Sechler Milo H, despatcher G R & I R R, rms 316 Calhoun.

Second Presbyterian Church, Berry bet Webster and Ewing.

Seeger Franklin F C, car inspector Penn Co, res 34 Chestnut.

Seele Henry A, machine hand Olds' Wagon Works, bds 10 McClellan.

Seelig Charles, baker Louis Fox & Bro, res e s Maysville n of city limits.

Seelig Conrad, clerk G H Wilson & Sons, bds e s Maysville road n of city limits.

Seelig Henry, foreman Louis Fox & Bro, res 20 Summit.

Seelig John, clerk Louis Fox & Bro, res w s Maysville road e of city limits.

Seely Albert J, cabinetmaker J M Miller, res 72 W Williams.

Seely Albert J jr, helper Kerr-Murray Mnfg Co, bds 72 W Williams.

Seemann, *see also Siemon.*

Seemann Charles, laborer J C Peters, res 395 W Main.

Seemeyer Caroline (wid Gottlieb C), res 118 W Jefferson.

Seemeyer Miss Lena, bds 118 W Jefferson.

Seemeyer Theodore G, clerk Carnahan & Co, bds 118 W Jefferson.

Segur Charles A, clk Mossman, Yarnelle & Co, bds 309 W Washington.

Seibert, *see also Siebert and Seybert.*

Seibert Douglas G, teamster, res 69 Hamilton.

Seibert Frank M, carpenter, res 106 W Creighton ave.

Seibert Henry W, laborer Penn Co, res 65 W Williams.

Seibert John C, bds 106 W Creighton ave.

Seibert Mrs Mary, bds 29 John.

Seibold, *see also Seabold, Seybold and Siebold.*

Seibold Andrew, car repairer Wabash R R, res 77 Huestis.

Seibold Catherine (wid Gottlieb), res 43 Walnut.

Seibold Charles F, stopmaker Fort Wayne Organ Co, res 173 W DeWald.

Seibold Henry J, sec and treas Fort Wayne City Bill Posting Co and manager J O Keller, res 168 Ewing.

Seibold Jacob, res 18 Miner.

Seibold John J, laborer, res 35 Huestis ave.

Seibold Joseph A, cabinetmaker Fort Wayne Organ Co, res 61 Home ave.

Seibold Margaret (wid David), res 148 Wells.

Seibold Olive M, seamstress, bds 107 N Cass.

Seibt Charles B, laborer, res e s Lafayette 3 s of Pontiac.

Seibt Charles W H, machinist Bass Foundry and Machine Works, bds C B Seibt.

Seibt Louis, machinist, bds C B Seibt.
Seidel Arthur, clerk, bds 52½ Calhoun.
Seidel Block, 52 Calhoun.
Seidel Conrad, blacksmith, res 86 Hayden.
Seidel Edmund (Wm C Seidel & Bro), rms 52½ Calhoun.
Seidel Edward, Insurance, Real Estate and Loan
    Agent, 52½ Calhoun, res same.
Seidel Miss E Rosa, cashier Wm C Seidel & Bro, rms 52½
    Calhoun.
Seidel Mrs Lizzie, bds 90 Maumee road.
Seidel Otto, waiter Wm C Seidel & Bro, rms 52½ Calhoun.
Seidel Wm C (Wm C Seidel & Bro), rms 52½ Calhoun.
Seidel Wm C & Bro (Wm C and Edmund), Proprs
    Nickel Plate Restaurant and Ice Cream Parlors, Nickel
    Plate Depot.
Seifert Herman, laborer, res 85 Holman.
Seifert Wm F, driver M F Kaag, res 39 W 4th.
Seiler August, baker L P Scherer, bds 53 Walnut.
Seiling Diedrich, car builder Penn Co, res 171 Fairfield ave.
Seipp Frederick, stone mason Fort Wayne Steam Stone Wks,
    res 71 Hoffman.
Seitz David, carpenter, res 8 Elm.
Selbst Mary, operator S M Foster, bds 33 St Martin.
Selbst Mary A (wid Jacob), res 33 St Martin.
Selix Alice, domestic George H Baldwin.
Selix Patrick, bds 60 W Williams.
Selkmann John A, machine hand Fort Wayne Organ Co, bds
    199 S Broadway.
Sellers Wm, trimmer Jenney Electric Light and Power Co,
    bds 22 E Columbia.
Senniger John, laborer Penn Co, res 22 John.
Sergeant, *see also Sargent.*
Sergeant James E, harnessmaker, res 106 Wells.
Sesseman Mary, bds 52 Elm.
Sesseman Wm, carpenter, res 52 Elm.
Sessions Frank L, draughtsman Fort Wayne Electric Co, bds
    50 W Washington.
Sessler Charles E, bds 55 Grand.
Sessler Peter, res 55 Grand.
Seybert, *see Seibert and Siebert.*
Seybold, *see also Seabold, Seibold and Siebold.*
Seybold Miss Lillian H, teacher Harmer School, bds 149
    Griffith.
Seybold Wm, tuner Ft Wayne Organ Co, bds 158 W DeWald.
Seymoure Horace A, draughtsman H W Matson, bds 34 W
    Superior.

Seys John, clerk Rich's Hotel.

Shack, *see Schack.*

Shackelford Rev Nathan D, pastor Trinity M E Church,'res 106 N Cass.

Shadle, *see Schaedle.*

Shafer, *see also Schaefer, Schafer, Schaffer, Scheffer and Shaffer.*

Shafer George, blacksmith, res 212 Thomas.

Shafer John R, driver, res 122 W Washington.

Shafer Mrs Sadie, res 26 Harrison.

Shaffer, *see also Schaefer, Schafer, Schaffer, Scheffer and Shafer.*

Shaffer Allen C, blacksmith L C Zollinger, res 10 Ewing.

Shaffer George, res 169 Broadway.

Shaffer Harry L, brakeman Penn Co, res 131 Horace.

Shaffer Orville S, hostler Ft Wayne Transfer and Baggage Line, res cor Columbia and Barr.

Shambaugh Henry, carpenter, bds 84 Gay.

Shambaugh Wm H, lawyer, 11 Bank Block, bds Hotel Randall.

Shane Henry C, laborer Penn Co, res 305 S Harrison.

Shane John R, farmer, res 305 S Harrison.

Shane Rudolph, carpenter, bds 305 S Harrison.

Shane Wm J, carpenter, bds 305 S Harrison.

Shanks, *see also Schank.*

Shanks Rev Ernest H, pastor Church of God, res 96 De Wald.

Shanline David, barber, bds n s Howell 2 w of Rumsey ave.

Shannon George, laborer, bds S P Shannon.

Shannon Jennie, domestic 251 Calhoun.

Shannon Samuel P, carpenter, res e s Piqua ave opp Rudisill.

Shannon Thomas, cook Rich's Hotel.

Sharp Miss Carrie B, Principal Westminster Seminary, res 251 W Main.

Sharp Henry, res 25 Jackson.

Sharp Louis P, Notions, 15 Court, res 296 W Jefferson.

Sharp Ralph P, clerk F P Mensch, res 174 W Superior.

Sharp Wesley J, rms 15 Foster block.

Shaughnessey, *see also O'Shaughnessy.*

Shaughnessey W M E, machine hand Ft Wayne Organ Co, res 108 Fairfield ave.

Shaw Albert P, flagman, bds 23 Smith.

Shaw Charles H, painter L C Zollinger, res 74 W 4th.

Shaw David J, meats, 28 Smith, res 26 same.

Shaw George A, molder Bass Foundry and Machine Works, bds 135 E De Wald.

Shaw Mrs Robert H, grocer, 121 Fairfield ave, res 129 same.

Shaw Robert H, mach E B Kunkle & Co, res 129 Fairfield.

John Pressler, Galvanized Iron Cornices and Slate Roofing
Columbia, Barr and Dock Streets.

482   R. L. POLK & CO.'S

Shaw Thomas, laborer Bass Foundry and Machine Works, res 135 E De Wald.
Shaw Vincent B, machine hand American Wheel Co, res 23 Smith.
Shay Maggie, domestic McKinnie House.
Shay Mary (wid Cornelius), bds 36 Hayden.
Shayne David, barber Mathias Momper, bds Howell 3 e of Runnion road.
Shea Mrs Catherine, res 7 Walnut.
Shea Hannah, seamstress, bds 7 Walnut.
Shea John F, tinsmith Penn Co, res 41 Hugh.
Shea Joseph, messenger, bds 41 Hugh.
Shea Julia, bds 41 Hugh.
Shea Kate A, seamstress, bds 7 Walnut.
Shea Loretto, bds 41 Hugh.
Shea Michael, barber E Collins, bds Sullivan House.
Shea Michael F, engineer, res 421 Calhoun.
Shea Nellie, bds 41 Hugh.
Shea Patrick, fireman, res 44 Melita.
Shea Thomas, laborer Penn Co, bds 32 Chicago.
Shea Thomas E, brakeman, res 108 Boone.
Shea Timothy, res 41 Hugh.
Shea Wm H, switchman Penn Co, res 41 Hugh.
Shedd Arthur B, bds 575 Fairfield ave.
Sheehan John D, res rear 223 Calhoun.
Sheehan J Martin, conductor Penn Co.
Sheehan M C, conductor Penn Co, bds Sullivan House.
Sheets Gertrude, domestic 24 W Berry.
Sheetz, see also Scheetz.
Sheetz Charles, tailor, res 87 Pritchard.
Sheetz Johanna (wid Gottfried), res 201 Hanna.
Shefler, see also Scheffler.
Shefler Conrad B, conductor Penn Co, res n e cor Harrison and Brackenridge.
Shelbey Thomas J, clerk, bds 72 Nelson.
Shelby Harry, fireman, rms 23 Baker.
Sheldon Charles H, bleacher, 57 Clinton, res same.
Shell, see also Schell.
Shell Ella, domestic 19 W De Wald.
Shell E Clarence, mngr Old Fort Mnfg Co, res 68 W Main.
Shell Jennie (wid Frank), res 68 W Main.
Shellaberger Edwin, polisher American Wheel Co, res 313 S Clay.
Sheller Samuel, carpenter, res 307 W Washington.
Shelley Joseph, engineer, rms 14 Chicago.
Shelton Cora, clerk Diamond Hotel.

Shepard Abram L, brakeman, res 71 Taylor.
Shepard James A, bookkeeper American Wheel Co, res 168 W Jefferson.
Shepard Martin L, bds 71 Taylor.
Shepard Wm, helper Penn Co, res 71 Taylor.
Shepler John F, conductor, res 296 E Creighton ave.
Shepley George A, engineer Fort Wayne Organ Co, bds 518 Fairfield ave.
Sheppard Thomas, drill pressman Penn Co, bds 189 Montgomery.
Sheppo Wm, painter Penn Co, bds 89 Shawnee ave.
Sherbondy Edward M, laborer Fort Wayne Electric Co, bds 240 W De Wald.
Sherbondy George L, machine hand, bds 240 W De Wald.
Sherbondy Susannah R (wid Abraham), res 240 W De Wald.
Sherbondy Wm H, dynamo man Penn Co, bds 240 De Wald.
Sherer, *see Schearer and Scherer.*
Sheridan Annie B (wid John), res 19 Taylor.
Sheridan Catherine, janitor Bloomingdale School, bds 75 E Superior.
Sheridan Charles L, laborer, bds 19 Taylor.
Sheridan Ella, works Troy Steam Laundry, bds 53 Oliver.
Sheridan James, fruit trees, res 76 Montgomery.
Sheridan Mamie, bds 76 Montgomery.
Sherin Eliza (wid John), res 15 W Main.
Sherin Miss Mary L, dressmaker, 15 W Main, bds same.
Sherland Mark P, conductor, res 17 Boone.
Sherland Nathaniel, bds 17 Boone.
Sherman Miss Anna, bds 344 E Wayne.
Sherman Joseph (Sherman & Owens), res 130 Erie.
Sherman Josephine, bds 422 E Washington.
Sherman Tassie (wid John), res 422 E Washington.
Sherman & Owens (Joseph Sherman, Michael J Owens), barbers, 249 Calhoun.
Sherwin Cornelia (wid Wm C), res 159 Barr.
Sherwin Hattie G, dressmaker, bds 159 Barr.
Sherwin Millard D, laborer, res 159 Barr.
Sherwin Wilbur H, laborer, bds 159 Barr.
Sheviron Frank, fireman, res 22 Laselle.
Shick, *see Schick.*
Shidel Charles A, barber, 21 Calhoun, res 182 E Wayne.
Shideler Irvin P, helper Penn Co, bds 234 Harmer.
Shields Miss Addie J, bds Sylvester Lewis.
Shields Andrew, laborer, bds 67 Baker.
Shilling, *see Schilling.*
Shingler Wm H, gasfitter, res 211 E Wayne.

Shinn John, bds 64 W Wayne.
Shipman Frank I, baggage master L S & M S Ry, rms same.
Shisler, *see also Schisler.*
Shisler George, painter, res 126 E Creighton ave.
Shivers George B, bookkpr A L Johns & Co, res 29 N Cass.
Shmidt, *see Schmidt, Schmit and Smith.*
Shneider, *see Schneider, Snider and Snyder.*
Shoaff James B, agent, res 157 E Berry.
Shoaff John A, Photographer, 23 W Berry, res e s
     Spy Run ave 4 n of Riverside ave.
Shoaff Orin L, bds 157 E Berry.
Shoaff Samuel H, res 84 E Berry.
Shoaff Uriah S, traveling agent, res 50 W Superior.
Shober Viola (wid John), res 99 W Superior.
Shock Emma, dressmaker Mary L Sherin, bds 168 W Main.
Shoda Melinda, domestic 16 Lincoln ave.
Shoemaker, *see also Schumacher.*
Shoemaker Andrew, laborer, res 81 Brackenridge.
Shoemaker Eldora, domestic Grand Central Hotel.
Shoemaker Frank, machinist Fort Wayne Iron Works, bds 71
     Harrison.
Shoemaker John, laborer, bds 139 Holman.
Shoemaker Lizzie (wid James S), res e s Spy Run ave 9 n of
     Wagner.
Shoemaker Mary (wid Adam), res 23 Baker.
Shoemaker Rosa, bds 81 Brackenridge.
Shoemaker Wm W, gardener, bds Lizzie Shoemaker.
Shondel George, engineer, res 243 Clay.
Shondel Louisa, bds 241 E Wayne.
Shondel Mary, bds 243 Clay.
Shondel Wm, res 241 E Wayne.
Shook Maggie, dressmaker, bds 88 Wells.
Shookman John, engineer Winch & Son, res 420 Hanna.
Shoph, *see Schoepf.*
Shordon Daniel (Shordon & Alderman), restaurant, 61 E
     Columbia, res same.
Shordon & Alderman (Daniel Shordon, Dayton Alderman),
     farm implements, 63 E Columbia.
Shores John W, lab, bds s s Wayne Trace 5 e of Walton av.
Shorey George W, foreman, res 18 Butler.
Shorey I Herbert, clerk Wabash R R, res 18 Butler.
Shorey Wm H, baggageman, res 55 Butler.
Shorray August, lather, rms 27 Baker.
Short Gideon H, carpenter, res 19 St Michael's ave.
Short Henry A, conductor, res 19 St Michael's ave.
Short James, sawyer Hoffman Bros, res 193 W Superior.

Short James C, engineer, res 15 St Michael's ave.

Shrader, *see Schrader and Schroeder.*

Shrimpton Alfred, Builder, 152 W Main, rms same.

Shrock Wm, driver Fort Wayne Street Railway Co, res 412 E Washington.

Shroyer James, car builder Penn Co, res 63 Winter.

Shroyer Martin D, carpenter, res 365 E Lewis.

Shryock Wm W, Dentist, 27 W Berry, res same.

Shuder Susan, bds 67 Boone.

Shuey John, laborer, bds 137 Holman.

Shuey Joseph S, feeder The Press, bds 496 S Harrison.

Shuler, *see Schuler.*

Shultz, *see also Schultz and Schulz.*

Shultz Miss Wilhelmina, clk County Recorder, bds 103 Wilt.

Shulze, *see also Schultz and Schulz.*

Shulze Charles E, clerk Root & Co, res 333 S Webster.

Shulze Charles H, clerk G DeWald & Co, bds 333 S Webster.

Shulze Elliott G, stenographer Hoffman Bros, res 39 E Butler.

Shuman, *see also Scheiman, Scheumann and Schumann.*

Shuman Block, n s Main bet Barr and Clinton.

Shuman Erastus (E Shuman & Sons), res 56 E Wayne.

Shuman E & Sons (Erastus, Frank G, Gilbert E and George W), Wholesale Notions and General Store Supplies, 41 and 43 E Main.

Shuman Frank G (E Shuman & Sons), bds 56 E Wayne.

Shuman George W (E Shuman & Sons), bds 56 E Wayne.

Shuman Gilbert E (E Shuman & Sons), bds 56 E Wayne.

Shunk Frank, painter F H Treep, bds 19 Lafayette.

Shunk Nye, cornicemkr John Pressler, bds 19 Lafayette.

Shunk Theresa (wid Frank R), rms 19 Lafayette.

Shuster, *see also Schuster.*

Shuster John, laborer Penn Co, res s s New Haven road 3 e of toll gate.

Sible Henry B, laborer The Herman Berghoff Brewing Co, bds 101 Glasgow ave.

Sible John E, driver Fred Eckert, bds 91 E Wayne.

Siboni Miss Anna, music teacher, bds August Crull.

Sibray Mary E, clerk Root & Co, bds 230 W Wayne.

Sibray Nathan, carpenter Wabash R R, res 230 W Wayne.

Siebert, *see also Seibert.*

Siebert Otto, teamster J E Remus, bds 442 S Broadway.

Siebert Otto W, saloon, 303 W Main, res 305 same.

Siebold, *see also Seabold, Seibold and Seybold.*

Siebold Caspar, teamster, res 83 Barthold.

Siebold Christian, foreman Louis Rastetter, res 34 Pritchard.

Siebold Christopher W, horseshoer Geary & Perrey, bds n s
Howell e of Rumsey ave.

Siebold Edward F, finisher The Peters Box and Lumber Co,
bds 83 Barthold.

Siebold George H, clerk McKinnie House, bds 83 Barthold.

Siebold Henry F, blacksmith Fleming Mnfg Co, res 81 Barthold.

Siebold John P, policeman, res 216 W DeWald.

Siebold Samuel P, machine hand The Peters Box and Lumber
Co, bds 83 Barthold.

Siebold Sophia (wid Bernard), res 7 Pine.

Siebold Wm, framemaker Siemon & Bro, bds 7 Pine.

Siebold Wm C, laborer, bds 34 Pritchard.

Siebold Wm C, teamster John Orff, res 81 Barthold.

Siefert, *see Seifert.*

Siegmund Charles, clerk E Vordermark & Sons, rms 60 E
Washington.

Siegmund Herman, tailor Leonhardt Jaxtheimer, res s s
Pontiac 1 s of Abbott.

Siemon, *see also Seemann.*

Siemon August W, clerk Isidore Lehman, bds 27 Madison.

Siemon Carl F, mngr The Siemon Wall Paper Co, res 47
Elizabeth.

Siemon Carl F jr, bookkeeper Pfeiffer & Schlatter, bds 47
Elizabeth.

Siemon Charles A, tinsmith C F Graffe & Co, bds 75 Madison.

Siemon Conrad, expressman, res 19 Jones.

Siemon Ferdinand J, carpenter, bds 82 E Jefferson.

Siemon Helena (wid August F), res 27 Madison.

Siemon Henry R (Siemon & Brother), bds 27 Madison.

Siemon Herman T (Siemon & Brother), bds 27 Madison.

Siemon Otto, teacher latin and history Concordia college,
res College grounds.

Siemon Paul, res 82 E Jefferson.

Siemon Rudolph, propr The Siemon Wall Paper Co, 191 Calhoun, res 23 E Jefferson.

Siemon Wall Paper Co The (Formerly The Wayne
Wall Paper Co), Rudolph Siemon Propr, George W.
Schiefer and Carl Siemon Mngrs; Dealers in All Grades
of Wall Paper, Window Shades, Room Moldings, Artists'
Materials; and Sole Agents of Soule's (Boston) Photo-
graphic Reproductions of Works of Art, 191 Calhoun.
(*See left bottom lines.*)

Siemon & Brother (Henry R and Herman T), Books,
Stationery, Wall Paper, Picture Frames etc, 50 Calhoun.
(*See back cover.*)

Sievers Lena (wid Frederick W), res 203 E Wayne.
Sievers Louis H, carpenter, bds 110 High.
Sigler Edward F, laborer Penn Co, res 24 Huron.
Sigrist Wm E, springmaker The Peters Box and Lumber Co, res 21 Barthold.
Silbermann Wm R, lab Kerr-Murray Mnfg Co, res 231 Barr.
Silvers Helen (wid Allen), res 190 Montgomery.
Simmons Peter, laborer Penn Co, res 593 S Calhoun.
Simmons Wm H, night watchman, res 158 Madison.
Simon Julius, machinist Penn Co, res 18 Pine.
Simons Gordon, bds 72 Calhoun.
Simons James, bds 63 Winter.
Simons Joseph R, car builder Penn Co, res 63 Winter.
Simons Winfield M, vice-pres First National Bank, res Plymouth, Ind.
Simonson James H (Rhinesmith & Simonson), sec and treas Anthony Wayne Mnfg Co, res 61 W Berry.
Simonton Frank, laborer, res 156 Taylor.
Simonton George W, saloon, 161 Wells, res same.
Simpson M E Church, cor Harrison and Dawson.
Simpson Wm, teamster, res 204 E Wayne.
Sims Clifford S, asst engineer Penn Co, bds Rich's Hotel.
Sims Rev George H, pastor Christian Chapel, res s s W Jefferson 2 e of Griffith.
Sinclair Miss Frances C, res 332 W Jefferson.
Sinclair Miss Susan, principal Nebraska School, res 332 W Jefferson.
Sinclair Thomas, machinist Wabash R R, res 109 W DeWald.
Sinclair Thomas H, clk D L Harding, bds 109 W DeWald.
Sine Sherman E, fireman, res 469 Lafayette.
Singer Mnfg Co The, N H Bledsoe Mngr, 4 Aveline House Block.
Singleton Michael T, policeman, res 33 Baker.
Singleton Michael T jr, porter F C Boltz, bds 33 Baker.
Singleton Philip J, machinist Penn Co, res 27 Baker.
Singmaster Joseph, res 177 Jackson.
Singmaster Joseph M, flue welder Penn Co, res 177 Jackson.
Singrey Frank E, res 252 S Hoagland ave.
Sink, *see also Szink.*
Sink Elizabeth W (wid Elijah), bds 514 Broadway.
Sink Miss Florence E, bds 514 Broadway.
Sinnigen Albert, tinsmith, res 26 John.
Sinnigen Henry, bds 22 John.
Sinnigen John, laborer Penn Co, res 22 John.
Sipes Abner, wagonmkr Chauvey Bros, bds 130 Clinton.
Siple John, laborer, bds 46 E Columbia.

Sircle Emanuel J, fireman, res Fairfield ave s of organ factory.
Sites David, wheel inspector American Wheel Co, res 17 Miner.
Sites Edward F, Dentist, 86 Calhoun, res 206 W Wayne. (*See right top lines.*)
Sites Emory A, res 670 Broadway.
Sites George W, action maker Ft Wayne Organ Co, res 229 Indiana ave.
Sites Henry C, Dentist, 82 Calhoun, res 15 W Lewis.
Sites John, laborer, res 670 Broadway.
Sithens Stevens G K, millwright, res 120 W Superior.
Siver Emett L, physician, 5 Schmitz blk, res 150 Clinton.
Sivits Alaska A, laborer, bds Racine Hotel.
Skatulla Charles patternmaker Bass Foundry and Machine Works, res w s Hanna 5 s of Pontiac.
Skeer Adolphus G, painter, res 60 W 5th.
Skelley Philip S, constable, res 11 McClellan.
Skelton Benjamin W, cracker mnfr, 209 Calhoun, res 126 W Jefferson.
Skelton Edward, laborer B W Skelton, bds 126 W Jefferson.
Skelton Wanda E, bookkeeper B W Skelton, bds 126 W Jefferson.
Skelton Wm W, clerk B W Skelton, bds 126 W Jefferson.
Skinner Benjamin C, engineer, res 367 Hanna.
Slager Henry L, clerk Carnahan & Co, rms 183 Calhoun.
Slagle Arthur M, laborer Penn Co, bds e s Metz 1 n of Wabash R R.
Slagle Cecil B, draughtsman Fort Wayne Electric Co, bds 232 W Jefferson.
Slagle Estella (wid John H), res 232 W Jefferson.
Slagle James, laborer, res 67 Baker.
Slagle Levi H, engineer, res 22 Fisher.
Slagle Louisa (wid John), res 104 Butler.
Slagle Nora E, bds 142 Fairfield ave.
Slagle Wm S, engineer, res 64 Charles.
Slater Edward, laborer Penn Co, bds 184 Francis.
Slater George A, machinist Penn Co, res 184 Francis.
Slater John, blacksmith Penn Co, res 196 Fairfield ave.
Slater Joseph, blacksmith, res 19 Bass.
Slater Monroe I, wood turner J Klett & Son, res 24 Barthold.
Slater Sarah T (wid Isaac A), bds 24 Barthold.
Slater Wm M, letter carrier, bds 175 Fairfield ave.
Slattery Marmaduke M, electrician, res 302 W Washington.
Slattery Michael, watchman, res 65 Melita.
Slaudraff Theodore, expressman, bds 181 Taylor.
Slaughteroff Peter, res 273 W Main.

Slinker Betsey, domestic 271 W Wayne.
Sloat Henry, bds 232 E Jefferson.
Sloat H, laborer Penn Co, res 82 Montgomery.
Sloat Rolandus S, harnessmaker, 360½ Calhoun, res same.
Slocum Samuel, electrician Ft Wayne Electric Co, res 73 Brackenridge.
Small, *see also Schmoll.*
Small John E, works J O Keller, res 69 Archer ave.
Smaltz, *see also Schmalz.*
Smaltz Francis M, grocer, 307 W Main, res 353 same.
Smaltz John, clk F M Smaltz, bds 353 W Main.
Smart Carlos M, printer The Press, bds 35 E Wayne.
Smead Albert, truckman, res 439 E Washington.
Smead Miss Fannie, bds 44 Webster.
Smead Frank K, mngr Union Pacific Tea and Coffee Store, res 44 Webster.
Smead John, laborer, res 252 E Wayne.
Smead John H, laborer res 43 W Superior.
Smenner Catherine (wid Henry), res rear 122 Madison.
Smenner Charles H, carpenter Ft Wayne Iron Works, res 117 Madison.
Smenner Edmund, foreman Pearse & Loag, res 227 Barr.
Smenner Frederick D, brewer, bds rear 122 Madison.
Smenner Phœbe, bds 117 Madison.
Smenner Maggie (wid George), janitor 94 Calhoun, res 224 Lafayette.
Smenner Theodore, carpenter, res 92 Montgomery.
Smethers John H, machine hand American Wheel Co, res 183 Lafayette.
Smick Manford M, coal, 80 E Columbia, res 88 W Main.
Smick Solomon S, res 526 E Wayne.
Smick Wm P, clerk, res 44 Pontiac.
Smidt John F, carpenter, res s e cor Diamond and Euclid.
Smith, *see also Schmidt and Schmit.*
Smith Mrs Abbie, bds n s Spring 1 w of Franklin ave.
Smith Alice, domestic Windsor Hotel.
Smith Amelia A, market stall 60, res s s Illinois road 3 from Court House.
Smith Andrew, machinist Wabash R R, bds 100 Butler.
Smith Anna A, dressmaker Mrs G J Stier, bds 236 E Lewis.
Smith Anna M, milliner A Mergentheim, bds 115 Gay.
Smith Arthur E, bookkeeper E C Smith, bds 11 Monroe.
Smith Ashland F, brakeman, bds 163 Wells.
Smith Ashley J, machinist Indiana Machine Works, bds 163 Wells.
Smith Benjamin D, student, bds 126 N Cass.

Election Slips. Headquarters for PERFECT SLIPS
at JOHN F. EBY & CO.'S, DETROIT.

490   R. L. POLK & CO.'S

Smith Calvin L, clerk Penn Co, res s w cor Washington and Barr.

Smith Miss Carrie A, bds 38 Douglas ave.

Smith Caspar A, engineer, res 100 Butler.

Smith Catherine (wid Charles), bds 88 W Washington.

Smith Mrs Celia, res 2 Madison.

Smith Charles, painter Charles Rivers & Son, bds 64 E Berry.

Smith Charles, stone mason, res 132 Chicago.

Smith Charles A, clerk Ft Wayne Electric Co, res 40 Hendricks.

Smith Charles P, student, bds s w cor Washington and Barr.

Smith Christian D, finisher American Wheel Co, res 113 Boone.

Smith Clarence E, teacher, rms 27 Pritchard.

Smith Clarence G, mngr Business Guide Co, and bookkeeper Fort Wayne Newspaper Union, res 344 W Washington.

Smith Cora A, bds James L Smith.

Smith Cornelius S, physician, 38 Douglas ave, res same.

Smith C Percy, student S B Brown, bds 166 Barr.

Smith Mrs C L, supt Fort Wayne City Hospital.

Smith Daniel E, miller, res 122 Fairfield ave.

Smith Edward, porter Rich's Hotel, bds same.

Smith Edward C, carriage trimmer, 16 Lafayette, res 11 Monroe.

Smith Egan H, taxidermist, 21 Calhoun, rms same.

Smith Elisha J, farmer, res 92 W Superior.

Smith Emma J, bds s w cor Washington and Barr.

Smith Esther (wid Samuel), res 53 W Lewis.

Smith Eugene B, foreman printer Fort Wayne Newspaper Union, res 38 McClellan.

Smith Eugenie, bds 38 McClellan.

Smith Ewald, wood turner Fort Wayne Organ Co, bds 50 Home ave.

Smith Ezra D, driver Fort Wayne Street Railroad Co, res 225 Lafayette.

Smith Fernando, laborer Penn Co, res 154 Broadway.

Smith Frank C, fireman, res 46 Elm.

Smith Frank M, laborer A Hattersley & Sons, res 12 Madison.

Smith Franklin H, laborer, bds 57 Hoffman.

Smith Fred M (F M Smith & Co), bds 50 W Superior.

Smith Frederick S, machinist Fort Wayne Electric Co, res w s Hanna 9 s of Pontiac.

Smith F M & Co (Fred M Smith), Hardware, 22 Calhoun.

Smith George, fireman, res 45 Hurd.

Smith George B, molder Bass Foundry and Machine Works, bds 343 E Lewis.

Smith George B, laborer, res 6 St Mary's ave.
Smith George E, stone mason, res 16 Gay.
Smith George G, well driver, bds 91 Franklin ave.
Smith George H, cigarmaker Christian Wenninghoff, res 63 Madison.
Smith George M, blacksmith Fleming Mnfg Co, res 85 Barthold.
Smith George W, carpenter, res 21 W Williams.
Smith George W, coil winder Fort Wayne Electric Co, res 13 Wall.
Smith George W, asst engineer City Water Works, res 39 Brackenridge.
Smith Harry A, bds 11 Monroe.
Smith Henry, clerk Penn Co, res 186 W De Wald.
Smith Henry, engineer, res 106 W De Wald.
Smith Henry, laborer Fred Eckart, res 43 Elm.
Smith Henry, machine hand Fort Wayne Organ Co, bds 19 Walnut.
Smith Henry C, laborer Fort Wayne Electric Co, res 10 Pritchard.
Smith Henry I, lawyer, 18 Schmitz block, res 342 Broadway.
Smith Henry J, clerk D N Foster Furniture Co, res 301 W Jefferson.
Smith Henry W, clerk, bds 106 W De Wald.
Smith Hiram, plasterer, res e s Calhoun 2 n of Cour.
Smith Homer T, tel operator, res 67 W Main.
Smith Ida M (wid George W), hair goods, 170 Calhoun, res 24 E Washington.
Smith Isaac, bds 388 E Wayne.
Smith Isaac M, car builder Penn Co, res cor Lumbard and McDonald.
Smith Jacob, laborer, res 87 Home ave.
Smith Mrs James, res 114 W Berry.
Smith James (col'd), barber Jerome Peters, rms cor Columbia and Barr.
Smith James, carpenter, res 16 Winch.
Smith James (col'd), cook Rich's Hotel, res 227 W Washington.
Smith James, foreman American Wheel Co, res 236 E Lewis.
Smith James, laborer A McKernan, bds Wm A Smith.
Smith James A, salesman Singer Mnfg Co, bds 196 Barr.
Smith James L, carpenter, res e s Lumbard 1 n of Wabash R R.
Smith James M, sawyer J C Peters, res 95 Franklin ave.
Smith James S, plumber Robert Ogden, bds 104 Barr.
Smith John, laborer, res 55 Wabash ave.
Smith John, molder Bass Foundry and Machine Works, res 343 E Lewis.

Smith John, porter Rich's Hotel.
Smith John C, laborer Wabash R R, bds 116 Butler.
Smith John E, driver J C Peters, bds 2 De Groff.
Smith John J, molder Bass Foundry and Machine Works, bds 16 Gay.
Smith John W, laborer, bds 119 Fairfield ave.
Smith John W, laborer The Herman Berghoff Brewing Co, res 1 Dwenger ave.
Smith Joseph, laborer, res 163 Wells.
Smith Joseph C, clerk, bds 9 N Cass.
Smith Joseph D, laborer, res 120 W 3d.
Smith J Sion, asst supt, res 96 Butler.
Smith Kate (wid Charles), bds 88 W Washington.
Smith Kelley, laborer, res 87 Pritchard.
Smith Lewis, lab Penn Co, res 53 Walton ave.
Smith Lizzie, seamstress D S Redelsheimer & Co, bds 115 Gay.
Smith Louis, porter Rich's Hotel.
Smith Miss Lucy C, bds 37 Douglas ave.
Smith Manning, bookkeeper, res 353 E Wayne.
Smith Margaret (wid Caleb), res 233 John.
Smith Margaret S (wid J McNutt), res 37 Douglas ave.
Smith Mary, bds 16 Winch.
Smith Mary, bds 63 Madison.
Smith Miss Mary, bds 236 E Lewis.
Smith Mary, domestic Richard Smith.
Smith Miss Mary J, tchr Miner School, bds 38 McClellan.
Smith Millard F, cigarmkr Schele Bros, bds 225 Calhoun.
Smith Minerva (wid Elliott), bds 87 Wilt.
Smith Murray U, bds 37 Douglas ave.
Smith Nathaniel, musician, res 19 Lafayette.
Smith Odis, painter City Carriage Works, bds 63 Columbia.
Smith Payton, laborer H W Bond, res 97 Riverside ave.
Smith Philip B, mach Bass Foundry and Machine Works, res 14 Wall.
Smith Reader P, lumber, bds 37 Douglas ave.
Smith Reuben H, baggageman, res 59 E 3d.
Smith Richard, laborer, res e s Piqua ave 4 n of Rudisill ave.
Smith Richard C, clerk Windsor Hotel.
Smith Roy R, clerk Fort Wayne Electric Co, bds 21 W Williams.
Smith Rufus H D, hostler Fort Wayne Transfer and Baggage Line, res 41 Monroe.
Smith Samuel, stone mason, bds 16 Winch.
Smith Samuel jr, laborer, bds 16 Winch.
Smith Sarah A, laundress, rms 191 Calhoun.
Smith Sylvester, canvasser, rms rear 262 Calhoun.

Smith Susan E (wid Anthony), bds 211 St Mary's ave.

Smith Thomas B, machinist American Wheel Company, bds 236 E Lewis.

Smith Thomas C, painter Penn Co, res 154 Montgomery.

Smith Vernon, carpenter, bds 29 Buchanan.

Smith Walter C, conductor, res 9 N Cass.

Smith Willard D, truckman, bds 41 Monroe.

Smith Wm, laborer J C Peters, res 2 DeGroff.

Smith Wm, farmer, res 27 Oliver.

Smith Wm, laborer, bds 14 Force.

Smith Wm, laborer, bds 50 Smith.

Smith Wm A, foreman A McKernan, res w s Burd ave 1 n of Wabash R R.

Smith Wm B, bookkeeper Bass Foundry and Machine Works, res cor Calhoun and Grace.

Smith Wm C, plumber A Hattersley & Sons, bds 25 Charles.

Smith Wm E, canvasser Indiana Installment Co, bds 32 Brackenridge.

Smith Wm H, coil winder Fort Wayne Electric Co, res 35 Hood.

Smith Wm L, trav agent American Wheel Co, res 79 Brackenridge.

Smith Wm M, mngr Hunter Mnfg Co, bds 10 W Superior.

Smithers John, lab Olds' Wagon Works, res 183 Lafayette.

Smitley Homer B, carp, res w s Piqua ave 1 s of Marchell.

Smitley Charles, brakeman, res 367 Lafayette.

Smock, see also Schmuck.

Smock Frank L (G E Bursley & Co), res 171 Clinton.

Smoscie Charles, laborer M Orr, bds 112 Mechanic.

Smyser Daniel F, clerk S Bash & Co, bds 253 W Berry.

Smyser Frank D, res 253 W Berry.

Smyser Miss Mary, tchr Jefferson School, bds 253 W Berry.

Smyser Mary A (wid Jacob), bds 253 W Berry.

Smyser Peter D (S Bash & Co), res 246 W Berry.

Smyth Robert W, electrician Fort Wayne Electric Co, bds 50 W Washington.

Snider, see also Schneider and Snyder.

Snider Alberta, milliner A C Keel, bds n s Propect ave 5 e of Spy Run ave.

Snider Allen B, dentist A J Rauch, res n s Prospect ave 5 e of Spy Run ave.

Snider George, carpenter, bds 57 Barr.

Snider Jeremiah, brakeman, bds 12 St Mary's ave.

Snider Kate, domestic Hamilton homestead.

Snider Lois M (wid Evan), res n s Prospect ave 5 e of Spy Run ave.

Snider Oscar, rimmer, res 203 Lafayette.

Snider Rufus M, clerk F H Treep, bds 342 Broadway.

Snively Miss Carrie A, teacher Washington School, bds 36 Butler.

Snively Catherine (wid Henry), res 36 Butler.

Snook Thomas, carpenter, bds 110 W Main.

Snowberger Clyde, painter J Snowberger, bds 372 E Washington.

Snowberger John, painter, 372 E Washington, res same.

Snowberger Laura E, bds 372 E Washington.

Snowberger Mrs Mary, res 216 Lafayette.

Snyder, see also Schneider and Snider.

Snyder Augustus G, machinist Fort Wayne Electric Co, res 107 Wilt.

Snyder Boyd W, clerk Bass Foundry and Machine Works, res 138 Franeis.

Snyder Carrie, domestic 336 W Washington.

Snyder Charles A, laborer, bds 320 Calhoun.

Snyder Charles W, wheelmaker American Wheel Co, bds 213 E Wayne.

Snyder Clarence , bds 205 E Washington.

Snyder Edward P, laborer Olds' Wagon Works, bds 137 Holman.

Snyder Eli, carpenter, res 204 High.

Snyder Emma, bds 204 Hanna.

Snyder Harriet (wid Wm), res 205 E Washington.

Snyder Henry, fireman, res 143 Griffith.

Snyder Henry J, clk Frederick Weidel, res 323 W Jefferson.

Snyder Herman, laborer, bds 34 Chicago.

Snyder Isaac L, conductor Penn Co, res 46 Butler.

Snyder James A, baker Markey & Mungovan, bds 312 S Harrison.

Snyder Jennie, operator S M Foster, bds 205 E Washington.

Snyder John, laborerer A Hattersley & Sons, bds 31 Wilt.

Snyder John, laborer, res 66 Oliver.

Snyder John, nurse Fort Wayne City Hospital.

Snyder John H, teamster, res 23 Hoffman.

Snyder John R, hub selector Winch & Son, res e s Lumbard n of Piqua rd.

Snyder John T, laborer Penn Co, res 320 Calhoun.

Snyder Joseph, clerk S E Hayden, bds 204 Hanna.

Snyder Joseph A, carpenter, bds 36 Oak.

Snyder Mary (wid Henry), bds 99 W Superior.

Snyder Mary, bds 66 Oliver.

Snyder Mary A, seamstress E C Smith, bds 31 Wagner.

Snyder Maud, operator S M Foster, bds 205 E Washington.

Builders' Hardware, PFEIFFER & SCHLATTER, 38 and 40 EAST COLUMBIA ST.

FORT WAYNE DIRECTORY. 495

Snyder Minnie, seamstress E C Smith, bds 31 Wagner.
Snyder Sadie J, bds 23 Hoffman.
Snyder Samuel, bds 104 Barr.
Snyder Simon, res 145 Pfeiffer ave.
Snyder Wm C W, wheelmaker American Wheel Co, res 213
    E Wayne.
Snyder Wm F, carpenter, bds 23 Hoffman.
Soest Christian, laborer Penn Co, res 87 Madison.
Soest Henry W (Soest, Nickey & Co), rms 493 Calhoun.
Soest, Nickey & Co (Henry W Soest, Alfred J
    Nickey), Druggists, 360 Calhoun.
Soliday Bros (Solomon D and George W), second-hand store,
    71 E Main.
Soliday George W (Soliday Bros), res 432 E Wayne.
Soliday John A, letter carrier, res 98 N Harrison.
Soliday Solomon D (Soliday Bros), res 29 Elizabeth.
Somers, *see also Sommers and Summers.*
Somers Charles M, driver Wm E Meiner, bds 30 E Columbia.
Somers Emma (wid Calvin), res 30 E Columbia.
Somers Lydia, bds 77 Holman.
Somers Minnie, works Troy Steam Laundry, bds 22 Harrison.
Somers Wm M, fireman, res 325 W Jefferson.
Somiski Frank, laborer, bds e s Franklin ave 2 n of Lake.
Somiski Maria (wid Charles), res e s Franklin ave 2 n of Lake.
Sommer Carl, photographer, 30 Calhoun, res 41 Putnam.
Sommer Josephine L C, photographer, bds 41 Putnam.
Sommers, *see also Somers and Summers.*
Sommers Henry, machinist Penn Co, res 55 W Jefferson.
Sommers Henry G, drugs, 35 Calhoun, res 22 E Washington.
Sommers John F, conductor, res 196 Broadway.
Sommers Peter J, conductor, res 418 S Clinton.
Sonazin, *see Sarrazin.*
Sonnenberg Frederick, laborer Bass Foundry and Machine
    Works, res 136 Force.
Sonnenburg August, bds 45 Smith.
Sonnenburg Daniel, coremkr Bass Foundry and Machine
    Works, res 45 Smith.
Sontag Louis, tailor F Hardung, bds 185 Calhoun.
Sordelet Charles P, clerk Pfeiffer & Schlatter, bds 19 E
    Washington.
Sordelet Eliza, bds 16 Clay.
Sordelet Emil L, lab American Wheel Co, bds 57 Charles.
Sordelet Frank L, clk L Wolf & Co, res 212 E Jefferson.
Sordelet Pauline (wid Louis), res 57 Charles.
Sorg Barbara M, waitress J A Sorg, bds 61 E Main.
Sorg Eva (wid Joseph), res 61 E Main.

Sorg John, laborer, res 2 Glasgow ave.
Sorg John P, laborer Louis Diether & Bro, res 68 Maumee rd.
Sorg Joseph A, restaurant, 61 E Main, res same.
Sorg Mary B, presser, bds 68 Maumee rd.
Sosenheimer Charles J, City Treasurer, City Hall, res 49 Charles.
Sosenheimer John, res 52 Charles.
Sosenheimer Mary (wid Benjamin), bds 33 St Martin.
Souder Daniel W, res e s Spy Run ave 5 n of Wagner.
Souers Philip, hostler Hoffman Bros, res 213 W Superior.
Sourbrine Amos J, brakeman Nickel Plate, bds 20 Huron.
South Wayne Brick Co, Henrietta Thompson, Byron S Thompson and Chester Scotton Proprs, w s Thompson ave n of Wabash R R.
South Wayne Greenhouse, B L Auger Propr, cor Creighton ave and Webster.
Southern James, engineer, res 278 Webster.
Sovin Emanuel, carpenter, res 20 W 4th.
Spain John, laborer American Wheel Works, res 155 Hayden.
Spalding Christian, laborer, bds 100 Montgomery.
Spalding Thomas R, cigarmkr F J Gruber, res 256 E Wayne
Spalding Willard W, dairy w s Calhoun s of city limits, res same.
Spangler Amanda E, bds 26 Harrison.
Spangler Daniel D, cooper, res e s Spy Run ave opp Randolph.
Spangler George W, farmer, res 270 Hoagland ave.
Spangler John, bds 8 W Wayne.
Spanla Louis, lab Indiana Machine Works, bds 101 Wells.
Spanla Louis jr, laborer, bds 101 Wells.
Spanley Martin, market stall 16, res s s Taylor w of city limits.
Spear John, fruit stand, bds 51 E Main.
Spearing Henry, engineer, res 8 Locust.
Speath Louis, ticket receiver Penn Co, bds Diamond Hotel.
Speckman Charles, driver Michael Baltes, res 3 N Harrison.
Speckman Lizzie, domestic 309 W Washington.
Speece Samuel P, fireman, bds 11 Butler.
Speidel Anthony, armature winder Fort Wayne Electric Co, bds 272 E Jefferson.
Speidel Frank, molder Bass Foundry and Machine Works, res 272 E Jefferson.
Speidel Herman, helper Penn Co, res 272 E Jefferson.
Spekert Caspar, mach hand Louis Rastetter, res 11 Caroline.
Spencer Calvin W, meat market, 13 Highland, res 15 same.
Spencer Cyrus, marshal, res 21 Huestis ave.
Spencer Cyrus M, laborer, bds 21 Huestis ave.

Spencer David J, cigars, 39 Calhoun, bds Aldine Hotel.

Spencer Ellen J, clerk Root & Co, bds 216 W Wayne.

Spencer Frederick I, cigarmaker Schele Bros, bds 88 Montgomery.

Spencer George E, compositor Fort Wayne Gazette, bds 58 E Wayne.

Spencer George W, train dispatcher Nickel Plate, res 90 E Berry.

Spencer Martin V B, lawyer, 33 Calhoun, res 216 W Wayne.

Spencer Samuel W, driver, bds 21 Huestis ave.

Spereisen Crescentia, domestic 261 W Berry.

Spereisen Jacob A, blksmith, 165 Fairfield ave, res 56 Taylor.

Spice Elmer W, bookkpr Robert Spice, rms 74 W Main.

Spice Kate, bds 21 Pine.

Spice Robert, Dealer in Pumps and Windmills, Lightning Rods, also Water Works and General Plumbing and Natural Gas Fitting, 48 W Main and 11 Pearl, res 171 Jackson. Tel 261. (*See left top lines.*)

Spiegel August F, clerk, bds 36 Nirdlinger ave.

Spiegel August F jr, clerk Ernest Spiegel, bds 36 Nirdlinger.

Spiegel Bernard, boilermkr Wabash R R, res 233 W DeWald.

Spiegel Carl B, clk Meyer Bros & Co, res 13 Jones.

Spiegel Ernest, stopmaker Ft Wayne Organ Co, bds 233 W DeWald.

Spiegel Mrs F C, milliner, 106 Broadway, res same.

Spiegel George, clerk, bds 233 W DeWald.

Spiegel Gottfried E, Grocer, 183 Broadway, res 36 Nirdlinger ave.

Spiegel Gustave, boots and shoes, 132 Broadway, res 15 Jones.

Spiegel Minnie, milliner, bds 36 Nirdlinger ave.

Spiegel Wm A, tuner Ft Wayne Organ Co, res 315 W Jefferson.

Spielmann Lizzie, bds 206 Madison.

Spielmann Mary (wid Peter), res 206 Madison.

Spielmann Victor, bds 206 Madison.

Spillnar Charles, engineer, res 261 Hanna.

Spindler August, machine hand Horton Mnfg Co, res 104 Mechanic.

Spindler Augusta, domestic 496 Harrison.

Spindler Jacob, laborer, res 176 E Jefferson.

Spitz Michael, market stall 37, res s s Leo road e of city limits.

Spollitz Frederick, laborer Wm Miller, res 236 Gay.

Sponhauer Edward, carpenter, bds 57 Barr.

Sponhauer Weidler S (Mossman, Yarnelle & Co), res 43 Union.

Sprague Miss Aurelia, dressmaker, 39 Wilt, res same.

John Pressler, Hot Air and Hot Water Furnaces.
Columbia, Barr and Dock Streets.

498   R. L. POLK & CO.'S

Sprandel Wm F, clerk Aveline House, res 55 E Wayne.
Sprandel Wm F jr, porter Aveline House, bds 55 E Main.
Springer Lavinia (wid Jacob), res 103 Mechanic.
Springer Monroe, engineer Ranke & Yergens, res 46 Wall.
Springman Charles, sawyer American Wheel Co, res 21 Charles.
Sprinkle Edward E, wagonmaker, bds 63 W Main.
Sprinkle John, barber, bds 63 W Main.
Sprinkle Milton O, car builder Penn Co, res 415 Lafayette.
Sproat Alexander, salesman, res 135 Broadway.
Sproat Clarence E, laborer Penn Co, bds 135 Broadway.
Sproat Edward, driver, bds 135 Broadway.
Sproat Miss Lizzie, bds 135 Broadway.
Spuhler Mary, domestic 220 W Jefferson.
Spurgeon Henry D, stone mason, res 129 Wells.
Spurrier Dennis D, tinsmith, res 141 Force.
Squire Grant, helper Ft Wayne Iron Works.
Squires Frank, clerk Rich's Hotel.
Stace Alfred W, grocer, 253 E Lewis, res same.
Stack Michael J, flagman Penn Co, res 293 W Main.
Stack Patrick, bds 18 McClellan.
Stackhouse John W, fireman Nickel Plate, res 24 Boone.
Stadtler Christian P, res 73 W 4th.
Stafford Martin, engineer, res 273 E Lewis.
Stager Emma, works Model Steam Laundry, bds 71 W 3d.
Stagle Wm S, engineer, res 64 Charles.
Stahl Charles C, carpenter, bds 29 E DeWald.
Stahl Christian, laborer Penn Co, res 49 St Martin.
Stahl Christian F jr, machinist Penn Co, bds 442 Lafayette.
Stahl Harvey A, carpenter, bds 29 E DeWald.
Stahl J Henry, carpenter, bds 29 E DeWald.
Stahl Mary, seamstress, bds 49 St Martin.
Stahl Metter, laborer, bds 50 Smith.
Stahl Reuben, contractor, res 29 E DeWald.
Stahl Sarah J (wid John), teacher Bloomingdale School, res 59 Brackenridge.
Stahl Wm, painter Olds' Wagon Works, bds 49 Francis.
Stahl Wm G, letter carrier, res 440 Lafayette.
Stahlhut Charles, clerk F P Mensch, bds 145 Ewing.
Stahlhut Frederick, policeman, res 145 Ewing.
Stahlhut Frederick jr, teamster, bds 145 Ewing.
Stahlhut John, driver Engine Co No 2, rms Engine Hous No 2.
Stahlhut Lizzie, bds 145 Ewing.
Stahlhut Wm, teamster, res 82 Maumee road.
Stahn George, draughtsman Penn Co, bds 85 Monroe.

Stahn & Heinrich, Dealers in BOOKS and FINE STATIONERY, Blank Books, Etc. 116 Calhoun Street.

FORT WAYNE DIRECTORY. 499

Stahn Oswald (Stahn & Heinrich), res 151 Montgomery.

Stahn' & Heinrich (Oswald Stahn, Louis Heinrich), Books and Stationery, 116 Calhoun. (*See right top lines.*)

Stakemyer Jacob, carpenter, bds 22 W Main.

Staley Edward, foreman Ryan Bros, bds 84 Fairfield ave.

Staley John, conductor, res 172 W Superior.

Staley Lizzie, domestic 44 S Wayne ave.

Stalf Leonard, res 122 Clay.

Stalf Louis, carpenter, bds 183 Calhoun.

Standard Medical and Surgical Institute, J W Younge, A M, M D, Pres, W J Carter, A M, M D, General Mngr, 210 Calhoun. (*See adv, p 4.*)

Standard Hall, 40 W Berry.

Standard Oil Co, John Gilbert mngr, cor Columbia City rd and Nickel Plate R R.

Staneky Mary (wid John), res 17 Brandriff.

Staneky Millard, miller, bds 17 Brandriff.

Stanford Caroline, bds 244 Erie.

Stanford Jeremiah M, laborer Penn Co, res 244 Erie.

Stanford John, bottle washer, bds 244 Erie.

Stanford Lewis, laborer, bds 244 Erie.

Stanger, *see also Stenger.*

Stanger Alexander, laborer, bds 599 Lafayette.

Stanger Charles W, painter Olds' Wagon Works, bds 599 Lafayette.

Stanger Eliza, domestic 599 Lafayette.

Stanger George, molder, bds 599 Lafayette.

Stanger Henry, laborer, res 599 Lafayette.

Stanger Kate, domestic 599 Lafayette.

Stanley Agnes, dressmaker, bds 45 Miner.

Stanley Chauncey, carriagemaker, res 45 Miner.

Stanley Miss Emma, teacher Bloomingdale School, bds 45 Miner.

Stanley Joseph, molder, bds 1 Lumbard.

Stanley Marian, bds 45 Miner.

Stanton Clark, special pension examiner, bds 113 W Wayne.

Stanton Eliza A (wid Charles F), res 382 Lafayette.

Stanton John W, machine hand, bds 382 Lafayette.

Stanton Luella, clerk, bds 382 Lafayette.

Stanton Wm O, wks Winch & Son, res 382 Lafayette.

Stantz Charles, butcher Fred Eckart, bds M L Stantz.

Stantz Martin L, boarding house, cor Clinton and Superior.

Stapleford Charles E, laborer Nickel Plate, res s s Baker ave 1 mile from city limits.

Stapleford Francis A, tinsmith Penn Co, bds 248 Calhoun.

Stapleford Henry T, trav agt, res 226 W Creighton ave.
Stapleford Lucien P (Stapleford & Co), res 152 E Wayne.
Stapleford Thomas A, tinner, bds 248 Calhoun.
Stapleford & Co (Lucien P Stapleford), livery and coal, 1 Lafayette.
Stapleton Charles, teamster, res 217 Broadway.
Stapleton John, laborer, res 240 Erie.
Stapleton Robert, teamster, bds 240 Erie.
Star Iron Tower Co, J H Bass pres, H G Olds vice-pres, R T McDonald sec, P A Randall treas, mnfrs of towers for electric lighting and publrs American Electrical Directory, cor Plum and Nickel Plate R R.
Starbuck Lincoln A, switchman, bds 251 Calhoun.
Stark Christian, carpenter Penn Co, res 14 West.
Stark Erasmus, porter A C Trentman, res 23 Nirdlinger ave.
Stark Frank J, bartender Ulrich Stotz, bds 10 Force.
Stark John, bds 10 Force.
Stark Martin, laborer Penn Co, res 10 Force.
Stark Miss Tena, teacher, bds 177 Calhoun.
Starkel Frank H, clerk L S & M S Ry, res 155 Wells.
Starkey Frederick, blacksmith Penn Co, res 6 Orchard.
Starkey Frederick W, helper Penn Co, bds 6 Orchard.
Starkey Mrs Hannah A (wid Orlando L), res 102 E Main.
Starkey Mary, seamstress D S Redelsheimer & Co, bds 6 Orchard.
Staub Alexander H (Staub Bros), res 31 Lincoln ave.
Staub Bros (Alexander H and George W), tinners, 18 W Columbia.
Staub George W (Staub Bros), res 130 W Main.
Staudacher George, res 43 Wilt.
Stauffer Ellis, butcher Leikauf Bros, bds 101 Glasgow ave.
Stauffer Emil, tailor Gottlieb Stauffer, bds 182 Calhoun.
Stauffer Gottlieb, merchant tailor, 182 Calhoun, res same.
Stauffer Henry H, butcher, res rear 537 E Wayne.
Staus Conrad, packer F Eckart, bds 43 Elm.
Stauter John L, res 141 E Berry.
Stayner Bernard L, clk Dozois, Beadell & Co, bds 96 E Wayne.
Steadley Charles, bds 115 (old No) Gay.
Steadley James, huckster, res 115 (old No) Gay.
Steadley Wm P, helper Bass Foundry and Machine Works, bds 115 (old No) Gay.
Stecher Charles J, engineer, res 54 Buchanan.
Stecher Frederick C, helper Olds' Wagon Works, bds 54 Buchanan.
Steel Martin, laborer, res 286 E Jefferson.
Steel Martin, laborer, res s w cor Lillie and Maumee road.

Steele Johnson W, driver, res 276 E Washington.
Steele Retta, domestic 99 Grant ave.
Steen, *see also Stein.*
Steen Elizabeth (wid Joseph), res 84 Fairfield ave.
Steer, *see Stier.*
Steffey Alexander, foreman S Bash & Co, res 82 Hoagland ave.
Stege August, laborer Penn Co, res 7 Summit.
Steger Albert, bookkeeper R Steger & Co, res Dawson.
Steger Gustav C E, clk R Steger & Co, bds 150 Montgomery.
Steger Rudolph (R Steger & Co), res 150 Montgomery.
Steger R & Co (Rudolph Steger), Hardware, Rasps, Mill Picks and Stonecutters' Tools, 126 Calhoun.
Stegner Charles A, clerk Root & Co, res 350 E Washington.
Steib Jacob, molder Kerr-Murray Mnfg Co, bds 334 Lafayette.
Steib Joseph, lab Kerr-Murray Mnfg Co, bds 334 Lafayette.
Steib Philip, cupola tender Kerr-Murray Mnfg Co, res 334 Lafayette.
Steichler Frederick, laborer, res 441 Hanna.
Steichler Jacob, laborer, res n s High 2 w of St Mary's ave.
Steichler Joseph, machine hand American Wheel Co, bds 441 Hanna.
Steigerwald John, turner American Wheel Co, res w s Walton ave 4 s of Pontiac.
Steigerwald John A, turner American Wheel Co, res 63 Madison.
Stein, *see also Steen.*
Stein Anthony, machine hand American Wheel Co, bds 44 Butler.
Stein Arthur C, laborer B L Auger, bds 57 Winter.
Stein Charles F A, lab Horton Mnfg Co, res 300 E Wayne.
Stein Charles F A jr, machinist Bass Foundry and Machine Works, res 57 Winter.
Stein Daniel L, car builder Penn Co, res 318 Harrison.
Stein Freda, milliner W Malloy, bds 25 Boone.
Stein Henry W, lab Bass Foundry and Machine Works, res 8 Hough.
Stein Joseph N, car builder Penn Co, res 333½ Hanna.
Stein Mary, operator S M Foster, bds 333½ Hanna.
Stein Peter, laborer, res 122 Maumee road.
Stein Peter, molder Bass Foundry and Machine Works, res 157 Hanna.
Stein Robert J, car builder Penn Co, res s s Howell bet Runnion and Rumsey aves.
Stein Sophie, clerk H H Barcus, bds same.
Stein Wilhelmina (wid Jacob), res 44 Butler.
Steinacker Benjamin T, laborer, bds 112 Fairfield ave.

Steinacker Mrs Frances, res 112 Fairfield ave.
Steinacker Frank, Meat Market, 134 Fairfield ave, bds 112 same.
Steinacker Henry, lab American Wheel Co, bds 112 Fairfield.
Steinau Charles B, shoemkr C Schiefer & Son, res 71 Wells.
Steinau Edward, clk Renner, Cratsley & Co, bds 71 Wells.
Steinbach John W, clk Dozois, Beadell & Co, res 57 Pixley & Long bldg.
Steinbach Michael, mason, bds 29 E Main.
Steinborn John, brickmaker, res 223 Walton ave.
Steinborn Theodore, lab Bass Foundry and Machine Works, bds 6 Edgerton.
Steinbrenner, *see also Stoneburner.*
Steinbrenner Frederick J, stock cutter Fort Wayne Organ Co, res 105 Fairfield ave.
Steinbrunner Anna M, clk Daniel Klotz, bds 24 W Williams.
Steinbrunner Kate, bookkeeper Zoeller & Merz, bds 24 W. Williams.
Steinbrunner Robert, foreman Penn Co, res 24 W Williams.
Steinbrunner Rosa, dressmaker, bds 24 W Williams.
Steiner Joseph C, barber John Munich, bds 41 Locust.
Steinhauser John, helper Penn Co, res cor E Lewis and Ohio.
Steinhauser Mary (wid Henry), res 31 Taylor.
Steinhauser May, operator S M Foster, bds 31 Taylor.
Steinhauser Nicholas, sawyer Louis Rastetter, res 21 Bell av.
Steinhauser Tillie, works Troy Steam Laundry, bds 31 Taylor.
Steinhauser Wm J, blacksmith Olds' Wagon Works, bds 31 Taylor.
Steinkaemper Anthony, carpenter, res 19 Rockhill.
Steinke August R, machine hand Fort Wayne Organ Co, bds 61 Oakley.
Steinke Edward J, wiper Penn Co, res 61 Oakley.
Steinmann Abraham J, car bldr Penn Co, res 346 Broadway.
Steinwalt John, laborer Joseph Fremion, res Walton ave.
Steiss Charles, barber, bds 45 Pfeiffer ave.
Steiss John, cooper, res 45 Pfeiffer ave.
Steiss John G jr, barber, 41 W Main, bds 45 Pfeiffer ave.
Stellhorn Charles, Mnfr and Dealer in Boots and Shoes; also Books and Stationery, 146 Calhoun, res 133 W Superior.
Stellhorn Charles, gardener Montgomery Hamilton, bds 213 Madison.
Stellhorn Frederick, bds 133 W Superior.
Stellhorn Henry J, laborer Penn Co, res 22 Madison.
Stellhorn Sophia (wid Henry), res s s New Haven road 1 w of toll gate.

Stellhorn Wm, carpenter, bds 133 W Superior.

Stellhorn Wm L, clerk Peter Morganthaler, bds 22 Madison.

Stemen Christian, brakeman, res 65 Boone.

Stemen Christian B (Stemen & Stemen), Pres Taylor University of Fort Wayne, and Dean Fort Wayne College of Medicine, res 25 Broadway.

Stemen Elizabeth, bds 25 Broadway.

Stemen George B, physician, 311 W Main, res 292 same.

Stemen George C (Stemen & Stemen), res 493 Calhoun.

Stemen Harriet, bds 25 Broadway.

Stemen Lawrence W, canvasser Indiana Installment Co, bds Windsor Hotel.

Stemen Wm E, clerk, bds 25 Broadway.

Stemen & Stemen (Christian B and George C), physicians, 74 Calhoun.

Stemmler Henry, cigarmaker F J Gruber, bds 115 Gay.

Stempel Guido H, local editor Fort Wayne Gazette, bds 21 W Jefferson.

Stenger, *see also Stanger.*

Stenger Frank, blacksmith, res 111 Force.

Stenner Bernard, plumber H J Ash.

Stenz, *see also Stantz.*

Stenz Henry, cigarmaker, bds 132 Lafayette.

Stephan, *see also Stevens.*

Stephan Anthony F, foreman Louis Diether & Bro, res 99 St Mary's ave.

Stephan Augusta, clerk Alexander Goodman, bds 32 Wall.

Stephan Edward, clerk, bds 32 Wall.

Stephan Emily, seamstress, bds Wm Stephan.

Stephan George P, carpenter, res 26 Union.

Stephan Julius C, checker, res 32 Wall.

Stephan Wm, chief draughtsman Penn Co, res n e cor Winter and Pontiac.

Stephan Wm, mach Penn Co, bds cor Winter and Pontiac.

Stephens Emma A, seamstress, bds 304 E Creighton ave.

Stephens James, laborer, bds Jacob Sanger.

Stephens Philip, res 26 Union.

Stephenson, *see also Stevenson.*

Stephenson Taylor, pipeman Salimonie Mining and Gas Co, bds 22 E Columbia.

Steps Walter (col'd), waiter Hotel Randall.

Stern Raph S (Sam, Pete and Max), res Cleveland, Ohio.

Sternberger Martin, laborer Fort Wayne Steam Stone Works, res 32 W 5th.

Stetter Frederick J, stopmaker Fort Wayne Organ Co, bds 42 Nirdlinger ave.

Stetter John P, lab American Wheel Co, res 42 Nirdlinger av.
Stetter Louis J, carpenter Penn Co, res 46 Nirdlinger ave.
Stetter Mary (wid Louis), bds 42 Nirdlinger ave.
Stetzer Caroline S, bds 352 E Washington.
Stetzer Emma, bds 352 E Washington.
Stetzer Helen, clerk, bds 352 E Washington.
Stetzer Katie, dressmkr L A Worch, bds 352 E Washington.
Stetzer Maggie, dressmaker, bds 352 E Washington.
Stetzer Peter, laborer Penn Co, res 352 E Washington.
Steup H C Gottlieb, clerk F Hardung, res 106 W Jefferson.
Steup Louis, driver Chemical Engine Co, rms Engine house
    No 1.
Stevens, see also Stephan.
Stevens Arbor C, brakeman, res 92 Oliver.
Stevens Edwin F, bds 92 Oliver.
Stevens George H, engineer, res 106 Jackson.
Stevens James, bartender Belger & Lennon, bds 70 Dawson.
Stevens James D, clerk, bds 125 Fairfield ave.
Stevens John K, molder Bass Foundry and Machine Works,
    res 60 Hugh.
Stevens Lizzie (wid Wm), res 52 Hamilton.
Stevens Nelson, blacksmith H A Rose, bds 36 Oak.
Stevens Rufus L, upholsterer Penn Co, res 129 Holman.
Stevens Thomas, res 173 W Wayne.
Stevens Wm L, laborer B W Skelton, bds 248 Calhoun.
Stevenson, see also Stephenson.
Stevenson Wm L (Mommer & Stevenson), bds 60 E Colum-
    bia.
Stewart Annie (wid Charles J), res 37 E De Wald.
Stewart Annie (wid James), res 205 E Washington.
Stewart Calvin M, carpenter Louis Diether & Bro, res n s
    High s of city limits.
Stewart Charles, car builder Penn Co, res 301 Calhoun.
Stewart Charles, blacksmith Penn Co, res 149 Holman.
Stewart Charles A, molder, bds 149 Holman.
Stewart Frank, clerk Root & Co, bds 432 E Wayne.
Stewart Rev John P, res 292 E Lewis.
Stewart Joseph H, fireman, bds 149 Holman.
Stewart Joseph H (col'd), laborer Bass Foundry and Machine
    Works, res 61 Garden.
Stewart Miss Lockey, bds 292 E Lewis.
Stewart Mattie (wid Samuel C), res 40 Bass.
Stewart Mattie A (wid Robert M), bds 62 Wilt.
Stewart Miss Octavia, stenographer Ft Wayne Electric Co,
    bds 228 W Jefferson.
Stewart Theresa (wid Wm D), res 228 W Jefferson.

Stewart Thomas (Stewart & Hahn), res 136 E Berry.
Stewart Wm D, trav agent McDonald, Watt & Wilt, res 58 Nelson.
Stewart Wm F, machine hand American Wheel Co, bds 149 Holman.
Stewart Wm H, awningmaker, res 432 E Wayne.
Stewart & Hahn (Thomas Stewart, Wm Hahn), dry goods, 28 Calhoun.
Sthair Archie S, blacksmith Theodore Tuttle, res 42 W Main.
Sthair Frank, hostler, bds 309 W Washington.
Sthair Frank W, blacksmith, bds 26 Harrison.
Sthair George A, saloon, 108 Broadway, res same.
Sthair John H, driver Coverdale & Archer, bds 26 Harrison.
Sthair Mary A (wid Henry), res 26 Harrison.
Sthair Wm, apprentice, bds 26 Harrison.
Stieb Philip, res 334 Lafayette.
Stiegerwald Adam, res 63 Madison.
Stier Bros (George A and John A), barbers, 324 Lafayette.
Stier Charles J, clerk James Madden, bds 32 Clinton.
Stier Christina, dressmaker, bds 94 Buchanan.
Stier Clara, bds 32 Clinton.
Stier Frank G, molder Bass Foundry and Machine Works, res 508 E Lewis.
Stier George A (Stier Bros), res 324 Lafayette.
Stier George J, clerk Dozois, Beadell & Co, res 32 Clinton.
Stier Mrs George J, milliner, 32 Clinton, res same.
Stier Henry, foreman, res 106 Lafayette.
Stier Henry A, bartender, res 94 Buchanan.
Stier Henry J jr, clerk Dozois, Beadell & Co, bds 106 Lafayette.
Stier Jacob J, foreman Bass Foundry and Machine Works, res 337 E Lewis.
Stier John, res 188 E Washington.
Stier John A (Stier Bros), res 180 Hanna.
Stier Julius A, laborer, bds 94 Buchanan.
Stier Kate, bds 188 E Washington.
Stier Louisa, bds 188 E Washington.
Stier Rosa, bds 188 E Washington.
Stier Sophia, bds 106 Lafayette.
Stier Wm A, barber Stier Bros, bds 94 Buchanan.
Stierheim Miss Stella, bds 50 Harrison.
Stierheim Valeria (wid Jacob), res 50 Harrison.
Sties Edward J, carpenter, res 52 Walnut.
Stiles Frank M, carpenter J A Crow & Co, bds 54 Hamilton.
Still Smith, machinist, res 135 Madison.
Stillgus James D (col'd), cook, res 68 Murray.

Stillhorn, *see Stellhorn.*

Stilson Ivy, domestic 111 Force.

Stimmel Charles, boilermaker Kerr-Murray Mnfg Co, res s w cor Eliza and Chute.

Stimmel Mark G, Agent Adams Express Co, res 27 Broadway.

Stine, *see Steen and Stein.*

Stiner Bernard, plumber H J Ash, bds Fox's Restaurant.

Stinson Morris A, brakeman, res 67 Boone.

Stirk Harry W, bookkeeper Coombs & Co, bds 16 Hoffman.

Stirk Marion A, clerk, bds 18 Hoffman.

Stirk Samuel W, collector Nickel Plate, res 16 Hoffman.

Stirling John, feed stable, 29 N Clinton.

Stoach Wm, laborer, res 507 E Lewis.

Stock George A, laborer Hoffman Bros, res 206 High.

Stockbridge Charles A, books, 15 E Columbia, res 225 W Wayne.

Stockbridge Miss Mary P, bds 45 Shawnee ave.

Stockbridge Nathaniel P, newsdealer, 15 E Columbia, res 45 Shawnee ave, S Wayne.

Stockbridge Nathaniel P jr, clerk M Clark & Co, bds 45 Shawnee ave, S Wayne.

Stocking Miss Alice M, bkkpr S M Foster, bds 126 Ewing.

Stocking Henry K, engineer, res 126 Ewing.

Stocking John W, engineer, bds 126 Ewing.

Stockmann Charles H, cooper, 101 N Harrison, res 44 E 4th.

Stockmann Charles P F, clk Fleming Mnfg Co, bds 44 E 4th.

Stocks John, machinist, bds 318 S Broadway.

Stockwell James S, engineer, res 184 Montgomery.

Stoehr Frederick, carpenter, res 502 Hanna.

Stoehr John, Saloon and Boarding House, 199 Broadway, res same.

Stokes Edward M, engineer, res 44 McClellan.

Stoll Anthony, carpenter Frederick Kraft, res 74 Nelson.

Stoll Carrie G, dressmaker, bds 29 Wefel.

Stoll Conrad, res 29 Wefel.

Stoll Emil, cabinetmkr Ft Wayne Organ Co, bds 24 Murray.

Stoll Frederick, clerk, bds 46 Walnut.

Stoll Frederick, coppersmith Wabash R R, res 46 Walnut.

Stoll George J, mach Wabash R R, bds 46 Walnut.

Stoll Henry, res 25 E 2d.

Stoll Henry, policeman, res 11 Ohio.

Stoll Jacob, bartender Aldine Hotel, bds 25 E 2d.

Stoll Otto H, helper Bass Foundry and Machine Works, bds 40 Allen.

Stoll Wm H, helper Penn Co, bds 371 W Main.

Stahn & Heinrich, Leading Dealers in ARTISTS' MATE-
RIALS AND DRAUGHTING INSTRU-
MENTS. 116 Calhoun Street.

FORT WAYNE DIRECTORY. 507

Stolte Charles, coachman, 122 W Wayne.

Stone Lester E, painter, res s s New Haven road 1 e of toll gate.

Stonebrook Thomas G, painter Penn Co, bds 233 Lafayette.

Stoneburner, *see also Steinbrenner.*

Stoneburner Elias, painter, res 137 Walton ave.

Stoneburner Frank, harnessmaker A L Johns & Co, bds 137 Walton ave.

Stonecifer Benjamin F, conductor, res 43 E DeWald.

Stonemiller G, laborer Penn Co, res 68 Walton ave.

Stoner Archibald, brakeman, rms 376 W Main.

Stoner Harry, brakeman, rms 376 W Main.

Stookey Oliver, packer Fort Wayne Electric Co, res 14 E Columbia.

Stoppenhagen Charles, car builder Penn Co, res 33 Hugh.

Stoppenhagen Emily, domestic 335 Harrison.

Storch Wm, baker, res 507 E Lewis.

Stork Owen C, baker J H Schwieters, bds 41 E Columbia.

Storm Joseph A M, General Hardware, Mechanics' Tools and Farm Implements, 7 E Columbia, res 302 W Washington.

Story Harriet (wid James), res 16 W Superior.

Stotz Ulrich, saloon, 21 E Main, res 23 same.

Stouder, *see also Studer.*

Stouder Frank E, business manager Masonic Temple, bds 30 E Wayne.

Stouder Harvey F, bds S Current.

Stouder Henry G, fireman, res 21 Pritchard.

Stouder Jacob H, flagman Nickel Plate, res 30 E Wayne.

Stouder Jacob M, salesman Pfeiffer & Schlatter, res s w cor Runnion ave and Howell.

Stouder Leon, assistant ticket agent, bds 30 E Wayne.

Stouder Wallace W, foreman Olds' Wagon Works, res 30 W Williams.

Stouder Wm, brickmaker A McKernan, bds Wm A Smith.

Stouder Wm W, laborer, res 21 Buchanan.

Stough George A, foreman John Pressler, bds 99 E Jefferson.

Stout Charles A, carriage painter M L Albrecht, res 105 W Williams.

Stout Frederick P, insurance agent, bds 126 Harrison.

Stover George, foreman, res 335 W Main.

Stow Eliakim, bds 119 E Main.

Strack Charles H, machine hand American Wheel Co, res 36 Buchanan.

Strack Miss Desdemona, bds 237 W Berry.

Strack Edward W (Strack & Angell), res 237 W Berry.

Strack Emma, dressmaker Mary Strack, bds 131 Broadway.

Strack Miss Mary, dressmaker, 131 Broadway, res same.

Strack & Angell (Edward W Strack, Byron D Angell), lumber, 52 Calhoun.

Strader Isaac, driver Ryan Bros, res 191 Lafayette.

Strain Charles S, clerk J O Keller, bds 154 E Berry.

Strangmann Conrad, carpenter, bds 123 Madison.

Strangmann Herman, porter Gross & Pellens, bds 123 Madison.

Strangmann Louisa, bds 123 Monroe.

Strangmann Wilhelmina (wid Conrad), res 123 Madison.

Strasburg Augusta (wid Frederick W), res 74 Wilt.

Strasburg Christopher (C Strasburg & Sons), res 119 Wilt.

Strasburg Christopher jr (C Strasburg & Sons), bds 119 Wilt.

Strasburg C & Sons (Christopher, Wm and Christian), rags, etc, 106 E Columbia.

Strasburg Ferdinand W, clerk Root & Co, bds 74 Wilt.

Strasburg Frederica, clerk, bds 74 Wilt.

Strasburg Maria, clerk, bds 74 Wilt.

Strasburg Wilhelmina, bds 74 Wilt.

Strasburg Wm (C Strasburg & Sons), bds 119 Wilt.

Strasburg Wm, machine hand Louis Diether & Bro, res 74 Wilt.

Strass Carrie, clerk L Wolf & Co, bds 50 Douglas ave.

Strass Emanuel, trav agt J Nathan & Co, res 106 Webster.

Strass Emma, cashier Frank & Co, bds 106 Webster.

Strass Isaac, mngr D S Redelsheimer & Co, bds 50 Douglas.

Strass Julia, bds 50 Douglas ave.

Strass Kate, bds 50 Douglas ave.

Strass Minnie, clerk Alexander Goodman, bds 106 Webster.

Strass Rev Samuel, res 50 Douglas ave.

Strasser Felix, laborer Penn Co, bds 131 Taber.

Strasser George J, machinist Fort Wayne Electric Co, bds 95 Buchanan.

Strasser Henry, fireman, res 17 Colerick.

Strasser Rupert, res e s Winter 1 s of Pontiac.

Stratton George M, painter L O Hull, res Columbia House.

Straub Anton, candymaker Louis Fox & Bro, bds 60 E Williams.

Straughan Jesse R, civil engineer, res 87 E Berry.

Strauss Mrs Ella, clerk A Mergentheim, res 120 N Harrison.

Strawbridge Charles T, stenographer Bass Foundry and Machine Works, res 355 E Wayne.

Strawn Byron A, photographer, 2 E Columbia, res 150 Broadway.

Strebe Christian, machine hand Horton Mnfg Co, bds 375 W Main.

E. F. Sites, 🦷 Dentist, 86 Calhoun St., Four Doors North of Wayne.

FORT WAYNE DIRECTORY. 509

Strebe Frank E, saloon, 375 W Main, res same.
Strebe George A, boilermaker Ft W, C & L R R, res 419 W Main.
Strebig Charles V, engineer, res 446 E Washington.
Strebig Isaac, finisher Winch & Son, bds 465 E Washington.
Strebig Wm, cooper, res 101 Hayden.
Street Commissioner's Office, D O'Brien commissioner, office 68 Barr.
Streetmeyer Caroline (wid Mathias), res 30 Laselle.
Streicher Anna (wid Andrew), res 35 Wefel.
Streicher George, barber S G Hubbard, bds 35 Wefel.
Streicher John, bartender P Certia, res 131 Wells.
Streicher Wm J, bartender C W Kline, res 13 Chestnut.
Streng Edward H, packer Olds' Wagon Wks, bds 17 Baker.
Strengtman Dickinson, teamster, bds 140 E Washington.
Streubel August, wagonmkr Fleming Mnfg Co, res 61 W 5th.
Stribley Lillian, domestic 9 Chestnut.
Stribley Nancy (wid Murray), res 16 Union.
Strickland Wm H, clerk L O Hull, res 148 W Jefferson.
Strieder Christopher J, teacher St Paul's German Lutheran School, res 166 Barr.
Strieder Gottlieb, clerk Gross & Pellens, bds 166 Barr.
Striker Christian, cabinetmaker Fort Wayne Organ Co, res 120 W Creighton ave.
Striker Tunis V, regulator Fort Wayne Organ Co, res 49 Shawnee ave.
Stringer Elza T, merchant, res 76 W DeWald.
Stringer Miss Estella C, bds 76 W DeWald.
Stringer Miss Helen F, bds 76 W DeWald.
Stritmatter Angust, laborer, bds 531 E Wayne.
Stritmatter Henry, laborer, bds 118 Maumee rd.
Stritmatter John, laborer, bds n w cor Coombs and Cochran.
Strobel Wm, clerk Custer House.
Strodel Albert, cigar maker, bds 40 W 4th.
Strodel Annie B (wid Mathias), res 40 W 4th.
Strodel Catherine (wid August), saloon, s s Bluffton rd 2 w of St Mary's river, res same.
Strodel Christian G, washer L Brames & Co, bds 40 W 4th.
Strodel John G, saloon, 54 E Main, res 111 W 3d.
Strodel J George, harness maker, bds 40 W 4th.
Strohm Christina, domestic 133 Barr.
Strohm Jacob, baggageman Wabash R R depot, bds 15 Poplar.
Strohm John, car builder, res 15 Poplar.
Strohm Mary (wid George), res 15 Poplar.
Strong Harriet E (wid Melzar), res 258 W Wayne.

Strong Henry, confectioner, 73 Webster, res same.
Strong Jared C, res 128 E Main.
Strong Josephine, bds 128 E Main.
Strong Miss Lourie E, teacher Clay School, bds 128 E Main.
Strong Thomas M, laborer W W Spalding, bds same.
Strouse Matilda (wid David), res 20 Francis.
Strube Adolph, patternmaker, res 28 Scott ave.
Strubey G Charles, music teacher, 83 E Jefferson, res same.
Strucken Edward, laborer American Wheel Company, res 383 Lafayette.
Struckmann Charles, lab American Wheel Co, res 229 John.
Struger Frank, tool dresser Penn Co, bds 111 Force.
Strunk Amidore M, flagman Penn Co, rms Monroe House.
Strunz Christian, grocer, 72 Barr, res 99 E Berry.
Struver Louisa, bds 66 E Main.
Struver Wm, grocer, 66 E Main, res same.
Struver Wm F, clk Wm Struver, bds 66 E Main.
Stuart, *see Stewart.*
Stubnatzy Bettie (wid Ernest), bds 222 E Washington.
Stuck Jay, driver, bds 234 Indiana ave.
Stuck Levi A, notions, 67½ McCulloch, bds 67 same.
Stuck Martin, carpenter, bds 239 Madison.
Stuck Solomon K, teamster, res 234 Indiana ave.
Stuckey Walter S, student Stemen & Stemen, bds Taylor University.
Studer, *see also Stouder*
Studer Block, 228 W Main.
Studer H Leopold, saloon, 232 W Main, res same.
Studer Jerome J, clk L Wolf & Co, res 15 E Washington.
Studer Joseph, engineer, res 84 W 3d.
Studer Mary A (wid Bernard), bds 189 E Wayne.
Stuermer Adelina, dressmaker, bds 108 Maumee road.
Stuermer Julius, clerk Klinkenberg & Detzer, bds 108 Maumee road.
Stuermer Matilda, bds 108 Maumee road.
Stuermer Wm, boilermaker, res 108 Maumee road.
Stuhlmueller George, laborer Penn Co, res 68 Walton ave.
Stull Martin, laborer J A Koehler, res 56 Smith.
Stults Charles E, physician, 81 Wells, res same.
Stults Ernest, teacher, rms 27 Pritchard.
Stump Louis, car repairer Penn Co, res 33 Wall.
Stumpf Miss Martha, teacher Holton Avenue School, bds 389 Calhoun.
Sturgis Louis T, physician, 275 Hanna, res 132 Wallace.
Sturgis Mary (wid Wm E), bds w s Spy Run ave 1 n of Elizabeth.

Sturgis Miss Sadie L, teacher Hanna School, bds 275 Hanna.
Sturm Commodore P, soap presser Summit City Soap Works, res e s Glasgow ave bet E Washington and Maumee rd.
Sturmar Wm F, machinist Bass Foundry and Machine Wks, res 108 Maumee road.
Stuter Ferdinand, laborer, res 69 Home ave.
Stuter Frederick, truckman Wabash R R, bds 215 W Main.
Stutz John A, Physician, 50 W Washington, res same.
Stutzenberger Josephine (wid Frank), res 383 E Washington.
Stutzenberger Lena, labeler Summit City Soap Works, bds 383 E Washington.
Subkowski Henry, laborer, res 30 Smith.
Such Charles, Saloon, Billiard and Pool Room; Best Brands of Wines, Liquors and Cigars, 303 Lafayette and 358 Calhoun, bds 24 Leith.
Such Emil, bartender Charles Such, res 24 Leith.
Sudbrink Wm H, car builder Penn Co, res 445 Hanna.
Suedhoff Ernest H, clerk Frank & Co, res 210 W Jefferson.
Suell Irvin, cook, rms 65 Baker.
Suelzer John, carpenter, res 418 Hanna.
Suelzer John W, meat markets, 281 Hanna and 422 Lafayette, res 287 Hanna.
Suelzer Wm, clerk John Suelzer, bds 287 Hanna.
Suetterlin Reinhard, blacksmith Bass Foundry and Machine Works, res 35 Maumee road.
Sukup Andrew, res 27 Laselle.
Sukup Joseph A, molder Kerr-Murray Mnfg Co, bds 27 Laselle
Sukup Mary, operator Hoosier Mnfg Co, bds 27 Laselle.
Sukup Peter, molder Bass Foundry and Machine Works, bds 27 Laselle.
Suleg John, vegetables, market stall 2, res s s Maysville rd. e of city limits.
Sulfer Charles O, brakeman, res 59 W Superior.
Sullivan Andrew, res n e cor Grant and Oliver.
Sullivan Cornelius, watchman, res 23 Taylor.
Sullivan Hannah, dressmkr, bds 50 Melita.
Sullivan Henry J C, musician, bds 347 Hanna.
Sullivan House, Warren Rogers propr, 2 Thomas.
Sullivan James J, flue cleaner Penn Co, bds 23 Taylor.
Sullivan John, laborer J A Koehler, bds same.
Sullivan John, brakeman Penn Co, res 76 Chicago.
Sullivan Mrs Kittie, res 92 Calhoun.
Sullivan Maggie, housekeeper McKinnie House.
Sullivan Mary (wid Patrick), res 50 Melita.
Sullivan Mrs Mary, res 174 E Berry.
Sullivan Mary A, dressmaker, bds 23 Taylor.

Sullivan Michael, engineer, res 401 Hanna.
Sullivan Michael, truck rivetter Penn Co, res 118 E Creighton.
Sullivan Nathaniel, pedler, res 10 Hensch.
Sullivan Nellie M, converter worker Fort Wayne Electric Co, bds 50 Melita.
Sullivan Nonie, bds 401 Hanna.
Sullivan Nora, laundress McKinnie House.
Sullivan Patrick J, brakeman Penn Co, bds 50 Melita.
Sullivan Patrick S, helper Wabash R R, res 23 Taylor.
Sullivan Thomas, brakeman Penn Co, res 69 Grand.
Sullivan Timothy, laborer, bds 91 E Washington.
Sullivan Timothy J, flagman Penn Co, bds 50 Melita.
Sult George, laborer Fort Wayne Gas Light Co, res w s Spy Run ave 2 n of St Mary's bridge.
Sulzer, *see Suelzer.*
Summers Anna (wid John), res 331 Lafayette.
Summers Bridget, bds 49 Grand.
Summers George T, bds 17 Burgess.
Summers James, saloon, 262 Calhoun, res 47 Douglas ave.
Summers Mary (wid John), res 49 Grand.
Summit City Galvanized Iron Works, John Pressler Propr; also Plumbing, Gas and Steam Fitting, Columbia, Barr and Dock Streets. Telephone 249. (*See left top lines.*)
Summit City Green House, B L Auger propr, n e cor Creighton ave and Webster.
Summit City Soap Works (P A Randall, A L Griebel, B S O'Connor, H C Graffe), C P Coy mngr, 12 Glasgow ave.
Summit City Steel Works, John Rupp Propr, n end of Barr.
Summit City Woolen Mills, French & Jefferds proprs, 96 E Superior.
Sunday, *see Sontag.*
Sunderland Charles S, machinist Fort Wayne Iron Works, res 27 W 4th.
Sunderland John W, flagman Penn Co, res 7 Duryea.
Sunderland Joseph E jr, clk Wabash R R, res 175 W DeWald.
Sunderland Joseph R, baggageman Wabash R R depot, res 177 W DeWald.
Sunderland Mary A, clk T J Fleming, bds 177 W DeWald.
Sundermann John, res 197 Lafayette.
Sunley George T, bds 17 Burgess.
Sunley Mrs Margaret, boarding house, 17 Burgess.
Superior Court of Allen Co, Court House.
Supple Mary, seamstress, bds 74 Montgomery.
Suter Albert S, carpenter, bds 509 Broadway.

Suter Edward, carpenter, cor Ferguson ave and Broadway, res 509 Broadway.

Suter Wm E, carpenter Edward Suter, bds 509 Broadway.

Sutermier Carl F, boilermkr Wabash R R, bds 47 W Lewis.

Sutley Harry, res 22 Fairfield ave.

Sutorius Gottlieb, washer L Brames & Co, bds 176 Oakland.

Sutorius Jacob, laborer Fort Wayne Steam Stone Works, res 176 Oakland.

Suttenfield A Moore, teamster, res 102 Fairfield ave.

Suttenfield Bird, teamster, bds 102 Fairfield ave.

Suttenfield Laura, dressmkr L E Burnett, bds 102 Fairfield av.

Suttenfield Wm, driver, res 183 W Jefferson.

Sutter Daniel, laborer, bds 24 E Williams.

Sutton Rev Benjamin A, pastor First United Brethren Church, res 54 Division.

Sutton David C, machine hand, res 212 W Creighton ave.

Sutton Harry E, machine hand Fort Wayne Furniture Co, res 210 W Creighton ave.

Sutton John, machinist, bds 13 N Calhoun.

Sutton Joseph S, brakeman, bds 104 St Mary's ave.

Swager August, laborer A McKernan, bds Wm A Smith.

Swager John, carpenter, res n s Cochran 2 e of Coombs.

Swaidner Jacob W, propr Hedekin House, 25 Barr.

Swaidner John L, telegraph operator, bds Hedekin House.

Swain, see also Swayne.

Swain Benjamin F, laborer Penn Co, res 57 Grand.

Swain Carl P, res 53 Walter.

Swain Charles, teamster, bds 118 W Creighton ave.

Swain Charlotte (wid Jackson), bds 73 W De Wald.

Swain Elizabeth (wid Caleb), res 53 Walter.

Swain George W, driver patrol wagon, res 134 E Main.

Swain George W, plasterer, res 118 W Creighton ave.

Swain John D, plasterer, res 191 Jackson.

Swander James, laborer, res 240 Erie.

Swank Alonzo D, coil winder Ft Wayne Electric Co, res 21 Lincoln ave.

Swank Jennie, bds 168 E Jefferson.

Swank Jesse, wagonmkr Olds' Wagon Works, bds 3 Dawson.

Swann Clarence S, clerk postoffice, bds 19 W De Wald.

Swann Emmet, res 178 E Washington.

Swann J W Scott, trav agent Olds' Wagon Works, res 19 W De Wald.

Swart Meinhard F C, laborer, bds 91 W Williams.

Swart Wm, engineer Penn Co, res 91 W Williams.

Swartz, see Schwartz, Schwarz and Schwarze.

Swartzel Oliver J, helper, bds 109 John.

Swartzel Wm J, wheel molder Bass Foundry and Machine Works, res 109 John.

Swayne, *see also Swain.*

Swayne Miss Margaret J, teacher and stenographer McDermut & Whiteleather, bds 278 W Berry.

Swayne Rhoda A (wid Samuel F), bds 278 W Berry.

Swayne Samuel F (Swayne & Doughman), res 278 W Berry.

Swayne & Co (Samuel F Swayne, Newton D Doughman), insurance, real estate and loan agents, 16 W Main.

Swayne & Doughman (Samuel F Swayne, Newton D Doughman), Attorneys-at-Law, 16 W Main.

Sweedler John, laborer, bds Washington House.

Sweeney Abraham, carpenter, res 45 Harrison.

Sweeney Alexander, machine hand American Wheel Co, res 77 Laselle.

Sweeney Cornelius, watchman, res 19 Brandriff.

Sweeney Julia, bds 19 Brandriff.

Sweeney Maggie, bds 19 Brandriff.

Sweeney Philip, laborer Penn Co, bds 19 Brandriff.

Sweeney Wm J, hostler Ft Wayne Street Railroad Co, bds 290 Calhoun.

Sweer John H, tinsmith Penn Co, res 259 Calhoun.

Sweer Philip, laborer, bds 408 W Main.

Sweet Edward R, res 183 Jackson.

Sweet Frank E, clerk L S & M S Ry, bds 25 Brackenridge.

Sweet Miss Jessie M, bds 25 Brackenridge.

Sweet Samuel B, asst genl frt agt, res 25 Brackenridge.

Sweetser Miss Fannie, bds 115 W Main.

Swenson Robert, painter L O Hull, res 58 Smith.

Sweny Charles F, engineer, res s e cor Lafayette and DeWald.

Sweny Louis D, engineer, res 481 Lafayette.

Sweringen Frank H, car builder Penn Co, res 197 W Wayne.

Sweringen George, laborer Penn Co, bds 197 W Wayne.

Sweringen Lucinda (wid George W), res 197 W Wayne.

Sweringen Hiram V, physician, 197 Wayne, res same.

Swick Minnie, domestic 235 W Main.

Swick Peter D, Merchant Tailor, 50 Harrison, res cor Lafayette and Madison.

Swift Bayless, rms 105 E Washington.

Swift Frank, hostler Jenson & Sargent, bds Racine Hotel.

Swift Frank M, laborer, bds Isabella Dodge.

Swinehart Isaac J, barber Edward Schele, res 255 E Lewis.

Swinehart Sherman, truckman L S & M S Ry, res 129 W 3d.

Swinney Block, 11, 13 and 15 E Main.

Swinney Miss Carrie, bds Miss Theresa Swinney.

Swinney Miss Frances, bds Miss Theresa Swinney.
Swinney's Park, *see Allen County Fair Grounds.*
Swinney Miss Theresa, res W Jefferson and County Fair Gds.
Szink, *see also Sink.*
Szink George A, blacksmith Penn Co, res 471 Harrison.

T

Tag Catherine (wid Christian), res 99 E Washington.
Tagtmeyer, *see also Tegtmeyer.*
Tagtmeyer Amelia, bds 274 W Washington.
Tagtmeyer Conrad H, foreman David Tagtmeyer, res 42 Breck.
Tagtmeyer David, Lumber Mnfr, n w cor Webster and N Y, C & St L R R, res 77 W Superior.
Tagtmeyer Henry W, carpenter, bds 42 Breck.
Tagtmeyer Lena C, dressmaker, bds 42 Breck.
Tagtmeyer Wm, engineer H Volland & Sons, res 47 Wells.
Tagtmeyer Wm, machinist Indiana Machine Works, res 274 W Washington.
Tagtmeyer Wm C, clk G H Kuntz, bds 77 W Superior.
Tait, *see also Tate.*
Tait Frank (Frank Tait & Sister), res 26 E Wayne.
Tait Frank & Sister (Frank Tait, Mrs Florence Reynolds), millinery, 26 E Wayne.
Talbot Burt B, brakeman Nickel Plate, res 324 W Main.
Talbot John E, electrical engineer Fort Wayne Electric Co, res 237 W Wayne.
Talbot Samuel L, tuner Fort Wayne Organ Co, res 108 E Berry.
Talmage Charles H, store keeper Indiana School for Feeble-Minded Youth.
Tancey Hugh, plumber James Madden, bds 138 Fulton.
Tancey Michael, Justice and Real Estate, 1 Bank Block, res 138 Fulton.
Tanner Edward E, brakeman, res 36 Hamilton.
Tanner James, stone cutter Wm & J J Geake, bds 312 W Main.
Tanner John, stone cutter Wm & J J Geake, bds 312 W Main.
Tape Wm, sawyer, res rear 33 Elm.
Tapp Almina, bds 13 Ohio.
Tapp Ferdinand, bridge builder, res 13 Ohio.
Tapp Herman W, bridge contractor, 227 E Lewis, res same.
Tapp Robert W, bridge builder, res 146 Maumee road.
Tarbaugh Oliver C, machine hand American Wheel Co, bds 77 Huestis ave.

Tarmon Harry, machinist Fort Wayne Music Co, bds Henry A Tarmon.

Tarmon Henry A, carpenter, res e s Spy Run ave 4 n of Riverside ave.

Tassler August, carpenter Penn Co, res 19 Wall.

Tassler Frederick, laborer Penn Co, res 365 Lafayette.

Tate, *see also Tait.*

Tate Ellen, domestic Rich's Hotel.

Tate Frank A, well digger Frederick Weidel, res 348 Broadway.

Tate Lizzie, domestic Rich's Hotel.

Tate Wm J, blacksmith helper Penn Co, bds 299 Harrison.

Taylor Alonzo R (col'd), restaurant, 62 E Columbia, res same.

Taylor Andrew, brass molder, Wabash ave, res 84 S Wayne.

Taylor Beal F, carpenter Nickel Plate, res n s Howell 2 w of Rumsey ave.

Taylor Bristol W, machinist, res 413 Calhoun.

Taylor Bros Piano Co, Samuel R Taylor pres, Isaac N Taylor sec, 138 Calhoun.

Taylor Charles E, machinist Bass Foundry and Machine Works, res 50 Summit.

Taylor Charles N, conductor, res 90 Wells.

Taylor Edward E, bookkeeper, bds 407 Fairfield ave.

Taylor Frank B, student, bds 391 Fairfield ave.

Taylor Frank P, laborer, res 312 Lafayette.

Taylor Hayes E, clerk Union Pacific Tea and Coffee Store, res 132 W 3d.

Taylor Henry C, res 131 Lafayette.

Taylor Henry J, bookkeeper Hamilton National Bank, bds 131 Lafayette.

Taylor Hubert G, conductor, res 40 E 2d.

Taylor Isaac N, sec Taylor Bros Piano Co, res 407 Fairfield.

Taylor James M, insurance, 20 Schmitz blk, bds 101 Calhoun.

Taylor Jesse M, teamster, res 11 Hoffman.

Taylor John, res e s Hanover bet E Washington and E Wayne.

Taylor John M, laborer Hoffman Bros, res s s Howell near Rumsey ave.

Taylor John W (col'd), barber J H Roberts, res 203 Calhoun.

Taylor Joseph, painter, bds 55 Barr.

Taylor Joseph M, rivetter American Wheel Co, res 66 Oakley.

Taylor Mary (wid Philo), bds C L Hill.

Taylor Peter, kiln setter, res 525 E Lewis.

Taylor Robert S, Lawyer, 34 E Berry, res 391 Fairfield ave.

Taylor Samuel M, train despatcher Penn Co, res 79 Holman.

Taylor Samuel R, pres Taylor Bros Piano Co, res 274 Webster.

Taylor Susan, bds 525 E Lewis.

Taylor University of Fort Wayne, Successor to Fort Wayne College, C B Stemen A M, M D and L L D Pres, Charles McCulloch Treas, H C Schrader Sec, foot of Wayne.

Taylor Wm, butcher, bds 525 E Lewis.

Taylor Wm C, clerk, res s w cor Howell and Runnion ave.

Taylor Wm J, clerk, bds 131 Lafayette.

Teagarden Claude A, gasfitter H J Ash, bds 111 W Superior.

Teagarden Marion F, engineer, res 111 W Superior.

Teaman Mary (wid Andrew), bds 138 Fulton.

Tearman Thomas, car repairer Penn Co, res 73 Madison.

Teepe Wm, laborer J C Peters, res 33 Elm.

Teeters, see also Teters.

Teeters Wilson, electrician Jenney Electric Light and Power Co, res 111 Franklin.

Tefft Charles W, car builder Penn Co, res 8 Hoagland ave.

Tegeder Eliza, bds 22 W Wayne.

Tegeder Frederick, carpenter, res 68 Wall.

Tegeder Frederick, laborer American Wheel Co, res e s Lafayette 6 s of Pontiac.

Tegtmeyer, see also Tagtmeyer.

Tegtmeyer Andrew, machinist Penn Co, bds 77 Brackenridge.

Tegtmeyer Charles D, machinist, res 25 Clark.

Tegtmeyer Elizabeth K, seamstress, bds F W, Tegtmeyer.

Tegtmeyer Ernst, laborer Penn Co, res 77 Brackenridge.

Tegtmeyer Ernst jr, machinist, bds 77 Brackenridge.

Tegtmeyer Frederick, bolt cutter Penn Co, bds 12 Summit.

Tegtmeyer Frederick jr, molder, bds 12 Summit.

Tegtmeyer Frederick, machine hand Horton Mnfg Co, res 24 Wilt.

Tegtmeyer Frederick B H, flagman Penn Co, bds 70 W Williams.

Tegtmeyer Frederick H, lab Penn Co, bds F W Tegtmeyer.

Tegtmeyer Frederick W, shoes, 352½ Calhoun, res w s Calhoun junction Piqua ave.

Tegtmeyer Henry W, clerk C E Heaton, bds 12 Summit.

Tegtmeyer Louis F, cigarmaker L Dessauer & Co, bds 181 Calhoun.

Tegtmeyer Martin C, molder Bass Foundry and Machine Works, rms 181 Calhoun.

Tegtmeyer Wm, candymkr Louis Fox & Bro, bds 12 Summit.

Tegtmeyer Wm, fireman, res 3 Brandriff.

Tehart Abraham, res 43 Wall.

Tehl Eugene, helper Kerr-Murray Mnfg Co, bds 21 Force.

Teiman Henry, hostler A C Perrin, bds 217 E Washington.

Telger Henry, market stall 52, res nr County Poor House.

Telgmann John, laborer, res 120 Eliza.

Telle George, machinist Fort Wayne Electric Co, res 189 Broadway.

Telley George W, asst foreman Penn Co, res 43 W Williams.

Telley Thomas, engineer, res 13 W Williams.

Telley Thomas H jr, messenger Penn Co, bds 13 W Williams.

Tellmann John W, molder Bass Foundry and Machine Wks, bds 119 Force.

Temme Lena, bds 21 Erie.

Temme Mary (wid Bernard), res 21 Erie.

Temperance Hall, 94 Harrison.

Templar Harry, shipping clerk Fort Wayne Electric Co, res 66 Wilt.

Tenbrook George W, works Indiana School for Feeble-Minded Youth.

Tenney Edwin L, engineer, res 309 W Jefferson.

Tenney Edwin L jr, machinist Wabash R R, bds 309 W Jefferson.

Tensing Sophie (wid Wm), bds n e cor Liberty and Coombs.

Terhl John, laborer, res 77 Hayden.

Terry George H, conductor, res 92 Dawson.

Terry John F, conductor, res 59 W DeWald.

Terry Walter, brakeman, res 25 Elm.

Tesher Maggie, domestic 36 W Wayne.

Texton Hannah, works Indiana School for Feeble-Minded Youth.

Thackeray Harry, bds Clifton House.

Thailer Herman, molder Bass Foundry and Machine Works, bds 25 Force.

Thain Anna, dressmkr M C Hagan, bds 273 W Washington.

Thain Mrs Caroline, bds 26 Baker.

Thain Charles C, upholsterer P E Wolf, res 36 Boone.

Thain George, barber, 130 Calhoun, bds 273 W Washington.

Thain John, res 273 W Washington.

Thain John jr, clerk, bds 273 W Washington.

Thain Miss Kate, bds 273 W Washington.

Thain Miss Minnie, bds 273 W Washington.

Thain Wm, mach Kerr-Murray Mnfg Co, bds 262 Calhoun.

Thallen Adam, laborer Winch & Son, res 150 Wilt.

Thavenet Alexander, switchman, res 512 Harrison.

Thayer Frederick, propr Lying-in Institution and Sanitarium, 57 Walton ave, res same.

Thayer Leonard E, traveling agent Fort Wayne Organ Co, res 35 E Jefferson.

Thiebolt George W, switchman, res 100 W Superior.

Thiel Wm, wagonmkr, 146 W Main, res 336 Main.

Thiel Wm jr, clk Keller & Brown, bds 366 W Main.

Thiele Diedrich, machinist Penn Co, res 84 Wilt.

Thiele Diedrich jr, carpenter, bds 84 Wilt.

Thiele Frederick, clk Wm Meyer & Bro, bds 84 Wilt.

Thiele Henry W, clerk J Wilding & Son, bds 84 Wilt.

Thiele Louise M, dressmkr Wm Malloy, bds 84 Wilt.

Thiele Minnie, bds 84 Wilt.

Thiele Wm, clk Gottlieb Niemann, bds 84 Wilt.

Thieme Andrew, watchman, bds 169 Van Buren.

Thieme Bros (John A and J Gottlieb Jr), Merchant Tailors, 12 W Berry.

Thieme Charles F W, saloon, 17 W Main, res same.

Thieme Ella (wid George), res 36 Baker.

Thieme Ernest, helper, res n s Liberty 1 w of Coombs.

Thieme Frederica (wid Andreas), res 169 Van Buren.

Thieme Frederick, laborer J A Koehler, res 72 Gay.

Thieme Frederick J, trav salesman, bds 216 W Berry.

Thieme Gottlieb C (J G Thieme & Son), bds 53 E Wayne.

Thieme J Gottlieb jr (Thieme Bros), res 216 W Berry.

Thieme Hugo P, bds 216 W Berry.

Thieme John, machinist, res 51 Ferguson ave.

Thieme John A (Thieme Bros), res 310 W Washington.

Thieme John A, saloon, 170 Broadway, res 172 same.

Thieme John G (J G Thieme & Son), res 53 E Wayne.

Thieme J G & Son (John G and Gottlieb C), Merchant Tailors and Clothiers, 37 E Columbia.

Thieme Miss Leonie C, res 216 W Berry.

Thieme Miss Matilda, bds 216 W Berry.

Thieme Miss Paulina A, teacher Westminster Seminary, bds 216 W Berry.

Thieme Theodore F, bds 216 W Berry.

Thieme & Gross Block, s w cor Calhoun and Wayne.

Thiesen Charles M, tinner Pickard Bros, res 56 Wells.

Thiesmann Henry, vegetables, market stall No 93, res w s New Haven road 5 miles.

Thing Samuel B (S B Thing & Co), res Boston, Mass.

Thing S B & Co (S B Thing, J W Emery, W A Prior), Proprs Massachusetts Shoe Co, 36 Calhoun.

Third Presbyterian Church, n e cor Calhoun and Holman.

Tholen George H, teamster The Herman Berghoff Brewing Co, res 28 Grant ave.

Tholen John G, molder Bass Foundry and Machine Works, res 393 E Lewis.

Thomas Archer L, mach Indiana Mach Wks, res 405 W Main.

Thomas Charles D, brakeman, bds 17 Burgess.
Thomas Eugene S, cigars, 178 Calhoun, res 105 Lafayette.
Thomas Harvey, car builder Penn Co, res 300 E Creighton av.
Thomas Herman, lab American Wheel Co, bds 177 Maumee.
Thomas James R, laborer, res 533 E Wayne.
Thomas John, carpenter, res 409 W Main.
Thomas Liverton D, plasterer, bds 77 N Cass.
Thomas Louis T, machinist Indiana Machine Works, bds 110 W Wayne.
Thomas Sarah (wid Calvin), res 173 Jackson.
Thomma Jacob A, lab, res e s Franklin 1 n of Wabash R R.
Thompkins Owen, carpenter, res 348 Calhoun.
Thompson Adelbert, traveling agent A L Johns & Co, res 283 E Washington.
Thompson Anna (wid John), res 49 E Main.
Thompson Benjamin F, res 132 W DeWald.
Thompson Benjamin F jr, engineer, bds 132 W DeWald.
Thompson Byron S, traveling agent, res 474 Broadway.
Thompson Charles C, gas regulator, bds 26 Harrison.
Thompson Charles F, converter worker Fort Wayne Electric Co, bds 407 S Clinton.
Thompson Charles O, telegraph operator Nickel Plate, bds 288 W Main.
Thompson Ella, bds 49 E Main.
Thompson Frank, cigarmkr George Reiter, res 311 S Harrison.
Thompson Frank M, confectioner, 205 Lafayette, bds 290 E Lewis.
Thompson Frank S, laborer Penn Co, res 225 Calhoun.
Thompson George W, wheel molder Bass Foundry and Machine Works, res 246 E Lewis.
Thompson Henrietta, res 474 Broadway.
Thompson John, bds 329 E Wayne.
Thompson John R, foreman American Wheel Co, res 17 Grant ave.
Thompson Joseph, laborer American Wheel Co, bds 204 Lafayette.
Thompson J Harry, lineman N Y, C & St L R R, rms 20 W Superior.
Thompson Milton M, County Recorder, Office Court House, res 241 W Washington.
Thompson Miss Minnie E, bds 474 S Broadway.
Thompson Nelson, foreman Coombs & Co, res 329 E Wayne.
Thompson Nelson W, carpenter, res 111 Gay.
Thompson Oliver, laborer Penn Co, res 16 Holman.
Thompson Owen, carpenter Ft W, C & L R R, res 348 S Calhoun.

Thompson Peter A, clerk Jenney Electric Light and Power Co, bds 329 E Wayne.

Thompson Peter W, cement, bds Frederick Zimmendorf.

Thompson Richard, ticket agt Wabash R R, bds 9 E Wayne.

Thompson Miss Susan L, music teacher, 474 Broadway.

Thompson Thomas, laborer American Wheel Co, res 59 Gay.

Thompson Thomas D, molder, res 290 E Lewis.

Thompson Wm, driver Ryan Bros, res n s Chestnut bet Wabash R R and New Haven road.

Thompson Wm E, finisher, bds 17 Grant ave.

Thompson Wm L, watchman Penn Co, bds 132 W DeWald.

Thompson Wm W, porter G E Bursley & Co, res 204 Lafayette.

Thompson & Scotton (Henrietta and Byron Thompson, Chester Scotton), proprs South Wayne Brick Co, w s Thompson ave n of Wabash R R.

Thornburg Avide W, carpenter, bds Adam McClish.

Thornton Edward, flagman Penn Co, bds 70 Murray.

Thorp Edward, conductor Penn Co, bds 130 E Lewis.

Thorp Mrs Elizabeth, res 130 E Lewis.

Thorp Henry D, bds 91 W Washington.

Thorp Jacob, brakeman, bds 130 E Lewis.

horward Theodore, deputy oil inspector, res 33 Miner.

Threadgall George A, wheel molder Bass Foundry and Machine Works, res 3 Dawson.

Threadgall Harry E, wheel molder Bass Foundry and Machine Works, res 41 Laselle.

Threadgall John W, res 356 Calhoun.

Throckmorton John A, tool dresser Penn Co, res 132 Monroe.

Throckmorton Sidney G, cigarmaker F J Gruber, bds 132 Monroe.

Thum Margaret W, housekeeper 111 Putnam.

Thumb Jacob, clerk E Shuman & Sons, bds 61 E Main.

Thurman Charles, clerk, res 89 W Jefferson.

Thurston Wm R, machinist, res 105 W Williams.

Tibbals Miss Martha E, teacher Taylor University, bds same.

Tibbles Frank E, despatcher, res 166 Lafayette.

Tibbles John H, cabinetmaker, res 177 Griffith.

Tice Henry, hostler J C Brinsley, bds Clifton House.

Tiedmann Mary, bds 245 W Wayne.

Tiekenbrook Kate, bds n e cor Tons and Dwenger aves.

Tielker Frederick W, porter Penn Co, res 17 Barthold.

Tiemann Annie, bds 217 E Washington.

Tiemann Frederick H, carpenter, bds 424 S Broadway.

Tiemann Frederick W, carpenter Louis Diether & Bro, res 83 Wall.

Tiemann Henry, hostler, bds 217 E Washington.
Tiemann John F W, laborer, bds 424 S Broadway.
Tiemann J Frederick, contractor, 424 S Broadway, res same.
Tiemann J Henry, carpenter, bds 424 S Broadway.
Tiemann Louisa, seamstress, bds 424 S Broadway.
Tiemann Wm, machinist Penn Co, res 217 E Washington.
Tiernan Agnes, clerk Frank & Co, bds 73 Madison.
Tiernan Mary (wid Wm H), bds 247 S Webster.
Tiernan Thomas, car repairer Penn Co, res 73 Madison.
Tierney Michael C, engineer Penn Co, res 23 Baker.
Tigar, *see also Tyger.*
Tigar Wm H, despatcher Penn Co, res 147 E Berry.
Tigges Anna, operator S M Foster, bds 177 Ewing.
Tigges Ernest W, checker Penn Co, res 177 Ewing.
Tigges Frederick R, lab L S & M S Ry, res 154 Greely.
Tigges George R, cigarmaker L C Heck, bds 177 Ewing.
Tilbury Charles, laborer, bds 546 E Wayne.
Tilbury Harrison, laborer, bds 544 E Wayne.
Tilbury John J, finisher, res 546 E Wayne.
Tilbury Robert, machine hand Ft Wayne Organ Co, rms 223 Calhoun.
Tilbury Scott, fitter Ft Wayne Furniture Co, res 70 E Main.
Tilbury Wayde, engineer, bds 4 Kansas.
Tilkens Frederick, carpenter, bds 72 Thomas.
Tillier John E, bds 104 Barr.
Tillo Charles D, Mngr Ft Wayne Newspaper Union, res 153 E Berry.
Timberlake Dora M, bds 301 Calhoun.
Timmerman David B, fireman, bds 111 Wells.
Timmis Alonzo, laborer Joseph Fremion, res s s Eckart 4 e of Hanna.
Timmis Harry, rivet heater Penn Co.
Timmis Rosa, domestic 138 Horace.
Timmis Wm, flagman Penn Co, res 150 Horace.
Timmis Wm, teamster, res n s Eckart 4 e of Hanna.
Tine Wm, helper, bds rear 262 Calhoun.
Tinkham Benjamin F, trav agent, res 24 Home ave.
Tinkham Clyde P, dentist, res 144 W De Wald.
Tinkham Miss Cora, clerk, bds 219 W Main.
Tinkham Frank, clerk J P Tinkham, bds 219 W Main.
Tinkham John P, coal, 120 W Main, res 219 same.
Tinkham Melvin W, student, bds 24 Home ave.
Tirk Edward, pipe liner Salamonie Mining and Gas Co, bds 43½ Columbia.
Titus Charles H, fireman, res e s Franklin ave 1 s of High.
Titus Philip, engineer, res 32 Gay.

Stahn & Heinrich, Leading Dealers in ARTISTS' MATE-RIALS AND DRAUGHTING INSTRU-MENTS. 116 Calhoun Street.

FORT WAYNE DIRECTORY. 523

Titus Roger, plasterer, bds 248 Calhoun.
Titus Theodore, engineer, res 130 Buchanan.
Tivoli Garden, cor Spy Run ave and Emily.
Tobias Isaac W, driver Fort Wayne Street Railroad Co, res 4 Melita.
Tobias Oscar, carpenter, bds 192 E Wayne.
Todd Charles S, fireman, bds 103 Wilt.
Todd Frederick E, clerk J J Jenkinson, bds 186 Jackson.
Todd Ida, domestic 251 W Main.
Todd James, teamster, res 64 W Wayne.
Todd John S, flagman Penn Co, res 58 John.
Todd Mills, domestic 127 E Washington.
Todd Samuel L, res s s New Haven road near Section line.
Todd Warner W, genl car inspector Penn Co, bds Aveline House.
Todd W J, laborer Penn Co, res 230 Lafayette.
Toedtman Christina (wid Henry C), res 292 S Harrison.
Toedtman Frederick C, clerk L Schmidt & Co, bds 292 S Harrison.
Toedtman Henry F, clk B R Noll & Co, bds 292 S Harrison.
Toedtman Miss Lizzie, bds 292 S Harrison.
Toenges, *see also Tonges.*
Toenges Frederick, laborer, res 63 Buchanan.
Toenges Frederick W, shoemaker H Busking, res 17 Summit.
Toenges Henry, car builder Penn Co, res 212 E Lewis.
Toensing Henry E (Meinzen & Toensing), res e s Canal 2 n of E Wayne.
Toerge Wm, toolmaker Ft Wayne Electric Co, res 83 Nirdlinger ave.
Tolan Miss Alice, bds 62 W De Wald.
Tolan Brentwood S, architect, 108 Calhoun, bds 62 De Wald.
Tolan Charles B, clerk Kerr-Murray Mnfg Co, bds 62 W De-Wald.
Tolan Frank C, printer Ft Wayne News, bds 62 W DeWald.
Tolan Hattie T (wid Thomas J), res 62 W De Wald.
Toler Jefferson E, laborer, res cor Lafayette and Piqua ave.
Toler Jefferson V, teamster, bds J E Toler.
Tombaugh Daniel, laborer, res 38 Miner.
Tombaugh Thomas C, laborer, res 108 W Creighton ave.
Tomkinson Albert, plumber Robert Ogden, res s s Cochran 2 w of Coombs.
Tonges, *see also Toenges.*
Tonges Wm, mason, res n w cor Holton ave and Maud.
Tonk August, laborer, res 84 Van Buren.
Tonne Frederick W J, foreman boiler shop Fort Wayne Iron Works, res 354 E Washington.

Tonne Helen, bds 354 E Washington.
Tonne Julius, foreman, res 354 E Washington.
Tons Gustav A, coil winder Fort Wayne Electric Co, res w s Miner 3 n of Ferguson ave.
Tons Miss Lydia, clerk L P Sharp, bds 75 W DeWald.
Tons Minnie (wid Henry), bds 75 W DeWald.
Tonsing Henry, helper Penn Co, bds 98 Montgomery.
Tonsing Henry E (Borcherding & Tonsing), res s e cor Canal and Erie.
Tonsing Wm, carpenter, bds 1 Tam.
Toohy Patrick, res 43 Melita.
Toomey Thomas, laborer, res 44 Baker.
Torrence George K, real estate and notary public, 80 Calhoun, res 41½ W Berry.
Touey Anna A, domestic 15 Holman.
Tourge Wm, engineer, res 60 Greene.
Tousley Abner B, brakeman, bds 104 Ewing.
Tower Alexander M, machinist Penn Co, res 25 Williams.
Tower Floyd, machinist Penn Co, res 164 Brackenridge.
Tower Miss Frances E, teacher, bds 103 W Berry.
Tower Frank M, paperhanger Renner, Cratsley & Co, res 126 W Main.
Towns Nelson, wks Jenney Electric Light and Power Co, bds 84 W Main.
Towns Sylvester, foreman Jenney Electric Light and Power Co, res 84 W Main.
Towsley Edgar A, foreman East End Street Car Barn, res 419 E Washington.
Tracey Thomas, fireman, bds 12 St Mary's ave.
Tracy Asbury, section hand, res cor Queen and Abbott.
Tracy John A, section hand, res s s Pontiac 3 e of Walton.
Tracy Rosa J, boxmaker W H Davis, bds 248 E Jefferson.
Trader August, stone cutter, res 525 E Wayne.
Trader Clara, seamstress, bds 525 E Wayne.
Trainer George J, helper, res 208 E Lewis.
Trainer John, rms 36 Baker.
Trarbach Charles, res 568 Lafayette.
Trarbach Frederick, machine hand, bds 568 Lafayette.
Trarbach Gustav A, blacksmith helper Penn Co, bds 568 Lafayette.
Tratschz Herman, laborer Hoffman Bros, bds 168 N Main.
Traub Carrie, clerk Frank & Co, bds 221 E Wayne.
Traub Louis, cutter A L Johns & Co, res 221 E Wayne.
Traub Louisa, packer Louis Fox & Bro, bds 221 E Wayne.
Traub Rose, clerk Eleanor Kratzch, bds 102 Butler.
Traub Sophia, dressmaker, 17 Duryea, bds same.

E. F. Sites, Dentist, 86 Calhoun St., Four Doors North of Wayne.

FORT WAYNE DIRECTORY. 525

Traub Tillie, clerk Frank & Co, bds 221 E Wayne.
Trauerman Isaac (L Dessauer & Co), res 92 W Main.
Trautmann Emma, bds 120 E Wayne.
Trautmann Frederick J, expressman, res 115 Wilt.
Trautmann George, hack driver Fort Wayne Transfer and Baggage Line, bds 120 E Wayne.
Trautmann Henry J W, driver Fort Wayne Transfer and Baggage Line, bds 120 E Wayne.
Trautmann John, policeman, res 120 E Wayne.
Trautmann Louisa, clk B Gutermuth, bds 120 E Wayne.
Trautmann Wm, laborer, bds 115 Wilt.
Travers Martin, machinist Penn Co, res 133 Holman.
Travers Mary, domestic Hanna homestead.
Travis James A, brakeman Penn Co, res s e cor Winter and E Creighton ave.
Travis Patrick, real estate, res 161 Holman.
Travis Peter C, conductor Penn Co, bds 58 Baker.
Traxler Daniel C, clk Adams Exp Co, res 400 E Washington.
Traxler Wm, rms 26 Court.
Trainer John W, foreman, res 279 W Creighton ave.
Trainer Roy, bds 279 W Creighton ave.
Treaster Harry R, wagonmkr Olds' Wagon Works, bds 137 Calhoun.
Treat James W, engineer, res 275 W Washington.
Trebra Lizzie, domestic 38 Summit.
Trebra Robert, blksmith helper Penn Co, bds 194 Madison.
Treep Frank H, wall paper, 68 E Main, res 250 E Jefferson.
Treese Annie, wks Troy Steam Laundry, bds 396 Broadway.
Treese George A, checker Wabash R R, bds 396 Broadway.
Treese James, truckman Wabash R R, res 396 Broadway.
Treese Rosa, wks Troy Steam Laundry, bds 396 Broadway.
Treiber Susan, domestic Hamilton homestead.
Tremble Anna M (wid Jacob), res 556 Hanna.
Tremble Jacob, laborer, bds 241 Barr.
Tremmel Anna, operator Hoosier Mnfg Co, bds 34 Force.
Tremmel August, driver Hook and Ladder Co No 2, res 120 Wallace.
Tremmel Charles, driver Philip Graf, bds 401 Lafayette.
Tremmel Conrad, teamster, res 515 Hanna.
Tremmel John, molder Kerr-Murray Mnfg Co, bds 515 Hanna.
Tremmel John, policeman, res n w cor Berry and Griffith.
Tremmel Peter, driver, bds 556 Hanna.
Tremmel Philip, conductor Penn Co, res 106 Wallace.
Tremmel Rickie, operator Hoosier Mnfg Co, bds 34 Force.
Trenam Miss Anna M, teacher Hoagland School, bds 162 W Main.

Trenam George E, clerk Penn Co, bds 162 W Main.

Trenam Mary (wid George), res 162 W Main.

Trenary Broad, driver Fort Wayne City Railroad Co, bds 101 Glasgow ave.

Trenkley Celestine (Trenkley & Scherzinger), res 106 W Washington.

Trenkley & Scherzinger (Celestine Trenkley, Primus Scherzinger), Watches, Clocks and Jewelry, 78 Calhoun.

Trentman August C, Wholesale Groceries, Notions and Liquors, 111 to 119 Calhoun, res 72 W Wayne.

Trentman Bernard, shipping clerk A C Trentman, res 330 Calhoun.

Trentman Bernard H, res 161 E Wayne.

Trentman Bernard J, grocer, res e s Calhoun 2 s of Pontiac.

Trentman Block, e s Calhoun bet Berry and Wayne.

Trentman Miss Carrie, bds 72 W Wayne.

Trentman Edward A, bds 161 E Wayne.

Trentman Miss Mary, bds 72 W Wayne.

Trepera Jarolim, jeweler, 140 Broadway, res same.

Treseler Henry, dry goods, 108 Barr, res 152 Ewing.

Tresselt Charles A, bookkeeper Meyer Bros & Co, res 88 E Jefferson.

Tresselt Christian (C Tresselt & Sons), res 55 E Jefferson.

Tresselt C & Sons (Christian, Oscar W and Herman C), Proprs City Flouring Mills and Elevator; Dealers in Grain, Flour, Seeds, Salt, etc, cor Clinton and Nickel Plate R R.

Tresselt Frederick T, clerk C Tresselt & Sons, bds 55 E Jefferson.

Tresselt Henry, car builder Penn Co, res 53 Melita.

Tresselt Herman, taxidermist, 83 N Cass, bds same.

Tresselt Herman C (C Tresselt & Sons), res 50 Oak.

Tresselt Oscar W (C Tresselt & Sons), bds 55 E Jefferson.

Tribus Joseph, bookkeeper Louis Wolf, res e s Ewing 2 s of Pearl.

Trier John C, driver Pfeiffer & Schlatter, bds 294 E Lewis.

Trier Wm, carpenter, bds 77 W Superior.

Trimble E Rebecca, seamstress, bds 397 S Broadway.

Trimble Marion, conductor, res 138 E Lewis.

Trimble Maud, bds 138 E Lewis.

Trimble Samuel, res 397 S Broadway.

Trinity English Lutheran Church, Rev Samuel Wagenhals Pastor, s w cor Clinton and Wayne.

Trinity Episcopal Church, s w cor W Berry and Fulton.

Trinity M E Church, n e cor Cass and 4th.

Trisch I J, dressmaker, 96 Wells, res same.

Triskett Charles A, clerk McDonald, Watt & Wilt, res 2 Piqua road.

Tri-State Building and Loan Association, George W Pixley pres, A D Cressler vice-pres, C A Wilding sec, Joseph W Bell treas, 13 and 14 Pixley & Long bldg.

Tritschler Charles, plumber, bds 7 Fulton.

Tritschler John P, res 7 Fulton.

Trone Henry, boarding house, 43½ E Columbia.

Trosen Harry, helper, res 225 John.

Trott Harry, machine hand American Wheel Co, bds 197 Jackson.

Trott Rudolph, painter, res 197 Jackson.

Trout John, laborer, bds 27 E 1st.

Trout Monroe, lab South Wayne Brick Co, bds 26 Thompson.

Troutner John, farmer, res 320 E Jefferson.

Troutner Nettie, bds 320 E Jefferson.

Trowbridge Addison, res 75 E Jefferson.

Trowbridge George E, stereotyper Fort Wayne Newspaper Union, bds 75 E Jefferson.

Trowbridge Wm M, carpenter, bds Lake Shore Hotel.

Troxell Charles O, miller Monning & Baker, res 24 E Washington.

Troy Steam Laundry, F L Jones & Co Proprs, 48 and 50 Pearl. (*See left bottom lines.*)

True Frederick C, teamster, bds G J True.

True George J, teamster, res w s Piqua ave 1 s of Rudisill av.

Truebenbach Henry, butcher, res 170 Brackenridge.

Truebenbach Moritz, carpenter, res 98 Harrison.

Truesdale Richard, fireman, res 104 Fairfield ave.

Trumbauer James M, cigarmkr C A Berndt, res 93 E Lewis.

Trumbull Charles, laborer, res s s Rebecca w of Runnion av.

Trythall James, forgeman Penn Co, res 43 E Butler.

Tuckey Gardner J, conductor, res 306 Hanna.

Tuerschmann Paul, coremaker Bass Foundry and Machine Works, bds 89½ Force.

Tulley George W, foreman, bds 43 W Williams.

Tumbleson Eliza (wid Joseph), bds 164 Harrison.

Tumbleson Walter H, insurance agent, res 164 Harrison.

Tunghans Edwin, carpenter, res n w cor Harrison and Allen.

Turkopp August, waiter C Entemann.

Turman Furney (col'd), waiter, res s s Hayden bet Ohio and Chute.

Turner Annie E (wid Wm W), bds 177 W Superior.

Turner Charles W, laborer Penn Co, bds 377 Hanna.

Turner Delia, bds 65 W Lewis.

Turner Frank, clerk, bds 377 Hanna.
Turner George, res 18 Chicago.
Turner James A, bookkeeper L C Zollinger, bds 65 W Lewis.
Turner John, res 23 Elm.
Turner Levi, res 65 W Lewis.
Turner Wm, engineer, res 377 Hanna.
Turner Wm H, laborer C L Centlivre, bds Edsall House.
Tuttle Myron E, train despatcher Penn Co, res 333 Lafay-ette.
Tuttle Theodore, blacksmith, w s Spy Run ave 2 n of Ran-dolph, res 21 W 4th.
Tuttle Worthy E, musician, bds 21 W 4th.
Twimiller Joseph, brewer, bds 30 Schick.
Twomey Edward J, deputy county clerk, rms 159 E Lewis.
Tyger, *see also Tigar.*
Tyger Charles W, clk Charles Falk & Co, bds 69 N Cass.
Tyger Kate A, bds 69 N Cass.
Tyger Morton B, student, bds 69 N Cass.
Tyger Philip C, engineer, res 69 N Cass.
Tyler Miss Anna O, bds John Orff.
Tyler Charles J, carriage painter M Albrecht, bds 31 Pritchard.
Tyler Frank, driver, bds 31 Pritchard.
Tyler James F, carpenter, res 31 Pritchard.
Tyler John L, teacher in writing Public Schools, res 391 Hanna.
Tyler Percy A, flagman Penn Co, bds 31 Pritchard.
Tyler Royal A, laborer G K Hubbard, bds 31 Pritchard.
Tyrrell Frank D, asst supt Wabash R R shops, res 250 W Creighton ave.
Tyson Caroline (wid Enoch), bds 54 Oliver.

U

Uebelhoer Frederick, bds 169 Brackenridge.
Uebelhoer John, tinsmith Penn Co, res 169 Brackenridge.
Uebelhoer Louise E (wid Philip), res 68 E Main.
Uebelhoer Mollie, dressmaker, bds 68 E Main.
Uebelhoer Roland W, watches, 68 E Main, bds same.
Uebelhoer Sophia, dressmaker, bds 68 E Main.
Ueber Joseph, helper Penn Co, bds 231 Barr.
Uetrecht Frederick, carpenter, bds 230 Harmer.
Uhl Albert, molder Kerr-Murray Mnfg Co, bds 252 E Wayne.
Ulenhake Henry, switchman, res 43 Boone.
Ulery Eliza (wid John), res 332 W Main.
Ulmer Christian, driver, bds Theodore S Ulmer.
Ulmer Christian, laborer Wm & J J Geake, res 191 Oakland.

Ulmer Christopher F, driver Fort Wayne Street Railroad Co, res 73 Melita.

Ulmer Emma, domestic 200 W Berry.

Ulmer Gustav, driver Adams Exp Co, bds 106 Lafayette.

Ulmer Theodore S, engineer Root & Co, res n s Prospect ave 3 e of Spy Run ave.

Ulrecht Herman, carpenter, bds 203 Gay.

Ulrecht J Henry, car builder Penn Co, res 203 Gay.

Ulrey Mrs Sophie, bds 37 Wilt.

Ulrich Emil, lab Bass Foundry and Machine Works, res 16 University.

Ulrich John, laborer Penn Co, res 237 Gay.

Umstead Elizabeth (wid John), res 509 E Washington.

Umstead Ellen, bds 509 E Washington.

Umstead Harry D, Mnfr and Dealer in Men's and Boys' Fine Shoes; Repairing a Specialty, 283 Calhoun, res 18 Murray. (*See adv in classified Boots and Shoes.*)

Umstead Mary, tailor, bds 509 E Washington.

Underhill Alonzo E, driver Foster Furniture Co, res s w cor Maud and Holton ave.

Underhill Elliot S, with Underhill's Monumental Works, res 159 Hanna.

Underhill Frank W, mngr Underhill's Monumental Works, res 87 Wilt.

Underhill Harriet O (wid Phineas S), bds 109 W Washington.

Underhill's Monumental Wks, F W Underhill mngr, 82 Barr.

Underwood Thomas J, laborer, res 204 Francis.

Ungemach J Henry, teacher St Paul's German Lutheran School, res 15 Madison.

Unger Ferdinand, tinsmith Penn Co, res s s W Creighton ave 2 e of Broadway.

Unger Frank A, laborer, bds 288 Calhoun.

Unger Frederick G, laborer, bds Ferdinand Unger.

Unger Gottlieb, meter repairer Fort Wayne Gas Light Co, res 117 Wells.

Unger John G, machine hand Fort Wayne Electric Co, bds Ferdinand Unger.

Unger John S, engineer Western Gas Construction Co, rms 26 Pixley & Long bldg.

Ungerer George, carpenter, res 49 Stophlet.

Ungerer George L, pressman Fort Wayne News, bds 49 Stophlet.

Ungerer Wm F, feeder Archer, Housh & Co, bds 49 Stophlet.

Union Block, n w cor Main and Clinton.

Union Cigar Box Mnfg and Job Printing Co, Ruesewald & Didion Proprs, 49 E Main.

Union Line, F N Kollock Agent, 79 Calhoun.
Union Pacific Tea and Coffee Store, 102 Calhoun.
United Brethren Church, s w cor Boone and Fry.
United States Baking Co, The Fox Branch, Louis Fox Mngr, n e cor Calhoun and Jefferson.
United States Express Co, C B Beaver Agent, 79 Calhoun.
Unker Ludwig, laborer Weil Bros & Co, bds 1 Oak.
Updegraff Miss Josephine, teacher Washington School, bds 34 Douglas ave.
Updegraff Miss Sarah, asst Central Grammar School, bds 34 Douglas ave.
Uplegger, *see also Oppliger.*
Uplegger Charles, guard city jail, res 146 Broadway.
Uplegger Louis, barber, 45 Wells, bds 9 Marion.
Upmeyer Henry H G, clerk Henry Treseler, res 108 Barr.
Upmeyer Mrs Mary J, bds 294 W Washington.
Upmeyer Wm, laborer Jenney Electric Light and Power Co, bds 43½ E Columbia.
Uran John G, conductor, res 47 St Mary's ave.
Urbahns August E, flagman, bds 282 W Berry.
Urbahns C Emil, tel operator N Y, C & St L R R, bds 282 W Berry.
Urbahns Elizabeth (wid John), res 282 W Berry.
Urbahns Ferdinand D, bds 282 W Berry.
Urbahns F Wm, despatcher N Y, C & St L R R, bds 282 W Berry,
Urban Philip, servant J F W Meyer.
Urbine Addie, wks Troy Steam Laundry, bds 19 W Jefferson.
Urbine James, clerk Meyer Bros & Co, res 52 E Williams.
Urbine Nora, wks Troy Steam Laundry, bds 19 W Jefferson.
Usler Christian, machine hand Fort Wayne Organ Co, bds 518 Fairfield ave.

Vachon Frank A, teamster, res 22 W 3d.
Vachon John, laborer, res 135 Wallace.
Vachon Joseph, laborer, bds 89 W DeWald.
Vachon Richard, bds 292 Hanna.
Vachon T Alfred, machine hand Olds' Wagon Works, bds 91 E Washington.
Vachon Wm H, car builder Penn Co, bds 292 Hanna.
Vachon Zachariah, res 292 Hanna.
Valenti Anton, fruits, res 12 Lafayette.
Valentine Charles F, car builder Penn Co, res 16 Bass.

Valroff August, plumber A Hattersley & Sons, res 90 E Main.
Van Allen John, laborer, res 127 W Superior.
Van Allen John H, hackman, res 48 N Cass.
Van Alstine Ellen (wid Wm), res 17 Jones.
Van Alstine Miss Lettie A, teacher Washington School, bds
    17 Jones.
Van Alstine Perry, brakeman, res 241 Barr.
Van Ausdall Garret, barnman Bass Foundry and Machine
    Works, res 33 Gay.
Van Ausdall Mamie, bds 33 Gay.
Van Buskirk Aaron E, physician, 416 Calhoun, res same.
Van Camp Mrs Henrietta, res 36 Hamilton.
Vance Charles, bds 186 W Berry.
Vance Mary J (wid Lawrence M), bds 186 W Berry.
Vancura Jacob, machine hand Fort Wayne Organ Co, res 25
    Taylor.
Vanderford Charles E, carpenter Louis Diether & Bro, res
    106 Madison.
Vanderlast Herman, painter Rear & Bugert, bds 199 Broad-
    way.
Van Der Water Charles, laborer, res 129 Wells.
Vandewater Mary, domestic 391 Fairfield ave.
Van Fleet Ralph A, trav salesman, res 56 Douglas ave.
Vangorder Charles H, engineer, res 182 Greely.
Van Meter Eugene, laborer, res e s Grant ave 2 s of Penn.
Van Meter Mary (wid Wm), res 431 E Washington.
Vanosdale Benjamin, lab Heller & Bottenberg, res 33 Smith.
Van Osdale George, section hand, bds 33 Smith.
Van Osdale Laura, dressmaker, 33 Smith, bds same.
Van Osdale Wm M, fireman, res 361 Lafayette.
Van Slyke Ira M, conductor, res 51 Butler.
Van Slyke Rev Wm M, pastor Berry Street M E Church, res
    26 W Berry.
Van Tilburg Emmons, engineer, res 407 W Main.
Van Tilburg Gaerie, molder Indiana Machine Works, bds 407
    W Main.
Van Valkenburg Frank H, trav agent, bds Aldine Hotel.
Van Vleet Miss Lanie, bds 66 W Jefferson.
Van Winkle Charles B, traveling agent, res 114 Lafayette.
Van Winkle Isaac, res 114 Lafayette.
Van Winkle Miss Mary E, bds 114 Lafayette.
Varner George W, painter, res 23 Holman.
Vasemar Sophie, domestic 248 W Wayne.
Vasen Philip, plumber James Madden, bds 177 Griffith.
Vaughan Warren, res 45 Grand.
Vaughn Martin C, painter, res 3 Bass.

Vegalies Catherine (wid Jacob), res w s Franklin ave 1 n of
  Spring.
Veidel Conrad, helper Kerr-Murray Mnfg Co, res 86 Hayden.
Veit August, carpenter, bds 37 Wabash ave.
Veit Charles, laborer, bds 37 Wabash ave.
Veit Minnie, bds 37 Wabash ave.
Veit Philip, res 37 Wabash ave.
Veith Frank, horseshoer, 50 Barr, res same.
Veith's Hall, 267 E Wayne.
Veith Joseph, bds 265 E Wayne.
Veith Mary, bds 265 E Wayne.
Veith Peter, res 265 E Wayne.
Veith Wm, laborer Penn Co, bds 265 E Wayne.
Verdilla George, cigarmaker, bds 11 Melita.
Vernetzki Joseph, laborer, res 61 John.
Vernor, see Vorner.
Vesey Wm J (Randall & Vesey), res 90 Thompson ave.
Vetter Andrew, baker J H Schwieters, bds 41 E Columbia.
Viberg Augusta (wid Harmon), res 23 Douglas ave.
Viberg George H, Sheriff, Court House, res County Jail.
Viberg George L, machinist Kerr-Murray Mnfg Co, bds 23
  Douglas ave.
Viberg Miss Mattie, teacher, bds 23 Douglas ave.
Viberg Mollie H, clerk G De Wald & Co, bds 23 Douglas.
Vincent Edward L, laborer C L Centlivre, res 37 Barr.
Vincent Fannie (wid Gustav), janitor, 20 W Berry, res 28 E
  Columbia.
Vincent Frank M, painter, L O Hull, res 16 Laselle.
Vincent James, finisher French, Hanna & Co, bds 105 Lafay-
  ette.
Vincent John, laborer, bds 28 Melita.
Vincent Wm, laborer Wm Moellering & Co, res w s Lafay-
  ette 12 s of Pontiac.
Vining John, bds John Vining jr.
Vining John jr, brickmaker A McKernan, res n w cor Glas-
  gow ave and Maumee road.
Violand Joseph, carpenter, res 11 Euclid ave.
Violand Milla (wid Louis), res 340 E Wayne.
Violet Henry, laborer, res 19 Penn.
Virgil Rev Almon, bds 70 Harrison.
Virgil Anna E (wid Thomas S), res 70 Harrison.
Vizard Anthony, blacksmith Kerr-Murray Mnfg Co, bds 47
  Barr.
Vizard Thomas, laborer, bds 30 Melita.
Vobay Victor, market stall 49, res e s Auburn road n of city
  limits.

Fine Commercial Printing, **M. CLARK & CO.,**
16 W. COLUMBIA STREET.

FORT WAYNE DIRECTORY. 533

Vodde Bernardina (wid Frederick F), res 430 E Washington.
Vodde Wm, laborer, bds 55 Lillie.
Vodenheimer Samuel, works Liggett Bros, rms 5 N Harrison.
Voelker Frederick, car inspector Penn Co, res s s Chestnut 1
e of Warren.
Vogel Henry A, asst supt Fort Wayne Organ Co, bds Aldine
Hotel.
Vogel Veronica (wid Frank B), bds 324 Calhoun.
Vogel Wm C, tuner Fort Wayne Organ Co, res 160 W
Washington.
Vogelgesang Ferdinand, laborer, res 1 Hanover.
Vogely Andrew, blacksmith, s w cor Maumee road and Ohio,
res 52 Oak.
Vogely Wm, stone rubber Ft Wayne Steam Stone Works,
res 157 W Main.
Vogler Mrs Albertina, res 159 Madison.
Vogler Miss Anna, bds 159 Madison.
Vogler Edward, tailor Thieme Bros, bds 22 W Main.
Vogler Julius, washing machines, bds 159 Madison.
Vogler Theodore P, grocer, 231 E Jefferson, res 161 same.
Vogtlin Henry, butcher Bernhard Weber, bds 121 Calhoun.
Voigt Herman, mason, res 72 Oakley.
Voirol Edward G, porter G E Bursley & Co, res 24 W 5th.
Voirol Emma, bds 244 Calhoun.
Voirol Frank A, watchmaker F J Voirol, res 244 Calhoun.
Voirol Frank J, watches, 244 Calhoun, res n s Suttenfield 2 e
of Clinton.
Voirol John J, laborer C L Centlivre, bds 244 Calhoun.
Voirol Joseph, fireman, res 147 E Jefferson.
Voirol Louis, cigarmaker, bds Lake Shore Hotel.
Voirol Mary, bds 244 Calhoun.
Volland Charles H, clerk, bds 279 W Washington.
Volland Henry (H Volland & Sons), res 279 W Washington.
Volland Henry J (H Volland & Sons), res 17 Sturgis.
Volland H & Sons (Henry, John G, Wm G and Henry J)
proprs Volland Mills and dealers in flour, grain and mill
feed, 14 W Columbia.
Volland John G (H Volland & Sons), bds 279 W Washington.
Volland Mills, H Volland & Sons proprs, 14 W Columbia.
Volland Wm G (H Volland & Sons), bds 279 W Washington.
Vollmer Emma, clerk L Wolf & Co, bds 195 W Main.
Vollmer Frederick C (Fremion & Vollmer), res 166 Holman.
Vollmer Louisa (wid Daniel), res 195 W Main.
Vollmer Wm, clerk Renner, Cratsley & Co, bds 195 W Main.
Vollmer Wm F, painter, res 168 Holman.
Vollmerding Frederick, clerk Root & Co, res 63 Hugh.

Vollriede Christian, night watchman J C Peters, res 3 Polk.

Volz Anthony, laborer, res e s Hanna 2 s of Eckart.

Volz Anthony, polisher, res 558 Hanna.

Volz Baltzer, laborer, bds 558 Hanna.

Volz Henry, laborer Penn Co, res 19 Chestnut.

Volz Henry jr, molder Bass Foundry and Machine Works, bds Henry Volz.

Volz Jacob, machine hand American Wheel Co, res 150 E Creighton ave.

Volz Ulrich, laborer, bds 558 Hanna.

Von Behrens Ferdinand, carpenter, res 68 Nelson.

Vonfange Henry, cigarmaker H W Ortmann, bds 63 Baker.

Voorheis Peter V, agent Prudential Life Insurance Co, res 200 E Washington.

Voors Edward, machine hand, bds 175 Wells.

Voors John G, res 175 Wells.

Voors John G jr, saloon, 574 E Washington, res 572 same.

Vordermark Alice, teacher, bds 301 E Washington.

Vordermark Annie, bds 301 E Washington.

Vordermark Christina (wid Ernest), res Vordermark homestead.

Vordermark Ernest, rimmer, res n w cor Warren and New Haven ave.

Vordermark E & Sons (John W and Henry P), boots and shoes, 32 Calhoun.

Vordermark's Grove, s s Maumee road 1 e of Glasgow ave.

Vordermark Harry, bds s e cor Walton ave and Maumee rd.

Vordermark Henry P (E Vordermark & Sons), res s e cor Maumee road and Walton ave.

Vordermark John W (E Vordermark & Sons), res 301 E Washington.

Vordermark Kate, bds 301 E Washington.

Vordermark Miss Lillie, bds cor Walton ave and Maumee rd.

Vore Cara, laborer, bds 27 E 1st.

Vore Wm A, mach Indiana Machine Works, bds 2 Centre.

Voss Louis, bds 99 Summit.

Votrie Albert, laborer A McKernan, bds Wm A Smith.

Votrie Frank J, laborer Wm Moellering & Co, res w s Lafayette 6 s of Pontiac.

Votrie James, laborer, bds w s Lafayette 6 s of Pontiac.

Votry Alexander, laborer, res 206 Broadway.

Voughley Peter, drayman, bds 53 Walnut.

Vought John, bds 389 E Wayne.

Vought Wm S, real estate, 18 Schmitz blk, res 389 E Wayne.

Vreeland Henry S, mngr carpet dept Root & Co, res 186 Clay.

Vreeland Maud, bds 186 Clay.

W

Wabash Railroad, master mechanic's office cor Fairfield ave and Wabash R R; passenger and freight depot cor Calhoun and Wabash R R.

Wacker Anton, molder Bass Foundry and Machine Works, res s s Pontiac 1 w of Hanna.

Wackerman John M (Wackerman & Wilkin), bds 91 Montgomery.

Wackerman & Wilkin (John M Wackerman, Oliver P Wilkin), barbers, 222 Calhoun.

Wackmiller John, tool keeper Fort Wayne Electric Co, res 51 Home ave.

Waddington Benjamin C, painter, res 158 Holman.

Waddington Rosanna (wid Wm), bds 158 Holman.

Wade Bridget, bds 172 Holman.

Wade Frederick M, clerk Wabash R R, bds 378 Calhoun.

Wade John, machinist, bds 172 Holman.

Wade Julia, bds 172 Holman.

Wade Miss Margaret A, teacher Hanna School, bds 172 Holman.

Wade Maria (wid James), res 172 Holman.

Wade Patrick S, messenger, res 140 Holman.

Wadge Etta (wid Richard), bds 143 Montgomery.

Wadge George, wool sorter, res 170 Montgomery.

Wadge Miss Georgina, teacher Clay School, bds 170 Montgomery.

Wadge Minnie, bds 143 Montgomery.

Wadge Wm, carpenter, res 143 Montgomery.

Wadge Wm H, clerk, bds 137 E Berry.

Waener George, baker, res 85 Buchanan.

Wafel, see also Wefel.

Wafel Wm, carpenter, bds 32 Colerick.

Wageman Bernard, car repairer Penn Co, res Strawberry ave.

Wageman George, painter, res 165 Wells.

Wageman Henry, car repairer Penn Co, res Strawberry ave.

Wageman John, laborer, res 133 Franklin ave.

Wagenhals Rev Samuel, Pastor Trinity English Lutheran Church, res 54 E Wayne.

Waggoner Robert T, driver Hook and Ladder Co No 1, res 65 Clinton.

Wagner Catherine (wid John), res 140 W Jefferson.

Wagner Charles, hostler, bds 309 W Washington.

Wagner Christina, domestic A Aehnelt.

Wagner Edward F, carpenter, bds 45 Butler.

Wagner Ella J, bds 140 W Jefferson.
Wagner Eva, domestic 207 W Berry.
Wagner Frederick, laborer C L Centlivre, res 27 Randolph.
Wagner George E, engineer, res 154 E Lewis.
Wagner Henry, laborer Bass Foundry and Machine Works, res 5 Edgerton.
Wagner Henry E, carpenter, res 109 E Creighton ave.
Wagner Herman, laborer, bds Washington House.
Wagner John, carpenter, 45 Butler, res same.
Wagner John B, machinist, bds 140 W Jefferson.
Wagner John C, pianos, 27 W Main, bds 238 E Jefferson.
Wagner John C, road master, res 35 N Calhoun.
Wagner John H, fireman, bds 35 N Calhoun.
Wagner John T, Propr Union Saloon, Coffee House and Restaurant; Orders Served at All Hours; All Kinds of Wines and Liquors, 7 E Main, res 186 W Main.
Wagner Julian, carpenter, res w s Piqua ave 3 s of Rudisill.
Wagner Louis, laborer Bass Foundry and Machine Works, res 238 Gay.
Wagner Philip, bartender J T Wagner, bds 186 W Main.
Wagner Philip, molder Bass Foundry and Machine Works, res e s Lake ave nr Tecumseh.
Wagner Rudolph, laborer, res 330 Force.
Wagner Susan, packer Louis Fox & Bro, bds 186 W Main.
Wagner Wm C, helper A Hattersley & Sons, bds 35 N Calhoun.
Wagner Wm W, telegraph operator G R & I R R, rms 209 Harrison.
Wagoner Austin E, carpenter Penn Co, res s s Leith 1 w of Calhoun.
Wagoner Franciska (wid Henry G), res 26 E Washington.
Wah Thomas, machinist, bds Monroe House.
Wah Kee & Co (Wah Kee, James Lanyon), Chinese Goods and Laundry, 8 W Wayne. (*See adv, p 67.*)
Wahl Henry, turner, res Leikauf's Packing House.
Wah Lung, laundry, 104 Broadway, res same.
Wahrenburg Frederick, car builder Penn Co, res 12 Union.
Wahrenburg Henry, bricklayer, res 506 E Lewis.
Waibel George, clerk G W Seavey, res 226 W Jefferson.
Waibel Placidus, cabinetmaker Fort Wayne Organ Co, res 226 W Jefferson.
Waite Florence, bds 188 Hanna.
Wakefield Elmer, machine hand Fort Wayne Organ Co, bds 851 Broadway.
Wakefield John F, carriagemaker, res 851 Broadway.
Wakefield Roscoe, cigarmaker, bds 851 Broadway.

Walbaum Eliza (wid Henry), dressmaker L A Worch, res 63 Summit.

Walbaum Frederick, machinist Bass Foundry and Machine Works, bds 63 Summit.

Walbaum Henry W, molder Bass Foundry and Machine Works, bds 63 Summit.

Walborn Nancy J (wid John H), bds s e cor Creighton and Walton ave.

Walch, *see Walsh, Welch and Welsh.*

Walda, *see also Waldo.*

Walda Amelia, bds 331 E Washington.

Walda Charles, carpenter Penn Co, res 329 E Washington.

Walda Charles F W, painter, res 47 Walter.

Walda Christian, machine hand Horton Mnfg Co, res 325 W Washington.

Walda Christian C, carpenter, res n e cor Erie and Canal.

Walda Christopher F, carpenter Bass Foundry and Machine Works res Ridge rd Wayne twp.

Walda Frederick, tailor, res s e cor Pontiac and Webster.

Walda Hannah, operator, bds Frederick Walda.

Walda Henry, laborer J C Peters, res 382 W Main.

Walda Henry, upholsterer, bds 325 W Washington.

Walda Henry B (H B Walda & Bro), res 331 E Washington.

Walda Henry B & Bro (Henry B and Wm C), Carpenters and Joiners, Jobbers and General Contractors; Store and Office Fixtures Made to Order on Short Notice, Shop Erie bet Canal and Schick. (*See adv, p 69.*)

Walda Herman, painter, bds 325 W Washington.

Walda John F, saloon, 5 Fairfield ave, res same.

Walda Louisa, operator, bds Frederick Walda.

Walda Mattie, operator, bds Frederick Walda.

Walda Wm, carpenter, res s s Erie 3 w of Schick.

Walda Wm, wheelmaker American Wheel Co, res 361 Lafayette.

Walda Wm C (H B Walda & Bro), res 26 Schick.

Waldmann Charles, helper Penn Co, bds 312 Lafayette.

Waldo George, painter, res 71 Hamilton.

Waldo Miss Grace M, teacher Hoagland School, bds 99 E Washington.

Waldo Henry, teamster, res 590 Calhoun.

Waldo Mrs Mary S, principal Harmer School, res 99 E Washington.

Waldo Susan M (wid George W), bds 294 W Washington.

Waldschmidt George, laborer Penn Co, res 94 Walton ave.

Waldschmidt George jr, clerk G W Seavey, bds 94 Walton.

Waldschmidt Jacob, machinist Penn Co, bds 94 Walton ave.

Waldschmidt Kate, domestic 96 E Washington.

Wales Edward A, paymaster, res 254 W Jefferson.

Walker, *see also Welker*.

Walker Andrew, clerk Penn Co, res 214 Francis.

Walker Anthony, molder, res s s Pontiac 2 e of Lafayette.

Walker Frank, finisher Ft Wayne Organ Co, bds s s Pontiac 2 e of Lafayette.

Walker Frank R, clerk Penn Co, bds 306 Harrison.

Walker John A, tank builder, bds 130 W Wayne.

Walker Leonard S, farmer, res 57 Miner.

Walker Mary C (wid Louis J), res 130 W Wayne.

Walker Peter, carver Fort Wayne Organ Co, bds 518 Fairfield.

Walkey Frank, carpenter, bds Monroe House.

Walla George, teamster, bds 120 Union.

Wallace Miss Fanny, res n s Cochrane 3 e of Coombs.

Wallace Harry H, clerk Randall Hotel.

Wallace Henry H (col'd), waiter, rms 67 W Superior.

Wallace Jeremiah, res 233 Lafayette.

Wallace John, boilermaker Penn Co, res 140 E Lewis.

Wallace Lucidia A, bds 140 E Lewis.

Wallace Wm, painter, bds 233 Lafayette.

Wallies G Frederick, carpenter, res 124 Harrison.

Walsh, *see also Welch and Welsh*.

Walsh Annie, tailoress L J Feist, bds 165 Gay.

Walsh Carl, laborer, bds Washington House.

Walsh Garrett, watchman, res 165 Gay.

Walsh James M, laborer, rms 183 Calhoun.

Walsh John F, brakeman Penn Co, rms 183 Calhoun.

Walsh Miss Mary E, bds 85 E Jefferson.

Walsh Michael V, clerk Aveline House, rms 41½ W Main.

Walsh Patrick H, laborer, bds 165 Gay.

Walsh Thomas A, laborer, bds 165 Gay.

Waltemath Amelia, bds 43 W Lewis.

Waltemath Charles H (C H Waltemath & Sons), res 325 Lafayette.

Waltemath Charles H, apprentice G F Yergens, bds 201 Lafayette.

Waltemath C H & Sons (Charles H, Wm H and Louis F), Dry Goods, Groceries, Bakery, Flour, Feed and Grain, 321 to 325 Lafayette.

Waltemath Emma A, dressmaker, 12 W Jefferson, res same.

Waltemath Henry F, car repairer Penn Co, res 43 W Lewis.

Waltemath Lazette (wid Henry), res 201 Lafayette.

Waltemath Lena, dressmaker J M Gould, bds 43 W Lewis.

Waltemath Miss Lizzie, clerk C H Waltemath & Sons, bds 325 Lafayette.
Waltemath Louis, machine hand Olds' Wagon Works, bds 43 W Lewis.
Waltemath Louis F (C H Waltemath & Sons), bds 325 Lafayette.
Waltemath Louis H, pressman Fort Wayne News, bds 259 E Lewis.
Waltemath Minnie, bds 259 E Lewis.
Waltemath Sophia, tailoress, bds 201 Lafayette.
Waltemath Sophie (wid Louis), res 259 E Lewis.
Waltemath Wm F C, laborer Penn Co, res 50 Maumee rd.
Waltemath Wm H (C H Waltemath & Sons), bds 325 Lafayette.
Waltemath Wm L F, clerk J D Lewis, bds 201 Lafayette.
Walter Amos R, trav agt McDonald, Watt & Wilt, res 274 W Creighton ave.
Walter August, laborer American Wheel Co, bds 149 Force.
Walter David, butcher Robert Hood, res 51 Barr.
Walter Jacob (Walter & Ellert), res 28 E Wayne.
Walter Jacob, laborer Penn Co, res 149 Force.
Walter Jennie I, operator Wooster Mnfg Co, bds 51 Barr.
Walter John A, boots and shoes, 40 Harrison, res 22 Huron.
Walter Lillie, seamstress E C Smith, bds 51 Barr.
Walter Margaret (wid Frank), bds 12 Pine.
Walter & Ellert (Jacob Walter, Benoit Ellert), barbers, 105 Calhoun.
Walters David B, rms 35 E Wayne.
Walters Edward, painter Charles Rivers & Son, bds 305 Harrison.
Walthour Louis, brakeman, bds 51 W Superior.
Waltke George, miller Monning & Baker, res 78 E Columbia.
Waltke Sophia, domestic A Aehnelt.
Waltke Wm H, laborer, bds 78 E Columbia.
Walton Charles E, train master Penn Co, res 43 Brackenridge.
Walton Clinton H, bds 131 E Wayne.
Walton Horace B, flagman Penn Co, res 26 Colerick.
Walton Joseph R, store keeper Penn Co, res 43 Brackenridge.
Waltsmith Julia, domestic Aveline House.
Wambach Mathias, painter Olds' Wagon Works, bds 332 Hanna.
Wambach Peter, laborer Penn Co, res 332 Hanna.
Warburton Anson L, patternmaker Kerr-Murray Mnfg Co, bds 69 N Cass.
Ward Alice, binder C E Davis, bds 233 W Berry.
Ward Ambrose G, brakeman, bds 20 Leith.

Election Slips. Headquarters for PERFECT SLIPS
at JOHN F. EBY & CO'S., DETROIT

540   R. L. POLK & CO.'S

Ward Amos M, carpenter, bds 91 E Washington.
Ward Miss Annie, bds 233 W Berry.
Ward Charles C, fireman, bds 20 Leith.
Ward Charles L, clerk Fred Eckert.
Ward Daniel G, stripper G F Sorge, bds 71 W 3d.
Ward Emma K, seamstress, bds 71 W 3d.
Ward Horatio N, crockery, 8 W Columbia, res 233 W Berry.
Ward John, stone cutter Wm & J J Geake, bds 312 W Main.
Ward John, section foreman Wabash R R, res 8 Bass.
Ward Loran D, binder C E Davis, res 71 Laselle.
Ward Michael, fireman, bds 12 St Mary's ave.
Ward Robert, brakeman, res 71 W 3d.
Ward Samuel M, pedler, res 25 Euclid ave.
Ward Wm A, brakeman, res 40 Pontiac.
Ward Wm H, supt, res 20 Leith.
Ward Wm H jr, clerk J D Gumpper, bds 20 Leith.
Warner, see also Werner and Woerner.
Warner Charles A, cabinetmaker Fort Wayne Organ Co, bds
   Windsor Hotel.
Warner George, blacksmith L C Zollinger, res n s Wagner 7
   w of St Joseph river.
Warner George F, machinist Penn Co, res 38 Pritchard.
Warner Henry, laborer, bds Samuel Hinkson.
Warner Joseph, baker Christian Hoffner, bds same.
Warner Thomas C, printer Fort Wayne News, res 90 E Lewis.
Warnock Jane (wid Cory), bds 76 E Columbia.
Warren Perry S, shoemaker, res 44 Centre.
Warrick Charles A, fireman, res 396 Hanna.
Warrick Lee A, lab American Wheel Co, bds 396 Hanna.
Warriner Arthur F, clerk G W Seavey, bds 336 Broadway.
Warsthorn Anton, laborer, res 19 Laselle.
Warsthorn Anthony, laborer American Wheel Company, res
   337 Lafayette.
Wartenbe Amanda (wid Ephraim), res 25 Hough.
Wartenbe Charles M, bds 25 Hough.
Wartenbe Wm E, laborer Penn Co, res 25 Hough.
Waser Carl R, instrument maker Fort Wayne Electric Co, res
   68 Miner.
Washington House, Bernhard Weber Propr, 121 and
   123 Calhoun.
Wass Samuel L, foreman, res 290 E Creighton ave.
Wasserbach Charles C, laborer, res 68 Oakley.
Wasserbach John, Merchant Tailor, 38 Harrison, res
   same.
Wasserman Emma, opr Hoosier Mnfg Co, bds 305 W Main.
Wassman Philip, music tchr, 305 W Main, bds same.

Waterbeck John C, butcher Kabisch & Son, res 68 Oakley.
Waterbeck John Z, machine hand American Wheel Co, bds 68 Oakley.
Waterhous Edward (Waterhous & Bro), res w s Spy Run ave 2 n of St Mary's bridge.
Waterhous John H (Waterhous & Bro), res 55 Barr.
Waterhous & Bro (John H and Edward), blacksmiths, s e cor Columbia and Clay.
Waterhouse Arthur E, lumber, res 145 W Berry.
Waterhouse Margaret (wid John), bds Mary Dolan.
Waterman George H, traveling agt G E Bursley & Co, res 41 Home ave.
Waterman John H, res 234 W Washington.
Waters Clara, domestic 377 Fairfield ave.
Waters James, farmer, res 63 Elizabeth.
Waters Kendall R, printer Fort Wayne Newspaper Union, res 78 Wells.
Waters Mary E, nurse, bds 142 Jackson.
Waters Robert K, compositor, res 78 Wells.
Waters Sarah W (wid John A), res cor Thompson and Wabash R R.
Watkins John A, carpenter, res 35 Grand.
Watkins Lewis T, switchman Nickel Plate, res 368 W Main.
Watkins Sylvester E, carpenter, res 581 S Broadway.
Watkins Wm W, barber N C Browand, bds Robert S Swenson.
Watson James, machinist Penn Co, res 28 Stophlet.
Watson Maria (wid Henry), res 135 Madison.
Watson Walter W, despatcher G R & I R R, res 113 E Washington.
Watt Wm H (McDonald, Watt & Wilt), res 229 W Berry.
Watterson David W, conductor, res 66 Wells.
Watterson Wm F, conductor, res n e cor Howell and Rumsey.
Waugh Charles R, brakeman, res 459 Lafayette.
Waugh J Edward, dentist, 74 Calhoun, res 295 W Wayne.
Wavada Mary (wid Louis), res 14 Brandriff.
Wayne Paint and Painting Co, James Wilding & Son proprs, 193 Calhoun.
Wayne Stables, John G Hooper Propr, 13 and 15 Pearl. Telephone 41.
Wayne Street M E Church, s w cor Broadway and W Wayne.
Wayne The, Wm M McKinnie & Co Proprs, Columbia bet N Calhoun and Harrison.
Weaver Mrs Carrie, res 356 Calhoun.
Weaver Charles, carpenter, res 12 Clark.

Weaver Charles, teamster Winch & Son, res e s Grant ave 1
s of Maumee road.

Weaver Charles W, trav agent B W Skelton, res 89 W Jefferson.

Weaver Ephraim, teamster, res Maumee rd 1 e of Glasgow av.

Weaver Equa C, laborer White's Wheel Works, res Euclid
ave 2 s of Maumee road.

Weaver Frank, bds 110 W Main.

Weaver Freedom G, tinsmith Penn Co, res 146 E Lewis.

Weaver James F, fireman A Hattersley & Sons, bds 2 Madison.

Weaver John, fireman, bds 164 Broadway.

Weaver John F jr, helper A Hattersley & Sons, res 2 Madison.

Weaver Louis, brakeman Penn Co, res 28 John.

Weaver Mattie, domestic Clifton House.

Weaver Sarah, dressmaker, rms 145 Holman.

Weaver Theodore A, brakeman, res n w cor Pontiac and
Winter.

Weaver Wm F, watchman Fort Wayne Furniture Co, res
w s Spy Run ave 2 s of Elizabeth.

Webb Charles P, ticket broker, 92 Calhoun, res Indianapolis,
Ind.

Webb Marion A, trav agent, res 305 W Washington.

Webb Reuben (Kimball & Webb), res cor Jackson and
Wayne.

Webb Rhoda A (wid Augustus M), res 238 W Wayne.

Webb Samuel L, laborer, bds 211 St Mary's ave.

Webber Henry, molder Bass Foundry and Machine Works,
res 30 Oliver.

Webber Mary E (wid Benjamin), bds 787 Broadway.

Webber Milton N, saloon, 3 E Main, res 95 Fulton.

Webber Sophie, domestic 75 Maumee road.

Weber Adam (McNulty & Weber), res 81 Montgomery.

Weber Miss Amelia S, teacher Bloomingdale School, bds 344
E Washington.

Weber Andrew, foreman Penn Co, res 167 Clinton.

Weber Bernard, laborer Penn Co, res 26 Buchanan.

Weber Bernard, Propr Washington House, 121 and
123 Calhoun, and Meat Market 224 Lafayette, res Washington House.

Weber Carl J, deputy city treasurer, bds 167 Clinton.

Weber Charles L (John Weber & Sons, bds 54 W Main.

Weber Clement, clerk G DeWald & Co, bds 81 Montgomery.

Weber Edward, clerk Wm Moellering & Sons, bds 81 Montgomery.

Weber Emma, bds 54 W Main.

Weber Miss Emma C, principal East German School, bds 344 E Washington.

Weber Ferdinand T, foreman molding dept Ft Wayne Iron Works, res 391 E Lewis.

Weber Frank, cigarmaker, res 275 E Wayne.

Weber Frank A, assistant street commissioner, res 123 Maumee road.

Weber Frederick, carpenter, res e s Comparet, bet E Wayne and E Washington.

Weber Frederick, laborer, res 55 Hugh.

Weber Frederick J, cabinetmaker Ft Wayne Furniture Co, res 358 E Wayne.

Weber George, car builder Penn Co, res 5 Fletcher.

Weber Heinrika (wid John J), res 344 E Washington.

Weber Henry, molder Kerr-Murray Mnfg Co, bds Henry Gardt.

Weber Henry, tuner Ft Wayne Organ Co, res 56 Nelson.

Weber Jacob, wiper Penn Co, res 108 John.

Weber John (John Weber & Sons) res 54 W Main.

Weber John, molder, bds 289 Hanna.

Weber John, res 275 E Wayne.

Weber John jr, driver John Ruppel, bds 275 E Wayne.

Weber John B (John Weber & Sons), res Decatur, Ind.

Weber John F, painter Olds' Wagon Works, bds 108 John.

Weber John & Sons (John, John B and Charles L), sale stable, 21 Pearl.

Weber Joseph, helper, bds 231 Barr.

Weber Lena, bds 54 W Main.

Weber Linus, stone cutter George Jaap, res 64 Chicago.

Weber Louis, helper A Hattersley & Sons, bds 37 Colerick.

Weber Miss Louisa, bds 344 E Washington.

Weber Mark, machine hand G K Hubbard, bds 37 Colerick.

Weber Minnie, domestic 270½ Calhoun.

Weber Noah, hostler John Weber & Sons, bds 54 W Main.

Weber Peter, stone mason, res 308 W Jefferson.

Weber Pierce, plumber, bds 37 Colerick.

Weber Rosa, bds 54 W Main.

Weber Rosa, converter worker Ft Wayne Electric Co, bds 37 Colerick.

Weber Tegla (wid Louis), res 37 Colerick.

Weber Theodore G A, bds 344 E Washington.

Weber Theresa, bds 81 Montgomery.

Weber Valentine, molder Fort Wayne Iron Works, bds 81 Montgomery.

Weber Wm, cigarmaker H W Ortmann, res 80 N Harrison.

Weberruss John J, shoemaker, n s Wagner 5 w of St Joseph river, res same.

Webster Wm H, laborer The Remington-Lawton Co, res 202 E DeWald.

Wechterman Frederick, boilermaker, bds 368 E Lewis.

Wechterman Wm, carpenter, res 368 E Lewis.

Wechterman Wm jr, coremaker, bds 368 E Lewis.

Wedler Herman J, laborer, res 150 Smith.

Weedler Gustav, painter Olds' Wagon Works, res n w cor Hayden and Division.

Weedler Theodore, helper, res n s Hayden nr Harmer.

Weeks George H, car painter Penn Co, res 149 Wallace.

Weers Alonzo S, laborer, res 574 Lafayette.

Weesner Samuel, driver Fort Wayne Transfer and Storage Co, bds 125 Harrison.

Wefel Adolph J, tinsmith Penn Co, res 21 E Washington.

Wefel Anna, domestic 271 W Wayne.

Wefel August, carriage painter M L Albrecht, bds 161 High.

Wefel Charlotte (wid Frederick W), res 161 High.

Wefel Edward, laborer, res 91 W Jefferson.

Wefel Frederick W, blacksmith, res 41 Barthold.

Wefel Frederick W A, car repairer Wabash R R, res 163 High.

Wefel Gibson, works J H Adams, bds 21 E Washington.

Wefel John, laborer, res 73 W 4th.

Wefel John W, carpenter J Wagner, res 168 High.

Wefel Martin H, Druggist, 314 Hanna, res 297 same.

Wefel Wilhelmina (wid John H), res 41 Barthold.

Wehler Charles F, timber buyer Hoffman Bros, res 19 Burgess.

Wehnert Charles F, cabinetmaker Fort Wayne Furniture Co, res 43 Wagner.

Wehnert Frederick, shoemaker, 283 W Main, res same.

Wehnert Frederick E, shoemaker Gottlieb Knobel, res 295 W Main.

Wehnert Johanna, domestic 252 W Wayne.

Wehnert Wm, shoemaker 317½ W Main, res same.

Wehr Frederick, carpenter, res 391 W Main.

Wehr Henry, laborer Horton Mnfg Co, res 391 W Main.

Wehrmister August, laborer, res 187 John.

Wehrmister Emil, laborer, bds 187 John.

Wehrmister Robert, helper Bass Foundry and Machine Wks, bds 187 John.

Wehrs Annie M (wid Frederick), res 122 W Jefferson.

Wehrs Henry H, laborer, res 56 E Main.

Wehrs John, laborer, res 144 High.

Wehrs Wm H, machinist Penn Co, res 35 Hough.

Wehrs Wm J D, res 133 E Lewis.

Weibel Frederick, windmills and pumps, 9 Harrison, res 479 S Broadway.

Weichselfelder Charles, bds e s Franklin ave 1 n of Lake.

Weichselfelder George J, tallyman N Y, C & St L R R, res n w cor Lake and Franklin ave.

Weick Jacob, car builder Penn Co, res 71 Buchanan.

Weick Philip M, laborer, res 173 Wells.

Weidemann, *see Wiedemann.*

Weidenmier Peter, baker, rms 362 W Main.

Weidke Henry, cooper, res 84 Lewis.

Weidner Michael, clerk Philip Graf, bds 401 Lafayette.

Weidner Nicholas, teamster Standard Oil Co, res s s Jessie e of Runnion ave.

Weigant John, laborer Bass Foundry and Machine Works, bds 88 Hayden.

Weiger F, laborer Penn Co, res 363 E Lewis.

Weigman Henry, car repairer Penn Co, res Adams twp.

Weigmann Frederick H, clerk, res 200 E Jefferson.

Weihe Emil, clerk Meyer Bros & Co, 123 Madison.

Weik Edward, deliverer A J Dittoe & Co, bds 266 E Washington.

Weik Joseph, deliverer A J Dittoe & Co, bds 266 E Washington.

Weikart Curtis, works Indiana School for Feeble-Minded Youth.

Weikart Jacob, bartender George Noirot, rms 49 E Main.

Weikart James, carpenter, res 25 Wagner.

Weikart James T, clerk F D Paulus, res n s Wagner 10 e of Spy Run ave.

Weiker Jacob J, cabinetmaker Fort Wayne Organ Co, res 144 Taber.

Weil, *see also Wile.*

Weil Abraham (Weil Bros & Co), bds 53 W Wayne.

Weil Bros & Co (Abraham and Isaac), hides, 92 E Columbia.

Weil George, cabinetmaker Fort Wayne Organ Co, res 314 Broadway.

Weil Isaac (Weil Bros & Co), res 47 W Wayne.

Weil Jacob, res 53 W Wayne.

Weil Jennie, bookkeeper Weil Bros & Co, bds 53 W Wayne.

Weil John, bartender G Geller, res 96 Broadway.

Weil Wm, machinist Penn Co, res 305 Calhoun.

Weiler Charles, agent Prudential Life Ins Co, res 70 W 3d.

Weiler Charles J, cabinetmaker Louis Diether & Bro, res 129½ W 3d.

Weiler Martin, lab Kerr-Murray Mnfg Co, res 133 Madison.

Weils Henry J, teamster, res 14 Barthold.

John Pressler, Hot Air and Hot Water Furnaces.
Columbia, Barr and Dock Streets.

546   R. L. POLK & CO.'S

Weimar Charles, carpenter, res 144 E Creighton.

Weimer Frank, bds 46 E Jefferson.

Weimer George A, baker C H Waltemath & Sons, res 85 Buchanan.

Weimer John, painter, res 154 E Creighton ave.

Weimester August, lab Bass Foundry and Machine Works, res 187 John.

Weinder Michael, res 173 Wells.

Weininger Joseph, laborer, res 206 Broadway.

Weipert August, laborer Ranke & Yergens, bds 99 Hoffman.

Weipert Frederick, carpenter, res 101 Hoffman.

Weipert Michael J, carpenter, res 99 Hoffman.

Weipert Reinhard, engineer Ranke & Yergens, res 59 Pfeiffer.

Weis Annie, dressmaker, bds 67 Charles.

Weis Justin, laborer, res e s Coombs n of Nickel Plate R R.

Weisbaker George, bartender Peter Certia, res 73 3d.

Weise Emanuel, pedler, res 74 Maumee rd.

Weise Flora, grocer, 74 Maumee rd, res same.

Weise Gottlieb, laborer Bass Foundry and Machine Works, res 80 John.

Weise Henrietta, clerk Flora Weise, bds 74 Maumee rd.

Weise Richard, mach hand American Wheel Co, bds 80 John.

Weisell Miss Carrie, bds 311 W Jefferson.

Weisell David D (D D Weisell & Son), res 311 W Jefferson.

Weisell D D & Son (David D and W Ellis), Dentists, 34 Calhoun.

Weisell Gearis, bds 311 W Jefferson.

Weisell W Ellis, M D (D D Weisell & Son), bds 311 W Jefferson.

Weisenberger Daniel, musician, res 44 Charles.

Weisenberger Valentine, laborer, res s e cor Wiebke and Lafayette.

Weisenburger Catherine (wid Valentine), res 44 Charles.

Weisenburger Benjamin, teamster, res 126 W 3d.

Weismantel Frank, driver F M Smith & Co, bds 100 Union.

Weismantel Mary M, tailoress A F Schoch, bds 100 Union.

Weist Frances, domestic 519 E Washington.

Weist Ursula (wid Henry), bds 26 Buchanan.

Weitzmann Miss Clara, bds 182 Jackson.

Weitzmann Felix T, tailor F T Weitzmann, res 13 Nirdlinger ave.

Weitzmann F Theobald, Merchant Tailor, 162 Calhoun, res 182 Jackson.

Weitzmann Miss Ida, bds 182 Jackson.

Weitzmann Miss Maggie, bds 182 Jackson.

Weitzmann Max O, tailor F T Weitzman, bds 182 Jackson.
Weitzmann Paul T, tailor F T Weitzman, bds 182 Jackson.
Welch, *see also Walsh and Welsh.*
Welch Alice, bds 130 Erie.
Welch Charles E, roofer J H Welch, bds 84 W Creighton av.
Welch Charles H, fireman, bds 175 Fairfield ave.
Welch Daniel L, trimmer City Carriage Works, res 71 Maumee road.
Welch George F, laborer, bds 84 W Creighton ave.
Welch Hannah, domestic Wayne Hotel.
Welch John, boilermaker Nickel Plate, res 8 Orchard.
Welch John, laborer Penn Co, res 36 Bass.
Welch John H, roofer, 190 Calhoun, res 84 W Creighton ave.
Welch John J, machinist Kerr-Murray Mnfg Co, bds 84 W Creighton ave.
Welch John S, brakeman, res 298 E Creighton ave.
Welch Joseph, brakeman, res 19 Euclid ave.
Welch Louis, laborer, res 31 Duck.
Welch Mary E (wid George W), res 175 Fairfield ave.
Welch Michael, laborer, res 130 Erie.
Welch Michael, laborer, res 174 Hoffman.
Welch Miss Ricka, bds 22 Brackenridge.
Weldon Francis R, clerk Penn Co, res 395 S Calhoun.
Welker, *see also Walker.*
Welker Charles J, clerk Stewart & Hahn, bds 21 W Jefferson.
Welker Daniel, carpenter, res 19 Hoffman.
Welker George J, upholsterer P E Wolf, res 67 Garden.
Welker Henry, cabinetmaker, res 59 Wall.
Welker Louis, finisher Fort Wayne Furniture Co, res n w cor Oakland and Spring.
Welker Maria (wid Ernst), bds 59 Wall.
Welkin John jr, brakeman, res 44 Taylor.
Welkin Mary A (wid John), bds 44 Taylor.
Weller Barbara (wid Christian), res 76 E Wayne.
Weller Charles W, meat market 92 W Jefferson, res same.
Weller Christopher C, operator W U Tel Co, bds 121 Harrison.
Weller Elizabeth D, bds 76 E Wayne.
Weller G Richard, clerk S W Harmon, bds 121 Harrison.
Weller John, res 121 Harrison.
Weller John jr, cigarmaker G F Yergens, bds 121 Harrison.
Weller Rosa, bds 121 Harrison.
Wellick August, laborer, res 43 Putnam.
Welling Frank, clerk, res 149 W Washington.
Wellman Emma, clerk Stewart & Hahn, bds 112 Jackson.
Wellman Charles, helper Penn Co, res 100 Wilt.

Wellman Frederick H, time keeper Kerr-Murray Mnfg Co, bds 112 Jackson.
Wellman Henry (Schone & Wellman), res 44 Pritchard.
Wellman Lizzie, bds 44 Pritchard.
Wellmann Sophie (wid Frederick), res 112 Jackson.
Wellmeier Frederick W, laborer Hoffman Bros, res 229 W Superior.
Wells Miss Alice, music teacher, 205 W Jefferson, bds same.
Wells Mrs Delphine B, Principal Westminster Seminary, res 251 W Main.
Wells George R, harnessmkr, 69 E Main, res same.
Wells James A, mason, res e s Webster 1 s of Marchell.
Wells Jennie, miller Wm Malloy, bds 366 Calhoun.
Wells John T, laborer, res 68 Gay.
Wells John W, fireman, res 1 Pape ave.
Wells Judson W, bookkeeper S F Bowser & Co, res 100 W DeWald.
Wells Julian B, switchman, res 35 Chestnut.
Wells La Motte, tuner Fort Wayne Organ Co, res 111 W Williams.
Wells Maria (wid Arnold), bds 205 W Jefferson.
Wells Martin A, patternmkr Kerr-Murray Mnfg Co, bds 366 Calhoun.
Wells Rachel (wid George), res 26 Grant ave.
Wells Richard, blacksmith American Wheel Co, res w s Harrison 1 s of Killea.
Wells Walter W, clerk Carnahan & Co, bds 251 W Main.
Wells Warren D, Book and Job Printer, 9 and 10 Foster Blk, rooms same. (*See left bottom lines.*)
Welsh, *see also Walsh and Welch.*
Welsh Catherine (wid John), res 73 Grand.
Welsh Ella, domestic 270½ Calhoun.
Welsh Howard G, bds 292 E Lewis.
Welsh James, driver Fort Wayne Transfer and Baggage Line, bds 75 E Superior.
Welsh Mary (wid Joseph), w s Indiana ave 3 s of Home.
Welsh Mary (wid Patrick), res 75 E Superior.
Welsh Michael, laborer, bds 182 E Jefferson.
Welsh Patrick T, engineer, res 441 Lafayette.
Welsh Richard J, trav agt S A Maxwell & Co, Chicago, bds 75 E Superior.
Welsh Thomas, wiper Penn Co, res 100 Montgomery.
Welsheimer Catherine (wid Daniel), bds 158 Madison.
Welsheimer Tillie (wid John M), res 240 W Washington.
Welsheimer Wm T, lawyer, res n w cor Howell and Runnion.
Welten Bertha E, clk A E C Becker, bds 38 Butler.

Welten Carrie E, bookkeeper Gottlieb Haller, bds 38 Butler.

Welten Frederick, engineer, bds 38 Butler.

Welten John, machinist Penn Co, bds 38 Butler.

Welten John B jr, machine hand Fort Wayne Organ Co, bds 38 Butler.

Wendell Ferdinand J, pres The Press, res Columbus, Ohio.

Wendelen Henry, laborer Bass Foundry and Machine Works, res 347 E Washington.

Wendelen Mary, operator Hoosier Mnfg Co, bds 347 E Washington.

Wendt Wm, shoemaker n e cor Gay and E Creighton ave, bds same.

Weninger Agnes (wid Joseph), rms 135 Lafayette.

Weninger Mrs Lilla, res 214 E Jefferson.

Wenker B, car builder Penn Co, res 67 Lillie.

Wenninghoff Christian, Cigar Mnfr, 110 W Jefferson, res same.

Wenninghoff Mollie, bds 18 Fairfield ave.

Wenninghoff Rudolph H, cigarmaker Christian Wenninghoff, res 18 Fairfield ave.

Wenninghoff Miss Sadie, bds 110 W Jefferson.

Wente Christian, plasterer, res 137 John.

Wente Wilhelmina (wid Wm), res 90 Barr.

Wenzel Emma, cook 248 Calhoun.

Wenzel Frederick, clerk Salimonie Mining and Gas Co, res 18 Maiden Lane.

Wenzel Tena, cook 248 Calhoun.

Werd Thomas, helper Wabash R R, bds 224 Calhoun.

Werges Peter, laborer, res 17 St Martin.

Werkmann Edward, cow herder, bds 92 Walton ave.

Werkmann Ernest V, machinist Penn Co, res 44 Charles.

Werkmann Gertrude, domestic Andrew Baepler.

Werkmann John A C, barber Christian Fuchs, bds 92 Walton ave.

Werkmann Philip E, finisher Fort Wayne Organ Co, res 3 Walnut.

Werkmann Philip H, blacksmith Olds' Wagon Works, res 92 Walton ave.

Werkmann Valentine, section hand, res 161 Hayden.

Werkmann Valentine jr, painter Olds' Wagon Works, bds 161 Hayden.

Werkmann Wm F, painter Olds' Wagon Works, res 92 Walton ave.

Wermuth Charles R, carpenter, res 172 Suttenfield.

Werne Gottlieb, bds 47 Buchanan.

Werner, see also Warner and Woerner.

Werner Adolph, laborer American Wheel Co, bds 55 John.

Werner Charles, fireman The Peters Box and Lumber Co, res 112 St Mary's ave.

Werner Henry C, fireman, res 24 Locust.

Werner Louis, cleaner, res 55 John.

Werstein Philip H, clerk Root & Co, res 13 Chestnut.

Wertman Samuel L, sawyer The Peters Box and Lumber Co, res 34 Hoffman.

Wertz Gustave, machinist Indiana Machine Works.

Wery, *see also Whery.*

Wery Charles, carpenter, bds 130 W Williams.

Wery Henry, carpenter, bds 130 W Williams.

Wery John H, medicine mnfr, 132 W Williams, res 130 same.

Wesemann Wm, helper Wabash R R, res 12 Union.

Wesemann Wm H F, molder Bass Foundry and Machine Works, res 262 E Jefferson.

Weshelmann Casper, laborer, bds 164 Harmer.

Wesling August, carpenter, bds 68 Nelson.

Wesner Augustus, engineer, res 42 Thomas.

Wesner Laura A, works Troy Steam Laundry, res 42 Thomas.

Wessel Wm, laborer, res 206 Thomas.

Wessell John, res 401 Lafayette.

Wesson Frederick, gardener, n s St Joe road 3 e of St Joe bridge, res same.

Wesson George, driver Hose Co No 1, res 63 Clinton.

Wesson James, works Indiana School for Feeble-Minded Youth, res w s Parnell ave 1 n of St Joe road.

West Allen T, tel opr Penn Co, res n e cor Barr and Butler.

West German School, e s Webster bet W Washington and W Jefferson.

Westenfeld Ferdinand H, res 138 Force.

Westenfeld Wm F C, clerk F C & J M Parham, res 39 W Williams.

Westerman Harry A, barber, Hotel Randall, res 188 W Superior.

Westerman Harry J, engineer, res 20 Buchanan.

Westermann Frederick W H, boilermaker Bass Foundry and Machine Works, bds 368 E Lewis.

Westermann Wm, coremaker Bass Foundry and Machine Works, bds 368 E Lewis.

Western Gas Construction Co, Olaf N Guldlin Pres, Gordon W Lloyd Vice-Pres and Treas, Detroit, Mich, Frank H Adams Sec, John S Unger Engineer; Gas Engineers and Builders of Coal, Water and Fuel Gas Works and Apparatus, Office 24 to 27 Pixley & Long Bldg.

Western Union Telegraph Co, Oscar L Perry Mngr, Aveline House Block.

Westhoff Wm, bricklayer, res 38 Summit.

Westminster Seminary, Miss Carrie B Sharp and Mrs Delphine B Wells Principals, 251 W Main.

Westminster Seminary Annex for Boys, n w cor W Berry and Griffith.

Westover Addie, operator S M Foster, bds 414 Hanna.

Westphal Frederick, res 173 Montgomery.

Westrumb Henry C F, teamster, res 415 E Washington.

Wetta Herman, laborer, res 141 W 3d.

Wetter Abraham, carpenter, bds 192 E Wayne.

Wetter John, carpenter, bds 192 E Wayne.

Wetzel John W, teamster, res 70 Nirdlinger ave.

Wetzel Wm, helper Winch & Son, res 74 John.

Weyer Anthony, plumber, bds 10 Hoffman.

Weyer Benjamin D, tinsmith Penn Co, res cor 3d and Cass.

Woyer Hattie, bds 10 Hoffman.

Weyer Martin, wiper Penn Co, res 10 Hoffman.

Weyer Mary, bds 10 Hoffman.

Whalen Annie, domestic 33 E Williams.

Whalen Bridget, dressmaker, res 44 Melita.

Whalen John S, molder A Hattersley & Sons, res 222 Hugh.

Whan Joseph, draughtsman, res 43 Baker.

Wharton Charles S, clerk G W Seavey, res 15 Clay.

Wheeler Augustina R, Propr Gospel Tidings Publishing Co, 9 Foster Block, res 24 same.

Wheeler Charles, laborer, res 19 Burgess.

Wheeler Charles, plumber Robert Ogden, res 131 E Washington.

Wheeler Charles A, teamster, res 158 Taylor.

Wheeler Joshua C, market stall No 70, res w s Bluffton road 4 miles n.

Wheeler Nelson, rms 105 W Wayne.

Wheeler Robert B, mach Hoosier Mnfg Co, res 70 Taylor.

Wheelock Kent K, physician, 94 Calhoun, res same.

Whelan Thomas, engineer, res 290 W Main.

Whery, *see also Wery.*

Whery Mary A, Physician and Surgeon; Specialty Womens' Diseases, 26 Madison, res same.

Whery Wm P, physician and sec Fort Wayne College of Medicine, 94 Calhoun, res 26 Madison.

Whistler Robert, machinist, bds 196 Hanna.

Whitacre Mary, dressmaker, 87 N Cass, bds same.

Whitaker Maggie, domestic Windsor Hotel.

White Alexander B, propr A B White Cycle Co, bds 60 Barr.

White Amanda, seamstress D S Redelsheimer & Co, bds 90 Thomas.
White Mrs Anna, dressmaker, 94 Barr, res same.
White A B Cycle Co, A B White propr, 86 Clinton.
White's Block, s e cor Wayne and Calhoun.
White Charles F, trav agt, bds 94 Barr.
White Miss Edith, bds 76 S Wayne ave.
White Edward, clerk J B White and pres Allen County Loan and Savings Association, bds 60 Barr.
White Edward, finisher, bds Matilda Armstrong.
White Edwin B, mach White's Wheel Wks, res 89 E Lewis.
White Enos H, janitor Government bldg, res 76 S Wayne av.
White George I, finisher American Wheel Co, bds 158 Wallace.
White Harry R, cook Randall Hotel.
White Ira C, mach hand Olds' Wagon Works, bds 76 S Wayne.
White James B (White's Wheel Works), Fruit House and Dealer in General Merchandise, 8, 10 and 12 E Wayne, and 97 Calhoun res 60 Barr.
White Jefferson, bds Matilda Armstrong.
White Jesse, bds Matilda Armstrong.
White John, bds Matilda Armstrong.
White John jr, laborer, bds s w cor Glasgow ave and Wayne,
White John I, sec Bass Foundry and Machine Works, bds Aveline House.
White John W (White's Wheel Works), res 128 E Wayne.
White Joseph D, blksmith Penn Co, res e end of New Yards.
White Mrs Kate, bds 73 Grand.
White Luther, flagman Penn Co, res 90 Thomas.
White Roderick W, miller John Orff, res 38 Ewing.
White Taylor, brakeman, res 90 Thomas.
White's Wheel Works (James B and John W White), east end of E Wayne on N Y, C & St L R R.
White Wm, bds Matilda Armstrong.
White Wm J, machinist Penn Co, res 49 E Lewis.
Whitehead Arthur, engineer G R & I R R, res 316 Calhoun.
Whitehead Richard A, bookkeeper Central Mutual Fire Ins Co, rms 196 Calhoun.
Whiteleather James F, teacher, res 469 Harrison.
Whiteley George, bds 106 E Main.
Whiteley Mary (wid Thomas), bds 24 Jones.
Whiteley Thomas R, tailor, 172 W Jefferson, res 24 Jones.
Whiteman Emmet A, apprentice W S Harrison, bds 23 Holman.
Whiteman George W, driver Ft Wayne Street Railroad Co, bds 23 Holman.

Whiteman Hiram, bds 23 Holman.
Whitfield Robert H (col'd), barber, 37 E Columbia, rms same.
Whiting Henry, laborer, bds Hyer House.
Whitlock May, bds 26 Rockhill.
Whitlock Solomon, res 26 Rockhill.
Whitlock Wm P, watchman P, Ft W & C Ry, res 26 Rockhill.
Whitman Louisa, operator, bds 220 Lafayette.
Whitman Maggie, operator Hoosier Mnfg Co, bds 220 Lafayette.
Whitman Mary (wid Sebastian), res 220 Lafayette.
Whitmer Miss Blanche, bds 209 Harrison.
Whitmer Daniel, agent, res 209 Harrison.
Whitmore Merritt, lab Ft Wayne Organ Co, bds 38 Walnut.
Whitney Frank H, engineer, res 36 McClellan.
Whitney J Irving, porter Adams Ex Co, bds 142 Jackson.
Whitney Miranda P (wid Washington I), 142 Jackson.
Whitney Nancy T (wid David), bds 78 Douglas ave.
Whittenberger Wm, canvasser Ft Wayne Gazette, res Clayton.
Whittles Joab, machinist Nickel Plate, res 342 W Main.
Wibke Anna, domestic 27 W Berry.
Wible Mary (wid Thomas), dressmaker, bds 209 Harrison.
Wicher Jacob J, cabinetmaker, res 144 Taber.
Wichman Adolph F, machinist Bass Foundry and Machine Works, bds John Betzinger.
Wichman Agnes, bds 30 Schick.
Wichman Albert C F, supt Anthony Wayne Mnfg Co, res 219 Madison.
Wichman Albert O, bricklayer, bds 219 Madison.
Wichman Miss Emma, milliner, 164 Calhoun, bds 219 Madison.
Wichman Herman, machinist, res 42 Division.
Wichman John T, machinist Bass Foundry and Machine Works, res 27 Schick.
Wichman Lena, clerk Stewart & Hahn, bds 219 Madison.
Wichman Theodore G, laborer, bds 26 Dubois.
Wick Philip, harnessmaker G H Kuntz, res 8 Ewing.
Wickliff Isaac, painter, bds Lake Shore Hotel.
Wickliffe Branson B, plasterer, res n s Grace ave 2 w of Miner.
Wickliffe Franklin P, car builder Penn Co, res 226 Hugh.
Wickliffe Frederick, laborer Fort Wayne Transfer and Storage Co, bds 28 W Main.
Wickliffe Jane B, propr Oliver House, 107 E Columbia.
Wickliffe John, carpenter, res 103 Wells.
Wickliffe Prince A, painter Olds' Wagon Works, bds 103 Wells.

Wideman Anna, domestic 401 Lafayette.
Wiebke August H, feeder Archer, Housh & Co, bds 92 Barr.
Wiebke Henry, laborer Ranke & Yergens, res 92 Barr.
Wiebke Henry A (Mannix & Weibke), bds 92 Barr.
Wiebke Sophie, domestic 322 Fairfield ave.
Wiebke Wm C, bartender, bds 92 Barr.
Wiebke Wm H, bookkeeper Fort Wayne Organ Co, res s s
    Richardsville ave bet Broadway and Fairfield ave.
Wiedburck Desdemona A (wid Christian), res 90 Barr.
Wiedelman Henry, machine hand White's Wheel Works,
    bds 16 Liberty.
Wiedelman Louisa, domestic Rudolph Bischoff.
Wiedelman Wm, lab, bds E Liberty bet Begue and Coombs.
Wiedemann Caspar, foreman Bass Foundry and Machine
    Works, res 370 E Washington.
Wiedemann Frederick H, machine hand J C Peters, res n s
    Rebecca 2 n of Tyler.
Wiedemann Herman, laborer, res n s Rebecca w of Runnion.
Wiedemann Joseph, laborer Penn Co, res 347 Lafayette.
Wiedemann Ulrich, whitewasher, res 347 Lafayette.
Wiedemeier Frank, laborer, res 38 Wall.
Wiedemeier Joseph, tailor, bds 38 Wall.
Wiedman Charles, bds G W Beberstine.
Wiedman Charles, car builder Penn Co, res 130 Walton ave.
Wiedman Charles, carpenter, bds Washington House.
Wiedman John, wagonmaker, bds Washington House.
Wiedman Martin A, car builder Penn Co, res s s Rudisill
    ave 2 w of Piqua ave.
Wiedman Mary (wid Sebastian), res 220 Lafayette.
Wiegand Frank, car builder Penn Co, res 118 Eliza.
Wiegand Henry, mantel setter John Pressler, res 219 E Jef-
    ferson.
Wiegand John W, pattern maker Fort Wayne Electric Co,
    res 343 Lafayette.
Wiegand Lizzie, operator S M Foster, bds 343 Lafayette.
Wiegand Otto H, draughtsman Wing & Mahurin, bds 343
    Lafayette.
Wiegand Regina, bds 343 Lafayette.
Wiegand Sebastian, carpenter, res 343 Lafayette.
Wiegand Wm F, finisher Fort Wayne Organ Co, bds w s
    Brooklyn ave w of St Mary's River.
Wieger Frederick, laborer Penn Co, bds 363 E Lewis.
Wiegmann Charles (H Wiegmann & Sons), bds Henry Wieg-
    mann.
Wiegmann Frederick, clk G DeWald & Co, res 200 E Jeffer-
    son.

Stahn & Heinrich, **Booksellers and Stationers,**
Schmitz Block News Stand, 116 Calhoun Street.

FORT WAYNE DIRECTORY. 555

Wiegmann Henry (H Wiegmann & Sons), res n s Mayville
rd 1 mile e of Maumee bridge.
Wiegmann Henry jr (H Wiegmann & Sons), bds 199 La-
fayette.
Wiegmann Hermann W (Wiegmann & Franke), res 399 W
Main.
Wiegmann H & Sons (Henry, Henry Jr, Charles and
Wm), Grocers and Bakers, 199 Lafayette.
Wiegmann Matilda M, tailoress G Scheffler, bds 403 W Main.
Wiegmann Michael, janitor, res 30 Rockhill.
Wiegmann Wm (H Wiegmann & Sons), bds Henry Wieg-
mann.
Wiegmann Wm, laborer, res 403 W Main.
Wiegmann & Franke (Herman W Wiegmann, Charles Franke),
carpenters, s e cor Broadway and Taylor.
Wiehe Charles, core maker Bass Foundry and Machine Wks,
res 84 Gay.
Wiehe Emil, clerk, res 294 E Lewis.
Wiehe Minnie, domestic A Aehnelt.
Wiehl John, harness maker G H Kuntz, bds 81 Holman.
Wiekman Wm, machine hand Horton Mnfg Co, res 403 W
Main.
Wieman Kate (wid Wm), res 102 E Lewis.
Wieman Wm E, bds 102 E Lewis.
Wieneke Charles, harnessmaker G H Kuntz, bds 12 Rockhill.
Wieneke Frederick, shoemaker, 317½ W Main, res 12 Rock-
hill.
Wieneke Herman, broommaker Robert Gage, bds 12 Rockhill.
Wieneke Wm F, sorter, res 31 Laselle.
Wies, *see also Weis and Wise.*
Wies Annie, bds 6 Gay.
Wies Jacob, carpenter, res 6 Gay.
Wiese Henry A, engineer C Tresselt & Sons, res 367 W
Main.
Wiese Henry A jr, bookkeeper Salimonie Mining and Gas Co,
bds 367 W Main.
Wiesenberg August, janitor St Paul German Lutheran
Church, res 45 Hugh.
Wiesmann Eugene, clerk Wm Hoch, bds 313 Lafayette.
Wiesmantle Lena (wid Frank), res 104 Barr.
Wiesner Edward, butcher, bds 313 Lafayette.
Wiesner Peter N, lab Olds' Wagon Works, bds 327 Hanna.
Wigand John, laborer, res 73 Smith.
Wiggins Albert D, brakeman Penn Co, res 75 Smith.
Wiggins Jennie, domestic 58 Thomas.
Wigmann Miss Sophia, bds 23 Wilt.

Wikel Samuel A, gen'l freight agent Ft W, C & L R R, res 287 W Berry.

Wilbert David H, fireman, res 334 Calhoun.

Wilcox Clarence H, mach Fort Wayne Electric Co, bds 322 Broadway.

Wilcox O Royal, brakeman, bds 219 Lafayette.

Wilcox Pauline M (wid Isaac), res 322 Broadway.

Wilde Jacob, res 103 Wallace.

Wilder Amelia (wid August), bds 324 E Washington.

Wilder Joseph H, res 127 W Wayne.

Wilder Wm, fireman, rms 36 Baker.

Wilder Wilson W, switchman, res 78 Baker.

Wildermood Jennie, domestic 9 E Wayue.

Wilding Charles A, sec Tri-State Building and Loan Association, bds 260 W Wayne.

Wilding Miss Emma, bds 100 Fairfield ave.

Wilding James (James Wilding & Son), res 260 W Wayne.

Wilding James W (James Wilding & Son), res 132 Fairfield.

Wilding James & Son (James and James W), Wood and Coal; also Painters and Painters' Supplies, 193 Calhoun.

Wildtman Jacob, laborer George DeWald, bds same.

Wile, *see also Weil.*

Wile Isaac (Isaac Wile & Co), bds Aveline House.

Wile Isaac & Co (Isaac Wile), liquors, 8 Calhoun.

Wiley, *see also Willey.*

Wiley Lewis, laborer, res n w cor Lillie and Maumee road.

Wiley O Bird, city engineer, office 68 Barr, bds McKinnie House.

Wiley Sarah J (wid Alexander), res e s Savannah 2 n of Pontiac.

Wilhelm George S, clk Nickel Plate, res 220 W Washington.

Wilhelm George W, teamster, res 12 Short.

Wilhelm Henry, salesman, res 259 E Washington.

Wilhelm Mrs M L, Mnfr of Madame Cosper's Reliable Hair Preparation, 259 E Washington, res same.

Wilkens Bros (Charles, Christian and Jacob V), butchers, 112 Broadway and w s of Broadway nr Huestis ave.

Wilkens Catherine (wid Christian), res 116 Broadway.

Wilkens Charles (Wilkens Bros), bds 116 Broadway.

Wilkens Christian (Wilkens Bros), bds 116 Broadway.

Wilkens Herman, laborer, res s e cor Oakland and Aboit.

Wilkens Jacob V (Wilkens Bros), res 73 Wilt.

Wilkens John, clerk Wilkens Bros, bds 116 Broadway.

Wilkie Joseph, car builder Penn Co, res 27 Walton ave.

Wilkins Elizabeth, domestic 493 Calhoun.

Wilkins Emma (wid Wm), res 39 Wilt.
Wilkins Oliver P (Wackerman & Wilkins), res n e cor St Martin and Lafayette.
Wilkins Wm, section hand, bds s s New Haven ave 2 e of Lumbard.
Wilkins Wm H, laborer Winch & Son, res s s New Haven av ¼ mile e of junction.
Wilkinson Charity (wid Thomas), res 225 E Wayne.
Wilkinson Edward H, retoucher Felix Schanz, res 68 Walton.
Wilkinson Miss Elvina, clerk, bds s e cor Maumee road and Walton ave.
Wilkinson Frank, chief of police, office City Hall, res 91 Cass.
Wilkinson James, Justice of Peace 231 Calhoun, and Propr Diamond Hotel 233 Calhoun, res same.
Wilkinson John, student, bds 91 N Cass.
Wilkinson John, supt Allen County Asylum, res same.
Wilkinson John E, gate keeper New Haven and Ft Wayne pike, res same.
Wilkinson Mary E, bds 225 E Wayne.
Wilkinson Maude L, bds 113 Lafayette.
Wilkinson Michael, watchman L S & M S Ry, bds Lake Shore House.
Wilkinson Miss Minnie, bds Diamond Hotel.
Wilkinson Thomas A, deputy sheriff, res 113 Lafayette.
Wilkinson Wm, laborer A Hattersley & Sons, res 21 W 4th.
Wilkinson Wilmer W, clerk Police Dept, bds 113 Lafayette.
Will Frank, fireman, bds 126 Calhoun.
Will Thomas H, blacksmith Kerr-Murray Mnfg Co, res 126 Calhoun.
Willett Charles G, clerk Dreier & Bro, res 98 E Jefferson.
Willey George B, editorial writer Daily News, bds 316 E Jefferson.
Williams Miss Addie H, tchr Hanna School, bds 61 Douglas.
Williams Allen H, bds Hamilton homestead.
Williams Benjamin, bricklayer, res 25 Duck.
Williams Charles, cigarmaker, bds 86 Montgomery.
Williams Creighton, bds Hamilton homestead.
Williams Dan N, insptr Hoffman Bros, res 5 Fulton.
Williams Daniel D, clerk Isaac Lauferty, res 46 W Lewis.
Williams David M, bds 50 W Washington.
Williams Edward, paver, bds 29 E Main.
Williams Edward P, office s w cor Clinton and Berry, bds 96 W Wayne.
Williams Effingham T (George DeWald & Co), res 132 E Main.
Williams Henry C, barber J W Brown, bds 87 Wells.

38

Williams Henry M (Beaver, Miller & Co), office s w cor Clinton and Berry, bds s e cor Lewis and Clinton.

Williams James B, real estate and insurance, 8 Schmitz blk, rms same.

Williams James H, brakeman, res 167 High.

Williams Jefferson, farmer, rms 52 Barr.

Williams Jeremiah, janitor Medical College, res 52 Barr.

Williams John A, laborer, res 87 Wills.

Williams John W, filer Hoffman Bros, bds 5 Fulton.

Williams Jordan D, auditor, res 50 W Washington.

Williams Joshua J, tie inspector, res 29 Butler.

Williams Lewis S, lumber inspector Fort Wayne Organ Co, res 197 W De Wald.

Williams Mrs Lizzie (Rowe & Williams), res 50 W Washington.

Williams Mary (wid David), bds 143 Force.

Williams Mrs Mary H, bds Hamilton homestead.

Williams Park, s s W Creighton ave bet Webster and Hoagland ave.

Williams Peter, laborer, res 5 Pine.

Williams Samuel, clerk Custer House.

Williams Susan C (wid Jesse L), res 96 W Wayne.

Williams Thomas, blacksmith, res 74 Maumee road.

Williams Thomas, helper Penn Co, res 109 Hayden.

Williams Thomas (col'd), waiter, rms 227 W Washington.

Williams Wm D, driver Troy Steam Laundry, res 49 W Jefferson.

Williamson Andrew J, cooper, s e cor Wheeler and Runnion ave, res same.

Williamson Charles, cigarmaker Schele Bros, bds 86 Montgomery.

Williamson Edward J, paperhanger L O Hull, bds Columbia House.

Williamson Henry L, foreman job office Fort Wayne Gazette, bds 120 Harrison.

Williamson James S, cooper, bds A J Williamson.

Williamson Jennie, bds A J Williamson.

Williamson Jessie A, bds A J Williamson.

Williamson John R, machinist, bds 29 E Main.

Williamson Louis E, sawyer Old Fort Mnfg Co, res 332 Hanna.

Williard Miss Ella R, teacher Harmer School, bds 45 Madison.

Williard Joseph C, trav agt, bds 45 Madison,

Williard Miss Mary, teacher, bds 45 Madison.

Williard Rachel A (wid Bianchinia L P), res 45 Madison.

Willis Augustus, pedler, res 137 High.

Willson Harry L, clerk, bds 59 Oakley.

Willson Martin S, dynamo tester Fort Wayne Electric Co, res 59 Oakley.

Willson Oscar J, chief clerk Wabash R R, res 217 W Wayne.

Wilsey Wm C, laborer, res 76 E Columbia.

Wilson Alexander, steam fitter Penn Co, res 46 Park ave S Wayne.

Wilson Miss Carrie A, bds 221 W Berry.

Wilson Clarence E, laborer Penn Co, bds 42 Miner.

Wilson Columbus T, barber Beninghoff & Futter, bds 13 Colerick.

Wilson David, brakeman Penn Co, res 58 Smith.

Wilson Mrs Delia F, teacher, res 42 Miner.

Wilson Edward M (Schrader & Wilson), bds 149 Griffith.

Wilson Frank, painter, bds Monroe House.

Wilson Frank P, driver, res 52 Hillside ave.

Wilson Frank W, train despatcher G R & I R R, res 76 Brackenridge.

Wilson George, saw repairer, 177 Calhoun, res 238 W Creighton ave.

Wilson George jr, saw repairer George Wilson, bds 238 W Creighton ave.

Wilson George C, carpenter, res 23 W 4th.

Wilson George H (George H Wilson & Sons), res 221 W Berry.

Wilson George H, checker Penn Co, res 42 Miner.

Wilson George H & Sons (George H and George W), stoves, 31 E Columbia.

Wilson George M, telegraph operator, bds Aldine Hotel.

Wilson George W (George H Wilson & Sons), bds 221 W Berry.

Wilson Hattie A, bds 118 Hanna.

Wilson Henry D, laborer, bds 59 Grand.

Wilson Jacob L, fireman, res 59 Grand.

Wilson John (John Wilson & Sons), res 117 Hanna.

Wilson John, laborer, bds 64 E Berry.

Wilson John, lab Hoffman Bros, bds s s Hoffman 4 w of Short.

Wilson John C (John Wilson & Sons), res 25 Hamilton.

Wilson John W, teamster David Tagtmeyer, res 81 W Superior.

Wilson John & Sons (John, Walter B and John C), Dealers in Coal, Coke, Kindling, Wood, Charcoal, Drain Tile and Lumber, Chestnut and Railroad near Calhoun.

Wilson Miss Julia E, bds 221 W Berry.

Wilson Miss Laura A, bds 221 W Berry.

Wilson Louisa (wid Judson), res 62 Wilt.

Wilson Miss Mary, bds 217 W Wayne.
Wilson Mrs Mary L, dressmaker, 16 Hamilton, res same.
Wilson Orra L, brakeman, res 91 W Main.
Wilson Oscar J, clerk, res 217 W Wayne.
Wilson Miss Sarah E, bds 67 Brackenridge.
Wilson Talbot M, carpenter, bds 13 Colerick.
Wilson Thomas W, lawyer 31 Calhoun, res 13 Colerick.
Wilson Walter B (John Wilson & Sons), res 118 Harrison.
Wilson Miss Winifred M, bds 217 W Wayne.
Wilt Franklin P (McDonald, Watt & Wilt), res 306 S Cal-
    houn.
Wiman, see Wiemann.
Wimmer Frank L, printer Fort Wayne Sentinel, bds 46 E Jef-
    ferson.
Wimmer Henry, molder Bass Foundry and Machine Works,
    bds 56 Smith.
Winans Theodore O, agent Metropolitan Mnfg Co, rms 93 W
    Berry.
Winbaugh Bertha, bookkeeper City Book Bindery, bds 1
    Jennison.
Winbaugh George W, Propr City Book Bindery and
    Paper Box Mnfr, 13 E Main, res 117 Gay.
Winbaugh Miss Henrietta, teacher Harmer School, bds 248
    E Lewis.
Winbaugh John F, printer Fort Wayne Sentinel, bds 1 Hol-
    ton ave.
Winbaugh Minnie, converter worker Fort Wayne Electric
    Co, bds Arminda M McCaffery.
Winch Calvin J (Winch & Son), res 300 Maumee road.
Winch Miss Daisy M, bds 300 Maumee road.
Winch Fanny M, bds 300 Maumee road.
Winch Homer D (Winch & Son), res 306 Maumee road.
Winch Howard T, clerk Winch & Son, bds 300 Maumee rd.
Winch Jessie M, bds 300 Maumee road.
Winch Mildred, bds 300 Maumee road.
Winch Sherman P, bookkeeper Winch & Son, bds 300 Mau-
    mee road.
Winch Willard E, rms 306 Maumee road.
Winch & Son (Calvin J and Homer D), Hub and Spoke
    Mnfrs, s w cor Wabash R R and Winch.
Winck Helena (wid John), res 121 Madison.
Windsor Bertha, bds 40 McClellan.
Windsor Clara, bds 40 McClellan.
Windsor Hotel, Mary A Franz propr, 302 Calhoun.
Windsor Wm H, engineer, res 40 McClellan.
Wineke Wm F, foreman American Wheel Co, res 31 Laselle.

Wineken Ferdinand J L, with Underhill's Monumental Wks, res 133 Wallace.

Wing John F (Wing & Mahurin), res 37 W Creighton ave.

Wing & Mahurin (John F Wing, Marshall S Mahurin), architects, 41 and 42 Pixley & Long bldg.

Wingate Catherine (wid John), bds 11 Gay.

Winget Fremont, fireman, res 336 Harrison.

Winget Wm, watchman P, Ft W & C R R, res 114 W Creighton.

Winkelmeyer Bros (Henry jr and Wm F), livery, 44 W Main.

Winkelmeyer Charles, clerk, rms 94 Calhoun.

Winkelmeyer Henry, bds 81 W Superior.

Winkelmeyer Henry jr (Winkelmeyer Bros), res 81 W Superior.

Winkelmeyer Wm F (Winkelmeyer Bros), res 84 W Jefferson.

Winkle Thomas, boilermkr Bass Foundry and Machine Wks, bds 418 W Washington.

Winkler Charles, lab Bass Foundry, res s s Hartman cor Evans.

Winkler Charles H, laborer Penn Co, res 3 Pine.

Winslow Miss Annie, res 20 Francis.

Winslow Gerney (col'd), barber 176 Broadway, res 68 Chicago.

Winslow Kate M, bds 35 Fairfield ave.

Winstanley Jasper, cash Empire Line, bds 293 W Jefferson.

Winston Miss Clark, teacher Indiana School for Feeble-Minded Youth.

Winte Henry D, collector Fort Wayne Sentinel, bds 342 Calhoun.

Winte John C, blacksmith 216 Fairfield ave, res 213 same.

Winte John D, car repairer Penn Co, res 342 Calhoun.

Winte Minnie, bds 342 Calhoun.

Winter Amelia, clerk Frederick Winter, bds 103 Maumee rd.

Winter Frederick, grocer 105 Maumee rd, res 103 same.

Winter Stella, teacher, bds 3 Riverside ave.

Winter Wm P, teacher Taylor University, res 277 W Washington.

Winters Jacob, laborer, bds 235 Barr.

Winters Moses, plater n w cor Main and Clinton, res 3 Riverside ave.

Wintle Wm, clerk Dozois, Beadell & Co, bds 343 E Wayne.

Winton George W, gasfitter, res 44 Harrison.

Wirges Peter, laborer Bass Foundry and Machine Works, res 17 St Martin.

Wirsse Catherine (wid Peter), res 174 Jackson.

Wirsse Paulina, bds 174 Jackson.

Wirth George J, tel operator Penn Co, res 322 E Jefferson.
Wirtz John, watchmaker, bds 22 E Columbia.
Wise, *see also Weis and Wies.*
Wise Frank E, clerk, bds 228 W Berry.
Wise Gustav, blacksmith, res 8 Force.
Wise Harry O, bds 228 W Berry.
Wise Isaac, carpenter Penn Co, res 13 Smith.
Wise John, constable, bds 46 Hoagland ave.
Wise Platt J, deputy sheriff, res 228 W Berry.
Wise Wm, Blacksmith, Horseshoer and General Jobber, 363 Calhoun, bds 13 Smith. (*See adv in classified Horseshoers.*)
Wisemer Nicholas, res 112 E Creighton ave.
Wisemer Nicholas jr, machine hand American Wheel Co, bds 112 E Creighton ave.
Wishart Robert, helper Wabash R R, res 242 W De Wald.
Witmer Elias F, cabinetmaker Ft Wayne Furniture Co, res 131 W 3d.
Witmer John, carpenter, res 73 Gay.
Witte Augusta, dressmaker Mary L Sherin, bds 27 Charles.
Witte Christian, car builder Penn Co, res 27 Charles.
Witte Christian, tailor Thieme Bros, res 77 Maumee rd.
Witte Christian J, laborer American Wheel Co, res 203 E Washington,
Witte Clara (wid Frederick), res 203 E Washington.
Witte Edward, clerk Henry Busching, bds 148 Wallace.
Witte Frank, watchman, res 49 Locust.
Witte Frederick, car builder Penn Co, res 178 W Creighton.
Witte Frederick, laborer, res 77 Shawnee ave.
Witte Herman, oiler Penn Co, res 133 W 3d.
Witte Lena, bds 27 Charles.
Witte Louis, wheel molder Bass Foundry and Machine Works, res 130 John.
Witte Wm, brakeman, bds 12 St Mary's ave.
Witte Wm, helper Fort Wayne Electric Co, res 59 Maud.
Wittmack Wm, brakeman, rooms 12 St Mary's ave.
Witzigreuter Max, druggist, 361 W Main, res 27 Elm.
Witzigreuter Max jr, painter City Carriage Works, bds 12 Elm.
Wobrock Oscar, barber, 10 W Berry, res same.
Woebbeking Christian, clerk Fort Wayne Iron Works, bds 195 S Broadway.
Woebbeking Henry C F, tailor Gottlieb Stauffer, bds 195 Broadway.
Woebbeking Wm, clerk Adams & Armstrong, bds 195 Broadway.

Woehnker Benjamin J, bds 209 E Washington.

Woehnker Frank H, armature winder Fort Wayne Electric Co, res 134 Fulton.

Woehnker Frederick, res 263 E Washington.

Woehnker Frederick H, coil winder Fort Wayne Electric Co, res 209 E Washington.

Woehnker Henry J, laborer Penn Co, bds 209 E Washington.

Woehnker Herman T, molder Bass Foundry and Machine Works, res 224 E Wayne.

Woehnker Wm C, coffee roaster Monning & Baker, res 14 Francis.

Woenker Bernard, car builder Penn Co, res 67 Lillie.

Woenker Christian, teamster, res 21 Oak.

Woenker Frank, shoemaker, bks 21 Oak.

Woenker Henry, bds 21 Oak.

Woenker Joseph B, carpenter, res 67 Lillie.

Woerner, *see Warner and Werner.*

Wohlers Sophia, domestic 35 Stophlet.

Wohlfort Miss Martha E, teacher Hanna School, bds 389 Calhoun.

Wohlfort Martha E (wid Rosemund W), res 389 Calhoun.

Wohlfrom Leopold, butcher N B Rowe, res 309 Broadway.

Wolf, *see also Woulfe and Wulf.*

Wolf Abraham, laborer, res 73 W Main.

Wolf August, laborer, bds w s Hanover 3 n of Erie.

Wolf Bessie (wid Leopold), res 1 Dawson.

Wolf Daniel H, carpenter, res 612 E Wayne.

Wolf Edward F, engineer, res 309 W Main.

Wolf Edward W, laborer, bds 612 E Wayne.

Wolf Ella, clerk McKinnie House.

Wolf Frederick H, wheelmaker American Wheel Co, res 87 Force.

Wolf George V, hostler, res 429 E Washington.

Wolf Henry, laborer, res 29 Stophlet.

Wolf Henry, laborer, bds w s Hanover 3 n of Erie.

Wolf Jasper E, conductor Penn Co, res East yards.

Wolf Jasper E jr, asst foreman Winch & Son, bds 612 E Wayne.

Wolf John, brakeman, res n w cor Milan and Savannah.

Wolf Katie, domestic 94 W Wayne.

Wolf Levi, laborer, res 354 W Main.

Wolf Louis (Louis Wolf & Co), res 204 W Berry.

Wolf Louis & Co (Louis Wolf), Dry Goods and Carpets, 54 Calhoun.

Wolf Michael, laborer, res s s Columbia bet Clay and Lafayette.

Wolf Paul E, Mnfr Upholstered Furniture, Mattresses and Awnings and Propr Fort Wayne Carpet Beating Works, 33 and 35 Clinton, res n e cor Liberty and Canal.

Wolf Samuel, clk L Wolf & Co, bds 73 W Main.

Wolf Victor E, Propr Parisian Millinery and Cloak House, 26 Calhoun, res 72 W Jefferson.

Wolf Wm, laborer, res 127 Fairfield ave.

Wolfe Charles H, brakeman, res 237 Barr.

Wolfe Fredericka (wid Edmund), res 105 Fairfield ave.

Wolfe Henry R, machinist Fort Wayne Electric Co, res 105 W Jefferson.

Wolff Albert A, wks Jenney Electric Light and Power Co, res 18 W 3d.

Wolff C Henry, shoemaker, bds 18 W 3d.

Wolff Ella, dressmaker, rms 53 W Lewis.

Wolff Henry, laborer, res w s Hanover nr Leikauf's Packing House.

Wolford Charles H, teamster, res 228 Lafayette.

Wolford Dennis A, punchman Penn Co, res 48 Miner.

Wolford George L, finisher Fort Wayne Organ Co, res 134 Fairfield ave.

Wolford James, machine hand, res 250 Erie.

Wolford Rush R, helper Penn Co, bds 408 Hanna.

Wolford Wm A, machinist Penn Co, res 408 Hanna.

Wolfrum Adam W, carpenter, bds Edward Waterhous.

Wolfrum John, carpet weaver, 92 Fairfield ave, res same.

Wolfrum John A, fireman, bds 92 Fairfield ave.

Wolfsifer Alfred, clk C W Weller, bds 92 W Jefferson.

Wolke Block, s w cor Calhoun and Wayne.

Wolke Wm, laborer George Jaap, bds 78 Plum.

Wolke Wm F, carpenter, res 19 Wall.

Wollert Rudolph, car repairer, res 147 High.

W C T U Hall, w s Harrison 1 s of W Wayne.

Women's Free Reading Room (1,300 Volumes), Laura Goshorn Librarian ; Open from 9 a m to 9 p m, 23½ W Wayne.

Wonderland The, F D Clarke Propr, J S McKenzie Mngr; Wholesale and Retail Dealer in Notions, Crockery, Glassware, Tinware, Woodenware, Jewelry, Furnishing Goods, Hats and Caps, etc, 5 E Main.

Wood Frank C, clerk Coombs & Co, res s s Grace ave nr Broadway.

Wood George, carpenter, bds 29 Buchanan.

Wood Hester A (wid George W), res 50 W Superior.

Woodard Caroline M (wid Wm), bds 50 W Superior.

Woodard John W, frescoe painter S O Hull, res 320 Calhoun.

Woodruff Wm H, grocer, s e cor Creighton ave and Winter, res same.

Woods George, carpenter, bds 301 Calhoun.

Woods James, painter, bds 10 E Berry.

Woods Robert, laborer, bds 408 W Main.

Woods Wm, slater J H Welch, bds Washington House.

Woodward Edwin S, bartndr James Lannen, bds 106 E Main.

Woodward Miss Grace T, stenographer Olds' Wagon Works, bds 106 E Main.

Woodward Miss Jennie S, tchr Clay School, bds 106 E Main.

Woodward John, painter, bds 320 Calhoun.

Woodward Marcus E, clerk Pixley & Co, res 106 E Main.

Woodworth Miss Alida, bds 234 W Berry.

Woodworth Alonzo O, blacksmith Penn Co, res 38 Lillie.

Woodworth Benjamin S, physician, 234 W Berry, res same.

Woodworth Charles B (C B Woodworth & Co), pres Fort Wayne City Bill Posting Co, res 254 W Wayne.

Woodworth C, B & Co (Charles B Woodworth), Druggists, 1 Aveline House ; Dental Supplies, Room 28 Pixley & Long Block.

Woodworth James C, asst cash Old National Bank, res 224 W Wayne.

Woodworth James P, laborer Penn Co, res 38 Lillie.

Woodworth John, bds 38 Lillie.

Woodworth James W, boilermaker Penn Co, res 30 Melita.

Woodworth Miss Laura, with C B Woodworth & Co, bds 234 W Berry.

Woodworth Mrs Mary, res 30 Melita.

Wooff Joseph F, machinist Penn Co, res 127 Holman.

Woolford Charles H, brakeman, res 41 Duck.

Woolsey Hiram B, foreman American Wheel Co, res 25 W Creighton ave,

Woolsey Isaac B, finisher, res 42 W Jefferson.

Worch Louis A, traveling agent, res 95 E Jefferson.

Worch Louise A, dressmaker, 95 E Jefferson, res same.

Worden Anna (wid James L), res 209 Barr.

Worden Charles H (Worden & Morris), res 279 Fairfield ave. S Wayne.

Worden James W, clerk Penn Co, bds 209 Barr.

Worden Miss Littie, bds 38 Chicago.

Worden & Morris (Charles H Worden, John Morris jr), lawyers, 34 E Berry.

Work Alexander S, supt motive power Nickel Plate, res 250 W Jefferson.

Work Hannah M (wid Robert), res 337 W Jefferson.

Work Robert, bds 337 W Jefferson.

Workman, *see Werkman.*

World's Museum The, James P Geary propr and mngr, n s E Berry bet Clinton and Barr.

Worley Elmer, carpenter, bds 99 Madison.

Worley Richard H, carpenter, res 99 Madison.

Wormcastle Hugh, laborer Wm Bruns, bds 130 Gay.

Worman Jacob, engineer, res 143 Force.

Worman Samuel O, brakeman, bds 143 Force.

Worrell Wm A, painter, res 72 E Columbia.

Worry, *see Wery and Whery.*

Wort John M, foreman Fort Wayne Gas Light Co, res 122 E Main.

Woulfe, *see also Wolf and Wulf.*

Woulfe James, res 28 Baker.

Woulfe Michael, res 36 Melita.

Woy George, engineer B W Skelton, res 55 Madison.

Wren Mary M (wid Joseph), bds 64 Charles.

Wright, *see also Reidt.*

Wright Miss Annie, bds 241 W Washington.

Wright Charles, carpenter, bds 101 Franklin ave.

Wright Charles, machinist, res 57 W Superior.

Wright Daniel, night watchman, res 77 Home ave.

Wright Delbert, finisher American Wheel Co, res 580 S Lafayette.

Wright Frank, engineer, res 13 McClellan.

Wright Frank D, paperhanger, res s s New Haven road 4 e of toll gate.

Wright Luther, watchman, res 41 Pritchard.

Wright L Isaac, laborer, bds 24 E Williams.

Wright Mary E, converter worker Fort Wayne Electric Co, res 37 Wilt.

Wright Mary J (wid Edward), res 120 Clinton.

Wright Norman W, letter carrier, res 67 W De Wald.

Wright Philip L, bds 77 Home ave.

Wright Robert, machinist Penn Co, res 181 Calhoun.

Wright Thomas B, clerk Hoffman Bros, bds 67 W De Wald.

Wright Wm U, stopmkr Fort Wayne Organ Co, res 22 Park.

Wulf, *see also Wolf and Woulfe.*

Wulf Christian J, shoemaker, 96 Barr, rms same.

Wulle Charles, wks Liggett Bros, bds 43 W Superior.

Wunderland Emil, bridge carp, bds 68 Smith.

Wunderlin John, carpenter, bds rear 3 Oak.

Wunderlin Madeline (wid Peter), bds 136 Franklin ave.

Wunderlin Peter, laborer Fort Wayne Steam Stone Works, bds 136 Franklin ave.

Wunderlin Peter jr, laborer, res 136 Franklin ave.

MILLINERY GOODS — LATEST STYLES — MRS. E. A. FLAGLER, 14 W. BERRY STREET.

FORT WAYNE DIRECTORY. 567

Wunderlin Wm, laborer Weil Bros & Co, bds 81 Summit.
Wursch Wm, laborer, res 54 John.
Wursten Sabine E (wid Samuel), res 64 Barthold.
Wurtle Wm G, machinist Fort Wayne Electric Co, res 481
    Broadway.
Wyatt Henry M, meat market, 21 Francis, res 19 same.
Wyatt Marion A, painter F H Treep, bds 19 Francis.
Wyatt Spencer B, teamster The Peters Box and Lumber Co,
    bds 73 High.
Wyatt Thomas, waiter, bds 19 Francis.
Wybourn Christopher, helper Penn Co, bds 96 E Lewis.
Wyckliff Frederick, carpenter, bds 28 W Main.
Wyckoff Oren C (Griebel, Wyckoff & Becker), res 67 College.
Wygalak John, mach hand Fort Wayne Organ Co, res s s
    Rudisill ave 4 w of Piqua ave.
Wyge Ferdinand, painter, res 19 Union.
Wylie, see Wiley and Willey.
Wyman Bert, switchman, bds 251 Calhoun.
Wysong Edward, lab American Wheel Co, bds 670 Broadway.
Wysong Wm C, painter, res 99 W Superior.
Wyss Albrecht, laborer, res n s Killea 3 e of Hoagland ave.
Wyss Philip, carp, bds w s Lumbard 3 s of Wabash R R.

Y

Yaeger, see also Yager, Yeager and Jaeger.
Yaeger Jacob, laborer, res 97 Summit.
Yaeger Lizzie, bds 97 Summit.
Yager, see also Yaeger, Yeager and Jaeger.
Yager August, carpet weaver, 93 Franklin ave, res same.
Yager George, teamster, bds 301 Calhoun.
Yagerlehner Charles, coil winder Fort Wayne Electric Co,
    bds 24 Poplar.
Yagle George, turner Old Fort Mnfg Co, bds 393 E Wayne.
Yahney Frank L, canvasser Indiana Installment Co, res 87
    W Superior.
Yant Abbie B, domestic 152 Wells.
Yant Frederick, carpenter, bds 63 High.
Yarnelle Edward F (Mossman, Yarnelle & Co), res 276 W
    Wayne.
Yates Andrew, laborer, bds 22 Allen.
Yates Ida M, seamstress, bds 22 Allen.
Yates Mary (wid John), res 22 Allen.
Yates Olive L, dressmaker, 114 W Williams, bds same.
Yates Wm, engineer, res 114 W Williams.

Yates Wm L, boilermaker Kerr-Murray Mnfg Co, bds 114 W Williams.

Yautz, *see also Jautz.*

Yautz Conrad, car repairer, res 65 High.

Yeager, *see also Yaeger, Yager and Jaeger.*

Yeager August, carpet weaver, res 150 Franklin ave.

Yeager David, driver, bds 91 Montgomery.

Yeager George O, clerk Master Builders' Association, res 91 Montgomery.

Yeakley Charles, barber Oscar Wobrock, bds 168 Griffith.

Yeark Charles, molder, res 435 Hanna.

Yenney Mrs Mary M, bds 87 E Lewis.

Yenney Robert, laborer American Wheel Co, res 87 E Lewis.

Yergen August, laborer Wm Miller, res w s Lafayette 13 s of Pontiac.

Yergens August H, paperhanger Keil & Keil, bds Grand Central Hotel.

Yergens Gustav F, cigar mnfr, 123 E Lewis, res 96 E Washington.

Yergens Sophie, domestic Aveline House.

Yergens Wm (Ranke & Yergens), res 87 W Washington.

Yergens Wm jr, paperbanger, res 70 W Washington.

Yergens Wm F A, fireman Wabash R R, res 87 Montgomery.

Yerick Edward H, engineer, res 13 N Calhoun.

Yesse John F T, carpenter, res 27 Chute.

Ynklevetch Frank, pedler, res 138 Maumee road.

Yoast, *see also Yost and Joost.*

Yoast Charles W, conductor Penn Co, res 202 Hanna.

Yobst, *see also Dobst.*

Yobst Bruno, res 85 N Cass.

Yobst Dora, bds 189 E Jefferson.

Yobst Elizabeth (wid Amand), res 189 E Jefferson.

Yobst Henry, plumber, bds 85 N Cass.

Yobst John, butcher Edwin Rich, res 47 Wilt.

Yobst Joseph, meats, 232 Calhoun, bds 189 E Jefferson.

Yobst Louis, butcher Josph Yobst, bds 189 E Jefferson.

Yobst Maggie C, cashier Joseph Yobst, bds 189 E Jefferson.

Yobst Wm, butcher Joseph Yobst, bds 189 E Jefferson.

Yoder Amos F, clerk Coombs & Co, res 51 Miner.

Yohey Addie A, bookkeeper M R Yohey, bds 19 Miner.

Yohey Charles C, clerk M R Yohey, bds 19 Miner.

Yohey Joseph M, mngr M R Yohey, res 19 Miner.

Yohey Maggie R, paper 59 E Columbia, res 19 Miner.

Yohn, *see Jahn and John.*

Yokel Mary L, converter worker Fort Wayne Electric Co, bds 118 W DeWald.

Yokel Mathias, mason, res 118 W DeWald.

Yoquelet Hubert, teamster The Herman Berghoff Brewing Co, res 110 Grant ave.

York Sarah A (wid Cyrus T), res 22 W 4th.

Yost, *see also* Yoast *and* Joost.

Yost George F, draughtsman Bass Foundry and Machine Works bds Windsor Hotel.

You Adolph, engineer res 20 Van Buren.

Young Alfred W, printer, 21 Schmitz blk, bds 171 W Washington.

Young Alma, bds 31 Hough.

Young Amos J, machine hand Louis Diether & Bro, res s s Spring nr city limits.

Young Andrew L, plasterer, res 132 Wells.

Young A Ford, caller Nickel Plate, bds 99 N Harrison.

Young Bessie N, tobacco stripper John Gronendyke, bds 31 Hough.

Young Charles, carpenter, res 80 Oakley.

Young Charles, trav agent S F Bowser & Co, res 146 W Main.

Young Charles F, clerk Heilbroner & Brown, bds 80 Oakley.

Young Clara E, bds 26 Union.

Young Edgar S, clerk Nickel Plate, bds s w cor Wayne and Clinton.

Young Edward, machine hand Louis Diether & Bro, res n s Howell 3 e of Rumsey ave.

Young Edward, plasterer, bds 320 Calhoun.

Young Frank A. messenger, bds 563 E Washington.

Young Frederick, rms 60 E Columbia.

Young George, carpenter, 20 Howell, res same.

Young George, laborer Salimonie Mining and Gas Co, bds 22 E Columbia.

Young George A, laborer Kerr-Murray Mnfg Co, bds 94 Buchanan.

Young Harry E, mach Ft Wayne Electric Co, bds 31 Hough.

Young Henry, clerk John Christen, bds 58 W 3d.

Young Henry, carver Fort Wayne Organ Co, bds 268 Metz.

Young James W, section hand Penn Co, bds 164 Walton ave.

Young Jennie (col'd), domestic 332 W Jefferson.

Young John, carpenter George Young, bds 20 Howell.

Young John, laborer, res e s Rumsey ave nr Richardson.

Young John, yard conductor, res 31 Hough.

Young John B, res 563 E Washington.

Young John T, engineer Government bldg, res 99 N Harrison.

Young Joseph, machine hand American Wheel Co, bds 74 Leith.

Election Slips. Headquarters for PERFECT SLIPS at JOHN F. EBY & CO.'S, DETROIT.

570   R. L. POLK & CO.'S

Young Josephina, bds 563 E Washington.
Young Louis, laborer Penn Co, res 186 Metz.
Young Louis, well digger, res 58 W 3d.
Young Mary, milliner Mrs G J Stier, bds 262 E Jefferson.
Young Men's Christian Association (City Department), D F Bower Genl Sec, 103 and 105 Calhoun.
Young Men's Christian Association (R R department), C H Newton pres, Z T Esmond genl sec, 245 Calhoun.
Young Men's Christian Association Building, 105 Calhoun.
Young Peter, shoemaker, res 37 Ewing.
Young Ransom H (col'd), brakeman, res 72 Murray.
Young Rastes, carpenter, res s s Richardson 2 e of Rumsey.
Young Stephen, lab J C Peters, res n s Howell e of Rumsey.
Young Stephen, market stall 15, res e s Coldwater rd n of city limits.
Young Wm, carpenter, bds n w cor E Lewis and Hanna.
Young Wm, car builder Penn Co, res s e cor Home and Raymond.
Young Wm C, stonecutter Underhill's Monumental Works, res 171 W Washington.
Young Wm G, clerk The Pape Furn Co, res 130 Wilt.
Young, plasterer, bds 320 Calhoun.
Younge John W, A M, M D, President and Consulting Surgeon Standard Medical and Surgical Institute, Office 135 Calhoun, res s e cor Webster and Taber.
Youngker George W, painter, res 85 Summit.
Youngker Isaac C, teamster, res n s Wagner nr Spy Run.
Yunk John P, market stall 67, res s s Taylor rd w city limits.

Z

Zafstone John, cigarmaker, bds Hedekin House.
Zagel Andrew J, teacher Zion German Lutheran School, res e s Hanna 3 s of Creighton ave.
Zagel August L, clerk Stahn & Heinrich, bds A J Zagel.
Zagel Henry C, laborer, bds A J Zagel.
Zahn Catharine (wid Andrew), res 27 Erie.
Zahn Elizabeth, bds 27 Erie.
Zahn Frederick, car builder Penn Co, res 173 Hanna.
Zahn Mathias, helper Indiana Machine Works, res 241 E Jefferson.
Zahn Wm, bds 173 Hanna.
Zahniser George, foreman Salimonie Mining and Gas Co, bds Monroe House.
Zartman Rev Allen K, pastor Grace Reformed Church, res 96 E Washington.

Zauner, *see also Sahner and Sayner.*
Zauner Amelia, operator Hoosier Mnfg Co, bds 33 Force.
Zauner Clara, operator Hoosier Mnfg Co, bds 33 Force.
Zauner Henry, machinist, bds 33 Force.
Zauner Louis, machinist, bds 33 Force.
Zauner Mathias, engineer, Bass Foundry and Machine Works, res 33 Force.
Zegenfus Margaret (wid David), res 23 Hough.
Ziegler Charles, bds 64 W Wayne.
Zeller, *see also Zoeller.*
Zeller Anthony, harness maker, bds 98 Pfeiffer ave.
Zeller Bertha, operator Hoosier Mnfg Co, bds 98 Pfeiffer av.
Zeller Josephine, operator Hoosier Mnfg Co, bds 98 Pfeiffer.
Zeller Kilian, laborer C L Centlivre, res 98 Pfeiffer ave.
Zellers Wm, wheelmaker American Wheel Co, res 56 Charles.
Zelt Catherine, bds 58 Division.
Zeplin Wm, baker H H Barcus, bds Grand Central House.
Zepp Frederick, stonecutter, res 71 Hoffman.
Zern Gregory A, student, bds 342 Hanna.
Zern John, Grocer and Cigar Mnfr, 342 Hanna, res same.
Zern Justina (wid Xavier), res 342 Hanna.
Zerull John, laborer, res n s Howell 3 w of Rumsey ave.
Zerull Julius, harnessmaker A L Johns & Co, bds n s Howell 3 e of Runnion ave.
Ziegenfelder Mary, dressmaker Mrs G J Stier, bds 260 E Jefferson.
Ziegler Adam, wagonmaker, res 113 Wilt.
Ziegler Adam jr, molder, bds 113 Wilt.
Ziegler Caroline, bds 113 Wilt.
Ziegler Charles, clerk, bds 113 Wilt.
Ziegler Charles W, res 16 Huron.
Ziegler George, machine hand, bds 113 Wilt.
Ziegler George F, res 35 Lincoln ave.
Ziegler Henry, laborer, bds 113 Wilt.
Ziegler John A, molder Borcherding & Tonsing, bds 113 Wilt.
Ziegler Sarah (wid Jeremiah), bds 16 Huron.
Ziegler Wm C, clerk S W Hull, res 113 Wilt.
Ziegler Wm, fireman G R & I R R, res 61 Grand.
Ziegmond Herman, tailor, res w s Abbott 1 s of Pontiac.
Zigroef Gabriel, lab C L Centlivre, bds Albert Eckerle.
Zigroff Louis, night watch C L Centlivre, res 22 Koch.
Zimm John W, switchman, res 2 Holton ave.
Zimmendorff Frederick, res n s Wagner 1 e of Spy Run ave.
Zimmendorff Wm, laborer, bds Frederick Zimmendorff.
Zimmerly Frederick J, machinist Penn Co, res 78 Dawson.
Zimmerly John W, painter Penn Co, res 78 Dawson.

Zimmerly Wm A (Harr & Zimmerly), res 55 W Wayne.
Zimmermann Anton, machine hand Fort Wayne Organ Co, res 552 Fairfield ave.
Zimmermann Anton, shoemaker, 40 Pritchard, res same.
Zimmermann Augusta, dressmaker M A Fletcher, bds nr gas well No 2.
Zimmermann Charles, bds Windsor Hotel.
Zimmermann David, laborer, res 25 W 5th.
Zimmermann Denorah, bds 77 Baker.
Zimmermann Erhardt, shoemaker, 289 W Jefferson, res same.
Zimmermann Frank E, clerk L Wolf & Co, res 77 Baker.
Zimmermann Frank L, clerk Heller & Frankel, bds 77 Baker.
Zimmermann Hannah (wid John), res 100 Summit.
Zimmermann John, druggist, 200 Broadway, res same.
Zimmermann John, spoke culler White's Wheel Works, res n e cor Dwenger ave and Tons.
Zimmermann Julia, domestic 96 E Berry.
Zimmermann Justina, nurse, rms 59 E Wayne.
Zimmermann Kate, opr Hoosier Mnfg Co, bds 40 Pritchard.
Zimmermann Martin S, machine hand, res 294 Broadway.
Zimmermann Mary, opr Hoosier Mnfg Co, bds 40 Pritchard.
Zimmermann Minnie, opr Hoosier Mnfg Co, bds 40 Pritchard.
Zimmermann Paul J, clerk L O Hull, bds 200 Broadway.
Zimmermann Stephen, shoemaker, res 141 Wells.
Zimmermann Wm, boilermaker Bass Foundry and Machine Works, bds 40 Pritchard.
Zinc John W, painter, 55 Smith, res same.
Zion German Lutheran School, s w cor Creighton ave and Force.
Zipperling Christopher, cupola tender, res 138 John.
Zipperling Lizzie, bds 138 John.
Zitzmann Henry J, helper Monning & Baker, bds 24 Cass.
Zitzmann John, engineer Monning & Baker, res 24 Cass.
Zitzman Margaret M (wid Peter), bds 69 Wall.
Zoeller, *see also Zeller.*
Zoeller Roman (Zoeller & Merz), res 368 Calhoun.
Zoeller & Merz (Roman Zoeller, Louis Merz), grocers, 368-370 Calhoun.
Zollars Hon Allen, Attorney-at-Law, MacDougal Block, n w cor Calhoun and Berry, res 17 Brackenridge.
Zollars Miss Clara, bds 17 Brackenridge.
Zollars Frederick E, clerk Mossman, Yarnelle & Co bds 17 Brackenridge.
Zoller George, laborer, res 17 W 5th.
Zollinger August, saloon, 562 E Washington, res 618 E Wayne.

E. F. Sites, 🦷 **Dentist,** 86 Calhoun St., Four Doors North of Wayne.

FORT WAYNE DIRECTORY. 573

Zollinger Charles A, res 248 W Wayne.
Zollinger Charles C, boilermaker Wabash R R, res 60 Chicago.
Zollinger Christian, bds 618 E Wayne.
Zollinger Christian jr, clerk A Zollinger, bds 618 E Wayne.
Zollinger George C, blacksmith A Vogely, bds 154 Clay.
Zollinger Henry, car builder Penn Co, res 289 Hanna.
Zollinger Louis C, Blacksmith and Wagonmaker, 13 and 15 E Superior, res 15 same.
Zollinger Miss Mamie, bds 248 W Wayne.
Zollinger Wm, carpenter Christian Doenges, bds 289 Hanna.
Zongker Rosa M, dressmaker, bds 16 W Jefferson.
Zook Miss Francis L, teacher, bds 193 W De Wald.
Zook John H, painter, res 193 W De Wald.
Zook Zella M, seamstress, bds 193 W De Wald.
Zuber Frederick, res 15 Monroe.
Zuber H R, laborer Leikauf Bros, res 527 Wayne.
Zuber Jacob, plasterer, res Bluffton road 1 w St Mary's river.
Zuber John, carpenter, bds w s Lumbard 3 s of Wabash R R.
Zuber Lulu, opr Hoosier Mnfg Co, bds 203 E Washington.
Zuber May, bds 15 Monroe.
Zuber Nicholas, plasterer, res 91 Maumee road.
Zuber Philip, Carpenter, Contractor and Practical Builder, cor Lumbard and Chestnut, res same. (*See adv, p 7.*)
Zuber Rony, butcher, res 527 E Wayne.
Zuber Wm D, laborer Wm Moellering & Co, res e s Piqua ave 1 s of Rudisill ave.
Zucker Frederick, teacher Concordia College, res 49 Walter.
Zumbro Harry, teamster, bds 349 W Washington.
Zumbro Henry, carpenter, bds 349 W Washington.
Zundermann John, laborer, res 197 Lafayette.
Zurbrugg John H, bartender Charles Liebenguth, rms cor Calhoun and Railroad.
Zurbuch Mrs Carrie, bds 38 Oak.
Zurbuch George I, clk, bds s w cor Pontiac and Webster.
Zurbuch Henry A, clk L Wolf & Co, bds Pontiac and Webster.
Zurbuch John H, clk W D Henderson, res 188 E Suttenfield.
Zurbuch Joseph F, horseshoer, 387 W Main, res same.
Zurbuch Peter, clk H F Beverforden, bds s w cor Pontiac and Webster.
Zur Muehlen Henry, clk H N Ward, res 52 W Lewis.
Zuttermeister Wm D, coil winder Fort Wayne Electric Co, res 18 McClellan.
Zwahlen Frank B, mngr F M Zwahlen, res 254 E Lewis.
Zwahlen Frank M, grocer, 254 E Lewis, res same.
Zweigle John, laborer, bds Washington House.

FORT WAYNE DIRECTORY.

1890-91.

CLASSIFIED BUSINESS DIRECTORY,

Names appearing under headings marked thus * are only inserted when specially contracted for.

ABSTRACTS OF TITLE.

Abstract Office The, 19 Court.
Crane G D, s w cor Clinton and Berry.
Dreibelbiss Abstract of Title Co The, 3 and 4 Pixley & Long
  building.
Graham J E & Son, 26 Bank block.
Jones G W, 33 Calhoun.
Kuhne & Co, 19 Court.

ADVERTISING AGENTS.

Fort Wayne Advertising Co, 55 and 57 E Columbia.

AGRICULTURAL IMPLEMENTS.

(See also Hardware.)

Clausmeier E F & Co, 50 E Columbia.
Collins G W, 47 E Columbia.
Edgerton J K, 57 W Main.
Heller & Bottenberg, 58 E Columbia.
Hohnholz Herman, 46 W Main.
Morgan & Beach, 19 and 21 E Columbia.
Newhouse Henry, 56 E Columbia.
Parham F C & J M, 29 Barr.
Paulus F D, 24 E Columbia.
Pfeiffer & Schlatter, 38 and 40 E Columbia. *(See
  right top lines.)*

AGRICULTURAL IMPLEMENTS—Continued.

Shordon & Alderman, 63 E Columbia.
Storm J A M, 7 E Columbia.

ALE AND BEER BOTTLERS.

See Bottling Works.

AMUSEMENTS—PLACES OF.

See Theatres, Halls, etc.

ARCHITECTS.

Kendrick F B, rooms 24 to 26 Schmitz Block. (*See back cover.*)
Matson H W, 40 to 44 W Berry. (*See front cover.*)
Riedel J M E, 112 Calhoun. (*See front cover.*)
Tolan B S, 108 Calhoun.
Wing & Mahurin, 41 Pixley and Long building.

*ARCHITECTURAL IRON WORKS.

Kerr-Murray Mnfg Co, cor Calhoun and Murray.

*ART REPRODUCTIONS.

Siemon Wall Paper Co The, Sole Agents of Soule's (Boston) Photographic Reproductions of Works of Art, 191 Calhoun. (*See left bottom lines.*)

ARTISTS.

Covington Miss P K, 11 Schmitz block.
Dornbusch Henry J, 14 Schmitz block.
Schanz Felix, 112 Calhoun.

ARTISTS' MATERIALS.

Hull L O, 90 Calhoun. (*See right top lines.*)
Renner, Cratsley & Co, 56 Calhoun. (*See front cover.*)
Siemon Wall Paper Co The, Formerly The Wayne Wall Paper Co, 191 Calhoun. (*See left bottom lines.*)
Siemon & Bro, 50 Calhoun. (*See back cover.*)
Stahn & Heinrich, 116 Calhoun. (*See right top lines.*)

ASHERIES.

See Potash Mnfrs.

ATTORNEYS-AT-LAW.

See Lawyers.

AWNINGS AND TENTS.

Beach F J, 171 Broadway.
Stewart Wm H, 302 E Wayne.
Wolf P E, 33 and 35 Clinton.

AUXILIARY PUBLISHERS.

Fort Wayne Newspaper Union, 55 E Columbia.

BAKERS AND CONFECTIONERS.

(See also Fruits and Confectionery, also Confectioners.)

Barcus H H, 96 Calhoun.
Barthold L E, 37 W Berry.
Braun George, 135 Fairfield ave.
Geller W F, 98 Broadway.
Gumpper C C, 238 Calhoun.
Gutermuth Benjamin, 29 W Columbia.
Haffner Christian, 105 E Lewis.
Jacobs C W, 62 E Main.
Kiesling F W, 142 Broadway.
Klippert George, 393 Lafayette.
Lange J H & Sons, 327 Calhoun.
Lauer John, 152 Barr.
Markey & Mungovan, 256 Calhoun.
Ross J P & Sons, 25 and 27 W Columbia.
Scherer L P, 99 Maumee road.
Schwieters J H, 41 E Columbia.
Shaw D J, 28 Smith.
Wiegman H & Sons, 199 Lafayette.
Waltemath C H & Sons, 325 Lafayette.

BAKING POWDER MNFRS.

Monning J B & Co, 73 and 75 E Columbia.

*BAND SAW MILLS.

Bass Foundry and Machine Works, Hanna s of railroad crossing.
Fort Wayne Iron Works, s e cor Superior and Harrison.
Hoffman J R & Co, 200 W Main.
Peters Box and Lumber Co The, 79 to 105 High.
  (See adv, p 6.)

BANDS OF MUSIC.

See page 31.

John Pressler, Mantels, Grates and Tile Floor.
Columbia, Barr and Dock Streets.

578   R. L. POLK & CO.'S

BANKS AND BANKERS.

First National Bank, s e cor Main and Court.
Hamilton National Bank, 44 Calhoun.
Nuttman & Co, 32 E Main.
Old National Bank, s w cor Calhoun and Berry.

BAR GOODS.

Kaag M F, 5 E Columbia. (*See left bottom lines.*)

BARBERS' SUPPLIES.

Gross & Pellens, 94 Calhoun.

BARBERS.

Bailey Alexander, 21 Grand.
Bass Alfred, 32 E Columbia.
Beninghoff & Futter, Hotel Pearse.
Brooks Bryant, 48 E Columbia.
Browand N C, 192 Calhoun.
Brown J W, 42 E Columbia.
Brunskill John, 318 Lafayette.
Collins Edward, n e cor Buchanan and Thomas.
Ehrman & Geller, 12 W Main.
Fink J B, 56 E Main.
Fuchs Christian, 76 Barr.
Gardt Henry, 271 Hanna.
Guenther Henry, 318 E Washington.
Guffin Elmer, 200 Broadway.
Halstead Charles, 70 Barr.
Hubbard S G, 21 W Columbia.
Jully Louis, 112 St Mary's ave.
Kabisch J H, 137 Fairfield ave.
Kime & Brown, 352 Broadway.
Lauer Henry, 562 E Washington.
Lauer John, 154 Barr.
Lichtenwalter & Butler, 272 Calhoun.
Marks Simon, 47 Maumee rd.
Miner S R, 311½ W Main.
Mommer & Stevenson, Aveline House.
Momper Mathias, 24 W Main.
Munich John, 352 Calhoun.
Nichter G J, 153 Broadway.
Pegg L B, 136 Broadway.
Peters Jerome, cor Columbia and Barr.
Roberts J H, 205 Calhoun.
Roos George, 377 E Washington.

Schele Edward, 121 E Lewis.
Sherman & Owens, 249 Calhoun.
Shidel C A, 21 Calhoun.
Steiss J G jr, 41 W Main.
Stier Bros, 324 Lafayette.
Thain George, 130 Calhoun.
Uplegger Louis, 45 Wells.
Wackerman & Wilkin, 222 Calhoun.
Walter & Ellert, 105 Calhoun.
Whitfield R H, 37 E Columbia.
Westerman H A, Hotel Randall.
Wilkins O P, 333 Lafayette.
Winslow Gerney, 176 Broadway.
Wobrock Oscar, 10 W Berry.

BATHS.

McCaskey G & W, 38 W Wayne.

BEE HIVES—MNFRS.

Hubbard G K, 277 Harrison.

BELTING AND PACKING.

Morgan & Beach, 19 E Columbia.
Pfeiffer & Schlatter, 38 and 40 E Columbia. (*See right top lines.*)

BICYCLES.

Edgerton C W, 57 W Main.
White A B Cycle Co, 86 Clinton.

BILL POSTERS.

Fort Wayne City Bill Posting Co, 1 Aveline House blk.

*BILLIARD HALLS.

(*See also Saloons.*)

Centlivre L A, Harmony court bet Berry and Main.
Kirkendall J G, 26 E Columbia.

*BILLIARD HALLS—Continued.

Kline C W, 242 Calhoun. (*See adv, p 579.*)
Klingenberger J M, 9 E Main.
Schiemer Frank, 264 Calhoun.

*BIRCH BEER MNFRS.

Brames L & Co, 123, 125 and 127 Clay. (*See adv, p 3.*)

BIRD STORES.

Lade M G, 58 E Main.

*BLACK WALNUT LUMBER.

(*See also Lumber Dealers.*)

Peters Box and Lumber Co The, 79 to 101 High.
  (*See adv, p 6.*)

BLACKSMITHS.

(*See also Carriage and Wagonmakers; also Horseshoers.*)

Becker Fred & Bro, 13 E Washington.
Ehrmann Charles, 149 W Main.
Flinn & Jackson, 81 E Columbia.
Freistoffer Henry, 41 W Main.
Harter Joseph, 170 W Main.
Israel Bros, 5 Pearl.
Meier Ferdinand, 123 Wallace.
Roesener Frederick, 356 Broadway.
Rose H A, 10 N Calhoun.
Schwartz Louis, 84 Barr.
Spereisen J A, 165 Fairfield ave.
Tuttle Theodore, w s Spy Run ave 2 n of Randolph.
Vogely Andrew, s w cor Maumee road and Ohio.
Waterhous Edward, 5 Lafayette.
Winte J C, 216 Fairfield ave.
Wise Wm, 363 Calhoun. (*See adv in Horseshoers.*)
Zollinger L C, 13 E Superior.
Zurbach J F, 387 W Main.

*BLACKSMITHS' TOOLS.

Coombs & Co, 38 E Main.

BLANK BOOK MNFRS.

Davis C E, 84 Calhoun.

BLEACHERS AND PRESSERS.

Sheldon C H, 57 Clinton.

BOARDING HOUSES.

Bartley J S, 137 Holman.
Brokaw L T, 251 Calhoun.
Brown J D, 12 Harrison
Byers C E, 57 Barr.
Casteel Mrs Mary, 28 Chicago.
Didion Martin, 71 Harrison.
Fletter W S, 182 E Jefferson.
Fitzgerald Ellen, 39 W Washington.
Fitzpatrick Michael, 12 Chicago.
Hamilton House, 103 W Berry.
Heckler George, 15 Pearl.
Henry J A, 34 Chicago.
Johnson F M, 248 Calhoun.
Koehlinger Peter, 64 E Berry.
Miller J A, 49 W Main.
Motsch F J, 518 Fairfield ave.
Payne W C, 290 Calhoun.
Robinson C B, 301 Calhoun.
Rossington Mrs Linnie, 96 E Wayne.
Sawyer J T, 27 E 1st.
Stantz M L, cor Clinton and Superior.
Stoehr John, 199 Broadway.
Sundley Margaret, 17 Burgess.
Trone Henry, 43½ E Columbia.
Waterhous J H, 55 Barr.

*BOILER MNFRS.

Bass Foundry and Machine Works, Hanna s of R R crossing.
Fort Wayne Iron Works, s e cor Superior and Harrison.
Kerr-Murray Mnfg Co, cor Calhoun and Murray.
Miller M A, e s Barr 2 n of E Superior.

BOOK BINDERS AND BLANK BOOK MNFRS.

City Book Bindery, 13 E Main.
Davis C E, 84 Calhoun.
Siemon & Bro, 50 Calhoun. (*See back cover.*)

BOOKS AND STATIONERY.

(*See also Newsdealers.*)

Jocquel Louis, 168 Calhoun.
Katt A C, 82 Calhoun.

BOOKS AND STATIONERY—Continued.

Renner, Cratsley & Co, 56 Calhoun. (*See front cover.*)
Siemon & Bro, 50 Calhoun. (*See back cover.*)
Stahn & Heinrich, 116 Calhoun. (*See right top lines.*)
Stellhorn Charles, 146 Calhoun.
Stockbridge C A, 15 E Columbia.

BOOT AND SHOE MNFRS.

Foellinger Bros, 36 Calhoun.

BOOTS AND SHOES—WHOLESALE.

Carnahan & Co, 76 Clinton.

BOOTS AND SHOES—RETAIL.

App Matthias, 106 Calhoun.
Bauer Henry, 321 Lafayette.
Braeuer Conrad, 358 S Broadway.
Buesking Conrad, 302 Hanna.
Busking Henry, 90 Harmer.
Fitch O B, 52 Calhoun.
Fleming T J, 25 Calhoun.
Fortriede Louis, 19 Calhoun.
Helmke F W E, 212½ Calhoun.
Helmke Herman, 45 W Main.
Klug Gregor, 194 Hanna.
Lehman Isidor, 17 Calhoun.
Massachusetts Shoe Co, 36 Calhoun.
Mommer Joseph jr, 76 Calhoun.
Nestel A G, 189 Lafayette.
Nickels Wm, 71 Smith.
Noll J F, 22 Clinton.
Puff Bros, 338 Hanna.
Puff C B, 134 Maumee road.
Redlich Bros, 20 Calhoun.
Schiefer C & Son, 8 E Columbia.
Spiegel Gustave, 132 Broadway.
Stellhorn Charles, 146 Calhoun.
Tegtmeyer F D, 352½ Calhoun.
Umstead H D, 283 Calhoun. (*See adv opp.*)
Vordermark E & Sons, 32 Calhoun.
Walter J A, 40 Harrison.
White J B, 8 to 12 E Wayne.

BOOT AND SHOEMAKERS.

Albrecht Peter, 117 Broadway.
Bauer Henry, 321 Lafayette.
Baumann John, 374 Calhoun.
Buesking Conrad, 302 Hanna.
Bronenkant Diónysius, 14 Nirdlinger ave.
Campbell E T, 156½ Fairfield ave.
Eggemann Peter, 17 E Main.
Etzold Henry, 110 Webster.
Fortriede Louis, 19 Calhoun.
Getz J C, 174 Fairfield ave.
Geye Henry, 424 E Wayne.
Graham J W, 174 Calhoun.
Havens Nathaniel, cor Calhoun and Railroad.
Heilbronner S A, 27 Pearl.
Henry August, 24 Barr.
Henry J H, s e cor Creighton and Oliver.
Henz Wm, 102 Wells.
Huser L P, 178 Broadway.
Knobel Gottlieb, 110 Wells.
Krauhs Charles, 169 Jackson.
Lerch Joseph, 127 Fairfield ave.
Lordier Philip, 37 Baker.
McNulty & Weber, 211 Lafayette.
Muller August, n s New Haven ave 5 w of Lumbard.
Nill George, 191 Broadway.
Nix Valentine, 80 E Jefferson.
Robel John, 15½ Grand.
Schmoe Louis, 161 Ewing.
Schnieders B H, 197 Calhoun.
Umstead H D, 283 Calhoun. (*See adv below.*)
Weberruss J J, n s Wagner 5 w of St Joseph river.
Wehnert Frederick, 283 W Main.
Wehnert Wm, 317½ W Main.
Wendt Wm, n e cor Gay and E Creighton ave.
Wieneke Frederick, 317½ W Main.
Wulf C J, 96 Barr.

BOOT AND SHOEMAKERS—Continued.

Zimmermann Anton, 40 Pritchard.
Zimmermann Erhardt, 289 W Jefferson.

BOTTLING WORKS.

(See also Mineral Water Mnfrs.)

Berghoff Herman Brewing Co The, e s Grant ave near E Washington.
Brames L & Co (Mineral Water), 123, 125 and 127 Clay. *(See adv, p 3.)*
Centlivre C L, n end Spy Run ave.
Christen John, 100 Calhoun.
Fort Wayne Bottling Works, 9 N Harrison.
Hahn Wm (beer), 148 W Main.
Riedmiller J M (beer), s e cor Taylor and Eagle.
Schafer Christian, foot E Main.
Studer H L, 232 W Main.

BOX MNFRS—CIGAR.

Empire Box Factory, 3d floor Bank block.
Ruesewald & Didion, 49 E Main.

BOX MNFRS—PACKING.

Peters Box and Lumber Co The, 79 to 105 High. *(See adv, p 6.)*

BOX MNFRS—PAPER.

Empire Box Factory, 3d floor Bank blk.
Winbaugh G W, 13 E Main.

BRASS FOUNDERS.

Hattersley A & Sons, 48 E Main. *(See embossed line, front cover.)*

*BRASS GOODS.

Ogden Robert, 26 E Berry. *(See back cover and opp Plumbers.)*

BREWERS.

Berghoff Herman Brewing Co The, e s Grand ave nr E Washington.
Centlivre C L, n end Spy Run ave.

BRICK MNFRS.

Fremion Joseph, w s Hanna 10 s of Pontiac.
Koehler J A, w s Lafayette 10 s of Pontiac.
Koehler Paul, cor Rudisill ave and Webster.
McKernan Alexander, w s Burd ave 1 n of Wabash R R.
Miller Wm, e s Hanna s of city limits.
Moellering Wm, 53 to 59 Murray. (*See front edge and p 5.*)
Moellering Wm & Co, w s Calhoun s of Rudisill ave.
Ormiston Alexander, w s Piqua ave 4 s of Rudisill ave.
South Wayne Brick Co, w s Thompson ave n of Wabash R R.

BROKERS—REAL ESTATE AND LOAN.

Curtice J F, 1 and 2 Pixley & Long Bldg. (*See front cover and p 63.*)

BROKERS—TICKET.

Blitz M J, 5 Aveline House block.
Webb C P, 92 Calhoun.

BROOM MNFRS.

Bechtold Louis, 152 Maumee road.
Cartwright C A, s e cor E Lewis and Lillie.
Didier John & Co, 102 Maumee road.
Gage Robert, 318 W Main.
Rombke Henry, 68 Madison.

*BUGGY BOW MNFRS.

Ranke & Yergens, s e cor Superior and Griffith.
Rastetter Louis, s w cor Broadway and P, Ft W & C Ry.

*BUGGY TOPS AND CUSHIONS.

Horstman Louis, 9 E Superior. (*See adv, p 65.*)

BUILDERS.

See Carpenters, Contractors and Builders.

*BUILDERS' SUPPLIES.

Muhler Charles F & Son, 1 N Calhoun. (*See adv, top edge and p 59*).

BUILDING MATERIAL.

Moellering Wm, 53 to 59 Murrray. (*See front edge and p 5.*)

BUILDING MATERIAL—Continued.

Muhler Charles F & Son, 1 N Calhoun. (*See adv, top edge and p 59.*)

BUILDING AND LOAN ASSOCIATIONS.
See p 31.

*BUSINESS COLLEGES.
(*See also Colleges, Schools, etc.*)

McDermut W E (Late McDermut & Whiteleather), n w cor Calhoun and Berry. (*See back cover and p 8.*)

BUTCHERS.
See Meat Markets.

CABINETMAKERS.
See Furniture.

CAR WHEEL MNFRS.
Bass Foundry and Machine Works, Hanna s of R R crossing.

CARPENTERS, CONTRACTORS AND BUILDERS.
Allen C W, 324 W Washington.
Bertels John, 160 Harmer.
Bley George W, 152 Hanna.
Boester Frederick, 164 Griffith.
Boseker C F, 62 McClellan.
Breimeier & Son, 22 W Creighton ave.
Brokaw Robert, 69 Lillie.
Brooks H C, 187 W DeWald.
Crow J A, 82 Fairfield ave. (*See adv, p 65.*)
Doenges Christian, 126 Maumee road.
Doenges Wm, n w cor Grant and Oliver.
Drebert Frank, 91 W DeWald.
Franke Henry, 362 E Lewis.
Gallmeier Wm, 136 Francis.
Griffith & Son, 77 W Williams.
Grotholtman H A & Co, 48 W Jefferson.
Hall J E, 254 W Creighton ave.
Hiler J V, 470 Fairfield ave.
Hilgemann E H & Son, s e cor Baker and Fairfield ave. (*See adv, p 67.*)
Hilgemann J W, 216 E Washington. (*See adv, p 67.*)
Hoffman H A, 52 W Creighton ave.

Kraft Frederick, n s Montgomery 4 e of Lafayette.
Krock John, 416 E Wayne.
Lallow L J, 61 Pontiac.
Lauer Joseph, 1 University.
Lauer Justin, 151 Hanna.
Lauman H J, 127 W 3d.
Lehman Conrad, 608 Calhoun.
Liebman & Henry, s e cor W Jefferson and Fulton. (*See adv, p 67.*)
McBennett Frank, 410 Lafayette.
McMullen John, 70 Charles.
Miller Frederick, 8 Summit.
Moellering Wm, 53 to 59 Murray. (*See front edge and p 5.*)
Pranger J H, 226 E Washington.
Pressler George, 52 W DeWald.
Ross Lewin E A, 181 E Lewis.
Ruchel Wm, 209 E Lewis. (*See adv, p 69.*)
Schroeder Herman, n w cor Walnut and Fox.
Shrimpton Alfred, 152 W Main.
Stahl Reuben, 29 E DeWald.
Suter Edward, cor Ferguson ave and Broadway.
Tiemann J F, 424 S Broadway.
Wagner John, 45 Butler.
Walda H B & Bro, Erie bet Canal and Schick. (*See adv, p 69.*)
Wiegmann & Franke, s e cor Broadway and Taylor.
Young George, 20 Howell.
Zuber Philip, cor Lumbard and Chestnut. (*See adv, p 7.*)

*CARPET CLEANERS.

Fort Wayne Carpet Beating Works, 33 and 35 Clinton.

CARPET SWEEPERS.

Fowler Mnfg Co, 152 Calhoun.

CARPET WEAVERS.

Bayer J M, 34 Sherman.
Beck Leopold, 136 Barr.
Birk J G, 58 Elm
Buchmann J F, 110 Broadway.
Claus J A, 16 University.
Helwig Julia, 227 Gay.
Hertwig Paul, 287 E Lewis.

CARPET WEAVERS—Continued.

Hickman J W, 157 Wells.
Poch M E, 165 Broadway.
Pomper Herman, 229 Lafayette.
Riedel G J, 338½ Force.
Schoen Wm, 76 Maumee road.
Wolfrum John, 92 Fairfield ave.
Yager August, 93 Franklin ave.

CARPETS, OIL CLOTHS, ETC.
(See also Dry Goods; also Furniture.)

Foster D N Furniture Co, 11 Court.
Root & Co, 46 and 48 Calhoun and 15 W Main.
Wolf L & Co, 54 Calhoun.

CARRIAGE AND WAGONMAKERS.
(See also Blacksmiths; also Wagonmakers.)

Albrecht M L, cor Main and Barr. *(See adv, p 63.)*
Baker B H, 16 Lafayette.
Chauvey Bros, 35 E Superior.
Dudenhoefer, Bueker & Scherer, 11 and 13 Clay.
Ehrmann Charles, 149 W Main.
Olds' Wagon Works, s s Murray bet Calhoun and Lafayette.
Rose H A, 10 N Calhoun.
Spereisen J A, 165 Fairfield ave.
Thiel Wm, 146 W Main.
Vogely Andrew, s w cor Maumee road and Ohio.
Zollinger L C, 13 and 15 E Superior.

*CARRIAGE AND WAGON MATERIAL.

American Wheel Co, s e cor Lafayette and W,St L & P R R.
Coombs & Co, 38 to 42 E Main.
Rastetter Louis, s w cor Broadway and P, Ft W & C R R.

CARRIAGE TRIMMERS.

Smith E C, 16 Lafayette.

*CELERY GROWERS.

Hays C A, 13 E Main.

*CHAIR STUFF MNFRS.

Peters Box and Lumber Co The, 79 to 101 High.
 (See adv, p 6.)

*CHARCOAL.

Wilson John & Sons, Chestnut and Railroad.

CHINA WARE.

See Crockery and Glassware.

CIDER AND VINEGAR MNFRS.

(See also Vinegar Mnfrs.)

Brames L & Co, 123 to 127 Clay. (*See adv, p 3.*)
Hoffmann C A, 183 to 187 Calhoun.

CIGAR MNFRS.

Baker A C, 31 E Main.
Bender Louis, 166 E Washington.
Berndt C A, 176 Calhoun.
Bender Reuben, 19 Grand.
Bolman A F, 138½ Broadway.
Boltz F C, 92 Calhoun. (*See adv, p 2.*)
Dessauer L & Co, 23 Calhoun.
Ehle A N, 178 Broadway.
Gronendyke John, 214 Calhoun.
Gruber F J, 110 Calhoun.
·Heck L C, 79 E Washington.
Hollister A J, 104 W Williams.
Kasten & Kohlmeyer, 173 Broadway.
Lohman J & Co, 137 Calhoun.
Ortmann H W, 26 Clinton.
Rahe F H, 241 Broadway.
Reiter George, 30 Calhoun.
Schele Bros, 52 Barr.
Schneider Wm, 104 Webster.
Sorge G F, 43 Wells.
Wenninghoff Christian, 110 W Jefferson.
Yergens G F, 123 E Lewis.
Zern John, 342 Hanna.

CIGARS AND TOBACCO.

Boltz F C, 27 Calhoun. (*See adv, p 2.*)
Carl John, 259 Calhoun.
Falk & Lamley (whol), 24 E Columbia.
Goodman F X, 139 E Jefferson.
Gouty T A, 252 Calhoun.
Gruber F J, 110 Calhoun.
Heilbronner & Brown, 18 W Berry.
Kimball & Webb, 81 Calhoun.

CIGARS AND TOBACCO—Continued.

Mergel Rheinhard, 17½ W Main.
Meyer Henry, 88½ Barr.
Motz George, 47 W Main.
Mulligan J W, 272 Calhoun.
Spencer D J, 39 Calhoun.
Thomas E S, 178 Calhoun.

CIVIL ENGINEERS AND SURVEYORS.

Goshorn J S, 26 Court.
Wiley O B, 68 Barr.

*CLAIM AGENTS.

Graham J E, 26 Bank block.

CLOTHING.
(See also Merchant Tailors.)

Friend A I & H, 62 Calhoun.
Heller & Frankel, 40 Calhoun.
Lauferty Isaac, 73 Calhoun.
Lehman Benjamin, 72 Calhoun.
Morganthaler Peter, 52½ Calhoun.
Pixley & Co, 16 and 18 E Berry.
Sam, Pete & Max, 58 Calhoun.
Thieme J G & Son, 37 E Columbia.

COAL AND WOOD.
(See also Wood.)

City Coal Co, 80 E Columbia.
Krudop C F, n e cor Harmer and Hayden.
Moderwell J M, 10 Wells.
Quicksell Peter, 196 Jackson.
Scheele Henry, 68 Murray.
Smick M M, 80 E Columbia.
Stapleford & Co, 1 Lafayette.
Tinkham J P, 120 W Main.
Wilding J & Son, 193 Calhoun.
Wilson John & Sons, Chestnut and Railroad.

COFFEE AND SPICE MILLS.

Monning J B & Co, 73 and 75 E Columbia.

*COKE.

Wilson John & Sons, Chestnut and Railroad.

*COLLECTION AGENTS.

Branner C B, 4 Schmitz block.
Graham J E, 26 Bank block.
Haiber Frederick, 64 Wells.

COLLEGES, SCHOOLS, ETC.

Academy of Our Lady of the Sacred Heart, 6 miles n of
    Court House.
Fort Wayne College of Medicine, foot of Wayne.
McDermut W E, 62 and 64 Calhoun. (*See back cover
    and p 8.*)
Taylor University of Ft Wayne, ft of Wayne.
Concordia College (German Lutheran), e s Schick bet Wash-
    ington and Maumee road.
Westminster Seminary, 251 W Main.

COMMISSION.

Bash S & Co, 22 W Columbia.
Bond H W, 65 E Columbia.
Clutter & Purcell, 37 E Main.
Comparet D F, 76 E Columbia.
Gumpper J D, 240 Calhoun.
Pottlitzer Bros, 25 E Columbia.
Ryan Thomas, 406 S Clinton.

CONFECTIONERS—WHOLESALE.

Barcus H H, 96 Calhoun.
Fox Louis & Bro, n e cor Calhoun and Jefferson.

CONFECTIONERS—RETAIL.

Barcus H H, 96 Calhoun.
Fox J V, 25 E Main.
Geller Wm F, 98 Broadway.
McAfee Rose, 331 Hanna.
Mintch Martin, 172 Calhoun.
Morrey A R, 322 Calhoun.
Rentschler Mrs Mollie, 138 Brodway.
Strong Henry, 73 Webster.
Thompson F M, 205 Lafayette.

CONTRACTORS.

(*See also Carpenters, Contractors and Builders.*)

Crow J A, 82 Fairfield ave. (*See adv, p 65.*)
Derheimer Joseph, 55 Clinton. (*See adv, p 592.*)

CONTRACTORS—Continued.

Ehle E H (brick), 529 Broadway.

Fort Wayne Steam Stone Works (Stone), 86 to 98 Pearl. (*See adv, p 7.*)

Geary Charles (sewers), 287 E Washington.

Hensel Peter (brick and stone), 37 Miner.

Hilgemann E H & Son, s e cor Baker and Fairfield ave. (*See adv, p 67.*)

Hilgemann J W, 216 E Washington. (*See adv, p 67.*)

Jaap George, 79 and 81 E Columbia. (*See left bottom lines and card in Cut Stone Contractors.*)

Liebman & Henry, s e cor W Jefferson and Fulton. (*See adv, p 67.*)

Moellering Wm (Brick and Stone), 53 to 59 Murray. (*See front edge and p 5.*)

Muhler C F & Son (Stone), 1 N Calhoun. (*See top edge and p 59.*)

Remington-Lawton Co The (roofing and paving), 19 and 20 Pixley and Long bldg.

Rippe Frederick (brick), 176 Madison.

Ruchel Wm, 209 E Lewis. (*See adv, p 69.*)

Schultz Frederick (sewer), 140 Francis.

Shrimpton Alfred, 152 W Main.

Tapp H W (bridge), 227 E Lewis.

Walda H B & Bro, Erie bet Canal and Schick. (*See adv, p 69.*)

Zuber Philip, cor Lumbard and Chestnut. (*See adv, p 7.*)

COOPERS.

Brucker F X, n s Butler 2 w of Calhoun.

Hergenrother Henry, 76 Murray.

L.O. Hull, Artists' Materials, Studies, Etc.
AT 90 CALHOUN STREET.

FORT WAYNE DIRECTORY. 593

Hoffmeister Henry, 12 W 3d.
Sauertieg Frederick, 17 E Superior.
Stockmann C H, 101 N Harrison.
Williamson A J, s e cor Wheeler and Runnion ave.

CORN PLANTER MNFRS.

Horton Mnfg Co, w s Osage n of Main.

*CRACKER MNFRS.

Fox Louis & Bro, n e cor Calhoun and Jefferson.
Skelton B W, 209 Calhoun.

CROCKERY AND GLASSWARE.
(See also Glassware.)

Fleming T J, 25 Calhoun.
Kaag M F, 5 E Columbia. *(See left bottom lines.)*
Lintz T L, 12 E Columbia.
Pierre C J, s w cor Wells and 2d.
Poppel H D F, 302 E Washington.
Ward H N, 8 W Columbia.
Wonderland The, 5 E Main.

*CUT STONE CONTRACTORS.

Fort Wayne Steam Stone Works, 86 to 98 Pearl. *(See adv, p 7.)*
Jaap George, 79 and 81 E Columbia. *(See left bottom lines and adv below.)*

*CUTLERY.

Kaag M F, 5 E Columbia. *(See left bottom lines.)*

DAIRIES.

Bassett W H & Son, n e cor Runnion ave and Rebecca.
Hamilton R J, n s Bluffton road 1 w of St Mary's river.

John Pressler, Hot Air and Hot Water Furnaces.
Columbia, Barr and Dock Streets.

594   R. L. POLK & CO.'S

DAIRIES—Continued.

Hazard Wm, e s Lumbard 1 s of Wabash R R.
Newcomer George, e s Smith 1 s of Pontiac.
Pleasant Hill Dairy, n s Maysville rd 2 miles n e of city limits.
Reilly J A, 58 Walton ave.
Schilling Charles F, n s Howell e of Rumsey.
Spalding W W, w s Calhoun s of city limits.

*DECORATORS.

(See also Painters.)

Hull L O, 90 Calhoun. *(See right top lines.)*
Kramer Ernest, 247 Calhoun.
Muldoon J W, 12 E Berry. *(See embossed line back cover.)*

DENTISTS.

Adams J H, 106 Calhoun.
Brown S B, 15 Bank block.
Coyle J D, 84 Calhoun.
Hartman S B, 1 Schmitz block.
McCullough Gustine, 27 Calhoun.
McCurdy J S, 15 Bank block.
Mommer B H, 76 Calhoun.
Loag & Mungen, 2 E Columbia.
Rauch A J, 48 Harrison.
Schirmeyer W T, 27 Calhoun.
Shryock W W, 27 W Berry.
Sites E F, 86 Calhoun. *(See right top lines.)*
Sites H C, 82 Calhoun.
Waugh J E, 74 Calhoun.
Weisell D D & Son, 34 Calhoun.

DENTISTS' SUPPLIES.

Woodworth C B & Co, 28 Pixley & Long block,

*DIAMONDS.

Graffe H C, cor Calhoun and Columbia.
Trenkley & Scherzinger, 78 Calhoun.

DINING ROOMS.

See Restaurants.

DIRECTORY PUBLISHERS.

Polk R L & Co, 50 Calhoun.

DOG BREEDERS.

Cooper Fanny, 787 S Broadway.

*DRAIN TILE.

Wilson John & Sons, Chestnut and Railroad.

DRESS AND CLOAK MAKERS.

(*See also Milliners.*)

Aker Mrs A J, 178 W Washington.
Allen Mrs Maggie, 204 Hanna.
Belvick M R, 303 Calhoun.
Bercot E F, 37 Barr.
Bitsberger Mrs E F, 102 Wallace.
Blynn Harriet, 23 W Wayne.
Brink E M, 320 E Washington.
Brossard Tracy, 33 Wefel.
Burnett L E, 148 Fairfield ave.
Campbell Mrs Bessie, 259 W Jefferson.
Driscoll M E, 274 Calhoun.
Druhot Sisters, 324 E Jefferson.
Eakin Ella, 28 Clinton.
Edmonds Mary, 131 Jackson.
Ferguson A J, 289 W Washington.
Fessenden Mrs S C, 128 Calhoun.
Fitzgerald Bridget, 27 W Columbia.
Fletcher M A, 48 Barr.
Freer L A, 19 N Cass.
Gibson Mary, 194 W DeWald.
Gindlesparger I B, s w cor Pearl and Maiden Lane.
Gould Mrs J M, 47 W Main.
Gouty Mary, 179 W Superior.
Green Sisters, 179 Jackson.
Hagan M C, 46 Harrison.
Hawthorne Miss Ida, 140 Calhoun.
Hutchinson Blanche, 130 W 3d.
Jackson Emma, 197 E Jefferson.
Julliard Frances, 103 Broadway.
Krull Sisters, 268 E Washington.
McGee Maria, 175 Clinton.
McKeag A T, 149 Fairfield ave.
Malloy Wm, 16 Calhoun.
Martz Susan, 176 W Washington.
Miller Mrs C C, 101 Lafayette.
Mischo Kate, bds 33 Pritchard.
Palmer Jennie, 57 E Main.

DRESS AND CLOAK MAKERS—Continued.

Patton Alice 10 W Superior.
Perry Emma, 2 Oak.
Pierson U D, 153 Hanna.
Rahe Mrs Catherine, 241 Broadway.
Reilly Annie, 58 Walton Ave.
Schaich M J, 190 Taber.
Scherer Lizzie, 28 Lillie.
Schiemer Pauline, 43 N Calhoun.
Sherin Miss M L, 15 W Main.
Sprague Aurelia, 39 Wilt.
Stoll C G; 29 Wefel.
Strack Mary, 131 Broadway.
Traub Sophia, 17 Duryea.
Trisch I J, 96 Wells.
Van Osdale Laura, 33 Smith.
Waltemath E A, 12 W Jefferson.
White Mrs Anna, 94 Barr.
Whitacre Mary, 87 N Cass.
Wilson M L, 16 Hamilton.
Worch Mrs L A, 95 E Jefferson.
Yates O L, 114 W Williams.

*DRESSMAKING SCHOOLS.

Chalat Miss L R, s w cor Calhoun and Highland.

*DRUGGISTS—WHOLESALE.

Meyer Bros & Co, s w cor Calhoun and Columbia.
(*See adv, p 59.*)

DRUGGISTS—RETAIL.

Beneke W F, 443 Broadway.
Beneke & Co, 210 Calhoun.
Beverforden H F, 286 Calhoun.
Boecker F W, 108 Fairfield ave.
Brink J J, 44 Wells.
Byall C A, 52 Oliver.
Detzer Martin, 260 Calhoun.
Dreier & Bro, 10 Calhoun.
Frankenstein M L, n w cor Barr and Washington.
Gross & Pellens, 94 Calhoun.
Heaton C E, 36 E Berry.
Hetrick J & Co, 303 E Washington.
Hoham F D, 298 Calhoun.
Keller A J, 97 Broadway.

Klinkenberg & Detzer, 80 Calhoun.
Lepper C O, 66 W Jefferson.
Lewis J D, 434 Calhoun.
Loesch G H, 96 Barr.
Meyer Bros & Co, s w cor Calhoun and Columbia.
 (*See adv, p 59.*)
Miller A W & Co, 210 Calhoun.
Miller F J, 327 Lafayette.
Moellering W L, n w cor Lewis and Lafayette.
Mordhurst H W, 72 Calhoun.
Noll B R & Co, 10 E Columbia and 128 Broadway.
Schafer E A, 277 E Washington.
Schmidt Louis & Co, 120 Calhoun.
Schroeder Bros, 97 Broadway.
Soest, Nickey & Co, 360 Calhoun.
Sommers H G, 35 Calhoun.
Wefel M H, 314 Hanna,
Witzigreuter Max, 361 W Main.
Woodworth C B & Co, 1 Aveline House blk.
Zimmermann John, 200 Broadway.

DRY GOODS—WHOLESALE.

De Wald George & Co, n e cor Columbia and Clinton.
Root & Company, 46 Calhoun.

DRY GOODS—RETAIL.

Becker A E C, 160 Fairfield ave.
Bond W J, 376 Calhoun.
De La Grange F J E, 273 Hanna.
De Wald George & Co, n e cor Columbia and Clinton.
Dozois, Beadell & Co, 22 E Berry.
Fleming T J, 25 Calhoun.
Frank M & Co, 60 Calhoun.
Gerke J F & Co, 191 Lafayette.
Haiber G W, s w cor Hanna and E De Wald.
Irwin G B, 125 Broadway.
Kalbacher Anton, 13 and 15 Grand.
Klotz Daniel, 372 Calhoun.
Pierre C J, s w cor Wells and 2d.
Pierre Peter, 166 Broadway.
Root & Co, 46 Calhoun.
Scherer C W, 56 Walton ave.
Smaltz F M, 307 W Main.
Stewart & Hahn, 28 Calhoun.

DRY GOODS—RETAIL—Continued.

Treseler Henry, 108 Barr.
Waltemath C H & Sons, 321 Lafayette.
Wolf Louis & Co, 54 Calhoun.

DYERS AND SCOURERS.

Baumann Paul, 51 E Main.
Flagler Mrs E A, 14 W Berry.   (*See right top lines.*)
Whiteley T R, 172 W Jefferson.

DYNAMO ELECTRIC MACHINE MNFRS.

Fort Wayne Electric Co, Broadway and P, Ft W & C Ry.

*ELECTRIC LAMP MNFRS.

Fort Wayne Electric Co, Broadway and P, Ft W & C Ry.

ELECTRIC LIGHT AND APPARATUS.

Fort Wayne Electric Co, Broadway and P, Ft W & C Ry.
Jenney Electric Light and Power Co, 38 and 39 Pixley & Long building.
Star Iron Tower Co, cor Plum and Nickel Plate R R.

*ELECTRIC MOTOR MNFRS.

Fort Wayne Electric Co, Broadway and P, Ft W & C Ry.

ELECTRICIANS.

Binkley F C, Room 17 Foster Block.   (*See right side lines.*)

*EMBALMERS.

Peltier J C, 17 W Wayne.

EMPLOYMENT AGENCIES.

Fitzgerald Mrs Ellen, 39 W Washington.

*ENGINE BUILDERS.

(*See also Founders and Machinists.*)

Bass Foundry and Machine Works, Hanna s of R R crossing.
Fort Wayne Iron Works, s e cor Superior and Harrison.
Kerr-Murray Mnfg Co, cor Calhoun and Murray.

ENGRAVERS—WOOD.

Close E C, n w cor Main and Clinton.

EXCAVATORS—ODORLESS.

Koenemann John, 32 Colerick.

EXPRESS COMPANIES.

Adams Express Co, 95 Calhoun.
American Express Co, 52 Court.
Pacific Express Co, 79 Calhoun.
United States Express Co, 79 Calhoun.

EYE AND EAR INFIRMARIES.

Guardian Medical and Surgical Institute, 13 W Wayne.

*FANCY GOODS.

Stahn & Heinrich, 116 Calhoun. (*See right top lines.*)

FARM MACHINERY.

See Agricultural Implements.

FEED MILLS.

Collins L D, 21 N Harrison.

FEED YARDS.

(*See also Livery Stables.*)

Brinsley J C, 24 Pearl.
Draker J J, 42 Pearl.
Huguenard V A, 62 E Superior.
Kelsey Joseph, 40 Pearl.
Lintlag Jacob, 10 Pearl.
Melching W A, 20 N Harrison.
Schroeder Henry, n e cor Duck and Calhoun.
Stirling John, 29 N Clinton.

FIRE BRICK AND CLAY.

Baltes Michael, cor Harrison and Nickel Plate Track.
Moellering Wm, 53 to 59 Murray. (*See front edge and p 5.*)
Muhler Charles F & Son, 1 N Calhoun. (*See top edge and p 59.*)

FIRE WORKS—WHOLESALE.

Fox Louis & Bro, n e cor Calhoun and Jefferson.

*FISH, OYSTERS AND GAME.

Ake & McQuown, 154 Calhoun.
Gumpper J D, 240 Calhoun.
Niswonger G D, 17½ W Berry.

*FISHING TACKLE.

Miller C H, 20 W Main.

FLORISTS.

Auger B L, 16 E Washington and Creighton ave cor
    Webster.
Covington T E, Charlotte n of Asylum for Feeble-Minded.
Doswell G W, n s W Main near Lindenwood Cemetery.
Flick G W, 132 Thompson ave.
Knecht F J, 301 E Wayne.
Markey Bros, 117 W Jefferson.

FLOUR AND FEED.

Bond H W, 65 E Columbia.
Doehrmann & Hitzeman, 56 Barr.
Hartman J H, 126 E Washington.
Hartman & Bro, 63 E Wayne.
Henderson W D, 69 E Columbia.
Kalbacher A & Co, 296 Calhoun.
La Vanway C J, 20 Harrison.
Mayflower Mills, 20 W Columbia.
Miner W E, 45 E Columbia.
Tresselt C & Sons, cor Clinton and Nickel Plate R R.
Volland H & Sons, 14 W Columbia.
Waltemath C H & Sons, 321 to 325 Lafayette.

*FLOUR MILL MACHINERY.

Bass Foundry and Machine Works, Hanna s of R R crossing.

FLOUR MILLS.

(*See also Grain Dealers.*)

Bloomingdale Mills, cor Wells and 6th.
Empire Flour Mills, nr W Main St bridge.
Globe Flour Mills, 73 and 75 E Columbia.
Mayflower Mills, 20 W Columbia.
Pilliod & Brown, cor Wells and 6th.
Tresselt C & Sons, cor Clinton and Nickle Plate R R.
Volland H & Sons, 14 W Columbia.

*FOREIGN EXCHANGE.

Siemon & Bro, 50 Calhoun. (*See back cover.*)

FOREIGN PASSAGE AGENTS.

See Steamship Agents.

FOUNDERS AND MACHINISTS.

(*See also Engine Builders.*)

Bass Foundry and Machine Works, Hanna s s of R R crossing.
Borcherding & Toensing, n e cor Superior and Barr. (*See adv below.*)
Fort Wayne Iron Works, s e cor Superior and Harrison.
Kerr-Murray Mnfg Co, cor Calhoun and Murray.

*FRUITS—WHOLESALE.

Clutter & Purcell, 37 E Main.
Fox Louis & Bro, n e cor Calhoun and Jefferson.
Gumpper J D, 240 Calhoun.
Pottlitzer Bros, 25 E Columbia.
White J B, 8, 10 and 12 E Wayne and 97 Calhoun.

FRUITS AND CONFECTIONERY.

(*See also Bakers and Confectioners; also Confectioners.*)

Carles H W, 40 W Berry.
Casso F A, 156 Calhoun.
White J B, 8 to 12 E Wayne and 97 Calhoun.

*FUNERAL DIRECTORS.

Schone & Wellman, 39 W Berry.

FUR DEALERS.

Perry G H, 22 W Columbia.

*FURNACES—HOT AIR.

Carter & Son, 29 Clinton. (*See bottom edge and p 61.*)

John F. Eby & Co, BOOK AND JOB PRINTERS
65 and 67 W. CONGRESS ST., DETROIT.

602   R. L. POLK & CO.'s

FURNITURE.

Baals & Co, 59 E Main.
Fort Wayne Furniture Co The, e end E Columbia.
Foster D N Furniture Co, 11 Fort.
Griebel & Son, 44 E Main.
Hayden S E, 184 Calhoun.
Houk F E, 36 Clinton.
Lund H M, 172 W Creighton ave.
Miller J M, 50 and 52 E Main.
Nogal L H, 246 Calhoun.
Pape Furniture Co The, 28 E Berry.
Peters Box and Lumber Co The, 79 to 105 High.
 (*See adv, p 6.*)
Rahe J H, 34 Clinton.
Shuman E & Sons, 43 E Main.
Wolf P E, 33 and 35 Clinton.

*FURNITURE MNFRS.

Fort Wayne Furniture Co The, e end E Columbia.
Peters Box and Lumber Co The, 79 to 105 High.
 (*See adv, p 6.*)

GALVANIZED IRON CORNICES.

Baker John & Co, rear 377 Lafayette.
Pressler John, Columbia, Barr and Dock sts. (*See left top lines.*)
Welch J H, 190 Calhoun.

GAS COMPANIES.

Fort Wayne Gas Light Co, s e cor Superior and Barr.

GAS ENGINEERS AND CONTRACTORS.

Western Gas Construction Co, 24 to 27 Pixley & Long bldg.

GAS FIXTURES.
See Plumbers.

*GAS WORKS MACHINERY.

Kerr-Murray Mnfg Co, cor Calhoun and Murray.

GENTS' FURNISHING GOODS.
(*See also Clothing.*)

Dozois, Beadell & Co, 22 E Berry.
Durfee S A, 258 Calhoun.

Stahn & Heinrich, Booksellers and Stationers, Schmitz Block News Stand, 116 Calhoun Street.

FORT WAYNE DIRECTORY. 603

Fleming T J, 25 Calhoun.
Golden & Monahan, 68 Calhoun.
Goodman Alexander, 38 Calhoun.
Lauferty Isaac, 73 Calhoun.
Meyer Wm & Bro, 34 Calhoun.
Meyer & Niemann, 142 Calhoun.
Morganthaler Peter, 52½ Calhoun.
Ohnhaus & Co, 86 Calhoun.
Pierre C J, s w cor Wells and 2d.
Pixley & Co, 16 and 18 E Berry.
Rust H F C, 126 Broadway.
Sam, Pete & Max, 58 Calhoun.
Wonderland The, 5 E Main.

*GERMAN BOOKS AND PERIODICALS.

Stahn & Heinrich, 116 Calhoun. (*See right top lines.*)

*GINGER ALE MNFRS.

Brames L & Co, 123 to 127 Clay. (*See p 3.*)

*GLASSWARE.

(*See also Crockery and Glassware.*)
Kaag M F, 5 E Columbia. (*See left bottom lines.*)

*GOLD AND SILVER PLATERS.

Winters Moses, n w cor Main and Clinton.

GRAIN DEALERS.

(*See also Flour Mills.*)
Henderson Wm D, 69 E Columbia.
Tresselt C & Sons, cor Clinton and Nickel Plate R R.
Volland H & Sons, 14 W Columbia.

GRAIN ELEVATORS.

Bash S & Co, 22 and 24 W Columbia.

GRAINING AND HARD OIL FINISHING.

Muldoon J W, 12 E Berry. (*See line back cover*).

*GRATES AND MANTELS.

Carter & Son, 29 Clinton. (*See bottom edge and p 61.*)

GROCERS—WHOLESALE.

Bursley G E & Co, 129 to 133 Calhoun.
McDonald, Watt & Wilt, 141 and 143 Calhoun.
Moellering W & Sons, 215 and 217 Lafayette.
Trentman A C, 111 to 119 Calhoun.
White J B, 8 to 12 E Wayne and 97 Calhoun.

GROCERS—RETAIL.

Arens John, 122 Madison.
Aurentz S A, 31 W Main.
Baade C H, 2 Fairfield ave.
Ball Magdalena, 172 W Main.
Bangert Bonifacius, 34 Fairfield ave.
Barr Bros, 32 W Main.
Bechtold Louis, 152 Maumee road.
Becker A E C, 160 Fairfield ave.
Becker Lorenz, 91 John.
Beckman George, 56 Thomas.
Berthold Emil, s w cor Hanna and E Creighton ave.
Brase A C, 73 W Jefferson.
Brauneisen Joseph, 137 Fairfield ave.
Brinkroeger H P W, 48 Harrison.
Broeking Charles, n e cor Gay and E Creighton ave.
Brossard John, 84 Wells.
Busching Henry, 272 Hanna.
Butke Henry, 141 Broadway.
Butler L F, 7 N Calhoun.
Carles H W, 40 W Berry.
Carson J K, s e cor Spy Run and Riverside aves.
Certia Jacob, 116 Wells.
Coverdale & Archer, 24 Harrison.
Crance G W, s w cor Smith and Creighton ave.
Currier C H, 72 E Main.
De La Grange F J E, 273 Hanna.
Dicke Frederick, 29 Smith.
Dicke Henry, 119 E Lewis.
Dittoe A J & Co, 20 W Berry.
Dodane A L, 92 Wells.
Doehrmann & Hitzeman, 56 Barr.
Ernsting C H jr, 121 Wells.
Figel J C, 54 Wells.
Figel Robert, 53 Wells.
Fox W W, 325 W Main.
Frank Mendel, 208 Hanna.
Freese & Fehling, 184 Fairfield ave.

Frese Frederick, 379 E Washington.
Gaffney Wm, 378 Calhoun.
Gerow T D, 120 Fairfield ave.
Glaser E F, 195 Hanna.
Goldstine Herman, 401 E Wayne.
Graf Philip, 337 Lafayette.
Gumpper J D, 240 Calhoun.
Haiber C F, 122 Wells.
Haiber G W, s w cor Hanna and E DeWald.
Hammerle Xavier, 297 W Main.
Harmsdorfer G A, 279 W Jefferson.
Hartman J H, 126 E Washington.
Hartman & Bro, 63 E Wayne.
Henkenius G J, s w cor St Mary's ave and Spring.
Hermsdorfer J A, 281 W Jefferson.
Hilgemann F, 123 W Jefferson.
Huguenard J C, 107 Maumee rd.
Huxoll August, 92 Barr and 65 E Wayne.
Jacobs Andrew, 354 Broadway.
Johnson L H, rear 262 Calhoun.
Jourdain C J, 98 Maumee road.
Kalbacher Anton, 13 Grand.
Kayser & Baade, 129 Broadway.
Kiefer P F, 16 Wilt.
Kline Jacob, 30 E Columbia.
Klippert George, 393 Lafayette.
Koenig C F, 89 Harmer.
Korn August, 194 Broadway.
Korn John, 136 Fairfield ave.
Langard John, 70 E Columbia.
Lange J H & Sons, 327 Calhoun.
Leykauf Nicholas, 209 Broadway.
Limecooly L F, 546 Calhoun.
Litt G W, 132½ Broadway.
Loos Henry, 421 Lafayette.
Malone Peter, 167 Broadway.
Markey & Mungovan, 256 Calhoun.
Mensch F P, 23 W Columbia.
Meyers C W, n w cor W Creighton ave and Miner.
Meyer W D, 227 Lafayette.
Miller Mrs C H, s w cor E Lewis and Walton ave.
Miller E W, 2 Lincoln ave.
Miller G C, 230 W Main.
Miller Isaac, 406 Calhoun.
Moellering Wm & Sons, 215 and 217 Lafayette.

41

GROCERS—RETAIL—Continued.

Morton Thomas, 302 E Wayne.
Mulharen Thomas, 117 Fairfield ave.
Myers Mary, 1 St Mary's ave.
Neumeier Adam, 38 Maumee road.
Niebergall Henry, 201 E Washington.
Nieman Theodore, 272 E Washington.
Niemann Gottlieb, 148 Calhoun.
Noll U W, s w cor E Creighton ave and Lillie.
Oddou J F, 44 E Columbia.
Pfleiderer Jacob, 529 E Wayne.
Pierre C J, s w cor Wells and 2d.
Poppel H D F, 302 E Washington.
Reehling Henry, 220 Madison.
Reinkensmeier C F, 124 Broadway.
Rekers Gerhard, 116 W Washington.
Riethmiller G & Son, 139 Taylor.
Romy Louis, 142 Maumee road.
Rose Charles, 75 E Wayne.
Rosenberger Charles, 342 Force.
Ross J P & Sons, 25 and 27 W Columbia.
Ruppel John, 268 E Wayne.
Sallier Francis, 66 E Columbia.
Schaefer J H W jr, rear 147 W 3d.
Scheffer & Geiger, 292 Calhoun.
Scheiman Wm, 362 Calhoun.
Scherer C W, 56 Walton ave.
Schirmeyer Louis, 122 E Washington.
Schwier C & Son, 176 Montgomery.
Shaw Mrs R H, 121 Fairfield ave.
Smaltz F M, 307 W Main.
Spiegel G E, 183 Broadway.
Stace A W, 253 E Lewis.
Strunz Christian, 72 Barr.
Struver Wm, 66 E Main.
Vogler T P, 231 E Jefferson.
Waltemath C H & Sons, 321 to 325 Lafayette.
Weise Flora, 74 Maumee road.
White J B, 8 to 12 Wayne and 97 Calhoun.
Wiegman H & Sons, 199 Lafayette.
Winter Frederick, 105 Maumee road.
Woodruff W H, s e cor Creighton ave and Winter.
Zern John, 342 Hanna.
Zoeller & Merz, 368 Calhoun.
Zwahlen F M, 254 E Lewis.

GUNS AND AMMUNITION.

Krohne Herman, 13 W Berry.
Lade M G, 58 E Main.
Leonard Wm, 71 W Superior.
Miller C H, 20 W Main.

GUNSMITHS.

Blakely Wm F, 88 Broadway.
Lade M G, 58 E Main.
Leonard Wm, 71 W Superior.

HAIR DRESSERS.

Bartele Sisters, 167 Harmer.

HAIR GOODS.

Allen Mrs Maggie, 204 Hanna.
Cramp W S, 128 Calhoun.
Smith I M, 170 Calhoun.
Wilhelm M L (hair preparation), 259 E Washington.

*HAIR—PLASTERING.

Baltes Michael, cor Harrison and Nickel Plate track.

HARDWARE—WHOLESALE.

Coombs & Co, 38 to 42 E Main.
Morgan & Beach, 19 E Columbia.
Mossman, Yarnelle & Co, 10 and 12 W Columbia.
Pfeiffer & Schlatter, 38 and 40 E Columbia. (*See right top lines.*)
Seavey G W, 19 and 21 W Main.

HARDWARE—RETAIL.

(*See also Stoves and Tinware.*)

Ash H J, 9 E Columbia.
Gerding & Aumann Bros, 115 Wallace.
Graffe C F & Co, 132 Calhoun.
Gray J P, 364 Calhoun.
Griffiths W E, 120 Broadway.
Morgan & Beach, 19 E Columbia.
Pfeiffer & Schlatter, 38 and 40 E Columbia. (*See right top lines.*)
Seavey G W, 19 W Main.
Smithy F M & Co, 22 Calhoun.
Steger R & Co, 126 Calhoun.
Storm J A M, 7 E Columbia.

HARDWOOD LUMBER MNFRS.
(See also Lumber Mnfrs—Hardwood.)
Peters Box and Lumber Co The, 79 to 105 High.
(See adv, p 6.)

HARNESS—WHOLESALE.
Johns A L & Co, 51 E Columbia.

HARNESSMAKERS.
Hilt Frederick, 18½ E Columbia.
Johns A L & Co, 51 E Columbia.
Kuntz F B, 14 Pearl.
Kuntz G H, 11 Harrison.
Neireiter C B, 28 Clinton.
Schafer Wm, 20 N Harrison.
Sloat R S, 360½ Calhoun.
Wells G R, 69 E Main.

HATS, CAPS AND FURS.
Fleming T J, 25 Calhoun.
Golden & Monahan, 68 Calhoun.
Lauferty Isaac, 73 Calhoun.
Meyer Wm & Bro, 34 Calhoun.
Meyer & Niemann, 142 Calhoun.
Ohnhaus & Co, 86 Calhoun.
Pixley & Co, 16 and 18 E Berry.
Sam, Pete & Max, 58 Calhoun.
Wonderland The, 5 E Main.

*HAY AND STRAW.
Miner W E, 45 E Columbia.

HIDES, PELTS AND FURS.
Bash G & Co, 22 and 24 W Columbia.
Perry G H, 22 W Columbia.
Weil Bros & Co, 92 E Columbia.

HORSE COLLAR MNFRS.
Racine Aime, cor 1st and N Cass.
Racine F L, 36 N Cass.

HORSESHOERS.
(See also Blacksmiths.)
Becker F & Bro, 13 E Washington.

Freistroffer Henry, 41 W Main.
Geary & Perrey, 5 Harrison.
Rose H A, 10 N Calhoun.
Schwartz Louis, 84 Barr.
Veith Frank, 50 Barr.
Wise Wm, 363 Calhoun. (*See adv below.*)
Zurbuch J F, 387 W Main.

*HOT AIR FURNACES.

Carter & Son, 29 Clinton. (*See adv, p 61.*)
Pressler John, Columbia, Barr and Dock sts. (*See left top lines.*)

HOT WATER HEATERS.

Madden James, 101 Calhoun. (*See right side lines.*)
Pressler John, Columbia, Barr and Dock Sts. (*See left top lines.*)

HOTELS.

Aldine Hotel, n s E Berry bet Clinton and Barr.
Aveline House, s e cor Calhoun and E Berry.
Brokaw House, 31 W Columbia.
Clifton House, 12 Harrison.
Columbia House, 25 and 27 W Columbia.
Custer House, 16 and 18 W Main. (*See adv, p 61.*)
Darrow House, 248 Calhoun.
Diamond Hotel, 233 Calhoun.
Fritz Hotel, 10 E Berry.
Grand Central Hotel, 101 Calhoun.
Hedekin House, 25 Barr.
Hotel Pearse, n w cor Calhoun and Chicago.
Hotel Randall, cor Harrison and Columbia.
Hyer House, 3 Railroad.
Imperial Hotel, s e cor Clinton and E Superior.
Jewel House, 225 Calhoun.
Lake Shore Hotel, 6 N Cass.
McKinnie House, Penn Depot.
Monroe House, 224 Calhoun.

HOTELS—Continued.

Nickel Plate Hotel, 31 W Columbia,
Oliver House, 107 E Columbia.
Racine Hotel, n e cor Cass and 1st.
Rich's Hotel, n w cor Calhoun and Douglas ave.
Riverside Hotel, 2 N Cass.
Washington House, 121 and 123 Calhoun.
Wayne The, s s W Columbia bet N Calhoun and Harrison.
Windsor Hotel, 302 Calhoun.

HOUSE FURNISHING GOODS.

Ash H S, 9 E Columbia.
Pickard Bros, 29 E Columbia.
Seavey G W, 19 and 21 W Main.
Wilson George H & Sons, 31 E Columbia.

HOUSE MOVERS AND RAISERS.

Boerger C R & Bro, 194 E Washington. (*See adv, p 65.*)
Martin Wm, 225 Broadway.

HUB AND SPOKE MNFRS.

Winch & Son, s w cor Wabash R R and Winch,

ICE CREAM PARLORS.

Seidel Wm C & Bro, Nickel Plate Depot.

ICE MNFRS.

Fort Wayne Artificial Ice Co, cor Wells and Cass.

ICE DEALERS.

Gerberding August, 103 Erie.
Helling F W, 189 Griffith.
Moran P A, 201 E Wayne.

INSTALLMENT GOODS.

Indiana Installment Co, 127 Calhoun.
Fowler Mnfg Co, 152 Calhoun.
Metropolitan Mnfg Co, 19 W Wayne.
N Y Installment Co, 43 E Columbia.

INSURANCE AGENTS.

Aikins H J W, 80 Calhoun.
Argo M E, n w cor Calhoun and Berry.

Ball J L, 7 Schmitz block.
Barkley I L, 18 Schmitz block. (*See left top lines.*)
Buchman A O, 83 Force.
Douglass W V, 3 Schmitz block.
Eme & Son, 1 and 2 Foster block.
Fairbank Clark, 19 Court.
Fisher D C, 32 E Berry.
Glutting & Bauer, 55 Clinton.
Graham J E & Son, 26 Bank block.
Hunt H B, 1 Trentman block.
Komp & Scarlet, 27 Bank block.
Kuhne & Co, 19 Court.
Lumbard S C, 3 Aveline House block.
Malone J W, 16 W Main.
Miller & Dougall, 4 Foster block.
Miner W E & G E, 45 E Columbia.
Neireiter Conrad, 269 W Washington.
Ohnhaus J E, 10 Pixley & Long building.
Randall F P & Son, 24 Clinton.
Reed Louis, 12 E Berry.
Sauer Charles, 30 Pixley & Long building.
Schrader & Wilson, 46 Harrison.
Schuhler F X, 4 Pixley & Long building.
Seidel Edward, 52½ Calhoun,
Siemon & Brother, 50 Calhoun. (*See back cover.*)
Swayne & Co, 16 W Main.
Taylor J M, 20 Schmitz block.

INSURANCE COMPANIES—ACCIDENT.

Travelers' of Hartford, Conn, 46 Harrison.

INSURANCE COMPANIES—FIRE AND MARINE.

American of Philadelphia, 46 Harrison.
Central Mutual, Aldine Hotel bldg.
Continental of New York, 46 Harrison.
Detroit of Detroit, Mich, 55 Clinton.
Farmers of York, Penn, City Hall.
Fireman's Fund of California, of San Francisco, Cal, 55 Clinton.
Girard of Philadelphia, 46 Harrison.
Guardian of London, Eng, 24 Clinton.
Hartford of Hartford, Conn, 24 Clinton.
Merchants of Newark, N J, City Hall.
Milwaukee Mechanics', City Hall.
Newark of Newark, N J, City Hall.
New Hampshire of New Hampshire, 46 Harrison.

INSURANCE COMPANIES—FIRE AND MARINE—
Continued.

North Western National, of Milwaukee, City Hall.
Northern Assurance, of London, 46 Harrison.
Orient of Hartford, Conn, 24 Clinton.
Phœnix of Hartford, Conn, City Hall.
Phœnix of London, Eng, 55 Clinton.
Reading of Reading, Pa, 55 Clinton.
St Paul of St Paul, Minn, 45 E Columbia.
Sun Fire Office, of London, Eng, City Hall.
Teutonia of Dayton, O, 55 Clinton.
Union of San Francisco, Cal, 24 Clinton.
Westchester of New York, 46 Harrison.
Western Assurance of Toronto, 46 Harrison.

INSURANCE COMPANIES—LIFE.

Ætna Life Insurance Co, of Hartford, Conn, I L
  Barkley, Agent, 18 Schmitz Block. (*See left top lines.*)
Barkley I L, 18 Schmitz Block. (*See left top lines.*)
New York Life, of New York, 46 Harrison.

INSURANCE COMPANIES—PLATE GLASS.
Metropolitan of New York, 46 Harrison.

*IRON.
Coombs & Co, 38 to 42 E Main.

*IRON DOORS AND SHUTTERS.
Bass Foundry and Machine Works, Hanna s of R R crossing.

JEWELERS.
See Watches, Clocks and Jewelry.

JUNK DEALERS.
Bottenberg & Miller, 3 Canal.
Strasburg C & Sons, 106 E Columbia.

JUSTICES OF THE PEACE.
France H F, 13 E Main.
Hays C A, 13 E Main.
McDaniel Alexander, w s Spy Run ave 6 n of St Mary's
  bridge.
Romy R L, 4 Bank block.
Ryan Daniel, 24 E Berry.

Tancey Michael, 1 Bank block.
Wilkinson James, 231 Calhoun.

*LAMPS AND CHANDELIERS.

Kaag M F, 5 E Columbia. (*See left bottom lines.*)
Ogden Robert, 26 E Berry. (*See adv in Plumbers.*)

LAUNDRIES.

Hadley W P, 63 Barr.
Hop Lee Henry, 154½ and 180 Calhoun.
Kee Wah, 203 Calhoun.
Model Steam Laundry, cor Superior and Wells. (*See right side lines.*)
Phillabaum A J, 168 Francis.
Troy Steam Laundry, 48 and 50 Pearl. (*See left bottom lines.*)
Wah Kee & Co, 8 W Wayne. (*See adv, p 67.*)
Wah Lung, 104 Broadway.

LAWYERS.

Abel John C, 19 Court.
Alden S R, 18 Bank block.
Bell & Morris, 32 E Berry.
Bittenger J R, 26 Court.
Bittinger & Edgerton, 27 Bank block.
Brackenridge Joseph, 20 W Berry.
Branner C B, 4 Schmitz block.
Breen W P, 44 Calhoun.
Calvert B T, n w cor Calhoun and Berry.
Colerick W G, 22 Court.
Colerick & France, 17 Pixley & Long building.
Colerick & Oppenheim, 506 Pixley & Long building.
Crane G D, s w cor Clinton and Berry.
Dawson C M, 5 Bank block.
Denny W P, 34 E Berry.
Edsall C W, 5 Bank block.
Ellison T E, 23 Bank block.
France H F, 13 E Main.
Graham J E, 26 Bank block.
Hanna H C, 8 Bank block.
Harper B F, 10 Pixley and Long building.
Harper J B, 12 Bank block.
Hartman H C, 32 W Berry.
Hayden J W, 22 Bank block.
Hays C A, 13 E Main.
Heaton O N, 44 Calhoun.

LAWYERS—Continued.

Hench S M, 31 E Main.
Henderson C F, 204 E Wayne.
Jenkinson J J, 15 and 16 Pixley & Long building.
Kerr W J, 13 E Main.
Kuhne C W, 19 Court.
Leonard W & E, 25 Bank block.
Lowry Robert, 5 Court.
Miller & Dougall, 4 Foster block.
Morris & Barrett, 52½ Calhoun.
Ninde L M & H W, 42 W Berry.
Purman A A, 1 and 2 Foster block.
Randall & Vesey, 19 Bank block.
Robertson R S, 20 W Berry.
Robinson H H, 56 Pixley & Long building.
Robinson J M, s w cor Main and Calhoun.
Rodabaugh J F, 5 Foster block.
Ryan Daniel, 24 E Berry.
Schaden P W, n w cor Calhoun and Berry.
Shambaugh W H, 11 Bank block.
Smith H I, 18 Schmitz block.
Spencer M V B, 33 Calhoun.
Swayne & Doughman, 16 W Main.
Taylor R S, 34 E Berry.
Wilson T W, 31 Calhoun.
Worden & Morris, 34 E Berry.
Zollars Allen, n w cor Calhoun and Berry.

LEATHER AND FINDINGS.

Boerger G W, 39 E Main.
Freiburger S & Bro, 24 E Main.

LETTER FILE MNFRS.

Davis Wm H, 3d floor Bank block.

LIBRARIES.

Women's Free Reading Rooms, 23½ W Wayne.

LIGHTNING RODS.

Spice Robert, 48 W Main and 11 Pearl.   (*See left top lines.*)

LIME MNFRS.

Baltes Michael, cor Harrison and Nickel Plate track.

LIME, PLASTER AND CEMENT.

Baltes Michael, cor Harrison and Nickel Plate track.

Jaap George, 79 E Columbia.

Moellering Wm, 53 to 59 Murray. (*See front edge and p 5.*)

Muhler Charles F & Son, 1 N Calhoun. (*See adv, p 59.*)

LIQUORS.

See Wines and Liquors.

*LIVE STOCK.

Curtice J F, 1 and 2 Trentman Block. (*See front cover and p 63.*)

Dimon John, s s Huntington road near Lindenwood Cemetery.

Rockhill Bros & Fleming, s s Huntington road near Lindenwood Cemetery.

LIVERY, BOARDING AND SALE STABLES.

Barnum G P, 91 E Columbia.

Brinsley J C, cor Pearl and Maiden Lane.

Carpenter A L, n e cor Duck and Clinton.

Fletcher J F, 32 Barr. (*See adv, p 65.*)

Freistroffer & Jasper, n e cor Clinton and Nickel Plate R R.

Gerding Bros, 66 Harrison.

Hunt J T, 14 Randolph.

Jenson & Sargent, 16 Wells.

Lee & Fulton, 18 W Wayne.

Liggett Bros, 5 N Harrison.

McAfee Mary, 36 E 1st.

Myers Frederick, 62 E Wayne.

Pearse & Loag, 18 Holman.

Perrin A C, 88 E Main. (*See adv, p 63.*)

Rippe & Son, 84 Broadway.

Rippe & Sons, 111 Broadway.

Stapleford & Co, 1 Lafayette.

Wayne Stables, 13 and 15 Pearl.

Weber John & Sons, 21 Pearl.

Winkelmeyer Bros, 44 W Main.

LOAN AGENTS.

Barkley I L, 18 Schmitz Block. (*See left top lines.*)

Breidenstein Simpson, 25 W Wayne.

Harding D L, City Hall.

Curtice J F, 1 and 2 Trentman Block. (*See front cover and p 63.*)

LOAN AGENTS—Continued.

Eme & Son, 152 Foster block.
Fisher D C, 32 E Berry.
Glenn T M, 352½ Calhoun.
Graham J E & Son, 26 Bank block.
Hayden & Grier, 22 Bank block.
Komp & Scarlet, 27 Bank block.
Kretsinger H R, 20 Schmitz block.
Kuhne & Co, 19 Court.
Lumbard S C, 3 Aveline House block.
Michael Herman, 19 Court.
Potter P L, 28 Bank block.
Romy & Porter, 4 Bank block.
Schrader & Wilson, 46 Harrison.
Seidel Edward, 52½ Calhoun.
Swayne & Co, 16 W Main.

LOCKSMITHS AND BELL-HANGERS

Reiling August, 66 Pearl.

*LOOKING GLASSES.

Kaag M F, 5 E Columbia. (*See left bottom lines.*)
Siemon & Brother, 50 Calhoun. (*See back cover.*)

LUMBER—HARDWOOD.

Baker Kilian, cor Superior and Lafayette.
Cromwell J C, 261 W Wayne.
Hoffman Lumber Co, 200 W Main.
Peters Box and Lumber Co The, 79 to 105 High.
    (*See adv, p 6.*)
Peters J C, w s Osage n of Main.
Root, Vandoren & Co, 22 W Columbia.
Strack & Angell, 52 Calhoun.

LUMBER MNFRS.

Baker Kilian, cor Superior and Lafayette.
Cromwell J C, 261 W Wayne.
Cromwell J W, 224 W Berry.
Diether Louis & Bro, Office and Yard bet City Mills
    and Gas Works on E Superior; Factory 100 Pearl. (*See
    right side lines.*)
Fort Wayne Lumber Co, 106 W Main.
Hoffman Bros, 200 W Main.
Peters Box and Lumber Co The, 79 to 105
    High. (*See adv, p 6.*)

Rhinesmith & Simonson, cor Lafayette and Wabash R R.
Tagtmeyer David, n w cor Webster and N Y, C & St L R R.

LUMBER DEALERS.

Beaver, Miller & Co, n e cor Francis and Hayden.
Bruns Wm, east end Buchanan.
Cromwell C W, 244 W Berry.
Diether Louis & Bro, Office and Yard bet City
    Mills and Gas Works on E Superior; Factory 100 Pearl.
    (*See right side lines.*)
Fee F F, 181 W Wayne.
Fort Wayne Lumber Co, 106 W Main and 796 S Broadway.
Hoffman Lumber Co, 200 W Main.
Klett J & Son, 54 Pearl.
Peters Box and Lumber Co The, 79 to 105
    High. (*See adv, p 6.*)
Rhinesmith & Simonson, cor Lafayette and Wabash R R.
Smith Reader, 37 Douglas ave.
Wilson John & Sons, Chestnut and Railroad.

*LUMBER, LATH AND SHINGLES.

Diether Louis & Bro, Office and Yard bet City
    Mills and Gas Works on E Superior; Factory 100 Pearl.
    (*See right side lines.*)

*LYING-IN INSTITUTES.

Thayer Frederick, 57 Walton ave.

*MANTELS AND GRATES.

Carter & Son, 29 Clinton. (*See adv, p 61.*)
Pressler John, Columbia, Barr and Dock Sts. (*See
    left top lines.*)

MARBLE WORKS.

(*See also Stone Yards.*)

Brunner & Haag, 126 W Main.
Griebel, Wyckoff & Becker, 74 W Main.
Underhill's Monumental Works, 82 Barr.

MARKET GARDENERS.

Covington T E, Charlotte n of Asylum for Feeble-Minded.
Durnell Luke, e s Spy Run ave 1 n of brewery.
Fricke Joseph, n s St Joe road 4 e of St Joe bridge.
Jautz Christian, 3 Polk.
Knedeler Frederick, 815 Broadway.

MARKET GARDENERS—Continued.

Parrant F E, e s Walton ave 2 s of Wayne Trace.
Piepenbrink Charles, w s Lumbard 1 s of New Haven road.
Wesson Frederick, h s St Joe road 3 e of St Joe bridge.

MASONS.

Grund Frederick (stone), 59 Melita.
Yokel Matthias (stone), 118 DeWald.

*MATTRESS MNFRS.

Wolf P E, 33 and 35 Clinton.

MEATS—WHOLESALE.

Fort Wayne Beef Co, 4 Calhoun.

MEAT MARKETS.

(*See also Pork Packers.*)

Bruns G W, 350 Calhoun.
Carson J K, s e cor Spy Run and Riverside aves.
Cutshall W H, 61 Wells.
Duncker Ernest, 139 Force.
Eckart Frederick, 35 W Main.
Fox H A, 319 W Main.
Frank Mendel, 208 Hanna.
Gessler A F, 60 E Main.
Gombert & Piepenbrink, 94 Maumee road.
Haiber C F, 122 Wells.
Haiber G W, s w cor Hanna and E DeWald.
Haiber Lorenz, 15 High.
Haller Gottlieb, 366 Calhoun and 277 Hanna.
Haller Wm, 109 E Lewis.
Hoch Wm, 121 Wallace.
Hood Robert, 98 Barr.
Huguenard J C, 107 Maumee road.
Jacobs Charles, 197 E Washington.
Kabisch & Son, 156 Fairfield ave.
Kelsey Bros, 17 Grand.
Kohn Charles, 42 Maumee road.
Korn John, 134 Fairfield ave.
La Vanway & Le Graw, 68 E Columbia.
Lenk George, 198 Broadway.
Lenz Frederick, 170 Hanna.
Leutweiler Wm, 544 Calhoun.
Miller J L, 109 Maumee road.
Miller W L, 228 W Main.

Noll Theresa, 109 Barthold.
Ofenloch Frank, 100 Barr.
Parrot Frank, 28 E Columbia.
Pfleiderer Jacob, 529 E Wayne.
Rich Edwin, 22 Harrison.
Rich & Karn, 254 Calhoun.
Ross J P & Sons, 25 and 27 W Columbia.
Rousseau & Pfeiffer, 44 W Berry.
Rowe N B, 189 Broadway.
Schwab John, n e cor Buchanan and Thomas.
Scott S B, 352 Broadway.
Shaw D J, 28 Smith.
Spencer C W, 13 Highland.
Steinacker Frank, 134 Fairfield ave.
Suelzer John W, 281 Hanna and 422 Lafayette.
Weber Bernard, 224 Lafayette.
Weller C W, 92 W Jefferson.
Wilkens Bros, 112 Broadway.
Wyatt H M, 21 Francis.
Yobst Joseph, 232 Calhoun.

MECHANICS' TOOLS.

Storm J A M, 7 E Columbia.

MEDICAL AND SURGICAL INSTITUTES.

Guardian Medical and Sur ical Institute, 13 W Wayne.
Standard Medical and Surgical Institute, 210 Calhoun. (*See adv, p 4.*)

MEDICINE MNFRS.

Haines H H, 120 E Lewis.
Keller J O, e s Barr 1 n of Wayne.
Markley Medicine Co, 46 Harrison.
Meyer Bros & Co, s w cor Calhoun and Columbia. (*See adv, p 59.*)
Wery J H, 132 W Williams.

MERCANTILE AGENCIES.

Dun R G & Co, 21 Pixley & Long building.

MERCHANT TAILORS.

(*See also Tailors.*)

Clark J M & Co, 34 E Berry.
Feist L J, 226 Lafayette.

MERCHANT TAILORS—Continued.

Foster Andrew, 15 W Wayne. (*See left top lines.*)
Fowles J W, 64 Barr.
Friend A I & H, 26 Calhoun.
Hardung Frederick, 35 E Main.
Hunter Mnfg Co, 15 W Columbia.
Jaxtheimer Leonhard, 83 Calhoun.
Kruse Charles, 13 Harrison.
Meinzen & Toensing, 227 Calhoun.
Meyer Adolph, 54 W Wayne.
Meyer H C, 44 Harrison.
Oestermeier Charles, s e cor Calhoun and Montgomery.
Rabus John, 16 W Berry.
Schmidt & Bro, 70 E Main.
Schoch A F, 41½ W Main.
Stauffer Gottlieb, 182 Calhoun.
Swick P D, 50 Harrison.
Thieme Bros, 12 W Berry.
Thieme J G & Son, 37 E Columbia.
Wasserbach John, 38 Harrison.
Weitzmann F T, 162 Calhoun.

MIDWIVES.

(*See also Nurses.*)

Linnemeier Minnie, 131 Monroe.
Rathert Mrs Amelia, 51 Wilt.

MILLINERY—WHOLESALE.

Adams & Armstrong, 109 Calhoun.

MILLINERY—RETAIL.

Carroll J L, 222 Calhoun.
Chapman M B, 150 Fairfield ave.
Flagler Mrs E A, 14 W Berry. (*See right top lines.*)
Hall S B, 31 W Main.
Keel Mrs A C, 22 W Berry.
Koch Margaret, 74 Barr.
Kratzch Eleanor, 114 Calhoun.
Krudop A F, 33 E Main.
Krull Sisters, 268 E Washington.
Lau M M, 31 E Main.
Malloy Wm, 16 Calhoun.
Mergentheim Alexander, 38 Calhoun.
Proegler Carl, 137 Broadway.
Quinn Mrs E, 119 Fairfield ave.

Raab Christina, 175 E Washington.
Reitze Minnie, 118 Calhoun.
Rowe & Williams, 84 Calhoun.
Ruch Clara, 339 W Main.
Schulte Mrs Adolph, 332 Calhoun.
Seaney C E, 164 Calhoun.
Spiegel Mrs F C, 106 Broadway.
Stier Mrs G J, 32 Clinton.
Tait Frank & Sister, 26 E Wayne.
Wichmann Emma, 164 Calhoun.
Wolf V E, 26 Calhoun.

MINERAL LANDS.

Curtice J F, 1 and 2 Trentman Block. (*See front cover and p 63.*)

*MINERAL WATER MNFRS.

Brames L & Co, 123, 125 and 127 Clay. (*See adv, p 3.*)

*MIRRORS.

Junk L, 181 Calhoun. (*See left bottom lines.*)

MITTEN MNFRS.

Hutchinson O G, s e cor Cherry and Boone.

*MOULDINGS—MNFRS.

Diether Louis & Bro, Office and Yards Between City Mills and Gas Works on E Superior; Factory 100 Pearl. (*See right side lines.*)
Junk L, 181 Calhoun. (*See left bottom lines.*)

*MUSIC DEALERS.

Baldwin D H & Co, 98 Calhoun.
Kyle Wm D, 82 Calhoun.

MUSIC TEACHERS.

Albert Miss J A, 15 E Washington.
Anderson & Large, 36 W Wayne.
Baughman J R, 63 W 4th.
Bellamy C A, 135 N Cass.
Chambers J C, 16 Brackenridge.
Dawson G W, 187 E Jefferson.
Ferguson W H, 851 Broadway.
Fort Wayne Conservatory of Music, 22 to 26 E Main.

Robert Spice, Waterworks and General Plumbing. 48 West Main and 11 Pearl Streets.

622   R. L. POLK & CO.'S

MUSIC TEACHERS—Continued.

Getty L I, 97 E Jefferson.
Goebel Frederick, 32 W Main.
Gouty E S, 252 Calhoun.
Hartman Josephine, 65 Maple ave.
Joost Albert, 132 W Jefferson.
Lindemann Matilda, 81 Wilt.
Merrell E D, 26 Chute.
Miller Louise, 145 Broadway.
Nonnamaker Lizzie, 205 W Jefferson.
Orff Henry, 233 S Webster.
Pyke Miss Lillie M, 144 E Berry.
Rodabaugh Rosa, 286 W Washington.
Rogers Adelbert, 102 E Jefferson.
Schrader Miss C B, w s Rockhill bet Berry and W Main.
Strubey G C, 83 E Jefferson.
Thompson Miss S A, 474 Broadway.
Wassman Philip, 305 W Main.
Wells Alice, 205 W Jefferson.

MUSIC AND MUSICAL INSTRUMENTS.

(See also Organ Mnfrs; also Pianos and Organs.)

Baldwin D H & Co, 98 Calhoun.
Diem Charles, 75 Harrison.
Fort Wayne Music Co, 212 Calhoun.
Kyle W D, 82 Calhoun.

MUSICAL MERCHANDISE.

Dawson G W, 27 W Main.
Fort Wayne Music Co, 212 Calhoun.

NATURAL GAS.

Salimonie Mining and Gas Co, 50 Clinton.

*NATURAL GAS FITTERS.

Hattersley A & Sons, 48 E Main. *(See embossed line front cover.)*
Ogden Robert, 26 E Berry. *(See back cover and p 631.)*

NEWSDEALERS.

(See also Books and Stationery.)

Katt A C, 82 Calhoun.
Siemon & Brother, 50 Calhoun. *(See back cover.)*
Stahn & Heinrich, 116 Calhoun. *(See right top lines.)*
Stockbridge N P, 15 E Columbia.

NEWSPAPERS—DAILY.

Fort Wayne Freie Presse, n e cor Calhoun and Main.
Fort Wayne Gazette, 41 E Berry.
Fort Wayne Journal, 30 E Main.
Fort Wayne News, 19 E Main.
Fort Wayne Sentinel, 107 Calhoun.
Indiana Staats Zeitung, n e cor Columbia and Clinton.
Press The, 17 Court.

NEWSPAPERS—WEEKLY.

Fort Wayne Dispatch, 24 Clinton.
Fort Wayne Gazette, 41 E Berry.
Fort Wayne Journal, 30 E Main.
Fort Wayne News, 19 E Main.
Indiana Deutsche Presse, n e cor Calhoun and Main.
Indiana Staats Zeitung, n e cor Columbia and Clinton.
Press The, 17 Court.

NEWSPAPERS—MONTHLY.

American Farmer, 107 Calhoun.
Business Guide The, 55 and 57 E Columbia.
Gospel Tidings The, 9 Foster block.
Poultry and Pets, 19 E Main.
Watchman The, 575 Fairfield ave.

NEWSPAPERS—QUARTERLY.

Fort Wayne Journal of Medical Science, 74 Calhoun.

*NOTARIES PUBLIC.

Bittinger A H, 27 Bank block.
Fisher D C, 32 E Berry.
Haiber Frederick, 64 Wells.
Kerr W W, 13 E Main.
Potter P L, 28 Bank block.
Schrader H C, 46 Harrison.
Torrence G K, 80 Calhoun.

NOTIONS—WHOLESALE.

(*See also Dry Goods— Wholesale.*)

DeWald George & Co, cor Columbia and Clinton.
Falk Charles & Co, 23 W Main.
Trentman A C, 111 to 119 Calhoun.

NOTIONS—RETAIL.

Bond Wm J, 376 Calhoun.
Clarke F D, 5 E Main.
Colmey Mrs C R & Ripley, 201 Calhoun.
De LaGrange F J E, 273 Hanna.
DeWald George & Co, cor Columbia and Clinton.
Dozois, Beadell & Co, 22 E Berry.
Fleming T J, 25 Calhoun. .
Frank M & Co, 60 Calhoun.
French E M, 87 Maumee road.
Gerke J F & Co, 191 Lafayette.
Hills A R, 15 E Main.
Irwin G B, 125 Broadway.
Kane J M, 24 Calhoun.
Koch Margaret, 74 Barr.
Pierre C J, s w cor Wells and 2d.
Pierre Peter, 166 Broadway.
Renner, Cratsley & Co, 56 Calhoun. (*See front cover.*)
Rich & Hoadley, 170 Calhoun.
Root & Company, 46 Calhoun.
Sharp L P, 15 Court.
Shuman E & Sons, 41 E Main.
Siemon & Brother, 50 Calhoun.   (*See back cover.*)
Stuck L A, 67½ McCulloch.
Wonderland The, 5 E Main.

*NOVELTY MNFRS—WOODEN.

Horton Mnfg Co The, w s Osage n of Main.

NURSES.

(*See also Midwives.*)

Bagby Mrs M N, 302 W Jefferson.
Bernard Mrs Nancy J, 48 W Williams.
Cramer Miss Jennie, 21 Melita.
Groner Mrs Elsie, 32 Butler.
Lobdill Effie, 94 W Main.
McDaniel Anna, w s Spy Run ave 6 n of St Mary's bridge.
McDaniel Jennie, w s Spy Run ave 6 n of St Mary's bridge.
McQuarie Samantha, 115 Barr.
Zimmermann Justina, 59 E Wayne.

NURSERYMEN.

(*See also Florists.*)

Covington F E, Charlotte n of Asylum for Feeble-Minded.
Nestel Daniel, w s Broadway opp W Creighton ave.

OCULISTS AND AURISTS.

(*See also Physicians.*)

Seaton John, 10 Calhoun.

ODORLESS EXCAVATORS.

See *Excavators— Odorless.*

*OIL STOVES.

Pickard Bros, 29 E Columbia.

*OIL TANK AND PUMP MNFRS.

Bowser S F & Co, 260 E Creighton ave.

OILS.

(*See also Paints, Oils and Glass.*)

Brinsley G C & Son, cor Pearl and Maiden Lane.
Meyer Bros & Co, s w cor Calhoun and Columbia.
(*See adv, p 59.*)
Morgan G W, 184 E Jefferson.
Standard Oil Co, cor Columbia City road and Nickel Plate.

*OMNIBUS AND HACK LINES.

Powers & Barnett, 18 E Wayne.

ORGAN MNFRS.

Fort Wayne Organ Co, e s Fairfield av ½ mile s of city limits

*OVERALL MNFRS.

Hoosier Mnfg Co, 28 and 30 E Berry.
Redelsheimer D S & Co, 30 Clinton.

*PAINTERS—FRESCO.

Hull L O, 90 Calhoun. (*See right top lines.*)
Kelley Wm, 158 Holman.

PAINTERS—HOUSE AND SIGN.

Alter Bros, 20 Wilt.
Brimmer J H, 33 W Main.
Brunners J L, 79 Nirdlinger ave.
Harrison W S, 32 E Columbia.
Hild Henry, 149 W Main.
Hull L O, 90 Calhoun. (*See right top lines.*)
Hull S W, 27 Clinton.
Johnson L H, rear 262 Calhoun.

John Pressler, Mantels, Grates and Tile Floor. Columbia, Barr and Dock Streets.

626   R. L. POLK & CO.'S

PAINTERS—HOUSE AND SIGN—Continued.

Kappel J H & Bro, 180 E Washington.
Kramer Ernest, 247 Calhoun.
Muldoon J W, 12 E Berry. (*See embossed line back cover.*)
Nestel E P, 115 E Lewis.
Ott Frank, 90 E Main.
Rear & Bugert, 185 Broadway.
Rivers & Son, 70 Calhoun.
Robinson F W, 68 Wells.
Snowberger John, 372 E Washington.
Treep F H, 68 E Main.
Wilding James & Son, 193 Calhoun.
Zinc J W, 55 Smith.

*PAINTERS AND PAPERHANGERS' SUPPLIES.

Wilding James & Son, 193 Calhoun.

PAINTS, OILS AND GLASS.

(*See also Druggists; also Hardware.*)

Hull L O, 90 Calhoun. (*See right top lines.*)
Meyer Bros & Co, s w cor Calhoun and Columbia. (*See adv, p 59.*)
Morgan & Beach, 19 E Columbia.
Pfeiffer & Schlatter, 38 and 40 E Columbia. (*See right bottom lines.*)
Robinson F W, 68 Wells.

PAPER—WHOLESALE.

Fisher Bros, 23 E Columbia.
Fort Wayne Newspaper Union, 55 and 57 E Columbia.
Siemon & Brother, 50 Calhoun. (*See back cover.*)
Yohey M R, 59 E Columbia.

*PAPER HANGERS.

(*See also Painters.*)

Hull L O, 90 Calhoun. (*See right top lines.*)
Muldoon J W, 12 E Berry. (*See embossed line back cover.*)
Siemon Wall Paper Co The, Formerly The Wayne Wall Paper Co, 191 Calhoun. (*See left bottom lines.*)
Siemon & Brother, 50 Calhoun. (*See back cover.*)

*PATENT MEDICINE MNFRS.

(See also Medicine Mnfrs.)

Meyer Bros & Co, s w cor Calhoun and Columbia. *(See adv, p 59.)*

*PATENT OFFICE DRAWINGS.

Riedel J M E, 112 Calhoun. *(See front cover.)*

PAVERS—ASPHALT.

Remington-Lawton Co The, 19 and 20½ Pixley & Long bldg.

PAWNBROKERS.

Mariotte Horace, 20 E Columbia.

PENSION CLAIM AGENTS.

Graham J E, 26 Bank block.
Kerr W J, 13 E Main.
Miller & Dougall, 4 Foster block.

PERFUME MNFRS.

Biddle C I, 169 Ewing.

PHOTOGRAPHERS.

Austin D S, 156 Horace.
Barrows C V, 16 W Berry.
Barrows F R, 62 Calhoun.
Barry C V, 16 W Berry.
Jarrard H R, 86 Calhoun.
Salzmann Wm, 164 Calhoun.
Schanz Felix, 112 Calhoun.
Shoaff J A, 23 W Berry.
Sommer Carl, 30 Calhoun.
Strawn B A, 2 E Columbia.

*PHOTOGRAPHERS' SUPPLIES.

Jones M L, 44 Calhoun.
Klinkenberg & Detzer, 80 Calhoun.

PHYSICIANS.

Barnett W W, 434 Calhoun.
Bartele Michael, 167 Harmer.
Bergk Charles, 52 W 4th.
Boswell A C, 96 Barr.

PHYSICIANS—Continued.

Boswell A J, 96 Barr.
Bower G B M, 72 Harrison.
Bowen G W, 12 W Main.
Buchman A P, 94 Calhoun.
Caldwell James, 20 Schmitz block.
Carter W J, 210 Calhoun.
Cary D B, 200 E Washington.
Chambers J D, 16 Brackenridge.
Coblentz J W, 41 W Berry.
Deppeller Rudolph, 18 E Columbia.
Dills T J, 42 W Berry.
Dinnen J M, 67 W Wayne.
Enslen W M, 286 Calhoun.
Ferguson W T, 82 W Berry.
Gard Brookfield, 13 W Wayne.
Green M Francis, 139 W Main.
Greenawalt George L, 151 E Wayne.
Harris E F, 148 Calhoun.
Harris L P, 148 Calhoun.
Heaton C E, 36 E Berry.
Hetrick Jacob, 303 E Washington.
Jones C A, 87 Maumee road.
Jones J H, 320 W Jefferson.
Kesler A J, s e cor Wallace and Monroe.
Laubach A J, n w cor Barr and Washington.
Lemon A M, 80 Calhoun.
Leonard P M, 61 Brackenridge.
McCaskey G W, 38 W Wayne.
McCausland J W, 113 E Lewis.
McCormick T H, 7, 8 and 9 Pixley & Long bldg.
McCullough Howard, 42 W Berry.
McCullough T P, 180 Harrison.
McOscar E J, 16 W Jefferson.
Magnus C W B, 124 Buchanan.
Mann J E, 37 Pixley & Long bldg.
Martz Christian, 15 W Jefferson.
Metcalf S C, 10 Calhoun.
Miller James E, 210 Calhoun.
Myers H S, 12 Schmitz block.
Myers W H, 157 W Wayne.
Neier O C, 113 E Lewis.
Neiswonger H W, 284 E Jefferson.
Nieschang C C F, 298 Calhoun.
Ogle John J, 13 W Wayne.
Phelps Whitcomb, 367 E Lewis.

Phillips S P, 123 E Main.
Porter M F, 80 Calhoun.
Poyneer G W, 114 Calhoun.
Proegler Carl, 137 Broadway.
Rauch A J, 48 Harrison.
Rosenthal I M, 96 W Berry.
Ross G A, 84 Calhoun.
Schilling Carl, 15 E Washington.
Siver E L, 5 Schmitz block.
Smith C S, 38 Douglas ave.
Stemen G B, 311 W Main.
Stemen & Stemen, 74 Calhoun.
Stults C E, 81 Wells.
Sturgis L T, 275 Hanna.
Stutz John A, 50 W Washington.
Sweringer H V, 197 W Wayne.
Thayer Frederick, 57 Walton ave.
Van Buskirk A E, 416 Calhoun.
Wheelock K K, 94 Calhoun.
Whery M A, 26 Madison.
Whery W P, 94 Calhoun.
Woodworth B S, 234 W Berry.
Younge J W, 210 Calhoun.

PIANO TUNERS.

Baldwin D H & Co, 98 Calhoun.
Blinn J N, 23 Butler.
Orff Henry, 233 S Webster.

PIANOS AND ORGANS.

(*See also Organ Mnfrs; also Music and Musical Instruments.*)

Baldwin D H & Co, 98 Calhoun.
Hill C L, 38 Clinton.
Karn S A, 118 Calhoun.
Taylor Bros Piano Co, 138 Calhoun.
Wagner J C, 27 W Main.

PICTURES AND PICTURE FRAMES.

Frentzel J A N, 90 E Main.
Henry Jacob, 379 Lafayette.
Junk L, 181 Calhoun. (*See left bottom lines.*)
Keil & Keil, 116 Calhoun.
Siemon & Brother, 50 Calhoun. (*See back cover.*)

PLANING MILLS.

(See also Sash, Doors and Blinds.)

Diether Louis & Bro, Office and Yard bet City Mills and Gas Works on E Superior ; Factory 100 Pearl. *(See right side lines.)*
Hoffman Bros, 200 W Main.
Peters Box and Lumber Co The, 79 to 105 High. *(See adv, p 6.)*
Rhinesmith & Simonson, cor Lafayette and Wabash R R.

PLASTERERS.

Nahrwold Charles, 265 E Lewis.

*PLATE GLASS.

Seavey G W, 19 and 21 W Main.

*PLOW MNFRS.

(See also Agricultural Implements.)
Edgerton J K, 57 W Main.

PLUMBERS, STEAM AND GAS FITTERS.

Ash H J, 9 E Columbia.
Bruns C W & Co, 166 Calhoun.
Cox P E, 29 W Main.
Fox Charles, 123 Broadway.
Hattersley A & Sons, 48 E Main. *(See embossed line front cover.)*
Madden James, 101 Calhoun. *(See right side lines.)*
Murray James, 63 E Main.
Ogden Robert, 26 E Berry. *(See back cover and opp.)*
Pressler John, Columbia, Barr and Dock Sts. *(See left top lines.)*
Spice Robert, 48 W Main and 11 Pearl. *See left top lines.)*

*PLUMBERS' SUPPLIES.

Hattersley A & Sons, 48 E Main. *(See embossed line on front cover.)*
Madden James, 101 Calhoun. *(See right side lines.)*
Ogden Robert, 26 E Berry. *(See back cover and opp.)*

*POP MNFRS.

Brames L & Co, 123 to 127 Clay. *(See adv, p 3.)*

PORK AND BEEF PACKERS.

(See also Meat Markets.)

Eckart Frederick, 35 W Main.
Leikauf Bros, 94 Barr.

POTASH MNFRS.

Strasburg C & Sons, 106 E Columbia.

POWDER.

Hercules Powder Co, 18 W Columbia.

PRINTERS—BOOK AND JOB.

Archer, Housh & Co, 82 Clinton.
Clark M & Co, 16 W Columbia. *(See right top lines.)*
Indiana Staats Zeitung Co, n e cor Columbia and Clinton.
Rayhouser R C F, 34 E Berry.
Ruesewald & Didion, 86 Barr.
Wells W D, 9 Foster block. *(See left bottom lines.)*
Young A W, 21 Schmitz block.

PRINTERS—NEWSPAPER AND MAGAZINE.

Fort Wayne Newspaper Union, 55 and 57 E Columbia.

*PRINTERS' SUPPLIES.

Fort Wayne Newspaper Union, 55 and 57 E Columbia.

PRODUCE.

Bash S & Co, 22 W Columbia.

*PUBLISHERS.

Archer, Housh & Co, 82 Clinton.
Pettit J S, 19 Schmitz block.

*PULLEY MNFRS.

Old Fort Mnfg Co, 3 and 4 Pixley & Long building.

PUMP MNFRS AND DEALERS.

Bufford Edward, 88 E Columbia.
Spice Robert, 48 W Main and 11 Pearl. *(See left top lines.)*
Weidel Frederick, 9 Harrison.

RAILROADS.

See page 48.

*RANGES.

Carter & Son, 29 Clinton. *(See adv, p 61.)*

REAL ESTATE.

Abbott W T, 1 and 2 Foster block.
Archer John, 82 Clinton.
Barkley I L, 18 Schmitz block. *(See left top lines.)*
Bossler H H, 34 Clinton.
Breidenstein Simpson, 25 W Wayne.
Carver J F, 320 W Washington.
Craw E L, 71 W Main.
Curtice J F, 1 and 2 Trentman block. *(See front cover and p 63.)*
Douglass W V, 3 Schmitz block.
Edgerton J K, 57 W Main.
Eme & Son, 1 and 2 Foster block.
Fairfield C K, 7 Bell ave.
Fisher D C, 32 E Berry.
Forbing John, 28 Bank block.
Glenn T M, 352½ Calhoun.
Glutting & Bauer, 55 Clinton.
Graham J E & Son, 26 Bank block.
Harding D L, City Hall.
Hayden & Grier, 22 Bank block.
Hays C A, 13 E Main.
Jones G W, 33 Calhoun.
Komp & Scarlet, 27 Bank block.
Kowiansky Max, 28 Bank block.
Kretsinger H R, 20 Schmitz block.
Kuhne & Co, 19 Court.
Lumbard S C, 3 Aveline House block.
Michael H P, 19 Court.
Miller Wm, 5 W Main.
Miller & Dougall, 4 Foster block.

Miner W E & G E, 45 E Columbia.
Potter P L, 28 Bank block.
Randall F P & Son, 24 Clinton.
Romy & Porter, 4 Bank block.
Schrader & Wilson, 46 Harrison.
Schroeder & Sons, 99 Broadway.
Seidel Edward, 52½ Calhoun.
Swayne & Co, 16 W Main.
Tancey Michael, 1 Bank block.
Torrence G K, 80 Calhoun.
Vought W S, 18 Schmitz block.
Williams J B, 8 Schmitz block.

RESTAURANTS.

Cline J F, 99 Calhoun. (*See left bottom lines.*)
Entemann Christian, 13 E Main.
Fox J V, 25 E Main.
Harmon S W, 278 Calhoun.
Hill David, 29 E Main.
Hinton J C, 270½ Calhoun.
Hutzell Daniel, 378 W Main.
McKinnie G B, Penn depot.
Nickel Plate Restaurant, Nickel Plate depot.
Pease W H, 11 W Columbia.
Rich Edwin, 16 W Main.
Seabold G H, 22 W Main.
Siedel W C & Bro, Nickel Plate depot.
Shordon Daniel, 61 E Columbia.
Sorg J A, 61 E Wayne.
Stoehr John, 199 Broadway.
Strodel J G, 54 E Main.
Taylor A R, 62 E Columbia.
Wagner J T, 7 E Main.

ROAD MACHINE MNFRS.

Fleming Mnfg Co, 78 High. (*See adv, p 6.*)

ROOFERS—ASPHALT.

Remington-Lawton Co The, 19 and 20 Pixley & Long bldg.

ROOFERS—SLATE.

Baker John & Co, rear 377 Lafayette.
Pressler John, Columbia, Barr and Dock Sts. (*See left top lines.*)
Welch J H, 190 Calhoun.

ROOFERS—TIN AND IRON.

Gray J P, 364 Calhoun.

SADDLE AND HARNESSMAKERS.

See Harnessmakers.

SADDLERY—HARDWARE.

Bell J W, 13 E Columbia.
Johns A L & Co, 51 E Columbia.

*SAFES.

Pfeiffer & Schlatter, 38 and 40 E Columbia. (*See right top lines.*)

SAFETY VALVE MNFRS.

Kunkle E B & Co, 87 Barr.

SALOONS.

(*See also Wines and Liquors.*)

Ahern T W, 226 Calhoun.
Auprecht C F, 36 W Main.
Baker J L, 34 E Columbia.
Banet L E, 72 E Columbia.
Baum Joseph, 14 E Columbia.
Bauss Conrad, 36 Fairfield ave.
Becker A E C, 160 Fairfield ave.
Beckes Jacob, 221 Lafayette.
Beckman George, 56 Thomas.
Belger & Lennon, 140 Calhoun.
Bernhardt F J, 27 E Main.
Beugnot J E, 65 E Main.
Beverforden Rudolph, 294 Calhoun.
Bickford S D, 11 N Harrison.
Bicknese F C, 86 Barr.
Boltz F C, 27 Calhoun. (*See adv, p 2.*)
Bothner J G, 136 Calhoun.
Brooks Robert, 52 W Main.
Buesching Henry, 207 Lafayette.
Buhr J W, 202 Broadway.
Busching Henry, 272 Hanna.
Bush J L, 36 E Columbia.
Butler L F, 7 N Calhoun.
Centlivre L A, Harmony court bet Berry and Main.
Certia Jacob, 116 Wells.
Certia Peter, 70 Calhoun.

Christen John, 100 Calhoun.
Clark J A, 213 Lafayette.
Clark Thomas, 102 E Columbia.
Conway Frank, 55 E Main.
Crance G W, s w cor Smith and Creighton ave.
Cummerow R M, 276 Calhoun.
Dedolph Wm, 61 Wells.
De La Grange F J E, 273 Hanna.
Dierstein Henry, 24 E Berry.
Doehrmann & Hitzeman, 56 Barr.
Dornberg Wm, 91 Harmer.
Doudrick C A, 250 Calhoun.
Douglas J H, 284 Calhoun.
Dratt J A, 36 Barr.
Drew S A, 317 W Main.
Ehrman Coleman, 64 E Main.
Entemann Christian, 13 E Main.
Ernsting C H jr, 121 Wells.
Ferckel Martin, 31 Clinton.
Figel J C, 54 Wells.
Figel Robert, 53 Wells.
Frank Mendel, 208 Hanna.
Freese & Fehling, 184 Fairfield ave.
Gaetje John, 179 Calhoun.
Geiger F J, 288 Calhoun.
Geller Gottlieb, 96 Broadway.
George Runel, 28 W Main.
Gerardin Hippolyte, 70 Barr.
Gerow T D, 120 Fairfield ave.
Glessner Charles, 192 Griffith.
Goodfellow Bros, 274 Calhoun.
Graf Philip, 337 Lafayette.
Hahn Wm, 148 W Main.
Hake Frank, 26 Wells.
Hammerle Xavier, 297 W Main.
Hammill H B, 60 Calhoun.
Hartman Jacob, 267 E Wayne.
Hartman J H, 126 E Washington.
Hartman & Bro, 63 E Wayne.
Heilbroner & Brown, 18 W Berry.
Hilgemann H F, 121 W Jefferson.
Hoch Wm, 313 Lafayette.
Hollenbeck F W A, 144 Calhoun.
Howey W T, 354 Calhoun.
Hunziker Jacob, 25 Force.
Hutzell Daniel, 378 W Main.

SALOONS—Continued.

Huxoll August, 92 Barr and 65 E Wayne.
Jacobs Andrew, 354 Broadway.
Jacobs George, 30 W Main.
Jourdain C J, 98 Maumee road.
Kah George, 41 Harrison.
Keinz Philip, 307 Lafayette.
Kiefer P F, 16 Wilt.
Kirkendall J G, 26 E Columbia.
Klerner George, 156 E Washington.
Kline C W, 242 Calhoun. (*See adv, p 579.*)
Klingenberger J M, 9 E Main.
Koch Wm, 117 E Lewis.
Korn August, 194 Broadway.
Kuntz & Bro, 548 Calhoun.
Laible & Muehlfeith, 10 W Main.
Langard John, 70 E Columbia.
Langohr A J, 144 Broadway.
Lannan Edward, 7 Harrison.
Lannen James, 268 Calhoun.
Lauer John, 150 Barr.
Lazzerini Amadeo, 37 Barr.
Lill Martin, 150 Calhoun.
Liebenguth Charles, cor Calhoun and Railroad.
Loos Henry, 421 Lafayette.
Loos Joseph, 162 Holman.
Lowry J W, 6 E Columbia.
Mannix & Wiebke, 33 Calhoun.
Martin A A, 74 E Columbia.
Mayer J T, 6 Force.
Meyer F H, 104 Calhoun.
Meyer W D, 227 Lafayette.
Michael Frederick, 20 Clinton.
Neuenschwander I M, 46 E Columbia.
Neumeier Adam, 38 Maumee road.
Noirot Charles, 64 E Columbia.
Noirot George, 49 E Main.
Nolan J H, 330 Lafayette.
Oetting F D, 186 Fairfield ave.
Ortlieb J G, 88 Calhoun.
Pease W H, 11 W Columbia.
Post B L, 308 W Main.
Puff Bros, 340 Hanna.
Ranke Henry, 37 Calhoun.
Riedmiller C J, 16 Harrison.
Riegel & Bougher, 12 Calhoun.

Riethmiller G & Son, 139 Taylor.
Roeger Charles, 26 W Main.
Roeger Christian, n w cor Spy Run ave and Randolph.
Rosenberger Charles, 342 Force.
Rosselot Frederick, 22 E Columbia.
Ryan & Gebert, 60 E Columbia.
Schafer Christian, 99 Calhoun and 201 Lafayette.
Scheffer & Geiger, 292 Calhoun.
Schele Frank, 14 Harrison.
Schele J H, 26 Harrison.
Schiemer Frank, 264 Calhoun.
Schirmeyer Louis, 122 E Washington.
Schmidt Philip, 168 W Main.
Schmueckle Frederick, 10 E Berry.
Schneider George, e s Piqua ave 1 n of Rudisill ave.
Schoppman Wm, 209 Hanna.
Schuler T J, 35 W Columbia.
Seacrist Harvey, 223 Calhoun.
Siebert Otto W, 303 W Main.
Simonton G W, 161 Wells.
Spiegel G E, 183 Broadway.
Sthair G A, 108 Broadway.
Stoehr John, 199 Broadway.
Stotz Ulrich, 21 E Main.
Strebe F E, 375 W Main.
Strodel Catherine, s s Bluffton road 2 w of St Mary's river.
Strodel J G, 54 E Main.
Studer H L, 232 W Main.
Such Charles, 358 Calhoun.
Summers James, 262 Calhoun.
Thieme C F W, 17 W Main.
Thieme J A, 170 Broadway.
Voors J G jr, 574 E Washington.
Wagner J T, 7 E Main.
Walda J F, 5 Fairfield ave.
Webber M N, 3 E Main.
Winter Frederick, 105 Maumee road.
Zern John, 342 Hanna.
Zoeller & Merz, 368 Calhoun.
Zollinger August, 562 E Washington.

SALT.

Tresselt C & Sons, cor Clinton and Nickel Plate R R.

*SANITARY PLUMBING.

Madden James, 101 Calhoun. (*See right side lines.*)
Ogden Robert, 26 E Berry. (*See back cover and p 631.*)

43

Robert Spice, Pumps, Pipe, Hose, Fittings and Brass Goods
48 WEST MAIN and 11 PEARL STS.

638 , R. L. POLK & CO.'S

SASH, DOORS AND BLINDS.

(See also Planing Mills.)

Diether Louis & Bro, Office and Yard between City Mills and Gas Works on E Superior ; Factory 100 Pearl. *(See right side lines.)*

Pfeiffer & Schlatter, 38 and 40 E Columbia. *(See right top lines.)*

Rhinesmith & Simonson, s w cor Lafayette and Wabash R R.

*SAUSAGE MNFRS.

Haller Gottlieb, 366 Calhoun and 277 Hanna.

*SAW MILL MACHINERY.

Bass Foundry and Machine Works, Hanna s of R R crossing.
Hoffman J R & Co, 200 W Main.

*SAW MILLS.

(See also Lumber Mnfrs.)

Peters Box and Lumber Co The, 79 to 105 High. *(See adv, p 6.)*

Peters J C, w s Osage n of Main.
Tagtmeyer David, n w cor Cass and N Y, C & St L R R.

SAW REPAIRERS.

Bowman Charles, 18 Harrison. *(See left top lines.)*
Gorham M D L F, 19 W Berry.
Wilson George, 177 Calhoun.

SAW WORKS.

Bowman Charles, 18 Harrison. *(See left top lines.)*

*SAWS—CIRCULAR, MILL AND CROSS-CUT.

Pfeiffer & Schlatter, 38 and 40 E Columbia. *(See right top lines.)*

*SCHOOL FURNITURE.

Siemon & Brother, 50 Calhoun. *(See back cover.)*

SCHOOLS AND COLLEGES.

See Colleges, Schools, Etc.

SCHOOLS OF TELEGRAPHY.

Binkley F C, Rooms 17 to 20 Foster Block. *(See right side lines.)*

Builders' Hardware, PFEIFFER & SCHLATTER, 38 and 40 EAST COLUMBIA ST.

FORT WAYNE DIRECTORY. 639

SECOND-HAND GOODS.

Horn J L & Co, 13 W Berry.
Klinger J E, 67 E Columbia.
Nogal L H, 246 Calhoun.
Soliday Bros, 71 E Main.

*SEEDS.

Bash S & Co, 22 W Columbia.
Tresselt C & Sons, cor Clinton and Nickel Plate R R.

SEWER BUILDERS.

Hettler Gottlieb, 84 Charles.
Polson John, 148 Wells.

*SEWER PIPE.

Boltes Michael, cor Harrison and Nickel Plate R R.
Jaap George, 79 and 81 E Columbia. (*See left bottom lines and p 593.*)
Moellering Wm, 53 to 59 Murray. (*See front edge and p 5.*)
Muhler Charles F & Son, 1 Calhoun. (*See top edge and p 59.*)

SEWING MACHINES.

Davis Amos, 138 Calhoun.
Manth J G, 27 W Main.
Pfeiffer & Schlatter, 38 and 40 E Columbia. (*See right bottom lines.*)
Singer Mnfg Co The, 4 Aveline House block.

SHINGLES.

Diether Louis & Bro, Office and Yard bet City Mills and Gas Works on E Superior; Factory 100 Pearl. (*See right side lines.*)

SHIRT MNFRS.

Comparet C M & Co, 34 E Berry.
Foster S M, n end Lafayette.
Kuttner P G, 144 Calhoun.

SHOEMAKERS.

See Boot and Shoe Makers.

*SIGN WRITERS.

Harrison W S, 32 E Columbia.
Kramer Ernest, 247 Calhoun.

SKATING RINKS.

Princess Roller Skating Rink, s e cor W Main and Fulton.

SOAP MNFRS.

Fort Wayne Soap Works, 91 to 95 Glasgow ave.
Summit City Soap Works, 2 to 12 Glasgow ave.

*SPORTING GOODS.

Lade M G, 58 E Main.

SPRING BEDS.

Fowler Mnfg Co, 152 Calhoun.
Metropolitan Mnfg Co, 19 W Main.

*STAIR BUILDERS.

Rhinesmith & Simonson, cor Lafayette and Wabash R R.

STAVE MNFRS.

Ranke & Yergens, s e cor Superior and Griffith.

STEAMSHIP AGENTS.

Graham J E & Son, 26 Bank block.
Kuhne & Co, 19 Court.
Siemon & Brother, 50 Calhoun. (*See back cover.*)

STEAMSHIP LINES.

Anchor Line, Siemon & Bro Agents, 50 Calhoun.
American Line, Siemon & Bro Agents, 50 Calhoun.
Baltic Line, Siemon & Bro Agents, 50 Calhoun.
Bordeaux Line, Siemon & Bro Agents, 50 Calhoun.
Hamburg-American Packet Co, Siemon & Bro Agents, 50 Calhoun.
Inman Line, Siemon & Bro Agents, 50 Calhoun.
Italian Line, Siemon & Bro Agents, 50 Calhoun.
North German Lloyd, Siemon & Bro Agents, 50 Calhoun.
Red Star Line, Siemon & Bro Agents, 50 Calhoun.
Rotterdam Line, Siemon & Bro Agents, 50 Calhoun.
Siemon & Bro, 50 Calhoun. (*See back cover.*)
State Line, Siemon & Bro Agents, 50 Calhoun.
Union Line, Siemon & Bro Agents, 50 Calhoun.

STEEL MNFRS.

Rupp John, n end of Barr.

*STENOGRAPHERS.

Goodrich Janette, 49 Pixley & Long building.
Logan T J, 16 W Main.
McDermut W E, 62 Calhoun. (*See back cover and p 8.*)

STEREOTYPERS.

Fort Wayne Newspaper Union, 55 and 57 E Columbia.

*STONE—ARTIFICIAL.

Remington-Lawton Co The, 19 and 20 Pixley & Long bldg.

STONE CUTTERS' TOOLS.

Steger R & Co, 126 Calhoun.

STONE YARDS.

(*See also Marble Works.*)

Baltes Michael, cor Harrison and Nickel Plate track.
Fort Wayne Steam Stone Yards, 86 to 98 Pearl.
(*See adv, p 67.*)
Geake Wm & J J, 76 Pearl.
Jaap George, 79 and 81 E Columbia. (*See left bottom lines and p 593.*)
Moellering Wm, 53 to 59 Murray. (*See front edge and p 5.*)
Muhler Charles F & Son, 1 N Calhoun. (*See top edge and p 59.*)

STORAGE.

Fort Wayne Transfer and Storage Co, 47 E Columbia.

STOVES AND TINWARE.

(*See also Hardware.*)

Ash H J, 9 E Columbia.
Freiburger J J, 139 Broadway.
Gerding & Aumann Bros, 115 Wallace.
Gray J P, 364 Calhoun.
Nogal L H, 246 Calhoun.
Pickard Bros, 29 E Columbia.
Seavey G W, 19 W Main.
Wilson G H & Sons, 31 E Columbia.

John Pressler, Hot Air and Hot Water Furnaces.
Columbia, Barr and Dock Streets.

642   R. L. POLK & CO.'S

SURVEYORS.

See Civil Engineers and Surveyors.

TAILORS.

(See also Merchant Tailors.)

Barnett Simon, 152 Calhoun.
Feist L J, 226 Lafayette.
Hitzemann G H, 133 Broadway.
Horstmann F H, 351 Calhoun.
Kayser Frederick, 42 Harrison.
Koenig F G, 58 W Main.
Koenig F H, 176 Greely.
Kruse Charles, 13 Harrison.
Luhman F H, 125 Calhoun.
Meyer Adolph, 54 W Wayne.
Meyer H C, 44 Harrison.
Motz George, 47 W Main.
Oestermeier Charles, s e cor Calhoun and Montgomery.
Scheffler Gustav, 43 W Main.
Schoch A F, 41½ W Main.
Stauffer Gottlieb, 182 Calhoun.
Whiteley T R, 172 W Jefferson.

TALLOW RENDERERS.

Falls D M, east end of Dwenger ave 1 mile e of city limits.

TANNERS.

Hutchinson O G, s e cor Cherry and Boone.

TAXIDERMISTS.

Schroeder A H, 38 Clinton. *(See adv, p 69.)*
Smith E H, 21 Calhoun.
Tresselt Herman, 83 N Cass.

TEAS AND COFFEES.

Union Pacific Tea and Coffee Store, 102 Calhoun.

TELEGRAPH COMPANIES.

Edison Mutual Telegraph Co, The Wayne Hotel.
Western Union, Aveline House block.

TELEGRAPH POLES.

Gilmartin Edward, 31 W Williams.

*TELEPHONE COMPANIES.

Central Union Telephone Co, 34 Calhoun.

TICKET BROKERS.

See Brokers—Ticket.

THEATRES, HALLS, ETC.

Arion Hall, cor Main and Harrison.
Masonic Temple, n e cor Clinton and Wayne.

*TILE FLOOR.

Pressler John, Columbia, Barr and Dock Streets. (*See left top lines.*)

TINNERS' STOCK.

Ash H J, 9 E Columbia.
Seavey G W, 19 W Main.
Wilson G H & Sons, 31 E Columbia.

TIN, COPPER AND SHEET IRON WORKERS.

(*See also Stoves and Tinware.*)

Ash H J, 9 E Columbia.
Baker John & Co, rear 377 Lafayette.
De Wald Henry, 80 Barr.
Freiburger G W, 55 Thomas.
Freiburger J J, 139 Broadway.
Fischer Jacob, 125 Fairfield ave.
Gerding & Aumann Bros, 115 Wallace.
Graffe C F & Co, 132 Calhoun.
Gray J P, 364 Calhoun.
Scharf C A, 195 Lafayette.
Seavey G W, 19 W Main.
Staub Bros, 18 W Columbia.
Staub G W, 16 E Columbia.

*TOBACCO PAIL MNFRS.

Peters Box and Lumber Co The, 79 to 105 High. (*See p 6.*)

*TOBACCONISTS.

See Cigars and Tobacco.

TOOL MNFRS.

Schmidt F W, 181 W Jefferson.

*TOYS, ETC.

(See also Notions.)

Renner, Cratsley & Co, 56 Calhoun. *(See front cover.)*

TRANSFER AND BAGGAGE LINES.

Fort Wayne Transfer and Storage Co, 47 E Columbia.

TRANSPORTATION COMPANIES.

Empire Line, 26 Court.
Merchants' Despatch, 3 Schmitz block.
Union Line, 79 Calhoun.

TRUCKMEN.

Fort Wayne Transfer and Storage Co, 47 E Columbia.
Himbert Michael, 14 Pritchard.
Ryan Bros, 21 W Wayne.

TRUNKS AND VALISES.

Fisher Bros, 23 E Columbia.

TRUSS HOOP MNFRS.

Bitler S D, cor E Wayne and Schick.

*TUBULAR WELLS.

Spice Robert, 48 W Main and 11 Pearl. *(See left top lines.)*

TYPE WRITERS.

McDermut W E, 62 and 64 Calhoun. *(See back cover and p 8.)*

TYPE WRITING MACHINES.

Kuhne & Co, 19 Court.

UNDERTAKERS.

Scheumann & Klaehn, 39 W Main.
Schone & Wellman, 39 W Berry.

UPHOLSTERERS.

See Furniture Mnfrs and Dealers.

VARNISH MNFRS.

Millet W C, 149 Barr.

VAULT CLEANERS.
See Excavators— Odorless.

*VENEER SAW MILLS.
Peters Box and Lumber Co The, 79 to 105 High. (*See adv, p 6.*)

VETERINARY SURGEONS.
Barnum G P, 91 E Columbia.
Dodge Arthur, cor Pearl and Maiden lane.
Gaskill & Kyle, 159 Hoffman.
Langtry Walter, 7 N Harrison.
Myers W F, 112 Webster.
Read H A, 66 Harrison.

VINEGAR MNFRS.
(*See also Cider and Vinegar Mnfrs.*)
Hoffmann C A, 183 to 187 Calhoun.

WAGONMAKERS.
(*See also Carriage and Wagonmakers.*)
Olds' Wagon Works, s s Murray bet Calhoun and Lafayette.
Zollinger L C, 13 and 15 E Superior.

*WAGONS.
Pfeiffer & Schlatter, 38 and 40 E Columbia. (*See right bottom lines.*)

WALL PAPER.
Hull L O, 90 Calhoun. (*See right top lines.*)
Hull S W, 134 Broadway.
Keil & Keil, 116 Calhoun.
Kreibaum Frederick, 90 Barr.
Long H M, 11 W Berry.
Renner, Cratsley & Co, 56 Calhoun. (*See front cover.*)
Robinson F W, 68 Wells.
Siemon Wall Paper Co The (Formerly The Wayne Wall Paper Co), 191 Calhoun. (*See left bottom lines.*)
Siemon & Brother, 50 Calhoun. (*See back cover.*)
Treep F H, 68 E Main.
Wilding James & Son, 193 Calhoun.

WASHING MACHINE MNFRS.

Anthony Wayne Mnfg Co, cor Lafayette and Wabash R R.
Diether & Barrows, 100 Pearl. (*See right side lines.*)
Horton Mnfg Co The, w s Osage n of Main.
Lewis Jonathan, 142 Pearl.

WATCHES, CLOCKS AND JEWELRY.

Bruder August, 98 Calhoun.
Fort Wayne Music Co, 212 Calhoun.
Garman J W, 207 Calhoun.
Graffe H C, cor Calhoun and Columbia.
Koenig August, 176 Calhoun.
Krull R L, 128 E Washington.
McKee C W, 120 Calhoun.
Pietz J F, 138 Calhoun.
Sauser Louis, 188 Calhoun.
Trenkley & Scherzinger, 78 Calhoun.
Trepera Jarolim, 140 Broadway.
Uebelhoer R W, 68 E Main.
Voirol F J, 244 Calhoun.

WELL BORERS.

Hopkins Zelous, 30 Huron.
McMillan J B, n s Richardson 1 w of Runnion ave.
Spice Robert, 48 W Main and 11 Pearl. (*See left top
lines.*)
Young Louis, 58 W 3d.

WHEEL MNFRS.

American Wheel Co, s e cor Lafayette and W, St L & P R R.
White's Wheel Works, e end of E Wayne on N Y, C & St L
R R.

*WIND MILLS.

Spice Robert, 48 W Main and 11 Pearl. (*See left top
lines.*)
Weidel Frederick, 9 Harrison.

WINES AND LIQUORS—WHOLESALE.

Boltz F C, 27 Calhoun. (*See adv, p 2.*)
Falk & Lamley, 17 E Columbia.
Meyer Bros & Co, s w cor Calhoun and Columbia.
(*See adv, p 59.*)
Nathan J & Co, 137 Calhoun.
Trentman A C, 111-119 Calhoun.

Sallier Francis, 66 E Columbia.
Wile Isaac & Co, 8 Calhoun.

WINES AND LIQUORS—RETAIL.

Boltz F C, 27 Calhoun. (*See adv, p 2.*)
Christen John, 100 Calhoun.
Meyer W D, 227 Lafayette.
Sallier Francis, 66 E Columbia.

WOOD.

(See also Coal and Wood.)
Carroll J M, 58 W 5th.
Ryan & Lake, n e cor Grant and Oliver.

WOOD ENGRAVERS.

See Engravers— Wood.

WOODEN NOVELTIES.

Horton Mnfg Co, w s Osage n of Main.

WOOD WORKING MACHINERY.

Indiana Machine Works, Osage near Main.

WOOL.

Bash S & Co, 22 and 24 W Columbia.

WOOLEN MILLS.

Summit City Woolen Mills, 96 E Superior.

YEAST.

Fleischmann & Co, n e cor Calhoun and Jefferson.

CAUTION.

Pay no money in advance to itinerant Directory Canvassers. We are led to mention this from the fact that certain parties have been fraudulently using our publications as specimens, and by that means collecting moneys in advance. *Before signing an order, see that it has the name of R. L. POLK & CO. printed thereon.* We ask no payment until the work is delivered, and our solicitors have strict orders not to take payment for either advertisements or subscriptions.

R. L. POLK & CO.

R. L. POLK & CO.'S
ALLEN COUNTY DIRECTORY.

1890-91.

ABBREVIATIONS.

f, farmer; f lab, farm laborer; f t, farm tenant; lab, laborer; carp, carpenter; mnfr, manufacturer.

Following each name are given: First, business; second, number of section upon which person resides; third, number of acres; fourth, assessed value of farm; fifth, name of township; sixth, postoffice address.

A

Abbott Frank H, Adams, Fort Wayne.

Abbott W T & R B, Adams, Fort Wayne.

Abel George W, f, 14, 80, $1570, Aboite, Fort Wayne.

Abel Mrs Mary, Aboite, Fort Wayne.

Adair Alexander, f, 31, 167, $2490, Madison, Hoagland.

Adair Alexander jr, Madison, Monroeville.

Adair Anna M, Madison, Haogland.

Adair George, f t, Madison, Hoagland.

Adair Jonathan, f, 29, 76, $1570, Madison, Hoagland.

Adair Margaret, Madison, Hoagland.

Adair Philip, f, t, Madison, Monroeville.

Adair Samuel, f, 26, 40, $550, Madison, Monroeville.

Adam Israel, Wayne, Fort Wayne.

Adams Augustus, Aboite, Aboite.

Adams Charlotte, f, 18,¾,$10, Jefferson, New Haven.

Adams Earl, f, 17, 70, $1250, Jefferson, New Haven.

Adams Gabriel, Madison, Monroeville.

Adams Henry, lab, Aboite, Aboite.

Adams Jacob, f, 34, 100, $2140, Adams, Soest.

Adams Jennie, f, 7, 108, $2185, Jefferson, New Haven.

Adams Josiah, f, 4, 26, $375, Jefferson, New Haven.

Adams Mary E, f, 13, 40, $495, Madison, Monroeville.

Adams Samuel G, f, Cedar Creek, Cedarville.

Adams Seth, Jefferson, New Haven.

Adams Wm, Adams, Fort Wayne.

Adams Wm, f, 34, 100, $2520, Adams, Soest.

Adkins Arthur, lab, Aboite, Dunfee.

Ætna Life Insurance Co, 34, 80, $1145, Monroe, Monroeville.

Ahlersmeyer Wm, Adams, Fort Wayne.

Ahlinger Peter, f t, Maumee, Woodburn.

Ahrens Henry, f, 34, 178, $3810, Adams, Soest.

Aiken James A,f,t,Lafayette, Myhart.

Ainsworth John M, f, 3, 8, $820, Wayne, Fort Wayne.

Ake Elias, f, 8,80,$1045,Madison, Maples.

Ake James, f, 35, 180, $2870, Adams, Maples.

Ake Jesse, f, 19, 77, $1500, Marion, Poe.

Ake Marion, f, 11, 81, $1505, Pleasant, Poe.

Ake Samuel, f, 63, $1220, Pleasant, Poe.

Ake Zedekiah, f, 12, 148, $3065, Pleasant, Poe.

Akers John, f, 20, $1580, Lafayette, Myhart.

Albauch Eli, f, 14, 16, $215, Madison, Monroeville.

Albaugh A C, Madison, Monroeville.

Alderman Frank, f, 13, 40, $4460, Wayne, Fort Wayne.

Alderman Wm, f, 4, 112, $2550, Milan, Harlan.

Aldrich Charles H, f, 4, 1, $5, Lafayette, Myhart.

Aldrich Frederick, Jefferson, Maples.

Aldrich H M, f, 15, 7, $1820, Wayne, Fort Wayne.

Aldrich & Barrett, attys, 3, $655,Monroe, Fort Wayne.

Alfeld Wm, f, 22, 80, $1030, Madison, Hoagland.

Allen Alfred, f, Scipio, Hicksville.

Allen Arthur, f, Scipio, Hicksville.

Allen Thomas, f, 5, 182, $3145, Scipio, Hicksville.

Allgeier Daniel, f, 16, 39, $1330, Adams, Fort Wayne.

Allgeier Edward, Adams, Fort Wayne.

Allgeier John, f,16 59, $1660, Adams, Fort Wayne.

Alliger John D, editor, 18, 8, $145, Monroe, Monroeville.

Allschenede Christian, f, 25, 39, $780, Adams, Soest.

Altekruse Emma, Adams, Fort Wayne.

Alterkruse Fred C, Lake, Fort Wayne.

Alterkruse Henry, Adams, Fort Wayne.

Alway Edward and Esther, Wayne, Fort Wayne.

Ambler Christian D, f, 33, 80, $1410, Aboite,Fort Wayne.

Ambler David, f, 24, 80, $1340, Lafayette, Nine Mile.

Ambler George W, laborer, Pleasant, Sheldon.

Ambler John, laborer, Pleasant, Sheldon.

Ambler Samuel, lumber, 33, 2, $85, Pleasant, Sheldon.

Ambrose Patrick, f, 20, 170, $2365, Lake, Arcola.

Amstultz Jacob, f, 35, 40, $710, Cedar Creek, Leo.

Amstultz John, f,9,240,$3910, Cedar Creek, Leo.

Anderson Andrew, Jackson, Dawkins.

Anderson A H, laborer, Monroe, Monroeville.

Anderson D B, f, Lake, Duke.

Anderson Elizabeth, f, 36, 40, $610, Eel River, Wallen.

Anderson Elizabeth, f, 8¾, $3595, Wayne,FortWayne.

Anderson Hannah A, f, 18, ¾, $200, Monroe, Monroeville.

Anderson John, f, 36, 40, $745, Eel River, Wallen.

Anderson John M, f t, Madison, Monroeville.

Anderson J P, f, 26, ½, $45, Monroe, Monroeville.

Anderson Mary, f, 4, 40, $455, Monroe, Monroeville.

Anderson Oliver, f, 24, 40, $760, Lake, Fort Wayne.

Anderson Stephen, f, 35, 79, $1040, Eel River, Wallen.

Anderson Thomas P, f, 1, 2, $550, Wayne, Fort Wayne.

Anderson Wm, Jackson,Dawkins.

Anderson William, f, 36, 40, $475, Eel River, Wallen.

Anderson William G, Lake, Duke.

Anderson William W, f, 25, 160, $3150, Eel River, Wallen.

Anderson W B et al, Adams, Fort Wayne.

Andoffer Jacob, ft, Pleasant, Sheldon.

Andoffer Joseph, f, 25, 80, $1485,Pleasant, Poe.

Andoffer Paul, f, 25, 40,$740, Pleasant, Poe.

Andre James & L M, f, 11, 1½, $120, Adams, Fort Wayne.

Andrew John H, f, 35, 20, $130, Lake, Duke.

Andrews D B, f, 2, 140, $1620, Eel River, Wallen.

Andrews Harry S, Milan, Chamberlain.

Andrews M E, painter, Jefferson, Maples.

Andrews Sidney D, f, 7, 7, $920, Perry, Huntertown.

Andrews Theron M, f, 7, 211, $4455, Perry, Huntertown.

Andrews Wm H, f, 8, 1, $30, Milan, Chamberlain.

Ankenbrook Martin,f, 17, 40, $1920,Adams, Fort Wayne.

Ankrim Jeremiah, Jefferson, Maples.

Ankrim Richard, Milan, Chamberlain.

Anspach George W, f,34,122, $560, Maumee, Jackson.

Antrum W S, St Joseph, Goeglein.

Antrup Frederick N, f, 279, $8090, St Joseph, Fort Wayne.

Antrup Henry, f, 91, $2500, St Joseph, Fort Wayne.

Applegate John H, f, 10, 187, $2015, Maumee, Ohio.

Applegate Orlando D, f, 3, 15, $110, Maumee, Ohio.

Archer George, Lake, Arcola.

Election Slips. Headquarters for PERFECT SLIPS
at JOHN F. EBY & CO'S., DETROIT

652 R. L. POLK & CO.'S

Archer John D, Lake, Arcola.

Archibald A B, f t, Pleasant, Nine Mile.

Argo Martin E, ins agt, 7, 242, $3785, Monroe, Angola.

Armbruster Charles, f t, Maumee, Woodburn.

Armbruster C H, f t, Maumee, Woodburn.

Armbruster John G, f, 3, 30, $210, Maumee, Ohio.

Armestring M G, Adams, Fort Wayne.

Armitage Wm, f, 27, 80, $1070, Jefferson, Maples.

Armstrong David, Perry, Huntertown.

Arney Scott, Adams, Fort Wayne.

Arney & Sturm, f t, Cedar Creek, Cedarville.

Arnke Ernest, f, 31, 82, $1525, Milan, New Haven.

Arnold Albert, f, 28, 15, $250, Eel River, Heller's Corners.

Arnold Charles, f, 1, 80, $1130, Lake, Wallen.

Arnold Eli, f, 11, 80, $1105, Cedar Creek, Leo.

Arnold Frederick, f, 27, 40, $595, Madison, Monroeville.

Arnold Henry, f, 27, 100, $2065, Eel River, Heller's Corners.

Arnold John J, Cedar Creek, Cedarville.

Arnold Martha A, f, 3, 3, $20, Monroe.

Arnold Wm, f, 1, 54, $790, Lake, Wallen.

Artis James, Adams, Fort Wayne.

Ash James N, Perry, Leo.

Ashbaugh Charles H, Aboite.

Ashcroft Homer C, Minister M E Church, Cedar Creek, Leo.

Ashler Loraine & Lottie, f, 16, 20, $445, Aboite, Fort Wayne.

Ashley Emma V, f, 30, 8, $105, Cedar Creek, Fort Wayne.

Ashley Frederick H, f, 74, $2080, St Joseph, Fort Wayne.

Ashley George L, f, 74, $2250, St Joseph, Fort Wayne.

Ashley Theodore H, f, 6, $245 St Joseph, Fort Wayne.

Ashman Albert, laborer, Cedar Creek.

Ashten Ambrose, f, 5, 282, $3005, Maumee, Harlan.

Ashton Eliza, f, 6, 20, $115, Maumee, Harlan.

Ashton George F, f t, Maumee, Harlan.

Ashton Jacob, f t, Maumee, Harlan.

Atchison Hannah G, f, 12, 80, $1343, Aboite, Fort Wayne.

Auer Anthony, f, 22, 40, $430, Jackson, Monroeville.

Auer August, laborer, Jackson, Monroeville.

Auer Eliza, f, 22, 40, $410, Jackson, Smiley.

Auer Jacob, f, 22, 120, $2750, St Joseph, Fort Wayne.

Auer John, Wayne, Fort Wayne.

Auer Nicholas, f, 22, 40, $300, Jackson, Monroeville.

Auer Wm, St Joseph, Goeglein.

Aukenbruck, John, Adams, Fort Wayne.

Aulls Silas, f, 40, Pleasant, Nine Mile.

Aulrey Emelia, gardener, 2½, $735, Wayne, Fort Wayne.

Aulrey James B, gardener, ½, $110, Wayne, Fort Wayne.

Aulrey Joseph, Wayne, Fort Wayne.

Auman Ellis, f, 7, 62, $1630, St Joseph, Fort Wayne.

Aurand Daniel, f, 21, 56, $795, Monroe, Monroeville.

Aurand Robert, teacher, Monroe, Monroeville.

Auras George, f, 7, 40, $840, Cedar Creek, Collingwood.

Ausbach George W, f, 10, 234, $2175, Jackson, Edgerton.

Austin B A, canvasser, Wayne, Fort Wayne.

Austin Charles E, Lake, Arcola.

Auth Joseph, f, 5, 80, $1640, Marion, Poe.

Auth Joseph jr, f, Marion, Poe.

Axt August H et al, Adams, Fort Wayne.

Ayers James, St Joseph, Goeglein.

Aylesworth N J, $105, Wayne, Fort Wayne.

B

Baade Christian, f, 83, $8490, Wayne, Fort Wayne.

Baade H Frederick, laborer, Wayne, Fort Wayne.

Baals John, f, 16, 80, $1480, Wayne, Fort Wayne.

Baals Wm, laborer, Wayne, Fort Wayne.

Baatz C, St Joseph, Goeglin.

Baatz Wm, f, 31, 5, $235, St Joseph, Fort Wayne.

Babcock Edwin B, St Joseph, Fort Wayne.

Babcock O L, St Joseph, Fort Wayne.

Bachman John, St Joseph, Fort Wayne.

Bachman Wm, St Joseph, Goeglein.

Backopen Julius, Wayne, Fort Wayne.

Bacon Henry, f, 35, 133, $2705, Cedar Creek, Harlan.

Bacon Lewis J, Milan, Gar Creek.

Bacon Samuel, Jefferson, Maples.

Badiac Charles, f, 33, 12, $180, Perry, Academy.

Bahde Augusta, St Joseph, Fort Wayne.

Bahde Frederick, St Joseph, Goeglein.

Bahde Frederick, f, 23, 80, $1740, St Joseph, Fort Wayne.

Bahrat Christopher, f, 28, 40, $745, Adams, Soest.

Bahrdt Christopher, Wayne, Fort Wayne.

Baierlein George, f, 11, 40, $705, Lake, Fort Wayne.

Bailey J C, f, 1, 75, $1410, Cedar Creek, Spencerville.

Bailey L M, f, Monroe, Dixon, O.

Bailey Nelson, f, 27, 40, $565, Lafayette, Zanesville.

Bailey Wm B, f, 25, 40, $765, Perry, Fort Wayne.

Bainbridge William et al, f, 17, 99, $1255, Lake, Arcola.

Bair Christian, f, Cedar Creek, Spencerville.

Bair John, f, Cedar Creek, Spencerville.

Bair Rudolph, f, 6, 156, $3115, Cedar Creek, Speucerville.

Bair Simon, f, 6, 166, $3305, Cedar Creek, Spencerville.

Baird David H, attorney, Eel River, Wallen.

Baird Robert D, f, 36, 148 $2545, Eel River, Wallen.

Baird R E and W H, f t, Eel River, Wallen.

Baker Adam, f, 32, 60, $680, Monroe, Monroeville.

Baker Albert S, Milan, Gar Creek.

Baker Alexander, f t, Maumee, Woodburn.

Baker Barbara, f, 26, 40, $825, Lafayette, Zanesville.

Baker Belinda, f, 26, 37, $735, Lafayette, Zanesville.

Baker Cain, f t, Maumee Woodburn.

Baker Cain jr, f t, Maumee Woodburn.

Baker David, f, 26, 15, $210, Lafayette, Zanesville.

Baker Edward, lab, Monroe, Monroeville.

Baker Frank, St Joseph, Ft Wayne.

Baker George, f, 20, 8, $340, Wayne, Fort Wayne.

Baker Jacob, f, 25, 200, $2040, Milan, Gar Creek.

Baker Jacob H, f, Monroe, Monroeville.

Baker John, f, 26, 55, $1005, Lafayette, Zanesville.

Baker J W, St Joseph, Ft Wayne.

Baker John & Susannah, f, 35, 80, $1535, Lafayette, Zanesville.

Baker Kilian, f, 9, 40, $730, Pleasant, Nine Mile.

Baker Mary A, f, 26, 16, $230, Lafayette, Zanesville.

Baker Samuel, f t, Lafayette, Zanesville.

Baker Sarah, f t, Lafayette, Zanesville.

Baker Simon S, f, 10, 40, $455, Monroe, Monroeville.

Baker Sylvanus, f, 27, 270, $4005, Monroe, Dixon, O.

Baker W H, carpenter, Monroe, Dixon, O.

Baldwin Abel, f, 31, 56, $2160, St Joseph, Ft Wayne.

Baldwin Joseph, f, 27, 80, $765, Jackson, Baldwin.

Baldwin Timothy, f, 35, 40, $455, Jackson, Baldwin.

Balentine W M, Perry, Huntertown.

Ball Samuel L, f, Monroe, Monroeville.

Ballard Paul, f t, Maumee, Woodburn.

Ballou James E, f, 17, 10, $325, Perry, Huntertown.

Ballou Jane E, Perry, Huntertown.

Balzer V & B, Wayne, Ft Wayne.

Bandelier Charles, Jefferson, New Haven.

Bandolier Emmett, f, 8, 76, $1105, Jefferson, New Haven.

Bandolier Ferdinand, f, 9, 80, $1180, Jefferson, New Haven.

Bandolier Henry L, f, 9, 74, $970, Jefferson, New Haven.

Bandolier Paul, f, 8, 80, $1000, Jefferson, New Haven.

Banett James M, Adams, Ft Wayne.

Sewing Machines, Shears and Pocket Knives, Pfeiffer & Schlatter 38 & 40 E. Columbia.

ALLEN COUNTY DIRECTORY. 655

Banks Creed F, f, 9, 77, $3015, Wayne, Ft Wayne.

Barber Alfred, Adams, Ft Wayne.

Barber Francis, f, 19, 40, $615, Jackson, Zulu.

Barfell Thomas J, f t, Madison, Monroeville.

Barjarow Augustus J, Adams, Ft Wayne.

Barkdoll Charlotte, f, 9, 29, $450, Aboite, Ft Wayne.

Barkley Abraham, f, 1, $245, Monroe, Monroeville.

Barkley Ira L, f t, 26, 100, $1885, Marion, Hoagland.

Barkley Jacob, f, 26, 170, $1385, Marion, Root.

Barkley Jesse, f t, Madison, Monroeville.

Barkley John H, f, 29, 80, $1275, Monroe, Monroeville.

Barkley Joseph D, f, 33, 40, $570, Monroe, Monroeville.

Barnes E H, f, 12, 16, $1100, Adams, Ft Wayne.

Barnett Jacob F, f, 33, 35, $900, Lafayette, Zanesville.

Barnett Joseph, f, 6, 139, $3340, St Joseph, Ft Wayne.

Barnhart Capitola, f, 18, 17, $580, Monroe, Monroeville.

Barnhart C W, f, Monroe, Monroeville.

Barnhart Harriet, f, 18, 30, $1020, Monroe, Monroeville.

Barnhart Peter, f, 6, 40, $680, Madison, Maples.

Barnhouse Wm, f, 27, 20, $320, Lafayette, Zanesville.

Baroe John B, sawmiller, Cedar Creek, Cedarville.

Barr James S, f, 5, 40, $775, Pleasant, Nine Mile.

Barrand Hubert, f, 28, ⅔, $15, Lake, Arcola.

Barraud Louis, f, 6, 5, $50, Monroe, Monroeville.

Barrett George W, f, 2, 120, $1515, Perry, Collingwood.

Barrett Marion, Adams, Ft Wayne.

Barrett Wm H, f, 18, 168 $2730, Cedar Creek, Leo.

Barrett W H & R M, f, 24, 47, $635, Perry, Collingwood.

Barron Henry, f, 32, 66, $1255, Milan, Ft Wayne.

Barron John, f, 32, 50, $810, Milan, Fort Wayne.

Barrone Amos, lab, Jackson, Edgerton.

Barrone George W, f, Monroe, Monroeville.

Barrone Polly, f, 6, 20, $405, Monroe, Monroeville.

Barrows Jacob, lab, Maumee, Woodburn.

Barrus Timothy, Adams, Ft Wayne.

Bart Nelson O, f, 36, 102, $1255, Pleasant, Nine Mile.

Bartels Henry, f, 7, 62, $1710, St Joseph, Ft Wayne.

Bartels John H et al, f, 14, 40, $815, St Joseph, Ft Wayne.

Barthold Frederick L, f, 9, 19, $900, Maumee, Ft Wayne.

Barthold Sophia D, f, 15, $525, Wayne, Ft Wayne.

Bartholomew John H, f, 29, 40, $580, Scipio, Hall's Corners.

Bartholomew W H, lab, Scipio, Hall's Corners.

Barto Milton, Marion, Hoagland.

Barve Benjamin R, St Joseph Ft Wayne.

Barve Joseph T, f t, Cedar Creek, Leo.

Base Frederick W, Adams, Ft Wayne.

Baselman Henry J, Milan, Goeglin.

Bash Charles S, f, 4, 56, $5, Lafayette, Ft Wayne.

Bassett H W, dairy, Wayne, Ft Wayne.

Batdorf Edward, Perry, Huntertown.

Bates Alfred H, f, 5, 150, $2745, Aboite, Arcola.

Battenberg Daniel, f, 22, 160, $2700, Monroe, Monroeville.

Bauer Charley, St Joseph, Ft Wayne.

Bauet Justin, f, 30, 80, $780, Jackson, Zulu.

Baumgardner S H, lab, Maumee, Woodburn.

Baumgratz Charles, Wayne, Ft Wayne.

Bauserman George, f, 9, 36, $380, Monroe, Monroeville.

Bauserman G W, f, 10, 2, $25, Madison, Monroeville.

Bauserman Leal, f, 9, 4, $130, Monroe, Monroeville.

Bauserman L & E D, f, 4, 79, $1040, Monroe, Monroeville.

Bauserman Wm H, f, 3, 27, $355, Madison, Monroeville.

Baxter David D, f, 19, 80, $1485, Monroe, Monroeville.

Baxter D J, f, 32, 40, $545, Monroe, Monroeville.

Baxter James, blksmth, 31, 93, $1875, Eel River, Arcola.

Bayer Jacob, Wayne, Ft Wayne.

Beaber D L, f, 31, 5, $380, St Joseph, Ft Wayne.

Beaber Jennie, Lake, Arcola.

Beahes John, Adams, Ft Wayne.

Beam Henry, f, Cedar Creek, Spencerville.

Beaman Frederick, f, 31, 39, $590, Jefferson, Maples.

Beams Henry W, f, 1, 80, $1735, Cedar Creek, Spencerville.

Beams John W, f, 1, 80, $1365, Cedar Creek, Spencerville.

Bear George, M f, 20, 176, $2970, Eel River, Churubusco.

Bear George & Joseph, f, 17, 40, $650, Eel River, Churubusco.

Bear Isaac, f, 21, 160, $3150, Aboite, Ft Wayne.

Bear Levi, f, 30, 120, $2250, Eel River, Churubusco.

Beard Charles E, Lake, Arcola.

Beard Joseph (estate of), f, 9, 30, $490, Eel River, Ari.

Beard Milo, f, 36, 60, $705, Pleasant, Nine Mile.

Beard Warren M, f, 34, 40, $685, Lake Arcola.

Beard W A, Wayne, Ft Wayne.

Beardsher Samuel, f, 5, 80, $1015, Monroe, Monroeville.

Beardsley J O & Mary J, f, 18, 20, $335, Perry, Huntertown.

Bearing Oscar, Jefferson, Maples.

Bearman Charles, Adams, Soest.

Bearman Theodore, Adams, Soest.

Beaty Theodore, f, 32, 80, $1300, Monroe, Monroeville.

Beauchot August, Jefferson, Maples.

Beaushot Louis, f, 6, 35, $470, Monroe, Monroeville.

Beaushot Margaret, f, 6, 20, $290.

Beaushot Peter, f, 6, 40, $465, Monroe, Monroeville.

Beber E W, Perry, Huntertown.

Beber Michael, Perry, Huntertown.

Beck Mary P, Wayne, Ft Wayne.

Becker Wm F A, f, 24, 80, $1900, Adams, New Haven.

Beckman Frederick, f t, 1, 160, $3200, Marion, Soest.

Beckman Henry, Milan, Gar Creek.

Beckman Louis, f, 27, 95, $1780, Pleasant, Sheldon.

Beckman Nicholas F, f t, 15, 197, $3815, Marion, Hoagland.

Beckman Regina, Marion, Poe.

Beckstine John, f, 29, 80, $2380, St Joseph, Ft Wayne.

Beckstine John jr, St Joseph, Ft Wayne.

Becquett Jacob, tile mill, Aboite, Aboite.

Beebe Elizabeth, f, 16, 12, $170, Milan, Chamberlain.

Beeber E & G W, f, 3, 18, $405, Perry, Huntertown.

Beeching Charles, Aboite.

Beem Finley, f t, Pleasant, Poe.

Beerbower Peter M, f, 20, 80, $1435, Scipio, Lima, O.

Beerman Henry, f, 6, 40, $1340, Wayne, Ft Wayne.

Beers Jennie F, f, 18, 235, $2620, Perry, Huntertown.

Beers Wm P, Adams, Ft Wayne.

Beeson Roburn W, f t, Aboite, Ft Wayne.

Behrman Justina, f, 36, 160, $2715, Adams, Soest.

Behrman Wm, Jefferson, Maples.

Behrmann Wm, f t, Maumee, Woodburn.

Behrns Henry, Wayne, Ft Wayne.

Beighler John, f, 24, 160, $3270, Lafayette, Nine Mile.

Beightte George F, Perry, Huntertown.

Bell Archibald, f, 34, 40, $3485, Lafayette, Zanesville.

Bell C E, f, Monroe, Monroeville.

Bell Delia B, Adam, New Haven.

Bell Elmer, f t, Lafayette, Zanesville.

Bell H M, f, Monroe, Monroeville.

Bell James, grocer, Marion, Poe.

Bell John, f, 17, 7, $135, Monroe, Monroeville.

Bell Martha E, Pleasant, Sheldon.

Bell R C (trustee), 14, 2, $110, Wayne, Ft Wayne.

Bell Taylor, f t, Lafayette, Zanesville.

Bell Wm E, f, 32, 114, $2220, Lafayette, Zanesville.

Bellot Jacob, f, 23, 120, $1675, Perry, Huntertown.

Bellot Jacquot F, f, 14, 250, Perry, Huntertown.

Belot Francis J, Perry, Huntertown.

Bemseiter Joseph, f, 24, 46, $615, Milan, New Haven.

Bence Wm C, f, 7, $155, Adams, Ft Wayne.

Bender George, Perry, Collingwood.

Bender Lewis, f, 35, 74, $1340, Adams, Soest.

Bender Wm, f, 7, 48, $660, Cedar Creek, Collingwood.

Benjamin Charles, lab, Monroe, Dixon, O.

Benjamin James, Jefferson, New Haven.

Benneke Henry, lab, Maumee, Antwerp, O.

Bennett Anna, f, 7, 48, $485, Maumee, Antwerp, O.

Bennett Henrietta, f, 22, 6, $120, Eel River, Heller's Corners.

Bennett Jesse, lab, Eel River, Heller's Corners.

Bennett N F, carpenter, Eel River, Heller's Corners.

Benninghoff Solomon, f, 4, 102, $1925, Milan, Death.

Benton Charles, Adams, Fort Wayne.

Benward Commodore, lab, Eel River, Wallen.

Benward E C, f t, Eel River, Wallen.

Benward John E, lab, Eel River, Wallen.

Benward John S, f, 26, 180, $2495, Eel River, Wallen.

Benzinger John F, f t, 10, 39, $2650, Marion, Soest.

Beorger Wm, Aboite.

Bercot Felix, Lake, Arcola.

Bercot Francis, f, 6, 19, $520, St Joseph, Fort Wayne.

Bercot Frank, Lake, Arcola.

Bercot Henry, St Joseph, Ft Wayne.

Bercot Louis, f, 24, 80, $4680, Wayne, Fort Wayne.

Bercot S Frank, lab, Wayne, Fort Wayne.

Berest Claude, f, 15, 1, $15, Lake, Arcola.

Berg Anna M, Wayne, Fort Wayne.

Berg Philip F, f t, 16, 78 $1830, Marion, Poe.

Bergermer Nicholas, f 13, 3½, $860, Wayne, Ft Wayne.

Berghoff Henry C, Adams, Fort Wayne.

Bergman George D, f, 8, 80, $1165, Madison, Maples.

Bergman H R & C A, f, 14, ½, $200, Wayne, Ft Wayne.

Bernhardt John, Adams, New Haven.

Bering Charles W, f t, 35, 120, $2705, Marion, Hoagland.

Berman Henry, f, 6, 100, $1475, Madison, Maples.

Bernadine Constant, f, 15, 26, $525, St Joseph, Ft Wayne.

Bernadine Hortense, f, 15, 53, $900, St Joseph, Ft Wayne.

Berning Charlotte, f, 20, 40, $785, St Joseph, Fort Wayne.

Berning Conrad, f, 20, 40, $985, St Joseph, Ft Wayne.

Berning Ferd, Marion, Poe.

Berning Henry, f, 20, 40, $1020, St Joseph, Fort Wayne.

Berning Wm, f, 20, 40, $920, St Joseph, Fort Wayne.

Bernreiter John, f, 11, 5⅔, $220, Adams, New Haven.

Bertch John, f, 23, 45, $915, Cedar Creek, Leo.

Berthend Amiel, Jefferson, New Haven.

Berthend Annabel, Jefferson, New Haven.

Berthend Cæsar, Jefferson, New Haven.

Berthend Leon, Jefferson, New Haven.

Berthend Louis, f, 30, 80, $580, Jackson, New Haven.

Berthland Joseph et al, f, 8, 159, $1975, Monroe, Monroeville.

Bertsch Andrew, Milan, Chamberlain.

Bertsch Henry, f t, Cedar Creek, Leo.

Bertsch John, f, 5, 40, $785, Milan, Chamberlain.

Bertsch John W, Milan, Chamberlain.

Bethel Walter, teamster, Pleasant, Sheldon.

Betzel Henry, Lake, Arcola.

Beverstein George et al, f, 14, ½, $385, Wayne, Fort Wayne.

Beyerlein Anna A, Wayne, Fort Wayne.

Beyerlein Susan B, f, 4, 6½, $390, Wayne, Fort Wayne.

Beyers Charles, f, 11, 61, $960, Lake, Fort Wayne.

Beyers John, Lake, Fort Wayne.

Beyers Wm, f, 14, 59, $1110, Lake, Arcola.

Bice Adam D, f, 6, 50, $925, Scipio, Hicksville, Ohio.

Bice David, f, 6, 30, $530, Scipio, Hall's Corners.

Bickel Henry, f, 6, 40, $795, Milan, Chamberlain.

Bidlack Martin, f, 31, 40, $605, Scipio, Harlan.

Bidwell Moses V, Adams, Fort Wayne.

Bieber Allen, Milan, Gar Creek.

Bieber Eli, Milan, Gar Creek

Bieber Jonathan, f, 34, 60, $1180, Milan, Gar Creek.

Biegel Mary, f, 10, 10, $170, Jefferson, Gar Creek.

Biehold Gottlieb, Wayne, Fort Wayne.

Bienend A B C, Adams, Fort Wayne.

Bienend Sophia, Adams, Fort Wayne.

Bierbaum Frederick, Adams, Fort Wayne.

Biddle Henry F, f, 34, ¾, $240, Lafayette, Zanesville.

Bidwell Wm F, f t, Maumee, Antwerp, Ohio.

Biggs Jeremiah, Madison, Hoagland.

Bilser Jacob, driver express, Wayne, Fort Wayne.

Bilser John, laborer, Wayne Fort Wayne.

Binkley Abraham, f, 13, 127, $2255, Lake, Arcola.

Binkley Levi, f, 14, 80, $835, Lake, Arcola.

Bird Elmira, f, 2, 80, $1660, Aboite, Ft Wayne.

Bird James, f, 7, 1, $100, Adams, Ft Wayne.

Bireley Margaret A, f, 16, 11, $195, St Joseph, Fort Wayne.

Bischoff Diedrich, f, 30, 118, $2245, Milan, Goeglein.

Bischoff Henry, f, 31, 59, $1195, Milan, Goeglein.

Bishop Henry, Pleasant.

Bishop John, f, 28, 39, $1805, Wayne, Ft Wayne.

Bishop Wm F, f, 18, 80, $1630, Pleasant, Nine Mile.

Bisson John B, f, 31, 10, $490, St Joseph, Ft Wayne.

Bitner John B, Adams, Ft Wayne.

Bixler Margaret, f, 3, 15, $220, Jefferson, Gar Creek.

Bixler Samuel, Jefferson, Gar Creek.

Bixler Wm, f, 34, 40, $685, Milan, Gar Creek.

Black Calvin & Wm, f, 22, 80, $11,30, Milan, Goeglein.

Black Frank E, Adams, Ft Wayne.

Black George, f t, Aboite, Ft Wayne.

Black John, f, 26, 154, $4815, St Joseph, Ft Wayne.

Black Joseph, f, 18, 122, $2355, Milan, Goeglein.

Black J F, f, 6, 80, $1630, Milan, Goeglein.

Black Oliver, Adams, Fort Wayne.

Black Sophia, f, 32, 40, $805, Monroe, Monroeville.

Black Wm, f, 18, 93, $2125, Milan, Harlan.

Blackburn Jane, 20, 40, $460, Scipio, Hall's Corners.

Blackburn Leonard, f, 19, 40, $745, Scipio, Hall's Corners.

Blackburn Leroy, lab, 19, 20, $300, Scipio, Hall's Corners.

Blackburn Maria, Scipio, Hall's Corners.

Blackburn Richard, Jefferson, Zulu.

Blackburn Samuel, Jefferson, New Haven.

Blackburn Sylvia, f, 17, 74, $1345, Jefferson, New Haven.

Blain Charles, lab, Cedar Creek, Leo.

Blair Ben F, Adams, Ft Wayne.

Blake Carl, f, 1, 49, $985, Wayne, Ft Wayne.

Blakley B, f, 35, 13, $65, Aboite.

Blakely Emmet, lab, Aboite, Ft Wayne.

Blakely Jasper, lab, Cedar Creek, Hursh.

Blakely Mary C, Adams, Ft Wayne.

Blakely Truman, lab, 1, $140, Cedar Creek, Hursh.

Blauser Martha, f, 27, 60, $1150, Lafayette, Zanesville.

Blauser Noah, f,35,120,$2470, Lafayette, Zanesville.

Bleekman Jerome, Wayne, Ft Wayne.

Bleitchan John, Lake, Arcola.

Bleke Charles, f t,6, 45,$1055, Marion, Ft Wayne.

Bleke Charles F, f, 30, 368, $6890, Perry, Huntertown.

Bleke Christian, f t, 6, 42, $605, Marion, Ft Wayne.

Bleke Diederich, f, 14, 4¼, $655, Wayne, Ft Wayne.

Bleke Edward, Marion, Poe.

Bleke Frederick, f, 19, 92, $3160, St Joseph, Ft Wayne.

Bleke Louisa, Perry, Huntertown.

Bleke Wm, Perry, Huntertown.

Bleke Wm, f, 19, 22, $365, St Joseph, Ft Wayne.

Blem Mary A, f, 26, 40, $375, Jackson, Baldwin.

Blessing Catherine, f, 23, 40, $340, Lake, Fort Wayne.

Blessing George, f, 15, 80, $1590, St Joseph, Ft Wayne.

Blessing George L, f, 20, 80, $1325, Lake, Arcola.

Blessing John, Lake, Arcola.

Blessing Peter, f, 24, 438, $5195, Lake, Ft Wayne.

Blessing Wm, Lake, Arcola.

Bloenhuff Catherine, f, 9, 2, $70, Adams, Ft Wayne.

Bloese Wm, f, 33, 78, $2020, Adams, Ft Wayne.

Blondiot Felix, f, 7, 7, $1075, Adams, Ft Wayne.

Blosser John, ins agt, 5, 40, $695, Scipio, Hicksville, O.

Blum Andrew, St Joseph, Ft Wayne.

Blum August, f, 20,160, $3700, St Joseph, Ft Wayne.

Blum August, f, 103, $2100, Cedar Creek, Cedarville.

Blum August S, f t, Cedar Creek, Cedarville.

Blumbach Louis, St Joseph, Goeglein.

Blum Martin, f, 11,347, $7340, St Joseph, Ft Wayne.

Blum Martin jr, f, 3, 158, $3385, St Joseph, Fort Wayne.

Blume Wm, Adams, Ft Wayne.

Bly Abraham O, f, 5, 40, $705, Pleasant, Nine Mile.

Bly Elizabeth, f, 35, 40, $740, Lafayette, Zanesville.

Bly Theodore, Adams, Fort Wayne,

Blythe Samuel W, Adams, Fort Wayne.

Boals Mary, f, 4, 80, $1325, Madison, Maples.

Boals Rebecca, f, 4, 2, $15, Madison, Maples.

Bobay Adeline, f, 5, 16, $290, St Joseph, Fort Wayne.

Bobay Alfred L, St Joseph, Fort Wayne.

Bobay Celina, f, 34, 20, $375, Perry, Academy.

Bobay Frank, St Joseph, Fort Wayne.

Bobay John A, f, 34, 40, $710, Perry, Academy.

Bobay John B, f, 14, 80, $1405, St Joseph, Ft Wayne.

Bobay Joseph, St Joseph, Goeglein.

Bobay Paul, Perry, Academy.

Bobay Peter, f, 6, 138, $2645, St Joseph, Fort Wayne.

Bobay Philip, f, 5, 45, $670, St Joseph, Fort Wayne.

Bobay Victor, St Joseph, Ft Wayne.

Bobilya E L, f, 34, 34, $355, Madison, Monroeville.

Bode August, f, 15, 70, $1400, St Joseph, Fort Wayne.

Bode Henry, f, 21, 80, $1855, St Joseph, Fort Wayne.

Bode Henry jr, f, 22, 40, $670, St Joseph, Fort Wayne.

Bode John B, f, 14, 40, $720, St Joseph, Fort Wayne.

Bodeker Wm, Milan, Gar Creek.

Bodine Tisha A, Cedar Creek, Cedarville.

Body Peter W, lab, Maumee, Woodburn.

Boeger Wm, f, 18, $1500, Wayne, Fort Wayne.

Boerger Frederick, f, 34, 80, $1145, Madison, Monroeville.

CHARLES BOWMAN, No. 18 Harrison Street. **Saw Gumming,** FILING and SETTING.

662   R. L. POLK & CO.'S

Boerger Louis C, f t, Madison, Decatur.

Boese Frederick, Adams, Ft Wayne.

Boeuf August, Lake, Arcola.

Boeuf Henry, Lake, Arcola.

Boeuf Octave, f, 27, 200, $3110, Lake, Arcola.

Boevell John, f, 17, 12, $110, Maumee, Woodburn.

Bohlinger Clement L, f t, 23, 40, $650, Lafayette, Zanesville.

Bohlinger Joseph, f, 16, 90, $1700, Lafayette, Myhart.

Bohlinger Lincoln, f, 18, 53, $945, Lafayette, Myhart.

Bohlinger Mary A, f t, Lafayette, Myhart.

Bohlman August, f, 22, 60, $1300, St Joseph, Ft Wayne.

Bohlman Henry, St Joseph, Goeglein.

Bohnart Donates, f, 28, $15, Pleasant, Nine Mile.

Bohnke Frederick, f, 7, 152, $1522, Maumee, Adams.

Bohnke W F, f, 52, 160, $1965, Madison, Hoagland.

Boisuet Charles, f, 24, 40, $440, Jefferson, Zulu.

Boiteaux Felician et al, f, 15, 40, $515, Jefferson, New Haven.

Boiteaux Gustave, f, 15, 40, $505, Jefferson, New Haven.

Boiteaux P H & F, f, 22, 109, $1675, Jefferson, New Haven.

Boisenet Julian, Jefferson, Maples.

Boitet Celina, f, 15, 70, $1155, Jefferson, New Haven.

Boitet Francis, f, 23, 166, $2015, Jefferson, New Haven.

Boitet Francis jr, Jefferson, New Haven.

Boitet Joseph, Jefferson, New Haven.

Boknecht John F, f, 35, 77, $1345, Madison, Decatur.

Boley Francis, f, 10, 99, $2065, St Joseph, Ft Wayne.

Boley John N, Adams, Ft Wayne.

Bolinger Frederick D, Cedar Creek.

Bolinger Jacob J, f, 7, 205, $1340, Jackson, Hoagland.

Bollman Henry, f, 23, 57, $755, Milan, Gar Creek.

Bolton George, f, 17, 51, $595, Scipio, Hall's Corners.

Bolton Joseph, f, 17, 120, $1900, Scipio, Hall's Corners.

Boltz Alexander, f, 3, 11, $110, Perry, Huntertown.

Boltz Ferdinand C, Adams, Ft Wayne.

Boltz John, Perry, Huntertown.

Boltz Kate, Adams, Ft Wayne.

Bolyard Andrew, Jefferson, Maples.

Bolyard John, Jefferson, Maples.

Bolyard Levi, f t, Madison, Monroeville.

Bolyard Samuel, f, 32, 82, $1045, Jackson, Monroeville.

Bond Charles E, Adams, Ft Wayne.

Bond Mahlon H, f, 7, 120, $925, Jackson, Ft Wayne.

Bond Stephen B, f, 32, 80, $2780, St Joseph, Ft Wayne

Boner Benjamin, lab, Scipio, Hall's Corners.

Bonyour Louis, f, 19, 39, $415, Jackson, Zulu.

Boone John L, f, 32, 140, $2710, Wayne, Ft Wayne.

Boone John S, f, 32, 45, $860, Wayne, Fort Wayne.

Borden Melvin, saw mill, Scipio, Hall's Corners.

Borden Reuben, f t, Scipio, Hall's Corners.

Boschet Catherine, Aboite, Fort Wayne.

Boschet John M, f, 12, 120, $2160, Lake, Arcola.

Boschet John M jr, Lake, Ft Wayne.

Boseker Catherine, f, 32, 40, $785, Milan, Fort Wayne.

Boshler Franklin, clk, Pleasant, Nine Mile.

Boshler Frederick, f, 8, 80, $1785, Pleasant, Nine Mile.

Bosler A H, lab, Eel River, Ari.

Bosler John A, f, 15⅓, $1270, Wayne, Milwaukee, Wis.

Bott Joseph, lab, Aboite, Ft Wayne.

Bott Stephen, f, 11, 3, $25, Jefferson, Dawkins.

Bottenburg J E, lab, Monroe, Monroeville.

Bottenburg T J, lab, Monroe, Monroeville.

Botteron Ann C, f, 13, 58, $1050, St Joseph, Fort Wayne.

Botteron Frederick, f, 9, 51, $945, Milan, Chamberlain.

Botteron Frederick L, f, 13, 20, $530, St Joseph, Fort Wayne.

Botteron Frederick W, f, 13, 58, $1130, St Joseph, Fort Wayne.

Botteron Mary J, f, 9, 40, $620, Milan, Chamberlain.

Botts Francis, f, 23, 80, $1715, Aboite, Fort Wayne.

Boulton Henry, f, 1, 112, $1500, Milan, Harlan.

Bouserman Delbert, Milan, Chamberlain.

Bouvier Peter, f, 33, 40, $400, Jackson, Monroeville.

Bovine F D, Wayne, Fort Wayne.

Bower Harry, Adams, Fort Wayne.

Bowerman Edson P, f, 12, 40, $340, Milan, Harlan.

Bowerman E G, Milan, Gar Creek.

Bowers Adam M, f, 2, 51, $720, Madison, Monroeville.

Bowers David, f, 30, 2, $25, Lake, Arcola.

Bowers David B, f, 29, 80, $750, Jackson, Maples.

Bowers David S, Wayne, Ft Wayne.

Bowers Henry, f, 15, 60, $765, Monroe, Monroeville.

Bowers Jacob, f, 21, 160 $2715, Monroe, Ft Wayne.

Bowers Jacob W, f, 10, 40, $410, Monroe, Monroeville.

Bowers John, f, 22, 80, $815, Monroe, Monroeville.

Bowers John F, f, 33, 86, $1515, Pleasant, Nine Mile.

Bowers John W, lab, 31, 1, $50, Monroe, Monroeville.

Bowers L N, f, 21, 40, $280, Jackson, Baldwin.

Bowers Mary, f, 30, 40, $445, Lake, Arcola.

Bowers Peter, Lake, Arcola.

Bowers Warren N, f, 27, 40, $420, Jackson, Baldwin.

Bowersock Andrew, f, 8, 191, $3435, Lafayette, Aboite.

Bowman A M, f, 32, 46, $1020, Lafayette, Zanesville.

Bowman Calvin, f t, 5, ¼ $15, Lafayette, Aboite.

Bowman Clark, f, 4, 34, $645, Eel River, Lastle.

Bowman D P, f, 34, 82, $1705, Lafayette, Zanesville.

Bowman Eliza, f, 26, 160, $2845, Lafayette, Zanesville.

Bowman Elizabeth, f, 36, 40, $650, Lafayette, Zanesville.

Bowman Henry (reserve), 577, $7140, Lafayette, Aboite.

Bowman John M, f t, Lafayette, Nine Mile.

Bowman Lycurgus, f, 5, 80, $1835, Eel River, Ari.

Bowman Ruth C (reserve), 108, $2410, Lafayette, Aboite.

Bowman R M, f, 36, 80, Lafayette, Zanesville.

Bowman Samuel, f, 36, 20, $330, Lafayette, Zanesville.

Bowman Sarah E, f, 36, 40, $680, Lafayette, Zanesville.

Bowman Wm B, f, 36, 180, $1500, Lafayette, Zanesville.

Bowman Wm J (reserve), 13, $220, Lafayette, Aboite.

Bowser Ann, f, 28, 40, $1435, Perry, Huntertown.

Bowser David B, f, 27, 180, $3300, Jefferson, Maples.

Bowser George, f, 27, 60, $1085, Perry, Huntertown.

Bowser Henry C, f, 28, 80, $1295, Jefferson, Maples.

Bowser Sylvester, Perry, Academy.

Bowser Theodore, f, 21, 78, $1205, Perry, Huntertown.

Boyd James, Adams, Ft Wayne.

Boyer Solomon, Perry, Huntertown.

Boyle Edward B, Marion.

Brace Alonzo, f t, Scipio, Hicksville, O.

Brace Deborah, Scipio, Hicksville, O.

Brace Ellary, lab, 6, 80, $1365, Scipio, Hicksville, O.

Brackenridge Eliza, f, 10, 47, $3525, Wayne, Indianapolis.

Brackenridge George W, f, 30, 215, $7220, St Joseph, Ft Wayne.

Brackenridge Joseph, f, 10, 5, $650, Wayne, Ft Wayne.

Bradbury Jane, f, Lafayette, Nine Mile.

Bradbury John, f, 5, 80, $1565, Pleasant, Nine Mile.

Bradbury Sherod, f, 33, 90, $2930, Wayne, Ft Wayne.

Braden David, Adams, Ft Wayne.

Bradtmiller Charles, f, 21, 112, $2930, Adams, Ft Wayne.

Bradtmiller Ernst, f, 27, 85, $2275, Adams, Ft Wayne.

Bradtmiller Frederick, f, 21, 80, $2225, Adams, Ft Wayne.

Bradtmiller Wm, f, 15, 110, $3035, Adams, Ft Wayne.

Brady Wm H, clerk, 13, 1, $440, Wayne, Ft Wayne.

Brahs J C, Wayne, Ft Wayne.

Brames Henry, Adams, Fort Wayne.

L. O. HULL, Paints, Oils, Varnishes and Glass at 90 Calhoun Street.

ALLEN COUNTY DIRECTORY. 665

Brames Joseph H, Adams, Ft Wayne.

Brames Wm, f, 18, 120,$4800, Adams, Ft Wayne.

Brandeberry Abraham, f, 7, 32, $1320, Monroe, Monroeville.

Brandeberry George W, tile mnfr, 7, 43, $1900, Monroe, Monroeville.

Branning Ernst, f, 40, $3840, Wayne, Ft Wayne.

Branning Henry E, f, Wayne, Ft Wayne.

Branstratter Amos, lab, Aboit, Ft Wayne.

Branstratter Ida C, f,reserve, 52, $1020, Lafayette, Fort Wayne.

Branstratter James M, f, reserve, 38, $770, Lafayette, Fort Wayne.

Branstratter John, lab, Aboite, Fort Wayne.

Branstratter Mary A, f, reserve, 90, $1800, Lafayette, Fort Wayne.

Branstratter William,reserve, 362, $5830, Lafayette, Ft Wayne.

Braun Henry B, f, 14, 80, $1600, Aboite, Ft Wayne.

Bremer John, f, 35, 41, $660, Milan, Gar Creek.

Bremer John F, f, 31, 98, $1515, Milan, New Haven.

Bremer Martin F, Jefferson, New Haven.

Brenkman Henry, lab, Cedar Creek, Leo.

Brenneke August, f, 18, 100, $810, Maumee, Antwerp, O.

Brewer George, f, 16, 200, $2785, Madison, Maples.

Brewer George jr, f, 8, 83, $1325, Madison, Maples.

Brewer Henry, f,12, 50,$1125, St Joseph, Thurman.

Brewer Henry, f, 9, 77,$1725, Madison, Maples.

Brewer Jacob (est), 17, 80, $1625, Madison, Maples.

Brewer Martin, f t, 1, 150, $2430, Marion, Soest.

Brewer W D, f, 12, 40, $670, St Joseph, Thurman.

Brick John, f, 28, 120, $2730, Adams, Soest.

Bricknell Ila G, f, 1, 40, $720, Madison, Monroeville.

Briggemann H W, Adams, Fort Wayne.

Brindle Daniel, f, 36, 40, $700, Lafayette, Sheldon.

Brindle William, f, 25, 120, $2275, Lafayette, Sheldon.

Brintzenhofe Amon S, Wayne, Fort Wayne.

Brockman Frederick, f, 33, 68,$1280, Milan, Gar Creek.

Brockmeyer Henry, Madison, Hoagland.

Brockmeyer Henry, f t, 11, 80, $1510, Marion, Soest.

Brockmeyer William, f, 32, 105, $1715, Madison, Hoagland.

Brodbeck August L, f,10,160, $1360, Lake Arcola.

Broderick Daniel, Jefferson, Gar Creek.

Broderick T W, tel opr, Pleasant, Sheldon.

Brodmiller Henry, Madison, Hoagland.

Bronsen Mary, 30, 40, $455, Scipio, Harlan.

Bronson Wm, f t, Scipio, Hall's Corners.

Brooks Albert W, f 17, 80, $1510, Milan, Chamberlain.

Election Slips. Headquarters for PERFECT SLIPS at JOHN F. EBY & CO.'S, DETROIT.

666   R. L. POLK & CO.'S

Brooks Charles A, Milan, Chamberlain.

Brooks Edson A, f, 15, ¾, $90, Milan, Chamberlain.

Brooks Mills B, f, 9, 120, $2310, Milan, Chamberlain.

Brooks Robert & Mary, Wayne, Fort Wayne.

Brosius Henry, f, 10, 80, $1410, Aboite, Ft Wayne.

Brosius Jesse, f, 6, 50, $1000, Aboite, Dunfee.

Brosoosks Martin, Adams, Ft Wayne.

Brothers Gideon, f, 35, 40, $395, Milan, Gar Creek.

Brothers John, Milan, Gar Creek.

Brouwer Elizabeth, Madison, Maples.

Brower George, Wayne, Fort Wayne.

Brower G & E, f, 6, 20, $245, Madison, Monroeville.

Brown Albert N, Madison, Monroeville.

Brown Amanda, Adams, Ft Wayne.

Brown Amos, f, 14, 80, $1210, Lake, Arcola.

Brown A M, lab, Monroe, Dixon, O.

Brown C D, Marion, Poe.

Brown David C, f, 21, 67, $1450, Eel River, Heller's Corners.

Brown George, Madison, Hoagland.

Brown Henry, f, 35, 80, $1455, Adams, Soest.

Brown James A & L, f, 23, 80, $795, Madison, Monroeville.

Brown James E, Adams, Ft Wayne.

Brown Jessie W, f, 25, 40, $630, Madison, Monroeville.

Brown John, Lake, Arcola.

Brown John, f, 36, 80, $1275, Madison, Monroeville.

Brown John, f, 33, 54, $1625, St Joseph, Ft Wayne.

Brown John C, St Joseph, Ft Wayne.

Brown John J, Lake, Arcola.

Brown John J, f, 25, 40, $675, Madison, Monroeville.

Brown John M, grocer, Marion, Poe.

Brown John M, f, 35, 40, $620, Madison, Monroeville.

Brown John M, f t, 29, $70, Marion, Poe.

Brown John W, Adams, Ft Wayne.

Brown John W, Lake, Arcola.

Brown Louis, Adams, Soest.

Brown Maria A, Marion, Poe.

Brown Michael, f, 32, 79, $1235, Lake, Arcola.

Brown Nathan, Lake, Arcola.

Brown N P, f, 25, 40, $670, Madison, Monroeville.

Brown R L, Milan, Gar Creek.

Brown Samuel, f, 14, 50, $710, Lake, Arcola.

Brown Samuel K, f t, Lafayette, Zanesville.

Brown Stanley, f, 21, 15, $315, Eel River, Heller's Corners.

Brown Valorus, f, 31, 40, $615, Eel River, Churubusco.

Brown William, Lake, Arcola.

Brown William, Marion, Poe.

Brown William, f, 27, 80, $1810, Adams, Soest.

Brown Wm, f, 25, 80, $995, Madison, Monroeville.

Brown Wm M, Adams, Ft Wayne.

Bruck Henry, f, 36, 60, $1470, Adams, Soest.

Brude Joseph et al, f, 3, 46, $520,Madison, New Haven.

Brudi Charles, f, 13, 20, $465, Adams, New Haven.

Brudi G, f, 10, 80, $3130, Adams, New Haven.

Brudi J H (estate of), f, 12, 20¾, $540, Adams, New Haven.

Brueback George T, Adams, Fort Wayne.

Bruick Adam, f, 6, 143, $3125, Adams, New Haven.

Bruick August, Adams,Soest.

Bruick Diana, f, 13, ½, $10, St Joseph, Goeglein.

Bruick Henry J, f, 23, 80, $1980, St Joseph, Goeglein.

Bruick John, f, 23, 60, St Joseph, Goeglein.

Bruick Martin, St Joseph, Goeglein.

Bruick Moritz, f, 196, $3180, Milan, Death.

Bruick Wm, St Joseph, Goeglein.

Brumback O L, f, $500, Wayne, Fort Wayne.

Brundage Homer, f, 12, 80, $750, Milan, Harlan.

Brunkhart Samuel, f, 2, 56, $1285, Milan, Harlan.

Brunner John F, f, 6, 22, $615,Jefferson,New Haven.

Bryant Ira S, f, 4, 68, $1200, Jefferson, New Haven.

Bryant Mary E, Adams, Fort Wayne.

Bryhe Francis, f, 7, 44, $625, Eel River, Churubusco.

Bubb Anthony, 21, 20, $505, Marion, Poe.

Bubb George, thresher, Pleasant, Sheldon.

Buchanan Arza W, Madison, Monroeville.

Buchanan David T, f t, Madison, Monroeville.

Buchanan John H, Madison, Monroeville.

Bucher Frederick, Adams, Ft Wayne.

Buchfink John M, f, 13, 41, $760, Lafayette, Nine Mile.

Buchner Conrad, Wayne, Ft Wayne.

Buck Charles W, f, 1, 85, $795, Madison.

Bueter Bernhard, f, 8, 85, $3390, Adams, New Haven.

Bueter John B, f, 8, 90, $3650, Adams, New Haven.

Bueter J Herman, Adams, Ft Wayne.

Buetter John, Adams, Fort Wayne.

Buffington Jesse, Wayne, Ft Wayne.

Bugbee Catherine, Adams, Ft Wayne.

Bugbee John, Adams, Fort Wayne.

Buhler Jacob, f, 31, 5, $255, Adams, Fort Wayne.

Buhr Frederick, f, 20, 80, $1020, Milan, Goeglein.

Buhr Frederick, f, 27, 80, $1970,St Joseph, Goeglein.

Buhr Frederick E, f, 20, 170, $2515, Milan, Goeglein.

Buhr Henry, f, 77, $2085, St Joseph, Goeglein.

Buhr Henry F, St Joseph, Goeglein.

Buhr Wm, St Joseph, Goeglein.

Bullerman Christian, St Joseph, Goeglein.

Bullerman Frederick, f, 22, 120, $2675, St Joseph, Ft Wayne.

Bullerman Henry jr, f, 28, 39, $690, St Joseph, Ft Wayne.

Bullerman Henry F, Adams, Ft Wayne.

Bullord George, f, 13, 230, $3585, Aboite, Ft Wayne.

Bulmahn Ernst, Adams, Ft Wayne.

Bulmahn Sophia, Adams, Ft Wayne.

Bump Cyrus, f t, Lafayette, Zanesville.

Bump Noel, f, 29, 21, $375, Lafayette, Zanesville.

Bundy Joseph, Wayne, Ft Wayne.

Bunn Harmon, f t, Lafayette, Nine Mile.

Bunn Lydia, Cedar Creek, Cedarville.

Bunnell John H, Lake, Arcola

Bunsold Samuel B, teacher, Aboite.

Bunting Eliza, et al, f, 8, 100, $2470, Jefferson, New Haven.

Burchardt John, St Joseph, Goeglein.

Burg Adolph, St Joseph, Goeglein.

Burgart Peter, f, 6, 8, $1085, Monroe, Monroeville.

Burkholder David, f, 18, 47, $1125, Milan, Thurman.

Burkholder John, Milan, Chamberlain.

Burnier Peter A, f, 4, 1, $15, Eel River, Ari.

Burns Mary M, f, 31, 20, $650 Wayne, Ft Wayne.

Burns Wm F, f, 9, 4, $125, Adams, New Haven.

Burrier George, f t, Scipio, Hall's Corners.

Burrier Isaac, f, 29,120,$1430, Scipio, Hall's Corners.

Burrier Joseph W, f t, Scipio, Hall's Corners.

Burrier Philip f,31, 80,$1030, Scipio, Harlan.

Burrier Wm, f, 19, 60, $850, Scipio, Hall's Corners.

Busche Anton, f, 27, 161, $3985, St Joseph,Goeglein.

Busche Ernest, f, 19, 100, $1170, Milan, Goeglein.

Busche Henry, f, 25, 40, $400, Milan, Gar Creek.

Busche Henry W, Milan, Gar Creek.

Busching Frederick, f, 31, 8, $485, St Joseph, Goeglein.

Busching Mary, f, 29, 74, $2125, St Joseph, Goeglein.

Busching Wm, f, 31, 5, $500, St Joseph, Goeglein.

Buschman Edward, f, 30, 200, $3890, Wayne, Ft Wayne.

Bush Amos L, f, 21, 80, $1615, Lafayette, Myhart.

Bush Frank, f t, Lafayette, Zanesville.

Bush George, f, 21,160,$2925, Lafayette, Myhart.

Bush Jacob W, Wayne, Fort Wayne.

Bush James, f, 30, 22, $525, St Joseph, Goeglein.

Bush Nathan E, f, 17, 80, $1445, Lafayette, Myhart.

Bush W E, f t, Lafayette, Myhart.

Busick Frederick, f, 26, 150, $2110, Madison, Decatur.

Buskirk Daniel, f, Pleasant, Sheldon.

Buskirk Dorothea, f, 25, 40, $675, Lafayette, Nine Mile.

Buskirk George F, f, Pleasant, Nine Mile.

Buskirk George W, mercht, 6, 131, $3185, Pleasant, Nine Mile.

Buskirk John (est), f, 19, 98, $1800, Pleasant, Nine Mile.

Buskirk John W, f, 24, 180, $3130, Lafayette, Nine Mile.

Buskirk J F, f t, Lafayette, Nine Mile.

Busse Charles, f, 29, 80, $945, Milan, Goeglein.

Busse Frederick, Milan, Gar Creek.

Busse Henry, f, 33, 78, $1610, Milan, Gar Creek.

Butke Henry, Wayne, Fort Wayne.

Butler David, Lake, Duke.

Butler Eliza H, f, 6, 10, $400, Jefferson, New Haven.

Butler Elizabeth, Cedar Creek.

Butler Fannie, Cedar Creek.

Butler George, Lake, Duke.

Butler H, Jefferson, Maples.

Butler Ira, Jefferson, New Haven.

Butler Jacob & M, f, 5, 50, $1015, Jefferson, New Haven.

Butler John, f, 30, 80, $1310, Jefferson, Maples.

Butler Silas, Jefferson, Maples.

Butt B F, f, 19, 80, $1025, Lake, Arcola.

Butt Hannah, f, 20, 40, $680, Lake, Arcola.

Butt James F, f, 4, 200, $2765, Maumee, Antwerp, O.

Butt Wm W, f, 4, 120, $1100, Lake, Arcola.

Buttemeier Ferdinand, 33, 127, $2155, Marion, Poe.

Buttemeier Louis, 36, 160, $3035, Marion, Hoagland.

Butterfield George, Lake, Arcola.

Butterfield Sophronia, Lake, Arcola.

Buttner, Joseph, St Joseph, Fort Wayne.

Butz Frederick, Wayne, Ft Wayne.

Byall Howard S, f t, Aboite, Fort Wayne.

Byall, Israel, f, 9, 160, $2995, Aboite, Fort Wayne.

Byers Andrew, f, 25, 179, $3005, Perry, Huntertown.

Byers Enos, Perry, Huntertown.

Byers Franklin, f, 14, 20, $200, Milan, Chamberlain.

Byers Franklin F, f, 14, 20, $290, Milan, Chamberlain.

Byers George W, grocer, Lafayette, Aboite.

Byers Jonathan E, f, 10, 80, $1135, Milan, Harlan.

Byers John W, f, 14, 20, $195, Milan, Gar Creek.

Byers Phœbe, f, 16, 14, $235, Milan, Chamberlain.

Byers Samuel, Perry, Huntertown.

Byers Wm, Milan, Gar Creek.

Byers Wm, Perry, Huntertown.

Byrd Nelson, f t, Lafayette, Myhart.

Byrd William, f, 15, 2, $105, Lafayette, Myhart.

Byroads Alfred, f, Scipio, Antwerp, O.

Byroads Mary J, f, 29, 80, $970, Scipio, Antwerp, O.

C

Cagnot Allen, f, 11, 180, $2475, Madison, Monroeville.

Robert Spice, WINDMILLS AND DRIVE WELLS, LIGHTNING RODS AND FIXTURES, 48 West Main and 11 Pearl Streets.

670   R. L. POLK & CO.'S

Cahill Edward, St Joseph, Goeglein.

Cahill John E, f, 36, 80,$1250, St Joseph.

Cahill J M, Perry, Huntertown.

Caillie August, f, 36, 49,$800, Perry, Fort Wayne.

Caldwell Albert S, Wayne, Fort Wayne.

Caldwell D, 6, 40, $465, Marion.

Caldwell Robert W, Adams, Fort Wayne.

Callagan John, f, 11, 2, $90, Adams, New Haven.

Calvin Elbert, Adams, Fort Wayne.

Cameron James, f, 9, 50, $1095, Milan, Harlan.

Camick James, Perry, Huntertown.

Campbell Isaac W, lab, Eel River, Heller's Corners.

Campbell John, f t, Cedar Creek, Cedarville.

Campbell John (est), f, 90, $2360, St Joseph, Fort Wayne.

Campbell J J, Perry, Huntertown.

Campbell Stephen, Milan,Gar Creek.

Campbell W G, St Joseph, Ft Wayne.

Cane Wm, Wayne, Ft Wayne.

Carbaugh Albert, Lake, Wallen.

Carbaugh Wm H, f, 24, 40, $660, Lafayette, Nine Mile.

Carey Ira L, Aboite.

Carey J W, Perry, Huntertown.

Carey L M, Wayne, Ft Wayne.

Carey W B, f, 5, 17, $185, Lake, Ft Wayne.

Carles Horace W, f, 24, 98, $1700, Pleasant, Nine Mile.

Carles John, f, 24, 98, $1770, Pleasant, Nine Mile.

Carles Martha E, f, 24, 13, $1390, Pleasant, Nine Mile.

Carll Dinah, 13, 1, $110, Wayne, Ft Wayne.

Carlton John, f, 1, 44, $715, St Joseph, Ft Wayne.

Carnahan W D, Perry, Huntertown.

Carns Rebecca, 10, $105, Cedar Creek, Leo.

Carpenter Addison A, f t, Madison, Monroeville.

Carpenter Enoch, Lafayette, Zanesville.

Carpenter John B, f t, Madison, Monroeville.

Carpenter John D, f, 31, 40, $440, Jackson,Monroeville.

Carpenter Mary, f, 26, 40, $725, Lafayette,Zanesville.

Carpenter Mary A, f, 26, 8, $185,Lafayette, Zanesville.

Carpenter M J, f, Monroe, Monroeville.

Carpenter Samuel, Lafayette, Zanesville.

Carrier H H, f, 7, 17, $380, St Joseph.

Carrier H & C, Adams, Ft Wayne.

Carrier Preston & Henry, f, 34, 40, $375, Monroe, Monroeville.

Carroll Alfred A, f, 29, 160, $2935, Cedar Creek, Cedarville.

Carroll George E, Adams, Ft Wayne.

Carroll John, f, Lafayette.

Carroll Louis, f t, Cedar Creek, Cedarville.

Carroll Michael, f, 28, 79, $1125, Perry, Huntertown.

Carroll Thomas J, f, 28, 80, $1240, Perry, Huntertown.

Carruth Cornelius C, f, 1, 93, $1420, St Joseph, Ft Wayne.

Carruthers F (estate of), f, 4, 92, $1845, Eel River, Churubusco.

Cartwright Alfred, laborer, Wayne, Ft Wayne.

Cartwright Anna L, f, 11, $350, Wayne, Ft Wayne.

Cartwright Elizabeth, f, 1, 28, $515, Lake, Ft Wayne.

Cartwright James, laborer, Wayne, Ft Wayne.

Cartwright James S, Adams, Ft Wayne.

Cartwright James W, f, 2 4-5, $80, Wayne, Ft Wayne.

Cartwright John, f, 5, $205, Wayne, Ft Wayne.

Cartwright Lewis A, f, Aboite, Ft Wayne.

Cartwright Mary M, 31, 120, $2320, Marion, Poe.

Cartwright P. & O M, f, 8⅔, $1110, Wayne, Ft Wayne.

Cartwright Rollin, Marion, Poe.

Cartwright Samuel, laborer, Wayne, Ft Wayne.

Cartwright Samuel, f, 4, 180, $5385, Aboite, Ft Wayne.

Cartwright Silas W, laborer, Wayne, Ft Wayne.

Cartwright Warren, Lake, Wallen.

Cartwright Wm, Lake, Arcola.

Carver John F, Adams, Ft Wayne.

Case David, Wayne, Fort Wayne.

Casteel Henry, f, 29, 80, $1520, Pleasant, Sheldon.

Casteel Thomas, f, 1, 40, $590, St Joseph, Ft Wayne.

Castle John, Jefferson, Maples.

Castle Robert, Adams, Ft Wayne.

Castleman Henry, Jefferson, Zulu.

Caston Harvey, f, 33, 40, $545, Marion, Poe.

Cattez Julia, Adams, Ft Wayne.

Cavilier Victor, f, 33, 182, $2835, Lake, Arcola.

Cayotte Francis, f, 26, 49, $555, Jefferson, Zulu.

Ceffel Charles, f, 30, 20, $365, Aboite, Aboite.

Certia Sarah, f, 11, 40, $1130, Adams, New Haven.

Challanger Margaretta, f, 31, 30, $2370, St Joseph, Ft Wayne.

Chaney John, f t, Maumee, Antwerp, O.

Chapin Augustus A, Adams, Ft Wayne.

Chapman Charles L, Madison, Hoagland.

Chapman Frank M, Adams, Ft Wayne.

Chapman John, Adams, Ft Wayne.

Chapman John W, f, 24, 50, $690, Madison, Hoagland.

Chapman Minerva A, f, 20, 20, $370, Perry, Huntertown.

Chapman Preston, f, 10, $280, Pleasant, Ft Wayne.

Chapman Solomon, f, 23, 200, $3590, Perry, Huntertown.

Chapman Sylvester G, f, 20, 20, $370, Perry, Huntertown.

Chapman S (estate), f, 19, 62, $700, Perry, Huntertown.

Chapman S G, f, 28, 20, $360, Perry, Huntertown.

Chapman Wm, f, 58, $1160, Pleasant, Sheldon.

Chapman William E, Madison, Hoagland.

Chapman Wm G, f t, Eel River, Heller's Corners.

Chapman Wm S, Pleasant.

Chase Levi, f, 27, 144, $2020, Eel River, Heller's Corners.

Chausse Alfred, f, 30, 40, $405, Jackson, Monroeville.

Chausse Charles, f, 30, 40, $455, Jackson, Monroeville.

Chausse Edward, St Joseph, Thurman.

Chaussee Aimee, f, 62, $1455, St Joseph, Thurman.

Chaussee Amade jr, Jefferson, Monroeville.

Chaussee Amanda, f, 25, 80, $1065, Jefferson, Monroeville.

Cheney James, f, 8, 165, $3285, Lafayette, Myhart.

Cheney Otto R, f, 34, 2, $330, Lafayette, Zanesville.

Chester Charles E, St Joseph, Thurman.

Chester John H, f, 17, 80, $555, Maumee, Woodburn.

Chevillot Emilie, f, 17, 80, $550, Jackson, Zulu.

Chevillot Josephine, f, 9, 78, $965, Jefferson, New Haven.

Chevillot Jules, Jefferson, New Haven.

Chevillot Philip, Jefferson, New Haven.

Chinnoweth Jane R, Wayne, Ft Wayne.

Chresten G, Adams, Ft Wayne.

Christen Anthony, f, 13, 2½, $530, Wayne, Ft Wayne.

Christen Joseph, lab, Wayne, Ft Wayne.

Christian John, St Joseph, Ft Wayne.

Christianer Henry W, f, 34, 120, $1910, Madison, Decatur.

Christlieb George W, f t, Eel River, Huntertown.

Christlieb Samuel, f, 8, 20, $420, Eel River, Heller's Corners.

Christman Jacob, Pleasant.

Christman Jacob L, f, 32, 80, $1175, Lake, Arcola.

Christman Lewis, f, Pleasant, Poe.

Christman Nicholas, f, 27, 239, $4300, Pleasant, Sheldon.

Christman Peter, f, 34, 95, $1815, Pleasant, Sheldon.

Clark E W, Wayne, Ft Wayne.

Clark James H, Aboite.

Clark Jane (est), 18, 7, $35, Wayne, Ft Wayne.

Clark John A, Aboite, Ft Wayne.

Clark Sophia, Lafayette, Zanesville.

Clark Thomas R, f t, Aboite.

Clark Wm, f, 22, 2, $20, Maumee, Woodburn.

Clark Wm F, lab, Aboite, Ft Wayne.

Clark Wilson, f, 14, 80, $1405, Aboite, Ft Wayne.

Clark W E, non r, 28, 40, $880, Aboite, Ft Wayne.

Clark Zaccheus, f, 33, 160, $2835, Pleasant, Sheldon.

Clarke Thomas, f, 5, 39, $685, Aboite, Ft Wayne.

Clarke Victoria, f, 5, 39, $735, Aboite, Ft Wayne.

Clarke Wm, Cedar Creek.

Claxton Wm, lab, Eel River, Churubusco.

Clayton Enoch, f, 24, 40, $630, Madison, Monroeville.

Clayton Henry, f, 8, 40, $580, Eel River, Churubusco.

Clayton J M, f, 23, 60, $740, Madison, Monroeville.

Clayton Leander, Madison, Monroeville.

Clayton M E et al, $170, Wayne, Ft Wayne.

Clayton Robert, f t, Eel River, Churubusco.

Clem Adam, f, 27, 40, $530, Monroe, Dixon, O.

Clem A J, f, Monroe, Monroeville.

Clem Bell, f, 9, 20, $180, Monroe, Monroeville.

Clem David, f, 27, 79, $1350, Monroe, Monroeville.

Clem Jeremiah, f, 34, 50, $710, Monroe, Dixon, O.

Clem John, f, 33, 160, $2650, Monroe, Monroeville.

Clem Joseph, f, 34, 120, $1565, Monroe, Monroeville.

Clem Noah, Monroe, Monroeville.

Clem Samuel jr, f, 9, 80, $1155, Monroe, Monroeville.

Clem Sarah A, f, 34, 80, $1220, Monroe, Dixon, O.

Clem Wm, f, 20, 280, $5505, Monroe, Monroeville.

Clemmens John, Wayne, Ft Wayne.

Click George W, f, 14, 120, $2410, Aboite, Ft Wayne.

Clifford James, coal burner, Aboite, Ft Wayne.

Clifford James, f, 29, 160, $1920, Lake, Arcola.

Clifford Joseph, f, 31, 123, $1765, Lake, Arcola.

Cline Adeline, f, 32, 80, $870, Jackson, Monroeville.

Clinger Isaac, Aboite.

Clopsattle George A, Lake, Fort Wayne.

Clopsattle John G, f, 27, 80, $1415, Lake, Arcola.

Clopsattle W A et al, f, 22, 20, $365, Lake, Arcola.

Close John W, Aboite.

Clossen Josiah M, f, 7, 5, $60, Maumee, Woodburn.

Clutter Clara M, f, 29, 40, $540, Perry, Huntertown.

Clutter W M, Perry, Huntertown.

Coblenz Ephraim, f, 21, 80, $1485, Aboite, Ft Wayne.

Cochoit Francis, Jefferson, New Haven.

Cochoit Hortense & James, f, 20, 50, $730, Jefferson, New Haven.

Cochoit Joseph, f, 20, 20, $260, Jefferson, New Haven.

Cocoran Thomas, driver exp, Wayne, Fort Wayne.

Coder A J, Cedar Creek.

Codier Joseph, f, 18, ⅛, $15, Wayne, Ft Wayne.

Cody Bridget, 29, 3, $580, Marion.

Cody Maurice, Marion, Fort Wayne.

Coleman Albert, lab, Aboite, Fort Wayne.

Coleman David E, St Joseph, Fort Wayne.

Coleman George, f, 23, 80, $1565, Aboite, Ft Wayne.

John Pressler, Hot Air and Hot Water Furnaces, Columbia, Barr and Dock Streets.

674   R. L. POLK & CO.'S

Coleman Hiram, f, 24, 60, $1175, Aboite, Ft Wayne.

Coleman Isaiah, f, 17, 65, $1460, St Joseph, Fort Wayne.

Coleman Jacob, Aboite, Fort Wayne.

Coleman Sylvester S, f t, Aboite, Fort Wayne.

Coleman S S, f, 18, 7¾, $300, Wayne, Fort Wayne.

Coleman Wm, Aboite, Fort Wayne.

Coleman Wm, Lake, Arcola.

Colerick Charles E, Adams, Fort Wayne.

Colerick C F (est), f, 7, 5¾, $920, Adams, Fort Wayne.

Colerick J & Maria C, Adams, Fort Wayne.

Colerick Thomas W, Adams, Fort Wayne.

Coles Edmond, lab, Scipio, Hall's Corners.

Coles Jesse, f, 19, 78, $2050, St Joseph, Fort Wayne.

Collins George, f, 26, 80, $1115, Aboite, Ft Wayne.

Collins Joseph & Mary, f, 24, 70, $685, Jefferson, Zulu.

Colvin Joseph, Wayne, Fort Wayne.

Comer Marion C, 31, 40, $535, Marion, Poe.

Comer Wm, f, 31, 40, $625, Marion, Poe.

Comer Wm (est), f, 36, 100, $1745, Pleasant, Sheldon.

Comer Wm jr, Pleasant.

Comer Winifred, f, 5, 50, $690, Monroe, Monroeville.

Comincavish Felix, gardener, 15, 3 2-5, $540, Wayne, Fort Wayne.

Comment Justin, Jefferson, New Haven.

Comparet T Louis, St Joseph, Fort Wayne.

Compton Ira, Lake, Arcola.

Cone A J, f, 7, 9, $175, Perry, Huntertown.

Cone Charlotte, f, 17, 1, $175, Perry, Huntertown.

Conklin Elizabeth, f, 10, 53, $760, Eel River, Ari.

Connell Dennis P, Wayne, Fort Wayne.

Connelly Michael, Perry, Huntertown.

Connelly Wm A, physician, 18, ½, $30, Monroe, Monroeville.

Conner Frank, Lake, Arcola.

Conner Wilhelmina, Lake, Duke.

Conners Margaret, f, 30, 6, $115, Lake, Arcola.

Connett Allen, lab, Wayne, Fort Wayne.

Connett Caroline, f, 16, 31¾, $1830, Wayne, Ft Wayne.

Connett David S, f, 16, 25, $1100, Wayne, Ft Wayne.

Connett George, lab, Wayne, Fort Wayne.

Connett Isaac, f, 16, 33½, $1960, Wayne, Ft Wayne.

Connett John, lab, Wayne, Fort Wayne.

Connett Narcissus, Wayne, Fort Wayne.

Connor Matthias, Pleasant.

Conrad Henry P, Milan, New Haven.

Conrad Jacob, f, 23, 25, $315, Cedar Creek, Leo.

Conrad John, Adams, New Haven.

Conrad John, f, 22, 102, $2440, Cedar Creek, Leo.

Conrad Peter G, f 9, 24, $1070, Adams, New Haven.

Stahn & Heinrich, Leading Dealers in ARTISTS' MATE-RIALS AND DRAUGHTING INSTRU-MENTS. 116 Calhoun Street.

ALLEN COUNTY DIRECTORY. 675

Conrad Wm, Wayne, Ft Wayne.

Converset August, Jefferson, Maples.

Converset Marie, f, 29, 40, $630, Jefferson, Maples.

Conway David M, f, 2, 80, $1380, Milan, Gar Creek.

Conway Wm, f, 11, 40, $345, Milan, Harlan.

Cook Arthur P, f, 28, 1, $20, Lake, Arcola.

Cook Cynthia, f, 28, 2½, $820, Cedar Creek, Cedar-ville.

Cook Eugene, miller, Cedar Creek, Cedarville.

Cook Jacob, f, 4, 147, $3445, St Joseph, Ft Wayne.

Cook J George, St Joseph, Ft Wayne.

Cook Reuben, f t, Cedar Creek, Leo.

Cook Samuel, f, 3, 20, $380, Jefferson, Gar Creek.

Cook Wellington, Wayne, Ft Wayne.

Coolman Adam, et al, Wayne, Ft Wayne.

Coolman George W, Wayne, Ft Wayne.

Coolman John H, Wayne, Ft Wayne.

Coolman J H & M J, Lake, Ft Wayne.

Coolman Mary J, Wayne, Ft Wayne.

Cooper Wm, f, 21, 120, $2800, Perry, Huntertown.

Copley Peter, Lake, Ft Wayne.

Corbat Alphonse & Frank, f, 4, 46, $645, Aboite, Arcola.

Corbat Vandolia, f, 3, 118, $2770, Aboite, Arcola.

Cordevey Adelaide, f, 36, 60, $1045, Perry, Ft Wayne.

Cordevey J B, f, 24, 80, $1695, Perry, Huntertown.

Cordrey Francis, f, 1, 120, $2340, Aboite, Ft Wayne.

Cordrey John A, lab, Aboite, Ft Wayne.

Core Eliza E, f, 20, 4, $60, Maumee, Woodburn.

Core Henry, Maumee, Wood-burn.

Corey John N, f, 18, 160, $3425, Aboite, Ft Wayne.

Corine Horace, f, 4, 30, $235, Maumee, Woodburn.

Corine Myron, f t, Maumee, Harlan.

Corneille A L, f, 7, 8, $1535, Adams, Ft Wayne.

Corneille Louis, 25, 80, $1460, Marion, Hoagland.

Corson John, f, 16, 47, $1015, Pleasant, Sheldon.

Corson Jonah, f, 35, 37, $655, Lake, Duke.

Corson Silas, Lake, Arcola.

Corvill Amzi, Marion, Hoag-land.

Corvill George C, Marion, Hoagland.

Corvill J H, Marion, Hoag-land.

Corville Lewis (estate of), 29, 40, $470, Madison, Monroe-ville.

Cosgrove Frank K, Adams, Ft Wayne.

Cotton Eliza, f, 31, ½, $10, Eel River, Churubusco.

Cotton John (estate of), f, 31, 147, $3085, Eel River, Ari.

Cotton Other, f t, Eel River, Churubusco.

Coulardot Frank, f, 13, 22, $220, Jefferson, Zulu.

Coulardot Henrietta, f, 13, 20, $210, Jefferson, Zulu.

Coulardot Hypolite, f, 13, 38, $495, Jefferson, Zulu.

Coulardot H & F, f, 13, 40, $260, Jefferson, Zulu.

Coulardot James, f, 13, 13, $145, Jefferson, Zulu.

Coulardot Juliette, f, 21, 14, $190, Jefferson, Zulu.

Coulardot Maria, f, 21, 14, $210, Jefferson, Zulu.

Coulardot Narcissa, f, 13, 20, $210, Jefferson, Zulu.

Coulardot Virginia, f, 21, 59, $945, Jefferson, Maples.

Coulter Jacob, f, 28, 2, $545, Lake, Arcola.

Coulter & Smith, f, 23, 158, $3360, Adams, Arcola.

Couples Joseph, lab, Monroe, Dixon, O.

Cour Anna G E, Wayne, Ft Wayne.

Courdevey Peter jr, f, 16, 79, $1285, Lake, Duke.

Courdevy Louis, Wayne, Ft Wayne.

Coverdale, George, f, 12, 76, $1575, Lafayette, Nine Mile.

Coverdale George W, f, 12, 38, $670, Lafayette, Nine Mile.

Coverdale Martha, Lafayette, Roanoke.

Coverdale Sarah, f, 18, 70, $1275, Pleasant, Nine Mile.

Covington Thomas, f, 13, 120, $2675, Aboite, Ft Wayne.

Cowell John W, f, Monroe, Monroeville.

Cowell Mary, f, 34, 40, $400, Monroe, Dixon, O.

Cox James D, f, 26, 7, $170, Monroe, Dixon, O.

Crabbs Harry, Lafayette, Roanoke.

Crabbs Jacob M, f, 19, 40, $725, Lafayette, Roanoke.

Crabbs Jane, f, 15, $325, Lafayette, Roanoke.

Crabbs John S, Lafayette, Roanoke.

Crabbs William R, f, 19, 113, $2340, Lafayette, Roanoke.

Crabill B R, carpenter, Monroe, Monroeville.

Crabill D H, f, 8, 80, $1495, Monroe, Monroeville.

Crabill Francis, f, 8, 50, $845, Monroe, Monroeville.

Crabill George W, f, 28, 60, $680, Monroe, Dixon, O.

Crabill Jacob, f, 33, 100, $1455, Monroe, Monroeville.

Craft Wm P, f t, Maumee, Woodburn.

Craig Aurilla, Lafayette, Roanoke.

Craig Enoch B, f, reserve, 36, $735, Lafayette, Roanoke.

Craig James, f, 15, 140, $2925, Aboite, Ft Wayne.

Craig James T, St Joseph, Ft Wayne.

Craig Thomas E, f, Aboite, Ft Wayne.

Craig Wm J, f, 27, 80, $1175, Monroe, Dixon, O.

Crall Henry A, Milan, Gar Creek.

Crance, George & Mary, f, 13, 2½, $325, Wayne, Ft Wayne.

Crater Levi, f, 31, 160, $2625, Monroe, Monroeville.

Craw Anna M, Wayne, Ft Wayne.

Craw Catherine, Wayne, Ft Wayne.

Crawford Andrew, f, 24, 160, $3055, Perry, Huntertown.

Crawford A C, Jefferson, Maples.

Crawford Allen & Lucy, f, 21, 32, $615, Lake, Arcola.

Crawford Henry A, Aboite, Arcola.

Crawford John, f, reserve, 127, $2405, Lafayette, Roanoke.

Crawford John (estate of), f, 33, 80, $1315, Lake, Duke.

Crawford John W, f, 24, $3540, Perry, Huntertown.

Crawford Louisa L, f, 28, 80, $1490, Cedar Creek, Cedarville.

Crawford Martin H, Adams, Ft Wayne.

Crawford Mary, Lake, Arcola.

Crawford Nelson, Adams, Ft Wayne.

Crawford S S, Adams, Ft Wayne.

Crawford Thomas G, f, 8, 80, $1645, Lafayette, Roanoke.

Crawford Wm J, f, 20, 50, $705, Scipio, Hall's Corners.

Creekmoore Henry, lab, Pleasant, Sheldon.

Creekmoore L A, lab, Pleasant, Sheldon.

Creekmoore Thomas, lab, Pleasant, Sheldon.

Creekmore Sherman, lab, Pleasant, Sheldon.

Cressler Alfred D, f, 19, 93, $3100, St Joseph, Ft Wayne.

Cresswell A J, f, 21, 40, $645, St Joseph, Fort Wayne.

Cresswell Elmer E, f t, Cedar Creek, Cedarville.

Cresswell Wm, f, 34, 92, $1560, Cedar Creek, Cedarville.

Crim George W, Madison, Hoagland.

Crippen James A, f, 14, 20, $470, Adams, New Haven.

Criswell Sarah, 19, 97, $1640, Marion, Poe.

Criswell W C, Marion, Poe.

Cronkite John, f, 32, 39, $1515, St Joseph, Ft Wayne.

Crosby P H, Wayne, Ft Wayne.

Crouse Charles F, Adams, Ft Wayne.

Crouse David, f, 27, 80, $1840, Aboite, Ft Wayne.

Crouse George H, lab, Aboite, Ft Wayne.

Crouse Jesse, f, 19, 103, $2080, Aboite, Ft Wayne.

Crow Benjamin, Lafayette, Zanesville.

Crow Calvin, Lafayette, Zanesville.

Crow George, f, 29, 22, $310, Lafayette, Zanesville.

Crow James, f, 27, 117, $2255, Lafayette, Zanesville.

Crow John, f, 28, 40, $860, Lafayette, Zanesville.

Crow Jonathan, f, 31, 70, $1300, Wayne, Ft Wayne.

Crow Joseph, f, Monroe, Monroeville.

Crow Julian J, f, 32, 25, $390, Wayne, Ft Wayne.

Crow Martin, f, 27, 83, $1715, Lafayette, Zanesville.

Crow M M, tel opr, Monroe, Monroeville.

Crow T E, tel, opr, Monroe, Monroeville.

Crowe Neil, St Joseph, Ft Wayne.

Croxton N E, Adams, Ft Wayne.

Croy Henry A, f, 9, 60, $670, Lake, Fort Wayne.

Croy Sarah, f, 9, 40, $680, Lake, Fort Wayne.

Crozier James E, Madison, Maples.

Crozier Samuel, f, 4, 82, $1230, Madison, Maples.

Crozier Samuel H, f, 4, 32, $330, Madison, Maples.

Crozier Stephen, f t, Madison, Maples.

Crull August, Adams, Ft Wayne.

Cruthers Mary E, f t, Eel River, Churubusco.

Cuber Jacob, Wayne, Fort Wayne.

Culver Henry, f, 27, 100, $960, Jackson, New Haven.

Cunningham D F, f, 14, 113, $785, Maumee, Ohio.

Cunningham Michael, R R section, Aboite, Dunfee.

Cunningham N, f, 15, 40, $515, Lake, Fort Wayne.

Cunnison Alexander, Pleasant

Cunnison George, lab, Wayne, Fort Wayne.

Cunnison James, f, Wayne, Ft Wayne.

Cunnison James, f, 4, 196, $4015, Pleasant, Nine Mile.

Cunnison Ruth, f, 33, 40, $1235, Wayne, Ft Wayne.

Cunnison R W (est), 34, 76, $2350, Wayne, Ft Wayne.

Current Carrie, f, 7, 3½, $465, Adams, Fort Wayne.

Current S S, Adams, Fort Wayne.

Curry D, Perry, Huntertown.

Curry E H, Perry, Huntertown.

Curtis Margaret, Jefferson, Maples.

Cutler E L, Adams, Fort Wayne.

Cutler W M, Adams, Fort Wayne.

Cutschan George W, Lake, Arcola.

Cutshall Samuel, f, 36, 83, $1395, Eel River, Wallen.

D

Daffon John, f, 33, 107, $2445, Eel River, Fort Wayne.

Daffon Wm M, f, 17, 80, $1750, Pleasant, Nine Mile.

Dahms John, Adams, Fort Wayne.

Dailey Charles, f, Cedar Creek, Leo.

Dailey Samuel, f, 23, 100, $2320, Cedar Creek, Leo.

Daily Alexander, Lafayette, Zanesville.

Daily George, Lafayette, Zanesville.

Daler John, Adams, Fort Wayne.

Dales Lewis P, f, 9, 12, $630, Adams, Fort Wayne.

Dalman Charles, f, 3, 65, $1540, Pleasant, Sheldon.

Dalman David, f, 33, 57¾, $1890, Wayne, Ft Wayne.

Dalman Frederick, f, 18, 60, $930, Pleasant, Nine Mile.

Dalman James H, Pleasant.

Dalman Jesse, f, 33, 62, $2435, Wayne, Fort Wayne.

Dalman John, f, 3, 334, $6775, Pleasant, Fort Wayne.

Dalman Mary, f, 8, 81, $1615, Pleasant, Fort Wayne.

Dalman Wm (estate of), f, 3, 60, $1275, Pleasant, Fort Wayne.

Dalman Wm jr, f, 28, 75, $1345, Pleasant, Sheldon.

Dalton Tim, Adams, Fort Wayne.

Dammeier Hannah, f, 28, 75, $1435, Perry, Fort Wayne.

Dammier Catharine, Wayne, Fort Wayne.

Daner Henry H, Madison, Hoagland.

Daniels Harriet, 32, 40, $415, Scipio, Antwerp, O.

Daniels Joseph L, f, 3, 4, $30, Maumee, Seifris.

Daniels Martin, f, 36, 80, $1535, St Joseph, Fort Wayne.

Daniels Wm, St Joseph, Ft Wayne.

Dannenfelser Conrad, f, 69, $2770, St Joseph, Goeglein.

Dannenfelser Ernst, Adams, New Haven.

Dannenfelser George, St Joseph, Goeglein.

Darby Ann, f, 23, 40, $730, Lake, Arcola.

Darby Aurelia, f, 4, 40, $405, Lake, Arcola.

Darby George H, f, 14, 25, $395, Lake, Arcola.

Darby Henry, Lake, Arcola.

Darby John jr, f, 16, 60, $840, Lake, Arcola.

Dargon L O, Adams, New Haven.

Darling A G, f, 1, 30, $525, Milan, Harlan.

Darling Eli, Milan, Harlan.

Darling George W, f, 2, 56, $1250, Milan, Gar Creek.

Darr Frederick, Madison, Monroeville.

Darr John, f, 27, 45, $925, Madison, Monroeville.

Darroch A M, f t, Aboite.

Daseler Christian, f, 16, 40, $840, St Joseph, Ft Wayne.

Dauer Henry, f, 36, 40, $710, Adams, Soest.

Daugherty Alvin, f, 32, 40, $525, Madison, Hoagland.

Daugherty Elizabeth, f, 29, 40, $670, Madison, Hoagland.

Davidson George H, f, 19, 160, $1650, Lake, Arcola.

Davidson Richard, Jefferson, Zulu.

Davis Henry, f, 33, 1, $30, Wayne, Fort Wayne.

Davis Samuel H, f, 16, 80, $1660, St Joseph, Fort Wayne.

Davis Samuel T, f, 3, 64, $1445, St Joseph, Fort Wayne.

Davis S C, St Joseph, Fort Wayne.

Davisy W H, lab, Pleasant, Nine Mile.

Davis W W, clk, 22, 29, $380, Monroe, Monroeville.

Dawer Henry, f, 30, 12, $200, Jefferson, Maples.

Dawkins Henry G, f, 7, 245, $4325, Jefferson, New Haven.

Dawkins James, f, 12, 77, $865, Jefferson, Dawkins.

Dawkins James W, Jefferson, New Haven.

Dawkins John, f, 17, 80, $1535, Jefferson, New Haven.

Dawkins John jr, Jefferson, Maples.

Dawkins John R, f, 19, 12, $210, Jefferson, Maples.

Dawkins Sheldon, Jefferson, Dawkins.

Dawkins Wm, f, 19, 80, $1580 Jefferson, Maples.

Dawson Amariah, f, 22, 39, $315, Eel River, Heller's Corners.

Deahl Edward H, carpenter, Pleasant, Fort Wayne.

Deardorf Anna E, f, 5, 37, $930, Wayne, Ft Wayne.

Deatsman Jerusha, 4, 56, $1235, Scipio, Hicksville,O.

Decker Charles F, f t, Aboite, Fort Wayne.

Decker Daniel,f,22, 80, $1940, Aboite, Fort Wayne.

Decker Daniel jr, f, 22, 80, $1385, Aboite, Ft Wayne.

Decker John, f, 5, 10, $590, Adams, Fort Wayne.

Decker John C, f, 21, 159, $3005, Aboite, Ft Wayne.

Deel James M, 31, 40, $645, Marion, Poe.

Deel Samuel J, Marion.

Deeph Philip, Adams, Fort Wayne.

Deffenderfer Isabella,Adams, Fort Wayne.

Deffriant Francis, St Joseph, Fort Wayne.

Deininger J E & Julia, f, 25, 80, $2530, Wayne, Fort Wayne.

Deister Wm, f, 8, 133, $1135, Maumee, Woodburn.

Delagrange Constant, f, 27, 199, $3995,Perry,Academy.

Delagrange F C, Perry.

Delagrange Joseph, f, 6, 81, $1470, Milan, Thurman.

Delagrange L S, Perry, Academy.

Delagrange Victor, f, 27,175, $3205, Cedar Creek, Leo.

Delagrange Victor W, f, Cedar Creek, Leo.

DeLong E L, lab, Eel River, Ari.

DeLong Isaac, f, 14, 5, $130, Aboite, Fort Wayne.

Demoney Joseph, f, 18, 40, $575, Lake, Arcola.

Denges Christian, f, 35, 158, $2320, Milan, Gar Creek.

Denges Christian jr, Milan, Gar Creek.

Denges Henry, Milan, Gar Creek.

Denner John, f t, Aboite, Ft Wayne.

Denner Matthew, lab, Aboite Ft Wayne.

Denney Rolandus, f, 27, 69, $1385,Lafayette,Zanesville.

Denney Walter, f, 27, 11, $190, Lafayette, Zanesville.

Dennis Eliza, f, 15, 40, $665, Lafayette, Myhart.

Dennis George G, Adams, Ft Wayne.

Dennis Henry, f, 19, 57, $1385, Aboite, Ft Wayne.

Dennis Isaac, f, 30, 40, $575, Jefferson, New Haven.

Dennis Jacob, f, 9, 290, $5215, Lafayette, Myhart.

Dennis J H, Lafayette, Myhart.

Dennis Milton, Lafayette, Zanesville.

Dennis Wm H, f, 20, 80, Lafayette, Myhart.

Denny Watts P, Wayne, Ft Wayne.

Dentlebeck George A, f, 15, 30, $560, Lafayette,Myhart.

Denzell Francis, f, 10, 20, $840, Adams, New Haven.

Denzell Joseph, f, 10, 81, $2595, Adams, New Haven.

Denzell Mathias, f, 10, 56, $1985, Adams, New Haven.

Deppler John, Aboite.

Deshong Abel, Pleasant.

Deturk David, Wayne, Ft Wayne.

Detzer Adam, Adams, Ft Wayne.

Devaugh David, f, 13, 30, $640, St Joseph, Ft Wayne.

Devaugh Louis, f, 13, 40, $695, St Joseph, Ft Wayne.

Devaux Annie, f, 11, 40, $365, Milan, Harlan.

Devaux John, f, 20, 100, $1405, Milan, Goeglein.

Devender Frederick, f, 15, 15, $420, Cedar Creek, Cedarville.

Deveraux Alfred, St Joseph, Goeglein.

Dewey Charles H, f, 23, 53, $500, Maumee, Antwerp, O.

Dewey James B, f, Maumee, Antwerp, O.

DeWitt Daniel W, f, reserve, 74, $1485, Lafayette, Roanoke.

Dice Henry, f, 22, 99, $1715, Eel River, Heller's Corners.

Dice John, f, 22, 20, $460, Eel River, Churubusco.

Dick Charles, Adams, Soest.

Dicke Diederich, f, 13, 120, $2340, Aboite, Ft Wayne.

Dickerson H P, Adams, Ft Wayne.

Dickison Gideon, lab, Maumee, Antwerp, O.

Dickover Jacob, carpenter, Cedar Creek, Cedarville.

Didier Frank, merchant, Wayne, Latta, O.

Didier F H, f, 32, 30, $460, Perry, Fort Wayne.

Didier Peter, Lake, Arcola.

Didier Thiebaut, f, 20, $680, Wayne, Fort Wayne.

Didier Victor, f, 15, 40, $460, Jefferson, New Haven.

Diebold Benjamin, f, 36, 38, $735, Perry, Fort Wayne.

Diederich H W, Adams, Ft Wayne.

Diederich Jacob, f, 11, 80, $1635, Aboite, Ft Wayne.

Diederich John, f t, Marion, Poe.

Diehl Eli, f, 11, 160, $3225, Aboite, Fort Wayne.

Dietrich Alfred, f, 4, 15, $515, Milan, Chamberlain.

Dietrich Lourenia, Milan, Chamberlain.

Dietrich R S, Milan, Chamberlain.

Diffendorfer George W, f, 134, ½, $225, Lafayette, Zanesville.

Diffendorfer Henry, f, 20, $1330, Wayne, Ft Wayne.

Diffendorfer John, f, 4, 108, $1415, Lake, Arcola.

Diffendorffer Catherine, f, Lake, Arcola.

Diffendorffer H C, f, 33, ¾, $10, Lake, Arcola.

Diffendorffer John A, Lake, Arcola.

Dignan Hannah, f, 32, 113, $1690, Jefferson, Maples.

Dignan Jane C, f, 144, $3710, Cedar Creek, Leo.

Dignan John O, f, 31, 80, $995, Jefferson, Maples.

Dihem Henry, Wayne, Fort Wayne.

Dinger F C, f t, Madison, Maples.

Dinger John, Milan, Gar Creek.

Dinger Robert, f, 9, 80, $1280, Madison, Maples.

Dingman A J, f, reserve, 20, $150, Maumee, Antwerp, O.

Dinkslager Barney, Adams, Fort Wayne.

Dinkslager Eliza, f, 7, 5, $520, Adams, Fort Wayne.

Dinnen John, Wayne, Fort Wayne.

Dishler Agnes, f, 9, 65, $970, Eel River, Ari.

Disler A C, justice, 3, ¼, $130, Eel River, Ari.

Dishong Charles, Lake, Arcola.

Disler Frank P, f, 20, 26, $195, Cedar Creek, Leo.

Disler Henry, f, 20, 50, $960 Cedar Creek, Leo.

Disler J W, f, Cedar Creek, Leo.

Disler Mary A, f, 21, 60, $1380, Cedar Creek, Cedarville.

Disler Samuel, f, 2, 75, $1470. Cedar Creek, Cedarville.

Disler Timothy F, f, 28, 10¾ $185, Cedar Creek, Cedarville.

Ditmar H A & Mary, f, 4, 79, $1435, Eel River, Ari.

Ditzell, Wm, f, 29, 72, $1135, Jefferson, Maples.

Ditzell Wm jr, Jefferson, Maples.

Dobbins Henry, f, 30, 40, $615, Pleasant, Sheldon.

Doctor Charles, f, 33' 80, $1895, Adams, Soest.

Doctor Frederick, Marion.

Doctor George, 2, 224, $4270, Marion, Soest.

Doctor Henry, f, 33, 60, $1035, Adams, Soest.

Doctor Henry G, f, 4, 354, $6265, Marion, Soest.

Doctor Henry J, Marion.

Doctor Louis, f, 22, 70, $1305, Marion, Soest.

Doctor Nathan C, f, 11, 153, $1330, Maumee, Antwerp, O.

Doctor Wm, Marion.

Dodane Edward, f, 16, 59, $985, Jefferson, New Haven.

Dodane Francis, f, 16, 88, $1145, Jefferson, New. Haven.

Dodane Frank, Jefferson, Maples.

Dodane Joseph, f, 16, 31, $450, Jefferson, New Haven.

Dody J C, St Joseph, Fort Wayne.

Doenger Peter, Adams, Fort Wayne.

Doenger Philip, Adams, Fort Wayne.

Doenges John, f, 32, 80, $1925, Adams, Ft Wayne.

Doerhman Frederick, Wayne, Fort Wayne.

Doermer Peter, Adams, Ft Wayne.

Dolan Cynthia A, f, 18, 46, $1390, Wayne, Ft Wayne.

Dolan Lucretia, f, 36, 40, $750, Eel River, Wallen.

Dolan Mary, f, 31, 80, $1270, Wayne, Fort Wayne.

Dolan Susan, f, 22, 28, $240, Eel River, Churubusco.

Dole Frank B, f t, Eel River, Churubusco.

Dollerhite Alexander, f, 1, 47, $705, Milan, Harlan.

Dollerhite Emsley, f, 17, 21, $235, Maumee, Woodburn.

Dollerhite Isam, f, 20, 58, $555, Maumee, Woodburn.

Dollerhite John, f, 20, 22, $210, Maumee, Woodburn.

Donahue Bridget et al, f, 34, 79, $1295, Lake, Arcola.

Donaldson Joseph, f, 16, 160, $3600, Eel River, Heller's Corners.

Donn Robert, St Joseph, Ft Wayne.

Dooley Charles F, f, 29, 114, $1220, Lake, Arcola.

Dooley John, Lake, Arcola.

Donot Julius, f, 7, 4, $655, Adams, New Haven.

Dorcat Felix, f, 15, 40, $530, Jefferson, New Haven.

Dornk Wm H, Adams, Ft Wayne.

Dorsey Allen, f t, Scipio, Hall's Corners.

Dorsey Benjamin P, f t, Scipio, Hicksville, O.

Dorsey George, f, 7, 375, $5725, Scipio, Hall's Corners.

Dorsey George J, Scipio, Hicksville, O.

Dorsey Joseph J, f, Scipio, Hicksville, O.

Dorsey Leonard, f, 17, 40, $480, Scipio, Hall's Corners.

Dorsey Leonard, f, Scipio, Hicksville, O.

Dorsey N A & M, 7, 80, $1305, Scipio, Harlan.

Dorsey Polly, Scipio, Hall's Corners.

Dorsey Robert, f, 7, 289, $4520, Scipio, Hall's Corners.

Doswell A E, Wayne, Ft Wayne.

Doswell George, lab, Wayne, Ft Wayne.

Doswell John H, f, 3, 1¼, $910, Wayne, Ft Wayne.

Doty Solomon, f, 17, 123, $2295, Milan, Chamberlain.

Doty Willis P, Adams, Ft Wayne.

Double David, Pleasant.

Double Haran, carp, Marion, Poe.

Double John W, f, Wayne, Ft Wayne.

Double Wm, f, 11, 37, $880, Pleasant, Poe.

Doughman A & D, f, 1, 146, $3040, Aboite, Ft Wayne.

Doughman Franklin, Aboite, Ft Wayne.

Douglas James W, lab, Cedar Creek, Leo.

Douglas John, f, 18, 140, $2990, Cedar Creek, Leo.

Douglass Joseph, f, 12, 40, $715 St Joseph, Thurman.

Dove Albert, Perry, Huntertown.

Dove John, Perry, Huntertown.

Dove Margaret M, f, 34, 30, $485, Cedar Creek, Cedarville.

Dower August, Adams, Soest.

Dowie Albert, lab, Aboite, Aboite.

Dowie Catharine, f, 30, 82, $735, Aboite, Aboite.

Dowie John M, lab, Aboite, Aboite.

Dowie Thomas, lab, Aboite, Aboite.

Dowling Bartholomew, f, 28, 80, $1155, Jefferson, New Haven.

Downing J B, f, 25, 80, $2430, Wayne, Ft Wayne.

Doyle Jeremiah, Jefferson, New Haven.

Doyle Martin, Jefferson, New Haven.

Doyle Wm, f, 8, 160, $2680, Jefferson, New Haven.

Drage Charlotte, 34, 100, $2330, Marion, Hoagland.

Drage Edwin, Marion.

Drage Ellen M (guar), Marion.

Drage Frederick, f, 25, 80, $1445, Marion, Hoagland.

Drage Frederick (estate of), f, 34, 112, $2455, Marion, Hoagland.

Drage Henry, f, 34, 100, $1925, Marion, Poe.

Drage Lillie F, Marion.

Draker James L, f, 8, 6⅔, $490, Adams, Ft Wayne.

Draker John, f, 15, 53,$1235, St Joseph, Ft Wayne.

Drebert Frank, Adams, Ft Wayne.

Drebert Henry, f, 5, 100, $2070, Marion, Soest.

Drebert John, Marion.

Drebert John K, f, 5, 100, $2125, Marion, Soest.

Dreibelbiss Robert B, f, 16, 5, $95, St Joseph,Goeglein.

Dreibilbis Anna, f, 21, 40, $1845, Wayne, Ft Wayne.

Dreibilbis Charles G, f, 2, $615, Wayne, Ft Wayne.

Dressler August, f, 27, 40, $1005, St Joseph,Goeglein.

Dressler August C, f, 22, 80, $2100, St Joseph,Goeglein.

Driver Ambrose, Madison, Maples.

Driver Charles, f, 4, 40, $740, Madison, Maples.

Driver Charles jr, Madison, Maples.

Driver David D, f, 4, 59, $1665, Madison, Maples.

Driver Ira L, f, 17, 40,$1070, Scipio, Hall's Corners.

Driver John, Jefferson, Maples.

Driver John W, f, 6, 91, $1040, Maumee, Harlan.

Driver Oscar, Madison, Maples.

Driver Ulysses, Madison, Maples.

Druley E S, St Joseph, Ft Wayne.

Dudenhoefer Louis, Marion, Soest.

Dudenhoefer Philip, f, 10, 143, $2755, Marion, Soest.

Dudgeon Charles H, f, 30, 160, $1780, Scipio, Harlan.

Duemling Herman, Adams, Ft Wayne.

Duglay Fletcher, f, 7, 180, $3580, Eel River, Churubusco.

Duglay Loraine, f, 18, 124, $2620, Eel River, Churubusco.

Duly James W, f, 5, 1, $5, Lafayette, Zanesville.

Duly Solomon, f, 26, 80, $1700, Perry, Huntertown.

Dunfee A L, Perry, Huntertown.

Dunfee Elijah, Perry, Huntertown.

Dunfee Isaac, f t, Eel River, Ari.

Dunn Charles W, Lake, Wallen.

Dunn Wm, f, 12, 80, $1245, Lake, Wallen.

Dunten Allen G, f, 18, 1⅛, 55, Perry, Huntertown.

Dunten A W, Perry, Huntertown.

Dunten Ellis, f, 17, 40, $845, Perry, Huntertown.

Dunten Elmer N, f, 17, 3, $305, Perry, Huntertown.

Dunten Emma, f, 16, 117, $1850, Perry, Huntertown.

Dunten E H, Perry, Huntertown.

Dunten George W, f, 20, 280, $4990, Perry, Huntertown.

Dunten Hannah J, f, 18, 22, $255, Perry, Huntertown.

Dunten Henry C, f, 17, 20, $440, Perry, Huntertown.

Dunten Horace, f, 16, 192, $3560, Perry, Huntertown.

Dunten Hulda (estate), f, 20, 80, $700, Perry, Huntertown.

Dunten Manville N, f, 7, 113, $1975, Perry, Huntertown.

Dunten Mary J, f, 19, 6, $105, Perry, Huntertown.

Dunten Paul G, Perry, Huntertown.

Dunten S M, Perry, Huntertown.

Dunten Washington, f, 18, 20, $215, Perry, Huntertown.

Duodick August, f, 7, 9, $290, St Joseph, Fort Wayne.

Dupont Marcellus, f, 36, 70, $1030, Perry, Ft Wayne.

Dupont Peter, f, 7, 21, $370, St Joseph, Fort Wayne.

Dupeyrone Celeste, f, 24, 40, $555, Jefferson, Zulu.

Dupeyrone John B, f, 24, 40, $275, Jefferson, Zulu.

Dupeyrone Raymond, Jefferson, Zulu.

Durbin Honora, f, 3, 80, $1265, Milan, Harlan.

Durbin J J, Milan, Harlan.

Durbin Legaria B, Milan, Harlan.

Durnell Luke et al, gardener, 20, 44, $725, Wayne, Fort Wayne.

Dush Jeremiah B, f 10, 20, $160, Monroe, Monroeville.

Dyer Millard C, Madison, Hoagland.

E

Eager Thomas, f t, Scipio, Hall's Corners.

Eagy C E, Madison, Monroeville.

Eagy Wm M, f, 27, 80, $1385, Madison, Monroeville.

Earnest Andrew, f, 20, 100, $1965, Monroe, Monroeville.

Eberle John M, Lake, Arcola.

Eby Andrew, f, 15, 40, $460, Milan, Chamberlain.

Eby Daniel, f, 3, 40, $725, St Joseph, Fort Wayne.

Eby Eli, f, 2, 40, $645, St Joseph, Fort Wayne.

Eby Henry, f, 2, 40, $710, St Joseph Ft Wayne.

Eby Louisa, f, 26, 40, $685, Eel River, Wallen.

Eby Mark, St Joseph, Fort Wayne.

Eby Rufus F, St Joseph, Ft Wayne.

Eby Samuel, Eel River, Wallen.

Echner Robert, Adams, Ft Wayne.

Eckert Frederick, Adams, Ft Wayne.

Eckhart W W, Wayne, Ft Wayne.

Eckles James & Mary, Perry, Huntertown.

Eckles John H, Milan, Harlan.

Edsall Simon S, f, 7, 15, $1590, Adams, Ft Wayne.

Edward Lucinda, f, 25, 45, $565, Madison, Monroeville.

Edwards John W, f, 25, 29, $360, Madison, Monroeville.

Edwards Lewis, f, 25, 28, $350, Madison, Monroeville.

Eggeman David, Aboite, Ft Wayne.

Eggeman Frederick, f, 31, 2¼, $160, Adams, Ft Wayne.

Eggeman Lavina, f, 16, 16, $340, Aboite, Ft Wayne.

Eggeman Theodore, f, 23, 116, $2445, Adams, Fort Wayne.

Eggeman Wm, f, 32, 39, $1150, Adams, Ft Wayne.

Ehinger Carl, f, 8, 75, $1655, Jefferson, New Haven.

Ehinger Frank, Jefferson, Gar Creek.

Ehinger John, f, 4, 76, $1075, Jefferson, Gar Creek.

Ehinger J R, f, 7, 4¾, $340, Adams, Ft Wayne.

Ehle Wm, f, 10, 281, $4155, Milan, Harlan.

Ehling Adam, f, Monroe, Monroeville.

Ehling Christian, f, 28, 80, $1255, Monroe, Monroeville.

Ehrman John W, Adams, Ft Wayne.

Eicher Andrew, Milan, Harlan.

Eicher Joseph, f, 12, 40, $395, Milan, Harlan.

Eickkoff Rev F H, Maumee, Woodburn.

Eigenberg Frederick, f, 21, 100, $605, Madison, Hoagland.

Eigenberg Henry, f, 15, 40, $430, Madison, Hoagland.

Eigenberg William, f, 21, 10, $140, Madison, Hoagland.

Eix Charlotte, f, 29, 80, $2005, St Joseph, Ft Wayne.

Eix Christian, St Joseph, Ft Wayne.

Eizinger Andrew, Wayne, Ft Wayne.

Eizinger George E, f, 13, 10, $1190, Wayne, Ft Wayne.

Elaph Henry, f, 15, 27, $420, Aboite, Ft Wayne.

Elett Herman, f, 33, 2, $85, Adams, Soest.

Ellett Christian, Adams, Ft Wayne.

Elliott Mary J, Adams, Ft Wayne.

Ellison Daniel M, Madison, Maples.

Ellison Thomas S, f, 4, 30, $285, Lafayette, Fort Wayne.

Elsner Alert, St Joseph, Ft Wayne.

Elson John O, Cedar Creek.

Ely Adam F, f, 84, $1220, Cedar Creek, Cedarville.

Ely David, f, 12, 55, $1105, Cedar Creek, Cedarville.

Ely Edward, f, 4, 148, $3245, St Joseph, Ft Wayne.

Eme Eugene, Lake, Arcola.

Eme Ferdinand, f, 33, 80, $1560, Lake, Arcola.

Eme Frank, Lake, Arcola.

Eme Louis J, Wayne, Ft Wayne.

Emerich Wm, f, 6, 21, $260, Perry, Huntertown.

Emerick Adam, f, 13, 80, $1505, Marion, Hoagland.

Emerick Augustina, f, 12, 160, $2290, Lake, Arcola.

Emerick A J, f, 12, 120, $2300, Pleasant, Poe.

Emerick Barbara, f, 19, ⅛, $65, Madison, Hoagland.

Emerick George, f, 12, 40, $630, Cedar Creek, Hurst.

Builders' Hardware, PFEIFFER & SCHLATTER, 38 and 40 EAST COLUMBIA ST.

ALLEN COUNTY DIRECTORY. 687

Emerick Henry, f, 13, 38, $955, Marion, Hoagland.

Emerick Jacob, f, 13, 203, $3425, Pleasant, Poe.

Emerick Jacob L, f, Pleasant, Poe.

Emerick James B, f t, Marion, Poe.

Emerick John, Perry, Huntertown.

Emerick John P, f, 13, 82, $1675, Pleasant, Poe.

Emerick Judson B, f, Pleasant, Poe.

Emerick Martin, Perry, Huntertown.

Emerick Melville, Marion, Poe

Emerick Preston S, Wayne, Ft Wayne.

Emerick Wm, f, 8, 110, $2420, Perry, Huntertown.

Emerick Wm H, Madison, Maples.

Emmenheiser Catherine, Madison, Hoagland.

Emmenheiser Joseph, f, 29, 138, $2115, Madison, Hoagland.

Emmenheiser Joseph W, f, 30, 78, $865, Madison, Hoagland.

Emmenheiser J A, f, 31, 78, $1080, Monroe, Monroeville.

Emmenheiser Stephen, Madison, Hoagland.

Empie Thomas B, Adams, Ft Wayne.

Endinger Frederick, Milan, Chamberlain.

Endinger George, f, 15, 20, $265, Milan, Chamberlain.

Engelbrecht Wm, Adams, Ft Wayne.

Engle Amiel, f, 35, 79, $1230, Madison, Monroeville.

Engle Edward, Adams, Ft Wayne.

Engle George, f, 21, 1, $25, Wayne, Ft Wayne.

Engle John F, f, 14, 1⅓, $450, Wayne, Ft Wayne.

Engle Margaret, f, 21, 64, $3370, Wayne, Ft Wayne.

Engle Mary A, f, 35, 40, $510, Madison, Monroeville.

Engle Warren, Wayne, Ft Wayne.

English Alice, f, 2, 40, $705, St Joseph, Ft Wayne.

English James, f, 19, 129, $2180, Madison, Hoagland.

English Thomas, f, 22, 40, $440, Milan, Chamberlain.

Enyard Matilda, f t, Maumee, Antwerp, O.

Enz Frederick, Wayne, Ft Wayne.

Erdel Valentine, f, 11, 80 $2000, Aboite, Ft Wayne.

Erdman Frederick, Wayne, Fort Wayne.

Erick George, f, 30, 193, $4270, Perry, Wallen.

Ernest U G, St Joseph, Fort Wayne.

Erskine A S, f, Cedar Creek, Collingwood.

Erwin Marie E, f, 10, 4, $70, Aboite, Ft Wayne.

Erwin Richard K, f, 10, 35, $825, Aboite, Fort Wayne.

Erwin Richard M, Wayne, Fort Wayne.

Essig James M, Marion, Poe.

Essig John G, f, 20, 186, $3900, Marion, Poe.

Esterline Wm J, f, 19, 149, $2920, Aboite, Ft Wayne.

Evans Nathan, f, 18, 12½, $800, Adams, Ft Wayne.

Evans Regina, Wayne, Fort Wayne.

Evard Ami C, f, 2, $165, St Joseph, Thurman.

Evard Clement, Milan, Thurman.

Evard David E, Milan, Thurman.

Evard Frederick, Milan, Thurman.

Evard James, f, 24, 79,$2210, St Joseph, Thurman.

Evard John A, f, 7, 74, $1195, Milan, Thurman.

Evard Jules, f, 12, 80, $1320, St Joseph, Thurman.

Evard Julius, f, 7, 100, $2080, Milan, Thurman.

Evard Justin, Jefferson, Monroeville.

Evard Mary L, f, 29, 80, $1271, Milan, Goeglein.

Evard Sophia, f, 36, 80, $810, Jefferson, Monroeville.

Everett Samuel W, Perry, Huntertown.

Evry A & S T, Adams, Fort Wayne.

Ewart David J, f, reserve, 106, $1580, Lafayette, Nine Mile.

Ewart Robert & Mary, f, 10, 106, $1735, Lafayette, Nine Mile.

Ewing George W, f, 5, 3½ $185, Adams, Ft Wayne.

Eyly Jacob, f, 2, 40, $540, Milan, Harlan.

Eyson John A, f, 6, 4, $470, Adams, Fort Wayne.

F

Fachs Francis A, f, 22, 100, $1855, Pleasant.

Fackler Elias, f, 17, 40, $525, Madison, Hoagland.

Fackler Michael, f, 17, 80, 1085, Madison, Hoagland.

Fahl Ada, f, 19, 22, $500, Lafayette, Zanesville.

Fahl Charles F, Lafayette, Roanoke.

Fahl Henry, f, 19, 40, $775, Lafayette, Roanoke.

Fahlsing Christian, driver, Wayne, Fort Wayne.

Fahlsing Conrad, f, 8, 333, $3645, Maumee, Woodburn.

Fahlsing Frederick, f, 4, 7, $420, Wayne, Ft Wayne.

Fahlsing Frederick W, f, 30, 400, $2790, Maumee, Fort Wayne.

Fahlsing Frederick W, f, 4 123, $4980, Wayne, Fort Wayne.

Fahner Wm, lab, Aboite, Ft Wayne.

Failor Jacob, f, 24, 13¾, $615, Wayne, Ft Wayne.

Failour Wilson, Wayne, Ft Wayne.

Fair Gabriel, f, 26, 160, $2-495, Eel River, Wallen.

Fairfield A W, Wayne, Ft Wayne.

Fairfield Charles, f, 29, 370, $7745, Wayne, Ft Wayne.

Fairfield Charles W, f, 28, 100, $2765, Wayne, Fort Wayne.

Fairfield James, f, 36,35,$470, Lake, Duke.

Falkenberg Wm, lab, Eel River, Heller's Corners.

Fall D M & Mary, f, 5, 5, $215, Adams, Ft Wayne.

Falls Joseph, f, 21, 110, $2720, Marion, Poe.

Falls Margaret, f, 5, 6¾, $775, Adams, Ft Wayne.

Falls Owen, f, 30, 61, $610, Jackson, Monroeville.

Fark Edward, f, 14, 20, $345, St Joseph, Ft Wayne.

Fark Frederick, f, 16, 40, $770, St Joseph, Ft Wayne.

Fark Henry, f, 15, 30, $530, St Joseph, Ft Wayne.

Fark Louis, f, 15, 20, $320, St Joseph, Ft Wayne.

Farmer Christian, f, 2, 58, $955, Milan, Harlan.

Farmer Cyrus, Milan, Harlan.

Farrand Deliloh, f, 17, ⅔, 105, Perry, Huntertown.

Farrand Richard S, saloon, Cedar Creek, Cedarville.

Farre Joseph, Wayne, Fort Wayne.

Farrell Andrew J, lab, Pleasant, Sheldon.

Farrell Austin, f, 26, 25, $355, Lafayette, Zanesville.

Farrell Cornelius, lab, Pleasant, Sheldon.

Farrell George B, f t, Pleasant, Sheldon.

Farrell James W, lab, Pleasant, Sheldon.

Farrell Jonas, lab, Pleasant, Sheldon.

Faulkner Charles W, Perry, Huntertown.

Faulkner Elijah J, f t, Aboite, Ft Wayne.

Faulkner Frank C, f t, Maumee, Harlan.

Faulkner Joseph A, f t, Maumee, Woodburn.

Faulkner W H, tel opr, Maumee, Woodburn.

Faust Anthony, f, 11, 71, $1815, Cedar Creek, Hursh.

Faveret John, Jefferson, Maples.

Faveret Louis, Jefferson, Maples.

Faveret Venus, f, 33, 18, $260, Jefferson, Maples.

Favery Frank, Madison.

Favret Lucas, lab, 18, 1, $115, Monroe, Monroeville.

Favrier Claude S, f, 15, 40, $535, Jefferson, New Haven.

Feaser Alva M, lab, Aboite, Ft Wayne.

Feaser Jacob, lab, Aboite, Ft Wayne.

Feaser Nicholas, f, 16, 10, $290, Aboite, Ft Wayne.

Featon Franklin, f, 32, 40, $580, Monroe, Monroeville.

Federspiel John, f, 27, 129, $1975, Milan, Death.

Federspiel Joseph, f, 2, 57, $1625, Adams, New Haven.

Federspiel Magdalen, f, 1, 60, $2075, Adams, New Haven.

Federspiel Michael, f, 28, 53, $940, Milan, New Haven.

Federspiel, Michael, jr, Milan, Gar Creek.

Federspiel Peter B, f, 13, 63, $1060, Milan, New Haven.

Feichter Charles, f, 14, 80, $1300, Lafayette, Nine Mile.

Feichter Jacob, f, 14, 40, $830, Lafayette, Nine Mile.

Feighley Matilda (estate of), 6, 91, $1000, Maumee.

Feighner Adam, f, Lafayette, Zanesville.

Feighner Mary, f, 28, 10, $270, Lafayette, Nine Mile.

Feighner Solomon R, f, 15, 159, $2650, Lafayette, Nine Mile.

Feighner Wm, Lafayette, Zanesville.

Feightley Theodore, f t, Maumee, Harlan.

John Pressler, Hot Air and Hot Water Furnaces.
Columbia, Barr and Dock Streets.

690   R. L. POLK & CO.'S

Feigner Daniel, Pleasant, Nine Mile.

Felger Christian F, Lake, Arcola.

Felger Christopher, f, reserve, 170, $3625, Marion, Poe.

Felger Dorothea, f, 3, 136, $2115, Marion, Soest.

Felger Frederick E, Lake, Arcola.

Felger Gottlieb, f, 22, 144, $2080, Lake, Arcola.

Felger Gottlieb, f, 34, 99, $1815, Milan, Gar Creek.

Felger George F, f, 28, 80, $1255, Lake, Arcola.

Felger Henry W, Marion, Soest.

Felger Jacob H jr, f, 15, 107, $1730, Lake, Arcola.

Felger John, f, 11, 97, $1820, Marion, Soest.

Felger John A, Lake, Arcola.

Felger John C, f, 15, 144, $2410, Lake, Arcola.

Felger John W, f, 28, 80, $1600, Lake, Arcola.

Felger Louisa, f, 34, 40, $450, Milan, Gar Creek.

Felger Rosina et al, f, 28, 58, $1100, Lake, Fort Wayne.

Felger Sophia, f, 28, 22, $575, Lake, Fort Wayne.

Felger Wm C, f, 22, 80, $1200, Lake, Arcola.

Felker Jesse B, 34, 2, $190, Wayne, Fort Wayne.

Fell Christian, f, 2, 100, $2080, Pleasant.

Fell James F, f, 9, 80, $1575, Pleasant, Fort Wayne.

Felt Charles, Adams, Fort Wayne.

Felt Owen, Aboite.

Felt Wm, Marion.

Feltz W H, Wayne, Fort Wayne.

Fenker Conrad, Adams, Ft Wayne.

Fensee Henry, f, 6, 84, $555, Maumee, Woodburn.

Ferber Conrad P, blksmith, 3, 2, $260, Marion, Soest.

Ferguson John, f, 9, 800, $5935, Pleasant, Sheldon.

Fetters David, Monroe, Monroeville.

Feuker Rudolph G, Adams, Ft Wayne.

Feusner Henry, Milan, Goeglein.

Fick Michael, Pleasant, Nine Mile.

Fiedler Albert, Milan, Gar Creek.

Fields Amos, f t, Pleasant, Nine Mile.

Fields Francis B, f, 18' 77, $1560, Pleasant, Nine Mile.

Fields George T, f, Pleasant, Nine Mile.

Figel Charles G, f, 4, 18, $220, Madison, Maples.

Figel Margaret & Charles, f, 4, 47, $755, Madison, Hoagland.

Fillen K, lab, Monroe, Dixon, O.

Finan Edward, f, 3, 78, $1090, Monroe, Monroeville.

Fink Jacob, wagon mnfr, 11, $20, Cedar Creek, Leo.

Finkey Wm, Adams, Ft Wayne.

Firestine Charles, St Joseph, Ft Wayne.

Firestine George, f, 31, 10, $425, St Joseph, Ft Wayne.

Firestine Lyman, St Joseph, Ft Wayne.

Fisher Abel, Adams, Ft Wayne

FisherB G,Wayne,Ft Wayne

Fisher Frank, Pleasant.

Fisher Henry, f, 18, ¾, $45, Eel River, Churubusco.

Fisher Henry W, f, 22, 80, $1220, Lafayette, Myhart.

Fisher Jacob, f, 14, 79, $1505, Pleasant.

Fisher Mary E, f, 7, 76, $1750, Eel River, Churubusco.

Fisher Samuel, f, 7, 160, $2845, Lafayette, Aboite.

Fisher Thomas, lab, Eel River, Ari.

Fitch David, f, 9, 160, $2550, Perry, Huntertown.

Fitch Harvey, f, 15, 160, $2380, Perry, Huntertown.

Fitch Matthias, f, 4, 226, $4590, Perry, Huntertown.

Fitch Nancy, f, 19, 19, $395, Perry, Huntertown.

Fitch Sarah, f, 4, 18, $325, Perry, Huntertown.

Fitzgerald Ellen,CedarCreek, Leo.

Fitzgerald Henry, f, 1, 10, $165, St Joseph, Thur-man.

Fitzgerald H, f, 6, 56, $950, Milan, Thurman.

Fitzgerald James, Wayne, Ft Wayne.

Fitzgerald Mary R, f, 5, 80, $1880, Milan, Thurman.

Fitzgerald Michael, Milan, Chamberlain.

Fitzgerald Patrick, Pleasant, Sheldon.

Fitzgerald Wm, f, 6, 210, $3915, Milan, Thurman.

Fitzmaurice Ellen, 13, 5, $600, Wayne, Ft Wayne.

Fitzsimmons Nathaniel, f, 17, 157, $3610, Perry, Hunter-town.

Flack Charles R, f, 14, 40, $760, Aboite, Ft Wayne.

Flack Robert, tinsmith, 3, $145, Wayne, Ft Wayne.

Flaig Frederick, lab,Pleasant, Sheldon.

Flaig Jacob, f, 12, 40, $837, Lafayette, Nine Mile.

Flanigan John, f, 12, 40, $735, Perry, Collingwood.

Flaugh Jacob, Jefferson, Maples.

Flaugh Jacob (estate of), f, 18,30,$415,Madison, Maples

Flaugh John M, f, 18, 37, $545, Madison, Hoagland.

Flaugh Marion, f, 6, 106, $2555, Wayne, Ft Wayne.

Fleming James W, f, 30, 155, $2880, Perry,Collingwood.

Fleming Oliver, f, 17, 40, $300, Maumee, Ft Wayne.

Fleming Theodore,Lafayette, Myhart.

Fleming Thomas H, Perry, Wallen.

Fleming Wm, f, 15, 115,$605 Jackson, Ft Wayne.

Fleming Wm, f, 26, 80, $875, Milan, Harlan.

Fleming Wm (estate of), 253, $7660, Wayne, Ft Wayne.

Fleming & Brackenridge, f, 28, 19, 110, Maumee, Fort Wayne. -

Fletcher C C, Adams, Fort Wayne.

Fletcher John T, Jefferson, Maples.

Fletter James M, f, 12, 80, $1220, St Joseph, Thurman

Fletter Wm B, St Joseph, Fort Wayne.

Flickinger John, f, 7, 80, $1745, Milan, Chamberlain.

Flickinger John F, f, 14, 20, $195, Milan, Chamberlain.

Flickinger J L, Milan, Chamberlain.

Flickinger Sylvester, f, 14, 80, $910, Milan, Harlan.

Flowers Menno S, f, 12, 9, $270, Adams, New Haven.

Flum Albert, Lafayette, Zanesville.

Flum Joseph, f t, Pleasant, Sheldon.

Flutter Sarah, f, 20, 22¼, $700, Wayne, Ft Wayne.

Foerster John, Adams, Soest.

Fogel Delano, f, 10, 80, $1125, Eel River, Ari.

Fogel Frank, f, 16, 20, $340, Eel River, Churubusco.

Fogel John, lab, Eel River, Ari.

Fogel Nancy J, f t, Eel River, Ari.

Fogel Orrin, f, 7, 2, $25, Eel River, Churubusco.

Fogel Winton, f, 3, 80, $1020, Eel River, Ari.

Fogwell David, f, 1, 75, $1405, Pleasant.

Fogwell George, f t, Pleasant, Nine Mile.

Fogwell George F, f, 1, 29, $415, Lafayette, Nine Mile.

Fogwell Wm, f, 1, 194, $3765, Lafayette, Nine Mile.

Foltz Anton, Wayne, Fort Wayne.

Foltz Christian, f, 12, 116, $2310, Lafayette, Nine Mile.

Foltz Henry, f, 4, 49, $870, Aboite, Arcola.

Foltz Isaiah, Aboite, Arcola.

Foltz Martha, f, 35, 9, $145, Lake, Arcola.

Fonner David, f, 34, 6½, $110, Marion, Poe.

Fonner David M, f, 34, 48, $1050, Marion, Poe.

Fonner Wm, f, 33, 129, $2350, Marion, Poe.

Fonner Wm H, Marion, Poe.

Foote Harvey B, f, 29, 95, $1405, Scipio, Hall's Corners.

Forbes Frank, Milan, Gar Creek.

Forbing Harrison, Lake, Arcola.

Forbing Joseph, f, 18, 86, $1050, Lake, Arcola.

Fordham Louis, Wayne, Ft Wayne.

Forsythe David H, f t, Aboite, Fort Wayne.

Forsythe Frank, lab, Aboite, Fort Wayne.

Forsythe Wesley H, f, 7, 80, $1850, Aboite, Ft Wayne.

Forthmiller Henry, f, 6, 160, $2965, Jefferson, New Haven.

Forthmiller Jacob, f, 17, 160, $3205, Jefferson, New Haven.

Fortmiller Alice & Catherine, Jefferson, New Haven.

Fortriede Louis, Adams, Ft Wayne.

Fosnight Hiram, lab, Scipio, Hall's Corners.

Foster Edgar C, Perry, Huntertown.

Foster Frederick, f, 35, 79, $1470, Adams, Soest.

Foster Jesse, f, 21, 125, $1695, Monroe, Monroeville.

Foster Joel D, f, 9, 78, $945, Maumee, Antwerp, O.

Foster J B, Monroe, Monroeville.

Foster Levi, f, 21, 31, $390, Monroe, Monroeville.

Foulks Charles S, f, Pleasant, Nine Mile.

Foulks Harriet, f, 29, 25, $370, Pleasant, Sheldon.

Foulks Morgan, f, Pleasant, Sheldon.

Foust Martha E, f, 11, 40, $415, Milan, Antwerp, O.

Fowler Ben B, f, 1, ⅘, $240, Wayne, Ft Wayne.

Fowzer R B, Adams, Fort Wayne.

Fox Alexander, Adams, Fort Wayne.

Fox August, f, 16, 160, $3520, Cedar Creek, Leo.

Fox Charles, f t, Cedar Creek

Fox Francis, f, 9, 10, $230, Adams, Ft Wayne.

Fox Gilbert S, Perry, Huntertown.

Fox Henry, f, 27, 120, $2880, Adams, Ft Wayne.

Fox Henry, f, 33, 44 ⅔, $710, Cedar Creek, Cedarville.

Fox J & A M, f, 34, 77, $1205, Lake, Arcola.

Fox Louis, Adams, Fort Wayne.

Fox Mary, f, 30, 67, $705, Lake, Arcola.

Fox Mary, Perry, Huntertown.

Fox Philander, f, 34, 22, $465, Lake, Arcola.

Fox Valentine, gardener, 21, 14, $500, Wayne, Fort Wayne.

Fradenburg Rachael, f, 1, $30, St Joseph, Fort Wayne.

Frame Ingraham, f, 16, 80, $1820, Aboite, Ft Wayne.

Frame Norris, f t, Aboite, Arcola.

France Abraham, Adams, Ft Wayne.

France August, St Joseph, Thurman.

France Christian, f, 35, 55, $660, Madison, Decatur.

France Delilah, f, 15, 20, $225, Madison, Monroeville.

France Francis, f, 19, 8, $160, Milan, Thurman.

Franee J E K, Adams, Ft Wayne.

France Macey, Adams, Ft Wayne.

France Mary, f, 23, 40, $520, Jefferson, Zulu.

Francis Caroline, f, 14, 1¾, $120, Wayne, Ft Wayne.

Francis Francis, f, 13, 68, $1230, St Joseph, Thurman.

Francis Sarah A, f, 9, 3½, $385, Wayne, Ft Wayne.

Francis Wm F, f, 7, 51, $1035, Lafayette, Aboite.

Frank Mendace, $50, Adams, Ft Wayne.

Frank Wilhelm, f, 1, 83, $855, Lake, Ft Wayne.

Franke A, Wayne, Ft Wayne.

Franke Frederick, f, 16, 99, $1405, Madison, Hoagland.

Franke Frederick W, f, 20, 80, $1015, Madison, Hoagland.

Franke Herman, f, 20, 80, $1275, Madison, Hoagland.

Franklin Zachariah, lab, Maumee, Antwerp, O.

Frantz Thiebaut, f, 19, 25, $300, Jackson, Zulu.

Franzler Isaiah, saw mill, 19, 4, $85, Scipio, Hall's Corners.

Frary Francis, Wayne, Ft Wayne.

Frauenfelder Anna, Wayne, Ft Wayne.

Frazier G W, f t, Eel River, Churubusco.

Frederick Amos, Perry, Collingwood.

Frederick Samuel, f, 2, 78, $1720, Perry.

Frederickson George, St Joseph, Ft Wayne.

Fredline J W, miller, Lafayette, Zanesville.

Freeland C J, Adams, Ft Wayne.

Freeman Mary S, f, 3, ½, $100, Eel River, Ari.

Freeman R L, f, 14, 99, $1575, Eel River, Huntertown.

Freeman Wm D, f, 11, 60, $970, Eel River, Ari.

Freemion John, Wayne, Ft Wayne.

Freemion Joseph, brick mnfr, 13, 4½, $385, Wayne, Ft Wayne.

Freemion Philippi, St Joseph, Ft Wayne.

Freemion Sarah, 13, $220, Wayne, Ft Wayne.

Freemion Seraphine, 13, 6½, $1560, Wayne, Ft Wayne.

Freiburg Simon, Wayne, Ft Wayne.

Freiburger Ignatius, f, 5, 121, $2265, Pleasant.

Freiburger John, f t, Pleasant, Sheldon.

Freistoffer John, f, 4, 56, $1280, Marion, Poe.

Freistoffer Simon, f, 9, 80, $1570, Marion, Poe.

French Francis H, lieut U S A, 14, 1½, $190, Wayne, Ft Wayne.

Fresch Henry J, f, 23, 80, $1815, Aboite, Ft Wayne.

Friday Henry, gardener, 3, 5, $505, Wayne, Ft Wayne.

Friedline Emanuel, f, 29, 160, $2875, Monroe, Monroeville.

Friedline John, Monroe, Monroeville.

Friedline John D, f, 30, 339, $5400, Monroe, Monroeville.

Friedline M J, farmer, Monroe, Monroeville.

Frisby Ann E, f, 3, 75, $2570, Adams, Ft Wayne.

Frisinger S P, St Joseph, Ft Wayne.

Fritche Henry, Wayne, Ft Wayne.

Fritcher Bernard, f, 27, 60, $1100, Milan, Gar Creek.

Fritcher Henry, f, 27, 82, $995, Milan, Gar Creek.

Fritcher Julian C, f, 26, 80, $720, Milan, Gar Creek.

Fritz August, Lake, Wallen.

Fritz Henry, f, 2, 21, $255, Lake Wallen.

Fritz John D, f, 2, 95, $1490, Lake, Wallen.

Fritz Mary, f, 1, 107, $1280, Lake, Wallen.

Fritz Michael, f, 11, 80, $945, Lake, Ft Wayne.

Fritz Wm, Lake, Wallen.

Froesch Conrad C, f, 30, 80, $2395, Adams, Ft Wayne.

Froesch Martin, f, 29, 80, $1825, Adams, Ft Wayne.

Fromuth Herman, Jefferson. Maples.

Frousfield John, f, 14, 160, $1730, Lake, Wallen.

Frost J S, Adams, Ft Wayne.

Fruechtenicht Francis, f, 31, 110, $3095, Adams, Ft Wayne.

Fruechtenicht Frank, f, 31, 69, $1415, Adams, Ft Wayne.

Fruechtenicht Frederick, Adams, Ft Wayne.

Fruechtenicht John H, f, 31, 107, $3275, Adams, Ft Wayne.

Fruechtenicht Wm, Adams, Ft Wayne.

Fry Abraham, f, 10, 100, $1510, Madison, Monroeville.

Fry Conrad, Madison, Maples.

Fry Frederick, Jefferson, Maples.

Fry Frederick G, Madison, Hoagland.

Fry George, f, 14, 100, $1510, Madison, Monroeville.

Fry George M, Madison, Monroeville.

Fry Henry P, f, 3, 40, $420, Madison, Monroeville.

Fry Jacob G, f, 3, 65, $795, Madison, Monroeville.

Fry James, f, 3, 10, $105, Madison, Monroeville.

Fry John, f, 3, 38, $440, Madison, Monroeville.

Fry John (estate of), f, 17, 160, $2600, Lake, Wallen.

Fry John L, Madison, Maples.

Fry Martin, f, 3, 49, $540, Madison, Maples.

Fry Mary A, f, 9, 80, $880, Madison, Maples.

Fry Oscar, Lake, Arcola.

Fry Philip, f, 16, 99, $1635, Madison, Monroeville.

Fry Sarah F, f, 15, 80, $715, Madison, Maples.

Fudge James O, Lake, Arcola.

Fuelling H F W, f, 33, 40, $605, Madison, Bingen.

Fuelling John F, f, 12, 116, $1430, Milan, Woodburn.

Fuhrman Christian, f, 33, 54, $1280, Marion, Poe.

Fuhrman John J, f, 33, 80, $1420, Marion, Poe.

Fuiling John T, f, 6, 84, $675, Maumee, Woodburn.

Fulke Benjamin jr, lab, Eel River, Ari.

Fulkerson D L, f, 30, 80, $1605, Cedar Creek, Cedarville.

Fulkerson Hulda B, Cedar Creek, Cedarville.

Fuller Charles, teamster, Cedar Creek, Leo.

Fuller Jacob jr, lab, Eel River, Ari.

Fulmer Jacob, Milan, Gar Creek.

Fulmer James, f, 25, 170, $1985, Milan, Gar Creek.

Fulmer Wm, Milan, Gar Creek.

Fultz Wm J, f, 29, 40, $860 Lafayette, Roanoke.

Funk Jacob, f, 28, 40, $760, St Joseph, Ft Wayne.

Funk Leonard, f, 29, 64, $1855, St Joseph, Fort Wayne.

Funk Samantha, f 28, 120, $1145, Jackson, Monroeville.

Furnish Thomas E, f, 2, 80, $1985, Cedar Creek, Hursh.

Fusehober John F, Pleasant, Sheldon.

Fulke George F, f, 6, 40, $635, Eel River, Churubusco.

Fulke Jacob, f, 6, 40, $800, Eel River, Churubusco.

Fulke Jacob jr, lab, Eel River, Ari.

Fulke John C, f, 5, 120, $1555, Eel River, Churubusco.

G

Gable Daniel, f, 30, 60, $980, Jefferson, Maples.

Gable Frederick L, f, 5, 80, $1115, Madison, Maples.

Gable Jacob, dairy, 25, 28, $930, Wayne, Ft Wayne.

Gable Peter, St Joseph, Goeglein.

Gable Peter jr, St Joseph, Goeglein.

Gaetze John, Adams, Fort Wayne.

Gailey Galvin, Madison, Monroeville.

Gailey James M, Madison, Monroeville.

Gailey John, f t, Madison, Monroeville.

Galler Andrew, Madison, Monroeville.

Gallmeier Ernest, f, 36, 78, $1460, Marion, Hoagland.

Gallmeyer Conrad, f, 26, 40, $715, Adams, Ft Wayne.

Gallmeyer Diederich, f, 26, 168, $2530, Milan, Gar Creek.

Gallmeyer Frederick, f, 33, 155, $2890, Milan, Gar Creek.

Gallmeyer Frederick jr, Milan, Gar Creek.

Gallmeyer Wm, f, 26, 80, $2110, Adams, Ft Wayne.

Galloway David H, f t, Eel River, Heller's Corners.

Galloway John H D, f, 14, 640, $7370, Eel River, Huntertown.

Gandy Oscar, f, 9, 322, $6395, Eel River, Churubusco.

Garboden Henrietta, 13, $25, Wayne, Fort Wayne.

Gard Brookfield, phys, 12, $650, Wayne, Ft Wayne.

Gard Margaret C, Adams, Ft Wayne.

Garman B F, f, 10, 302, $5120, Perry, Huntertown.

Garman Eli H, Perry, Collingwood.

Garman Enoch, f, 5, 80, $1140, Cedar Creek, Collingwood.

Garman Enoch, f, 1, 275, 5035, Perry, Collingwood.

Garman Mary, f, 12, 26, $140, Perry, Huntertown.

Garman W H, f, 1, 50, 950, Perry, Collingwood.

Garrett George, lab, Cedar Creek, Cedarville.

Garrett John, 28, 10, $260, Cedar Creek, Cedarville.

Garrett Z T, gen store, Cedar Creek, Cedarville.

Garton James B, sawmill, Marion, Poe.

Garver Alfred, Milan, Gar Creek.

Garver Charles, Milan, Chamberlain.

Garver David, f, 24, 60, $795, Milan, Gar Creek.

Garver Henry J, Lake, Arcola.

Garver Matilda, f, 13, 15, $320, St Joseph, Fort Wayne.

Garver Sarah E, f, 24, 90, $975, Milan, Gar Creek.

Garver Wm, Milan, Chamberlain.

Gaskill Ann L, f, 29, 25, $425, Lafayette, Roanoke.

Gassert Agnes, Wayne, Ft Wayne.

Gassert Frederick, Wayne, Ft Wayne.

Gates Abraham, Adams, Ft Wayne.

Gault George S, f, 26, 58, $755, Madison,Monroeville.

Gay J C, Perry, Huntertown.

Gay Martin, Adams, Fort Wayne.

Gay Millard F, Adams, Fort Wayne.

Gaylord Eliza, Adams, Fort Wayne.

Gaylord Henry, f t, Madison, Hoagland.

Gearin Cornelius, f, 30, 72, $855, Lake, Arcola.

Gearin John, f, 31, 80, $1155, Lake, Arcola.

Gearin Peter, Wayne, Fort Wayne.

Gebert Christian L, f, 19, 38, $485, Milan, Thurman.

Gebhard Charles, gardener, 16, 39, $2090, Wayne, Ft Wayne.

Gebhard D, lab, Wayne, Ft Wayne.

Gebhard J C & M, gardener, 22, 11, $610, Wayne, Fort Wayne.

Gehant Francis, f, 22, 40, $630, Lake, Arcola.

Gehring Jacob, f, 10, 80, $525, Lake, Arcola.

Gehring J W & Bros, brickmakers, Cedar Creek, Leo.

Gehring Mary, Lake, Arcola.

Geiger Hettie, f, 8, 99, $1920, Eel River, Churubusco.

Geiger John, f t, Eel River, Churubusco.

Geiner Henry, 14, ¼, $350, Wayne, Ft Wayne.

Geiser Joseph, f, 13, 102, $11,455,Wayne, Ft Wayne.

Geisking John, f, 32, 242, $4915, Eel River, Churubusco.

Geisman R, 5, 13¾, $345, Wayne, Ft Wayne.

Genth Ann M, Lafayette, Nine Mile.

Genth Eli, f, 13, 40, $765, Lafayette, Nine Mile.

Genth George, f, 23, 40, $700, Lafayette, Nine Mile.

Genth John, f, 12, 40, $775, Lafayette, Nine Mile.

Genth John A, f, 15, 120, $1990,Lafayette,Nine Mile.

Genth John P, f, 24, 100, $1805,Lafayette,Nine Mile.

Genth Wm A, f, 9, 59, $1055, Lafayette, Nine Mile.

Geofford Bernhart, f, 13, 2, $430, Wayne, Ft Wayne.

George Lillie, f, 1, 48, $625, Milan, Harlan.

Gerardot Louis, f, 26, 40, $525, Jefferson, Maples.

Gerberding August, Wayne, Fort Wayne.

Gerding Charles, Lake, Duke.

Gerding Christian L, Lake, Duke.

Gerding Frederick, f, 35, 77, $1475, Lake, Duke.

Gerding Henry, Lake, Duke.

Gerding John H, f, 35, 231, $3620, Lake, Duke.

Gerding Louis & G, f, 34, 38, $655, Lake, Duke.

Gerig Andrew, f, 4, 90,$1555, Cedar Creek, Leo.

Gerig Andrew jr, f, 14, 69, $1795, Cedar Creek, Leo.

Gerig B S, f, 14, 35, $605, Cedar Creek, Leo.

Gerig Christian, f, 17, 66, $1260, Milan, Chamberlain.

Gerig Eli, lab, Cedar Creek, Leo.

Gerig Enoch G, f, 11, 60, $645, Milan, Harlan.

Gerig John, f, 25, 60, $1280, Cedar Creek, Leo.

Gerig Joseph, f, 24, 80, $1400, Cedar Creek, Collingwood.

Gerig Rev Joseph, 14, 160, $2965, Cedar Creek, Leo.

Gerig Joseph, Milan, Chamherlain.

Gerig Joseph K, lab, Cedar Creek, Leo.

Gerig Joseph W, f, 10, 220, $3530, Cedar Creek, Collingwood.

Gerig Josephine, f, 3, 160, $2965, Cedar Creek, Leo.

Gerig Peter, f, 10, 200, 3645, Cedar Creek, Leo.

Gerke Christian S, Wayne, Ft Wayne.

Gerke Frederick, f, 26, 160, $3970, St Joseph, Ft Wayne.

Gerke F D W, f, 2, 117, $1320, Maumee, Adams.

Gerke F J, f, 22, 80, $1475, St Joseph, Ft Wayne.

Gerke F W, St Joseph, Ft Wayne.

Gerke H F A, f, 25, 132, $3900, Wayne, Ft Wayne.

Gerke John H, f, 26, 104, $4515, Wayne, Ft Wayne.

Gerke J H L, f, 25, 303, $8435, Wayne, Ft Wayne.

Gerken George, f, 21, 80, $1860, St Joseph, Goeglein.

Gerker Wm jr, Adams, Ft Wayne.

Gerlach Emil, Wayne, Ft Wayne.

Germain R M, engineer, Wayne, Ft Wayne.

Gersline Maria B, Wayne, Ft Wayne.

Gertros Wm H, f, 31, 80, $745, Scipio, Hall's Corners.

Getz Charles, Wayne, Ft Wayne.

Getz Henry, Wayne, Ft Wayne.

Getz John, f, 18, 8, $665, Adams, Ft Wayne.

Getz John W, Adams, Ft Wayne.

Gevers Henry, f, 27, 81, $1325, Milan, Gar Creek.

Geyer Charles A, f, 7, 28, $755, Monroe, Monroeville.

Geyer Ferdinand, f, 7, 11, $320, Monroe, Monroeville.

Geyers Charles, f, 12, 20, $325, Monroe, Monroeville.

Giant Franklin, Jefferson, Zulu.

Giant Jacob, f, 36, 130, $1490, Jefferson, Monroeville.

Giant Jacob jr, Jefferson, Zulu.

Giant James, Jefferson, Zulu.

Giant Joseph, f, 36, 10, $115, Jefferson, Zulu.

Giant Joseph jr, Jefferson, Zulu.

Giant Josephine, f, 36, 10, $90, Jefferson, Zulu.

Giant Nicholas, Jefferson, Maples.

Giant Peter, Jefferson, Zulu.

Gibb W H, Perry, Huntertown.

Gibbons Charles jr, laborer, Scipio, Hall's Corners.

Gibbons John, f, 16, 40, $715, Monroe, Monroeville.

Gibert •Frederick, f, 13, 60, $1305, St Joseph, Goeglein.

Gibert John F, f, 14, 60, $1140, St Joseph, Goeglein.

Gibson Arthur M, f t, Pleasant, Sheldon.

Gibson David W, f, 16, 70, $1720, Marion, Poe.

Gibson Edward, Marion, Poe.

Gibson George, f, 4, 40, $590, Monroe, Monroeville.

Gibson Henry, f, 20, 142, $3130, Marion, Poe.

Gibson John, f, 14, 80, $1575, Pleasant, Sheldon.

Gibson John C, f, 36, 200, $3500, Pleasant, Sheldon.

Gibson John D, f t, Pleasant, Sheldon.

Gibson John W, f, 26, 55, $915, Madison, Monroeville.

Gibson Joseph, lab, Maumee, Woodburn.

Gibson Sarah A, f, 26, 67, $1090, Madison, Monroeville.

Gibson Sedelia, f, 26, 40, $475, Madison, Monroeville.

Gibson Wm, f, 3, 30, $310, Monroe, Monroeville.

Gichman August, Adams, Ft Wayne.

Gick Conrad, Adams, Soest.

Gick Conrad W, Adams, Soest.

Gick John, Adams, Soest.

Giddings F S & Co, f (reserve), 78, $615, Lafayette, Myhart.

Gieseking Wm, f, 3, 285, $4040, Lake, Churubusco.

Giffeth Levi & Sarah, f, 24, 23½, $1080, Wayne, Ft Wayne.

Gilbert Charles W, f, 19, 160, $1170, Jackson, Smiler, O.

Gilbert J V, Adams, Fort Wayne.

Gill Joshua S, Adams, Fort Wayne.

Gill Martin E, Adams, Fort Wayne.

Gilleron Louis J, St Joseph, Ft Wayne.

Gilleron Louis V, f, 11, 119, $2050, St Joseph, Fort Wayne.

Gillett Charles M, f, 29, 80, $1340, Cedar Creek, Cedarville.

Gillett Taylor M, f, 18, 20, $655, Milan, Thurman.

Gillmartin Edward, Adams, Fort Wayne.

Gilman J M, Jefferson, Zulu.

Gilmore D W, Monroe, Monroeville.

Gilmore J S, f t, Madison, Monroeville.

Gingrich Jacob, Wayne, Ft Wayne.

Ginther George E, f, 36, 40, $400, Jefferson, Monroeville.

Ginther, Samuel, f t, Madison, Monroeville.

Girard August, f, 28, 52, $500, Jackson, Monroeville.

Girard Felicia, f, 22, 39, $675, Jefferson, New Haven.

Girard Jules, f, 18, 40, $135, Jackson, New Haven.

Girard Louis, f, 21, 40, $580, Jefferson, New Haven.

Girardot Anthony, f, 29, 88, $1175, Jefferson, Maples.

Girardot August, lab, Jackson, Monroeville.

Girardot Charles, f, 21, 220, $3030, Jefferson, New Haven.

Girardot Edward, f, 33, 90, $1235, Jefferson, Maples.

Girardot H, f, 22, 80, $1105, Jefferson, Zulu.

Girardot Joseph, f, 33, 68, $1045, Jefferson, Maples.

Girardot Jules, f, 12, 80, $605, Jefferson, Dawkins.

Girardot Louis, f, 32, 20, $390, Jefferson, Maples.

Girardot Louis jr, f, 35, 80, $1310, Jefferson, Monroeville.

Girardot Louis C, Jefferson, Zulu.

Girardot Louis J, Jefferson, Dawkins.

Girardot Louis L, Jefferson, Maples.

Girardot Louisa, f, 19, 15, $355, Jefferson, Maples.

Girardot, Mary, f, 12, 40, $585, Jefferson, Dawkins.

Girardot Peter, f, 4, 40, $490, Madison, Maples.

Girardot Rosa S, Jefferson, Maples.

Gish Eva, f, 13, 3, $450, Wayne, Ft Wayne.

Gladbach Gottfried, Wayne, Fort Wayne.

Gladieaux Celestine, f, 31, 357, $4985, Jefferson, Zulu.

Gladieaux C F, Jefferson, Zulu.

Gladieaux Francis, f, 25, 490, $5355, Jefferson, Zulu.

Gladieaux Francis C, f, 25, 1, $60, Jefferson, Zulu.

Gladieaux Louis, Jefferson, Zulu.

Gladieaux Louis J, f, 23, 40, $585, Jefferson, Zulu.

Gladieaux Mary, f, 25, 10, $155, Jefferson, Zulu.

Glasier Nathan C, f, 17, $\frac{1}{4}$, $45, Perry, Huntertown.

Glass Emery, f, 9, 60, $1985, Adams, Fort Wayne.

Glass E & S, Milan, Chamberlain.

Glass J W, f, Pleasant, Nine Mile.

Glasser Francis, f, 26, $565, St Joseph, Fort Wayne.

Glaze Wm, Wayne, Fort Wayne.

Gleason John, St Joseph, Ft Wayne.

Gleen Wm, f, 11, 80, $1545, Aboite.

Glenn Wm, f t, Aboite, Ft Wayne.

Gloyd Edward G, f, 14, 100, $1180, Perry, Huntertown.

Gloyd George B, f, 25, 80, $1975, Perry, Fort Wayne.

Gloyd Jerome D, f, 26, 160, $2875, Perry, Fort Wayne.

Gloyd Wm S, f, 26, 80, $1560, Perry, Fort Wayne.

Gobel Jacob, f, 30, 75, $1960, Adams, Fort Wayne.

Gocke Francis, f, 36, 190, $2725, Lake, Duke.

Gocke Joseph, f, 36, 92, $1840, Lake, Duke.

Godfrey Aldine, f, 11, 100, $1720, Lake, Duke.

Godfrey George, f, 7¾, $220, Wayne, Fort Wayne.

Godfrey James, f, 19½, $555, Wayne, Fort Wayne.

Goeal John jr, Jefferson, New Haven.

Goeglein Anna, f, 25, 79, $2945, St Joseph, Goeglein.

Goeglein George, Adams, Ft Wayne.

Goeglein George, f, 31, 26, $425, Milan, Goeglein.

Goeglein George, f, 26, 129, $1530, St Joseph,Goeglein.

Goeglein George A, St Joseph, Goeglein.

Goeglein Jacob, f, 229,$6180, St Joseph, Goeglein.

Goeglein John, St Joseph, Goeglein.

Goeglein John H, f, 25, 22, $400, St Joseph, Goeglein.

Goeglein Valentine, St Joseph, Goeglein.

Goepfert Francis G, Lake, Arcola.

Goerline Gustav, Marion,Poe.

Goers August, Wayne, Fort Wayne.

Goers Wm, Wayne, Fort Wayne.

Goethe Conrad, f t, Madison, Hoagland.

Goetz John, f, 18, 4, $250, Adams, Fort Wayne.

Goff Orange, Eel River, Ari.

Goheen Charles J, f t, Eel River, Wallen.

Goheen Sarah J, f, 25, 40, $980, Eel River, Wallen.

Goheen Wm. f, 11,160, $2315, Lake, Arcola.

Goings Francis, f t, Pleasant, Sheldon.

Goings James, f,28, 49,$1255, Perry, Fort Wayne.

Golden Henry, f t, Eel River, Wallen.

Golden Samuel, St Joseph, Goeglein.

Goldsmith Amos, f, 12, 40, $1140, Cedar Creek, Hursh.

Goldsmith C, Cedar Creek.

Goldsmith Jacob, f, 12, 120, $3250, Cedar Creek, Hursh.

Goldsmith Joseph jr, f, 13, 100, $1965, Cedar Creek, Hursh.

Goldsmith Nicholas, f, 3, 121, $1985, Cedar Creek, Hursh.

Goldsmith Henry, f, 12, 73, $2545, Cedar Creek, Hursh.

Golliver Henry, lab,Pleasant, Sheldon.

Good Henry, f, 35,160, $2395, Milan, Gar Creek.

Good Henry jr, Milan, Gar Creek.

Goodwin Isaac, f, 27, 80, $1910, Aboite, Ft Wayne.

Gordon Catherine, f, 17, 26, $495,Eel River,Churubusco.

Gordon James W, f, 6, 42, $840,Eel River,Churubusco

Gordon Jasper,lab,Eel River, Churubusco.

Gordon John S, f, 17, 53, $965,Eel River,Churubusco

Gorham Jeremiah, f, 6, 19, $355, Aboite, Dunfee.

Gorman Dennis, f, 29, 60, $810, Lake, Fort Wayne.

Gorman Thomas, f, 29, 60, $1280, Lake, Arcola.

Gorrell Cyrus, Milan, Harlan.

Gorrell John, f, 19, 42, $840, Jefferson, New Haven.

Gorrell John, f, 1, 83, $1405, Milan, Harlan.

Gorrell Martha M, f, 12, 20, $195, Milan, Harlan.

Gorrell Milo R, f,17, 40, $580, Scipio, Hall's Corners.

Gorrell Wm F, Milan, Harlan.

Goshom J S, Adams, Fort Wayne.

Goshom Laura, Adams, Fort Wayne.

Gotte Conrad, Adams, Fort Wayne.

Gouty Benjamin F, Wayne, Ft Wayne.

Grabemeier Wm, f t, Maumee, Woodburn.

47

Graber Daniel, f, 3' 80, $1680, Milan, Chamberlain.

Graber John, f, 5, 84, $1665, Milan, Chamberlain.

Graber Joseph, f, 5, 80, $1785, Milan, Chamberlain.

Graber Peter jr, f, 3, 80, $1545, Milan, Chamberlain.

Grabner John, lab, Jackson, Monroeville.

Grace John, f, 7, 39, $705, Aboite, Ft Wayne.

Grace Simon, f, reserve, 38, $775, Lafayette, Roanoke.

Grace Simon L, Aboite, Fort Wayne.

Graham Jacob, Wayne, Fort Wayne.

Graham Samuel, f, 18, ¾, $275, Monroe, Monroeville.

Gramaud Joseph (est of), f, 6, 60, $1325, Jefferson, New Haven.

Gratz David, f t, Cedar Creek, Hursh.

Gratz Eliza, f, 2, 80, $1310, Cedar Creek, Hursh.

Gratz Silas S, f t, Cedar Creek, Spencerville.

Graves A J, f, 15, 25, $395, Milan, Chamberlain.

Gravey Frederick, f t, Pleasant, Sheldon.

Grayless Charles, Lake, Arcola.

Grayless George, f, 7, 49, $690, Lake, Arcola.

Grayless J W, lab, Eel River, Heller's Corners.

Grayless Nancy, f, 18, 15, $180, Lake, Arcola.

Greek Dallas, f t, Pleasant, Nine Mile.

Greek John W, f, 30, 29, $565, Pleasant, Nine Mile.

Greek Wm, f, 25, 32, $420, Lafayette, Sheldon.

Greek W W, f, Pleasant, Nine Mile.

Green Elisha W, f, 12, 82, $2975, Adams, New Haven.

Green Elisha & J A, f, 12, 117, $4105, Adams, New Haven.

Green Henry L, lumber mnfr, Eel River, Ari.

Green Judson E, f t, Eel River, Ari.

Green Silas, Adams, New Haven.

Green Stanley, lab, Eel River, Ari.

Green S A D, lab, Monroe, Dixon, O.

Greenawalt Edgar, f t, Eel River, Ari.

Greenawalt Eliza, f, 17, 160, $2785, Eel River, Churubusco.

Greenawalt L C, f, 11, 80, $1115, Eel River, Churubusco.

Greenewald John E, f, 8, 100, $1180, Scipio, Hicksville, O.

Greenewald Mary D, f, 8, 120, $440, Scipio, Hicksville, O.

Greenwell Christian L, f, 14, 47, $1155, Eel River, Huntertown.

Greenwell Edward L, Perry, Huntertown.

Greenwell Frank, f, 17, 41, $1010, Perry, Huntertown.

Greenwell F & M J, Perry, Huntertown.

Greenwell George, f, 15, 40, $760, Eel River, Huntertown.

Greenwell G W, f, Eel River, Huntertown.

Sewing Machines, Shears and Pocket Knives, Pfeiffer & Schlatter 38 & 40 E. Columbia.

ALLEN COUNTY DIRECTORY. 703

Greenwell Mary J, f, 17, 13, $10, Perry, Huntertown.

Greer Chester, f t, Pleasant, Nine Mile.

Greer Thomas, f, 5, 95, $2020, Pleasant, Nine Mile.

Gregg Austin W, f, 6, 15, $95, Jackson, Dawkins.

Greider Finley, f t, Pleasant, Nine Mile.

Greider Martin, f t, Pleasant, Sheldon.

Gremaux Frank, f, 19, 80, $911, Jackson, Zulu.

Gremaux Victor, f, 30, 80, $765, Jackson, Zulu.

Gresley Jacob, Madison, Hoagland.

Gresley John, f, 13, 159, $3555, Marion, Hoagland.

Gresley John A, f, 27, 53, $820, Madison, Hoagland.

Gresley John E, Marion, Hoagland.

Gresley Noah, Marion, Hoagland.

Gresley Peter, f, 28, 70, $965, Madison, Hoagland.

Gresley Solomon, f, 13, 60, $1245, Marion, Hoagland.

Greutert Henry, Lake, Duke.

Greve M J, Wayne, Ft Wayne

Grew Wm, Marion, Poe.

Grice Jesse, f, 7, 100, $1940, Milan, Harlan.

Grider David, f, 34, 118, $2635, Wayne, Ft Wayne.

Grider John, Wayne, Ft Wayne.

Grider Samuel, Wayne, Ft Wayne.

Griebel Amelia, gravel pit, 10, $1700, Wayne, Ft Wayne.

Griebel A L, f, 19, 80, $615, Maumee, Ft Wayne.

Griebel Frederick, St Joseph, Fort Wayne.

Griebel George, f, 11, 270, $6270, Marion, Soest.

Griebel George & Mary R, Wayne, Ft Wayne.

Griebel Louis, Marion, Soest.

Griebel Maria, Wayne, Fort Wayne.

Griebel Wm, Marion, Soest.

Grieg Dora, Aboite, Fort Wayne.

Grieg Frederick, lab, Aboite, Fort Wayne.

Griese John, f t, 8, 80, $1665, Marion, Poe.

Grieser Wm, Wayne, Fort Wayne.

Griest A B, Lafayette, Roanoke.

Griffin Alanson, f, 2, 80, $2170, Perry, Collingwood.

Griffith John, f, 16, 80, $1295, Monroe, Monroeville.

Griffith John C, Adams, Ft Wayne.

Griffith M E, clerk, Monroe, Monroeville.

Grim Charles A, lab, Eel River, Ari.

Grime Carl, f, 34, 79, $1400, Milan, Gar Creek.

Gristdowfer Wm, Wayne, Ft Wayne.

Grobner Henry, Jefferson, Maples.

Grobner Peter J, f, 29, 80, $645, Jackson, Monroeville.

Grobner Peter M, f, 29, 80, $922, Jackson, Monroeville.

Grobner Samuel, Jefferson, Maples.

Grodrian August W, f, 8, 160, $2465, Madison, Maples.

Grodrian Charles, f, 6, 139, $1205, Madison, Maples.

Grodrain Charles A, f t, Madison, Maples.

Grodrain Wm, f, 8, 80, $1150, Madison, Maples.

Groman Andrew, f, 20, 230, $3060, Marion, Poe.

Groman Andrew jr, Marion, Poe.

Groman Geo A, Marion, Poe.

Gronan F W, Adams, Fort Wayne.

Gronauer George F, Jefferson, New Haven.

Gronauer Joseph (est of), f, 34, 41, $695, Milan, New Haven.

Groove David, f, 21, 120, $2590, Aboite, Ft Wayne.

Grosh Henry, f, 11, 37, $520, Cedar Creek, Hursh.

Grosh Isaac, f, 11, 10, $200, Cedar Creek, Hursh.

Grosjean Bros & Co, Lake, Arcola.

Grosjean B E & J, f, 28, 1, $25, Lake, Arcola.

Grosjean John B, f, 28, 65, $1190, Lake, Arcola.

Grosjean John & Mary, Lake, Arcola.

Grotean Fred, Jefferson, Maples.

Grothaus Henry, f t, 33, 80, $510, Maumee, Woodburn.

Grover Albert H, f, 34, 80, $805, Milan, Gar Creek.

Grover Alfred, Jefferson, New Haven.

Grover Alfred S, f, 3, 45, $1000, Jefferson, Gar Creek.

Grover Benjamin, f, 17, 80, $1425, Jefferson, New Haven.

Grover Julia C, f, 20, 80, $1615, Jefferson, New Haven.

Grover Mahala, f, 20, 40, $685, Jefferson, New Haven.

Grover Martin S, f, 20, 40, $665, Jefferson, New Haven.

Grover Samuel, f, 21, 20, $325, Jefferson, New Haven.

Grover Samuel J, f, 17, 80, $1585, Jefferson, New Haven.

Grover Sidney, f, 7, 43, $490, Maumee, Woodburn.

Grubaugh Margaret, f, 97, $1810, Cedar Creek, Cedarville.

Grubaugh M A, f, 69, $1345, Cedar Creek, Cedarville.

Grubb James L, f t, Cedar Creek, Leo.

Grubb Job, Milan, Chamberlain.

Grubb Michael, f, 13, 30, $590, St Joseph, Goeglein.

Grube Daniel, Madison, Hoagland.

Gruber John H, Milan, Chamberlain.

Gruber John W, f, 17, 53, $1040, Lafayette, Myhart.

Gruber Milton, f t, Scipio, Hall's Corners.

Grunar L & Augusta, Adams, Fort Wayne.

Grush Andrew, f, 27, 40, $435, Jackson, Baldwin.

Guck Casper, f, 26, 40, $815, Adams, Soest.

Guck John, f, 26, 80, $1665, Adams, Soest.

Guenin Edward, Madison, Monroeville.

Guenin Francis, f, 13, 40, $640, Madison, Monroeville.

Guenin Frank, f t, Madison, Monroeville.

Guenther Stephen A D, f, 3, 20, $365, Milan, Harlan.

Guhlke Wm, Adams, Fort Wayne.

Guibler Adam, Lake, Arcola.

Guibler Felicite, f, 28, 52, $1285, Lake, Arcola.

Guibler J, Lake, Arcola.

Guife Joseph, St Joseph, Ft Wayne.

Guiley John, Jefferson, New Haven.

Guilford Derick, f t, Maumee, Woodburn.

Guilford Russell, f t, Maumee, Harlan.

Guillaume Florence, Milan, Thurman.

Guillaume James, f, 5, 40, $785, Milan, Chamberlain.

Guillaume Louis, Milan, Thurman.

Gumbert Charles, f, 28, 40, $1015, Adams, Ft Wayne.

Gumbert John, Adams, Ft Wayne.

Gummieaux Arsene, f, 24, 80, $850, Jefferson, Zulu.

Gump Albert N, f, 9, 40, $855, Eel River, Ari.

Gump C T, lab, Eel River, Ari.

Gump George, f, 15, 184, $3660, Perry, Huntertown.

Gump Henry M, Perry, Huntertown.

Gump H E, lab, Eel River, Ari.

Gump Jacob, f, 3, 120, $2860, Perry, Collingwood.

Gump Jeremiah, f, 9, 220, $3990, Eel River, Ari.

Gump Jesse A, lab, Eel River, Ari.

Gump L E, Perry, Huntertown.

Gump Perry A, f, 3, 40, $1230, Perry, Collingwood.

Gunther Susannah, f, 18, ½, 40, Perry, Huntertown.

Gusching Joseph, Adams, Ft Wayne.

Gushman Edward V, f, 9, 240, $3305, Lake, Arcola.

Gustin Harvey, f t, Scipio, Hall's Corners.

Gustin John, f, 8, 20, $190, Maumee, Woodburn.

Gustin Joseph H, f, 16, 40, $275, Maumee, Woodburn.

Gustin Marvin, f, Scipio, Hall's Corners.

Gustin Milo, f t, Scipio, Hall's Corners.

Gutermuth H & Mary, f, 18, 80, $1645, Pleasant, Nine Mile.

Guyer Rolla, Milan, Chamberlain.

Guyer Rudolph, St Joseph, Goeglein.

H

Haag A C, Adams, Ft Wayne.

Habbel Charles, 10, 3, $245, Wayne, Ft Wayne.

Habecker Alice M, Adams, Ft Wayne.

Habecker Martin, f, 17, 27, $1075, Adams, Ft Wayne.

Habecker Wm H, Adams, Ft Wayne.

Hack John, Wayne, Fort Wayne.

Hadsell Austin, f, 11, 40, $870, Pleasant, Sheldon.

Hadsell Cyrus, f t, Pleasant, Sheldon.

Hadsell James, f t, Pleasant, Sheldon.

Haench August, Wayne, Ft Wayne.

Hagan John, f, 6, 180, $2485, Lake.

John Pressler, Mantels, Grates and Tile Floor..
Columbia, Barr and Dock Streets.

706   R. L. POLK & CO.'S

Hagan Michael G, Lake, Arcola.

Hagan Wm jr, f, 16, 40, $685, Lake, Arcola.

Hagerfeldt Frederick, f t, Madison, Hoagland.

Hagerman Joseph, f, 7, 4, $420, Adams, Fort Wayne.

Haifley Elmore, lab, Maumee, Woodburn.

Haifley Joseph B, postmaster and druggist, Cedar Creek, Leo.

Haifley Uriah, f t, Maumee, Woodburn.

Haines Benjamin, f t, Aboite, Fort Wayne.

Haines Wm, lab, Aboite, Ft Wayne.

Hair Augusta, Lake, Arcola.

Hake Frank, f, 24, 80, $1590, Marion, Hoagland.

Hake George, f, 14, 120, $2060, Marion, Hoagland.

Hake Henry, f, 24, 120, $2520, Marion, Hoagland.

Hake Jacob, f, 14, 120, $2175, Marion, Hoagland.

Hake John, f, 24, 38, $595, Marion, Hoagland.

Hale Charles, lab, Aboite, Ft Wayne.

Halfeldt Henry, Marion, Poe.

Hall Alvin, f, 18, 99, $2305, Milan, Chamberlain.

Hall Eliza, Perry, Huntertown.

Hall Ernest, $15, Perry, Huntertown.

Hall Franklin, Milan, Gar Creek.

Hall Sarah A, f, 26, 80, $795, Milan, Gar Creek.

Hall Wm, Adams, Ft Wayne.

Haller Lucy, f, 18, 62, $1310, Eel River, Churubusco.

Hallerman H J, 13, 5, $810, Wayne, Fort Wayne.

Hallien George, f, 19, 58, $1050, Pleasant, Nine Mile.

Hallien John, f, 21, 40, $825, St Joseph, Ft Wayne.

Halter Caroline, f, 122, $2415, Cedar Creek, Cedarville.

Halter Henry L, lab, Cedar Creek, Cedarville.

Hamilton Allan (est), f, 35, 400, $9660, St Joseph, Fort Wayne.

Hamilton Ellen, f, 3, 173, $6400, Adams, Ft Wayne.

Hamilton Holman, f, 290, $9100, Adams, Ft Wayne.

Hamilton James, f, 28, Lafayette, Zanesville.

Hamilton John A, lab, Aboite, Fort Wayne.

Hamilton John B, Lafayette, Zanesville.

Hamilton John C, f, 16, 80, $1250, Milan.

Hamilton John W, f, 28, 40, $820, Lafayette, Zanesville.

Hamilton Michael, f, 27, 170, $3200, Lafayette, Zanesville

Hamilton Michael C, f, Lafayette, Zanesville.

Hamilton Peter, f, 13, 6⅓, $1400, Wayne, Ft Wayne.

Hamilton Phœbe, f, 6, 69, $6885, Adams, Ft Wayne.

Hamilton Robert J, f, 15, 14, $1425, Wayne, Ft Wayne.

Hamilton Wm A, f, 17, 206, $3980, Aboite, Ft Wayne.

Hamilton Wm F, lab, Aboite, Fort Wayne.

Hamm Adam & Rebecca, f, 5, 160, $2930, Cedar Creek, Leo.

Hamm Joseph, f t, Cedar Creek, Leo.

Hammond Charles, Jefferson, Maples.

Hammond Charles S, f, 31, 40, $600, Jefferson, Maples.

Hammond Wm, f, 9, 40,$600, Madison, Maples.

Hand George W, f, 25, 200, $2500, Eel River, Huntertown.

Hand W E, f, 25, 80, $1445, Eel River, Churubusco.

Haney John C, Adams, Fort Wayne.

Haney Melinda, f, 34, 6, $170, Lafayette, Zanesville.

Hank Zachariah, f t, Maumee, Antwerp, O.

Hankel Jacob, f, 34, 50, $965, Adams, Soest.

Hanna A B, f, 7, $1025, Adams, Fort Wayne.

Hanna Charles H, f, 15, 80, $550, Jackson, Ft Wayne.

Hanna Eliza, f, 30,100,$4660, St Joseph, Fort Wayne.

Hanna James T, f, 31, 240, $1295, Maumee, Fort Wayne.

Hanna Oliver E, f, 28, 254, $1465, Maumee, Ft Wayne.

Hanna Samuel D, f, 9, 154, $1155, Jackson, Ft Wayne.

Hanschild Heinrich, St Joseph, Fort Wayne.

Harber Adam, f t, Pleasant, Sheldon.

Harber Daniel, f, Pleasant, Sheldon.

Harber Frank J, f, 15, 90, $1725, Pleasant, Sheldon.

Harber George J, f, 16, 90, $1730, Pleasant, Sheldon.

Harber Gerhardt, f, 20, 157, $2350, Pleasant, Sheldon.

Harber Gerhard jr, f, 15, 98, $1810, Pleasant, Sheldon.

Harber Henry, f t, Pleasant, Sheldon.

Harder Jacob, f t, Pleasant, Sheldon.

Harber John, f t, Pleasant, Sheldon.

Harber John jr, f, 29, 80, $1270, Pleasant, Sheldon.

Harber John H, f, 15, 90, $1340, Pleasant, Sheldon.

Harber Joseph, f, 21, 80, $1455, Pleasant, Sheldon.

Harber Kaspar, f t, Pleasant, Sheldon.

Harber Martin, f, 21, 212, $3840, Pleasant, Sheldon.

Harber Nicholas, f, 15, 379, $7600, Pleasant, Sheldon.

Hardesty Edward, f, 20, 80, $1080, Cedar Creek, Cedarville.

Hardesty John f t, Cedar Creek, Cedarville.

Hardin Dennis, f t, Maumee, Antwerp, O.

Harding Charles R, f t, Aboite, Aboite.

Harding James, f, 24, 86, $2020, St Joseph, Fort Wayne.

Harding John, f, 9, 70, $1470, Milan, Chamberlain.

Harding Joseph, f, 8, 80, $1870, Milan, Chamberlain.

Harding Robert, Milan, Chamberlain.

Hardung Frederick, Adams, Fort Wayne.

Hargenroether Mathias, Adams, Fort Wayne.

Hargrave Hannah, Adams, New Haven.

Hargrave Wm, Adams, New Haven.

Harkenreider A M, f, 28, 80, $1125, Pleasant, Sheldon.

Harkenreider M J, f t, Pleasant, Sheldon.

Harkey Catherine, f, 10, 73, $1030, Perry, Collingwood.

Harkey John N, f, 10, 57, $805, Perry, Collingwood.

Harp Henry (est), f, 4, 82, $1640, Milan, Chamberlain.

Harp Polly, f, 3, ½, $40, Milan, Chamberlain.

Harper Edward, f,11,74,$685, Jefferson, New Haven.

Harper Hamilton, f, 11, 77, $690, Jefferson, Gar Creek.

Harper Isaiah, f, 6, 60, $1140, Aboite, Dunfee.

Harper John, f, 32, 80, $1420, Milan, Gar Creek.

Harper Mary E, f, 5, 58, $855, Jefferson, New Haven.

Harper Melissa, f, 32, 50, $825, Milan, Gar Creek.

Harper Robert E, f, 5, 100, $2325, Jefferson, New Haven.

Harper Wm,Milan,Gar Creek.

Harries G, Adams,Ft Wayne.

Harring Leness, lab, Aboite.

Harris Ella F, Adams, Fort Wayne.

Harris Frederick, f, 32, 60, $1715, Adams, Ft Wayne.

Harris Frederick, f, 6, 26, $470, Marion, Soest.

Harris George, f, 5, 94, $1695, Marion, Soest.

Harris George W, f, Lafayette, Roanoke.

Harris John, Jackson, Baldwin.

Harris Wesley, f, 34, 20,$180, Jackson, Baldwin.

Harris Wm & H, f, 17, 80, $1450, Lafayette, Myhart.

Harrison Henrietta, f, 19, 56, $990, Jefferson, New Haven.

Harrison Jose h T, f, 1, 95, $1170, Lake Wallen.

Harrison M, Jefferson, New Haven.

Harrod Clay, Marion, Hoagland.

Harrod C E, Madison, Hoagland.

Harrod Enos, f t, Madison, Hoagland.

Harrod Eunice,Marion,Hoagland.

Harrod Isaac (est), 24, 344, $5525, Marion, Soest.

Harrod Joseph, f, 19, 128, $2045, Madison, Hoagland.

Harrod Lucinda, Marion, Hoagland.

Harrod Mills, Marion, Hoagland.

Harrod Morgan, f, 26, 80, $1850, Marion, Hoagland.

Harrod Newton, Madison, Hoagland.

Harrod Wm D, Marion, Hoagland.

Hart Oliver T, f, 15, 40, $433, Monroe, Monroeville.

Hart Mrs R T, f,15, 4½,$890, Wayne, Fort Wayne.

Hart Sarah W, f, 16, 80, $1695,Monroe,Monroeville.

Hart Wayne M, f, 10, 40, $385, Monroe, Monroeville.

Harter Frederick, Wayne, Fort Wayne.

Harter G M, lab, Eel River, Churubusco.

Harter Joseph, lab,Eel River, Churubusco.

Harter M J, Wayne, Fort Wayne.

Harter Wm H, f, 7, 60, $1025, Scipio, Hall's Corners.

Hartle Samuel jr, lab, Scipio, Hicksville, O.

Hartman Anna, f, 7, 2½, $390, Adams, Ft Wayne.

Hartman August, f, 2, 39, $595, Jefferson, Gar Creek.

Hartman Charles, St Joseph, Ft Wayne.

Hartman David H, Lafayette, Myhart.

Hartman Henry, f, 16, 160, $5580, Adams, Ft Wayne.

Hartman John, Wayne, Ft Wayne.

Hartman John, f, 2, 70, $835, Jefferson, Gar Creek.

Hartman John F, f, 13, 36, $2255, Wayne, Ft Wayne.

Hartman John G, Marion.

Hartman John H, f, 3, 80, $1420, Jefferson, Gar Creek.

Hartman Joseph, f, 2, 100, $2150, Marion, Soest.

Hartman Nancy, f, 18, 4, $280, Adams, Ft Wayne.

Hartman Wm, f, 109, $7860, Wayne, Ft Wayne.

Hartraugh L M, Adams, Ft Wayne.

Hartzell Allen & Warren, f, 11, 73, $1790, Adams, New Haven.

Hartzell Elias, Marion.

Hartzell Ida M, f, 27, 57 $1070, Marion, Hoagland.

Hartzell John R, f, 14, 120, $2695, Adams, New Haven.

Hartzell Mary, f, 14, 160, $4730, Adams, New Haven.

Hartzell Warren, Adams, New Haven.

Hartzell Warren S, f, 11, 160, $1680, Milan, Harlan.

Harvey Aaron R, f, 22, 12, $145, Monroe, Dixon, O.

Haswell A M, Perry, Huntertown.

Hatch Brenton, f, 12, 130, $2180, Eel River, Huntertown.

Hatch Lewis, f, 23, 40, $910, Pleasant, Ft Wayne.

Hatch Mary D, f, 9, 16, $680, Perry, Huntertown.

Hatch Newman V, f, 17, 19, $960, Perry, Huntertown.

Hatch Samuel, f t, Pleasant, Sheldon.

Hatch Theodore, f, 9, 33, $495, Perry, Huntertown.

Hatch Theron V, f, 12, 105, $2115, Eel River, Huntertown.

Hatfield Amos, f t, Aboite, Ft Wayne.

Hatfield Lincoln, f t, Aboite, Ft Wayne.

Hatfield Malinda J, f, 14, 80, $955, Milan, Harlan.

Hathaway Frank, lab, Eel River, Heller's Corners.

Hathaway Josephine, f, 8, 9½, $295, Wayne, Ft Wayne.

Hathaway Mary E, Eel River, Heller's Corners.

Hathaway Philip, postmaster, Eel River, Heller's Corners.

Hathaway Stephen & Mary, f, 6⅖, $160, Wayne, Fort Wayne.

Hattersley Alfred, Adams, Ft Wayne.

Hauck John, f, 11, 84, $755, Perry, Huntertown.

Hauck John E, f, 3, 40, $765, Perry.

Hauschild Henry, f, 21, 62, $1060, Milan, Goeglein.

CHARLES BOWMAN, Saw Gumming, FILING and SETTING.
No. 18 Harrison Street.

710   R. L. POLK & CO.'S

Hauser Bros, lumber mnfrs, Madison, Hoagland.

Hauser Joseph, Madison, Hoagland.

Hausmann C, Wayne, Fort Wayne.

Haverstock Wm, f, 32, 180, $3300, Lafayette, Zanesville.

Havert Theodore, Jefferson, Maples.

Hawk Catherine, f, 10, 50, $550, Maumee, Antwerp, O.

Hawkins, Wm, f t, Madison, Monroeville.

Hay James, lab, Cedar Creek, Hursh.

Hay Samuel, lab, Eel River, Huntertown.

Hay Wm H, Madison, Monroeville.

Hayden F J, f, 31, 71, $3150, St Joseph, Ft Wayne.

Hayes Clara W, Wayne, Ft Wayne.

Hayes George, Jefferson, Gar Creek.

Hayes John, f, 18, 68, $1685, Monroe, Monroeville.

Hayes Wm, Jefferson, New Haven.

Hays Daniel B, f, 21, 160, $3075, Lafayette, Roanoke.

Hays Hulda R, f, 21, 45, $825, Lafayette, Roanoke.

Hays Valentine, lab, Cedar Creek, Hursh.

Haywood Charles, lab, Eel River, Huntertown.

Hazen Mrs W S, Adams, New Haven.

Hazlett James H, Milan, Thurman.

Hazlett John, f, 13, 38, $810, St Joseph, Ft Wayne.

Hazlett Wm, f, 18, 50, $1165, Milan, Thurman.

Hazlett Wm, f, 12, 20, $380, St Joseph, Ft Wayne.

Head Irving F, Adams, Fort Wayne.

Heath Curtis, Milan, Chamberlain.

Heath Rachel C, f, 8, 81, $1900, Milan, Chamberlain.

Heath Stephen f, 8, 60, $1220, Milan, Thurman.

Heaton Charles E, Marion, Ft Wayne.

Heaton Henrietta, f, 22, 40, $615, Marion, Ft Wayne.

Heaton Jesse, f t, 28, 210, $3570, Marion, Poe.

Heckbur Theodore, f t, Pleasant, Sheldon.

Heckert David, f, 2, 44, $400, Monroe, Monroeville.

Heckler Daniel, Jefferson, Maples.

Heckler Frank, Marion.

Heckman George S, f, 26, 7, $100, Adams, Zulu.

Heckvur Elizabeth, Pleasant, Sheldon.

Hedekin Mary C, Adams, Ft Wayne.

Heffelfinger Alexander, f, 30, 15, $230, Perry, Huntertown.

Heffelfinger C L, lab, Eel River, Heller's Corners.

Heffelfinger Elizabeth, f, 30, 23, $480, Perry, Huntertown.

Heffelfinger Martin G, f t, Eel River, Heller's Corners.

Hegersfeld Wm, Wayne, Ft Wayne.

Heiber Charles, laborer, Eel River, Ari.

Heiber George, f, 4, 86, $1350, Eel River, Ari.

Heiber Lane, Perry, Huntertown.

Heiber Samuel, Wayne, Ft Wayne.

Heiber Wm, lab, Eel River, Ari.

Heidenrich Christian, f, 34, 28, $365, Lake, Arcola.

Heiderhorst Louisa, f, 17, 17, $230, Madison, Hoagland.

Heidrick Francis, Adams, Ft Wayne.

Heidrick Frank, Lake, Arcola.

Heine August, Jefferson, New Haven.

Heine Christian, f, 33, 160, $1070, Maumee, Woodburn.

Heine Christian H, f, 13, 80, $1995, Adams, New Haven.

Heine Frederick J, f, 17' 77, $2335, Adams, Ft Wayne.

Heine Frederick W, f, 18, 75, $1495, Adams, New Haven.

Heine Henry F W, f, 18, 94, $1915, Adams, New Haven.

Heine J F & M C L, f, 19, 70, $1450, Adams, New Haven.

Heine Wm, Wayne, Fort Wayne.

Heine Wm, f, 18, 188, $4170, Adams, New Haven.

Heine Wm, f, 33, 40, $485, Milan, New Haven.

Heiner Wm, St Joseph, Ft Wayne.

Heining George, laborer, Eel River, Heller's Corners.

Heintzelman Susan S, Wayne, Fort Wayne.

Heintzelman W J, teacher, Wayne, Fort Wayne.

Heiser David jr, f t, Pleasant, Sheldon.

Heiser George, f, 25, 77, $1375, Pleasant, Sheldon.

Heiser Jackson B, f, 19, 10, $210, Lafayette, Roanoke.

Heiser Jacob, saloon, 9, $300, Wayne, Ft Wayne.

Heiser Jacob, f, 26, 143, $2555, Pleasant, Sheldon.

Heiser John, f, 18, $1010, Lafayette, Roanoke.

Heiser Judson, f, 19, 40, $715, Lafayette, Roanoke.

Heiser Wm, f, 18, 40, $850, Lafayette, Roanoke.

Heiser Wm H, f, 16, 155, $2940, Pleasant, Sheldon.

Heisner John, Madison, Maples

Heisner Lenie, f, 5, 40, $675, Madison, Maples.

Heller Carrie M, Adams, Ft Wayne.

Hellman Edward, f, 7, 40, $1065, Adams, New Haven.

Hellworth Michael, f, 1, 71, $2470, Adams, New Haven.

Helmick Henry C, f, 18, 117, $2515, Adams, New Haven.

Helmke F W E, Wayne, Ft Wayne.

Henchen Wm, f, 34, 80, $1690, Lake, Fort Wayne.

Henderson George W, f, 31, 153, $2650, Cedar Creek, Cedarville.

Henderson Isabella, Adams, Fort Wayne.

Henderson Wm, Milan, Chamberlain.

Hendry David, f, 22, 390, $7065, Pleasant, Sheldon.

Hendry Horace G, f t, Pleasant, Sheldon.

Hendry James, f, 35, 153, $2600, Pleasant, Sheldon.

Henline Elizabeth, f, 13, 80, $1520, Lake, Fort Wayne.

Henry Aaron, f, 22, 46, $665, Pleasant, Sheldon.

Henry Andrew M, f, 18, 74, $400, Monroe.

Henry Francis, f,23,96,$1955, St Joseph, Fort Wayne.

Henry John B, St Joseph, Ft Wayne.

Henry Joseph, St Joseph, Ft Wayne.

Henry Peter, f, 12, 97, $1845, St Joseph, Fort Wayne.

Henry Samuel, lab, Pleasant, Sheldon.

Henschen Adam M, Adams, Fort Wayne.

Henschen Henry, Adams, Ft Wayne.

Henscil Laura, f, 13, 5, $95 Aboite, Fort Wayne.

Henscil Manford, f t, Aboite, Fort Wayne.

Hensinger Harrison, f, 11, 110, $1755, Perry, Collingwood.

Hensinger John, f, 11, ½, $45, Perry, Collingwood.

Hensinger Michael, Perry, Collingwood.

Herber Anton N, f, 16, 80, $1190, Marion, Poe.

Herber Frank A,Marion,Poe.

Herber John, f, 16, 80, $1780, Marion, Poe.

Herber John jr, f, 20, 85, $1700, Marion, Poe.

Herber Nicholas, f, 15, 158, $3155, Marion, Poe.

Herber Veronica, f, 21, 68, $1370, Marion, Poe.

Herchenroether Wm f, 24, 80, $1455,Pleasant,Sheldon

Herman Adolph, St Joseph, Fort Wayne.

Herman Jacob, f, 9, 40, $550, Madison, Maples.

Herman Valentine, f, 35, 80, $2165, St Joseph, Fort Wayne.

Hermeler Ernst F, f, 7, 43, $875, St Joseph, Ft Wayne.

Hermsoth Herman, f, 29, 60, $850, Milan, Goeglein.

Herres Mathias, Adams, Ft Wayne.

Herrick H N, f, 80, $1495, Milan, Thurman.

Herrick Wm, f, 18,10, $1315, Milan, Death.

Herrin D E O, f, 11, 119, $2160, Cedar Creek, Leo.

Herrin James & J R, f ts, Cedar Creek, Leo.

Herrington Catherine, f, 26, 1¾, $220, Wayne, Fort Wayne.

Herrod U & E W, Lake, Arcola.

Hesler James, f, 34, 67, $1225, Lafayette, Zanesville.

Hess Jacob, Marion.

Hess John W, f t, Madison, Monroeville.

Hester James, f, Lafayette, Zanesville.

Hetzfield Louis,Milan, Chamberlain.

Hewen Maria & J, f, 27, 80, $1050, Eel River, Heller's Corners.

Hewitt George, Adams, Fort Wayne.

Hibler Anthony, f, 13, 1⅘, $295, Wayne, Fort Wayne.

Hibler Bernard, f, 13, 1⅘, $645, Wayne, Ft Wayne.

Hibler John B, Wayne, Ft Wayne.

Hicks Wm, Wayne, Fort Wayne.

Hieder Wm, Wayne, Fort Wayne.

Hifflefinger Jeremiah, f, 21, 200, $3880, Eel River, Heller's Corners.

Hiffleffinger Margaret, f, 16, 140, $2730, Eel River, Heller's Corners.

Higgins C E, Adams, Fort Wayne.

Higgs Martin, Pleasant, Sheldon.

High Daniel, Marion, Hoagland.

High Elizabeth, f, 36, 10, $115, Adams, Monroeville.

Hildebrand August, f, 10, 160, $2760, Marion, Soest.

Hildebrand Wm, f, 9, 76, $1230, Marion, Soest.

Hiler John, carp, 4, $320, Wayne, Fort Wayne.

Hiler J N, Wayne, Fort Wayne.

Hiler Salathiel, f, 2, $105, Aboite, Fort Wayne.

Hiler Wm A, f t, Aboite, Ft Wayne.

Hilgeman Frederick, Adams, Fort Wayne.

Hilgeman Frederick W, Adams, Fort Wayne.

Hill Adam D, f, 12, 80, $1630, Lafayette, Nine Mile.

Hill Cynthia A, f, 4, 11, $990, Wayne, Fort Wayne.

Hill David, hotel, f, 18, 80, $1415, Pleasant, Ft Wayne.

Hill Elizabeth, f, reserve, 12, $230, Lafayette, Nine Mile.

Hill Jacob, f, 5, $5, Lafayette, Aboite.

Hill John D, lab, Maumee, Woodburn.

Hill Michael, Lake, Arcola.

Hill Nathan, Milan, Gar Creek.

Hill S C, Wayne, Ft Wayne.

Hille John F W, f, 23, 40, $680, Lake, Fort Wayne.

Hille John H, f, 23, 39, $655, Lake, Fort Wayne.

Hillegass Hezekiah, f, 8, 74, $1665, Perry, Huntertown.

Hillegass Jacob, f, 17, 296, $6530, Perry, Huntertown.

Hillegass Lucy A, f, 18, 18, $135, Perry, Huntertown.

Hilme Charles W, f, 12, 40, $460, Madison, Maples.

Hilzeman Frederick, f, 31, 40, $540, Marion.

Himbert John & Helen, f, 17, 80, $1220, Milan, Thurman.

Himes Caroline, f, 21, 83, $1760, Eel River, Heller's Corners.

Hine Frederick, Adams, Ft Wayne.

Hinen Frank, f t, Pleasant, Sheldon.

Hinksen Samuel, Wayne, Ft Wayne.

Hinterwinkle John, f t, Cedar Creek, Leo.

Hintzelman S S et al, f, 16½, $145, Wayne, Ft Wayne.

Hippenhamer C O, f, 17, $95, Perry, Huntertown.

Hippenhamer Helen I, f, 17, ⅓, $5, Perry, Collingwood.

Hippenhamer Isaac L, f, 17, ½, $50, Perry, Huntertown.

Hippenhamer John, f, 17, ½, $90, Perry, Huntertown.

Hippenhammer Charles E, f t, Eel River, Wallen.

Hippenhammer Ellsworth, teacher, Eel River, Huntertown.

Hire Elias, Wayne, Ft Wayne.

Hire Elisha, f, 5, 158, $2095, Lake, Arcola.

Hire Wm, S Madison, Maples.

Hirschey Jacob, f, 21, 80, $2235, Cedar Creek, Cedarville.

Hiser George, f, 31, 80,$1450, Marion, Poe.

Hiser George D, Wayne, Ft Wayne.

Hiser Wm H, Wayne, Ft Wayne.

Hisner Frederick, Jefferson, Maples.

Hissong David, lab, 32, 20, $215, Scipio, Antwerp, O.

Hissong Wm, laborer, Scipio, Antwerp, O.

Hite George, Jefferson, Maples.

Hite John, f, 32, 80, $1485, Jefferson, Maples.

Hite Samuel, Wayne, Fort Wayne.

Hite Samuel, f, 5, 33, $305, Jefferson, Maples.

Hitzeman Frederick J, Wayne Ft Wayne.

Hitzeman Frederick L, Adams, Ft Wayne.

Hitzman Frederick, f, 36, 119, $2305, Marion, Hoagland.

Hitzman Frederick H, f, 24, 80, $1525, Lake, Fort Wayne.

Hitzman Frederick W, f, 15, 120, $3495, Adams, Ft Wayne.

Hitzman George, f, 6, 40, $430, Maumee, Ft Wayne.

Hoadley Oscar, lab, Eel River, Huntertown.

Hoagland James E, f, 2, 206, $4740, Adams, Ft Wayne.

Hoagland Merica, f, 2, $25, Adams, Ft Wayne.

Hobbs Alfred, Milan, Chamberlain.

Hobbs Amanda M, f, 33, 8, $125, Jefferson, Maples.

Hobbs Charles I, Milan, Chamberlain.

Hobbs Daniel J, Jackson, Dawkins.

Hobbs Elmer M, Milan, Chamberlain.

Hobbs George H, f, 16, 30, $610, Milan, Chamberlain.

Hobbs Henry, Jefferson, Maples.

Hobbs J A, Adams, Ft Wayne.

Hobbs Thomas W, Madison, Monroeville.

Hobbs Wm H, Jackson, Dawkins.

Hobbs Wm R, f, 16, 60, $1110, Milan, Chamberlain.

Hobel Charles, Wayne, Ft Wayne.

Hobel John, Wayne, Fort Wayne.

Hober Anthony, Lake, Arcola.

Hobrock John C, Jefferson, Maples.

Hobron Walter M, f, 31, 10, $360, St Joseph, Ft Wayne.

Hobson George L, f, 31, 10, $395, St Joseph, Ft Wayne.

Hobson Jacob E, f, 31, 5, $270, St Joseph, Ft Wayne.

Hochhouse George, Wayne, Ft Wayne.

Hochman Frederick, Adams, Ft Wayne.

Hochstetter Wm, f, 5, 61, $2835, Wayne, Ft Wayne.

Hockemeyer Frederick, f, 28, 52, $1855, Adams, Fort Wayne.

Hockemeyer Frederick, f, 27, 40, $610, Madison, Hoagland.

Hockemeyer Frederick, f, 8, 161, $3175, Marion, Soest.

Stahn & Heinrich, Dealers in BOOKS and FINE STATIONERY, Blank Books, Etc. 116 Calhoun Street.

ALLEN COUNTY DIRECTORY. 715

Hockemeyer Herman, f t, Madison, Hoagland.

Hockemeyer Wilhelmina, Marion.

Hockemeyer Wm, f, 27, 170, $2220, Madison, Hoagland.

Hockmeyer Charles, Wayne, Ft Wayne.

Hockmeyer C, Adams, Fort Wayne.

Hockmeyer Henry, f, 28, 143, $2835, Milan, Gar Creek.

Hodle Frederick, Cedar Creek

Hoevel Henry, f, 19, 140, $4485, Adams, Ft Wayne.

Hoevel Henry J, f, 20, 80, $1950, Adams, Ft Wayne.

Hoevel Henry L, f, 20, 40, $1350, Adams, Ft Wayne.

Hoevel John H, f, 21, 160, $4355, Adams, Ft Wayne.

Hoevel Wm C, f, 16, 80, $2335, Adams, Ft Wayne.

Hofer Andrew, Wayne, Ft Wayne.

Hoffman Charles A, Adams, Ft Wayne.

Hoffman Christ, f, 21, 79, $1155, Monroe, Monroeville.

Hoffman Daniel, Wayne, Ft Wayne.

Hoffman Edward E, f, 9, 1, $40, Wayne, Ft Wayne.

Hoffman Elizabeth, f, 16, 40, $400, Madison, Monroeville.

Hoffman Ervin, f, Lafayette, Roanoke.

Hoffman George B, f, 6, 48, $710, Madison, Soest.

Hoffman Henry, f, 23, 40, $1000, Adams, Ft Wayne.

Hoffman Henry, f, 10, 318, $4305, Madison, Monroeville.

Hoffman Jacob, f, 7, 79, $1650, Lafayette, Aboite.

Hoffman Jacob, f, 11, 175, $3485, Marion, Soest.

Hoffman John, f, 2, 100, $1265, Madison, Monroeville.

Hoffman John F, Marion, Soest.

Hoffman John W, Madison, Monroeville.

Hoffman M A & R, Adams, Fort Wayne.

Hoffman Nicholas, f, 10, 225, $2630, Madison, Monroeville.

Hoffman Nicholas jr, f, 2, 100, $1285, Madison, Monroeville.

Hoffman Rudolph, f, 19, 80, $980, Madison, Hoagland.

Hoffman Theresa, Adams, Fort Wayne.

Hoffman Wm, f, 1, 40, $710, Perry, Collingwood.

Hoffman W H, Adams, Ft Wayne.

Hoffmeyer Caroline, f, 24, 80, $1495, Lake, Fort Wayne.

Hoffmeyer Charles, Lake, Fort Wayne.

Hoffmeyer Wm, Lake, Fort Wayne.

Hoffner John, Lake, Arcola.

Hoffner Moses, Lake, Arcola.

Hoffner Wilhelmina, Lake, Arcola.

Hogan Timothy (est), 14, 1½, $245, Wayne, Ft Wayne.

Hohm John, Adams, Fort Wayne.

Hohmeyer Christian, f, 94, 91, $910, Maumee, Adams.

Hoke Charles L, f t, Pleasant, Sheldon.

Hoke John B, f, 23, 80, $1390, Pleasant, Sheldon.

Hoke Warren, f t, Pleasant, Sheldon.

Holbrock Caroline, Adams, Ft Wayne.

Holbrock John H, Adams, Fort Wayne.

Holder Charles, lawyer, Monroe, Monroeville.

Holesapple B F, f, 29, 80, $930, Jackson, Monroeville.

Holesapple Wm, f, 29, 80, $985, Jackson, Monroeville.

Holle Frederick, Marion.

Holliday L H, f, 6½, $235, Adams, New Haven.

Hollipeter Israel, f, 22' 76, $1455, Eel River, Heller's Corners.

Hollopeter Avery A, f, 34, 20, $150, Jackson, Maysville.

Hollopeter E, lab, Eel River, Heller's Corners.

Hollopeter George W, f, 28, 105, $2150, Cedar Creek, Cedarville.

Hollopeter H J, f, 34, 20, $180, Jackson, Baldwin.

Hollopeter John W, f, 22, 80, $2400, Cedar Creek, Leo.

Hollopeter Marion S, f, 19, 25, $295, Cedar Creek, Leo.

Hollopeter Mathias, f, 28, 109, $2445, Cedar Creek, Cedarville.

Hollopeter Rev Seldon, 2, 44, $270, Monroe, Monroeville.

Hollopeter Wm C, f, 12, 40, $590, Perry, Collingwood.

Hollopeter Wm H & A, f, 19, 44, $750, Cedar Creek, Cedarville.

Hollopeter W C, f, 7, 160, $2350, Cedar Creek, Leo.

Hollopeter & Stevick, sawmillers, Cedar Creek, Leo.

Holman Frank, f, 6, 120, $2575, Marion, Soest.

Holman Susannah, f, 13, 40, $745, St Joseph, Ft Wayne.

Holman Wm, f, 13, 39, $890, St Joseph, Fort Wayne.

Holmes C W, Jefferson, Maples.

Holmes Exter D, Jefferson, Maples.

Holmes George W, f, 19, ½, $10, Madison, Hoagland.

Holmes James M, f, 1, 28, $240, Lake, Wallen.

Holmes John M, f, 1, 28, $240, Lake, Wallen.

Holmes John W, f, 35, 160, $1715, Eel River, Wallen.

Holmes Joshua, 6, 40, $1225, Wayne, Fort Wayne.

Holmes Roland, f, 6, 40, $1215, Wayne, Ft Wayne.

Holmes Simon, Wayne, Fort Wayne.

Holmes Wm P, Jefferson Maples.

Holt A H, f, 17, 163, $2635, Lake, Arcola.

Holt Wm, Lake, Arcola.

Holtzman Samuel M, Wayne, Fort Wayne.

Honeck Henry, Wayne, Fort Wayne.

Hood Florence M, f, 1, 48, $625, Milan, Harlan.

Hood Frank, f, 1, 43, $558, Milan, Harlan.

Hood Frank, teacher, Eel River, Churubusco.

Hood H G, f, 18, 52, $660, Springfield.

Hood James W, f, 1, 43, $860, Milan, Harlan.

Hood Joseph & Margaret, f, 32, 120, $1965, Eel River, Churubusco.

E. F. Sites, Dentist, 86 Calhoun St., Four Doors North of Wayne.

ALLEN COUNTY DIRECTORY. 717

Hood Lavina, f, 7, 50, $455, Springfield.
Hood Thomas, f, 12, 40, $375, Milan, Harlan.
Hoodley Wm, Perry, Huntertown.
Hook John, f, 16, 36, $440, Scipio, Hicksville, O.
Hook John H, f, 17, 20, $425, Perry, Huntertown.
Hoopingorner G A, f, Lafayette, Zanesville.
Hoopingorner Solomon, f, 32, 80, $1685, Lafayette, Zanesville.
Hoops Reuben B, f, 23, 40, $570, Jefferson, Maples.
Hoover Sarah A, f, 8, 44, $400, Maumee, Woodburn.
Hoppe Frederick, Marion, Hoagland.
Hopple Edward, f, 3, 156, $2040, Lake, Wallen.
Hopple Henry, f, 36, 90, $1860, Marion, Hoagland.
Horley Catherine, f, 9, 40, $720, Monroe, Monroeville.
Horman Diederich, Marion, Poe.
Horman Frederick, f, 17, 1, $365, Adams, Ft Wayne.
Horman George, f, 26, 95, $1985, Adams, Ft Wayne.
Horman George, f, 26, 80, $810, Milan, Gar Creek.
Horman Henry, f, 17, 346, $7210, Marion, Poe.
Horman Henry jr, Marion, Poe.
Horman Henry S, f, 26, 80, $1135, Milan, Gar Creek.
Horman Wm, Marion, Poe.
Horn John C, f, Cedar Creek, Leo.
Horschburger Sylvester, Lake, Arcola.

Hort Jacob, Marion, Poe.
Horter Asa, Lake, Arcola.
Horz John, f, 13, 99, $1825, Lake, Fort Wayne.
Horz Rosanna, f, 11, 20, $320, Lake, Ft Wayne.
Hosler Polly, f, 1, 60, $840, St Joseph, Ft Wayne.
Hosler R, Eel River, Heller's Corners.
Hossler Edward, St Joseph, Fort Wayne.
Hossler Elizabeth, Cedar Creek, Leo.
Hossler Frank, f t, Cedar Creek, Leo.
Hossler Henry, f t, Cedar Creek, Leo.
Hossler John, f, 16, 10, $1225, Cedar Creek, Leo.
Hossler Maria, f, 16, 110, $2630, Cedar Creek, Leo.
Hossler Mary E, f, 15, 40, $965, Cedar Creek, Leo.
Hostmeyer Wm, f, 14, 55, $1005, Aboite, Ft Wayne.
Houch Peter, Marion.
Hough Sarah D, f, 20, 20, $440, Wayne, Ft Wayne.
Houghton Lloyd, Perry, Huntertown.
Houk Elijah, f, 33, 130, $2260, Madison, Bingen.
Houk Samuel, f, 32, 120, $1745, Madison, Bingen.
Hourigan Daniel H, f, 10, 79, $1545, Pleasant, Sheldon.
Houser Charles, f t, Pleasant, Sheldon.
Houser Charles, f, 19, 1, $285, Madison, Hoagland.
Houser Henry, f, 13, $425, Wayne, Fort Wayne.
Houser Joseph, Madison, Hoagland.

Houser J & C, f, 19, 1, $260, Madison, Hoagland.

Houser Washington, lab, Eel River, Huntertown.

Howard Arthur, f, 29, 40, $555, Monroe, Monroeville.

Howard Austin D, f, 29, 40, $710, Monroe, Monroeville.

Howard Wm P, f, 29, 40, $495, Monroe, Monroeville.

Howe Charles B, f, 22, 20, $155, Jackson, Edgerton.

Howe George B, f, 22, 20, $160, Jackson, Edgerton.

Howe Williard, Jackson, Edgerton.

Howell Cedar, f t, Madison, Monroeville.

Howell Emma F, f, 26, 15, $240, Lafayette, Ft Wayne.

Howell Emma M, f, 10, 35, $410, Madison, Monroeville.

Howell Hannah M, f, 26, 14, $250, Lafayette, Zanesville.

Howell James L, Monroe, Monroeville.

Howell John M, Madison, Monroeville.

Howell John W, f, Lafayette, Zanesville.

Howell Lydia, f, 26, 65, $1185, Lafayette, Zanesville.

Howell Martha J, f, 26, 15, $260, Lafayette, Zanesville.

Howell Minda E, f, 26, 15, $225, Lafayette, Nine Mile.

Howell Rosa B, f, 26, 15, $260, Lafayette, Zanesville.

Howell Wm, f, 13, 40, $555, Madison, Monroeville.

Howey C W, Cedar Creek, Leo.

Howey John K, f, 1, 5, $100, Cedar Creek, Hursh.

Howey Wm, f, 1, 30, $315, Cedar Creek, Hursh.

Howriezen Jacob, f t, Eel River, Huntertown.

Hoy Charles, Lake, Arcola.

Hubbard John H, Adams, Ft Wayne.

Huber Frederick, Adams, Ft Wayne.

Huber Samuel M, f, 49, $880, Marion.

Huber Ulrich, Wayne, Fort Wayne.

Hubert Richard, Marion.

Hubertus Catharine, f, 31, 10, $500, St Joseph, Ft Wayne.

Hubler Curtis F, f, 22, 80, $1600, Marion, Hoagland.

Hubler Henry, f, 26, 190, $4095, Marion, Hoagland.

Hubler John, f, 6, 51, $925, Marion, Hoagland.

Hubler John, f, 36, 80, $1640, Wayne, Fort Wayne.

Hubler Samuel M, f, 25, 79, $1760, Marion, Hoagland.

Hubler Wm H, f, 25, 119, $2145, Marion, Hoagland.

Hudson James (est), f, 18, 80, $2335, St Joseph, Fort Wayne.

Huff Ernest, Aboite.

Huffard Eliza J, f, 3, 1, $80, Eel River, Ari.

Huffman Charles V, f, 1, 42, $1155, Cedar Creek, Hursh.

Huffman Christian S, f, 21, 15, $170, Monroe, Monroeville.

Huffman Edward, lab, Pleasant, Sheldon.

Huffman G W, f, 5, 95, $770, Springfield.

Huffman Johanna, f, reserve, 16, $300, Pleasant, Sheldon.

Huguenard August, f, 1, 40, $730, Aboite, Fort Wayne.

Huguénard Claude, f, 36, 40, $595, Perry, Fort Wayne.

Huguenard Edward, Jefferson, Gar Creek.

Huguénard Felicia, f, 10, 120, $1430, Jefferson, Gar Creek.

Hull Adam, f, 19, 125, $2415, Eel River, Churubusco.

Hull Charles E, f, 29, 29, $490, Eel River, Churubusco.

Hull Henry, lab, Eel River, Churubusco.

Hull S P, lab, Eel River, Churubusco.

Hullinger J W, Jefferson, Monroeville.

Humbert George, f, 5, 80, $1305, Eel River, Churubusco.

Humbert Justin, f, 16, 79, $1140, Jefferson, New Haven.

Humbold Henry, Jackson, Zulu.

Humphrey Jane, Wayne, Ft Wayne.

Hunter Amy, Perry, Huntertown.

Hunter Henry, f, 18, 2, $45, Perry, Huntertown.

Hunter H P, Perry, Huntertown.

Hunter J C, f, 17, 17, $455, Perry, Huntertown.

Hunter J P, Perry, Huntertown.

Hunter Lewis C, Adams, Ft Wayne.

Hunter L C, f, 32, 159, $2750, Perry, Huntertown.

Hunter Mahala, f, 18, 10, $455, Perry, Huntertown.

Hunter Mary J, f, 17, ½ $160, Perry, Huntertown.

Hunter Wm C & G, f, 18, 10, $290, Perry, Huntertown.

Hunter Wm T, Perry, Huntertown.

Hursh Catherine, f, 16, $385, Cedar Creek, Hursh.

Hursh Enoch (estate), Cedar Creek, Hursh.

Hursh Harriet, f, 19, 15, $150, Cedar Creek, Hursh.

Hursh Hiram, f, 19, 40, $525, Cedar Creek, Cedarville.

Hursh Isaac W, lab, Cedar Creek, Hursh.

Hursh Jacob, f, 24, 146, $2330, Perry, Huntertown.

Hursh John C, Cedar Creek, Hursh.

Hursh John W, f, 24, 53, $925, Perry, Huntertown.

Huss E O, f t, Pleasant, Sheldon.

Huss Hiram, lab, Pleasant, Sheldon.

Husted George & James, f, 3, 20, $130, Maumee, Antwerp, O.

Husted G W, f, 3, 89, $555, Maumee, Antwerp, O.

Husted Louis, f, 3, 80, $825, Maumee, Antwerp, O.

Huston James F, f, 8, 114, $2240, Jefferson, New Haven.

Hutchins David, Lake, Arcola.

Hutchinson Charles W, f, 19, 120, $550, Perry, Huntertown.

Hutchinson C W, f, 36, 200, $2075, Milan, Ft Wayne.

Huth Carl, Adams, Ft Wayne.

Hutker Bernhart, f, 15, 118, $1395, Milan, Chamberlain.

Hutson James W, Jefferson, New Haven.

Hyde Charles L, Adams, Ft Wayne.

Hyde Frederick,f t, Pleasant, Sheldon.

Hyde F C, Jefferson, Maples.

Hyndman G B, f, 30, 110, $1870, Eel River, Churubusco.

Hyndman Joseph, f, 19, 141, $2630, Eel River, Churubusco.

Hyndman Mary A, f, 19, 60, $915, Eel River, Churubusco.

Hyndman Nelson, f, 18, 160, $2690, Eel River, Churubusco.

Hyndman Samuel, f, 30, 49, $1430, St Joseph, Ft Wayne.

I

Iliff John W, Adams, Ft Wayne.

Imberger S A & Mary B, f, 15, 80, $955, Monroe, Monroeville.

Imler John, farmer, Monroe, Dixon, O.

Ireland E H, Jefferson, Zulu.

Ireland Isam, Jackson, Edgerton.

Ireland John C, Jackson, Dawkins.

Irving Alexander, f, 23, 172, $2460, Milan, Harlan.

Irwin John, Lake, Arcola.

Irwin Mary I, Lake, Arcola.

Isabel Charles, Perry, Huntertown.

Isabey George, Adams, Fort Wayne.

Isabey Joseph A, Adams, Ft Wayne.

Isabey Louis C, f, 9, ¾, $20, Adams, Ft Wayne.

Isliff David H, Adams, Ft Wayne.

J

Jackemeyer Henry, Adams, New Haven.

Jackman Conrad, f, 24, 80, $2045, Adams, New Haven.

Jackson Abraham, f, 5, 240, $4190, Scipio, Hicksville, O.

Jackson Albert, f, 8, 40, $530, Scipio, Hicksville, O.

Jackson Charles, f t, Scipio, Hicksville, O.

Jackson Elizabeth, f, 29, 20, $460, Lafayette, Zanesville.

Jackson Frank A, blksmith, Marion, Poe.

Jackson Henry, Adams, New Haven.

Jackson Henry W, f, 16, 40, $615, Milan, New Haven.

Jackson John, farmer, Monroe, Monroeville.

Jackson John H, f, 29, 29, $325, Lafayette, Zanesville.

Jackson Joseph, farmer, Monroe, Monroeville.

Jackson Lewis, f t, Eel River, Heller's Corners.

Jackson Louis, f, 1, 7, $80, Lake, Arcola.

Jackson Martin, f, 12, 40, $725, Eel River, Huntertown.

Jackson Mary J, f, 5, 46, $1040, Scipio, Hicksville, O.

Jackson Peter, lab, Aboite, Aboite.

Jackson P W, f, 21, 120, $2685, Perry, Huntertown.

Jackson Sarah E, f, 9, 235, $3780, Scipio, Hicksville, O.

Jackson Silas, f, 8, 12, $275, Wayne, Ft Wayne.

Jackson Theodore, f, 5, 36, $450, Scipio, Hicksville, O.

Jackson Thomas, Aboite.

Jackson Wallace, f t, Scipio, Hicksville, O.

Jacob Elizabeth, Wayne, Ft Wayne.

Jacobs Charles W, Adams, Fort Wayne.

Jacobs Henry, Wayne, Fort Wayne.

Jacquay Hugo, f, 26,40,$655, Jefferson, Maples.

Jacquay Lemuel, f, 2, 43, $1565, Adams, New Haven.

Jacquay Louis S, f, 27, 20, $295, Jefferson, Maples.

Jacquay Martha A, f, 26, 40, $445, Jefferson, Maples.

James Jonathan, f, 26, 120, $1940, Lake, Fort Wayne.

James Joseph M, f, 6, 45, $540, Maumee, Harlan.

Jamey Francis, f, 22, 68, $890, Lake, Fort Wayne.

Jamey Frederick, f, 36, ½, $10, Lake, Fort Wayne.

Jamison Curtis C, f, 22, 46, $795, Marion, Hoagland.

Jamison O E, f, 23, 240, $4520, Marion, Hoagland.

Janarschke Frank, Wayne, Fort Wayne.

Jarchon Wm, Marion.

Jeanmongin Charles, f, 22,80, $1495, Lake, Arcola.

Jeanmongin Frank, f, 22, 57, $840, Lake, Arcola.

Jefferds Mary C, Adams, Ft Wayne.

Jeffries Adam, f, 4, 1, $155, St Joseph, Fort Wayne.

Jenkinson Joseph J, Adams, Fort Wayne.

Jenness C H, Milan, Chamberlain.

Jennings David W, f, 4, 78, $1620, Eel River, Ari.

Jetmore John J, lab, Aboite, Fort Wayne.

Jetmore Levi, Perry, Huntertown.

Jillet Alva, Perry, Churubusco.

Jobes James M, lab, Maumee, Woodburn.

Jobs Wm, f, 17, 120, $2355, Lafayette, Myhart.

Johnell Henry, f, 1, 10, $200, Aboite, Fort Wayne.

Johnell Lawrence, f, 36, 6, $105, Lake, Fort Wayne.

Johns John, Wayne, Fort Wayne.

Johns Nicholas, Wayne, Fort Wayne.

Johnson Belinda, f, 28, 27, $755, Eel River, Heller's Corners.

Johnson Benjamin, lab, Maumee, Antwerp, O.

Johnson B F (est of), f, 7, 35, $955, Eel River, Heller's Corners.

Johnson B H, Monroe, Monroeville.

Johnson Catherine, f, 7, 9, $140, Eel River, Churubusco.

Johnson Catherine, f, 26, 80, Pleasant, Sheldon.

Johnson Charles, f, 34, 39, $820, Milan, Gar Creek.

Johnson David, f, 27, 88, $1545, Eel River, Heller's Corners.

Johnson David A, f, 15, 57, $830, Milan, Chamberlain.

Johnson Elmira, f, 7, 8, $180, Eel River, Churubusco.

Johnson E M, f, Monroe, Monroeville.

Johnson Francis A, f, 31, 120, $1700, Scipio, Harlan.

Johnson Frank M, f, 16, 40, $280, Maumee, Ft Wayne.

Johnson F M, Adams, Fort Wayne.

Johnson Harvey, f, Pleasant, Sheldon.

Johnson Isaac C, f, 10, 79, $1070, Lake, Arcola.

Johnson Jacob, f, Maumee, Antwerp, O.

Johnson John A, f, 19, 34, $610, Pleasant, Nine Mile.

Johnson John C, f, 80, Pleasant, Sheldon.

Johnson John K, Jackson, Edgerton.

Johnson John P, Perry, Huntertown.

Johnson Joseph B, lab, Maumee, Antwerp, O.

Johnson Joseph B, f, 8, 40, $795, Monroe, Monroeville.

Johnson J C, Adams, Fort Wayne.

Johnson J H, lab, Scipio, Harlan.

Johnson Lewis, Lafayette, Sheldon.

Johnson Mamie, f, 7, 8, $180, Eel River, Churubusco.

Johnson Martin, f, 8, 59, $980, Eel River, Churubusco.

Johnson Myron A, laborer, Scipio, Harlan.

Johnson Nathan H, f, 8, 65, $1430, Eel River, Churubusco.

Johnson Perry, f, 21, 137, $2745, Eel River, Heller's Corners.

Johnson R M, f, Maumee, Antwerp, O.

Johnson Sherman, f, Eel River, Eel River.

Johnson Uriah, f, 27, 80, $1510, Perry, Deealle.

Johnson Wesley, f, 20, 174, $3450, Eel River, Churubusco.

Johnson Wm, f, 28, 7, $130, Eel River, Eel River.

Johnson Wm A, teacher, Eel River, Churubusco.

Johnson Wm F, lab, Maumee, Antwerp, O.

Johnson Wm H, f, 28, 24, $410, Eel River, Heller's Corners.

Johnson Wm R, f, 5, 40, $670, Eel River.

Joker John L, f t, Aboite, Ft Wayne.

Jolly Constantine, Perry, Huntertown.

Joly Francis, f, 22, 57, $1215, Perry, Huntertown.

Joly Louis C F, f, 32, ½, $40, Jefferson, Maples.

Jones Benjamin, f, 23, 39, $540, Lake, Arcola.

Jones Charles, lab, Monroe, Monroeville.

Jones David, Jefferson, New Haven.

Jones David, St Joseph, Ft Wayne.

Jones Edgar B, f t, Aboite, Fort Wayne.

Jones Emma, f, 8, 10, $1310, Adams, Fort Wayne.

Jones George W, f, 5, 40, $510, Monroe, Monroeville.

Jones H S, farmer, Monroe, Monroeville.

Jones Jackson, Jackson, Edgerton.

Jones Jasper W, f, 16, 160, $1385, Jackson, Monroeville.

Jones John A, f, 32, 157, $1950, Jackson, Monroeville.

Jones L M, Adams, Fort Wayne.

Jones Owen G, lab, Aboite, Fort Wayne.

Jones Thomas S, clk, 9, 200, $2985, Monroe, Monroeville.

Jones Wm, St Joseph, Fort Wayne.

Jones W M, Lafayette, Zanesville.

Jones W O, Adams, Fort Wayne.

Jordan Alonzo, Wayne, Fort Wayne.

Jordan George, Milan, Chamberlain.

Jordan John, lab, Wayne, Fort Wayne.

Jordan Mary A, f, 5, 78, $3025, Wayne, Ft Wayne.

Jourdain Mary J, f, 20, 235, $3400, Perry, Huntertown.

Juiff Emily, f, 12, 40, $400, Milan, Harlan.

Juiff Francis, f, 12, 80, $1275, St Joseph, Fort Wayne.

Juiff Frank, f, 29, 40, $435, Perry, Huntertown.

Juiff John, f, 6, 100, $2115, Eel River, Churubusco.

Juiff Julius, Eel River, Eel River.

Juiff Paul, f, 33, 108, $2085, Perry, Academy.

Juiff Victor, f, 33, 109, $2270, Perry, Ft Wayne.

Juliard Louisa, f, 30, 80, $1260, Wayne, Ft Wayne.

Jump Levi, f, 8, 60, $1015, Scipio, Hicksville, O.

Jump Oscar, f, 4, 63, $1435, Milan, Chamberlain.

Jump T M, f, 31, 18, $275, Scipio, Harlan.

Junge August, f, 50, $1430, Adams, Ft Wayne.

Junk J P, f, Wayne, Fort Wayne.

Junks Catherine, f, 8, 30, $585, Wayne, Ft Wayne.

Jurgens Henry, f, 28, 40, $900, St Joseph, Fort Wayne.

Jurgens Henry A, Wayne, Ft Wayne.

Jurgens Louis, f, 14, 80, $1485, St Joseph, Fort Wayne.

Jurgens Louisa, f, 15, 45, $770, St Joseph, Ft Wayne.

Justis Lewis S, f, 32, ½, $40, Pleasant, Sheldon.

Justice Sophia, f, 29, 40, $650, Pleasant, Sheldon.

K.

Kaiser Christian, Madison, Soest.

Kaiser Edward, f t, 28, 64, $1200, Marion, Poe.

Kaiser Ernst, f, 28, 96, $2000, Marion, Poe.

Kaiser Eve C, Madison, Soest.

Kaiser Frederick, f, 36, 70, $1590, Marion, Hoagland.

Kaiser Jacob, f, 2, 75, $1255, Marion, Soest.

Kaiser John F, f, 1, 80, $1545, Marion, Soest.

Kaiser John G, f, 1, 60, $1015, Marion, Soest.

Kaiser John G jr, f, 20, 122, $1755, Madison, Hoagland.

I. L. Barkley, General Agent ÆTNA LIFE INSURANCE CO.
18 SCHMITZ BLOCK.

724　　　　R. L. POLK & CO.'S

Kaiser John H, Madison, Soest.

Kaiser Wm, f, 28, 107, $2290, Marion, Poe.

Kalen Peter, Wayne, Fort Wayne.

Kalmeier Charles, f, 24, 80, $1470, Adams, New Haven.

Kallmeyer Henry, Adams, New Haven.

Kammeyer Conrad, gardener, Wayne, Ft Wayne.

Kamphus Henry, Wayne, Ft Wayne.

Kane Mary, f, 32, 12, $205, Lake, Arcola.

Kanger Andrew, f, 2, 35, $630, Milan, Harlan.

Kanning Henry, f, 25, 80, $1535, Adams, Soest.

Kaough James, f, 3, 80, $1795, Aboite, Ft Wayne.

Karber James H, Adams, Ft Wayne.

Karder Valentine, f, 13, 80, $1415, Lake, Fort Wayne.

Kariger Samuel, Adams, Ft Wayne.

Kasbaum Charles, Wayne, Ft Wayne.

Kasmire John, wagon mnfr, Cedar Creek, Leo.

Kaumlaup Cyrus, Perry, Huntertown.

Kaus Mary, 1, 35, $495, Cedar Creek.

Keadle Arthur, Aboite.

Keaft Frederick, Wayne, Ft Wayne.

Keck Alfred, Lake, Wallen.

Keck Jacob, Lake, Wallen.

Keck Mary E, f, 1, 41, $260, Lake, Wallen.

Keck Mary R, f, 1, 32, $390, Lake, Wallen.

Keeber David, St Joseph, Ft Wayne.

Keef Catherine, lab, Pleasant, Sheldon.

Keef Wm jr, Pleasant, Sheldon.

Keeler Mary E, 25, 20, $405, St Joseph, Fort Wayne.

Keesler Henry, Milan, Chamberlain.

Keever Edward M, f, 31, 5, $275, St Joseph, Ft Wayne.

Keever Isabella, f, 15, 40, $460, Monroe, Dixon, O.

Keever Meinrad, lab, Jackson, Edgerton.

Kehler B D, Wayne, Fort Wayne.

Kehler C F, Wayne, Fort Wayne.

Kehles Joseph W, Wayne, Fort Wayne.

Kehn Wm, Wayne, Fort Wayne.

Keiler Charles H, f, 20, 120, $2015, Lake, Wallen.

Keiler Minnie, f, 29, 40, $470, Lake, Arcola.

Keim Daniel, f, 18, 201, $2490, Lake, Arcola.

Keim George W, Lake, Fort Wayne.

Keim Solomon D, Lake, Arcola.

Keingle Wm, Lake, Fort Wayne.

Keintz Valentine, gard, 21, 40, $1390, Wayne, Fort Wayne.

Keiser George, f t, Pleasant, Sheldon.

Keiser John, St Joseph, Fort Wayne.

Keiser Peter, f, Pleasant, Sheldon.

Fine Commercial Printing, **M. CLARK & CO.,** 16 W. COLUMBIA STREET.

ALLEN COUNTY DIRECTORY. 725

Kelicker Jacob, St Joseph, Goeglein.

Kelicker John, St Joseph, Goeglein.

Kell George V, f, 12, 100, $1655, Eel River, Huntertown.

Kell Jacob, f, 16,698, $13,835, Perry, Huntertown.

Kell Solomon, f, 21,80,$1850, Perry, Huntertown.

Keller Albert, Lafayette, Myhart.

Keller Charles, Adams, Fort Wayne.

Keller Ferris, f, Lafayette, Zanesville.

Keller Frederick, f t, Pleasant, Nine Mile.

Keller Frederick, f, 23, 160, $2720, Lafayette, Fort Wayne.

Keller Frederick (estate of) f, 8, 80, $1545, Pleasant, Nine Mile.

Keller Harriet, f, 8, 40, $690, Pleasant, Nine Mile.

Keller Henry, f, 17, 80, $720, Maumee, Woodburn.

Keller Henry, f, 8, 80, $1800, Pleasant, Nine Mile.

Keller John L, f, 18, 160, $3365, Pleasant, Sheldon.

Keller Jonathan F, f t, Pleasant, Nine Mile.

Keller Joseph, f t, Pleasant, Sheldon.

Keller Sebastian, f, 33, 233, $3990, Lake, Arcola.

Keller Wm, f t, Pleasant, Nine Mile.

Keller Wm N, f, 31, 99, Jackson, Monroeville.

Kellermeier John, Wayne, Ft Wayne.

Kellermeer Ludwig, f, 16, 40, $1750, Wayne, Ft Wayne.

Kelley Abraham, f, 1, 43, $760, Milan, Harlan.

Kelley Thomas, f, 23, 80, $1485, Pleasant, Nine Mile.

Kelsey Abner, f, 29, 103, $2005, Lafayette, Roanoke.

Kelsey Ambrose B, f, 18, 78, $1395, Aboite, Aboite.

Kelsey A R, f, Lafayette, Zanesville.

Kelsey Benjamin D, f, 30, 57, $945, Aboite, Aboite.

Kelsey David. H, f, 19, 116, $2410, Aboite, Ft Wayne.

Kelsey Elizabeth, f, 18, 1, $220, Aboite, Ft Wayne.

Kelsey Elva C, f, 34, 29, $645, Lafayette, Fort Wayne.

Kelsey Henry S, f, 18, 144, $2680, Lafayette, Roanoke.

Kelsey James H, f, 28, 80, $1595, Lafayette, Fort Wayne.

Kelsey John M, f, Lafayette, Zanesville.

Kelsey Otto J, lab, Aboite, Aboite.

Kelsey Sarah E, f, 28, 40, $815, Lafayette, Ft Wayne.

Kelsey Sarah M, f, 29, 28, $540, Lafayette, Ft Wayne.

Kelsey Wm A, f, 18, 74, $1460, Aboite, Ft Wayne.

Kelspler S C, Adams, Fort Wayne.

Kemp Bernard, f, 1, 99, $2635, Adams, Ft Wayne.

Kemp Mathias F, Adams, Ft Wayne.

Kennark Edward J, f, 10, 79, $1570, Pleasant, Sheldon.

Kennark Frisbie T, f, Pleasant, Sheldon.

CHARLES BOWMAN, No. 18 Harrison Street. **Saw Gumming,** FILING and SETTING.

726   R. L. POLK & CO.'S

Kennark John E, Marion, Hoagland.

Kennark Selina, f, 4, 160, $3185, Pleasant, Sheldon.

Kennark Timothy, f, 23, 185, $3770, Marion, Hoagland.

Kennark Wm, f, 10,84,$1810, Pleasant, Sheldon.

Kennedy Sophia, f, 10, 80, $1755, Aboite, Ft Wayne.

Kennison John W, Milan, Harlan.

Kenraede Frank, St Joseph, Goeglein.

Kensinger D, Perry, Huntertown.

Kensinger L W, Perry, Huntertown.

Kent Robert C, teacher, Eel River, Churubusco.

Kent Rev Wm S, Eel River, Churubusco.

Keplinger Daniel, f, 16, 80, $555, Maumee, Wells.

Keplinger J L, f, 23, 40, $805, Lafayette, Nine Mile.

Keplinger Margaret, f, Lafayette, Zanesville.

Keplinger Woodworth, f, Lafayette, Zanesville.

Kepner Amos, f, 16, 40, $325, Maumee, Cass.

Kerkhoff Louis, f t, 22, 80, $1405, Pleasant, Sheldon.

Kern Charles, St Joseph, Ft Wayne.

Kern Elizabeth, f, 2, 104, $3995, Adams, New Haven.

Kern E B, genl store, Pleasant, Sheldon.

Kern John T, Adams, Ft Wayne.

Kerns Martha, Maumee, Woodburn.

Kerns Ulysses S, lab, Maumee, Woodburn.

Kerns Wm, lab, Maumee, Woodburn.

Kerr Hugh, f, 29, 77, $1010, Madison.

Kerr Wm E, Wayne, Ft Wayne.

Kertwaight Charles M, f, 17, 55, $785, Lake, Arcola.

Ketchum Andrew, f, 16, 5, $80, Perry, Huntertown.

Ketchum A J, f, 16, 14, $220, Perry, Huntertown.

Ketchum Mary M, f, 7, 4, $20, Perry, Huntertown.

Ketchum Wm, Perry, Huntertown.

Kever Kasper, 84, $2530, St Joseph, Ft Wayne.

Kever Samuel, Wayne, Ft Wayne.

Kew Hugh, f, 24, 156, $2785, Marion, Hoagland.

Keyser Henry N, f, 10, 61, $1255, Lafayette, Nine Mile.

Keyser Jacob F, f, 36, 40, $1520, Lafayette, Zanesville.

Keyser Peter F, f, 15, 40, $735, Lafayette, Nine Mile.

Kidd John, Adams, Fort Wayne.

Kiefer Henry, Adams, Fort Wayne.

Kieffe Edward, f, 10, 160, $2320, Jefferson, Dawkins.

Kieler George, Lake, Arcola.

Kignerey Angelique et al, Adams, Ft Wayne.

Kile Edward, Adams, Fort Wayne.

Killian Ella, f, 18, 32, $345, Maumee, Woodburn.

Killian Frank, f, 17, 20, $200, Maumee, Woodburn.

Mrs. E. A. Flagler, Cheapest, Best and Most Fashionable MILLINERY STORE in Town. 14 West Berry Street.

ALLEN COUNTY DIRECTORY. 727

Killworth John, Adams, Ft Wayne.

Kimball Desdemona, f, 19, 80, $485, Wayne, Ft Wayne.

Kimmel David, f, 17, 80, $1575, Pleasant, Nine Mile.

Kimmel Jacob H, f, 6, 212, $4260, Pleasant, Nine Mile.

Kimmel Robert J, f t, Pleasant, Nine Mile.

Kimmell John, f, 31, 100, $2195, Wayne, Ft Wayne.

Kimmell Newton, f, 28, 40, $660, Wayne, Ft Wayne.

Kindell Elizabeth, Adams, Ft Wayne.

Kinder Michael, f, 24, 40, $625, Pleasant, Sheldon.

Kinder Nicholas, f, 26, 80, $1405, Pleasant, Sheldon.

Kinder Nicholas jr, f t, Pleasant, Sheldon.

Kinder Paul, f, 14, 80, $1570, Pleasant, Sheldon.

King Asa, f, 36, 124, $2175, Pleasant, Sheldon.

King Diamond, f, 25, 106, $2235, Pleasant, Sheldon.

King Freeman, f, 25, 80, $1420, Pleasant, Sheldon.

King John, Marion.

King Josiah D, f, 25, 9, $140, Pleasant, Sheldon.

King Merica C, f, 19, 141, $2720, Pleasant, Sheldon.

King Thomas, f, 17, 52, $1035, Pleasant, Nine Mile.

Kingsley Julia, Adams, Fort Wayne.

Kinsey Emma H, Wayne, Ft Wayne.

Kipfer John, f, 26, 80, $1385, Cedar Creek, Leo.

Kirbach E, Wayne, Fort Wayne.

Kirchner Ferdinand, Adams, Ft Wayne.

Kirkwood C C, Adams, Fort Wayne.

Kistler A J, Perry, Collingwood.

Kistler L E, Perry, Collingwood.

Kistler Michael, f, 1, 110, $2285, Perry, Collingwood.

Kite Archibald, Aboite, Fort Wayne.

Klaehn Frederick, f, 11, 126, $2850, Aboite, Ft Wayne.

Klaehn Frederick jr, f, 12, 40, $945, Aboite, Fort Wayne.

Klaehn John R, Adams, Ft Wayne.

Klaehn Wm R, Adams, Fort Wayne.

Klanke Frederick, Jefferson, Maples.

Klaper John, Marion.

Kleber Christian, f, 8, 134, $2920, Marion, Poe.

Klein Bernhard, f, 32, 118, $2410, Wayne, Ft Wayne.

Klein John, f, 32, 53, $1545, Wayne, Ft Wayne.

Klein Joseph, Wayne, Fort Wayne.

Klein Thomas, Wayne, Fort Wayne.

Kleine Charles, Aboite, Fort Wayne.

Kleine Henry, Marion.

Kleinzeicher John, Marion, Poe.

Klenke August, Wayne, Ft Wayne.

Klenke Christian, f, 31, 60, $755, Jefferson, Maples.

Klenke Frederick (estate of), f, 29, 40, $645, Jefferson, Maples.

Kline Charles, Jefferson, Maples.

Kline Eliza, 3, 40, $580, St Joseph, Ft Wayne.

Kline Henry, St Joseph, Ft Wayne.

Kline Jacob, f, 32, 99, $1130, Lake, Arcola.

Kline Jacob, f, 10, 80, $1065, Milan, Ft Wayne.

Kline James, f, 20, 20, $315, Jefferson, Maples.

Kline John, 3, 45, $825, St Joseph, Ft Wayne.

Kline John, f, 20, 20, $310, Jefferson, Maples.

Kline John F, f, 35, 134, $2930, Marion, Hoagland.

Kline Mary, lab, Pleasant, Sheldon.

Kline Susan, Cedar Creek, Cedarville.

Klinger Caroline, 32, 10, $470, St Joseph, Ft Wayne.

Klinger Isaac, f, 7, 7, $1000, Adams, Ft Wayne.

Klinger Jacob, Wayne, Fort Wayne.

Klinger Wm, St Joseph, Ft Wayne.

Klingman Joseph, Adams, Fort Wayne.

Klintzel Christian, f, 12, 20, $275, Lake, Arcola.

Klopfenstein Christian, f, 24, 80, $1835, Cedar Creek, Leo.

Klopfenstein David M, f, Cedar Creek, Leo.

Klopfenstein Emanuel, f, 23, 71, $1880, Cedar Creek, Leo.

Klopfenstein Jacob, sawmiller and f, 23, 65, $1365, Cedar Creek, Leo.

Klopfenstein Jerry, f, Cedar Creek, Leo.

Klopfenstein Joseph, f, 24, 130, $2970, Cedar Creek, Leo.

Klopfenstein Joseph M, tile mnfr, 25, 80, $1455, Cedar Creek, Leo.

Klopfenstein J, f, 14, 160, $3570, Cedar Creek, Leo.

Klopfenstein J P, f, 13, 20, $260, Cedar Creek, Leo.

Klopfenstein J S, f, Cedar Creek, Leo.

Klopfenstein Michael, f, 24, 185, $3675, Cedar Creek, Leo.

Klopfenstein Michael jr, tile mnfr, 23, 40, $760, Cedar Creek, Leo.

Klotz Herman, 14, $\frac{1}{2}$, $855, Wayne, Fort Wayne.

Knapp John R, f, 31, 120, $1885, Scipio, Harlan.

Knapp Thomas W, lab, Lafayette, Myhart.

Knapp Wm, lab, Scipio, Harlan.

Knepper Caleb, Aboite, Fort Wayne.

Knepper Joseph, f t, Wayne, Fort Wayne.

Knepper Margaret, f, 9, 80, $1585, Aboite, Ft Wayne.

Knepper Noah, f, 15, 80, $1695, Aboite, Fort Wayne.

Knight Christian, f, 8, 39, $1215, Milan, Chamberlain.

Knight Conrad, f, 31, 233, $3775, Lafayette, Zanesville.

Knight H, Lafayette, Zanesville.

Knight Lewis, f, 8, 40, $750, Milan, Chamberlain.

Knight Wm, Wayne, Fort Wayne.

Knipstein Frederick, f, 27,40, $615, Madison, Hoagland.

Kniseley Barbara, f,11,20,$195 Milan, Harlan.

Kniseley David, f,11,20,$200, Milan, Harlan.

Knisley George M, f, 3, 18, $130, Monroe, Monroeville.

Knisley John W, f, 3,18, $125, Monroe, Monroeville.

Kniss Emma, Eel River, Huntertown.

Knoblauch Otto, f, 33, 440, $3055, Maumee, Woodburn.

Knode Lucy B, f, 18, 11¼, $1400, Adams, New Haven.

Knoll George, f,16, 38,$1545, Wayne, Fort Wayne.

Knoll John, f, 20, 24¾, $460, Wayne, Fort Wayne.

Knouse John, f, 30, 80,$1385, Scipio, Hall's Corners.

Knouse Maria, f, 24, 39, $725, Madison, Monroeville.

Knowlton Charles L, Lafayette, Roanoke.

Knowlton G H, f, 8,79,$1395, Lafayette, Roanoke.

Knox Jane, f, 7, 24, $485, Jefferson, New Haven.

Koble Catherine, Cedar Creek, Leo.

Koble Christian, lab, Cedar Creek, Leo.

Koch Gottlieb, f,29,80,$1000, Scipio, Hall's Corners.

Koch Henry, f, 33, 80, $510, Maumee, Woodburn.

Koch Wm, f, 20, 140, $1805, Scipio, Hall's Corners.

Koehlhepp Moritz, f, 7, 2½, $245, Adams, Ft Wayne.

Koehlinburg Conrad, f, 25, 238, $5165, Adams, Fort Wayne.

Koehlinger Christian, Marion.

Koehlinger Frederick, f, 35, 92, $1800, Adams, Soast.

Koehlinger George, f, 1, 70, $1385, Marion, Soest.

Koehlinger George H, f, 35, 35, $855, Adams, Soest.

Koehlinger Henry, Marion.

Koehlinger J H, f, 13, 100, $3025, Adams, New Haven.

Koehlinger Philip, f, 35, 80, $1960, Adams, Soest.

Koelinger Jacob, f, 11, 197, $3755, Marion, Soest.

Koeneman August, f,20, 100, $1435, Madison, Hoagland.

Koenig Edward, Wayne, Ft Wayne.

Koenig Frederick (estate of), f, 27, 105, $2435, Adams, Ft Wayne.

Koeper Nicholas, St Joseph, Ft Wayne.

Koepf Jacob, Adams, Fort Wayne.

Koerdt Ferdinand, f t, Pleasant, Sheldon.

Koerdt Ferdinand jr, f t, Pleasant, Sheldon.

Koerdt Mary M, f t, Pleasant, Sheldon.

Koert Ernst C, f, 66, $4515, Wayne, Ft Wayne.

Koester Christian jr, 24, 150, $4090, St Joseph, Thurman.

Kohlbach John, Wayne, Ft Wayne.

Kohlbach Louisa, Wayne, Ft Wayne,

Kohlenberg August, Adams, Ft Wayne.

Kohlenberg Conrad, Adams, Ft Wayne.

Kohlenberg Wm, Wayne, Ft Wayne.

Kohlmeier Angeline, f, 6, 41, $655, Marion, Ft Wayne.

Kohlmeyer Anton, 22, 80, $1980, St Joseph, Goeglein.

Kohr Elias, f, 33, 40, $805, Lafayette, Zanesville.

Koker Joseph, St Joseph, Ft Wayne.

Koons Edgar L, f t, Pleasant, Sheldon.

Koons Ellen M, f, 33, 98, $2570, Wayne, Ft Wayne.

Koons Foster, Wayne, Fort Wayne.

Koons George, f, 3, 80, $1610, Pleasant, Nine Mile.

Koons Irvin E, f t, Pleasant, Nine Mile.

Koons Michael, f, 3, 20, $515, Pleasant, Nine Mile.

Koontz Ezra, grocer, Scipio, Hall's Corners.

Koop Henry, St Joseph, Goeglein.

Koop Sophia, 15, 80, $1765, St Joseph, Fort Wayne.

Koop Wm, St Joseph, Goeglein.

Koovansky Hannah, Wayne, Fort Wayne.

Koppel Herman G, Adams, Fort Wayne.

Korte Conrad, 14, 60, $1135, St Joseph, Ft Wayne.

Korte Henry, f t, Wayne, Ft Wayne.

Korte John G, Wayne, Ft Wayne.

Kover Edward, Wayne, Ft Wayne.

Kover Emeline, Wayne, Ft Wayne.

Kowianskey Hannah, 29, 16, $350, St Joseph, Ft Wayne.

Kowianski Simon, Adams, Ft Wayne.

Kramer Albert, Jackson, Dawkins.

Kramer Catherine, f, 7, 80, $895, Jackson, Dawkins.

Kramer Charles, 247, $6120, St Joseph, Ft Wayne.

Kramer Florence, Jackson, Dawkins.

Kramer Frank, Jackson, Dawkins.

Kramer Frederick, f, 36, 40, $680, Lake, Arcola.

Kramer John, Wayne, Fort Wayne.

Kramer Wm, St Joseph, Goeglein.

Krauskoff George J, Adams, Fort Wayne.

Krauskoff Henry, f, 5, 66, $2330, Adams, Ft Wayne.

Krauskoff Jacob, f, 5, 20, $935, Adams, Ft Wayne.

Krauskoff Peter, f, 5, 60, $2360, Adams, Ft Wayne.

Krauskoff Peter jr, f, 5, 20, $660, Adams, Ft Wayne.

Krauskoff Philip, Adams, Ft Wayne.

Krauter George F, f, 34, 40, $765, Pleasant, Sheldon.

Krauter George H, f, 34, 10, $115, Pleasant, Sheldon.

Krewson Andrew, Jackson, Monroeville.

Krewson A G, f, Monroe, Dixon, O.

Krewson M K, painter, Monroe, Monroeville.

Krewson Sarah E, Monroe, Monroeville.

Krenbuhler Frederick, f, 4, 80, $590, Maumee, Harlan.

Kress Eliza A, f, Lafayette, Nine Mile.

Kress George, lab, Wayne, Ft Wayne.

Kress 'Henry, f, Lafayette, Nine Mile.

Kress Joseph, f t, Wayne, Ft Wayne.

Kretzinger Barbara A, Wayne, Ft Wayne.

Kretzinger Constantine, Wayne, Ft Wayne.

Krick Adam, f, 6, 80, $855, Monroe, Monroeville.

Krick Elijah, f, 10, 40, $395, Monroe, Monroeville.

Krick Henry, f, 14, 80, $1085, Monroe, Monroeville.

Krick J A, f, Monroe, Monroeville.

Krick Minor, Madison, Monroeville.

Krick Philip, f, 11, 80, $1350, Madison, Monroeville.

Krick & McIntosh, saloon, Monroe, Monroeville.

Krickenberg August, Adams, Soest.

Krider John, f, 5, 116, $1975, Eel River, Ari.

Krill David, f, 34, 63, $1825, Wayne, Ft Wayne.

Krill Samuel F, f, 34, 55, $1540, Wayne, Ft Wayne.

Krill Sophia, Wayne, Fort Wayne.

Krill Wm, f, 34, 63, $2530, Wayne, Ft Wayne.

Krim G & C, f, 28, 73, $2040, Cedar Creek, Cedarville.

Kriss George, f, 11, 80, $1260, Eel River, Huntertown.

Kritzman Valentine, Adams, Ft Wayne.

Kroh John H, Adams, Fort Wayne.

Krommaker Wm, St Joseph, Ft Wayne.

Kronmiller Elizabeth, f, 13, 3, $1670, Wayne, Ft Wayne.

Kronmiller George, f, 13, 120, $1810, Lake, Fort Wayne.

Krouse Cosmos D, f, 34, 80, $1335, Pleasant, Sheldon.

Krouse Herman, f, 28, 155, $2880, Pleasant, Sheldon.

Kruckberg August, f, 25, 150, $3065, Adams, Soest.

Kruckeberg Christian, 20, 60, $1325, St Joseph, Fort Wayne.

Kruckeberg O & L, 20, 20, $400, St Joseph, Ft Wayne.

Kruger Reinhold H, Adams, Fort Wayne.

Krum Frederick, f t, Scipio, Hicksville, O.

Krumbigle Henry, f, 27, 70, $1270, Cedar Creek, Cedarville.

Krumma Andrew, f, reserve, 80, $1550, Lafayette, Nine Mile.

Krumma Anthony, f, 12, 20, $345, Lafayette, Nine Mile.

Kruse Christian, 31, 6, $650, St Joseph, Fort Wayne.

Kruse Henry F, f, 33, 80, $7530, Milan, Gar Creek.

Kryder Albert W, f t, Cedar Creek, Cedarville.

Kryder Harrison W, f, 22, 65, $1950, Cedar Creek, Leo.

Kryder John, f, 28, 71, $1795, Cedar Creek, Cedarville.

Kryder John L, physician, Cedar Creek, Cedarville.

Kryder M J & J L, f, 32, 165, $3365, Cedar Creek, Cedarville.

Kryder W, f t, Cedar Creek, Cedarville.

Kuckbuck Louis, 28, 80, $2010, St Joseph, Fort Wayne.

Kuehn Herman, f, 30, 189, $3550, Milan·

Kuhl Martin, Adams, Fort Wayne.

Kuhne F W et al, Adams, Ft Wayne.

Kumfer Benjamin, f, 31, 20, $380, Pleasant, Sheldon.

Kumfer Martin, Wayne, Ft Wayne.

Kunkle G W, lab, Eel River, Huntertown.

Kunkle Nathaniel, f t, Eel River, Huntertown.

Kuntz Adam, 2, $50, Wayne, Fort Wayne.

Kurz Catherine, f, 13, 21, $355, Lake, Fort Wayne.

Kurtz Henry, Milan, Chamberlain.

Kurtz John, f, 4, 113, $2625, Milan, Chamberlain.

Kurz John C, f, 14, 40, $735, Lake, Fort Wayne.

Kurz John M, f, 13, 70, $1240, Lake, Fort Wayne.

Kyler Basil, Jackson, Edgerton.

Kyburz, f t, Maumee, Antwerp, O.

L

Lackey Homer, Perry, Huntertown.

La Croix Louis, 6, 138, $3170, St Joseph, Fort Wayne.

Ladig Christian, f, 16, 72, $970, Lake, Arcola.

Ladig Felix, f, 9, 48, $280, Lake, Arcola.

Ladig John, Jackson, Edgerton.

Ladig Nicholas, Jefferson, New Haven.

Ladig Sarah M, f, 18, 146, $2590, Jefferson, New Haven.

Ladow Frank, St Joseph, Ft Wayne.

Lafevre Samuel, Lake, Wallen.

Lagerman Henry, f, 6, 40, $435, Maumee, Woodburn.

Lahman Catherine, f, 4, 20, $290, Lafayette, Myhart.

Lahman George, f, 9, 319, $5855, Marion, Poe.

Lahman Geo jr, Marion, Poe.

Lahman Jacob, f, Lafayette, Myhart.

Lahman Wm, Marion, Poe.

Lahmeyer Henry, f, 30, 97, $2455, Adams, Ft Wayne.

Lahmeyer John P, 22, 20, $380, St Joseph, Goeglein.

Lahmeyer J F C, f, 30, 98, $2585, Adams, Ft Wayne.

Lahrman Charles, f, 14, 40, $830, Pleasant, Sheldon.

Lahrman George, f t, Pleasant, Sheldon.

Lahrman Jacob, f, 23, 160, $3075, Pleasant, Sheldon.

Lake Chauncey H, f, 2, 30, $330, Milan, Harlan.

Lake Curtis, f, 3, 31, $1780, Milan, Harlan.

Lake John, f, 1, 50, $695, Milan, Harlan.

Lakey Ephraim, f t, Pleasant, Sheldon.

Lallow August H, f, 34, 39, $1035, Eel River, Heller's Corners.

Lallow Margaret, f, 7, 24, $485, Jefferson, New Haven.

Lamblin Eliza J, f, 34, 20, $180, Jackson, Baldwin.

Lamblin Jacob, Jackson, Zulu.

Lamblin James, Jackson, Baldwin.

Lamle Catherine, f, 2, 20, $210, Lake, Arcola.

Lamle Christian, Lake, Wallen.

Lamle George, f, 15, 40, $445, Lake, Wallen.

Lamle Gottlieb, f, 12, 252, $3940, Lake, Wallen.

Lamle Gottlieb jr, f, 11, 103, $1500, Lake, Wallen.

Lamle Hannah, Adams, Fort Wayne.

Lamle Wm A, f, 2, 98, $1365, Lake, Wallen.

Lamont Alphonse, f, 10, 217, $3165, Jefferson, Dawkins.

Lamont Cecil F, f, 16, 31, $545, Jefferson, New Haven.

Lamont Francis, f, 16, 80, $1420, Jefferson, New Haven.

Lamont Frank E, Jefferson, New Haven.

Lamont Louisa & Laura, Jefferson, Gar Creek.

Lamont Pauline, f, 14, 120, $1840, Jefferson, Dawkins.

Lampe Diederich, 33, 40, $910, St Joseph, Goeglein.

Lampe Wm, Milan, Goeglein.

Lancaster John, Wayne, Ft Wayne.

Lancaster Peter, f, 4, 37, $690, Milan, Goeglein.

Lander Ernst, f, 21, 80, $945, Marion.

Lander Wm, f, 1, 65, $1680, Adams, Ft Wayne.

Landermeier Joseph, f, 7, 5, $1540, Adams, New Haven.

Landin Jacob, f, 148, $2570, Milan, Goeglein,

Landre Dorothea, Marion, Hoagland.

Landre Ernst, f, 36, 40, $930, Marion, Hoagland.

Landstaffer George, f, 22, 140, $2510, Pleasant, Sheldon.

Lang Jacob, Lake, Arcola.

Lang W, Wayne, Ft Wayne.

Langacher Jacob, f, 25, 80, $1680, Cedar Creek, Harlan.

Langacher John, f, 25, 107, $2225, Cedar Creek, Harlan.

Langacher Samuel, f, 36, 109, $2225, Cedar Creek, Harlan.

Langan Edward, Wayne, Ft Wayne.

Langardner John W, f, 2, 75, $650, Jefferson, Gar Creek.

Langardner Joseph, f, 2, 80, $1010, Jefferson, Gar Creek.

Langardner Mary B, f, 2, 40, $700, Jefferson, Gar Creek.

Lange Frederick, Adams, Ft Wayne.

Lange Henry, Adams, Ft Wayne.

Lange John H, f, 31, 185, $4990, Adams, Ft Wayne.

Langham Amiel, lab, Scipio, Hall's Corners.

Langham John, f, 28, 22, $320, Scipio, Harlan.

Langham Wm, f, 33, 33, $250, Scipio, Hall's Corners.

Langher J W jr, teamster, 10, $1155, Wayne, Ft Wayne.

Langle Thomas, 13, 31, $570, St Joseph, Ft Wayne.

Langley Wm, 13, 32, $540, St Joseph, Ft Wayne.

Langson Richard, 29, 41, $1405, St Joseph, Fort Wayne.

Lanninger Benjamin, lab, Eel River, Heller's Corners.

Lanoir Aristede, St Joseph, Ft Wayne.

Lanoir Francis, f, 36, 50, $700, Perry, Ft Wayne.

Lanoir Francis J, 7, 47, $945, St Joseph, Ft Wayne.

Lanpe Diederich, f, 19, 154, $2185, Milan, Goeglein.

Lansdown Job, Wayne, Fort Wayne.

Lanstoffer Wm, f t, Pleasant, Sheldon.

Lanternier A J, Adams, Fort Wayne.

Lantz Frederick, grocer, Cedar Creek, Leo.

La Point George C, Wayne, Fort Wayne.

Lapp Arna, Milan, Goeglein.

Lapp George, St Joseph, Ft Wayne.

Lapp Henry, f, 34, 119, $2180, Cedar Creek, Cedarville.

Lapp Martin, Milan, Goeglein.

Lapp Valentine, 33, 100, $2890, St Joseph, Fort Wayne.

Lardier John, 36, 80, $2105, St Joseph, Ft Wayne.

Lardier Michael J, 36, 80, $2250, St Joseph, Fort Wayne.

Larimore Albert et al, f, 9, 60, $790, Lake, Arcola.

Larimore Eli, Lake, Arcola.

Larimore John, f, 2, 37, $575, Lake, Wallen.

Larimore Levi B, Wayne, Ft Wayne.

Larimore Thomas, f, 8, 400, $4740, Lake, Arcola.

Larwell John C, Adams, Ft Wayne.

Lasalle Caroline E, Wayne, Fort Wayne.

Latham Mary E, Perry, Huntertown.

Latham Ralph, Perry, Huntertown.

Latham Wm, Perry, Huntertown.

Latournette James jr, f, 28, 80, $1415, Eel River, Heller's Corners.

Latournette W H, genl store, 4, 1, $350, Eel River, Ari.

Latt Charles W, f, 16, 40, $280, Maumee, Cass.

Latta Charles S, Adams, Fort Wayne.

Lauer John G, Adams, Fort Wayne.

Lauer Gustave, f, 22, 80, $1565, Pleasant, Sheldon.

Lauer John G, Wayne, Fort Wayne.

Lauer Martin, Pleasant, Sheldon.

Lauferty Minnie E, Adams, Fort Wayne.

Laughlin James O, farmer, Monroe, Monroeville.

Laurent Frederick, f, 36, 80, $1520, Lake, Ft Wayne.

Laurentz Alexander, Adams, Fort Wayne.

Lautell Kate, Wayne, Fort Wayne.

Lautz Christian, f, 28, 22, $420, Milan, Goeglein.

Lautz Jacob, f, 8, 6, $200, Milan, Chamberlain.

Lavan Samuel, f, 13, 16, $2795, Lafayette, Nine Mile.

Lavanway Josephine, Wayne, Fort Wayne.

Lavitt Ormeal, Adams, Fort Wayne.

Builders' Hardware, PFEIFFER & SCHLATTER, 38 and 40 EAST COLUMBIA ST.

ALLEN COUNTY DIRECTORY. 735

Lawoer George W, f, 31, 103 $2065, Lafayette, Roanoke.

Lawrence Amos, f, 10, 97, $1905, Lafayette, Myhart.

Lawrence David, f, 10, 163, $3235, Lafayette, Myhart.

Lawrence George E, f, Lafayette, Myhart.

Lawrence G B, f, 9, 257, $4870, Lafayette, Myhart.

Lawrence John, f, Lafayette, Myhart.

Lawrence John F, f, 20, 47, $735, Lafayette, Roanoke.

Lawrence Mary A, f, 30, 114, $2560, Lafayette, Roanoke.

Lawrence Oliver, f, 5, 102, $3215, Wayne, Ft Wayne.

Lawrence Wm J, Wayne, Ft Wayne.

Lawyer Francis, f,3,76,$1000, Monroe, Monroeville.

Lawyer Joseph,Monroe, Monroeville.

Layman George, Wayne, Ft Wayne.

Leach Edward, Wayne, Fort Wayne.

Leach Wm, Wayne, Fort Wayne.

Lederman Peter, f, 26, 40, $1235, Cedar Creek, Leo.

Lee Henry,Wayne,Ft Wayne

Lee Joseph, lab,Cedar Creek, Leo.

Lee Mary, Cedar Creek, Cedarville.

Lee Thomas A, Madison, Maples.

Leech Wm H, Aboite.

Lefevre George H, Lake, Wallen.

Leheke Frederick, Lake, Arcola.

Lehman Anna L, Wayne, Ft Wayne.

Lehman Conrad, Wayne, Ft Wayne.

Lehman Ferdinand, f, 35, 20, $220, Madison, Decatur.

Lehman Theodore, f, reserve, 30, $485,Lafayette,Myhart.

Lehman Verona, f, 35, 40, $465, Madison.

Lehneke Catherine, f, 17,124. $1720, Lake, Arcola.

Lehneke Leonard, Lake, Arcola.

Lehrman Henry, Madison, Decatur.

Lehrman Jacob D, 14, 1, $680, Wayne, Fort Wayne.

Leichner Frank, f, 18, 80, $1385, Scipio, Hall's Corners.

Leichty C S, f t, Cedar Creek, Leo.

Leichty John, f, 26, 180, $3150, Cedar Creek, Leo.

Leichty Nicholas, f, 13, 80, $1810, Cedar Creek, Leo.

Leichty Peter, f,Cedar Creek, Leo.

Lenhart George, Madison, Maples.

Lenhart Henry C, f, 14, 80, $865, Madison,Monroeville.

Lenhart Joseph R, Jefferson, Maples.

Lenhart Lineas A, Madison, Maples.

Lenhart Peter, f, 4, 95, $1425, Madison, Maples.

LeMay Sarah E, Wayne, Ft Wayne.

Lemon E P, f, Monroe, Dixon, O.

Lemon Wm, lab, Monroe, Dixon, O.

Lenhart Peter, f, 33, 22, $245, Jefferson, Maples.

Lenninger Jacob, Jackson, Monroeville.

Lenninger Theobald, f, 33, 120, $1120, Jackson, Monroeville.

Lennington A B, f, Lafayette, Nine Mile.

Lennington Jacob, f, 34, 80, $1485, Lafayette, Zanesville.

Lentz Jacob, f, 26, 100, $1645, Marion, Hoagland.

Lentz Samuel, St Joseph, Ft Wayne.

Lenz Wm, Wayne, Ft Wayne.

Leonberger Gottlieb, f, 14, 54, $500, Madison, Monroeville.

Lepp Wm, Adams, Fort Wayne.

Leppard Christian, Madison, Hoagland.

Lepper Charles, Marion, Soest.

Lepper Charles W, Marion, Soest.

Lepper Charlotte, f, 3, 120, $2370, Marion, Soest.

Lepper George, f, 3, 79, $1535, Marion, Soest.

Lepper George jr, f, 1, 40, $715, Marion, Soest.

Lepper Henry, f, 16, 80, $1515, Madison, Hoagland.

Lepper Henry W, Adams, Soest.

Lepper John, f, 3, 107, $1735, Marion, Soest.

Lepper Peter, f, 2, 25, $395, Marion, Soest.

Lesh Emmet, Jefferson, Zulu.

Lesh Isaac C, f, 26, 120, $1680, Jefferson, Zulu.

Lesh John, lab, 36, 3, $105, Cedar Creek, Cedarville.

Leutwein Joseph, shoemaker, Cedar Creek, Leo.

Leutwein M, shoemaker, 3, 19, $310, Cedar Creek, Leo.

Levack John, Wayne, Fort Wayne.

Levan Delilah, f, Lafayette, Nine Mile.

Levan Frank, f, Lafayette, Nine Mile.

Levans Franklin, f, 4, 74, $1630, Pleasant, Sheldon.

Ley Martin, f, 32, 40, $600, Lake, Arcola.

Lichtenwalter Clark, f, 29, 152, $3380, Marion, Poe.

Lichtenwalter Solomon, f, 24, 101, $1790, Pleasant, Sheldon.

Lichtsin Henry, Wayne, Ft Wayne.

Liedolf Henry, f, 27, 80, $1810, Adams, Soest.

Liehering Frederick J, Aboite.

Liggett Daniel, f, Lafayette, Myhart.

Liggett Elizabeth, f, Lafayette, Myhart.

Lilley M B, Adams, Fort Wayne.

Lillie John W, Adams, Ft Wayne.

Limecooly Frederick W, Wayne, Fort Wayne.

Linden George W, f, 13, 452, $3275, Milan, New Haven.

Linder G W, f, 6, 225, $4425, Jefferson, New Haven.

Lindermuth Albert C, f, 2, 64, $465, Maumee, Antwerp, O.

Lindermuth Clayton, f and teacher, 31, 5, $85, Scipio, Hall's Corners.

Lindermuth Edward, lab, Scipio, Hall's Corners.

Lindermuth James B, f, 19, 36, $670, Scipio, Hall's Corners.

Lindermuth Sarah, !Scipio, Hall's Corners.

Lindermuth Vance, lab, Scipio, Hall's Corners.

Lindsey Wesley, f, 7, 40, $675, Cedar Creek, Leo.

Lingel Daniel, Wayne, Fort Wayne.

Lingenfelser Juliette, Adams, New Haven.

Link H E, f, 6, $140, Wayne, Fort Wayne.

Link John, Wayne, Fort Wayne.

Link Margaret, Wayne, Fort Wayne.

Link Mary, Wayne, Fort Wayne.

Linker Charles, Madison, Maples.

Linker David, Madison, Maples.

Linker John, f, 5, 40, $550, Madison, Maples.

Linker Philip, Madison, Maples.

Linnamier H, f t, Wayne, Ft Wayne.

Linton Eliza, Aboite, Dunfee.

Linton Jacob, Adams, Fort Wayne.

Linton Lewis, Lake, Arcola.

Linton Samuel, Aboite, Dunfee.

Lintz Delia, Adams, Fort Wayne.

Lipes Anna D, f, 31, 49, $965, Eel River, Churubusco.

Lipes A F, physician, Eel River, Churubusco.

Lipes David H, f, 4, 296, $3035, Lake, Arcola.

Lipes John M, f, 29, 155, $3025, Marion, Poe.

Lipp John, f, 14, 40, $665, Lafayette, Zanesville.

Lippar Henry, f, 36, 40, $865, Adams, Soest.

Lippar Wm (est of), f, 34, 40, $730, Adams, Soest.

Lipper Frederick, f, 36, 40, $725, Adams, Soest.

Lipper Theodore, f, 36, 50, $945 Adams, Soest.

Litchfield D B, f, 12, 86, $2365, Lake, Arcola.

Litchfield Edwin G, Lake, Wallen.

Litol George A, f, 27, 95, $1645, Pleasant, Sheldon.

Litterman Daniel, f t, Cedar Creek, Leo.

Little Andrew, f, 7, 5, $60, Maumee, Woodburn.

Little Elizabeth, f, 7, 35, $500, Maumee, Antwerp, O.

Little Horatio N, f, 18, 111, $1475, Maumee, Woodburn.

Little James, f, 32, 60, $1355, Lafayette, Zanesville.

Little Oliver, f, 15, 80, $535, Jackson, Edgerton.

Lochner Conrad, f, 9, 80, $1445, Cedar Creek, Leo.

Lochner David, lab, Cedar Creek, Leo.

Lochner George, f t, Cedar Creek, Leo.

Lochner John, f, 10, 160, $3170, Cedar Creek, Leo.

Lochner Peter (est), 2, 40, $585, Cedar Creek, Leo.

Lochner Samuel, lab, Cedar Creek, Leo.

Logan Adaline, f, 21, 11, $155, Lafayette, Zanesville.

Logan Alice E, f, 21, 11, $175, Lafayette, Zanesville.

John Pressler, Hot Air and Hot Water Furnaces.
Columbia, Barr and Dock Streets.

738   R. L. POLK & CO.'S

Logan Ann, f, 21, 47, $1045, Lafayette, Zanesville.

Logan Guilford, f t, Pleasant, Sheldon.

Logan Jacob, f, 21, 11, $190, Lafayette, Zanesville.

Logan James, f, 29, 80, $1430, Pleasant, Sheldon.

Lolome Guisseppe, Milan, Harlan.

Lomas Edward, 20, 30, $750, St Joseph, Ft Wayne.

Lomas Elizabeth, 19, 82, $2550, St Joseph, Ft Wayne.

Long Cyrus, Adams, Fort Wayne.

Long John, St Joseph, Fort Wayne.

Long J W, Madison, Monroeville.

Lopshire George, f, 12, 136, $2595, Lafayette, Nine Mile.

Lopshire George A, f, reserve, 114, $1775, Lafayette, Nine Mile.

Lopshire George L, f, Lafayette, Nine Mile.

Lopshire Hamlin, f, Lafayette, Roanoke.

Lopshire Oliver J, f, 1, 80, $1500, Lafayette, Nine Mile.

Lopshire Sarah, Marion, Poe.

Lopshire Wm, f, 9, 184, $3825, Lafayette, Myhart.

Lopshire Wm W, wagonmkr, Marion, Poe.

Lorain Charles, Jefferson, Maples.

Lorain Frank, Jefferson, New Haven.

Lorain J B, f, 20, 39, $690, Jefferson, Maples.

Lorain Michael jr, f, 28, 20, $230, Jefferson, Maples.

Lordier August, 2, 94, $1610, St Joseph, Ft Wayne.

Lordier Malinda, 7, 2, $90, St Joseph, Ft Wayne.

Lorimore Albert, Lake, Arcola.

Lortie Charles, f, 15, 80, $520, Jackson, Edgerton.

Lortie Dominick, f, 15, 120, $785, Jackson, Edgerton.

Lose Cyrus J, Adams, Fort Wayne.

Lothamer Andrew, Jackson, Smiley, Ohio.

Lothamer Henry, Jackson, Monroeville.

Lothamer Theobald, f, 23, 54, $650, Jackson, Monroeville.

Louks Oscar, f, 15, 4, 75, Milan, Chamberlain.

Lovall Harriet, f, 3, 35, $700, Adams, New Haven.

Lovall Samuel, f, 3, 75, $2530, Adams, New Haven.

Lovall Wm, f, 7, 40, $340, Maumee, Woodburn.

Loveland, H W, f, 11, 147, $4210, Adams, New Haven.

Lowmiller Elroy, f, 15, 40, $520, Monroe, Dixon, O.

Lowmiller John, f, 27, 80, $1405, Monroe, Dixon, O.

Lowry Abraham, f, 7, 9, $210, Jefferson, New Haven.

Lowry Jesse, Jefferson, Gar Creek.

Luce Grant, lab, Aboite, Fort Wayne.

Luce John, f, 28, 80, $1425, Aboite, Aboite.

Luce Joseph, Madison, Monroeville.

Luce Lydia, Aboite, Fort Wayne.

ALLEN COUNTY DIRECTORY. 739

Luckey James, f, 12, 40, $715, Aboite, Ft Wayne.

Luckey Wm E, lab, Aboite, Ft Wayne.

Ludwick Joseph, f t, Pleasant, Sheldon.

Ludwig Esdras, f t, Pleasant, Sheldon.

Lueke Christian, Marion, Poe.

Lugbull John, f, 17, 113, $1810, Cedar Creek, Leo.

Lugbull J C, f, Cedar Creek, Leo.

Luhrs Carl, f, 36, 80, $1010, Milan, Ft Wayne.

Luke David V, St Joseph, Ft Wayne.

Luman Wm, f, 27, 77, $665, Maumee, Whitby.

Lumbard C C, Adams, Fort Wayne.

Lumm Charles, lab, Cedar Creek, Leo.

Luntz John G, f, 21, 103, $2570, Wayne, Ft Wayne.

Luntz Wm, St Joseph, Fort Wayne.

Lunz George, 79, $2250, St Joseph, Ft Wayne.

Lunz George H, Adams, Ft Wayne.

Lunz John G, f, 199, $6500, Adams, New Haven.

Lunz John V, Adams, Fort Wayne.

Lupkin Laborius, f, 25, 237, $4085, Adams, New Haven.

Luther Israel, f t, Eel River, Churubusco.

Luttman Wm, Madison, Decatur.

Lutz David, 23, 40, $900, St Joseph, Ft Wayne.

Lutz Ephraim, Maumee, Antwerp, O.

Lutz Frederick, f t, Pleasant, Nine Mile.

Lutz Jacob, f, 14, 2, $25, Maumee, Antwerp, O.

Lutz Samuel, f, 31, 160, $3645, Marion, Poe.

Lutz Wm, Marion, Poe.

Lyman R C, Perry, Huntertown.

Lynch Thomas, f, Lafayette, Myhart.

Lyne Rebecca, Wayne, Fort Wayne.

Lyon S K, f t, Eel River, Huntertown.

Lyon W S, lab, Eel River, Huntertown.

M

McArdle James, f, Monroe, Monroeville.

McArdle Peter, f, 31, 160, $3255, Monroe, Monroeville.

McBratney Henry, St Joseph, Fort Wayne.

McBratney Margaret, 40, $780, St Joseph, Ft Wayne.

McBride James, f, 22, 40, $630, Eel River, Heller's Corners.

McBride Mitchell, f, 10, 40, $820, Eel River, Ari.

McBride Wm, f, 10, 83, $1575, Eel River, Ari.

McBride Wm, f, 16, 59, $1225, Lafayette, Myhart.

McCamick Joseph, Jefferson, Zulu.

McCann Amelia F, Adams, Fort Wayne.

McCarthy D, Adams, New Haven.

McCarthy C (heirs), f, 14, 80, $1730, Adams, New Haven.

McCarthy John, Adams, Ft Wayne.

McCarthy Julia, f, 11, $155, Adams, New Haven.

McCartney John, f, 6, 24, $160, Lake, Arcola.

McCartney Louis, f t, Cedar Creek, Leo.

McCarty Eunice E, f, 1, 56, $770, Eel River, Huntertown.

McCarty F C, Wayne, Fort Wayne.

McCarty James, f, 22, 86, $1450, Cedar Creek, Leo.

McCarty John (estate of), f, 1, 191, $2860, Eel River, Huntertown.

McCarty J H, f t, Eel River, Huntertown.

McCarty Samuel, f, 9, 77, $1165, Eel River, Ari.

McClare John, f, 20, 213, $3875, Lafayette, Roanoke.

McClare Samuel P, f, 24, 80, $1405, Lafayette, Roanoke.

McClaren Eliza, gardener, 22, 2⅘, $215, Wayne, Fort Wayne.

McClish George, Jackson, Dawkins.

McCollen Wm, Jackson, Edgerton.

McComb James, f, 23, 200, $4075, Perry, Huntertown.

McComb John S, f, 28 20, $340, Perry, Huntertown.

McComb Meliae, f, 28, 20, $400, Perry, Huntertown.

McComb R S, Perry, Huntertown.

McComb Thomas C, Perry, Huntertown.

McConaghey James, f, 30, 40, $535, Madison, Hoagland.

McConahey Louisa A, Wayne, Fort Wayne.

McConnell B A, f, 30, 80, $930, Jackson, Monroeville.

McConnell John, f, 16, 120, $900, Jackson, Edgerton.

McCord Wm, f, 29, 40, $435, Scipio, Hall's Corners.

McCormick Eliza, f, 23, 40, $475, Jefferson, Zulu.

McCormick Florence, Adams, Fort Wayne.

McCormick F A, lab, Monroe, Monroeville.

McCormick J D, f, 23, 16, $175, Monroe, Monroeville.

McCormick J T, vet surgeon, Eel River, Churubusco.

McCormick Louisa, f, 1, 53, $315, Lake, Wallen.

McCormick Martha, 14, 60, $1100, Cedar Creek, Leo.

McCormick Monroe, f, 34,40, $890, Eel River, Fort Wayne.

McCormick Patrick, f, 36, 80, $745, Jefferson, Monroeville

McCormick Samuel, Lake, Arcola.

McCormick Thomas H, Marion, Hoagland.

McCormick W H, f, 26, 100, $1715, Lake, Arcola.

McCormick W M, f, 34, 40, $630, Eel River, Ft Wayne.

McCormick & Moran, Aboite.

McCoy Charles O, Adams, Ft Wayne.

McCoy George W, f, 6, 177, $7940, Adams, Ft Wayne.

McCoy Jennie, f, 6, 40, $1955, Adams, Fort Wayne.

McCracken Harvey, contr, 70, $5740, Wayne, Ft Wayne.

McCrory David, f, 8, 80, $1360, Cedar Creek, Leo.

McCrory George S, f t, Cedar Creek, Leo.

McCrory James, f, 11, 340, $5590, Cedar Creek, Hursh.

McCrory O D, meats, Cedar Creek, Leo.

McCrory Samuel, f t, Cedar Creek, Leo.

McCurdy Eliza, f, 16, 80, $1430, Eel River, Ft Wayne.

McCurdy Miles C, lab, Eel River, Ari.

McDonald Daniel, lab, Aboite, Fort Wayne.

McDonald David, f, 24, 40, $760, Lake, Arcola.

McDonald Nelson, Lake, Arcola.

McDonald R V, 32, 306, $11,660, St Joseph, Fort Wayne.

McDougall M C, f, 7, 2, $365, Adams, Fort Wayne.

McDougall Theodore, Milan, Gar Creek.

McDowell Anne, Lake, Arcola.

McDowell Frank, butcher, Pleasant, Sheldon.

McDowell George H, teamster, Pleasant, Sheldon.

McDowell Sarah A, f, 34, 80, $1625, Pleasant, Sheldon.

McDowell Wm W, live stock, Pleasant, Sheldon.

McDuffy Horace G, f, 6, 78, $1520, Eel River, Churubusco.

McDuffy James, f, 6, 56⅔, $1515, Eel River, Churubusco.

McFadden Henry, Lafayette, Myhart.

McFadden W H, Lafayette, Myhart.

McGinniss Darius, Lafayette, Myhart.

McGinniss Esther, f, 17, 80, $1525, Lafayette, Myhart.

McGirk John, Marion, Hoagland.

McGoogan Wm, f, 33, 40, $915, Lafayette, Zanesville.

McGoogin George, Lake, Arcola.

McGrath John, f, 31, 120, $1530, Lake, Arcola.

McGuire Samuel C, carp, Cedar Creek, Cedarville.

McIntosh Alexander, Jefferson, Maples.

McIntosh Ann, f, 19, 30, $550, Jefferson, Maples.

McIntosh Benjamin, f, 19, 80, $1225, Madison, Hoagland.

McIntosh Benjamin C, Madison, Hoagland.

McIntosh Charles L, f, 30, 90, $1245, Jefferson, Maples.

McIntosh Henry, Jefferson, Maples.

McIntosh John, f, 19, 80, $1145, Madison, Hoagland.

McIntosh John W, Madison, Hoagland.

McIntosh Wm, f, 9, 64, $2825, Adams, Ft Wayne.

McInturff Robert H, merchant, 26, ½, $110, Monroe, Dixon, O.

McKague Douglas M, Madison, Hoagland.

McKee John, f, 33, 95, $1830, Pleasant, Sheldon.

McKee John (estate of) f, 21, 77, $1465, Eel River, Eel River.

McKee Mary, f, 21, 20, $345, Eel River, Eel River.

McKee Thomas L, f, 20, 298, $4980, Eel River, Heller's Corners.

McKee Warren, lab, Pleasant, Sheldon.

McKeenan James, Madison, Hoagland.

McKeenan Margaret, f, 18,80, $910, Madison, Hoagland.

McKernan Alexander, f, 7, 12, $1225, Adams, Fort Wayne.

McKeving John, Jefferson, Dawkins.

McKinley John W, Aboite, Aboite.

McKinney Frank, f, 11, 2¾, $115, Adams, New Haven.

McKinnie Emeline, Cedar Creek.

McKinsey Mary, f, 29, 80, $1305, Aboite, Aboite.

McKinzie Benson, lab, Aboite, Aboite.

McKinzie George H, f t, Aboite, Aboite.

McKinzie J I, f, 3, 80, $1445, Milan, Harlan.

McKinzie Wm, f t, Aboite, Aboite.

McLain George H, $100, Wayne, Ft Wayne.

McLain Zerinah, $1055, Wayne, Ft Wayne.

McMahan Mary A, Wayne, Ft Wayne.

McMahan Thomas, f, 26, 168, $2720, Monroe, Dixon, O.

McMahon Sylvester, f, 16, 160, $2440, Lake, Fort Wayne.

McMaken J C F, Lake, Arcola

McMakin Deborah, f, 29, 52, $1320, Wayne, Ft Wayne.

McMakin Henry C, f, 8, 62, $1980, Wayne, Ft Wayne.

McMakin Joseph H, Adams, Ft Wayne.

McMakin J G (estate of), f, 90, $3110, Adams, Fort Wayne.

McMakin Wm B, f, 29, 48, $155, Wayne, Ft Wayne.

McMillan J B, Wayne, Ft Wayne.

McMunn Marion, Lake, Arcola.

McNabb W C, f t, Cedar Creek, Hursh.

McNabb W J, f, 1, 47, $965, Cedar Creek, Hursh.

McNair Mary N, f, 28, 63, $1240, Wayne, Ft Wayne.

McNair Sarah R, f, 11, 37, $870, Pleasant, Poe.

McNally E A, Jefferson, New Haven.

McNally John, Adams, Ft Wayne.

McNamara Robert, f, 10, $220, Wayne, Ft Wayne.

McNearn Emelia, f, 30, 40, $925, Eel River, Churubusco.

McNulty John, 14, ¼, $20, Wayne, Ft Wayne.

McNutt Wm, Jackson, Edgerton.

McPhail Janet, Adams, Ft Wayne.

McPhail Morgan, Adams, Ft Wayne.

McPherson Samuel, f, 20, 2, Lake, Ft Wayne.

McQuiston Sarah A, f, 32, 80, $1680, Perry, Huntertown.

McRieder John, f, 7, 96, $2175, Cedar Creek, Hursh.

McRieder Rosanna, 6, 7½, $105, Cedar Creek, Hursh.

McSorley Henry, Jackson, Dawkins.

McTigue James, f, 4, 77, $1260, Lake, Arcola.

McWhinnery Frank, f, 30, 80, $485, Wayne, Fort Wayne.

McWhirter Hugh, Madison, Hoagland.

McWhirter Margaret, Madison, Hoagland.

M

Mackay James, Wayne, Ft Wayne.

Madden John, f, 5, 80, $990, Eel River, Churubusco.

Madden Martha, f, 2,35, $680, Eel River, Churubusco.

Madden Mary A, 16, 10, $95, St Joseph, Fort Wayne.

Madden Mary J, f, 14, 20, $265, Milan, Harlan.

Madden Michael, f, 5, 57, $1200, Eel River, Churubusco.

Madden Nicholas, f, 6, 76, $1145, Eel River, Churubusco.

Madden W R, f, 8, 75, $1235, Eel River, Churubusco.

Madden W W, f, 5, 80, $920, Lake, Arcola.

Madden & Schmidt, f, 29,127, $1775, Eel River, Churubusco.

Maddox Frank, f t, Pleasant, Nine Mile.

Magner Eli E, Madison, Monroeville.

Magner Isaiah, f, 31, 40,$735, Monroe, Monroeville.

Magner Joshua, lab, Monroe, Dixon, O.

Magner Wright, Jackson, New Haven.

Mahew Joseph, St Joseph, Ft Wayne.

Mahew Sarah, 44, $1310, St Joseph, Fort Wayne.

Mahl John, Adams, Fort Wayne.

Mahon George W, lab, Eel River, Heller's Corners.

Mahoney John, f, 6, 98,$1490, Eel River, Churubusco.

Main Christopher, f, 13, 85, $1230, Milan, Harlan.

Main Clarence W, Jefferson, New Haven.

Main John G, f, 5, 20, $415, Jefferson, New Haven.

Main Malinda, Milan, Harlan.

Maire Mary J, f, 16,80,$1345, Jefferson, New Haven.

Maire Peter, f, 14, 40, $505, Jefferson, Zulu.

Major B H, Monroe, Monroeville.

Malcolm Emily S, Perry, Huntertown.

Malcolm James, Perry, Huntertown.

Malcolm John, f, 18, 3, $70, Perry, Huntertown.

Malding Mary, f, 29, 38,$490, Jefferson, Maples.

Malin John W, lab, Monroe, Monroeville.

Mallen George, f, 6, 126, $2620, Pleasant, Sheldon.

Malloy Patrick, f, 36, 80, $1260, Pleasant, Sheldon.

Maloney James, f t, Eel River, Ari.

Maloney James, f, 11, 7, $245, Adams, Ft Wayne.

Maloney John (trustee), Eel River, Churubusco.

Manier Joseph W, f, 28, 170, $2945, Lake, Arcola.

Manier Michael, Lake, Arcola.

Manley Maggie, Adams, Fort Wayne.

Manning Amos, f, 9, 77, $1475, Eel River, Ari.

Manning Clara, Aboite.

Manning Elias, Aboite.

Manning George, f t, Eel River, Ari.

Manning Mary, f, Lake, Arcola.

Manning Samuel, Aboite.

Manning Sarah E, Cedar Creek, Leo.

Manning Wm, painter, Cedar Creek, Leo.

Manor David, Lake, Arcola.

Manor Joseph, f, 17, 86, $1270, Lake, Arcola.

Manor Joseph P, Lake, Arcola.

Mansdorf George J, Wayne, Ft Wayne.

Mansdorfer Emelia, 14, 1¾, $120, Wayne, Ft Wayne.

Manweiler John C, f, 4, 18, $1335, Aboite, Ft Wayne.

Maples Charles, Jefferson, Maples.

Maples Frank B, Jefferson, Maples.

Maples George O, Jefferson, Maples.

Maples Lewis S, f, 32, 113, $1455, Jefferson, Zulu.

Marble M C, ins agt, 27, 40, $575, Monroe, Van Wert, O.

March Augustus, Wayne, Ft Wayne.

March John, lab, Pleasant, Sheldon.

Marchal Peter, Adams, Fort Wayne.

Marhenke August, f, 22, 80, $2095, Adams, Ft Wayne.

Marhenke Christian, Adams, Ft Wayne.

Marhenke Henry, f, 15, 40, $1155, Adams, Ft Wayne.

Mark John A, Marion, Fort Wayne.

Markell Charles, f, 24, 82, $1940, Cedar Creek, Leo.

Marker John, lab, Eel River, Heller's Corners.

Marquardt Adam, f, 14, 180, $2845, Madison, Monroeville.

Marquardt Adam jr, Madison, Monroeville.

Marquardt George, Lafayette, Roanoke.

Marquardt Isaac, f, 1, 40, $505, Madison, Monroeville.

Marquardt Jacob, f, 11, 276, $3760, Madison, Monroeville.

Marquardt John F, Madison, Monroeville.

Marquardt J J, f, 10, 2, $30, Madison, Monroeville.

Marquardt Louisa, f, 2, 56, $965, Madison, Monroeville.

Marquadt Philip, f, 11, 313, $4405, Madison, Monroeville.

Marshall Charles, Perry, Huntertown.

Marshall George, Adams, Ft Wayne.

Marshall W S, f, 35, 10, $85, Eel River, Ari.

Martin Anthony, f, 9, 40, $550, Madison, Maples.

Martin August G, f, 35, 320, $6560, Perry, Ft Wayne.

Martin August J, f, 35, 80, $1300, Perry, Ft Wayne.

Martin A E, Perry, Fort Wayne.

Martin David, f, 9, 80, $900, Monroe, Monroeville.

Martin Delphos F, f, 14, 282, $4795, Perry, Huntertown.

Martin Edward, Adams, Fort Wayne.

Martin Francis C, 11, 170, $2370, St Joseph, Fort Wayne.

Martin Frederick, Jackson, Edgerton.

Martin Henry, Jefferson, Maples.

Martin Honora, f, 31, 60, $625, Jackson, Monroeville.

Martin Isaiah, f 22, ¾, $10, Milan, Harlan.

Martin John, Jefferson, Maples.

Martin John (estate), f, 35, 54, $820, Perry, Ft Wayne.

Martin John F, f, 24, 80, $790, Milan, Harlan.

Martin Joseph C, Perry, Huntertown.

Martin Julian, f, 31, 60, $655, Jackson, Monroeville.

Martin Julian, Perry, Fort Wayne.

Martin Malinda, f, 16, 80, $1160, Monroe, Monroeville.

Martin Victor, Adams, Ft Wayne.

Martin Wm, Perry, Fort Wayne.

Martz Philip, f, 18, 3, $100, Monroe, Monroeville.

Mason Arsene, Perry, Fort Wayne.

Mason Catherine A, f, 28, 241, $6545, Wayne, Ft Wayne.

Mason Charles, f, 30, 106, $2730, Wayne, Ft Wayne.

Mason Mrs Charles, Wayne, Fort Wayne.

Mason Ella & Anna, Wayne, Fort Wayne.

Mason Eugene, Lake, Arcola.

Mason George, Lake, Wallen.

Mason George E, f, 3, 242, $4105, Lafayette, Fort Wayne.

Mason George L, f, 15, 10, $150, Lafayette, Zanesville.

Mason G L & M, f, 15, 30, $495, Lafayette, Ft Wayne.

Mason John B, f, 35, 80, $2060, Perry, Ft Wayne.

Mason John N, 11, 80, $1535, St Joseph, Ft Wayne.

Mason Joseph, f, 27, 80, $1485, Lake, Arcola.

Mason Joseph A, barber, Pleasant, Sheldon.

Mason Joseph A, Perry, Fort Wayne.

Mason Joseph F, Lake, Arcola.

Mason Josephine S, f, 29, 20, $70, Wayne, Ft Wayne.

Mason Julius, Perry, Fort Wayne.

Mason J B, 5, 48, $895, St Joseph, Ft Wayne.

Mason J N, Perry, Ft Wayne.

Mason Mary, f, 34, 20, $375, Perry, Ft Wayne.

Mason Peter & Mary, f, 35, 10, $250, Perry, Ft Wayne.

Mason Philomena, Lake, Arcola.

Mason Pierre, f, 35, 40, $845, Perry, Ft Wayne.

Mason & Flynn, Wayne, Ft Wayne.

Massmunster Emil, Cedar Creek, Leo.

Mastbaum Bernard, f, 22, 118, $2695, Adams, Ft Wayne.

Masterson Laughlin, Adams, Fort Wayne.

Mathais Caroline, f, 17, 80, $1370, Lafayette, Myhart.

Mathews Alfred, f, 3, 100, $1675, Eel River, Huntertown.

Mathews Commodore, lab, Eel River, Huntertown.

Mathews John (estate of), Adams, Ft Wayne.

Mathews Samuel, f, 1, 295, $4625, Eel River, Huntertown.

Mathews Samuel J, f, 11, 40, $520, Eel River, Huntertown.

Matters Nicholas, f, 2, 77, $1450, Aboite.

Matthais Daniel, Lafayette, Myhart.

Matthais Jacob, Lafayette, Myhart.

Matthais Louis L, Lafayette, Myhart.

Matthew Joseph, Adams, Ft Wayne.

Maunal M C, attorney, Cedar Creek, Leo.

Maurer James, Perry, Collingwood.

Maxfield Orange, miller,$105, Cedar Creek, Leo.

Maxfield & Dever, millers, 15, 8, $840, Cedar Creek, Leo.

Maxheimer Wm, f, 29, 40, $660, Monroe, Monroeville.

Maxwell Abraham, f t, Eel River, Churubusco.

Maxwell Abraham (est of), f, 19, 10, $280, Eel River, Churubusco.

Maxwell Adam, f, 18, 138, $2425, Eel River, Churubusco.

Maxwell George, f, 19, 40, $630,Eel River,Churubusco

Maxwell George W, f, 19, 113, $2220, Eel River,Churubusco.

Maxwell Jacob,f t,Eel River.

Maxwell John S, Adams, Ft Wayne.

Maxwell Wm, lab, Eel River, Churubusco.

May Wm, f, 33, 1,$15, Lafayette, Zanesville.

Mayer Lizzie C, Adams, Fort Wayne.

Mayhew Allen, Cedar Creek, Cedarville.

Mayhew J H & C, threshers, Cedar Creek, Cedarville.

Mayland Carl, f, 245, $5045, Marion, Poe.

Mayland Charles, f, 27, 41, $1545, Marion, Poe.

Mayland Charles J, Marion, Hoagland.

Mayland Ferdinand, Marion, Hoagland.

Mayland Henry, Marion, Hoagland.

Mayo Anna E, f, 27, 30,$245, Eel River, Heller's Corners.

Mayo Hannah J, f, 28, 40, $610, Eel River, Heller's Corners.

Mayo Lewis T, f, 28, 45,$660, Eel River, Heller's Corners.

Mayo Wm J, f, 28, 80,$1570, Eel River, Heller's Corners.

Mays Bernard T, f, 18, 150, $2910, Jefferson, New Haven.

Mays Joseph, f, 12, 3, $35, Milan, Harlan.

Meads Betty, f, 27, 60, $575, Jackson, Monroeville.

Meads Frederick, f, 28, 160, $1635,Jackson, Monroeville

Meeker Henry W, f t, Aboite, Fort Wayne.

Meeks Nancy, f, 4, 160, $2550, Monroe, Monroeville.

Meeks Thomas, Monroe, Monroeville.

Meese John, St Joseph, Fort Wayne.

Meiser Benjamin, Wayne, Ft Wayne.

Meisner Fiatta, Wayne, Ft Wayne.

Meler N H jr, f, 3, 40, $475, Madison.

Mendarfer Mary A, f, 27, 40, $965, Adams, Ft Wayne.

Mengerson Carl H, 21, 120, $2755, St Joseph, Goeglein.

Mengerson Charles, 21, 40, $555, St Joseph, Goeglein.

Menges Emanuel K, f, 29, 40, $520, Lake, Arcola.

Mensing Charles, f, 25, 78, $1440, Lake, Ft Wayne.

Mensing Mary, Wayne, Ft Wayne.

Mercer Robert, Madison, Monroeville.

Merchant R B, mason, Pleasant, Sheldon.

Mercier Elizabeth, f, 33, 40, $415, Jackson, Toledo, O.

Meredith M W, f, 21, 30, $580, Lake, Arcola.

Merillot August, f, 25, 120, $1220, Jefferson, Zulu.

Merillot John, Jefferson, Dawkins.

Merillot Mary I, Jefferson, Zulu.

Meritt Milan H, Milan, Harlan.

Merrett Mary L, 4, 40, $1000, St Joseph, Goeglein.

Merriam Edward, Madison, Hoagland.

Merriam V S, Madison, Hoagland.

Merriman Amasa (est), f, 27, 20, $400, Marion, Hoagland.

Messler Israel, f, reserve, 38, $635, Lafayette, Ft Wayne.

Messler Mary A, f, reserve, 17, $205, Lafayette, Fort Wayne,

Metcalf John, Perry, Huntertown.

Metcalf Martin, f, 26, 80, $1670, Perry, Ft Wayne.

Metcalf Vatchel, f, 34, 136, $2400, Perry, Ft Wayne.

Mettert Frederick, lab, Eel River, Churubusco.

Mettert Henry C, Lake, Arcola.

Mettert Henry L, f, 4, 15, $120, Maumee, Harlan.

Mettert James P, f, Maumee, Harlan.

Mettert Levi, f, 31, 47, $750, Scipio, Antwerp, O.

Mettert Martin, f, 31, 15, $455, Eel River, Churubusco.

Mettert Martin G, f, 31, 4½, $25, Eel River, Churubusco.

Mettert Samuel G, f, 32, 60, $865, Scipio, Antwerp, O.

Metzer Harry M, Adams, Ft Wayne.

Meyer August, St Joseph, Ft Wayne.

Meyer August, Wayne, Ft Wayne.

Meyer Barney, Adams, Fort Wayne.

Meyer Charles, f, 3, 59, $1410, Marion, Soest.

Meyer Charles, 29, 100, $2715, St Joseph, Goeglein.

Meyer Charles F, St Joseph, Fort Wayne.

Meyer Clara C, f, 29, 43, $640, Pleasant, Fort Wayne.

Meyer Diederich, f, 29, 90, $1905, Marion, Poe.

Election Slips. Headquarters for PERFECT SLIPS
at JOHN F. EBY & CO'S., DETROIT

748   R. L. POLK & CO.'S

Meyer Dorothy, 20, 80, $2010, St Joseph, Goeglein.

Meyer Eliza, f, 24, 60, $745, Jefferson, Zulu.

Meyer Elizabeth, Madison, Bingen.

Meyer Ernest, St Joseph, Ft Wayne.

Meyer Francis, 33, 44, $705, Cedar Creek, Cedarville.

Meyer Frederick, Marion, Hoagland.

Meyer Frederick, St Joseph, Fort Wayne.

Meyer Frederick, f, 35, 60, $810, Adams, Ft Wayne.

Meyer Frederick G, Milan, Harlan.

Meyer Frederick W, f, 16, 159, $2710, Adams, Ft Wayne.

Meyer Frederick W, 21, 100, $2015, St Joseph, Goeglein.

Meyer H C W, 25, 118, $3310, St Joseph, Goeglein.

Meyer John, f, 8, 60, $2150, Adams, Fort Wayne.

Meyer John jr, 25, 168, $4145, St Joseph, Goeglein.

Meyer John A, 29, 100, $2680, St Joseph, Goeglein.

Meyer John C, f, reserve, 363, $7655, Pleasant, Ft Wayne.

Meyer John F, St Joseph, Ft Wayne.

Meyer Julia, Wayne, Fort Wayne.

Meyer Margaret, f, 9, 60, $2145, Adams, Ft Wayne.

Meyer Mathias, f, reserve, 21, $565, Pleasant, Fort Wayne.

Meyery Valentine, f, 2, 16, $245, Marion, Soest.

Meyer Wm, Wayne, Fort Wayne.

Meyer Wm, f, 21, 80, $1380, Madison, Hoagland.

Meyer Wm L, St Joseph, Ft Wayne.

Meyer W T, carp, Madison, Hoagland.

Meyers C E, Perry, Collingwood.

Meyers Fred C, tile mnfr, 18, 8, $670, Monroe, Monroeville.

Meyers Henry, f, 7, 187, $3275, Milan, Goeglein.

Meyers Henry, f, 11, 75, $1540, Perry.

Meyers Henry W, Milan, Goeglein.

Meyers Israel, Perry, Collinwood.

Meyers John, f, 20, 80, $1230, Milan, Goeglein.

Meyers John F, f, 31, 80, $1385, Perry, Wallen.

Meyers John H, f, 31, 40, $500, Jackson, Monroeville.

Meyers J F W, Milan, Goeglein.

Meyers Michael & M A, fs, 7, 28, $335, Jackson, Dawkins.

Meyers M F, f, 1, 40, $615, Perry, Collingwood.

Meyers Nathan (estate), Perry, Collingwood.

Meyers Orlando D, f, 31, 40, $360, Jackson, Monroeville.

Meyers Soloman, f, 11, 60, $1560, Perry, Collingwood.

Meyers Wm, Milan, Thurman.

Meyers Wm, Perry, Collingwood.

Meyers Wm H, f, 3, 40, $700, Perry, Collingwood.

Michael E H & Hattie, f, 30, 30, $210, Maumee, Harlan.

Michael John C, f, 21, 16, $530, Wayne, Ft Wayne.

Michael John G (estate of), Lafayette, Zanesville.

Michael Jonathan, Lafayette, Zanesville.

Michael Linor, Perry, Huntertown.

Michael Philip, St Joseph, Ft Wayne.

Michael & Hamilton, Lafayette, Zanesville.

Middaugh A J, f, 35, 140, $2620, Lafayette, Zanesville.

Middaugh A S, Lafayette, Zanesville.

Middaugh S R, f, 23, 40, $740, Lafayette, Zanesville.

Middleton Amanda, Jefferson, Maples.

Middleton Ambrose C, Jefferson, Maples.

Middleton Thomas, Jefferson, Maples.

Mikle John, f, 29, 80, $1355, Jefferson, Maples.

Milburn B F, f t, 20, 15, $215, Scipio, Hall's Corners.

Milledge Wm, Milan, Gar Creek.

Miller Abraham, f, 14, 38, $445, Jefferson, Zulu.

Miller Albert, carp, 18, ⅟₅, $185, Monroe, Ft Wayne.

Miller Amherst, Milan, Chamberlain.

Miller Amherst W, f, 8, 119, $2175, Milan, Chamberlain.

Miller Andrew, Milan, Chamberlain.

Miller Andrew, lab, Pleasant, Sheldon.

Miller Andrew, f, 21, 40, $805, Pleasant, Sheldon.

Miller Ann, f, 23, 80, $1390, Lafayette, Zanesville.

Miller Anson, f, 15, 49, $935, Milan, Chamberlain.

Miller August, Adams, New Haven.

Miller Augusta H, 5, 18, $315, Scipio, Hicksville, O.

Miller A, f, 25, 40, $810, Lake, Arcola.

Miller A E, Wayne, Fort Wayne.

Miller Barbara E, f, 13, 10, $1315, Wayne, Ft Wayne.

Miller Benjamin E, Madison, Hoagland.

Miller Catherine, f, 20,9,$185, Wayne, Fort Wayne.

Miller Charles, Marion,Hoagland.

Miller Charles, Milan,Harlan.

Miller Charles, Wayne, Fort Wayne.

Miller Charles E, Lake, Arcola,

Miller Charlotte, Adams, Ft Wayne.

Miller Christian, f, 31, 160, $3020, Monroe,Monroeville.

Miller Christian, f, 28, 111, $1935,Pleasant, Ft Wayne.

Miller Christian H F,Marion.

Miller Conrad, f, 23, 24⅘, $1695, Wayne, Ft Wayne.

Miller Daniel, f, 25, 40, $730, Cedar Creek, Harlan.

Miller David A, f t, 31, 40, $520, Scipio, Antwerp, O.

Miller D W (estate of), f, 11, 9, $435, Adams, Ft Wayne.

Miller D W, lab, Monroe, Monroeville.

Miller Edward L, f, Scipio, Hicksville, O.

Miller Edward R, Milan, Chamberlain.

Miller Edwin N, f, 17, 30, $545, Milan, Chamberlain.

Miller Elizabeth, f, 20, 24⅔, $450, Wayne, Fort Wayne.

Miller Elizabeth A, f, 21, 40, $675, Monroe, Monroeville.

Miller Emma, f, 17, 40, $825, Eel River, Eel River.

Miller Ethan D, Jefferson, Zulu.

Miller E D, Madison, Monroeville.

Miller E J, Jefferson, Monroeville.

Miller Frank, f, 8, 2, $35, Milan, Chamberlain.

Miller Frank J, f, 28, 40, $755, Pleasant, Sheldon.

Miller Franklin, f, Monroe, Monroeville.

Miller F W, Wayne, Fort Wayne.

Miller George, f, 22, 10, $135, Milan, Chamberlain.

Miller George J, f, 36, 25, $230, Jefferson, Monroeville.

Miller George W, Adams, Ft Wayne.

Miller George W, f, 17, 60, $980, Eel River, Churubusco.

Miller George W, f, 17, 109, $2395, Milan, Chamberlain.

Miller George W jr, Milan, Chamberlain.

Miller Hannah, f, 8, 30, $375, Monroe, Monroeville.

Miller Henry, Lafayette, Zanesville.

Miller Henry, f, 15, 40, $465, Milan, Chamberlain.

Miller Henry M, Adams, Ft Wayne.

Miller Henry N, Wayne, Ft Wayne.

Miller H F C, f, 1, 76, $1455, Madison, Monroeville.

Miller H S, lab, Cedar Creek, Cedarville.

Miller Jacob, Marion, Hoagland.

Miller Jacob, butcher, Pleasant, Sheldon.

Miller Jacob D, f, 25, 80, $1375, Marion, Hoagland.

Miller Jacob F, Milan, Chamberlain.

Miller Jacob W, f, 27, 80, $655, Jackson, Monroeville.

Miller James, Marion, Hoagland.

Miller James, Wayne, Fort Wayne.

Miller Jeremiah, f t, Cedar Creek, Cedarville.

Miller Joel, f, 36, 64, $1375, Cedar Creek, Harlan.

Miller John, f, 25, 40, $620, Cedar Creek, Harlan.

Miller John, Lake, Arcola.

Miller John, f, 7, 80, $1625, Milan, Chamberlain.

Miller John, f, 27, 155, $2735, Pleasant, Sheldon.

Miller John (est of), f, 14, $330, Wayne, Ft Wayne.

Miller John jr, Adams, Fort Wayne.

Miller John A, f, 20, 26⅔, $110, Wayne, Ft Wayne.

Miller John D, Wayne, Ft Wayne.

Miller John H, Adams, Ft Wayne.

Miller John H, f, 10, 60, $1240, Marion, Soest.

Miller John M, f, 8, 104, $3960, Adams, Ft Wayne.

Miller John R, f, 29, 80, $1090, Jefferson, Maples.

Miller Joseph, f, 3, 120, $2065, Milan, Chamberlain.

Sewing Machines, Shears ¿Pfeiffer & Schlatter
—and Pocket Knives,——⸗38 & 40 E. Columbia.

ALLEN COUNTY DIRECTORY. 751

Miller Joseph, f, 28, 9, $195, Pleasant, Ft Wayne.
Miller Joseph (estate of), f, 21, 87, $1545,Pleasant, Poe.
Miller Joseph E,Milan,Chamberlain.
Miller Julia A, f, 20, 52, $1235, Wayne, Ft Wayne.
Miller Lavina M, f, 21, 40, $740, Milan, Chamberlain.
Miller Levi, f, 1, 40, $350, Madison, Hoagland.
Miller Lewis D, f, 30, 4, Madison, Hoagland.
Miller Lucy A, f, 17, 65, $1515, Eel River.
Miller Margaret,Cedar Creek.
Miller Mary A, f, 14, 3¾,$925, Wayne, Ft Wayne.
Miller Michael, Eel River, Heller's Corners.
Miller Milo A, f, 36, 20, $205, Jefferson, Monroeville.
Miller Nancy, f, 18, 5, $345, Monroe, Monroeville.
Miller Nelson J, Jefferson, Monroeville.
Miller Newton,Marion, Hoagland.
Miller Nicholas, f t, Pleasant, Sheldon.
Miller Noah, f, 36, 64, $1340, Cedar Creek, Harlan.
Miller N A, f, 35, 200, $2445, Jefferson, Monroeville.
Miller N H W, Jefferson, Monroeville.
Miller Paul, Wayne, Fort Wayne.
Miller Phœbe A, f, 26, 14, $240, Lafayette, Zanesville.
Miller Robert, f, 5, $680, Wayne, Ft Wayne.
Miller Samuel M, f, 36, 20, $190, Jefferson, Monroeville.

Miller Samuel T, f, 36, 60, $620, Jefferson, Monroeville.
Miller Sarah A, f, 11, 7, $510, Adams, New Haven.
Miller Silas, f, 19, 4, $75, Madison, Hoagland.
Miller Warren, lab, Pleasant, Sheldon.
Miller Wm, Adams, Fort Wayne.
Miller Wm, Lake, Wallen.
Miller Wm, f, 31, 28, $475, Eel River.
Miller Wm, f, 6, 378, $5780, Lake, Arcola.
Miller Wm, f, 11, 199, $4045, Pleasant, Sheldon.
Miller Wm, f, 13, 2½, $325, Wayne, Ft Wayne.
Miller Wm E, Wayne, Fort Wayne.
Miller Wm W, Milan, Chamberlain.
Miller Willis, Jackson, Monroeville.
Miller W C, lab, Monroe, Monroeville.
Miller W H, f, 20, 18, $520, Wayne, Ft Wayne.
Miller & Ashley, f, 28, 40, $945, Cedar Creek, Cedarville.
Millhouse Samuel, Adams, Ft Wayne.
Milliman Herman J, f, 11, 80, $835, Milan, Thurman.
Milliman Steward, f, 18, 40, $875, Milan, Thurman.
Milliman Wm, f, 18, 72, $1465, Milan, Thurman.
Mills A & L J, Wayne, Ft Wayne.
Mills George W, f, 9, 103, $1975, Lafayette, Myhart.
Mills John, Aboite.

Mills J C, Lafayette, My-hart.

Mills Milton G, Wayne, Fort Wayne.

Mills R B, Lafayette, My-hart.

Mills W S, Lafayette, My-hart.

Miner D L, Monroe, Dixon, O.

Miner Henry, f, 15, 80, $1220, Monroe, Dixon, O.

Miner James, Monroe, Dixon, O.

Miner John, f, 14, 73, $1135, Monroe, Dixon, O.

Miner Wm E, f t, Wayne, Ft Wayne.

Minster John, Madison, Monroeville.

Miracle Enoch, f, 17, 105, $1925, Eel River, Churubusco.

Miracle George K, 7, 25, $625, St Joseph, Ft Wayne.

Miracle John, lab, Eel River, Churubusco.

Mitchell Frank, Lafayette, Myhart.

Mitchell George, f, 7, 2, $110, Adams, Ft Wayne.

Mitchell George W, f, 2, 74, $1470, Milan, Harlan.

Mitchell Margaret, f, 17, 94, $2010, Pleasant, Sheldon.

Mitchell Philander, f, 34, 20, $230, Eel River, Heller's Corners.

Mitchell & Henning, f, 34, ⅓, $15, Eel River, Eel River.

Mix Sylvester, Jefferson, New Haven.

Mix Thomas D, f, 7, 51, $850, Jefferson, New Haven.

Mock Jacob, f, 32, 151, $2450, Madison, Bingen.

Mock Jane, 16, 80, $1080, Cedar Creek, Hursh.

Mock Lemuel, Madison, Bingen.

Mock Wesley M, f, 13, 80 $1660, Madison, Monroeville.

Moderwell Mary D, Wayne, Ft Wayne.

Moehnring Henry, 14, 39, $490, St Joseph, Ft Wayne.

Moeller Charles, f, 16, 1, $25, Adams, Ft Wayne.

Moeller Charles C, f, 16, 56, $1785, Adams, Ft Wayne.

Moellering Charles F, 25, 80, $2655, Wayne, Ft Wayne.

Moellering Wm, Adams, Fort Wayne.

Moellering W H F, foreman, 24, $1765, Wayne, Ft Wayne.

Moellering W L, Adams, Fort Wayne.

Moffat Hamilton, f, 16, 39, $915, Aboite, Ft Wayne.

Moffett Ellen F, Adams, Ft Wayne.

Mohr Louis, Wayne, Fort Wayne.

Moldham Wm, f, 28, 80, $910, Madison, Hoagland.

Moldham Wm J, f, 20, 180, $2750, Madison, Hoagland.

Mollet Henry G, f, 30, 160, $1750, Wayne, Ft Wayne.

Mollet Peter, f t, Wayne, Ft Wayne.

Molliter A, Wayne, Ft Wayne.

Mommer Anthony, Perry, Huntertown.

Mommer Joseph, f, 21, 76, $705, Perry, Huntertown.

Moneysmith John, f, 31, 40, $470, Jackson, Monroeville.

Moneysmith Henry (est of), 27, 444, $995, Marion, Root.

Monghan John, lab, Pleasant, Sheldon.

Monnier Eli, Jefferson, Monroeville.

Monnier John P, f, 35, 89, $1090, Jefferson, Monroeville.

Monnot Edward, Jefferson, Zulu.

Monnot Eugene, Jefferson, New Haven.

Monnot Jules, Jefferson, Zulu.

Monnot Mary, f, 21, 100, $1600, Jefferson, New Haven.

Monnot Nancy, f, 24, 110, $1420, Jefferson, Zulu.

Mooney Benjamin J, f, 21,55, $595, Jackson,Monroeville.

Mooney Johnson, Madison, Maples.

Mooney J C, f, 10, 160,$2710, Eel River, Ari.

Mooney Mary, Jefferson, Maples.

Mooney Mary R, f, 5, 159, $1870, Madison, Maples.

Mooney Sarah,f, 21, 35, $480, Jackson, Monroeville.

Mooney W F, lab, Eel River, Ari.

Moore Eliza L, f, 34,6½, $135, Wayne, Fort Wayne.

Moore Frank, lab, Cedar Creek, Leo.

Moore Henrietta, 20, 30, $440, Scipio, Hall's Corners.

Moore Matthew L, f, Scipio, Hall's Corners.

Moore Moses, f, 18,159,$2615, Scipio, Hall's Corners.

Moore W H, Adams, New Haven.

Moos Frederick, f, 5, ½, $55, Lafayette. Aboite.

Moos Frederick E, Wayne, Fort Wayne.

Morell Eleanor, f, 21, 81, $2635, Wayne, Ft Wayne.

Morell E & C, f, 15, 4⅛, $1065, Wayne, Ft Wayne.

Morgan John H, lab, Monroe, Monroeville.

Morgan Dr Joseph D, f, 26, 15, $310, Monroe, Dixon, O.

Morrison Sarah, f, 31, 1, $200, Eel River, Churubusco.

Morse John (estate of), f, 20, 31, $490, Jefferson, New Haven.

Morss Samuel E, Wayne, Indianapolis, Ind.

Morton George, f, 28, 133, $2630, Marion, Poe.

Morton George A jr, f, 34, 62, $1045, Marion, Poe.

Morton James, lab, Eel River, Churubusco.

Morton John A, f, 34, 61, $1385, Marion, Poe.

Morton Wm A, Marion, Poe.

Morton W H & Lucca, fs, 16, 40, $325, Jackson, Fort Wayne.

Moses Aaron B, barber, Pleasant, Sheldon.

Moses George, lab, Pleasant, Sheldon.

Moses Henry, Pleasant, Sheldon.

Moshammer John L, f, 35, 24, $510, Pleasant, Poe.

Moss Alexander, f, 19, 113, $1415, Cedar Creek, Leo.

Moss Franklin, f, 11, 83, $1090, Cedar Creek, Leo.

Moss George W, f, 19, 40, $490, Cedar Creek, Cedarville.

Moss Willard, Perry, Fort Wayne.

Mosshamer John B, f, 15, 1, $350, Wayne, Ft Wayne.

Moudy H L, f, Cedar Creek, Cedarville.

Moudy John W, f, 30, 160, $1530, Cedar Creek, Cedarville.

Moudy J R, f, Cedar Creek, Cedarville.

Moudy Martin, miller, Cedar Creek, Hursh.

Move George W, f, 11, 5½, $325, Adams, New Haven.

Mowery Andrew, lab, Aboite, Fort Wayne.

Mowery Arthur, lab, Aboite, Fort Wayne.

Mowery Louis, lab, Aboite, Fort Wayne.

Mowery O, lab, Aboite, Ft Wayne.

Mowrer Isaac, 14, 220, $4810, St Joseph, Fort Wayne.

Mowrey Paul, f, 19, 80, $800, Jackson, New Haven.

Mowry Paul, f, 14, 40, $820, Jefferson, Dawkins.

Much & Sons, f, 23, 80, $3490, Wayne, Ft Wayne.

Mueller Conrad, Wayne, Ft Wayne.

Mueller Gustave, Wayne, Ft Wayne.

Mueller Rudolph, Adams, Ft Wayne.

Mueller Sebastin, Wayne, Ft Wayne.

Mullen Thomas, Marion, Poe.

Mullen Wm, Jackson, Edgerton.

Muller E W E, gen store, Cedar Creek, Leo.

Muller Francis, planing mill, Cedar Creek, Leo.

Muller Herman, fireman, Cedar Creek, Leo.

Muller Joseph, lab, Cedar Creek, Leo.

Muller Michael W, Cedar Creek, Leo.

Muller Victor H, hotel, 20, 127, $1115, Cedar Creek, Leo.

Muller Wm, 21, 80, $1770, Cedar Creek, Leo.

Muller W S, tinner, Cedar Creek, Ft Wayne.

Muhler Catherine, f, 18, 40, $1890, Adams, Ft Wayne.

Muhn Bernard, f, 6, 40, $555, Cedar Creek, Collingwood.

Muhn B W, lab, Cedar Creek, Collingwood.

Muhn Michael, f, 6, 37, $440, Cedar Creek, Collingwood.

Muhn Wm, f, 6, 10, $185, Cedar Creek, Collingwood.

Muhn W F, f, Cedar Creek, Collingwood.

Muldoon Charles, Marion, Poe.

Muldoon Elliott, Marion, Poe.

Muldoon Jane, reserve, 203, $5460, Marion, Poe.

Muldoon Wm, Marion, Poe.

Muldoon W Henry, f, 19, 120, $2720, Marion, Poe.

Mum James, St Joseph, Fort Wayne.

Mumma George W, f, 32, 115, $2090, Monroe, Monroeville.

Mumma Nancy J, Monroe, Dixon, O.

Mumma Washington, Monroe, Dixon, O.

Munch Catherine, f, 7, 80, $965, Madison, Hoagland.

Munch Charles, Marion, Soest.

Munch Elizabeth, f, 12, 95, $1890, Marion, Hoagland.

Munch Francis, f, 7, 81, $1225, Jefferson.

Munch Frank, Madison, Hoagland.

Munch Frank J, f, 18, 80, $1070, Madison, Hoagland.

Munch Henry, Monroe, Dixon, O.

Munch Henry, f, 13, 39, $650, Marion, Hoagland.

Munch Herman, f, 12, 80, $1210, Marion, Hoagland.

Munch Jacob (est of), f, 12, 99, $2110, Marion, Hoagland.

Munch John B, Madison, Hoagland.

Munch Julian, Madison, Hoagland.

Munch Nicholas, f, 18, 169, $2780, Madison, Hoagland.

Munch Nicholas, f, 19, 160, $2195, Monroe, Monroeville.

Munch Wm, Madison, Hoagland.

Munsell Charles, Aboite.

Munson Charles A, f, 7, 8, $870, Adams, Fort Wayne.

Murchland Abel, f, Monroe, Monroeville.

Murchland Anderson, Monroe, Monroeville.

Murchland Samuel C, foreman, 22, 5, $80, Monroe, Dixon, O.

Murchland Wm, foreman, 15, 80, $875, Monroe, Monroeville.

Murfield Daniel, Monroe, Monroeville,

Murphy Dennis, f, 34, 40, $545, Lake, Arcola.

Murphy Edward, Wayne, Ft Wayne.

Murphy Dr George, Cedar Creek, Leo.

Murphy James & Bridget, 7, $280, Monroe, Dixon, O.

Murphy Robert R, Milan, Harlan.

Murray George S, Adams, Ft Wayne.

Murray Lucian E, f, 28, 40, $760, Lafayette, Zanesville.

Musser Jacob, f, 35, 97, $2135, Marion, Hoagland.

Müster Henry, Wayne, Fort Wayne.

Myer August, f, 8, 160, $1205, Jackson, Zulu.

Myer Mary M, f, 31, 40, $450, Jackson, Monroeville.

Myers George B, Jackson, Monroeville.

Myers Isaac N, Jefferson, Maples.

Myers John W, f, Cedar Creek, Cedarville.

Myers Louis, Cedar Creek, Leo.

Myers Mary C, 19, 4⅔, $230, Cedar Creek, Cedarville.

Myers Nelson, lawyer, Cedar Creek, Leo.

Mygrant Isaac, lab, Aboite, Dunfee.

Mynton Honora, f, 16, 40, $555, Monroe, Dixon, O.

Mynton Joseph, f, 5, 30, $390, Monroe, Dixon, O.

N

Nahrwald Ernst, f, 25, 39, $765, Adams, Soest.

Nahrwald F C, f, 24, 80, $1435, Adams, Ft Wayne.

Nahrwald Henry, f, 36, 140, $1300, Milan, Goeglein.

Nail Daniel B, f, 28, 60, $740, Jefferson, Maples.

Nail John, f, 22, 190, $3435, Jefferson, Maples.

Nail John W, Jefferson, Maples.

Nare George, f t, Eel River.

Naylor George, Cedar Creek, Cedarville.

Neadstine Frank, f t, Madison, Hoagland.

Need John, f, 34, 80, $1045, Monroe, Dixon, O.

Neff Jacob, f, 17, 40, $570, Madison, Hoagland.

Neff Jacob P, f, 17, 40, $750, Madison, Hoagland.

Neff Peter, f, 9, 40, $605, Madison, Maples.

Neff Rebecca, f, 3, 2, $490, Wayne, Ft Wayne.

Neher Joseph, Adams, Fort Wayne.

Nehrhood Jacob, f, 18, 80, $895, Lake, Arcola.

Neibel Joseph, f t, Eel River, Churubusco.

Neireiter Caspar, f, 14, 80, $1845, Marion, Hoagland.

Neireiter Christian, f, 28, 50, $1180, Wayne, Ft Wayne.

Neireiter Daniel, Madison, Hoagland.

Neireiter George, Marion, Hoagland.

Neireiter Henry, f, 14, 80, $1375, Marion, Hoagland.

Neireiter Henry N, Marion, Hoagland.

Nelson Charles, Perry, Huntertown.

Nesbit Isaac, Jefferson, Monroeville.

Nesbit James, f, 36, 120, $1420, Jefferson, Monroeville.

Nesbit Jeremiah, Madison, Monroeville.

Nesbitt John, Jefferson, Monroeville.

Nettlehorst Charles C, f t, Madison, Hoagland.

Nettlehorst Louis, f, 17, 80, $1610, Cedar Creek, Leo.

Nettlehorst L W, lab, Cedar Creek, Leo.

Neunschwander B, f, 13, 80, $1590, Cedar Creek, Leo.

Newcomb George, Wayne, Ft Wayne.

Newhouse Wm, Lake, Fort Wayne.

Newhouser Christian, f, 6, 75, $1935, Milan, Thurman.

Newhouser Christian W, f, 9, 80, $1415, Cedar Creek, Leo.

Newhouser Peter, Cedar Creek, Leo.

Newland T J, lab, Maumee, Woodburn.

Ney Ann, Lake, Ft Wayne.

Nichols Otis S, f, 16, 20, $320, Milan, Chamberlain.

Nicholson John, Milan, Harlan.

Nicholson John L, f, 23, 40, $770, Lafayette, Zanesville.

Nicholson Wm E, f, 28, 100, $1990, Lafayette, Nine Mile.

Nickey A B, f, 22, 140, $2415, Eel River, Ari.

Nickey David W, f, 31, 133, $2550, Eel River, Ari.

Nickey Orpha L, f, 6, 290, $4200, Lake, Fort Wayne.

Nickol Irenus, Jefferson, New Haven.

Nicodemus Caroline, f, 12, 2, $70, Lafayette, Nine Mile.

Nicodemus Oscar, Lafayette, Myhart.

Nicodemus Peter, f, 11, 60, $1095, Lafayette, Nine Mile.

Niehoff Anna, Adams, Fort Wayne.

Nieman Samuel, Perry, Huntertown.

Niemann Buella, Adams, Ft Wayne.

Niemeyer Christian, Adams, Fort Wayne.

Niemeyer Wm, f, 17, 80, $2360, Adams, Ft Wayne.

Nieter H C, Jefferson,Maples.

Nietert Christian, f, 21, 160, $4125, Adams, Ft Wayne.

Nietert Frederick, Adams, Fort Wayne.

Nietert Frederick, f, 29, 20, $245, Milan, Goeglein.

Nietert Henry, f, 29, 190, $2730, Milan, Goeglein.

Nietert Sophia, f, 28, 69, $1760, Adams, Ft Wayne.

Nietert Wilhelmina, f, 28, 28, $630, Adams, Ft Wayne.

Nieth Frank R, Lafayette, Myhart.

Nieth Joseph, f, 17, 80, $1790, Lafayette, Myhart.

Ninde James W, f, 26, 20, $265, Lake, Ft Wayne.

Ninde J W, 33, 102, $2370, St Joseph, Fort Wayne.

Nistel Martha, 13, $550, Wayne, Ft Wayne.

Nizn Mary M & L B, f, 30, 32, $410, Monroe, Monroeville.

Noble C & J, Adams, Fort Wayne.

Nobley Edward H, Perry, Huntertown.

Noble Hanna, f, 8, 39, $1850, Adams, Ft Wayne.

Noble Jennie, Adams, Fort Wayne.

Noble J M, physician, Pleasant, Zanesville.

Noble Lyman, Adams, Fort Wayne.

Noisler John, Adams, Fort Wayne.

Nolton J T & Co, Adams, Ft Wayne.

Nommany Philomona, ⅔,$180, Wayne, Fort Wayne.

Nonamaker James P, f, 14, 80, $1345, Lafayette, Nine Mile.

Nonamaker John, f, 24, 80, $1600, Lafayette, Nine Mile.

Nonamaker Jonathan, f t, Pleasant, Sheldon.

Noonan James, f, 17, 1, $380, Perry, Huntertown.

Noonan Josephine, Adams, Fort Wayne.

Nord Catherine, f, 2, 30, $770, Marion, Soest.

Nord Henry, f, 2, 84, $1315, Marion, Soest.

Nord Louis, Marion, Soest.

Nord Wm, Marion, Soest.

North Charles, lab, Maumee, Woodburn.

North Hinson, lab, Maumee, Woodburn.

Norton Chester K, f, 12, 52, $910, Aboite, Fort Wayne.

Norton John T, Adams, Fort Wayne.

Norton Sophia R, f, 12, 52, $910, Aboite, Fort Wayne.

Norton Wm C, lab, Aboite, Fort Wayne.

Notestine Daniel, f, 32, 80, $1930, Cedar Creek, Cedarville.

Notestine Eliza A, 3, 20, $470, St Joseph, Fort Wayne.

Notestine J A, St Joseph, Ft Wayne.

Notestine Peter, 3, 50, $1165, St Joseph, Fort Wayne.

Notestine Uriah, 3, 47, $1145, St Joseph, Fort Wayne.

Noyer Elizabeth, Aboite, Dunfee.

Noyer John W, f, 6, 30, $605, Aboite, Dunfee.

Noyer L H, f t, Madison, Monroeville.

Null Daniel E, f, 20,72,$1345, Jefferson, New Haven.

Null Susan, f, 14, 40, $1405, Adams, Fort Wayne.

Null Susan W, f, 14, 35,$810, Adams, Fort Wayne.

Nuttle Amanda, f, 16, 6, $85, Milan, Chamberlain.

Nuttle A D, f, 10, 63, $1505, Milan, Chamberlain.

Nuttle Daniel, f, 16, 5, $85, Milan, Chamberlain.

Nuttle Dora, f, 16, 6, $85, Milan, Chamberlain.

Nuttle George W, f, 16, 6, $85, Milan, Chamberlain.

Nuttle Hannah, f, 16, 18, $430, Milan, Chamberlain.

Nuttle James M, Milan, Chamberlain.

Nuttle Mary J, f, 16, 6, $85, Milan, Chamberlain.

Nuttman Catherine, f, 10,141, $6505, Adams, Ft Wayne.

Nycum Wm, 28, 80, $1755, St Joseph, Ft Wayne.

Nye Emauuel, Jackson, Edgerton.

O

Ober W A, Lafayette, Myhart.

Oberlin John, Marion, Poe.

Oberlin Wm, f, 32, 80, $1445, Marion, Soest.

Oberly Frank, f, 19, 40, $350, Jackson, Dawkins.

O'Brien Charles, Lafayette, Aboite.

O'Brien James, lab, Cedar Creek, Collingwood.

O'Brien Jane, f, 6, 40, $635, Milan, Ft Wayne.

O'Brien Thomas, f, 6, 40, $1415, Milan, Ft Wayne.

O'Brien Wm, lab, 18, 5, $145, Monroe, Monroeville.

Occleston Hannah, f, 20, 73, $1850, Aboite, Ft Wayne.

Occleston John S, f t, Aboite, Ft Wayne.

O'Connor Bernard et al, Adams, Ft Wayne.

Odam Henry, Jackson, Edgerton.

Odam Oliver L, f, 21, 80, $765, Jackson, Edgerton.

Oddow Louis, 6, 57, $1050, St Joseph, Ft Wayne.

O'Dea Dennis, f, 35, 92, $1945, Lake, Duke.

O'Donnell Catherine, 29, 80, $2160, St Joseph, Fort Wayne.

Oesch Christian, f, 11, 40, $400, Milan, Harlan.

Oesch Daniel, f, 11, 40, $565, Milan, Harlan.

Oetting Carl, f, 36, 120, $3025, Wayne, Ft Wayne.

Oetting Henry, f, 36, 40, $825, Wayne, Ft Wayne.

Oetting H W, f t, Wayne, Ft Wayne.

Oetting Louis, f, 36, 120, $4975, Wayne, Ft Wayne.

Ogden Benjamin F, f 25, 40, $1175, Wayne, Ft Wayne.

O'Grady Daniel, f, 17, 157, $2090, Lake, Arcola.

O'Grady Michael, Lake, Arcola.

O'Harra John, St Joseph, Ft Wayne.

Ohler John, f, 6, 40, $605, Madison, Soest.

Ohler Lewis, Madison, Soest.

Ohneck Bernard, f, 25, 40, $750, Lake, Duke.

Olcott Frederick P, f, 36, $4040, Wayne, Ft Wayne.

Olsmutz Frederick, Adams, Ft Wayne.

Oman Wm, f t, Pleasant, Sheldon.

O'Neal Wm, St Joseph, Ft Wayne.

O'Neil Lawrence, 18, 64, $1620, St Joseph, Ft Wayne.

Onspacher Daniel, Lafayette, Nine Mile.

Opdyke A W, f t, Cedar Creek, Leo.

Opdyke David F, f, 20, 56, $1195, Cedar Creek, Leo.

Opdyke Ellen, 17, 55, $1390, Cedar Creek, Leo.

Opleiger Wm, Lake, Arcola.

Opple Frederick, f, 4, $270, Wayne, Ft Wayne.

Ormiston Elizabeth, Wayne, Ft Wayne.

Ormiston Levi et al, f, 14, 7, $1035, Wayne, Ft Wayne.

Ormiston Mary, Wayne, Ft Wayne.

Ormiston & Eby, 10, 2, $40, St Joseph, Ft Wayne.

Orr Eleanor N, 2, 57, $1020, St Joseph, Ft Wayne.

Ort Louis, Milan, Gar Creek.

Ort Wm G, Milan, Gar Creek.

Osborn L F, 15, 10, $310, Cedar Creek, Leo.

Oser Wm, f t, Aboite, Arcola.

O'Shaughnessy Wm, f, 5, 80, $1015, Monroe, Monroeville.

O'Shea Elizabeth, Adams, Ft Wayne.

Oster Francis, f t, Aboite, Ft Wayne.

Osterman J B, f, 34, 48, $790, Lake, Ft Wayne.

Ostermeyer Henry, f, 35, 45, $535, Madison, Decatur.

Ostman August, Wayne, Ft Wayne.

Otenneller John, Marion, Poe.

Ott G W, f t, Eel River, Huntertown.

Otto Abraham, f, 22, 68, $1085, Perry, Huntertown.

Otto Franklin, f, 6, 75, $915, Cedar Creek, Collingwood.

Otto Henry, f, 23, 10, $205, Perry, Huntertown.

Otto James L, Perry, Huntertown.

Otto Matthias, f, 23, 12, $220, Perry, Huntertown.

Outhier Frank, R R lab, 6, 1, $50, Aboite, Dunfee.

Overmeyer Edward, f t, Maumee, Antwerp, O.

Overmeyer George E, f, Maumee, Antwerp, O.

Overmyer Frank, Jackson, Edgerton.

Owens Wm, lab, Maumee, Woodburn.

P

Pachin John P, f, 26, 79, $1640, Perry, Ft Wayne.

Paff George W, 4, 100, $1875, St Joseph, Ft Wayne.

Page Hiram, f, 24, 21, $435, Cedar Creek, Leo.

Page, Taylor & Co, Adams, Ft Wayne.

Paine James D, Adams, Ft Wayne.

Paine James D, f, 4, 31, $420, Eel River.

Paine Henrietta, f, 25, 80, $1570, Marion, Hoagland.

Paine Lemuel C, 1, 80, $1340, St Joseph, Fort Wayne.

Palmer Albert D, 14, 67 100, $435, Wayne, Ft Wayne.

Palmer David & Jane, f, 8, 160, $3025, Aboite, Fort Wayne.

Palmer Ira, Pleasant, Poe.

Palmer James V, f t, Aboite, Fort Wayne.

Palmer Joseph, lab, Aboite, Fort Wayne.

Palmer L C, f, 7, 115, $2260, Scipio, Hicksville, O.

Palmer Wm, f, 28, 37, $945, Wayne, Fort Wayne.

Pancake George, f, 32, 80, $1215, Monroe, Monroeville.

Pape Louis, f, 12, 40, $390, Milan, Fort Wayne.

Par Franklin E, Milan, Harlan.

Parent F A, Adams, Fort Wayne.

Parent F E, f, 7, 4, $1190, Adams, Ft Wayne.

Parent P J, Adams, Fort Wayne.

Parker Abraham, 20, 59, $1755, St Joseph, Fort Wayne.

Parker Belle, Perry, Huntertown.

Parker Catherine, 21, $420, St Joseph, Fort Wayne.

Parker Charles, St Joseph, Fort Wayne.

Parker Charles H, f, 8, 35, $640, Perry, Huntertown.

Parker Edward N, St Joseph, Fort Wayne.

Parker Eli, f, 28, $105, Pleasant, Sheldon.

Parker E H & L, Perry, Huntertown.

Parker Francis A C, Adams, Fort Wayne.

Parker George, 2½, $50, St, Joseph, Ft Wayne.

Parker George A, St Joseph, Fort Wayne.

Parker James, St Joseph, Ft Wayne.

Parker James & Fannie, Wayne, Ft Wayne.

Parker John M, St Joseph, Ft Wayne.

Parker L E, f t, Pleasant, Sheldon.

Parker Maria, f, 7, 7, $540, Perry, Huntertown.

Parker Oliver P, 20, 160, $4750, St Joseph, Ft Wayne.

Parker Omroi, f, 8, 115, $1900, Perry, Huntertown.

Parker Peter, St Joseph, Ft Wayne.

Parker Polly, 9, 100, $1605, Scipio, Hicksville, O.

Parker Sanford, f, 8, 80, $1760, Perry, Huntertown.

Parker Sheldon B, Perry, Huntertown.

Parker Washington, f t, Eel River, Wallen.

Parker Wellington, f, 9, 72, $1720, Scipio, Hicksville, O.

Parker Willard, f t, Eel River, Wallen.

Parker Wm, St Joseph, Fort Wayne.

Parker Wm, 20, 23, $585, St Joseph, Ft Wayne.

Parker W D & D, f, 8, 27, $365, Perry, Huntertown.

Parks Joseph, f, 16, 70, $1030, Eel River, Churubusco.

Parks Lewis, lab, Eel River, Churubusco.

Parks Volney, Adams, Fort Wayne.

Parnin Adolph, f, 21, 240, $4760, Aboite, Ft Wayne.

Parnin August, Jackson, Monroeville.

Parnin August, f, 16, 80, $1255, Lake, Arcola.

Parnin Eugene, f, 27, 120, $2230, Perry, Ft Wayne.

Pernin Francis, f, 32, 160, $1920, Jackson, Monroeville.

Parnin Frank, teacher, Aboite, Ft Wayne.

Parnin Gabriel, f, 4, 60, $1150, Aboite, Arcola.

Parnin James E, lab, Aboite, Ft Wayne.

Parnin Louis E, lab, Aboite, Ft Wayne.

Parnin Victor, f, Monroe, Monroeville.

Parrent Hiram, f, 32, 146, $3020, Milan, Goeglein.

Parrent Wm, Milan, Goeglein.

Partner H E, f, 7, 138, $4025, Wayne, Ft Wayne.

Patten Bridget, f, 9, 80, $730, Lake, Arcola.

Pauline Mathias, f, 8, 80, $1025, Cedar Creek, Leo.

Paulman Francis, 53, $1175, St Joseph, Ft Wayne.

Payne Isaac, Jackson, Edgerton.

Payton John, Wayne, Fort Wayne.

Pearson Albert P, f, 20, 25, $295, Scipio, Hall's Corners.

Pearson J S, f, 20, 20, $300, Scipio, Hall's Corners.

Pearson Philena, 20, 20, $285, Scipio, Hall's Corners.

Peckham Peter, f, 25, 40, $780, Madison, Monroeville.

Peckham Rebecca, f, 25, 40, $515, Madison, Monroeville.

Peckham Wm, f, 26, 86, $1495, Madison, Monroeville.

Pefler Jacob (estate of), f, 36, 40, $630, Adams, Fort Wayne.

Pepe August, f, 22, 79, $1545, Jefferson, New Haven.

Pepe A J, f t, Eel River, Churubusco.

Pepe Jane B, f, 11, 40, $560, Jefferson, New Haven.

Pepe Julian, Jefferson, New Haven.

Pepe Louis, f, 28, 115, $1315, Perry, Ft Wayne.

Pepe Melissa W, f, 16, 40, $890, Eel River, Churubusco.

Pepler Louis, f, 31, 56, $945, Jefferson, Ft Wayne.

Pequignot Abel, Adams, Ft Wayne.

Pequignot August, Perry, Huntertown.

Pequignot Francis F, f, 13, 80, $925, Perry, Huntertown.

Pequignot Randolph, Perry, Huntertown.

Pequinot August C, f, 34, 217, $2495, Eel River, Wallen.

Pequinot Charles, f t, Eel River, Wallen.

Pequinot Charles jr, lab, Eel River, Wallen.

Pequinot Claude, f, 35, 50, $735, Eel River, Wallen.

Pequinot Frank, f, 35, 120, $1785, Eel River, Wallen.

Peregua Peter, f, 7, 3¼, $1140, Adams, Ft Wayne.

Perriguey Felix, brick mnfr, 90, $3270, Wayne, Fort Wayne.

Perriguey Frank, Wayne, Ft Wayne.

Perkins Daniel, St Joseph, Goeglein.

Perkins G W, f, 6, 85, $830, Maumee, Harlan.

Perkins Lafayette, St Joseph, Goeglein.

Perkins Nancy A, f, 31, 23, $265, Scipio, Harlan.

Perkins O A & L B, Adams, Ft Wayne.

Perkins Whitley, lab, Scipio, Hall's Corners.

Perkins Wm, f, Maumee, Harlan.

Perkins Wm, St Joseph, Goeglein.

Pernot Constant, f, 18, 120, $1040, Jackson, Dawkins.

Pernot Francis, Jackson, Dawkins.

Perry Ella R, f, 2, 80, 1190, Eel River, Churubusco.

Perry Martin, f, 15, 17, $295, Lafayette, Myhart.

Perry O L, f, 2, 60, $885, Eel River, Wallen.

Perry Wm J, lab, Maumee, Woodburn.

Peteram C, Wayne, Fort Wayne.

Peters Daniel, Milan, Harlan.

Peters Ernst, f, 29, 120, $2415, Adams, Ft Wayne.

Peters John, Adams, Fort Wayne.

Peters Samuel, f, 11, 51, $385, Jefferson, Dawkins

Peters Simon J, Adams, Fort Wayne

Peters Wm, f, 29, 120, $2865, Adams, Ft Wayne.

Petzinger Frederick, f, 13, 2⅘, $1080, Wayne, Ft Wayne.

Petzold Adam, Marion, Hoagland.

Petzold John H, f, 13, 20, $545, Marion, Hoagland.

Pfeidner Jacob, f, 6, 5, $625, Adams, Ft Wayne.

Pfleger Peter, Wayne, Fort Wayne.

Pflegin Joseph, Wayne, Fort Wayne.

Pfleiderer Mary, f, 33, 79, $1205, Eel River, Churubusco.

Pfleidner Mary P, f, 2, 158, $1740, Lake, Ft Wayne.

Philips Frank, Wayne, Fort Wayne.

Philley Charles, f, 24, 88, $3940, Wayne, Ft Wayne.

Philley Hiram A, clk, Wayne, Fort Wayne.

Philley Morton W, Wayne, Fort Wayne.

Phillips Jacob, f, 32, 71, $1160, Scipio, Antwerp, O.

Phillips John F, f, 32, 143, $3235, Wayne, Ft Wayne.

Phillips Ogden E, f, 20, $655, Wayne, Ft Wayne.

Pichon Alexander C, f, 29, 80, $1810, Cedar Creek, Ft Wayne.

Pichon Frank, carp, Cedar Creek, Cedarville.

Pichon F J, St Joseph, Fort Wayne.

Pichon John, f t, Cedar Creek, Cedarville.

Picket Benjamin C, Adams, Fort Wayne.

Piehl John, Adams, Fort Wayne.

Piepenbrink Charles, f, 7, 10, $1705, Adams, Ft Wayne.

Piepenbrink Conrad, f, 21, 80, $2055, Adams, Ft Wayne.

Piepenbrink Louis, Adams, Fort Wayne.

Pierce Eli, f, 6, 1, $15, Lake, Fort Wayne.

Pierce James S, f, 18, 70, $2030, Wayne, Ft Wayne.

Pierce John E, f, 6, 124, $1990, Lake, Fort Wayne.

Pierson Annie, f, 14, 1¾,$120, Wayne, Fort Wayne.

Pierson Nicholas, St Joseph, Fort Wayne.

Pierson Wm S (est of), 7⅔, $570, Wayne, Fort Wayne.

Piggott Edward, lab, Eel River, Churubusco.

Piggott Margaret, f, 30, 76, $1550, Eel River, Churubusco.

Piggott Thomas, f t, Eel River, Churubusco.

Pine George, f, Monroe, Monroeville.

Pine Patrick, f, Monroe, Monroeville.

Pio Frank D, Jefferson, Dawkins.

Pio W J & Mary, f, 7, 40, $250, Jackson, Dawkins.

Piou Claude F, f, 22, 80, $1270, Perry, Huntertown.

Piou Franklin, Perry, Huntertown.

Piou Mary & John, f, 22, 55, $795, Perry, Huntertown.

Plants Isaac, f, 30, 37, $735, Eel River, Churubusco.

Platter M J, f, 22, 41, $580, Milan, Death.

Plenge George C, f, 17, 240, $1030, Lake, Fort Wayne.

Plicard Freeman, f t, Aboite, Fort Wayne.

Plicard Joseph, lab, Aboite, Fort Wayne.

Plogstart Adam, Adams, Ft Wayne.

Plow Christian F, Adams, Fort Wayne.

Pluis Herman, Adams, Fort Wayne.

Pocock Elias, Lafayette, Myhart.

Poehler Charles, f, 36, 40, $1125, Wayne, Ft Wayne.

Poehler Charles J C, f, 36, 95, $1895, Wayne, Ft Wayne.

Poehler Christian, f, 36, 140, $5350, Wayne, Ft Wayne.

Poehler John, f t, Wayne, Ft Wayne.

Poepler John F, f, 32, 80, $1830, Adams, Ft Wayne.

Poeppel John J, f, 29, 160, $2350, Milan, Goeglein.

Poff Andrew J, St Joseph, Fort Wayne.

Pohl George, Adams, Fort Wayne.

Poinsette Edward, f, 2, 80, $1385, Aboite, Ft Wayne.

Poinsette Joseph, f, 16, 80, $1425, Aboite, Ft Wayne.

Poinsette Wm, f, 16, 116, $1825, Aboite, Ft Wayne.

Pollock Charles, Wayne, Ft Wayne.

Pollock Wm, carp, 26,2,$305, Wayne, Fort Wayne.

Pompey Joseph, Marion, Poe.

Pompey Mary E, Marion, Poe.

Pool Francis Y, Wayne, Fort Wayne.

Pool George W, f t, Wayne, Fort Wayne.

Pool George W, f, 32, 40, $780, Wayne, Ft Wayne.

Pool James F, f, 31, 140, $2800, Wayne, Ft Wayne.

Poorman M D & I, f, 3, 40, $380, Monroe, Monroeville.

Popitz Frederick, f, 19, 40, $435, Milan, Goeglein.

Popp Frederick, f, 25, 40, $690, Perry, Leo.

Popp Frederick, f, 30, 115, $2435, Cedar Creek, Cedarville.

Popp Henry, lab, Cedar Creek, Cedarville.

Porter Allen, f, 31, 151, $3185, Perry, Wallen.

Porter Crawford, f, 7, 60, $1045, Scipio, Hall's Corners.

Porter Daniel, f, 18, 60, $865, Scipio, Hall's Corners.

Porter Hiram, 115, $3065, St Joseph, Fort Wayne.

Porter Joseph, 2, 137, $2490, St Joseph, Fort Wayne.

Porter Samuel, f, 27, 80, $1635, Aboite, Fort Wayne.

Potter F J & M J, Wayne, Fort Wayne.

Potter James, f, 3, 165, $3620, Eel River, Ari.

Potter Newton G, f, 4, 6, $105, Eel River, Ari.

Potts Hiram, f, 28, 40, $440, Madison, Monroeville.

Potts Wm A, f, 27, 26, $510, Madison, Monroeville.

Poulson B, Wayne, Fort Wayne.

Poulson Wm, $1145, Wayne, Fort Wayne.

Powell Daniel, lab, Scipio, Hall's Corners.

Powell Harriet, Pleasant, Sheldon.

Powell Isaac B, Pleasant, Sheldon.

Powell Joseph, f, 3, 80, $1250, Scipio, Hall's Corners.

Powell Nancy, Pleasant, Sheldon.

Powers Charles, lab, Pleasant, Sheldon.

Powers James, Jefferson, New Haven.

Powers L D, Jefferson, New Haven.

Poyneer Hugh V, f, 30, 80, $595, Maumee, Woodburn.

Pratt Augusta, St Joseph, Ft Wayne.

Pratt Margaret M, 3, $105, St Joseph, Ft Wayne.

Prange Charles, Wayne, Ft Wayne.

Prange Christian, f, 21, 80, $2190, Adams, Ft Wayne.

Prange Frederick, f, 27, 107, $2425, Adams, Ft Wayne.

Prange F M, f, 80, $6015, Wayne, Ft Wayne.

Prange Henry, f, 25, 40, $630, Lake, Ft Wayne.

Prange Herman, f, 24, 80, $2400, Adams, Ft Wayne.

Prange John H, f, 9, 36, $1650, Adams, Ft Wayne.

Prange Wm, Adams, Fort Wayne.

Prange Wm, f, 19, 110, $1885, Milan, Goeglein.

Prange Wm F, Wayne, Fort Wayne.

Pranger Charles, Adams, Ft Wayne.

Pranger Frederick, Adams, Ft Wayne.

E. F. Sites, 🦷 Dentist, 86 Calhoun St., Four Doors North of Wayne.

ALLEN COUNTY DIRECTORY. 765

Prepsing Bernard, f, 10, 80, $2780, Adams, New Haven.

Preston Edward, f, 7, 83, $1695, Perry, Huntertown.

Preston Frederick, f, 7, 22, $540, Perry, Huntertown.

Preston James, f, 7, 16, $435, Perry, Huntertown.

Preston Nancy, f, 2, 5, $75, Milan, Harlan.

Presuhn Francis, f, 26, 80, $1100, Madison, Decatur.

Presune James, Monroe, Monroeville.

Pretzinger J R, Wayne, Ft Wayne.

Price Mahlon, f, 21, 70, $770, Scipio, Hicksville, O.

Price Moses B, f, 6, 100, $1225, Maumee, Harlan.

Priest Edward, gardener, 6, 7, $45, Jackson, Dawkins.

Prill Benjamin F, Lake, Arcola.

Prill Emanuel, f, 29, 73, $1180, Lake, Arcola.

Prill Thomas, Lake, Arcola.

Prince George, Wayne, Fort Wayne.

Prince John, Wayne, Fort Wayne.

Prince Wm, Pleasant, Sheldon.

Pring Elbridge, f t, Cedar Creek, Cedarville.

Pring James, f t, Cedar Creek, Cedarville.

Prophet Abraham, f, Monroe, Monroeville.

Prophet L M & F E, f, 16, 40, $440, Monroe, Monroeville.

Pruse Ernst, f, 6, 49, $1020, Marion, Poe.

Pulver Franklin, f, 21, 80, $1215, Perry, Huntertown.

Pulver Louisa, f, 17, ¼, $70, Perry, Huntertown.

Purdy George W, Marion, Hoagland.

Putt Elizabeth, f, 34, 120, $940, Jackson, Baldwin.

Putt John, f, Pleasant, Nine Mile.

Putt Mary, f, 7, 28, $660, Pleasant, Nine Mile.

Putt Wm, genl store, Pleasant, Nine Mile.

Q

Quandt Anna B, f, 18, $195, Madison, Hoagland.

Quandt Charles, f, 7, 80, $1255, Madison, Soest.

Quandt Charles jr, f, 7, 37, $430, Madison, Soest.

Quandt Henry, f, 7, 40, $390, Madison, Soest.

Quandt Louis, f, 17, 80, $1050, Madison, Hoagland.

Quinlan John, f, 21, 46, $1035, Monroe, Monroeville.

Quinte Charles, 7, 6, $100, St Joseph, Ft Wayne.

R

Raal John, meat mkt, 10, $315, Wayne, Ft Wayne.

Rabbitt Jack, carp, Monroe, Monroeville.

Rabbitt W B, f, 32, 80, $1090, Monroe, Monroeville.

Racht Joseph, 14, 1⅘, $1150, Wayne, Ft Wayne.

Racine John F jr, 2, 40, $695, St Joseph, Ft Wayne.

Racine Louis, Lake, Wallen.

Rackewig Charles, f, 50, $1315, Wayne, Ft Wayne.

Robert Spice, Pumps, Pipe, Hose, Fittings and Brass Goods
48 WEST MAIN and 11 PEARL STS.

766   R. L. POLK & CO.'S

Rademacher Joseph, Wayne, Ft Wayne.

Rahman John, reserve, 75, $1125, Milan, Goeglein.

Ralus Gustave B, f, 31, 160, $925, Maumee, Ft Wayne.

Ramsey James, 4, ½, $85, Wayne, Ft Wayne.

Randall David, lab, Wayne, Ft Wayne.

Randall Mary J,31, 53,$3430, St Joseph, Ft Wayne.

Rank Ezra & Palmer, 30, $705, St Joseph,Ft Wayne.

Rank Mary, St Joseph, Fort Wayne.

Ranke & Yergens, f, 14, 119, $950, Jackson, Ft Wayne.

Ranner George M, f, 21, 40, $995, Marion, Poe.

Ranner Marcellus, f, 21, 13, $265, Marion, Poe.

Ranner Mary A, f, 21, 26, $450, Marion, Poe.

Rapp George, f, 2, 100,$1635, Eel River, Churubusco.

Rapp George, f, 20,86, $2535, Wayne, Ft Wayne.

Rapp Henry, f t, Wayne, Ft Wayne.

Rapp Jacob, f, 27, 102, $1655, Lake, Arcola.

Rapp John jr, f, 19, 157, $1995, Lake, Arcola.

Rapp John H, f, 20, 40, $555, Lake, Arcola.

Rapp Louis, f t, Wayne, Ft Wayne.

Rapp Philip, f, 21, 40, $500, Wayne, Ft Wayne.

Rathfon Catherine, Lafayette, Roanoke.

Rathfon Frank, Lafayette, Roanoke.

Rathmall Peter, 9, 54, $1165, St Joseph, Ft Wayne.

Ratledge Wm M, Jackson, Edgerton.

Rauch Wm, f, 15, $405, Wayne, Ft Wayne.

Rauhaus Albert, f, 13, 100, $2340, Cedar Creek, Leo.

Rauner George J, lab, Pleasant, Ft Wayne.

Rauner Isadore, lab, Pleasant, Ft Wayne.

Rauner Joseph, lab, f, 6, 40, $860, Pleasant, Ft Wayne.

Rausis Francis, f, 19, 30, $505, Jefferson, Maples.

Rawley Andrew, f, 34, 40, $545, Lake, Arcola.

Rawley James, f, 32, 28, $450, Lake, Arcola.

Rawley Wm, f, 32, 89, $1280, Lake, Arcola.

Rawson S A, f, 15, 25, $395, Milan, Chamberlain.

Razet Peter, Jackson, Monroeville.

Read Abbie W, gardener, 22, 7, $390, Wayne, Fort Wayne.

Reader D M, carp, Cedar Creek, Leo.

Ream C W, Perry,Academy.

Ream Jacob, f, 34, 120,$1945, Perry, Academy.

Ream Mercia M, f, 34, 20, $275, Perry, Academy.

Ream Wm O, f, 34, 20, $275, Perry, Academy.

Rebber Christian, Adams, Ft Wayne.

Rebber Christopher, f, 22, 80, $2025, Adams, Ft Wayne.

Rebber Christopher jr, Adams, Ft Wayne.

Rebber Frank F, Adams Ft Wayne.

Rebber F W & E, Adams, Ft Wayne.

Rebber Gerhard, f, 23, 339, $6915, Adams, Ft Wayne.

Rebber Henry, Adams, Fort Wayne.

Rebber Henry, f, 23, 80, $1725, Adams, Ft Wayne.

Rebber Louis, Adams, Fort Wayne.

Reber George, Wayne, Fort Wayne.

Reckeway Diederich, f, 14, 80, $1020, Milan, Harlan.

Reckeway W, f, 30, 40, $595, Milan, Harlan.

Reddin Alpheus, f, 21, 1, $15, Lafayette, Zanesville.

Reddin Catherine, f, 29, 75, $1200, Lafayette, Zanesville.

Reddin George, f, 35, 80, $1335, Lafayette, Zanesville.

Reddin Isaiah, f, 21, 159, $2875, Lafayette, Zanesville.

Reddin Isaiah jr, f, 29, 20, $350, Lafayette, Zanesville.

Reddin Joseph, f, 35, 2, $135, Lafayette, Zanesville.

Reddin Joshua S, f, 35, 77, $1460, Lafayette, Zanesville.

Reddin Sylvester, Lafayette, Zanesville.

Reddin S Q, f, Lafayette, Zanesville.

Reddin Wm J, f, 29, 81, $1610, Lafayette, Ft Wayne

Redelsheimer D S, merchant, 5, 160, $1625, Monroe, Monroeville.

Reed Arthur H, lab, Wayne, Ft Wayne.

Reed Clarence B, lab, Wayne, Fort Wayne.

Reed George, f, 25, 40, $715, Lafayette, Sheldon.

Reed George W, f, 30, 40, $760, Pleasant, Sheldon.

Reed Harvey, f t, Pleasant, Sheldon.

Reed John A, Marion.

Reed John M, Lafayette, Zanesville.

Reed Matilda, Marion, Poe.

Reed Samuel, painter, Marion, Poe.

Reed Sidney A, Marion, Poe.

Reed S S, f, 25, 40, $880, Lafayette, Sheldon.

Reed Wm, f t, Eel River, Churubusco.

Reed Wm B, f, 5, 120, $3640, Adams, Fort Wayne.

Reed Wm J, Adams, Fort Wayne.

Reeks Charles F, Adams, Ft Wayne.

Reemer Wm H, Aboite, Aboite.

Rees M J & W H, f, 5, ¾, $10, Lafayette, Aboite.

Rees Wm, Lafayette, Aboite.

Refner Calvin, lab, Eel River, Wallen.

Rehla Mary A, f, 23, 20, $375, Pleasant, Sheldon.

Rehling Ernest, 21' 40, $840, St Joseph, Ft Wayne.

Rehling Henry P, f t, Pleasant, Poe.

Rehling John G jr, f t, Pleasant, Poe.

Rehling John J, f, reserve, 117, $2210, Pleasant, Sheldon.

Reiber John G, Wayne, Ft Wayne.

Reichart Frederick, f, 4, 40, $820, Jefferson, Gar Creek.

Reicher Christian, f, 6, 62, $1615, Milan, Chamberlain.

Reid Adam D, f, 9⅜, $250, Wayne, Ft Wayne.

Reid Rodantia, f, 4, 6, $155, Wayne, Ft Wayne.

Reiler Henry, Adams, Fort Wayne.

Reilly John, Jefferson, New Haven.

Reiney, Hedges & Walter, Adams, Ft Wayne.

Reinhard Henry, Wayne, Ft Wayne.

Reinhold Cora, Perry, Collingwood.

Reinhold Henry, f, 18, 298, $6265, Perry, Huntertown.

Reinhold John, f, 12, 80, $1785, Perry, Collingwood.

Reinhold Lafayette, f, 12, 40, $480, Perry, Collingwood.

Reinhold Perry, Perry, Collingwood.

Reinmeyer John, Adams, Ft Wayne.

Reiter Diederich, f, 31, 124, $1730, Madison, Bingen.

Reiter Frederick, Madison, Bingen.

Reiter Harman, Madison, Bingen.

Reiter Henry, Madison, Bingen.

Reiter John, f, Monroe, Monroeville.

Reiter Walter, f, Monroe, Monroeville.

Reiter Wm, f, Monroe, Monroeville.

Remenschneider August, Adams, New Haven.

Reminger Frederick, f, 7, 80, $1080, Madison, Soest.

Remmey John F, f, 17, 40, $610, Milan, Chamberlain.

Remus John, Milan, Goeglein.

Remus Julius & John, 30, 54, $1550, St Joseph, Fort Wayne.

Reninger Henry, Marion, Hoagland.

Reninger Jacob, Marion, Hoagland.

Rennecher P S, f t, Eel River, Wallen.

Rennerson James A, St Joseph, Ft Wayne.

Rennkemp Henry, Adams, Fort Wayne.

Reppert Louisa, 3, $75, Wayne, Fort Wayne.

Reuge Fred B, f, 30, 80, $760, Jackson, Monroeville.

Reuille Adolph, f, 13, 80, $815, Jefferson, Dawkins.

Reuille Joseph, f, 14, 160, $2445, Jefferson, Zulu.

Reuille Louis J, f, 23, 40, $560, Jefferson, Zulu.

Reuille Peter, Jefferson, Zulu.

Reuillo Jules H, saloon, 7, 80, $1405, Monroe, Monroeville.

Reuss John B, Adams, New Haven.

Revert Frank, St Joseph, Ft Wayne.

Revert Henry, 1, 60, $990, St Joseph, Fort Wayne.

Revert Jacob, f t, Cedar Creek, Cedarville.

Rex Henry, St Joseph, Fort Wayne.

Reynolds Albert, f, Monroe, Monroeville.

Reynolds C O, Monroe, Monroeville.

Reynolds George M, f, 28, 159, $2380, Monroe, Monroeville.

Reynolds Jefferson, Milan, Chamberlain.

Reynolds Newton, f, 15, 20. $455, Milan, Chamberlain,

Reynolds Wm A, Milan, Chamberlain.

Reynolds Wm E, f, Monroe, Monroeville.

Rhein Jacob, Wayne, Fort Wayne.

Rhine John, Adams, Ft Wayne.

Rhine Lavinia, Adams, Fort Wayne.

Rhoades Catherine, f t, Eel River, Churubusco.

Rhoades Daniel J, f, 8, 119, $2295, Aboite, Ft Wayne.

Rhoades D W, Adams, Fort Wayne.

Rhoades Isaac, Wayne, Fort Wayne.

Rhoades Isaiah, Aboite, Fort Wayne.

Rhoades John (estate of), f, 18, 62, $1310, Eel River.

Rhoades John F, f t, Eel River, Heller's Corners.

Rhoades Martha E, Adams, Fort Wayne.

Rhoades Mary A, f, 35, 5, $115, Pleasant, Sheldon.

Rhodenbaugh Gilbert, f, 18, 93, $1565, Cedar Creek, Leo.

Rhodenbaugh James, teamster, Cedar Creek, Leo.

Rhodin Victor, Adams, Fort Wayne.

Rhorback Magnus G, f t, Madison, Maples.

Rhyne Gustave, Wayne, Ft Wayne.

Ribbet John P K, Adams, Ft Wayne.

Rice Calvin F, Adams, Fort Wayne.

Rice Catherine G, f, 15, 40, $785, Lafayette, Aboite.

Rice Frank B, lab, Eel River, Huntertown.

Rice Frederick, Pleasant, Sheldon.

Rice George W, f, 30, 100, $1825, Pleasant, Nine Mile.

Rice Harvey, f, 12, 70, $1550, Eel River, Huntertown.

Rice James, f, Pleasant, Nine Mile.

Rice Jesse, f, 20, 80, $1635, Pleasant, Nine Mile.

Rice Mary, Pleasant, Sheldon

Rich A A, f t, Eel River, Ari.

Rich A J, f t, Eel River, Ari.

Rich B L, f, 11, $370, $2765, Eel River, Ari.

Rich B L & Co, Eel River.

Rich Casper, 1, 44, $680, St Joseph, Fort Wayne.

Richard Charles H, Jefferson, Maples.

Richard D J, Perry, Leo.

Richard Francis, Milan, Gar Creek.

Richard Frank, lab, Cedar Creek, Leo.

Richard F D C & E, f, 34, 27, $415, Cedar Creek, Leo.

Richard Ira, Milan, Gar Creek.

Richard John, f, 36, 50, $1125, Perry, Fort Wayne.

Richard John M, f, 34, 27, $440, Cedar Creek, Leo.

Richard Joseph, f, 22, 110, $1875, Milan, Gar Creek.

Richard Joseph jr, f, 23, 75, $795, Milan, Gar Creek.

Richard W S, Milan, Gar Creek.

Richards Allen & A, f, 4, 100, $2330, Milan, Chamberlain.

Richards Charles E, f, 12, 76, $1130, Madison, Monroeville.

Richards David, f t, Eel River, Churubusco.

Richards Elizabeth, f, 28, 36, $590, Jefferson, Maples.

Richards James L, f, 20, 100, $1720, Jefferson, New Haven.

Richards Joseph, f t, Eel River, Churubusco.

Richards Laura J, Marion.

Richards Rebecca, f, 18, 40, $815, Eel River, Ari.

Richards Wm, f, 27, 40, $425, Jefferson, Maples.

Richardson Austin H, f, 19, 80, $680, Lake, Arcola.

Richardson George, Wayne, Fort Wayne.

Richardson Hannah, Adams, Fort Wayne.

Riche Joseph, St Joseph, Ft Wayne.

Richter Frederick E, Wayne, Fort Wayne.

Rickett George E, f, 18, 2, $225, Perry, Huntertown.

Ridenour Adam L, Madison, Monroeville.

Ridenour Ephraim, f, 33, 94, $1205, Monroe, Monroeville

Ridenour Esther, f, 33, 225, $3775, Monroe, Monroeville

Ridenour Marcus, f, 22, 160, $2405, Madison, Monroeville.

Rider Jacob, lab, 14, ¼, $30, Wayne, Ft Wayne.

Riedmiller John M, Wayne, Ft Wayne.

Riedmiller J G, grocer, 10, 1, $480, Wayne, Ft Wayne.

Rieman Mary, Adams, Ft Wayne.

Riley Jesse F, Madison, Monroeville.

Riley John, f, 15, 40, 465, Madison, Monroeville.

Riley Peter, lab, Monroe, Monroeville.

Riley Sarah, lab, Pleasant, Sheldon.

Rimenschneider August, f, 22, 60, $1140, Milan, New Haven.

Rinehart Louis, f, 9, 160, $2935, Milan, Ft Wayne.

Rinehart Mary, f, 15, 110, $1535, Milan, Chamberlain.

Ring John (estate of), f, 9, 61, $2620, Adams, Fort Wayne.

Ringgenberger Christian, Milan, Chamberlain.

Ringgenberger John, f, 12, 20, $210, Milan, Harlan.

Ringgenberger Peter, f, 5, 100, $2210, Milan, Chamberlain.

Ringgenberger Peter jr, Milan, Chamberlain.

Ringwalt Eli, f, 17, 80, $1670, Milan, Chamberlain.

Ringwalt George P, Milan, Chamberlain.

Ringwalt Wm H, f, 20, 40, $450, Scipio, Hall's Corners.

Ringwalt Wm S, Milan, Chamberlain.

Rinhart Phoebe, f, 30, 22, $325, Lafayette, Aboite.

Rinker Henry, f, 17, 76, $2045, Adams, Ft Wayne.

Ritter Wm, Madison, Maples.

Roach John, f, 7, 41, $335, Lake, Ft Wayne.

Roach John, Madison, Monroeville.

Stahn & Heinrich, Leading Dealers in ARTISTS' MATE-RIALS AND DRAUGHTING INSTRU-MENTS. 116 Calhoun Street.

ALLEN COUNTY DIRECTORY. 771

Roach John J, f t, Madison, Monroeville.

Roadebush James, f, 27, 60, $1075, Madison, Hoagland.

Roamer Charles, Milan, Harlan.

Robb Mary, lab, Pleasant, Sheldon.

Robel Catherine, Wayne, Ft Wayne.

Roberson Elijah, f t, Eel River, Churubusco.

Roberson Ellen, f t, Eel River, Churubusco.

Roberson Harvey W, f, 30, 19, $290, Eel River, Churubusco.

Roberson Uriah, f, 30, 40, $990, Eel River, Churubusco.

Robert W H, Milan, Chamberlain.

Roberts George W, f, 2, 61, $1005, Milan, Harlan.

Roberts Hiram, f,31, 40, $350, Jackson, Poe.

Roberts R S, Jackson, Monroeville.

Roberts Sylvester, f, 24, 10, $185, Madison,Monroeville.

Roberts W W, f, 32, 1, $20, Jefferson, Maples.

Robertson Eliza H, f, 30, 34, $1120, Lafayette, Roanoke.

Robertson Frank P, f, 30, 44, $650, Lafayette, Roanoke.

Robertson H H, f, 30, 60, $1030, Lafayette, Aboite.

Robertson Susan, f, 29, 80, $1800, Wayne, Ft Wayne.

Robinet James, f, 5, 40, $860, Aboite, Dunfee.

Robinson Amanda, f, 26, 20, $370, Pleasant, Sheldon.

Robinson Amasa, f, 17, 112, $1980, Monroe,Monroeville.

Robinson A W, undertaker, f, 30, 167, $3665, Eel River, Churubusco.

Robinson Caroline, hotel, 28, 30, $625, Pleasant, Sheldon.

Robinson David, f, 10, 160, $1260, Lake, Arcola.

Robinson D A, f, 30, 40,$1195, Eel River, Churubusco.

Robinson Elijah, f, 34, 120, $1865, Eel River, Churubusco.

Robinson Jacob C, Pleasant, Sheldon.

Robinson James B, f, 29, 92, $1670, Pleasant, Nine Mile.

Robinson James M, lawyer, 3, 40, $385, Monroe, Fort Wayne.

Robinson John & Ulysses, Milan, Chamberlain.

Robinson L C, f t, Eel River, Heller's Corners.

Robinson Nelson, f t, Eel River, Heller's Corners.

Robinson Parker, f, 30, 235, $4565, Eel River, Churubusco.

Robinson Warren, f t, Pleasant, Nine Mile.

Robinson Warren, f, 26, 201, $4015, Pleasant, Nine Mile.

Robinson Wm, f, 97, $1975, Lafayette, Myhart.

Robinson Wm M, f, 29, 67, $1090, Pleasant, Sheldon.

Robinson Wm S, f, 20, 220, $3825, Pleasant, Sheldon.

Robinson W H, f, 22, 89, $1485, Eel River, Churubusco.

Robinson W L, Adams, Fort Wayne.

Robison James M, Madison, Hoagland.

Robison John W, f t, Madison, Hoagland.

Robison Jonathan L, Madison, Hoagland.

Rockhill Edward W, Lake, Arcola.

Rockhill Emily, f, 18, 1, $85, Adams, Ft Wayne.

Rockhill Henry A, Lake, Arcola.

Rockhill Howell C, live stock, 9, 147, $7180, Wayne, Fort Wayne.

Rockhill H C, Adams, Fort Wayne.

Rockhill H W, live stock, Wayne, Ft Wayne.

Rockhill Jesse, live stock, Wayne, Ft Wayne.

Rockhill Joseph, f, 35, 166, $2545, Lake, Arcola.

Rockhill Wm, f, 28, 314, $4395, Lake, Arcola.

Rodabaugh John, Adams, Ft Wayne.

Rodabaugh John F, f, 9, 160, $1205, Jackson, Ft Wayne.

Rodenbeck Diederich, f, 15, 120, $3430, Adams, Fort Wayne.

Rodenbeck D, f, 32, 120, $2385, Perry, Ft Wayne.

Rodenbeck D jr, Adams, Ft Wayne.

Rodenbeck Ernest, f, 32, 76, $1600, Perry, Ft Wayne.

Rodenbeck Henry, Adams, Fort Wayne.

Rodenbeck Henry, f, 15, 120, $3705, Adams, Ft Wayne.

Rodenbeck Wm, Perry, Fort Wayne.

Rodenwald John (estate of), f, 32, 80, $2100, Adams, Fort Wayne.

Rodenwold George, Wayne, Fort Wayne.

Rodewald Herman, Adams, Fort Wayne.

Rodgers Lamont, f, 16, 160, $1090, Jackson, New Haven.

Roe Adam, f, 21, 80, $640', Jackson, Poe.

Roemke Conrad, Malin, Goeglein.

Roemke Wm, Malin, Goeglein.

Roepke Frederick, Adams, Fort Wayne.

Rogers L M, f, 11, 46, Adams, New Haven.

Rogge Wilhelmina, Adams, Fort Wayne.

Rohe H, lab, Wayne, Fort Wayne.

Rohrback Jacob, Jefferson, Dawkins.

Rohrback John W, f, 31, 60, $805, Jefferson, Maples.

Rohrback Magnus, f, 6, 159, $2080, Madison, Maples.

Rolland Frederick, f, 29, 160, $2680, Perry, Huntertown.

Roller Jacob, f t, Pleasant, Nine Mile.

Roller John, f, 18, 82, $1735, Pleasant, Nine Mile.

Roller Josiah, miller, 28, 2½ $820, Cedar Creek, Cedarville.

Roller Wm, f t, Pleasant, Sheldon.

Romara A, Wayne, Ft Wayne

Romary August, Lake, Arcola.

Romary John J, f, 23, 10, $155, Perry.

Romick John W, Aboite, Dunfee.

Romick W & Jane, f, 6, 40, $800, Aboite, Dunfee.

Romine Herby, f t, Cedar Creek, Leo.

Romine Perry, f, 4, 80, $1480, Cedar Creek, Leo.

Romy E, Wayne, Ft Wayne.

Romy Frederick, f, 5, 39, $1265, Wayne, Ft Wayne.

Romy John, Wayne, Fort Wayne.

Romy Peter, Wayne, Ft Wayne.

Rondot Charles, Wayne, Ft Wayne.

Rondot Julius A, f, 20, 106⅔, $1770, Cedar Creek, Cedarville.

Rondot P, f t, Cedar Creek, Cedarville.

Roose Charles, f, 3, 1155, $11040, Jackson, Edgerton.

Roose Herman, Jackson, Edgerton.

Root Clara, 10, $660, Wayne, Ft Wayne.

Root F W, f t, Pleasant, Sheldon.

Root Jesse E, f, 32, 40, $580, Perry, Wallen.

Root Palmer C, St Joseph, Ft Wayne.

Root W H, Perry, Ft Wayne.

Rorick John K, f, 14, 40, $715, Jefferson, Dawkins.

Rorick Wm J, f, 2, 60, $790, Jefferson, Gar Creek.

Rose Anton (estate of), f, 20, , 139, $3535, Adams, Fort Wayne.

Rose Benjamin F, f, 5, 40, $725, Scipio, Hicksville, O.

Rose Christian F, 18, 232, $6735, St Joseph, Fort Wayne.

Rose C H, St Joseph, Fort Wayne.

Rose Daniel B, f, 6, 40, $810, Scipio, Hicksville, O.

Rose Frank, Adams, New Haven.

Rose Frederick, St Joseph, Ft Wayne.

Rose H, St Joseph, Ft Wayne.

Rose K, f, 28, 35, $525, Milan, Ft Wayne.

Rose L A, lab, Monroe, Monroeville.

Rose Mathias, f, 2, 125, $2975, Adams, New Haven.

Rose Maurice W, f, 27, 80, $1150, Jefferson, Maples.

Rose Wm, f, 35, 80, $1000, Milan, Ft Wayne.

Rose Wm J, Milan, New Haven.

Roselot James F, 18, 79, $2435, St Joseph, Fort Wayne.

Roselot Julia A, 18, 79, $2275, St Joseph, Fort Wayne.

Roselot Louis G, St Joseph, Ft Wayne.

Roselot Wm, St Joseph, Ft Wayne.

Rosener Christian, genl store, Maumee, Woodburn.

Ross Enoch, f, 27, 26, $420, Eel River, Heller's Corners.

Ross John L, f, 27, 40, $430, Eel River, Churubusco.

Rosseau Anna B, f, 9, 80, $1515, Aboite, Ft Wayne.

Rosseau Martha J, f, 17, 45, $1095, Wayne, Ft Wayne.

Rosseau R Daniel, f, 17, 40, $1525, Wayne, Ft Wayne.

Roth Benedict, f, 35, 295, $5735, Cedar Creek, Leo.

Roth Henry, f t, Cedar Creek, Leo.

Roth Jacob, f, 26, 119, $3205, Cedar Creek, Leo.

Roth Simon, f t, Cedar Creek, Leo.

Rothenberg Wm, St Joseph, Ft Wayne.

Rothgeb Amos, f, 20, 15, $220, Jefferson, New Haven.

Rothgeb Chase, Jefferson, Gar Creek.

Rothgeb Daniel, Adams, Ft Wayne.

Rothgeb Daniel, Jefferson, Gar Creek.

• Rothgeb Eby, f, 4, 30, $530, Jefferson, Gar Creek.

Rothgeb George, f, 35, 40, $380, Milan, Gar Creek.

Rothgeb Henry, Jefferson, Gar Creek.

Rothgeb Hezekiah, f, 4, 43, $755, Jefferson, Gar Creek.

Rothgeb Jesse, f, 34, ¾, $210, Milan, Gar Creek.

Rothgeb John, Jefferson, Gar Creek.

Rothgeb Margaret, f, 3, 77, $1660, Jefferson, Gar Creek.

Rothgeb Michael, f, 1, 80, $660, Jefferson, Gar Creek.

Rothgeb Solomon, Jefferson, Gar Creek.

Rothgeb Wm, Milan, Gar Creek.

Rothgeb Wm, f, 34, 60, $1090, Milan, Gar Creek.

Rothget Wm, St Joseph, Ft Wayne.

Rothman John, St Joseph, Ft Wayne.

Rothman Joseph, St Joseph, Fort Wayne.

Roudebush Wm A, Madison, Monroeville.

Roussey August, f, 12, 40, $395, Jefferson, Dawkins.

Roussey Elizabeth, f, 13, 20, $580, Adams, New Haven.

Roussey Elizabeth, f, 19, 38, $625, Jefferson, Zulu.

Roussey Francis, f, 13, 179, $1995, Jefferson, Zulu.

Roussey Frank A, Jefferson, Zulu.

Roussey John, Jefferson, Zulu

Roussey Joseph M, Adams, New Haven.

Roussey Louis A, Jefferson, Zulu.

Roussey Louis E, Jefferson, Zulu.

Roux George, Adams, Fort Wayne.

Row Margaret, f, 10, 80, $1130, Monroe, Monroeville.

Rowan Jennie, Adams, Fort Wayne.

Rowan M H, Adams, Fort Wayne.

Rowe Melissa, f, 1, 1½, $155, Adams, New Haven.

Roy Charles, Perry, Huntertown.

Roy Charles J, Perry, Fort Wayne.

Roy C A, Jefferson, Zulu.

Roy Emma, f, 26, 45, $630, Jefferson, Zulu.

Roy Felix, f, 28, 117, $2285, Perry, Huntertown.

Roy Florentine, f, 33, 170, $5020, Perry, Fort Wayne.

Roy Frank, Perry, Huntertown.

Roy Henry, Perry, Huntertown.

Roy James & Mary B, hardware, 6, 80, $900, Monroe, Monroeville.

Roy Jean B, f, 23, 80, $1110, Jefferson, Zulu.

Roy John, Perry, Wallen.

Roy John B, Adams, Fort Wayne.

Roy Julian, f t, Cedar Creek, Leo.

Roy Louis, f, 27, 15, $220, Jefferson, Zulu.

Roy Louis F, Perry, Huntertown.

Ruar Lawrence, f, 21, 80, $1190, Lake, Arcola.

Ruble George W, Jackson, Monroeville.

Ruble Julia A, gardener, 33, 5, $75, Jackson, Monroeville.

Ruby A M, f, 20, 120, $1570, Lake, Arcola.

Ruby Franklin, Lake, Arcola.

Ruch George, f, 15, 160, $1445, Jackson, Edgerton.

Ruch George A, Adams, Ft Wayne.

Ruch Joshua, f, 22, 40, $280, Jackson, Fort Wayne.

Ruch J G, Madison, Hoagland.

Ruchel Caroline, 14, 1, $350, Wayne, Fort Wayne.

Rudisill F H, Perry, Wallen.

Rudisill John A, f, 31, 105, $1700, Perry, Wallen.

Rudisill T M, Perry, Wallen

Rudolph Julius, Cedar Creek, Leo.

Ruffing Martin, f, 24, 60, $650, Milan, Gar Creek.

Ruhl Barbara, f, 30, 20, $265, Madison, Hoagland.

Ruhl Charles R, f, 30, 72, $860, Madison, Hoagland.

Ruhl James H, f, 27, 71, $1550, Marion, Hoagland.

Ruhl John C, f, 26, 40, $570, Madison, Monroeville.

Ruhl Julia, f, 14, 22, $805, Adams, New Haven.

Ruhl Dr Mary L, f, 28, 5, $80. Pleasant, Sheldon.

Ruhl O C, f, 23, 40, $485, Madison, Monroeville.

Ruhl W O, physician, Pleasant, Sheldon.

Ruhling Conrad, Adams, Ft Wayne.

Ruhling Wm, Adams, Fort Wayne.

Ruls John, Adams, New Haven.

Rumsey Helen, f, 10, 315, $2090, Jackson, Ft Wayne.

Rumsey Rebecca K, Wayne, Fort Wayne.

Rundalls John J, f, 9, 241, $4210, Perry, Wallen.

Runnion Harriet, f, 19, 106, $2045, Eel River, Churubusco.

Runnion Joseph, f t, Eel River, Churubusco.

Runser John, Wayne, Fort Wayne.

Rupert John I, Jackson, Edgerton.

Rupert Manasseh, f, Maumee, Woodburn.

Rupp John, Adams, Fort Wayne.

Rupp Sophia, Adams, Fort Wayne.

Rush Henry, f, 23, 92, $725, Maumee, Antwerp, O.

Rushart Andrew, f, 35, 68, $835, Milan, Gar Creek.

Rushart Catherine, f, 4, 50, $920, Jefferson, Gar Creek.

Russey Justin, Jefferson, Zulu.

Ruth Julius, Lake, Wallen.

Ryan Bridget, Lake, Fort Wayne.

Ryan George W, Adams, Ft Wayne.

Ryan John, f, 21, 40, $600, Jefferson, New Haven.

Ryan Michael & Matilda, Wayne, Fort Wayne.

Ryan Patrick, Milan, Chamberlain.

Ryan Patrick, f, 24, 80, $1315, Lake, Arcola.

Ryan Patrick jr, f, 3, 80, $1375, Jefferson, Gar Creek.

Ryan Thomas, f, 34, 74, $1450, Milan, Gar Creek.

S

Sack Henry, f, 9, 64, $885, Marion, Soest.

Sack Henry jr, f, 9, 160, $2745, Marion, Soest.

Sackman D, Adams, Fort Wayne.

Safford Charles P, Milan, Harlan.

Safford G W T, f, 9, 120, $2385, Milan, Chamberlain.

Safford Wm H, Milan, Harlan.

Salfrank Frederick, Marion, Soest.

Salfrank Henry, f, 10, 80, $1450, Marion, Soest.

Salfrank Henry jr, Marion.

Salfrank John H, f, 15, 180, $3325, Marion, Soest.

Salfrank Louis, Marion, Soest.

Salfrank Wm, Marion, Soest.

Salge Ferdinand, 16, 79, $1450, St Joseph, Ft Wayne.

Salge Ferdinand F, St Joseph, Ft Wayne.

Salway Eliza, f, 16, 40, $550, Monroe, Monroeville.

Salway James, f, 22, 88, $900, Monroe, Monroeville.

Salway John, lab, 9, 40, $445, Monroe, Monroeville.

Salzbrenner Gottlieb, f, 3, 20, $1045, Jefferson, Gar Creek.

Sander John, f, 30, 84, $1380, Jefferson, Maples.

Sander Wilhelmina, Wayne, Ft Wayne.

Sanders Ann, f, 26, 40, $610, Scipio, Hall's Corners.

Sanders Cyrenus, lab, Scipio, Hall's Corners.

Sanders Elmer, f t, Scipio, Hall's Corners.

Sanders Oscar, lab, Scipio, Hall's Corners.

Sandford Philip, lab, Wayne, Ft Wayne.

Sanford Barbara, f, 14, 1, $400, Wayne, Ft Wayne.

Sanscotte George, f, 17, 80, $450, Jackson, Zulu.

Sanscotte John B, f, 19, 80, $760, Jackson, Zulu.

Sapp Daniel, f, 2, 26, $420, Milan, Harlan.

Sapp Levi, f, 2, 52, $850, Milan, Harlan.

Sapp Samuel, f, 2, 18, $420, Milan, Harlan.

Sargent Charlotte, f, 29, 40, $1150, Marion, Poe.

Sargent John, Marion, Poe.

Sarninghausen D, Adams, Ft Wayne.

Sarrazin August, 16, 83, $1745, St Joseph, Ft Wayne.

Sarrazin Francis, 10, 53, $995, St Joseph, Ft Wayne.

Sarrazin Julius, St Joseph, Ft Wayne.

Sarrazin Orzine, f, 33, 80, $1250, Perry, Academy.

Satowres Theodore, Lake, Ft Wayne.

Sauer Benjamin, f, 6, 70, $1335, Scipio, Hall's Corners.

Sauer Christian, f, Scipio, Hicksville, O.
Sauer George H (estate of), f, 25, 50, $945, Lake, Arcola.
Sauers Elvina, f, 13, 44, $880, St Joseph, Ft Wayne.
Sauers John M, f, 12, 20, $305, St Joseph, Ft Wayne.
Sauvage M A, St Joseph, Ft Wayne.
Sauvain Samuel, f, 5, 3⅖, $380, Adams, Ft Wayne.
Savage John E, f, 28, 3, $40, Milan, Harlan.
Saviot Caroline, f, 33, 10, $130, Jefferson, Maples.
Saviot Francis, f, 33, 58, $820, Jefferson, Maples.
Saviot Frederick, f, 13, 40, $625, Madison, Monroeville.
Saviot James, f t, Madison, Monroeville.
Saviot Michael E, f, 33, 50, $705, Jefferson, Maples.
Sayler John W, f t, Scipio, Hall's Corners.
Saylor D E & A E, Perry, Huntertown.
Saylor Elizabeth, f, 4, 15, $305, Milan, Chamberlain.
Saylor Frank, f, 3, 6, $190, Maumee, Antwerp, O.
Saylor Harland, f, 17, 3, $415, Perry, Huntertown.
Saylor Henry, Milan, Harlan.
Saylor Jacob, f, 10, 174, $2225, Maumee, Antwerp, O.
Saylor Jane A, f, 3, 34, $295, Maumee, Antwerp, O.
Saylor Lyman, Perry, Huntertown.
Saylor Wm, Milan, Harlan.
Scarlet Chester, Adams, Fort Wayne.

Scarlet John, f, 28, 120, $2815, Monroe, Monroeville.
Scarlet Malinda, Wayne, Ft Wayne.
Scarlet Washington C, Wayne, Ft Wayne.
Schaaf Frederick, Milan, Gar Creek.
Schafenaker T, Adams, Fort Wayne.
Schafer Charles, Wayne, Ft Wayne.
Schafer Christian, f, 20, 120, $3395, Adams, Ft Wayne.
Schafer Christian F, f, 13, 99, $9165, Wayne, Ft Wayne.
Schafer Frederick, f, 19, 75, $2655, Adams, Ft Wayne.
Schafer Frederick W, f, 12, 83, $2370, Wayne, Fort Wayne.
Schafer Gottlieb, f, 28, 117, $3095, Adams, Ft Wayne.
Schafer Mary, f, 19, 180, $5930, Adams, Ft Wayne.
Schaffer Gottlieb, f, 19, 155, $2040, Milan, Goeglein.
Schaffer Henry, f, 1, 80, $1680, Cedar Creek, Hursh.
Schaffer Wm, f, 29, 79, $1305, Milan, Goeglein.
Schafter David & Mary, 10, 19, $310, St Joseph, Fort Wayne.
Schafter Pacific, f t, Cedar Creek, Cedarville.
Schaick Christian, 12, 80, $1455, St Joseph, Fort Wayne.
Schambaugh John, contr, Cedar Creek, Hursh.
Schamerle Henry, f, 20, 62, $1470, Marion, Poe.
Schanebeck Daniel, f, 24, 80, $1900, Cedar Creek, Hursh.

Schanebeck David, lab, Cedar Creek, Harlan.

Schanebeck John, f t, Cedar Creek, Harlan.

Schaper Louisa, Adams, Ft Wayne.

Scharpenberg Henry, f, 25, 79, $1245, Adams, Soest.

Scharpenberg Henry jr, Adams, Soest.

Scheiman Eliza, Madison, Bingen.

Scheiman Wm, f, 31, 135, $2185, Madison, Bingen.

Schele August, f, 7, 5, $1470, Adams, Fort Wayne.

Schele Carrie, f, 7, 1, $205, Adams, Fort Wayne.

Schele Catherine, f, 7, 1⅘, $600, Adams, Ft Wayne.

Schele Henry, Adams, Fort Wayne.

Schele Theresa, f, 7, 9, $1180, Adams, Fort Wayne.

Schellhammer Charles, Wayne, Fort Wayne.

Schellhammer Rupert, Wayne, Fort Wayne.

Schepelman Henry, brick mnfr, 5, 244, $1980, Maumee, Woodburn.

Scherpenberger H E, f, 30, 9, $140, Jefferson, Maples.

Scherschal Louis, f, 35, 40, $585, Milan, Gar Creek.

Scheuler Margaret, f, 3, 2, $105, Eel River, Ari.

Scheuman Carl, Marion, Poe.

Scheuman D F W, f, 27, 213, $4180, Marion, Hoagland.

Scheuman E Diederich, f, 36, 119, $2195, Marion, Hoagland.

Schever Amanda, f, 30, 80, $2110, Marion, Poe.

Schever Henry, f, 7, 52, $970, Pleasant, Sheldon.

Schever Herbert, f, 30, 113, $1860, Marion, Poe.

Schever Jacob, f, 8, 160, $3205, Pleasant, Sheldon.

Schiefer Caroline, Adams, Ft Wayne.

Schiefer Charles, Adams, Ft Wayne.

Schiefer George W, Adams, Fort Wayne.

Schilling David, f, 21, 116, $2610, Eel River, Eel River.

Schilling Adolph, Wayne, Ft Wayne.

Schilling Camilla, Wayne, Ft Wayne.

Schilling Charles, Wayne, Ft Wayne.

Schilling C (est of), f, 3, 8, $1415, Wayne, Ft Wayne.

Schilling Martin, f, 20, 18, $385, Wayne, Fort Wayne.

Schirschel John, Marion, Poe.

Schlagel Augusta, Marion, Soest.

Schlagel Henry, Milan, Gar Creek.

Schlandrauff Christian, Adams, Fort Wayne.

Schlandrauff George, Wayne, Fort Wayne.

Schlandrauff Henry, f, 12, 75, $1590, Marion, Soest.

Schlandrauff John, Adams, Fort Wayne.

Schlandrauff Louis, f, 7, 41, $590, Madison, Maples.

Schlandrauff Ludwig, f, 33, 249, $6575, Adams, Soest.

Schlandrauff Wm, Adams, Ft Wayne.

Schlatter Benedict, f, 9, 239, $3860, Cedar Creek, Leo.

Stahn & Heinrich, Booksellers and Stationers,
Schmitz Block News Stand, 116 Calhoun Street.

ALLEN COUNTY DIRECTORY. 779

Schlatter Benedict J, f, 21, 120, $2575, Cedar Creek, Leo.

Schlatter Benjamin, f, 15, 309, $7170, Cedar Creek, Leo.

Schlatter B B, f, 14, 142, $3520, Cedar Creek, Leo.

Schlatter B O, f, 15, 15, $1225, Cedar Creek, Leo.

Schlatter B S, f, 13, 100, $2015, Cedar Creek, Leo.

Schlatter Christian D, f, 17, 260, $4370, Cedar Creek, Leo.

Schlatter C B, f, Cedar Creek, Leo.

Schlatter D D, f, 32, 23, $1230, Cedar Creek, Leo.

Schlatter Henry C, Adams, Fort Wayne.

Schlatter John, f, 17, 157, $3315, Cedar Creek, Leo.

Schlatter Jonas, f t, Cedar Creek, Leo.

Schlatter Joseph G, f, 15, 81, $2640, Cedar Creek, Leo.

Schlatter Josephine, Cedar Creek, Leo.

Schlatter J, f, 12, 111, $2975, Cedar Creek, Hursh.

Schlatter Magdalene, Cedar Creek, Leo.

Schlatter Rebecca, f, 32, 126, $2685, Cedar Creek, Leo.

Schlegel Gottlieb, St Joseph, Fort Wayne.

Schlegel John, f, 33, 80, $1370, Milan, Gar Creek.

Schlegel Wm, Adams, Fort Wayne.

Schlemer Philip, f, 20, 40, $660, Monroe, Monroeville.

Schlink George, f, 28, 125, $2370, Milan, Goeglein.

Schlink Joseph, f, 29, 61, $840, Milan, Goeglein.

Schlup Frederick, f t, Aboite, Fort Wayne.

Schmick Frederick, St Joseph, Fort Wayne.

Schmidt August, f, 10, 80, $790, Monroe, Monroeville.

Schmidt Christian, f, 23, 80, $1060, Lake, Fort Wayne.

Schmidt Elizabeth T, f, 8, 39, $630, Marion, Poe.

Schmidt George, f, 1, 76, $1580, Marion, Soest.

Schmidt Jacob, Jefferson, New Haven.

Schmidt John, Adams, Fort Wayne.

Schmidt John, f, 5, 53, $850, Marion, Poe.

Schmidt Louis, Adams, Fort Wayne.

Schmidt Wm, Lake, Arcola.

Schmidt Wm, Jefferson, New Haven.

Schmitt John, Wayne, Fort Wayne.

Schmitt J G jr, Adams, Fort Wayne.

Schmucker John, f, 3, 72, $1600, Milan, Chamberlain.

Schneider Caroline, f, 2, 30, $770, Perry, Collingwood.

Schneider Carolus, f, 6' 100, $2100, Cedar Creek, Collingwood.

Schneider Christian, f, 26, 40, $550, Lake, Ft Wayne.

Schneider Christian W, f, 26, 40, $755, Lake, Arcola.

Schneider E C, Cedar Creek, Leo.

Schneider Frederick, f, 27, 80, $1245, Lake, Arcola.

Schneider Gottlieb, f, 26, 100, $2090, Lake, Arcola.

Schneider Ida A, f, 26, 40, $480, Lake, Arcola.

John F. Eby & Co., BOOK AND JOB PRINTERS
65 and 67 W. Congress St., DETROIT.

780   R. L. POLK & CO.'S

Schneider John, f, 36, 50, $945, Adams, Soest.

Schneider John, f, 26, 120, $1590, Lake, Arcola.

Schneider John jr, Adams, Soest.

Schnelker B (heirs), f, 17, 160, $1415, Maumee, New Haven.

Schnelker H, f, 12, 240, $8720, Adams, New Haven.

Schnelker H F, f, 17, 80, $1060, Maumee, New Haven.

Schnelker Mary G, f, 23, 158, $2065, Milan, New Haven.

Schnitzer Adam, f, 26, 40, $695, Pleasant, Sheldon.

Schnurr George, Wayne, Ft Wayne.

Schnurr Gerominhus, Wayne, Fort Wayne.

Schoaf Jacob, Wayne, Fort Wayne.

Schoene Peter W, f t, Aboite, Fort Wayne.

Schoenfeld Henry, f, 12, 12, $360, Adams, New Haven.

Schoenfeld H & W, f, 13, 10, $270, Adams, New Haven.

Schoenle John, Adams, Fort Wayne.

Schoenle Joseph, Adams, Ft Wayne.

Schoerpf Barbara, Cedar Creek, Leo.

Schoerpf Fredolin, saloon, Cedar Creek, Leo.

Schoerpf John, saloon, 17, 80, $1470, Cedar Creek, Leo.

Schofer & Ohr, Adams, Fort Wayne.

Schoper E C Gottlieb, Adams, Fort Wayne.

Schoper Gottlieb jr, Adams, Fort Wayne.

Schoper Henry, Adams, Fort Wayne.

Schopman Ernest, 29, 40, $1080, St Joseph, Fort Wayne.

Schopman Louis, 32, 40, $1030, St Joseph, Ft Wayne

Schopman Wm, 28,120,$3175, St Joseph, Fort Wayne.

Schopman Wm jr, 28, 40, $1095, St Joseph, Ft Wayne.

Schoppman Diederich, f, 31, 105, $1610, Madison, Hoagland.

Schoppman Ferdinand, Madison, Hoagland.

Schoppman Frederick, f, 25, 40, $505, Marion, Hoagland.

Schoppman Henry, St Joseph, Fort Wayne.

Schott George J, Adams, Ft Wayne.

Schroeder August, f, 17, 112, $2325, Marion, Poe.

Schroeder Edmund, Adams, Fort Wayne.

Schroeder Edward, f, 21, 55, $2175, Adams, Ft Wayne.

Schroeder Eliza, Adams, Fort Wayne.

Schroeder Frederick, f, 35, 100, $2090, Marion, Hoagland.

Schroeder Henry, f, 35, 100, $2200, Marion, Hoagland.

Schroeder Henry jr, Marion, Poe.

Schroeder Wm, f, 17, 80, $1640, Marion, Poe.

Schroeder Wm G, Marion.

Schroeder Wm L, Marion.

Schuckman Alexius, Adams, New Haven.

Schuckman Anna, f, 1, 58, $1615, Adams, New Haven.

Schuckman Frederick, Adams, New Haven.

Schuler Casper, St Joseph, Ft Wayne.

Schuler Frank, Wayne, Ft Wayne.

Schuler Henry, f t, Pleasant, Sheldon.

Schuler John, f, 35, 156, $2745, Pleasant, Sheldon.

Schuler John, f, 20, 46, $575, Cedar Creek, Cedarville.

Schuler Lorenzo, 16, 59, $1260, St Joseph, Ft Wayne.

Schultz Dora C, f, 29, 48, $655, Lake, Arcola.

Schuman John, f, 33, 80, $1400, Milan, Harlan.

Schunker August, Wayne, Ft Wayne.

Schurk Charles, f t, Cedar Creek, Leo.

Schuster John, Adams, Fort Wayne.

Schutt Cora A, Perry, Huntertown.

Schutt Charles, Perry, Huntertown.

Schutt J E, Perry, Huntertown.

Schutz Henry, Marion, Poe.

Schwalm Margaret, f, 6, 46, $880, Aboite, Dunfee.

Schwalm Philip, 21, 120, $2560, St Joseph, Ft Wayne.

Schwartz Benawell, f, 5, 80, $1360, Cedar Creek, Collingwood.

Schwartz Carl, f, 7, $\frac{2}{5}$, $475, Adams, Ft Wayne.

Schwartz Charles, Adams, Ft Wayne.

Schwartz C R, f t, Cedar Creek, Leo.

Schwartz Elizabeth, f, 12, 26$\frac{2}{3}$, $455, St Joseph, Ft Wayne.

Schwartz Henry, f, 7, 186, $5665, Wayne, Ft Wayne.

Schwartz Jacob, f, 10, 277, $5745, Cedar Creek, Leo.

Schwartz Jacob B, f, 22, 25, $880, Cedar Creek, Leo.

Schwartz Joel, f t, Cedar Creek, Leo.

Schwartz John C, f t, Cedar Creek, Leo.

Schwartz Joseph, f, 20, 40, $575, Milan, Chamberlain.

Schwartz Katie, f, 24, 28, $550, Cedar Creek, Leo.

Schwartz Louisa, Adams, Ft Wayne.

Schwartz Reuben, 12, 53, $835, St Joseph, Ft Wayne.

Schwartz Rudolph, f, 23, 40, $1015, Cedar Creek, Leo.

Schwell Adam, Wayne, Fort Wayne.

Schwier C H, Wayne, Fort Wayne.

Scott David W, f, 33, 80, $1650, Lafayette, Zanesville.

Scott George, f, 28, 80, $1760, Lafayette, Zanesville.

Scott George, f, 16, 20, $240, Monroe, Monroeville.

Scott George A, f t, Aboite, Ft Wayne.

Scott Harry, lab, Monroe, Monroeville.

Scott John, f, 10, 280, $5590, Aboite, Ft Wayne.

Scott John jr, f, 20, 120, $2020, Aboite, Ft Wayne.

Scott John J, f t, Aboite, Ft Wayne.

Scott Leonide B, f, 24, 80, $1160, Madison, Monroeville.

Scott Martin, f, 28, 40, $595, Lafayette, Zanesville.

52

Scott Mary A, f, 28, 20, $370, Aboite, Ft Wayne.

Scott Mary E, f, 7, 17, $615, Monroe, Monroeville.

Scott Michael, f, 34, ½, $5, Lafayette, Zanesville.

Scott M, f, 21, 11, $160, Lafayette, Zanesville.

Scott Samuel, f, 16, 40, $630, Monroe, Monroeville.

Scott Sarah, f, 24, 40, $455, Madison, Monroeville.

Scott Wm, f, 11, 80, $1395, Aboite, Ft Wayne.

Scott Wm, f, 27, 80, $1730, Lafayette, Zanesville.

Scott Wm, f, 4, 40, $635, Monroe, Monroeville.

Scott Wm M, f, 23, 10, $180, Aboite, Ft Wayne.

Scott Winfield, f, 16, 20, $270, Monroe, Monroeville.

Scoville Herman, f, 9, 127, $1690, Maumee, Antwerp, O.

Scranton James, lab, Scipio, Hicksville, O.

Screen John, lab, Wayne, Ft Wayne.

Seaman Joseph, f, 34, ¾, $280, Lafayette, Zanesville.

Sear Margaret, f, 32, 20, $175, Monroe, Monroeville.

Sear Nicholas, butcher, 17, 2, $35, Monroe, Monroeville.

Sear Peter, f, Monroe, Monroeville.

Sechler Catherine, f, 20, 141, $2255, Perry, Huntertown.

Sedlemeyer H R, f, 30, 80, $2480, Adams, Ft Wayne.

Seeds Thomas, Wayne, Fort Wayne.

Seegar Adam, f, 14, 94, $1595, Lake, Arcola.

Seegar George, f, 14, 30, $420, Lake, Arcola.

Seel John, Adams, Fort Wayne.

Seeley Conrad, Adams, Ft Wayne.

Seeley John, Adams, Fort Wayne.

Seeley Marguerite, f, 6, 5, $600, Adams, Ft Wayne.

Seenot John, St Joseph, Ft Wayne.

Seibt Carl B, f, 13, 2½, $905, Wayne, Ft Wayne.

Seibt Charles A, Wayne, Ft Wayne.

Seibt Louis, Wayne, Fort Wayne.

Seidel Edward, f, 34, 40, $285, Jackson, Ft Wayne.

Seifferlein Charles, lab, Pleasant, Sheldon.

Seigel Richard, f, 28, 80, $1685, Monroe, Monroeville.

Seiler Barbara, f, 22, 67, $2040, Adams, Ft Wayne.

Seiler Frank, f, 22, 20, $405, Adams, Ft Wayne.

Seiler John, f, 3, 144, $4295, Adams, Ft Wayne.

Seiler Joseph, Adams, Fort Wayne.

Seiler Joseph, f, 12, 81, $1520, Marion, Soest.

Seiler Peter, f, 22, 63, $1650, Adams, Ft Wayne.

Seilert J D, St Joseph, Fort Wayne.

Selking Conrad, f, 21, 140, $2105, Madison, Hoagland.

Sell G A, St Joseph, Fort Wayne.

Sewell John W, f, 19, 123, $2165, Lafayette, Roanoke.

Sexton Wm, Jackson, Dawkins.

Shaff Nellie, f, 33, ¾, $30, Lake, Arcola.

Sewing Machines, Shears) Pfeiffer & Schlatter
—and Pocket Knives,—) 38 & 40 E. Columbia.

ALLEN COUNTY DIRECTORY. 783

Shaffer Amasa, f, 35, 59, $910, Madison, Monroeville.

Shaffer Jabez, f t, Madison, Monroeville.

Shaffer Jacob, f, 22, 151, $2370, Lake, Arcola.

Shaffer John, f, 36, 80, $1275, Madison, Monroeville.

Shaffer Lydia E, f, 30, 67, $850, Monroe, Monroeville.

Shaffer Valentine F, f, 20, 72, $1170, Monroe, Monroeville.

Shaffer V L, f, Monroe, Monroeville.

Shambaugh Daniel, f, 110, $2140, Cedar Creek, Hursh.

Shank George, f, 20, 49, $710, Lafayette, Roanoke.

Shank John M, Lafayette, Roanoke.

Shannen P S, Wayne, Fort Wayne.

Sharpy Williard, Jefferson, Dawkins.

Sharp Wm, Jefferson, Dawkins.

Shatzer Wm, f (reserve), 80, $1590, Lafayette, Nine Mile.

Shaughnessy Michael, lab, Pleasant, Sheldon.

Shaughnessy Thomas, f, 14, 80, $1650, Pleasant, Nine Mile.

Shaw D J, Adams, Ft Wayne.

Sheafer Charles H, f t, Aboite, Ft Wayne.

Sheaver Atwell, f (reserve), 80, $1650, Pleasant, Nine Mile.

Sheehan Charles, Jackson, Monroeville.

Sheehan Daniel, f, 4, 60, $610, Monroe, Monroeville.

Sheehan James (heirs), f, 27, 40, $355, Jackson, Payne, O.

Sheehan John, justice, 8, 40. $940, Monroe, Monroeville.

Sheehan Louisa, f, 26, 81, $690, Jackson, Payne, O.

Sheehan Wm, f, 4, 60, $720, Monroe, Monroeville.

Sheffield Edwin & Henry, f, 8, 200, $1525, Jackson, Dawkins.

Sheldon Cyrus A, f t, 7, 20, $445, Eel River, Ari.

Sheldon Rev D C, 28, 26, $300, Scipio, Fort Wayne.

Shelner Rebecca, f, 17, ¼, $30, Perry, Huntertown.

Shepler Frank P, f, 34, 100, $1685, Lafayette, Zanesville.

Shereisen Victor, Adams, Ft Wayne.

Sherer Christian, f, 15, 72, $1425, Lafayette, Myhart.

Sheridan Catherine, f, 9, 17, $585, Adams, Fort Wayne.

Sheridan Ermine, 7, ½, $25, St Joseph, Fort Wayne.

Sheridan Frank, St Joseph, Fort Wayne.

Sheridan Michael, f, 9, 19, $730, Adams, Fort Wayne.

Sherman E W, Lafayette, Zanesville.

Sherman Herman, Milan, Gar Creek.

Sherpenberger August, f, 31, 40, $535, Jefferson, Maples.

Sherrard Marion, Jackson, Monroeville.

Sherrard Martha, f, 21, 30, $305, Jackson, Monroeville.

Sherwin Millard, St Joseph, Fort Wayne.

Shever Frederick, Lafayette, Zanesville.

Shevrer Frederick, f, 35, 80, $1100, Madison, Decatur.

Shiery John, Wayne, Fort Wayne.

Shilling A B, justice, Eel River, Heller's Corners.

Shilling Charles B, lab, Eel River, Heller's Corners.

Shilling Eli, Eel River, Heller's Corners.

Shilling Martin, f, 20, 3, $70, Wayne, Fort Wayne.

Shippy Angelina M, f, 27, 40, $750, Aboite, Aboite.

Shira Peter (est of), 2, 18, $290, St Joseph, Ft Wayne.

Shirey G W, stonemason, Cedar Creek, Cedarville.

Shirey John, stonemason, Cedar Creek, Cedarville.

Shirey Lewis, stonemason, Cedar Creek, Cedarville.

Shirley Dora, Maumee, Woodburn.

Shirley George W, Jefferson, Monroeville.

Shirley John, f, 3, 20, $180, Maumee, Antwerp, O.

Shirley Robert B, f, 7, 270, $2960, Maumee, Woodburn.

Shive Chester, f, 9, 117, $2315, Pleasant, Nine Mile.

Shive John & Jane, f, 10, 24, $455, Pleasant, Nine Mile.

Shive John M, f, 10, 67, $1640, Pleasant, Nine Mile.

Shive Wm, f, 5, 50, $1035, Pleasant, Nine Mile.

Shively Wallace B, lab, Aboite, Ft Wayne.

Shoaff David M, f, 7, 80, $2005, Perry, Huntertown.

Shoaff David W, Perry, Huntertown.

Shoaff Eliza J, f, 24, 160, $2330, Eel River, Huntertown.

Shoaff James B, f, 14, 174, $2650, Eel River, Fort Wayne.

Shoaff John F, f, 13, 634, $11200, Eel River, Churubusco.

Shoaff J F, lab, Eel River, Churubusco.

Shoaff Wm W, f, 13, 262, $3835, Eel River, Huntertown.

Shoaff W S, f, 15, 440, $6430, Eel River, Heller's Corners.

Shoof Peter, f, 27, 80, $1065, Milan, Gar Creek.

Shook J N, Marion, Poe.

Shook Philip, f, 31, 116, $2300, Marion, Poe.

Shook P S, Marion, Poe.

Shookman Benjamin, Madison, Hoagland.

Shookman George, f, 27, 60, $1270, Marion, Hoagland.

Shookman Jacob, Jackson, Maples.

Shoonover Daniel, f, 33, 33, $575, Lafayette, Zanesville.

Shorden George, 35, 110, $3540, St Joseph, Goeglein.

Shorden Lillie, St Joseph, Goeglein.

Shorden Wm, 35, 90, $2750, St Joseph, Goeglein.

Shorden Wm, f, 13⅛, $385, Wayne, Fort Wayne.

Shores J W, Adams, Fort Wayne.

Short Joseph C, f, 13, 60, $1210, Cedar Creek, Hursh.

Shortly Louis, St Joseph, Ft Wayne.

Shoup Wm H, Lafayette, Zanesville.

Shreeve Sherman, lab, Scipio, Hicksville, O.

Shrimp Richard, f, 5, 80, $1815, Milan, Chamberlain.

Shugar Wm, f, 31, 136, $810, Milan, Chamberlain.

Shull Charles, 30, 100, $1700, Scipio, Hall's Corners.

Shull Jonathan, 29, 31, $260, Scipio, Hall's Corners.

Shull Leonora, 19, 90, $1485, Scipio, Hall's Corners.

Shull Nellie, 29, 29, $255, Scipio, Hall's Corners.

Shuman George W, Adams, Ft Wayne.

Shy Peter, f, 33, 80, $810, Monroe, Monroeville.

Sibel Clark, lab, Eel River, Ari.

Sibel Wm, f, 16, 100, $2090, Eel River, Churubusco.

Sibits Henry, f, 34, 61, $910, Cedar Creek, Leo.

Siebold Adam, f, 25, 70, $1465, Lake, Ft Wayne.

Siebold Bernard, f, 24, 40, $785, Lake, Ft Wayne.

Siebold Christopher, Wayne, Ft Wayne.

Siebold Henry, Lafayette, Nine Mile.

Siebold John, f, 6, 24, $465, Pleasant, Nine Mile.

Siebold Samuel, f, 33, 40, $865, Lafayette, Zanesville.

Siegel George, f, Monroe, Monroeville.

Siegel Philip, f, Monroe, Monroeville.

Sieger Frederick, Adams, Ft Wayne.

Siegmund Henry & J, Adams, Ft Wayne.

Siegmund H J, Adams, Fort Wayne.

Siegmund Jennie, Adams, Ft Wayne.

Silking Conrad jr, f t, Madison, Hoagland.

Silking Frederick, Madison, Hoagland.

Silvers Edward, Jackson, Edgerton.

Simcoe David, f t, Aboite, Aboite.

Simcoe Sarah, f, 30, 10 $140, Aboite, Aboite.

Simmer Calvin, f, 4, 40, $440, Monroe, Monroeville.

Simmerman Lydia, f, 27, 42, $715, Aboite, Ft Wayne.

Simmers Daniel W, f, 22, 80, $1900, Aboite, Ft Wayne.

Simon Solomon, f, 5, 225, $5005, Perry, Huntertown.

Simons Eli, f, 18, 48, $1385, Milan, Thurman.

Simons G L, Perry, Huntertown.

Simons Jacob, f, 18, 1, $180, Monroe, Monroeville.

Simons James, Perry, Huntertown.

Simons John V, f, 22, 20, $195, Monroe, Monroeville.

Simons L H, Monroe, Monroeville.

Simons M W, f, 23, 89, $5610, Wayne, Plymouth.

Simons Oscar A (est of), 13, 16½, $1540, Wayne.

Simons Wm R, f, Monroe, Monroeville.

Simonton Catherine, Lafayette, Zanesville.

Simonton Frederick, Lafayette, Zanesville.

Sims Thomas W, Lake, Arcola.

Sims Wm, f, 8, 80, $1065, Madison, Maples.

John Pressler, Mantels, Grates and Tile Floor.
Columbia, Barr and Dock Streets.

Sims W S, Madison, Maples.

Sinel John F, Lake, Arcola.

Sinel Stephen, f, 22, 97, $1315, Lake, Arcola.

Singmaster Joseph,. f, 18, 69, $1920, Wayne, Ft Wayne.

Sinram Frederick, f, 26, 97, $2220, Adams, Soest.

Sites Albert, Lafayette, Roanoke.

Sites Emanuel, Lake, Arcola.

Sites Milton, lab, Wayne, Ft Wayne.

Sites Malachi, f, 8, 235, $4395, Lafayette, Aboite.

Sitten Joseph, Adams, Fort Wayne.

Sitten Joseph, f, 7, 40, $325, Jackson, New Haven.

Skatulla Charles, $815, Wayne, Ft Wayne.

Skellinger Sylvester, Milan, Harlan.

Slater Alfred, Wayne, Fort Wayne.

Slater John, f, 31, ½, $80, Eel River, Churubusco.

Slater Wm H, f t, Pleasant, Sheldon.

Slatoper Felician, f, 7, 20, $3505, Adams, Ft Wayne.

Slatoper F & D L, f, 7, 1, $280, Adams, Ft Wayne.

Slattery Arthur, f, Monroe, Monroeville.

Slattery M & Rebecca, f, 22, 100, $900, Monroe, Dixon, O.

Slaugh John, Wayne, Fort Wayne.

Sledd Martha B, f, 110, $4285, Wayne, Ft Wayne.

Sledd Samuel D, f, 12, ½, $380, Lafayette, Nine Mile.

Slemmer Henry, f, Monroe, Monroeville.

Slemmer Philip W, f, Monroe, Monroeville.

Sloffer Aaron, f, 1, 80, $1220, Eel River, Ari.

Sloffer Aaron jr, f, 1, 154, $2240, Eel River, Ari.

Sloffer Aaron J, f, 6, 12, $210, Perry, Huntertown.

Sloffer B F, f t, Eel River, Ari.

Sloffer Henry, f, 3, 40, $100, Eel River, Ari.

Sloffer John, f t, Eel River, Ari.

Sloffer Rebecca, f, 1, 28, $505, Eel River, Ari.

Sloffer Wm, f, 1, 40, $815, Eel River, Ari.

Sloffer Wm H & C W, f, 1, 28, $370, Eel River, Ari.

Small Albert J, f, Maumee, Woodburn.

Small Alberta E, f, 21, 55, $960, Jackson, New Haven.

Small Almira, Marion, Poe.

Small Daniel L, Marion, Hoagland.

Small Franklin, Marion, Poe.

Small John, Adams, Fort Wayne.

Small John, f, 21, 426, $2880, Maumee, Woodburn.

Small John E, f t, Pleasant, Poe.

Small Lucy C, f, 21, 55, $960, Jefferson, New Haven.

Small Marion F, f, 19, 4, $230, Madison, Hoagland.

Small Robert, f, 26, 80, $1905, Marion, Poe.

Smaltz George H, f t, 22, 80, $1700, Aboite, Ft Wayne.

Smaltz Noah A, lab, Aboite, Ft· Wayne.

Smith Mrs Amelia, Wayne, Ft Wayne.

Smith Amherst P, Milan, Chamberlain.

Smith Andrew B, f, Maumee,· Antwerp, O.

Smith Andrew J, f, 13, 80, $1255, Lake, Ft Wayne.

Smith Anna A, gardener, 21, 101, $2945, Wayne, Fort Wayne.

Smith Asa, Milan, Chamberlain.

Smith B W, Wayne, Fort Wayne.

Smith Catherine, f, 31, 20, $300, Monroe, Monroeville.

Smith Charles H, f, 26, 77, $1785, Adams, Ft Wayne.

Smith Charles H, Lake, Arcola.

Smith David, gen store, Cedar Creek, Hursh.

Smith David C, Adams, New Haven.

Smith David P, f, 15, 40, $655, Milan, Chamberlain.

Smith David S, f t, Eel River, Ari.

Smith Dean, Lake, Arcola.

Smith Elisha, f, 4, 157, $2050, Lake, Ft Wayne.

Smith Enoch, Pleasant, Sheldon.

Smith Ephraim, f t, Aboite, Aboite.

Smith Finley, f, 30, 180, $3015, Pleasant, Sheldon.

Smith Francis E, f t, Pleasant, Poe.

Smith Franklin, Lake, Arcola.

Smith Franklin A, Milan, Chamberlain.

Smith Frederick, saloon, ¾, $285, Wayne, Ft Wayne.

Smith George, f, 31, 95, $1230, Jefferson, Maples.

Smith George T, lab, Pleasant, Sheldon.

Smith Henry, f, 8, 80, $1560, Marion, Poe.

Smith Henry, Milan, Chamberlain.

Smith Henry A, Adams, Ft Wayne.

Smith Henry W, Lafayette, Roanoke.

Smith Hulda, Eel River, Wallen.

Smith Jacob, f, 32, 40, $790, Pleasant, Sheldon.

Smith Jacob, f, 17, 5, $185, Perry, Huntertown.

Smith Jacob A, f, 30, 40, $610, Pleasant, Sheldon.

Smith James B, Wayne, Ft Wayne.

Smith James L, Adams, Fort Wayne.

Smith James W, f, 14, 10, $165, Madison, Monroeville.

Smith Jarvis M, f, 31' 45, $675, Eel River, Churubusco.

Smith John, Cedar Creek, Cedarville.

Smith John, f, 34, 106, $2475, Adams, Ft Wayne.

Smith John C, Marion, Poe.

Smith John F, Milan, Chamberlain.

Smith John K, Lafayette, Myhart.

Smith John M, f, 36, 280, $4035, Madison, Monroeville.

Smith John W, f, 19, 18, $240, Lafayette, Aboite.

Smith Jonas, Pleasant, Sheldon.

Smith Joseph, Milan, Chamberlain.

Smith Joseph, f, 9, 80, $1485, Marion, Poe.

Smith Joseph L, f, 30, 65, $1265, Madison, Hoagland.

Smith Josiah, f, 7, 58, $1050, Eel River, Churubusco.

Smith J, lab, Monroe, Monroeville.

Smith J W, Adams, Fort Wayne.

Smith J W F, f, 36, 40, $765, Lafayette, Sheldon.

Smith L O, genl store, Pleasant, Sheldon.

Smith Margaret, Adams, Ft Wayne.

Smith Margaret, f, 36, 80, $1520, Lake, Arcola.

Smith Maria, Madison, Hoagland.

Smith Marion, f, 33, 115, $2075, Marion, Poe.

Smith Mary, f, 5, 15, $210, Lake, Arcola.

Smith Mary A, f, 31, 59, $1040, Eel River, Churubusco.

Smith Matthias, Milan, Chamberlain.

Smith Milton A, Madison, Hoagland.

Smith Minnie, Wayne, Fort Wayne.

Smith Nathan, f, 5, 120, $1885, Lake, Arcola.

Smith Otis B, f t, Eel River, Churubusco.

Smith O C, f, 30, 40, $675, Pleasant, Sheldon.

Smith Peter, lab, Monroe, Monroeville.

Smith Peter, f, 32, 80, $1885, Adams, Ft Wayne.

Smith Philip P, Adams, New Haven.

Smith R, Wayne, Ft Wayne.

Smith Samuel, Adams, Fort Wayne.

Smith Samuel, f, 12, 160, $3270, Perry, Collingwood.

Smith Suddo, Lake, Arcola.

Smith S S, f, 21, 88, $1365, Lake, Arcola.

Smith Theodore, Milan, Chamberlain.

Smith Wm, gardener, Wayne, Ft Wayne.

Smith Wm, f, 8, 80, $1660, Marion, Poe.

Smith Wm E, f t, Eel River, Churubusco.

Smith Wm V, f, 4, 29, $675, Eel River, Ari.

Smith Wilson W, f, 32, 147, $2865, Marion, Poe.

Smith W A, Adams, Fort Wayne.

Smith W A, Perry, Huntertown.

Smith & Giddings, f, 11, 480, $8985, Lafayette, Myhart.

Smithers Charles, Lake, Arcola.

Smithey Homer, Marion, Hoagland.

Smithley Ann, f, 22, 110, $2050, Marion, Hoagland.

Smithley Enos C, f, 22, 46. $895, Marion, Hoagland.

Smithley F W & W, 21, 20, $250, Scipio.

Smithley George, Marion, Poe.

Smithley George, f, 27, 6, $115, Marion, Hoagland.

Smithley George E, f, 27, 42, $885, Marion, Hoagland.

Smithley Warren, Madison, Hoagland.

Snearly George F, Lafayette, Myhart.

Snearly John, Lafayette, Myhart.

Snider Harry, Lake, Arcola.

Snider Herman, Jackson,
Edgerton.

Snider W J, Perry, Hun-
tertown.

Snisher Solomon (est of), f,
2, 95, $825, Maumee, Ant-
werp, O.

Snitzler Peter, f t, Pleasant,
Sheldon.

Snyder Ann M, f, 28, 10,
$210, Pleasant, Sheldon.

Snyder A & J M, 2, 40, $725,
St Joseph, Fort Wayne.

Snyder Benjamin, f, 26, 80,
$1205, Jefferson, Monroe-
ville.

Snyder Charles, Milan, Harlan.

Snyder Daniel, f, 9, 7, $100,
Milan, Chamberlain.

Snyder Devid, f, 35, 40,
$430, Jefferson, Monroe-
ville.

Snyder Edward, f, 10, 32,
$645, Eel River, Ari.

Snyder Elizabeth, f, 34, 21,
$370, Pleasant, Sheldon.

Snyder George, f, 3, 164,
$3595, Aboite, Arcola.

Snyder Harrison, f, 11, 27,
$585, Perry, Collingwood.

Snyder Harry, f t, Aboite, Ft
Wayne.

Snyder Henry, f, 2, 35, $590,
Milan, Harlan.

Snyder John W, f, 35, 80,
$1465, Pleasant, Sheldon.

Snyder Jonathan, Milan, Harlan.

Snyder Louisa M, Wayne, Ft
Wayne.

Snyder Marietta, f, 9, 6, $80,
Milan, Chamberlain.

Snyder Mary, f, 30, 6, $120,
Eel River, Ari.

Snyder Mary, f, 30, 6, $95,
Jefferson, Monroeville.

Snyder Monroe, f, 2, 5, $30,
Maumee, Antwerp, O.

Snyder Nicholas, f, 13, 60,
$1575, Adams, New Haven.

Snyder Philip, Marion, Poe.

Snyder Philip, f, 22, 280,
$4355, Marion, Poe.

Snyder Preston H, f, 32, 151,
$2880, Marion, Poe.

Snyder Samuel, f, 30, 77,
$1035, Lake, Arcola.

Snyder Samuel E, f t, Aboite,
Fort Wayne.

Snyder Solomon(reserve),163,
$3455, Marion, Poe.

Snyder Solomon jr, f, 29, 89,
$1765, Marion, Poe.

Snyder Susan, f, 2, 17, $245,
Milan, Harlan.

Soest Christian, f, 10, 120,
$2375, Marion, Soest.

Soest George, Marion, Soest.

Soest Louis, f, 3, 2, $190,
Marion, Soest.

Soest Wm, f, 11, 10, $1020,
Marion, Soest.

Soest Wm jr, Marion, Soest.

Solgy Conrad, Perry, Huntertown.

Soliday Lucy, f, 22, 23, $340,
Lake, Arcola.

Solomon Christian, f, 32, 33,
$530, Perry, Academy.

Solon George P, Lake, Ar-
cola.

Solon John, f, 20, 120, $2175,
Lake, Arcola.

Solon John W, Lake, Arcola.

Solway Charles, lab, Monroe,
Monroeville.

Somers John W, Madison,
Monroeville.

CHARLES BOWMAN, No. 18 Harrison Street. **Saw Gumming,** FILING and SETTING.

790   R. L. POLK & CO.'S

Somers Joseph, f, 30, 97, $1485, Madison, Hoagland.
Sommers Ambrose D, f, 6, 33, $790,Eel River,Churubusco
Sommers Caroline J, f, 24, 40, $505, Cedar Creek, Harlan.
Sommers Charles F, f, 3, 38, $645, Lafayette, Nine Mile.
Sommers Christian, f, Cedar Creek, Harlan.
Sommers Christian jr, f, 36, 160, $2835, Cedar Creek, Harlan.
Sommers C F, f, 13, 20, $285, Lafayette, Nine Mile.
Sommers Eli, f, 36, 131, $2755, Cedar Creek, Harlan.
Sommers Henry, f, 36, 59, $1205, Pleasant, Poe.
Sommers James B, f, 27, 131, $2205, Cedar Creek,Harlan.
Sommers Levi, f, 25,60,$1100, Pleasant, Poe.
Sommers Perry, f t, Pleasant, Poe.
Sommers Simon, f, 21, 40, $800, Marion, Poe.
Sordelet August, f, 23, 80, $1520, Lake, Arcola.
Sordelet A & F J, f, 35, 49, $950, Perry, Ft Wayne.
Sordelet Frank, 5, 55, $815, St Joseph, Ft Wayne.
Sordelet Jacques, f, 11, 40, $295, Jefferson, Dawkins.
Soren Rev E S, 7, 113, $2575, St Joseph, Ft Wayne.
Sorg Anton, Marion, Hoagland.
Sorg Charles, Marion, Poe.
Sorg Henry, Marion, Poe.
Sorg John (estate of), f, 8, 79, $1465, Marion, Poe.
Sorg John (reserve), 88,$1730, Marion, Poe.

Sorg John B, f, 8, 20, $330, Marion, Poe.
Sorg John G, f, 11, 116, $2390, Pleasant, Sheldon.
Sorg John W, f, 16, 570, $8440, Marion, Poe.
Sorg John M jr, Marion, Poe.
Sorg John M A, Marion, Poe.
Sorg Joseph L, f (reserve), 80, $1555, Pleasant, Sheldon.
Sorg Joseph L, f, 19, 121, $2580, Marion, Poe.
Sorg Peter, f, 20, 160, $2225, Pleasant, Sheldon.
Sorg Theodore, f, 11, 97, $1915, Pleasant, Sheldon.
Sorgen Frederick B, f, 9, 60, $695, Monroe, Monroeville.
Sorgen James F, f, 4, 80, $1040,Monroe, Monroeville.
Souder Elizabeth, 14, 30, $610, Cedar Creek, Leo.
Souder Henry, f, 23, 100, $2105, Cedar Creek, Leo.
Souder Jacob, f, 10, 181, $3210, Cedar Creek, Leo.
Souder Jacob jr, f, 34, 46, $630, Cedar Creek, Leo.
Souder Jonas, f, 2, 60, $990, Cedar Creek, Leo.
Souder Samuel, lab, Cedar Creek, Leo.
Soule Wm T, f t, Cedar Creek, Leo.
Souser Oliver, f, 14, 20, $245, Milan, Harlan.
Sovine Eudora, 32, 41, $1760, St Joseph, Ft Wayne.
Sovine Frederick, f, 34, 35, $1005, Eel River, Fort Wayne.
Sowers Daniel, f, 8, 76, $1125, Scipio, Hicksville, O.
Sowers Wm, f, 6, 50, $875, Scipio, Hicksville, O.

Spacht Mary M, 15, $20, Wayne, Ft Wayne.

Spangler Frederick, f, 30, 80, $1665, Marion, Poe.

Spangler George B, f, 30, 80, $1905, Marion, Poe.

Spangler Mary, 14 1¼, $25, Wayne, Ft Wayne.

Spangler Nancy, Marion, Poe.

Spaulding Adeline S, dairy, Wayne, Ft Wayne.

Spaulding N R, f, Monroe, Monroeville.

Spaulding Sarah, f, 5, 120, $1575, Monroe, Monroeville.

Speaker Frank, f, Maumee, Woodburn.

Speaker Rosa, Maumee, Woodburn.

Spear A, Wayne, Ft Wayne.

Spencer Leverette L, f, 14, 20, $205, Milan, Harlan.

Spencer Wm H, f, 5, 25, $445, Pleasant, Sheldon.

Spenly Frank, f, 16, 26, $865, Wayne, Ft Wayne.

Spenly Martin, f, 16, 14, $925, Wayne, Ft Wayne.

Spenly Martin J, f, 16, 15, $565, Wayne Ft Wayne.

Spereisen Joseph (estate of), f, 22, 42, $1145, Adams, Ft Wayne.

Spice John, Perry, Huntertown.

Spindler Nelson S, Milan, Chamberlain.

Spindler Wm A, f, 16, 80, $1700, Milan, Chamberlain.

Spitler Henry, f, 30, 80, $1415, Cedar Creek, Cedarville.

Spitler John, f t, Cedar Creek, Cedarville.

Spitler Levi, f, 29, 40, $505, Scipio, Linx, O.

Spitler Morton, f, Scipio, Hall's Corners.

Sprague Isaac C, f t, Madison, Monroeville.

Sprague Isaac E, f t, Madison, Monroeville.

Sprague Leroy, f, 21, 95, $1875, Milan, Chamberlain.

Sprague Lewis L, Madison, Monroeville.

Sprague Rundalla, f, 34, 126, $2005, Madison, Monroeville.

Sprague Wm R, f, 4, 40, 310, Monroe, Monroeville.

Spran Charles, f, 34, 100, $1195, Eel River, Fort Wayne.

Sprang Philip G, Marion.

Sprang Sarah, f, 36, 163, $2645, Pleasant, Sheldon.

Sprankle J C F, f, 8, 20, $650, Wayne, Fort Wayne.

Sprankle Martha, f, 28, 230, $2420, Aboite, Ft Wayne.

Springer Charles, f t, Pleasant, Sheldon.

Springer Charles A, lab, Pleasant, Sheldon.

Springer Daniel, f t, Pleasant, Sheldon.

Springer Ella & W S, 1, 20, $305, St Joseph, Ft Wayne.

Springer F A, f t, Pleasant, Sheldon.

Springer George D, lab, Pleasant, Sheldon.

Springer George F, f, 34, 60, $1060, Pleasant, Sheldon.

Springer George L, f, 34, 198, $3095, Pleasant, Sheldon.

Springer George W, f, 34, 129, $2005, Pleasant, Sheldon.

Springer Harry, 15, 40, $780, St Joseph, Fort Wayne.

Springer Henry, lab, Cedar Creek, Cedarville.

Springer H C, f, 33, 40, $905, Pleasant, Sheldon.

Springer Jacob (heirs), f, 20, 40, $550, Lake, Arcola.

Springer John F, f t, Pleasant, Sheldon.

Springer John W, f, 34, 179, $2805, Pleasant, Sheldon.

Springer Lavina, Lake, Arcola.

Springer Philopena, f t, Pleasant, Poe.

Squier J W, Perry, Wallen.

Squire Lafayette, f, 16, 116, $1415, Scipio, Linx, O.

Squire Platt E, lab, Scipio, Hall's Corners.

Sriner John, f, 3, 50, $1075, Aboite, Fort Wayne.

Stack James, Lake, Arcola.

Stahl Frederick, f, 3, 109, $2360, Aboite, Fort Wayne.

Stahlhut Charles, f, 23, 80, $1050, Lake, Arcola.

Stahlker John G, f, 15, 46, $3400, Wayne, Ft Wayne.

Staick Emil, St Joseph, Fort Wayne.

Stalder Christian, f, 13, 60, $1560, Cedar Creek, Leo.

Stalder C G, f t, Cedar Creek, Leo.

Stalder Jules, Jefferson, Dawkins.

Stalder Louis, Jefferson, Dawkins.

Stalder Peter, Jefferson, Dawkins.

Staley Bradley & Laura, f, 18, ¾, $10, Maumee, Woodburn.

Stanger Henry, f, 13, 2½, $655, Wayne, Fort Wayne.

Stapleton Frank, f t, Cedar Creek, Leo.

Stapleton Joshua, 4, 50, $1030, St Joseph, Fort Wayne.

Stapleton J & Ann, f, 33, 68, $1425, Cedar Creek, Cedarville.

Starehine Michael, f, Monroe, Monroeville.

Stark A L, Adams, New Haven.

Stark Mary, f, 1, ¾, $35, Adams, New Haven.

Starkweather Susan, f, 6, 90, $1480, Lake, Fort Wayne.

State Line Hoop Co, Jackson, Edgerton.

Stauder Amelia, f, 3, 168, $1920, Perry, Huntertown.

Staufer Absalom, f, 17, 79, $1515, Milan, Chamberlain.

Staufer Daniel, f, 16, 40, $750, Milan, Chamberlain.

Staufer David, f, 11, 60, $600, Milan, Chamberlain.

Staufer Elizabeth, f, 16, 40, $770, Milan, Chamberlain.

Staufer Solomon, Milan, Harlan.

Steager John, f, 16, 120, $965, Jackson, Edgerton.

Stearns N L, Wayne, Fort Wayne.

Steegerwald John, Wayne, Fort Wayne.

Steel Malinda, f, 8, 60, $1090, Cedar Creek, Leo.

Steel Wm, f, Monroe, Monroeville.

Stein Polycarp, f, 17, 60, $1185, Pleasant, Sheldon.

Stein Robert J & Jane, Wayne, Fort Wayne.

Steinbacher John, f t, Pleasant, Sheldon.

Steinback Christian jr, Adams, Fort Wayne.

Steinbacher Anna, f, 35, 105, $1620, Pleasant, Sheldon.

Steinbacher Michael, f t, Pleasant, Sheldon.

Steinborn John, Adams, Ft Wayne.

Steinborn Justin, Adams, Ft Wayne.

Steinbrenner Robert, Wayne, Fort Wayne.

Steiner Eli, f, 27, 52, $1420, Cedar Creek, Cedarville.

Steiner Lydia, 27, 16, $345, Cedar Creek, Cedarville.

Steinkemper A, 26, 80, $2270, St Joseph, Fort Wayne.

Stellhorn August, f, Wayne, Ft Wayne.

Stellhorn Charles, f, Wayne, Ft Wayne.

Stellhorn Frederick, f, 26, 192, $5720, Wayne, Fort Wayne.

Stellhorn Henry, f, 7, 2, $1100, Adams, Ft Wayne.

Stellhorn Henry, f, 20, 120, $1700, Milan, Goeglein.

Stellhorn John H, f, 35, 30, $870, Wayne, Ft Wayne.

Stellhorn Louis, Milan, Goeglein.

Stellhorn Wm, Adams, Fort Wayne.

Stephan Ellen, f, 25, 40, $665, Lafayette, Nine Mile.

Stephan Margaret, f, 26, 8, $115, Lafayette, Nine Mile.

Stephen Andrew, Milan, Gar Creek.

Stephen John, Lafayette, Zanesville.

Stephen John, f, 24, 60, $530, Milan, Gar Creek.

Stephen Samuel, Milan, Gar Creek.

Stephenson A L, f, Monroe, Monroeville.

Stephenson E & A, f, 8, 80, $1515, Monroe, Monroeville.

Stephenson James, f, Monroe, Monroeville.

Stephenson John M, f, 9, 80, $1055, Monroe, Monroeville.

Stephenson Mary E, f, 3, 80, $1060, Monroe, Monroeville.

Stephenson T L, f, Monroe, Monroeville.

Stephenson Wm, f, Monroe, Monroeville.

Sterling Alexander, f, 17, 80, $1390, Cedar Creek, Cedarville.

Sterling Allen, Perry, Huntertown.

Sterling Charles E, Perry, Huntertown.

Sterling Edgar, Perry, Ft Wayne.

Sterling George, Perry, Fort Wayne.

Sterling James C, f, 6, 660, $970, Cedar Creek, Collingwood,

Sterling Nancy, Perry, Huntertown.

Sterling Stephen, f, 1, 40, $455, Madison, Monroeville.

Sterling Wm J, Perry, Huntertown.

Sternheime Arthur S, f, 20, 92, $1405, Monroe, Monroeville.

Sterve Robert, Lake, Arcola.

Steury Albert, lab, Cedar Creek, Leo.

Steury Christian, lab, Cedar Creek, Leo.

Steury John, f, 25, 80, $1915, Cedar Creek, Leo.

Steury Peter, lab, Cedar Creek, Leo.

Stevens W H, f, 28, 1, $110, Lake, Arcola.

Stevenson A C, Maumee, Antwerp, O.

Stevenson George W, f, Maumee, Antwerp, O.

Stevenson W H, Maumee, Antwerp, O.

Stevick Jacob,f, Cedar Creek, Leo.

Stevick Jacob W, f, 20, 80, $1710, Cedar Creek, Cedarville.

Stevick John L, blacksmith, Cedar Creek, Cedarville.

Stevick Wm C, f, 80, $1470, Cedar Creek, Cedarville.

Stevick Wm W, saw mill, Cedar Creek, Leo.

Stevick & Hollopeter, saw mill, Cedar Creek, Leo.

Steward Benjamin, Maumee, Woodburn.

Stewart Jacob, f, 28, 80, $1455, Aboite, Ft Wayne.

Stewart John W, f, 16, 10, $225, Eel River, Heller's Corners.

Stewart J A, f t, Eel River, Churubusco.

Stiles Clifford, Adams, Fort Wayne.

Stirling Alexander, f, 25, 532, $10,425, Perry, Fort Wayne,

Stirling Eliza J, f, 18, 37, $1440, Perry, Huntertown.

Stirling Harriet L, f, 32, 80, $1375, Perry, Ft Wayne.

Stirling Jackson, f, 32, 80, $2035, Perry, Academy.

Stirling John G, Lake, Arcola.

Stirling J & C, f, 21, 39, $830, Perry, Collingwood.

Stirling Wilson R, f, 15, 163, $2705, Lake, Arcola.

Stock Ferdinand, f, 16, 57, $1320, Adams, Ft Wayne.

Stokes Mathew, Milan, Chamberlain.

Stoler Jacob, f, 5, 31, $925, Wayne, Ft Wayne.

Stoll Jacob, f t, Wayne, Ft Wayne.

Stolze Christian, f, 31, 67, $1495, Milan, Goeglein.

Stone I N & John R, f, 8, 106, $2480, Milan, Chamberlain.

Stone L E, Adams, Fort Wayne.

Stone Richard D, Adams, Ft Wayne.

Stone Solon, f, 23, 37, $805, Adams, New Haven.

Stone Thaddeus, f, 8, 34, $705, Milan, Chamberlain.

Stonebruck T A G, f t, Pleasant, Sheldon.

Stoneman Jacob, Jefferson, Maples.

Stoner Daniel W, Adams, Fort Wayne.

Stoop Samuel W, Adams, Ft Wayne.

Stopenhagan Charles, Adams, Fort Wayne.

Stoppenhagen F Christian, f, 5, 84, $690, Maumee, Woodburn.

Stouder Charles, f t, Aboite, Fort Wayne.

Stouder H T, Adams, Fort Wayne.

Stouder James H, f t, Aboite, Fort Wayne.

Stouder Simon W, f, 10, 80, $1905, Aboite, Ft Wayne.

Stouder Solomon B, f, 10, 119, $2600, Aboite, Fort Wayne.

Stout George W, f t, Madison, Hoagland.

Stout John, lab, Maumee, Woodburn.

Stover John, miller, Cedar Creek, Hursh.

Stover Wm F, Wayne, Fort Wayne.

Strack C F, sand, 2½, $75, Wayne, Fort Wayne.

Strass Morris, furniture, 18, ½, $20, Monroe, Monroeville.

Strasser Rupert, f, 13, 12½, $1370, Wayne, Ft Wayne.

Stratton J Q, Wayne, Fort Wayne.

Stratton Robert, Adams, Ft Wayne.

Stratton Robert L, 33, 1, $30, St Joseph, Fort Wayne.

Straughan Caroline J, f, 17, 86, $910, Monroe, Fort Wayne.

Straughan James C, f, 17, 73, $1280, Monroe, Ft Wayne.

Straughan Jesse R, f, 17, 252, $3930, Monroe, Ft Wayne.

Streeter Benjamin, f, 30, 34, $455, Scipio, Hall's Corners.

Streeter James, f t, Scipio, Antwerp, O.

Streetmatter S, Adams, Fort Wayne.

Strine Samuel, f t, Maumee, Woodburn.

Striver Jacob N, f, 19, 58, $970, Scipio, Hall's Corners.

Striver John E, f t, Scipio, Hall's Corners.

Striver Samuel, f, 32, 89, $850, Scipio, Hall's Corners.

Strodel John G, Adams, Fort Wayne.

Strodel Kate, saloon, Wayne, Fort Wayne.

Strong Amelia, f, 19, 3, $195, Eel River, Churubusco.

Strong Lewis, f t, Eel River, Churubusco.

Strong Mary, 6, 5, $95, St Joseph, Fort Wayne.

Stroup Elmer, lab, Eel River, Ari.

Stroup James, Lafayette, Roanoke.

Stuck Wm, Wayne, Fort Wayne.

Stuckey Christian, f, Cedar Creek, Leo.

Stuckey John, lab, Cedar Creek, Leo.

Stuckey Joseph, f, 3, 80, $1460, Cedar Creek, Leo.

Stuckey Moses, f t, Cedar Creek, Leo.

Stump Elmer W, Lafayette, Myhart.

Stump Jesse H, f, 18, 50, $1270, Lafayette, Myhart.

Stump Jonathan, f, 18, 50, $1605, Lafayette, Myhart.

Sturem C P, Adams, Fort Wayne.

Sturgeon A F, f, 17, 199, $4080, Eel River, Churubusco.

Sturgeon J K, Eel River, Churubusco.

Sturgis Mary C, f, 4, 9, $835, Wayne, Fort Wayne.

Sturm James, 33, 16, $315, St Joseph, Fort Wayne.

Election Slips. Headquarters for PERFECT SLIPS at JOHN F. EBY & CO'S., DETROIT

796   R. L. POLK & CO.'S

Sturm John, 33' 64, $1360, St Joseph, Fort Wayne.

Sturm John L, St Joseph, Ft Wayne.

Sullenborger C, Adams, Fort Wayne.

Sult George, Wayne, Fòrt Wayne.

Summers Caroline, f, 5, 80, $1515, Milan, Chamberlain.

Summers Charles, barber, Monroe, Monroeville.

Summers Frank, barber, Monroe, Monroeville.

Summers Harrison, f, 13, 80, $1155, Madison, Monroeville.

Summers Lewis,f t, Eel River, Churubusco.

Summers Mary C, milliner, Monroe, Monroeville.

Sunderland Ellen, f t, Aboite, Fort Wayne.

Surface Andrew, f, 17, 140, $4560, Perry, Huntertown.

Surface George, f, 3, 80, $1930, Perry, Collingwood.

Surface John W, f, 2, 120, $2830, Perry, Collingwood.

Surface Samuel, f, 2, 160, $3185, Perry, Collingwood.

Surface Stephen, f, 6, 80, $1495, Cedar Creek, Collingwood.

Sutorius Christian, Wayne, Fort Wayne.

Sutters Daniel, f, 14, 40, $700, Lafayette, Nine Mile.

Sutters Edward, f, 23, 160, $3045, Lafayette, Ft Wayne

Sutters Jacob, f, 14, 40, $660, Lafayette, Nine Mile.

Swain Nettie F, $1015, Wayne, Fort Wayne.

Swander John J, f, 8, 40, $785, Eel River, Churubusco.

Swank Anna A, f, 16, 32, $625, Pleasant, Sheldon.

Swank Christian, f, 25, 40, $645, Lafayette, Sheldon.

Swank Christian, f, Pleasant, Sheldon.

Swank Daniel, f, 16, 80, $1545, Pleasant, Sheldon.

Swank Irving, Perry, Huntertown.

Swank Mason, lab, Pleasant, Sheldon.

Swank Thomas, f, 22, 220, $3455, Pleasant, Sheldon.

Swank Thomas C, f, 33, $5, Pleasant, Sheldon.

Swartz Christian, f, 21, 82, $1485, Milan, Chamberlain.

Swartz David, Milan, Chamberlain.

Swartz Jacob S, Milan, Chamberlain.

Swartz John, f, 21, 81, $1670, Milan, Chamberlain.

Swartz John J, Milan, Chamberlain.

Swayne Samuel T, Adams, Fort Wayne.

Sweeny Joseph, f, 23, 10, $75, Maumee, Antwerp, O.

Sweeney Lucy J, f, 2, 20, $180, Jefferson, Gar Creek.

Sweet Daniel, f, 3, 40, $360, Maumee, Antwerp, O.

Sweet Francis, Lake, Arcola.

Sweet Joseph D, f t, Maumee, Woodburn.

Sweet Julian, f, Maumee, Antwerp, O.

Sweet Mary, f, 10, 40, $490, Maumee, Antwerp, O.

Sweet M, Marion, Root.

Sweet Warren, Madison, Hoagland.

Sweetzer James, f, 23, 618, $5890, Aboite.

Swift Alpheus, f, 8, 268, $5500, St Joseph, Fort Wayne.

Swift Catherine, f, 7, 30, $720, St Joseph, Ft Wayne.

Swift Isabella, f, 10, $190, St Joseph, Ft Wayne.

Swineheart Daniel, lab, Aboite, Ft Wayne.

Swineheart George W, f t, Aboite, Ft Wayne.

Swisher John, f, 32, 40, $630, Scipio, Hall's Corners.

Syndram Charles, f t, Wayne, Fort Wayne.

T

Taber Rosa A, f, 6, 40, $3985, Adams, Ft Wayne.

Taflinger George F, Wayne, Fort Wayne.

Taflinger Thomas, dairy, Wayne, Ft Wayne.

Tait George W, f, 31, 5⅔, $350, St Joseph, Ft Wayne.

Tam Jane, f, 13, 5, $450, Wayne, Ft Wayne.

Tapp John F F, f, 33, 146, $3465, St Joseph, Fort Wayne.

Tarr Elizabeth, f, 12, 20, $200, Madison, Monroeville.

Taylor Andrew J, lab, Pleasant, Sheldon.

Taylor Beal F, Wayne, Fort Wayne.

Taylor Charles, Jackson, Monroeville.

Taylor Charles, St Joseph, Fort Wayne.

Taylor Charles W, lab, Monroe, Dixon, O.

Taylor Edward, Jackson, Monroeville.

Taylor Fannie W, Adams, Ft Wayne.

Taylor George, f, 26, 190, $5610, Aboite, Ft Wayne.

Taylor Henry, lab, 18, 1, $130, Monroe, Monroeville.

Taylor H C, livery, Monroe, Monroeville.

Taylor Isaac Y, f, 12, 83, $985, Madison, Monroeville.

Taylor John, f, 32, 80, $790, Jackson, Monroeville.

Taylor John, f, 22, 29, $355, Monroe, Monroeville.

Taylor John, f, 23¼, $670, Wayne, Fort Wayne.

Taylor John M, f, 29, 548, $8470, Eel River, Churubusco.

Taylor J W, lab, Monroe, Monroeville.

Taylor Luther, lab, Monroe, Dixon, O.

Taylor Mahala A, Wayne, Ft Wayne.

Taylor Mary V, f, 24, 160, $3795, St Joseph, Thurman.

Taylor Nash, lab, Monroe, Dixon, O.

Taylor Oliver, f, 18, 2¾, $250, Monroe, Monroeville.

Taylor Susan W, lab, Pleasant, Sheldon.

Taylor Thomas, Monroe, Monroeville.

Taylor Wm C, Wayne, Fort Wayne.

Taylor Wm H, f, 19, 85, $1690, Monroe, Monroeville.

Taylor W W, f, 24, 40, $440, Madison, Monroeville.

Teegeder Frederick, lab, 13, 1⅘, $490, Wayne, Fort Wayne.

Tegeder Frederick, St Joseph, Fort Wayne.

Tegmeyer Anna et al, Wayne, Fort Wayne.

Teisman Gustave, Adams, Ft Wayne.

Ternet Amile, Jefferson, New Haven.

Ternet Charles, Jefferson, New Haven.

Ternet John, Jefferson, New Haven.

Teuchtenhagen A, f, 33, 40, $600, Milan, Gar Creek.

Tevis Henry, f, Pleasant, Poe.

Theye Ferdinand, f, 27, 80, $920, Milan, Gar Creek.

Thiebault J A, f t, Eel River, Heller's Corners.

Thiele Conrad, f, 26, 485, $7520, Pleasant, Sheldon.

Thiele Frederick, f, 23, 80, $1210, Lake, Fort Wayne.

Thiele Frederick O, f, 23,120, $1930, Pleasant, Sheldon.

Thiele Henry, f, 30, 79, $1245, Milan, Goeglein.

Thiele Wm, f, Pleasant, Poe.

Thimlar Charles, f, 10, 30, $435, Milan, Chamberlain.

Thimlar John, f, 9,112, $1850, Milan, Harlan.

Thimlar Theodore, f, 15, 107, $1700, Milan, Chamberlain.

Thomas A D, St Joseph, Ft Wayne.

Thomas Clarence, 30, 8, $105, Cedar Creek, Cedarville.

Thomas C L, f, 5, 38, $1890, Wayne, Ft Wayne.

Thomas Elizabeth, f, 1, 40, $620, Milan, Harlan.

Thomas Evelyn M, teacher, 30, 8, $105, Cedar Creek, Cedarville.

Thomas John, Milan, Harlan.

Thomas Levi, Jackson, Baldwin.

Thomas Magdalene, f, 1, 40, $595, Milan, Harlan.

Thomas Mahlon, f, Maumee, Harlan.

Thomas Mary L, f, 7, 40, $340, Maumee, Harlan.

Thomas Morgan, f, 8, 140, $1835, Jefferson, New Haven.

Thomas Morgan H, Jefferson, New Haven.

Thomas Nancy, 30, 48, $925, Cedar Creek, Cedarville.

Thomas Wm S & L, 29, 79, $1135, Cedar Creek, Cedarville.

Thompkinson Albert, Wayne, Ft Wayne.

Thompson Charles, lab, Maumee, Antwerp, O.

Thompson Frank J, Perry, Ft Wayne.

Thompson George E, Marion, Poe.

Thompson James, f, 6, 80, $1730, Marion, Poe.

Thompson Joseph O, f, 16, 40, $780, Lafayette, Myhart.

Thompson Mary, Lafayette, Myhart.

Thompson Wm, f t, Cedar Creek, Cedarville.

Thompson Wm, f, Maumee, Harlan.

Thompson Willis E, Jackson, Monroeville.

Thompson W H, f, 5, 80, $1755, Marion, Poe.

Thomson John, Milan, Gar Creek.

Thornton Stephen A, f, 18, 15, $1900, Perry, Wallen.

Thornton S A, f, 17, $150, Perry, Huntertown.

Builders' Hardware, PFEIFFER & SCHLATTER, 38 and 40 EAST COLUMBIA ST.

ALLEN COUNTY DIRECTORY. · 799

Thornton S H, Perry, Huntertown.

Threvey Charles W, f, 2, 20, $350, Pleasant, Sheldon.

Threvey John J (estate of), f, 24, 99, $1880, Pleasant, Sheldon.

Thurber Lewis E, f t, Pleasant, Sheldon.

Thurber Mark, f, 25, 40, $775, Pleasant, Sheldon.

Tibbett Barney, f, 11, 19, $680, Adams, New Haven.

Tibbett Herman, f, 11, 161, $4920, Adams, New Haven.

Tiegner Perry, Jackson, Edgerton.

Tielker Conrad, f, 16, 84, $2950, Wayne, Ft Wayne.

Tielker Henry, f, 16, 60, $1305, Wayne, Ft Wayne.

Tielker Henry F C, f, 16, 12, $710, Wayne, Ft Wayne.

Tielker Wm, f, 27, 100, $1225, Lake, Ft Wayne.

Tielking Frederick, Adams, Ft Wayne.

Tierman Thomas, f, 35, 146⅔, $2675, Cedar Creek, Leo.

Tierman Wm, lab, Cedar Creek, Leo.

Tilbury Henry, f, 80, $2715, Adams, Ft Wayne.

Tilbury Jasper, Adams, Fort Wayne.

Tilbury Margaret, f, 33, 55, $1210, St Joseph, Fort Wayne.

Tilbury Mary J, f, 29, 36, $505, Milan, Goeglein.

Tilden Charles L, f, 31, 80, $1500, Perry, Wallen.

Tilden E M, f, 31, 111, $1900, Perry, Wallen.

Till Michael, Lake, Duke.

Tillman John, f, 25, 120, $1715, Jefferson, Monroeville.

Tilton Sophia J, f, 25, 200, $1960, Milan, Gar Creek.

Timbrook James, saw mill, Cedar Creek, Cedarville.

Timme Henry, f, 18, 47, $915, Jefferson, New Haven.

Timmis Alonzo, mach, Wayne, Ft Wayne.

Timmis Jesse, Wayne, Fort Wayne.

Timmis Wm, gardener, Wayne, Ft Wayne.

Tinkham J P, f, 15, 26⅔, $615, St Joseph, Goeglein.

Tirsman Henry, f, 9, 20, $805, Adams, Ft Wayne.

Todd Abigail, f t, 18, 12, $220, Monroe, Monroeville.

Todd Asbury B, f, 24, 50, $650, Madison, Hoagland.

Todd Eli, f, 4, 39, $680, Madison, Maples.

Todd Elizabeth, Madison, Hoagland.

Todd Elmira, Madison, Hoagland.

Todd George B, Marion, Poe.

Todd James, f, 12, 40, $790, Aboite, Ft Wayne.

Todd Jesse W, Madison, Hoagland.

Todd John W, Madison, Monroeville.

Todd Martha W, f, 24, 10, $185, Madison, Ft Wayne.

Todd Martin, Jackson, Edgerton.

Todd Morgan, f, 19, 2, $230, Madison, Hoagland.

Todd Philip, Adams, New Haven.

Todd Samuel, Adams, New Haven.

Todd Wm W, f, 24, 10, $185, Madison, Monroeville.

Toler Jefferson, Wayne, Ft Wayne.

Tonkel August, Perry, Fort Wayne.

Tonkel Frank, St Joseph, Ft Wayne.

Tonkel George, f t, Cedar Creek, Cedarville.

Tonkel Henry, f, 30, 80, $1660, Cedar Creek, Cedarville.

Tonkel Henry, f, 25, 40, $695, Perry, Fort Wayne.

Tonkel H L, Perry, Fort Wayne.

Tonkel Joseph, f, 4, 50, $1060, St Joseph, Fort Wayne.

Tools Thomas E, Adams, Ft Wayne.

Toomey Patrick, Lake, Arcola.

Tope George W, Aboite.

Tourney August, f, 28, 90, $1635, Perry, Fort Wayne.

Townsend Caleb, f, 25, 62, $910, Jefferson, Zulu.

Townsend George jr, Jefferson, Zulu.

Townsend George D, f, 20, 160, $1275, Jackson, Zulu.

Townsend Josephine, f, 23, 80, $1185, Jefferson, Zulu.

Townsend Wm, Jefferson, Zulu.

Townsend Wm S, f, 25, 40, $440, Jefferson, Zulu.

Tracy David A, Adams, Ft Wayne.

Tracy George, Lake, Arcola.

Tracy Jacob W, Adams, Ft Wayne.

Tracy John, Adams, Fort Wayne.

Tracy John A, Adams, Fort Wayne.

Tracy Mary, f, 32, 160, $2225, Lake, Arcola.

Tracy Mary A, Lake, Arcola.

Trahin Jules, f, 21, 40, $850, Lake, Arcola.

Trahin Matilda, f, 21, $650, Lake, Arcola.

Trainor David H, Lafayette, Myhart.

Trainor Wm, f, 16, 90, $1630, Lafayette, Myhart.

Trautman Edward, f, 7, 43, $590, Madison, Maples.

Trautman Frederick, f t, Aboite, Fort Wayne.

Trautman Jacob, f, 29, 80, $1465, Aboite, Ft Wayne.

Trautman John, lab, Aboite, Fort Wayne.

Travelbee Henry, Milan, Ft Wayne.

Treace Franklin, f, 19, 84, $1715, Cedar Creek, Cedarville.

Treace George A, f, 32, 53, $1125, Cedar Creek, Cedarville.

Treace George C, Cedar Creek, Cedarville.

Treace George H, f, 24, 32, $190, Perry, Fort Wayne.

Treace George W, f, 31, 228, $4170, Cedar Creek, Cedarville.

Treace G W & J L, f, 32, 84, $1800, Cedar Creek, Cedarville.

Treace Henry A, f, 24, 120, $1555, Perry, Ft Wayne.

Treace John L, f t, Cedar Creek, Cedarville.

Treace Robert, f, 24, 80, $1145, Perry, Ft Wayne.

Treace Wm W, f, 21, 80, $2125, Cedar Creek, Cedarville.

Trease Dayton S, St Joseph, Ft Wayne,

Trease G W, f, 4, 93, $1945, St Joseph, Ft Wayne.

Tresh Michael A, f, 36, 40, $665, Pleasant, Sheldon.

Treuchet Frank, Jefferson, Zulu.

Treuchet Joseph, Jefferson, Zulu.

Treut Thomas S, Jefferson, New Haven.

Trew George, 14, 1, $160, Wayne, Ft Wayne.

Trick George M, f, 9, 40, $710, Pleasant, Sheldon.

Trick John, f, 9, 78, $1850, Pleasant, Sheldon.

Trier Herman, f, 29, 160, $3335, Adams, Ft Wayne.

Trier Martin, f, 17, 89, $1645, Jefferson, New Haven.

Trier Paul, f, 32, 159, $3670, Adams, Ft Wayne.

Trier Peter, f, 27, 80, $1870, St Joseph, Goeglein.

Trimple Jacob, Wayne, Fort Wayne.

Trimple Peter, Wayne, Ft Wayne.

Triskett Charles A, Wayne, Ft Wayne,

Trougott Victor, f, 31, 20, $160, Jackson, Monroeville.

Troutman Peter, f, 9, 40, $770, Marion, Soest.

Troutner Henry, f, 34, 40, $735, Adams, Ft Wayne.

Troutner John, f, 12, 2½, $325, Adams, New Haven.

True Frederick, Wayne, Ft Wayne.

True George, Wayne, Fort Wayne.

True John, Wayne, Fort Wayne.

Truman James N, Lake, Arcola.

Trutwig Herman, Wayne, Ft Wayne.

Tschanner Christian, f, 6, 80, $1875, Aboite, Ft Wayne.

Tucker E G, Perry, Huntertown,

Tucker George W, f, 11, 41, $810, Perry, Huntertown.

Tucker George W, lab, Eel River, Ari.

Tucker Isaac T, f, 36, 79, $1130, Eel River, Wallen.

Tucker Jacob B, f, 15, 80, $1680, Perry, Huntertown.

Tucker Solomon, f, 4, ⅔, $35, Eel River, Wallen.

Tucker Thomas, f, 16, 96, $2240, Perry, Huntertown.

Tulbert Charles, Jackson, Edgerton.

Turner Asa, f, 33, 77, $1660, Aboite, Ft Wayne.

Turner Daniel, lab, Eel River, Huntertown.

Turner H R, f, 19, 285, $7550, Marion, Poe.

Tussing Rev A H, Cedar Creek, Cedarville.

Tustison Henry, f and tile mill, 5, 10, $180, Scipio, Hicksville, O.

Tustison Oliver, f, 2, 48, $1875, Adams, New Haven.

Tustison Sarah, f, 2, 48, $225, Adams, New Haven.

Tyler Justin A, 14, 1, $105, Wayne, Ft Wayne.

Tytus M E, f, 5, 6⅘, $340, Adams, Ft Wayne.

John Pressler, Hot Air and Hot Water Furnaces; Columbia, Barr and Dock Streets.

802 R. L. POLK & CO.'S

U

Ulery John, Marion, Hoagland.

Ulery Levi, f, 23, 160, $2985, Marion, Hoagland.

Ulery Nelson, Marion, Hoagland.

Ullery John, f, 30, ¾, $5, Madison, Hoagland.

Ullery Joseph, Madison, Hoagland.

Ulmer Henry, Jefferson, New Haven.

Ulmer Theodore, Wayne, Ft Wayne.

Umstead Elizabeth, f, 5, $585, Wayne, Ft Wayne.

Urbine Cassimer, f, 19, 160, $2670, Jefferson, Maples.

Urbine Ellen, f, 33, 40, $515, Jefferson, Maples.

Urbine Frank, Perry, Huntertown.

Urbine Joseph D, f, 33, 85, $1130, Perry, Academy.

Urbine Joseph N, f, 27, 160, $3170, Perry, Ft Wayne.

Urbine Louis, Jefferson, Maples.

Urbine May, f, 26, 38, $545, Jefferson, Maples.

Urbine Peter, f, 27, 22, $290, Jefferson, Zulu.

Utley Della, f, 1, 40, $725, St Joseph, Ft Wayne.

V

Vachon E, Pleasant, Sheldon.

Vachon Thomas, f, 25, 20, $445, Pleasant, Sheldon.

Vachon Vidal, Pleasant, Sheldon.

Vachon Vidal jr, f t, Pleasant, Sheldon.

Vachon Zaccheus, f t, Pleasant, Sheldon.

Vainet John L, f, 7, 1, $105, St Joseph, Fort Wayne.

Valdemeier Peter, f, 10, 70, $1105, St Joseph, Fort Wayne.

Valentine Charles, lab, Monroe, Monroeville.

Valentine Jackson, f, 33, 199, $3820, Eel River, Heller's Corners.

Valentine J W, f, 2, 224, $2390, Lake, Wallen.

Valentine Marie, Wayne, Ft Wayne.

Valentine Peter, Adams, Ft Wayne.

Valkert Samuel, f, 20, 60, $755, Scipio, Hall's Corners.

Vallmer Frederick, f, 23, 80, $2055, St Joseph, Ft Wayne.

Van Alstine Frank, Aboite, Ft Wayne.

Vanator Jasper, f, 14, 72, $1470, Cedar Creek, Leo.

Van Buskirk Dr A E, 18, ¼, $15, Monroe, Ft Wayne.

Van Buskirk Herman, Madison, Hoagland.

Van Buskirk John W, Madison, Monroeville.

Van Buskirk Joseph, Madison, Hoagland.

Van Buskirk Lenford, f, 24, 70, $1030, Madison, Monroeville.

Van Buskirk M E and J N, f, 25, 27, $545, Madison, Monroeville.

VanCamp Henry, harnessmaker, Cedar Creek, Leo.

VanCamp James, Cedar Creek, Leo.

Vanderly George J, f, 19, 80, $825, Jackson, Zulu.

Stahn & Heinrich, Leading Dealers in ARTISTS' MATE-RIALS AND DRAUGHTING INSTRU-MENTS. 116 Calhoun Street.

ALLEN COUNTY DIRECTORY.   803

Vanderpool John, f, 28, 5, $105, Lake, Arcola.

Vandevau Christian, St Joseph, Goeglein.

Vandevau Frederick, St Joseph, Goeglein.

Vandevau Herman, f, 24, 80, $1700, St Joseph, Goeglein.

Vandevau Jacob, f, 4, 168, $1555, Milan.

Vandevau Jacob, f, 36, 160, $4190, St Joseph, Goeglein.

Vandevau Peter W, f, Maumee, Woodburn.

Vandewater Eliza J, f, 29, 80, $985, Lake, Arcola.

Vandewater James, f, Lake, Arcola.

Vandolah Benjamin, f, 14, 180, $2375, Perry, Huntertown.

Vandolah James, f, 15, 160, $2350, Perry, Huntertown.

Vandolah Thomas, f, 12, 40, $660, Perry, Huntertown.

Vandolah Thomas J, f, 13, 245, $3485, Perry, Huntertown.

Van Dorn Abraham C, f, 31, 72, $840, Lake, Arcola.

Van Hoozen George, f, 18, 40, $1190, Aboite, Ft Wayne.

Van Hoozen John, Aboite, Aboite.

Van Hoozen Nathaniel, f, 17, 160, $3245, Aboite, Fort Wayne.

Van Horn Albert, St Joseph, Fort Wayne.

Van Horn George, f, 36, 80, $1270, Adams, Maples.

Van Horn George, Marion, Hoagland.

Van Horn George, St Joseph, Fort Wayne.

Van Horn Isaac, Madison, Monroeville.

Van Horn John, Jackson, Zulu.

Van Horn Mary, Marion, Poe.

Van Horn M C, Marion, Poe.

Van Horn Sarah C, f, 36, 40, $790, Madison, Monroeville.

Van Horn Silas, Adams, Maples.

Van Horn Wm, Jefferson, Maples.

Van Horn Wm, f, 15, 40, $425, Madison, Monroeville.

Van Horn Wm H, Marion, Hoagland.

Van Horn Wilson, Marion, Hoagland.

Van Meter Eugene, Adams, Fort Wayne.

Vanmeter George, Wayne, Fort Wayne.

Vanopen Barney, f, 1, 80, $665, Jefferson, Gar Creek.

Van Wormer Wm A, f, 29, 33, $570, Lafayette, Zanesville.

Vanzile Alexander, f, 12, 164, $3255, Cedar Creek, Hursh.

Vanzile Azariah, f, 6, 60, $1404, Cedar Creek, Hursh.

Vanzile Daniel, f, 7, 120, $1710, Cedar Creek, Hursh.

Vanzile David, f t, Cedar Creek, Hursh.

Vanzile J M, f, 18, 18, $275, Cedar Creek, Hursh.

Vanzile Thomas J, f, 18, 18, $275, Cedar Creek, Leo.

Vardaman Walter, Pleasant, Sheldon.

Vaughan Charles L, Aboite, Arcola.

Vaughan James M, f, 5, 37, $780, Aboite, Ft Wayne.

Vaughn Henry, Lake, Arcola.

Vaughn John, Marion, Poe.

Vaughn Lucinda, f, 28, 30, $670, Marion, Poe.

Vaughn Marietta, f, 28, 30, $580, Marion, Poe.

Vaughn Simon J, f, 28, 29, $545, Marion, Poe.

Veit Philip, f, 5, 136, $2075, Madison, Ft Wayne.

Veit Philip J, Adams, Fort Wayne.

Velley Aaron, f t, Cedar Creek, Leo.

Velley George, f t, Cedar Creek, Leo.

Venderly Louis, Jackson, Zulu.

Verner Edwin E, Adams, Ft Wayne.

Vernon Edward E, Adams, Fort Wayne.

Vesey Allen J, f, 4, 147, $1510, Lake, Arcola.

Viberg Conrad, f, 8, 219, $3775, Cedar Creek, Leo.

Vieland Frederick, Jackson, Edgerton.

Vincent Wm, Wayne, Fort Wayne.

Vining James W, f, 19, 82, $2785, St Joseph, Fort Wayne.

Violand Adelaide, Adams, Fort Wayne.

Violand Joseph, Adams, Ft Wayne.

Violet Henry, Adams, Fort Wayne.

Vizard Wm, f, 27, 95, $1165, Monroe, Dixon, O.

Vodde Bernard J, f, 13, 70, $1965, Adams, New Haven.

Voelker F, Adams, Fort Wayne.

Voetter Julius, f, 6, 126, $4005, Wayne, Ft Wayne.

Vogel Andrew, f, 7, 6, $245, Adams, Ft Wayne.

Vogel Frank B, Adams, Fort Wayne.

Vogley Andrew, f, 7, 2, $290, Adams, Ft Wayne.

Voinet Francis, Perry, Huntertown.

Voirol August, f, 9, $560, Jefferson, New Haven.

Voirol Florence, f, 18, 120, $910, Jackson, Zulu.

Voirol Frank, f, 17, 80, $455, Jackson, Zulu.

Voirol Jules, f, 19, 40, $520, Jackson, New Haven.

Voirol Melicia, f, 9, 39, $645, Jefferson, New Haven.

Voirol Wm, f, 30, 80, $695, Jackson, Zulu.

Volrider Christian, Wayne, Fort Wayne.

Voltz Emanuel, f, 22, 80, $1265, Lafayette, Zanesville.

Voltz John, Lafayette, Nine Mile.

Volz Anton, Wayne, Fort Wayne.

Volz Balthaser, Wayne, Fort Wayne.

Volz Franz, Wayne, Fort Wayne.

Volz Henry, Adams, Fort Wayne.

Vordermark Christian (est of), f, 7, 12⅔, $2310, Adams, Fort Wayne.

Vordermark E, Adams, Fort Wayne.

Votrie Frank J, Wayne, Ft Wayne.

Votrie James, Madison, Hoagland.

Vuilmine Eugene C, f, 6, 40, $760, St Joseph, Ft Wayne.

W

Wacker Anton, 13, 2⅘, $1185, Wayne, Fort Wayne.

Waddington Benjamin C, Adams, Fort Wayne.

Wagner Annetta, 33, 52, $490, Scipio, Hicksville, O.

Wagner Eliza, Adams, Fort Wayne.

Wagner George, f, 36, 40, $610, Adams, Maples.

Wagner George, Jefferson, New Haven.

Wagner Jacob, f, 1, 40, $530, Madison, Monroeville.

Wagner Jacob, f t, Wayne, Fort Wayne.

Wagner Joseph B, lab, Pleasant, Sheldon.

Wagner Josiah B, Perry, Huntertown.

Wagner Julian, Wayne, Ft Wayne.

Wagner Martin, f, 30, 100, $2040, Pleasant, Sheldon.

Wagner Peter, f, 24, 160, $5175, Wayne, Ft Wayne.

Wagner Philip, St Joseph, Ft Wayne.

Wagner Wm D, f t, Pleasant, Sheldon.

Wake Daniel, lab, Pleasant, Sheldon.

Wake Francis M, lab, Pleasant, Nine Mile.

Wake John, f, 19, 34, $605, Pleasant, Nine Mile.

Wake Loretta, f, 19, 34, $570, Pleasant, Nine Mile.

Wake Wm, tel operator, Pleasant, Sheldon.

Walbold George, f t, Cedar Creek, Cedarville.

Walbold John, f, 74, $1945, Cedar Creek, Cedarville.

Walbold John W, f t, Cedar Creek, Cedarville.

Walbott John, f, 2, 20, $305, St Joseph, Fort Wayne.

Walch Thomas C, Lafayette, Zanesville.

Walda H P & W C, Adams, Fort Wayne.

Walke Christian, St Joseph, Fort Wayne.

Walke John, St Joseph, Fort Wayne.

Walker Charles, lab, $50, Scipio, Hall's Corners.

Walker E M, f, Monroe, Monroeville.

Walker Frank, lab, Pleasant, Sheldon.

Walker John, f, 17, 40, $460, Scipio, Hall's Corners.

Walker John M, Lafayette, Zanesville.

Walker Luther, f, $40, Scipio, Hall's Corners.

Walker Marian, f, 19, 40, $670, Scipio, Hall's Corners.

Walker Noah, Lafayette, Zanesville.

Walker Samuel, f, 19, 20, $420, Scipio, Hall's Corners.

Walker Wallace, lab, 50, Scipio, Hall's Corners.

Walker Wm M, lab, Pleasant, Sheldon.

Wallace Fanny, Wayne, Ft Wayne.

Wallace Harvey, lab, Pleasant, Nine Mile.

Wallace Jesse S, f, 5, 15, 28, $415, Lafayette, Myhart.

Wallace John, carp, Pleasant, Nine Mile.

Wallace Noah, lab, 23, ¼, $5, Monroe, Dixon, O.

Wallace Wm, f t, 7, 1, $380, Pleasant, Sheldon.

Wallace W P, f, 28, 40, $885, Aboite, Ft Wayne.

Wallick Henry, f, 22, 160, $2880, Lafayette, Zanesville.

Wallick H N, Lafayette, Zanesville.

Walsh Michael V, 14, 1½, $245, Wayne, Ft Wayne.

Waltemoth Henry, f, 31, 7½, $470, St Joseph, Ft

Walter Euphemia, ⅔, $2500, Wayne, Ft Wayne.

Waltke Ferdinand, f, Maumee, Woodburn.

Waltke Henry, f, 4, 92, $625, Maumee, Woodburn.

Waltke Wm, f, 34, 51½, $1470, St Joseph, Fort Wayne.

Walton Charles E, f, 7, ½, $110, Adams, Ft Wayne.

Walton Walker, f, 10, 81, $895, Monroe, Monroeville.

Walworth Chester, f, 7, 13, $1285, Adams, Ft Wayne.

Wamsley Horace B, f, 18, 1, $540, Perry, Huntertown.

Wannamaker John, f, Monroe, Monroeville.

Wappes George, f, 3, 180, $2805, Eel River, Ari.

Wappes Joseph, lab, Eel River, Huntertown.

Wappes Wm, lab, Eel River, Ari.

Warcup Ellen J, Perry, Huntertown.

Warcup Ellen M, f, 18, 20, $370, Perry, Huntertown.

Warcup George A, f, 18, 72, $1335, Perry, Huntertown.

Warcup Wm, f, 7, 112, $2665, Perry, Huntertown.

Ward Andrew J, f, 12, 20, $200, Milan, Harlan.

Ward Elizabeth, f, 34, 1, $65, Lafayette, Zanesville.

Ward Joseph M, Lafayette, Zanesville.

Ward Sarah, f, 11, 40, $425, Milan, Harlan.

Ward S M, Adams, Fort Wayne.

Warner Albert H, Perry, Collingwood.

Warner Alexander, f, 5, 56, $735, Cedar Creek, Collingwood.

Warner Amos, f, 6, 104, $1675, Cedar Creek, Collingwood.

Warner C H, Perry, Collingwood.

Warner Daniel W, f, Springfield, Harlan.

Warner George, Wayne, Ft Wayne.

Warner George, f, 12, 131, $1855, Perry, Collingwood.

Warner George W, f, 18, 329, $6200, Scipio, Hall's Corners.

Warner Howard, lab, $1, Scipio, Hall's Corners.

Warner James, f, 12, 40, $1070, Perry, Collingwood.

Warner John, f, 11, 42, $505, Perry, Collingwood.

Warner John A, f, 2, 50, $1020, Perry, Collingwood.

Warner Joseph, f, 11, 148, $2850, Perry, Collingwood.

Warner Lincoln, Perry, Collingwood.

Warner Samuel, f, 10, 147, $2105, Perry, Collingwood.

Warner Samuel S, f, 7, 20, $260, Cedar Creek, Collingwood.

Warner Samuel W, f, 7, 6½, $45, Cedar Creek, Collingwood.

Warner Wesley G, f, 5, 2, $30, Cedar Creek, Collingwood.

Warner Wm, f, Springfield, Harlan.

Warner W jr, lab, Pleasant, Sheldon.

Warren John H, Adams, Ft Wayne.

Wass Josephine, f, 18, 8, $155, Monroe, Monroeville.

Wass Samuel W, f, 18, 14, $355, Monroe, Monroeville.

Wass Wm E, f, Monroe, Monroeville.

Waterhouse Amelia, ½, $900, Wayne, Ft Wayne.

Waters James, f, 33, 56, $840, Perry, Ft Wayne.

Waters John, f, 27, 130, $1810, Perry, Academy.

Waters John, f, 105½, $2050, St Joseph, Ft Wayne.

Waters Martin, f, 28, 65, $860, Scipio, Hall's Corners.

Waters Oliver M, f, 49, $1035, St Joseph, Ft Wayne.

Waters Stephen, f, 33, 73, $1160, Perry, Academy.

Waters Sylvester, lab, $25, Scipio, Hall's Corners.

Waters S P, huckster, Cedar Creek, Leo.

Waters Wesley, f, 3, 18, $390, St Joseph, Ft Wayne.

Watson David, f t, Cedar Creek.

Watson John S, f, 16, 80, $970, Cedar Creek, Leo.

Watson John W, Jefferson, Monroeville.

Watson M C, f, Monroe, Monroeville.

Watson Samuel, f, 1, 40, $490, Cedar Creek, Leo.

Watson Sarah A, f, 36, 5, $35, Jefferson, Monroeville.

Watson Shannon, Jackson, Monroeville.

Watson Sylvanus, Jackson, Edgerton.

Watson Wm J, f, 1, 120, $2125, Cedar Creek, Hursh

Watterson B F, Wayne, Fort Wayne.

Watterson Samuel P f, 20, 98, $1830, Eel River, Heller's Corners.

Watterson W E, lab, Eel River, Wallen.

Waugh Hanna, Lake, Arcola.

Waugh John W, Lake, Arcola.

Waugh Milton, f, 19, 80, $865, Lake, Arcola.

Waxenfelder John T, Aboite, Ft Wayne.

Weaver Alonzo, f, 34, 1, $295, Lafayette, Zanesville.

Weaver Benjamin, f, 33, 121, $1915, Pleasant, Sheldon.

Weaver Benjamin, laborer, Pleasant, Sheldon.

Weaver B F, Lafayette, Zanesville.

Weaver Cornelius, f, 33, 19, $390, Pleasant, Sheldon.

Weaver E C, Adams, Fort Wayne.

Weaver George, f, Lafayette, Zanesville.

Weaver George E, f, 31, 53, $1045, Lafayette, Zanesville.

Weaver Isaiah, gardener, 28, 31, $1285, Wayne, Fort Wayne.

Weaver Jacob A, f, 32, 80, $1575, Lafayette, Zanesville.

Weaver James, f, 16, 40, $665, Lafayette, Myhart.

Weaver James, saloon, Pleasant, Sheldon.

Weaver James M, lab, Pleasant, Nine Mile.

Weaver John, Perry, Huntertown.

Weaver John C, f, 16, 70, $1400, Lafayette, Zanesville.

Weaver John R, f, 36, 20, $195, Jefferson, Monroeville.

Weaver Oliver P, lab, Pleasant, Nine Mile.

Weaver Susannah, Lafayette, Zanesville.

Weaver S H, Lafayette, Zanesville.

Webb Louis, f, 7¾, $220, Wayne, Fort Wayne.

Webb Reuben M, 4, 8⅓, $1290, Wayne, Ft Wayne.

Webber Milton N, Adams, Fort Wayne.

Weber Frederick, f, 31, 7, $360, St Joseph, Ft Wayne.

Weberruz J J & D, Wayne, Fort Wayne.

Webster Alzina H, f, 17, 40, $700, Pleasant, Sheldon.

Webster B H, f, 17, 40, $1000, Pleasant, Sheldon.

Webster George, lab, Pleasant, Nine Mile.

Webster Hiram, f, 14, 52, $615, Jefferson, Zulu.

Webster John K, Jefferson, Zulu.

Webster Nathan, Jefferson, Maples.

Webster Warren B, Jefferson, Zulu.

Webster Wm H, f, 20, 100, $2085, Pleasant, Nine Mile.

Weers Albert W, Milan, Harlan.

Wegiman Henry, Aboite.

Wegint Chauncey G, Lake, Arcola.

Wehnert Carl, Wayne, Fort Wayne.

Wehrs John W, f, 31, 4, $375, St Joseph, Ft Wayne.

Weibel Frederick, f, 22, 80, $1275, Lafayette, Fort Wayne.

Weichers Henry, Milan, Gar Creek.

Weichselfelder George, f, 27, 40, $955, Aboite, Fort Wayne.

Weick Eliza, f, 13, 40, $2045, Wayne, Fort Wayne.

Weickart W H, f, 30, $955, St Joseph, Fort Wayne.

Weideman Aloysius, St Joseph, Fort Wayne.

Weighman Frederick H, Madison, Decatur.

Weighman Lizette, Madison, Hoagland.

Weiker Silas D, f, 9, 79, $1785, Perry, Huntertown.

Weilman Jacob, Jefferson, New Haven.

Weilman Rudolph, Jefferson, New Haven.

Weirich John, f t, Eel River, Churubusco.

Weirich Joseph H, f t, Eel River, Churubusco.

Weirich S A, f t, Eel River, Churubusco.

Weisel John A, Lake, Wallen.

Weisenberger C C, f, 24, 42, $865, Lake, Fort Wayne.

Weisenberger George, f, 14, 179, $3565, Aboite, Fort Wayne.

Weisenberger Jacob, St Joseph, Fort Wayne.

Weisenberger Valentine, Wayne, Fort Wayne.

Weishert Henry, f, 17, 120, $3655, Adams, Ft Wayne.

Weissel Elzira, f, 34, 5, $45, Eel River, Heller's Corners.

Weisser Emanuel, Wayne, Fort Wayne.

Weitz Henry, Adams, Fort Wayne.

Welbaum David, f, 5, 124, $2605, Pleasant, Nine Mile.

Welbaum F H, f t, Wayne, Fort Wayne.

Welch J E, Adams, Fort Wayne.

Welch Mary A, f, 23, 40, $405, Madison, Monroeville.

Welch Patrick, Perry, Huntertown.

Welkers Daniel, f, 5, 37, $670, Aboite, Ft Wayne.

Wellbaum C A, lab, Pleasant, Nine Mile.

Wellbaum Marshall, lab, Pleasant, Nine Mile.

Welling Elizabeth, f, 33, 90, $1955, Milan, New Haven.

Welling Henry, f, 11, 60, $2430, Adams, New Haven.

Welling Henry jr, Adams, New Haven.

Wellington R S, Wayne, Ft Wayne.

Wells Aaron, Lake, Arcola.

Wells Anna C, f, 31, 7, $395, St Joseph, Ft Wayne.

Wells Charles, tile mnfr, Aboite, Aboite.

Wells David, f t, Eel River, Wallen.

Wells E B, lab, Eel River, Wallen.

Wells George, f, 8, 24½, $560, Wayne, Ft Wayne.

Wells Jane, Wayne, Fort Wayne.

Wells John, f, 2, 10, $130, Jefferson, Gar Creek.

Wells John E, f, 33, 2, $60, Wayne, Ft Wayne.

Wells Julian B, Adams, Ft Wayne.

Wells Warren D, Lake, Arcola.

Wells Wm D & Francis, f, 21, 76, $1275, Perry, Huntertown.

Welph John, f, 10, 212, $6830, Adams, Ft Wayne.

Welsheimer Eliza A, f, 4, 7, $575, Wayne, Ft Wayne.

Welsheimer E L, Lake, Wallen.

Welsheimer Frank G, Lake, Wallen.

Welsheimer Ludwig, f, 3, 223, $3850, Lake, Wallen.

Welsheimer Otto, Lake, Wallen.

Wenger E A, Wayne, Fort Wayne.

Werling Henry, f, 14, 100, $3425, Adams, New Haven.

Wersnetski Emily, f, 12, 40, $375, Milan, Harlan.

Werts Joseph F, f, 3, 109, $2415, Milan, Harlan.

Wesling August, Adams, Ft Wayne.

West Columbia H, f, 5, 256, $2415, Perry, Huntertown.

West Curtis C, f, 3, 120, $2680, Perry, Huntertown.

West Fisher C, f, 4, 527, $10,585, Perry, Huntertown.

West P D, Perry, Hunter-town.

Westenfield Carl, Marion, Soest.

Westenfield Charles, f, 16, 40, $660, St Joseph, Ft Wayne.

Westenfield Conrad, f, 5, 53, $1260, Marion, Soest.

Westman Daniel, f, 7, 80, $1775, Milan, Chamberlain.

Wetherby George, f, 22, 12, $205, Eel River, Churubusco.

Wetzell Henry A, St Joseph, Fort Wayne.

Wetzell John, f, 3, 20, $465, St Joseph, Fort Wayne.

Wetzell Wm, f, 3, 103, $2580, St Joseph, Ft Wayne.

Weyer Emanuel A, lab, Monroe, Monroeville.

Weyleman Elizabeth, f, 20, 80, $1165, Jefferson, New Haven.

Weyleman W & Jacob, f, 21, 120, $1795, Jefferson, Maples

Weyman H, Adams, Fort Wayne.

Wheeler Almira, f 6, 135, $2100, Perry, Huntertown.

Wheeler Commodore, f, 5, 115, $1520, Perry, Hunter-town.

Wheeler C J, Wayne, Fort Wayne.

Wheeler Julia, f, 6, 97, $1240, Perry, Huntertown.

Wheeler Lydia, f, 6, 254, $3780, Perry, Huntertown.

Wheeler Wm, Jackson, Edgerton.

Wheelock E G, capitalist, Cedar Creek, Leo.

Wheelock E G, f, 2, 200, $3420, St Joseph, Fort Wayne.

Wherry George W, f, 32, 40, $505, Monroe, Monroeville.

Whetten Margaret, Pleasant, Sheldon.

Whipkey Sarah A, Monroe, Monroeville.

Whitcomb Charles, Madison, Hoagland.

White Andrew, f, 25, 160, $1470, Eel River, Wallen.

White August L, Lake, Arcola.

White Edward, Jackson, Dawkins.

White Edwin T, Adams, Ft Wayne.

White Elmer, f, 6, 40, $280, Jackson, Fort Wayne.

White Grace, Adams, Fort Wayne.

White James B, f, 34, 40, $280, Jackson, Ft Wayne.

White John W, f, 18, 40, $175, Jackson, Ft Wayne.

White J B, f, 18, 32, $260, Maumee, Fort Wayne.

White J D, Adams, Fort Wayne.

White Robert, St Joseph, Ft Wayne.

Whitehead Arthur, f, 32, 90, $2200, Wayne, Ft Wayne.

Whiting Anna M, gardener, 22, 6⅝, $785, Wayne, Fort Wayne.

Whitman Edward, f, 25, 120, $1855, Lafayette, Fort Wayne.

Whitmore Delia, St Joseph, Fort Wayne.

Whitmore Edward, f, 15, 76, $6160, Wayne, Ft Wayne.

Whitmore H E, Wayne, Fort Wayne.

Whitmore W E, f t, Wayne, Fort Wayne.

Whitney Alanson, f, 22, 170, $2750, Jefferson, Maples.

Whitney Calvin, lab, Pleasant, Sheldon.

Whitney George W, Lake, Arcola.

Whitney James E, f, 1, 160, $1915, Madison, Monroeville.

Whitney Rebecca, Eel River, Churubusco.

Whitney Wm J, Jefferson, Maples.

Whittern Charles, f, 18, 167, $4870, Monroe, Monroeville.

Whittern Margaret, f, 27, 70, $2520, Wayne, Ft Wayne.

Whittern N H, f, 13, 80, $1080, Madison, Monroeville.

Whittern R & C A, f, 13, 80, $880, Madison, Monroeville

Whitwright L A, f, Monroe, Monroeville.

Whitwright Samuel, f, Monroe, Monroeville.

Whyburn Maria C, f, 18, 11, $95, Madison, Monroeville.

Whyburn Wm T, f, 12, 56, $825, Madison, Monroeville.

Wickey August, f, 21, 40, $900, Milan, Chamberlain.

Wickey Samuel, Milan, Chamberlain.

Wickliffe Edward, f, 22, 40, $795, Aboite, Fort Wayne.

Wickliffe Francis, lab, Pleasant, Sheldon.

Wickliffe Frank, Lafayette, Zanesville.

Wickliffe George, Lafayette, Zanesville.

Wickliffe John, carp, Pleasant, Fort Wayne.

Wickliffe Martin, Lafayette, Zanesville.

Wickliffe N W, f, Lafayette, Zanesville.

Wickliffe Rebecca, f, 25, 40, $920, Lafayette, Sheldon.

Wickliffe Richard, f, 25, 40, $750, Lafayette, Sheldon.

Wickliffe & Mathews, f, 13, 3⅔, $255, Wayne, Fort Wayne.

Widner Amos, f, 3, 5, $145, St Joseph, Ft Wayne.

Widner Eliza A, f, 3, 2½, $50, St Joseph, Ft Wayne.

Wiebke Diederich, f, 25, 120, $2075, Lake, Ft Wayne.

Wiebke Ferdinand, f, 25, 80, $1645, Lake, Ft Wayne.

Wiebke Frederick, f, 58, $1640, Wayne, Ft Wayne.

Wiebke Frederick jr, Wayne, Ft Wayne.

Wiebke Henry, f, 40, $3390, Wayne, Ft Wayne.

Wiebke Wm H, Wayne, Ft Wayne.

Wiecher Frederick, f, 25, 40, $435, Milan, Gar Creek.

Wiedeman Herman, Wayne, Ft Wayne.

Wiedeman H & E, Wayne, Ft Wayne.

Wiedner Nicholas, Wayne, Ft Wayne.

Wiegand Wm, Wayne, Fort Wayne.

Wiegman Henry, f, 32, 98, $5150, St Joseph, Fort Wayne.

Wiegman Wm, f, 16, 60, $685, Madison, Hoagland.

Wieke August, f, 23, 40, $785, Adams, Ft Wayne.

Wieke Diederich, f, 11, 40, $615, Marion, Soest.

Wieke Elizabeth, f, 10, 60, $1255, Marion, Soest.

Wiekert Maurice, Milan, Chamberlain.

Wiese Christian, f, 15, 110, $3255, Adams, Ft Wayne.

Wiess August, f, Maumee, Woodburn.

Wiest Horatio, lab, Pleasant, Nine Mile.

Wiest Sarah A, f, 8, 62, $1335, Pleasant, Nine Mile.

Wietfield Henry, 35, 44, $705, Madison, Decatur.

Wiggins Archibald, Jackson, Edgerton.

Wigman Henry jr, f, 21, 130, $1810, Madison, Hoagland.

Wilber Arilla & Inez, f, 4, 41, $935, Milan, Chamberlain.

Wilberr George W, f, 4, 210, $4230, Milan, Chamberlain.

Wilcoxen Meredith, lab, Pleasant, Sheldon.

Wildman Martin, 14, ¼, $135, Wayne, Ft Wayne.

Wilds Jacob W, lab, Eel River, Ari.

Wiley O A W, Adams, Fort Wayne.

Wiley O B, f, 7, 28, $4150, Adams, Ft Wayne.

Wilfried Nancy B, Adams, Ft Wayne.

Wilhelm Henry, Wayne, Ft Wayne.

Wilkerson Charles, f, 15, 1, $15, Lafayette, Roanoke.

Wilkerson Charles H, lab, Pleasant, Nine Mile.

Wilkerson George N, f, 30, 60, $850, Lafayette, Roanoke.

Wilkerson Thomas J, f, 30, 60, $1315, Lafayette, Roanoke.

Wilkie Wm, f, 15, 160, $3175, Pleasant, Nine Mile.

Wilkie Wm W, f, 28, 20, $455, Pleasant, Nine Mile.

Wilkins Sidney E, Adams, Ft Wayne.

Wilkins Wm, Adams, Fort Wayne.

Wilkinson Charity, Wayne, Ft Wayne.

Wilkinson George, lab, $20, Scipio, Hall's Corners.

Wilkinson J E, Adams, Fort Wayne.

Willard Rachel A, Adams, Ft Wayne.

Willens Wm F, Lake, Arcola.

Williams Helen T, Adams, Ft Wayne.

Williams Henry M, f, 29, 400, $3145, Jackson, Ft Wayne.

Williams Jesse L (estate of), 4, 127, $12,660, Wayne, Ft Wayne.

Williams John, f, 19, 15, $140, Jackson, Zulu.

Williams John, Jackson, Zulu.

Williams J A, Wayne, Fort Wayne.

Williams Rosina, Wayne, Ft Wayne.

Williams Stephen, lab, $10, Scipio, Hall's Corners.

Williams W, Wayne, Fort Wayne.

Wills George, f t, Aboite, Aboite.

Wilock J D, St Joseph, Fort Wayne.

Wilson George, Adams, Fort Wayne.

Wilson George H, f, 31, 15¾, $650, St Joseph, Ft Wayne.

E. F. Sites, ☞ Dentist, 86 Calhoun St., Four Doors North of Wayne.

ALLEN COUNTY DIRECTORY. 813

Wilson Isaac A, f, 30, 151, $2730, Lafayette, Roanoke.

Wilson John, St Joseph, Ft Wayne.

Wilson John F, lab, Eel River.

Wilson J W, Lafayette, Roanoke.

Wilver Henry D, 1½, $110, Wayne, Ft Wayne.

Winch Calvin, 7, 2, $1710, Adams, Ft Wayne.

Winch C J & Sons, Adams, Ft Wayne.

Winch Howard, Adams, Fort Wayne.

Winch Jesse M, Adams, Fort Wayne.

Winch Mary C, 7, $40, Adams, Ft Wayne.

Winch Mildred D, Adams, Ft Wayne.

Winch Sherman P, Adams, Ft Wayne.

Winch Tanner M, Adams, Ft Wayne.

Winegart Frank, Lake, Arcola.

Winegart John A, Adams, Fort Wayne.

Winkler Carl W, f, 18, 1, $50, Adams, Ft Wayne.

Winkler John, Jefferson, Gar Creek.

Winter August, Pleasant, Sheldon.

Winter Charles, f, 16, 30, $595, Pleasant, Nine Mile.

Winter Christian (estate of), f, 16, 125, $2455, Pleasant, Nine Mile.

Winter Frank, Pleasant, Sheldon.

Winter Henry, Jefferson, Maples.

Winter Peter, f, 8, 2, $80, Pleasant, Nine Mile.

Winters Frederick, f, 27, 80, $1030, Jefferson, Maples.

Winters Philip, f, 34, 80, $1060, Jefferson, Maples.

Wisely Isaac, f t, Madison, Monroeville.

Wiseman Jacob, f, 32, 20, $220, Scipio, Hall's Corners.

Withers Martha, Wayne, Ft Wayne.

Witmer Christian, f, 27, 220, $4470, Cedar Creek, Leo.

Witmer Christian, f, 6, 78, $1255, Milan, Chamberlain.

Witmer Daniel, f t, Cedar Creek, Leo.

Witmer John, lab, Cedar Creek, Leo.

Witmer Peter, f, 22, 58, $1820, Cedar Creek, Leo.

Witt August C, Madison, Maples.

Witte August, f, 9, 40, $500, Madison, Maples.

Witte Caroline, f, 9, 80, $1375, Madison, Maples.

Witte Julius, f, 4, 38, $625, Madison, Maples.

Witzgall Lewis, f, 14, 160, $2325, Lafayette, Nine Mile.

Witzgall Lewis F, Lafayette, Nine Mile.

Witzgall Wm, f, 11, 58, $950, Lafayette, Nine Mile.

Woebeking Henry, f, 8, 202, $2155, Maumee, Woodburn.

Woebeking Theodore, f, Maumee, Woodburn.

Woebling Conrad, f, 7, 1, $125, Adams, Ft Wayne.

Woehr Henry, Wayne, Fort Wayne.

Wolf Elizabeth, Adams, Fort Wayne.

Wolf George, f, 5, 40, $885, Jefferson, New Haven.

Wolf H J, f, 11, 40, $980, Aboite, Ft Wayne.

Wolf John W, Adams, Fort Wayne.

Wolf Martha J, f, 32, 40, $570, Milan, New Haven.

Wolf Samuel, f, 4, 70, $1105, Jefferson, New Haven.

Wolford Ira L, Perry, Huntertown.

Wonling Henry, f, 19, 47, $835, Jefferson, New Haven.

Wood Albert, f, 13, 40, $610, Eel River, Huntertown.

Wood Albert W, f, 19, 67, $840, Perry, Huntertown.

Wood Commodore, Perry, Huntertown.

Wood J A, Lafayette, Zanesville.

Wood Oscar, f, 17, 25, $105, Perry, Huntertown.

Wood Oscar, f, 29, 80, $660, Jackson, Zulu.

Wood Wm, Perry, Huntertown.

Woods Alexander, Pleasant, Sheldon.

Woods Clemens, f t, Pleasant, Sheldon.

Woods Emery, lab, Pleasant, Sheldon.

Woods Francis, lab, Pleasant, Sheldon.

Woods George, f, 31, 100, $1455, Pleasant, Sheldon.

Woods George A, Pleasant, Sheldon.

Woods Hester A, f, 9, 40, $1695, Wayne, Ft Wayne.

Woods Jacob, f, 31, 90, $1290, Pleasant, Sheldon.

Woods James, f, 32, 200, $3230, Pleasant, Sheldon.

Woods John B, f, 31, 60, $1030, Pleasant, Sheldon.

Woods John M, f, 29, 160, $3430, Adams, Ft Wayne.

Woods John W, f, 3, 5, $45, Monroe, Monroeville.

Woods J M, f, 22, 80, $1730, Aboite.

Woods Mary A, f, 3, 5, $40, Monroe, Monroeville.

Woods Milton, f, 36, 120, $2020, Lafayette, Sheldon.

Woods Samuel, f, 32, 160, $2650, Pleasant, Sheldon.

Woolman Wm, Jackson, Edgerton.

Worden Ezra, f, 4, 44, $475, Springfield, Harlan.

Worden J W, f, 31, 40, $485, Scipio, Harlan.

Work Charles, lab, Pleasant, Nine Mile.

Work George, lab, Pleasant, Sheldon.

Work Philip H, f, 5, 30, $755, Wayne, Fort Wayne.

Workman Herman, f t, Cedar Creek, Leo.

Worley George N, physician, Marion, Poe.

Worley Serepta F, Marion, Poe.

Wormcastle Jane, f, 23, 80, $850, Madison, Monroeville.

Wormcastle Joseph H, Madison, Monroeville.

Wright Charles, clerk, 18, ⅕, $25, Monroe, Monroeville.

Wright Franklin, f, Monroe, Monroeville.

Wright F D, Adams, Fort Wayne.

Wright George, Lafayette, Zanesville.

Wright Ida M, f, 18, ¼, $190, Monroe, Monroeville.

Wright Jesse, Jackson, Edgerton.

Wright L W, Lafayette, Myhart.

Wright Maria, f, 23, 40, $690, Lafayette, Nine Mile.

Wright Wm H, brick mnfr, 17, 5, $165, Monroe, Monroeville.

Wright Wm W, Wayne, Ft Wayne.

Wyatt Andrew, lab, Eel River.

Wyatt Daniel, f, 6, 11, $265, Perry, Huntertown.

Wyatt Ephraim, f t, Cedar Creek, Cedarville.

Wyatt James, f, 8, 152, $3055, Perry, Huntertown.

Wyatt Joseph, Perry, Huntertown.

Wyatt Mandana, f, 30, 4, $80, Eel River, Churubusco.

Wyatt Miles, f, 7, 3, $90, Perry, Huntertown.

Wyatt Spencer, lab, Eel River, Churubusco.

Wyatt Wm T, f, 2, 80, $1555, Cedar Creek, Leo.

Wyckoff James H, f, 33, 155, $1810, Jackson, Monroeville.

Wygralok Stanislaus, lab, 14, ½, $500, Wayne, Ft Wayne.

Wysong Isaac, f, 20, 102, $2120, Lafayette, Roanoke.

Wysong John M, Lafayette, Roanoke.

Wysong Julia A, Lafayette, Roanoke.

Wysong L C, Lafayette, Roanoke.

Wyss Albrecht, Wayne, Ft Wayne.

Wyss Bernard S, Marion, Poe.

Wyss Frank J, f, 72, $1510, Marion, Poe.

Wyss Franz, f, 16, 200, $3840, Marion, Poe.

Wyss John B, reserve, 99, $2075, Marion, Poe.

Wyss Nicholas J, f, 13, 77, $1670, Marion, Hoagland.

Y

Yaggy Andrew, f, Cedar Creek, Leo.

Yaggy Andrew B, lab, Cedar Creek, Leo.

Yaggy Henry, f t, Cedar Creek, Leo.

Yanguelet Alfred, f, 12, 120, $1260, Jefferson, Dawkins.

Yanguelet Louis S, f, 11, 78, $865, Jefferson, Dawkins.

Yargens & Ranke, f, 16, 200, $1345, Maumee, Ft Wayne.

Yaut Cornelius, f, 28, 80, $1660, Aboite, Ft Wayne.

Yearin Elijah, f, 5, 80, $1635, Eel River, Ari.

Yergens August, f, 28, 40, $985, St Joseph, Ft Wayne.

Yerks Franklin, Jackson, Monroeville.

Yerks James M, f, 16, 40, $1050, Milan, Chamberlain.

Yevington Wm, f, Maumee, Harlan.

Yoder Christian, f t, Cedar Creek, Leo.

Yoder Elias, f, 9, 80, $1595, Cedar Creek, Leo.

Yoder John, f, 9, 40, $800, Cedar Creek, Leo.

Young Amos, Wayne, Fort Wayne.

Young Anna, Wayne, Fort Wayne.

Young C C, f, 22, 40, $685, Lafayette, Zanesville.

Young David S, Aboite.

Young Edward, Wayne, Ft Wayne.

Young Erastus, Wayne, Fort Wayne.

Young George, Jackson, Edgerton.

Young George, Wayne, Fort Wayne.

Young George F, Lafayette, Zanesville.

Young Henry, f, 26, 335, $6540, St Joseph, Fort Wayne.

Young James M, f, 32, 90, $1760, Lafayette, Zanesville.

Young John, Lafayette, Myhart.

Young John H, St Joseph, Ft Wayne.

Young John S, f, 5, 38, $755, Eel River, Ari.

Young Julius, f, 10, 120, $2475, St Joseph, Fort Wayne.

Young J A, Jackson, Edgerton.

Young J C, St Joseph, Fort Wayne.

Young Margaret, Wayne, Ft Wayne.

Young Samuel, Lafayette, Myhart.

Young S J, f, 17, 21, $345, Lafayette, Myhart.

Young Wm H, Wayne, Fort Wayne.

Young W G, f, 11, 40, $560, St Joseph, Ft Wayne.

Younke John P, Wayne, Ft Wayne.

Younker T C, Wayne, Fort Wayne.

Youse Christian, f, 33, 554, $7170, Madison, Bingen.

Youse Edward E, Madison, Bingen.

Youse John L, f, 29, 160, $2525, Marion, Hoagland.

Youse Nelson, Madison, Bingen.

Youse Wm A, f, 23, 100, $935, Madison, Monroeville.

Z

Zallmeyer Frederick, f, 3, 65, $1490, Marion.

Zehnder George W, f, 10, 80, $1470, Cedar Creek, Leo.

Zehnder James, f, 34, 165, $3445, Cedar Creek, Cedarville.

Zehnder John, f, 10, 80, $1675, Cedar Creek, Leo.

Zehr Michael, f, 10, 20, $335, Milan, Harlan.

Zelt Jacob, f, 24, 160, $4605, Adams, Ft Wayne.

Zelt John, Adams, Fort Wayne.

Zentner Emanuel, lab, Cedar Creek, Cedarville.

Zerull J & Ernestine, Wayne, Ft Wayne.

Ziegler Harriet, Cedar Creek, Leo.

Ziegler Harriet M, Jackson, Monroeville.

Ziegler John J, Marion, Poe.

Ziegler Martin, f, 20, 40, $885, Marion, Poe.

Ziegler Mattie, Cedar Creek, Leo.

Ziemendorf Ann & Mary, Wayne, Ft Wayne.

Zimmerman Abram W, lab, Cedar Creek, Leo.

Zimmerman Charles, laborer, Cedar Creek, Cedarville.

Zimmerman Elias, f, 19, 80, $415, Jackson, Edgerton.

Zimmerman F D, f, 18, 80, $1680, Eel River, Churubusco.

Zimmerman Herman, Jackson, Edgerton.

Zimmerman John, Adams, Ft Wayne.

Zimmerman Samuel, f, 21,38, $1205, Cedar Creek, Cedarville.

Zollars Allen, lawyer, 18, ¾, $30, Monroe, Fort Wayne.

Zollars George, f, 2, 20, $320, St Joseph, Fort Wayne.

Zollars George E, f, 65, $1045, Cedar Creek, Cedarville.

Zollars Charles, lab, Cedar Creek, Cedarville.

Zollinger Christian, f, 23, $50, Adams, Fort Wayne.

Zollinger C A, f, 14, 22, $525, Adams, Fort Wayne.

Zollinger H C, f, 22, 112, $2615, Adams, Fort Wayne

Zollinger M F, Adams, Fort Wayne.

Zollinger Valentine, f, 6, 50, $765, Madison, Maples.

Zolman Clarence, lab, Eel River, Churubusco.

Zolman David, lab, Eel River, Churubusco.

Zolman James P, f, 7, 98, $1885, Eel River, Churubusco.

Zolman John, lab, Eel River, Churubusco.

Zolman Johnston, f, 7, 49, $870, Eel River, Churubusco.

Zook Daniel, Cedar Creek.

Zschoche Charles, Marion, Soest.

Zuber Barbara, Wayne, Fort Wayne.

Zuber Henry S, f, 33, 40, $785, Adams, Fort Wayne.

Zuber John, Adams, Fort Wayne.

Zuber Joseph,, f, 28, 40, $875 Adams, Fort Wayne.

Zuber Lucinda, Wayne, Fort Wayne.

Zuber Mary A, f, 28, 39, $1040, Adams, Ft Wayne.

Zuber Michael, f, 32, 40, $830, Adams, Fort Wayne.

Zuber Philip, f, 7, 1, $125, Adams, Fort Wayne.

Zubrick B, f, 5, 80, $1040, Monroe, Monroeville.

Zurbuch Francis J, f, 1, 147, $3255, Adams, Ft Wayne.

Zurbuch John, Adams, New Haven.

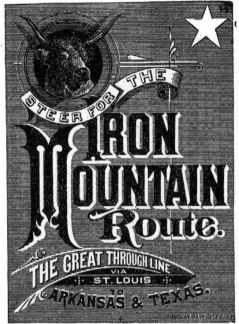

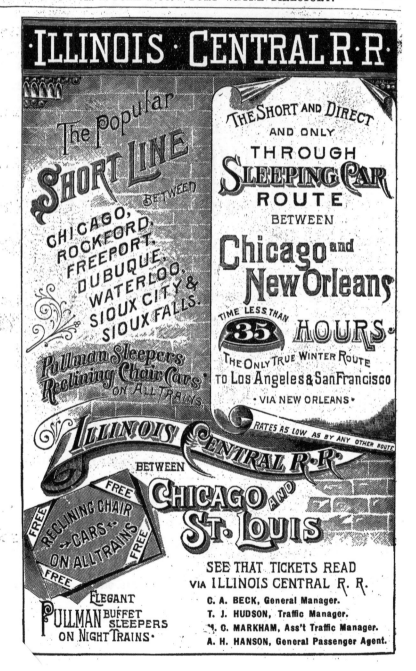